STATUTORY INSTRUMENTS 1968

PART II
(in two Sections)

SECTION 2

Published by Authority

LONDON
HER MAJESTY'S STATIONERY OFFICE
1968

NOL.

SBN 11 840011 8

Contents of the Volume

PART I, Section 1

PART I, Section 2

PART II, Section 1

PART II, Section 2

PART III

Contents of the Volume

PART I, Section 1

PART I, Section 2

PART II, Section 1

PART II, Section 2

PART III

STATUTORY INSTRUMENTS

1968 No. 1101

INCOME TAX

The Double Taxation Relief (Taxes on Income) (Malawi) Order 1968

Laid before the House of Commons in draft

Made - - - - *12th July* 1968

At the Court at Buckingham Palace, the 12th day of July 1968

Present,

The Queen's Most Excellent Majesty in Council

Whereas a draft of this Order was laid before the Commons House of Parliament in accordance with the provisions of section 347(6) of the Income Tax Act 1952(a), and an Address has been presented to Her Majesty by that House praying that an Order may be made in the terms of this Order:

Now, therefore, Her Majesty, in exercise of the powers conferred upon Her by section 347(1) of the said Income Tax Act 1952, as amended by section 64 of the Finance Act 1965(b) and of all other powers enabling Her in that behalf, is pleased, by and with the advice of Her Privy Council, to order, and it is hereby ordered, as follows:—

1. This Order may be cited as the Double Taxation Relief (Taxes on Income) (Malawi) Order 1968.

2. It is hereby declared—

(*a*) that the arrangements specified in the Agreement set out in the Schedule to this Order have been made with the Government of the Republic of Malawi with a view to affording relief from double taxation in relation to income tax or corporation tax and taxes of a similar character imposed by the laws of Malawi varying the arrangements set out in the Schedule to the Double Taxation Relief (Taxes on Income) (Federation of Rhodesia and Nyasaland) Order 1956(c), as adapted for continuance in force in relation to Malawi by the arrangements set out in the Schedule to the Double Taxation Relief (Taxes on Income) (Malawi) Order 1964(d); and

(*b*) that it is expedient that those arrangements should have effect.

W. G. Agnew.

(a) 15 & 16 Geo. 6 & 1 Eliz. 2. c. 10.   (b) 1965 c. 25.
(c) S.I. 1956/619 (1956 I, p. 1072).   (d) S.I. 1964/1401 (1964 III, p. 3275).

SCHEDULE

AGREEMENT SUPPLEMENTARY TO AND AMENDING THE AGREEMENT BETWEEN THE GOVERNMENT OF THE UNITED KINGDOM OF GREAT BRITAIN AND NORTHERN IRELAND AND THE GOVERNMENT OF THE REPUBLIC OF MALAWI FOR THE AVOIDANCE OF DOUBLE TAXATION AND THE PREVENTION OF FISCAL EVASION WITH RESPECT TO TAXES ON INCOME

The Government of the United Kingdom of Great Britain and Northern Ireland and the Government of the Republic of Malawi,

Desiring to amend the Agreement between the Government of the United Kingdom of Great Britain and Northern Ireland and the Government of the former Federation of Rhodesia and Nyasaland for the avoidance of double taxation and the prevention of fiscal evasion with respect to taxes on income signed at London on 25 November, 1955, (hereinafter referred to as "the 1955 Agreement") which continued with effect from the dissolution of the Federation of Rhodesia and Nyasaland on 1 January, 1964, in force, subject to certain modifications, between the Government of the United Kingdom and the Government of Nyasaland and from 6 July, 1964, when Nyasaland attained Independence under the name of Malawi, between the Government of the United Kingdom and the Government of Malawi and from 1 July, 1966, when Malawi became a Republic, between the Government of the United Kingdom and the Government of the Republic of Malawi,

Have agreed as follows:

ARTICLE 1

The 1955 Agreement shall be amended—

(a) by the addition at the end of Article VI of the following new paragraph—

"(3) If the recipient of a dividend is a company which owns 10 per cent. or more of the class of shares in respect of which the dividend is paid then paragraph (1) shall not apply to the dividend to the extent that it can have been paid only out of profits which the company paying the dividend earned or other income which it received in a period ending twelve months or more before the relevant date. For the purposes of this paragraph the term "relevant date" means the date on which the beneficial owner of the dividend became the owner of 10 per cent. or more of the class of shares in question. Provided that this paragraph shall not apply if the beneficial owner of the dividend shows that the shares were acquired for *bona fide* commercial reasons and not primarily for the purpose of securing the benefit of this paragraph."; and

(b) by the substitution for paragraphs (1) and (2) of Article XIII of the following two new paragraphs—

"(1) Subject to the provisions of the law of the United Kingdom regarding the allowance as a credit against United Kingdom tax of tax payable in a territory outside the United Kingdom (which shall not affect the general principle hereof)—

(a) Malawi tax payable under the laws of Malawi and in accordance with this Agreement, whether directly or by deduction, on profits or income from sources within Malawi shall be allowed as a credit against any United Kingdom tax computed by reference to the same profits or income by reference to which the Malawi tax is computed. Provided that in the case of a dividend the credit shall only take into account such tax in respect thereof as is additional to any tax payable by the company on the profits out of which the dividend is paid and is ultimately borne by the recipient without reference to any tax so payable.

(b) Where a company which is a resident of Malawi pays a dividend to a company resident in the United Kingdom which controls directly or indirectly at least 10 per cent. of the voting power in the first-mentioned company, the credit shall take into account (in addition to any Malawi tax for which credit may be allowed under sub-paragraph (a)) the Malawi tax payable by that first-mentioned company in respect of the profits out of which such dividend is paid.

(2) Subject to the provisions of the law of Malawi regarding the allowance as a credit against Malawi tax of tax payable in a territory outside Malawi (which shall not affect the general principle hereof)—

(a) United Kingdom tax payable under the laws of the United Kingdom and in accordance with this Agreement, whether directly or by deduction, on profits or income from sources within the United Kingdom shall be allowed as a credit against any Malawi tax computed by reference to the same profits or income by reference to which the United Kingdom tax is computed. Provided that in the case of a dividend the credit shall only take into account such tax in respect thereof as is additional to any tax payable by the company on the profits out of which the dividend is paid and is ultimately borne by the recipient without reference to any tax so payable.

(b) If Malawi tax is payable in respect of a dividend paid by a company which is a resident of the United Kingdom to a company resident in Malawi which controls directly or indirectly at least 10 per cent. of the voting power in the first-mentioned company, the credit shall take into account (in addition to any United Kingdom tax for which credit may be allowed under sub-paragraph (a)) the United Kingdom tax payable by that first-mentioned company in respect of the profits out of which such dividend is paid."

ARTICLE 2

(1) This Agreement shall enter into force when the last of all such things shall have been done in the United Kingdom and Malawi as are necessary to give the Agreement the force of law in the United Kingdom and Malawi respectively.

(2) Upon the entry into force of this Agreement in accordance with paragraph (1) the new paragraph (3) of Article VI of the 1955 Agreement shall have effect immediately and the new paragraphs (1) and (2) of Article XIII thereof shall have effect—

(a) in the United Kingdom:

(i) as respects income tax and surtax, for any year of assessment beginning on or after 6 April, 1968; and

(ii) as respects corporation tax, for any financial year beginning on or after 1 April, 1968;

(b) in Malawi: as respects income tax, for any year of assessment beginning on or after 1 April, 1968.

IN WITNESS WHEREOF the undersigned, duly authorised thereto, have signed this Agreement.

DONE in duplicate at Zomba this Second day of April 1968.

For the Government of the
United Kingdom of Great Britain
and Northern Ireland:

For the Government of
the Republic of Malawi:

T. S. TULL

JOHN TEMBO

EXPLANATORY NOTE

(This Note is not part of the Order.)

This Agreement makes two amendments to the Agreement between the United Kingdom and the Federation of Rhodesia and Nyasaland, subsequently continued in force with Malawi, which is scheduled to the Double Taxation Relief (Taxes on Income) (Federation of Rhodesia and Nyasaland) Order 1956.

First it provides that the exemption of dividends from any tax chargeable in addition to the tax on the paying company's profits is not to be allowed in certain cases where the shareholder is a company having a substantial holding in the paying company. The restriction does not apply to dividends on shares acquired for *bona fide* commercial reasons.

Secondly, it amends Article XIII of the 1956 Agreement in its application to dividends by providing that credit for tax on the profits out of which dividends are paid, whether that tax is deducted from the dividends or not, is to be given only where the recipient is a company which holds not less than 10 per cent of the voting power in the paying company. So far as United Kingdom income tax is concerned this provision takes effect from the year of assessment 1968/69.

STATUTORY INSTRUMENTS

1968 No. 1102

INCOME TAX

The Double Taxation Relief (Taxes on Income) (St. Lucia) Order 1968

Laid before the House of Commons in draft

Made - - -   *12th July* 1968

At the Court at Buckingham Palace, the 12th day of July 1968

Present,

The Queen's Most Excellent Majesty in Council

Whereas a draft of this Order was laid before the Commons House of Parliament in accordance with the provisions of section 347(6) of the Income Tax Act 1952(a), and an Address has been presented to Her Majesty by that House praying that an Order may be made in the terms of this Order :

Now, therefore, Her Majesty, in exercise of the powers conferred upon Her by section 347(1) of the said Income Tax Act 1952, as amended by section 64 of the Finance Act 1965(b), and of all other powers enabling Her in that behalf, is pleased, by and with the advice of Her Privy Council, to order, and it is hereby ordered, as follows :—

1. This Order may be cited as the Double Taxation Relief (Taxes on Income) (St. Lucia) Order 1968.

2. It is hereby declared—
   (a) that the arrangements specified in the Agreement set out in the Schedule to this Order have been made with the Government of St. Lucia with a view to affording relief from double taxation in relation to income tax or corporation tax and taxes of a similar character imposed by the laws of St. Lucia varying the arrangements set out in the Schedule to the Double Taxation Relief (Taxes on Income) (St. Lucia) Order 1949(c) ; and

   (b) that it is expedient that those arrangements should have effect.

W. G. Agnew.

(a) 15 & 16 Geo. 6 & 1 Eliz. 2. c. 10.   (b) 1965 c. 25.   (c) S.I. 1949/366 (1949 I, p. 2289).

SCHEDULE

AGREEMENT AMENDING THE ARRANGEMENT BETWEEN THE GOVERNMENT OF THE UNITED KINGDOM OF GREAT BRITAIN AND NORTHERN IRELAND AND THE GOVERNMENT OF ST. LUCIA FOR THE AVOIDANCE OF DOUBLE TAXATION AND THE PREVENTION OF FISCAL EVASION WITH RESPECT TO TAXES ON INCOME

The Government of the United Kingdom of Great Britain and Northern Ireland and the Government of St. Lucia,

Desiring to amend the Arrangement for the avoidance of double taxation and the prevention of fiscal evasion with respect to taxes on income made in 1949 between His Majesty's Government and the Government of St. Lucia (hereinafter referred to as "the Arrangement"),

Have agreed as follows:

ARTICLE 1

The Arrangement shall be amended—

(a) by the deletion of paragraph 2(1)(b);

(b) by the substitution for the references therein to "the Colony", "Colonial enterprise" and "Colonial tax" of references to "St. Lucia", "St. Lucia enterprise" and "St. Lucia tax" respectively;

(c) by the addition at the end of paragraph 6 of the following new sub-paragraph—

"(3) If the recipient of a dividend is a company which owns 10 per cent. or more of the class of shares in respect of which the dividend is paid then sub-paragraph (1) shall not apply to the dividend to the extent that it can have been paid only out of profits which the company paying the dividend earned or other income which it received in a period ending twelve months or more before the relevant date. For the purposes of this sub-paragraph the term "relevant date" means the date on which the beneficial owner of the dividend became the owner of 10 per cent. or more of the class of shares in question. Provided that this sub-paragraph shall not apply if the beneficial owner of the dividend shows that the shares were acquired for *bona fide* commercial reasons and not primarily for the purpose of securing the benefit of this paragraph."; and

(d) by the substitution for sub-paragraphs (1) and (2) of paragraph 13 of the following two new sub-paragraphs—

"(1) Subject to the provisions of the law of the United Kingdom regarding the allowance as a credit against United Kingdom tax of tax payable in a territory outside the United Kingdom (which shall not affect the general principle hereof)—

(a) St. Lucia tax payable under the laws of St. Lucia and in accordance with this Arrangement, whether directly or by deduction, on profits or income from sources within St. Lucia shall be allowed as a credit against any United Kingdom tax computed by reference to the same profits or income by reference to which St. Lucia tax is computed. Provided that in the case of a dividend the credit shall only take into account such tax in respect thereof as is additional to any tax payable by the company on the profits out of which the dividend is paid and is ultimately borne by the recipient without reference to any tax so payable.

(b) Where a company which is a resident of St. Lucia pays a dividend to a company resident in the United Kingdom which controls directly or indirectly at least 10 per cent. of the voting power in the first-mentioned company, the credit shall take into account (in addition to any St. Lucia tax for which credit may be allowed under (a) of this sub-paragraph) the St. Lucia tax payable by that first-mentioned company in respect of the profits out of which such dividend is paid.

(2) Subject to the provisions of the law of St. Lucia regarding the allowance as a credit against St. Lucia tax of tax payable in a territory outside St. Lucia (which shall not affect the general principle hereof)—

(a) United Kingdom tax payable under the laws of the United Kingdom and in accordance with this Arrangement, whether directly or by deduction, on profits or income from sources within the United Kingdom shall be allowed as a credit against any St. Lucia tax computed by reference to the same profits or income by reference to which the United Kingdom tax is computed. Provided that in the case of a dividend the credit shall only take into account such tax in respect thereof as is additional to any tax payable by the company on the profits out of which the dividend is paid and is ultimately borne by the recipient without reference to any tax so payable.

(b) Where a company which is a resident of the United Kingdom pays a dividend to a company resident in St. Lucia which controls directly or indirectly at least 10 per cent. of the voting power in the first-mentioned company, the credit shall take into account (in addition to any United Kingdom tax for which credit may be allowed under (a) of this sub-paragraph) the United Kingdom tax payable by that first-mentioned company in respect of the profits out of which such dividend is paid."

Article 2

(1) This Agreement shall enter into force when the last of all such things shall have been done in the United Kingdom and St. Lucia as are necessary to give the Agreement the force of law in the United Kingdom and St. Lucia respectively.

(2) Upon the entry into force of this Agreement in accordance with paragraph (1) the new sub-paragraph (3) of paragraph 6 of the Arrangement shall have effect immediately and the new sub-paragraphs (1) and (2) of paragraph 13 thereof shall have effect—

(a) in the United Kingdom:
  (i) as respects income tax (including surtax), for any year of assessment beginning on or after 6 April, 1968 ; and
  (ii) as respects corporation tax, for any financial year beginning on or after 1 April, 1968 ;

(b) in St. Lucia:
  as respects income tax, for any year of assessment beginning on the first day of January, 1968 and subsequent years.

IN WITNESS WHEREOF the undersigned, duly authorised thereto, have signed this Agreement.

DONE in duplicate at Castries this fifth day of April 1968.

For the Government of the United Kingdom of Great Britain and Northern Ireland:

For the Government of St. Lucia:

DESMOND M. KERR

JOHN G. M. COMPTON

EXPLANATORY NOTE

(This Note is not part of the Order.)

This Agreement makes two amendments to the Arrangement between the United Kingdom and St. Lucia which is scheduled to the Double Taxation Relief (Taxes on Income) (St. Lucia) Order 1949.

First it provides that the exemption of dividends from any tax chargeable in addition to the tax on the paying company's profits is not to be allowed in certain cases where the shareholder is a company having a substantial holding in the paying company. The restriction does not apply to dividends on shares acquired for *bona fide* commercial reasons.

Secondly, it amends paragraph 13 of the 1949 Arrangement in its application to dividends by providing that credit for tax on the profits out of which dividends are paid, whether that tax is deducted from the dividends or not, is to be given only where the recipient is a company which holds not less than 10 per cent of the voting power in the paying company. So far as United Kingdom income tax is concerned this provision takes effect from the year of assessment 1968/69.

STATUTORY   INSTRUMENTS

1968 No. 1103

INCOME TAX

The Double Taxation Relief (Taxes on Income) (St. Vincent) Order 1968

Laid before the House of Commons in draft

Made - - - *12th July* 1968

At the Court at Buckingham Palace, the 12th day of July 1968

Present,

The Queen's Most Excellent Majesty in Council

Whereas a draft of this Order was laid before the Commons House of Parliament in accordance with the provisions of section 347(6) of the Income Tax Act 1952(**a**), and an Address has been presented to Her Majesty by that House praying that an Order may be made in the terms of this Order :

Now, therefore, Her Majesty, in exercise of the powers conferred upon Her by section 347(1) of the said Income Tax Act 1952, as amended by section 64 of the Finance Act 1965(**b**), and of all other powers enabling Her in that behalf, is pleased, by and with the advice of Her Privy Council, to order, and it is hereby ordered, as follows :—

1. This Order may be cited as the Double Taxation Relief (Taxes on Income) (St. Vincent) Order 1968.

2. It is hereby declared—

(*a*) that the arrangements specified in the Agreement set out in the Schedule to this Order have been made with the Government of St. Vincent with a view to affording relief from double taxation in relation to income tax or corporation tax and taxes of a similar character imposed by the laws of St. Vincent varying the arrangements set out in the Schedule to the Double Taxation Relief (Taxes on Income) (St. Vincent) Order 1949(**c**) ; and

(*b*) that it is expedient that those arrangements should have effect.

W. G. Agnew.

(**a**) 15 & 16 Geo. 6 & 1 Eliz. 2. c. 10.   (**b**) 1965 c. 25.
(**c**) S.I. 1949/367 (1949 I, p. 2296).

SCHEDULE

AGREEMENT AMENDING THE ARRANGEMENT BETWEEN THE GOVERNMENT OF THE UNITED KINGDOM OF GREAT BRITAIN AND NORTHERN IRELAND AND THE GOVERNMENT OF SAINT VINCENT FOR THE AVOIDANCE OF DOUBLE TAXATION AND THE PREVENTION OF FISCAL EVASION WITH RESPECT TO TAXES ON INCOME

The Government of the United Kingdom of Great Britain and Northern Ireland and the Government of Saint Vincent,

Desiring to amend the Arrangement for the avoidance of double taxation and the prevention of fiscal evasion with respect to taxes on income made in 1949 between His Majesty's Government and the Government of Saint Vincent (hereinafter referred to as "the Arrangement"),

Have agreed as follows:

ARTICLE 1

The Arrangement shall be amended—

(a) by the deletion of paragraph 2(1)(b);

(b) by the substitution for the references therein to "the Colony", "Colonial enterprise" and "Colonial tax" of references to "Saint Vincent", "Saint Vincent enterprise" and "Saint Vincent tax" respectively;

(c) by the addition at the end of paragraph 6 of the following new sub-paragraph—

"(3) If the recipient of a dividend is a company which owns 10 per cent. or more of the class of shares in respect of which the dividend is paid then sub-paragraph (1) shall not apply to the dividend to the extent that it can have been paid only out of profits which the company paying the dividend earned or other income which it received in a period ending twelve months or more before the relevant date. For the purposes of this sub-paragraph the term "relevant date" means the date on which the beneficial owner of the dividend became the owner of 10 per cent. or more of the class of shares in question. Provided that this sub-paragraph shall not apply if the beneficial owner of the dividend shows that the shares were acquired for *bona fide* commercial reasons and not primarily for the purpose of securing the benefit of this paragraph.";

(d) by the substitution for sub-paragraphs (1) and (2) of paragraph 13 of the following two new sub-paragraphs—

"(1) Subject to the provisions of the law of the United Kingdom regarding the allowance as a credit against United Kingdom tax of tax payable in a territory outside the United Kingdom (which shall not affect the general principle hereof)—

(a) Saint Vincent tax payable under the laws of Saint Vincent and in accordance with this Arrangement, whether directly or by deduction, on profits or income from sources within Saint Vincent shall be allowed as a credit against any United Kingdom tax computed by reference to the same profits or income by reference to which Saint Vincent tax is computed. Provided that in the case of a dividend the credit shall only take into account such tax in respect thereof as is additional to any tax payable by the company on the profits out of which the dividend is paid and is ultimately borne by the recipient without reference to any tax so payable.

(b) Where a company which is a resident of Saint Vincent pays a dividend to a company resident in the United Kingdom which controls directly or indirectly at least 10 per cent. of the voting power in the first-mentioned company, the credit shall take into account (in addition to any Saint Vincent tax for which credit may be allowed under (*a*) of this sub-paragraph) the Saint Vincent tax payable by that first-mentioned company in respect of the profits out of which such dividend is paid.

(2) Subject to the provisions of the law of Saint Vincent regarding the allowance as a credit against Saint Vincent tax of tax payable in a territory outside Saint Vincent (which shall not affect the general principle hereof)—

(*a*) United Kingdom tax payable under the laws of the United Kingdom and in accordance with this Arrangement, whether directly or by deduction, on profits or income from sources within the United Kingdom shall be allowed as a credit against any Saint Vincent tax computed by reference to the same profits or income by reference to which the United Kingdom tax is computed. Provided that in the case of a dividend the credit shall only take into account such tax in respect thereof as is additional to any tax payable by the company on the profits out of which the dividend is paid and is ultimately borne by the recipient without reference to any tax so payable.

(*b*) Where a company which is a resident of the United Kingdom pays a dividend to a company resident in Saint Vincent which controls directly or indirectly at least 10 per cent. of the voting power in the first-mentioned company, the credit shall take into account (in addition to any United Kingdom tax for which credit may be allowed under (*a*) of this sub-paragraph) the United Kingdom tax payable by that first-mentioned company in respect of the profits out of which such dividend is paid." ; and

(*e*) by the addition after paragraph 13 of the following new paragraph—

"13A. This Arrangement shall not apply to companies entitled to any special tax benefit under the Saint Vincent International Business Companies (Exemption from Income Tax) Ordinance, 1966, as in effect on 9 February, 1967, or any substantially similar law enacted by Saint Vincent after that date."

ARTICLE 2

(1) This Agreement shall enter into force when the last of all such things shall have been done in the United Kingdom and Saint Vincent as are necessary to give the Agreement the force of law in the United Kingdom and Saint Vincent respectively.

(2) Upon the entry into force of this Agreement in accordance with paragraph (1) the new sub-paragraph (3) of paragraph 6 and the new paragraph 13A of the Arrangement shall both have effect immediately and the new sub-paragraphs (1) and (2) of paragraph 13 thereof shall have effect—

(*a*) in the United Kingdom:

(i) as respects income tax (including surtax), for any year of assessment beginning on or after 6 April, 1968 ; and

(ii) as respects corporation tax, for any financial year beginning on or after 1 April, 1968 ;

(*b*) in Saint Vincent:

as respects income tax, for any year of assessment beginning on or after 1 January, 1968.

IN WITNESS WHEREOF the undersigned, duly authorised thereto, have signed this Agreement.

DONE in duplicate at Kingstown this 1st day of April 1968.

For the Government of the United Kingdom of Great Britain and Northern Ireland :	For the Government of Saint Vincent :
DESMOND M. KERR	S. E. SLATER

EXPLANATORY NOTE

(*This Note is not part of the Order.*)

This Agreement makes three amendments to the Arrangement between the United Kingdom and St. Vincent which is scheduled to the Double Taxation Relief (Taxes on Income) (St. Vincent) Order 1949.

First it provides that the exemption of dividends from any tax chargeable in addition to the tax on the paying company's profits is not to be allowed in certain cases where the shareholder is a company having a substantial holding in the paying company. The restriction does not apply to dividends on shares acquired for *bona fide* commercial reasons.

Secondly, it amends paragraph 13 of the 1949 Arrangement in its application to dividends by providing that credit for tax on the profits out of which dividends are paid, whether that tax is deducted from the dividends or not, is to be given only where the recipient is a company which holds not less than 10 per cent of the voting power in the paying company. So far as United Kingdom income tax is concerned this provision takes effect from the year of assessment 1968/69.

Thirdly, it provides that the Arrangement is not to apply to certain St. Vincent companies which enjoy special privileges under St. Vincent tax law.

STATUTORY INSTRUMENTS

1968 No. 1104

INCOME TAX

The Double Taxation Relief (Taxes on Income) (Sierra Leone) Order 1968

Laid before the House of Commons in draft

Made -   -   -   -   12*th July* 1968

At the Court at Buckingham Palace, the 12th day of July 1968.

Present,

The Queen's Most Excellent Majesty in Council

Whereas a draft of this Order was laid before the Commons House of Parliament in accordance with the provisions of section 347(6) of the Income Tax Act 1952(a), and an Address has been presented to Her Majesty by that House praying that an Order may be made in the terms of this Order:

Now, therefore, Her Majesty, in exercise of the powers conferred upon Her by section 347(1) of the said Income Tax Act 1952, as amended by section 64 of the Finance Act 1965(b), and of all other powers enabling Her in that behalf, is pleased, by and with the advice of Her Privy Council, to order, and it is hereby ordered, as follows:—

1. This Order may be cited as the Double Taxation Relief (Taxes on Income) (Sierra Leone) Order 1968.

2. It is hereby declared—

   (*a*) that the arrangements specified in the Agreement set out in the Schedule to this Order have been made with the Government of Sierra Leone with a view to affording relief from double taxation in relation to income tax or corporation tax and taxes of a similar character imposed by the laws of Sierra Leone varying the arrangements set out in the Schedule to the Double Taxation Relief (Taxes on Income) (Sierra Leone) Order 1947(c); and

   (*b*) that it is expedient that those arrangements should have effect.

W. G. Agnew.

(a) 15 & 16 Geo. 6 & 1 Eliz. 2. c. 10.   (b) 1965 c. 25.
(c) S.R. & O. 1947/2873 (Rev. X, p. 492: 1947 I, p. 1171).

SCHEDULE

AGREEMENT AMENDING THE ARRANGEMENT BETWEEN THE GOVERNMENT OF THE UNITED KINGDOM OF GREAT BRITAIN AND NORTHERN IRELAND AND THE GOVERNMENT OF SIERRA LEONE FOR THE AVOIDANCE OF DOUBLE TAXATION AND THE PREVENTION OF FISCAL EVASION WITH RESPECT TO TAXES ON INCOME

The Government of the United Kingdom of Great Britain and Northern Ireland and the Government of Sierra Leone,

Desiring to amend the Arrangement for the avoidance of double taxation and the prevention of fiscal evasion with respect to taxes on income in force between Her Majesty's Government and the Government of Sierra Leone immediately before 27 April, 1961, when Sierra Leone attained fully responsible status and continued in force since that date between the Government of the United Kingdom and the Government of Sierra Leone (hereinafter referred to as "the Arrangement"),

Have agreed as follows:

ARTICLE 1

The Arrangement shall be amended—

(a) by the deletion of paragraph 2(1)(b);

(b) by the substitution for the references therein to "the Colony", "Colonial enterprise" and "Colonial tax" of references to "Sierra Leone", "Sierra Leone enterprise" and "Sierra Leone tax" respectively;

(c) by the addition at the end of paragraph 6 of the following new sub-paragraph—

"(3) If the recipient of a dividend is a company which owns 10 per cent. or more of the class of shares in respect of which the dividend is paid then sub-paragraph (1) shall not apply to the dividend to the extent that it can have been paid only out of the profits which the company paying the dividend earned or other income which it received in a period ending twelve months or more before the relevant date. For the purposes of this sub-paragraph the term "relevant date" means the date on which the beneficial owner of the dividend became the owner of 10 per cent. or more of the class of shares in question. Provided that this sub-paragraph shall not apply if the beneficial owner of the dividend shows that the shares were acquired for *bona fide* commercial reasons and not primarily for the purpose of securing the benefit of this paragraph."; and

(d) by the substitution for sub-paragraphs (1) and (2) of paragraph 13 of the following new sub-paragraphs—

"(1) Subject to the provisions of the law of the United Kingdom regarding the allowance as a credit against United Kingdom tax of tax payable in a territory outside the United Kingdom (which shall not affect the general principle hereof)—

(a) Sierra Leone tax payable under the laws of Sierra Leone and in accordance with this Arrangement, whether directly or by deduction, on profits or income from sources within Sierra Leone shall be allowed as a credit against any United Kingdom tax computed by reference to the same profits or income by reference to which the Sierra Leone tax is computed. Provided that in the case of a dividend the credit shall only take into account such tax in respect thereof as is additional to any tax payable by the company on the profits out of which the dividend is paid and is ultimately borne by the recipient without reference to any tax so payable.

(b) Where a company which is a resident of Sierra Leone pays a dividend to a company resident in the United Kingdom which controls directly or indirectly at least 10 per cent. of the voting power in the first-mentioned company, the credit shall take into account (in addition to any Sierra Leone tax for which credit may be allowed under (a) of this sub-paragraph) the Sierra Leone tax payable by that first-mentioned company in respect of the profits out of which such dividend is paid.

(2) Subject to the provisions of the law of Sierra Leone regarding the allowance as a credit against Sierra Leone tax of tax payable in a territory outside Sierra Leone (which shall not affect the general principle hereof)—

(a) United Kingdom tax payable under the laws of the United Kingdom and in accordance with this Arrangement, whether directly or by deduction, on profits or income from sources within the United Kingdom shall be allowed as a credit against any Sierra Leone tax computed by reference to the same profits or income by reference to which the United Kingdom tax is computed. Provided that in the case of a dividend the credit shall only take into account such tax in respect thereof as is additional to any tax payable by the company on the profits out of which the dividend is paid and is ultimately borne by the recipient without reference to any tax so payable.

(b) Where a company which is a resident of the United Kingdom pays a dividend to a company resident in Sierra Leone which controls directly or indirectly at least 10 per cent. of the voting power in the first-mentioned company, the credit shall take into account (in addition to any United Kingdom tax for which credit may be allowed under (a) of this sub-paragraph) the United Kingdom tax payable by that first-mentioned company in respect of the profits out of which such dividend is paid."

ARTICLE 2

(1) This Agreement shall enter into force when the last of all such things shall have been done in the United Kingdom and Sierra Leone as are necessary to give the Agreement the force of law in the United Kingdom and Sierra Leone respectively.

(2) Upon the entry into force of this Agreement in accordance with paragraph (1) the new sub-paragraph (3) of paragraph 6 of the Arrangement shall have effect immediately and the new sub-paragraphs (1) and (2) of paragraph 13 of the Arrangement shall have effect—

(a) in the United Kingdom:

(i) as respects income tax (including surtax), for any year of assessment beginning on or after 6 April, 1968; and

(ii) as respects corporation tax, for any financial year beginning on or after 1 April, 1968;

(b) in Sierra Leone:

as respects income tax (including surtax), for any year of assessment beginning on or after 1 April, 1968.

IN WITNESS WHEREOF the undersigned, duly authorised thereto, have signed this Agreement.

DONE in duplicate at Freetown this 18th day of March 1968.

For the Government of
the United Kingdom
of Great Britain and
Northern Ireland:

For the Government of Sierra Leone:

S. J. G. FINGLAND

A. T. JUXON SMITH

EXPLANATORY NOTE

(This Note is not part of the Order.)

This Agreement makes two amendments to the Arrangement between the United Kingdom and Sierra Leone which is scheduled to the Double Taxation Relief (Taxes on Income) (Sierra Leone) Order 1947.

First it provides that the exemption of dividends from any tax chargeable in addition to the tax on the paying company's profits is not to be allowed in certain cases where the shareholder is a company having a substantial holding in the paying company. The restriction does not apply to dividends on shares acquired for *bona fide* commercial reasons.

Secondly, it amends paragraph 13 of the 1947 Arrangement in its application to dividends by providing that credit for tax on the profits out of which dividends are paid, whether that tax is deducted from the dividends or not, is to be given only where the recipient is a company which holds not less than 10 per cent of the voting power in the paying company. So far as United Kingdom income tax is concerned this provision takes effect from the year of assessment 1968/69.

STATUTORY INSTRUMENTS

1968 No. 1105

INCOME TAX

The Double Taxation Relief (Taxes on Income) (Sweden) Order 1968

Laid before the House of Commons in draft

Made - - - *12th July* 1968

At the Court at Buckingham Palace, the 12th day of July 1968

Present,

The Queen's Most Excellent Majesty in Council

Whereas a draft of this Order was laid before the Commons House of Parliament in accordance with the provisions of subsection (6) of section 347 of the Income Tax Act 1952(a), and an Address has been presented to Her Majesty by that House praying that an Order may be made in the terms of this Order:

Now, therefore, Her Majesty, in exercise of the powers conferred upon Her by subsection (1) of the said section 347, as amended by section 64 of the Finance Act 1965(b), and of all other powers enabling Her in that behalf, is pleased, by and with the advice of Her Privy Council, to order, and it is hereby ordered, as follows:—

1. This Order may be cited as the Double Taxation Relief (Taxes on Income) (Sweden) Order 1968.

2. It is hereby declared—

(a) that the arrangements specified in the Protocol set out in the Schedule to this Order have been made with the Government of the Kingdom of Sweden with a view to affording relief from double taxation in relation to income tax or corporation tax and taxes of a similar character imposed by the laws of Sweden varying the arrangements set out in the Schedule to the Double Taxation Relief (Taxes on Income) (Sweden) Order 1961(c); and

(b) that it is expedient that those arrangements should have effect.

W. G. Agnew.

(a) 15 & 16 Geo. 6 & 1 Eliz. 2. c. 10.   (b) 1965 c. 25.
(c) S.I. 1961/577 (1961 I, p. 1265).

SCHEDULE

PROTOCOL AMENDING THE CONVENTION BETWEEN THE GOVERNMENT OF THE
UNITED KINGDOM OF GREAT BRITAIN AND NORTHERN IRELAND AND
THE GOVERNMENT OF THE KINGDOM OF SWEDEN FOR THE AVOIDANCE OF
DOUBLE TAXATION AND THE PREVENTION OF FISCAL EVASION WITH
RESPECT TO TAXES ON INCOME SIGNED AT LONDON ON THE 28th JULY, 1960

The Government of the United Kingdom of Great Britain and Northern
Ireland and the Government of the Kingdom of Sweden;

Desiring to conclude a Protocol to amend the Convention between the
Contracting Parties for the Avoidance of Double Taxation and the
Prevention of Fiscal Evasion with respect to Taxes on Income, signed
at London on the 28th July, 1960 (hereinafter referred to as " the
Convention ");

Have agreed as follows:

ARTICLE I

(1) The proviso to paragraph (1) of Article XXIII of the Convention
(which proviso begins with the words " Where such income is an ordinary
dividend " and ends with the words " the dividend exceeds that fixed rate ")
shall be deleted and the following substituted;

" Where such income is a dividend paid by a company which is a resident
of Sweden to a company resident in the United Kingdom which controls
directly or indirectly not less than one-tenth of the voting power in the
former company, the credit shall take into account (in addition to any
Swedish tax payable in respect of the dividend) the Swedish tax payable
by that former company in respect of its profits."

(2) The proviso to paragraph (2) of Article XXIII of the Convention (which
proviso begins with the words " provided that where such income is a dividend "
and ends with the words " the dividend so charged ") shall be deleted and the
following substituted:

" provided that in the case of a dividend paid by a company which is
a resident of the United Kingdom to a resident of Sweden, not being a
company which is exempt from Swedish tax according to the provisions
of paragraph (2) of Article VII, tax may be imposed on the dividend by
Sweden."

ARTICLE II

(1) This Protocol shall be ratified and the instruments of ratification
shall be exchanged at Stockholm as soon as possible.

(2) This Protocol shall enter into force after the expiration of a month
following the date on which the instruments of ratification are exchanged(a)
and shall thereupon have effect:

(a) Instruments of ratification were exchanged on 20th June 1968.

(*a*) in the United Kingdom in relation only to dividends due and payable on or after 6th April, 1966 or on or after the date of entry into force of this Protocol (whichever is the later); and

(*b*) in Sweden in relation only to dividends due and payable on or after 6th April, 1966.

(3) This Protocol shall in relation to such dividends be regarded as an integral part of the Convention.

In witness whereof the undersigned, duly authorised thereto, have signed this Protocol.

Done in duplicate at London this 25th day of March, 1966, in the English and Swedish languages, both texts being equally authoritative.

For the Government of the United Kingdom of Great Britain and Northern Ireland:

WALSTON

For the Government of the Kingdom of Sweden:

GUNNAR HÄGGLÖF

EXPLANATORY NOTE
(This Note is not part of the Order.)

Paragraph (1) of Article XXIII of the Convention between the United Kingdom and Sweden which is scheduled to the Double Taxation Relief (Taxes on Income) (Sweden) Order 1961 provides that where an ordinary dividend is received from a Swedish company by a United Kingdom resident, credit is to be given for the Swedish tax borne by the company on the profits out of which it is paid. The Protocol provides that credit for the Swedish tax on the profits out of which the dividend is paid shall in future be given only where the dividend is received by a United Kingdom company which controls not less than one-tenth of the voting power in the Swedish company paying the dividend.

The proviso to paragraph (2) of Article XXIII of the Convention (which in general exempts from Swedish tax income taxed in the United Kingdom) permits, in certain cases, the taxation in Sweden of dividends from United Kingdom companies, but sets limits on the amount of tax that may be charged. The Protocol removes these limits.

The Protocol is expressed to take effect in the United Kingdom in relation to dividends due and payable on or after 6th April 1966 or on or after the entry into force of this Protocol, whichever is the later.

STATUTORY INSTRUMENTS

1968 No. 1106

INCOME TAX

The Double Taxation Relief (Taxes on Income) (Zambia) Order 1968

Laid before the House of Commons in draft

Made - - - *12th July* 1968

At the Court at Buckingham Palace, the 12th day of July 1968

Present,

The Queen's Most Excellent Majesty in Council

Whereas a draft of this Order was laid before the Commons House of Parliament in accordance with the provisions of section 347(6) of the Income Tax Act 1952(a), and an Address has been presented to Her Majesty by that House praying that an Order may be made in the terms of this Order :

Now, therefore, Her Majesty, in exercise of the powers conferred upon Her by section 347(1) of the said Income Tax Act 1952, as amended by section 64 of the Finance Act 1965(b), and of all other powers enabling Her in that behalf, is pleased, by and with the advice of Her Privy Council, to order, and it is hereby ordered, as follows :—

1. This Order may be cited as the Double Taxation Relief (Taxes on Income) (Zambia) Order 1968.

2. It is hereby declared—

(a) that the arrangements specified in the Agreement set out in the Schedule to this Order have been made with the Government of the Republic of Zambia with a view to affording relief from double taxation in relation to income tax or corporation tax and taxes of a similar character imposed by the laws of Zambia varying the arrangements set out in the Schedule to the Double Taxation Relief (Taxes on Income) (Federation of Rhodesia and Nyasaland) Order, 1956(c), as adapted and continued in force in relation to Zambia by the Double Taxation Relief (Taxes on Income) (Northern Rhodesia) Order 1964(d) ; and

(b) that it is expedient that those arrangements should have effect.

W. G. Agnew.

(a) 15 & 16 Geo. 6 & 1 Eliz. 2. c. 10.   (b) 1965 c. 25.
(c) S.I. 1956/619 (1956 I, p. 1072).   (d) S.I. 1964/1402 (1964 III, p. 3277).

SCHEDULE

AGREEMENT SUPPLEMENTARY TO AND AMENDING THE AGREEMENT BETWEEN THE GOVERNMENT OF THE UNITED KINGDOM OF GREAT BRITAIN AND NORTHERN IRELAND AND THE GOVERNMENT OF THE REPUBLIC OF ZAMBIA FOR THE AVOIDANCE OF DOUBLE TAXATION AND THE PREVENTION OF FISCAL EVASION WITH RESPECT TO TAXES ON INCOME

The Government of the United Kingdom of Great Britain and Northern Ireland and the Government of Zambia,

Desiring to amend the Agreement between the Government of the United Kingdom of Great Britain and Northern Ireland and the Government of the former Federation of Rhodesia and Nyasaland for the avoidance of double taxation and the prevention of fiscal evasion with respect to taxes on income signed at London on 25 November, 1955 (hereinafter referred to as "the 1955 Agreement") which continued with effect from the dissolution of the Federation of Rhodesia and Nyasaland on 1 January, 1964, in force, subject to certain modifications, between the Government of the United Kingdom and the Government of Northern Rhodesia and from 24 October, 1964, when Northern Rhodesia became an independent Republic under the name of Zambia, between the Government of the United Kingdom and the Government of Zambia,

Have agreed as follows:

ARTICLE 1

The 1955 Agreement shall be amended—

(a) by the addition at the end of Article VI of the following new paragraph—

"(3) If the recipient of a dividend is a company which owns 10 per cent. or more of the class of shares in respect of which the dividend is paid then paragraph (1) shall not apply to the dividend to the extent that it can have been paid only out of profits which the company paying the dividend earned or other income which it received in a period ending twelve months or more before the relevant date. For the purposes of this paragraph the term "relevant date" means the date on which the beneficial owner of the dividend became the owner of 10 per cent. or more of the class of shares in question. Provided that this paragraph shall not apply if the beneficial owner of the dividend shows that the shares were acquired for *bona fide* commercial reasons and not primarily for the purpose of securing the benefit of this paragraph." ; and

(b) by the substitution for paragraph (1) of Article XIII of the following new paragraph—

"(1) Subject to the provisions of the law of the United Kingdom regarding the allowance as a credit against United Kingdom tax of tax payable in a territory outside the United Kingdom (which shall not affect the general principle hereof)—

(a) Zambia tax payable under the laws of Zambia and in accordance with this Agreement, whether directly or by deduction, on profits or income from sources within Zambia shall be allowed as a credit against any United Kingdom tax computed by reference to the same profits or income by reference to which the Zambia tax is computed. Provided that in the case of a dividend the credit shall only take into account such tax in respect thereof as is additional to any tax payable by the company on the profits out of which the dividend is paid and is ultimately borne by the recipient without reference to any tax so payable.

(b) Where a company which is a resident of Zambia pays a dividend to a company resident in the United Kingdom which controls directly or indirectly at least 10 per cent. of the voting power in the first-mentioned company, the credit shall take into account (in addition to any Zambia tax for which credit may be allowed under sub-paragraph (*a*)) the Zambia tax payable by that first-mentioned company in respect of the profits out of which such dividend is paid."

ARTICLE 2

(1) This Agreement shall enter into force when the last of all such things shall have been done in the United Kingdom and Zambia as are necessary to give the Agreement the force of law in the United Kingdom and Zambia respectively.

(2) Upon the entry into force of this Agreement in accordance with paragraph (1) the new paragraph (3) of Article VI of the 1955 Agreement shall have effect immediately and the new paragraph (1) of Article XIII thereof shall have effect—

(*a*) in the United Kingdom:

(i) as respects income tax (and surtax), for any year of assessment beginning on or after 6 April, 1968 ; and

(ii) as respects corporation tax, for any financial year beginning on or after 1 April, 1968 ;

(*b*) in Zambia:

as respects income tax, for any charge year beginning on or after 1 April, 1968.

IN WITNESS WHEREOF the undersigned, duly authorised thereto, have signed this Agreement.

DONE in duplicate at Lusaka this sixth day of April 1968.

For the Government of the United Kingdom of Great Britain and Northern Ireland:

J. L. PUMPHREY

For the Government of the Republic of Zambia:

R. KAMANGA

EXPLANATORY NOTE

(This Note is not part of the Order.)

This Agreement makes two amendments to the Agreement between the United Kingdom and the Federation of Rhodesia and Nyasaland, subsequently continued in force with Zambia, which is scheduled to the Double Taxation Relief (Taxes on Income) (Federation of Rhodesia and Nyasaland) Order 1956.

First it provides that the exemption of dividends from any tax chargeable in addition to the tax on the paying company's profits is not to be allowed in certain cases where the shareholder is a company having a substantial holding in the paying company. The restriction does not apply to dividends on shares acquired for *bona fide* commercial reasons.

Secondly, it amends Article XIII(1) of the 1956 Agreement in its application to dividends by providing that credit for Zambia tax on the profits out of which dividends are paid, whether that tax is deducted from the dividends or not, is to be given only where the recipient is a company resident in the United Kingdom which holds not less than 10 per cent of the voting power in the paying company. This provision takes effect from the year of assessment 1968/69.

STATUTORY INSTRUMENTS

1968 No. 1108 (C. 14)

MERCHANT SHIPPING

SAFETY

The Merchant Shipping (Load Lines) Act 1967 (Commencement) Order 1968

Made - - -	*12th July* 1968
Laid before Parliament	*18th July* 1968
Coming into Operation	*21st July* 1968

At the Court at Buckingham Palace, the 12th day of July 1968

Present,

The Queen's Most Excellent Majesty in Council

Her Majesty, in pursuance of the power conferred upon Her by section 34(3) of the Merchant Shipping (Load Lines) Act 1967(a), is pleased, by and with the advice of Her Privy Council, to order, and it is hereby ordered, as follows:—

1. The Merchant Shipping (Load Lines) Act 1967, except section 25 and Schedule 1, shall come into operation on 21st July 1968.

2. This Order may be cited as the Merchant Shipping (Load Lines) Act 1967 (Commencement) Order 1968, and shall come into operation on 21st July 1968.

W. G. Agnew.

EXPLANATORY NOTE

(*This Note is not part of the Order.*)

This Order brings into operation on 21st July 1968 the Merchant Shipping (Load Lines) Act 1967, except section 25 and Schedule 1 which came into force on the passing of the Act. The Act enables the United Kingdom to give effect to the International Convention on Load Lines 1966 (Cmnd. 3070) which comes into force on that date.

(a) 1967 c. 27.

STATUTORY INSTRUMENTS

1968 No. 1109

MERCHANT SHIPPING

SAFETY

The Merchant Shipping (Load Lines Convention) (Various Countries) Order 1968

Made - - - -	*12th July* 1968
Laid before Parliament -	*18th July* 1968
Coming into Operation	*21st July* 1968

At the Court at Buckingham Palace, the 12th day of July 1968

Present,

The Queen's Most Excellent Majesty in Council

Whereas by section 31(1) of the Merchant Shipping (Load Lines) Act 1967(a) it is enacted that Her Majesty may, if satisfied that the Government of any country has accepted or acceded to the International Convention on Load Lines 1966, by Order in Council make a declaration to that effect:

And Whereas Her Majesty is satisfied that the Governments of the countries specified in the Schedule hereto have accepted or acceded to the said Convention:

Now, therefore, Her Majesty in pursuance of the powers conferred upon Her by the said section 31(1) and of all other powers enabling Her in that behalf is pleased, by and with the advice of Her Privy Council, to order, and it is hereby ordered, as follows:—

1. It is hereby declared that the Governments of the countries specified in the Schedule to this Order have accepted or acceded to the International Convention on Load Lines 1966.

2. This Order may be cited as the Merchant Shipping (Load Lines Convention) (Various Countries) Order 1968, and shall come into operation on 21st July 1968.

W. G. Agnew.

(a) 1967 c. 27.

SCHEDULE

The United Kingdom of Great Britain and Northern Ireland
Kingdom of Denmark
French Republic
Republic of India
State of Israel
Italian Republic
Republic of Liberia
Malagasy Republic
Maldive Islands
Islamic Republic of Mauritania
Kingdom of Morocco
Kingdom of the Netherlands
    Surinam and Netherlands Antilles
Kingdom of Norway
Republic of Panama
Republic of Peru
Somali Republic
Republic of South Africa
Kingdom of Sweden
Swiss Confederation
Trinidad and Tobago
Tunisian Republic
United States of America
Union of Soviet Socialist Republics

STATUTORY INSTRUMENTS

1968 No. 1110

MERCHANT SHIPPING

SAFETY

The Merchant Shipping (Load Line Certificates) (Various Countries) Order 1968

Made - - - -	12*th July* 1968
Laid before Parliament	18*th July* 1968
Coming into Operation	21*st July* 1968

At the Court at Buckingham Palace, the 12th day of July 1968

Present,

The Queen's Most Excellent Majesty in Council

Whereas by section 28(3) of the Merchant Shipping (Load Lines) Act 1967(a) (hereinafter called "the Act") it is enacted that if, in the case of any country or territory outside the United Kingdom, it appears to Her Majesty in Council:—

(*a*) that the provisions which, as part of the law of that country or territory, have effect for marking ships with load lines, and for the issue of certificates in respect of ships so marked, are based on the same principles as the corresponding provisions of the Act and are equally effective, and

(*b*) that provision has been or in pursuance of any agreement will be made by the law of that country or territory for recognising United Kingdom load line certificates as having the like effect in ports of that country or territory as certificates issued under the said first-mentioned provisions,

Her Majesty may by Order in Council direct (subject to section 28(4) of the Act) that certificates issued under those provisions shall have the like effect for the purposes of the Act as if they were United Kingdom load line certificates:

And whereas it appears to Her Majesty in Council that the above-mentioned conditions are satisfied in relation to each of the countries specified in the Schedule to this Order:

Now, therefore, Her Majesty in pursuance of the powers conferred upon Her by the said section 28(3) and of all other powers enabling Her in that behalf, is pleased, by and with the advice of Her Privy Council, to order, and it is hereby ordered, as follows:—

1. A load line certificate issued in respect of a ship registered in or flying the flag of a country specified in the Schedule to this Order being a certificate issued in pursuance of the aforesaid provisions in force as part of the law of that country for marking ships with load lines and for the issue of certificates in respect of ships so marked, shall, subject to the provisions of section 28(4) of the Act, have the like effect for the purposes of the Act as if it was a United Kingdom load line certificate.

2.—(1) The Interpretation Act 1889(b) shall apply to the interpretation of this Order as it applies to the interpretation of an Act of Parliament.

(a) 1967 c. 27.   (b) 1889 c. 63.

(2) This Order may be cited as the Merchant Shipping (Load Line Certificates) (Various Countries) Order 1968 and shall come into operation on 21st July 1968.

W. G. Agnew.

SCHEDULE

Kingdom of Denmark

French Republic

Republic of India

Kingdom of the Netherlands
    Surinam and Netherlands Antilles

Kingdom of Norway

Kingdom of Sweden

EXPLANATORY NOTE

(This Note is not part of the Order.)

This Order is made under section 28(3) of the Merchant Shipping (Load Lines) Act 1967 and provides for the recognition of load line certificates issued by the countries specified in the Schedule. The Order is subject to section 28(4) of the Act. This precludes its application to ships to which the International Convention on Load Lines 1966 applies, and for which separate provision is made in the Act.

STATUTORY INSTRUMENTS

1968 No. 1111

ROAD TRAFFIC

The Motor Vehicles (International Circulation) (Amendment) Order 1968

Laid before Parliament in draft

Made - - -	*12th July* 1968
Coming into Operation	*(On a date to be notified in the London Gazette)*

At the Court at Buckingham Palace, the 12th day of July 1968

Present,

The Queen's Most Excellent Majesty in Council

Whereas a draft of this Order has in pursuance of section 1(5) of the Motor Vehicles (International Circulation) Act 1952(a) been laid before Parliament and approved by resolution of each House of Parliament :

Now, therefore, Her Majesty, in pursuance of section 1 of the Motor Vehicles (International Circulation) Act 1952 is pleased, by and with the advice of Her Privy Council, to order, and it is hereby ordered, as follows :—

Citation and commencement

1. This Order may be cited as the Motor Vehicles (International Circulation) (Amendment) Order 1968 and shall come into operation on the same date on which the Goods Vehicles (Exemption from Duties) Agreements are both first in force for the United Kingdom, which date shall be notified in the London Gazette.

Interpretation

2.—(1) In this Order—

"the principal Order" means the Motor Vehicles (International Circulation) Order 1957(b), as varied by the Motor Vehicles (International Circulation) (Amendment) Order 1962(c) ;

"Goods Vehicles (Exemption from Duties) Agreements" means agreements between the United Kingdom and Sweden or Turkey whereby provision is made on a reciprocal basis for exempting a vehicle registered in one country

---

(a) 15 & 16 Geo. 6. & 1 Eliz. 2. c. 39.   (b) S.I. 1957/1074 (1957 II, p. 2154).
(c) S.I. 1962/1344 (1962 II, p. 1483).

party to the agreement from taxes and charges payable in respect of the circulation or the possession of the vehicle while temporarily used for the purpose of the carriage of goods in the other country party to the agreement.

(2) The Interpretation Act 1889(a) shall apply for the interpretation of this Order as it applies for the interpretation of an Act of Parliament.

Amendment of principal Order

3. In relation to a vehicle registered in a country outside the United Kingdom with which country there is in force a Goods Vehicles (Exemption from Duties) Agreement, Article 5 of the principal Order, as substituted by the Motor Vehicles (International Circulation) (Amendment) Order 1962, shall have effect as though in sub-paragraph (iv) of paragraph (2) of that Article there were omitted the words from "and shall be used" to the end of that sub-paragraph.

W. G. Agnew.

EXPLANATORY NOTE

(*This Note is not part of the Order.*)

Article 5 of the Motor Vehicles (International Circulation) Order 1957, as amended, inter alia grants exemption from duty under the Vehicles (Excise) Act 1962 of goods vehicles brought temporarily into Great Britain, subject to certain conditions, one of which is that such a vehicle shall not be used for reward or in connection with a trade or business. This Order amends Article 5 so as to exempt from compliance with the last mentioned condition vehicles registered in a foreign country with which there is in force a Goods Vehicles (Exemption from Duties) Agreement as defined in Article 2 of this Order. The Agreement between the United Kingdom and Sweden has been issued as Cmnd. 3606 and the Agreement between the United Kingdom and Turkey has been issued as Cmnd. 3672.

(a) 52 & 53 Vict. c. 63.

STATUTORY INSTRUMENTS

1968 No. 1116

MERCHANT SHIPPING

SAFETY

The Merchant Shipping (Load Lines) (Exemption) Order 1968

Made - - -		*12th July* 1968
Laid before Parliament		*19th July* 1968
Coming into Operation		*21st July* 1968

The Board of Trade in exercise of their powers under section 18(2) of the Merchant Shipping (Load Lines) Act 1967(a) and of all other powers enabling them in that behalf hereby make the following Order:—

1.—(1) Ships under 80 tons register engaged solely in the coasting trade, being ships of the following classes, shall be exempt from the provisions of the Act while not carrying cargo:—

    (a) tugs and salvage ships;

    (b) ships engaged in the surveying of harbours or the approaches thereto;

    (c) hopper barges and dredgers;

    (d) ships which are pilot boats within the meaning of section 38 of the Pilotage Act 1913(b);

    (e) ships used by or on behalf of—

        (i) a general or local lighthouse authority for the purpose of the authority's functions as such;

        (ii) a Government department for fishery protection purposes, or a local fishery committee for the regulation of sea fisheries within its district;

        (iii) a Government department for fishery or scientific research;

        (iv) the Secretary of State for Defence for the purpose of ensuring safety in the use of firing ranges or weapons at sea;

    (f) sailing ships;

    (g) ships in respect of which passenger steamer certificates are in force specifying limits beyond which the ship must not ply, and which operate solely within those limits;

    (h) ships carrying not more than 12 passengers on voyages in the course of which they are at no time more than 15 miles (exclusive of any smooth waters) from the point of departure or more than 3 miles from land.

(2) Ships coming within class (g) in paragraph (1) of this Article shall also be exempt from the provisions of the Act while carrying cargo in accordance with the terms, if any, of the ship's passenger steamer certificate expressly authorising the carriage of cargo.

(a) 1967 c. 27.   (b) 1913 (2 & 3 Geo. 5) c. 31.

2.—(1) In this Order—

"local fisheries committee" means a local fisheries committee constituted under the Sea Fisheries Regulation Act 1966**(a)**;

"sailing ship" means a ship designed to carry sail, whether as the sole means of propulsion or as a supplementary means;

"smooth waters" has the meaning assigned to it in the rules **(b)** made under section 1 of the Merchant Shipping (Safety Convention) Act 1949**(c)** as amended by section 8 of the Merchant Shipping Act 1964**(d)**.

(2) The Interpretation Act 1889**(e)** shall apply to the interpretation of this Order as it applies to the interpretation of an Act of Parliament.

(3) This Order may be cited as the Merchant Shipping (Load Lines) (Exemption) Order 1968 and shall come into operation on 21st July 1968.

12th July 1968

William Rodgers,
Minister of State,
Board of Trade.

EXPLANATORY NOTE
(*This Note is not part of the Order.*)

This Order exempts from the provisions of the Merchant Shipping (Load Lines) Act 1967 classes of ships under 80 tons register engaged solely in the coasting trade, while not carrying cargo, and passenger steamers under 80 tons register so engaged while carrying cargo in accordance with the terms of their passenger steamer certificates.

(a) 1966 c. 38.   **(b)** See S.I. 1965/1103 (1965 II, p. 2826).
     (c) 1949 c. 43.   **(d)** 1964 c. 47.
       (e) 1889 c. 63.

STATUTORY INSTRUMENTS

1968 No. 1117

MERCHANT SHIPPING

SAFETY

The Merchant Shipping (Load Lines) (Fees) Regulations 1968

Made - - -		12*th July* 1968
Laid before Parliament		19*th July* 1968
Coming into Operation		21*st July* 1968

The Board of Trade with the approval of the Treasury and in exercise of their powers under section 26 of the Merchant Shipping (Load Lines) Act 1967(a) and of all other powers enabling them in that behalf hereby make the following Regulations :—

1. The fee payable in respect of—

(1) the survey of a ship carried out pursuant to the Merchant Shipping (Load Line) Rules 1968(b) with a view to the issue of a load line certificate or a load line exemption certificate ; and

(2) the periodical inspection pursuant to the said rules of a ship for which such a certificate is in force

shall, subject to Regulation 4, be the appropriate standard fee specified in the table in Part I of the Schedule to these Regulations.

2. The fee payable in respect of the inspection of a ship with a view to the issue of a load line certificate under Regulation 3 of the Merchant Shipping (Load Lines) (Transitional Provisions) Regulations 1968(c) shall be the same as that for a periodical inspection specified in Regulation 1(2).

3. The fee in the case of a survey specified in Regulation 1(1) or an inspection specified in Regulation 2 shall cover the issue of a load line certificate or a load line exemption certificate following the survey or inspection, as the case may be, and in the case of a periodical inspection specified in Regulation 1(2) shall cover the endorsement of a certificate following the inspection.

4. The standard fee shall be adjusted in accordance with Part II of the Schedule to these Regulations.

5.—(1) In these Regulations—

"the Act" means the Merchant Shipping (Load Lines) Act 1967 ;
"the 1932 Act" means the Merchant Shipping (Safety and Load Line Conventions) Act 1932(d) ;
"Assigning Authority" means a body which is an Assigning Authority for the purpose of the load line rules for the time being in force under the Act ;
"a classed ship" means a ship which has been surveyed by or on behalf of an Assigning Authority (other than the Board) and has, following such survey, been classified by that authority in accordance with standards set for ships by it and remains so classified at the date of the survey or inspection for which the relevant fee is payable ;

(a) 1967 c. 27. (b) S.I. 1968/1053 (1968 II, p. 2774).
(c) S.I. 1968/1052 (1968 II, p. 2769). (d) 1932 c. 9.

"unclassed ship" means a ship which is not a classed ship ;

"tons" means tons gross tonnage and the gross tonnage of ships having alternative gross tonnages shall be taken to be the larger of those tonnages.

(2) The Interpretation Act 1889(a) shall apply to the interpretation of these Regulations as it applies to the interpretation of an Act of Parliament.

6. These Regulations may be cited as the Merchant Shipping (Load Lines) (Fees) Regulations 1968 and shall come into force on 21st July 1968.

William Rodgers,
Minister of State,
Board of Trade.

12th July 1968.

We approve the making of these Regulations.

B. K. O'Malley,
J. McCann,
Two of the Lords Commissioners of
Her Majesty's Treasury.

12th July 1968.

SCHEDULE

PART I

TABLE OF STANDARD FEES

	Fees			
	Classed Ships		Unclassed Ships	
	1	2	3	4
Ship's Tonnage	Survey	Periodical Inspection	Survey	Periodical Inspection
	£ s.	£ s.	£ s.	£ s.
Under 50 tons	15 3	6 18	34 10	5 10
50 tons and under 150	17 18	6 18	68 15	9 13
150 „ „ „ 300	27 10	9 13	92 5	12 8
300 „ „ „ 500	34 10	12 8	124 0	16 10
500 „ „ „ 1,000	42 15	15 3	160 0	22 0
1,000 „ „ „ 1,500	53 15	19 5	207 0	27 10
1,500 „ „ „ 2,000	60 10	20 13	237 0	33 0
2,000 „ „ „ 2,500	67 10	23 8	270 0	33 0
2,500 „ „ „ 3,000	74 5	26 3	302 0	37 5
3,000 „ „ „ 4,000	78 10	27 10	333 0	42 15
4,000 „ „ „ 5,000	88 0	27 10	366 0	42 15
5,000 „ „ „ 6,000	95 0	27 10	399 0	42 15
6,000 „ „ „ 7,000	102 0	29 0	429 0	42 15
7,000 „ „ „ 8,000	106 0	29 0	462 0	42 15
8,000 „ „ „ 9,000	110 0	30 5	495 0	42 15
9,000 „ „ „ 10,000	113 0	33 0	528 0	42 15
10,000 tons and above ...	113 0	33 0	561 0	42 15
			Plus £33 for every 1,000 tons or part of 1,000 tons by which the tonnage exceeds 10,999 tons.	

(a) 1889 c. 63.

PART II

ADJUSTMENTS OF STANDARD FEES

A. SURVEYS

Periodical surveys of ships which have previously held certificates

1.—(1) In the case of a periodical survey of a classed ship the standard fee shall, except in a case to which sub-paragraph (2) of this paragraph applies, be reduced by one half.

(2) Where the periodical survey of a classed ship is carried out by a surveyor on behalf of an Assigning Authority other than the Board at the same time as a special survey of the ship for classification purposes for which a fee is charged by that Authority, the standard fee shall be that which would be appropriate for a periodical inspection of the ship.

(3) In this paragraph "periodical survey" means a survey of a ship in respect of which there is in force at the time of the survey, or was in force immediately before that time, a load line certificate or a load line exemption certificate issued by or on behalf of the Board under the Act or the 1932 Act.

Survey carried out concurrently with other surveys

2.—(1) Where a survey of a ship is carried out by a surveyor appointed by the Board concurrently with—

    (*a*) a survey of the ship for a Passenger Steamer Certificate or a Passenger and Safety Certificate—
        (i) in the case of a classed ship, no fee shall be payable ;
        (ii) in the case of an unclassed ship the fee shall be one half that which would otherwise be payable ;

    (*b*) a survey of the ship (whether classed or unclassed) for the issue of a Cargo Ship Safety Construction Certificate, the fee shall be one half that which would otherwise be payable.

(2) No additional fee shall be payable under paragraph 5 or paragraph 6 of this Schedule in any case to which sub-paragraph (1)(*a*) of this paragraph applies.

Survey where alterations do not necessitate a complete survey

3. Where, in the case of a survey of a ship (whether classed or unclassed) in respect of which a load line certificate under the 1932 Act or under the Act, or a load line exemption certificate is in force, alterations have been made to the ship which involve the assignment of new freeboards but are not such as to necessitate a complete survey of the ship for that purpose, the standard fee shall be that which would be appropriate for a periodical inspection of the ship, and as if the ship had, in any event, been a classed ship.

Partial survey carried out afloat for issue of short-term certificates

4. Where a survey other than a complete survey is carried out on a ship afloat (whether classed or unclassed) for the purpose of the issue in respect of the ship of a certificate valid for a period not exceeding 12 months, the standard fee shall be reduced by one half.

Additional fee when survey involves inquiry into stability

5.—(1) In the case of the survey of a ship which is required to comply with the requirements of Schedule 4 to the Merchant Shipping (Load Line) Rules 1968 relating to stability there shall, subject to sub-paragraph (2) of this paragraph, be paid an additional fee of £60 plus £1 for every metre, if any, by which the length of the ship exceeds 24 metres subject to a maximum additional fee of £400.

(2) No additional fee shall be paid under this paragraph if—
    (*a*) the ship has been previously surveyed under the said rules and was at the time of that survey required to comply with the above-mentioned requirements relating to stability, and

(*b*) no changes have been made in the ship since that survey which involve a re-examination of whether the ship continues to comply with those requirements.

Additional fee where survey involves calculations relating to floodability

6. Where in the case of a ship of more than 100 metres in length a survey involves calculations for the purposes of Schedule 5 of the Merchant Shipping (Load Line) Rules 1968 as to the ability of the ship to withstand the flooding of compartments, there shall be paid an additional fee of £150.

B. PERIODICAL INSPECTIONS

Additional fees for periodical inspections

7.—(1) Where the periodical inspection of a ship of over 300 tons (whether classed or unclassed) is completed in one operation but requires two or more visits to the ship by the surveyor, there shall be paid an additional fee of £11.

(2) Where the periodical inspection of a ship (whether classed or unclassed) is not completed in one operation there shall be paid—
    (*a*) an additional fee of £11 for each part of the inspection, and
    (*b*) if the ship is over 300 tons and any part of the inspection requires two or more visits to the ship by the surveyor, a further additional fee of £11 in respect of each such part.

(3) An inspection shall be taken for the purposes of this paragraph to be completed in one operation if it is completed within one day, or within a period of successive days (excluding Sundays or public holidays) on each of which one or more visits to the ship are paid by the surveyor.

(4) Where for the purposes of an inspection it is necessary for the surveyor to revisit the ship for the sole purpose of checking the rectification of defects found at an earlier stage of the inspection and on that visit those defects are found to be rectified, such visit shall not be taken into account for the purposes of this paragraph.

(5) Where the periodical inspection of a ship is not completed in one operation but the fact that it is not so completed is in no way attributable to failure by the owner to have the ship available for inspection at any time after the commencement of the inspection, sub-paragraph (2) of this paragraph shall not be applicable.

Remission of fee where periodical inspection carried out concurrently with certain surveys

8. Where the periodical inspection of a ship is carried out by a surveyor appointed by the Board at the same time as—
    (1) survey of the ship for the issue of a Passenger Steamer Certificate or a Passenger and Safety Certificate, or
    (2) any intermediate survey of the ship required under the cargo ship construction and survey rules made under the Merchant Shipping Act 1964(**a**)
no fee shall be payable in respect of that inspection.

EXPLANATORY NOTE
(*This Note is not part of the Regulations.*)

These Regulations prescribe the fees payable for inspections and surveys carried out in pursuance of the Merchant Shipping (Load Lines) Act 1967 and the Rules made thereunder.

(**a**) 1964 c. 47.

STATUTORY INSTRUMENTS

1968 No. 1118

SOCIAL SECURITY

The Supplementary Benefit (Determination of Requirements) Regulations 1968

Laid before Parliament in draft

Made	-	-	-	-	15*th July* 1968
Coming into Operation				7*th October* 1968

Whereas a draft of the following regulations was laid before Parliament and approved by resolution of each House of Parliament:

Now, therefore, the Minister of Social Security, with the consent of the Treasury, in exercise of the powers conferred by section 5 of the Ministry of Social Security Act 1966(a), and of all other powers enabling her in that behalf, hereby makes the following regulations:—

Citation, commencement and interpretation

1.—(1) These regulations may be cited as the Supplementary Benefit (Determination of Requirements) Regulations 1968 and shall come into operation on 7th October 1968.

(2) In these regulations, unless the context otherwise requires, "the Act" means the Ministry of Social Security Act 1966(a) and other expressions have the same meaning as in the Act.

(3) The rules for the construction of Acts of Parliament contained in the Interpretation Act 1889(b) shall apply for the purpose of the interpretation of these regulations as they apply for the purpose of the interpretation of an Act of Parliament.

Amendment of calculation of requirements

2.—(1) Schedule 2 to the Act shall be varied in accordance with the following provisions of this regulation.

(2) For paragraph 9 of the said Schedule, as varied(c), (which provides the scale for computing normal requirements) there shall be substituted the following paragraph:—

" 9. Requirements of persons other than blind persons—

	£	s.	d.
(*a*) husband and wife or other persons falling within paragraph 3(1) of this Schedule	7	9	0
(*b*) person living alone or householder not falling within sub-paragraph (*a*) of this paragraph who is directly responsible for household necessities and rent (if any)	4	11	0
(*c*) any other person aged—			
(i) not less than 21 years	3	14	0
(ii) less than 21 but not less than 18 years ...	3	1	0
(iii) less than 18 but not less than 16 years ...	2	13	0
(iv) less than 16 but not less than 13 years ...	2	1	0
(v) less than 13 but not less than 11 years ...	1	19	0
(vi) less than 11 but not less than 5 years ...	1	12	0
(vii) less than 5 years	1	7	0 "

(a) 1966 c. 20.   (b) 1889 c. 63.   (c) S.I. 1967/1127 (1967 II, p. 3287).

(3) For paragraph 10 of the said Schedule, as varied(**a**), (which provides the scale for computing the requirements of blind persons) there shall be substituted the following paragraph :—

" 10. Requirements of persons who are or include blind persons—

	£	s.	d.
(*a*) husband and wife or other persons falling within paragraph 3(1) of this Schedule—			
(i) if one of them blind	8	13	6
(ii) if both of them blind	9	9	6
(*b*) any other blind person aged—			
(i) not less than 21 years	5	15	6
(ii) less than 21 but not less than 18 years ...	4	1	0
(iii) less than 18 but not less than 16 years ...	3	9	0
(iv) less than 16 but not less than 13 years ...	2	1	0
(v) less than 13 but not less than 11 years ...	1	19	0
(vi) less than 11 but not less than 5 years ...	1	12	0
(vii) less than 5 years	1	7	0 "

(4) In paragraphs 11 and 12 of the said Schedule (which provide for additional requirements respectively of persons in receipt of supplementary pension and certain persons in receipt of supplementary allowance) for the sum " 9s. 0d." there shall be substituted the sum " 10s. 0d.".

(5) In paragraph 13(1)(*b*) of the said Schedule (which provides for an increase in the requirements of non-householders aged 18 or over) for the sum " 10 shillings " there shall be substituted the sum " 11 shillings ".

Judith Hart,
Minister of Social Security.

12th July 1968.

We consent,

Harry Gourlay,
Joseph Harper,
Two of the Lords Commissioners
of Her Majesty's Treasury.

15th July 1968.

EXPLANATORY NOTE

(This Note is not part of the Regulations.)

These regulations provide for increases in the weekly sums allowed in calculating requirements for the purpose of determining entitlement to supplementary pension or allowance.

(a) S.I. 1967/1127 (1967 II, p. 3287).

STATUTORY INSTRUMENTS

1968 No. 1120

PENSIONS

The Superannuation (Teaching and Public Boards) Interchange Rules 1968

Made - - -	*12th July* 1968
Laid before Parliament	*24th July* 1968
Coming into Operation	*25th July* 1968

The Secretary of State for Education and Science, with the consent of the Treasury, in exercise of the powers conferred on him by sections 2 and 15 of the Superannuation (Miscellaneous Provisions) Act 1948(**a**), as amended by the Superannuation (Miscellaneous Provisions) Act 1967(**b**), hereby makes the following Rules:—

PART I

GENERAL

Citation and Commencement

1. These Rules may be cited as the Superannuation (Teaching and Public Boards) Interchange Rules 1968 and shall come into operation on 25th July 1968.

Revocation

2.—(1) The Superannuation (Teaching and Public Boards) Interchange Rules 1965(**c**) are hereby revoked:

Provided that the Rules hereby revoked shall continue to apply in relation to any person who, before the beginning of April 1967, became employed in contributory service or in public board employment within the meaning of those Rules in like manner as they would have applied if these Rules had not been made.

(2) Section 38(2) of the Interpretation Act 1889(**d**) (which relates to the effect of repeals) shall have effect in relation to the Rules revoked by this rule as if they were an enactment repealed by an Act.

Interpretation

3.—(1) In these Rules, unless the context otherwise requires—

" the Act of 1948 " means the Superannuation (Miscellaneous Provisions) Act 1948;

" contributing service ", " non-contributing service " and " contributory employee " have the same respective meanings as in the Local Government Superannuation Acts 1937 to 1953(**e**);

(**a**) 1948 c. 33. (**b**) 1967 c. 28.
(**c**) S.I. 1965/1023 (1965 I, p. 2483). (**d**) 1889 c. 63.
(**e**) 1937 c. 68; 1939 c. 18; 1953 c. 25.

" national service " means, in relation to any person, service which is relevant service within the meaning of the Reserve and Auxiliary Forces (Protection of Civil Interests) Act 1951(a) and any similar service immediately following relevant service entered into with the consent of the body or person by whom he was last employed before undertaking the service;

" operative date " means the date of the coming into operation of these Rules;

" pension " has the meaning assigned to it by the Act of 1948;

" pension authority " means the persons or body administering the public board pension scheme to which a person either becomes subject after ceasing to be employed in teaching service or, as the case may be, was last subject before he became employed in teaching service;

" prescribed period " has the meaning assigned to that expression by rule 4;

" public board " means a body named in a Schedule to these Rules;

" public board employment " means employment in respect of which a public board pension scheme makes provision for pensions;

" public board pension scheme " means a scheme by which provision is made for pensions for persons employed by a public board;

" reckonable service " means such service as is by virtue of the Teachers' Regulations reckonable service for all the purposes of Part I of the Teachers' Superannuation Act 1967(b);

" repaid contributions " means any sum paid to a person under the Teachers (Superannuation) Acts 1918 to 1956, the Teachers' Regulations or a public board pension scheme by way of repayment of contributions (other than voluntary contributions and contributions made or deemed to be made for the purpose of securing benefits for a widow, children or other dependants); and includes both any interest included in such sum and any amount deducted therefrom in respect of income tax;

" the Secretary of State " means the Secretary of State for Education and Science;

" the Teachers' Regulations " means the Teachers' Superannuation Regulations 1967(c);

" teaching service " means—

    (a) reckonable service;

    (b) service which for the purposes of the Teachers' Regulations is service as an organiser, a teacher in an admitted school, a services civilian teacher or a services education officer; and

    (c) service as a part-time teacher within the meaning of the Teachers' (Part-time) Superannuation Regulations 1967(d);

" the Transfer Value Regulations " means the Local Government Superannuation (Transfer Value) Regulations 1954(e);

" voluntary contributions " means—

    (a) in relation to employment in teaching service, additional contributions being paid under section 19 of the Teachers (Superannuation) Act 1956(f) or regulation 32 of the Teachers' Regulations in respect of a period of previous employment and any contributions being paid as a condition of actual service being increased by the addition thereto

---

(a) 1951 c. 65.   (b) 1967 c. 12.
(c) S.I. 1967/489 (1967 I, p. 1562).   (d) S.I. 1967/1286 (1967 II, p. 3721).
(e) S.I. 1954/1212 (1954 II, p. 1723). (f) 1956 c. 53.

of any other period (not being a period of war service or national service); and

(b) in relation to public board employment, payments (other than completed payments, that is to say, payments made in respect of a liability which has been wholly discharged) being made as a condition of—

(i) any period (not being a period of war service or national service) being added to actual employment and treated as pensionable; or

(ii) any period of employment being reckoned for the purpose of calculating benefits or being so reckoned at a value greater than that at which it would otherwise be reckonable.

(2) For the purposes of these Rules a person to whom a public board pension Scheme applies shall be deemed to be employed by the public board for persons employed by which that scheme makes provision for pensions.

(3) Any reference in these Rules to the provisions of any enactment, rules, regulations or other instrument shall, unless the context otherwise requires, be construed as a reference to those provisions as amended, modified, affected or re-enacted by any subsequent enactment, rules, regulations or instrument.

(4) Any reference in these Rules to a rule, a Part or a Schedule shall, unless the context otherwise requires, be construed as a reference to a rule or a Part of, or a Schedule to, these Rules, as the case may be.

(5) The Interpretation Act 1889 shall apply for the interpretation of these Rules as it applies for the interpretation of an Act of Parliament.

Prescribed Period

4.—(1) For the purposes of these Rules, subject as hereafter in this rule provided, the expression " prescribed period " shall mean—

(a) in the case of a person who, immediately after ceasing to be employed in teaching service or in public board employment became engaged in national service, a period of six months after the date of termination of the national service; and

(b) in the case of any other person, a period of twelve months after the date on which he ceased to be employed in teaching service or in public board employment.

(2) The Secretary of State in the case of a person becoming employed in teaching service and the pension authority in the case of a person becoming employed in public board employment may, with the agreement of the other, in any particular case extend the period of six months or twelve months, whichever is appropriate, specified in paragraph (1) above.

(3) Subject as in paragraph (4) below provided—

(a) in reckoning the periods of six months and twelve months specified in paragraph (1) above no account shall be taken of any period spent by a person on a course of study or training which he undertook after leaving his former employment;

(b) if a person left his former employment in order to undertake a course of study or training and on completion of that course became engaged in national service, he shall be deemed for the purposes of paragraph (1) above to have left his former employment at the time when he completed the said course of study or training.

(4) The provisions of paragraph (3) above shall not apply—

    (*a*) to a person to whose new employment a public board pension scheme applies unless the pension authority are satisfied that by reason of his having undertaken the said course of study or training he is better fitted for the duties of his new employment; or

    (*b*) to a person who in his new employment is in teaching service unless—

        (i) before leaving his former employment (or, if between leaving that employment and undertaking the said course of study or training he was engaged in national service, before the end of that service) he gave notice in writing to the pension authority of his intention to undertake the said course of study or training; and

        (ii) the Secretary of State is satisfied that by reason of his having undertaken the said course of study or training he is better fitted for the duties of his new employment.

Equivalent Pension Rights

5. A transfer value shall not be paid or received by the Secretary of State under these Rules in respect of a person transferring to or from public board employment unless the Secretary of State is satisfied that that person's pension rights in respect of that employment are, or will be, at least substantially equivalent to those in respect of reckonable service.

PART II

TRANSFER FROM TEACHING SERVICE TO PUBLIC BOARD EMPLOYMENT

Application

6.—(1) Subject as in paragraph (2) below and in rule 7 provided, this Part shall apply to a person who within the prescribed period after ceasing to be employed in teaching service—

    (*a*) becomes on or after the operative date employed in public board employment;

    (*b*) after the beginning of April 1967 and before the operative date became employed in public board employment by a body named in Schedule 1; or

    (*c*) before the operative date became employed in public board employment—

        (i) by a body named in Schedule 2; or

        (ii) by a body named in Schedule 3 after having ceased to be employed in teaching service on or after the date one year before that specified against the name of that body.

(2) This Part shall not apply to—

    (*a*) a person who has become entitled to any pension (other than repayment of contributions) under the Teachers (Superannuation) Acts 1918 to 1956 or the Teachers' Regulations; or

    (*b*) a person by virtue of paragraph (1)(*c*) above unless the Secretary of State and the pension authority consent.

Conditions for Application

7.—(1) This Part shall not apply to a person unless—

    (*a*) within the period specified in paragraph (2) below, or within such longer period as the pension authority may with the agreement of the Secretary of State in any particular case allow, he notifies that authority in writing that he desires this Part to apply to him and furnishes that authority with particulars in writing of his teaching service; and

(b) within the period defined in paragraph (2) below, or within such longer period as the pension authority may in any particular case allow, he pays to that authority an amount equal to any repaid contributions paid to him after he last ceased to be employed in teaching service, together with compound interest thereon of an amount determined in accordance with paragraph (3) below.

(2) For the purposes of paragraph (1) above the period shall be—

(a) in a case to which rule 6(1)(a) applies, three months after becoming employed in public board employment;

(b) in a case to which rule 6(1)(b) applies, three months after the operative date; and

(c) in a case to which rule 6(1)(c) applies, six months after the operative date.

(3) For the purposes of paragraph (1)(b) above—

(a) compound interest shall not be payable unless the period between a person's ceasing to be employed in teaching service and becoming employed in public board employment exceeds one year;

(b) if the aforesaid period exceeds one year, compound interest shall be calculated on the amount of the repaid contributions at three per cent. per annum with yearly rests from the date one year after that on which the person ceased to be employed in teaching service to the date on which he became employed in public board employment; and

(c) if the amount of compound interest calculated as aforesaid exceeds a sum equal to one half of the difference between the amount of the transfer value payable under rule 8 and the amount of the transfer value which would have been so payable if calculated by reference to the person's age on ceasing to be employed in teaching service, it shall be reduced to that sum.

Transfer Value

8.—(1) In respect of a person to whom this Part applies the Secretary of State shall, out of moneys provided by Parliament, pay to the pension authority a transfer value of an amount calculated in accordance with the following provisions of this rule.

(2) Subject as hereafter in this rule provided, the transfer value shall be an amount equal to the transfer value which would have been payable under the Transfer Value Regulations if the person, at the date when he ceased to be employed in teaching service, had ceased to be a contributory employee under one local authority and had become such an employee under another local authority and had been entitled to reckon as contributing service his reckonable service and his service reckonable for the purposes of Parts VII, IX and X of the Teachers' Regulations at the length at which it is so reckonable.

(3) For the purposes of paragraph (2) above service which is reckoned as contributing service shall be deemed to have been affected or modified in accordance with regulations applicable to contributing service made under section 110 of the National Insurance Act 1965(a), or under any provision corresponding thereto contained in an enactment repealed by that Act, in like manner and to the like extent, as nearly as may be, as it was affected or modified by other such regulations.

_____

(a) 1965 c. 51.

(4) In calculating the amount of a transfer value there shall be excluded—

  (a) any period of war service within the meaning of the Teachers Super-annuation (War Service) Act 1939(a) and of national service within the meaning of the Teachers Superannuation (National Service) Rules 1949(b) in respect of which, at the time the transfer value is paid, the contributions remain unpaid; and

  (b) any period in respect of which the person was immediately before ceasing to be employed in teaching service paying voluntary contributions and in respect of which, at the time the transfer value is paid, he has not elected to continue to pay such contributions.

(5) The amount of the transfer value payable in respect of a person shall, in lieu of being reduced in accordance with the proviso to paragraph 2 of the First Schedule to the Transfer Value Regulations, be reduced by

  (a) an amount equal to the sum of any repaid contributions paid to him after he last ceased to be employed in teaching service and any compound interest thereon payable in accordance with rule 7(3);

  (b) an amount equal to any sum which remained to be paid by him on his ceasing to be employed in teaching service towards the discharge of a fixed sum as a condition of any period of service being reckoned for the purposes of the Teachers' Regulations;

  (c) an amount equal to the capital value of any voluntary contributions which on his ceasing to be employed in teaching service remained to be paid by him in respect of any period not excluded from the calculation of the amount of the transfer value by paragraph (4)(b) above; and

  (d) an amount equal to any sum payable by the Secretary of State by way of income tax by reason of its payment.

(6) In respect of a person who ceased to be employed in teaching service more than one year before the operative date the amount of the transfer value shall, except in a case to which paragraph (7) below applies, be calculated by reference to his age on that date.

(7) In respect of a person who became employed in public board employment on or after the operative date and to whom either paragraph (2) or paragraph (3) of rule 3 applies the amount of the transfer value shall be calculated by reference to his age on the date on which he became employed in public board employment.

Benefits under Teachers' Regulations

9.—(1) Subject to the provisions of Part III and any provisions similar thereto contained in other rules made under the Act of 1948, no payment of any pension shall be made under the Teachers' Regulations to any person or his personal representatives in respect of any service which is taken into account in calculating the amount of a transfer value under rule 8.

(2) If a person to whom this Part applies ceases to be employed in public board employment and becomes re-employed in teaching service in circumstances in which neither the provisions of Part III nor any provisions similar thereto contained in other rules made under the Act of 1948 apply to him, any service in respect of which a transfer value was paid under this Part shall be qualifying service for the purposes of regulation 41 of the Teachers' Regulations.

(a) 1939 c. 95.   (b) S.I. 1949/468 (1949 I, p. 1533).

PART III

TRANSFER FROM PUBLIC BOARD EMPLOYMENT TO TEACHING SERVICE

Application

10.—(1) Subject as in paragraph (2) below and in rule 11 provided, this Part shall apply to a person who—

    (*a*) becomes on or after the operative date employed in teaching service within the prescribed period after ceasing to be employed in public board employment;

    (*b*) after the beginning of April 1967 and before the operative date became employed in teaching service within the prescribed period after ceasing to be employed in public board employment by a body named in Schedule 1; or

    (*c*) before the operative date became employed in teaching service within the prescribed period after ceasing to be employed in public board employment—

        (i) by a body named in Schedule 2; or

        (ii) by a body named in Schedule 3 on or after the date specified against the name of that body.

(2) This Part shall not apply to—

    (*a*) a person who has become entitled to any pension (other than repayment of contributions) under a public board pension scheme; or

    (*b*) a person by virtue of paragraph (1)(*c*) above unless the Secretary of State consents.

Conditions for Application

11.—(1) This Part shall not apply to a person unless—

    (*a*) within the period defined in paragraph (2) below, or within such longer period as the Secretary of State may with the agreement of the pension authority in any particular case allow, he notifies the Secretary of State in writing that he desires this Part to apply to him and furnishes the Secretary of State with particulars in writing of his public board employment;

    (*b*) within the period specified in paragraph (2) below, or within such longer period as the Secretary of State may in any particular case allow, he pays to the Secretary of State an amount equal to any repaid contributions paid to him after he last ceased to be employed in public board employment; and

    (*c*) in respect of him the Secretary of State receives from the pension authority a transfer value of an amount determined in accordance with the provisions of rule 12.

(2) For the purposes of paragraph (1) above the period shall be—

    (*a*) in a case to which rule 10(1)(*a*) applies, three months after becoming employed in teaching service;

    (*b*) in a case to which rule 10(1)(*b*) applies, three months after the operative date; and

    (*c*) in a case to which rule 10(1)(*c*) applies, six months after the operative date.

Transfer Value

12.—(1) Subject as hereafter in this rule provided, the amount of the transfer value receivable by the Secretary of State from the pension authority in respect of a person to whom this Part applies shall be equal to the transfer value which would have been payable under the Transfer Value Regulations if the person, at the date when he ceased to be employed in public board employment, had ceased to be a contributory employee under one local authority and had become such an employee under another local authority and had been entitled to reckon—

    (*a*) as non-contributing service, any service which was originally non-contributing service and which, under the public board pension scheme last applicable to him, was treated in like manner as non-contributing service is treated under the Local Government Superannuation Acts 1937 to 1953 and regulations made thereunder; and

    (*b*) as contributing service, any service (other than that specified above) which he was entitled to reckon for the purpose of computing benefits under the public board pension scheme last applicable to him.

(2) For the purposes of paragraph (1) above service which is reckoned as contributing or non-contributing service shall be deemed to have been affected or modified in accordance with regulations applicable to such service made under section 110 of the National Insurance Act 1965, or under any provision corresponding thereto contained in an enactment repealed by that Act, in like manner and to the like extent, as nearly as may be, as it was affected or modified by provisions in connection with national insurance contained in or relating to a public board pension scheme.

(3) The amount of the transfer value shall be reduced by an amount equal to any sum payable by the pension authority by way of income tax by reason of its payment.

(4) In respect of a person who ceased to be employed in public board employment more than one year before the operative date the amount of the transfer value shall, except in a case to which paragraph (5) below applies, be calculated by reference to his age on that date.

(5) In respect of a person who became employed in teaching service on or after the operative date and to whom either paragraph (2) or paragraph (3) of rule 4 applies the amount of the transfer value shall be calculated by reference to his age on the date on which he became employed in teaching service.

Reckoning of Service

13.—(1) Subject as hereafter in this rule provided, in respect of a person to whom this Part applies—

    (*a*) there shall be reckoned as reckonable service—

        (i) any period of service treated as contributing service for the purpose of calculating the amount of the transfer value payable under this Part; and

        (ii) one-half of any period of service treated as non-contributing service for the said purpose; and

    (*b*) there shall be reckoned as class C external service for the purposes of the Teachers' Regulations any period of service treated as non-contributing service for the said purpose, except in so far as that service is reckoned under this rule or those Regulations as reckonable service or external service for the purposes of those Regulations.

(2) The whole of any period of service to which paragraph (1) above applies shall, for the purpose of calculating under section 4(3) of the Teachers'

Superannuation Act 1967 the average salary of a person to whom this Part applies, be reckoned as a period of employment in reckonable service.

(3) Notwithstanding anything in this rule before contained, any service of a person to whom this Part applies which under the public board pension scheme last applicable to him was at the time he ceased to be employed in public board employment reckonable only for the purpose of calculating the amount of any pension payable to or in respect of him or only for the purpose of determining whether he was entitled to any pension shall be reckoned only for the corresponding like purpose under the Teachers' Regulations.

Voluntary Contributions

14.—(1) A person to whom this Part applies may, within three months of becoming employed in teaching service or within such longer period as the Secretary of State may in any particular case allow, elect to continue to pay voluntary contributions being paid by him immediately before ceasing to be employed in public board employment.

(2) If a person elects as aforesaid and—

    (*a*) within three months of becoming employed in teaching service, or within such longer period as the Secretary of State may in any particular case allow, pays to the Secretary of State a sum equal to the sum of any payment made to him on or after ceasing to be employed in public board employment by way of return of voluntary contributions, any interest added thereto and any deduction therefrom in respect of income tax; and

    (*b*) thereafter pays to the Secretary of State any amounts outstanding in respect of voluntary contributions at the times at which they would have been payable if he had remained in public board employment

his teaching service shall be affected in the same manner, as nearly as may be, as his public board employment would have been affected if he had completed payment of the voluntary contributions immediately before ceasing such employment.

(3) The provisions of paragraphs (5)(*b*), (6), (7), (8) and (12) of regulation 32 and of regulation 38 of the Teachers' Regulations shall apply to voluntary contributions payable under this rule as if they were additional contributions payable in respect of previous employment within the meaning of these Regulations.

(4) If a person does not elect as aforesaid or if voluntary contributions are repaid to him under regulation 38 of the Teachers' Regulations, as applied by this rule, the period in respect of which such contributions were paid shall be reckoned for the purposes of the Teachers' Regulations only to the extent, if any, to which it would have been so reckoned if no such payments or contributions had been made in respect thereof.

Commencement of Employment

15. For the purposes of regulation 41(1)(*a*)(ii) of the Teachers' Regulations the date on which a person to whom this Part applies became employed in public board employment shall be deemed to be a date on which he became employed in teaching service.

Return of Contributions

16.—(1) Where a person to whom this Part applies ceases to be employed in teaching service or dies, then, in computing the sum to which he or his personal representatives shall be entitled under the Teachers' Regulations, there shall be included a sum in respect of contributions paid by him in respect of service which by virtue of these Rules is reckoned as reckonable service and, in the case of a person who has elected in pursuance of rule 14 to continue paying voluntary contributions, in respect also of voluntary contributions paid by him before becoming employed in teaching service which have either not been returned to him, or if returned, have been paid to the Secretary of State under rule 14 and have not subsequently been again returned.

(2) In computing the amount of the sum so included for the purposes of this rule compound interest shall be calculated—

(a) as respects the period ending immediately before the date on which the person became employed in teaching service, in the manner in which such interest, if any, would have been calculated if the occasion for making the calculation had occurred immediately before that date; and

(b) as respects the period beginning with that date, in accordance with the provisions of Part IV of the Teachers' Regulations.

Modification of Contributions and Benefits by reason of National Insurance

17.—(1) In relation to a person to whom this Part applies the provisions of this rule shall have effect for the purpose of determining whether the following provisions of Schedule 5 of the Teachers' Regulations shall apply, that is to say—

paragraph 2 (which provides for the reduction of contributions),

paragraph 4 (which provides for the reduction of pensions by fixed annual amounts specified therein), and

paragraph 5 (which provides for the reduction of pensions by annual amounts ascertained by reference to a table and age at a given date).

(2) Paragraphs 2, 4 and 5 of the said Schedule 5 shall not apply to a person in respect of whom—

(a) the service to be reckoned as teaching service under rule 13 commenced on or before 5th July 1948; and

(b) the transfer value received by the Secretary of State is not reduced in accordance with Part IV of the Transfer Value Regulations.

(3) Paragraphs 2 and 5 of the said Schedule 5 shall apply—

(a) to a person in respect of whom—

(i) the service to be reckoned as teaching service under rule 13 includes service which commenced on or before 5th July 1948 and in respect of which the benefits under the public board pension scheme last applicable to him were subject to modification by reason of national insurance; and

(ii) the transfer value received by the Secretary of State is reduced in accordance with Part IV of the Transfer Value Regulations; and

(b) to a person to whom, before he became employed in public board employment, either paragraphs 2 and 5 of the said Schedule 5 applied or the modification of the Teachers (Superannuation) Acts 1918 to 1956 prescribed by the National Insurance (Modification of Teachers Pensions) Regulations 1948(a), as amended by the National Insurance (Modification of Teachers Pensions) Amending Regulations 1956(b), applied as to an existing teacher within the meaning of those Regulations.

(a) S.I. 1948/889 (Rev. XVI, p. 298: 1948 I, p. 2851).
(b) S.I. 1956/1482 (1956 I, p. 1643).

(4) Paragraphs 2 and 4 of the said Schedule 5 shall apply to a person to whom neither paragraph (2) nor paragraph (3) above applies.

(5) For the purposes of paragraph 5 of the said Schedule 5 the date of modification in relation to a person shall—

(a) in a case to which paragraph (3)(a) above applies, be the date on which he was first affected by provisions modifying a public board pension scheme by reason of national insurance; and

(b) in a case to which paragraph (3)(b) above applies, the date of modification in relation to him for the purposes of the Regulations therein mentioned.

Payment into Exchequer

18. All sums received by the Secretary of State in relation to a person to whom this Part applies whether by way of transfer value or otherwise shall be paid into the Exchequer.

Rules 3, 6 and 10	SCHEDULE 1

The Agricultural Research Council

The British Broadcasting Corporation

The British Council

The British European Airways Corporation

The British Overseas Airways Corporation

The Central After-Care Association (England and Wales)

The Commonwealth Institute

The Commonwealth War Graves Commission

The Crown Agents for Oversea Governments and Administrations

The Electricity Council

An Electricity Board in England and Wales

The South of Scotland Electricity Board

The North of Scotland Hydro-Electric Board

The Forestry Commission

The Gas Council

An Area Gas Board

The Independent Television Authority

The Kingston upon Hull Telephone Undertaking

The Metropolitan Water Board

The National Association of Discharged Prisoners' Aid Societies (Incorporated)

The National Coal Board

The National Dock Labour Board

The National Industrial Fuel Efficiency Service

The Port of London Authority

The United Kingdom Atomic Energy Authority

Rules 3, 6 and 10	SCHEDULE 2

The Natural Environment Research Council

The Welsh Industrial Estates Corporation

SCHEDULE 3   Rules 3, 6 and 10

The Science Research Council	1st April 1965
The Social Science Research Council	1st December 1965
An Industrial Training Board established under section 1 of the Industrial Training Act 1964(a) which executed the Trust Deed dated 20th July 1967 regulating the Industrial Training Boards Pension and Retirement Benefits Funds or has executed a Deed of Adherence to that Trust Deed.	The date of the establishment of the Board.

Given under the Official Seal of the Secretary of State for Education and Science on 26th June 1968.

(L.S.)

Edward Short,
Secretary of State for Education and Science.

We concur,

J. McCann,
B. K. O'Malley,

Two of the Lords Commissioners
of Her Majesty's Treasury.

12th July 1968.

EXPLANATORY NOTE
(This Note is not part of the Rules.)

The purpose of the Rules is to continue arrangements made by earlier Rules for the preservation of superannuation rights upon changes of employment between teaching and Public Boards named in the Schedules, and to extend the scope of those arrangements. Schedules 2 and 3 list the Boards now included for the first time.

In accordance with Section 2(5) of the Superannuation (Miscellaneous Provisions) Act 1948 the Rules may apply retrospectively to past transfers to or from employments newly included, subject to the agreement of the employee and the former employer and to certain restrictions indicated by the Rules.

(a) 1964 c. 16.

STATUTORY INSTRUMENTS

1968 No. 1122 (S.123)

COURT OF SESSION, SCOTLAND

Act of Sederunt (Form of Extract Decree of Divorce) 1968

Made - - - 11th July 1968
Coming into Operation 12th July 1968

The Lords of Council and Session, under and by virtue of the powers conferred upon them by Section 16 of the Administration of Justice (Scotland) Act 1933(a) and of all other powers competent to them in that behalf do hereby enact as follows:—

1. An Extract Decree of Divorce shall, as nearly as possible, be in the form contained in the Schedule appended hereto.

2. This Act of Sederunt may be cited as the Act of Sederunt (Form of Extract Decree of Divorce) 1968 and shall come into operation on 12th July 1968.

And the Lords appoint this Act of Sederunt to be inserted in the Books of Sederunt.

Edinburgh,   *J. L. Clyde*
11th July 1968.   I.P.D.

SCHEDULE
COURT OF SESSION, SCOTLAND
Extract Decree of Divorce

In Causa

                                                                  Pursuer
against
                                                                  Defender

At Edinburgh the   day of   19 :
SITTING IN JUDGMENT the Lords of Council and Session pronounced an Inter-locutor:

(1)   divorcing the Defender from the Pursuer on the ground of the Defender's   :

* (2)   awarding custody to the Pursuer/Defender of the following child/children

* (3)   ordaining payment:

(a) by the   to the   of £ : : per   as aliment for each of said child/children until sixteen years of age:

(b) by the Defender to the Pursuer of a periodical allowance of £ : : per   payable until her death or remarriage:

(c) by the Defender to the Pursuer of a capital sum of £ : :

(a) 1933 c. 41.

(d) by the   to the   of £   :   :   of expenses and £   :   : dues of Ext-
    ract

*and (4) granting leave to either party to apply to the Court for any order required
anent custody and aliment until   19   :

And the said Lords Grant Warrant for a lawful execution hereon.
Extracted at Edinburgh this   day of   19   by me

                                  Extractor of the Court of Session

*Delete where inapplicable.

EXPLANATORY NOTE

(*This Note is not part of the Act of Sederunt.*)

This Act of Sederunt prescribes the form of an Extract Decree of Divorce.

STATUTORY INSTRUMENTS

1968 No. 1124

SUGAR

The Sugar (Rates of Surcharge and Surcharge Repayments) (No. 4) Order 1968

Made - - - -	*15th July* 1968
Laid before Parliament	*16th July* 1968
Coming into Operation	*17th July* 1968

The Minister of Agriculture, Fisheries and Food, in exercise of the powers conferred on him by sections 7(4), 8(6) and 33(4) of the Sugar Act 1956(a) having effect subject to the provisions of section 3 of, and Part II of Schedule 5 to, the Finance Act 1962(b), and of all other powers enabling him in that behalf, with the concurrence of the Treasury, on the advice of the Sugar Board, hereby makes the following order:—

1.—(1) This order may be cited as the Sugar (Rates of Surcharge and Surcharge Repayments) (No. 4) Order 1968; and shall come into operation on 17th July 1968.

(2) The Interpretation Act 1889(c) shall apply for the interpretation of this order as it applies for the interpretation of an Act of Parliament.

2. Notwithstanding the provisions of Article 2 of the Sugar (Rates of Surcharge and Surcharge Repayments) (No. 3) Order 1968(d), the rates of surcharge payable under and in accordance with the provisions of section 7 of the Sugar Act 1956, having effect as aforesaid, in respect of sugar and invert sugar imported or home produced or used in the manufacture of imported composite sugar products shall on and after 17th July 1968 be those rates specified in Schedule 1 to this order.

3. For the purpose of section 8(3)(b) of the Sugar Act 1956, having effect as aforesaid, the rates of surcharge repayments in respect of invert sugar produced in the United Kingdom from materials on which on or after 17th July 1968 sugar duty has been paid or, by virtue of paragraph 1 of Part II of Schedule 5 to the Finance Act 1962, is treated as having been paid shall, notwithstanding the provisions of Article 3 of the Sugar (Rates of Surcharge and Surcharge Repayments) (No. 3) Order 1968 be those specified in Schedule 2 to this order.

(a) 1956 c. 48.   (b) 1962 c. 44.
(c) 1889 c. 63.   (d) S.I. 1968/999 (1968 II, p. 2656).

In Witness whereof the Official Seal of the Minister of Agriculture Fisheries and Food is hereunto affixed on 15th July 1968.

(L.S.)

R. P. Fraser,
Authorised by the Minister.

We concur.

15th July 1968.

Harry Gourlay,
Joseph Harper,
Two of the Lords Commissioners of
Her Majesty's Treasury.

SCHEDULE 1

PART I

SURCHARGE RATES FOR SUGAR

Polarisation	Rate of Surcharge per cwt.	
	s.	d.
Exceeding—		
99°	35	0
98° but not exceeding 99°	33	0
97° „ „ „ 98°	32	2·4
96° „ „ „ 97°	31	4·3
95° „ „ „ 96°	30	6·2
94° „ „ „ 95°	29	8·1
93° „ „ „ 94°	28	10
92° „ „ „ 93°	28	0
91° „ „ „ 92°	27	1·9
90° „ „ „ 91°	26	3·8
89° „ „ „ 90°	25	5·7
88° „ „ „ 89°	24	7·6
87° „ „ „ 88°	23	11·2
86° „ „ „ 87°	23	2·8
85° „ „ „ 86°	22	7·3
84° „ „ „ 85°	21	11·7
83° „ „ „ 84°	21	4·2
82° „ „ „ 83°	20	8·6
81° „ „ „ 82°	20	1·9
80° „ „ „ 81°	19	7·2
79° „ „ „ 80°	19	0·4
78° „ „ „ 79°	18	5·7
77° „ „ „ 78°	17	11
76° „ „ „ 77°	17	4·3
Not exceeding 76°	16	9·6

PART II
SURCHARGE RATES FOR INVERT SUGAR

Sweetening matter content by weight	Rate of Surcharge per cwt.
	s. d.
70 per cent. or more	22 2
Less than 70 per cent. and more than 50 per cent.	15 11
Not more than 50 per cent.	7 10

SCHEDULE 2
SURCHARGE REPAYMENT RATES FOR INVERT SUGAR

Sweetening matter content by weight	Rate of Surcharge Repayment per cwt.
	s. d.
More than 80 per cent.	26 3
More than 70 per cent. but not more than 80 per cent.	22 2
More than 60 per cent. but not more than 70 per cent.	15 11
More than 50 per cent. but not more than 60 per cent.	12 8
Not more than 50 per cent. and the invert sugar not being less in weight than 14 lb. per gallon	7 10

EXPLANATORY NOTE
(*This Note is not part of the Order.*)

This order prescribes—

    (*a*) increases equivalent to 2s. 4d. per cwt. of refined sugar in the rates of surcharge payable on sugar and invert sugar which become chargeable with surcharge on or after 17th July 1968;

    (*b*) correspondingly increased rates of surcharge repayment in respect of invert sugar produced in the United Kingdom from materials on which surcharge has been paid.

STATUTORY   INSTRUMENTS

1968 No. 1125

SUGAR

The Composite Sugar Products (Surcharge and Surcharge Repayments—Average Rates) (No. 4) Order 1968

Made - - - -	*15th July* 1968
Laid before Parliament	*16th July* 1968
Coming into Operation	*17th July* 1968

Whereas the Minister of Agriculture, Fisheries and Food (hereinafter called " the Minister ") has on the recommendation of the Commissioners of Customs and Excise (hereinafter called " the Commissioners ") made an order(a) pursuant to the powers conferred upon him by sections 9(1) and 9(4) of the Sugar Act 1956(b), having effect subject to the provisions of section 3 of, and Part II of Schedule 5 to, the Finance Act 1962(c) and to the provisions of section 52(2) of the Finance Act 1966(d), providing that in the case of certain descriptions of composite sugar products surcharge shall be calculated on the basis of an average quantity of sugar or invert sugar taken to have been used in the manufacture of the products, and that certain other descriptions of composite sugar products shall be treated as not containing any sugar or invert sugar, and that in the case of certain descriptions of goods in the manufacture of which sugar or invert sugar is used, surcharge repayments shall be calculated on the basis of an average quantity of sugar or invert sugar taken to have been so used:

Now, therefore, the Minister, on the recommendation of the Commissioners and in exercise of the powers conferred upon him by sections 9(1), 9(4) and 33(4) of the Sugar Act 1956, having effect as aforesaid, and of all other powers enabling him in that behalf, hereby makes the following order:—

1.—(1) This order may be cited as the Composite Sugar Products (Surcharge and Surcharge Repayments—Average Rates) (No. 4) Order 1968; and shall come into operation on 17th July 1968.

(2) The Interpretation Act 1889(e) shall apply for the interpretation of this order as it applies for the interpretation of an Act of Parliament.

2. Surcharge payable on or after 17th July 1968 under and in accordance with the Sugar Act 1956, having effect as aforesaid, in respect of sugar and invert sugar used in the manufacture of the descriptions of imported composite sugar products specified in column 2 of Schedule 1 to this order shall, notwithstanding the provisions of the Sugar (Rates of Surcharge and Surcharge Repayments) (No. 4) Order 1968(f) and the Composite Sugar Products (Surcharge and Surcharge Repayments—Average Rates) (No. 3) Order 1968(a), be calculated by reference to the weight or value, as the case may be, of the products at the rates specified in relation thereto in column 3 of the said Schedule.

(a) S.I. 1968/1000 (1968 II, p. 2659).   (b) 1956 c. 48.   (c) 1962 c. 44.
(d) 1966 c. 18.   (e) 1889 c. 63.   (f) S.I. 1968/1124 (1968 II, p. 3092).

3. Imported composite sugar products other than those of a description specified in Schedules 1 and 2 to this order shall be treated as not containing any sugar or invert sugar for the purposes of surcharge payable on or after 17th July 1968.

4. Surcharge repayments payable on and after 17th July 1968 under and in accordance with the provisions of section 8 of the Sugar Act 1956, having effect as aforesaid, in respect of sugar and invert sugar used in the manufacture of the descriptions of goods specified in column 1 of Schedule 3 to this order shall, notwithstanding the provisions of the Sugar (Rates of Surcharge and Surcharge Repayments) (No. 4) Order 1968(a) and the Composite Sugar Products (Surcharge and Surcharge Repayments—Average Rates) (No. 3) Order 1968(b), be calculated by reference to the quantity of the goods at the rates specified in relation thereto in column 2 of the said Schedule.

In Witness whereof the Official Seal of the Minister of Agriculture, Fisheries and Food is hereunto affixed on 15th July 1968.

(L.S.)

R. P. Fraser,
Authorised by the Minister.

SCHEDULE 1

In this Schedule:—

" Tariff heading " means a heading or, where the context so requires, a subheading of the Customs Tariff 1959 (see paragraph (1) of Article 1 of the Import Duties (General) (No. 4) Order 1968(c)).

" Per cent." means, where it occurs in relation to any rate of surcharge, per cent. of the value for customs duty purposes of the product to which it relates.

Tariff heading	Description of Imported Composite Sugar Products	Rate of Surcharge per cwt. s. d.
04.02	Milk and cream, preserved, concentrated or sweetened containing more than 10 per cent. by weight of added sweetening matter	15 6
17.02 (B) (2) and 17.05 (B)	Syrups containing sucrose sugar, whether or not flavoured or coloured, but not including fruit juices containing added sugar in any proportion:— containing 70 per cent. or more by weight of sweetening matter	22 3
	containing less than 70 per cent., and more than 50 per cent., by weight of sweetening matter...	16 0
	containing not more than 50 per cent. by weight of sweetening matter	7 9

(a) S.I. 1968/1124 (1968 II, p. 3092).   (b) S.I. 1968/1000 (1968 II, p. 2659).
(c) S.I. 1968/679 (1968 I, p. 1519).

Tariff heading	Description of Imported Composite Sugar Products	Rate of Surcharge
		per cwt. s.　d.
17.02 (F)　...	Caramel:—	
	Solid　...　...　...　...　...　...　...	35　0
	Liquid　...　...　...　...　...　...	24　6
17.04 ...　...	Sugar confectionery, not containing cocoa ...　...	28　6
18.06 ...　...	Chocolate and other food preparations containing cocoa:—	
	Chocolate couverture not prepared for retail sale; chocolate milk crumb, liquid ...　...	15　6
	Chocolate milk crumb, solid　...　...　...	19　2
	Other　...　...　...　...　...　...	20　3
		per cent.
19.08 ...　...	Pastry, biscuits, cakes and other fine bakers' wares containing added sweetening matter:—	
	Biscuits　...　...　...　...　...　...	7½
	Other　...　...　...　...　...　...	4½
20.01 ...　...	Vegetables and fruit, prepared or preserved by vinegar or acetic acid, containing added sweetening matter　...　...　...　...　...　...	10½
20.03 ...　...	Fruit preserved by freezing, containing added sugar	3¾
		per cwt. s.　d.
20.04 ...　...	Fruit, fruit-peel and parts of plants, preserved by sugar (drained, glacé or crystallised)　...　...	23　0
20.05 ...　...	Jams, fruit jellies, marmalades, fruit purée and fruit pastes, being cooked preparations, containing added sweetening matter　...　...　...	22　0
		per cent.
20.06	Fruit otherwise prepared or preserved, containing added sweetening matter:—	
	Ginger　...　...　...　...　...　...	15
	Other　...　...　...　...　...　...	3¾

SCHEDULE 2

Tariff heading	Description of Imported Composite Sugar Products
17.05 (A) and (B)	Sugar and invert sugar, flavoured or coloured.

SCHEDULE 3

Description of goods	Rate of surcharge repayment per bulk barrel of 36 gallons
Lager	1s. 5·5d.
All beer other than lager	1s. 3·6d.

EXPLANATORY NOTE

(This Note is not part of the Order.)

This order provides for increases on and after 17th July 1968 in the average rates of surcharge payable on imported composite sugar products of the descriptions specified in Schedule 1 and in the average rates of surcharge repayment in respect of exported goods of the descriptions specified in Schedule 3. These correspond to the increases in surcharge rates effected by the Sugar (Rates of Surcharge and Surcharge Repayments) (No. 4) Order 1968 (S.I. 1968/1124). Provision is also made for certain imported composite sugar products to be treated as not containing any sugar or invert sugar.

STATUTORY INSTRUMENTS

1968 No. 1126 (S.124)

CUSTOMS AND EXCISE
The Methylated Spirits (Sale by Retail) (Variation of Fees) (Scotland) Order 1968

Made - - -		10*th July* 1968
Coming into Operation		2*nd September* 1968

In exercise of the powers conferred on me by section 2(4) as read with section 6 of the Methylated Spirits (Sale by Retail) (Scotland) Act 1937(a), and of all other powers enabling me in that behalf, I hereby make the following Order:—

1. This Order may be cited as the Methylated Spirits (Sale by Retail) (Variation of Fees) (Scotland) Order 1968 and shall come into operation on 2nd September 1968.

2. The Methylated Spirits (Sale by Retail) (Scotland) Order 1937(b), article 2, (which relates to fees payable to a local authority under section 2(4) of the Methylated Spirits (Sale by Retail) (Scotland) Act 1937(a) by every person whose name is entered in the list kept by that authority) shall be amended by substituting for the fees specified in the said article as set out in the second column of the Schedule to this Order, the fees specified in the third column thereof.

3. The Interpretation Act 1889(c) shall apply for the interpretation of this Order as it applies for the interpretation of an Act of Parliament.

William Ross,
One of Her Majesty's Principal
Secretaries of State.

St. Andrew's House,
Edinburgh, 1.
10th July 1968.

(a) 1937 c. 48   (b) S.R. & O. 1937/993 (Rev. XXI, p. 474; 1937, p. 1713).
(c) 1889 c. 63.

SCHEDULE

Amendments to the Methylated Spirits (Sale by Retail) (Scotland) Order 1937, Article 2.

1 Matter to which fee relates	2 Old fee	3 New fee
(a) in respect of the entry of a person's name in the list	5s. 0d.	15s. 0d.
(b) in respect of the making of any alteration in the list in relation to the premises on which a person is entitled to sell or in relation to the kind of spirit he is entitled to sell on such premises	1s. 0d.	5s. 0d.
(c) in respect of the retention of a person's name on the list in any year subsequent to the year in which his name is first entered therein	2s. 6d.	7s. 6d.
(d) in respect of the issue of a certificate that a person's name is entered on the list	1s. 0d.	5s. 0d.
For each additional set of premises on which a person is entitled to sell methylated or surgical spirits:		
(i) in respect of an entry in the list	5s. 0d.	15s. 0d.
(ii) in respect of the retention of a person's name on the list	2s. 6d.	7s. 6d.
(iii) in respect of the issue of a certificate	1s. 0d.	5s. 0d.

EXPLANATORY NOTE

(This Note is not part of the Order.)

This Order increases the fees payable to a local authority by every person whose name is entered in a list of retailers of methylated or surgical spirits kept by that authority in accordance with the provisions of Article 2 of the Methylated Spirits (Sale by Retail) (Scotland) Order 1937.

STATUTORY INSTRUMENTS

1968 No. 1130

WAGES COUNCILS

The Wages Regulation (Road Haulage) Order 1968

Made - - - -	15*th July* 1968
Coming into Operation	16*th August* 1968

Whereas the Secretary of State has received from the Road Haulage Wages Council the wages regulation proposals set out in the Schedule hereto;

Now, therefore, the Secretary of State in exercise of her powers under section 11 of the Wages Councils Act 1959(a), and of all other powers enabling her in that behalf, hereby makes the following Order:—

1. This Order may be cited as the Wages Regulation (Road Haulage) Order 1968.

2.—(1) In this Order the expression "the specified date" means the 16th August 1968, provided that where, as respects any worker who is paid wages at intervals not exceeding seven days, that date does not correspond with the beginning of the period for which the wages are paid, the expression " the specified date " means, as respects that worker, the beginning of the next such period following that date.

(2) The Interpretation Act 1889(b) shall apply to the interpretation of this Order as it applies to the interpretation of an Act of Parliament and as if this Order and the Orders hereby revoked were Acts of Parliament.

3. The wages regulation proposals set out in the Schedule hereto shall have effect as from the specified date and as from that date the Wages Regulation (Road Haulage) Order 1966(c) and the Wages Regulation (Road Haulage) (Amendment) Order 1968(d) shall cease to have effect.

Signed by order of the Secretary of State.

15th July 1968.

A. A. Jarratt,
Deputy Under Secretary of State,
Department of Employment and Productivity.

(a) 1959 c. 69.
(c) S.I. 1966/554 (1966 II, p. 1142).

(b) 1889 c. 63.
(d) S.I. 1968/123 (1968 I, p. 343).

ARRANGEMENT OF SCHEDULE

MINIMUM REMUNERATION AND HOLIDAYS

PART I

SCHEDULE

The following minimum remuneration and provisions as to holidays and holiday remuneration shall be substituted for the statutory minimum remuneration and provisions as to holidays and holiday remuneration set out in the Wages Regulation (Road Haulage) Order 1966(a) (hereinafter referred to as "Order R.H.(84)") as amended by the Wages Regulation (Road Haulage) (Amendment) Order 1968(b) Order (R.H.(86)).

STATUTORY MINIMUM REMUNERATION

PART I

REGULAR WORKERS OTHER THAN MILK WORKERS

This Part of this Schedule applies to regular workers (as defined in paragraph 38) other than milk workers (as defined in paragraph 43).

1. Subject to the provisions of this Part and of Parts III and V of this Schedule, the minimum remuneration of regular workers other than milk workers shall be as follows:—

(1) All workers except those employed on the Carriage of Indivisible Loads to whom sub-paragraph (2) of this paragraph applies:—

Occupation	Carrying capacity of vehicle (as defined in paragraph 34)	Age of worker	Remuneration per week	
			Workers whose home depot is situated in the London Area (as defined in para. 35)	Workers whose home depot is situated outside the London Area (as defined in para. 35)
			s.　d.	s.　d.
(a) Drivers of vehicles other than (i) tractors not exceeding two tons unladen weight used exclusively for furniture removal work and (ii) tractors which operate from a depot in the London Area (as defined in paragraph 35).	Of 1 ton or less	Under 19 years ... 19 and under 21 years 21 years or over ...	151　9 181　6 223　6	149　9 179　6 218　6
	Over 1 ton and up to and including 5 tons ” 5 tons ” ” 10 ” ” 10 ” ” ” 15 ” ” 15 ” ” ” 18 ” Over 18 tons ” ” 21 ” ” 21 ”	All ages	223　6 232　9 240　6 249　9 261　3 271　0	218　6 227　9 235　6 244　9 256　3 266　0
(b) Drivers of tractors not exceeding two tons unladen weight used exclusively for furniture removal work.	—	All ages	223　6	218　6

(a) S.I. 1966/554 (1966 II, p. 1142).　　　(b) S.I. 1968/123 (1968 I, p. 343).

Occupation	Carrying capacity of vehicle (as defined in paragraph 34)	Age of worker	Remuneration per week	
			Workers whose home depot is situated in the London Area (as defined in para. 35)	Workers whose home depot is situated outside the London Area (as defined in para. 35)
			s. d.	s. d.
(c) Drivers of tractors, other than tractors not exceeding two tons unladen weight used exclusively for furniture work, which operate from a depot in the London Area (as defined in paragraph 35).	Up to and including 8 tons ...	All ages ...	234 0	—
	Over 8 tons and up to and including 12 tons ...		242 3	—
	Over 12 tons ...		251 0	—
(d) Workers in the Furniture Warehousing and Removing Industry employed as:	—	21 years or over ...		
Foremen ...			222 6	218 0
Removal packers ...			215 6	213 0
Porters ...			213 0	210 6
(e) Statutory attendants ...	—	Under 18 years ...	128 6	125 9
(f) Other road haulage workers ...	—	Under 16 years ...	86 9	84 6
		16 and under 17 years	94 9	92 6
		17 ,, ,, 18 ,,	103 0	101 9
		18 ,, ,, 19 ,,	138 6	135 9
		19 ,, ,, 20 ,,	151 0	147 3
		20 ,, ,, 21 ,,	166 9	162 6
		21 years or over ...	215 6	212 6

(2) Workers employed on the Carriage of Indivisible Loads.

(a) Workers on vehicles whilst used in connection with the movement of loads, other than live or dead cattle, which by reason of indivisibility require mechanical loading or unloading equipment carried on the vehicle and operated upon the responsibility of the driver, or

(b) Workers employed on vehicles authorised for the carriage of abnormal indivisible loads as defined in the Motor Vehicles (Authorisation of Special Types) (Amendment) Order 1968(a):—

Occupation	Class of Vehicle	Carrying capacity of vehicle (as defined in paragraph 34)	Remuneration per week	
			Workers whose home depot is situated in the London Area (as defined in para. 35) s. d.	Workers whose home depot is situated outside the London Area (as defined in para. 35) s. d.
Drivers	Vehicles referred to in (a) above	Over 6 tons and up to and including 10 tons " 10 " " " " " 16 "	241 0 251 6	237 0 247 6
	Vehicles referred to in (b) above	" 16 " " " " " 20 " " 20 " " " " " 25 " " 25 " " " " " 45 " Over 45 tons " " " " 65 " " 65 "	267 0 273 3 280 0 312 6 327 6	263 0 269 3 276 0 308 6 323 6
Mates	Vehicles referred to in (a) above	Over 6 tons and up to and including 16 tons	215 6	212 6
	Vehicles referred to in (b) above	" 16 " " " " " 20 " Over 20 tons	217 9 224 6	214 9 221 6
Heavy brakesmen and steersmen (as defined in paragraph 41)	Vehicles referred to in (b) above	—	241 3	238 3

A worker who on any day is employed in the circumstances specified in this sub-paragraph shall be paid at the rate appropriate to the vehicle for all hours worked by him on that day notwithstanding that he may be employed on other work during some part of that day.

(a) S.I. 1968/438 (1968 I, p. 1146).

COMPUTATION OF HOURS OF WORK

2. The following provisions shall apply to regular workers, other than milk workers, to whom the guaranteed weekly remuneration provisions apply:—

(1) a five-day worker who works on any day other than Saturday or Sunday shall be deemed to have worked for 8 hours on any such day notwithstanding that he was employed for less than 8 hours;

(2) a six-day worker who works on any day other than Sunday shall, subject to the provisions of paragraph 25 and the proviso to paragraph 44(1)(a), be deemed to have worked for 7¼ hours on any day Monday to Thursday, for 7 hours on Friday and for 4 hours on Saturday notwithstanding that he was employed for less than 7¼, 7 or 4 hours respectively:

Provided that a worker who is instructed to report for duty and presents himself for duty but does not commence work shall be deemed to have commenced work.

OVERTIME

3. Subject to the provisions of paragraphs 24, 25 and 44 the following shall be regarded as overtime:—

(1) Time worked in excess of 7¼ hours on any day Monday to Thursday and 7 hours on Friday (subject to the proviso to paragraph 44(1)(a)) in the case of a six-day worker and in excess of 8 hours on any day Monday to Friday in the case of a five-day worker.

(2) Time worked on Saturdays:—

(a) in the case of a six-day worker, in excess of 4 hours, provided that all time worked after 12.30 p.m. by a worker other than a film transport worker shall be regarded as overtime;

(b) in the case of a five-day worker, all time worked, provided that a five-day worker who works for less than 4 hours shall be deemed to have worked for 4 hours.

(3) Time worked on Sunday.

A worker who works for less than 5½ hours on Sunday shall be deemed to have worked for 5½ hours:

Provided that a worker whose hours entail a spell of duty commencing on Saturday and finishing on Sunday before 5.30 a.m. or commencing on Sunday after 6.30 p.m. and finishing on Monday, shall not, unless the Sunday duty is less than 3 hours, be deemed to have worked on Sunday in excess of the hours actually worked. If the Sunday duty is less than 3 hours he shall be deemed to have worked 3 hours on Sunday:

Provided also that a worker commencing work on Saturday who finishes work between midnight and 1 a.m. on Sunday shall be deemed to have worked one hour on Sunday.

(4) Time worked in any week in excess of 40 hours.

4.—(1) In determining the time to be regarded as overtime, time worked shall include time deemed to have been worked under the provisions of paragraphs 2, 3(3) and 24.

(2) Time worked on a customary holiday in accordance with paragraph 27(2)(b) or paragraph 28(2)(b) or on a day in the circumstances set out in the proviso to paragraph 27(4)(a) or paragraph 28(4)(a), paragraph 27(3) or paragraph 28(3) shall not be included in the calculation of overtime.

(3) When a worker's hours of duty or any part thereof entail employment between 9 p.m. and 6 a.m., a day shall, for the purpose of paragraph 3(1) and paragraph 3(2), be deemed to be any period of 24 hours commencing at 12 noon.

PAYMENT FOR OVERTIME

5. The following are the rates payable for overtime:—

in any week (exclusive of Sunday)   ...   .   time-and-a-half
on Sunday   ...   .   double time.

PART II

MILK WORKERS

This Part of this Schedule applies to milk workers (as defined in paragraph 43)

6. Subject to the provisions of this Part and of Parts III and V of this Schedule, the minimum remuneration of milk workers shall be as follows:—

Occupation	Carrying capacity of vehicle (as defined in paragraph 34)	Age of worker	Remuneration per week	
			Workers whose home depot is situated in the London Area (as defined in para. 35)	Workers whose home depot is situated outside the London Area (as defined in para. 35)
			s. d.	s. d.
(1) Drivers of vehicles other than tractors which operate from a depot in the London Area (as defined in paragraph 35).	Of 1 ton or less	Under 19 years ... 19 and under 21 years 21 years or over ...	151 9 181 6 223 6	149 9 179 6 218 6
	Over 1 ton and up to and including 5 tons ,, 5 tons ,, ,, ,, ,, 10 ,, ,, 10 ,, ,, ,, ,, ,, 15 ,, ,, 15 ,, ,, ,, ,, ,, 18 ,, Over 18 tons ,, ,, ,, ,, 21 ,, ,, 21 ,,	All ages	223 6 232 9 240 6 249 9 261 3 271 0	218 6 227 9 235 6 244 9 256 3 266 0
(2) Drivers of tractors which operate from a depot in the London Area (as defined in paragraph 35). ...	Up to and including 8 tons ... Over 8 tons and up to and including 12 tons ... Over 12 tons	All ages	234 0 242 3 251 0	— — —
(3) Statutory attendants	—	Under 18 years ...	128 6	125 9
(4) Other road haulage workers ...	—	Under 16 years ... 16 and under 17 years 17 ,, ,, 18 ,, 18 ,, ,, 19 ,, 19 ,, ,, 20 ,, 20 ,, ,, 21 ,, 21 years or over ...	86 9 94 9 103 0 138 6 151 0 166 9 215 6	84 6 92 6 101 9 135 9 147 3 162 6 212 6

SUNDAY WORK

7. A milk worker shall be paid time-and-a-half for 6 hours 40 minutes for any time worked or deemed to have been worked not exceeding 6 hours 40 minutes on Sunday not being the worker's normal day of rest and, thereafter, in accordance with paragraph 11.

COMPUTATION OF HOURS OF WORK

8. A milk worker to whom the guaranteed weekly remuneration provisions apply who works on any day shall be deemed to have worked for 6 hours 40 minutes notwithstanding that he was employed for less than 6 hours 40 minutes:

Provided that a milk worker who is instructed to report for duty and presents himself for duty but does not commence work shall be deemed to have commenced work.

OVERTIME

9. Subject to the provisions of paragraphs 25 and 44 the following shall be regarded as overtime:—

(1) Time worked in excess of 6 hours 40 minutes on any day other than the milk worker's normal day of rest, and all time worked on the milk worker's day of rest.

(2) Time worked in any week in excess of 40 hours.

10.—(1) In determining the time to be regarded as overtime, time worked shall include time deemed to have been worked under the provisions of paragraphs 8 and 24.

(2) Time worked on a customary holiday in accordance with paragraph 27(2)(b) or paragraph 28(2)(b) or on a day in the circumstances set out in the proviso to paragraph 27(4)(a) or paragraph 28(4)(a), paragraph 27(3) or paragraph 28(3) shall not be included in the calculation of overtime.

(3) When a worker's hours of duty or any part thereof entail employment between 9 p.m. and 6 a.m., a day shall, for the purpose of paragraph 9(1), be deemed to be any period of 24 hours commencing at 12 noon.

PAYMENT FOR OVERTIME

11. The following are the rates payable for overtime:—

in any week exclusive of the milk worker's normal day of rest and Sunday	time-and-a-half
on Sunday not being the milk worker's normal day of rest—	
for all time worked in excess of 6 hours 40 minutes ...	double time
on the milk worker's normal day of rest—	
for any time worked not exceeding 6 hours 40 minutes ...	double time for 6 hours 40 minutes
for all time worked in excess of 6 hours 40 minutes ...	double time.

Part III

REGULAR WORKERS INCLUDING MILK WORKERS

This Part of this Schedule applies to regular workers including milk workers.

WORKERS TEMPORARILY TRANSFERRED

12. A worker who is temporarily transferred away from his normal home depot and stationed in another locality (beyond reasonable daily travelling distance from his home) for more than one week shall be paid either the rates of wages appropriate to the locality in which his normal home depot is situated, or those appropriate to the new locality in which he has been stationed, whichever is more favourable to the worker.

HOURLY RATE

13. For the purpose of calculating the hourly rates of regular workers, the rates of wages specified in paragraphs 1 and 6 shall be divided by 40.

GUARANTEED WEEKLY REMUNERATION

14.—(1) Notwithstanding the provisions of the other paragraphs of this Schedule, where in any week a worker has performed some road haulage work for the employer and the total remuneration payable for time worked and time deemed to have been worked (excluding overtime and special payments as defined in sub-paragraph (4) of this paragraph is less than the guaranteed weekly remuneration provided under this paragraph, the minimum remuneration payable to that worker for that week shall, subject to the provisions of this paragraph, be that guaranteed weekly remuneration with the addition of any amount which may be payable in respect of overtime and by way of special payments.

(2) The guaranteed weekly remuneration is the pay for 40 hours, reduced by any time not reckonable by reason of sub-paragraph (3) of this paragraph and excluding special payments, calculated as follows:—

(a) for the time worked and time deemed to have been worked at the rate or rates applicable to such work (but excluding overtime) and

(b) for the remaining time at the time rate normally applicable to the worker.

(3) In calculating the guaranteed weekly remuneration no account shall be taken of (a) any time during which the worker is absent from work with or without leave of the employer or on account of sickness or (b) any time during which the worker is suspended from work following the expiry of any notice given to him in any of the following manners and circumstances:—

(i) flood, snow, ice or other climatic conditions of such a nature as to preclude the operation of the vehicle, provided that not less than 24 hours' notice of the suspension of work shall be given individually to the worker and by the posting of a notice in the depot or other mutually convenient place;

(ii) where the employer is unable to carry on his business by reason of a strike or lock-out, provided that not less than 4 days' notice of such inability is given to the worker;

(iii) where the employer is unable to operate a vehicle or vehicles owing to the restriction of his fuel supply under any enactment or regulation made thereunder, provided that not less than 24 hours' notice of such inability is given to the worker or workers concerned:

Provided that the foregoing notices shall not be given when the worker is away from his home depot, and the suspension shall not operate until the required notice has been given to the worker on his return to his home depot.

(4) For the purposes of sub-paragraphs (1) and (2) of this paragraph:—

(a) in addition to any time deemed to have been worked under the other provisions of this Schedule;

(i) where a worker is allowed a day as a customary holiday or in lieu of a customary holiday or an annual holiday he shall be deemed to have worked the number of hours (excluding overtime) ordinarily worked by him on that day of the week;

(ii) where a worker is required to work on a day of customary holiday he shall be deemed to have worked the number of hours (excluding overtime) ordinarily worked by him on that day of the week notwithstanding that he was employed for less than that number of hours:

Provided that if a worker works on a customary holiday in accordance with the provisions of paragraph 27(2)(b) or paragraph 28(2)(b) or on a day in the circumstances set out in the proviso to paragraph 27(4)(a) or paragraph 28(4)(a) he shall be deemed only to have worked double the number of hours worked by him on that day (part of an hour being counted as an hour).

(b) " Special payments " means the following amounts:—

(i) Any additional payment for night work payable under paragraph 21.

(ii) Any amount payable under paragraph 23 (payment for telephoning for instructions whilst off duty).

(iii) Any subsistence allowance (other than payment for hours during which the worker is deemed to be on duty) payable under paragraph 24.

(iv) Any amount payable in respect of customary holidays occurring on the worker's weekly half-holiday or, in the case of a five-day worker, on a Saturday, or, in the case of a milk worker, on his normal day of rest, under provisos (a) (b) and (c) of paragraph 27(1) or under provisos (i), (ii) and (iii) of paragraph 28(1).

(5) The provisions of this paragraph shall not apply to a worker whose normal employment in the service of the employer substantially includes other work as well as road haulage work. Such a worker shall be paid in respect of the road haulage work at the appropriate rate for the time actually spent on such work.

A worker not normally a road haulage worker, but who occasionally performs road haulage work, shall be paid the rates of wages appropriate to a road haulage worker for the time actually spent on such work.

GUARANTEED MINIMUM REMUNERATION

15.—(1) Where in any week a worker has worked, or under the provisions of paragraphs 2, 3(3), 8, 14(4)(a) and 24 is deemed to have worked, on road haulage work for the employer for not less than 40 hours and the total remuneration payable to that worker for that week for time worked and time deemed to have been worked (including overtime but excluding special payments as defined in paragraph 14(4)(b)) is not less than the guaranteed weekly remuneration provided for by sub-paragraph (2) of paragraph 14 but is less than 300s. 0d., then, notwithstanding anything contained in this Schedule, the minimum remuneration payable to that worker shall be the guaranteed minimum remuneration provided for by sub-paragraph (2) of this paragraph, with the addition of any amount which may be payable by way of special payments.

(2) The guaranteed minimum remuneration shall be the total remuneration increased by the amount provided for either in (a) or (b) of this sub-paragraph whichever is the lesser:—

(a) (i) *by twenty shillings in the case of a worker aged 21 years or over or whose rate of remuneration per week is not related to his age;*

(ii) *by fifteen shillings in the case of a worker aged under 21 years of age and whose rate of remuneration per week is related to his age;*

(b) *by an amount equal to the difference between the total remuneration and 300s. 0d.*

PART IV

WORKERS OTHER THAN REGULAR WORKERS

This Part of this Schedule applies to workers other than regular workers.

16. Subject to the provisions of this Part and of Part V of this Schedule, the minimum remuneration of workers other than regular workers shall be the hourly rates applicable to regular workers under Part I or Part II of this Schedule increased by 4d. per hour.

GUARANTEED DAY

17. Subject to the provisions of paragraph 25 (relating to the alternative weekly half-holiday) and sub-paragraphs (6) and (7) of paragraphs 27 and 28 (relating to work on customary holidays), a worker other than a regular worker shall be paid not less than the wages due for 7¼ hours in respect of work done, or deemed to have been done, by him on any day Monday to Thursday, for 7 hours in respect of work done, or deemed to have been done, on Friday, and not less than the wages due for 4 hours in respect of work done, or deemed to have been done, by him on Saturday:

Provided that—

    (1) where a spell of duty commences before midnight and continues thereafter, a worker shall not be entitled, by that fact alone, to two guaranteed payments in respect of that spell of duty;

    (2) a worker who is engaged for a day of not less than $7\frac{1}{4}$ hours on any day Monday to Thursday, of not less than 7 hours on Friday, or for not less than 4 hours on Saturday, for work other than road haulage work, but who may perform some road haulage work, shall be paid for the time actually spent on road haulage work at the hourly rate or rates, calculated in accordance with the provisions of paragraph 16; and

    (3) a worker who is instructed to report for duty, and presents himself for duty but does not commence work, shall be deemed to have commenced work.

Subject to the provisions relating to overtime, a worker other than a regular worker shall, when the number of hours worked or payable under the guarantee provided in this paragraph, is $7\frac{1}{4}$ on any day Monday to Thursday, 7 on Friday or 4 on Saturday, be paid the wages applicable to a regular worker for $7\frac{1}{4}$ hours, 7 hours or 4 hours as the case may be, plus 2s. 8d.

In all other circumstances, he shall be paid at an hourly rate, which is 4d. per hour above the hourly rate applicable to a regular worker.

OVERTIME

18. Subject to the provisions of paragraphs 24 and 25, the following shall be regarded as overtime:—

    (1) Time worked in excess of $7\frac{1}{4}$ hours on any day Monday to Thursday, in excess of 7 hours on Friday and in excess of 4 hours on Saturday.

    (2) Time worked on Sunday.

A worker who works for less than $5\frac{1}{2}$ hours on Sunday shall be deemed to have worked for $5\frac{1}{2}$ hours:

Provided that a worker whose hours entail a spell of duty commencing on Saturday and finishing on Sunday before 5.30 a.m. or commencing on Sunday after 6.30 p.m. and finishing on Monday, shall not, unless the Sunday duty is less than 3 hours, be deemed to have worked on Sunday in excess of the hours actually worked. If the Sunday duty is less than 3 hours he shall be deemed to have worked 3 hours on Sunday:

Provided also that a worker commencing work on Saturday who finishes work between midnight and 1 a.m. on Sunday shall be deemed to have worked one hour on Sunday.

19.—(1) In determining the time to be regarded as overtime, time worked shall include time deemed to have been worked under the provisions of paragraphs 18(2) and 24.

(2) Time worked on a customary holiday in accordance with paragraph 27(2)(b) or paragraph 28(2)(b) or on a day in the circumstances set out in the proviso to paragraph 27(4)(a) or paragraph 28(4)(a) shall not be included in the calculation of overtime.

(3) When a worker's hours of duty or any part thereof entail employment between 9 p.m. and 6 a.m., a day shall, for the purpose of paragraph 18(1), be deemed to be any period of 24 hours commencing at 12 noon.

PAYMENT FOR OVERTIME

20. The following are the rates payable for overtime:—

on any day (other than Sunday)	time-and-a-half
on Sunday	double time.

Part V

ALL WORKERS—ADDITIONAL PROVISIONS

This Part of this Schedule applies to all workers except where otherwise stated.

NIGHT WORK

21. A worker whose hours of duty or any part thereof entail employment between 7 p.m. and 6 a.m. shall be paid the appropriate rates of wages specified in paragraph 1, paragraph 6, or paragraph 16 and, in addition, in each spell of duty, 11d. for each hour, or part of an hour, worked between 7 p.m. and 6 a.m. provided that where a spell of duty commences before 7 p.m. and finishes not later than 9 p.m. the additional payment shall not be payable. Where overtime is payable in respect of hours worked between 7 p.m. and 6 a.m., this additional payment remains payable but is not to be included for the purpose of calculating the overtime rate payable in respect of those hours.

TRAVELLING

22. When a worker is required to travel in, or on, or to accompany a vehicle for the purpose of doing road haulage work he shall, in determining the wages payable, be deemed to be engaged on the road haulage work usually performed by him.

TELEPHONING FOR INSTRUCTIONS WHILE OFF DUTY

23.—(1) If a worker during the period between two spells of duty is required to telephone for instructions he shall be paid the wages due for one hour:

Provided that this provision shall not apply when the telephone call is made immediately following a spell of duty.

(2) On each subsequent occasion, during the same period between two spells of duty, on which the worker is required to telephone for instructions he shall be paid the wages due for 4 hours:

Provided that if when telephoning on any such occasion the worker is instructed to commence work within one hour of so telephoning, he shall be paid for one hour instead of the said 4 hours.

(3) The payments to be made under sub-paragraphs (1) and (2) of this paragraph shall be at the rate normally applicable to the worker and shall be in addition to the weekly wages otherwise due to him.

SUBSISTENCE

24.—(1)(a) When a worker's period of rest occurs away from his home depot he shall be paid 23s. 0d. in respect of each period of rest not exceeding 15 hours' continued duration. Subject to the provisions of sub-paragraph (1)(b) of this paragraph, when any such period of rest exceeds 15 hours the worker shall be deemed to be on duty and shall be entitled to be paid (in addition to the 23s. 0d.) at the time rate which would be payable if he were actually at work for the period he is resting in excess of 15 hours but not in excess of 24 hours or 23 hours according to whether he is a five- or six-day worker. If the period of rest exceeds 24 or 23 hours, as the case may be, these arrangements will continue to apply until the worker resumes actual duty;

(b) Where, following the first 15 hours of a period of rest for which sub-sistence is payable, deemed duty or actual duty commences on a Sunday, the worker shall be entitled (in addition to the 23s. 0d.) in respect of any deemed and any actual duty performed on the Sunday to not less than the wages due for 9 hours or 8 hours at double time, according to whether he is a five- or six-day worker.

(2) Notwithstanding the provisions of sub-paragraph (1) of this paragraph the following provisions shall apply in the case of a worker who is temporarily transferred away from his normal home depot and stationed in another locality (beyond reasonable daily travelling distance from his home) for more than one week:—

(a) after payment in respect of the first week in accordance with the provisions of sub-paragraph (1) of this paragraph a worker shall, in respect of the second and subsequent weeks, be paid a weekly subsistence allowance of 112s. 0d. (i.e., 16s. 0d. per day);

(b) if a worker already on temporary transfer is temporarily transferred to another new station beyond reasonable travelling distance from his home he shall (after payment in respect of the first week at such other new station in accordance with sub-paragraph (1) of this paragraph) be paid, in respect of the second and subsequent weeks, a weekly subsistence allowance of 112s. 0d. (i.e., 16s. 0d. per day);

(c) for any period of rest occurring away from a new station and from his home, he shall be paid in accordance with the provisions of sub-paragraph (1) of this paragraph and, in respect of any day for which payment is made to the worker under the provisions of that sub-paragraph, the subsistence allowances of 16s. 0d. per day (specified in (a) and (b) above) shall be reduced to 12s. 3d. per day.

ALTERNATIVE WEEKLY HALF-HOLIDAY

25. Where it is the established practice of any section of the industry to allow the weekly half-holiday on any weekday other than a Saturday, and that day is in the case of a six-day worker substituted for Saturday as the worker's weekly half-holiday the provisions of paragraphs 2, 3(1) and (2), 14, 17, 18(1) and 44, shall apply as if in these provisions that day were substituted for " Saturday " and " Saturday " for that day.

MEAL TIMES

26. The hours of work specified are, except for the purpose of paragraph 24, exclusive of meal times.

CUSTOMARY HOLIDAYS—ENGLAND AND WALES

27.—(1) Subject to the provisions of this paragraph, an employer in England and Wales shall allow the following days as holidays to regular workers to whom paragraphs 1 and 6 apply and who were in his employment on the day immediately prior to the day of holiday:—Christmas Day (or, if Christmas Day falls on a Sunday, such weekday as may be prescribed by national proclamation, or the next following Tuesday), Boxing Day, Good Friday, Easter Monday, Whit Monday (or where another day is substituted therefor by national proclamation, that day), August Bank Holiday and all nationally proclaimed holidays. Where in any place it is not the custom or practice to observe such days as holidays, other days (not fewer in number) may, by agreement between the employer and the worker, be substituted for the above-mentioned days. Each such day (i.e., one of the days specified above or a day substituted therefor—hereafter in this paragraph referred to as a " customary holiday ") taken as a holiday shall be paid for on the basis of the wages due for the number of hours (excluding overtime) ordinarily worked by the worker on that day of the week at the time rate normally applicable to the worker:

Provided that—

(a) in addition to the foregoing, in the case of a six-day worker, other than a milk worker, where the customary holiday falls on the worker's weekly half-holiday he shall be paid in respect of that day a sum equivalent to the wages due for 4 hours' work at the rate normally applicable to him;

(b) in the case of a five-day worker, where the customary holiday falls on a Saturday he shall be paid in respect of that day a sum equivalent to the wages due for 8 hours' work at the rate normally applicable to him;

(c) in the case of a milk worker, where the customary holiday falls on the worker's normal day of rest he shall be paid in respect of that day a sum equivalent to the wages due for 6 hours 40 minutes' work at the rate normally applicable to him.

(2) Notwithstanding the foregoing provisions of this paragraph, a regular worker may work for the employer on a customary holiday:—

(a) where by reason of the necessity of maintaining essential services the allowing of a customary holiday is rendered impracticable; or

(b) where the worker will work on the customary holiday for not more than 3 hours during a spell of duty commencing on the day before the customary holiday or ending on the day after the holiday:

Provided that this sub-paragraph shall not apply to women and young persons in whose cases work on the customary holiday would be illegal.

(3)(*a*) Where a worker works on a customary holiday by virtue of sub-paragraph (2)(*a*) of this paragraph he shall be paid for work on that day at not less than double the rate appropriate to such work for all time worked by him thereon or for the basic hours for that worker, whichever amount is the greater. For the purpose of this sub-paragraph basic hours means in the case of a milk worker 6 hours 40 minutes, and, in the case of any other worker, the number of hours (excluding overtime) ordinarily worked by him on the day of the week on which the customary holiday falls.

(*b*) Where a worker works on a customary holiday by virtue of sub-paragraph (2)(*b*) of this paragraph he shall be paid for work on that day at not less than double the rate appropriate to such work (part of an hour being counted as an hour) and, in addition, an amount equal to the holiday remuneration to which he would have been entitled under the provisions of this order if he had been allowed a customary holiday on that day.

(4)(*a*) Where a regular worker works on a customary holiday by virtue of the provisions of sub-paragraph (2)(*a*) of this paragraph he shall, within the period of eight weeks immediately following the customary holiday, be allowed a day's holiday (hereafter referred to as " a day in lieu of a customary holiday ") on a weekday (other than a weekly half-holiday) on which the worker normally works for the employer:

Provided that if on a weekday which is not a customary holiday or a weekly half-holiday within the said period of eight weeks the worker works for the employer for not more than 3 hours during a spell of duty commencing on the immediately preceding day or ending on the following day and the worker is paid for such work remuneration not less than the remuneration provided for work on a customary holiday under sub-paragraph (3)(*b*) of this paragraph, an employer is not required to allow to a worker a day in lieu of a customary holiday.

(*b*) For each day in lieu of a customary holiday allowed to a worker he shall be paid not less than the holiday remuneration to which he would have been entitled under the provisions of this Schedule if the day had been a customary holiday.

(*c*) For the purposes of this paragraph in the case of a worker who is employed on spells of duty which start before midnight and continue for more than 3 hours after midnight the day in lieu of a customary holiday shall include any period of 24 consecutive hours beginning and ending at noon on a weekday (other than a weekly half-holiday) on which the worker normally works.

(5) The holiday remuneration for a customary holiday or a day in lieu of a customary holiday shall be paid by the employer to the worker not later than the day on which the wages for the first working day following the customary holiday or day in lieu of the customary holiday are paid.

(6) Except as specified in sub-paragraph (7) of this paragraph a worker, other than a regular worker, who is employed on a customary holiday shall be paid for such work at double the rate otherwise appropriate thereto, and, notwithstanding that he may work for less than $7\frac{1}{4}$ hours on any such day, he shall be paid not less than twice the amount due, under the provisions of paragraph 17, for a guaranteed day of $7\frac{1}{4}$ hours.

(7) Where a worker, other than a regular worker, works for the employer on a customary holiday for not more than 3 hours during a spell of duty commencing on the immediately preceding day or ending on the following day, he shall be paid for such work at double the rate appropriate to such work, part of an hour being counted as an hour.

CUSTOMARY HOLIDAYS—SCOTLAND

28.—(1) Subject to the provisions of this paragraph, an employer in Scotland shall allow the following days as holidays to regular workers to whom paragraphs 1 and 6 apply and who were in his employment on the day immediately prior to the day of holiday:—

(a) New Year's Day (or the following day if New Year's Day falls on a Sunday), the local Spring Holiday, the local Autumn Holiday, and all nationally proclaimed holidays;

(b) Three other days in the course of a calendar year, to be fixed by the employer and notified to the workers not less than 21 days before the holiday;

(c) Where in any place it is not the custom or practice to observe the days mentioned in (a) above as holidays, other days (not fewer in number) may, by agreement between the employer and the worker, be substituted for the above-mentioned days.

Each such day (i.e., one of the days specified above or a day substituted therefor —hereafter in this paragraph referred to as a " customary holiday ") taken as a holiday shall be paid for on the basis of the wages due for the number of hours (excluding overtime) ordinarily worked by the worker on that day of the week at the time rate normally applicable to the worker:

Provided that—

(i) in addition to the foregoing, in the case of a six-day worker other than a milk worker, where the customary holiday falls on the worker's weekly half-holiday he shall be paid in respect of that day a sum equivalent to the wages due for 4 hours' work at the rate normally applicable to him;

(ii) in the case of a five-day worker, where the customary holiday falls on a Saturday he shall be paid in respect of that day a sum equivalent to the wages due for 8 hours' work at the rate normally applicable to him;

(iii) in the case of a milk worker, where the customary holiday falls on the worker's normal day of rest he shall be paid in respect of that day a sum equivalent to the wages due for 6 hours 40 minutes' work at the rate normally applicable to him.

(2) Notwithstanding the foregoing provisions of this paragraph, a regular worker may work for the employer on a customary holiday:—

(a) where by reason of the necessity of maintaining essential services the allowing of a customary holiday is rendered impracticable; or

(b) where the worker will work on the customary holiday for not more than 3 hours during a spell of duty commencing on the day before the customary holiday or ending on the day after the holiday:

Provided that this sub-paragraph shall not apply to women and young persons in whose cases work on the customary holiday would be illegal.

(3)(a) Where a worker works on a customary holiday by virtue of sub-paragraph (2)(a) of this paragraph he shall be paid for work on that day at not less than double the rate appropriate to such work for all time worked by him thereon or for the basic hours for that worker, whichever amount is the greater. For the purpose of this sub-paragraph basic hours means, in the case of a milk worker, 6 hours 40 minutes and, in the case of any other worker, the number of hours (excluding overtime) ordinarily worked by him on the day of the week on which the customary holiday falls.

(b) Where a worker works on a customary holiday by virtue of sub-paragraph (2)(b) of this paragraph he shall be paid for work on that day at not less than double the rate appropriate to such work (part of an hour being counted as an hour) and, in addition, an amount equal to the holiday remuneration to which he would have been entitled under the provisions of this order if he had been allowed a customary holiday on that day.

(4)(a) Where a regular worker works on a customary holiday by virtue of the provisions of sub-paragraph (2)(a) of this paragraph he shall, within the period of eight weeks immediately following the customary holiday, be allowed a day's holiday (hereafter referred to as " a day in lieu of a customary holiday ") on a weekday (other than a weekly half-holiday) on which the worker normally works for the employer:

Provided that if on a weekday which is not a customary holiday or a weekly half-holiday within the said period of eight weeks the worker works for the employer for not more than 3 hours during a spell of duty commencing on the immediately preceding day or ending on the following day and the worker is paid for such work remuneration not less than the remuneration provided for work on a customary holiday under sub-paragraph (3)(*b*) of this paragraph an employer is not required to allow a worker a day in lieu of a customary holiday.

(*b*) For each day in lieu of a customary holiday allowed to a worker he shall be paid not less than the holiday remuneration to which he would have been entitled under the provisions of this Schedule if the day had been a customary holiday.

(*c*) For the purposes of this paragraph in the case of a worker who is employed on spells of duty which start before midnight and continue for more than 3 hours after midnight the day in lieu of a customary holiday shall include any period of 24 consecutive hours beginning and ending at noon on a weekday (other than a weekly half-holiday) on which the worker normally works.

(5) The holiday remuneration for a customary holiday or a day in lieu of a customary holiday shall be paid by the employer to the worker not later than the day on which the wages for the first working day following the customary holiday or day in lieu of a customary holiday are paid.

(6) Except as specified in sub-paragraph (7) of this paragraph, a worker, other than a regular worker, who is employed on any of the days mentioned in sub-paragraph (1)(*a*) of this paragraph shall be paid for such work at double the rate otherwise appropriate thereto, and, notwithstanding that he may work for less than 7¼ hours on any such day, he shall be paid not less than twice the amount due, under the provisions of paragraph 17, for a guaranteed day of 7¼ hours.

(7) Where a worker, other than a regular worker, works for the employer on a customary holiday for not more than 3 hours during a spell of duty commencing on the immediately preceding day or ending on the following day, he shall be paid for such work at double the rate appropriate to such work, a part of an hour being counted as an hour.

ANNUAL HOLIDAY AND HOLIDAY REMUNERATION

29.—(1) In addition to the holidays provided for in paragraphs 27 and 28 (and subject to the provisions of sub-paragraphs (3) and (6) of this paragraph) an employer shall between the date on which this Schedule becomes effective and 15th October 1968, and in each succeeding year between 1st May and 15th October allow a holiday (hereinafter referred to as an " annual holiday ") to every worker in his employment for whom statutory minimum remuneration has been fixed under paragraphs 1, 6 or 16 and who was during the 12 months immediately preceding the commencement of the holiday season in that year (hereinafter referred to as the " qualifying period ") in his employment for any of the periods of employment specified below, and the duration of a worker's annual holiday shall be related to the period of his employment during the qualifying period as follows:—

Six-day workers		Five-day workers	
Period of employment	Duration of annual holiday	Period of employment	Duration of annual holiday
At least 48 weeks	12 days	At least 48 weeks	10 days
„ „ 44 „	11 „	„ „ 43 „	9 „
„ „ 40 „	10 „	„ „ 38 „	8 „
„ „ 36 „	9 „	„ „ 33 „	7 „
„ „ 32 „	8 „	„ „ 28 „	6 „
„ „ 28 „	7 „	„ „ 24 „	5 „
„ „ 24 „	6 „	„ „ 19 „	4 „
„ „ 20 „	5 „	„ „ 14 „	3 „
„ „ 16 „	4 „	„ „ 9 „	2 „
„ „ 12 „	3 „	„ „ 4 „	1 day
„ „ 8 „	2 „		
„ „ 4 „	1 day		

(2) For the purpose of calculating a period of employment in respect of annual holiday and accrued holiday remuneration " employment " means employment on road haulage work specified in paragraphs 45 and 46 and also employment partly on that work and partly on work other than such road haulage work, and a worker shall be treated as in the employment of the employer when absent from work in any of the following circumstances:—

> (*a*) absences of the worker arising from suspension in accordance with paragraph 14(3)(*b*);
>
> (*b*) absences of the worker owing to proved illness or accident up to but not exceeding 16 weeks in the aggregate during the qualifying period;
>
> (*c*) suspension from employment owing to shortage of work or mechanical breakdown up to but not exceeding 16 weeks in the aggregate during the qualifying period;
>
> (*d*) absences of the worker arising from the allowance of holidays provided for in paragraph 27 or paragraph 28 and annual holiday allowed under the provisions of this paragraph;
>
> (*e*) other absences with reasonable cause during the qualifying period;
>
> (*f*) absence for not more than 7 days during the qualifying period for reasons other than those specified in (*a*) to (*e*) above.

(3) Notwithstanding the provisions of sub-paragraphs (1) and (2) of this paragraph, a worker who has been absent for more than 7 days during the qualifying period for reasons other than those specified in (*a*) to (*e*) of sub-paragraph (2) of this paragraph shall not be entitled to any annual holiday in respect of such period.

(4) The duration of the worker's annual holiday during the holiday season ending on 15th October 1968, shall be reduced by any days of annual holiday duly allowed to him by the employer under the provisions of Order R.H. (84) as amended by Order R.H. (86) between 1st May 1968 and the date on which the provisions of this Schedule become effective.

(5) In this Schedule the expression " holiday season " means in relation to an annual holiday during the year 1968, the period commencing on 1st May 1968 and ending on 15th October 1968, and in relation to each subsequent year, the period commencing on 1st May and ending on 15th October in that year.

(6) Notwithstanding the provisions of sub-paragraphs (1) and (5) of this paragraph, where before 1st October in any holiday season, at the written request of a worker his employer has agreed in writing that the worker shall be allowed after the end of the holiday season and before 1st May in the following year, the annual holiday, or any part thereof, for which he has qualified under this paragraph, any such days of annual holiday may, subject to the provisions of paragraph 33, be allowed in accordance with the agreement and if so allowed shall be treated for the purposes of this Schedule as having been allowed during the holiday season.

30.—(1) In respect of an annual holiday allowed under paragraph 29, holiday remuneration shall be paid as follows:—

Period of annual holiday Column 1	Holiday remuneration for—		Column 4
	Six-day workers Column 2	Five-day workers Column 3	
12 days	Twice the amount in Col. 4	—	The amount which the worker would be entitled to receive from his employer at the date of the annual holiday for 40 hours' work (exclusive of overtime) at the time rate normally applicable to him under this Schedule, *together with an addition, in the case of a regular worker, where the amount so calculated is less than 300s. 0d. of whichever of the following amounts is the lesser:—* *(a) the difference between the amount so calculated and 300s. 0d.* *OR* *(b) (i) twenty shillings in the case of a worker aged 21 years or over or whose rate of remuneration per week is not related to his age:* *(ii) fifteen shillings in the case of a worker aged under 21 years of age and whose rate of remuneration per week is related to his age,*
11 days	One and five-sixths times the amount in Col. 4	—	
10 days	One and two-thirds times the amount in Col. 4	Twice the amount in Col 4	
9 days	One and half times the amount in Col. 4	One and four-fifths times the amount in Col. 4	
8 days	One and one-third times the amount in Col. 4	One and three-fifths times the amount in Col. 4	
7 days	One and one-sixth times the amount in Col. 4	One and two fifths times the amount in Col. 4	
6 days	The amount in Col 4	One and one-fifth times the amount in Col. 4	
5 days	Five-sixths of the amount in Col. 4	The amount in Col. 4	
4 days	Two-thirds of the amount in Col. 4	Four-fifths of the amount in Col. 4	
3 days	One-half of the amount in Col. 4	Three-fifths of the amount in Col. 4	
2 days	One-third of the amount in Col. 4	Two-fifths of the amount in Col. 4	
1 day	One-sixth of the amount in Col. 4	One-fifth of the amount in Col. 4	

(2) Holiday remuneration shall be paid on the last pay day preceding the annual holiday:

Provided that where in accordance with the proviso to paragraph 33(1) an annual holiday is allowed in two or three periods the holiday remuneration shall be apportioned accordingly.

31. Where any accrued holiday remuneration has been paid by the employer to the worker under paragraph 32(1) in respect of any period of employment in the qualifying period preceding the holiday season current when the annual holiday is allowed, the amount to be paid in respect of the period of such holiday is the appropriate amount payable under paragraph 30 less the accrued holiday remuneration previously paid as aforesaid.

32.—(1) Where a worker ceases to be employed, accrued holiday remuneration shall, immediately on the termination of the employment, be paid to him by his employer in accordance with sub-paragraph (2) of this paragraph for periods of employment in respect of which he has not been allowed or has not become entitled to be allowed an annual holiday under this Schedule:

Provided that—

(a) where a worker ceases to be employed after being allowed a part of the annual holiday for which he has qualified by reason of his employment during any of the periods of 12 months referred to in the next following sub-paragraph but before being allowed the rest of the annual holiday for which he has so qualified, the accrued holiday remuneration payable to him in respect of his employment during the said period of 12 months shall be reduced by the amount of holiday remuneration received by him in respect of the part of the annual holiday he has been allowed;

(b) the amount of any accrued holiday remuneration payable in respect of any period of employment shall be reduced by the amount of any previous payment of accrued holiday remuneration in respect of that period made by the employer to the worker under the provisions of this Schedule or of Order R.H. (84) and Order R.H. (86).

(2) For the purpose of sub-paragraph (1) of this paragraph, during the period of 12 months commencing on 1st May 1967, and thereafter during each successive period of 12 months commencing on 1st May, accrued holiday remuneration shall be payable as follows:—

Six-day workers		Five-day workers		
Period of employment Column 1	Accrued holiday remuneration Column 2	Period of employment Column 3	Accrued holiday remuneration Column 4	Column 5
After 48 weeks	Twice the amount in Col. 5	After 48 weeks	Twice the amount in Col. 5	The amount which the worker would be entitled to receive from his employer at the date of the termination of his employment for 40 hours' work (exclusive of overtime) at the time rate normally applicable to him under this Schedule, *together with an addition, in the case of a regular worker where the amount so calculated is less than 300s. 0d. of whichever of the following amounts is the lesser:—* (a) *the difference between the amount so calculated and 300s. 0d.* OR (b) (i) *twenty shillings in the case of a worker aged 21 years or over or whose rate of remuneration per week is not related to his age:* (ii) *fifteen shillings in the case of a worker aged under 21 years of age and whose rate of remuneration per week is related to his age.*
After 44 weeks	One and five-sixths times the amount in Col. 5	After 43 weeks	One and four-fifths times the amount in Col. 5	
After 40 weeks	One and two-thirds times the amount in Col. 5	After 38 weeks	One and three-fifths times the amount in Col. 5	
After 36 weeks	One and a half times the amount in Col. 5	After 33 weeks	One and two-fifths times the amount in Col. 5	
After 32 weeks	One and one-third times the amount in Col. 5	After 28 weeks	One and one-fifth times the amount in Col. 5	
After 28 weeks	One and one-sixth times the amount in Col. 5	After 24 weeks	The amount in Col. 5	
After 24 weeks	The amount in Col. 5	After 19 weeks	Four-fifths of the amount in Col. 5	
After 20 weeks	Five-sixths of the amount in Col. 5	After 14 weeks	Three-fifths of the amount in Col. 5	
After 16 weeks	Two-thirds of the amount in Col. 5	After 9 weeks	Two-fifths of the amount in Col. 5	
After 12 weeks	One-half of the amount in Col. 5	After 4 weeks	One-fifth of the amount in Col. 5	
After 8 weeks	One-third of the amount in Col. 5			
After 4 weeks	One-sixth of the amount in Col. 5			

(3) Accrued holiday remuneration shall not be payable to a worker in respect of a qualifying period during which he was absent for more than 7 days for reasons other than those specified in (a) to (e) of paragraph 29(2).

33.—(1) An annual holiday under paragraph 29 shall be allowed on consecutive working days being days upon which the worker is normally called upon to work, and days of holiday shall be treated as consecutive notwithstanding that a Sunday or any of the holidays allowed under paragraph 27 or paragraph 28 intervenes:

Provided that where the duration of an annual holiday for which a worker is qualified exceeds the period of his normal working week, the holiday may, at the written request of the worker and with the agreement of the employer, be allowed in two or three periods, one of which shall be not less than the period of his normal working week.

(2) An employer shall give to a worker reasonable notice of the commencing date or dates and of the duration of his annual holiday. Such notice may be given individually to a worker or by the posting of a notice in the worker's home depot.

PART VI

DEFINITIONS

Carrying capacity

34.—(1) The carrying capacity of a vehicle is the weight of the maximum load normally carried by the vehicle, and such carrying capacity when so established shall not be affected either by variations in the weight of the load resulting from collections or deliveries or emptying of containers during the course of the journey, or by the fact that on any particular journey a load greater or less than the established carrying capacity is carried.

(2) Where a trailer is attached to the vehicle, the load shall be the loads of the vehicle and trailer combined.

LONDON AREA

35. London Area means the localities named below, and these localities are, unless the context otherwise requires, those defined for local government purposes as at 1st August 1964.

Locality	Local Authority	Locality	Local Authority
City of London		Rainham (see Hornchurch UD)	Parish
Dartford	Borough	Romford	Borough
Dartford—Only Parish of Stone...	Rural District	Stone (see Dartford RD) ...	Parish
		Swanscombe	Urban
Gravesend	Borough		District
Hornchurch—Only Parishes of Rainham, Wennington, and such other parts as are within 2 miles, in a straight line, of the north bank of the River Thames	Urban District	Thurrock—Only that part which is within 2 miles, in a straight line, of the north bank of the River Thames, except those parts which were, prior to 1st April 1936, known as the Parishes of Corringham, Fobbing, Mucking, Stanford-le-Hope, in the Rural District of Orsett	Urban District
Metropolitan Police District as existing on 1st August 1964— Except that part of the Borough of Watford which is included therein, and except the UD of Bushey	—		
Northfleet	Urban District	Wennington (see Hornchurch UD)	Parish

Note: In case of doubt as to the grading applicable to a particular depot, an enquiry should be addressed to the Clerk of the appropriate Local Authority as to the title of the Local Government administrative area, as it existed on 1st August 1964, in which the depot is situated.

Overtime expressions

36. The expressions time-and-a-half and double time mean respectively one and a half times and twice the rate of wages otherwise applicable.

Vehicle

37. Vehicle means a mechanically driven goods vehicle.

Regular worker

38. A regular worker is a worker employed by the week or longer period.

Driver

39. A driver is a worker employed in driving a vehicle and in performing when so required any other road haulage work.

Foremen and removal packers in the Furniture Warehousing and Removing Industry

40.—(1) A foreman in the Furniture Warehousing and Removing Industry is a worker who has charge of a removal and who has authority to issue instructions to two or more persons.

(2) A removal packer in the Furniture Warehousing and Removing Industry is a skilled worker who packs china and other articles.

Heavy brakesman and steersman

41. A heavy brakesman and steersman is a person operating the steering and braking equipment of a heavy trailer used for the carriage of abnormal indivisible loads.

Film transport worker

42. A film transport worker is a worker engaged exclusively in the collection and delivery of films for the cinematograph industry:

Provided that a worker shall not cease to be a film transport worker solely by reason of the fact that he collects from and delivers to cinemas cinematograph accessories and equipment which are carried at the same time as the films are normally carried.

Milk Worker

43. A milk worker is a regular worker who is employed on 6 days a week and who is exclusively engaged in the collection of milk from farms and its delivery to dairies:

Provided that a worker shall not cease to be a milk worker solely by reason of the fact that, exceptionally, he is required to work on the duties specified above on the remaining day of the week.

Ordinary working hours

44. The expression "number of hours (excluding overtime) ordinarily worked by the worker on that day of the week" means—

(1) in the case of a regular worker other than a milk worker:—

    (a) in respect of a six-day worker (subject to the provisions of paragraph 25), $7\frac{1}{4}$ hours on any day Monday to Thursday, 7 hours on Friday and 4 hours on Saturday:

        Provided that $7\frac{1}{4}$ hours may be substituted for 7 hours on Friday if 7 hours is substituted for $7\frac{1}{4}$ hours on one other day from Monday to Thursday.

    (b) in respect of a five-day worker, 8 hours on any day Monday to Friday;

(2) in the case of a milk worker, 6 hours 40 minutes.

PART VII

WORKERS TO WHOM THIS SCHEDULE APPLIES

45. Subject to the provisions of this paragraph and to the provisions of paragraph 48 hereof, this Schedule applies to road haulage workers in respect of road haulage work performed in connection with any motor goods vehicle (including a trailer)

specified or deemed to be specified in an "A" licence or a "B" licence granted under the Road Traffic Act 1960(a):

Provided that the remuneration specified in this Schedule shall not apply to the following classes of road haulage work, namely, the employment of contractors' men on vehicles hired on a 24-hour stand-by basis by or on behalf of the Secretary of State for Defence in connection with manoeuvres, exercises, training or active service.

46. A person is a road haulage worker and is deemed to be employed on road haulage work if he is employed on all or any of the work described in (1) to (5) below or if his time is occupied as specified in (6) to (9) below, that is to say:—

(1) driving or assisting in the driving or control of the vehicle;

(2) collecting or loading goods to be carried in or on the vehicle;

(3) attending to goods while so carried;

(4) unloading or delivering goods after being so carried;

(5) acting as attendant to the vehicle;

and who is required to travel on or to accompany the vehicle for the purpose of doing any such work;

(6) in doing any work incidental to his employment in work mentioned in sub-paragraphs (1) to (5) hereof:

(7) in travelling in or on or accompanying a goods vehicle in connection with his employment in the work so mentioned;

(8) in holding himself under the orders or at the disposal of his employer while waiting in connection with his employment in the work so mentioned;

(9) in waiting (whether overnight or otherwise) in accordance with the instructions of his employer as a necessary consequence of his employment in any of the work so mentioned:

Provided that a person employed in loading goods to be carried in or on a goods vehicle or in unloading goods after being so carried and required to travel on or to accompany the vehicle partly for that purpose, shall not be deemed to be a road haulage worker by reason only of that employment, if the main purpose for which he is required to travel on or to accompany the vehicle is that of executing work other than road haulage work after its arrival at his destination.

47. For the purposes of this Schedule road haulage work includes road haulage work performed by a road haulage worker employed by a person carrying on the business of a goods transport clearing house, i.e., the business of arranging for the mechanical transport of goods by road.

48. This Schedule does not apply to workers:—

(1) for whom or in respect of whose work a minimum rate of wages is, for the time being, fixed by or under any other enactment; or

(2) for whom minimum remuneration has been fixed pursuant to proposals of any other Wages Council established under the Wages Councils Act 1959.

(a) 1960 c. 16.

EXPLANATORY NOTE

(This Note is not part of the Order.)

This Order, which has effect from 16th August 1968, sets out the statutory minimum remuneration payable and the holidays to be allowed in substitution for the statutory minimum remuneration and holidays set out in the Wages Regulation (Road Haulage) Order 1966 (Order R.H. (84)) as amended by the Wages Regulation (Road Haulage) (Amendment) Order 1968 (Order R.H. (86)), which Orders are revoked.

New provisions are printed in italics.

1968 No. 1132

AGRICULTURE

The Price Stability of Imported Products (Minimum Import Price Levels) Order 1968

Made - - -		*16th July* 1968
Laid before Parliament		*23rd July* 1968
Coming into Operation		*1st August* 1968

The Minister of Agriculture, Fisheries and Food and the Secretaries of State respectively concerned with agriculture in Scotland and Northern Ireland, acting jointly in exercise of the powers conferred upon them by section 1 (2), (4), (6) and (7) of the Agriculture and Horticulture Act 1964(a) and of all other powers enabling them in that behalf, with the approval of the Treasury, hereby make the following order:—

1. This order may be cited as the Price Stability of Imported Products (Minimum Import Price Levels) Order 1968; and shall come into operation on 1st August 1968.

2.—(1) In this order—
"the Act" means the Agriculture and Horticulture Act 1964;
"produce" and "related product" have the meaning respectively assigned to them by section 1 (10) of the Act;
"the Ministers" means the Minister of Agriculture, Fisheries and Food, and the Secretaries of State respectively concerned with agriculture in Scotland and Northern Ireland acting jointly;
"specified commodity" means any description of produce or related product in relation to which the powers conferred by section 1 (2) of the Act are for the time being exercisable by virtue of an order made by the Ministers under section 1 (1) of the Act;
"tariff heading" means a heading of the Customs Tariff 1959 (as provided under section 1 (4) of the Import Duties Act 1958(b)), and four-figure references of the type "10.01" are references to tariff headings.

(2) In interpreting and applying Schedule 1 to this order the prescribed standard moisture content wherever referred to shall be 14 per cent. by weight.

(3) The Interpretation Act 1889(c) shall apply to the interpretation of this order as it applies to the interpretation of an Act of Parliament and as if this order and the orders hereby revoked were Acts of Parliament.

(a) 1964 c. 28.   (b) 6 & 7 Eliz. 2. c. 6.   (c) 1889 c. 63.

3.—(1) The minimum price level for such imports into the United Kingdom of any specified commodity as are described in column 2 of Schedule 1 to this order in relation to the tariff heading indicated in column 1 of that Schedule shall be that specified in relation thereto in column 3 of that Schedule.

(2) In each case the minimum import price level prescribed by this order shall be taken to represent a price level at which goods would normally be delivered to a buyer at any port or place of importation in the United Kingdom including any duty of customs chargeable in the United Kingdom.

4. The orders specified in Schedule 2 to this order are hereby revoked.

In Witness whereof the Official Seal of the Minister of Agriculture, Fisheries and Food is hereunto affixed on 10th July 1968.

    (L.S.)

Cledwyn Hughes,
Minister of Agriculture,
Fisheries and Food.

Given under the Seal of the Secretary of State for Scotland on 11th July 1968.

    (L.S.)

William Ross,
Secretary of State for Scotland.

Given under the hand of the Secretary of State for the Home Department on 15th July 1968.

James Callaghan,
Secretary of State for the Home
Department.

Approved

16th July 1968.

Harry Gourlay,
E. Alan Fitch,
Two of the Lords Commissioners
of Her Majesty's Treasury.

SCHEDULE 1

Minimum Import Price Levels

1 Tariff Heading	2 Description of Imports	3 Minimum Import Price Level (per ton)
		£ s. d.
	Imports of:—	
10.01	*Wheat:—*	
	A. Denatured wheat	22 19 0
	B. Other wheat:—	
	1. E.E.C. milling; Swedish milling; Finnish milling; Greek milling; wheats of comparable quality ...	25 5 0
	2. Canadian Soft Eastern White; United States Soft White No. 2; United States Soft Red Winter No. 2; wheats of comparable quality	26 10 0
	3. Australian fair average quality; Canadian No. 5; wheats of comparable quality	27 10 0
	4. United States Hard and Dark Hard Winters Nos. 1 and 2 with in each case less than 14 per cent. by weight of protein at the prescribed standard moisture content; United States Hard White; Argentinian; wheats of comparable quality ...	28 10 0
	5. Canadian Manitoba Northern No. 4; United States Northern, Dark Northern and Red Springs Nos. 1 and 2 with in each case less than 14 per cent. by weight of protein at the prescribed standard moisture content; United States Hard and Dark Hard Winters Nos. 1 and 2 with in each case 14 per cent. or more by weight of protein at the prescribed standard moisture content; wheats of comparable quality	29 5 0
	6. Canadian Manitoba Northern Nos. 1, 2 and 3; United States Northern, Dark Northern and Red Springs Nos. 1 and 2 with in each case 14 per cent. or more by weight of protein at the prescribed standard moisture content; wheats of comparable quality	30 0 0
10.03	Barley	21 19 0
10.04	Oats	21 19 0

1 Tariff Heading	2 Description of Imports	3 Minimum Import Price Level (per ton)
		£ s. d.
10.05	*Maize other than sweet corn on the cob:—* A. Flat white maize	22 19 0
	B. Other	22 19 0
10.07	Grain Sorghum	22 9 0
11.01	*Cereal flours, other than rice flour:—* A. Wheat flours:	
	1. not containing any chalk and containing less than 12 per cent. by weight of protein, 1 per cent. or more by weight of natural ash and not more than 1 per cent. by weight of fibre, in each case at the prescribed standard moisture content	26 4 0
	2. not containing any chalk and containing 12 per cent. or more by weight of protein, 1 per cent. or more by weight of natural ash and not more than 1 per cent. by weight of fibre, in each case at the prescribed standard moisture content	29 5 0
	3. not containing any chalk and containing not less than 0.7 per cent. and not more than 0.9 per cent. by weight of natural ash at the prescribed standard moisture content	36 0 0
	4. containing chalk and not less than 0.7 per cent. by weight of natural ash and not more than 1 per cent. by weight of fibre, in each case at the prescribed standard moisture content	36 0 0
	5. other: (A) containing less than 10 per cent. by weight of protein at the prescribed standard moisture content	36 0 0
	(B) containing 10 per cent. or more but not more than 12 per cent. by weight of protein at the prescribed standard moisture content... ...	40 10 0
	(C) containing more than 12 per cent. by weight of protein at the prescribed standard moisture content	45 0 0
	B. Other flours: 1. of barley	25 4 0
	2. of maize	26 4 0
	3. of oats	25 4 0
	4. other	25 4 0

1 Tariff Heading	2 Description of Imports	3 Minimum Import Price Level (per ton)
		£ s. d.
11.02	*Cereal groats, cereal meal, other worked cereals and germ of cereals (other than any products of rice and any blocked, pot and pearl barley):*	
	A. Cereal groats:	
	1. of wheat	26 4 0
	2. of barley	25 4 0
	3. of maize	26 4 0
	4. of oats	25 4 0
	5. other	25 4 0
	B. Cereal meals:	
	1. of wheat:	
	(A) denatured wheat meal	26 4 0
	(B) other:	
	(1) containing less than 10 per cent. by weight of protein at the prescribed standard moisture content	36 0 0
	(2) containing 10 per cent. or more but not more than 12 per cent. by weight of protein at the prescribed standard moisture content	40 10 0
	(3) containing more than 12 per cent. by weight of protein at the prescribed standard moisture content	45 0 0
	2. of barley	25 4 0
	3. of maize:	
	(A) containing less than 9 per cent. by weight of fibre at the prescribed standard moisture content	26 4 0
	(B) containing 9 per cent. or more by weight of fibre at the prescribed standard moisture content	21 17 0
	4. of oats	25 4 0
	5. other	25 4 0
	C. Kibbled or cut cereals:	
	1. wheat	26 4 0
	2. barley	25 4 0
	3. maize...	26 4 0
	4. oats	25 4 0
	5. other	25 4 0
	D. Rolled, flaked, crushed or bruised cereals:	
	1. wheat	27 14 0
	2. barley	26 14 0
	3. maize:	
	(A) flaked	28 9 0
	(B) rolled, crushed or bruised	27 14 0
	4. oats	26 14 0
	5. other	26 14 0

1 Tariff Heading	2 Description of Imports	3 Minimum Import Price Level (per ton)
		£ s. d.
	E. Other processed cereals:	
	1. wheat	26 4 0
	2. barley	25 4 0
	3. maize...	26 4 0
	4. oats	25 4 0
	5. other	25 4 0
23.02	*Bran, sharps and other residues derived from the sifting, milling or working of cereals other than of rice:* Containing not more than 13 per cent. by weight of fibre at the prescribed standard moisture content ...	20 15 0

SCHEDULE 2

Orders revoked	References
The Price Stability of Imported Products (Minimum Import Price Levels) Order 1964.	S.I. 1964/687 (1964 II, p. 1305).
The Price Stability of Imported Products (Minimum Import Price Levels) (Operative Date) Order 1964.	S.I. 1964/810 (1964 II, p. 1715).
The Price Stability of Imported Products (Minimum Import Price Levels) (Amendment) Order 1964.	S.I. 1964/990 (1964 II, p. 2231).
The Price Stability of Imported Products (Minimum Import Price Levels) (Amendment) Order 1965.	S.I. 1965/5 (1965 I, p. 7).
The Price Stability of Imported Products (Minimum Import Price Levels) (Amendment No. 2) Order 1965.	S.I. 1965/1578 (1965 II, p. 4600).

EXPLANATORY NOTE
(This Note is not part of the Order.)

This order, which comes into operation on 1st August 1968, supersedes the Price Stability of Imported Products (Minimum Import Price Levels) Order 1964, as amended. It prescribes new minimum import price levels for imports into the United Kingdom of the cereals, cereal products and by-products described in Schedule 1 to the order.

STATUTORY INSTRUMENTS

1968 No. 1146

AGRICULTURE

AGRICULTURAL GRANTS, GOODS AND SERVICES

Grants for Guarantees of Bank Loans (Extension of Period) Order 1968

Made - - - - - -	*20th June* 1968
Laid before the House of Commons	*28th June* 1968
Coming into Operation- - -	*1st April* 1969

The Minister of Agriculture, Fisheries and Food in exercise of the powers conferred upon him by section 64(7) of the Agriculture Act 1967(a), with the approval of the Treasury, hereby makes the following order:—

1. This order may be cited as the Grants for Guarantees of Bank Loans (Extension of Period) Order 1968; and shall come into operation on 1st April 1969.

2. The period mentioned in subsection (2)(*a*) of section 64 of the Agriculture Act 1967 (being the period within which a guarantee must be given if expenditure incurred in fulfilling a guarantee given on or after 1st April 1966 is to attract grant under that section) is hereby extended by an additional period of five years beginning on 1st April 1969.

In Witness whereof the Official Seal of the Minister of Agriculture, Fisheries and Food is hereunto affixed on 19th June 1968.

(L.S.)

Cledwyn Hughes,
Minister of Agriculture
Fisheries and Food.

Approved.
20th June 1968.

B. K. O'Malley,
J. McCann,
Two of the Lords Commissioners of
Her Majesty's Treasury.

(a) 1967 c. 22.

EXPLANATORY NOTE
(This Note is not part of the Order.)

Section 64 of the Agriculture Act 1967 empowers the Minister of Agriculture, Fisheries and Food, with the approval of the Treasury, to make a grant in respect of expenditure incurred in fulfilling a guarantee given as security for a loan made in the course of a banking business to a person requiring the loan for the purposes of an agriculture or horticulture business carried on by him where the guarantee was given during the period of three years beginning on 1st April 1966. This order, made under section 64(7) of the Act, extends that period, within which the guarantee must have been given, by an additional period of five years beginning on 1st April 1969.

In accordance with section 64(7), this order was approved by a resolution of the House of Commons on 18th July 1968.

STATUTORY INSTRUMENTS

1968 No. 1147

TAXES

The Selective Employment Payments Variation Order 1968

Laid before Parliament in draft

Made - - -	*18th July* 1968

Coming into Operation—

Article 2	*5th August* 1968
Article 3	*2nd September* 1968

The Secretary of State with the consent of the Treasury in exercise of her powers under section 9(1) of the Selective Employment Payments Act 1966(a) (hereinafter referred to as " the principal Act ") and of all other powers enabling her in that behalf hereby makes the following order, a draft of which has been approved by resolution of each House of Parliament.

Citation, commencement and interpretation

1.—(1) This Order may be cited as the Selective Employment Payments Variation Order 1968.

(2) Article 2 of this Order shall come into operation on 5th August 1968 and Article 3 of this Order shall come into operation on 2nd September 1968.

(3) The Interpretation Act 1889(b) shall apply to the interpretation of this Order as it applies to the interpretation of an Act of Parliament.

(4) The references in this Order to sections are references to sections of the principal Act.

(5) In this Order the expressions " knacker's yard " and " slaughterhouse "—

(*a*) in relation to England and Wales shall respectively apply only to premises licensed as a knacker's yard or a slaughterhouse under section 62 of the Food and Drugs Act 1955(c);

(*b*) in relation to Scotland shall respectively apply only to premises licensed as a knacker's yard under section 33 of the Public Health (Scotland) Act 1897(d) or to premises registered as a slaughterhouse under section 9 of the Slaughterhouses Act 1954(e).

(a) 1966 c. 32.	(b) 1889 c. 63.
(c) 1955 c. 16.	(d) 1897 c. 38.
(e) 1954 c. 42.	

Additions to employments to which section 1 applies

2. Section 1 (which, subject to the provisions of the Revenue Act 1968(**a**) specifies employments as respects which an employer is entitled to selective employment premium) shall have effect as if to subsection (2)(*a*) thereof there were added the following:—

> " (v) testing manufactured products carried on for the manufacturer for the purpose of ascertaining whether or not they conform to a standard laid down in any statutory provision;
>
> (vi) slaughtering animals in a knacker's yard or slaughterhouse;"

Removals from employments to which section 2 applies

3.—(1) Section 2 shall not apply to the following:—

(*a*) employment (other than employment directed to be left out of account under paragraph (*c*) of section 4(3)) which under the provisions of section 4 is by, or is treated as by, an employer to whom that section applies;

(*b*) employment by a charity.

(2) In this Article the expression " charity "—

(*a*) in the application of this Order to England and Wales has the same meaning as in section 5(3); and

(*b*) in the application of this Order to Scotland means an employer who is for the time being certified by the Secretary of State, or on appeal from him found by the Court of Session, to be such a charity as is referred to in section 5(4).

Barbara Castle,

17th July 1968.

First Secretary of State and Secretary of State
for Employment and Productivity.

We consent.

Joseph Harper,
E. Alan Fitch,

18th July 1968.

Two of the Lords Commissioners of Her Majesty's Treasury.

(a) 1968 c. 11.

EXPLANATORY NOTE

(This Note is not part of the Order.)

This Order adds to the employments which may be eligible for payments under section 1 of the Selective Employment Payments Act 1966, employments in establishments engaged in certain activities relating to statutory testing and slaughtering animals.

The Order also removes from section 2 employments by local authorities and charities. Provision for payments to the local authorities is made by section 4 of the Act and charities are eligible for refunds under section 5 thereof.

STATUTORY INSTRUMENTS

1968 No. 1148

EDUCATION, ENGLAND AND WALES

The Direct Grant Schools (Amendment) Regulations 1968

Made - - -	19*th July* 1968
Laid before Parliament	25*th July* 1968
Coming into Operation	1*st August* 1968

The Secretary of State for Education and Science, in exercise of the powers conferred upon him by section 100 of the Education Act 1944(a) as amended by the Secretary of State for Education and Science Order 1964(b), hereby makes the following regulations :—

Citation, commencement and interpretation

1.—(1) These regulations may be cited as the Direct Grant Schools (Amendment) Regulations 1968 and shall come into operation on 1st August 1968.

(2) The Interpretation Act 1889(c) shall apply for the interpretation of these regulations as it applies for the interpretation of an Act of Parliament.

Definition

2. In these regulations the expression "the principal regulations" means the Direct Grant Schools Regulations 1959(d) as amended (e).

Capitation grant

3. Capitation grant shall be payable to the proprietors of a grammar school under regulation 4(1)(a) of the principal regulations at a rate not exceeding £32 and accordingly for the reference in that paragraph to £52 there shall be substituted a reference to £32.

Provision of milk

4. Regulation 13 of the principal regulations shall cease to have effect in so far as it requires the proprietors of a grammar school to provide for the supply of milk to day-pupils and accordingly there shall be omitted—

(a) in paragraph (1)(b) of that regulation the words "of milk to drink and" ; and

(b) in paragraph (2) of the regulation the words "or for the milk supplied to day-pupils".

(a) 1944 c. 31.   (b) S.I. 1964/490 (1964 I, p.800).
(c) 1889 c. 63.   (d) S.I. 1959/1832 (1959 I, p.1034).
(e) The relevant amending instruments are S.I. 1963/1379, 1964/1312, 1965/1978 (1963 II, p. 2385; 1964 II, p. 2985; 1965 III, p. 5852).

Dismissal and exclusion of teachers

5. For regulations 23 and 24 of the principal regulations there shall be substituted—

"Restriction on employment of teachers

23. A person who is on grounds of misconduct or conviction of a criminal offence determined by the Secretary of State to be unsuitable for employment as a teacher or suitable for employment as such only to a limited extent, shall not be employed as a teacher or, as the case may be, shall be employed as such only to the extent determined by the Secretary of State.

Reporting of termination of employment of teachers

24. If the engagement of a teacher is terminated whether by dismissal or resignation on account of misconduct or conviction of a criminal offence, the facts shall be reported to the Secretary of State."

Given under the Official Seal of the Secretary of State for Education and Science on 19th July 1968.

(L.S.) *Shirley Williams,*

Minister of State for Education and Science.

EXPLANATORY NOTE

(This Note is not part of the Regulations.)

These regulations amend the existing provisions relating to the payment of capitation grant to, and the provision of milk in, direct grant grammar schools and to the dismissal and exclusion of teachers from direct grant schools generally.

STATUTORY INSTRUMENTS

1968 No. 1149 (S.125)

SHERIFF COURT, SCOTLAND

Act of Sedurunt (Sheriff Court Procedure Amendment) 1968

Made	-	-	-	*18th July 1968*
Coming into Operation				*16th September 1968*

The Lords of Council and Session, under and by virtue of the powers conferred upon them by section 34 of the Administration of Justice (Scotland) Act 1933(a) and of all other powers competent to them in that behalf do hereby enact and declare as follows:-

1. The Sheriff Courts (Scotland) Act 1907(b) as amended (hereinafter referred to as "the Act") shall be further amended as follows:-

(1) In Section 45 of the Act there shall be inserted between the words "fifteen", and "seventeen" the words "fifteen A,".

(2) After Rule 15 in the First Schedule to the Act there shall be added a new Rule as follows:- "15A.
"Postal citation. In any cause in which it shall be competent to serve or intimate "any document or to cite any person by recorded delivery, such service intim- "ation or citation, when made by recorded delivery, shall only be competent "and effective by such mode if it is made by recorded delivery first class service".

2. This Act of Sedurunt may be cited as the Act of Sedurunt (Sheriff Court Procedure Amendment) 1968, and shall come into operation on 16th September 1968.

And the Lords appoint this Act of Sedurunt to be inserted in the Books of Sederunt.

Edinburgh,
18th July 1968.

J. L. Clyde,
I.P.D.

(a) 1933 c. 41.   (b) 1907 c. 51.

EXPLANATORY NOTE

(The Note is not part of the Act of Sederunt)

This Act of Sederunt amends the Rules of the Sheriff Court by providing that any service, intimation or citation by recorded delivery shall be made by recorded delivery first class service. It applies to all causes including small debt causes. It comes into operation on the date appointed by the Postmaster General for the introduction of recorded delivery first class service.

STATUTORY INSTRUMENTS

1968 No. 1150 (S.126)

COURT OF SESSION, SCOTLAND

Act of Sedurunt (Rules of Court Amendment No. 2) 1968

Made - - -	*18th July 1968*
Coming into Operation	*16th September 1968*

The Lords of Council and Session, under and by virtue of the powers conferred upon them by section 16 of the Administration of Justice (Scotland) Act 1933(a) and of all other powers competent to them in that behalf, do hereby enact and declare as follows:-

1. The Rules of Court (b) shall be amended by the addition of a new Section to follow Rule 68 in Chapter I as follows:-

SECTION 10.

Service, intimation and citation

"68A.   In any cause in which it shall be competent to serve or intimate any document or to cite any person by recorded delivery, such service, intimation or citation, when made by recorded delivery, shall only be competent and effective by such mode if it is made by recorded delivery first class service".

2. This Act of Sederunt may be cited as the Act of Sederunt (Rules of Court Amendment No. 2) 1968, and shall come into operation on 16th September 1968.

And the Lords appoint this Act of Sederunt to be inserted in the Books of Sederunt.

Edinburgh,	*J. L. Clyde,*
18th July 1968.	I.P.D.

(a) 1933 c. 41.   (b) S.I. 1965/321 (1965 I, p. 803).

EXPLANATORY NOTE

(This Note is not part of the Act of Sederunt)

This Act of Sederunt amends the Rules of Court by providing that any service, intimation or citation by recorded delivery shall be made by recorded delivery first class service. It comes into operation on the date appointed by the Postmaster General for the introduction of recorded delivery first class service.

STATUTORY INSTRUMENTS

1968 No. 1157

CUSTOMS AND EXCISE

The Import Duty Drawbacks (No. 6) Order 1968

Made - - - -	*22nd July* 1968
Laid before the House of Commons	*26th July* 1968
Coming into Operation	*1st August* 1968

The Lords Commissioners of Her Majesty's Treasury, by virtue of the powers conferred on them by sections 9 and 13 of, and Schedule 5 to, the Import Duties Act 1958(**a**), and of all other powers enabling them in that behalf, on the recommendation of the Board of Trade hereby make the following order:—

1.—(1) In Schedule 2 to the Import Duty Drawbacks (No. 6) Order 1966(**b**), (which relates to the drawbacks to be allowed on the exportation of goods produced or manufactured from imported articles),—

(*a*) in the entry relating to animal black, the rate of drawback specified in column 3 shall be amended by substituting £2 13s. 0d. per ton for £6 3s. 4d. per ton; and

(*b*) the entry relating to confectionery cases and baking cases of crimped paper shall be omitted.

(2) Paragraph 2 of Schedule 3 to the said Order of 1966 shall be amended by omitting the words " Confectionery cases ".

(3) In the Schedule to the Import Duty Drawbacks (No. 8) Order 1966(**c**), paragraph 1 is hereby revoked.

2.—(1) This Order may be cited as the Import Duty Drawbacks (No. 6) Order 1968.

(2) The Interpretation Act 1889(**d**) shall apply for the interpretation of this Order as it applies for the interpretation of an Act of Parliament.

(3) This Order shall come into operation on 1st August 1968.

Joseph Harper,
J. McCann,
Two of the Lords Commissioners
of Her Majesty's Treasury.

22nd July 1968.

EXPLANATORY NOTE

(*This Note is not part of the Order*)

This Order—

(i) revises the rate of drawback of import duty in respect of animal black manufactured from certain imported bones;

(ii) revokes the provision for the allowance of drawback of import duty in respect of confectionery cases and baking cases of crimped paper manufactured from certain descriptions of imported paper.

(**a**) 1958 c. 6. (**b**) S.I. 1966/921 (1966 II, p. 2207).
(**c**) S.I. 1966/1220 (1966 III, p. 3278). (**d**) 1889 c. 63.

STATUTORY   INSTRUMENTS

1968 No. 1158

CUSTOMS AND EXCISE

The Import Duties (General) (No. 7) Order 1968

Made - - - -	*22nd July* 1968
Laid before the House of Commons	*26th July* 1968
Coming into Operation	*1st August* 1968

The Lords Commissioners of Her Majesty's Treasury, by virtue of the powers conferred on them by sections 1, 2 and 13 of the Import Duties Act 1958(a), and of all other powers enabling them in that behalf, on the recommendation of the Board of Trade hereby make the following Order:—

1. In Schedule 1 to the Import Duties (General) (No. 4) Order 1968(b) (which Schedule by reference to the Customs Tariff 1959 sets out the import duties chargeable under the Import Duties Act 1958), the following shall be substituted for subheadings (A), (B) and (C) of heading 56.01 (man-made fibres, discontinuous, not carded, combed or otherwise prepared for spinning):—

" (A) Produced by a process mentioned in
    Note 1(*a*) to Chapter 51:

    (1) Of copolymerised vinyl chloride and   —   —
         vinyl acetate, in lengths not ex-
         ceeding ¾ inch

    (2) Other   ...   .   7·8d. per lb.   C. 85% of the
                                        full rate
                                E.   —

(B) Produced by a process mentioned in
    Note 1(*b*) to Chapter 51:

    (1) Of regenerated protein including   —   —
         casein

    (2) Other   ...   .   5·9d. per lb.   C. 85% of the
                                          full rate
                                E.   —   "

2.—(1) This Order may be cited as the Import Duties (General) (No. 7) Order 1968.

(2) The Interpretation Act 1889(c) shall apply for the interpretation of this Order as it applies for the interpretation of an Act of Parliament.

(3) This Order shall come into operation on 1st August 1968.

Joseph Harper,
J. McCann,
Two of the Lords Commissioners
of Her Majesty's Treasury.

22nd July 1968.

(a) 1958 c. 6.   (b) S.I. 1968/679 (1968 I, p. 1519).   (c) 1889 c. 63.

EXPLANATORY NOTE

(This Note is not part of the Order.)

This Order removes the import duty on discontinuous man-made fibres of regenerated protein including casein (not carded, combed or otherwise prepared for spinning).

STATUTORY INSTRUMENTS

1968 No. 1163

PENSIONS

The Pensions Commutation Regulations 1968

Made   *22nd July* 1968

Coming into Operation   *1st August* 1968

The Treasury, in exercise of the powers conferred on them by sections 4 and 7 of the Pensions Commutation Act 1871(a) and section 3 of the Pensions Commutation Act 1882(b) and of all other powers enabling them in that behalf, hereby make the following Regulations:—

Interpretation

1.—(1) In these Regulations, unless the context otherwise requires, the following expressions have the meanings hereby respectively assigned to them:—

"the appropriate Department" means:—

(a) in the case of a person whose pension was awarded by the Admiralty, the War Office, the Air Ministry or the Ministry of Defence: the Ministry of Defence;

(b) in the case of a person whose pension was awarded by the Ministry of Pensions and National Insurance or the Ministry of Social Security: the Ministry of Social Security;

(c) in the case of any other person: the Department to which that person belonged;

"the Board" means the Pensions Commutation Board;

"the commutation rate" means the amount by which a pension, or a portion of a pension, to be commuted is to be multiplied in order to determine the capital sum to be paid;

"pension" has the meaning assigned to it by section 2 of the Pensions Commutation Act 1871.

(2) The Interpretation Act 1889(c) shall apply for the interpretation of these Regulations as it applies for the interpretation of an Act of Parliament.

Application for commutation

2. A person desiring to commute a pension, or a portion of a pension, shall address an application in writing to the appropriate Department, and such application shall be deemed to be made on the date on which it is received by the Department during the hours of public business.

(a) 1871 c 36.   (b) 1882 c. 44.   (c) 1889 c. 63.

Action by appropriate Department

3.—(1) On receipt of an application, the appropriate Department may, if it thinks fit, forward it, accompanied as provided in paragraph (2) of this Regulation, to the Board, who shall thereupon inquire into the application with a view to reporting on it to the Treasury.

(2) The application shall be accompanied, in a case in which the Ministry of Defence is the appropriate Department, by the recommendation of the Defence Council, and, in any other case, by the recommendation of the appropriate Department.

Requirements as to medical examination etc.

4. The Board shall require the applicant to undergo a medical examination, and the applicant shall, if the Board so require, furnish proof of the date of his birth and such further information with regard to his application as the Board may think necessary.

Withdrawal before medical examination

5. The applicant may withdraw his application at any time before undergoing a medical examination on payment of any expense (not exceeding £2.10s.0d.) which may have been incurred by the Board.

Lapse on failure to attend for medical examination, etc.

6.—(1) If at the expiration of the relevant period, or such longer period as the Treasury may allow in the exceptional circumstances of any particular case, the applicant has failed to furnish information required by the Board or to attend for medical examination, the application shall be deemed to have been withdrawn, and no further action shall be taken with regard to it.

(2) In this Regulation, the expression "the relevant period" means:—

    (*a*) in the case of an applicant resident in the United Kingdom or the Irish Republic, the period of four months beginning on the day on which the application was made; or

    (*b*) in any other case, the period of six months beginning on such day.

Procedure where application approved by Treasury

7.—(1) If an application for commutation is approved by the Treasury, the Board shall, by means of a notice in writing addressed to the applicant at the address given by him, notify him of the amount of money which would be payable in respect of his application.

(2) The applicant may, upon receipt of such notice, notify the Board in writing that he wishes the commutation of his pension, or portion of his pension, to take place; and in that event the applicant shall within the prescribed period either:—

(a) give notice that he is desirous of having the cheque for the net amount sent through the post in accordance with Regulation 3(1) of the Pensions Commutation Payment Regulations 1958(a); or

(b) collect the said cheque in accordance with Regulation 3(2) of those Regulations.

(3) Within the prescribed period, the applicant may withdraw his application on payment of a fee of £2.10s.0d.

(4) If the applicant does not either comply with the provisions of paragraph 2(a) or (b) of this Regulation, or withdraw his application, the commutation of his pension, or portion of a pension, shall take place on the day following the expiration of the prescribed period, and from that day the net amount shall be available for payment in accordance with the provisions of the Pensions Commutation Payment Regulations 1958.

(5) In this Regulation, the following expressions have the meanings hereby respectively assigned to them:—

"the prescribed period" means:—

(a) in the case of an applicant resident in the United Kingdom or Irish Republic, the period of thirty days beginning with the day of the despatch by the Board of a notice under paragraph (1) of this Regulation; or

(b) in the case of an applicant not resident as aforesaid, the period of forty two days beginning with such day; or

(c) such longer period as the Treasury may allow in the exceptional circumstances of any particular case;

"the net amount" means the amount of money referred to in paragraph (1) of this Regulation subject to the deduction mentioned in Regulation 9(2) of these Regulations.

Commutation rate

8.—(1) The Table set out in the Schedule to these Regulations shall be used to determine the commutation rate.

(2) In determining the commutation rate by the use of the Table, the age of the applicant shall be reckoned as the aggregate of his age on his birthday next succeeding the date of his application and any years to be added to his age on account of his life being impaired.

Commutation fee

9.—(1) There shall be charged in respect of the commutation of any pension or any portion of a pension a fee of 1 per cent. on the amount awarded; provided that such fee shall not be less than £2.10s.0d. nor more than £20 in any case.

(2) The amount of the fee shall be deducted from the amount awarded.

_____

(a) S.I. 1958/2195 (1958 II, p. 1796).

Cessation of pension

10. A person whose application for commutation has been approved shall continue to draw the pension, or the portion of a pension, which he has applied to commute up to:—

(*a*) the day on which a cheque is posted to him under Regulation 7(2)(*a*) of these Regulations; or

(*b*) the day on which he collects a cheque under Regulation 7(2)(*b*) of these Regulations; or

(*c*) the day on which commutation takes place under Regulation 7(4) of these Regulations,

as the case may be.

Revocation

11. The Pensions Commutation Regulations 1955(**a**) and the Pensions Commutation (Amendment) Regulations 1962(**b**) are hereby revoked.

Citation and Commencement

12. These Regulations may be cited as the Pensions Commutation Regulations 1968, and shall come into operation on 1st August 1968.

E. Alan Fitch,
J. McCann,
**Two of the Lords Commissioners
of Her Majesty's Treasury.**

22nd July, 1968.

(a) S.I. 1955/1047 (1955 II, p. 1755).   (b) S.I. 1962/667 (1962 I, p. 699).

SCHEDULE

TABLE FOR DETERMINING THE COMMUTATION RATE

Age next Birthday	Commutation Rate	Capital Sum for each £100 of pension			Age next Birthday	Commutation Rate	Capital Sum for each £100 of pension		
		£	s.	d.			£	s.	d.
30	14·897	1,489	14	0	60	10·063	1,006	6	0
31	14·811	1,481	2	0	61	9·823	982	6	0
32	14·721	1,472	2	0	62	9·581	958	2	0
33	14.624	1,462	8	0	63	9·339	933	18	0
34	14·522	1,452	4	0	64	9·092	909	4	0
35	14·415	1,441	10	0	65	8·845	884	10	0
36	14·304	1,430	8	0	66	8·593	859	6	0
37	14·188	1,418	16	0	67	8·339	833	18	0
38	14·072	1,407	4	0	68	8·086	808	12	0
39	13·948	1,394	16	0	69	7·833	783	6	0
40	13·819	1,381	18	0	70	7·579	757	18	0
41	13·683	1,368	6	0	71	7·331	733	2	0
42	13·542	1,354	4	0	72	7·084	708	8	0
43	13·401	1,340	2	0	73	6·839	683	18	0
44	13·252	1,325	4	0	74	6·602	660	4	0
45	13·104	1,310	8	0	75	6·367	636	14	0
46	12·946	1,294	12	0	76	6·139	613	18	0
47	12·781	1,278	2	0	77	5·916	591	12	0
48	12·613	1,261	6	0	78	5·698	569	16	0
49	12·436	1,243	12	0	79	5·485	548	10	0
50	12·250	1,225	0	0	80	5·283	528	6	0
51	12·060	1,206	0	0	81	5·073	507	6	0
52	11·860	1,186	0	0	82	4·843	484	6	0
53	11·656	1,165	12	0	83	4·593	459	6	0
54	11.442	1,144	4	0	84	4·333	433	6	0
55	11.225	1,122	10	0	85	4·081	408	2	0
56	11·003	1,100	6	0	86	3·851	385	2	0
57	10·774	1,077	8	0	87	3·631	363	2	0
58	10·541	1,054	2	0	88	3·421	342	2	0
59	10·305	1,030	10	0	89	3·211	321	2	0
					90	3·000	300	0	0

EXPLANATORY NOTE

(This Note is not part of the Regulations.)

These Regulations supersede the Pensions Commutation Regulations 1955 (as amended). They set out the procedure to be adopted where retired officers of the Armed Forces, or certain former holders of civil offices, desire to commute their pensions, and the conditions under which commutation may be effected. The principal changes are as follows. Regulation 6 lays down new time limits within which applicants must furnish information required by the Pensions Commutation Board and attend for medical examination and Regulation 7 lays down a new time limit within which applicants resident outside the United Kingdom and Irish Republic may withdraw their applications. New fees are prescribed in Regulations 5 and 7(3), in respect of the withdrawal of an application, and in Regulation 9(1), in respect of the completion of an application. Regulation 10 provides a new definition of the date on which an applicant's pension is to cease to be payable.

STATUTORY INSTRUMENTS

1968 No. 1164

SEA FISHERIES

The Molluscan Shellfish (Control of Deposit) Amendment Order 1968

Made - - - -	17*th July* 1968
Coming into Operation	18*th July* 1968

The Minister of Agriculture, Fisheries and Food in exercise of the powers conferred upon him by sections 12 and 20 of the Sea Fisheries (Shellfish) Act 1967(a) and of all other powers enabling him in that behalf hereby makes the following Order:—

Citation and commencement

1. This order, which may be cited as the Molluscan Shellfish (Control of Deposit) Amendment Order 1968, shall be construed as one with the Molluscan Shellfish (Control of Deposit) Order 1965(b) as amended (c), in this order referred to as "the principal order"), and shall come into operation on 18th July 1968.

Amendment of principal order

2. The principal order shall be further amended by the insertion after Article 4(1) of the following paragraph:—

"(1) (A) No oysters taken from shellfish beds in (i) France or the territorial waters adjacent thereto, or (ii) that part of the county of Hampshire which comprises the districts of the Havant and Waterloo Urban District Council and the Chichester Rural District Council, shall be deposited in the designated waters or upon the designated land".

In witness whereof the Official Seal of the Minister of Agriculture, Fisheries and Food is hereunto affixed on 17th July 1968.

(L.S.)   *Cledwyn Hughes,*
                                    Minister of Agriculture, Fisheries and Food.

EXPLANATORY NOTE

(*This Note is not part of the Order.*)

This Order amends the provisions of the Molluscan Shellfish (Control of Deposit) Order 1965.

The deposit in tidal waters of England and Wales or in adjacent land of oysters taken from beds in France, or from beds in the district of the Havant and Waterloo Urban District Council and the Chichester Rural District Council, is prohibited except under the authority of a licence granted by the Minister of Agriculture, Fisheries and Food.

(a) 1967 c. 83.   (b) S.I. 1965/1971 (1965 III, p. 5829).
(c) The relevant amending instrument is S.I. 1966/1162 (1966 III, p. 2788).

STATUTORY INSTRUMENTS

1968 No. 1166 (S. 127)

SHERIFF COURT, SCOTLAND

Act of Sederunt (Alteration of Sheriff Court Fees) 1968

Made - - -	19*th July* 1968
Laid before Parliament	31*st July* 1968
Coming into Operation	1*st October* 1968

The Lords of Council and Session, under and by virtue of the powers conferred upon them by section 40 of the Sheriff Courts (Scotland) Act 1907(a), as amended by section 39 of the Administration of Justice (Scotland) Act 1933(b), and of all other powers competent to them in that behalf, do hereby enact and declare as follows :—

1. The General Regulations contained in the Schedule to the Act of Sederunt (Alteration of Sheriff Court Fees) 1967(c) shall apply to work done on or after 1st October 1968 with the substitution for the figure "10", in paragraph 12 thereof, of the figure "15".

2. This Act of Sederunt may be cited as the Act of Sederunt (Alteration of Sheriff Court Fees) 1968, and shall come into operation on 1st October 1968.

And the Lords appoint this Act of Sederunt to be inserted in the Books of Sederunt.

Edinburgh,
19th July 1968.

J. L. Clyde,
I.P.D.

EXPLANATORY NOTE

(This Note is not part of the Act of Sederunt)

This Act of Sederunt, which applies to work done on or after 1st October 1968, increases the charge for certain outlays from 10% to 15% of the taxed amount of fees.

(a) 1907 c. 51.   **(b)** 1933 c. 41.   **(c)** S.I. 1967/1294 (1967 II, p. 3744).

STATUTORY INSTRUMENTS

1968 No. 1168

ROAD TRAFFIC

The Goods Vehicles (Temporary Use in Great Britain) Regulations 1968

Made - - - -	*22nd July* 1968
Laid before Parliament	*30th July* 1968
Coming into Operation	(on a date to be notified in the London Gazette)

The Minister of Transport, in exercise of his powers under section 190 of the Road Traffic Act 1960(a) as amended by section 22 of the Road Traffic Act 1962(b), and of all other enabling powers, and after consultation with representative organisations in accordance with the provisions of section 260(2) of the Road Traffic Act 1960, hereby makes the following Regulations:—

1.—(1) These Regulations may be cited as the Goods Vehicles (Temporary Use in Great Britain) Regulations 1968 and shall come into operation on the date on which the Agreement between the Government of the United Kingdom of Great Britain and Northern Ireland and the Government of Sweden on the International Carriage of Goods by Road, dated 21st November 1967, first comes into force for Great Britain, which date shall be notified in the London Gazette.

(2) The Interpretation Act 1889(c) shall apply for the interpretation of these Regulations as it applies for the interpretation of an Act of Parliament.

2. Section 164 of the Road Traffic Act 1960 (which requires users of goods vehicles to hold carriers' licences) shall not apply to a goods vehicle—

(*a*) which is a motor vehicle, or which is a trailer which is being drawn by a motor vehicle in respect of which all the requirements of this Regulation are satisfied; and

(*b*) which (in the case of a motor vehicle) is registered in Sweden; and

(*c*) which is brought temporarily into Great Britain and does not remain in Great Britain for more than 90 days; and

(*d*) which is being used on roads in Great Britain for the purposes of the carriage of goods by road on a journey whose route has used, or will use, before the end of the journey, roads outside the United Kingdom; and

---

(a) 8 & 9 Eliz.2.c.16.   (b) 10 & 11 Eliz.2.c.59.   (c) 52 & 53 Vict.c.63.

(e) which is not used at any time during the said journey for the carriage of goods loaded at one place in the United Kingdom for delivery at another place in the United Kingdom.

Given under the Official Seal of the Minister of Transport the 22nd July 1968.

(L.S.)
Richard Marsh,
Minister of Transport.

EXPLANATORY NOTE

(This Note is not part of the Regulations.)

These Regulations exempt persons using goods vehicles registered in Sweden and brought temporarily into Great Britain for certain purposes from the requirement in section 164 of the Road Traffic Act 1960 to obtain a carrier's licence.

These Regulations will enable the Government of the United Kingdom of Great Britain and Northern Ireland to ratify the Anglo-Swedish agreement referred to in Regulation 1(1) (issued as Cmnd. 3611) and will come into operation when that agreement comes into force for Great Britain.

STATUTORY INSTRUMENTS

1968 No. 1169

ROAD TRAFFIC

The Goods Vehicles (Plating and Testing) (Amendment) Regulations 1968

Made - - -	*22nd July* 1968
Laid before Parliament	*30th July* 1968
Coming into Operation	*1st August* 1968

The Minister of Transport in exercise of his powers under section 9 of the Road Safety Act 1967(**a**) and of all other powers him enabling in that behalf, and after consultation with representative organisations in accordance with the provisions of section 260(2) of the Road Traffic Act 1960(**b**), as applied by section 29(6) of the said Act of 1967, hereby makes the following Regulations :—

1. These Regulations shall come into operation on the 1st August 1968, and may be cited as the Goods Vehicles (Plating and Testing) (Amendment) Regulations 1968.

2. The Goods Vehicles (Plating and Testing) Regulations 1968(**c**) shall have effect as though :—

(1) in Regulation 2(1), in the definition of "the standard lists" for paragraph (*b*) there were substituted the following paragraph—
"(*b*) published by Her Majesty's Stationery Office on the 21st February 1968, on the 12th and 29th March 1968 and on the following dates, namely, the 3rd May and 31st May 1968, and the 11th July and 22nd July 1968 ; and" ;

(2) in Schedule 2, in paragraph 13 for the word "that" there were substituted the word "than" ;

(3) in Part I of Schedule 3—

(*a*) in paragraph 6, at the end thereof there were added the words "and Regulation 49(2) (prohibition on fitting of recut pneumatic tyres)" ;

(*b*) in paragraph 9, at the end thereof there were added the words "in so far as that Regulation provides that a speedometer shall be fitted, correctly positioned and illuminated" ;

(*c*) in paragraph 16(*h*), at the end thereof there were added the words "contained in any windscreen or in or in any window forming part of the cab" ;

(*d*) in paragraph 25, at the end thereof there were added the words "other than in Regulation 5(*c*) and (*d*)" ;

(**a**) 1967 c. 30.   (**b**) 8 & 9 Eliz. 2. c. 16.   (**c**) S.I. 1968/601 (1968 I,p.1372).

(4) in Part II of Schedule 3—

(a) in paragraph 3, at the end thereof there were added the words "and Regulation 62(2) (prohibition on fitting of recut pneumatic tyres)" ;

(b) in paragraph 6, sub-paragraph "(d)" were omitted.

Given under the Official Seal of the Minister of Transport the 22nd July 1968.

(L.S.)

Richard Marsh,
Minister of Transport.

EXPLANATORY NOTE

(*This Note is not part of the Regulations.*)

These Regulations amend the Goods Vehicles (Plating and Testing) Regulations 1968 (hereinafter referred to as "the 1968 Regulations") by—

(1) extending the definition of "standard lists" contained in Regulation 2(1) of the 1968 Regulations so as to include in that definition lists published since the making of the 1968 Regulations ; and

(2) making certain changes in the list of the construction and use requirements in relation to which goods vehicles are to be examined.

STATUTORY INSTRUMENTS

1968 No. 1170

IRON AND STEEL

The Iron and Steel (Compensation to Employees) Regulations 1968

Laid before Parliament in draft

Made - - - -   *22nd July* 1968

Coming into Operation   *2nd August* 1968

ARRANGEMENT OF REGULATIONS

PART I

PRELIMINARY

PART II

ENTITLEMENT TO COMPENSATION

PART III

RESETTLEMENT COMPENSATION FOR LOSS OF EMPLOYMENT

PART IV

LONG-TERM COMPENSATION FOR LOSS OF EMPLOYMENT OR LOSS OR DIMINUTION OF EMOLUMENTS

PART V

RETIREMENT COMPENSATION FOR LOSS OR DIMINUTION OF PENSION RIGHTS

PART VI

ADJUSTMENT AND COMPOUNDING OF COMPENSATION

PART VII

PROCEDURE

PART VIII

MISCELLANEOUS

SCHEDULE

The Minister of Power in exercise of his powers under section 41 of the Iron and Steel Act 1949(a), as revived and amended by section 31 of the Iron and Steel Act 1967(b), and after consultation with the British Steel Corporation and such organisations as appear to him to be representative of persons concerned, hereby makes the following regulations, a draft of which has been laid before Parliament and has been approved by resolution of each House of Parliament in accordance with the said section 41:—

PART I

PRELIMINARY

Citation and commencement

1. These regulations may be cited as the Iron and Steel (Compensation to Employees) Regulations 1968, shall come into operation 14 days after they have been approved by resolution of each House of Parliament and shall have effect from 28th July 1967.

Interpretation

2.—(1) In these regulations—

"the Act" means the Iron and Steel Act 1949 as revived and amended by the Iron and Steel Act 1967;

"added years" means years purchased under the provisions of the last relevant pension scheme for the purpose of being reckoned as pensionable service;

"the Corporation" means the British Steel Corporation;

"enactment" means any Act or any instrument made under an Act;

"last relevant pension scheme" means the pension scheme to which a pensionable officer was last subject before suffering loss of employment or loss or diminution of emoluments or pension rights in consequence of a relevant event;

"long-term compensation" means compensation payable in accordance with Part IV of these regulations for loss of employment or loss or diminution of emoluments;

(a) 1949 c. 72.   (b) 1967 c. 17.

"material date" means in the case of a person to whom these regulations apply and—

   (a) who is or has been an officer of a company which came into public ownership under Part II of the Act, the date on which the relevant event occurred in consequence of which he suffered loss of employment or loss or diminution of emoluments or pension rights as the case may be;

   (b) who has been an officer of the Iron and Steel Board established under Part II of the Iron and Steel Act 1953(a), 27th August 1967;

"minimum pensionable age" means, in relation to a pensionable officer, the earliest age at which, under his last relevant pension scheme, he could have become entitled to the immediate payment of a pension, other than a pension payable in consequence of his redundancy or his incapacity to discharge efficiently the duties of his employment by reason of permanent ill-health or infirmity of mind or body;

"national service" means service which is relevant service within the meaning of the Reserve and Auxiliary Forces (Protection of Civil Interests) Act 1951(b), and includes service immediately following such service as aforesaid, being service in any of Her Majesty's naval, military or air forces pursuant to a voluntary engagement entered into with the consent of the person under whom an officer held his last relevant employment;

"net annual emoluments" in relation to any employment means, subject to the provisions of regulation 38, the annual rate of the emoluments of that employment less such part of those emoluments as the officer was liable to contribute under a pension scheme associated with his employment (but including any part of those emoluments payable in respect of additional voluntary contributions); and in relation to any employment which has been lost or the emoluments of which have been diminished, the expression means the annual rate of emoluments as aforesaid immediately before the loss or diminution, as the case may be;

"normal retiring age" means, in the case of a pensionable officer, in relation to whom his last relevant pension scheme prescribes an age at which he becomes or would have become entitled to receive a normal retirement pension, that age and, in any other case, the age of 65 years, if the officer is a male, or 60 years if the officer is a female;

"pensionable officer", in relation to a person to whom these regulations apply who has suffered loss of employment or loss or diminution of emoluments or pension rights in consequence of a relevant event, means such a person who immediately before such loss or diminution was subject to a pension scheme;

"reckonable service", in relation to a person to whom these regulations apply, means any period of any relevant employment which is not a period in respect of which a pension (other than a return of contributions) has been paid or will become payable otherwise than under the last relevant pension scheme, and includes any period of war service or national service undertaken on his ceasing to hold any such employment;

"relevant employment" means whole-time employment in the service of—

   (a) the Corporation; or

   (b) a publicly-owned company (including service before the coming into public ownership of that company); or

   (c) the Iron and Steel Board; or

(a) 1953 c. 15.   (b) 1951 c. 65.

(*d*) the Iron and Steel Corporation of Great Britain established under the Iron and Steel Act 1949; or

(*e*) a previous owner of an undertaking owned by a publicly-owned company; or

(*f*) any organisation representative of the interests of iron and steel producers as defined by section 47(2) of the Iron and Steel Act 1967; or

(*g*) a company, not being a publicly-owned company, which during the period of whole-time employment was wholly or mainly engaged in iron and steel activities as defined by subsection (4) of the said section 47; or

(*h*) an organisation wholly or mainly engaged in undertaking research in relation to iron and steel activities, as so defined, as a common service for iron and steel producers as so defined; or

(*i*) the Crown,

"relevant event", in the case of a person who is or has been an officer of a company which came into public ownership under Part II of the Act means—

(*a*) the company so coming into public ownership; or

(*b*) effect being given to conclusions reported under section 4 of the Iron and Steel Act 1967 to the Minister; or

(*c*) effect being given to a direction given by the Minister by virtue of section 7(2) of that Act,

and, in the case of a person who has been an officer of the Iron and Steel Board, means the dissolution of that Board;

"resettlement compensation" means compensation payable in accordance with Part III of these regulations for loss of employment;

"retirement compensation" means compensation payable in accordance with Part V of these regulations for loss or diminution of pension rights;

"tribunal" means a tribunal established under section 12 of the Industrial Training Act(**a**);

"war service" means war service within the meaning of the Local Government Staffs (War Service) Act 1939(**b**), the Teachers Superannuation (War Service) Act 1939(**c**), the Education (Scotland) (War Service Superannuation) Act 1939(**d**), the Police and Firemen (War Service) Act 1939(**e**) or employment for war purposes, within the meaning of the Superannuation Schemes (War Service) Act 1940(**f**) and includes any period of service in the first world war in the armed forces of the Crown or in the forces of the allied or associated powers if such service immediately followed a period of relevant employment and was undertaken either compulsorily or with the permission of the employer in that employment;

"whole-time employment" means employment after reaching the age of 18 years, being employment to which the employee is required to devote on the average not less than 30 hours per week.

(2)(*a*) Where under any provision of these regulations an annual value is to be assigned to a capital sum or a capital value to an annual amount, the annual or capital value shall be ascertained in accordance with the tables contained in the schedule hereto in so far as they provide for the particular case.

(*b*) For the purpose of determining the application of the said tables the headings and the note to each table shall be treated as a part of the table.

(**a**) 1964 c. 16.   (**b**) 1939 c. 94.
(**c**) 1939 c. 95.   (**d**) 1939 c. 96.
(**e**) 1939 c. 103.   (**f**) 1940 c. 26.

(c) Where the said tables do not provide for a case in which an annual value is to be assigned to a capital sum or a capital value to an annual amount, the annual or capital value shall be such as may be agreed between the Corporation and the person to whom the capital sum or annual amount is payable.

(3) Expressions used in these regulations shall, unless the contrary intention appears, have the same respective meanings as in the Act.

(4) Unless the context otherwise requires, references in these regulations to the provisions of any enactment shall be construed as references to those provisions as amended, re-enacted or modified by any subsequent enactment.

(5) The Interpretation Act 1889(a) shall apply to the interpretation of these regulations as it applies to the interpretation of an Act of Parliament.

PART II

ENTITLEMENT TO COMPENSATION

Persons to whom the regulations apply

3. These regulations apply to any person who—

(a) was employed immediately before 22nd March 1967 in whole-time employment either as an officer of a company which came into public ownership under Part II of the Act or of the Iron and Steel Board, or

(b) would have been so employed at that date but for any national service on which he was then engaged.

National Service

4.—(1) A person to whom these regulations apply by virtue of regulation 3(b) shall be deemed not to have suffered loss of employment or loss or diminution of emoluments or pension rights unless he gives notice in writing to the Corporation in accordance with paragraph (3) that he is available for employment and he is either not given or offered re-employment in his former office or in any reasonably comparable office, or is given or offered such re-employment with reduced emoluments or pension rights as compared with the emoluments and pension rights which he would have enjoyed had he continued in his former office.

(2) If the ground of a claim for compensation under paragraph (1) is for loss of employment or loss or diminution of pension rights that loss shall for the purposes of these regulations be treated as having occurred on the earlier of the two following dates, that is to say, the date of the refusal of re-employment or a date one month after the date on which the person gave notice that he was available for employment, and the person shall be deemed to have been entitled to the emoluments or the pension rights which he would have enjoyed or been entitled to at such earlier date had he continued in his former office.

(3) Notice shall be given in writing to the Corporation before the expiry of 2 months after ceasing to be engaged on national service or of 2 months after the coming into operation of these regulations, whichever is the later or, if prevented by sickness or other reasonable cause, as soon as practicable thereafter.

(a) 1889 c. 63.

PART III

RESETTLEMENT COMPENSATION FOR LOSS OF EMPLOYMENT

Persons to whom resettlement compensation is payable

5.—(1) The Corporation shall, subject to the provisions of these regulations, pay resettlement compensation to any person to whom these regulations apply who—

(a) has suffered loss of employment in consequence of a relevant event not later than 10 years after the material date;

(b) had not at the date of the loss reached normal retiring age;

(c) had been continuously engaged (disregarding breaks not exceeding in the aggregate 6 months) in relevant employment during the period beginning 3 years before the material date and ending at the date of the loss; and for this purpose the expression "relevant employment" includes any period of national service immediately following such employment;

(d) has made a claim for compensation in accordance with the provisions of Part VII of these regulations not later than 13 weeks after the loss of employment which is the cause of his claim or 13 weeks after the coming into operation of these regulations, whichever is the later.

(2) Resettlement compensation shall not, however, be paid—

(a) to a person who has suffered loss of employment in consequence of a relevant event, if his employment could have been terminated by reason of misconduct or incapacity to perform such duties as, immediately before the loss of employment, he was performing or might reasonably have been required to perform; or

(b) to a person who has been offered reasonably comparable employment under the Crown or in the service of the Corporation or of a publicly-owned company.

(3) In ascertaining for the purposes of paragraph (2) of this regulation whether a person has been offered employment which is reasonably comparable with the employment which he has lost, no account shall be taken of the fact that the duties of the employment offered involve a transfer of his employment from one place to another within Great Britain.

(4) No account shall be taken for the purposes of this regulation of an offer of employment where the Corporation are satisfied—

(a) that acceptance would have involved undue hardship to the person; or

(b) that he was prevented from accepting the offer by reason of ill-health or other circumstances beyond his control.

Amount of resettlement compensation

6.—(1) The amount of resettlement compensation payable to a person shall, for each week for which such compensation is payable, be a sum ascertained by taking two thirds of the weekly rate of the net annual emoluments which that person has lost and deducting therefrom such of the following items as may be applicable—

(a) unemployment, sickness or injury benefit under any enactment relating to National Insurance claimable by him in respect of such week (excluding any amount claimable by him in respect of a dependant); and

(b) two thirds of the net annual emoluments received by him in respect of such week from work or employment undertaken in place of the employment which he has lost.

(2) For the purposes of this regulation the weekly rate of a person's net annual emoluments shall be deemed to be seven three hundred and sixty-fifths of those emoluments.

(3) Nothing in this regulation shall prevent effect being given to any other provision of these regulations empowering the withholding or reduction of, or making deduction from, resettlement compensation.

Period for payment of resettlement compensation

7. Resettlement compensation shall be payable to a person only in respect of the period of 13 weeks next succeeding the week in which he lost the employment in respect of which the compensation is payable or, in the case of a person who has at the date of losing that employment reached the age of 45 years, the said 13 weeks extended by one additional week for every year by which his age then exceeds the age of 45 years, subject to a maximum addition of 13 such weeks.

Claimant for resettlement compensation to furnish particulars of employment and to register if unemployed

8. Every claimant for resettlement compensation shall (after as well as before the compensation begins to be paid)—

(a) forthwith supply the Corporation in writing with particulars of any employment which he obtains or of any change in his earnings from any such employment; and

(b) register with the Department of Employment and Productivity, so long as he is out of employment and is not receiving sickness or injury benefit, unless the Corporation has in writing notified him that he is not required by them so to register.

Additional provisions relating to resettlement compensation

9. Subject to the provisions of these regulations, resettlement compensation shall be payable to a person at intervals equivalent to those at which the emoluments of his employment were previously paid or at such intervals as may be agreed between the person and the Corporation, and shall forthwith be terminated by the Corporation if, on being requested to do so, he fails to satisfy the Corporation that, so far as he is able, he is seeking suitable employment.

PART IV

LONG-TERM COMPENSATION FOR LOSS OF EMPLOYMENT OR LOSS OR DIMINUTION OF EMOLUMENTS

Persons to whom long-term compensation is payable

10.—(1) The Corporation shall, subject to the provisions of these regulations, pay long-term compensation to any person to whom these regulations apply, who—

(a) has suffered loss of employment or loss or diminution of emoluments in consequence of a relevant event not later than 10 years after the material date;

(b) had not, save as is provided in regulation 15, at the date of the loss or commencement of the diminution reached normal retiring age;

(*c*) had been continuously engaged (without a break of more than 12 months at any one time) in relevant employment during the period beginning 8 years before the material date and ending at the date of the loss; and for this purpose the expression "relevant employment" includes any period of national service immediately following such employment;

(*d*) has made a claim for compensation in accordance with the provisions of Part VII of these regulations not later than 2 years after the date on which the loss of employment or emoluments took place or the commencement of the diminution of emoluments began in respect of which the claim is made or 2 years after the coming into operation of these regulations, whichever is the later.

(2) Long-term compensation shall not, however, be paid:—

(*a*) to a person who has suffered loss of employment in consequence of a relevant event, if his employment could have been terminated by reason of misconduct or incapacity to perform such duties as, immediately before that loss of employment, he was performing or might reasonably have been required to perform; or

(*b*) to a person who has been offered reasonably comparable employment under the Crown or in the service of the Corporation or of a publicly-owned company.

(3) Regulation 5(3) and (4) (which relate to offers of employment) shall apply for the purposes of this regulation as they apply for the purposes of regulation 5.

(4) Claims for long-term compensation for loss of employment shall in all respects be treated as claims for such compensation for the loss of emoluments occasioned thereby and the provisions of these regulations shall apply to all such claims accordingly.

Factors to be considered in assessing loss or diminution of emoluments

11.—(1) For the purpose of determining the amount of long-term compensation, if any, the loss or diminution of emoluments suffered by a person shall be regarded as the annual loss or diminution (if any) of net annual emoluments which he would have suffered had he taken all reasonable steps open to him to mitigate that loss or diminution, and in assessing the loss or diminution such of the following factors as are relevant to the particular case shall be taken into consideration:—

(*a*) the conditions upon which the person held the employment which he has lost or the emoluments of which have been lost or diminished, including in particular its security of tenure, whether by law or practice;

(*b*) the emoluments and other conditions, including security of tenure, whether by law or practice, of any work or employment undertaken by the person in place of the employment which he has lost;

(*c*) the period for which he might reasonably have been expected to have remained in the employment which he has lost, or to have remained in that employment without diminution of emoluments, as the case may be, but for the relevant event in consequence of which he has suffered the loss or diminution;

(*d*) the period for which he might reasonably have been expected to engage or remain in the work or employment undertaken in place of the employment which he has lost or the emoluments of which have been lost or diminished;

(e) the extent to which he has sought suitable employment or training for such employment and the emoluments which he might have acquired by accepting other suitable employment offered to him;

(f) all the other circumstances of the case.

(2) In ascertaining for the purposes of sub-paragraph (e) of paragraph (1) whether a person has been offered suitable employment, regulation 5(4) shall apply as it applies for the purposes of regulation 5.

Amount of long-term compensation payable for loss of emoluments

12.—(1) Subject to the provisions of these regulations, long-term compensation for loss of emoluments shall consist of an annual sum payable until the normal retiring age or death of a person to whom it is payable, whichever first occurs, and shall be the amount of the annual loss of emoluments which he has suffered assessed in accordance with regulation 11, not, however, exceeding the maximum annual sum provided for in the following provisions of this regulation.

(2) The said maximum annual sum shall, subject as hereinafter provided, be the aggregate of the following sums:—

(a) for every year of the person's reckonable service, one sixtieth of the annual loss of emoluments so assessed; and

(b) in the case of a person who has reached the age of 40 years at the date of the loss, a sum calculated in accordance with the provisions of paragraph (3) appropriate to his age at that date:

Provided that the said maximum annual sum shall in no case exceed two thirds of the annual loss of emoluments so assessed.

(3) The sum referred to in paragraph (2)(b) shall be:—

(a) in the case of a person who has reached the age of 40 years but has not reached the age of 50 years at the date of the loss, the following fraction of the annual loss of emoluments so assessed—

(i) where his reckonable service is less than 10 years, one sixtieth for each year of such service after reaching the age of 40 years; or

(ii) where his reckonable service amounts to 10 years but is less than 15 years, one sixtieth for each year of such service after reaching the age of 40 years and one additional sixtieth; or

(iii) where his reckonable service amounts to 15 years but is less than 20 years, one sixtieth for each year of such service after reaching the age of 40 years and two additional sixtieths; or

(iv) where his reckonable service amounts to 20 years or more, one sixtieth for each year of such service after reaching the age of 40 years and three additional sixtieths,

but the sum so calculated shall not in any case exceed one sixth of the annual loss of emoluments so assessed;

(b) in the case of a person who has reached the age of 50 years but has not reached the age of 60 years at the date of the loss, one sixtieth of the annual loss of emoluments so assessed for each year of his reckonable service after reaching the age of 40 years, up to a maximum of 15 such years; and

(c) in the case of a person who has reached the age of 60 years at the date of the loss, one sixtieth of the annual loss of emoluments so assessed for each year of his reckonable service after reaching the age of 45 years.

(4) Long-term compensation determined under this regulation shall be payable to a person by instalments at intervals equivalent to those at which the emoluments of his employment were previously paid or at such intervals as may be agreed between the person and the Corporation.

(5) Long-term compensation payable in respect of a period for which resettlement compensation is also payable shall be reduced by the amount of that resettlement compensation.

Long-term compensation for diminution of emoluments

13.—(1) Long-term compensation payable for diminution of emoluments shall, subject to the provisions of these regulations, consist of an annual sum payable until the normal retiring age or death of a person to whom it is payable, whichever first occurs, and shall be the amount of the annual diminution which he has suffered assessed in accordance with regulation 11, not however exceeding the annual sum which bears to the maximum annual sum which could have been awarded to him under regulation 12 if he had suffered loss of emoluments the same ratio as the amount by which his net annual emoluments have been diminished bears to his net annual emoluments before diminution, so however that no compensation shall be payable under this regulation if the ratio is less than $2\frac{1}{2}\%$.

(2) Long-term compensation determined under this regulation shall be payable to a person by instalments at intervals equivalent to those at which the emoluments of his employment are or were previously paid or at such intervals as may be agreed between the person and the Corporation.

Date from which long-term compensation is to be payable

14.—(1) Long-term compensation shall be payable with effect from the date on which the claim is received unless made payable from an earlier date under the succeeding provisions of this regulation.

(2) Where a claim for long-term compensation is made within 13 weeks of the occurrence of the loss or the commencement of the diminution which is the subject of the claim, or of the coming into operation of these regulations whichever is the later, the compensation shall be payable with effect from the date on which the loss occurred or the diminution commenced.

(3) Where a claim for long-term compensation is made after the expiry of the period mentioned in paragraph (2), the compensation may, at the discretion of the Corporation, be made payable with effect from a date not earlier than 13 weeks prior to the date on which the claim was received:

Provided that if the Corporation are satisfied that the failure to make the claim within the period mentioned in paragraph (2) was due to ill-health or other circumstances beyond the claimant's control, the compensation may be made payable with effect from a date not earlier than that on which the loss occurred or the diminution commenced.

Compensation payable to non-pensionable officers on reaching retiring age

15.—(1) Where a person to whom these regulations apply and who is not a pensionable officer is receiving long-term compensation for loss of employment and reaches normal retiring age, the Corporation shall, if satisfied that the person would, but for the loss, have continued in the employment he has lost for a substantial period beyond that age, continue to pay compensation to him for the remainder of his life at half its former rate.

(2) Where a person to whom these regulations apply and who is not a pensionable officer suffers loss of employment in consequence of a relevant event on or after reaching normal retiring age, the Corporation shall, if satisfied that the person would in the normal course have continued in the employment he has lost for a further substantial period, pay compensation to him for the remainder of his life at half the rate which would have been payable under regulation 12 had he not attained normal retiring age on or before the date on which he lost his employment.

PART V

RETIREMENT COMPENSATION FOR LOSS OR DIMINUTION OF PENSION RIGHTS

Persons to whom retirement compensation is payable

16.—(1) The Corporation shall, subject to the provisions of these regulations, pay retirement compensation to any pensionable officer to whom these regulations apply, who—

(a) has suffered loss or diminution of pension rights in consequence of a relevant event not later than 10 years after the material date;

(b) had not at the date on which the loss or diminution was occasioned reached normal retiring age;

(c) had been continuously engaged (without a break of more than 12 months at any one time) in relevant employment during the period beginning 8 years before the material date and ending at the date of the loss; and for this purpose the expression "relevant employment" includes any period of national service immediately following such employment;

(d) has made a claim for compensation in accordance with the provisions of Part VII of these regulations not later than 2 years after the date on which the loss or diminution was occasioned or 2 years after the coming into operation of these regulations, whichever is the later; and

(e) has reached normal retiring age or has elected to take retirement compensation earlier in accordance with the following provisions of this Part of these regulations.

(2) Retirement compensation shall not, however, be paid:—

(a) to a person who has suffered loss or diminution of pension rights which has been occasioned by loss of employment in consequence of a relevant event, if his employment could have been terminated by reason of misconduct or incapacity to perform such duties as, immediately before that loss of employment, he was performing or might reasonably have been required to perform; or

(b) to a person who has been offered reasonably comparable employment under the Crown or in the service of the Corporation or of a publicly-owned company and who would not have suffered a loss or diminution of pension rights had he accepted that employment; or

(c) to a person who has suffered a diminution of pension rights which has been occasioned by a diminution in his emoluments of less than $2\frac{1}{2}\%$.

(3) Regulation 5(3) and (4) (which relate to offers of employment) shall apply for the purposes of this regulation as they apply for the purposes of regulation 5.

(4) References in this Part of these regulations to the date on which a loss or diminution of pension rights was occasioned shall subject to regulation 4(2) be interpreted as references to the date on which the loss of employment or emoluments took place or on which the diminution of emoluments began or the change in the terms of service occurred which occasioned the loss or diminution of pension rights.

Factors to be considered in assessing loss or diminution of pension rights

17. For the purpose of determining the amount of retirement compensation, if any, the loss or diminution of pension rights suffered by a person shall be regarded as the loss, if any, (adjusted in the case of diminution as provided in the following regulation) which he would have suffered had the conditions specified in any of the three following regulations as being appropriate to his case obtained and had he taken all reasonable steps open to him to mitigate the loss or diminution, and in assessing the loss (so adjusted in case of diminution) such of the factors specified in regulation 11 as are relevant to the particular case shall be taken into consideration, and in particular the following shall be taken into consideration—

(*a*) the terms of any pension scheme associated with any new employment undertaken; and

(*b*) the extent to which the person in question has sought pensionable employment, and the terms of any pension scheme which would have applied if he had accepted other suitable employment offered to him.

Extent of retirement compensation payable at normal retiring age

18.—(1) Subject to the provisions of these regulations, retirement compensation to be paid pursuant to regulation 16 to a person who has reached normal retiring age without having elected under either regulation 19 or regulation 20 to take retirement compensation earlier shall consist of—

(*a*) in the case of a person who has suffered loss of pension rights—

(i) an annual sum equivalent to the loss of any sum which under the last relevant pension scheme would have become payable to him in each year after retiring at normal retiring age;

(ii) a lump sum equivalent to the loss of any lump sum which would have become payable under that scheme on retiring at that age;

assessed in accordance with regulation 17,

(*b*) in the case of a person who has suffered a diminution of pension rights under the last relevant pension scheme by reason of a diminution of emoluments, the annual sum and the lump sum which respectively bear the same ratio to the sums which would be payable under the preceding provisions of this paragraph, had he suffered a loss of pension rights, as the amount by which his net annual emoluments have diminished bears to his net annual emoluments before diminution, and

(*c*) in the case of a person who has suffered a diminution of pension rights for any other reason, the sums which would be payable under (*a*) of this paragraph, had he suffered a loss of pension rights, respectively reduced by the amount of any sum payable under the last relevant pension scheme in each year after retirement compensation becomes payable and by the amount of any lump sum paid or payable under that scheme.

(2) The condition appropriate to the case of a person claiming retirement compensation under this regulation (which in accordance with regulation 17 is to be regarded as having obtained for the purpose of assessing loss or diminution of pension rights) is that the pensionable service which is to be taken into account for the purposes of the last relevant pension scheme is the pensionable service which would have been taken into account if on the date immediately preceding that on which the loss or diminution of pension rights was occasioned—

(a) he had reached normal retiring age and had then retired;

(b) he had complied with any requirement of the last relevant pension scheme as to a minimum period of qualifying service or contribution;

(c) he had continued any additional voluntary contributions until normal retiring age and had completed any payments in respect of added years which he was in the course of making;

(d) he had served for any additional period provided for in regulation 23.

(3) The sum referred to in paragraph (1)(a) which under the last relevant pension scheme would have been payable to a person in each year after retiring at normal retiring age shall be calculated without taking account of any reduction falling to be made in that sum by reason of the provisions of any Act relating to National Insurance, until he reaches the age at which under the last relevant pension scheme that sum would have been so reduced.

Retirement compensation payable on being incapacitated or at minimum pensionable age

19.—(1) A person to whom retirement compensation will be payable pursuant to regulations 16 and 18 on his reaching normal retiring age (if he does not elect to take it earlier under this or the following regulation) may claim, before reaching that age and by notice in writing to the Corporation, to be paid retirement compensation in accordance with this regulation if since the date on which the loss or diminution of pension rights was occasioned he has either:—

(a) become incapacitated in circumstances in which, if he had continued to be a pensionable officer, he would by reason of that incapacity have become eligible for a pension under the last relevant pension scheme; or

(b) reached the minimum pensionable age;

such retirement compensation as from the date from which it is payable to be in lieu of all other compensation payable as from that date under these regulations.

(2) For the purpose of determining the retirement compensation payable to a person claiming under this regulation, regulation 18 shall apply as it applies to a person who has reached normal retiring age, but subject to the provisions as to determining compensation hereinafter in this regulation stated and in the case of such incapacity as is mentioned in paragraph (1)(a) subject to the substitution for (a) of regulation 18(2) of the following—

"(a) he had become incapacitated in circumstances in which he would by reason of that incapacity have become eligible for a pension under the last relevant pension scheme."

(3) Within 13 weeks of the receipt of a claim under paragraph (1) of this regulation the Corporation:—

(a) shall, if they do not consider that the claimant is eligible for payment of retirement compensation assessed under this regulation, so notify him in writing;

(*b*) shall, if they do consider that he is eligible, assess the retirement compensation to be paid and notify him in writing accordingly;

and any such notification shall for the purposes of these regulations be deemed to be a notification by the Corporation of a decision on a claim for compensation.

(4) The Corporation may require any person who makes a claim for retirement compensation under paragraph (1)(*a*) of this regulation to submit himself to a medical examination by a registered medical practitioner selected by the Corporation, and, if they do so, they shall also offer the person an opportunity of submitting a report from his own medical adviser as a result of an examination by him, and the Corporation shall take that report into consideration, together with the report of the medical practitioner selected by them when considering the claim.

(5) If a person elects to receive compensation under this regulation, he shall so inform the Corporation in writing within one month from the receipt of a notification under paragraph (3) or, where the claim has been the subject of an appeal, from the decision of the tribunal thereon, and if he fails to do so he shall be deemed to have elected not to receive such compensation.

(6) On a person electing to receive retirement compensation under this regulation in accordance with paragraph (5), such retirement compensation shall be payable as from the date on which the Corporation received notice in writing of the claim in accordance with paragraph (1) and if any compensation under these regulations has been paid in lieu of which by virtue of that paragraph retirement compensation under this regulation is payable, payments of such retirement compensation shall be withheld or reduced accordingly.

(7) The computation of compensation under this regulation shall be subject to the following conditions:—

(*a*) where the Corporation, by virtue of regulation 23 has taken into account a period of additional years, that period shall not include any additional years beyond the number of years which the person in question has served or could have served, had he not lost his employment, before the date on which the claim was received by the Corporation; and

(*b*) if, by reason of any provision of the last relevant pension scheme for a minimum benefit, the amount of the pension which would have been payable under that scheme is in excess of that attributable to the person's actual service, no account shall be taken of any such period of additional years except to the extent (if any) by which it exceeds the number of years represented by the difference between his actual service and the period by reference to which the minimum benefit has been calculated; and

(*c*) if the number of years of pensionable service taken into account in accordance with regulation 18 as applied by paragraph (2) of this regulation is less than the minimum number of years of qualifying service prescribed by the last relevant pension scheme, the annual sum and lump sum payable as retirement compensation under this regulation shall, notwithstanding any minimum benefit prescribed by the pension scheme, not exceed such proportion of such minimum benefit as the number of years of pensionable service so taken into account bears to that minimum number of years of qualifying service.

Premature retirement compensation

20.—(1) A person to whom retirement compensation will be payable pursuant to regulations 16 and 18 on his reaching normal retiring age (if he does not elect to take it earlier under this or the preceding regulation) by reason of his having lost employment as a pensionable officer, if at the date of the loss he had reached 50 years of age, may, before reaching normal retiring age and by notice in writing to the Corporation, claim to be paid retirement compensation assessed in accordance with this regulation, such retirement compensation as from the date on which it is payable to be in lieu of all compensation payable as from that date under these regulations other than resettlement compensation.

(2) No claim under this regulation shall be entertained if the claimant has also claimed long-term compensation and the claim under this regulation is made more than 2 years after the determination of the claim for long-term compensation or after any review of that determination.

(3) For the purpose of determining the retirement compensation payable to a person claiming under this regulation, regulation 18 shall apply as it applies to a person who has reached normal retiring age, but subject to the omission of (d) of regulation 18(2).

(4) Paragraphs (3), (5) and (6) of regulation 19 shall apply in relation to a claim made under this regulation as they apply in relation to a claim made under regulation 19.

Pension contributions

21.—(1) A person to whom retirement compensation will be payable shall pay to the Corporation an amount equal to any sum which was paid to him by way of return of pension contributions, including any interest, after ceasing to be employed, and the Corporation may at his request repay that amount to him at any time before retirement compensation is payable, but if that amount is not paid to the Corporation, or is repaid by them to the person, the retirement compensation payable to him shall be reduced by an annual amount the capital value of which is equal to the amount of the said pension contributions.

(2) For the purposes of this regulation the expression "pension contributions" shall include payments made by the person in respect of added years.

Retirement compensation payable to a person who obtains further pensionable employment

22. Where a pensionable officer to whom these regulations apply, after the date on which a loss or diminution of pension rights was occasioned in consequence of a relevant event, enters employment other than that in which he suffered that loss or diminution and for the purpose of a pension scheme associated with that new employment there falls to be taken into account any period of service which also falls to be taken into account as being service reckonable under the last relevant pension scheme for the purpose of assessing any retirement compensation payable to him, then:—

(a) subject as is in this regulation stated, the foregoing provisions of this Part of these regulations shall apply to him as if he had suffered a diminution in pension rights occasioned by an annual diminution of emoluments as a pensionable officer to whom these regulations apply which is equivalent to the amount by which his net annual emoluments, as they were immediately before the date on which the loss or diminution of pension rights in respect of which retirement compensation is payable was occasioned, exceed his net annual emoluments in his new employment immediately after entering that employment; and

(b) if his claim to retirement compensation is for diminution of pension rights by reason of his emoluments having diminished, the retirement compensation payable shall not exceed the retirement compensation which would have been payable if he had not entered new employment.

Adjustment for additional years

23.—(1) Subject as hereinafter stated, in calculating the maximum retirement compensation payable to a person who has reached the age of 40 years at the date on which the loss or diminution of pension rights was occasioned, in addition to the service taken into account as being reckonable for the purposes of his last relevant pension scheme, a period not exceeding the aggregate of the following shall also be taken into account as if it were so reckonable, and retirement compensation shall be adjusted accordingly, that is to say—

(*a*) 2 years, whether or not he has completed any years of service after reaching the age of 40 years; and

(*b*) 2 years for each complete year of reckonable service, not exceeding 4 years of reckonable service in all, which elapsed between the date of his reaching the age of 40 years and the date on which the loss or diminution of pension rights was occasioned; and

(*c*) one year for each such complete year after the fourth of reckonable service so elapsing:

Provided that the aggregate of the additional years taken into account shall not exceed any of the following:—

(i) the number of years reckonable for the purposes of the last relevant pension scheme for which he would have served after the date on which the loss or diminution of pension rights was occasioned had he continued to be employed as an officer subject to that scheme until normal retiring age; or

(ii) the number of years of his reckonable service on that date; or

(iii) 15 years.

(2) In applying the method of calculation prescribed by the last relevant pension scheme for the purposes of determining retirement compensation, any period added under this regulation shall be aggregated with any years of service which under that scheme entail reduction of a pension benefit because of a retirement pension payable under section 30 of the National Insurance Act 1965(**a**).

(3) This regulation shall not apply to retirement compensation payable in accordance with regulation 20.

Other adjustments

24. If retirement compensation is payable in respect of the loss or diminution of rights to a pension which under the last relevant pension scheme would have been increased or supplemented in specified circumstances, or might at the discretion of the body administering the scheme have been increased or supplemented to a specified extent, the Corporation shall in those circumstances, or may at their discretion, as appropriate, increase or supplement to a proportionate extent the corresponding component of retirement compensation, and in the exercise of this discretion the Corporation shall have regard to the terms of any relevant resolution of the body administering the pension scheme with regard to the increase of benefits.

Surrender to spouse

25. If under his last relevant pension scheme a person would have been entitled to surrender a proportion of any pension which might have become

(**a**) 1965 c. 51.

payable to him in favour of his spouse or any dependant, then, if he so desires and informs the Corporation by notice in writing accordingly within one month after becoming entitled to retirement compensation under these regulations, he may surrender a proportion of as much of the said compensation as is payable by way of an annual sum on the like terms and conditions and in consideration of the like payments by the Corporation as if the said annual sum were a pension to which he had become entitled under the said pension scheme.

Balances payable to personal representatives

26.—(1) If a person to whom retirement compensation is or will be payable dies before he has received by way of retirement compensation sums which in the aggregate are equivalent to the amount of any contributions repaid by him under regulation 21, together with compound interest thereon up to the date of his death calculated at the rate and in the manner specified in the last relevant pension scheme (or where no rate is so specified at the rate of 3 per cent. per annum with half-yearly rests as from 1st April or 1st October next following the half-year in which the amount was repaid), and no pension or gratuity falls to be paid to his personal representatives, or to his widow, or any dependant of his, by reason of his having been immediately or prospectively entitled to retirement compensation, there shall be paid to his personal representatives the difference between the aggregate amount which he has received by way of retirement compensation as aforesaid and the said equivalent sum with interest.

(2) For the purposes of this regulation a person who has surrendered any part of his retirement compensation under regulation 25 shall be deemed to have received during any period the amount of compensation for that period which he would have received but for any such surrender.

Payment of compensation under Part V

27. Retirement compensation payable as an annual sum to or in respect of any person shall be payable at intervals equivalent to those at which the corresponding benefit would have been payable under the person's last relevant pension scheme or at such intervals as may be agreed between the person entitled to receive the compensation and the Corporation.

PART VI

ADJUSTMENT AND COMPOUNDING OF COMPENSATION

Adjustment of compensation where pension benefit is also payable

28.—(1) Where any period of service of which account was taken in calculating the amount of any compensation payable under Part IV or V of these regulations is subsequently taken into account for the purpose of calculating the amount of any pension benefit payable to any person in accordance with a pension scheme associated with any employment undertaken subsequent to the loss or diminution of emoluments or of pension rights which was the subject of the claim for compensation, the Corporation may in accordance with this regulation withhold or reduce the compensation payable in respect of any period for which such pension benefit is being received.

(2) If the part of any pension benefit by way of annual amounts which is attributable to a period of service mentioned in paragraph (1) equals or exceeds the part of any compensation by way of annual amounts which is attributable to the same period, that part of the compensation may be withheld, or if such

part of the pension benefit is less than such part of the compensation, the compensation may be reduced by an amount not exceeding such part of the pension benefit.

(3) In addition to any reduction authorised by paragraph (2), if, in the circumstances mentioned in paragraph (1), compensation by way of annual amounts is attributable in part to any provision of the last relevant pension scheme for a minimum benefit, the compensation may be reduced by an amount not exceeding that part.

(4) In addition to any other reduction authorised by this regulation, where any period of additional years has been taken into account under regulation 23 compensation by way of annual amounts may be reduced—

(a) if the number of such years is equal to or less than the period spent in the subsequent employment mentioned in paragraph (1), by an amount not exceeding that attributable to the additional years so taken into account;

(b) if the number of such years is greater than the period spent in the subsequent employment so mentioned, by such proportion of that amount as the period spent in the subsequent employment bears to the number of additional years so taken into account.

(5) Where retirement compensation has been calculated in accordance with regulation 22 the provisions of this regulation shall apply only in relation to such part (if any) of the pension benefit as is attributable to annual emoluments in excess of those to which the person was entitled immediately after entering the new employment.

(6) Where compensation is payable in respect of diminution of emoluments or of diminution of pension rights in consequence of diminution of emoluments, the provisions of this regulation shall apply only in relation to such part (if any) of the pension benefit as is attributable to annual emoluments in excess of those to which the person was entitled immediately prior to the diminution.

Reduction of compensation in certain cases

29.—(1) If under a person's last relevant pension scheme any benefit for which the scheme provided would have been subject to reduction or suspension on his taking up other specified employment, any retirement compensation to which he is entitled for loss or diminution of pension rights shall, where such employment is taken up, be reduced or suspended in the like manner and to the like extent:

Provided that in calculating the amount of the reduction there shall be aggregated with the emoluments of the employment taken up the amount of any pension benefit by way of annual amounts payable under the last relevant pension scheme.

(2) There shall be deducted from the retirement compensation payable to any person any additional voluntary contributions remaining unpaid at the date when he suffered loss of employment; and any such payments not recovered at the date of his death shall be deducted from any balance payable under regulation 26.

(3) Where a person is entitled to any compensation under these regulations and the circumstances are such that he is eligible to receive one or more of the following payments—

(a) a redundancy payment under the Redundancy Payments Act 1965(a);

(a) 1965 c. 62.

(b) any payment to compensate for the loss of his employment made under a contract or arrangement with the Iron and Steel Board or the publicly-owned company by which he was employed or the Corporation, or in satisfaction of damages or compensation (otherwise than by virtue of these regulations) awarded or claimed against the Board, the company or the Corporation;

(c) any payment under or by virtue of the provisions of any enactment relating to the reinstatement in civil employment of persons who have been in the service of the Crown,

the compensation payable to the person, whether by instalments or lump sum or both, shall in the aggregate be reduced by the amount of the payments referred to in this paragraph.

(4) Where any resettlement or long-term compensation is payable under these regulations to any person who is also entitled to a pension benefit under the last relevant pension scheme any instalment of such compensation which is payable in respect of any period shall be reduced by the amount of the instalment of such pension benefit which is payable in respect of the same period.

(5) For the purposes of paragraph (4) no account shall be taken of any sum payable in consequence of the surrender by any person of part of his pension benefit under any provision in that behalf in his last relevant pension scheme with a view to obtaining or increasing allowances for his spouse or any dependant; and he shall be deemed to have received during any period the amount of pension benefit which he would have received but for any such surrender.

(6) Subject to the following provisions of this regulation, where in any week a person is entitled to long-term compensation and is also entitled to unemployment, sickness or injury benefit under any Act relating to National Insurance, other than a benefit claimable by him in respect of a dependant, there shall be deducted from the long-term compensation payable for that week a sum equal to the amount by which the aggregate of such National Insurance benefit claimable in respect of that week and the weekly rate at which the long-term compensation would be payable but for this regulation exceeds two-thirds of the weekly rate of the net annual emoluments of the employment which he has lost or in which the emoluments have been diminished.

(7) Paragraph (6) shall not apply in relation to any such sickness or injury benefit in so far as an equivalent sum is deducted from the emoluments of his current employment and such deduction from those emoluments has not occasioned an increase in his long-term compensation.

(8) In paragraph (6) the expression "weekly rate" means seven three hundred and sixty-fifths of the relevant annual rate.

Notification of change of circumstances

30. Where—

(a) a pensionable officer after suffering loss of employment or loss or diminution of emoluments or pension rights enters any employment referred to in regulation 22 or becomes entitled to any pension benefit on ceasing to hold such employment; or

(b) a person entitled to long-term compensation enters employment the remuneration whereof is payable by the Corporation or a publicly-owned company, or ceases to hold such employment, or receives any increase in his remuneration in such employment; or

(c) a person entitled to retirement compensation enters employment in which the compensation is subject to reduction or suspension under regulation 29, or ceases to hold such employment, or receives any increase in his remuneration in such employment; or

(d) a person entitled to long-term compensation starts to receive any benefit, any increase in benefit or any further benefit under any Act relating to National Insurance;

he shall forthwith give notice in writing thereof to the Corporation.

Compounding of Awards

31.—(1) In a case where an annual sum which has been or might be awarded under these regulations does not exceed £26, the Corporation may, at their discretion, compound their liability in respect thereof by paying a lump sum equivalent to the capital value of the annual sum, and, if any lump sum payment has been or might be awarded in addition to such annual sum under regulation 18, 19 or 20, the Corporation may likewise discharge their liability in respect thereof by an immediate payment.

(2) In any other case, if a person who has been awarded long-term or retirement compensation requests them to do so the Corporation may, after having regard to the state of health of that person and the other circumstances of the case, compound up to one quarter of their liability to make payments under the award by payment of an equivalent amount as a lump sum, or, where any compensation has been awarded as a lump sum, by increasing that compensation to such equivalent amount; and in calculating for this purpose the liability of the Corporation to make such payments, account shall be taken of the annual value of lump sum payments of compensation.

(3) The making of a composition under paragraph (2) in relation to an award of long-term or retirement compensation shall not prevent the subsequent making of a composition under paragraph (1) in relation to that award, but, subject as aforesaid, not more than one composition may be made in relation to any award.

PART VII
PROCEDURE

Procedure on making claims

32.—(1) Every claim for compensation under these regulations and every request for a review of an award of long-term or retirement compensation shall be made in accordance with this regulation.

(2) Every such claim and request shall be made to the Corporation in a form approved by them, and shall state whether any other claim for compensation has been made by the claimant under these regulations.

(3) Resettlement compensation may however be claimed separately from any other form of compensation claimable under these regulations.

(4) The Corporation shall, provided that the person making the claim or request has complied with the provisions of this Part of these regulations, notify him in writing of their determination—

(a) in the case of a claim for resettlement compensation, not later than one month after the receipt of the claim; and

(b) in the case of a claim for, or request for the review of an award of, compensation under Part IV or V of these regulations, not later than 13 weeks after the receipt of the claim or request; and

(c) in any other case, as soon as possible after the determination.

(5) A determination of the Corporation shall not be invalidated by reason of the fact that notice of the determination is given after the expiry of the period mentioned in paragraph (4) unless the claimant has meanwhile instituted an appeal in accordance with regulation 34 and that appeal is not withdrawn.

(6) For the purposes of an appeal under regulation 34 a failure of the Corporation to comply with the provisions of the preceding paragraph within the period there mentioned shall be treated as a rejection of the claim in question.

(7) Every notification of a determination by the Corporation granting or refusing compensation or reviewing an award, or otherwise affecting any compensation under these regulations shall contain a statement—

(a) giving reasons for the determination;

(b) showing how any compensation has been calculated and, in particular, showing the factors taken into account in assessing loss or diminution of emoluments or pension rights; and

(c) directing the attention of the claimant to his right under regulation 34, if he is aggrieved by the determination, to bring an appeal before a tribunal and giving him the address to which the application instituting an appeal should be sent.

Claimants to furnish information

33.—(1) Any person claiming or receiving compensation or whose award of compensation is being reviewed shall furnish all such information as the Corporation may at any time reasonably require; and he shall verify the same in such manner, including the production of books or of original documents in his possession or control, as may be reasonably so required.

(2) Any such person shall, on receipt of reasonable notice, present himself for interview at such place as the Corporation may reasonably require; and any person who attends for interview may, if he so desires, be represented by his adviser.

Right of appeal from determination of Corporation

34.—(1) A claimant who is aggrieved by any determination of the Corporation as to whether any or what compensation under these regulations is payable to him may within 13 weeks of the notification to him of the determination bring an appeal before a tribunal in accordance with the Industrial Tribunals (Employment and Compensation) Regulations 1967(a) or, in Scotland, the Industrial Tribunals (Employment and Compensation) (Scotland) Regulations 1967(b), and these regulations.

(2) For the purpose of any such proceedings a person or persons may be appointed to sit with the tribunal as assessor or assessors.

Review of awards of long-term or retirement compensation

35.—(1) The Corporation shall, within a period of 2 years after the date on which any determination on a claim for long-term or retirement compensation (other than compensation payable under regulation 20) is notified to a claimant

---

(a) S.I. 1967/361 (1967 I, p. 1205).   (b) S.I. 1967/362 (1967 I, p. 1220).

under regulation 32, review their determination or, where the claim has been the subject of an appeal, the decision of the tribunal, at intervals of not more than 6 months, and these regulations shall apply in relation to any such review as they apply in relation to the initial determination of the claim; and on such review, in the light of any material change in the circumstances of the case, compensation may be awarded, or compensation previously awarded may be increased, reduced or discontinued, subject to the limits set out in these regulations:

Provided that where the claimant ceases to hold the employment in which his emoluments were diminished a review shall be held within 3 months after that date.

(2) After the expiration of the period mentioned in paragraph (1) the Corporation may, at their discretion, carry out reviews in accordance with that paragraph at intervals of not less than 12 months.

(3) The person to whom the determination relates may, at any time, require the Corporation to carry out a review in accordance with paragraph (1) if he considers that there has been a change in the circumstances of his case which is material for the purposes of these regulations.

(4) Notwithstanding anything contained in the foregoing provisions of this regulation—

(a) the Corporation shall in accordance with paragraph (1) review a determination of the Corporation or a decision of the tribunal, as the case may be, on a claim for long-term compensation for loss of employment after the expiration of the period mentioned in the said paragraph if at any time subsequent to the loss of employment the person to whom the determination or decision relates enters employment (hereinafter referred to as his "current employment") the remuneration whereof is payable by the Corporation or a publicly-owned company; and

(b) the Corporation shall further review in accordance with paragraph (1) any determination or decision reviewed under the foregoing provisions of this paragraph whenever the emoluments of the current employment of the person in question are increased.

(5) The Corporation shall give to a person to whom a determination or decision relates not less than 14 days' notice of any review of that determination or decision to be carried out under this regulation unless the review is carried out at his request.

(6) Nothing in this regulation shall preclude the making of any adjustment of compensation required by regulation 28 or 29 or the withholding, reducing or deducting from compensation under any other provision of these regulations.

Procedure on death of claimant

36.—(1) In the event of the death of a claimant or of a person who, if he had survived, could have been a claimant, a claim for compensation under these regulations may be continued or made, as the case may be, by his personal representatives.

(2) Where any such claim is continued or made as aforesaid by personal representatives, the personal representatives shall, as respects any steps to be taken or thing to be done by them in order to continue or make the claim, be deemed for the purposes of these regulations to be the person entitled to claim, but, save as aforesaid, the person in whose right they continue or make

the claim shall be deemed for the purposes of these regulations to be such person, and the relevant provisions of these regulations shall be construed accordingly:

Provided that the Corporation may in any such case extend the period within which a claim is required to be made by regulation 5, 10, 16 or 20.

Part VIII
Miscellaneous

Calculation of service

37. For the purpose of making any calculation under these regulations in respect of a person's reckonable service, all periods of such service shall be aggregated and, except where reference is made to completed years of service, if the aggregated service includes a fraction of a year, that fraction shall, if it equals or exceeds 6 months, be treated as a year, and shall, in any other case be disregarded.

Emoluments

38.—(1) For the purposes of determining whether any and what compensation is payable under these regulations, emoluments in relation to any person shall not include payments for overtime, other than payments which are a usual incident of his employment, or any allowances payable to him to cover the cost of providing office accommodation or clerical or other assistance, or any travelling or subsistence allowance or other moneys to be spent, or to cover expenses incurred by him, for the purposes of his employment, or any fees paid otherwise than in respect of services rendered as an officer or any emoluments paid to him solely by reason of his being a director of a company.

(2) Where fees or other variable payments were paid to a person as part of his emoluments during any period immediately preceding the loss or diminution the amount in respect of fees or other variable payments to be included in the annual rate of emoluments shall be the annual average of the fees or other payments paid to him during the period of 3 years immediately preceding the loss or diminution, or such shorter period as may be reasonable in the circumstances.

(3) When calculating the net annual emoluments of any employment any amount by which the said emoluments exceed £8,000 shall be disregarded.

Temporary variation of emoluments

39. In assessing for the purposes of these regulations the amount of any emoluments or pension rights lost, or the amount by which any emoluments or pension rights have been diminished, and in determining net annual emoluments of any person who has suffered such a loss or diminution, no account shall be taken of any increase in the amount of the person's emoluments which is attributable to any temporary allowance made in consequence of his temporary occupation of an office to which he has not been substantively appointed or in respect of temporary responsibilities additional to those normally attaching to his office.

Accrual of compensation

40. Resettlement and long-term compensation, and retirement compensation payable as an annual sum, shall accrue from day to day and be apportionable accordingly.

Compensation not assignable

41. Subject to any statutory provision in that behalf, any compensation to which a person becomes entitled under these regulations shall be paid to or in trust for him, and shall not be assignable.

Effect of non-compliance with regulations

42. Except in so far as the Minister may otherwise direct, compensation under these regulations shall not be payable to a person for so long as he fails to comply with regulations 8, 30 or 33.

Recovery of payments in error

43. Without prejudice to any other right of recovery there may be, any sum or any part of a sum paid under these regulations to a person in error, including any sum or part of a sum paid notwithstanding that by virtue of regulation 42 it is not payable, may be recovered by the Corporation by deduction from any compensation payable to that person under these regulations.

Dated 22nd July 1968.

Roy Mason,
Minister of Power.

SCHEDULE

TABLE 1

Table showing the capital value of an annual amount of £1 payable for life

Age	Capital value of £1 per annum payable for life	
	Female	Male
	£ s. d.	£ s. d.
Under 35	15 11 0	15 3 0
35 and under 40	15 2 0	14 12 0
40 and under 45	14 11 0	13 19 0
45 and under 50	13 18 0	13 2 0
50	13 9 0	12 11 0
51	13 5 0	12 7 0
52	13 2 0	12 3 0
53	12 18 0	11 18 0
54	12 14 0	11 14 0
55	12 10 0	11 9 0
56	12 6 0	11 5 0
57	12 2 0	11 0 0
58	11 18 0	10 15 0
59	11 13 0	10 10 0
60	11 8 0	10 5 0
61	11 4 0	10 0 0
62	10 19 0	9 14 0
63	10 14 0	9 9 0
64	10 8 0	9 3 0
65	10 3 0	8 18 0
66	9 18 0	8 12 0
67	9 12 0	8 7 0
68	9 7 0	8 1 0
69	9 1 0	7 16 0
70	8 15 0	7 10 0

NOTE:—This table is for use in connection with regulation 31(1) and (2) for the compounding of annual retirement compensation which a person is currently entitled to receive under regulation 18, 19 or 20. Where the compensation is payable before age 60 (females), 65 (males) but will be reduced on reaching that age (in connection with National Insurance pension) the table should be used in conjunction with Table II, i.e. Table II should be used for valuing that part of the compensation which ceases to be payable at 60 (65) and this table should be used for valuing the remainder.

TABLE II

Table showing the capital value of an amount of £1 per annum ceasing
at age 60 (females), 65 (males)

Age	Capital Value	
	Female	Male
	£ s. d.	£ s. d.
Under 35	13 8 0	14 2 0
35 and under 40	12 5 0	13 3 0
40 and under 45	10 14 0	11 19 0
45 and under 50	8 13 0	10 8 0
50	7 3 0	9 6 0
51	6 12 0	8 18 0
52	6 0 0	8 9 0
53	5 7 0	7 19 0
54	4 13 0	7 10 0
55	3 18 0	6 19 0
56	3 3 0	6 8 0
57	2 6 0	5 17 0
58	1 9 0	5 4 0
59	10 0	4 11 0
60	—	3 17 0
61	—	3 2 0
62	—	2 6 0
63	—	1 8 0
64	—	10 0

NOTE:—This table is for use in connection with regulation 31(1) and (2) for the compounding of any part of annual retirement compensation which will cease to be payable on reaching age 60 (females), 65 (males). Table I should be used in relation to the remainder of such compensation, i.e. the part which is payable for life—see note on that table.

TABLE III

Table showing the annual amount payable for life equivalent in value
to a lump sum of £100

Age	Annual sum, payable for life, equal in value to a lump sum of £100	
	Female	Male
	£ s. d.	£ s. d.
Under 35	6 8 7	6 12 0
35 and under 40	6 12 5	6 17 0
40 and under 45	6 17 5	7 3 4
45 and under 50	7 3 11	7 12 8
50	7 8 8	7 19 4
51	7 10 11	8 1 11
52	7 12 8	8 4 7
53	7 15 0	8 8 1
54	7 17 6	8 10 11
55	8 0 0	8 14 8
56	8 2 7	8 17 9
57	8 5 3	9 1 10
58	8 8 1	9 6 0
59	8 11 8	9 10 6
60	8 15 5	9 15 1
61	8 18 7	10 0 0
62	9 2 8	10 6 2
63	9 6 11	10 11 8
64	9 12 4	10 18 7
65	9 17 0	11 4 9
66	10 2 0	11 12 7
67	10 8 4	11 19 6
68	10 13 11	12 8 5
69	11 1 0	12 16 5
70	11 8 7	13 6 8

NOTE:—This table is for use in connection with regulation 21(1) for ascertaining the annual amount by which retirement compensation under regulation 18, 19 or 20 is to be reduced where a claimant has not paid to the Corporation an amount equal to any sum paid to him by way of pension contributions or that amount has been repaid to him by the Corporation at his request. It should also be used in connection with regulation 31(2) for calculating for the purposes of that paragraph the annual value of retirement compensation awarded as a lump sum.

TABLE IV

Table showing, according to the outstanding period of long-term compensation, the capital value of each £100 of the total amount of long-term compensation compounded

Outstanding number of complete years of long-term compensation	Capital value of each £100 of the total amount of long-term compensation	
	Female	Male
	£ s. d.	£ s. d.
0	98 8 0	98 4 0
1	95 4 0	94 16 0
2	92 2 0	91 10 0
3	89 4 0	88 6 0
4	86 8 0	85 8 0
5	83 16 0	82 14 0
6	81 6 0	80 2 0
7	78 18 0	77 14 0
8	76 14 0	75 8 0
9	74 12 0	73 4 0
10	72 12 0	71 4 0
11	70 12 0	69 6 0
12	68 16 0	67 10 0
13	67 0 0	65 14 0
14	65 6 0	64 2 0
15	63 14 0	62 10 0
16	62 2 0	61 0 0
17	60 12 0	59 12 0
18	59 4 0	58 4 0
19	57 16 0	56 18 0
20	56 10 0	55 12 0
21	55 4 0	54 8 0
22	54 0 0	53 4 0
23	52 16 0	52 0 0
24	51 12 0	50 18 0
25	50 10 0	49 18 0
26	49 8 0	48 18 0
27	48 8 0	47 18 0
28	47 8 0	46 18 0
29	46 8 0	45 18 0
30	45 10 0	45 0 0

NOTE:—This table is for use in connection with regulation 31(1) and (2) for compounding awards of long-term compensation under Part IV. The total amount of the annual long-term compensation which is to be compounded must first be calculated, i.e. the amount which the person would receive on account of that compensation, or the part of it which is to be compounded if it were paid until "normal retiring age" (as defined in regulation 2(1)). For each £100 so calculated, the lump sum payment will be the amount shown in the table according to the number of complete years in the period between the date of compounding and "normal retiring age".

EXPLANATORY NOTE

(This Note is not part of the Regulations)

1. These regulations, made under section 41 of the Iron and Steel Act 1949 as revived and amended by the Iron and Steel Act 1967, provide for the determination and payment by the British Steel Corporation of compensation to persons who suffer loss of employment or loss or diminution of emoluments or pension rights in consequence of (*a*) companies coming into public ownership under the Acts; (*b*) subsequent organisational changes giving effect to conclusions in a formal report by the Corporation to the Minister of Power or a direction by the Minister to the Corporation; (*c*) or the dissolution of the Iron and Steel Board.

2. Part I of the regulations contains definitions. Part II applies the regulations to any person who was employed immediately before 22nd March 1967 as an officer of a company which came into public ownership under the Acts or of the Iron and Steel Board.

3. The compensation payable is:—

(*a*) resettlement compensation for loss of employment (Part III of the regulations);

(*b*) long-term compensation for loss of employment or loss or diminution of emoluments (Part IV);

(*c*) retirement compensation for loss or diminution of pension rights (Part V).

4. Resettlement compensation is payable for a period not exceeding 26 weeks to persons who have served continuously (disregarding breaks not exceeding in the aggregate 6 months) with a publicly-owned company or the Iron and Steel Board or in other relevant employment during the period beginning on a date three years before the date of the event which gave rise to the loss and ending with the date of the loss; and who have fulfilled the other qualifying conditions set out in regulation 5. It consists of a weekly payment of two thirds of the net emoluments lost reduced by certain National Insurance benefits, by two thirds of the net emoluments from alternative employment, by payments under the Redundancy Payments Act, 1965 and by certain other payments (Regulations 6 and 29).

5. Long-term compensation is payable to persons who have served continuously (without a break of more than 12 months at any one time) with a publicly-owned company, the Iron and Steel Board or in other relevant employment during the period beginning on a date eight years before the date of the event which gave rise to the loss and ending with the date of the loss; and who have fulfilled the other qualifying conditions set out in regulation 10. It consists, of the annual loss or diminution of net emoluments which the person would have suffered had he taken all reasonable steps to mitigate it and taking into consideration the factors set out in regulation 11. The maximum is a proportion not exceeding two thirds of the loss or diminution as the case may be. (Regulation 12). Long-term compensation is reduced by payments under the Redundancy Payments Act, 1965 and by the other payments specified in Regulation 29.

6. Long-term compensation is payable from a date determined under regulation 14 until death or normal retiring age, whichever is the earlier. In the case of non-pensionable officers who would have continued working beyond normal retiring age, long-term compensation is payable from that age for the remainder of their lives at one half of the assessed rate (regulation 15).

7. Retirement compensation is payable to a pensionable officer who has fulfilled the conditions set out in regulation 16. It is based on the loss of pension rights which he would have suffered if the conditions specified in regulations 18, 19 or 20 had obtained and if he had taken all reasonable steps to mitigate (regulation 17). Retirement compensation is ordinarily payable from normal retiring age (regulation 16) but it may be payable earlier in the circumstances specified in regulations 19 and 20.

8. Part VI provides for the adjustment and compounding of compensation in certain circumstances. Part VII contains procedural provisions. Regulation 34 gives a claimant who is aggrieved by a determination of the Corporation on compensation a right of appeal to a tribunal established under section 12 of the Industrial Training Act 1964. Regulation 35 provides for the review and variation of long-term and retirement compensation in the light of changing circumstances.

9. Part VIII contains miscellaneous provisions.

10. These regulations come into operation on 2nd August 1968.

STATUTORY INSTRUMENTS

1968 No. 1173

DEFENCE

The Rules of Procedure (Air Force) (Amendment) Rules 1968

Made	- - -		*23rd July* 1968
Laid before Parliament			*31st July* 1968
Coming into Operation			*1st September* 1968

The Secretary of State in exercise of the powers conferred upon him by sections 103, 104, 105 and 106 of the Air Force Act 1955(**a**) and of all other powers enabling him in that behalf hereby makes the following Rules :—

Citation and Commencement

1. These Rules may be cited as the Rules of Procedure (Air Force) (Amendment) Rules 1968 and shall come into operation on 1st September 1968.

Interpretation

2. The Interpretation Act 1889(**b**) shall apply to the interpretation of these Rules as it applies to an Act of Parliament.

Amendment to the Rules of Procedure (Air Force) 1956

3.—(1) The Rules of Procedure (Air Force) 1956(**c**) as amended (**d**) shall be further amended in accordance with the following provisions of this Rule.

(2) In paragraph (3) of Rule 22 :—

(*a*) for the words "Criminal Appeal Act 1964"(**e**) there shall be substituted the words "Courts-Martial (Appeals) Act 1968"(**f**) ;

(*b*) for the words "paragraph 2 of Schedule I to" there shall be substituted the words "sub-section (3) of section 19 of" ;

(*c*) for the words "paragraph 4 of the said Schedule" there shall be substituted the words "sub-section (4) of the said section" ;

(*d*) for the words "paragraph 8 of the said Schedule" there shall be substituted the words "Part II of Schedule I to the said Act".

(3) In paragraph (3)(*a*) of Rule 93 :—

After the word "president" where it twice occurs there shall be added the words "or judge advocate".

(**a**) 1955 c. 19.   (**b**) 1889 c. 63.   (**c**) S.I. 1956/163 (1956 II, p. 2020).

(**d**) The relevant amending instruments are S.I.s 1964/489, 1964/1282, 1964/1854 (1964 I p. 794, 1964 II p. 2955, 1964 III p. 4045).

(**e**) 1964 c. 43.   (**f**) 1968 c. 20.

(4) In paragraph (2) of Rule 101:—

(*a*) for the words "Courts-Martial (Appeals) Act, 1951"(a) there shall be substituted the words "Courts-Martial (Appeals) Act 1968";

(*b*) for the words "section 22" there shall be substituted the words "section 49".

(5) In Form (5) in the Fourth Schedule :—

After the words "signed by the president" wherever they occur in the said Form there shall be added the words "or judge advocate".

Denis Healey,
One of Her Majesty's Principal
Secretaries of State.

23rd July 1968.

EXPLANATORY NOTE

(This Note is not part of the Rules.)

These Rules amend the Rules of Procedure (Air Force) 1956 :—

(*a*) by substituting for the references in Rules 22(3) and 101(2) to the Criminal Appeal Act 1964, and the Courts-Martial (Appeals) Act, 1951, both repealed, references to the consolidating Courts-Martial (Appeals) Act 1968;

(*b*) by making provision in Rule 93 and Form (5) for a judge advocate to mark and sign exhibits whether sitting alone or with the president and members of the court-martial.

(a) 1951 c. 46.

STATUTORY INSTRUMENTS

1968 No. 1177 (S.128)

REGISTRATION OF BIRTHS, DEATHS, MARRIAGES, ETC.

The Registration of Births, Deaths and Marriages (Fees) (Scotland) Order 1968

Made - - -	*22nd July* 1968
Laid before Parliament	*1st August* 1968
Coming into Operation	*1st October* 1968

In exercise of the powers conferred on me by section 5 of the Public Expenditure and Receipts Act 1968(a), and of all other powers enabling me in that behalf, I hereby make the following order:—

Citation and commencement

1. This order may be cited as the Registration of Births, Deaths and Marriages (Fees) (Scotland) Order 1968 and shall come into operation on 1st October 1968.

Interpretation

2. The Interpretation Act 1889(b) shall apply for the interpretation of this order as it applies for the interpretation of an Act of Parliament.

Variation of Fees

3. The enactments specified in column 2 of the schedule to this order shall be amended by substituting for the fees specified therein (as shown in column 4 of that schedule) the fees specified in column 5 thereof.

Fee abolished

4. The fee not exceeding threepence, specified by subsection (3) of section 97 of the Friendly Societies Act 1896(c), shall cease to be payable, and the said subsection is hereby repealed.

William Ross,

One of Her Majesty's Principal Secretaries of State.

St. Andrew's House,
Edinburgh, 1.
22nd July 1968.

(a) 1968 c. 14.   (b) 1889 c. 63.   (c) 1896 c. 25.

SCHEDULE

1	2 Enactment specifying fees	3 Type of certificate, etc.	4 Old Fee	5 New Fee
1887 c.40	Savings Banks Act 1887 Section 10	Certificate of birth, death or marriage, for purposes of certain Acts	Sum not exceeding 1s.	2s.
1896 c.25	Friendly Societies Act 1896 Section 97(1)	Certificate of birth or death, for purposes of that Act	Sum not exceeding 1s.	2s.
	Section 97(2)	Further certificates under Section 97(1)	Sum not exceeding 6d.	2s.
1938 c.69	Young Persons (Employment) Act 1938 Section 5	Certified copy of entry in register of births, for purposes of that Act	6d.	2s.
1948 c.39	Industrial Assurance and Friendly Societies Act 1948 Schedule 1, paragraph 7	Certificate of death, for purposes of that Schedule	1s.	2s.
1950 c.28	Shops Act 1950 Section 35	Certified copy of entry in register of births, for purposes of that Act	6d.	2s.
1961 c.34	Factories Act 1961 Section 178(1)	Certified extract of entry in register of births, for purposes of that Act	6d.	2s.
1962 c.47	Education (Scotland) Act 1962 Section 99(1)	Certified copy of entry in register of births, for purposes of certain Acts	6d.	2s.
1965 c.51	National Insurance Act 1965 Section 91(2)	Certified copy of entry of particulars for the purposes of that Act— (a) of birth, and (b) of marriage or death	 6d. 1s.	 2s. 2s.

EXPLANATORY NOTE

(This Note is not part of the Order.)

This Order increases to two shillings the fee payable for a certificate of birth, death or marriage issued for special purposes under certain statutory provisions. It also abolishes a fee of threepence payable under the Friendly Societies Act 1896.

STATUTORY INSTRUMENTS

1968 No. 1180

DEFENCE

The Rules of Procedure (Army) (Amendment) Rules 1968

Made - - -	*24th July* 1968
Laid before Parliament	*31st July* 1968
Coming into Operation	*1st September* 1968

The Secretary of State in exercise of the powers conferred upon him by sections 103, 104, 105 and 106 of the Army Act 1955(**a**) and of all other powers enabling him in that behalf hereby makes the following Rules:—

Citation and Commencement

1. These Rules may be cited as the Rules of Procedure (Army) (Amendment) Rules 1968 and shall come into operation on 1st September 1968.

Interpretation

2. The Interpretation Act 1889(**b**) shall apply to the interpretation of these Rules as it applies to an Act of Parliament.

*Amendment to the Rules of Procedure (Army) 1956(**c**)*

3.—(1) The Rules of Procedure (Army) 1956, as amended (**d**), shall be further amended in accordance with the following provisions of this Rule.

(2) In paragraph (3) of Rule 22:—

(*a*) for the words "Criminal Appeal Act 1964(**e**)" there shall be substituted the words "Courts-Martial (Appeals) Act 1968(**f**)";

(*b*) for the words "paragraph 2 of Schedule I to" there shall be substituted the words "sub-section (3) of section 19 of";

(*c*) for the words "paragraph 4 of the said Schedule" there shall be substituted the words "sub-section (4) of the said section";

(*d*) for the words "paragraph 8 of the said Schedule" there shall be substituted the words "Part II of Schedule 1 to the said Act".

(3) In paragraph (3)(*a*) of Rule 93, after the word "president" where it twice occurs, there shall be added the words "or judge advocate".

(4) In paragraph (2) of Rule 101:—

(*a*) for the words "Courts-Martial (Appeals) Act, 1951(**g**)" there shall be substituted the words "Courts-Martial (Appeals) Act 1968";

(*b*) for the words "section 22" there shall be substituted the words "section 49".

(**a**) 1955 c. 18.   (**b**) 1889 c. 63.   (**c**) S.I. 1956/162 (1956 I, p. 213).
(**d**) The relevant amending instruments are S.I's 1964/489 (1964 I p. 794) and 1964/1864 (1964 III, p. 4170).   (**e**) 1964 c. 43.   (**f**) 1968 c. 20.   (**g**) 1951 c. 46.

(5) In Form (5) in the Fourth Schedule, after the words "signed by the president" wherever they occur in the said form there shall be added the words "or judge advocate".

Dated 24th July 1968.

Denis Healey,
One of Her Majesty's Principal
Secretaries of State.

EXPLANATORY NOTE
(This Note is not part of the Rules.)

These Rules amend the Rules of Procedure (Army) 1956:—

(a) by substituting for the references in Rules 22(3) and 101(2) to the Courts-Martial (Appeals) Act 1951 and the Criminal Appeal Act 1964, both repealed, references to the consolidating Courts-Martial (Appeals) Act 1968.

(b) by making provision in Rule 93 and Form 5 for a judge advocate to mark exhibits whether sitting alone or with the president and members of the court-martial.

STATUTORY INSTRUMENTS

1968 No. 1181 (S.129)

FOOD AND DRUGS

FOOD HYGIENE

The Imported Food (Scotland) Regulations 1968

Made - - - -	*22nd July* 1968
Laid before Parliament	*31st July* 1968
Coming into Operation	*1st August* 1968

In exercise of the powers conferred on me by sections 13 and 56 of the Food and Drugs (Scotland) Act 1956(a) and of all other powers enabling me in that behalf, after consultation with such organisations as appear to me to be representative of interests substantially affected by the regulations and after reference to the Scottish Food Hygiene Council under section 25 of that Act, I hereby make the following regulations:—

PART I

PRELIMINARY

Citation and commencement

1. These regulations may be cited as the Imported Food (Scotland) Regulations 1968 and shall come into operation on 1st August 1968.

Interpretation

2.—(1) In these regulations, unless the context otherwise requires—

"the Act" means the Food and Drugs (Scotland) Act 1956;

"area" means, in relation to a local authority, the area of that authority, including the waters of any customs port abutting on any part of their area but does not include any part of their area which lies within the area of a port local authority; and, in relation to a port local authority, means the area of that authority;

"competent authority" means an authority having power under the laws in force in any country to examine food and to certify as to its fitness for human consumption;

"country of origin" means—

(*a*) in relation to meat other than whale meat, the country where the mammal from which the meat is taken was slaughtered;

(*b*) in relation to any meat product other than a whale meat product, the country where the meat product was prepared;

(a) 1956 c. 30.

(c) in relation to any whale meat or whale meat product, the country whose competent authority has, in respect of the whale meat or product, responsibility for the matters for which an official certificate is recognised, and for this purpose the country shall be deemed to include a ship on which the whale meat or whale meat product was dressed, packed or otherwise prepared;

"enforcing authority" means the authority responsible for the enforcement and execution of these regulations under regulation 5;

"export" means remove to a place not in the United Kingdom;

"food" includes drink, chewing gum and other products of a like nature and use, and articles and substances used as ingredients in the preparation of food or drink or of such products, but does not include—

(a) water, live animals or birds;

(b) articles and substances used only as drugs;

(c) liquid cows' milk or any such milk which is separated or skimmed;

"fully cooked", in relation to any food, means so cooked as to render it unnecessary for the food to be subjected to any further processing or heat treatment before being used for human consumption;

"hover vehicle" means a vehicle designed to be supported on a cushion of air;

"importer", in relation to imported food, includes any person who, whether as owner, consignor, consignee, agent or broker, is in possession of the food or in any way entitled to the custody or control of it;

"local authority" has the meaning assigned to it by section 26 of the Act;

"master", in relation to a ship, aircraft or hover vehicle, includes the officer or any other person for the time being in charge or command of the ship, aircraft or hover vehicle;

"meat" means the flesh or other edible part of a mammal other than a rabbit or hare, and includes meat which has been cured or smoked;

"meat product" means any of the articles specified in schedule 1 and "whale meat product" means any such article which consists of, or contains, whale meat;

"officer of Customs and Excise" includes any person acting under the authority of the Commissioners of Customs and Excise;

"official certificate" means a certificate, label, mark, stamp or other voucher which—

(a) the competent authority has affixed, or caused to be affixed, in the country of origin to any meat or meat product or to a package containing or intended to contain any meat or meat product, or which, in the case of lard or any rendered animal fat transported unpackaged in the tank of a ship, aircraft or hover vehicle, the competent authority at the place of shipment has caused to be sent in that ship, aircraft or hover vehicle; and

(b) is for the time being recognised by the Secretary of State in accordance with regulation 3 or 12(1)(c) as showing—

    (i) that the meat to which it relates, or the meat from which the meat product to which it relates was prepared, was derived from mammals inspected before and after death, or in the case of mammals killed when wild, was derived from mammals inspected after death only, in the country of origin of the meat and passed in accordance with criteria satisfactory to the Secretary of State; and

    (ii) that the dressing, packing and other preparation of the meat, or meat product, was carried out with all necessary precautions for the prevention of danger to health;

"pig" includes a boar, sow and hog;

"port local authority" has the meaning assigned to it by section 172 of the Public Health (Scotland) Act 1897(a) and includes a joint port local authority;

and other expressions have the same meaning as in the Act.

(2) The Interpretation Act 1889(b) shall apply for the interpretation of these regulations as it applies for the interpretation of an Act of Parliament.

(3) Unless the context otherwise requires, references in these regulations to the provisions of any enactment or regulations shall be construed as references to those provisions as amended by any subsequent enactment or regulations.

(4) Any reference in these regulations to a numbered regulation or schedule shall, unless the reference is to a regulation or schedule of a specified Act or regulations, be construed as a reference to the regulation or schedule bearing that number in these regulations.

(5) Any reference in these regulations to a justice of the peace shall include a reference to the sheriff and to a magistrate.

Recognition of an official certificate

3.—(1) Recognition of an official certificate shall be effected by means of a notice published in the Edinburgh Gazette, and the recognition may be made subject to conditions which shall be specified in the notice; and any such recognition or condition may be varied or revoked by a subsequent notice so published.

(2) Any recognition of an official certificate which was in force for the purposes of the Public Health (Imported Food) (Scotland) Regulations 1937 to 1948(c) immediately before the commencement of these regulations shall continue in force and have effect as if it had been effected under these regulations and may be varied or revoked accordingly.

Presumption as to food commonly used for human consumption

4. For the purposes of these regulations, any food commonly used for human consumption shall, if imported for sale or for use in the preparation of food for sale, be presumed, until the contrary is proved, to have been imported for sale or, as the case may be, for use in the preparation of food for sale, for human consumption.

(a) 1897 c. 38.   (b) 1889 c. 63.
(c) S.R. & O. 1937/509; S.I. 1948/1434 (Rev.VIII, p. 127: 1937, p. 1951; 1948 I, p. 1221).

Enforcement

5.—(1) Subject to the provisions of this regulation and to such provisions of these regulations as prescribe functions to be exercised by officers of Customs and Excise, the authority responsible for the enforcement of these regulations shall be—

  (a) in relation to imported food which is in or unloaded in the area of a port local authority and—

    (i) which is liable to immediate customs examination, the port local authority; or

    (ii) where the customs examination is deferred until the food reaches a place of destination in Scotland, the local authority in whose area the place of destination lies;

  (b) in relation to imported food which is unloaded—

    (i) elsewhere than in the area of a port local authority, or

    (ii) in England and Wales or Northern Ireland,

  the local authority in whose area or district the food is deposited for customs examination.

(2) Where immediately prior to the commencement of these regulations the Public Health (Imported Food) (Scotland) Regulations 1937 to 1948 were enforced and executed by a local authority in any part of the area of a port local authority, these regulations shall to the same extent be enforced and executed by that authority or by any other authority to whom the functions of the first-named authority have been transferred.

(3) Where imported food is unloaded in the area of a port local authority or of a local authority and—

  (a) customs examination of the food has been completed; and

  (b) an authorised officer of such authority nevertheless considers it expedient (having regard to the nature of the container in which the food is imported) that—

    (i) any examination of the food for purposes of these regulations should be deferred until the food reaches a specified place of destination elsewhere in Scotland or

    (ii) any examination of the food should take place under England and Wales or Northern Ireland regulations when the food reaches a specified place of destination in England and Wales or Northern Ireland; and

  (c) the importer gives to the port local authority or local authority of the port or airport of entry an undertaking in writing that the container has been sealed and will not be opened until it reaches the place of destination specified in the undertaking,

the authorised officer shall, by the most expeditious means available, notify the receiving authority that the food (so described as to enable it to be identified) has not, by reason of the matters referred to in sub-paragraph (b) of this paragraph, been examined under these regulations at the port or airport of entry and send them a copy of the undertaking referred to in sub-paragraph (c) of this paragraph and where the receiving authority are a local authority within the meaning of these regulations that authority shall thereupon become responsible for the execution and enforcement of these regulations in relation to that food.

2f

(4) Where under any provision corresponding to the last foregoing paragraph contained in England and Wales or Northern Ireland regulations a local authority receive notification that imported food which has not been examined under those regulations has been or is being sent to a place of destination in their area, they shall thereupon become responsible for the execution and enforcement of these regulations in relation to that food.

(5) Where imported food is unloaded in the area of a local authority or port local authority and customs examination is deferred until the food reaches a place of destination elsewhere in the United Kingdom, the local authority or port local authority shall so inform the receiving authority.

(6) In this regulation—

"England and Wales or Northern Ireland regulations" means regulations with respect to imported food in force in England and Wales or Northern Ireland, as the case may be;

"receiving authority" means an authority within the United Kingdom in whose area or district is situated the place of destination of any imported food, being an authority with enforcement functions under these regulations or the England and Wales or Northern Ireland regulations, namely—

    (*a*) where that place is in Scotland, a local authority within the meaning of these regulations;

    (*b*) where that place is in England and Wales a local authority within the meaning of the Imported Food Regulations 1968**(a)**;

    (*c*) where that place is in Northern Ireland, a health authority within the meaning of the Imported Food (Northern Ireland) Regulations 1968**(b)**.

PART II

ALL IMPORTED FOOD

Prohibition on importation of unfit food

6.—(1) No person shall import into Scotland any food intended for sale for human consumption—

    (*a*) which has been rendered injurious to health by means of any operation described in section 1(1) of the Act; or

    (*b*) which has been examined by a competent authority and found at the time of examination not to be fit for human consumption; or

    (*c*) which is otherwise unfit for human consumption;

    (*d*) in the preparation of which any such food as aforesaid has been used.

(2) In any proceedings for an offence against paragraph (1)(*c*) of this regulation, it shall be a defence for the accused to prove that at the time when he imported the food he did not know, and could not with reasonable diligence have ascertained, that it was unfit for human consumption.

Examination of imported food

7.—(1) An authorised officer may at all reasonable times examine any food intended for sale for human consumption which is imported into Scotland, and where on examination it appears to the authorised officer that any such food is being or has been imported in contravention of regulation 6, he may by notice

---

    (a) S.I. 1968/97 (1968 I, p. 272).   **(b)** S.I. 1968/98 (1968 I, p. 285).

in writing to the importer and to any other person in possession of the food require that, until the food has been dealt with by a justice of the peace, it shall not, without the consent of the authorised officer, be moved from the place of examination or from any other place specified in the notice.

(2) If on such examination being made it appears to an authorised officer that the food is being or has been imported in contravention of regulation 6, he may deal with it as food falling within section 9(1) of the Act (which relates to the examination and seizure of suspected food); and subsections (2) to (5) of that section shall apply in relation to such food and to regulation 6 as they apply in relation to food seized under that section and to section 8 of the Act (which relates to offences).

Analysis of samples

8. In any case where under section 28 of the Act (which confers powers of sampling) a sample has been procured for the purposes of these regulations by an authorised officer of a port local authority and submitted for analysis to a public analyst, section 29 of the Act (which relates to the analysis of samples) shall apply as though the sample had been procured within the area of the local authority which appointed the public analyst to whom it is submitted.

Special examination

9.—(1) Where an authorised officer is of the opinion that special procedure is necessary for the examination of food, or where at the request of the importer he has recourse to such special procedure, the importer shall provide all such facilities as the authorised officer may reasonably require for the examination of such food.

(2) An authorised officer may by notice in writing to the importer or to any other person in possession of the imported food prohibit or restrict the removal or delivery of the food during any period, not exceeding six days (exclusive of Saturdays, Sundays and public holidays), which may reasonably be required for the examination of the food; and the notice shall specify the period and the procedure required for that examination.

(3) When a notice under paragraph (2) of this regulation has been given to an importer or to any other person in possession of the imported food he may appeal against the notice to a justice of the peace who may direct that the notice be withdrawn or that such shorter period be fixed as appears reasonable in the circumstances.

Consent of officer of Customs and Excise

10. Where the duties of an officer of Customs and Excise with regard to the examination of a cargo or consignment comprising food have not been wholly discharged, no examination of the food shall be made or sample procured for the purposes of these regulations without his consent; but every officer of Customs and Excise shall afford such facilities as the circumstances require for such examination of the food to be made or sample be taken.

Powers of officer of Customs and Excise

11.—(1) An authorised officer may request an officer of Customs and Excise (either orally or in writing) to prohibit the removal of imported food which has not been cleared from customs charge until it has been examined by an authorised officer, and such a request may be made in relation to a particular consignment of food or in relation to food of any class or description specified in the request. A request made orally under this paragraph shall be confirmed in writing.

(2) Where a request has been made under the last preceding paragraph, the officer of Customs and Excise shall by notice in writing given to the importer or master of the ship, aircraft or hover vehicle in which the food is imported require that, until the food has been examined by an authorised officer, it shall not be removed from the place specified in the notice, and he shall at the same time inform the enforcing authority of the effect of the notice.

(3) An authorised officer shall, without undue delay, examine any food in respect of which a notice has been given by an officer of Customs and Excise under this regulation and shall send to that officer a copy of any notice or certificate issued by him in accordance with these regulations, or a statement in writing of any action taken by him under any other provision of these regulations in respect of that food.

(4) Where an officer of Customs and Excise has given notice under paragraph (2) of this regulation forbidding removal of any food, such food shall not, prior to its inspection by an authorised officer, be removed by any person contrary to the terms of the notice except with the written permission of either such officer.

PART III

MEAT AND MEAT PRODUCTS

Regulation of imported meat

12.—(1) Except as provided in paragraph (5) of this regulation, no person shall import into Scotland for sale for human consumption—

(a) any meat, other than meat of a description set out in schedule 2 or any meat product, from any place elsewhere than the Republic of Ireland or the Channel Islands unless that meat or meat product is accompanied by an official certificate; or

(b) any meat, other than meat of a description set out in schedule 2 or any meat product, imported into the Republic of Ireland or the Channel Islands and re-exported, whether or not it has been subjected to any process or treatment while in either country, unless that meat or meat product is accompanied by an official certificate; or

(c) any meat of a description set out in schedule 2 unless it is accompanied by an official certificate in the recognition of which by the Secretary of State it is expressly indicated that that recognition extends to that description of meat.

(2) An official certificate required by this regulation shall be—

(a) so placed as to be legible and clearly visible, and

(b) affixed to any sides or quarters of meat or packages of meat or meat products packed inside a container as well as to the container in which they are packed.

(3) An official certificate in respect of lard or rendered animal fat transported unpackaged in a tank of a ship, aircraft or hover vehicle shall—

(a) indicate the position in the ship, aircraft or hover vehicle of the tank;

(*b*) state the quantity of lard or fat contained in the tank; and

(*c*) state that the tank was inspected and found to be clean before the lard or fat was loaded.

(4)(*a*) In any case where the importation of any meat or meat products described in paragraph (1) of this regulation is not permitted by an authorised officer, having regard to the foregoing provisions of this regulation, by reason of the absence of an official certificate or some deficiency or inaccuracy in the form of an accompanying official certificate, and that officer has reasonable cause to believe that such absence, deficiency or inaccuracy is due to a bona fide mistake or to the official certificate being lost or damaged in transit after being affixed in the country of origin, he may forthwith notify the Secretary of State to that effect, and in that case shall furnish him with all relevant information in his possession.

(*b*) On receipt of such notification and information the Secretary of State shall make such inquiries as he considers appropriate, and shall communicate the results of his inquiries to the authorised officer.

(*c*) If, after taking into consideration the results of the Secretary of State's inquiries, and after consultation with the Secretary of State the authorised officer is satisfied that—

(i) the meat or meat product originally came from a country the official certificate of whose competent authority is for the time being recognised by the Secretary of State pursuant to regulation 3;

(ii) the meat, or meat from which the meat product was prepared, was derived from mammals inspected before and after death or in the case of mammals killed when wild was derived from mammals inspected after death only, by the competent authority in the country of origin of the meat and passed in accordance with criteria satisfactory to the Secretary of State; and

(iii) the dressing, packing and other preparation of the meat or meat product were carried out with all necessary precautions for the prevention of danger to health,

and notifies the Secretary of State in writing to that effect, the foregoing provisions of this regulation shall have effect in relation to the meat or meat product as if it had been accompanied by an official certificate in compliance with the relevant requirements of paragraphs (1) to (3) of this regulation.

(5) This part of these regulations shall not apply to any article of food specified in schedule 3.

Disposal of meat imported contrary to the regulations

13.—(1) If upon examination of any food an authorised officer is of the opinion that it comprises any meat or meat product imported in contravention of the provisions of regulation 12 or that it comprises any meat or meat product to which regulation 12(4)(*a*) applies, he shall notify in writing the importer or master of the ship, aircraft or hover vehicle in which the food is imported that the food must not be removed for any purpose other than its exportation.

(2) Unless the authorised officer proposes to notify the Secretary of State under regulation 12(4)(*a*) of the absence, deficiency or inaccuracy of any official certificate relating to the food, he shall, when giving a notice under paragraph (1) of this regulation, notify the importer in writing that unless within a time specified in the notice, being not less then 24 hours after the notice is received,

he gives a written undertaking to the enforcing authority to export the food at his own expense within fourteen days from the date of the undertaking, or to prove in proceedings before a justice of the peace that its importation is not contrary to the provisions of regulation 12, it may be destroyed or disposed of so that it cannot be used for human consumption.

(3) In the case of food as to which the authorised officer proposes to notify the Secretary of State under regulation 12(4)(a) of the absence, deficiency or inaccuracy of an official certificate, the notice referred to in paragraph (2) of this regulation shall be given if, after the inquiries and consultation referred to in regulation 12(4)(c), the authorised officer does not notify the Secretary of State that he is satisfied as to the matters set out in regulation 12(4)(c)(i) to (iii).

(4) If within the time specified in any notice given under paragraph (2) or (3) of this regulation the enforcing authority have not received such written undertaking as is described in the notice, or if within that time they have received an undertaking that the importer will at his own expense export the food and the importer fails to export it within fourteen days after the receipt of the undertaking, the enforcing authority may cause it to be destroyed or disposed of under the supervision of an authorised officer by such means and in such manner as to prevent it from being used for human consumption.

(5) Where in pursuance of this regulation the importer has given an undertaking to prove that the importation of any food is not contrary to the provisions of regulation 12, the enforcing authority shall within 24 hours after the receipt of the undertaking take steps to obtain the decision of a justice of the peace with respect thereto.

(6) If upon examination of any food in respect of which an officer of Customs and Excise has given a notice under regulation 11 an authorised officer is of the opinion that its importation is not contrary to the provisions of regulation 12, he shall give a certificate authorising its removal unless he takes action in respect of it under any other provisions of these regulations.

(7) Where in pursuance of paragraph (1) of this regulation an authorised officer has given a notice forbidding the removal of any food, it shall not be removed by any person contrary to the terms of the notice except with the written permission of the authorised officer.

Powers of a justice of the peace

14.—(1) Where, in pursuance of regulation 13, an application is made to a justice of the peace in respect of any food and he is satisfied that the importer has failed to prove that the importation of the food was not contrary to the provisions of regulation 12, he shall condemn the food and order it to be destroyed or disposed of under the supervision of an authorised officer by such means and in such manner as to prevent it from being used for human consumption.

(2) Where on such application the justice of the peace is satisfied that the importation of the food is not contrary to the provisions of regulation 12 he shall order the rescission of the notice prohibiting its removal.

Prohibition on the importation of meat required to be exported

15. No person shall land in Scotland any meat or meat product in respect of which a notice has been given under regulation 13(1) or any other regulation to the like effect then in force in any part of the United Kingdom, the Channel Islands or the Isle of Man.

PART IV
GENERAL

Record to be kept of food destroyed

16. Where in pursuance of these regulations any food is destroyed or otherwise disposed of under the supervision of an authorised officer, the enforcing authority, before the destruction or other disposal of the food, shall cause a description of, and such other details as will suffice to identify, the food to be recorded and shall keep the record in their custody for a period of not less than 12 months from the date of destruction or other disposal of the food.

Penalties

17.—(1) If any person contravenes or fails to comply with any of the foregoing provisions of these regulations he shall be guilty of an offence under these regulations.

(2) Any person who is guilty of an offence under these regulations shall be liable—

   (*a*) on summary conviction to—

      (i) a fine not exceeding £100 or to imprisonment for a term not exceeding 6 months or to both such fine and imprisonment; and

      (ii) in the case of a continuing offence, to a further fine not exceeding £10 for every day during which the offence is continued; or

   (*b*) on conviction on indictment to—

      (i) a fine not exceeding £500 or to imprisonment for a term not exceeding one year or to both such fine and imprisonment; and

      (ii) in the case of a continuing offence, to a further fine not exceeding £50 for every day during which the offence is continued.

Court may include a justice who has examined the food

18. The justice of the peace before whom any food is brought under regulation 7 or 13 may, but need not, be a member of the court before which a person is charged with an offence under regulation 6 or 12, as the case may be, in relation to the food.

Disputes as to compensation

19. Any dispute as to compensation arising under these regulations shall be determined, and any compensation awarded thereunder shall be recoverable, in like manner as if the dispute had arisen or the award had been made under the Act, and section 48 of the Act (which relates to disputed compensation) shall apply accordingly.

Application of various sections of the Act

20.—(1) Sections 41 (2) and (5) (which relates to proceedings), 42(1), (2) and (3) (which relates to evidence of certificates of analysis), 44 (which relates to the power of a court to require analysis by the Government Chemist), 46(2) (which relates to the conditions under which a warranty may be pleaded as a defence) and 47 (which relates to offences in relation to warranties and certificates of analysis) of the Act shall apply for the purposes of these regulations as if references therein to proceedings, or a prosecution, under or taken under the Act included references to proceedings, or a prosecution as the case may be, taken for an offence against these regulations and in addition as if—

    (*a*) in the case of section 44(1) of the Act, the reference therein to section 41(5) of the Act included a reference to said section 41(5) as applied by these regulations; and

    (*b*) in the case of section 47(1) and (2) of the Act, the references therein to an offence against the Act included references to an offence against these regulations.

(2) Section 41(4) of the Act shall apply for the purposes of these regulations as if the reference therein to section 47 of the Act included a reference to said section 47 as applied by these regulations.

Revocation

21.—(1) The regulations specified in schedule 4 are hereby revoked.

(2) Section 38 of the Interpretation Act 1889 shall apply as if these regulations were an Act of Parliament and as if the regulations revoked by these regulations were Acts of Parliament repealed by an Act of Parliament.

William Ross,
One of Her Majesty's
Principal Secretaries of State.

St. Andrew's House,
Edinburgh, 1.
22nd July 1968.

SCHEDULE 1   Regulation 2(1)

Meat Products

1. Meat packed in hermetically sealed glass or metal containers.

2. Salami or other uncooked sausages of a similar kind or such cured meats as are commonly consumed without heat treatment or further processing.

3. Fully cooked meat, dried meat, fully cooked meat pies and puddings and fully cooked sausages.

4. Meat pastes, meat powders, meat essences, meat extracts and dried blood products.

5. Intestines and other parts prepared in the form of sausage casings.

6. Rendered animal fats, except in margarine.

SCHEDULE 2   Regulation 12(1)

Meat which is prohibited subject to the provisions of regulation 12(1) (c)

1. Meat comprising, or forming part of, the thorax or abdomen from which there has been detached any part of the pleura or (except in the case of pig meat) the peritoneum, other than a part whose removal is essential to the deboning process in the preparation of boneless meat.

2. (a) Any whole carcase (other than the whole carcase of a sheep) and any side or any quarter of meat from which a lymphatic gland has been removed;

   (b) any whole carcase of a sheep from which more than two lymphatic glands have been removed;

   (c) any portion of a carcase from which any lymphatic gland has been removed or which contains no associated lymphatic gland;

   (d) any offal (other than the tongue of a sheep or pig) from which any lymphatic gland has been removed;

   (e) any meat from which bones have been removed and which contains no associated lymphatic gland or from which there has been removed any lymphatic gland other than the presternal, suprasternal, xiphoid, subdorsal, intercostal, renal and sub-lumbar lymphatic glands.

3. Without prejudice to the generality of paragraph 2 of this schedule, meat comprising—

   (a) the liver of any mammal from which the lymphatic gland has been removed;

   (b) the head of a pig from which a submaxillary lymphatic gland has been removed;

   (c) a carcase, side or forequarter of pork from which a submaxillary lymphatic gland has been removed;

   (d) the tongue from any bovine animal from which a submaxillary lymphatic gland has been removed;

   (e) the lungs of any mammal from which the bronchial lymphatic glands have been removed;

   (f) any part of a carcase which has been chopped or minced, with or without the addition of any spices, cereal products, salt, flavouring, vegetables or other ingredient;

   (g) scraps and trimmings.

4. Boneless veal appearing to an authorised officer to be from calves less than three months old.

Regulation 12(5)   **SCHEDULE 3**

Articles of food exempt from Part III of the regulations

Whale oil.

Whale liver oil.

Vitamin concentrates containing meat.

Pharmaceutical products containing meat.

Gelatine.

Rennet.

Puddings and any other prepared food of which meat is not a principal ingredient
    but which contain small quantities of meat.

Regulation 21(1)   **SCHEDULE 4**

Column 1	Column 2
Regulations revoked	References
The Public Health (Imported Food) Regulations (Scotland) 1937.	S.R. & O. 1937/509 (Rev. VIII, p. 127: 1937, p. 1951).
The Public Health (Imported Food) Amendment (Scotland) Regulations 1948.	S.I. 1948/1434 (Rev. VIII, p. 127: 1948 I, p. 1221).
The Food and Drugs (Whalemeat) (Scotland) Regulations 1949.	S.I. 1949/870 (1949 I, p. 1760).
The Food and Drugs (Whalemeat) (Amendment) (Scotland) Regulations 1950.	S.I. 1950/198 (1950 I, p. 758).

EXPLANATORY NOTE

(This Note is not part of the Regulations.)

These Regulations contain measures for the protection of public health in relation to imported food. They replace the Public Health (Imported Food) (Scotland) Regulations 1937 to 1948.

Part I of the Regulations contains definitions and specifies the authorities by whom the Regulations are to be enforced. This will usually be the local authority of the port through which the food is imported; but may in certain circumstances be an inland local authority.

Part II deals with imported food generally. Regulation 6 makes it an offence to import food which is unfit for human consumption. Food imported in contravention of this requirement can be taken before a justice of the peace, who may order its condemnation. Regulations 7 to 9 deal with the examination of imported food by authorised officers of local authorities and port local authorities and with the submission of samples to the public analyst. Customs officers are empowered in certain circumstances to detain food for examination (Regulations 10 and 11).

Part III deals with imported meat and meat products. With certain exceptions, these cannot be imported without an official certificate from the country of origin which is recognised by the Secretary of State, as guaranteeing that the meat or meat product has been prepared in accordance with satisfactory standards of hygiene. Meat and meat products which do not satisfy these requirements can be re-exported; but if this is not done, the local authority or port local authority may require the destruction of the meat or meat product or disposal in such a manner that it will not be used for human consumption. The importer has a right of appeal to a justice of the peace.

Part IV deals with various supplementary matters and includes provisions—

(a) requiring records to be kept for twelve months of food which is destroyed (Regulation 16);

(b) prescribing penalties for offences against the Regulations (Regulation 17);

(c) applying sections of the Food and Drugs (Scotland) Act 1956 dealing with prosecutions, evidence of analysis and third party or warranty defences.

STATUTORY INSTRUMENTS

1968 No. 1183

SHOPS AND OFFICES

The Offices, Shops and Railway Premises Act 1963 (Exemption No. 6) Order 1968

Made	- - -		*24th July* 1968
Coming into Operation			*1st August* 1968

The Secretary of State—

(a) by virtue of her powers under section 45 of the Offices, Shops and Railway Premises Act 1963(**a**) (hereafter in this Order referred to as "the Act") and of all other powers enabling her in that behalf ; and

(b) after consulting, pursuant to section 45(4) of the Act, organisations appearing to her to be representative of workers concerned and employers concerned, respectively, and it appearing to her that there are no other persons concerned ;

hereby makes the following Order :—

1.—(1) This Order may be cited as the Offices, Shops and Railway Premises Act 1963 (Exemption No. 6) Order 1968.

(2) The Offices, Shops and Railway Premises Act 1963 (Exemption No. 4) Order 1966(**b**) is hereby revoked.

2.—(1) The Interpretation Act 1889(**c**) shall apply to the interpretation of this Order as it applies to the interpretation of an Act of Parliament, and as if this Order and the Order hereby revoked were Acts of Parliament.

(2) In this Order the expression "railway signal box" means a railway signal box which is, or is comprised in, railway premises to which the Act applies.

3. The Secretary of State hereby exempts the following classes of premises from the requirements of the Act specified in relation to each class of premises, that is to say—

(a) railway signal boxes the construction of which was completed before 1st August 1964 and which are so situated that there is no piped water supply available within a distance of 200 yards from them, from so much of section 10(1) (which relates to washing facilities) of the Act as requires water supplied to be running water ;

(b) railway signal boxes the construction of which was completed before 1st August 1964 and in the case of which—
  (i) there is a piped water supply available within a distance of 200 yards from them ; but
  (ii) there are no effective means of heating running water ;
from so much of the said section 10(1) as requires washing facilities provided thereunder to include a supply of clean, running hot and cold or warm water, subject to the conditions specified in Article 4 of this Order.

(a) 1963 c. 41.   (b) SI 1966/975 (1966 II, p. 2351).   (c) 1889 c. 63.

4. The conditions referred to in Article 3(*b*) of this Order are that in the case of premises of the class to which the said Article 3(*b*) applies washing facilities provided shall include—

    (*a*) a supply of clean, running cold water ; and

    (*b*) effective means of heating water for washing.

5. The exemptions granted by this Order shall be for the period of two years commencing with 1st August 1968.

Signed by order of the Secretary of State.

24th July 1968.

P. H. St. J. Wilson,
Deputy Under Secretary of State,
Department of Employment and Productivity.

EXPLANATORY NOTE
(This Note is not part of the Order.)

This Order continues for a period of two years commencing with 1st August 1968 the exemptions granted by the Offices, Shops and Railway Premises Act 1963 (Exemption No. 4) Order 1966 which were for a period of two years commencing with 3rd August 1966. The Order exempts railway signal boxes which were constructed before 1st August 1964 and which are more than 200 yards from a piped water supply, from the requirement of section 10 of the Offices, Shops and Railway Premises Act 1963 that water supplied for washing shall be running water. The Order also exempts railway signal boxes constructed before 1st August 1964 where there is a piped water supply within 200 yards but where there are no effective means of heating running water, from the requirements of the said section 10 that clean, running hot and cold or warm water shall be supplied for washing. The latter exemption is granted subject to the conditions that clean, running cold water and means of heating water for washing are provided.

STATUTORY INSTRUMENTS

1968 No. 1184

HOUSING, ENGLAND AND WALES
The Housing Subsidies (Representative Rates of Interest) Order 1968

Laid before the House of Commons in draft

Made - - - -   *25th July* 1968

Coming into Operation   *1st September* 1968

The Minister of Housing and Local Government, in exercise of his powers under sections 2(2), 2(5) and 21(1) of the Housing Subsidies Act 1967(a) and of all other powers enabling him in that behalf and after consultation with such recipient authorities, and such bodies representative of recipient authorities, as appear to him to be appropriate, hereby makes the following order in the terms of a draft approved by resolution of the Commons House of Parliament:—

Citation, commencement and interpretation

1.—(1) This order may be cited as the Housing Subsidies (Representative Rates of Interest) Order 1968 and shall come into operation on 1st September 1968.

(2) The Interpretation Act 1889(b) applies for the interpretation of this order as it applies for the interpretation of an Act of Parliament.

Representative rates of interest

2. The rates of interest to be specified for the purposes of section 2(2) of the Housing Subsidies Act 1967 in respect of approved dwellings provided in England and Wales shall be as follows:—

    (*a*) in relation to all local authorities and all housing associations, in respect of the financial year commencing on 1st April 1968   7.07 per cent.

    (*b*) in relation to all development corporations and the Commission for the New Towns, in respect of the financial year commencing on 1st April 1968   7.13 per cent.

Given under the official seal of the Minister of Housing and Local Government on 25th July 1968.

(L.S.)

Anthony Greenwood,
Minister of Housing and Local Government.

(**a**) 1967 c. 29.   (**b**) 1889 c. 63.

EXPLANATORY NOTE
(This Note is not part of the Order.)

This Order specifies representative borrowing rates for the year 1968/69 for the several bodies who receive housing subsidies under the Housing Subsidies Act 1967.   The main subsidy will meet the difference between the loan charges on the aggregate approved cost of dwellings completed in that year at the borrowing rates specified in the Order, and the loan charges which would have been incurred at a fixed borrowing rate of 4 per cent.

STATUTORY INSTRUMENTS

1968 No. 1188

PRICES AND INCOMES

The Awards and Settlements (Temporary Continuation of Standstill) (No. 1) (Amendment) Order 1968

Made - - - -	*26th July* 1968
Laid before Parliament	*26th July* 1968
Coming into Operation	*26th July* 1968

Whereas by virtue of the Awards and Settlements (Temporary Continuation of Standstill) (No. 1) Order 1968(a) section 15(2) of the Prices and Incomes Act 1966(b) continued to apply to forbid the implementation of clause 1 of the undermentioned agreement and the implementation of the undermentioned award up to and including 26th July 1968, that is to say—

(a) the agreement providing for increases with effect from the first full pay period following 14th December 1967 in the rates of pay of all adult employees in the road passenger transport industry previously covered by the National Joint Industrial Council for the road passenger transport industry, made on 14th December 1967 between the Federation of Municipal Passenger Transport Employers on the one hand and the Transport and General Workers' Union and the National Union of General and Municipal Workers on the other, and ratified by the National Joint Industrial Council for the road passenger transport industry on 11th January 1968 ; and

(b) the award made on 22nd January 1968 whereby the Nottingham City Council by its Transport Committee resolved to implement the terms of the said agreement referred to in paragraph (a) above with effect from the pay week beginning on 4th February 1968.

Now, therefore, the Secretary of State having given notice under section 3(4)(a) of the Prices and Incomes Act 1968(c) of a proposal to make this Order, and having taken into consideration representations duly made in pursuance of the said notice, in exercise of the powers conferred on her by section 3(4) of the said Act of 1968, and of all other powers enabling her in that behalf, hereby makes the following Order :—

1.—(1) This Order, which may be cited as the Awards and Settlements (Temporary Continuation of Standstill) (No. 1) (Amendment) Order 1968, shall come into operation on 26th July 1968.

(2) The Interpretation Act 1889(d) shall apply for the interpretation of this Order as it applies for the interpretation of an Act of Parliament.

(a) S.I. 1968/816 (1968 II, p. 2207).   (b) 1966 c. 33.   (c) 1968 c. 42.
(d) 1889 c. 63.

2. The Awards and Settlements (Temporary Continuation of Standstill) (No. 1) Order 1968 shall have effect as if in Article 2 thereof for " 26th July 1968 " there were substituted " 26th December 1968 ".

Signed by order of the Secretary of State.

26th July 1968.

Harold Walker,
Joint Parliamentary Under Secretary of State,
Department of Employment and Productivity.

EXPLANATORY NOTE

(This Note is not part of the Order.)

This Order, which has effect from 26th July 1968, amends the Awards and Settlements (Temporary Continuation of Standstill) (No. 1) Order 1968 by continuing until 26th December 1968 the standstill imposed by that Order on the implementation of part of an agreement and of an award relating to the pay of certain workers employed in municipal road passenger transport undertakings.

STATUTORY INSTRUMENTS

1968 No. 1196

ROAD TRAFFIC

The Pedestrian Crossings (Amendment) Regulations 1968

Made - - -	*23rd July* 1968
Laid before Parliament	*1st August* 1968
Coming into Operation	*2nd August* 1968

The Secretary of State (as respects Scotland, Wales and Monmouthshire) and the Minister of Transport (as respects England excluding Monmouthshire) in exercise of their powers under section 23 of the Road Traffic Regulation Act 1967(a), and of all other powers them enabling in that behalf, and after consultation with representative organisations in accordance with the provisions of section 107(2) of the said Act, hereby make the following Regulations:—

1.—(1) These Regulations shall come into operation on the 2nd August 1968 and may be cited as the Pedestrian Crossings (Amendment) Regulations 1968.

(2) The Interpretation Act 1889(b) shall apply for the interpretation of these Regulations as it applies for the interpretation of an Act of Parliament.

2. The Pedestrian Crossings Regulations 1954(c), as amended (d), shall have effect as though in Schedule 1 to those Regulations for sub-paragraph (4) of paragraph 6 there were substituted the following sub-paragraph:—

"(4) Where globes are mounted on or attached to posts specially provided for the purpose, every such post shall, in so far as it extends above ground level, be coloured black and white in alternate horizontal bands, the lowest band visible to approaching traffic being coloured black and not less than 11 inches nor more than 3 feet 3 inches in width and each other band being not less than 11 inches nor more than 13 inches in width:

Provided that nothing in this sub-paragraph shall apply to any container fixed on any such post which encloses the apparatus for providing the illumination of a globe".

Dated the 23rd July 1968

William Ross,
One of Her Majesty's Principal
Secretaries of State.

Dated the 23rd July 1968

George Thomas,
One of Her Majesty's Principal
Secretaries of State.

Given under the Official Seal of the Minister of Transport the 23rd July 1968

Richard Marsh,
(L.S.)   Minister of Transport.

(a) 1967 c. 76.   (b) 52 & 53 Vict. c. 63.   (c) S.I. 1954/370 (1954 II, p. 1948).
(d) There is no amendment which relates expressly to the subject matter of these regulations.

EXPLANATORY NOTE
(This Note is not part of the Order.)

These Regulations further amend the Pedestrian Crossings Regulations 1954 by providing that posts at pedestrian crossings on which globes are mounted need not be circular and by slightly altering the provision as to the colouring of such posts.

STATUTORY INSTRUMENTS

1968 No. 1198

OVERSEAS TERRITORIES

The Bermuda Supreme Court (Amendment No. 2) Rules Order 1968

Made - - - - *26th July* 1968

At the Court at Buckingham Palace, the 26th day of July 1968

Present,

The Queen's Most Excellent Majesty in Council

Her Majesty, by virtue and in exercise of the powers vested in Her by section 7 of the Colonial Courts of Admiralty Act 1890(**a**), is pleased, by and with the advice of Her Privy Council, to order, and it is hereby ordered, as follows:—

Citation. **1.** This Order may be cited as the Bermuda Supreme Court (Amendment No. 2) Rules Order 1968.

Approval of Rules of Court. **2.** The rules of court entitled the Supreme Court (Amendment No. 2) Rules, 1968, made on 12th June 1968 by the Chief Justice of Bermuda in exercise of the powers conferred by section 7 of the Colonial Courts of Admiralty Act 1890 and section 22 of the Supreme Court Act, 1905(**b**), of Bermuda and set out in the schedule to this Order are approved.

W. G. Agnew.

SCHEDULE

The Supreme Court (Amendment No. 2) Rules, 1968

1. Order 75 of the Rules of the Supreme Court, 1952, is amended by the deletion, from paragraph (3) of Rule 26 thereof, of the word and figures " Order 29 " and the substitution therefor of the word and figures " Order 19 ".

2. These Rules shall not come into operation until the date when the approval thereof by Her Majesty-in-Council is made known by a notification published in the Gazette.

Made this twelfth day of June 1968.

M. J. ABBOTT
Chief Justice.

(a) 1890 c. 27.   (b) Laws of Bermuda, Rev. 1965, Title 8, item 1.

EXPLANATORY NOTE

(*This Note is not part of the Order.*)

In pursuance of section 7 of the Colonial Courts of Admiralty Act 1890 this Order approves rules of court correcting a typographical error in existing rules of court regulating the procedure and practice of the Supreme Court of Bermuda in the exercise of the jurisdiction conferred by that Act.

STATUTORY INSTRUMENTS

1968 No. 1199

ARBITRATION

The Arbitration (International Investment Disputes) (Guernsey) Order 1968

Made - - -	*26th July* 1968
Coming into Operation	*1st September* 1968

At the Court at Buckingham Palace, the 26th day of July 1968

Present,

The Queen's Most Excellent Majesty in Council

Her Majesty, in exercise of the powers conferred upon Her by section 6 of the Arbitration (International Investment Disputes) Act 1966(**a**), is pleased, by and with the advice of Her Privy Council, to order, and it is hereby ordered, as follows:—

1. The provisions of the Arbitration (International Investment Disputes) Act 1966 shall extend to the Bailiwick of Guernsey subject to the exceptions, adaptations and modifications specified in the Schedule to this Order.

2. The Interpretation Act 1889(**b**) shall apply for the purpose of the interpretation of this Order as it applies for the purpose of the interpretation of an Act of Parliament.

3. This Order may be cited as the Arbitration (International Investment Disputes) (Guernsey) Order 1968 and shall come into operation on 1st September 1968.

W. G. Agnew.

SCHEDULE

Exceptions, Adaptations and Modifications

1. Any reference to the Arbitration (International Investment Disputes) Act 1966 shall be construed as a reference to that Act as extended to the Bailiwick of Guernsey by this Order.

2.—(1) In section 1(2) for the words " the High Court " there shall be substituted the words " the appropriate Bailiwick court ".

(2) For section 1(6) there shall be substituted the following subsection—

" ' (6) The Royal Court sitting as a Full Court may from time to time make rules of court—

(**a**) 1966 c. 41.   (**b**) 1889 c. 63.

(a) prescribing the procedure for applying for registration under this section, and requiring an applicant to give prior notice of his intention to other parties;

(b) prescribing the matters to be proved on the application and the manner of proof, and in particular requiring the applicant to furnish a copy of the award certified pursuant to the Convention;

(c) prescribing the manner in which awards shall be registered;

(d) providing for the service of notice of registration of the award by the applicant on other parties;

and in this and the next following section " prescribed " means prescribed by such rules of court.'''.

(3) In section 1(7), immediately before paragraph (a) thereof, there shall be inserted the following paragraph:—

" ' (a) " the appropriate Bailiwick court " means—

    (i) as respects the Islands of Guernsey, Herm and Jethou, the Royal Court sitting as an Ordinary Court,

    (ii) as respects the Island of Alderney, the Court of Alderney,

    (iii) as respects the Island of Sark, the Court of the Seneschal of Sark,''',

and the existing paragraphs (a) and (b) shall accordingly be respectively re-designated as paragraphs (b) and (c).

3.—(1) In section 2(1) for the words " the High Court ", wherever they occur, there shall be substituted the words " the appropriate Bailiwick court ".

(2) In section 2(2) for the words " Rules of court under section 99 of the Supreme Court of Judicature (Consolidation) Act 1925 " there shall be substituted the words " Rules of court under subsection (6) of the last preceding section ".

4. For section 3 there shall be substituted the following section:—

"Proceed-   3.—(1) The Bailiff may, by rules made under this subsection—
ings in the
Bailiwick   (a) make provision, in relation to such proceedings pursuant
of   to the Convention as are specified in those rules, being
Guernsey.   proceedings taking place in the Bailiwick of Guernsey, for the attendance of witnesses, the taking of evidence and the production of documents;

      (b) direct that any of the provisions of the Foreign Tribunals Evidence Act 1856(a) (which relates to the taking of evidence for the purpose of proceedings before a foreign tribunal) shall apply to such proceedings pursuant to the Convention as are specified in those rules, with or without any modifications or exceptions specified in those rules.

(2) Any rules made under subsection (1) of this section may be varied or revoked by subsequent rules so made.".

5. Sections 5, 6(1)(a) and (c), 7, 8 and 9(2) shall be omitted.

(a) 1856 c. 113.

EXPLANATORY NOTE

(This Note is not part of the Order.)

This Order extends to the Bailiwick of Guernsey, with exceptions, adaptations and modifications, the provisions of the Arbitration (International Investment Disputes) Act 1966 (which implements the Convention on the settlement of investment disputes between States and nationals of other States which was opened for signature in Washington on 18th March 1965).

STATUTORY INSTRUMENTS

1968 No. 1200

MINISTERS OF THE CROWN

The Transfer of Functions (Prohibited Weapons) Order 1968

Made - - - -	26th July 1968
Laid before Parliament	1st August 1968
Coming into Operation	1st November 1968

At the Court at Buckingham Palace, the 26th day of July 1968

Present,

The Queen's Most Excellent Majesty in Council

Her Majesty, in pursuance of the Ministers of the Crown (Transfer of Functions) Act 1946(a), as amended by the Defence (Transfer of Functions) (No. 1) Order 1964(b), is pleased, by and with the advice of Her Privy Council, to order, and it is hereby ordered, as follows—

Citation, interpretation and commencement

1.—(1) This Order may be cited as the Transfer of Functions (Prohibited Weapons) Order 1968.

(2) The Interpretation Act 1889(c) applies for the interpretation of this Order as it applies for the interpretation of an Act of Parliament.

(3) In this Order " instrument " (without prejudice to the generality of that expression) includes in particular Orders in Council, judgments, decrees, orders, rules, regulations, byelaws, agreements, authorities, notices, certificates and other documents.

(4) Any reference in this Order to an enactment or instrument is a reference thereto as amended, and includes a reference thereto as applied, by or under any other enactment or instrument.

(5) This Order shall come into operation on 1st November 1968.

Transfer to Secretary of State of functions with respect to prohibited weapons and ammunition.

2. There are hereby transferred to the Secretary of State the functions of the Defence Council under the following enactments—

(a) sections 5 and 12(2) of the Firearms Act 1968(d);

(b) section 6 of the Firearms Act 1920(e) and section 7 of the Firearms (Amendment) Act 1936(f) as those sections have effect in Northern Ireland.

(a) 1946 c. 31.
(c) 1889 c. 63.
(e) 1920 c. 43.

(b) S.I. 1964/488 (1964 I, p. 769).
(d) 1968 c. 27.
(f) 1936 c. 39.

Supplementary

3.—(1) Any enactment or instrument passed or made before the coming into operation of this Order (and in particular the enactments specified in Article 2 of this Order and the following provisions of the Firearms Act 1968, namely sections 31, 34(3) and 38(2) and Schedule 6, Part I) shall have effect, so far as may be necessary for the purpose or in consequence of the foregoing provisions of this Order, as if for any reference to the Defence Council (including any reference which is to be construed as such a reference) there were substituted a reference to the Secretary of State.

(2) This Order shall not affect the validity of anything done, or having effect as if done, by or in relation to the Defence Council before the coming into operation of this Order; and anything which, at the time of the coming into operation of this Order, is in process of being done by or in relation to the Defence Council may, if it relates to any functions transferred by this Order, be continued by or in relation to the Secretary of State.

(3) Any authority or notice given or other thing whatsoever done, or having effect as if given or done, for the purposes of any functions transferred by this Order shall, if in force at the coming into operation of this Order, continue in force and have effect as if similarly given or done by the Secretary of State.

W. G. Agnew.

EXPLANATORY NOTE

(This Note is not part of the Order.)

This Order in Council, made under the Ministers of the Crown (Transfer of Functions) Act 1946, transfers to the Secretary of State the functions of the Defence Council under sections 5 and 12(2) of the Firearms Act 1968 (and the corresponding provisions in force in Northern Ireland) with respect to prohibited weapons and prohibited ammunition within the meaning of those provisions.

STATUTORY INSTRUMENTS

1968 No. 1201

TERMS AND CONDITIONS OF EMPLOYMENT

The Redundancy Payments Exclusion of Merchant Seamen Order 1968

Laid before Parliament in draft

Made - - -		24th *July* 1968
Coming into Operation		5th *August* 1968

The Secretary of State in exercise of her powers under section 16(6) of the Redundancy Payments Act 1965(a) and of all other powers enabling her in that behalf hereby makes the following Order, a draft of which has been laid before Parliament and approved by resolution of each House of Parliament:—

Citation and commencement

1. This Order may be cited as the Redundancy Payments Exclusion of Merchant Seamen Order 1968 and shall come into operation on the 5th August 1968.

Interpretation

2.—(1) The Interpretation Act 1889(b) shall apply to the interpretation of this Order as it applies to the interpretation of an Act of Parliament.

(2) In this Order, unless the context otherwise requires, the following expressions have the meanings hereby assigned to them respectively, that is to say—

"the Act" means the Redundancy Payments Act 1965 ;

"employment" has the same meaning as in section 25(1) of the Act and cognate expressions shall be construed accordingly ;

"merchant seamen" does not include any person employed in the fishing industry or any person employed on board a ship otherwise than by the owner, manager or charterer of that ship except a person so employed as a radio officer but save as aforesaid includes a master or a member of the crew of any ship, an apprentice to the sea service, a person employed as a trainee undergoing training for the sea service, and a person ordinarily employed as a merchant seaman who is employed in or about a ship in port by the owner, manager or charterer of the ship to do work of a kind ordinarily done by a merchant seaman on such a ship while it is in port ;

(a) 1965 c. 62.   **(b)** 1889 c. 63.

"relevant employment" means employment as a merchant seaman of a person who—

(a) is neither domiciled nor has a place of residence in Great Britain ; or

(b) is serving in a ship under articles which include a requirement to observe terms and conditions of employment set out in any National Maritime Board agreement for the time being in force ; or

(c) is serving in any ship as a radio officer employed by a marine wireless company incorporated in Great Britain ; or

(d) is on leave (including leave in respect of incapacity for work due to sickness or injury) with or without pay, with the consent of his employer in accordance with express or implied terms of his contract of employment or apprenticeship ; or

(e) is undergoing a course of training under his contract of employment or apprenticeship ; or

(f) is employed in or about a ship in port by the owner, manager or charterer of the ship to do work of a kind ordinarily done by a merchant seaman on such a ship while it is in port.

Exclusion of seamen in relevant employment

3. Section 1 of the Act shall not apply to any person in respect of any relevant employment.

Relevant employment to be disregarded in the calculation of redundancy payments

4. Where a person has been in relevant employment that employment shall be disregarded—

(a) in ascertaining whether that person has been employed for the requisite period of one hundred and four weeks referred to in section 8(1) of the Act ; and

(b) in calculating under Schedule 1 to the Act the amount of any redundancy payment due to that person ;

but not so as to break the continuity of that person's period of employment.

24th July 1968.

Barbara Castle,
First Secretary of State and Secretary of State
for Employment and Productivity.

EXPLANATORY NOTE

(*This Note is not part of the Order.*)

This Order excludes certain employments as a merchant seaman from the operation of the Redundancy Payments Act 1965.

STATUTORY   INSTRUMENTS

1968 No. 1205

SOCIAL SECURITY

The Family Allowances, National Insurance and Industrial Injuries (Consequential) (No. 2) Regulations 1968

Made - - - -	*26th July* 1968
Laid before Parliament	*5th August* 1968
Coming into Operation	*7th October* 1968

The Minister of Social Security, in conjunction with the Treasury and in exercise of powers conferred by section 3(3) of and Schedule 3 to the Family Allowances and National Insurance Act 1968(**a**) and of all other powers enabling her in that behalf, in consequence of the passing of that Act hereby makes the following regulations :—

Citation, commencement and interpretation

1.—(1) These regulations may be cited as the Family Allowances, National Insurance and Industrial Injuries (Consequential) (No. 2) Regulations 1968, and shall come into operation on 7th October 1968.

(2) In these regulations, unless the context otherwise requires—

" the Insurance Act " means the National Insurance Act 1965(**b**) ;

" the Industrial Injuries Act " means the National Insurance (Industrial Injuries) Act 1965(**c**) ;

" the 1968 Act " means the Family Allowances and National Insurance Act 1968 ;

" family allowance " means an allowance payable under the Family Allowances Act 1965(**d**) ;

and other expressions have the same meaning as in the Insurance Act, the Industrial Injuries Act or the Family Allowances Act 1965, as the case may require.

(3) References in these regulations to any enactment shall, except in so far as the context otherwise requires, be construed as references to that enactment as amended or extended by or under any other enactment, order or regulation.

(4) The rules for the construction of Acts of Parliament contained in the Interpretation Act 1889(**e**) shall apply for the purpose of the interpretation of these regulations as they apply for the purpose of the interpretation of an Act of Parliament.

Continuation of previous rates of benefit

2.—(1) In this regulation—

" benefit " means a retirement pension, widow's allowance, widowed mother's allowance or child's special allowance under the Insurance Act or an allowance under section 21 of the Industrial Injuries Act (death benefit in respect of children) ;

(a) 1968 c. 40.   (b) 1965 c. 51.   (c) 1965 c. 52.
    (d) 1965 c. 53.   (e) 1889 c. 63.

" continuing beneficiary " means a person who, being entitled to receive any benefit in respect of any child or children immediately before the qualifying date, continues without a break to be entitled to receive benefit in respect of that child or both or all those children (as the case may be) and does not become so entitled in respect of any other child or children ;

" eldest child " means a child in respect of whom a continuing beneficiary is entitled to benefit at a rate applicable to an only, elder or eldest child ;

" old rate " means a rate of benefit or of family allowance in force at the passing of the 1968 Act ;

" payable " means payable to the continuing beneficiary or to any other person and, in relation to a family allowance, includes an allowance which would be, or would have been, so payable if duly claimed ;

" period " means a continuous period commencing with the qualifying date ; and

" qualifying date ", in relation to a continuing beneficiary, means the earliest day on which any weekly rate of benefit to which he is then entitled is, or but for the provisions of this regulation would be, reduced by the operation of section 1 of the 1968 Act.

(2) For any period during which the aggregate weekly rate of—

(a) the benefit in respect of children to which a continuing beneficiary would but for the provisions of this regulation be entitled, and

(b) the family allowances payable in respect of the same children,

is less than it would have been if the old rates had continued in force, the reductions in benefit rates under section 1 of the 1968 Act shall be excluded in his case to the extent necessary to enable effect to be given to the following paragraph :

Provided that this paragraph shall not, save in such cases as the Minister in his discretion may permit, have effect in relation to a person who does not before 8th April 1969 give to the Minister notice in writing that he is or claims to be a person entitled to the continuation of an old rate of benefit.

(3) During any period during which the foregoing paragraph has effect in relation to a continuing beneficiary, the weekly rate of benefit to which he is entitled in respect of each child (other than an eldest child) successively according to age shall be such sum as—

(a) does not exceed that which would have been applicable—

    (i) if the old rates had continued in force, and

    (ii) if he had not become entitled in respect of that child (where he has so become) to any benefit of which immediately before the qualifying date the rate was higher than that of the benefit to which he was then entitled, but had instead continued to be entitled to the benefit to which he was then entitled ; and

(b) suffices, so far as possible, to secure that the aggregate weekly rate of—

    (i) the benefit to which he is entitled in respect of that child and any older children, and

    (ii) the benefit to which he would be entitled in respect of any children younger than that child if this regulation did not affect the rate thereof, and

    (iii) the family allowances payable in respect of all the children in respect of whom he is entitled to benefit, is not less than the aggregate weekly rate of the benefit to which he would be entitled in respect of all those children and of the family allowances which would be payable in respect of them if the old rates had continued in force.

Effect of existing awards of family allowances

3. Where a family allowance previously awarded has not terminated by 8th October 1968, and the award does not provide for it to be paid as from that date at the rate provided for by the 1968 Act, it shall not become payable at that rate for any period before—

(*a*) the expiry of any book of allowance orders for the payment of sums on account of that allowance which is current at that date ; or

(*b*) 7th October 1969 if there is no such book ;

save in so far as sums on account thereof are made receivable before 8th April 1970.

Judith Hart,
Minister of Social Security.

25th July 1968.

J. McCann,
Harry Gourlay,
Two of the Lords Commissioners
of Her Majesty's Treasury.

26th July 1968.

EXPLANATORY NOTE

(*This Note is not part of the Regulations.*)

These Regulations are made in consequence of the Family Allowances and National Insurance Act 1968 and in accordance with Schedule 3 paragraph 7 of that Act have not been referred to the National Insurance Advisory Committee or the Industrial Injuries Advisory Council.

Regulation 2 contains provisions for the continuation of previous rates of benefit under the National Insurance and National Insurance (Industrial Injuries) Acts in special cases in which the amount payable by way of benefit and family allowances in respect of children would otherwise be reduced.

Regulation 3 makes provision as to the effect of awards of family allowances at rates in force before the coming into operation of the Family Allowances and National Insurance Act 1968.

STATUTORY INSTRUMENTS

1968 No. 1206

PENSIONS

The Personal Injuries (Civilians) (Amendment) (No. 2) Scheme 1968

Made - - -	*25th July* 1968
Laid before Parliament	*1st August* 1968

Coming into Operation

Article 2	- -	*9th October* 1968
Article 3	- -	*14th October* 1968
Remainder	- -	*5th August* 1968

The Minister of Social Security, with the consent of the Treasury, in exercise of the powers conferred upon her by section 2 of the Personal Injuries (Emergency Provisions) Act 1939(a), and of all other powers enabling her in that behalf, hereby makes the following Scheme :—

Citation, interpretation and commencement

1.—(1) This Scheme, which may be cited as the Personal Injuries (Civilians) (Amendment) (No. 2) Scheme 1968, amends the Personal Injuries (Civilians) Scheme 1964(b), as amended (c), (hereinafter referred to as "the principal Scheme").

(2) Subject to the provisions of the next following paragraph, this Scheme shall come into operation on 5th August 1968.

(3) Article 2 of this Scheme shall come into operation on 9th October 1968, and Article 3 of this Scheme shall come into operation on 14th October 1968.

Amendment of Schedule 3 to the principal Scheme, and transitional provisions

2.—(1) In Schedule 3 to the principal Scheme (rates of pension and allowances payable in respect of disablement) there shall be made the amendments set out in Part I of the Schedule hereto.

(2) Where, by virtue of the provisions of paragraph (1) of this Article, the aggregate rate of additional unemployability or treatment allowances and allowances, if any, under the Family Allowances Act 1965(d) or under any legislation in Northern Ireland or the Isle of Man corresponding to that Act, payable in respect of the children of a disabled person who qualify therefor at 7th October 1968 is, upon the coming into operation of the said paragraph, less than it was according to the rates in force on the said 7th October, then for the period for which the said aggregate rate in respect of those children or any remaining number of them continues to be less than it would have been had

---

(a) 2 & 3 Geo. 6.c.82.   (b) S.I. 1964/2077 (1964 III, p. 5187).

(c) The relevant amending Schemes are
S.I. 1967/1250, 1968/176 (1967 II, p. 3617; 1968 I, p. 425).

(d) 1965 c. 53.

the said rates remained in force, the rate of additional unemployability or treatment allowances payable in respect of those children may be varied to the extent required to exclude the reduction in the said aggregate rate.

Amendment of Schedule 4 to the principal Scheme

3. In Schedule 4 to the principal Scheme (rates of pensions and allowances payable in respect of death) there shall be made the amendments set out in Part II of the Schedule hereto.

Amendment of Article 19 of the principal Scheme, and consequential amendment

4. In the principal Scheme, in Article 19 (allowance for lowered standard of occupation) there shall be made the amendment set out in paragraph 1 of Part III of the Schedule hereto, and in Article 31 (temporary allowances to widows and unmarried dependants who lived as wives of severely disabled persons) there shall be made the amendments set out in paragraph 2 of the said Part.

Article added to the principal Scheme

5. In the principal Scheme, after Article 63 there shall be added the Article set out in paragraph 3 of Part III of the Schedule hereto.

Amendment of Article 64 of the principal Scheme

6. In Article 64 of the principal Scheme (payment of public claims out of pensions) there shall be made the amendment set out in paragraph 4 of the said Part.

Judith Hart,

Minister of Social Security.

23rd July 1968.

We consent.

E. Alan Fitch,

J. McCann,

Two of the Lords Commissioners of Her Majesty's Treasury.

25th July 1968.

SCHEDULE

PART I

Amendment of Schedule 3 to the principal Scheme

1. In Schedule 3 paragraph 6 (unemployability allowances) for head (iii) of sub-paragraph (b) there shall be substituted the following head:—

"(iii) increased allowance under Article 17(4)(f)—

(a) in respect of the child, or the elder or eldest of the children, of a disabled person .. .. .. 28s. per week

(b) in respect of the second child of a disabled person 10s. per week

(c) in respect of each other child of a disabled person .. 8s. per week"

2. In Schedule 3 paragraph 10 (treatment allowances) for sub-paragraph (d) there shall be substituted the following sub-paragraph:—

"(d) increased additional allowance under Article 21(4) proviso (b)—

(i) in respect of the child, or the elder or eldest of the children, of a disabled person .. .. 28s. per week

(ii) in respect of the second child of a disabled person .. .. 10s. per week

(iii) in respect of each other child of a disabled person .. .. 8s. per week"

PART II

Amendment of Schedule 4 to the principal Scheme

In Schedule 4—

(a) for paragraph (6) (allowance under Article 33 in respect of a child under the age of 15) there shall be substituted the following paragraph:—

"6. Allowances under Article 33 in respect of children under the age of 15—

(a) in respect of the child, or the elder or eldest of the children, of a deceased person .. .. 49s. 6d. per week

(b) in respect of each other child of a deceased person—

(i) where the child qualifies for a family allowance under the Family Allowances Act 1965 or under any legislation in Northern Ireland or the Isle of Man corresponding to that Act .. .. 39s. 6d. per week

(ii) where the child does not so qualify .. 46s. 6d. per week"

(b) for paragraph 7 (pension under Article 34(1) to a motherless or fatherless child under the age of 15) there shall be substituted the following paragraph:—

"7. Pensions under Article 34(1) to motherless or fatherless children under the age of 15—

(a) in respect of the child, or the elder or eldest of the children, of a deceased person, and in respect of each other child of a deceased person who does not qualify for a family allowance as aforesaid .. .. 49s. 6d. per week

(b) in respect of each other child of a deceased person who qualifies for a family allowance as aforesaid .. .. 39s. 6d. per week"

PART III

1. Amendment of Article 19 of the principal Scheme

In Article 19 (allowance for lowered standard of occupation) for paragraph (2) there shall be substituted the following paragraph:—

"(2) An allowance under this Article shall not be payable to a disabled person for any period in respect of which an allowance under Article 17(1)(i) is payable to him."

2. Amendment of Article 31 of the principal Scheme

In Article 31 (temporary allowances to widows and unmarried dependants who lived as wives of severely disabled persons) in paragraph (1) after the words "an allowance under Article 14 or Article 17(1)(i)" there shall be inserted the words "or, in the case of a disabled person who was concurrently eligible for an allowance under Article 17(1)(i), Article 19", and for the proviso to paragraph (2) there shall be substituted the following proviso:—

"Provided that—

(i) a personal allowance shall not be payable for any period after the death of the widow ;

(ii) in calculating the weekly rate of allowances for the purposes of the foregoing provisions of this Article, a disabled person who, being concurrently eligible for an allowance under Article 17(1)(i), was in receipt of an allowance under Article 19 shall be deemed in lieu thereof to have been in receipt of an allowance under Article 17(1)(i)."

3. Article to be added to the principal Scheme

"*Abatement of awards in respect of National Insurance and Industrial Injuries Benefits*

63A. Where a pension is awarded to or in respect of a person for any past period for which benefit under the National Insurance Acts 1965 to 1968 or the National Insurance (Industrial Injuries) Acts 1965 to 1968 or any legislation in Northern Ireland corresponding to those Acts has been paid to or in respect of that person, the total amount of pension so awarded may be abated by the amount by which the amount of benefit so paid exceeds what would have been payable for that period had the pension been concurrently payable."

4. Amendment of Article 64 of the principal Scheme

In Article 64 (payment of public claims out of pensions) for paragraph (2) there shall be substituted the following paragraph:—

"(2) Where payment in respect of a pension is in arrears for any period and benefit under the Ministry of Social Security Act 1966(a) or benefit similar to the aforesaid benefit under any legislation in Northern Ireland or the Isle of Man corresponding to that Act has been paid for that period by reference to the requirements of the person to whom the payment is due, the amount by which the amount of benefit paid exceeds what would have been paid had the said payment not fallen into arrears shall be deemed to have been an overpayment for the purposes of paragraph (1) of this Article, and in the case of benefit paid under legislation in Northern Ireland or the Isle of Man as aforesaid shall for the purposes of that paragraph be repayable to the authority administering that benefit."

(a) 1966 c. 20.

EXPLANATORY NOTE

(This Note is not part of the Scheme.)

This Scheme further amends the Personal Injuries (Civilians) Scheme 1964, which provides for compensation to or in respect of civilians injured or killed in the 1939-45 War.

Articles 2 and 3 make amendments which take account of the increases in family allowances made by the Family Allowances and National Insurance Act 1968 from 8th October 1968 and have the effect of adjusting the rates of children's pensions and allowances so that the pensions or allowances and (where payable) family allowances together will normally continue to provide the same total rate for each child as was payable immediately before the aforesaid increases came into force. Transitional provisions secure that the aggregate rate of existing awards will be maintained where this is more advantageous.

Article 4 makes amendments which enable an award of an allowance for lowered standard of occupation in payment to a pensioner who becomes unemployable to be continued if, exceptionally, it would be to his financial disadvantage, having regard to any national insurance benefit concurrently payable, to transfer to unemployability supplement, and extend entitlement to an award of temporary allowances, at the rate which would have been payable had the pensioner been in receipt of unemployability supplement, to the widow, or unmarried dependent who lived as a wife, of such a pensioner.

Article 5 makes provision for the prevention of overlapping payments of war pension or allowances and national insurance benefit.

Article 6 extends the provisions for preventing overlapping payments of war pension or allowances and supplementary benefit, to Northern Ireland and the Isle of Man.

STATUTORY INSTRUMENTS

1968 No. 1207

POLICE

ENGLAND AND WALES

The Police (Amendment) (No. 3) Regulations 1968

Made - - - -	*25th July* 1968
Laid before Parliament	*1st August* 1968
Coming into Operation	*12th August* 1968

In exercise of the powers conferred on me by section 33 of the Police Act 1964(a), and after consulting the Police Council for Great Britain in accordance with section 45(4) of that Act, I hereby make the following Regulations:—

1. At the end of paragraph 1 of Part I of Schedule 3 to the principal Regulations (which contains scales of pay for men) there shall be added the following sub-paragraph:—

"(2) Notwithstanding anything in sub-paragraph (1), except in the case of a member of the City of London or metropolitan police force, the scale of pay of a chief superintendent assigned to duties designated for the purposes hereof by the Secretary of State shall be—

(*a*) before completing 1 year of service in the performance of those duties, £2,620 a year;

(*b*) after 1 year of such service, £2,705 a year;

(*c*) after 2 years of such service, £2,800 a year.".

2. The second Table in paragraph 1 of Part II of Schedule 3 to the principal Regulations (which contains scales of pay for women) shall have effect as if there were inserted therein the entry contained in the following Table:—

Rank	Before completing 1 year of service in the rank	After 1 year of service in the rank	After 2 years of service in the rank
Chief superintendent	£2,140 a year	£2,205 a year	£2,280 a year

3. Where for any period beginning on or after 1st January 1968 and ending before the revocation of the Police Regulations 1965(b), as amended(c), by the principal Regulations, that is to say before 1st February 1968, the pay of—

(*a*) a man holding the rank of chief superintendent, or

(*b*) a woman holding the rank of chief superintendent, otherwise than in the City of London or metropolitan police force,

---

(a) 1964 c. 48.   (b) S.I. 1965/538 (1965 I, p.1555).
(c) The relevant amending instrument is S.I. 1967/923 (1967 II, p.2742).

was less than it would have been if the amendments made to the principal Regulations by these Regulations had been made to the said Regulations of 1965, then the member in question shall be entitled to the difference by way of an increase in pay for that period.

4. In these Regulations any reference to the principal Regulations is a reference to the Police Regulations 1968**(a)**, as amended**(b)**.

5.—(1) These Regulations shall come into operation on 12th August 1968 and shall have effect—

  (*a*) for the purposes of Regulations 1 and 2 thereof, as from 1st February 1968;

  (*b*) for the purposes of Regulation 3 thereof, as from 1st January 1968.

(2) These Regulations may be cited as the Police (Amendment) (No. 3) Regulations 1968.

James Callaghan,
One of Her Majesty's Principal
Secretaries of State.

Home Office,
  Whitehall.
25th July 1968.

EXPLANATORY NOTE
(*This Note is not part of the Regulations.*)

These Regulations provide that men holding the rank of chief superintendent and performing specially designated duties shall enjoy an enhanced scale of pay (Regulation 1). The scale of pay for women holding the rank of chief superintendent, otherwise than in the City of London and metropolitan police forces, is prescribed for the first time (Regulation 2(1)).

Regulations 1 and 2 amend the Police Regulations 1968 and, by virtue of Regulation 5(1)(*a*) (made in exercise of the power conferred by section 33(4) of the Police Act 1964), have effect as from 1st February 1968 when the Regulations of 1968 came into operation. Regulation 3 makes similar provision to that made by Regulations 1 and 2 as respects the period 1st January to 1st February 1968 (during which period the Police Regulations 1965 were in operation) and by virtue of Regulation 5(1)(*b*) has effect as from 1st January 1968.

(a) S.I. 1968/26 (1968 I, p.38).

(b) The amending Regulations are not relevant to the subject matter of these Regulations.

STATUTORY INSTRUMENTS

1968 No. 1210

PENSIONS

The Superannuation (English Teaching and Scottish Local Government) Interchange Rules 1968

Made - - - -	*25th July* 1968
Laid before Parliament	*7th August* 1968
Coming into Operation	*8th August* 1968

The Secretary of State for Scotland and, with the consent of the Treasury, the Secretary of State for Education and Science, in exercise of the powers conferred on them by sections 2 and 15 of the Superannuation (Miscellaneous Provisions) Act 1948(a), as amended by the Superannuation (Miscellaneous Provisions) Act 1967(b), hereby jointly make the following Rules:—

PART I

GENERAL

Citation and Commencement

1. These Rules may be cited as the Superannuation (English Teaching and Scottish Local Government) Interchange Rules 1968 and shall come into operation on 8th August 1968.

Interpretation

2.—(1) In these Rules, unless the context otherwise requires—

"the Act" means the Superannuation (Miscellaneous Provisions) Act 1948;

"the Act of 1909" means the Asylums Officers' Superannuation Act 1909(c);

"the Act of 1937" means the Local Government Superannuation (Scotland) Act 1937(d);

"the Act of 1953" means the Local Government Superannuation Act 1953(e);

"the Acts of 1937 to 1953" means the Local Government Superannuation (Scotland)Acts 1937 to 1953(f);

"the Teachers Acts" means the Teachers (Superannuation) Acts 1918 to 1956;

"added years" means, in relation to local government employment, any additional years of service reckonable under regulation 12 of the Benefits Regulations or any corresponding provision of a local Act scheme and includes any additional years of service which, having been granted under any such provision or under any similar provision contained in any other enactment or scheme, have subsequently become and are reckonable under or by virtue of rules made under sections 2 and 15 of the Act or any other enactment;

(a) 1948 c.33.	(b) 1967 c.28.
(c) 1909 c.48.	(d) 1937 c.69.
(e) 1953 c.25.	(f) 1937 c.69; 1939 c.18; 1953 c.25.

"the Benefits Regulations" means the Local Government Superannuation (Benefits) (Scotland) Regulations 1954(a);

"fund authority" means a local authority maintaining a superannuation fund to which a person either becomes a contributor after ceasing to be employed in teaching service or, as the case may be, was last a contributor before he became employed in teaching service;

"local authority" includes, in the case of a local authority which has ceased to exist, the local authority by whom the expenses of the first-mentioned local authority were defrayable;

"local government employment" means employment by virtue of which the person employed is or is deemed to be a contributory employee or local Act contributor within the meaning of the Act of 1937;

"Local Government Modification Regulations" means the National Insurance (Modification of Local Government Superannuation Schemes) (Scotland) Regulations 1947(b) and any provisions contained in the Benefits Regulations or in a local Act scheme or in a scheme made in relation to a local Act replacing wholly or in part the provisions of the first-mentioned Regulations;

"national service", in relation to any person, means service which is relevant service within the meaning of the Reserve and Auxiliary Forces (Protection of Civil Interests) Act 1951(c) and any similar service immediately following relevant service entered into with the consent of the authority or person by whom he was last employed or, as the case may be, appointed to an office before undertaking that service;

"operative date" means the date of the coming into operation of these Rules;

"pension" has the meaning assigned to it by the Act;

"prescribed period" has the meaning assigned to that expression by rule 3;

"reckonable service" means such service as is by virtue of the Teachers' Regulations reckonable service for all the purposes of Part I of the Teachers' Superannuation Act 1967(d);

"repaid contributions" means any sum paid to a person under the Teachers Acts, the Teachers' Regulations, the Acts of 1937 to 1953 or a local Act scheme by way of repayment of contributions (other than voluntary contributions and contributions made or deemed to be made for the purpose of securing benefits for a widow, children or other dependants); and includes both any interest included in such sum and any amount deducted therefrom in respect of liability to income tax arising by reason of the payment;

"the Secretary of State" means the Secretary of State for Education and Science;

"the Teachers' Regulations" means the Teachers' Superannuation Regulations 1967(e);

"teaching service" means—

(a) reckonable service;

(b) service which for the purposes of the Teachers' Regulations is service as an organiser, a teacher in an admitted school, a services civilian teacher or a services education officer; and

---

(a) S.I. 1954/1059 (1954 II, p.1632).
(b) S.R. & O. 1947/1697 (Rev. XVI, p.286: 1947 I, p.1509).   (c) 1951 c.65.
(d) 1967 c.12.   (e) S.I. 1967/489 (1967 I, p.1562).

(*c*) service as a part-time teacher within the meaning of the Teachers' (Part-time) Superannuation Regulations 1967(**a**);

"the Transfer Value Regulations" means the Local Government Superannuation (Transfer Value) (Scotland) Regulations 1954(**b**);

"voluntary contributions" means—

(*a*) in relation to employment in teaching service, additional contributions being paid under section 19 of the Teachers (Superannuation) Act 1956(**c**) or regulation 32 of the Teachers' Regulations in respect of a period of previous employment and any contributions being paid as a condition of any other period (not being a period of war service within the meaning of the Teachers Superannuation (War Service) Act 1939(**d**) or of national service) being reckoned as reckonable service; and

(*b*) in relation to local government employment, payments (other than completed payments, that is to say, payments made in respect of a liability which has been wholly discharged) of any of the following categories—

(i) additional contributory payments of the kind referred to in section 2(3) and (4) of the Act of 1953;

(ii) any similar payments made under a local Act scheme as a condition of reckoning any period of employment as service or as a period of contribution for the purposes of the scheme, or, where the local Act scheme provides for the reckoning of non-contributing service, as contributing service for the purposes of the scheme;

(iii) any payments made for the purpose of increasing the length at which any period of service or of contribution would be reckonable for the purpose of calculating a benefit under a local Act scheme; and

(iv) any payments made in respect of added years;

(2) Other expressions which have meanings assigned to them by the Acts of 1937 to 1953 or the Teachers' Regulations have, unless the context otherwise requires, the same respective meanings for the purposes of these Rules.

(3) Any reference in these Rules to the provisions of any enactment, rules, regulations or other instrument shall, unless the context otherwise requires, be construed as a reference to those provisions as amended, modified, affected or re-enacted by any subsequent enactment, rules, regulations or instrument.

(4) References in these Rules to a rule or to a Part shall, unless the context otherwise requires, be construed as references to a rule or to a Part of these Rules, as the case may be.

(5) The Interpretation Act 1889(**e**) shall apply for the interpretation of these Rules as it applies for the interpretation of an Act of Parliament.

Prescribed Period

3.—(1) For the purposes of these Rules, subject as hereafter in this rule provided, the expression "prescribed period" shall mean—

(*a*) in the case of a person who, immediately after ceasing to be employed in teaching service or local government employment, became engaged in national service, a period of six months after the date of termination of the national service;

(a) S.I. 1967/1286 (1967 II, p.3721).   (b) S.I. 1954/1256 (1954 II, p.1736).
(c) 1956 c.53.   (d) 1939 c.95.   (e) 1889 c.63.

(b) in the case of a person to whom section 6 of the Act has become applicable, a period of five years after the date on which he ceased to be employed in local government employment or such longer period as the Secretary of State for Scotland may in any particular case allow; and

(c) in the case of any other person, a period of twelve months after the date on which he ceased to be employed in teaching service or local government employment.

(2) The Secretary of State in the case of a person entering teaching service and the fund authority in the case of a person entering local government employment may, with the agreement of the other, extend the period of six months or twelve months, whichever is appropriate, specified in paragraph (1) above.

(3) Subject as in paragraph (4) below provided—

(a) in reckoning the periods of six months and twelve months specified in paragraph (1) above no account shall be taken of any period spent by a person on a course of study or training which he undertook after leaving his former employment; and

(b) if a person left his former employment in order to undertake a course of study or training and on completion of that course became engaged in national service, he shall be deemed for the purposes of paragraph (1) above to have left his former employment at the time when he completed the said course of study or training.

(4) The provisions of paragraph (3) above shall not apply to a person who in his new employment is in local government employment unless the authority employing him are satisfied, or to a person who in his new employment is in teaching service unless the Secretary of State is satisfied, that by reason of his having undertaken the said course of study or training he is better fitted for the duties of his new employment.

Part II

Transfer from Teaching Service to Local Government Employment

Application

4.—(1) Except as hereinafter provided, this Part shall apply to a person who—

(a) enters, or before the operative date entered, local government employment within the prescribed period after ceasing to be employed in teaching service;

(b) before or within three months after entering local government employment or within six months after the operative date, whichever period shall last expire, or within such longer period as the fund authority may with the agreement of the Secretary of State in any particular case allow, notifies that authority in writing that he desires this Part to apply to him and furnishes that authority with particulars in writing of any national service in which he has been engaged since ceasing to be employed in teaching service; and

(c) within three months after entering local government employment or within six months after the operative date, whichever period shall last expire, or within such longer period as the fund authority may in any particular case allow, pays to that authority an amount equal to any repaid contributions paid to him after he last ceased to be employed in teaching service, together with any compound interest thereon payable in accordance with paragraph (2) below.

(2) For the purposes of paragraph 1(c) above—

(a) compound interest shall not be payable unless the period between a person's ceasing to be employed in teaching service and entering local government employment exceeds one year;

(b) compound interest shall be calculated on the amount of the repaid contributions at three per cent per annum with half-yearly rests from the day one year after that on which the person ceased to be employed in teaching service or from the day on which repaid contributions were paid to him, whichever shall be the later, to the day on which he notified the fund authority as required by paragraph (1)(b) above; and

(c) if the amount of compound interest calculated as aforesaid exceeds a sum equal to one half of the difference between the amount of the transfer value payable under rule 6 and the amount of the transfer value which would have been so payable if calculated by reference to the person's age on ceasing to be employed in teaching service, it shall be reduced to that sum.

Excepted Cases

5. This Part shall not apply to a person who—

(a) has received payment of any pension (other than repayment of contributions) under the Teachers Acts or the Teachers' Regulations;

(b) is a person in respect of whom a transfer value has been paid otherwise than under these Rules by the Secretary of State since he last ceased to be employed in teaching service;

(c) last ceased to be employed in teaching service before 4th February 1948; or

(d) last ceased to be employed in teaching service on or after 4th February 1948 but before the operative date, unless—

　(i) he has been employed in local government employment without a break of twelve months or more at any one time from the date when he ceased to be employed in teaching service until the operative date or, if he ceased to be employed in local government employment before the operative date, until the date when he so ceased; and

　(ii) if he ceased to be employed in local government employment before the operative date, the Secretary of State and the local authority maintaining the fund to which he was last a contributor agree that this Part shall apply to him.

Transfer Value

6.—(1) In respect of a person to whom this Part applies the Secretary of State shall, out of moneys provided by Parliament, pay to the fund authority a transfer value of an amount calculated in accordance with the following provisions of this rule.

(2) Subject as hereafter in this rule provided, the transfer value shall be an amount equal to the transfer value which would have been payable under the Transfer Value Regulations if the person, at the date when he ceased to be employed in teaching service, had ceased to be a contributory employee under one local authority and had become such an employee under another local authority and had been entitled to reckon as contributing service his reckonable service and his service reckonable for the purposes of Parts VII, IX and X of the Teachers' Regulations at the length at which it is so reckonable.

(3) For the purpose of calculating the amount of a transfer value any period of service which, having originally been non-contributing service or non-contributing service for the purposes of regulations made under section 67 of the National Health Service Act 1946(a) or section 66 of the National Health Service (Scotland) Act 1947(b), became reckonable as reckonable service by virtue of such regulations or of rules made under section 2 of the Act shall be treated as non-contributing service.

(4) For the purposes of paragraph (2) above service which is reckoned as contributing service shall be deemed to have been affected or modified in accordance with regulations applicable to contributing service made under section 110 of the National Insurance Act 1965(c), or under any provision corresponding thereto contained in an enactment repealed by that Act, in like manner and to the like extent, as nearly as may be, as it was affected or modified by other such regulations.

(5) In calculating the amount of a transfer value there shall be excluded—

(*a*) any period of war service within the meaning of the Teachers Superannuation (War Service) Act 1939 and of national service within the meaning of the Teachers Superannuation (National Service) Rules 1949(d) in respect of which, at the time the transfer value is paid, the contributions remain unpaid; and

(*b*) any period of previous employment and any period additional to actual service in respect of which the person was immediately before ceasing to be employed in teaching service paying voluntary contributions and in respect of which, at the time the transfer value is paid, he has not elected to continue to pay such contributions.

(6) In respect of a person who ceased to be employed in teaching service more than one year before the operative date the amount of the transfer value shall, except in a case to which paragraph (7) below applies, be—

(*a*) calculated by reference to his age on the operative date; and

(*b*) where either paragraph (2) or paragraph (3) of rule 3 applies, reduced by the amount of any compound interest payable by him in accordance with rule 4(2).

(7) In respect of a person who became employed in local government employment on or after the operative date and to whom either paragraph (2) or paragraph (3) of rule 3 applies the amount of the transfer value shall be—

(*a*) calculated by reference to his age on the date on which he became employed in local government employment; and

(*b*) reduced by the amount of any compound interest payable by him in accordance with rule 4(2).

Reckoning of Service

7.—(1) Subject as hereafter in this rule provided, so much service as is taken into account under rule 6 for the purpose of calculating the amount of the transfer value payable in respect of a person shall be reckoned as contributing service or as service under a local Act scheme or a period of contribution for the purposes of such a scheme.

(2) So much service as is taken into account as non-contributing service under rule 6 for the purpose of calculating the amount of the transfer value payable in respect of a person shall be reckoned as non-contributing service.

(a) 1946 c.81. (b) 1947 c.27.
(c) 1965 c.51. (d) S.I. 1949/468 (1949 I, p.1533).

(3) Any service of a person to whom this Part applies which under the Teachers' Regulations is reckonable only for the purpose of calculating the amount of any pension payable to or in respect of him or only for the purpose of determining whether he is entitled to any pension shall be reckoned only for the corresponding like purpose under the Acts of 1937 to 1953 or a local Act scheme.

(4) Except as in this rule before provided, a person to whom this Part applies shall not be entitled under section 12(2) of the Act of 1937 or any corresponding provision of a local Act scheme to reckon as service any local government employment prior to the date on which he became employed in teaching service if a transfer value has been paid in respect of that local government employment under rule 17 or under any corresponding provision contained in other rules made under section 2 of the Act.

Voluntary Contributions

8.—(1) A person to whom this Part applies may elect to continue to pay voluntary contributions being paid by him immediately before ceasing to be employed in teaching service.

(2) If a person elects as aforesaid and—

    (*a*) within three months of becoming employed in local government employment, or within such longer period as the fund authority may in any particular case allow, pays to that authority a sum equal to the aggregate of any sum paid to him by way of return of voluntary contributions on or after ceasing to be employed in teaching service, any interest added thereto and any amount deducted therefrom in respect of liability to income tax by reason of the payment; and

    (*b*) thereafter pays to that authority any amounts outstanding in respect of those voluntary contributions at the times at which and in the manner in which they would have been payable if he had remained in teaching service

his local government employment shall be affected in the manner prescribed by the following provisions of this rule.

(3) In respect of voluntary contributions made in respect of any period of previous employment and any period additional to actual service, the person shall enjoy rights and be subject to liabilities as if those years were added years in respect of which payments are being made in his local government employment under regulation 12 of the Benefits Regulations or, if in his local government employment he is subject to a local Act scheme, under such provisions corresponding to the said regulation 12 or to regulation 5 of the Local Government Superannuation (Reckoning of Service on Transfer) (Scotland) Regulations 1954(a) as are contained in that scheme.

(4) In respect of voluntary contributions other than those to which paragraph (3) above applies, the person shall be treated as if those contributions had been completed immediately before he ceased to be employed in teaching service.

Computation of Contributions

9.—(1) Where a person to whom this Part applies ceases to be employed in local government employment or dies, then, in calculating any amount payable or in respect of him by way of return of contributions, the amount of his contributions in respect of service reckonable in accordance with rule 7(1) shall be taken to include such amount as would have been payable by way of

---

(a) S.I. 1954/1241 (1954 II, p.1680).

return of contributions under the Teachers Acts or the Teachers' Regulations if, on his ceasing to be employed in teaching service, he had been entitled to be repaid his contibutions without interest.

(2) Where an amount payable by way of return of contributions or by way of benefit is a sum equal to, or which falls to be calculated by reference to, the amount of a person's contributions with compound interest thereon, compound interest shall also be payable in respect of the amount by which those contributions are increased under the last preceding paragraph, calculated—

(a) as respects the period ending immediately before the day on which he entered local government employment, at the rate at which it would have been calculated under the Teachers Acts or the Teachers' Regulations, as the case may be, if on ceasing to be employed in teaching service he had been entitled to a return of contributions together with compound interest thereon; and

(b) as respects the period beginning with the date on which he entered local government employment, in accordance with the provisions of section 10 of the Act of 1937 or, as the case may be, the corresponding provisions of the relevant local Act scheme.

(3) Notwithstanding anything in this rule previously contained, the sum by which contributions are increased by virtue of paragraph (1) or (2) above shall not include—

(a) any sum in respect of contributions which, on or after the person's ceasing to be employed in teaching service, were returned to and retained by him; or

(b) any amount in respect of voluntary contributions which are not continued in pursuance of rule 8 of these Rules.

Benefits under Teachers' Regulations

10. Subject to the provisions of Part III and of other rules made under section 2 of the Act, no payment of any pension shall be made under the Teachers' Regulations to any person or his personal representatives in respect of any service which is taken into account in calculating the amount of a transfer value under rule 6.

Modification of Contributions and Benefits by reason of National Insurance

11.—(1) The modifications for which the Local Government Modification Regulations provide shall not apply to a person to whom this Part applies if either—

(a) he ceased to be employed in teaching service before 1st April 1967 and at the time of so ceasing was not subject to the modifications of the Teachers Acts made by the Teachers Modification Regulations; or

(b) he ceased to be employed in teaching service on or after 1st April 1967 and at the time of so ceasing was not subject to paragraph 2 of Schedule 5 to the Teachers' Regulations.

(2) Without prejudice to the operation of the National Insurance (Modification of Local Government Superannuation Schemes) No. 2 (Scotland) Regulations 1961(a), the modifications for which the Local Government Modification Regulations provide shall apply to any other person to whom this Part applies as if any service reckonable in accordance with rule 7(1) were service for the purposes of the Acts of 1937 to 1953 or service for the purposes of a local Act scheme, as the case may be, rendered on or after 5th July 1948.

(a) S.I. 1961/492 (1961 I, p.1125).

(3) Where any pension which might have become payable under the Teachers Acts or the Teachers' Regulations to a person to whom this Part applies would have been subject to modification under the Teachers Modification Regulations or Part III of Schedule 5 to the Teachers' Regulations by reference to a table and his age at a given date, the provisions of the Local Government Modification Regulations modifying pensions in similar manner shall apply to that person and for that purpose the relevant date shall be that which was relevant for the purposes of the Teachers Modification Regulations or the said Schedule 5, as the case may be.

(4) In this rule "the Teachers Modification Regulations" means the National Insurance (Modification of Teachers Pensions) Regulations 1948(a), as amended by the National Insurance (Modification of Teachers Pensions) Amending Regulations 1956(b).

Questions and Appeals

12. The provisions of section 30 of the Act of 1937 (which section relates to the decision of questions and appeals) shall have effect in relation to a person (not being a local Act contributor), to whom this Part applies as if the reference therein to regulations made under that Act included a reference to these Rules

Application of Section 11(3) of Act of 1953

13.—(1) Section 11(3) of the Act of 1953 (which sub-section enables certain persons who would otherwise be debarred on grounds of age from becoming contributory employees or local Act contributors to become such employees or such contributors and to reckon previous pensionable employment) shall apply to a person who before the operative date entered the employment of a local authority after ceasing to be employed in teaching service on or after 4th February 1948.

(2) For the purposes of paragraph (1) above section 11(3) of the Act of 1953 shall have effect as if for the references therein to the passing of that Act there were substituted references to the coming into operation of these Rules.

PART III

TRANSFER FROM LOCAL GOVERNMENT EMPLOYMENT TO TEACHING SERVICE

Application

14.—(1) Except as hereinafter provided, this Part shall apply to a person who—

(a) becomes, or before the operative date became, employed in teaching service within the prescribed period after ceasing to be employed in local government employment;

(b) before or within three months after becoming employed in teaching service or within six months after the operative date, whichever period shall last expire, or within such longer period as the Secretary of State may with the agreement of the fund authority in any particular case allow, notifies the Secretary of State in writing that he desires this Part to apply to him and furnishes the Secretary of State with particulars in writing of any national service in which he has been engaged since ceasing to be employed in local government employment; and

(a) S.I. 1948/889 (Rev. XVI, p.298: 1948 I p.2851).   (b) S.I. 1956/1482 (1956 I, p.1643).

(c) within three months after becoming employed in teaching service or within six months after the operative date, whichever period shall last expire, or within such longer period as the Secretary of State may in any particular case allow, pays to the Secretary of State an amount equal to any repaid contributions paid to him after he last ceased to be employed in local government employment, together with any compound interest thereon payable in accordance with paragraph (2) below.

(2) For the purposes of paragraph (1)(c) above—

(a) compound interest shall not be payable unless—

(i) the period between the person's ceasing to be employed in local government employment and his becoming employed in teaching service exceeds one year; and

(ii) the fund authority requires that it be paid.

(b) compound interest shall be calculated on the amount of the repaid contributions at three per cent per annum with half-yearly rests from the day one year after that on which the person ceased to be employed in local government employment or from the day on which repaid contributions were paid to him, whichever shall be the later, to the day on which he notified the Secretary of State as required by paragraph (1)(b) above; and

(c) if the amount of compound interest calculated as aforesaid exceeds a sum equal to one half of the difference between the amount of the transfer value payable under rule 17 and the amount of the transfer value which would have been so payable if calculated by reference to the person's age on ceasing to be employed in local government employment, it shall be reduced to that sum.

Excepted Cases

15. This Part shall not apply to a person who—

(a) has received payment of any pension (other than repayment of contributions) under the Acts of 1937 to 1953 or a local Act scheme;

(b) is a person in respect of whom a transfer value has been paid otherwise than under these Rules, by a fund authority since he last ceased to be employed in local government employment;

(c) last ceased to be employed in local government employment before 4th February 1948; or

(d) last ceased to be employed in local government employment on or after 4th February 1948 but before the operative date, unless—

(i) he is employed in teaching service on the operative date, or, if he is not so employed on that date, the Secretary of State agrees that this Part shall apply to him; and

(ii) the fund authority agrees that this Part shall apply to him.

Discretionary Increase of Benefits

16.—(1) The local authority by whom a person to whom this Part applies was last employed may, within three months after the date on which they are notified by the Secretary of State of such application, exercise in relation to that person any discretion which, with a view to increasing the pension payable to him, it would have been open to them to exercise at the time when he left their employment if he had then retired and had been entitled to a retirement pension under regulation 5 of the Benefits Regulations or, if that regulation was not applicable to him, to any corresponding benefit provided under the superannuation provisions which were applicable to him in his former employment.

(2) A decision made in the exercise of any discretion under paragraph (1) above shall be subject to the limitations and restrictions (if any) and to the right of appeal (if any) to which it would have been subject if the discretion had been exercised on the person's retirement in the circumstances aforesaid.

(3) Where a discretion has been exercised under paragraph (1) above the service reckonable, immediately before he ceased to be employed in local government employment, by the person in whose favour the discretion has been exercised shall be deemed to have been correspondingly increased.

(4) Any increase in service, if attributable to a decision under this rule to increase the pension payable to the person otherwise than by any notional increase or extension of the service reckonable for the purpose of calculating that pension or by treating any specified period of non-contributing service as contributing service, or, under a local Act scheme, by similarly converting service of one category to service of another category, shall be ascertained by converting the service in respect of which the higher rate of benefit is payable into contributing service or service for the purposes of the relevant local Act scheme in the manner in which non-contributing service is converted into contributing service under section 2(4) of the Act of 1953.

Transfer value

17.—(1) In respect of a person to whom this Part applies the fund authority shall, out of the superannuation fund maintained by them, pay to the Secretary of State a transfer value of an amount calculated in accordance with the following provisions of this rule.

(2) Subject as hereafter in this rule provided, the transfer value shall be an amount equal to the transfer value which would have been payable under the Transfer Value Regulations if the person, at the date when he ceased to be a contributory employee or local Act contributor, had become such an employee or contributor under another local authority.

(3) In calculating the amount of a transfer value—

(a) there shall be included any increase of service of the person by reason of the exercise under rule 16 of a discretion in his favour;

(b) there shall be excluded any added years in respect of which the person was immediately before ceasing to be employed in local government service paying voluntary contributions and in respect of which, at the time the transfer value is paid, he has not elected to continue to pay such contributions; and

(c) the Transfer Value Regulations shall be deemed to be modified—

(i) by the omission from sub-paragraph (a) of the definition of "service" in paragraph 1 of the First Schedule thereto of the words "not being such service as is mentioned in proviso (a) to that sub-section"; and

(ii) by the omission, in respect of a person who was an established officer or servant within the meaning of the Act of 1909, of sub-paragraph (c) of the said definition.

(4) In respect of a person who ceased to be employed in local government employment more than one year before the operative date the amount of the transfer value shall, except in a case to which paragraph (5) below applies, be—

    (a) calculated by reference to his age on the operative date; and

    (b) where either paragraph (2) or paragraph (3) of rule 3 applies, reduced by the amount of any compound interest payable by him in accordance with rule 14(2).

(5) In respect of a person who became employed in teaching service on or after the operative date and to whom either paragraph (2) or paragraph (3) of rule 3 applies the amount of the transfer value shall be—

    (a) calculated by reference to his age on the date on which he became employed in teaching service; and

    (b) reduced by the amount of any compound interest payable by him in accordance with rule 14(2).

(6) The amount of the transfer value shall be reduced by an amount equal to any sum payable by the fund authority by way of income tax by reason of its payment.

Supplementary Provisions as to Transfer Values

18.—(1) Where the amount of a transfer value payable under rule 17 is increased by reason of the exercise under rule 16 of a discretion by a local authority, that authority shall pay the amount of the increase to the superannuation fund out of which the transfer value is payable.

(2) When paying a transfer value under rule 17 a fund authority shall furnish to the Secretary of State and to the person in respect of whom it is paid the like particulars relating to that person's pensionable service as would have been given to him if instead of becoming employed in teaching service he had re-entered local government employment.

(3) The transfer value payable under rule 17 in respect of a person who had been an established officer or servant within the meaning of the Act of 1909 shall be calculated as if paragraph (c) had been omitted from the definition of "service" in paragraph 1 of Schedule 1 to the Transfer Value Regulations.

(4) Where—

    (a) a transfer value is payable under rule 17 by a fund authority in respect of a person who before entering local government employment has been subject ot the Act of 1909; and

    (b) the body by whom he was last employed while subject to that Act would, if he had become entitled to a superannuation allowance on leaving local government employment, have been liable to contribute to that allowance

that body shall pay to the fund authority a sum equal to the transfer value which that body would have been liable to pay to the Secretary of State for Scotland under regulation 52(4) of the National Health Service (Scotland) (Superannuation) Regulations 1950(a) if that regulation had become applicable to the person on the date on which he became employed in teaching service; and where that body would have had in respect of any such contribution a

---

(a) S.I. 1950/498 (1950 I, p.1458).

right of contribution from any other body, that other body shall pay to the fund authority a sum equal to the transfer value which that other body would have been liable to pay to the Secretary of State for Scotland under paragraph (5) of the said regulation 52 if that regulation had become applicable to the person when he became employed in teaching service.

(5) Where any body referred to in the last preceding paragraph has been dissolved or has ceased to exercise functions as such, references to that body shall be construed as references to the appropriate authority as defined in paragraph (15) of the regulation mentioned therein.

Reckoning of Service

19.—(1) Subject as hereafter in this rule provided, in respect of a person to whom this Part applies—

(a) there shall be reckoned as reckonable service—

(i) any period of service which, at the time of his ceasing to be employed in local government employment, is reckonable as contributing service or as service or a period of contribution for the purposes of a local Act scheme;

(ii) any period of national service after ceasing to be employed in local government employment which would have been reckonable as aforesaid if he had again become employed in local government employment after the termination thereof; and

(iii) one-half of any period of service which, at the time of his ceasing to be employed in local government employment, is reckonable as non-contributing service; and

(b) there shall be reckoned as class C external service for the purposes of the Teachers' Regulations any period of service which, at the time of his ceasing to be employed in local government employment, is reckonable as non-contributing service, except in so far as that service is reckoned under this rule or those Regulations as reckonable service or as class A or class B external service for the purposes of those Regulations.

(2) Where a person to whom this Part applies has, during his local government employment, been employed as a part-time employee, the period of his part-time service shall be treated—

(a) for the purpose of determining whether he has served for any minimum period prescribed by the Teachers' Regulations as necessary for any pension to be paid to or in respect of him as if it were whole-time service; and

(b) for the purpose of calculating the amount of any pension payable under the Teachers' Regulations, as if it were whole-time service for a proportionately reduced period.

(3) Where by virtue of a scheme modifying the Act of 1937 any period of service of a person to whom this Part applies is reckoned at a fraction of its actual length for the purpose of calculating the amount of the transfer value payable under rule 17, then, for the purpose of calculating the amount of any pension payable to or in respect of him under the Teachers' Regulations, only that fraction of that period of service shall be reckoned as reckonable service.

(4) In respect of a person to whom this Part applies there shall not by virtue of this Part be reckoned as reckonable service—

(a) any service which he is or was entitled to reckon as contributing or non-contributing service by virtue of section 15 of the Act of 1937 or the corresponding provisions of a local Act scheme if that service is reckonable as first class service under the Teachers Superannuation (Scotland) Regulations 1957(a) or as reckonable service within the meaning of regulations made under section 1 of the Teachers' Superannuation (Scotland) Act 1968(b); or

(b) any service which in his case is deemed to be service to which the said section 15 applies by virtue of the Local Government Superannuation (England and Scotland) Regulations 1948(c), if that service is reckonable as reckonable service otherwise than by virtue of these Rules; or

(c) any service which is the subject of a direction under section 17(3) of the Act of 1953 that all rights enjoyed by or in respect of the person with respect to that service shall be forfeited.

(5) The whole of any period of service to which paragraph (1) above applies shall, for the purpose of calculating under section 4(3) of the Teachers' Superannuation Act 1967 the average salary of a person to whom this Part applies, be reckoned as a period of employment in reckonable service and his salary during any period so reckoned shall be such amount as would under the Benefits Regulations be taken into account for the purpose of determining the annual average of his remuneration during that period.

(6) Notwithstanding anything in this rule before contained, any service of a person to whom this Part applies which under the Acts of 1937 to 1953 or a local Act scheme was at the time ceased to be employed in local government employment reckonable only of the purpose of calculating the amount of any pension payable to or in respect of him or only for the purpose of determining whether he was entitled to any pension shall be reckoned only for the corresponding like purpose under the Teachers' Regulations.

Voluntary Contributions

20.—(1) A person to whom this Part applies may elect to continue to pay voluntary contributions of any category being paid by him immediately before ceasing to be employed in local government employment.

(2) If a person elects as aforesaid and—

(a) within three months of becoming employed in teaching service, or within such longer period as the Secretary of State may in any particular case allow, pays to the Secretary of State a sum equal to the aggregate of any sum paid to him on or after ceasing to be employed in local government employment by way of return of voluntary contributions of any category he has elected to continue to pay, any interest added thereto and any amount deducted therefrom in respect of liability to income tax arising by reason of the payment; and

(b) thereafter pays to the Secretary of State any amounts outstanding in respect of voluntary contributions of any category he has elected to continue to pay at the times at which they would have been payable if he remained in local government employment

his teaching service shall be affected in the manner prescribed by the following provisions of this rule.

(3) In respect of voluntary contributions paid in respect of added years, those years shall be reckoned as reckonable service.

(4) In respect of voluntary contributions paid otherwise than in respect of added years, the service in respect of which they are paid shall be reckoned for the purposes of the Teachers' Regulations in the manner in which it would under

---

(a) S.I. 1957/356 (1957 I, p.733).   **(b)** 1968 c.12.
(c) S.I. 1948/1131 (Rev. XVII, p.813: 1948 I, p.3304).

rule 19 have been so reckoned if the payment of the contributions had been completed immediately before the person ceased to be employed in local government employment.

(5) The provisions of paragraphs (5)(*b*), (6), (7), (8) and (12) of regulation 32 and of regulation 38 of the Teachers' Regulations shall apply to voluntary contributions payable under this rule as if they were additional contributions payable in respect of previous employment within the meaning of those Regulations.

(6) If a person does not elect as aforesaid or if voluntary contributions are repaid to him under regulation 38 of the Teachers' Regulations, as applied by this rule, the period in respect of which such contributions were paid shall be reckoned for the purposes of the Teachers' Regulations only to the extent, if any, to which it would have been so reckoned if no such payments or contributions had been made in respect thereof.

Commencement of Employment

21. For the purposes of regulation 41(1)(*a*)(ii) of the Teachers' Regulations the date on which a person to whom this Part applies entered local government employment shall be deemed to be a date on which he became employed in teaching service.

Computation of Contributions

22.—(1) Where a person to whom this Part applies ceases to be employed in teaching service or dies, then, in computing the sum to which he or his personal representatives shall be entitled under the Teachers' Regulations, there shall be included a sum in respect of contributions paid by him in respect of service which by virtue of these Rules is reckoned as reckonable service and, in the case of a person who has elected in pursuance of rule 20 to continue paying voluntary contributions, in respect also of voluntary contributions paid by him before becoming employed in teaching service which have either not been returned to him or, if returned, have been paid to the Secretary of State under rule 20 and have not subsequently been again returned.

(2) In computing the amount of the sum so included for the purposes of this rule compound interest shall be calculated—

(*a*) as respects the period ending immediately before the date on which the person became employed in teaching service, in the manner in which such interest, if any, would have been calculated if the occasion for making the calculation had occurred immediately before that date; and

(*b*) as respects the period beginning with that date, in accordance with the provisions of Part IV of the Teachers' Regulations.

Benefits under Acts or Scheme

23. Subject as in Part II provided, no payment of any pension shall be made under the Acts of 1937 to 1953, the Benefits Regulations or a local Act scheme to any person or his personal representatives in respect of any local government employment which is reckoned as reckonable service under this Part.

Modification of Contributions and Benefits by reason of National Insurance

24.—(1) In relation to a person to whom this Part applies—

(*a*) the following paragraphs of Schedule 5 to the Teachers' Regulations, that is to say—

paragraph 2 (which provides for the reduction of contributions), paragraph 4 (which provides for the reduction of pensions by fixed annual amounts specified therein), and

paragraph 5 (which provides for the reduction of pensions by annual amounts ascertained by reference to a table and age at a given date)

shall not apply if, on the date on which he ceased to be employed in local government employment, the contributions payable by him as a contributory employee or local Act contributor were not subject to reduction by virtue of the Local Government Modification Regulations;

(b) paragraphs 2 and 4 of the said Schedule 5 shall apply if any pension payable to him under the Acts of 1937 to 1953 or a local Act scheme would, apart from the National Insurance (Modification of Local Government Superannuation Schemes) No. 2 (Scotland) Regulations 1961, have been subject to reduction by virtue of paragraph 2(3) of the Third Schedule to the Benefits Regulations; and

(c) paragraphs 2 and 5 of the said Schedule 5 shall apply if any pension payable to him under the Acts of 1937 to 1953 or a local Act scheme would, apart from the National Insurance (Modification of Local Government Superannuation Schemes) No. 2 (Scotland) Regulations 1961 have been subject to reduction by virtue of paragraph 2(2) of the Third Schedule to the Benefits Regulations.

(2) Where, by virtue of paragraph (1)(c) above, paragraph 5 of Schedule 5 to the Teachers' Regulations applies to a person the date of modification for the purposes of the latter paragraph shall be the date which was in relation to him the material date for the purposes of the Third Schedule to the Benefits Regulations.

Payment into Exchequer

25. All sums received by the Secretary of State in relation to a person to whom this Part applies whether by way of transfer value or otherwise shall be paid into the Exchequer.

Given under the seal of the Secretary of State for Scotland

on 18th June 1968.

(L.S.)

William Ross,
Secretary of State for Scotland.

Given under the Official Seal of the Secretary of State for Education
and Science on 19th June 1968.

(L.S.)

Edward Short,
Secretary of State for Education and Science.

We concur

25th July 1968.

J. McCann,
Harry Gourlay
Two of the Lords Commissioners of
Her Majesty's Treasury.

EXPLANATORY NOTE

(This Note is not part of the Rules)

These Rules provide for preservation of the superannuation rights of persons
who change their employment in either direction between pensionable teaching
service in England or Wales and pensionable local government employment in
Scotland.

Since provision for this purpose has not previously existed, the Rules apply
subject to certain conditions, under powers conferred by Section 2(5) of the
Superannuation (Miscellaneous Provisions) Act 1948, to changes of employment
before the date of their coming into operation but not earlier than 4th February
1948. The effect is thus that the Rules can be applied to changes of employment
at any time during the period already covered by similar Rules now in force both
in Scotland and in England and Wales.

STATUTORY INSTRUMENTS

1968 No. 1211

WELSH LANGUAGE

The Welsh Sunday Polls (Welsh Forms) Order 1968

Made - - -	*29th July* 1968
Laid before Parliament	*2nd August* 1968
Coming into Operation	*3rd August* 1968

In pursuance of the powers conferred on me by section 2(1) of the Welsh Language Act 1967(**a**), I hereby make the following Order :—

1. The form set out in the Schedule to this Order is hereby prescribed as the Welsh version which may be used in place of the corresponding form specified in the English language at the head of the translation, being a form set out in Schedule 8 to the Licensing Act 1964(**b**).

2. This Order may be cited as the Welsh Sunday Polls (Welsh Forms) Order 1968 and shall come into operation on 3rd August 1968.

James Callaghan,
One of Her Majesty's Principal
Secretaries of State.

Home Office,
Whitehall.
29th July 1968.

SCHEDULE

WELSH VERSION OF FORM A, THE FORM OF REQUISITION PAPER SET OUT IN
THE APPENDIX TO SCHEDULE 8 TO THE LICENSING ACT 1964

A. *Ffurflen papur hawlio*

Yr ydym ni sy'n torri ein henwau isod, gan ein bod yn etholwyr llywodraeth leol yn (sir   ) (bwrdeistref sirol   ) yn hawlio drwy hyn gynnal pleidlais o dan adran 66 y Licensing Act 1964 ar y cwestiwn a ddylai adeiladau trwyddedig yn y sir (bwrdeistref) agor ar Suliau i werthu diod feddwol.

(**a**) 1967 c. 66.   (**b**) 1964 c. 26.

Llofnod	Enw llawn	Cyfeiriad swyddogol ar gofrestr etholwyr llywodraeth leol	Rhif ar y gofrestr (gan gynnwys llythyren arbennig y dosbarth pleidleisio seneddol)

EXPLANATORY NOTE

(This Note is not part of the Order.)

This Order prescribes the Welsh version of the form of requisition paper for use in the Welsh Sunday polls.

STATUTORY INSTRUMENTS

1968 No. 1212

LAND CHARGES

The Local Land Charges (Amendment) Rules 1968

Made - - - -	*26th July* 1968
Coming into Operation	*2nd September* 1968

I, Gerald, Baron Gardiner, Lord High Chancellor of Great Britain, in exercise of the powers conferred on me by sections 15(6) and 19 of the Land Charges Act 1925(a), and with the concurrence of the Treasury as to fees, hereby make the following Rules:—

1.—(1) These Rules may be cited as the Local Land Charges (Amendment) Rules 1968 and shall come into operation on 2nd September 1968.

(2) The Interpretation Act 1889(b) shall apply to the interpretation of these Rules as it applies to the interpretation of an Act of Parliament.

2. No fee shall be payable for the registration, variation or cancellation of any entry in any part of the register of local land charges other than Part 11, and accordingly the Schedule set out in the Schedule to these Rules shall be substituted for Schedule 4 to the Local Land Charges Rules 1966(c).

Dated 24th July 1968.

Gardiner, C.

We, the undersigned, two of the Lords Commissioners of Her Majesty's Treasury, do hereby concur in Rule 2 of the above Rules and in the Schedule thereto.

Dated 26th July 1968.

J. McCann,
Harry Gourlay.

(a) 1925 c. 22.   (b) 1889 c. 63.   (c) S.I. 1966/579 (1966 II, p. 1318).

SCHEDULE   Rule 2

Substituted Schedule 4 to Local Land Charges Rules 1966

Fees

Item	Fee
	£ s. d.
1. Registration of a charge in Part 11 of the register	10 0 0
2. Filing a further certificate of the Lands Tribunal under Rule 16(3)	5 0
3. Filing a judgment or order, or written request for the variation or cancellation of any entry, in Part 11 of the register	10 0
4. Inspection of documents filed in the registry relating to an entry in Part 11 of the register, in respect of each parcel of land... ...	5 0
5. Variation or cancellation of any entry in Part 11 of the register	3 0
6. Personal search in the whole or any part of the register ...	4 0
And in addition, but subject to a maximum additional fee of 28s. in respect of each parcel of land above one, where the search extends to more than one parcel...	2 0
7. Official search (including issue of official certificate of search) in:	
(a) any one part of the register	4 0
(b) the whole of the register	10 0
And in addition, but subject to a maximum additional fee of 40s. in respect of each parcel of land above one, where several parcels are included in the same requisition under Rule 24(3), whether the requisition is for search in the whole or any part of the register	2 6
8. Office copy of any entry in the register (not including a copy or extract of any plan or document filed in the registry)	3 0
9. Office copy of any plan or other document filed in the registry...	such reasonable fee as may be fixed by the local registrar according to the time and labour involved.

EXPLANATORY NOTE

(This Note is not part of the Rules.)

These Rules, which amend the Local Land Charges Rules 1966, abolish the fees payable by local and central authorities for the registration, variation and cancellation of local land charges.

STATUTORY INSTRUMENTS

1968 No. 1213

AGRICULTURE

The Price Stability of Imported Products (Rates of Levy) Order 1968

Made - - -		*29th July* 1968
Coming into Operation		*1st August* 1968

The Minister of Agriculture, Fisheries and Food, in exercise of the powers conferred upon him by section 1(2), (4), (5) and (6) of the Agriculture and Horticulture Act 1964(a) and of all other powers enabling him in that behalf, hereby makes the following order :—

1. This order may be cited as the Price Stability of Imported Products (Rates of Levy) Order 1968 ; and shall come into operation on 1st August 1968.

2.—(1) In this order—

" the Principal Order " means the Price Stability of Imported Products (Levy Arrangements) Order 1966(b), as amended by any subsequent order and if any such order is replaced by any subsequent order the expression shall be construed as a reference to such subsequent order ;

AND other expressions have the same meaning as in the Principal Order.

(2) The Interpretation Act 1889(c) shall apply to the interpretation of this order as it applies to the interpretation of an Act of Parliament.

3. In accordance with and subject to the provisions of Part II of the Principal Order (which provides for the charging of levies on imports of certain specified commodities) the rate of general levy for such imports into the United Kingdom of any specified commodity as are described in column 2 of the Schedule to this order in relation to a tariff heading indicated in column 1 of the Schedule shall be the rate set forth in relation thereto in column 3 of the Schedule.

In Witness whereof the Official Seal of the Minister of Agriculture, Fisheries and Food is hereunto affixed on 29th July 1968.

(L.S.)

A. C. Sparks,
Authorised by the Minister.

(a) 1964 c. 28.   (b) S.I. 1966/936 (1966 II, p. 2271).   (c) 1889 c. 63.

SCHEDULE

1. Tariff Heading	2. Description of Imports	3. Rate of General Levy
	Imports of :—	per ton £ s. d.
11.02	Cereal meal— of maize	2 10 0

EXPLANATORY NOTE

(This Note is not part of the order.)

This order, which comes into operation on 1st August 1968, fixes a rate of general levy to be charged (in accordance with and subject to the provisions of the Principal Order) on imports of the specified commodity described in the Schedule to the order.

STATUTORY INSTRUMENTS

1968 No. 1214

CUSTOMS AND EXCISE

The Spirits (Imported Vodka and Aquavit) Regulations 1968

Made - - - -	*30th July* 1968
Laid before Parliament	*6th August* 1968
Coming into Operation	*12th August* 1968

The Commissioners of Customs and Excise, in exercise of the powers conferred upon them by section 1(3) of the Finance Act 1968(a) and of all other powers enabling them in that behalf, hereby make the following Regulations: —

1. Section 109(1) of the Customs and Excise Act 1952(b) shall not apply to the following kinds of imported compounded spirits, that is to say, vodka and aquavit.

2. The Interpretation Act 1889(c) shall apply for the interpretation of these Regulations as it applies for the interpretation of an Act of Parliament.

3. These Regulations may be cited as the Spirits (Imported Vodka and Aquavit) Regulations 1968 and shall come into operation on the 12th August 1968.

Dated this 30th day of July, 1968.

R. W. Radford,
Commissioner of Customs and Excise.

King's Beam House,
Mark Lane,
London, E.C.3.

EXPLANATORY NOTE

(This note is not part of the Order.)

The Regulations provide that section 109(1) of the Customs and Excise Act 1952 (which provides that no spirits shall be delivered for home use unless they have been warehoused for a period of at least three years) shall not apply to certain imported vodka and aquavit.

(a) 1968 c. 44.	(b) 1952 c. 44.	(c) 52 & 53 Vict. c. 63.

STATUTORY INSTRUMENTS

1968 No. 1217
TRANSPORT
PENSIONS AND COMPENSATION
The British Transport Docks Board
(Alteration of Pension Schemes)
Order 1968

Made - - -	*29th July* 1968
Laid before Parliament	*12th August* 1968
Coming into Operation	*1st September* 1968

The Minister of Transport, in exercise of his powers under section 74 of the Transport Act 1962(a) and of all other enabling powers, hereby makes the following Order:—

Commencement, Citation and Interpretation

1.—(1) This Order shall come into operation on the 1st September 1968 and may be cited as the British Transport Docks Board (Alteration of Pension Schemes) Order 1968.

(2) In this Order unless the context otherwise requires —

"the Board" means the British Transport Docks Board;

"funded scheme" means a pension scheme where the pensions are payable out of a fund held by any person for the purpose of the scheme;

" the Male Wages Grades Scheme " means the pension scheme established by the British Transport Commission (Male Wages Grades Pensions) Regulations 1954 (b), as amended (c), (as that scheme now has effect subject to the provisions of any Order made by the Minister under section 74 of the Transport Act 1962);

"the Minister" means the Minister of Transport;

"the New Fund" means the British Transport Docks Board (Wages Grades) Pension Scheme which has been established by the Board, with the consent of the Minister, under the terms of an Interim Trust Deed executed by the Board on the 25th June 1968 and which comprises a Pensions Fund and a Lump Sum Retirement Benefit Fund established by the Board with the like consent under the terms of the same Trust Deed;

"the persons administering", in relation to a pension scheme, means the persons responsible for administering the scheme under the terms thereof, and includes the trustees (if any) of the scheme;

"the service" means whole time employment with the Board or with a subsidiary of the Board; and

"term", in relation to a pension scheme to which this Order applies, includes any rule or provision of the scheme, or of any statutory provision relating to the scheme, or of any deed or other instrument made for the purposes of the scheme.

(a) 1962 c.46. (b) S.I.1954/898 (1954 I,p.175).
(c) S.I.1957/1455,1960/784(1957 I,p.177:1960 I,p.430).

(3) The Interpretation Act 1889 (a) shall apply for the interpretation of this Order as it applies for the interpretation of an Act of Parliament.

Application of Order

2.—(1) This Order shall apply to the Male Wages Grades Scheme, to the other pension schemes listed in the Schedule to this Order and to the London Midland and Scottish Railway (London North Western) Provident and Pension Society and Supplemental Pension Fund.

(2) A pension scheme to which this Order applies shall be construed and have effect as if the relevant provisions of this Order were terms of the scheme, any other term thereof, whether expressed or implied, to the contrary notwithstanding.

Alterations in the terms of the Male Wages Grades Scheme

3.—(1) This Article shall apply to the Male Wages Grades Scheme.

(2) The terms of the Male Wages Grades Scheme which require persons to become members of Section A of that Scheme shall not apply to—
- (a) any person who enters or has entered the service on or after the 6th May 1968, or
- (b) any person who has entered the service before the 6th May 1968 but who, because the age and length of service conditions of the Male Wages Grades Scheme have not been satisfied in relation to him, has not become a member of Section A of that Scheme before the 2nd September 1968 and who on or before the date on which those conditions are satisfied in relation to him is accepted for membership of the New Fund, or
- (c) any person who, being a member of a salaried staff superannuation fund or scheme, moves on or after the 2nd September 1968 within the service to a grade or class not eligible for membership of such salaried staff fund or scheme and who on or before ceasing to contribute to that fund or scheme is accepted for membership of the New Fund.

(3) The terms of the Male Wages Grades Scheme which require persons to become members of Section B of that Scheme shall not apply to—
- (a) any person referred to in paragraph (2) of this Article, or
- (b) any other person who becomes a member of the New Fund on or after the 2nd September 1968.

(4) Any person in the service who immediately before the 2nd September 1968 is a member of the Male Wages Grades Scheme and who becomes a member of the New Fund on or after that date shall, on becoming such a member, cease to be a member of the Male Wages Grades Scheme.

(5) Any person who becomes a member of the New Fund on or after the 2nd September 1968 shall at all times after becoming a member thereof be ineligible for membership of either Section of the Male Wages Grades Scheme.

(6) Where a person ceases to be a member of the Male Wages Grades Scheme under the foregoing provisions of this Article, the New Fund shall be credited with a sum equal to the contributions paid by such person to the Male Wages Grades Scheme.

(7) Where under the foregoing provisions of this Article a person who has a right of re-admission to the Male Wages Grades Scheme becomes ineligible for membership thereof, that right of re-admission shall terminate.

Alterations in the terms of certain schemes for providing pensions

4.—(1) This Article shall apply to the pension schemes listed in the Schedule to this Order.

(2) A person who becomes a member of the New Fund on or after the 2nd September 1968 shall be ineligible for admission to a pension scheme to which this Article applies.

(3) Where a member of a pension scheme to which this Article applies becomes a member of the New Fund on or after the 2nd September 1968 the following provisions shall have effect:—
- (a) upon the date of his admission to membership of the New Fund he shall cease to be a member of that pension scheme and (except as hereinafter provided) his liability if any to pay contributions to and his right to receive benefit from that scheme shall cease; and

_____

(a) 1889 c.63.

(b)as soon as may be after that date the persons administering that pension scheme shall pay to the New Fund an appropriate transfer value in respect of the accrued pension rights of that member in that scheme.

Alterations in the terms of a certain scheme for providing pensions and other benefits.

5.—(1) This Article shall apply to the London Midland and Scottish Railway (London North Western) Provident and Pension Society and Supplemental Pension Fund.

(2) Where a member of that pension scheme becomes a member of the New Fund on or after the 2nd September 1968 the following provisions shall have effect:—

(a)upon the date of his admission to membership of the New Fund he shall cease to be entitled to receive from that scheme any benefit payable on retirement or death in relation to that scheme and (subject to this Order) such adjustment as may be appropriate shall be made in respect of the liability of that member to pay contributions to that scheme after that date; and

(b)as soon as may be after that date the persons administering that pension scheme shall pay to the New Fund an appropriate transfer value in respect of the accrued pension rights of that member in that scheme to such benefits.

Ascertainment of Transfer Values

6.   Where under any of the foregoing provisions of this Order there falls to be paid in relation to a member of a pension scheme to which this Order applies a transfer value in respect of his accrued pension rights in that scheme, then —

(a)if the scheme is a funded scheme, the amount to be paid shall be ascertained by first determining the portion of the funds of that scheme properly attributable to the accrued pension rights of that member in that scheme and then by deducting therefrom such sum as may be necessary to cover the cost actually incurred by the persons administering that scheme in making the apportionment and the payment and also an amount equal to any income tax which may then become payable by virtue of regulations made under section 379 of the Income Tax Act 1952(a);

(b)if the scheme is not a funded scheme, the amount to be paid shall be ascertained by first determining a sum representing the value of the accrued pension rights of that member in that scheme and then by deducting therefrom such sum as may be necessary to cover the cost actually incurred by the persons administering that scheme in making the determination and the payment.

Consequential Provisions

7.—(1) Where under the foregoing provisions of this Order a person ceases to be a member of a pension scheme to which this Order applies or where under those provisions an adjustment falls to be made in respect of the liability of a member of such a pension scheme to pay contributions to that scheme, such cessation or adjustment (as the case may be) shall be without prejudice to the obligation of that person to pay any outstanding contributions to that scheme in respect of any period before such cessation or adjustment, and at the rate appropriate to that period, and to the right of his employer to deduct such contributions from his emoluments.

(2)   Where under the foregoing provisions of this Order a person ceases to be a member of a pension scheme to which this Order applies, his rights to benefit from that scheme shall, except as otherwise provided in this Order, terminate with the cessation of his membership of that scheme.

(a) 1952c.10.

2h

Determination of Questions

8. Where under the foregoing provisions of this Order any matter or thing is to be determined in relation to a member of a pension scheme to which this Order applies who becomes a member of the New Fund, that matter or thing shall be determined by agreement between the persons administering that pension scheme on the one hand and the persons administering the New Fund on the other hand or, in default of such agreement, by the Minister.

Sealed with the Official Seal of the Minister of Transport the   29th July   1968

(L.S.)

Richard Marsh,
Minister of Transport.

SCHEDULE

SCHEMES FOR PROVIDING PENSIONS ONLY

Aire and Calder Navigation Superannuation Fund
Great Eastern Railway New Pension Supplemental Fund
Great Western Railway Salaried Staff Supplemental Pension Fund
Great Western Railway Inspectors' and Foremen's Special Pension Fund
North Eastern Railway Servants' Pension Society (Tables A and B only).

EXPLANATORY NOTE

(This Note is not part of the Order)

This Order provides for termination of membership of, and rights in, the British Transport Commission (Male Wages Grades) Pension Scheme and certain other pension schemes, in the case of members in the service of the British Transport Docks Board who join the new British Transport Docks Board (Wages Grades) Pension Scheme. Provision is also made for relieving new entrants to the service of the Board and certain other persons of any obligation to enter the British Transport Commission (Male Wages Grades) Pension Scheme. The Order provides, in addition, for the ascertainment of transfer values and for certain other consequential matters.

STATUTORY INSTRUMENTS

1968 No. 1218

AGRICULTURE

AGRICULTURAL GRANTS, GOODS AND SERVICES

The Field Beans Scheme 1968

Laid before Parliament in draft

Made - - -	*26th July* 1968
Coming into Operation	*26th July* 1968

The Minister of Agriculture, Fisheries and Food and the Secretary of State, acting jointly, in pursuance of section 40 of the Agriculture (Miscellaneous Provisions) Act 1968(a) and all their other enabling powers, with the approval of the Treasury, hereby make the following scheme, a draft of which has been laid before Parliament and approved by both Houses of Parliament :—

Citation and extent

1. This scheme, which may be cited as the Field Beans Scheme 1968, shall apply to the United Kingdom.

Interpretation

2.—(1) In this scheme, unless the context otherwise requires—

"crop year" means a period of 12 months commencing with 1st July in any year ;

"declaration of acreage" and "declaration of harvesting" have the meanings given to them in paragraph 6 ;

"field beans" means beans of the species *Vicia faba* of the kind usually grown for feeding to stock, and includes horse beans and tick beans, but not broad beans ;

"the Minister", in relation to Scotland, means the Secretary of State, and in relation to any other part of the United Kingdom, the Minister of Agriculture, Fisheries and Food ;

"occupier", in relation to land in Scotland, means the person who has the right to use that land for growing a crop of field beans, and, in relation to land in Northern Ireland, includes a person who, by virtue of an agreement, whether written or otherwise, has the right to the use of the land.

(2) The Interpretation Act 1889(b) shall apply to the interpretation of this scheme as it applies to the interpretation of an Act of Parliament.

(a) 1968 c. 34.   (b) 1889 c. 63.

Grants for field beans

3.—(1) Subject to the provisions of this scheme, the Minister may make payments at the rate of £5 per acre in respect of crops of field beans which are grown for harvesting in any crop year during the period commencing with 1st July 1968 and ending with 30th June 1971.

(2) A payment under this scheme in respect of a crop of field beans grown in any crop year may be made to the person who at the end of 1st September in that crop year is the occupier of the land on which the crop is grown.

(3) Payment shall not be made to a person under this scheme in respect of—

(*a*) a self-sown crop ; or

(*b*) a crop which is grown mixed with any other crop ; or

(*c*) a crop of less than one acre.

(4) Fractions of an acre shall be rounded down to the nearest quarter of an acre.

(5) Normal-sized headlands, hedges and ditches attributable to the area on which the crop is grown shall be included in the acreage of the crop.

Harvesting conditions

4.—(1) Subject to sub-paragraph (2) below, no payment shall be made under this scheme in respect of a crop of field beans unless it has been harvested as grain or is available for harvesting as grain.

(2) If a crop or any part of a crop fails after 31st August in the crop year in which it was intended that it should be harvested, and the Minister is satisfied that the failure was not brought about by any fault on the part of the occupier, he may make a grant in respect of the crop notwithstanding the provisions of sub-paragraph (1) above.

Withholding and reduction of grant where crops are inadequate

5. Where in the opinion of the Minister, having regard to the weather and other natural conditions, a crop is unduly small in relation to the acreage of land on which it is grown, or has been adversely affected by the unsuitability of the land for growing the crop, the Minister may withhold payment in respect of the crop or reduce the amount of such payment to such extent as he considers reasonable.

Applications

6.—(1) No payment may be made under this scheme in respect of a crop of field beans unless the following applications for payment have been made to the Minister in such manner as he may direct :—

(*a*) a first application, in this scheme referred to as a declaration of acreage, stating the acreage of field beans sown ; and

(*b*) a second application, in this scheme referred to as a declaration of harvesting, stating the acreage of field beans harvested as grain or available for harvesting as grain.

(2) Unless the Minister otherwise directs, a declaration of acreage in respect of a crop of field beans grown in any crop year shall be made so as to be received by him not later than 31st July in that crop year, and a declaration of harvesting not later than 31st March in that crop year.

Information and inspection

7. It shall be a condition of payment under this scheme that any person who desires to be paid in respect of a crop shall to the best of his ability provide the Minister with such information about the crop as he may require, and shall, if requested, permit him to inspect the crop and the land on which it is grown.

In Witness whereof the Official Seal of the Minister of Agriculture, Fisheries and Food is hereunto affixed on 22nd July 1968.

(L.S.)   *Cledwyn Hughes,*
                     Minister of Agriculture, Fisheries and Food.

Given under the Seal of the Secretary of State for Scotland on 24th July 1968.

(L.S.)   *William Ross,*
                                Secretary of State for Scotland.

Approved on 26th July 1968.

                                         B. K. O'Malley,
                                         Joseph Harper,
                              Two of the Lords Commissioners of
                                    Her Majesty's Treasury.

EXPLANATORY NOTE
(*This Note is not part of the Scheme.*)

Section 40 of the Agriculture (Miscellaneous Provisions) Act 1968 enables grants to be paid for break crops. This United Kingdom scheme, which relates only to field beans, is the first to be made under that section. Grants of £5 per acre may be made in respect of field beans grown for harvesting in the three year period commencing on 1st July 1968. The crop must be harvested as grain or available for harvesting as grain, and grant is payable to the person who is the occupier of the land at the end of 1st September. The scheme provides for the making of applications, for the calculation of the acreage of a crop and for excluding payment on less than one acre. Payment may be reduced or withheld where a crop is inadequate. Applicants must if requested provide information about the crop and permit the Minister to inspect it and the land on which it is grown.

STATUTORY INSTRUMENTS

1968 No. 1219 (S. 131)

HOUSING, SCOTLAND

The Scottish Special Housing Association (Limit of Advances) (Scotland) Order 1968

Laid before the House of Commons in draft

Made - - - - -	*26th July* 1968
Coming into Operation	*19th August* 1968

In exercise of the powers conferred upon me by section 15(1) and (2) of the Housing (Financial Provisions, &c.) (Scotland) Act 1967(a) and of all other powers enabling me in that behalf, I hereby make the following order in terms of a draft which has been laid before the Commons House of Parliament and has been approved by resolution of that House:—

Citation, commencement and interpretation

1.—(1) This order may be cited as the Scottish Special Housing Association (Limit of Advances) (Scotland) Order 1968 and shall come into operation on 19th August 1968.

(2) The Interpretation Act 1889(b) shall apply for the interpretation of this order as it applies for the interpretation of an Act of Parliament.

Limit of advances to the Scottish Special Housing Association

2. The aggregate amount of the advances made under section 18(1) of the Housing (Scotland) Act 1962(c), as amended by section 15(1) of the Housing (Financial Provisions, &c.) (Scotland) Act 1967, together with any advances made under section 94(1) of the Housing (Scotland) Act 1950(d) shall not exceed one hundred and seventy million pounds.

William Ross,
One of Her Majesty's Principal
Secretaries of State.

St. Andrew's House,
Edinburgh, 1.
26th July 1968.

(a) 1967 c. 20. (b) 1889 c. 63. (c) 1962 c. 28. (d) 1950 c. 34.

EXPLANATORY NOTE
(This Note is not part of the Order.)

This Order provides for raising the aggregate amount of advances which may be made from the National Loans Fund to the Scottish Special Housing Association from £145m. to £170m. The present limit of £145m. is laid down by Section 15(1) of the Housing (Financial Provisions, &c.) (Scotland) Act 1967 (which amended Section 18(1) of the Housing (Scotland) Act 1962) and which provides that a higher limit of £170m. may be substituted by an Order made by the Secretary of State.

STATUTORY INSTRUMENTS

1968 No. 1220 (L.13)

LEGAL AID AND ADVICE, ENGLAND

The Legal Aid in Criminal Cases (Complaints Tribunal) Rules 1968

Made	- - -		*17th July* 1968
Coming into Operation			*1st October* 1968

I, Gerald, Baron Gardiner, Lord High Chancellor of Great Britain, in exercise of the powers vested in me by section 82 of the Criminal Justice Act 1967(**a**), hereby make the following Rules :—

Title, commencement and interpretation

1.—(1) These Rules may be cited as the Legal Aid in Criminal Cases (Complaints Tribunal) Rules 1968 and shall come into operation on 1st October 1968.

(2) The Interpretation Act 1889(**b**) shall apply to the interpretation of these Rules as it applies to the interpretation of an Act of Parliament.

(3) In these Rules, unless the context otherwise requires—

"the Applicant" means a person duly authorised by the Bar Council or the Council of The Law Society to make application under these Rules ;

"the Bar Council" means the General Council of the Bar ;

"the Clerk" means the clerk to the appropriate Complaints Tribunal or any deputy or person appointed temporarily to perform the duties of that Office ;

"The Law Society" means the Society incorporated and regulated by Royal Charter dated the 26th day of February 1845, and Royal Charters supplemental thereto and any reference to the Council of The Law Society shall be taken as a reference to the Council elected in accordance with the provisions of the said Charters ;

"the Tribunal" means a Complaints Tribunal constituted in accordance with these Rules.

(4) In these Rules a rule or form referred to by number means the rule or form so numbered in these Rules.

Complaints tribunals

2.—(1) For the purpose of hearing and determining complaints against any barrister or solicitor arising out of his conduct when acting in

---

(**a**) 1967 c. 80. (**b**) 1889 c. 63.

criminal proceedings for a legally assisted person or his professional conduct generally, there shall be constituted—

(a) in a case relating to a barrister, a Tribunal consisting of the Chairman or Vice-Chairman of the Bar Council, three practising barristers nominated by the Bar Council, and a person (not being a practising barrister or solicitor) nominated by the Lord Chancellor ;

(b) in a case relating to a solicitor, a Tribunal consisting of the President or Vice-President of The Law Society, three solicitors nominated by the Council of The Law Society, and a person (not being a practising barrister or solicitor) nominated by the Lord Chancellor.

(2) In a case relating both to a barrister and solicitor, the Tribunals shall have power at their discretion in any particular case to sit together for all or any of the following purposes—

(a) to hear evidence ;

(b) to make joint findings of fact ;

(c) to make orders in accordance with Rule 3.

(3) Three members of a Tribunal shall form a quorum of whom the person nominated by the Lord Chancellor shall be one, and any decision of a Tribunal shall be taken, in the event of a difference between members, by the votes of a majority.

(4) The Bar Council or, as the case may be, The Law Society, shall appoint Clerks to the Tribunals for barristers and solicitors respectively and provide premises and other facilities for hearing and determining complaints, and any expenses so incurred by them shall be expenses of the Tribunals.

Powers of a tribunal

3. Where a Tribunal determine that a complaint against a barrister or solicitor has been substantiated they shall have power—

(a) to exclude him from acting in criminal proceedings for legally assisted persons (whether permanently or temporarily) and, in the case of a solicitor, to exclude any other person who is for the time being a member of the same firm ;

(b) to reduce or cancel the remuneration otherwise payable under a Legal Aid Order to him or, in the case of a solicitor, payable under a Legal Aid Order to him or to his firm ;

(c) to order him to pay all or any of the costs of the proceedings on any such complaint.

Applications to tribunals

4.—(1) The Bar Council or, as the case may be, The Law Society, shall receive and consider any complaints concerning the conduct when acting in criminal proceedings for legally assisted persons of, respectively, a barrister or a solicitor.

(2) Where the Bar Council or The Law Society are of the opinion, as a result of any such complaint or by reason of his professional conduct generally, that there may be good reason for imposing upon the barrister or solicitor (as the case may be) any of the penalties set out in Rule 3, they shall apply to the appropriate Tribunal to hear and determine the matter.

Procedure

5. The provisions of the Schedule to these Rules shall have effect with respect to the proceedings of a Tribunal.

Dated 17th July 1968.

Gardiner, C.

SCHEDULE

Form of application

1. An application to a Tribunal shall be in writing under the hand of the applicant in such one of the forms annexed hereto and numbered 1 and 2 as shall be appropriate and shall be sent to the Clerk together with an affidavit by the applicant in such one of the forms set out in the Schedule hereto and numbered 3 and 4 stating the matters of fact on which he relies in support of his application.

Supplementary information

2. Before fixing a day for the hearing the Tribunal may require the applicant to supply such further information and documents relating to the application as they think fit.

Dismissal of application without hearing

3.—(1) In the case of an application where, in the opinion of the Tribunal, no *prima facie* case is shown in favour of the application, the Tribunal may dismiss the application without requiring the respondent to answer the allegations, and without hearing the applicant.

(2) If required so to do, either by the applicant or the respondent, the Tribunal shall make a formal order dismissing such application.

Parties

4. In the case of an application against a solicitor who is a member of a firm the parties to the proceedings shall be—

(i) the applicant,

(ii) the solicitor, and

(iii) if the Tribunal so direct, every solicitor who is for the time being a partner of such solicitor.

Fixing hearing

5.—(1) In the case of an application in which, in the opinion of the Tribunal, a *prima facie* case is shown in favour of the application, the Tribunal shall fix a day for the hearing, and the Clerk shall serve notice thereof on each party to the proceedings and shall serve on each party, other than the applicant, a copy of the application and affidavit.

(2) There shall be at least 21 days between the service of any such notice and the day fixed therein for the hearing.

(3) The notice shall be in such one of the forms annexed hereto and numbered 5, 6 and 7, as shall be appropriate and shall require the party to whom it is addressed to furnish to the Clerk and to every other party at least 14 days before the day fixed for the hearing, unless the Tribunal direct otherwise, a list of all documents on which he intends to rely.

6.—(1) Any party may inspect the documents included in the list furnished by any other party.

(2) A copy of any document mentioned in the list furnished by any party shall, on application and on payment of the proper charges therefor by the party requiring it, be furnished to that party by the other within 3 days after the receipt of such application.

7. If any party fails to appear at the hearing the Tribunal may, upon proof of service on such party of the notice of hearing, proceed to hear and determine the application in his absence.

8. The Tribunal may, in their discretion, either as to the whole case or as to any particular fact or facts, proceed and act upon evidence given by affidavit.

9. Where it appears that the application against the respondent is based on circumstances which have—

(a) in the case of a respondent who is a barrister, been considered by the Senate of the four Inns of Court ; or

(b) in the case of a respondent who is a solicitor, been considered in proceedings against him before the Disciplinary Committee constituted under the Solicitors Act 1957(a) ;

the Tribunal may—

(i) act on such evidence as they may think sufficient as to what was the decision of the Senate or were the Findings and Order of the Disciplinary Committee (as the case may be) ; and

(ii) accept as conclusive in the proceedings before the Tribunal any facts found by the Senate or Disciplinary Committee.

10. If the Findings and Order of the Tribunal are not pronounced on the day of the hearing, the Clerk shall give notice to the parties of the date when the Findings and Order will be pronounced.

11.—(1) The Clerk shall on the day of pronouncement, or on such other date as the Tribunal shall have ordered, send copies of the Findings and Order to the Lord Chancellor, the Secretary of State for the Home Department, the Secretary of the Bar Council and to the Secretary of The Law Society.

(2) Within 4 days of the date when the Findings and Order shall have been pronounced, the Clerk shall send a copy thereof to each party to the application.

12. The Tribunal shall hear all applications in private.

13.—(1) Unless the Tribunal direct otherwise, no application shall be withdrawn after it has been sent to the Clerk.

(2) Where a party has applied for leave to withdraw his original application the Tribunal may, upon such terms as to costs or otherwise as they shall think fit, grant such leave, or of their own motion or upon the application of any party adjourn the hearing.

14. The Tribunal may, of their own motion or upon the application of any party, adjourn the hearing upon such terms, as to cost or otherwise, as the Tribunal shall think fit.

(a) 1957 c. 27.

Amendments

15. If upon the hearing it shall appear to the Tribunal that the allegations in the affidavit require to be amended, or added to, the Tribunal may permit such amendment, or addition, or if in the opinion of the Tribunal such amendment or addition is not within the scope of the affidavit, may require the same to be embodied in a further affidavit, provided that if such amendment, or addition, shall be such as to take any party by surprise, or prejudice the conduct of his case, the Tribunal shall grant an adjournment of the hearing, upon such terms as to costs, or otherwise, as the Tribunal shall think fit.

Suspension of publication of Order

16.—(1) The Tribunal shall have power upon the application of any party to suspend the sending of a copy of any Order thereof to the Lord Chancellor, the Secretary of State for the Home Department, the Secretary of The Law Society and to the Secretary of the Bar Council.

(2) Where the Tribunal grant an application under the preceding sub-paragraph, the Order shall not take effect until it has been sent to the Secretary of State for the Home Department, and if the Order is an Order that a barrister or solicitor be excluded from a panel for a period, the period of exclusion shall be deemed to begin on the date when the Order is so sent to the Secretary of State for the Home Department.

Shorthand notes

17.—(1) Shorthand notes of proceedings may be taken by a person appointed by the Tribunal; and any party who appeared at the proceedings shall be entitled to inspect the transcript thereof.

(2) The shorthand writer shall, if required, supply to the Tribunal, to any person entitled to be heard upon an appeal against an Order of the Tribunal, to the Bar Council and to The Law Society, but to no other person, a copy of the transcript of such notes on payment of his charges.

(3) If no shorthand notes be taken the Chairman of the Tribunal shall take a note of the proceedings, and the provisions of this Rule as to inspection and taking copies shall apply to such note accordingly.

(4) In this paragraph any reference to a shorthand note of any proceedings shall be construed as including a reference to a record of the proceedings made by mechanical means and, in relation to such a record, the reference to the shorthand writer shall be construed as a reference to the person responsible for transcribing the record.

Service

18. Service of any notice or document may be effected under these Rules by post addressed, in the case of a barrister, to his last known place of business and to his place of abode and in the case of a solicitor, to his place of business appearing in the Register (commonly known as the Practising Roll) kept by the Registrar of Solicitors and to his place of abode (if known) and such service shall be deemed to be effected at the time when the letter would be delivered in the ordinary course of post.

Power to dispense with requirements of Schedule

19. The Tribunal may dispense with any requirements of the Schedule respecting notices, affidavits, documents, service, or time, in any case where it appears to the Tribunal to be just so to do.

Extensions of time

20. The Tribunal may extend any of the times fixed by the Schedule.

Custody of documents

21.—(1) All affidavits shall be filed with and kept by the Clerk.

(2) The Tribunal may order that any books, papers, or other exhibits, produced or used at a hearing, shall be retained by the Clerk until the time within which an appeal may be entered has expired, and, if notice of appeal is given, until the appeal is heard or otherwise disposed of.

22. The Evidence Act 1938(a), shall apply in relation to proceedings before the Tribunal in the same manner as they apply in relation to civil and criminal proceedings.

Application of Evidence Act

23. (1) Any party may, by notice in writing at any time not later than 9 days before the day fixed for the hearing, call upon any other to admit any document saving all just exceptions and if such other party desires to challenge the authenticity of the document he shall, within 6 days after service of such notice, give notice that he does not admit the document and requires it to be proved at the hearing.

Notice to admit

(2) If such other party refuses or neglects to give notice of non-admission within the time prescribed in the last preceding paragraph he shall be deemed to have admitted the document unless otherwise ordered by the Tribunal.

(3) Where a party gives notice of non-admission within the time prescribed by the sub-paragraph (1) of this paragraph and the document is proved at the hearing, the costs of proving the document shall be paid by the party who has challenged the document, whatever the Order of the Tribunal may be, unless in their Findings the Tribunal shall find that there were reasonable grounds for not admitting the authenticity of the document.

FORM 1

Form of Application against a Barrister

To the Clerk to the Complaints Tribunal constituted under the Legal Aid in Criminal Cases (Complaints Tribunal) Rules 1968

In the Matter of J.K., a Barrister

and

In the Matter of the Criminal Justice Act 1967

I, the undersigned A.B. a person duly authorised in this behalf by [the General Council of the Bar] [the Council of The Law Society] make application that J.K. of
barrister may be excluded from acting for legally assisted persons and that such other Order may be made as the Tribunal shall think right.

In witness whereof I have hereunto set my hand this   day of
19 .

.............................Signature

.............................Address

....

.............................⎫ Profession, business,
.............................⎭ or occupation.

(a) 1938 c. 28.

FORM 2

Form of Application against a Solicitor

To the Clerk to the Complaints Tribunal constituted under the Legal Aid in Criminal Cases (Complaints Tribunal) Rules 1968

In the Matter of C.D., [E.F. and G.H.] [a] Solicitor[s]

and

In the Matter of the Criminal Justice Act 1967

I, the undersigned A.B. a person duly authorised in this behalf by [the Council of the Law Society] [the General Council of the Bar] make application that C.D. of   solicitor [and E.F. of   and G.H. of   solicitors, partners of the said C.D.] may be excluded from acting for legally assisted persons and that such other Order may be made as the Tribunal shall think right.

In witness whereof I have hereunto set my hand this   day of
19

....................................Signature

....................................Address

....

....................................⎫ Profession, business,
....................................⎭ or occupation.

FORM 3

Form of Affidavit by Applicant (Application against a Barrister)

In the Matter of J.K., a Barrister

and

In the Matter of the Criminal Justice Act 1967

I, A.B. of
make oath and say as follows:—

1. I am duly authorised by [the General Council of the Bar] [the Council of The Law Society] to make application that C.D. of
(hereinafter called the respondent) may be excluded from acting for legally assisted persons and that such other Order may be made as the Tribunal shall think right.

2. The respondent was called to the Bar by
in   and is a practising barrister with Chambers at

3. [Here state the facts with regard to the complaint concisely in numbered paragraphs and show deponent's means of knowledge.]

FORM 4

Form of Affidavit by Applicant (Application against a Solicitor)

In the Matter of C.D., [E.F. and G.H.] [a] Solicitor[s]

and

In the Matter of the Criminal Justice Act 1967

I, A.B. of
make oath and say as follows:—

1. I am duly authorised by [the Council of The Law Society] [the General Council of the Bar] to make application that C.D. of
solicitor [and E.F. of
and G.H. of   solicitors, partners of the
said C.D.] may be excluded from acting for legally assisted persons and that such other Order may be made as the Tribunal shall think right.

2. The said C.D. (hereinafter called the [first] respondent) was admitted as a solicitor of the Supreme Court of Judicature in England on the
[The said E.F. (hereinafter called the second respondent)
was admitted on the   and the said G.H. (hereinafter called the third respondent) was admitted on the   ].

3. The first respondent practises as a solicitor at
[and according to the best of my knowledge, information and belief the second and third respondents practise in partnership with him] [under the style or firm of   ].

4. [Here state the facts with regard to the complaint concisely in numbered paragraphs and show deponent's means of knowledge.]
Sworn, etc.

FORM 5

Form of Notice to Applicant by the Clerk to the Complaints Tribunal constituted under the Legal Aid in Criminal Cases (Complaints Tribunal) Rules 1968

[Heading as in Form 1 or Form 2.]

To A.B. of

The   day of   is the day fixed by the Complaints Tribunal constituted under the Legal Aid in Criminal Cases (Complaints Tribunal) Rules 1968, for the hearing of your application in the matter of [barrister] [solicitor[s]].

The Tribunal will sit at
at   o'clock in the   noon.

*[The parties to the application are as follows:—]

You are required by the Legal Aid in Criminal Cases (Complaints Tribunal) Rules 1968 to furnish to every other party to the application and to the Clerk to the Tribunal at The General Council of the Bar, Carpmael Building, Temple, London, E.C.4, or The Law Society, Chancery Lane, London, W.C.2 as appropriate at least 14 days before the said   day of
a list of all the documents on which you intend to rely.

You are requested to acknowledge receipt of this notice without delay.

Dated this   day of   19

Clerk to the Tribunal

*To be deleted where the application is against a barrister.

FORM 6

Form of Notice to a Barrister by the Clerk to the Complaints
Tribunal constituted under the Legal Aid in Criminal Cases
(Complaints Tribunal) Rules 1968

[Heading as in Form 1]

To J.K. of   , a barrister.

Application has been made by A.B., a person duly authorised in that behalf
by [the General Council of the Bar] [the Council of The Law Society] that
you may be excluded from the panels maintained under the Legal Aid
Scheme, 1950 or from such of them as the Tribunal shall think fit, and that
such other Order may be made as the Tribunal shall think right.

A copy of the affidavit in support of this application accompanies this
notice.

The   day of   is the day fixed by the Tribunal for
the hearing of the application. The Tribunal will sit at
                              at   o'clock in the   noon.

If you fail to appear the Tribunal may, in accordance with the Legal Aid
in Criminal Cases (Complaints Tribunals) Rules 1968, proceed in your
absence.

You are required by the said Rules to furnish to every other party to the
application to the Clerk to the Tribunal at The General Council of the Bar,
Carpmael Building, Temple, London, E.C.4, at least 14 days before the said
          day of   a list of all the documents on which
you propose to rely.

Either party may inspect the documents included in the list furnished by
any other and a copy of any document mentioned in the list of any party
must, on application and on payment of the proper charges therefor by the
party requiring it, be furnished to that party by the other within 3 days
after receipt of such application.

You are requested to acknowledge receipt of this notice without delay.

Dated this   day of   19   .

Clerk to the Tribunal

[N.B.—A copy of the Legal Aid in Criminal Cases (Complaints Tribunals)
Rules, 1968, is sent herewith for your information and guidance.]

FORM 7

Form of Notice to Solicitor by the Clerk to the Complaints Tribunal
constituted under the Legal Aid in Criminal Cases (Complaints
Tribunal) Rules 1968

[Heading as in Form 2]

To C.D. of
[E.F. of
                                                   and G.H. of
                                                   ], solicitor[s].

Application has been made by A.B., a person duly authorised in that behalf
by [the Council of The Law Society] [the General Council of the Bar] that
you [and E.F. and G.H.] may be excluded from, acting for legally assisted
persons, and that such other Order may be made as the Tribunal shall think
right.

The parties to the application are as follows: —

A copy of the affidavit in support of this application accompanies this
notice.

The   day of   is the day fixed by the Tribunal for
the hearing of the application.   The Tribunal will sit at
                        at   o'clock in the   noon.

If you fail to appear the Tribunal may, in accordance with the Legal Aid
in Criminal Cases (Complaints Tribunals) Rules 1968, proceed in your
absence.

You are required by the said Rules to furnish to every other party to the
application and to the Clerk to the Tribunal at The Law Society, Chancery
Lane, London, W.C.2, at least 14 days before the said   day of
                    a list of all the documents on which you propose to rely.

Any party may inspect the documents included in the list furnished by
any other and a copy of any document mentioned in the list of any party
must, on application and on payment of the proper charges therefor by the
party requiring it, be furnished to that party by the other within 3 days
after receipt of such application.

You are requested to acknowledge receipt of this notice without delay.

Dated this   day of   19   .

[N.B.—A copy of the Legal Aid in Criminal Cases (Complaints Tribunals)
Rules 1968, is sent herewith for your information and guidance.]

EXPLANATORY NOTE

(This Note is not part of the Rules.)

These Rules constitute two Complaints Tribunals for hearing and
determining complaints against, respectively, barristers and solicitors
arising out of their conduct when acting in criminal proceedings for
legally aided persons or their professional conduct generally.

STATUTORY INSTRUMENTS

1968 No. 1222

PARTNERSHIP

The Partnerships (Unrestricted Size) No. 1 Regulations 1968

Made - - - - 30th July 1968

Coming into Operation 7th August 1968

The Board of Trade in pursuance of the powers conferred upon them by section 120(2) of the Companies Act 1967(a) hereby make the following Regulations:—

1. Section 434 of the Companies Act 1948(b) shall not apply to the formation—

(a) for the purpose of carrying on practice as patent agents, of a partnership consisting of persons each of whom is registered as a patent agent in the register of patent agents maintained pursuant to the Patents Act 1949(c);

(b) for the purpose of carrying on one or more of the activities mentioned in Part I of the Schedule hereto, of a partnership consisting of persons not less than three-quarters of the total number of whom are members of one or more of the bodies mentioned in Part II of that Schedule.

2. These Regulations may be cited as the Partnerships (Unrestricted Size) No. 1 Regulations 1968 and shall come into operation on 7th August 1968.

C. W. Jardine,
An Under-Secretary of
30th July 1968. the Board of Trade.

(a) 1967 c.81. (b) 1948 c. 38.
(c) 1949 c. 87.

SCHEDULE

Part I

1. Surveying.
2. Auctioneering.
3. Valuing.
4. Estate Agency.
5. Land Agency.
6. Estate Management.

Part II

1. The Royal Institution of Chartered Surveyors.
2. The Chartered Land Agents' Society.
3. The Chartered Auctioneers' and Estate Agents' Institute.
4. The Incorporated Society of Valuers and Auctioneers.

EXPLANATORY NOTE

(This Note is not part of the Regulations.)

Section 434 of the Companies Act 1948 prohibits the formation of partnerships consisting of more than 20 members. These Regulations exempt from that prohibition partnerships of the descriptions, and formed for the purposes, specified in the Regulations.

STATUTORY INSTRUMENTS

1968 No. 1223

CUSTOMS AND EXCISE

The Origin of Goods (Republic of Ireland) (Amendment No. 2) Regulations 1968

Made - - -	*31st July* 1968
Laid before the House of Commons - -	*7th August* 1968
Coming into Operation	*8th August* 1968

The Board of Trade, in pursuance of the powers conferred upon them by section 12(2) of the Import Duties Act 1958(a), as it has effect by virtue of section 7 of the Finance Act 1966(b), hereby make the following Regulations:—

1. The Origin of Goods (Republic of Ireland) Regulations 1966(c), as amended (d), shall have effect as if:—

(1) in regulation 1, after the words "the Import Duties Act 1958" there were inserted the words "and section 3 of the Finance Act 1968(e)";

(2) the entries set out in Schedule 1 hereto were included in Part I of Schedule 1 thereto;

(3) the entry set out in Schedule 2 hereto were included in Schedule 2 thereto.

2. The Interpretation Act 1889(f) shall apply to the interpretation of these Regulations as it applies to the interpretation of an Act of Parliament.

3. These Regulations may be cited as the Origin of Goods (Republic of Ireland) (Amendment No. 2) Regulations 1968 and shall come into operation on 8th August 1968.

31st July 1968.

Edmund Dell,
Minister of State,
Board of Trade.

(a) 6 & 7 Eliz. 2 c. 6.   (b) 1966 c. 18.
(c) S.I. 1966/667 (1966 II, p. 1463).
(d) The relevant amending Regulations are S.I. 1966/1098 (1966 III, p. 2699).
(e) 1968 c. 44.   (f) 1889 c. 63.

SCHEDULE 1

Entries to be included in Part I of Schedule 1 to S.I. 1966 No. 667

Column 1 Tariff Heading	Column 2 Description of Goods
22.06	Vermouths and other wines of fresh grapes flavoured with aromatic extracts.
ex 22.07	Other fermented beverages (for example, cider, perry and mead), the following:— Wine
ex 36.05 36.06 }	Matches (including Bengal matches)
ex 98.10	Mechanical lighters and similar lighters, including chemical and electrical lighters and parts thereof, excluding flints and wicks:—

Portable lighters, being portable mechanical, chemical, electrical or similar contrivances intended to provide a means of ignition, whether by spark, flame or otherwise, and parts thereof, the following:—

Portable lighters constructed solely for the purpose of igniting gas for domestic use, whether complete or incomplete (including stems of electrical lighters and rigid or spring frames of flint lighters)
Other portable lighters complete or incomplete (including bodies).

SCHEDULE 2

Entry to be included in Schedule 2 to S.I. 1966 No. 667

Column 1 Tariff Heading	Column 2 Description of Goods	Column 3 Qualifying process
24.02	Manufactured tobacco, tobacco extracts and essences	Manufacture from materials not falling in 24.02

EXPLANATORY NOTE

(This Note is not part of the Regulations.)

In conformity with the provisions of the Agreement establishing a Free Trade Area between the United Kingdom and the Republic of Ireland, the protective element in revenue duties on goods of the Republic of Ireland is removed by section 3 of the Finance Act 1968. These Regulations amend the Origin of Goods (Republic of Ireland) Regulations 1966 by laying down conditions which goods subject to such duties and manufactured in the Republic of Ireland must satisfy in order to qualify as goods of that country.

STATUTORY INSTRUMENTS

1968 No. 1224

AGRICULTURE

The Meat and Livestock Commission Levy Scheme (Confirmation) Order 1968

Laid before Parliament in draft

Made - - - -	*30th July* 1968
Coming into Operation	*31st July* 1968

The Minister of Agriculture, Fisheries and Food and the Secretary of State concerned with agriculture in Scotland (hereinafter referred to as "the Ministers"), acting jointly in exercise of the powers conferred on them by section 13 of the Agriculture Act 1967(a) and of all other powers enabling them in that behalf, being satisfied that the bringing into force of a Scheme for the imposition of charges submitted to them by the Meat and Livestock Commission for their confirmation under the said section (which Scheme is hereinafter referred to as "the said Scheme") is desirable, hereby make the following order, a draft whereof has been laid before Parliament and approved by resolution of each House of Parliament:—

1. This order may be cited as the Meat and Livestock Commission Levy Scheme (Confirmation) Order 1968; and shall come into operation on the day immediately following the day on which it is made.

2. The said Scheme is hereby confirmed with the following modifications:—

(*a*) in paragraph 4(2) thereof (which specifies the maximum charge leviable in respect of each head of livestock slaughtered) there shall be substituted for the maximum charges of "8/-" for cattle (other than calves not exceeding 150 lb. deadweight), "2/-" for calves not exceeding 150 lb. deadweight and "10d." for sheep the following maximum charges respectively, that is to say, "6/-", "1/-" and "6d.";

(*b*) in paragraph 5(2) thereof there shall be substituted for the words "any person on whose instructions he slaughtered the livestock by reference to which the sum was paid" the words "any person on whose instructions the livestock by reference to which the sum was paid were slaughtered".

3. The said Scheme as so modified and confirmed is set forth in the Schedule to this order, and it shall come into force on the day on which this order comes into operation.

(a) 1967 c. 22.

In witness whereof the Official Seal of the Minister of Agriculture, Fisheries and Food is hereunto affixed on 30th July 1968.

(L.S.)   *Cledwyn Hughes,*
                                    Minister of Agriculture, Fisheries and Food.

Given under the Seal of the Secretary of State for Scotland on 30th July 1968.

(L.S.)   *William Ross,*
                                            Secretary of State for Scotland.

SCHEDULE

MEAT AND LIVESTOCK COMMISSION LEVY SCHEME

Under sections 13 and 14 of the Agriculture Act 1967, for the imposition of charges.

1. This Scheme, which applies in Great Britain, may be cited as the Meat and Livestock Commission Levy Scheme 1968.

2.—(1) In this Scheme, except where the context otherwise requires, the following expressions have the meanings hereby respectively assigned to them, namely:—

"the Commission" means the Meat and Livestock Commission established under Part I of the Agriculture Act 1967;

"deadweight" means in relation to calves the weight of the carcase after the head, skin and tail and the offal (except the kidneys) have been removed;

"livestock" means cattle, sheep and pigs;

"livestock product" has the meaning assigned thereto by Section 25(2) of the said Act;

"slaughterer" means any person (including a local authority) having the control and management of a slaughterhouse in which livestock are slaughtered and includes a local authority providing slaughterhouse facilities under Part II of the Slaughterhouses Act 1954 or Part IV of the Food and Drugs Act 1955, or providing any similar facilities under any local enactment;

"slaughterhouse" has, in England and Wales, the meaning given by section 135(1) of the Food and Drugs Act 1955 and, in Scotland, the meaning given by section 16 of the Slaughterhouses Act 1954.

(2) The Interpretation Act 1889 shall apply to the interpretation of this Scheme as it applies to the interpretation of an Act of Parliament.

3. Slaughterers are hereby specified as the class of persons on whom charges may be imposed under this Scheme.

4.—(1) All charges leviable under this Scheme are for the purpose of enabling the Commission to meet their expenses (including any sums to be paid into their reserve fund) other than expenses which are to be met in some other way: they shall be leviable by reference to livestock slaughtered in a slaughterhouse and shall be recoverable by the Commission from the slaughterer having the control and management of the slaughterhouse where the livestock are slaughtered.

(2) The maximum charge leviable in respect of each head of livestock slaughtered shall be in the case of—

(a) Cattle (other than calves not exceeding 150 lb. deadweight)   6/-
(b) Calves not exceeding 150 lb. deadweight   1/-
(c) Sheep   6d.
(d) Pigs   2/-

(3) Subject to sub-paragraphs (1) and (2) of this paragraph, the Commission are hereby authorised to levy such amounts as they think fit from time to time or to suspend the levy for any period: Provided that no charges shall be levied under this Scheme in respect of livestock slaughtered under the Diseases of Animals Act 1950 or any order or arrangements made thereunder.

(4) Without prejudice to the generality of sub-paragraph (3) of this paragraph (but subject to the Proviso thereto and to sub-paragraphs (1) and (2) of this paragraph), the Commission are hereby authorised if they think fit from time to time to levy different amounts in respect of different classes of livestock, and all or any of such classes may be determined by reference to number, type or weight or to any one or more of those matters, as the Commission think fit.

5.—(1) Any charge duly levied under this Scheme shall, subject as mentioned in sub-paragraph (3) of this paragraph, be payable to the Commission on such date or dates and at such place or places as the Commission may from time to time require and shall be recoverable as a debt due to the Commission from the slaughterer.

(2) The slaughterer is hereby authorised to recover as a debt due to him any sum paid by him under this Scheme from any person on whose instructions the livestock by reference to which the sum was paid were slaughtered, provided that such person is a person engaged in the production, marketing (including marketing by a person concerned otherwise than as a buyer or seller) or distribution of livestock or livestock products.

(3) The slaughterer shall be entitled to make from his payments to the Commission deductions in respect of his expenses in exercising his right of recovery under sub-paragraph (2) of this paragraph but such deduction shall not in any case exceed 0.75d. for each head of livestock slaughtered or such higher amount as the Commission may from time to time determine as being reasonable.

(4) Where the slaughterer defaults in payment to the Commission of any sum due from him under this Scheme and would, if he had made payment, have been authorised to recover such sum from another person in accordance with sub-paragraph (2) of this paragraph, the Commission are hereby authorised, if they think fit, to recover directly from the last mentioned person as a debt due from him to the Commission the amount which would have been payable indirectly if the default had not occurred: Provided that this sub-paragraph shall not apply where the last-mentioned person satisfies the Commission that he has made payment to the slaughterer.

(5) Where in the opinion of the Commission (whose decision shall be final and conclusive) any sum which a slaughterer is authorised by sub-paragraph (2) of this paragraph to recover from another person ought reasonably to be treated as irrecoverable by the slaughterer, the Commission shall afford him relief either by permitting him to deduct such sum from payments to the Commission or by way of refund, whichever the Commission shall decide.

6.—(1) So far as is necessary for determining the liability of slaughterers to charges under this Scheme, the Commission may, by notice published in at least one newspaper having a national circulation in England and Wales and at least one newspaper having a national circulation in Scotland and in such other newspapers and other periodicals as the Commission consider appropriate to bring the matter to the notice of persons affected, from time to time require every slaughterer (or any class or classes of slaughterers specified in the notice) to be registered in a register kept for the purpose by the Commission.

(2) Without prejudice to the preceding sub-paragraph, the Commission may (so far as is necessary for the purpose mentioned in that sub-paragraph) by notice served upon any slaughterer require him to be registered as aforesaid.

(3) Any slaughterer who is required to be registered as aforesaid shall apply to the Commission to be registered upon such form as the Commission may from time to time prescribe; and any person so registered who has ceased to be a slaughterer and who desires that his name shall be removed from the register shall apply for such removal upon such form as the Commission may from time to time prescribe.

7. So far as is necessary for determining the liability of any slaughterer to charges under this Scheme, the Commission may from time to time by notice in writing served upon any slaughterer require him:—

    (*a*) to keep an accurate record in writing, to be duly completed and dated each day, specifying—

        (i) for each head of livestock slaughtered on the instructions of another person, the name and sufficient other information to identify that person and a sufficient description of the animal to enable the charge payable in respect of it to be ascertained;

        (ii) the total number of livestock slaughtered each day and sufficient information to enable the charges payable in respect thereof to be ascertained;

    (*b*) to retain any such record for such period (not exceeding two years) as may be specified in the notice;

    (*c*) to produce for examination on demand by an authorised officer in the whole-time employment of the Commission any such record and any other books or documents in the slaughterer's custody or under his control;

    (*d*) to furnish to the Commission at such address and at such time or times and in such form as may be specified in the notice such returns and other information as may be so specified.

8. For the purpose of establishing the liability of any person under this Scheme, the production of a certificate purporting to be signed by the Director, Deputy Director or other officer of the Commission authorised to give the certificate specifying the amounts levied by the Commission for any period shall be sufficient evidence of the facts so specified.

EXPLANATORY NOTE

(This Note is not part of the Order.)

By this order the Ministers confirm, with modifications, the Meat and Live-stock Commission's Scheme for the imposition of charges for enabling the Commission to meet their expenses and for the recovery of such charges (which must not exceed the maximum charges specified in the Scheme) by the Commission from slaughterers by reference to livestock slaughtered in the slaughterhouses in their control and management. The slaughterers are authorised to recover sums paid by them under the Scheme from persons on whose instructions the livestock were slaughtered and to deduct from payments to the Commission expenses in respect of such recovery.

The Scheme also provides for the registration of slaughterers, for the keeping of appropriate records by them and for the making of returns to the Commission.

The modifications referred to make reductions in the amounts of the maximum charges which may be levied under the Scheme in respect of cattle, calves and sheep (the maximum for pigs remains unchanged), and make a small textual alteration in paragraph 5(2) of the Scheme.

The order provides that the scheme shall come into force on the same day as the order comes into operation.

STATUTORY INSTRUMENTS

1968 No. 1225

AGRICULTURE

The Price Stability of Imported Products (Rates of Levy No. 2) Order 1968

Made	-	-	-	29*th July* 1968
Coming into Operation			1*st August* 1968

The Minister of Agriculture, Fisheries and Food, in exercise of the powers conferred upon him by section 1(2), (4), (5) and (6) of the Agriculture and Horticulture Act 1964(a) and of all other powers enabling him in that behalf, hereby makes the following order :—

1. This order may. be cited as the Price Stability of Imported Products (Rates of Levy No. 2) Order 1968 ; and shall come into operation on 1st August 1968.

2.—(1) In this order—

" the Principal Order " means the Price Stability of Imported Products (Levy Arrangements) Order 1966(b), as amended by any subsequent order and if any such order is replaced by any subsequent order the expression shall be construed as a reference to such subsequent order ;

AND other expressions have the same meaning as in the Principal Order.

(2) The Interpretation Act 1889(c) shall apply to the interpretation of this order as it applies to the interpretation of an Act of Parliament.

3. In accordance with and subject to the provisions of Part II of the Principal Order (which provides for the charging of levies on imports of certain specified commodities)—

(*a*) the rate of general levy for such imports into the United Kingdom of any specified commodity as are described in column 2 of Part I of the Schedule to this order in relation to a tariff heading indicated in column 1 of that Part shall be the rate set forth in relation thereto in column 3 of that Part ;

(*b*) the rate of country levy for such imports into the United Kingdom of any specified commodity as are described in column 2 of Part II of the Schedule to this order in relation to a tariff heading indicated in column 1 of that Part shall be the rate set forth in relation thereto in column 3 of that Part.

In Witness whereof the Official Seal of the Minister of Agriculture, Fisheries and Food is hereunto affixed on 29th July 1968.

(L.S.)

A. C. Sparks,
Authorised by the Minister.

(a) 1964 c. 28.   (b) S.I. 1966/936 (1966 II, p. 2271).
(c) 1889 c. 63.

SCHEDULE

PART I

1. Tariff Heading	2. Description of Imports	3. Rate of General Levy
		per ton £ s. d.
10.01	Imports of :— Any wheat (other than seed wheat the value of which is not less than £34 per ton and denatured wheat) for which a minimum import price level is prescribed	12 6

PART II

1. Tariff Heading	2. Description of Imports	3. Rate of Country Levy
		per ton £ s. d.
10.01	Imports of :— Any wheat (other than seed wheat the value of which is not less than £34 per ton and denatured wheat) which has been grown in the French Republic and consigned to the United Kingdom from that country or which has been grown in the Kingdom of Sweden and consigned to the United Kingdom from that country	12 6

EXPLANATORY NOTE

(This Note is not part of the Order.)

This order, which comes into operation on 1st August 1968, fixes rates of levy to be charged (in accordance with and subject to the provisions of the Principal Order) as follows :—

(a) a general levy on imports of wheat described in Part I of the Schedule to the order ; and

(b) a country levy on imports of wheat described in Part II of that Schedule which has been grown in France or Sweden and consigned to the United Kingdom from that country.

STATUTORY INSTRUMENTS

1968 No. 1226 (S.132)

HOUSING, SCOTLAND

The Housing Subsidies (Representative Rates of Interest) (Scotland) Order 1968

Laid before the House of Commons in draft

Made - - -	*26th July* 1968
Coming into Operation	*1st September* 1968

In exercise of the powers conferred upon me by section 2(2), (3) and (5) of the Housing (Financial ·Provisions, &c.) (Scotland) Act 1967(a) and of all other powers enabling me in that behalf and after consultation with certain recipient authorities and such associations of other recipient authorities as appeared to me to be concerned, I hereby make the following order in the terms of a draft which has been laid before the Commons House of Parliament and has been approved by resolution of that House:—

Citation, commencement and interpretation

1.—(1) This order may be cited as the Housing Subsidies (Representative Rates of Interest) (Scotland) Order 1968 and shall come into operation on 1st September 1968.

(2) The Interpretation Act 1889(b) shall apply for the interpretation of this order as it applies for the interpretation of an Act of Parliament.

Representative rates of interest

2. The rates of interest to be specified for the purposes of section 2(2) of the Housing (Financial Provisions, &c.) (Scotland) Act 1967 in respect of approved houses provided in Scotland shall be as follows:—

    (*a*) in relation to all local authorities and all housing associations (except the Scottish Special Housing Association), for the financial year commencing on 16th May 1968—6.78 per cent.;

    (*b*) in relation to the Scottish Special Housing Association, for the financial year commencing on 1st April 1968—6.60 per cent.; and

    (*c*) in relation to all development corporations, for the financial year commencing on 1st April 1968—7.06 per cent.

William Ross,
One of Her Majesty's Principal
Secretaries of State.

St. Andrew's House,
Edinburgh, 1.
26th July 1968.

(a) 1967 c. 20.   (b) 1889 c. 63.

EXPLANATORY NOTE

(This Note is not part of the Order.)

This Order specifies the representative borrowing rates for the year 1968/69 applicable to the several bodies who receive housing subsidies under Section 2 of the Housing (Financial Provisions, &c.) (Scotland) Act 1967. The subsidy meets the difference between the loan charges on the aggregate approved cost of houses completed in that year at the borrowing rate specified in the Order and the loan charges which would have been incurred at a fixed borrowing rate of 4 per cent.

STATUTORY INSTRUMENTS

1968 No. 1230

LEGAL AID AND ADVICE, ENGLAND

The Legal Aid in Criminal Proceedings (Fees and Expenses) Regulations 1968

Made - - -	*31st July* 1968
Laid before Parliament	*8th August* 1968
Coming into Operation	*1st October* 1968

ARRANGEMENT OF REGULATIONS

In pursuance of the powers conferred upon me by section 83 of the Criminal Justice Act 1967(**a**), I hereby make the following Regulations :—

General

1.—(1) Fees and expenses payable to a solicitor or counsel assigned to a legally assisted person shall be taxed by a taxing authority who shall, subject to the provisions of these Regulations, allow such fees and expenses as appear to him to be fair remuneration for work actually and reasonably done.

(2) In these Regulations any reference to "taxing" shall include the determining of fees or expenses by assessment or other means.

Basic, refresher and daily fees

2.—(1) Where a person is granted legal aid under the provisions of section 73 of the Criminal Justice Act 1967, hereinafter referred to as "the Act", his

---

(**a**) 1967 c. 80.

solicitor and counsel shall (subject to the following provisions of these Regulations) be allowed basic fees in accordance with the provisions of the Schedule to these Regulations.

(2) Where a hearing has not been concluded at the end of the first relevant period (as defined in paragraph (9) of this Regulation) thereof, there shall be allowed to counsel in respect of each relevant period or, in the case of an incomplete relevant period, part thereof, after the first, a refresher fee in accordance with the provisions of the Schedule to these Regulations.

(3) Where a hearing has not been concluded on the day on which it started, there shall be allowed to the solicitor, in respect of the second or every subsequent day or part thereof, a daily fee in accordance with the provisions of the Schedule to these Regulations.

(4) The taxing authority may take into consideration in assessing the fees to be paid in accordance with paragraph (1) above any work done in the preparation of a written application for bail or in the making of an oral application for bail, except an oral application to a judge in chambers (which expression shall not include a single judge exercising his powers under the Criminal Appeal Act 1968(a)).

(5) In all cases where legal aid provides for the services of two counsel, the solicitor and counsel shall each be allowed such fees as appear to be reasonable and proper in all the circumstances of the case and such fees may exceed those prescribed in Regulation 4 of, and the Schedule to, these Regulations.

(6) Where a legal aid order is made in respect of proceedings in a magistrates' court and does not provide for the services of counsel, a solicitor who employs counsel may not receive in fees and reimbursement of expenses an amount greater than that to which he would have been entitled if counsel had not been employed.

(7) In addition to the fees payable under the foregoing provisions of this Regulation, a solicitor shall be allowed—

(a) expenses actually and reasonably incurred by himself or his clerk in travelling to and from the court and to and from any place visited for the purpose of preparing or conducting the case ;

(b) any other out of pocket expenses actually and reasonably incurred :

Provided that—

(a) if the expenses are abnormally large by reason of the distance of the solicitor's place of business both from the court and from the legally assisted person, reimbursement of the expenses may be limited to what would otherwise, having regard to all the circumstances, be a reasonable amount ;

(b) in the case of an appeal to the Court of Appeal, the cost of a transcript of the proceedings in the court from which the appeal lies, or any part thereof, shall not be allowed except where such transcript was supplied by the Registrar or the taxing authority considers that it is reasonable in all the circumstances for such expense to be allowed.

(8) There shall be allowed to counsel, in addition to any fees allowed under the foregoing paragraphs of this Regulation—

(a) in respect of any conference or consultation lasting not more than half-an-hour, a fee of £2 7s. 0d. or, in the case of a conference or consultation with two counsel, where two counsel are assigned, such fees as appear to be proper in all the circumstances of the case ;

(a) 1968 c. 19.

(b) in respect of any conference or consultation lasting more than half-an-hour, such fee as appears to be proper in all the circumstances of the case ;

(c) in respect of any application to a court that a case which is in a list of cases to be heard on any particular day be heard on any other day or stand out of the list, such fees as appears to be proper in all the circumstances of the case ;

(d) for advice in writing, a fee not exceeding £11 0s. 0d., or, where two counsel are assigned and the advice is given by both counsel, such fees as appear to be proper in all the circumstances of the case.

(9) In this Regulation "relevant period" means, as the taxing authority may determine, any day on any part of which the hearing is going on, or any period of five hours, whether continuous or not, during which the hearing is going on.

Assignment to more than one legally assisted person

3.—(1) Where a solicitor or counsel represents two or more persons in respect of whom a court has ordered under section 73 of the Act that they shall be given legal aid and whose cases are heard together, the total fee to be allowed to solicitor or counsel, as the case may be, in respect of all such persons, shall be increased above the amount which would have been allowed to him if he had been representing only one such person (which amount is hereafter referred to in this Regulation as the "normal amount") by such amount as appears to be proper in all the circumstances of the case:

Provided that any increase allowed by virtue of this Regulation shall not exceed, in any case where the number of persons is two, 40% of the normal amount and, where the number of persons exceeds two, a further 20% of the normal amount in respect of each person in excess of two.

(2) In assessing the normal amount the taxing authority shall do so by reference to that person in respect of whom the highest fees would have been allowed if the cases of all the persons had been disposed of separately.

(3) In addition to the increased amount referred to in paragraph (1) above, counsel or solicitor may be allowed the fees or expenses, as the case may be, in respect of each legally assisted person, referred to in paragraphs (7) and (8) of Regulation 2 and in Regulation 4.

Fees for advising on appeal

4.—(1) Where any advice or assistance is given by a solicitor under sub-sections (5) to (8) of section 74 of the Act, there shall, in addition to the fees which may be allowed under the foregoing Regulations, be allowed sums in respect of such expenses as are referred to in paragraph (7) of Regulation 2 and a fee not exceeding £10 10s. 0d.

(2) Where any advice or assistance as aforesaid is given by counsel in a case where counsel is assigned, there shall, in addition to the fees which may be allowed under the foregoing Regulations, be allowed to counsel a fee not exceeding £11 in respect of the work done.

(3) Fees not exceeding those aforesaid may also be allowed to a solicitor or counsel, as the case may be, where advice or assistance is given under section 74(9) of the Act.

Abandonment of appeals

5. In the case of an appeal which is abandoned there shall be allowed to the solicitor and to counsel assigned to the appellant such fees as the Registrar or the clerk of the peace may direct, but not exceeding the sums mentioned in these Regulations.

Amendment or revocation of legal aid order

6. Where a legal aid order is amended or revoked, there shall be allowed to the solicitor and to counsel previously assigned to the legally assisted person such fees as the taxing authority may direct, but not exceeding the sums mentioned in these Regulations.

Assessment by taxing authority

7.—(1) Subject to the provisions of these Regulations, the taxing authority in taxing the sums payable to a solicitor or counsel under any of the provisions of these Regulations shall take into account all the relevant circumstances, including the nature, importance, complexity or difficulty of the work and the time involved, including time spent at the court on any day waiting for the case to be heard if the case was in that day's list.

(2) The taxing authority shall take into consideration any bill of costs submitted by a solicitor or counsel and may require a solicitor or counsel to submit a bill of costs together with any supporting documents.

(3) If the work done by a solicitor or counsel includes work done in relation to more than one indictment or in relation to a retrial, the taxing authority shall take account thereof in his taxation.

(4) In taxing as aforesaid, the taxing authority shall not allow any sum in respect of any conference, consultation, view, attendance or visit unless the taxing authority is satisfied that such conference, consultation, view, attendance or visit was reasonably necessary.

(5) In taxing as aforesaid the sums to be paid to a solicitor or to counsel in any case, the taxing authority shall take into account any payment which may be or has already been made to him under these Regulations in the same case in another court, and for such purpose may require a solicitor to provide for him a copy of any bill of costs submitted or to be submitted to any other taxing authority.

(6) If it appears to the taxing authority having taken into account all the relevant circumstances referred to in paragraph (1) of this Regulation that nevertheless owing to exceptional circumstances the sums payable by virtue of these Regulations or any of them would not provide fair remuneration for the work actually and reasonably done by the solicitor or counsel, as the case may be (whether in respect of the whole work or a particular item of work, including work done in respect of advice on appeal or giving notice of appeal or application for leave to appeal), he shall certify accordingly; and, where he so certifies, any limitation contained in these Regulations on the amount of any fee payable shall not apply.

Reviews by taxing authority

8.—(1) Any solicitor or counsel assigned to a person under a legal aid order (other than an order made in respect of proceedings in a magistrates' court), who is dissatisfied with the assessment by the taxing authority of the fees or disbursements to be allowed to him under these Regulations or with the refusal of the taxing authority to grant a certificate under Regulation 7(6) of these Regulations, may apply to the taxing authority for a review of his decision, by making to the taxing authority written representations within 14 days of the receipt by him of the taxing authority's assessment.

(2) Such written representations shall be accompanied by a bill of costs and full supporting documents, including counsel's brief and fee note (if any), if these have not already been furnished.

(3) The taxing authority shall consider the representations made to him and make such alterations, if any, in his assessment as may seem to him proper in the light of such representations and shall notify the solicitor or counsel, as the case may be, of the result of his review.

(4) The taxing authority shall permit oral representations to be made by or on behalf of counsel or solicitor and shall notify counsel or solicitor of the time at which he is prepared to hear such representations.

Appeals to Taxing Master

9.—(1) If a solicitor or counsel is dissatisfied with a review by the taxing authority (other than the Law Society), he may, within 14 days of receiving notification of the result of the review, request the taxing authority to furnish him in writing with the reasons for his decision and, if so requested, the taxing authority shall furnish the reasons for his decision in writing to the solicitor or counsel, as the case may be, and where the taxing authority has disallowed any items or has reduced the amount claimed in respect of any items, he shall give separate reasons for such decision in respect of each item.

(2) Where a solicitor or counsel is dissatisfied with the reasons given by the taxing authority, he may within 14 days of receipt of such reasons apply to the Chief Master of the Supreme Court Taxing Office for a review of the decision of the taxing authority in respect of the bill of costs or of specific items in such bill and shall inform the taxing authority of his application.

(3) Such application shall be accompanied by a copy of the representations made under Regulation 8(1) and of the taxing authority's reasons given under paragraph (1) of this Regulation, a bill of costs together with full supporting documents, a copy of the legal aid order and a fee of £2 for the review.

(4) Such review shall be by a Taxing Master and the solicitor may appear in person or be represented by an agent, and counsel may appear in person or be represented by the solicitor or the solicitor's agent, and any application under paragraph (2) shall state whether the counsel or solicitor wishes to appear or be represented, or whether he will accept a decision given in his absence.

(5) If the solicitor or counsel gives notice in his application of his intention to appear in person or be represented by an agent, the Taxing Master shall inform him or the agent (as the case may be) of the date on which the review will take place.

(6) In reaching his decision the Taxing Master may consult the presiding judge and the taxing authority, and may require the solicitor or counsel to provide any further information which he may require for the purpose of his review, and, unless the Taxing Master otherwise directs, no further evidence shall be received on the hearing of the review ; and no ground of objection shall be valid which was not raised on the review under Regulation 8 of these Regulations.

(7) In making his review, the Taxing Master shall have the same powers as the taxing authority under these Regulations and, in the exercise of such powers, may alter the assessment of the taxing authority in respect of any sum allowed, whether by increase or decrease.

(8) The Taxing Master shall communicate the result of his review to the solicitor or counsel and to the taxing authority.

Appeals to the High Court

10.—(1) If a solicitor or counsel is dissatisfied with the review of the decision of the taxing authority by the Taxing Master, he may, within 14 days of receiving notification of the result of the review, appeal to the High Court :

Provided that such appeal shall lie only where the Taxing Master certifies that the question to be decided involves a point of principle of general importance.

(2) The appeal shall be heard and determined by a single judge of the Queen's Bench Division, whose decision shall be final.

(3) An appeal shall be instituted by an originating summons to the Queen's Bench Division.

(4) Upon the hearing of an appeal the court shall have the same power as the taxing authority under these Regulations and may reverse, affirm or amend the decision appealed against or make such other order as it thinks fit.

Payment and repayment of fees and expenses

11.—(1) On making an assessment, the taxing authority shall make out and deliver to the solicitor or counsel, as the case may be, an order for payment by the treasurer of the appropriate local authority of the fees and expenses allowed, or, where the taxing authority is the Law Society, shall pay such fees and expenses as aforesaid.

(2) Where an assessment is increased, the taxing authority shall arrange for payment of the amount of the increase in the manner aforesaid.

(3) Where an assessment is decreased, the counsel or solicitor, as the case may be, shall repay any excess paid to him to the appropriate local authority, or the Law Society, as the case may be.

(4) Where the Taxing Master or the judge of the High Court increases an assessment, the £2 referred to in Regulation 9(3) shall be included in the fees and expenses allowed.

(5) A solicitor or counsel who incurs expense in connection with a review of an assessment by the Taxing Master or an appeal to the High Court shall, except where the decision of the taxing authority or Taxing Master, as the case may be, is affirmed or his assessment is decreased, be allowed a reasonable sum in respect of those expenses.

(6) In this Regulation the expression "appropriate local authority" means the local authority out of whose funds the costs of legal aid are payable in accordance with section 81(1) of the Act.

Bills of costs

12. Any bill of costs referred to in these Regulations shall contain a summary of the work done and, when appropriate, details of the following matters and the time involved in each : —

    (*a*) instructions to counsel ;

    (*b*) attendances at court ;

(c) work done in connection with advice on appeal, assistance in giving notice of appeal or making application for leave to appeal and with settling the notice and grounds of appeal or application for leave to appeal or for a case to be stated ;

(d) any extra work done in the same case on behalf of any other legally assisted person ;

(e) travelling expenses and other disbursements ;

(f) applications to the court (including applications for bail) ;

(g) conferences, consultations, views, attendances, visits, advice given in writing or documents settled or perused ;

(h) any special circumstances which should be drawn to the attention of the taxing authority ;

and may include against each item the amount which counsel or solicitor considers to be the proper fee in respect of that item.

Interpretation

13.—(1) In these Regulations—

"legal aid order" has the same meaning as in section 73(9) of the Act ;

"presiding judge" means the judge who presided at the hearing of the case in respect of which the fees in question are claimed ;

"Registrar" means the Registrar of Criminal Appeals ;
"taxing authority" means—

(1) subject to the provisions of Regulation 14 of these Regulations, in the case of a legal aid order made by the criminal division of the Court of Appeal, the Registrar ;

(2) in the case of proceedings in a court of assize or quarter sessions, the clerk of assize or of the peace, as the case may be ;

(3) in the case of proceedings in a magistrates' court, the Law Society ;

so however that where the fees to be assessed are in respect of work done under section 74(5), (6) or (7) of the Act, the taxing authority in respect of such fees means as follows :—

(a) where the proceedings in respect of which an appeal is being considered were in a court of assize or quarter sessions, then—

(i) if notice of appeal or application for leave to appeal to the Court of Appeal is given (whether or not such appeal is afterwards abandoned) and, where the applicant was legally assisted in the court of trial, such notice is given on the advice of the counsel or solicitor assigned, the Registrar;

(ii) in other cases, the clerk of assize or clerk of the peace, as the case may be ;

(b) where the proceedings in respect of which an appeal is being considered were in a magistrates' court, the Law Society ;

"Taxing Master" means a Master of the Supreme Court (Taxing Office).

(2) The Interpretation Act 1889(a) shall apply to the interpretation of these Regulations as it applies to the interpretation of an Act of Parliament.

(a) 1889 c. 63.

Taxation in the House of Lords

14.—(1) In the case of proceedings in the House of Lords, fees and expenses payable to a solicitor or counsel assigned to a legally assisted person shall be taxed by such officer as may be prescribed by order of the House of Lords.

(2) Subject to paragraph (1) of this Regulation, these Regulations shall not apply to proceedings in the House of Lords.

Citation and Commencement

15. These Regulations may be cited as the Legal Aid in Criminal Proceedings (Fees and Expenses) Regulations 1968 and shall come into operation on 1st October 1968.

James Callaghan,
One of Her Majesty's Principal
Secretaries of State.

Home Office,
  Whitehall.
  31st July 1968.

Regulation 2

SCHEDULE

Court	SOLICITOR		COUNSEL	
	Basic fee for hearing and preparation therefor	Daily Fee	Basic fee on hearing	Refresher Fee
Court of Appeal	Not less than £8 8 0 Not exceeding £78 15 0	Not exceeding £15 15 0	Not less than £11 0 0 Not exceeding £64 10 0	Such fee as represents fair remuneration for work actually and reasonably done but not exceeding one half of the basic fee unless the proportion borne by any refresher fee payable to counsel for the prosecution in the case to the fee payable to such counsel in the actual conduct of the prosecution in court at the hearing (exclusive of refresher fee) exceeds one half in which case the refresher fee allowed shall not exceed such amount as bears the like proportion to the basic fee.
Assizes or Quarter Sessions	Not less than £8 8 0 Not exceeding £78 15 0	Where solicitor may appear and no counsel instructed, not exceeding £21 0 0 In any other case not exceeding £15 15 0	Not less than £8 13 0 Not exceeding £64 10 0	
Magistrates' Courts.	Where no counsel assigned Not less than £6 6 0 Not exceeding £47 5 0	Not exceeding £9 9 0	Such fee as appears to the Law Society to represent fair remuneration for the work actually and reasonably done, provided that a refresher fee shall not exceed one half of the basic fee.	
	Where counsel assigned, fair remuneration for work actually and reasonably done.			

EXPLANATORY NOTE

(This Note is not part of the Regulations.)

Part IV of the Criminal Justice Act 1967 makes fresh provision for the granting of legal aid in criminal proceedings. These Regulations prescribe fees and expenses which may be paid to the legal representatives of a legally assisted person and provide for their taxation. Provision is made for appeals from the taxing authority.

STATUTORY INSTRUMENTS

1968 No. 1231

LEGAL AID AND ADVICE, ENGLAND

The Legal Aid in Criminal Proceedings (General) Regulations 1968

Made - - -	*31st July* 1968
Laid before Parliament	*9th August* 1968
Coming into Operation	*1st October* 1968

ARRANGEMENT OF REGULATIONS

28. Enforcement of orders for payment of costs.
29. Notification of fund into which costs are to be paid.
30. Legal aid records.
31. Interpretation.
32. Determination in private and in absence of legally assisted person.
33. Forms.
34. Citation and commencement.

In pursuance of the powers conferred upon me by section 83 of the Criminal Justice Act 1967(**a**), I hereby make the following Regulations :—

Proceedings in a magistrates' court

1.—(1) An application for a legal aid order in respect of proceedings in a magistrates' court under section 73(2) of the Act (magistrates' court proceedings) may be made to the justices' clerk in Form 1 in the Schedule to these Regulations.

(2) An application for a legal aid order may be made orally to the court.

(3) A legal aid order shall not be made until the court, a justice of the peace or the justices' clerk has considered the statement of means of the applicant.

(4) Subject to the provisions of this Regulation, the powers of the court to determine an application for a legal aid order may be exercised by the justices' clerk or a justice of the peace to whom the clerk has referred the application.

(5) Where an application for a legal aid order is made orally to the court, the court may refer it to the justices' clerk for determination.

(6) The justices' clerk considering an application for a legal aid order shall—

(*a*) make an order ; or

(*b*) refuse to make an order unless the applicant first makes a payment on account of any contribution towards costs which he may be liable to pay ; or

(*c*) refer the application to the court or a justice of the peace.

(**a**) 1967 c. 80.

(7) Where the justices' clerk refuses to make a legal aid order unless the applicant first makes a payment on account of any contribution towards costs which he may be liable to pay, the applicant shall be entitled, on request, to have the application determined by the court or a justice of the peace, as the clerk thinks fit.

(8) Where the court or a justice of the peace determines an application for a legal aid order by refusing to make a legal aid order, the justices' clerk shall not make a legal aid order except where the court or justice of the peace refused to make a legal aid order unless the applicant first made a payment as aforesaid and such payment is made.

(9) In this Regulation the expression "justice of the peace" means a justice of the peace who is entitled to sit as a member of the magistrates' court and "legal aid order" means a legal aid order within the meaning of paragraph (1) of this Regulation.

Proceedings in a court of assize or quarter sessions

2.—(1) An application for a legal aid order under section 73(3) or (4) of the Act (proceedings in a court of assize or quarter sessions) may be made in Form 2 in the Schedule to these Regulations to—

(a) the clerk of assize or clerk of the peace, as the case may be, or

(b) in the case of an appeal to quarter sessions, the justices' clerk.

(2) An application for a legal aid order may be made orally to the court of assize or quarter sessions, or to the magistrates' court at the conclusion of the proceedings in that court.

(3)(a) An application for a legal aid order under section 73(8) of the Act (retrial) may be made in Form 2 in the Schedule to these Regulations to the clerk of assize or clerk of the peace, as the case may be.

(b) An application for such an order may be made orally to the Court of Appeal or the House of Lords, as the case may be, immediately after the decision of the court.

(4) A legal aid order shall not be made until the court, a judge of the court, the proper officer of the court or, where the application is made to the magistrates' court or justices' clerk, a justice of the peace has considered the statement of means of the applicant.

(5) Subject to the provisions of this Regulation, the powers of the court to determine an application for a legal aid order may be exercised by a judge of the court, the proper officer of the court, or, where the application is made to the magistrates' court or justices' clerk, a justice of the peace.

(6) Where an application for a legal aid order is made orally to the court, the court may refer it to the proper officer of the court for determination.

(7) The proper officer of the court considering an application for a legal aid order shall—

(a) make an order ; or

(b) refuse to make an order unless the applicant first makes a payment on account of any contribution towards costs which he may be liable to pay ; or

(c) except where the proper officer of the court is a justices' clerk, refer the application to a judge of the court, or, if he is, to the magistrates' court or a justice of the peace.

(8) Where the proper officer of the court refuses to make a legal aid order unless the applicant first makes a payment on account of any contribution towards costs which he may be liable to pay, the applicant shall be entitled, on request, to have the application determined by a judge of the court or, if the proper officer of the court is a justices' clerk, the magistrates' court or a justice of the peace, as the justices' clerk thinks fit.

(9) Where the court or a judge of the court or a justice of the peace determines an application for a legal aid order by refusing to make a legal aid order, the proper officer of the court shall not make a legal aid order except where the court, judge or justice refused to make a legal aid order unless the applicant first made a payment as aforesaid and such payment is made.

(10) In this Regulation the expression "magistrates' court" means the court which committed or convicted the applicant, "justice of the peace" means a justice of the peace who is entitled to sit as a member of the magistrates' court, "justices' clerk" means the clerk to the magistrates' court, and "legal aid order" means a legal aid order within the meaning of paragraph (1) or (3) of this Regulation, as the case may be.

Proceedings in the House of Lords or Court of Appeal

3.—(1) Notice of application for a legal aid order under section 73(5) of the Act (appeal to the Court of Appeal) may be given in Form 3, and under section 73(7) of the Act (appeal to the House of Lords) may be given in Form 3A, in the Schedule to these Regulations and in either case may be given to the Registrar.

(2) An application for a legal aid order may be made orally to the Court of Appeal, a judge of the court or the Registrar.

(3) A legal aid order shall not be made until—

(a) a notice of appeal or application for leave to appeal to the Court of Appeal or the House of Lords, as the case may be, has been given, and

(b) the Court of Appeal, a judge of the court or the Registrar has considered the statement of means of the applicant for legal aid.

(4) Subject to the provisions of this Regulation, the powers of the Court of Appeal to determine an application for a legal aid order may be exercised by a judge of the court or the Registrar.

(5) Where an application for a legal aid order is made orally to the Court of Appeal, the court may refer it to a judge of the court or the Registrar for determination ; and where such an application is made orally to a judge of the court, he may refer it to the Registrar for determination.

(6) The Registrar considering an application for a legal aid order shall—

(a) make an order ; or

(b) refuse to make an order unless the applicant first makes a payment on account of any contribution towards costs which he may be liable to pay ; or

(c) refer the application to the Court of Appeal or a judge of the court.

(7) Where the Registrar refuses to make a legal aid order unless the applicant first makes a payment on account of any contribution towards costs which he may be liable to pay, the applicant shall be entitled, on request, to have the application determined by a judge of the court.

(8) Where a judge of the court refuses to make a legal aid order or refuses unless the applicant first makes a payment as aforesaid, the applicant shall be entitled, on request, to have the application determined by the Court of Appeal.

(9) Where the Court of Appeal or a judge of the court determines an application for a legal aid order by refusing to make a legal aid order, the Registrar shall not make a legal aid order except where the court or judge refused to make a legal aid order unless the applicant first made a payment as aforesaid and such payment is made.

(10) In this Regulation the expression "legal aid order" means a legal aid order within the meaning of paragraph (1) of this Regulation.

Statement of means

4.—(1) A statement of means submitted by an applicant shall be in Form 4 in the Schedule to these Regulations.

(2) Where the applicant is an infant, a statement of means submitted by any person other than the applicant shall be in Form 5 in the Schedule to these Regulations.

(3) If an applicant does not furnish a statement of means at the time that he makes an application for legal aid, he shall be required to do so by the proper officer of the court to whom or to whose court he is making the application, unless he has already submitted such a statement in pursuance of a previous application in respect of the same case.

General powers to make legal aid order

5. Subject to the provisions of Regulation 4 of these Regulations, nothing in Regulation 1, 2 or 3 of these Regulations shall affect the power of a court or a judge of the court or the Registrar (subject to the provisions of section 75 of the Act) to make a legal aid order, whether an application has been made for legal aid or not, or the right of an applicant whose application has been refused to apply to the court at the trial or other proceedings.

Legal aid orders

6.—(1) A legal aid order shall be in Form 6 in the Schedule to these Regulations.

(2) A copy of such order shall be delivered or sent to the solicitor assigned or to counsel (where counsel only is assigned).

(3) When a legal aid order has been made or an application for legal aid has been refused, the proper officer of the court to which the application is made shall forthwith notify the applicant.

(4)(*a*) An order amending a legal aid order under section 80(1) of the Act shall be in Form 7 in the Schedule to these Regulations.

(*b*) A copy of the amending order shall be sent or delivered to the solicitor assigned by such order or to counsel (where counsel only is assigned) and to the solicitor and counsel assigned by the order which is amended.

(*c*) A copy of the order which is amended shall be sent or delivered to the solicitor assigned by the amending order or to counsel (where counsel only is assigned by such order).

(*d*) The legally assisted person shall be notified that the order has been amended.

(5)(*a*) An order revoking a legal aid order under section 80(2) of the Act shall be in Form 8 in the Schedule to these Regulations.

(*b*) A copy of an order revoking a legal aid order shall be sent or delivered to the legally assisted person and to the solicitor and counsel assigned under the order which is revoked.

(6) Where a legal aid order is amended in accordance with paragraph (4) of this Regulation, counsel originally assigned shall send or deliver forthwith to the solicitor who instructed him, or (where counsel only was assigned) to the counsel newly assigned, all papers and other things in his possession relating to the proceedings and the solicitor originally assigned shall send or deliver all papers and other things in his possession relating to the proceedings to the solicitor newly assigned (or to counsel, if counsel only is assigned by the amending order).

(7) Where a legal aid order is revoked in accordance with paragraph (5) of this Regulation, the counsel assigned shall send or deliver all papers and other things in his possession relating to those proceedings to the solicitor assigned or (where no solicitor is assigned) to the legally assisted person and the solicitor assigned shall send or deliver all papers and other things in his possession relating to the proceedings to the legally assisted person.

Exclusion of solicitors and counsel

7.—(1) The proper officer of each court shall keep a list of solicitors and counsel, notified to him by the Secretary of State, who are for the time being excluded from acting for legally assisted persons under section 82 of the Act.

(2) Any reference in these Regulations to solicitors or counsel shall not apply to solicitors or counsel so excluded.

Assignment of solicitor

8. Subject to the provisions of Regulations 11 and 14 of these Regulations, any person in respect of whom a legal aid order is made, entitling him to the services of a solicitor, may select any solicitor who is willing to act and such solicitor shall be assigned to him.

Selection of counsel

9. Where a legal aid order is made in respect of the services of solicitor and counsel, the solicitor may instruct any counsel who is willing to act:

Provided that in the case of proceedings in the Court of Appeal or House of Lords, counsel may be assigned by the court or person making or amending the legal aid order.

Assignment of counsel only

10.—(1) Where a legal aid order in respect of proceedings in a court of assize or quarter sessions is made or amended so as to provide for representation by counsel only, counsel shall be assigned by the court or person making or amending the legal aid order.

(2) Where a legal aid order in respect of proceedings in the Court of Appeal is made or amended so as to provide for representation by counsel only, counsel shall be assigned by the court, a judge of the court or the Registrar.

Assignment of counsel for House of Lords or Court of Appeal

11. In assigning counsel or solicitor to a legally assisted person in respect of an appeal to the House of Lords or Court of Appeal, the court, the judge of the court or the Registrar shall have regard, as far as is reasonably practicable, to the wishes of the legally assisted person, the identity of the solicitor or counsel, if any, who represented him in any earlier proceedings and the nature of the appeal.

Commencement of legal aid order

12. In making a legal aid order in respect of proceedings in the Court of Appeal, the court, a judge of the court or the Registrar, as the case may be, may specify the stage of the proceedings at which the legal aid shall commence.

Assignment of two counsel

13.—(1) Except as provided by paragraph (2) of this Regulation, a legal aid order shall not provide for the services of more than one counsel.

(2) In trials at assizes or quarter sessions or appeals to the House of Lords or the Court of Appeal, an order may provide for the services of two counsel—

    (*a*) on a charge of murder; or

    (*b*) where it appears to the court or person making the legal aid order that the case is one of exceptional difficulty, gravity or complexity and that the interests of justice require that the legally assisted person shall have the services of two counsel.

(3) Where, in such case as is specified in paragraph (2) of this Regulation, a legal aid order provides for the services of one counsel, it may be amended to provide for the services of two counsel.

Assignment of one solicitor or counsel to more than one legally assisted person

14. A solicitor or counsel may be assigned to two or more legally assisted persons whose cases are heard together, unless the interests of justice require that such persons be separately represented.

Documents

15. Where a notice of application for leave to appeal or a notice of appeal has been given to the Court of Appeal, copies of documents (including transcripts) may be supplied by the Registrar in accordance with rules made under the Criminal Appeal Act 1968(a).

Notes of evidence and depositions

16. Where a legal aid order is made in respect of an appeal to quarter sessions, the justices' clerk shall supply, on the application of the solicitor assigned to the appellant or respondent on whose application such an order was made, copies of any notes of evidence or depositions taken in the proceedings in the magistrates' court.

Transfer of documents

17. Where a person is committed by a lower court to a higher court or appeals or applies for leave to appeal from a lower court to a higher court, the proper

---

(a) 1968 c. 19.

officer of the lower court shall send to the proper officer of the higher court the following documents (if any):—

(a) a copy of any legal aid order previously made in the same case;

(b) a copy of any contribution order previously made;

(c) a copy of any legal aid application which has been refused;

(d) any statement of means already submitted.

Payments on account of contributions

18.—(1) Where a person is ordered under section 75(3) of the Act, to make a payment on account of any contribution towards costs, such payment on account shall be made to the proper officer of the court ordering such payment unless that court directs otherwise.

(2) Where such payment is made otherwise than to the appropriate authority, the person receiving such payment shall forward it to the appropriate authority.

Delivery of contribution orders

19.—(1) Where a contribution order is made, it shall be in Form 9 in the Schedule to these Regulations, a copy shall be sent or delivered to the legally assisted person and, if the order is made by a court other than a magistrates' court, a copy shall be sent by the proper officer of the court making the order to the appropriate authority.

(2) Where a payment on account has been made and a contribution order is not made by the court or person empowered in that behalf, the proper officer of that court shall notify the appropriate authority and the legally assisted person.

Assessment of contribution as proportion of taxed costs

20.—(1) Where a contribution order is made in respect of proceedings in a court other than a magistrates' court on such terms that the amount payable by the legally assisted person cannot be assessed without reference to the actual legal aid costs, the proper officer of that court shall send to the appropriate authority particulars of the amount of taxed costs in that court.

(2) Where a contribution order on such terms as aforesaid is made in respect of proceedings in a magistrates' court, the appropriate authority shall notify the Law Society, which shall send the appropriate authority particulars of the legal aid costs payable out of the legal aid fund.

(3) The appropriate authority on receipt of the aforesaid particulars shall notify the legally assisted person of the amount of the contribution payable by him.

Reference to Supplementary Benefits Commission

21. Where a legally assisted person in respect of whom a contribution order may be or has been made wishes the Supplementary Benefits Commission (hereinafter referred to as "the Commission") to enquire into his means, application may be made to the court having power to make or vary the order, either in court, during or immediately after consideration by the court as to whether such an order should be made, or in writing to the proper officer of the court within one month of the contribution order being made.

LEGAL AID AND ADVICE, ENGLAND

Forms and procedure of Supplementary Benefits Commission

22.—(1) A request to the Commission to enquire into the means of any person shall be in Form 10 in the Schedule to these Regulations and be accompanied by—

(*a*) the statement of means of the legally assisted person;

(*b*) the statement of means of a person referred to in Regulation 4(2) of these Regulations, where one has been submitted.

(2) Where such a request is made, the Commission may require from the legally assisted person such further information (including any documents) as it may think necessary for a proper inquiry and may require such person to attend at an office of the Ministry of Social Security for this purpose.

Variation of contribution orders

23.—(1) Any power of a court to make a contribution order after receiving a report from the Commission or to revoke or otherwise vary a contribution order made before receiving such a report may be exercised by any person entitled to sit as a member of the court.

(2) Any power of a court to revoke or reduce the amount of a contribution order made before receiving such a report may, if the court so authorises either generally or in a particular case, be exercised by the proper officer.

(3) An order revoking or otherwise varying a contribution order shall be in Form 11 in the Schedule to these Regulations.

(4) A copy of such an order shall be sent to the appropriate authority and the legally assisted person.

(5) Where, after such a report as aforesaid has been received, a contribution order is not made, the proper officer shall inform the legally assisted person.

(6) Where a contribution order made before receiving such a report is not revoked or otherwise varied, the proper officer shall inform the legally assisted person and the appropriate authority.

Stay of enforcement of contribution orders

24. Where a reference is made to the Commission after a contribution order has been made, the proper officer of the court, other than a magistrates' court making the reference, shall inform the appropriate authority and no action shall be taken thereafter to enforce the order, until the appropriate authority has been informed of the result of the reference.

Refund of payments on account

25.—(1) Where a payment on account has been made and a court having power to make a contribution order does not do so or that court or the proper officer or a person entitled to sit as a member of that court revokes a contribution order, the payment made on account shall be refunded to the legally assisted person by the appropriate authority.

(2) Where a contribution order is made or varied so that the amount ordered to be paid is less than any amount paid on account, the difference between the said amounts shall be refunded to the legally assisted person by the appropriate authority.

Disposal of sums received from legally assisted persons after conviction

26. Where a legally assisted person is ordered to pay any sum adjudged to be paid by a conviction and is also ordered to make a contribution in respect of legal aid, any payment on account received by a magistrates' court shall, unless the person paying the money specifically appropriates such payment or any part of it to payment of the contribution, be applied in the first place in accordance with the provisions of section 114 of the Magistrates' Courts Act 1952(a) and any sums paid in addition to the sums adjudged to be paid by conviction shall be paid to the Secretary of State in accordance with section 79(8) of the Act.

Recovery of costs

27. Where a court makes an order that the costs of a legally aided person shall be paid by any other person, the proper officer of that court shall notify the authority from whose funds the costs of legal aid are to be paid, or, in the case of an order made by a magistrates' court, the Law Society, of the order and of the name and address of the person by whom the costs are to be paid.

Enforcement of orders for payment of costs

28. Where a person ordered to pay the costs of a legally aided person does not pay them in accordance with section 79(1) of the Act, they may be recovered summarily by the aforesaid authority referred to in Regulation 27 of these Regulations or the Law Society, as the case may be, as a sum adjudged to be paid as a civil debt by order of a magistrates' court.

Notification of fund into which costs are to be paid

29. Where any court makes such an order as is referred to in Regulation 27 of these Regulations, the court shall cause the person against whom the order is made to be informed of the fund into which the payment must be made in accordance with section 79(1) of the Act.

Legal aid records

30.—(1) The proper officer of each court shall keep a record, in the manner and form directed from time to time by the Secretary of State, of all cases in which an application for legal aid was made to the court or a legal aid order was made, under Regulation 5 of these Regulations, by the court without application; and shall send to the Secretary of State such information from such record as the Secretary of State shall from time to time direct.

(2) The proper officer of each court shall send to the Secretary of State a copy of every contribution order made by his court.

Interpretation

31.—(1) In these Regulations, unless the context otherwise requires—

"the Act" means the Criminal Justice Act 1967;

"appropriate authority" has the meaning assigned to it by section 84 of the Act";

"contribution order" means an order made by a court under section 76 of the Act;

(a) 1952 c. 55.

"Court of Appeal" means the criminal division of the Court of Appeal;

"judge of the court" means—

(i) in the case of the Court of Appeal, a Lord Justice of Appeal or a judge of the Queen's Bench Division of the High Court;

(ii) in the case of quarter sessions, the chairman or a deputy chairman or the recorder or a deputy or assistant recorder;

"legal aid fund" has the meaning assigned to it by section 84 of the Act;

"legal aid order" means an order made under section 73 of the Act and includes an order made solely for the purpose described in section 74(8) of the Act;

"legally assisted person" has the meaning assigned to it by section 73(9) of the Act;

"proper officer" means the Clerk of the Parliaments, the Registrar of Criminal Appeals, the clerk of assize or of the peace or the justices' clerk (as the case may be);

"Registrar" means the Registrar of Criminal Appeals;

"statement of means" means a statement of means submitted in accordance with Regulation 4 of these Regulations.

(2) The Interpretation Act 1889(a) shall apply to the interpretation of these Regulations as it applies to the interpretation of an Act of Parliament.

Determination in private and in absence of legally assisted person

32. Where it is provided by these Regulations that any matter may be determined otherwise than by a court, it may be determined in private and in the absence of the applicant or legally assisted person.

Forms

33. The forms set out in the Schedule to these Regulations may be used with such variation as the circumstances may require.

Citation and commencement

34.—(1) These Regulations may be cited as the Legal Aid in Criminal Proceedings (General) Regulations 1968.

(2) These Regulations shall come into operation on 1st October 1968.

James Callaghan,
One of Her Majesty's Principal
Secretaries of State.

Home Office,
  Whitehall.
31st July 1968.

(a) 1889 c. 63.

SCHEDULE

FORMS

FORM 1

Application for legal aid (magistrates' court)

(Criminal Justice Act 1967, s.73; General Reg. 1)

I, (a)..
apply for legal aid for the purpose of the following proceedings before the
(a) Full name in BLOCK letters. State whether Mr., Mrs., Miss.

....Magistrates' Court:

(b) ....
(b) State reason for your appearance in the magistrates' court, e.g., charge of theft, alleged failure to comply with a requirement of a probation order or a condition of a recognizance.

....

(c)My case is due to be heard on..

(d)Special circumstances..

....
(c) Insert date if known.

....
(d) Set out here any special circumstances which you feel might qualify you for legal aid.

My permanent address is..

....

My present address (where different from above) is...............................

....

....

My trade or occupation is..

I was born on..

I attach a statement of my means.

I understand that I may be required by the Supplementary Benefits Commission to supply further information about my means. I also understand that the court may order me to make a contribution to the costs of legal aid or to pay the whole costs if it considers that my means enable me to do so.

The solicitor whom I wish to act for me is(e)....................................
(e) If you do not wish to select a particular solicitor leave this space blank.

.... of ....

(Signed)..

FORM 2

Application for legal aid (assizes or quarter sessions)

(Criminal Justice Act 1967, s.73; General Reg. 2)

(a) Full name in BLOCK letters. State whether Mr., Mrs., Miss.

I, (a) ....
apply for legal aid for the following purpose:

(1) On............................I was committed for trial and need legal aid for my defence;

(b) Delete as necessary. If legal aid is required for a purpose not mentioned at (1), (2) or (3) describe this at (4). Insert date of conviction or committal if known.

(b)

(2) On............................I was convicted by the......................
Magistrates' Court and committed to assizes/quarter sessions for sentence or to be otherwise dealt with and need legal aid;

(3) I need legal aid for an appeal to quarter sessions against my conviction and/or sentence on...
by the ....Magistrates' Court;

(4) I need legal aid for...

....

(c) Set out here any special circumstances which you feel qualify you for legal aid.

(c)Special circumstances...

....

My permanent address is...

....

My present address (where different from above) is..............................

....

....

My trade or occupation is...

I was born on...

(d) Delete as necessary. If you have already furnished a statement of means at an earlier stage of the case, a further statement will not be required unless your financial position has changed.

I (d) attach a statement of my means.

have already furnished a statement of my means to the clerk to the justices...and there has been no change in my financial position.

I understand that I may be required by the Supplementary Benefits Commission to supply further information about my means. I also understand that the court may order me to make a contribution to the costs of legal aid or to pay the whole costs if it considers that my means enable me to do so.

(e) If you do not wish to select a particular solicitor leave this space blank.

The solicitor whom I wish to act for me is(e)......................................

.... of ....

(Signed)..

FORM 3

Notice of application for legal aid in Court of Appeal

(Criminal Justice Act 1967, s.73; General Reg. 3)

To the Registrar,
Criminal Appeal Office,
Royal Courts of Justice,
Strand,
London, W.C.2.

PART 1

Particulars of appellant:

| | Forenames | Surname | Age on conviction |

Full names:
(Block letters)
Address:
(If detained give address
where detained and, if
detained in prison, give
prison number).

Court where tried and/or sentenced:
Dates of appearances at the Court   Name of
including dates of conviction (if   Court
convicted at the Court) and sen-
tence.   Name of Judge

Particulars of offences of which convicted: whether convicted on indictment or
by a magistrates' court: particulars of sentences and orders:

Offences	Convicted on indictment or by magistrates' court	Sentences and orders
....	....	....
....	....	....
....	....	....
....	....	....
....	....	....
....	....	....

Offences taken into consideration when sentenced.
Total sentence.

PART 2

Particulars of application

I wish to apply for legal aid.

Signed...

Date..

FORM 3A

Notice of application for legal aid in the House of Lords

(Criminal Justice Act 1967, s.73; General Reg. 3)

To the Registrar,
Criminal Appeal Office,
Royal Courts of Justice,
Strand,
London, W.C.2.

Full names of the applicant..

Criminal appeal reference number...

Date of decision of the Criminal Division of the Court of Appeal

....

Name and address of place at which applicant detained or, if not detained, applicant's address.

....

....

....

I apply for legal aid for the purpose of—
    *(a) appealing to the House of Lords against the above decision;
    *(b) opposing the appeal by the prosecutor.

    *Delete as necessary.

                              Signed...

                              Date...

FORM 4

Statement of means (Criminal Justice Act 1967, s.75;
General Reg. 4)

IMPORTANT—You should study this form very carefully. Failure to answer any question may lead to delay in the consideration of your application for legal aid. The information given below may be verified by the Supplementary Benefits Commission. ANY PERSON WHO IN COMPLETING THIS FORM KNOWINGLY OR RECKLESSLY MAKES A STATEMENT WHICH IS FALSE IN A MATERIAL PARTICULAR OR KNOWINGLY FAILS TO DISCLOSE ANY MATERIAL FACT IS LIABLE TO PROSECUTION AND, ON CONVICTION, TO IMPRISONMENT FOR A TERM NOT EXCEEDING FOUR MONTHS, OR A FINE NOT EXCEEDING £100, OR BOTH.

If after you have applied for legal aid there is any material change in your resources before the conclusion of the case you are required to inform the court. *All* applicants must complete Part 1.

PART 1

1. Full Name...
   (Block letters)

2. Date of Birth.....................   3. (ª)Married/Widow/Widower/Single/   (a) Delete as
                               Married but living apart/Divorced.   necessary.

4. Occupation (if unemployed, state occupation when last employed and how
   long you have been unemployed)..

5. Present Address...
   ....
   ....
   ....

If you are under the age of twenty-one, are you being wholly or mainly maintained by your parents or guardian? (Yes or No).....................................

If your answer is "Yes", your parents or guardian should be asked to complete a separate statement of means on Form 5, in addition to the statement of your means on this form.

If you are single, or a widower/widow, or divorced or living apart from your husband/wife.

(a) Are you receiving a supplementary pension or allowance from the Supplementary Benefits Commission?
                                         (Yes or No)...............

   If your answer is "Yes", you need not complete the remainder of this form but you should sign the declaration at the end of Part 1 of this form.

(b) Was your income from all sources during the past twelve months, after deducting income tax and national insurance contributions, £250 or less?
                                         (Yes or No)............

(c) Is your capital, if any, £25 or less?   (Yes or No)............

   If your answer to *both* (b) and (c) is "Yes", you need not complete the remainder of this form but you should sign the declaration at the end of Part 1 of this form.

FORM 4—continued

If you are married and living with your wife/husband.

(d) Are you or your wife/husband receiving a supplementary pension or allowance from the Supplementary Benefits Commission?

(Yes or No)...............

If your answer is "Yes", you need not complete the remainder of this form
but you should sign the declaration at the end of Part 1 of this form.

(e) Was the joint income of your wife/husband and yourself from all sources
during the past twelve months after deducting any income tax or national
insurance contributions £450 or less?

(Yes or No)...............

(f) Is your joint capital, if any, £40 or less?

(Yes or No)...............

If your answer to *both* (e) and (f) is "Yes", you need not complete the remainder of this form but you should sign the declaration at the end of Part 1
of this form.

I declare that to the best of my knowledge and belief, the information given
above is correct.

Signature...

Date...

*If you or your wife/husband are not receiving a supplementary pension or
allowance, and your answer to either of the questions about your income or capital
is "No", you must complete the remainder of this form.*

FOR OFFICIAL USE ONLY

PART 2—INCOME

State below particulars of your income from all sources and (if you are married and living with your wife/husband) particulars of her/his income. State against each item of income whether the amount is a weekly, monthly or annual one. The income declared should be the *net* amount after deduction of income tax and national insurance contributions. If only the *gross* figure is known write GROSS against the amount concerned.

Description of Income	Amount		Remarks
	Your Income	Income of wife/husband	
1. Wages or salary including over-time, commission and bonuses			
2. If in business on your own account, average profit.			
3. Family allowances.			
4. National insurance benefit or pension.			
5. Income from sub-letting house, rooms etc.			
6. Other income (give details).			

1.

Write "None" where appropriate.

PART 3—CAPITAL OR SAVINGS

Give below particulars of all your capital or savings. If you are married and your wife/husband is living with you, give details of her/his capital and savings also.

	Yourself	Wife/husband
1. Do you or your wife/husband own house property? If so, state:— (a) the capital value (i.e. approximate selling price) (b) the amount of any outstanding mortgage. (c) whether you are living in the house.	Yes/No. .... Yes/No.	Yes/No. ....
2. Give particulars of all capital or savings belonging to you or your wife/husband. You should state the amount and description (e.g. Post Office Savings Bank or other Bank, National Savings Certificates, cash).		

2.

3.

Write "None" where appropriate.

PART 4—EXPENSES

In assessing your means for legal aid purposes the court will make allowances for your outgoings on the maintenance of your wife (husband) and family and other dependent relatives, the cost of your accommodation, reasonable expenses in connection with your employment and other special expenses such as hire purchase payments. You should give the necessary information below.

(1) *Maintenance of dependants* (*Wife, children and other dependent relatives*). A husband or a single person should set out the persons actually dependent on him. A wife living with her husband should include her husband and children dependent on him, but if she is not living with her husband she should include only such children as she is actually supporting.

(a) *Living with you.*

Name	Age	Relationship	Whether fully dependent on you; if not, state means of dependant
....	....	....	....
....	....	....	....
....	....	....	....
....	....	....	....

(b) *Not living with you.*

Name	Age	Relationship	Weekly amounts of your payments for maintenance
....	....	....	....
....	....	....	....
....	....	....	....

4.

(2) *Living accommodation.*
How much do you pay for your living accommmodation..........................
(Include rent, rates, mortgage payments and interest etc.)
If you neither pay rent nor own the house in which you live, what weekly payments do you make for the keep of yourself and any dependants
....

(3) *Expenses in connection with employment.*
State what expenses you incur in connection with your employment (e.g. travelling expenses)..........

(4) *Other special expenses.*
Give particulars below of any special expenses (other than ordinary living expenses) such as hire purchase payments, insurance premiums, repayment of outstanding debts. In the case of hire purchase, state amount of weekly or monthly payments and the date on which last payment is due and specify the nature of the goods. In the case of insurance premiums, in addition to stating amount of premium (and whether weekly, monthly or yearly), state sum insured and date policy taken out.

....
....
....

5.

6.

7.

8.

FOR OFFICIAL
USE ONLY

PART 5—ADDITIONAL INFORMATION

Give below any additional information which you think the court should
know about your financial circumstances, including any changes which are
likely to occur within the next twelve months.

....   9.

....

....

....

....

....   10.

PART 6—DECLARATION   11.

I DECLARE that, to the best of my knowledge and belief, the information
given above is a complete and correct statement of my financial position   12.
[and that of my spouse(a)] and that I have no income, savings or capital
except as shown.

(a) Delete
as nec-
essary.

Signature ....

Date ....   13.

14.

15.

FORM 5

Statement of means of person financially responsible for
applicant (*Criminal Justice Act* 1967, *s.*78(2);
General Reg. 4).

If you are the parent of an applicant for legal aid or have the care and control of or are otherwise liable to maintain the applicant, you are requested to complete this form and return it to the clerk of the court to which the applicant has applied for legal aid.

PART 1

1. Name and address of applicant...

....

....

2. Your full name and address...

....

....

3. Your relationship to applicant...

4. Your occupation (if unemployed state occupation when last employed and how long you have been unemployed)...

....

5. (a) Are you or your wife/husband receiving a supplementary pension or allowance from the Supplementary Benefits Commission?

(Yes or No) ....

If your answer is "Yes", you need not complete the remainder of this form but you should sign the declaration at the end of Part 1 of this form.

If you are living with your wife/husband.

(b) Was your joint income from all sources during the past twelve months, after deducting any income tax and national insurance contributions, £450 or less?

(Yes or No) ....

(c) Is your joint capital, if any, £40 or less?

(Yes or No) ....

If your answer to *both* (b) and (c) is "Yes", you need not complete the remainder of this form, but you should sign the declaration at the end of Part 1 of this form.

If you are single, or a widower/widow, or divorced or living apart from your husband/wife.

(d) Was your income from all sources during the past twelve months, after deducting any income tax and national insurance contributions, £250 or less?

(Yes or No) ....

(e) Is your capital, if any, £25 or less?

(Yes or No) ....

If your answer to *both* (d) and (e) is "Yes", you need not complete the remainder of this form, but you should sign the declaration at the foot of Part 1 of this form.

I declare that to the best of my knowledge and belief the information given above is correct.

Signature..

Date...

If you or your wife/husband are not receiving a supplementary pension or allowance, and your answer to either of the questions about your income or capital is "No", you should complete the remainder of this form.

PART 2—INCOME

State below particulars of your income from all sources and (if you are married and living with your wife/husband) particulars of her/his income. State against each item of income whether the amount is a weekly, monthly or annual one. The income declared should be the *net* amount after deduction of income tax and national insurance contributions. If only the *gross* figure is known write GROSS against the amount concerned.

| Description of Income | Amount | | Remarks |
	Your Income	Income of wife/husband	
1. Wages or salary including over-time, commission and bonuses.			
2. If in business on your own account, average profit.			
3. Family allowances.			
4. National insurance benefit or pension.			
5. Income from sub-letting house, rooms etc.			
6. Other income (give details)			1.

Write "None" where appropriate.

PART 3—CAPITAL OR SAVINGS

Give below particulars of all your capital or savings. If you are married and your wife/husband is living with you, give details of her/his capital and savings also.

	Yourself	Wife/husband	
1. Do you or your wife/husband own house property? If so, state:— (a) the capital value (i.e. approximate selling price) (b) the amount of any outstanding mortgage. (c) whether you are living in the house.	Yes/No. .... Yes/No.	Yes/No.	2.
2. Give particulars of all capital or savings belonging to you or your wife/husband. You should state the amount and description (e.g. Post Office Savings Bank or other Bank, National Savings Certificates, cash).			3.

Write "None" where appropriate.

PART 4—EXPENSES

In assessing your means for legal aid purposes the court will make allowances for your outgoings on the maintenance of your wife (husband) and family and other dependent relatives, the cost of your accommodation, reasonable expenses in connection with your employment and other special expenses such as hire purchase payments. You should give the necessary information below.

(1) *Maintenance of dependants* (*Wife, children and other dependent relatives*). A husband or a single person should set out the persons actually dependent on him. A wife living with her husband should include her husband and children dependent on him, but if she is not living with her husband she should include only such children as she is actually supporting.

(a) *Living with you.*

Name	Age	Relationship	Whether fully dependent on you; if not, state means of dependant
....	....	....	....
....	....	....	....
....	....	....	....
....	....	....	....

(b) *Not living with you.*

Name	Age	Relationship	Weekly amounts of your payments for maintenance
....	....	....	....
....	....	....	....
....	....	....	....
....	....	....	....

4.

(2) *Living accommodation.*
How much do you pay for your living accommodation...........................
(Include rent, rates, mortgage payments and interest etc.)
If you neither pay rent nor own the house in which you live, what weekly payments do you make for the keep of yourself and any dependants
....

(3) *Expenses in connection with employment.*
State what expenses you incur in connection with your employment (e.g. travelling expenses)...

(4) *Other special expenses.*
Give particulars below of any special expenses (other than ordinary living expenses) such as hire purchase payments, insurance premiums, repayment of outstanding debts. In the case of hire purchase, state amount of weekly or monthly payments and the date on which last payment is due and specify the nature of the goods. In the case of insurance premiums, in addition to stating amount of premium (and whether weekly, monthly or yearly), state sum insured and date policy taken out.
....
....
....

5.

6.

7.

8.

	FOR OFFICIAL USE ONLY

Part 5—Additional Information

Give below any additional information which you think the court should know about your financial circumstances, including any changes which are likely to occur within the next twelve months.

....   **9.**

....

....

....

....

....   **10.**

Part 6—Declaration   **11.**

I DECLARE that, to the best of my knowledge and belief, the information given above is a complete and correct statement of my financial position [and that of my spouse(a)] and that I have no income, savings or capital except as shown.

12.   (a) Delete as necessary.

Signature ....

Date ....

13.

14.

15.

FORM 6

Legal aid order (Criminal Justice Act 1967, ss.73, 75;

General Reg. 6).

In accordance with the provisions of sections 73 and 75 of the Criminal Justice Act 1967 the...

(a) Delete (1) to (8) as necessary.
Court hereby grants legal aid to... for the following purpose(a):

(b) State charge etc.
(1) Proceedings before a magistrates' court in connection with(b).....................

....

(2) Appealing to a court of quarter sessions against a decision of the .... Magistrates' Court on ....

(3) Resisting an appeal to a court of quarter sessions against a decision of the .... Magistrates' Court on...

(c) State nature of proceedings.
(4) Proceedings before a court of assize or quarter sessions in connection with(c)..

....

including, in the event of his being convicted or sentenced in those proceedings, advice and assistance in regard to the making of an appeal to the criminal division of the Court of Appeal as provided in section 74(7) of the Criminal Justice Act 1967.

(5) An appeal to the Court of Appeal and any proceedings preliminary or incidental thereto.

(6) Advice by counsel or solicitor assigned by the Court of Appeal on the question whether there appear to be reasonable grounds of appeal and assistance by that counsel or solicitor in the preparation of an application for leave to appeal or the giving of a notice of appeal.

(7) An appeal to the House of Lords and any proceedings preliminary or incidental hereto.

(8) A retrial by a court of assize or quarter sessions ordered by the Court of Appeal or the House of Lords.

Except as otherwise provided above, the legal aid granted shall consist of representation by a solicitor/solicitor and counsel/solicitor and two counsel/ counsel only(d), including advice on the preparation of the case for the proceedings.

The solicitor assigned is..
of ....

(d) Delete as necessary.
The legally aided person has paid the sum of £   s.   d. to..................... ....as a payment on account of any contribution which he may be ordered to make at the conclusion of the case.

The legally assisted person has been committed to................................ ....prison/released on bail and may be communicated with at(d) ....

....

(e) Signature and designation of clerk to court.
Dated this...............................day of................... 19......

(Signed)(e)...

FORM 7

Order amending legal aid order

(Criminal Justice Act 1967, *s.*80; *General Reg.* 6)

The...court hereby amends the order......

granting legal aid to...

....

of ....

by substituting for the solicitor(a) named in the order another solicitor, namely   (a) Where counsel only is assigned by the order, amend accordingly.

....

of ....

/and by authorising the instruction of counsel in place of the counsel already   (b) Delete as necessary.

instructed.(b)

Dated this....................................day of...............19......

Signed(c)...   (c) Signature and designation of clerk to court.

2j

FORM 8

Order revoking legal aid order

(*Criminal Justice Act* 1967, *s.*80, *General Reg.* 6)

The.. court hereby
revokes, as from this date, the order granting legal aid to...........................
....
of ....
....for the purpose of ....
....

Dated this.............................day of.....................19......

(a) Signature
and designation
of clerk to
court.

Signature(a)...

NOTE TO LEGALLY ASSISTED PERSON

You are no longer entitled to legal aid. Your solicitor and counsel (if any) will cease to act further for you unless you yourself re-employ them and if you do so you will be responsible for their costs from the above date. The court has power to order you to pay a contribution towards any legal aid costs already incurred on your behalf.

FORM 9

Contribution order

(*Criminal Justice Act* 1967, *s.* 76, *General Reg.* 19)

To(ᵃ) ....   (a) Name and
                                                                                                     address of
of ....   legally assisted
                                                                                                     person.
....

By virtue of the powers contained in section 76 of the Criminal Justice Act
1967 the..
....(name of court) hereby
orders you to pay in respect of the legal aid provided for you under legal aid
order(s) no.(s)............:—   (b) Delete as
                                                                                                     necessary.

(ᵇ) ⎰ a contribution of £...............towards the costs
    ⎱ the whole costs amounting to £...............
    ⎰ *the whole costs, or £............, whichever is less.

This sum should be paid to the Clerk to the Justices,..............................
Magistrates' Court..(ᵇ) on or before
....(ᵇ) in ....
instalments of ...., the first to be paid on or before
...., the
second and subsequent instalments to be paid ....
....

(ᶜ)Signed...   (c) Signature
                                                                                                     and designation
                                                                                                     of clerk to the
                                                                                                     court.
....

(Date)..

*You will be informed of the amount payable as soon as the legal aid costs
incurred are known.

FORM 10

Reference to Supplementary Benefits Commission

(*Criminal Justice Act* 1967, *s.*77; *General Reg.* 22)

To: The Manager,
Legal Aid Assessment
Office,
Ministry of Social
Security,
....
....
....
....
....
....

Name and
Address of Court

Date...
Reference...

Dear Sir,

Name of legally assisted person...
(or applicant)

Present address (if different from..
that shown in Form 4).   ....

Address of wife/husband where known..
(if different from above).   ....

The attached statement(s) of means is/are referred for enquiry and report as to means. This request is made:—

(a) Delete as appropriate.

(a) { on the application of the legally assisted person.
{ by the court without application by the legally assisted person.

(b) Leave blank if no assessment has yet been made.

(b) The legally assisted person's resources were assessed for the purpose of a contribution order on...(date).

....

Yours faithfully,

(c) Signature and designation of clerk to court.

(c)Signed ....

FORM 11

Variation or revocation of contribution order

(*Criminal Justice Act* 1967, *s.* 77; *General Reg.* 23)

To(ª) ....
of ....
....

(a) Name and address of legally assisted person.

Having considered a report on your means by the Supplementary Benefits
Commission the..
court hereby revokes/varies as follows(ᵇ) contribution order no.....................
made on...

(b) Delete as necessary.

(ᵇ)The total amount which you are required to pay towards the costs of legal
aid shall be.....................   This sum should be paid to the Clerk
to the Justices,..
Magistrates' Court,...on or before
....
in..................................instalments of.............................,
the first to be paid on or before..,
the second and subsequent instalments to be paid...............................

(ᶜ)Signed...

(c) Signature and designation of clerk to court.

....

(Date)...

EXPLANATORY NOTE

(*This Note is not part of the Regulations.*)

Part IV of the Criminal Justice Act 1967 makes fresh provision for the granting of legal aid in criminal proceedings. These Regulations relate to all matters not otherwise covered by regulations made under that Part. Regulations 1 to 4 set out the procedure to be adopted (including the submission of a statement of means) in applying for legal aid in the various courts. Regulation 6 relates to the contents and disposal of a legal aid order. Regulations 7 to 14 relate to the assignment of solicitors and counsel. Regulations 15 to 17 relate to the provision of documents to legally assisted persons and their legal representatives and to the forwarding of documents to courts. Regulations 18 to 20 relate to the making of orders requiring the legally assisted person to contribute to the legal aid costs. Regulations 21 to 24 set out the procedure to be adopted when the Supplementary Benefits Commission is requested to report on the means of an applicant or legally assisted person. Regulations 25 and 26 relate to the disposal of sums received by courts either as payments on account of contributions or as a result of contribution orders. Regulations 27 to 29 relate to the recovery of any costs ordered to be paid to a legally assisted person. Regulation 30 relates to the keeping of records.

STATUTORY INSTRUMENTS

1968 No. 1232

EXCHANGE CONTROL

The Exchange Control (Declarations and Evidence) Order 1968

Made - - - - 1st *August* 1968
Coming into Operation 8th *August* 1968

The Treasury, in exercise of the powers conferred upon them by sections 8(1), 9(1), 13(*a*), 15(5), 16(1), 36(5) and 42 of the Exchange Control Act 1947(**a**), hereby make the following Order :—

1.—(1) The prescribed evidence for the purposes of section 8(1)(*b*) of the Exchange Control Act 1947 (hereinafter called ' the said Act '), to be produced to the person issuing the security, is evidence that the person to whom the security is to be issued is not resident outside the scheduled territories and from facts known to the person giving the evidence or from enquiries made by that person is not to the best of his belief acquiring the security as the nominee of any person resident outside the scheduled territories.

(2) The evidence shall be given by a declaration in writing signed by or on behalf of the person to whom the security is to be issued.

2. The prescribed evidence for the purposes of section 13(*a*) of the said Act, to be produced to a person concerned with the keeping of a register in the United Kingdom or the Channel Islands, is—

(*a*) in the case of the issue of securities, the evidence prescribed by article 1 of this Order,

(*b*) in the case of the transfer of securities, the declaration prescribed by article 4 of this Order and evidence given by a declaration in writing signed by an authorised depositary that the transferee is not resident outside the scheduled territories and from facts known to the person giving the evidence or from enquiries made by that person is not to the best of his belief acquiring the security as the nominee of any person resident outside the scheduled territories, and

(*c*) in the case of the registration of securities transferable by means of bearer certificates, the evidence prescribed by article 1(1) of this Order given by a declaration in writing signed by an authorised depositary.

3. The prescribed evidence for the purposes of section 15(5) of the said Act, to be produced to an authorised depositary, is the evidence prescribed in the case of the transfer of securities by article 2(*b*) of this Order.

4. The prescribed declaration for the purposes of section 9(1)(*b*) of the said Act, to be delivered to the transferee at or before the time of the transfer, is a declaration in the form set out in Schedule 1 to this Order or in a form to the like effect made by an authorised depositary.

5. The prescribed declaration for the purposes of section 16(1)(*a*) of the said Act, to be delivered to an authorised depositary, is a declaration in the form set out in Schedule 2 to this Order or in a form to the like effect made by an authorised depositary.

(**a**) 1947 c. 14.

6. This Order shall extend to the Channel Islands, and any reference in this Order to the Exchange Control Act 1947 includes a reference to that Act as extended by the Exchange Control (Channel Islands) Order 1947(**a**).

7.—(1) In this Order the word ' securities ' has the meaning ascribed to it by section 42(1) of the Exchange Control Act 1947 as amended by section 55 of the Finance Act 1968(**b**) and includes secondary securities.

(2) The Interpretation Act 1889(**c**) shall apply for the interpretation of this Order as it applies for the interpretation of an Act of Parliament and as if this Order and the Orders hereby revoked were Acts of Parliament.

8. The Exchange Control (Declarations and Evidence) Order 1954(**d**) and the Exchange Control (Declarations and Evidence) (Amendment) Order 1968(**e**) are hereby revoked.

9. This Order may be cited as the Exchange Control (Declarations and Evidence) Order 1968, and shall come into operation on 8th August 1968.

Roy Jenkins,

Harry Gourlay,

Two of the Lords Commissioners
of Her Majesty's Treasury.

1st August 1968.

SCHEDULE 1

The holder of the above-mentioned security is not resident outside the scheduled territories and from facts known to us or from enquiries we have made is not to the best of our belief holding the security as the nominee of a person resident outside those territories.

SCHEDULE 2

We hereby declare that to our knowledge the security specified in the attached schedule—
    (i) is *not* included in the current ' List of Securities—The subject of claims by the Royal Netherlands Government or former Netherlands owners ' ; and
    (ii) is now and has always been since the 2nd September 1939 owned by a person resident in the United Kingdom.

EXPLANATORY NOTE

(This Note is not part of the Order.)

This Order consolidates and replaces the Orders revoked with one amendment, namely the incorporation of a definition of ' securities '. Section 55 of the Finance Act 1968 has the effect that certificates of deposit and Government bills (including Treasury bills) are now securities within the meaning of the Exchange Control Act 1947.

(**a**) S.R. & O. 1947/2034 (Rev. VI, p. 1001: 1947 I, p. 660).   (**b**) 1968 c. 44.
    (**c**) 1889 c. 63.   (**d**) S.I. 1954/1635 (1954 I, p. 818).
    (**e**) S.I. 1968/80 (1968 I, p. 264).

STATUTORY INSTRUMENTS

1968 No. 1233

EXCHANGE CONTROL

The Exchange Control (Specified Currency and Prescribed Securities) (Amendment) Order 1968

Made - - - -	*1st August* 1968
Laid before Parliament	*7th August* 1968
Coming into Operation	*8th August* 1968

The Treasury, in exercise of the powers conferred upon them by sections 17(1) and 36(5) of the Exchange Control Act 1947(a), hereby make the following Order:—

1. The Exchange Control (Specified Currency and Prescribed Securities) Order 1967(b) shall be amended by inserting the following article after article 3 thereof:—

"3A. In this Order the word 'securities' has the meaning ascribed to it by section 42(1) of the Exchange Control Act 1947 as amended by section 55 of the Finance Act 1968(c) and includes secondary securities."

2. This Order shall extend to the Channel Islands, and any reference in this Order to the Exchange Control Act 1947 includes a reference to that Act as extended by the Exchange Control (Channel Islands) Order 1947(d).

3. The Interpretation Act 1889(e) shall apply for the interpretation of this Order as it applies for the interpretation of an Act of Parliament.

4. This Order may be cited as the Exchange Control (Specified Currency and Prescribed Securities) (Amendment) Order 1968, and shall come into operation on 8th August 1968.

Roy Jenkins,
Harry Gourlay,
Two of the Lords Commissioners
of Her Majesty's Treasury.

1st August 1968.

(a) 1947 c. 14.   (b) S.I. 1967/556 (1967 I, p. 1771).   (c) 1968 c. 44.
(d) S.R. & O. 1947/2034 (Rev. VI, p. 1001: 1947 I, p. 660).   (e) 1889 c. 63.

EXPLANATORY NOTE

(This Note is not part of the Order.)

This Order amends the Exchange Control (Specified Currency and Prescribed Securities) Order 1967 by incorporating therein a definition of 'securities'. Section 55 of the Finance Act 1968 has the effect that certificates of deposit and Government bills (including Treasury bills) are now securities within the meaning of the Exchange Control Act 1947.

STATUTORY INSTRUMENTS

1968 No. 1234

SEA FISHERIES

The White Fish and Herring Subsidies (Aggregate Amount of Grants) Order 1968

Made - - -	*9th July* 1968
Laid before the House of Commons	*15th July* 1968
Coming into Operation	*24th July* 1968

The Minister of Agriculture, Fisheries and Food and the Secretary of State for Scotland (being the Secretary of State concerned with the sea fishing industry in Scotland) in exercise of the powers conferred on them by section 4 of the White Fish and Herring Industries Act 1957(a) (as amended by section 37 of, and paragraph 23 of Schedule 2 to, the Sea Fish Industry Act 1962(b)) and section 1(6) of the Sea Fish Industry Act 1962 and of all other powers enabling them in that behalf, with the approval of the Treasury, hereby make the following Order :—

Citation, commencement and interpretation

1.—(1) This Order may be cited as the White Fish and Herring Subsidies (Aggregate Amount of Grants) Order 1968 and shall come into operation on the date on which it is approved by a resolution of the Commons House of Parliament.

(2) The Interpretation Act 1889(c) shall apply to the interpretation of this Order as it applies to the interpretation of an Act of Parliament.

Extension of limit of aggregate amount of grants

2. The aggregate amount of the grants which may be made in pursuance of schemes under section 5 of the White Fish and Herring Industries Act 1953(d) (being schemes providing for grants in respect of white fish) and of schemes under section 3 of the White Fish and Herring Industries Act 1957 (being schemes providing for grants in respect of herring) is hereby increased to £51,500,000.

In witness whereof the official seal of the Minister of Agriculture, Fisheries and Food is hereunto affixed on 5th July 1968.

(L.S.)   *Cledwyn Hughes,*
                              Minister of Agriculture, Fisheries and Food.

(a) 1957 c. 22.   (b) 1962 c. 31.
(c) 1889 c. 63.   (d) 1953 c. 17.

Given under the seal of the Secretary of State for Scotland on 9th July 1968.

(L.S.)   *William Ross,*
                                             Secretary of State for Scotland.

Approved 9th July 1968.

                                             E. Alan Fitch,
                                             J. McCann,
                                             Two of the Lords Commissioners
                                             of Her Majesty's Treasury.

EXPLANATORY NOTE

(This Note is not part of the Order.)

The White Fish and Herring Industries Acts of 1953 and 1957, both as amended by the Sea Fish Industry Act 1962, provide that, with a view to promoting the landing in the United Kingdom of a continuous and plentiful supply of white fish and herring, schemes may be made for the payment of grants to the owners or charterers of fishing vessels engaged *inter alia* in catching white fish or herring. The Minister of Agriculture, Fisheries and Food and the Secretary of State for Scotland are empowered to make orders from time to time increasing the aggregate amount of grants which may be made in pursuance of the aforesaid schemes provided that no one such increase is to exceed £5,000,000.

By this Order the aggregate amount of grants which may be so made, which by virtue of Orders already made is £48,750,000, is increased to £51,500,000.

STATUTORY INSTRUMENTS

1968 No. 1235

SEA FISHERIES

The White Fish and Herring Subsidies (United Kingdom) Scheme 1968

Made - - - -	*9th July* 1968
Laid before Parliament	*15th July* 1968
Coming into Operation	*1st August* 1968

The Minister of Agriculture, Fisheries and Food and the Secretary of State for Scotland (being the Secretary of State concerned with the sea fishing industry in Scotland) in exercise of the powers conferred upon them by section 5 of the White Fish and Herring Industries Act 1953(a) (as amended by section 2 of the White Fish and Herring Industries Act 1957(b) and by section 37 of, and paragraph 18 of Schedule 2 to, the Sea Fish Industry Act 1962(c)), section 3 of the White Fish and Herring Industries Act 1957 (as amended by section 37 of, and paragraph 22 of Schedule 2 to, the Sea Fish Industry Act 1962) and sections 1 and 2 of the Sea Fish Industry Act 1962, and of all other powers enabling them in that behalf, being satisfied that special rates of grants are needed, as provided by this scheme, by reason of special circumstances relating to the classes of vessels in respect of which they are so provided, with the approval of the Treasury, hereby make the following scheme:—

Citation, extent, commencement and interpretation

1.—(1) This scheme, which may be cited as the White Fish and Herring Subsidies (United Kingdom) Scheme 1968, shall apply to the United Kingdom and shall come into operation on 1st August 1968.

(2) In this scheme, unless the context otherwise requires—

"the appropriate Minister" means, in relation to white fish or herring landed from vessels in England, Wales or Northern Ireland and voyages made by vessels for the purpose of catching white fish or herring and landing them in England, Wales or Northern Ireland, the Minister of Agriculture, Fisheries and Food; and in relation to white fish or herring landed from vessels in Scotland and voyages made by vessels for the purpose of catching white fish or herring and landing them in Scotland, the Secretary of State for Scotland;

"approved" means approved by the appropriate Minister for the purposes of this scheme;

(a) 1953 c. 17.   (b) 1957 c. 22.
(c) 1962 c. 31.

"gross proceeds" means the proceeds from the first-hand sale of all fish (including white fish, herring, salmon, migratory trout and shellfish) taken on a voyage less such deductions as may be determined by the appropriate Minister in respect of expenses incurred on services not normally undertaken on a vessel and in respect of the part of such proceeds which forms the perquisite of the crew of the vessel from which the fish were landed;

"length", in relation to a vessel, means its length as calculated for the purposes of registration under the Merchant Shipping Act 1894(a);

"month" means a calendar month;

"vessel" means a fishing vessel registered in the United Kingdom;

"white fish" means fish of any kind found in the sea, except herring, salmon, migratory trout and shellfish.

(3) The Interpretation Act 1889(b) shall apply for the interpretation of this scheme as it applies for the interpretation of an Act of Parliament.

General conditions of grant

2.—(1) A grant may be paid in accordance with the following provisions of this scheme to the owner (or his agent) or, where there is a charter-party, to the charterer (or his agent), of a vessel, in respect of—

(a) white fish landed from the vessel in the United Kingdom during the period beginning with 1st August 1968 and ending with 31st July 1969, (the payment in such a case being hereinafter referred to as a "white fish stonage payment");

(b) a voyage made by the vessel during the period last hereinbefore referred to for the purpose of catching white fish and landing them in the United Kingdom, (the payment in such a case being hereinafter referred to as a "white fish voyage payment");

(c) herring landed from the vessel in the United Kingdom during the period beginning with 1st August 1968 and ending with 31st July 1969, (the payment in such a case being hereinafter referred to as a "herring stonage payment"); or

(d) a voyage made by the vessel during the period last hereinbefore referred to for the purpose of catching herring and landing them in the United Kingdom, (the payment in such a case being hereinafter referred to as a "herring voyage payment"):

Provided that no grant shall be payable by virtue of this sub-paragraph in any case where the white fish or herring are landed in the Isle of Man or Channel Islands.

(2) Whether or not a grant is payable by virtue of sub-paragraph (1) of this paragraph, a grant may be paid as aforesaid in respect of herring landed from the vessel in the United Kingdom during the period beginning with 1st August 1968 and ending with 31st July 1969 and sold for conversion into oil, meal or other approved product, if the appropriate Minister is satisfied that the said herring could not have been sold for purposes other than such conversion:

Provided that no grant shall be payable by virtue of this sub-paragraph in respect of—

(a) 1894 c. 60.   (b) 1889 c. 63.

(i) herring landed at any port not specified in Part I of Schedule 3 to this scheme;

(ii) more than 20% of the total landings of herring in any month at any port specified as aforesaid or, where such port is comprised in any group of ports specified in Part II of the said Schedule, at any such group of ports, as the case may be.

3. The owner or charterer of a vessel or his duly authorised agent who applies for payment of a grant shall, within such time as may be specified by the appropriate Minister, supply such information and make such returns concerning fishing operations, costs and trading results as may be required by the appropriate Minister, including detailed accounts, for such period and in such form as the appropriate Minister may require, of the financial results of the operation of all such vessels of which he is the owner or charterer, and shall make any relevant books and records open to examination by any person authorised by the appropriate Minister.

4. Application for payment of a grant under this scheme shall be made by the owner or charterer or his duly authorised agent in such form as the appropriate Minister may from time to time require and shall be completed and certified in all respects as so required and shall be delivered to the appropriate Minister at such address as he may at any time specify for the purpose.

5. Application for payment of a grant under this scheme shall be made not later than one month after the landing of the white fish or herring or the completion of the voyage, as the case may be, or such longer period as the appropriate Minister may, in special circumstances, allow.

6. Notice that a person is authorised to make application for and receive payment of grants under this scheme on behalf of an owner or charterer shall be given in writing signed by the owner or charterer in such form as the appropriate Minister may from time to time require and shall be sent to the address specified by the appropriate Minister for the purpose of paragraph 4 of this scheme:

Provided that not more than one person shall be authorised as aforesaid at any one time at any one port for any one vessel in respect of grants under either paragraph 2(1) or paragraph 2(2) of this scheme.

7. Without prejudice to the discretion of the appropriate Minister in the payment of grants under this scheme, if any owner or charterer or any person acting on his behalf makes any false statement or furnishes false information in respect of any of the matters required to be disclosed in connection with an application for payment of grant under this scheme or if any of the conditions relating to the payment of grants under this scheme are not complied with by any owner or charterer or any person acting on his behalf, the payment of grants to that owner or charterer or any person acting on his behalf at any time may be refused.

8.—(1) For the purpose of determining the grant, if any, which may be paid under this scheme in the case of two or more vessels jointly operating the same gear, the weight of white fish or herring landed from the combined voyage, the proceeds from the sale of such white fish or herring and the gross proceeds of such voyage shall be deemed to be divided equally between the vessels concerned whether they are of the same length or of different lengths, and the grant, if any, shall be calculated separately for each vessel in accordance with the appropriate rates specified in paragraphs 10, 14 or 15 of this scheme.

(2) Notwithstanding the provisions of paragraphs 10, 14 and 15 of this scheme, any grant under this scheme shall be paid, if at any time after 1st September 1963 any structural alteration shall have been made to any vessel which has increased or decreased its length, at the rate appropriate to the length of the vessel before such alteration unless in any such case the appropriate Minister is satisfied that the alteration was likely to be conducive to the increased fishing efficiency of the vessel.

9. For the purpose of giving effect to, but subject to the provisions of, any agreement or arrangement for the remuneration of the officers or crew of a vessel—

(a) in a case where the vessel does not exceed 80 feet in length any grant paid under this scheme shall be deemed to be part of the gross proceeds of the catch;

(b) in the case of any other vessel—

(i) if the remuneration of the officers or crew is calculated wholly or partly by reference to the net earnings of the vessel, any grant paid under this scheme shall be deemed to be part of the gross proceeds of the catch;

(ii) if the remuneration of the officers or crew is calculated wholly or partly by reference to the gross earnings of the vessel, seven-tenths of any grant paid under this scheme shall be deemed to be part of the gross proceeds of the catch.

Conditions relating to payments for voyages

10.—(1) Subject to the provisions of this scheme—

(a) a white fish voyage payment may be made at the appropriate rate set out in Part I of Schedule 1 to this scheme in respect of each voyage made by a vessel falling within one of the categories specified in the said Part I;

(b) a white fish voyage payment at a basic rate may be made at the appropriate rate set out in Part II of Schedule 1 to this scheme in respect of each voyage made by a vessel falling within the category specified in the said Part II;

(c) a grant at a special rate may be paid at the appropriate rate set out in Part III of Schedule 1 to this scheme in respect of each voyage made during the period beginning with 1st August 1968 and ending with 31st January 1969 by a vessel falling within one of the classes specified in the said Part III;

(d) a herring voyage payment may be made at the appropriate rate set out in Part IV of Schedule 1 to this scheme in respect of each voyage made by a vessel falling within one of the categories specified in the said Part IV.

(2) A grant at a special rate may be paid in respect of a voyage made by a vessel, notwithstanding the fact that a grant at a basic rate may also be payable in respect of the same voyage by that vessel.

11.—(1) Subject to sub-paragraph (2) of this paragraph, for the purposes of paragraph 10 of this scheme—

(i) in computing the length of a voyage, the day of departure and the day of arrival of the vessel may each be reckoned as one day at sea;

(ii) in computing the length of a voyage by a vessel falling within one of the categories or classes specified in Parts I, II or III of Schedule 1 to this scheme, the day on which the first-hand sale of the catch commences (if that is different from the day of arrival of the vessel) and any day intervening between the day of arrival of the vessel and the day on which the said sale commences may, if the appropriate Minister is satisfied that the said sale commenced as soon as was reasonably practicable, each be reckoned as one day at sea:

Provided that—

(a) if the day of arrival of the vessel or, in a case where the appropriate Minister is satisfied as in sub-paragraph (1)(ii) of this paragraph, the day on which the first-hand sale of the catch commences or any day intervening between the day of arrival of the vessel and the day on which the first-hand sale of the catch commences is also the day of departure of the vessel upon a subsequent voyage whether made for the catching and landing in the United Kingdom of white fish or herring, then that day shall not be reckoned with the subsequent voyage;

(b) each period of 24 hours which is spent during a voyage in any port shall be excluded in calculating the number of days at sea on that voyage.

(2) Where reference is made in this scheme to a voyage made during a specified period the reference shall be construed, in the case of a voyage only part of which is made during that period, as a reference to that part.

(3) The calculation made by the appropriate Minister for the purpose of this scheme of the number of days at sea on any voyage and the length of such voyage shall be final.

(4) Where in connection with an application for payment of a grant at a special rate any question arises as to whether a vessel is ordinarily engaged in fishing from a specified port the determination of the appropriate Minister shall be conclusive.

12.—(1) In a case where, in respect of a voyage, both a white fish voyage payment and a herring voyage payment might otherwise have been made only one such payment shall be made, being, in a case where the gross proceeds from the sale of the white fish exceed the gross proceeds from the sale of the herring, a white fish voyage payment and, in a case where the gross proceeds from the sale of the herring exceed the gross proceeds from the sale of the white fish, a herring voyage payment.

(2) No white fish voyage payment or herring voyage payment shall be made if the proceeds from the sale of white fish and herring landed in consequence of the voyage, taken together, amount to less than half the gross proceeds of the voyage.

(3) Where by virtue of the last preceding sub-paragraph neither a white fish voyage payment nor a herring voyage payment may be made a claim may be made for a white fish stonage payment or for a herring stonage payment or for both in respect of fish landed in consequence of the voyage, notwithstanding that the vessel falls within one of the categories specified in Part I or Part IV of Schedule 1 to this scheme: Provided that a payment made in pursuance of this sub-paragraph shall in no case exceed the payment which would have been made but for the operation of the last preceding sub-paragraph.

13. No white fish voyage payment shall be made in respect of a voyage made for the purpose of catching and landing fish of a kind not normally sold for human consumption.

Conditions relating to payments for white fish and herring landed

14.—(1) Subject to the provisions of this scheme a white fish stonage payment may be made in the case of a vessel under 60 feet in length, not being a vessel falling within category 'A' of Part I of Schedule 1 to this scheme, in respect of white fish of legal size landed and sold at first-hand otherwise than by retail, at the appropriate rate set out in Part I of Schedule 2 to this scheme.

(2) No white fish stonage payment shall be made (*a*) in respect of fish (other than filleted fish, wings of ray and skate, skinned dogfish and monkfish tails) landed without heads or tails or from which any portion of the head or tail has been removed, or (*b*) in respect of fish which is determined by the appropriate Minister to form part of the perquisite of the crew of the vessel from which the fish were landed.

15. Subject to the provisions of this scheme—

(*a*) a herring stonage payment may be made, in the case of a vessel under 40 feet in length, not being a vessel falling within category D of Part IV of Schedule 1 to this scheme, in respect of herring landed, at the rate set out in Part II of Schedule 2 to this scheme;

(*b*) a grant may be paid at the rate set out in Part IH of Schedule 2 to this scheme in respect of herring landed from a vessel and sold for conversion into oil, meal or other approved product.

16.—(1) For the purpose of computing the amount of a white fish stonage payment or a herring stonage payment which may be made under paragraphs 14(1) and 15(*a*) of this scheme the weight of the white fish or herring, as the case may be, shall be the weight determined at the time of the first-hand sale.

(2) No white fish stonage payment shall be made in consequence of a voyage where a claim for a herring voyage payment is made in respect of the voyage and no herring stonage payment shall be made in consequence of a voyage where a claim for a white fish voyage payment is made in respect of the voyage.

(3) No white fish stonage payment shall be made in respect of white fish landed from a vessel where the voyage on which the fish was caught commences and terminates on one day, that day being also the day of arrival of the vessel from a voyage, or the day of the departure of the vessel upon a voyage, in respect of which a claim for a herring voyage payment is made.

In Witness whereof the official seal of the Minister of Agriculture, Fisheries and Food is hereunto affixed on 5th July 1968.

(L.S.) *Cledwyn Hughes,*
Minister of Agriculture, Fisheries
and Food.

Given under the seal of the Secretary of State for Scotland on 9th July 1968.

(L.S.) *William Ross,*
Secretary of State for Scotland.

Approved on 9th July 1968.

E. Alan Fitch,
J. McCann,
Two of the Lords Commissioners of
Her Majesty's Treasury.

SCHEDULE 1

Paragraph 10

PART I

CATEGORIES OF VESSELS AND RATES OF GRANT IN RESPECT OF VOYAGES FOR THE CATCHING AND LANDING OF WHITE FISH

Category A

Motor fishing vessels of 35 feet in length or over but under 60 feet in length, provided, in relation to any such vessel registered in the United Kingdom as a fishing vessel before 1st January 1968, that the appropriate Minister is satisfied that the grants payable in respect of:—

(*a*) white fish or herring landed from the vessel (not being grants in respect of herring landed and sold for conversion into oil, meal or other approved product), and/or

(*b*) voyages made by the vessel for the catching and landing of white fish or herring

amounted, or would but for special circumstances beyond the control of the owner or charterer have amounted, in the year 1965 to at least £500, in the year 1966 to at least £300 or in the year 1967 to at least £250.

	Rate of grant per day at sea £ s. d.
Vessels of 35 feet in length or over but under 40 feet in length ...	3 10 0
Vessels of 40 feet in length or over but under 45 feet in length ...	3 15 0
Vessels of 45 feet in length or over but under 55 feet in length ...	4 4 0
Vessels of 55 feet in length or over but under 60 feet in length ...	4 9 0

Category B

Motor fishing vessels of 60 feet in length or over but under 80 feet in length.

	Rate of grant per day at sea £ s. d.
Vessels of 60 feet in length or over but under 65 feet in length ...	4 9 0
Vessels of 65 feet in length or over but under 80 feet in length ...	5 5 0

Paragraph 10

PART II

CATEGORY OF VESSELS AND BASIC RATES OF GRANT IN RESPECT OF VOYAGES FOR THE CATCHING AND LANDING OF WHITE FISH

Category C

Fishing vessels of 80 feet in length or over.

	Rate of grant per day at sea £ s. d.
Vessels of 80 feet in length or over but under 110 feet in length ...	4 10 0
Vessels of 110 feet in length or over but under 140 feet in length ...	6 10 0
Vessels of 140 feet in length or over	7 10 0

Paragraph 10

PART III

CLASSES OF VESSELS AND RATES OF SPECIAL GRANT IN RESPECT OF VOYAGES MADE DURING THE PERIOD BEGINNING WITH 1ST AUGUST 1968 AND ENDING WITH 31ST JANUARY 1969

		Rate of grant per day at sea £ s. d.
Class A	Vessels of 80 feet in length or over but under 110 feet in length	2 14 0
Class B	Vessels of 110 feet in length or over but under 140 feet in length	3 18 0
Class C	Vessels of 140 feet in length or over	4 10 0

Paragraph 10

PART IV

CATEGORIES OF VESSELS AND RATES OF GRANT IN RESPECT OF VOYAGES FOR THE CATCHING AND LANDING OF HERRING

Category D

Motor fishing vessels of 35 feet in length or over but under 40 feet in length, provided, in relation to any such vessel registered in the United Kingdom as a fishing vessel before 1st January 1968, that the appropriate Minister is satisfied that the grants payable in respect of:—

(a) white fish or herring landed from the vessel (not being grants in respect of herring landed and sold for conversion into oil, meal or other approved product), and/or

(b) voyages made by the vessel for the catching and landing of white fish

amounted, or would but for special circumstances beyond the control of the owner or charterer have amounted, in the year 1965 to at least £500, in the year 1966 to at least £300, or in the year 1967 to at least £250.

	Rate of grant per day at sea £ s. d.
Vessels of 35 feet in length or over but under 40 feet in length ...	3 10 0

Category E

Fishing vessels of 40 feet in length or over.

	Rate of grant per day at sea £ s. d.
Vessels of 40 feet in length or over but under 60 feet in length ...	4 13 0
Vessels of 60 feet in length or over but under 80 feet in length ...	5 5 0
Vessels of 80 feet in length or over	6 10 0

SCHEDULE 2

Paragraph 14

PART I

RATES OF GRANT IN RESPECT OF WHITE FISH LANDED
Kind of Fish

	Rate of grant per stone d.
All whole gutted fish and filleted fish of a kind normally sold for human consumption (including roes and chitlings), wings of ray and skate, skinned dogfish and monkfish tails	11
Ungutted bass, dogfish, eels, mackerel, mullet (red and grey) and pilchards	11
All other whole ungutted fish, if the appropriate Minister is satisfied that such fish has been sold for human consumption ... ...,	8½
All other whole fish of a kind normally sold for human consumption	2¾

Paragraph 15

PART II

RATE OF GRANT IN RESPECT OF HERRING LANDED

	Rate of grant per stone d.
Herring landed	4

Paragraph 15

PART III

RATE OF GRANT IN RESPECT OF HERRING LANDED AND SOLD FOR CONVERSION INTO OIL, MEAL OR OTHER APPROVED PRODUCT

	Rate of grant per cran s. d.
Herring landed from vessels and sold for conversion into oil, meal or other approved product	21 0

SCHEDULE 3

Paragraph 2

PART I

Ports

Aberdeen
Annalong
Anstruther
Arbroath
Ardglass
Ardrossan
Ayr
Berwick on Tweed
Bridlington
Buckie
Eyemouth
Fort William
Fraserburgh
Gairloch
Girvan

Gourock
Greenock
Grimsby
Hartlepool
Holyhead
Inverness
Kilkeel
Kyle of Lochalsh
Leith
Lerwick
Lowestoft
Mallaig
Milford Haven
Newhaven
North Shields

Oban
Peterhead
Portavogie
Portpatrick
Scalloway
Scarborough
Seahouses
Stornoway
Tarbert (Harris)
Tarbert (Loch Fyne)
Ullapool
Whitby
Whitehaven
Yarmouth

PART II

Groups of Ports

1.
Aberdeen
Fraserburgh
Peterhead

2.
Anstruther
Arbroath
Eyemouth
Leith
Newhaven

3.
Annalong
Ardglass
Kilkeel
Portavogie

4.
Ardrossan
Ayr
Girvan
Gourock
Greenock
Tarbert (Loch Fyne)

5.
Berwick on Tweed
Hartlepool
North Shields
Seahouses

6.
Bridlington
Scarborough
Whitby

7.
Gairloch
Stornoway
Tarbert (Harris)
Ullapool

8.
Holyhead
Whitehaven

9.
Kyle of Lochalsh
Mallaig
Oban

10.
Lerwick
Scalloway

11.
Lowestoft
Yarmouth

EXPLANATORY NOTE
(This Note is not part of the Scheme.)

The White Fish and Herring Industries Act 1953 provides that schemes may be made for the payment of grants to the owners or charterers of fishing vessels engaged in catching white fish. The White Fish and Herring Industries Act 1957 makes a like provision as regards vessels engaged in catching herring.

This scheme provides for the payment of grants in respect of the catching of both white fish and herring, and special grants for vessels of 80 feet and over in respect of the catching of white fish, such grants being calculated by reference either to voyages made by vessels or to fish landed from them. The period in respect of which grants are payable is from the 1st August 1968 to the 31st July 1969 except that the special grants are payable in respect of the period from the 1st August 1968 to the 31st January 1969.

This scheme succeeds the White Fish and Herring Subsidies (United Kingdom) Scheme 1967 (S.I. 1967/1132) and a scheme amending it (S.I. 1968/200).

STATUTORY INSTRUMENTS

1968 No. 1239 (S. 133)

SEA FISHERIES

SEAL FISHERIES

The Grey Seals Protection (Scotland) (Suspension of Close Season) Order 1968

Laid before Parliament in draft

Made - - -	25th July 1968
Coming into Operation	25th July 1968

The Secretary of State, in exercise of the powers conferred on him by section 1 of the Grey Seals Protection Act 1932(**a**), and of all other powers enabling him in that behalf, hereby makes the following order, a draft whereof has been laid before Parliament in accordance with section 1(4) of the said Act as read with section 6(2) of the Statutory Instruments Act 1946(**b**) :—

Citation

1. This order may be cited as the Grey Seals Protection (Scotland) (Suspension of Close Season) Order 1968.

Interpretation

2.—(1) In this order—

"the Act" means the Grey Seals Protection Act 1932 ;

"grey seal" means a seal of the species known as Halichoerus grypus ;

"the normal close season" means the period in each year in respect of which a close season for grey seals is established by section 1(1) of the Act (apart from any order made under the proviso thereto), that is to say the period extending from 1st September to 31st December ;

"the prescribed area" means Scotland other than the following areas— The islands of Haskeir Mor and Haskeir Beig in the Outer Hebrides and any place within 3 miles of any part of the said islands: and the following national nature reserves—

Rhum, St. Kilda, Sula Sgeir, North Rona, Hermaness (Unst, Shetland), Isle of May.

"the suspense period" means the period of 12 months next following the making of this order.

(2) The Interpretation Act 1889(**c**) applies for the interpretation of this order as it applies for the interpretation of an Act of Parliament.

(**a**) 1932 c. 23. (**b**) 1946 c. 36.
(**c**) 1889 c. 63.

Suspension of close season for the prescribed area in 1968-69

3. The Secretary of State hereby directs that, notwithstanding anything (apart from the proviso) in section 1(1) of the Act, there shall be no close season in the prescribed area during the suspense period.

Regulations

4. The regulations contained in the Schedule to this order, being regulations providing for the grant and revocation of permits by the Secretary of State and prohibiting the killing of grey seals in the prescribed area during so much of the normal close season as falls within the suspense period except by persons holding permits and in such manner and by means of such weapon or instrument as is specified in those regulations, shall have effect.

William Ross,
One of Her Majesty's Principal
Secretaries of State.

St. Andrew's House,
Edinburgh, 1.
25th July 1968.

SCHEDULE

REGULATIONS

1. The killing of grey seals in the prescribed area during so much of the normal close season as falls within the suspense period except by a person holding a permit granted in accordance with these regulations, and except in such manner and by means of such weapon or instrument as is specified in these regulations, is hereby prohibited.

2.—(1) The Secretary of State may, if he thinks fit, grant to any person a permit under these regulations and he may revoke the permit at any time by giving notice to the person to whom it was granted.

(2) Any such permit shall specify—
    (*a*) the area within which the holder is authorised to kill grey seals, and

    (*b*) the manner of killing and the means which the holder may employ for that purpose, both of which shall be in accordance with regulation 3 of these regulations.

3. The only manner in which grey seals may be killed in the prescribed area by a person holding a permit, granted in accordance with these regulations, is by shooting in such a way that death is caused instantaneously. The only weapon to be employed for that purpose is a Webley ·32 humane killer or a rifle.

EXPLANATORY NOTE

(*This Note is not part of the Order.*)

The Grey Seals Protection Act 1932 establishes an annual close season for grey seals extending from 1st September to 31st December. This order, made by the Secretary of State under section 1 of the Act, directs that there shall be no close season in Scotland other than in certain excepted areas during the period of 12 months next following the making of this order which was made on 25th July 1968. The order will continue during the period of 12 months next following the making of the order the position created by the Grey Seals Protection (Scotland) (Suspension of Close Season) Order 1967.

In accordance with section 1(2) of the Act, the order contains regulations prohibiting the killing of grey seals during the period which would, apart from the provisions of this order, be the normal close season, except by persons holding permits granted by the Secretary of State. The regulations specify the conditions of permits generally and the means by which the seals are to be killed.

STATUTORY INSTRUMENTS

1968 No. 1240

CUSTOMS AND EXCISE
The Countervailing Duty Order 1968

Made - - -	*2nd August* 1968
Laid before the House of Commons	*9th August* 1968
Coming into Operation	*10th August* 1968

The Board of Trade in pursuance of the powers conferred upon them by sections 1, 2 and 3 of the Customs Duties (Dumping and Subsidies) Act 1957(**a**), as amended by the Customs Duties (Dumping and Subsidies) Amendment Act 1968(**b**), hereby make the following Order:—

1. There shall be charged on the import into the United Kingdom of any goods of a description specified in the second column in the Schedule hereto a duty of customs at the relevant rate specified in the third column.

2. Section 3 of the Customs Duties (Dumping and Subsidies) Act 1957 (which provides for giving relief from any duty imposed under that Act) shall apply in relation to the duty imposed by this Order.

3. This Order may be cited as the Countervailing Duty Order 1968 and shall come into operation on 10th August 1968.

Anthony Crosland,

President of the
Board of Trade.

2nd August 1968.

SCHEDULE

Relevant Tariff Heading	Description of Goods	Rate of Duty
84.15 (A)	Domestic electrically operated refrigerators with a storage capacity not exceeding 12 cubic feet, originating in Italy.	£1 4s. 3d. per cwt.

(**a**) 1957 c. 18
(**b**) 1968 c. 33; this Act does not affect the imposition of the duty effected by this Order.

EXPLANATORY NOTE
(This Note is not part of the Order.)

This Order imposes a countervailing duty of £1 4s. 3d. per cwt. on domestic electric refrigerators originating in Italy, to meet a subsidy on such goods.

STATUTORY INSTRUMENTS

1968 No. 1241

REGISTRATION OF BIRTHS, DEATHS, MARRIAGES, ETC.

ENGLAND AND WALES

The Registration (Births, Still-births, Deaths and Marriages) Amendment Regulations 1968

Made - - -	*1st August* 1968
Coming into Operation	*1st October* 1968

The Registrar General, in exercise of the powers conferred on him by sections 11(3), 14(3), 24(2) and (4) and 39 of the Births and Deaths Registration Act 1953(a), and of all other powers enabling him in that behalf, with the approval of the Minister of Health, hereby makes the following regulations:—

1. These regulations may be cited as the Registration (Births, Still-births, Deaths and Marriages) Amendment Regulations 1968 and shall come into operation on 1st October 1968.

2. The Interpretation Act 1889(b) shall apply to the interpretation of these regulations as it applies to the interpretation of an Act of Parliament.

3. The following provisions in the Registration (Births, Still-births, Deaths and Marriages) Consolidated Regulations 1954(c) as amended (d) are hereby revoked, namely—

   (*a*) regulation 49 (which prescribes a fee for re-registration of the birth of a legitimated person more than 3 months after legitimation);

   (*b*) paragraph (3) of regulation 67 (which prescribes a fee for a duplicate certificate as to registration of a still-birth);

   (*c*) regulation 89 (which prescribes a fee for a certificate that a death is not required to be registered);

   (*d*) regulation 93 (which prescribes a fee for a duplicate certificate as to registration of a death).

(**a**) 1953 c. 20.
(**b**) 1889 c. 63.
(**c**) S.I. 1954/1596 (1954 II, p. 1871).
(**d**) The amending Regulations are not relevant to the subject matter of these Regulations.

Given under my hand on 1st August 1968.

Michael Reed,
Registrar General.

I approve.

Kenneth Robinson,
Minister of Health.

1st August 1968.

EXPLANATORY NOTE

(This Note is not part of the Regulations.)

These Regulations revoke provisions in the Registration (Births, Still-births, Deaths and Marriages) Consolidated Regulations 1954 which prescribe certain fees. The fees relate to re-registration of the birth of a legitimated person, duplicate certificates as to registration of a still-birth or death, and certificates that a death is not required to be registered.

STATUTORY INSTRUMENTS

1968 No. 1242

REGISTRATION OF BIRTHS, DEATHS, MARRIAGES, ETC.

ENGLAND AND WALES

The Registration of Births, Deaths and Marriages (Fees) Order 1968

Made - - -	1st *August* 1968
Laid before Parliament	9th *August* 1968
Coming into Operation	16th *August* 1968

The Minister of Health, in exercise of the powers conferred on him by section 5 of and Schedule 3 to the Public Expenditure and Receipts Act 1968(**a**), and of all other powers enabling him in that behalf, hereby makes the following order :—

Title and commencement

1. This order may be cited as the Registration of Births, Deaths and Marriage (Fees) Order 1968 and shall come into operation on 16th August 1968.

Interpretation

2.—(1) The Interpretation Act 1889(**b**) shall apply to the interpretation of this order as it applies to the interpretation of an Act of Parliament.

(2) In this order, any reference to a provision of the Marriage Act 1949(**c**) specifying sums shall be construed as a reference to that provision as amended by section 23 of and schedule 1 to the Registration Service Act 1953(**d**) (which increased certain sums specified in the Marriage Act 1949 by 50 per cent.)

Variation of fees, etc.

3. The enactments specified in column 2 of schedule 1 to this order (which relate to the fees, etc., payable in respect of the matters mentioned in column 3 of that schedule) shall be amended by substituting for the sums specified in column 4 of that schedule the sums specified in column 5 thereof.

Fees ceasing to be payable, and repeal of superseded enactments

4.—(1) The sums payable under the enactments specified in column 2 of schedule 2 to this order (which relate to the fees, etc., payable in respect of the matters mentioned in column 3 of that schedule) shall cease to be payable ; and the said enactments shall be repealed to the extent specified in column 4 of that schedule.

(2) The fee payable for the issue of a certificate for marriage under section 32(5) of the Marriage Act 1949 (which specifies the fees for issue of a certificate and licence for marriage) shall cease to be payable.

(**a**) 1968 c. 14.	(**b**) 1889 c. 63.
(**c**) 1949 c. 76.	(**d**) 1953 c. 37.

Different provision for certain cases

5.—(1) The fee of three shillings and ninepence specified by section 63(1) of the Marriage Act 1949 for every certified copy of an entry in a marriage register book to which that section applies shall be increased—

(*a*) to five shillings where application for a copy is made—

(i) at the time of registering the marriage or

(ii) to a registrar by whom the book containing the entry is kept, and

(*b*) to eight shillings in any other case.

(2) The fee of ninepence specified by section 33(1) of the Births and Deaths Registration Act 1953(**a**) for obtaining a short certificate of birth—

(*a*) shall cease to be payable for a certificate obtained at the time of registering the birth (or, if more than one such certificate is obtained, the first of them) and

(*b*) shall be increased to three shillings in any other case.

SCHEDULE 1   Article 3

VARIATION OF FEES

1	2 Enactment specifying fees	3 Matter for which fee is payable	4 Old fee	5 New fee
1855 c.81	Places of Worship Registration Act 1855 Section 5	Certification of place of meeting for religious worship	2s. 6d.	£1
1887 c.40	Savings Bank Act 1887 Section 10	Certificate of birth, death or marriage, for purposes of certain Acts	1s.	2s.
1896 c.25	Friendly Societies Act 1896 Section 97(1)	Certificate of birth or death, for purposes of that Act	1s.	2s.
	Section 97(2)	Further certificates under section 97(1)	6d.	2s.
1938 c.69	Young Persons (Employment) Act 1938 Section 5	Copy of entry in birth register, for purposes of that Act	6d.	2s.
1944 c.31	Education Act 1944 Section 94(1)	Copy of entry in birth register, for purposes of certain Acts	6d.	2s.
1948 c.39	Industrial Assurance and Friendly Societies Act 1948 Schedule 1, paragraph 7	Certificate of death, for purposes of that Act	1s.	2s.

(**a**) 1953 c. 20.

1	2 Enactment specifying fees	3 Matter for which fee is payable	4 Old fee	5 New fee
1949 c.76	Marriage Act 1949 Section 27(6)	Entry in marriage notice book	1s. 6d.	15s.
	Section 41(6)	Registration of buildings for solemnisation of marriages	£4 10s.	£6
	Section 51	Fees of registrars for attending marriage	15s. 7s. 6d. }	£1
	Section 57(4)	Sum paid to incumbent, etc. for every entry contained in quarterly certified copies of entries of marriages	9d.	3s.
	Section 64(2)	General search of indexes of register books kept by superintendent registrars	7s. 6d.	£2
		Certified copy of entry issued under that subsection	3s. 9d.	8s.
	Section 65(2)	Certified copy of entry, following search of indexes kept at General Register Office	3s. 9d.	8s.
1950 c.28	Shops Act 1950 Section 35	Copy of entry in birth register, for purposes of that Act	6d.	2s.
1953 c.20	Births and Deaths Registration Act 1953 Section 13(2)	Issue of certificate of baptism	1s. 6d.	3s.
	Section 30(2)	Certified copy of entry, following search of indexes kept in General Register Office	3s. 9d.	8s.
	Section 31(2)	General search of indexes kept by superintendent registrars	7s. 6d.	£2
		Certified copy of entry issued under that subsection	3s. 9d.	8s.
	Section 32	Certified copy of entry in registers kept by registrars	3s. 9d.	5s.
1961 c.34	Factories Act 1961 Section 178(1)	Extract of entry in birth register, for purposes of that Act	6d.	2s.
1965 c.51	National Insurance Act 1965 Section 91(2)	Copy of entry of particulars of birth, death or marriage for purposes of that Act	6d. 1s. }	2s.

SCHEDULE 2   Article 4

FEES CEASING TO BE PAYABLE

1	2 Enactment specifying fees	3 Matter for which fee is payable	4 Extent of repeal
1855 c.81	Places of Worship Re- gistration Act 1855 Section 7	Inspection of list of places certified under the Act	The words "on payment to such superintendent registrar of a fee of one shilling".
1856 c.119	Marriage and Regis- tration Act 1856 Section 24	Search in returns of certi- fied places of worship, etc.	The words "on payment to him of the several fees herein-after mentioned" and the words from "and the Registrar General shall be entitled" onwards.
1874 c.88	Births and Deaths Re- gistration Act 1874 Section 28	Registrars' returns of deaths to local authori- ties	The words from "The registrar making such return" onwards.
1896 c.25	Friendly Societies Act 1896 Section 97(3)	Filling up by registrar of form of application for certificate of birth or death	The whole subsection.
1944 c.31	Education Act 1944 Section 94(2)	Registrars' returns of births and deaths to local education authorities	The words from "and in respect of every entry" onwards.
1949 c.76	Marriage Act 1949 Section 29(1)	Entry of caveat against issue of certificate or licence for marriage	The words "on payment of a fee of seven shillings and sixpence".
	Section 31(6)	Issue of certificate for marriage without licence	The whole subsection.
	Section 63(1)	Search in marriage re- gister books kept by in- cumbents, registrars, etc.	Sub-paragraph (a).
	Section 64(2)	Particular search of in- dexes of marriage register books kept by superinten- dent registrars	Sub-paragraph (b).
	Section 65(2)	General or particular search of indexes kept at General Register Office	Sub-paragraphs (a) and (b).
1953 c.20	Births and Deaths Re- gistration Act 1953 Section 5	Registration of birth if effected at a private house	The proviso.
	Section 6(3)	Registration between 3 and 12 months from birth	The whole subsection.

1	2 Enactment specifying fees	3 Matter for which fee is payable	4 Extent of repeal
	Section 7(2)	Registration after 12 months from birth	The whole subsection.
	Section 9(4)	Declaration of information concerning birth	The whole subsection.
	Section 11(3)	Duplicate certificate as to registration of still-birth	The words "on payment of the prescribed fee".
	Section 12	Certificate by registrar that he has registered a birth	The words "and upon payment to him by the informant of a fee not exceeding fourpence".
	Section 13(1)	Registration of name of child given or altered within 12 months of registration of birth	The words "and upon payment to him by the person procuring the name mentioned in the certificate to be entered of a fee of one shilling and sixpence".
	Section 14(3)	Re-registration of births of legitimated persons	The whole subsection.
	Section 20	Registration of death if effected at a private house	The proviso.
	Section 21(2)	Registration of death after 12 months	The whole subsection.
	Section 24(2)	Certificate that a death is not required to be registered in England or Wales	The words "and upon payment of the prescribed fee".
	Section 24(4)	Duplicate certificate as to registration of death	The words "on payment of the prescribed fee".
	Section 29(3)	Correction of certain errors in a register of live-births, still-births or deaths	The words "upon payment to him by the person requiring the error to be corrected of a fee of three shillings and ninepence and".
	Section 30(2)	General or particular search of indexes kept at General Register Office	Sub-paragraphs (a) and (b).
	Section 31(2)	Particular search of indexes kept by superintendent registrars	Sub-paragraph (b).
	Section 32	Search in registers kept by registrars	Sub-paragraphs (a) and (b).

Given under the official seal of the Minister of Health on 1st August 1968.

(L.S.)   *Kenneth Robinson*,
                                          Minister of Health.

EXPLANATORY NOTE

(This Note is not part of the Order.)

This Order alters various fees payable under the Acts relating to the registration of births, deaths and marriages and associated matters. The fees listed in Schedule 1 to the Order are increased ; those listed in Schedule 2 are abolished, and consequential repeals are made. In addition, Article 5 provides for certain differential fees.

The principal alterations are—

1. Fees for searches in records and registers of births, deaths and marriages are abolished, except in the case of a general search at a superintendent registrar's office, where the fee is increased to £2.

2. Fees for certified copies of entries are increased to 5s. on registration and 8s. subsequently.

3. The fee for entering notice of marriage is increased to 15s. ; but the fee for subsequent issue of a certificate for marriage is abolished. (The fee for issue of a licence is not affected.)

4. Fees for certifying places of worship and for registering buildings for marriage are increased to £1 and £6 respectively.

5. Fees for special procedures for registering births are abolished.

6. Fees for special certificates of birth, death or marriage for purposes of certain Acts are increased to 2s.

STATUTORY INSTRUMENTS

1968 No. 1244 (L. 14)

SUPREME COURT OF JUDICATURE, ENGLAND

PROCEDURE

The Rules of the Supreme Court (Amendment No. 1) 1968

Made - - -	*31st July* 1968
Laid before Parliament	*9th August* 1968
Coming into Operation	*1st September* 1968

We, the Rule Committee of the Supreme Court, being the authority having for the time being power under section 99(4) of the Supreme Court of Judicature (Consolidation) Act 1925(**a**) to make, amend or revoke rules regulating the practice and procedure of the Supreme Court of Judicature, hereby exercise those powers and all other powers enabling us in that behalf as follows :—

PART I

CITATION, COMMENCEMENT AND INTERPRETATION

1.—(1) These Rules may be cited as the Rules of the Supreme Court (Amendment No. 1) 1968 and shall come into operation on 1st September 1968.

(2) In these Rules an Order referred to by number means the Order so numbered in the Rules of the Supreme Court 1965(**b**), as amended (**c**).

(3) The Interpretation Act 1889(**d**) shall apply to the interpretation of these Rules as it applies to the interpretation of an Act of Parliament.

PART II

AMENDMENTS CONSEQUENTIAL ON THE MATRIMONIAL CAUSES ACT 1967

2. In the Arrangement of Orders at the beginning of the Rules of the Supreme Court 1965—

(*a*) Order 104 shall be re-entitled "Enforcement of maintenance orders", and

(*b*) the following entry shall be inserted after Order 111 : —
"112. Miscellaneous Proceedings in the Probate, Divorce and Admiralty Division".

3. Order 1 shall be amended as follows :—

(1) The following item shall be added to the Table in rule 2(2) :—

Proceedings	*Enactments*
"6. Matrimonial proceedings	Matrimonial Causes Act 1967(**e**), section 7."

(**a**) 1925 c. 49.
(**c**) The relevant amending instrument is S.I. 1967/829 (1967 II, p. 2476).
(**d**) 1889 c. 63.
(**b**) S.I. 1965/1776 (1965 III, p. 4995).
(**e**) 1967 c. 56.

(2) Paragraph (3) of rule 2 shall be omitted and paragraphs (4) and (5) shall be re-numbered (3) and (4) respectively.

(3) In rule 2(4), as so re-numbered, for the words "paragraphs (2), (3) and (4)" there shall be substituted the words "paragraphs (2) and (3)".

(4) In rule 4(1) the following definition shall be inserted after the definition of "master" :—

" 'the matrimonial causes rules' means rules made under section 7 of the Matrimonial Causes Act 1967".

4. In Order 30, rule 2(4), for the words from "an Admiralty cause" to "as the case may be" there shall be substituted the words "proceeding in the Admiralty Registry, the Principal Probate Registry or a district registry, in which case it must be filed in that registry".

5. In Order 32, rule 2(3), for sub-paragraph (*c*) there shall be substituted the following sub-paragraph :—

"(*c*) in relation to a summons in a cause or matter proceeding in the Principal Probate Registry, that registry".

6. In Order 41, rule 9, the following paragraph shall be substituted for paragraph (3) :—

"(3) Every affidavit used in a cause or matter proceeding in the Principal Probate Registry must be filed in that registry."

7. Order 55 shall be amended as follows :—

(1) The following paragraph shall be substituted for paragraph (2) of rule 1 :—

"(2) This Order shall not apply to an appeal by case stated".

(2) In rule 7(7), for the words "The appeal shall not succeed" there shall be substituted the words "The Court shall not be bound to allow the appeal".

8. Order 59 shall be amended as follows :—

(1) In rule 11(2) for the words "A new trial shall not be ordered" there shall be substituted the words "The Court of Appeal shall not be bound to order a new trial".

(2) The following paragraph shall be inserted in rule 16 after paragraph (2):—

"(2A) Where the decree was pronounced in a cause pending in a divorce county court, the notice of appeal must be served on the registrar of that court as well as on the party or parties required to be served under rule 3.

In this paragraph "a cause pending in a divorce county court" does not include a cause pending in the Principal Probate Registry which is treated by the matrimonial causes rules as pending in a divorce county court."

(3) In rule 16(3) for the words "the said period" there shall be substituted the words "the period mentioned in paragraph (2)."

(4) At the end of rule 19(1) there shall be added the words "other than an appeal against a decree nisi of divorce or nullity of marriage".

9. Order 62 shall be amended as follows :—

(1) In rule 1(1) at the end of the definition of "proceedings in the Probate, Divorce and Admiralty Division" there shall be added the words "or a matrimonial cause or matter".

(2) In rule 8(8) the words "before an official referee or master" shall be omitted.

10. Order 67 shall be amended as follows :—

(1) The Table in rule 1(2) shall be amended by inserting in paragraph (*d*) after the words "county court" the words "which does not fall within paragraph (*e*)" and by inserting in paragraph (*e*) after the word "begun" the words "or appeal set down".

(2) Rule 9 shall be revoked.

11. In Order 89, rule 1, for the words "the Matrimonial Causes Rules 1957" there shall be substituted the words "the matrimonial causes rules".

12. Order 104 shall be amended as follows :—

(1) For the title there shall be substituted the words "ENFORCEMENT OF MAINTENANCE ORDERS".

(2) For rules 1 to 6 there shall be substituted the following rules :—

"I. INTERPRETATION

Definitions

1. In this Order—

"the Act of 1920" means the Maintenance Orders (Facilities for Enforcement) Act 1920(**a**) ;

"the Act of 1925" means the Guardianship of Infants Act 1925(**b**) ;

"the Act of 1950" means the Maintenance Orders Act 1950(**c**) ;

"the Act of 1958" means the Maintenance Orders Act 1958(**d**) ;

"the Act of 1965" means the Matrimonial Causes Act 1965(**e**) ;

"the chief registrar" means the chief registrar of the Chancery Division ;

"the divorce registry" means the Principal Probate Registry ;

"the senior registrar" means the senior registrar of the divorce registry.

II. PROCEEDINGS UNDER THE ACT OF 1920

Registration, etc. of orders under Act of 1920

2.—(1) The prescribed officer for the purposes of section 1(1) of the Act of 1920 shall be the senior registrar, and on receiving from the Secretary of State a copy of a maintenance order made by a court in any part of Her Majesty's dominions outside the United Kingdom to which the Act of 1920

(a) 1920 c. 33.   (b) 1925 c. 45.
(c) 1950 c. 37.   (d) 1958 c. 39.
(e) 1965 c. 72.

extends he shall cause the order to be registered in the register kept for the purpose of that Act (in this rule referred to as "the register").

The copy of the order received from the Secretary of State shall be filed in the divorce registry.

(2) An application for the transmission of an English maintenance order under section 2 of the Act of 1920 shall be made to a registrar of the divorce registry by lodging in the registry a certified copy of the order and an affidavit by the applicant stating the applicant's reasons for believing that the person liable to make payments under the order is resident in some part of Her Majesty's dominions outside the United Kingdom to which the Act of 1920 extends, together with full particulars, so far as known to the applicant, of that person's address and occupation and any other information which may be required by the law of that part of Her Majesty's dominions for the purpose of the enforcement of the order.

(3) If it appears to the registrar mentioned in paragraph (2) that the person liable to make payments under the English maintenance order is resident in some part of Her Majesty's dominions outside the United Kingdom to which the Act of 1920 extends, he shall send the certified copy of the order to the Secretary of State for transmission to the Governor of that part of Her Majesty's dominions.

Particulars of any English maintenance order sent to the Secretary of State under the said section 2 shall be entered in the register and the fact that this has been done shall be noted in the court minutes.

(4) Where an English maintenance order has been made in a cause or matter proceeding in a district registry, an application for the transmission of the order under the said section 2 may be made to the district registrar, and paragraphs (2) and (3) of this rule shall have effect as if for references to a registrar of the divorce registry there were substituted references to the district registrar.

The district registrar shall send to the divorce registry for entry in the register particulars of any order sent by him to the Secretary of State.

(5) Any person who satisfies a registrar of the divorce registry that he is entitled to or liable to make payments under an English maintenance order or a maintenance order made by a court in any part of Her Majesty's dominions outside the United Kingdom to which the Act of 1920 extends or a solicitor acting on behalf of any such person or, with the leave of a registrar of the divorce registry, any other person may inspect the register and bespeak copies of any order which has been registered and of any document filed therewith.

(6) In this rule expressions used in the Act of 1920 have the same meanings as in that Act and "English maintenance order" means a maintenance order made by the High Court.

(7) In relation to a maintenance order made under the Act of 1925 this rule shall have effect as if—

(a) for the references to the senior registrar and (except in paragraphs (2) and (3) as applied by paragraph (4)) a registrar of the divorce registry there were substituted references to the chief registrar,

(b) for the references to the divorce registry there were substituted references to the Chancery Registrars' Office, and

(c) for the words "in the court minutes" in paragraph (3) there were substituted the words "on the original order and on the duplicate thereof".

III. PROCEEDINGS UNDER PART II OF THE ACT OF 1950

Interpretation of Part II

3. In this Part of this Order:—

"the clerk of the Court of Session" means the deputy principal clerk in charge of the petition department of the Court of Session ;

"English order" means a maintenance order made by the High Court ;

"guardianship order" means a maintenance order made under the Act of 1925 ;

"maintenance order" means a maintenance order to which section 16 of the Act of 1950 applies ;

"Northern Irish order" means a maintenance order made by the Supreme Court of Northern Ireland ;

"register" means the register kept for the purposes of the Act of 1950 ;

"the registrar in Northern Ireland" means the chief registrar of the Queen's Bench Division (Matrimonial) of the High Court of Justice in Northern Ireland ;

"registration" means registration under Part II of the Act of 1950 and "registered" shall be construed accordingly ;

"Scottish order" means a maintenance order made by the Court of Session.

Registration, etc. of English order

4.—(1) An application for the registration of an English order may be made—

(a) in the case of a guardianship order, by lodging with the chief registrar the duplicate and two plain copies of the order, or

(b) in any other case, by lodging with a registrar of the divorce registry a certified copy of the order,

together, in either case, with an affidavit by the applicant (and a copy thereof) stating—

(i) the address in the United Kingdom, and the occupation, of the person liable to make payments under the order ;

(ii) the date of service of the order on the person liable to make payments thereunder or, if the order has not been served, the reason why service has not been effected ;

(iii) the reason why it is convenient that the order should be enforceable in Scotland or Northern Ireland, as the case may be ;

(iv) the amount of any arrears due to the applicant under the order, and

(v) that the order is not already registered.

(2) If it appears to the registrar that the person liable to make payments under the order resides in Scotland or Northern Ireland and that it is convenient that the order should be enforceable there, he shall send a certified copy of the order and the applicant's affidavit to the clerk of the Court of Session or to the registrar in Northern Ireland, as the case may be.

(3) The prescribed officer for the purposes of the Act of 1950 shall be the chief registrar in the case of a guardianship order and the senior registrar in any other case.

(4) On receipt of notice of the registration of an English order in the Court of Session or the Supreme Court of Northern Ireland the chief registrar or the senior registrar, as the case may be, shall cause particulars of the notice to be entered in Part I of the register.

(5) The fact that the order has been registered in the Court of Session or the Supreme Court of Northern Ireland shall be noted—

    (a) in the case of a guardianship order, on the original order and on the duplicate thereof, and

    (b) in any other case, in the court minutes.

(6) Where a maintenance order other than a guardianship order has been made in a cause or matter proceeding in a district registry, an application for the registration of the order may be made to the district registrar, and in such a case the references in paragraphs (1) and (3) to a registrar and the senior registrar shall be construed as references to the district registrar.

(7) Where a district registrar receives notice of the registration of a maintenance order in the Court of Session or the Supreme Court of Northern Ireland, he shall send particulars of the notice to the divorce registry for entry in Part I of the register and shall note in the court minutes the fact that this has been done.

(8) Where an English order registered in the Court of Session or the Supreme Court of Northern Ireland is discharged or varied, the appropriate registrar shall give notice of the discharge or variation to the clerk of the Court of Session or to the registrar in Northern Ireland, as the case may be, by sending him a certified copy of the order discharging or varying the maintenance order.

In this paragraph "the appropriate registrar" means, in the case of a guardianship order, the chief registrar and, in any other case, the registrar or district registrar by whom the order is discharged or varied.

(9) Where the registration of an English order registered in the Court of Session or the Supreme Court of Northern Ireland is cancelled under section 24(1) of the Act of 1950, the prescribed officer to whom notice of the cancellation is to be sent under section 24(3) of that Act shall be the chief registrar in the case of a guardianship order and the senior registrar in any other case ; and on receipt of such notice the chief registrar or the senior registrar, as the case may be, shall cause particulars of it to be entered in Part I of the register and, if it is a guardianship order, on the original order.

Registration, etc. of Scottish and Northern Irish orders

5.—(1) In relation to a Scottish or Northern Irish order the prescribed officer for the purposes of section 17(2) of the Act of 1950 shall be the chief registrar in the case of a guardianship order and the senior registrar in any other case.

(2) On receipt of a certified copy of a Scottish or Northern Irish order for registration, the chief registrar or the senior registrar, as the case may be, shall—

    (a) cause the order to be registered in Part II of the register and notify the clerk of the Court of Session or the registrar in Northern Ireland, as the case may be, that this has been done ;

    (b) file the certified copy and any statutory declaration or affidavit as to the amount of any arrears due under the order.

(3) An application under section 21(2) of the Act of 1950 by a person liable to make payments under a Scottish order registered in the High Court to adduce before that Court such evidence as is mentioned in that section shall

be made by lodging a request for an appointment before the chief master in the case of a guardianship order and before a registrar of the divorce registry in any other case ; and notice of the day and time fixed for hearing shall be sent by post to the applicant and to the person entitled to payments under the order.

(4) The prescribed officer to whom notice of the discharge or variation of a Scottish or Northern Irish order registered in the High Court is to be given under section 23(2) of the Act of 1950 shall be the registrar to whom a certified copy of the order was sent for registration, and on receipt of the notice he shall cause particulars of it to be registered in Part II of the register.

(5) An application under section 24(1) of the Act of 1950 for the cancellation of the registration of a Scottish or Northern Irish order shall be made ex parte by affidavit to the chief registrar in the case of a guardianship order and to a registrar of the divorce registry in any other case, and the registrar, if he cancels the registration, shall note the cancellation in Part II of the register and send notice of the cancellation to the clerk of the Court of Session or the registrar in Northern Ireland, as the case may be.

(6) A person entitled to payments under a Scottish or Northern Irish order (other than a guardianship order) registered in the High Court who wishes to take proceedings for or with respect to the enforcement of the order in a district registry as defined by matrimonial causes rules may apply by letter to a registrar of the divorce registry who may, if satisfied that the order ought to be enforceable in the district registry, make an order accordingly on such terms, if any, as may be just.

Inspection of register

6.—(1) Any person who satisfies the registrar that he is entitled to or liable to make payments under a maintenance order of a superior court or a solicitor acting on behalf of any such person or, with the leave of the registrar, any other person may inspect the register and bespeak copies of any such order which is registered in the High Court under Part II of the Act of 1950 and of any statutory declaration or affidavit filed therewith.

(2) The registrar for the purposes of paragraph (1) shall be the chief registrar in the case of a guardianship order and a registrar of the divorce registry in any other case."

(3) Parts III and IV of Order 104 shall be re-numbered IV and V respectively and accordingly in rule 7 and the heading thereof for the references to Parts III and IV there shall be substituted references to Parts IV and V respectively.

13. The following Order shall be inserted after Order 111 :—

"ORDER 112

MISCELLANEOUS PROCEEDINGS IN THE PROBATE, DIVORCE AND ADMIRALTY DIVISION

Interpretation

1. In this Order "divorce registry" means the Principal Probate Registry and "registrar" means a registrar of that registry.

Assignment and commencement of proceedings

2. All proceedings to which this Order relates shall be assigned to the Probate Division and shall be begun in the divorce registry.

Application for declaration affecting matrimonial status

3.—(1) Where, apart from costs, the only relief sought in any proceedings is a declaration with respect to the matrimonial status of any person, the proceedings shall be begun by petition.

(2) The petition shall state—

(*a*) the names of the parties and the residential address of each of them at the date of presentation of the petition ;

(*b*) the place and date of any ceremony of marriage to which the application relates ;

(*c*) whether there have been any previous proceedings between the parties with reference to the marriage or the ceremony of marriage to which the application relates or with respect to the matrimonial status of either of them and, if so, the nature of those proceedings ;

(*d*) all other material facts alleged by the petitioner to justify the making of the declaration and the grounds on which he alleges that the Court has jurisdiction to make it ;

and shall conclude with a prayer setting out the declaration sought and any claim for costs.

(3) Nothing in the foregoing provisions shall be construed—

(*a*) as conferring any jurisdiction to make a declaration in circumstances in which the Court could not otherwise make it, or

(*b*) as affecting the power of the Court to refuse to make a declaration notwithstanding that it has jurisdiction to make it.

(4) This rule does not apply to proceedings to which rule 4 applies.

Application under s. 39 of Matrimonial Causes Act 1965

4.—(1) A petition under section 39 of the Matrimonial Causes Act 1965 shall, in addition to stating the grounds on which the petitioner relies, set out the date and place of birth of the petitioner and the maiden name of his mother, and, if the petitioner is known by a name other than that which appears in the certificate of his birth, that fact shall be stated in the petition and in any decree made thereon.

(2) The petition shall be supported by an affidavit by the petitioner verifying the petition and giving particulars of every person whose interest may be affected by the proceedings and his relationship to the petitioner :

Provided that if the petitioner is under 16, the affidavit shall, unless otherwise directed, be made by his next friend.

(3) An affidavit for the purposes of paragraph (2) may contain statements of information or belief with the sources and grounds thereof.

(4) On filing the petition, the petitioner shall issue and serve on the Attorney-General a summons for directions as to the persons, other than the Attorney-General, who are to be made respondents to the petition.

(5) It shall not be necessary to serve the petition on the Attorney-General otherwise than by delivering a copy of it to him in accordance with subsection (6) of the said section 39.

(6) The Attorney-General may file an answer to the petition within 21 days after directions have been given under paragraph (4) and no directions for trial shall be given until that period has expired.

(7) A respondent who files an answer shall at the same time lodge in the divorce registry as many copies of the answer as there are other parties to the proceedings and a registrar shall send one of the copies to each of those parties.

Further proceedings on petition under rule 3 or 4

5.—(1) Unless a judge otherwise directs, all proceedings on any petition to which rule 3 or 4 relates shall take place in London.

(2) Subject to rules 2, 3 and 4 and paragraph (1) of this rule, the matrimonial causes rules shall apply with the necessary modifications to the petition as if it were a petition in a matrimonial cause.

Appeals under the Matrimonial Proceedings (Magistrates' Courts) Act 1960

6.—(1) Every appeal to the High Court under the Matrimonial Proceedings (Magistrates' Courts) Act 1960(a) shall be entered by lodging two copies of the notice of motion in the divorce registry.

(2) Order 55, rule 4(2), shall apply to the appeal as if for the period of 28 days therein specified there were substituted a period of 6 weeks.

(3) Notwithstanding anything in Order 10, rule 5, notice of the motion need not be served personally.

(4) On entering the appeal or as soon as practicable thereafter, the appellant shall, unless otherwise directed, lodge in the divorce registry—

    (a) two certified copies of the summons and of the order appealed against,

    (b) two copies of the clerk's notes of the evidence,

    (c) two copies of the justices' reasons for their decision,

    (d) a certificate that notice of the motion has been duly served on the clerk and on every party affected by the appeal, and

    (e) where the notice of the motion includes an application to extend the time for bringing the appeal, a certificate (and a copy thereof) by the appellant's solicitor, or the appellant if he is acting in person, setting out the reasons for the delay and the relevant dates.

(5) The wife may apply for security for her costs of the appeal and a registrar shall ascertain what is a sufficient sum of money to cover those costs, and if, after taking all the circumstances into account, including the means of the husband and of the wife, he considers that the husband should provide security for all or some of the wife's costs of and incidental to the appeal, he may order the husband to pay the sum so ascertained or some part of it into court or to give security therefor within such time as he may fix and may direct a stay of appeal until the order is complied with.

(6) If the clerk's notes of the evidence are not produced, the Court may hear and determine the appeal on any other evidence or statement of what occurred in the proceedings before the magistrates' court as appears to the Court to be sufficient.

(7) The Court shall not be bound to allow the appeal on the ground merely of misdirection or improper reception or rejection of evidence unless, in the opinion of the Court, substantial wrong or miscarriage of justice has been thereby occasioned.

(a) 1960 c. 48.

(8) A registrar may dismiss an appeal to which this rule applies for want of prosecution or, with the consent of the parties, may dismiss the appeal or give leave for it to be withdrawn, and may deal with any question of costs arising out of the dismissal or withdrawal."

14. The Matrimonial Causes Rules 1957(**a**), as amended (**b**), so far as they are still in force, are hereby revoked.

Part III

MISCELLANEOUS AMENDMENTS

15. Order 11 shall be amended as follows :—

(1) In rule 5(5), after sub-paragraph (*b*), there shall be inserted the words "or (*c*) by any other authority designated in respect of that country under the Hague Convention".

(2) The following paragraph shall be added at the end of rule 5 :—

"(8) In this rule and rule 6 "the Hague Convention" means the Convention on the service abroad of judicial and extra-judicial documents in civil or commercial matters signed at The Hague on 15th November 1965."

(3) In rule 6(2) after the words "a Civil Procedure Convention" there shall be inserted the words "(other than the Hague Convention)".

(4) The following paragraph shall be inserted in rule 6 after paragraph (2) :—

"(2A) Where, in accordance with these rules, notice of a writ is to be served on a defendant in any country which is a party to the Hague Convention, the notice may be served—

(*a*) through the authority designated under the Convention in respect of that country ; or

(*b*) if the law of that country permits—

(i) through the judicial authorities of that country, or

(ii) through a British consular authority in that country."

(5) In rule 6(4) for the words from the beginning to "that person" there shall be substituted the words "A person who wishes to serve notice of a writ by a method specified in paragraph (2), (2A) or (3)".

(6) In rule 7(1) for the words "the Carriage by Air Act 1932" there shall be substituted the words "the Carriage by Air Act 1961, the Schedule to the Carriage by Air (Supplementary Provisions) Act 1962 or the Schedule to the Carriage of Goods by Road Act 1965".

16. The following rule shall be added at the end of Order 73 :—

"*Registration of awards under Arbitration (International Investment Disputes) Act* 1966

9.—(1) In this rule and in any provision of these rules as applied by this rule—

"the Act of 1966" means the Arbitration (International Investment Disputes) Act 1966(**c**) ;

(**a**) S.I. 1957/619 (1957 II, p. 2406). (**b**) The relevant amending instruments are S.I. 1961/1082, 1963/989 (1961 II, p. 2058; 1963 II, p. 1628); and see S.I. 1968/219 (1968 I, p. 665).
(**c**) 1966 c. 41.

"award" means an award rendered pursuant to the Convention ;

"the Convention" means the Convention referred to in section 1(1) of the Act of 1966 ;

"judgment creditor" and "judgment debtor" mean respectively the person seeking recognition or enforcement of an award and the other party to the award.

(2) Subject to the provisions of this rule, the following provisions of Order 71, namely rules 1, 3(1) (except sub-paragraphs (c)(iv) and (d) thereof) and (2), 7 (except paragraph (3)(c) and (d) thereof), 8 and 10(3), shall apply with the necessary modifications in relation to an award as they apply in relation to a judgment to which Part II of the Foreign Judgments (Reciprocal Enforcement) Act 1933(a) applies.

(3) An application to have an award registered in the High Court under section 1 of the Act of 1966 shall be made by originating summons to which no appearance need be entered.

(4) The affidavit required by Order 71, rule 3, in support of an application for registration shall—

(a) in lieu of exhibiting the judgment or a copy thereof, exhibit a copy of the award certified pursuant to the Convention, and

(b) in addition to stating the matters mentioned in paragraph 3(1)(c)(i) and (ii) of the said rule 3, state whether at the date of the application the enforcement of the award has been stayed (provisionally or otherwise), pursuant to the Convention and whether any, and if so what, application has been made pursuant to the Convention which, if granted, might result in a stay of the enforcement of the award.

(5) There shall be kept in the Central Office under the direction of the senior master a register of the awards ordered to be registered under the Act of 1966 and particulars shall be entered in the register of any execution issued on such an award.

(6) Where it appears to the Court on granting leave to register an award or on an application made by the judgment debtor after an award has been registered—

(a) that the enforcement of the award has been stayed (whether provisionally or otherwise) pursuant to the Convention, or

(b) that an application has been made pursuant to the Convention which, if granted, might result in a stay of the enforcement of the award,

the Court shall, or, in the case referred to in sub-paragraph (b), may, stay execution of the award for such time as it considers appropriate in the circumstances.

(7) An application by the judgment debtor under paragraph (6) shall be made by summons and supported by affidavit."

17. In Order 80, rule 13(2), the words "or in the district registry of Manchester" shall be omitted from sub-paragraph (a), and after the word "Liverpool" in sub-paragraphs (a) and (b) there shall be inserted the words "or Manchester".

(a) 1933 c. 13.

18. The following rule shall be added at the end of Order 93 :—

"Application under s.19 or 27 of Leasehold Reform Act 1967

15. Proceedings by which an application is made to the High Court under section 19 or 27 of the Leasehold Reform Act 1967(**a**) shall be assigned to the Chancery Division."

19. Order 94 shall be amended as follows :—

(1) At the end of rule 6(1) there shall be added the following sub-paragraph :—
"(*h*) section 82(3) of the Criminal Justice Act 1967(**b**)".

(2) In rule 6(4) for the words "under section 6(3) of the Legal Aid and Advice Act 1949" there shall be substituted the words "under the enactments mentioned in paragraph (1)(*c*) and (*h*)".

(3) The following item shall be added to the Table in rule 6(5) :—

(1)	(2)	(3)
"Criminal Justice Act 1967 s.82(3)	The appropriate tribunal set up under rule 2 of the Legal Aid in Criminal Cases (Complaints Tribunal) Rules 1968(**c**).	The clerk of the appropriate tribunal."

(4) For paragraph (3) of rule 8 there shall be substituted the following paragraph:—

"(3) Where such an appeal is against the decision of—

(*a*) the tribunal constituted under section 42 of the National Health Service Act 1946(**d**), or

(*b*) a tribunal established under section 12 of the Industrial Training Act 1964(**e**),

Order 55, rule 4(2), shall apply in relation to the appeal as if for the period of 28 days therein specified there were substituted, in the case of the tribunal mentioned in sub-paragraph (*a*), a period of 14 days and, in the case of a tribunal mentioned in sub-paragraph (*b*), a period of 42 days."

20. In Order 100, rule 2(5), for the words "The period prescribed by paragraph (4)" there shall be substituted the words "The period prescribed by Order 55, rule 4(2), in relation to an appeal to which paragraph (1) applies or the period prescribed by paragraph (4) in relation to an application or appeal to which that paragraph applies".

21. In the last paragraph of Form 53 in Appendix A to the Rules of the Supreme Court 1965 the square bracket at the end shall be omitted and inserted after the words "in person".

(**a**) 1967 c. 88. (**b**) 1967 c. 80.
(**c**) S.I. 1968/1220 (1968 II , p. 3268). (**d**) 1946 c. 81.
(**e**) 1964 c. 16.

Dated 31st July 1968.

> Gardiner, C.
> Parker of Waddington, C.J.
> Denning, M.R.
> J. E. S. Simon, P.
> Cyril Salmon, L.J.
> Fenton Atkinson, L.J.
> Geoffrey Cross, J.
> N. Browne-Wilkinson
> W. O. Carter
> Arthur J. Driver

EXPLANATORY NOTE
(This Note is not part of the Rules.)

Part II of these Rules incorporates in the Rules of the Supreme Court, with modifications, the provisions of the Matrimonial Causes Rules 1957 left unrevoked by the Matrimonial Causes Rules 1968. These provisions relate to the reciprocal enforcement of maintenance orders (rule 12), legitimacy proceedings and appeals under the Matrimonial Proceedings (Magistrates' Courts) Act 1960 (rule 13). A wider discretion is given to the Court to allow such an appeal on the ground of misdirection or improper reception or rejection of evidence and a corresponding alteration is made in the rules relating to appeals to the High Court (rule 7(2)) and the Court of Appeal (rule 8(1)). A new rule is introduced requiring an application for a declaration with respect to a person's matrimonial status to be made by petition in the Probate, Divorce and Admiralty Division (rule 13).   Part II also makes a number of other amendments consequential on the transfer of the rule-making powers in matrimonial causes to the authority mentioned in section 7 of the Matrimonial Causes Act 1967.

The miscellaneous amendments in Part III make provision for the service of foreign process in this country under the Convention signed at The Hague on 15th November 1965 (rule 15), the enforcement of awards under the Arbitration (International Investment Disputes) Act 1966 (rule 16), the assignment of applications under sections 19 and 27 of the Leasehold Reform Act 1967 to the Chancery Division (rule 18), the substitution of 42 days for 28 days as the time for appeal from an industrial tribunal (rule 19(4)), the extension by the registrar of the time for appeal under the Trade Marks Act 1938 (rule 20) and various other minor matters.

STATUTORY INSTRUMENTS

1968 No. 1247

ROAD TRAFFIC

The Road Vehicles Lighting (Amendment) Regulations 1968

Made - - - -	31*st July* 1968
Laid before Parliament	13*th August* 1968
Coming into Operation	3*rd September* 1968

The Minister of Transport, in exercise of his powers under sections 4, 5, 10 and 11 of the Road Transport Lighting Act 1957(a), Article 8 of the Visiting Forces and International Headquarters (Application of Law) Order 1965(b), and of all other powers him enabling in that behalf, and after consultation with representative organisations in accordance with the provisions of section 13 of the said Act of 1957, as amended by section 264 of, and Schedule 17 to, the Road Traffic Act 1960(c), hereby makes the following Regulations:—

1.—(1) These Regulations shall come into operation on the 3rd September 1968 and may be cited as the Road Vehicles Lighting (Amendment) Regulations 1968.

(2) The Interpretation Act 1889(d) shall apply for the interpretation of these Regulations as it applies for the interpretation of an Act of Parliament.

2. The Road Vehicles Lighting Regulations 1964(e), as amended (f), shall have effect as though—

(*a*) in Regulation 3, after paragraph (1), there were inserted the following paragraph:—
"(1A) A vehicle so constructed that it can be divided into two parts both of which are vehicles and one of which is a motor vehicle shall (when not so divided) be treated for the purposes of these Regulations as that motor vehicle with the other part attached as a trailer."

(*b*) for Part V thereof, there were substituted the following Part:—

"Part V
REGULATIONS GOVERNING OBLIGATORY REFLECTORS ON VEHICLES

Position of obligatory reflectors
20. In the case of a vehicle of a description specified in column 1 of Schedule 2 to these Regulations, the number of obligatory reflectors specified in column 2 of the said Schedule in relation to that description of vehicle shall be fixed on the vehicle in accordance with the requirements with respect to the lateral and longitudinal position of the said reflectors, their maximum and minimum

---

(a) 5 & 6 Eliz. 2. c. 51.   (b) S.I. 1965/1536 (1965 II, p.4462).
(c) 8 & 9 Eliz. 2.c. 16.   (d) 52 & 53 Vict.c. 63.
(e) S.I. 1964/205 (1964 I, p.345).
(f) The relevant amending instruments are S.I. 1965/870, 1966/30 (1965 I, p.2367; 1966 I, p.45).

height from the ground and otherwise, which are specified in relation to that description of vehicle in columns 3,4,5,6 and 7 of the said Schedule.

Character of reflectors

21.—(1) In this Regulation and in the following Regulations in this Part of these Regulations, the expression "approval mark" means a marking designated as an approval mark by the Motor Vehicles (Designation of Approval Marks) (No. 2) Regulations 1964(a).

(2) Every obligatory reflector shall comply in all respects with the following conditions:—

(a) except as provided in the following paragraph, the reflecting area shall, if circular, be not less than $1\frac{1}{2}$ inches in diameter or, if not circular, be of an area of not less than the area of a circle of $1\frac{1}{2}$ inches in diameter and of such a shape that a circle of 1 inch in diameter may be inscribed therein;

(b) except as provided in the following paragraph, the reflecting area shall be of such a shape as to be capable of lying wholly within a circle of 6 inches in diameter;

(c) the reflector shall be so fixed to the vehicle that the reflecting area of the reflector is in a vertical position and facing squarely to the rear; and

(d) the reflector shall be kept clean and shall be plainly visible from the rear.

(3) Nothing in sub-paragraphs (a) and (b) of paragraph (2) of this Regulation shall apply—

(a) in respect of a mechanically propelled vehicle or a trailer manufactured in Italy (not being a mechanically propelled vehicle or a trailer brought temporarily into Great Britain by a person resident outside the United Kingdom) carrying obligatory reflectors in accordance with Regulation 20 of these Regulations, such reflectors bearing a marking approved by the Italian Ministry of Transport, namely, one including two separate groups of letters consisting of the letters "IGM" and "C.1." or "C.2."; or

(b) to an obligatory reflector marked with an approval mark incorporating the roman numeral I, II or III or with the specification number of the British Standard for Reflex Reflectors for Vehicles, namely, AU40 followed by a marking "L I", "L IA", "L III" or "L IIIA".

(4) In this Regulation the expression "reflecting area" means, in relation to a reflector, the area of the orthogonal projection on a vertical plane at right angles to the longitudinal axis of the vehicle of that part of the reflector designed to reflect light.

22.—(1) Subject to Regulation 22A of these Regulations, every obligatory reflector to which this Regulation applies shall be marked—

(a) with the specification number of the British Standard for Reflex Reflectors for Vehicles, namely, B.S.2515, and "Grade 1" or "Grade 2" and with the name, trade mark or other means of identification of the manufacturer of the reflector, or

(b) with the specification number of the British Standard for Reflex Reflectors for Vehicles, namely, AU40 followed by a marking "L I" or "L IA" and with the registered trade name or trade mark of the manufacturer of the reflector, or

---

(a) 1964/1561 (1964 III,p.3509).

(c) with an approval mark incorporating the roman numeral I or II:

Provided that nothing in this paragraph shall require a reflector to be marked as aforesaid if it is carried on such a mechanically propelled vehicle as is mentioned in Regulation 21(3)(a) of these Regulations.

(2) The obligatory reflectors to which this Regulation applies are reflectors carried on every vehicle which is not a trailer.

(3) Nothing in this Regulation shall be taken to authorise any person to apply the said specification number B.S.2515 or AU40 or the said approval mark to any obligatory reflector to which this Regulation applies in contravention of the Merchandise Marks Acts 1887 to 1953(a).

22A. Nothing in Regulation 22 of these Regulations shall be taken as permitting an obligatory reflector to which that Regulation applies to be marked in accordance with paragraph (1)(a) of that Regulation or with an approval mark incorporating the roman numeral II in accordance with paragraph (1)(c) of that Regulation if it is carried on—

(a) a mechanically propelled vehicle first registered under the Vehicles (Excise) Act 1962 on or after the 1st July 1970;

(b) a mechanically propelled vehicle not required to be registered under the said Act and supplied by its manufacturer to the Crown or any person on or after the said date, or

(c) any other vehicle (not being a trailer) supplied as aforesaid.

23.—(1) Subject to Regulation 23A of these Regulations, every obligatory reflector to which this Regulation applies shall be marked—

(a) with the specification number of the British Standard for Reflex Reflectors for Vehicles, namely, B.S. 2515 and "Grade 1" or "Grade 2" and with the name, trade mark or other means of identification of the manufacturer of the reflector, or

(b) with the specification number of the British Standard for Reflex Reflectors for Vehicles, namely, AU40 followed by a marking "L III" or "L IIIA" and with the registered trade name or trade mark of the manufacturer of the reflector, or

(c) with an approval mark incorporating the roman numeral III:

Provided that nothing in this paragraph shall require a reflector to be marked as aforesaid if it is carried on such a trailer as is mentioned in Regulation 21(3)(a) of these Regulations.

(2) The obligatory reflectors to which this Regulation applies are reflectors carried on every trailer supplied to the Crown or any person.

(3) Nothing in this Regulation shall be taken to authorise any person to apply the said specification number B.S. 2515 or AU40 or the said approval mark to any obligatory reflector to which this Regulation applies in contravention of the Merchandise Marks Acts 1887 to 1953.

23A.—(1) Nothing in Regulation 23 of these Regulations shall be taken as permitting an obligatory reflector to which that Regulation applies to be marked in accordance with paragraph (1)(a) of that Regulation if it is carried on a trailer supplied by its manufacturer to the Crown or any person on or after the 1st July 1970.

(a) 50 & 51 Vict. c. 28, 54 & 55 Vict.c.15; 57 & 58 Vict. c.19; 1 & 2 Geo. 5. c. 31; 16 & 17 Geo. 5. c. 53; 1& 2 Eliz. 2. c. 48.

(2) Without prejudice to paragraph (1) of this Regulation, on and after the 1st July 1972 nothing in the said Regulation 23 shall be taken as permitting an obligatory reflector to which that Regulation applies to be marked in acordance with paragraph (1)(*a*) of that Regulation."; and

(*c*) in Regulation 40(3), for the words and figures "Regulations 21 and 22", there were substituted the words and figures "Regulations 21 to 23A".

Given under the Official Seal of the Minister of Transport the 31st July 1968.

(L.S.)   *Richard Marsh,*
                                                                Minister of Transport.

EXPLANATORY NOTE

(*This Note is not part of the Regulations.*)

These Regulations further amend the Road Vehicles Lighting Regulations 1964 by:—

(1) permitting vehicles (including trailers) to carry obligatory reflectors marked with the specification number of the British Standard for Reflex Reflectors for Vehicles, namely, AU40 (Regulations 22(1) and 23(1));

(2) requiring all vehicles, except trailers, registered or supplied on or after 1st July 1970 to carry obligatory reflectors marked either with the said specification number or with an approval mark designated by the Motor Vehicles (Designation of Approval Marks) (No. 2) Regulations 1964 incorporating the roman numeral I (Regulations 22 and 22A);

(3) requiring all trailers supplied by their manufacturers on or after 1st July 1970 and all other trailers as from 1st July 1972 to carry obligatory reflectors marked either with the said specification number or with an approval mark designated by the Motor Vehicles (Designation of Approval Marks) (No.2) Regulations 1964 incorporating the roman numeral III (Regulations 23 and 23A).

STATUTORY INSTRUMENTS

1968 No. 1248

ROAD TRAFFIC

The Motor Vehicles (Construction and Use) (Amendment) (No. 5) Regulations 1968

Made - - -	*31st July* 1968
Laid before Parliament	*13th August* 1968
Coming into Operation	*3rd September* 1968

The Minister of Transport, in exercise of his powers under section 64(1) of the Road Traffic Act 1960(a), as amended by section 51 of and Schedule 4 to the Road Traffic Act 1962(b), and of all other powers him enabling in that behalf, and after consultation with representative organisations in accordance with the provisions of section 260(2) of the said Act of 1960, hereby makes the following Regulations :—

1.—(1) These Regulations shall come into operation on the 3rd September 1968 and may be cited as the Motor Vehicles (Construction and Use) (Amendment) (No. 5) Regulations 1968.

(2) The Interpretation Act 1889(c) shall apply for the interpretation of these Regulations as it applies for the interpretation of an Act of Parliament.

2. The Motor Vehicles (Construction and Use) Regulations 1966(d), as amended (e), shall have effect as though, in Regulation 66(4), for sub-paragraph (g), there were substituted the following sub-paragraph :—

"(g) to any trailer carrying two obligatory reflectors in accordance with the Road Vehicles Lighting Regulations 1964(f), as amended (g), such reflectors being marked either "AU4OL III" or "AU4OL IIIA" or with an approval mark incorporating the roman numeral III by virtue of Regulation 23 of those Regulations and being either mounted on a white background forming part of the reflector or surrounded by a white border at least $\frac{1}{2}$ of an inch in width.".

Given under the Official Seal of the Minister of Transport the 31st July 1968.

(L.S.)

Richard Marsh,
Minister of Transport.

(a) 8 & 9 Eliz. 2. c. 16.   (b) 10 & 11 Eliz. 2. c. 59
(c) 52 & 53 Vict. c. 63.   (d) S.I. 1966/1288 (1966 III, p. 3493).
(e) There is no relevant amending Instrument.
(f) S.I. 1964/205 (1964 I, p. 345).
(g) The relevant amending Instruments are S.I. 1965/870, 1966/30, 1968/1247 (1965 I, p. 2367; 1966 I, p. 45).

EXPANATORY NOTE

(This Note is not part of the Regulations.)

These Regulations amend sub-paragraph *(g)* of Regulation 66(4) of the Motor Vehicles (Construction and Use) Regulations 1966 by adding further kinds of obligatory reflectors to those already specified in that sub-paragraph, which exempts certain trailers from the need to exhibit a trailer plate at their rear if they carry two obligatory reflectors as provided in that sub-paragraph.

STATUTORY INSTRUMENTS

1968 No. 1249

TRANSPORT

PENSIONS AND COMPENSATION

The British Transport (Male Wages Grades Pensions) (Amendment) Order 1968

Made - - - -	*1st August* 1968
Laid before Parliament	*13th August* 1968
Coming into Operation	*14th August* 1968

The Minister of Transport in exercise of his powers under Section 74 of the Transport Act 1962(**a**) and of all other enabling powers, hereby makes the following Order:—

1.—(1) This Order shall come into operation on the 14th August 1968, and may be cited as the British Transport (Male Wages Grades Pensions) (Amendment) Order 1968.

(2) The Interpretation Act 1889(**b**) shall apply for the interpretation of this Order as it applies for the interpretation of an Act of Parliament.

2. The Rules of the British Transport Commission (Male Wages Grades) Pension Scheme as set out in the Schedule to the British Transport Commission (Male Wages Grades Pensions) Regulations 1954(**c**) as amended(**d**) (and as those Rules and that Scheme now have effect subject to the provisions of any Orders made by the Minister of Transport under Section 74 of the Transport Act 1962) shall have effect from the 1st January 1968 inclusive as though there were inserted after Rule 17 thereof the following Rule:—

"Flat-rate supplement to certain pensions

17A. (*a*) This Rule applies to every person who—

(i) before the 1st January 1967 first became entitled to receive any age or ill-health retirement pension under the provisions of Rule 14, 15, 16(*b*) or 17(*b*) and

(ii) is so entitled on the date of the coming into operation of the British Transport (Male Wages Grades Pensions) (Amendment) Order 1968.

(*b*) Every person to whom this Rule applies shall be entitled to receive with effect from the 1st January 1968 a supplementary pension at a flat rate of 6s. 6d. a week to be paid as an addition to his existing pension and to be payable as long as his existing pension continues.

(*c*) For the purposes of Rule 31 the said supplementary pension shall be disregarded but, save as aforesaid, the provisions of these Rules about pensions payable under these Rules shall apply in relation to the said supplementary pension as they apply in relation to any pension payable under any of the Rules mentioned in paragraph (*a*) of this Rule.

(**a**) 10 & 11 Eliz. 2. c. 46.   (**b**) 52 & 53 Vict. c. 63.
(**c**) S.I. 1954/898 (1954 I, p. 175).   (**d**) There is no relevant amending instrument.

(*d*) Payment to or for the benefit of a person to whom this Rule applies of the said supplementary pension for the period beginning on the 1st January 1968 and ending immediately before the commencement of the first of the four-weekly periods specified in Rule 20 which begins after the date of the coming into operation of the said Order of 1968 shall be made as soon as possible after that date.

(*e*) In making any calculation of the sum to be paid to or for the benefit of any person in respect of the said supplementary pension for a fraction of a week such pension shall be treated as accruing due at the rate of 1s. 1d. a day except a Sunday which for the purpose of this paragraph shall be disregarded.

(*f*) In this Rule " existing pension ", in relation to a person to whom this Rule applies, means the pension, or aggregate of the pensions, to which he is entitled under any one or more of Rules 14, 15, 16(*b*) and 17(*b*) on the date of the coming into operation of the said Order of 1968."

Sealed with the Official Seal of the Minister of Transport the 1st August 1968.

(L.S.)

Richard Marsh,
Minister of Transport.

EXPLANATORY NOTE

(This Note is not part of the Order.)

This Order amends the Rules of the British Transport Commission (Male Wages Grades) Pension Scheme to provide for a supplementary pension of 6s. 6d. a week to be paid to those persons who first became entitled to a pension from the Scheme before 1st January 1967 and who remained so entitled on the date on which the Order came into operation. The supplementary pension is payable retrospectively to 1st January 1968.

STATUTORY INSTRUMENTS

1968 No. 1251

EDUCATION, ENGLAND AND WALES

The Provision of Milk and Meals (Amendment No. 2) Regulations 1968

Made - - -	*2nd August* 1968
Laid before Parliament	*15th August* 1968
Coming into Operation	*16th August* 1968

The Secretary of State for Education and Science, in exercise of the powers conferred upon him by section 49 of the Education Act 1944(a) as amended by the Secretary of State for Education and Science Order 1964(b), hereby makes the following regulations :—

Citation, commencement and interpretation

1.—(1) These regulations may be cited as the Provision of Milk and Meals (Amendment No. 2) Regulations 1968 and shall come into operation on 16th August 1968.

(2) The Interpretation Act 1889(c) shall apply for the interpretation of these regulations as it applies for the interpretation of an Act of Parliament.

Amendment of regulations

2. Regulation 14 of the Provision of Milk and Meals Regulations 1945(d) as amended (e) shall cease to have effect in so far as it enables a local education authority to require a teacher to supervise pupils during school meals and accordingly there shall be omitted—

(*a*) in regulation 13(2)(b) the words "having regard to the power given to the Authority by the next following regulation to require teachers to supervise pupils"; and

(*b*) in regulation 14 everything after the word "meals" where that word first occurs.

Given under the Official Seal of the Secretary of State for Education and Science on 2nd August 1968.

(L.S.)

Shirley Williams,
Minister of State for Education
and Science.

(a) 1944 c. 31.   (b) S.I. 1964/490 (1964 I, p. 800).
(c) 1889 c. 63.   (d) S.I. 1945/698 (Rev. VI p. 380: 1945 I p. 336).
(e) The amending Regulations are not relevant to the subject matter of this Regulation.

STATUTORY INSTRUMENTS

1968 No. 1252

LOCAL GOVERNMENT, ENGLAND AND WALES

The School Health Service (Amendment) Regulations 1968

Made - - -	*2nd August* 1968
Laid before Parliament	*15th August* 1968
Coming into Operation	*19th August* 1968

The Secretary of State for Education and Science, in exercise of the powers conferred upon him by section 3(4) of the Local Government Act 1958(a), hereby makes the following regulations:—

Citation, commencement and interpretation

1.—(1) These regulations may be cited as the School Health Service (Amendment) Regulations 1968 and shall come into operation on 19th August 1968.

(2) The Interpretation Act 1889(b) shall apply for the interpretation of these regulations as it applies for the interpretation of an Act of Parliament.

Amendment of regulations

2. In regulation 5A of the School Health Service Regulations 1959(c) as amended (d), after the word " physiotherapist " there shall be inserted the word " orthoptist ".

> Given under the Official Seal of the Secretary of State for Education and Science on 2nd August 1968.

Shirley Williams,
(L.S.) Minister of State for Education and Science.

EXPLANATORY NOTE
(This Note is not part of the Regulations)

These regulations provide that an orthoptist may not be employed in the school health service unless he is registered as such.

(a) 1958 c. 55.	(b) 1889 c. 63.
(c) S.I. 1959/363 (1959 I, p. 1582).	(d) S.I. 1966/72 (1966 I, p. 150).

STATUTORY INSTRUMENTS

1968 No. 1253

POST OFFICE

The Inland Post Regulations 1968

Made - - -	*5th August* 1968
Laid before Parliament	*20th August* 1968
Coming into Operation	*16th September* 1968

ARRANGEMENT OF REGULATIONS

47. Trade charge money orders—crossing.

48. Trade charge money orders—payment to bankers.

49. Discharge to Crown by payment.

50. Void trade charge money orders.

PART IX
MISCELLANEOUS AND GENERAL

51. Stamping of paper.

52. Jury summonses.

53. Variation of route.

54. Remission of postage.

55. Application of the regulations to packets to and from the Republic of Ireland.

56. Revocation and transitional provision.

57. Citation and commencement.

Schedule 1 : Rates of postage and limits of size and weight.

Schedule 2 : Postal facilities.

Schedule 3 : Express delivery services.

Schedule 4 : Registered postal packets.

Schedule 5 : Cash on delivery packets.

Schedule 6 : Fees for stamping paper for use as cards, covers or envelopes.

Schedule 7 : Rates of postage and limits of size and weight for postal packets to be transmitted to the Republic of Ireland.

I, The Right Honourable John Thomson Stonehouse, M.P., Her Majesty's Postmaster General, by virtue of the powers conferred upon me by sections 5, 6, 7, 8, 10, 15 and 81 of the Post Office Act 1953(a) (as amended or substituted by sections 21 and 28 of and the Schedule to the Post Office Act 1961(b)), section 9 of the Crown Proceedings Act 1947(c), section 11 of the Juries Act 1862(d) and all other powers enabling me in this behalf, do hereby make the following regulations :

PART I—INTERPRETATION AND APPLICATION

Interpretation

1.—(1) In these regulations, except so far as the contrary is provided or the context otherwise requires, the following expressions have the meanings hereby respectively assigned to them:

"the Act" means the Post Office Act 1953 ;

"articles for the use of the blind" has the meaning assigned to it by regulation 23 ;

(a) 1953 c. 36.   (b) 1961 c. 15.
(c) 1947 c. 44.   (d) 1862 c. 107.

"business reply packet" means a letter or printed packet, on which postage has not been prepaid, and which :

(a) is addressed to, or to the agent of, a person who has made provision to the satisfaction of the Postmaster General for the payment of the appropriate postage on letters or printed packets which are posted without prepayment of postage and are received by him or such agent, and

(b) is distinguished or marked in such manner as the Postmaster General may direct ;

"cash on delivery packet" means a registered letter, printed packet or registered newspaper or a registered or unregistered parcel upon which the Postmaster General undertakes at the request of the sender to collect or secure the collection of a sum of money (in these regulations referred to as a trade charge) on his behalf from the addressee of the packet as a condition of delivery and upon which the sender has paid the fee for the cash on delivery service ;

"coin" means coin (whether or not current) except such as is used or designed for purposes of ornament ;

"current registered newspaper" means a registered newspaper which is of current issue and is in course of distribution by the publisher, a wholesaler or a retailer and which is intended by the sender to be transmitted at the rate of postage specified in item 3 of Schedule 1 and includes a packet of such newspapers ;

"customs duty" includes purchase tax ;

"express delivery office" means any post office from time to time authorised by the Postmaster General for the reception of postal packets for conveyance and delivery by special messenger ;

"express packet" means a postal packet conveyed and delivered by special messenger, at the request of the sender or the addressee, throughout its whole course in the post or any part thereof ;

"first class letter" means :

(a) a letter upon which there is denoted in a manner provided by regulation 10(3) payment of postage at the rate specified in or fixed under Schedule 1 appropriate for its transmission as a first class letter ;

(b) a letter on which postage has not been prepaid and with respect to which the Postmaster General has entered into an arrangement with the sender for the grant of credit facilities and which is distinguished or marked in such manner as the Postmaster General may direct to indicate the intention of the sender that it is to be transmitted as a first class letter ;

(c) a business reply packet (being a letter) which is distinguished or marked in such manner as the Postmaster General may direct to indicate the intention that it is to be transmitted as a first class letter ;

(d) a letter transmitted under the provisions of regulation 32 which is distinguished or marked in such manner as the Postmaster General may direct to indicate the intention of· the sender that it is to be transmitted as a first class letter ;

"inland", when used in relation to any postal packet or any description of postal packet, means posted in the British postal area and addressed to some place in the British postal area, but does not include a postal packet addressed to a ship of the Royal Navy, notwithstanding that the name of a port in the British postal area or the words "c/o G.P.O. London" are included in the address, if the packet has to be sent abroad for delivery to the ship ;

"jewellery" means :

(a) gold, silver or platinum or other precious metal in a manufactured state ; that is to say, a state in which value is added to the raw material by skilled workmanship, and in this definition are included any coins used or designed for purposes of ornament ;

(b) diamonds and precious stones ;

(c) watches, the cases of which are entirely or mainly composed of gold, silver or platinum or other precious metal ; and

(d) any article of a like nature which, apart from workmanship, has an intrinsic or market value ;

"late posted packet" has the meaning assigned to it by regulation 4 ;

"letter", except where that expression is used in regulation 16, means any postal packet except a printed packet, a packet consisting of articles for the use of the blind, a current registered newspaper, a parcel, an unaddressed packet or a packet consisting of a petition or address of the kind referred to in the proviso to section 5(1) of the Act ;

"local parcel" means a parcel addressed to a place within the local parcel delivery area of the place at which the parcel is posted ;

"local parcel delivery area" means the area prescribed as such for the place at which a parcel is posted ;

"the minimum registration fee" means the fee referred to as such in the first column of Part I of Schedule 4 ;

"ordinary parcel" means a parcel which is not a local parcel ;

"paper money" means :

(a) bank notes or currency notes, being current in the British postal area or elsewhere ;

(b) money orders and postal orders ;

(c) unobliterated postage or revenue stamps available for current use in the British postal area or elsewhere (except revenue stamps embossed or impressed on an instrument which has been executed), and National Savings stamps ;

(d) exchequer bills, bills of exchange, promissory notes, cheques, credit notes which entitle the holder to money or goods and all orders and authorities for the payment of money, whether negotiable or not ;

(e) bonds and coupons relating thereto and other securities for money, whether negotiable or not ;

(f) coupons, vouchers, tokens, cards, stamps or similar documents, exchangeable (singly or with other such documents) for money, goods or services ;

"parcel" means a postal packet which is posted as a parcel in accordance with the provisions of these regulations ;

"postage forward parcel" means a parcel on which postage has not been prepaid, and which:

(a) is addressed to, or to the agent of, a person who has made provision to the satisfaction of the Postmaster General for the payment of postage on postage forward parcels which are posted without prepayment of postage and are received by him or such agent ; and

(b) is distinguished or marked in such manner as the Postmaster General may direct ;

"postal form" means a form issued by or under the authority of the Postmaster General ;

"postal packet" means and includes every packet or article transmissible by post except a telegram ;

"preferred envelope" means an envelope which is of the shape and within the limits of size specified in the third column of Schedule 1 for a preferred letter, has no open panel, and is made of paper weighing at least 63 grammes per square metre ;

"preferred letter" means a letter which is of the shape and within the limits of size and weight specified in the third and fourth columns of Schedule 1 for a preferred letter and which either:

(a) is enclosed in a preferred envelope ; or

(b) consists of an unfolded card not enclosed in an outer covering which complies with the provisions of regulation 15 ; or

(c) consists of a folded card or folded paper of a type approved by the Postmaster General which is sealed or secured in such manner as the Postmaster General may require ;

"prescribed" means prescribed by the Postmaster General ;

"printed packet" has the meaning assigned to it by regulation 16 ;

"railex service" means a service whereby a letter is conveyed by a special messenger from the express delivery office to the appropriate railway station, despatched from that station by the next available and suitable train and delivered to the addressee from the railway station to which it was despatched ;

"recorded delivery packet" means an unregistered postal packet which is sent by the recorded delivery service ;

"redirection" as applied to a postal packet includes re-posting ;

"second class letter" means any letter other than a first class letter ;

"trade charge" has the meaning assigned to it in the foregoing definition of "cash on delivery packet" ;

"trade charge form" has the meaning assigned to it by regulation 44 ;

"trade charge money order" means a money order in a special form for remitting the trade charge to the sender of a cash on delivery packet or to a person named by him to receive the amount ;

"unaddressed packet" means a postal packet, whether enclosed in a cover or not, which is not addressed to or intended for delivery to any specified addressee or address, and forms part of a consignment for general delivery within a particular area ;

(2) Any reference in these regulations to additional postage shall take effect in relation to a postal packet for which no rate of postage is specified as though for the words "additional postage" there were substituted the word "postage".

(3) Any reference in these regulations to the provisions of any enactment or regulations shall be construed, unless the context otherwise requires, as a reference to those provisions as amended re-enacted or replaced by any subsequent enactments or regulations.

(4) The Interpretation Act 1889(a) applies for the interpretation of these regulations as it applies for the interpretation of an Act of Parliament, and as if these regulations and the regulations hereby revoked were Acts of Parliament.

Application

2. These regulations shall apply exclusively to inland postal packets, except as provided in regulation 55 and except in so far as the provisions of these regulations are expressly made applicable to any other postal packets by any regulations relating to such postal packets.

PART II—POSTAGE

Rates of postage

3.—(1) There shall be charged and paid upon the postal packets specified in the first column of Schedule 1 (other than packets accepted for transmission under regulation 32) the rates of postage respectively specified in or fixed under the second column thereof, upon unaddressed packets the rates of postage fixed under regulation 24, and upon packets accepted for transmission under regulation 32 the rates of postage fixed under that regulation.

(2) The Postmaster General shall publish from time to time in the London, Edinburgh and Belfast Gazettes or in such other manner as he may determine the rates of postage fixed by him under Schedule 1.

Additional postage on late posted packets

4.—(1) In this regulation the expression "late posted packet" means a postal packet of such description as may be prescribed:

(*a*) which is posted in any special posting box which may be provided by the Postmaster General for the purpose, after the ordinary hour of collection for a particular despatch from the office of collection on a particular day in order that it may if possible be forwarded by that despatch,

or (*b*) which is posted at any time in any posting box which may be provided by the Postmaster General on a train,

or (*c*) which is posted at any time in any posting box which may be provided by the Postmaster General for the purpose at a railway station, in order that it may if possible be conveyed by a particular train departing from that station,

---

(a) 1889 c. 63.

or (d) which is posted as a registered postal packet or as a recorded delivery packet, after the hour up to which such postal packets are ordinarily accepted at the office of posting in order that they may if possible be forwarded by a particular despatch, but within such further time (if any) as the Postmaster General may from time to time appoint in relation to the office.

(2) There shall be charged and paid in respect of a late posted packet additional postage of such amount, not exceeding 1s. 6d., as the Postmaster General may fix either generally or in relation to the description of postal packet concerned or to the description of office of collection or posting or to the manner or time of posting.

(3) Where no part, or part only, of such additional postage is prepaid, the packet may at the discretion of the Postmaster General either:

(a) be forwarded as if it had not been posted as a late posted packet ; or

(b) be forwarded by the despatch referred to in sub-paragraph (a) or (d) of paragraph (1), or by the train referred to in sub-paragraph (b) or (c) of paragraph (1), as may be appropriate in the particular case ; and if the packet is posted as a registered postal packet or as a recorded delivery packet and is forwarded by the despatch referred to in sub-paragraph (d) of paragraph (1), the amount payable by the addressee or the sender under section 7(1) of the Act in respect of the deficiency shall be the amount of the deficiency.

Additional postage on certain parcels

5. Upon any parcel redirected by the Post Office as specified in the first column of paragraph 13 of Schedule 2 to an address served from a different delivery office (not being an address within the same local parcel delivery area), there shall be charged additional postage at the appropriate rate as if the transmission of the parcel to the new address were a fresh transmission by post.

PART III—GENERAL CONDITIONS

Prohibitions

6.—(1) Save as the Postmaster General may either generally or in any particular case allow, there shall not be conveyed or delivered by post any postal packet of a description referred to in paragraphs (a), (b) or (c) of section 11(1) of the Act.

(2) Subject to section 8(3) of the Act, there shall not be posted or conveyed or delivered by post any postal packet:

(a) containing :

(i) except as may be permitted by the Postmaster General either generally or in any particular case, any living creature ;

(ii) any imitation of a bank note within the meaning of section 38 of the Criminal Justice Act 1925(a) ;

(b) containing or bearing any fictitious stamp (not being a fictitious stamp which is authorised to be made by or under Post Office regulations) or any counterfeit impression of a stamping machine used under the

---

(a) 1925 c. 86.

direction or by the permission of the Postmaster General or any counterfeit of any other impression authorised by or under these regulations to be used to denote payment of postage or fees ;

(*c*) having thereon, or on the cover thereof, any words, letters or marks (used without due authority) which signify or imply, or may reasonably lead the recipient thereof to believe, that the postal packet is sent on Her Majesty's service ;

(*d*) of such a size, form or colour or so made up for transmission by post as to be likely in the opinion of the Postmaster General to embarrass the officers of the Post Office in dealing with the packet ;

(*e*) having anything written, printed or otherwise impressed upon or attached to any part of the postal packet which, either by tending to prevent the easy and quick reading of the address of the packet or by inconvenient proximity to the stamp or stamps used in the payment of postage, or in any other way, is in itself, or in the manner in which it is written, printed, impressed, or attached, likely in the opinion of the Postmaster General to embarrass the officers of the Post Office in dealing with the packet ;

(*f*) whereon the payment of any postage or fees purports to be denoted by any stamp or impression which has been previously used to denote payment of the postage or fees on any other postal packet or any other Revenue duty or tax.

Packets containing others for different persons

7.—(1) There shall not be posted or conveyed or delivered by post any postal packet consisting of or containing two or more postal packets addressed to different persons who are at different addresses.

(2) If any such postal packet be posted, or tendered for conveyance by post, each postal packet contained therein may be forwarded to the addressee subject to such charges as the Postmaster General may fix in the particular case, not exceeding the total of the charges which would have been payable in respect of each of the separate postal packets contained therein if they had been posted singly without prepayment of postage.

Packing

8. Every postal packet shall be made up and secured in such manner as in the opinion of the Postmaster General is calculated to prevent injury to any other postal packet in course of conveyance, or to any receptacle in which the same is conveyed, or to an officer of the Post Office or other persons who may deal with such packet.

Limits of size and weight

9. The limits of size and weight of the postal packets specified in the first column of Schedule 1 shall (except with special permission of the Postmaster General) be those respectively specified in the third and fourth columns of the said Schedule.

Payment of postage and fees

10.—(1) Except as the Postmaster General may otherwise direct, and subject to the provisions of these regulations, the postage and fees payable on every postal packet, and the fees payable in respect of postal facilities, shall be prepaid.

(2) The provisions of these regulations with reference to prepayment of postage and fees shall not apply to the postage payable on business reply packets or postage forward parcels, or to the postage and fees payable on postal packets with respect to which the Postmaster General has entered into an arrangement with the senders for the grant of credit facilities.

(3) Payment of postage or fees payable under these regulations may be denoted:

(*a*) by adhesive postage stamps; or

(*b*) by impressions of stamping machines working under the direction or by the permission of the Postmaster General; or

(*c*) by the use of a stamped envelope, cover, card, or other postal form; or

(*d*) by the use of an embossed or impressed stamp cut out of or otherwise detached from an envelope, cover, card or other postal form; or

(*e*) in such other manner as the Postmaster General may from time to time permit.

(4) No stamp or impression of a stamping machine which is imperfect or mutilated or defaced in any way, or across which anything is written or printed or otherwise impressed, shall be used to denote payment of postage or fees; but a stamp shall not be deemed to be imperfect or mutilated or defaced or to have anything written or printed or impressed across it within the meaning of this provision, by reason only that it is distinctly perforated with initials by means of a punch if the perforating holes are not larger than those dividing one stamp from another in a sheet of stamps.

(5) No stamp indicating on the face thereof payment of a registration fee as well as postage shall be used to denote payment of postage or fees on any unregistered postal packet.

(6) Packets bearing the impression of stamping machines or intended for impression by stamping machines shall be accepted only at such post offices, within such hours, and under and subject to such conditions and restrictions as the Postmaster General may consider appropriate.

(7) Subject to the provisions of these regulations, the stamp or impression denoting payment of postage or fees shall be placed in such position on the envelope, cover, card or other form as the Postmaster General may consider appropriate.

Treatment of irregular packets

11.—(1) If any postal packet which appears to have been intended for transmission as a packet of a particular description is found in the post or is left at a post office, and it does not comply, or its manner of posting did not comply, with the provisions of these regulations which are applicable to postal packets of its purported description, the Postmaster General may if he thinks fit treat it as if it had been posted as a postal packet of such description (including its purported description) as he considers appropriate; and the packet shall for all purposes be deemed to be a postal packet of such description.

(2) Where any postal packet is treated as a parcel under paragraph (1), there shall be payable by the addressee on the delivery of the packet, or, if the packet is refused or cannot for any other reason be delivered, by the sender, the appropriate postage at the rate applicable to parcels and the additional sum of 3d., less the amount of any postage prepaid.

Return of undeliverable postal packets (except parcels)

12.—(1) With regard to any postal packet (other than (i) a parcel, (ii) a preferred letter transmitted as a second class letter chargeable by law with a postage at the lowest rate of postage for the time being payable in respect of a preferred letter so transmitted, (iii) any other letter transmitted as a second class letter chargeable by law with a postage at the lowest rate of postage for the time being payable in respect of any other letter so transmitted or (iv) a current registered newspaper chargeable by law with a postage at the lowest rate of postage for the time being payable in respect of a current registered newspaper) which for any reason cannot be delivered, the following provisions shall apply:

(*a*) Where the full name and address of the sender appear legibly on the outside of the packet, the packet shall be returned to the sender unopened, but subject to payment of any charges to which it has become liable.

(*b*) Where the name and address of the sender do not appear on the outside of the packet or are illegible, the packet shall be opened by any officer of the Post Office duly authorised in that behalf, and if the name and address of the sender can be ascertained, the packet shall be returned to the sender, subject to payment of any charges to which it has become liable.

(2) With regard to (i) any preferred letter transmitted as a second class letter chargeable by law with a postage at the lowest rate of postage for the time being payable in respect of a preferred letter so transmitted and (ii) any other letter transmitted as a second class letter chargeable by law with a postage at the lowest rate of postage for the time being payable in respect of any other letter so transmitted, which for any reason cannot be delivered, the following provisions shall apply:

(*a*) Where the full name and address of the sender appear legibly on the outside of the letter, the letter shall (if the Postmaster General so decides) be charged with additional postage equal in amount to the rate of postage originally chargeable upon the letter exclusive of any postage paid by virtue of regulation 4, and any such additional postage shall be payable by the sender of the letter; and the letter shall upon payment of any such additional postage and any other charges to which it has become liable, be returned to the sender.

(*b*) Where the name and address of the sender do not appear on the outside of the letter or are illegible, and the letter was accepted for transmission under regulation 31, the letter may be dealt with or disposed of in such manner as the Postmaster General may think fit.

(*c*) Where the name and address of the sender do not appear on the outside of the letter or are illegible, and the letter was not accepted for transmission under regulation 31, the letter shall be opened by any officer of the Post Office duly authorised in that behalf and

　(i) if the letter is found to contain or consist of nothing except commercial advertising matter, newspapers and magazines, it may be dealt with or disposed of in such manner as the Postmaster General may think fit;

　(ii) if the letter is found to contain or consist wholly or partly of anything other than commercial advertising matter, newspapers and magazines, then if the name and address of the sender can be ascertained, the letter shall (if the Postmaster General so decides) be charged with additional postage equal in amount to the rate of postage originally chargeable upon the letter, exclusive of any postage paid by virtue of regulation 4, and any such additional postage shall be payable by the sender of the letter, and the letter shall, upon payment of any such additional postage and any other charges to which it has become liable, be returned to the sender.

(3) With regard to any current registered newspaper chargeable by law with a postage at the lowest rate of postage for the time being payable in respect of a current registered newspaper, which for any reason cannot be delivered, the following provisions shall apply:

(a) Where the full name and address of the sender appear legibly on the outside of the newspaper, the newspaper shall (if the Postmaster General so decides) be charged with additional postage equal in amount to the rate of postage originally chargeable upon the newspaper exclusive of any postage paid by virtue of regulation 4, and any such additional postage shall be payable by the sender of the newspaper; and the newspaper shall upon payment of any such additional postage and any other charges to which it has become liable, be returned to the sender.

(b) Where the name and address of the sender do not appear on the outside of the newspaper or are illegible, the newspaper may be dealt with or disposed of in such manner as the Postmaster General may think fit.

(4) With regard to any postal packet (other than a parcel) which for any reason cannot be delivered, if upon the tender of the packet to the sender he refuses or fails to pay the charges to which the packet has become liable by law, the packet may be dealt with or disposed of in such manner as the Postmaster General may think fit.

Return of undeliverable parcels

13. With regard to parcels which for any reason cannot be delivered, and parcels which are addressed to a place beyond the limits of the postal delivery of any town or district, or to a ship at any port in the British postal area, and which are not called for or delivered within such times as the Postmaster General considers reasonable, the following provisions shall apply:

(1) The parcel shall be retained at or forthwith forwarded to such place as the Postmaster General may from time to time appoint, and may, if necessary, be there opened and examined.

(2) Where the name and address of the sender can be ascertained from the parcel, then subject to paragraphs (4), (5) and (6):

(a) in the case of a postage forward parcel, the parcel shall be tendered to the sender charged with postage equal in amount to the prepaid rate of postage which would have been originally chargeable if the parcel had not been a postage forward parcel;

(b) in the case of any other parcel, the parcel shall be returned to the sender free of charge.

(3) Where the name and address of the sender cannot be ascertained from the parcel, the parcel shall be retained pending a claim from the sender or addressee. In default of any claim within a period of 3 months, the parcel shall be disposed of in such manner as the Postmaster General may think fit.

(4) Where, in the case of a parcel which cannot be delivered for want of a true direction, the sender corrects the address of the parcel, the parcel shall be forwarded to the corrected address subject to the following conditions:

(a) Where the corrected address of the parcel is served from the same delivery office as the original address, and the parcel is not, at the time of such correction, lying at a returned letter office, no new charge shall be made with respect to the delivery of the parcel ;

(b) Where the corrected address of the parcel is not served from the same delivery office as the original address, or the parcel at the time of such correction is lying at a returned letter office, the sender shall pay additional postage at the appropriate rate as if the transmission of the parcel to the corrected address were a fresh transmission by post.

(5) Where for any reason a parcel cannot be delivered, and paragraph (4) is not applicable, and

(a) the parcel is subsequently retransmitted to the addressee at the request of the sender or the addressee ; or

(b) the name and address of a substituted addressee has been furnished by the sender or the addressee and the parcel is transmitted to the substituted address ;

the addressee or, as the case may be, the substituted addressee, shall pay additional postage at the appropriate rate as if such retransmission or transmission were a fresh transmission of the parcel by post.

(6) Notwithstanding anything herein contained, a parcel shall not be given up or returned by post to the sender except upon payment by him of any charge to which the parcel has become liable under the provisions of any such regulations as are referred to in section 16 of the Act.

(7) The Postmaster General may require proof to his satisfaction that an applicant for a parcel is entitled to receive it.

(8) Where an applicant fails to prove to the satisfaction of the Postmaster General that he is entitled to receive the parcel, or refuses or fails to pay any charges to which the parcel has become liable, the parcel may be dealt with or disposed of in such manner as the Postmaster General may think fit.

(9) Any parcel in the possession of the Postmaster General which becomes offensive or injurious to any officer of the Post Office, or other person, or to other parcels, or which is likely from its character or conditions to become offensive or injurious as aforesaid, or to become valueless before it can be delivered or otherwise dealt with in accordance with the provisions of these regulations, may forthwith be dealt with or disposed of in such manner as the Postmaster General may think fit, notwithstanding that the provisions of these regulations as to the return of such parcel have not been, or have only partially been, complied with.

Treatment of packets addressed to deceased persons

14.—(1) Where the Postmaster General is satisfied that the addressee of postal packets is dead he may in his discretion :

(a) deliver or redirect such postal packets on the written application of any one or more of the executors named in the will of the addressee or of a person appearing to the Postmaster General to be entitled to take out letters of administration to the estate of the addressee, or in Scotland of a majority or quorum of the executors or (if there is no will) of the person whose appointment is being sought as executor dative ; or (*b*) deliver or redirect such postal packets on the written application of any person appearing to the Postmaster General to be conducting the affairs of the deceased addressee of the postal packets ; or

(*c*) retain such postal packets for such period as he may think fit and on production of probate of the will or letters of administration to the estate of the addressee together with the written application of one or more of the executors or administrators, or in Scotland on production of confirmation together with the written application of a majority or quorum of the executors or the executor dative, deliver or redirect the packets in accordance with such request ; or

(*d*) treat such postal packets in accordance with the provisions of these regulations as postal packets which cannot be delivered.

(2) The charges specified in paragraph 13 A of Schedule 2 shall be payable for redirection under this regulation, and regulation 5 shall apply to parcels so redirected.

PART IV

CONDITIONS RELATING TO PARTICULAR CLASSES OF POSTAL PACKETS

Cards

15. A letter consisting of a card not enclosed in an outer covering shall be made of material of such rigidity and thickness that its sorting and handling will not be hindered ; and no writing or printing, other than the name and address of the addressee, shall appear on the right hand half of the face thereof.

Printed packets

16.—(1) In these regulations the expression "printed packet" means a packet intended by the sender to be transmitted at the rate of postage specified in item 2 of Schedule 1 and which consists of or contains only articles or documents of the following descriptions :

(*a*) Books, magazines, newspapers, and other similar publications or works of a literary or technical character, whether containing written dedications or not ; sheet music ; catalogues ; almanacs ; and annual diaries ; in each case being printed on paper or on some other substance ordinarily used for printing ;

(*b*) Sketches, drawings, paintings, photographic prints, and engravings, on paper or on some other substance ordinarily used for the purpose, provided it is not a brittle or exceptionally fragile substance ;

(*c*) Maps, plans and charts, on paper or some other substance ordinarily used for the purpose, provided it is not a brittle or exceptionally fragile substance ;

(*d*) The binding or mounting of any article hereinbefore described, provided such binding or mounting be of a kind ordinarily used for the purpose, be not made of glass, or any brittle or exceptionally fragile substance, and be transmitted in the same packet with the article in respect of which it is used ;

(*e*) Letters and postcards which are out of date and have already fulfilled their original purpose ; tickets which may lawfully be sent through the post by virtue of section 45 of the Betting, Gaming and Lotteries Act 1963(**a**) or section 27 of the Betting and Lotteries Act (Northern Ireland) 1957(**b**) ; dress patterns and dress transfers ;

<hr>

(**a**) 1963 c. 2.   (**b**) 1957 c. 19 (N.I.).

(*f*) the following documents, whether containing matter in the nature of a letter or not, provided they respectively conform to the following conditions:

Description of Document	Conditions
(i) Commercial or business papers of a formal character, namely, invoices, orders for goods, or for work to be done, estimates for work, confirmations of orders, advice notes of the despatch or receipt of letters, documents, goods, or money (with or without instructions for their further treatment), waybills, bills of lading, receipts for goods or money, statements of account, price lists, prices current, market reports, delivery and shipping notes, tenders for goods or for advertisements, quotations for goods, inquiries for quotations, contract notes, confirmations of contracts, share transfer notices, applications for employment, and such other similar documents as the Postmaster General may from time to time permit.	(i), (ii) and (iii) That the documents consist of forms bearing printed matter clearly indicating the purpose for which the forms are intended to be used and that any writing refer solely to the subject-matter, or consist of a formula of courtesy or of a conventional character not exceeding five words or initials.
(ii) Notices, applications, certificates, reports and returns given or made to or by public officers and local authorities or other public bodies in the discharge of their public duties.	
(iii) Lists and tabular statements.	
(iv) Deeds, agreements, affidavits, Orders of Court, briefs from Solicitor to Counsel, proposals and policies of insurance, and formal papers necessarily incident to insurance, powers of attorney, proxy papers, licences, voting papers, testimonials and certificates. Copies of any of the foregoing documents.	(iv) That nothing appears in the documents in writing which does not form a necessary part thereof.
(v) Circulars (that is, printed notices and letters).	(v) That nothing appear in writing on the documents except: (1) Dates, hours and particulars of times. (2) The names, addresses and descriptions of parties. (3) The particulars of goods and of sums of money. (4) The mode of consignment or delivery of goods or money.

Description of Document	Conditions
(v) Circulars (that is, printed notices and letters,—*continued*	(5) The terms on which business is transacted. (6) Index or reference numbers and letters. (7) Corrections of errors in print. (8) The place, character and objects of meetings or appointments. (9) A formula of courtesy or of a conventional character not exceeding five words or initials.
(vi) Printed Christmas, New Year, Easter, Birthday, Greeting, Picture and Visiting Cards and Calendars.	(vi) That the documents be not sent as samples or for the purpose of sale, and that nothing appear in writing in the documents except: (1) Date of sending and names and addresses of sender and addressee. (2) A formula of courtesy or of a conventional character not exceeding five words or initials.
(vii) Manuscripts for press and printed proofs (including information for insertion in directories and similar publications) with corrections and instructions.	(vii) That any writing not forming part of the documents themselves refer solely to the arrangement or correction of the type or to the execution of the work.
(viii) Educational exercises and examination papers with comments, corrections and instructions.	(viii) That any writing not forming parts of the documents themselves refer solely to the subject-matter of the exercise or to the questions put or the answers thereto.
(ix) Addressed envelopes, cards, labels, or wrappers.	(ix) That not more than three such articles be enclosed in one packet, and that such articles be intended for return by post to the sender or a person designated by him.
(x) Blank forms.	(x) That the forms consist of paper bearing printed matter only, that not more than three forms of the same description be enclosed in one packet, that the forms be intended to be completed by the addressee, and that they be accompanied by a covering document which is transmissible in a printed packet.

(g) Anything necessary or convenient for the safe transmission of any of the before-mentioned articles by post when transmitted in the same packet with the article in respect of which it is so used:

Provided that:

(i) Any two or more documents coming within the definition of a printed packet may appear on the same sheet of paper, provided they are kept wholly distinct from one another;

(ii) On any printed packet or on its cover it is allowed to indicate, by hand or by a mechanical process, the name, description and address of the sender or of the addressee, and the date of despatch, the sender's signature, telephone number and telegraphic address and code ;

(iii) Any formula of courtesy or of a conventional character which may be written on any particular document may be written on the envelope, or on a fly leaf, or on a loose sheet accompanying the document, instead of on the document itself.

(2) In paragraph (1) expressions referring to print or printing shall be taken to refer to any species of type-printing easy to recognise as such, and to include lithography, hand stamping, or any mechanical process ordinarily used to produce a number of identical copies of written matter, and easy to recognise as such, but (except in relation to any article or document referred to in paragraph (1)(a) or to circulars) shall not be taken to include typeprinting after the fashion or in imitation of typewriting, or the reproduction of typewriting by the Mimeograph or any other mechanical process ordinarily used to produce a number of identical copies of written matter ; and expressions referring to writing shall be taken to include typewriting or any mechanical or other process ordinarily used to produce a single document.

(3) Every printed packet shall be subject to examination in the post, and if posted without a cover shall not be fastened or otherwise treated so as to prevent easy examination. A covered packet shall be unfastened or (save as the Postmaster General may either generally or in any particular case allow) so adapted that the contents can be easily examined without breaking any seal or tearing any paper or cutting any string or separating any adhering surfaces.

(4) No printed packet shall contain or bear any communication in the nature of a letter not being matter coming within the definition of such packet or being otherwise expressly allowed by these regulations.

(5) No circular which is reproduced from or produced after the fashion or in imitation of a typewritten document shall be sent by post as a printed packet save under such conditions as the Postmaster General may from time to time consider appropriate.

(6) No paper money shall be posted or conveyed or delivered by post in a printed packet:

Provided that this paragraph shall not apply to a single stamped proxy paper or to a single stamped and addressed card, wrapper or envelope forwarded by the sender of the packet in order that such card, wrapper or envelope may be returned through the post to such sender or some person designated by him.

Deferment of second class letters and printed packets

17. Any second class letter or printed packet may be withheld from despatch or delivery until any subsequent despatch or delivery.

Registration of newspapers under the Act

18. The fee for each registration of a newspaper under section 12 of the Act shall be 5s.

Conditions as to current registered newspapers

19.—(1) Every current registered newspaper or the cover or envelope thereof shall be prominently marked on the outside "Newspaper Post" and shall be subject to examination in the post, and if posted without a cover shall not be fastened or otherwise treated so as to prevent easy examination. The cover or envelope of a covered current registered newspaper shall be unfastened or (save as the Postmaster General may either generally or in any particular case allow) so adapted that the contents can be easily examined without breaking any seal or tearing any paper or cutting any string or separating any surfaces.

(2) Save as the Postmaster General may either generally or in any particular case allow, every current registered newspaper when posted shall be so folded and covered (if posted in a cover or envelope) as to permit the title and date of issue to be readily inspected.

(3) No article (not part of the newspaper) shall be posted in or in the cover or envelope with a current registered newspaper.

(4) No current registered newspaper and no cover or envelope in which it is enclosed shall bear anything (not being part of the newspaper) except :

(*a*) the names, addresses and descriptions of the sender and addressee with index or reference numbers and letters ;

(*b*) the words "With compliments", "Specimen copy" or "Voucher copy" ;

(*c*) the title of the newspaper, and a reference to its registration for transmission by post ; and

(*d*) a reference to any page of or place in the newspaper to which the attention of the addressee is directed.

Parcels

20.—(1) All parcels intended to be transmitted by post shall be posted : (*a*) by being handed in at a post office to an officer on duty at the counter, on the days and within the hours during which such office shall be open to the public for the posting of parcels, or (*b*) (in circumstances in which the Postmaster General permits that mode of posting) by being handed to an officer of the Post Office for the time being authorised to receive parcels for the post otherwise than at a post office.

(2) Every parcel shall be packed in such a manner as in the opinion of the Postmaster General is calculated to preserve the contents from loss or damage in the post and to prevent any tampering with its contents.

Parcels—Channel Islands and Isle of Man

21.—(1) Parcels which may be brought into or sent out of the United Kingdom by post from or to the Channel Islands or the Isle of Man shall not be posted conveyed or delivered except subject to such regulations as are referred to in section 16 of the Act.

(2) In respect of every parcel brought into or sent out of the United Kingdom by post from or to the Channel Islands to which such regulations as aforesaid apply, and upon the contents of which any customs duty is payable, there shall be charged and paid the further fee of 2s. 9d.

Parcels in bond

22.—(1) The Postmaster General may, on application being made in such manner as he may direct by the addressee of any parcel which is received in the United Kingdom by post from the Channel Islands and is in the custody of the Postmaster General at some place appointed by him and the Commissioners of Customs and Excise for customs examination :

(a) make a search for the parcel in order that it may if possible receive expedited customs examination ; or

(b) permit the addressee or his authorised agent, attending at the place where the parcel is, to inspect the parcel ; or

(c) re-address the parcel to any person either within or outside the British postal area ; or

(d) permit the addressee or his authorised agent, attending at the place where the parcel is, to re-address the parcel to any person either within or outside the British postal area.

(2) There shall be charged and paid in respect of the facilities provided for in this regulation :

(i) for each of the facilities mentioned in sub-paragraphs (a), (b) and (c) of paragraph (1), the fee appropriate to the number of parcels comprised in the application, according to the scale of fees set out in columns 1 and 2 of the table following ;

(ii) for the facility mentioned in paragraph (1)(d), the fee appropriate to the number of parcels comprised in the application, according to the scale of fees set out in columns 1 and 3 of the table following.

TABLE

Col. 1	Col. 2	Col. 3
	£ s. d.	£ s. d.
Number of packets:		
1	10 0	5 0
2	14 0	7 0
3	18 0	9 0
4	1 2 0	11 0
5	1 4 0	12 0
6 to 10 inclusive	1 8 0	14 0
11 to 20 ,, ...	1 16 0	18 0
21 to 30 ,, ...	2 4 0	1 2 0
31 to 40 ,, ...	2 12 0	1 6 0
41 to 50 ,, ...	3 0 0	1 10 0
Every additional 25 or part thereof	10 0	5 0

(3) Any fee charged under regulation 21(2) on a parcel which is re-addressed under this regulation shall be paid by the original addressee.

(4) There shall be charged and paid by the original addressee in respect of each parcel which is re-addressed under this regulation :

(a) to an address in the British postal area or the Republic of Ireland, such additional postage and fees (if any) as would have been payable thereon if it had been redirected under regulation 28 ;

(*b*) to an address elsewhere, such additional postage and fees (if any) as would have been payable thereon if it had been redirected under regulation 22 of the British Commonwealth and Foreign Parcel Post Regulations 1965(**a**), as amended (**b**).

(5) Where notice has been given under regulation 9(1) of the Postal Packets (Customs and Excise) Regulations 1966(**c**), as amended (**d**), requiring entry to be made of the goods in a parcel which is received in the United Kingdom by post from the Channel Islands and the parcel remains in the custody of the Postmaster General at some place appointed by him and the Commissioners of Customs and Excise for customs examination for a period of more than 28 days after the date of such notice, there shall be charged on the parcel (in addition to any other fees payable under these regulations) a fee, not exceeding 27s., calculated at the rate of 1s. for each day or part of a day in excess of the said period of 28 days during which the parcel remains in the custody of the Postmaster General as aforesaid ; and the fee shall be paid by the addressee.

Articles for the use of the blind

23.—(1) In these regulations the expression "articles for the use of the blind" means :

(i) Books and papers (including letters to or from blind persons) impressed or otherwise prepared for the use of the blind ;

(ii) Paper posted to any person for the purpose of being so impressed or prepared ;

and the following articles specially adapted for the use of the blind :

(iii) Relief maps ;

(iv) Machines, frames and attachments for making impressions for the use of the blind ;

(v) Pencil writing frames and attachments ;

(vi) Braillette boards and metal pegs therefor ;

(vii) De Braille instructional devices ;

(viii) Games (including card games) ;

(ix) Mathematical appliances and attachments ;

(x) Voice records on discs, film, tape or wire of readings from books, journals, newspapers, periodicals or other similar printed publications ;

(xi) Metal plates impressed, or posted for the purpose of being impressed, for the use of the blind ;

(xii) Wrappers and labels for use on postal packets for the blind—bulk supplies ;

(xiii) Braille watches, clocks, and timers ;

(xiv) Tools, aids and precision instruments ;

(xv) Rules and measures ;

(xvi) Sectional or collapsible walking sticks ;

(xvii) Harness for guide dogs.

(**a**) S.I. 1965/1734 (1965 III, p. 4859).
(**b**) The relevant amending instrument is S.I. 1966/913 (1966 II, p. 2190).
(**c**) S.I. 1966/66 (1966 I, p. 134).　　　　(**d**) S.I. 1968/931 (1968 II, p. 2440).

(2) The following provisions shall apply to postal packets consisting of articles for the use of the blind ;

(a) Every packet shall bear on the outside thereof the inscription "Articles for the blind" and the written or printed name and address of the sender.

(b) Every packet shall be subject to examination in the post.

(c) Every packet shall be posted either without a cover or in a cover which can be easily removed for the purposes of examination.

(d) No packet shall contain any article not being an article for the use of the blind (except a label which may bear the name and address of the person to whom the packet is to be returned).

(e) No packet shall contain any communication or inscription either in writing or printing (except the title, date of publication or manufacture, serial number, names and addresses of printer, publisher or manufacturer, price and table of contents of the book or paper, and any key to or instructions for the use of the special type or of any enclosed article).

(f) Articles (viii) to (xvii) (inclusive) mentioned in paragraph (1) may be sent only to blind persons by such institutions as have entered into special arrangements to the satisfaction of the Postmaster General with regard to the transmission of such articles, or to such institutions by blind persons.

Unaddressed packets

24.—(1) Subject to the following paragraphs of this regulation, unaddressed packets may be sent in a consignment for general delivery within an area in respect of which the unaddressed packet delivery service is available.

(2) The number of unaddressed packets in each consignment shall be such as the Postmaster General shall require, having regard to the number of delivery points in the delivery area.

(3) The packets comprised in a consignment of unaddressed packets shall be identical with each other in all respects, and the weight (which shall not exceed 2 lb.), dimensions and shape of each shall be such as the Postmaster General may approve.

(4) Every unaddressed packet shall be subject to examination in the post. Save as the Postmaster General may allow either generally or in respect of any category of unaddressed packets or in any particular case, a packet without a cover shall not be fastened or otherwise treated so as to prevent easy examination, and a covered or enveloped packet shall be so made up that the contents can be easily examined without breaking any seal or tearing any paper or cutting any string or separating any adhering surfaces.

(5) The sender shall comply with such conditions as the Postmaster General may consider appropriate either generally or in the particular case as to :

(a) the provision by the sender to the Post Office of a specimen of the unaddressed packets to be included in a proposed consignment before the consignment is posted ;

(b) the assembly of the individual unaddressed packets into groups or bundles by the sender, and their enclosure by him in mail bags or other containers ;

(c) the manner, time, day and office at which a consignment of un-addressed packets is to be posted ;

(d) any incidental or supplemental matters for which the Postmaster General may consider it expedient to provide.

(6) There shall be charged and paid on unaddressed packets such rates of postage as the Postmaster General may fix, and different rates may be fixed for different circumstances, including in particular the circumstance whether the packets are to be delivered in a town postal delivery area or a rural delivery area :

Provided that the rate of postage charged and paid on a consignment of unaddressed packets shall not exceed the total postage which would have been payable under these regulations on the individual packets comprised in the consignment if each had been posted singly, in the case of a packet not exceed-ing 1 lb. 8 oz. in weight as a second class letter and in the case of a packet exceeding 1 lb. 8 oz. as a printed packet.

(7) The Postmaster General shall publish in the London, Edinburgh and Belfast Gazettes or in such other manner as he may determine the rates of postage from time to time fixed by him under the last preceding paragraph.

(8) Postage on unaddressed packets shall be paid in such manner as the Postmaster General shall require.

(9) The Postmaster General may if he thinks fit refuse to accept any con-signment or part of a consignment of unaddressed packets for delivery.

(10) The Postmaster General may defer for such time as he thinks fit the delivery of any unaddressed packets.

(11) Any unaddressed packet which is not delivered may be dealt with or disposed of as the Postmaster General may think fit.

(12) The Postmaster General may provide as postal facilities in relation to unaddressed packets such incidental services as he may consider expedient, and the fees for any services so provided shall be such as the Postmaster General may fix either generally or in any particular case, and shall be paid in such manner as the Postmaster General shall require.

(13) (a) An unaddressed packet shall not be regarded as a printed packet for the purpose of these regulations.

(b) For the purpose of the definition of "inland" in regulation 1(1), an unaddressed packet shall be deemed to be addressed to a place within the area in which it is to be delivered.

(c) Regulations 10(3), 12, 33 and 40 shall not apply to unaddressed packets.

PART V—POSTAL FACILITIES

General

25.—(1) There shall be charged and paid for the postal facilities specified in the first column of Schedule 2 the charges specified or referred to in the second column of the said Schedule, and the said facilities shall be subject to the conditions and provisions contained in the body of these regulations.

(2) The postal facilities referred to in this Part of these regulations and in Schedules 2 and 3 may be provided by the Postmaster General at such times, during such periods, and at such post offices, in such circumstances, and on such conditions (not being inconsistent with the provisions of these regulations) as the Postmaster General may from time to time consider expedient.

Express delivery

26.—(1) There shall be charged and paid for the conveyance of an express packet conveyed in the manner specified in the first column of Schedule 3 fees at the rates specified in the second and fourth columns of the said Schedule. The facilities shall be subject to the limits of size and weight of the postal packets conveyed referred to in the third column of the said Schedule, to the provisions specified in the fourth column thereof and to the further provisions contained in the body of these regulations.

(2) An express packet (other than a packet to be conveyed by special messenger to an office of collection for transmission by ordinary post through the remainder of its course in the post) shall bear the word "Express" or such other words, and such lines or marks, as the Postmaster General may require.

(3) An express packet to be conveyed by special messenger throughout the whole of its course in the post shall be posted :

(*a*) by being handed in at a post office to an officer on duty at the counter, or

(*b*) (in circumstances in which the Postmaster General permits that mode of posting) by being handed to an officer of the Post Office for the time being authorised to receive such express packets otherwise than at a post office.

(4) The sender or addressee of an express packet may require the messenger who delivers the packet to convey an express packet by way of reply or further service. There shall be charged and paid in respect of the last mentioned packet the charges specified in Schedule 3.

(5) The Postmaster General may forward a packet as an express packet although the full postage and fees chargeable thereon are not prepaid, and if the addressee refuses to pay the amount payable in respect of the deficiency, it shall be paid by the sender. In no case shall the Postmaster General be bound to deliver any express packet not fully prepaid unless the addressee pays the amount payable thereon.

(6) Subject to the provisions of these regulations as to express delivery, all express packets shall be forwarded, conveyed, and delivered in all respects subject to the provisions of the Acts and regulations in force for the time being in relation to inland postal packets, so far as the same are applicable.

Railex service

27.—(1) A letter intended to be transmitted by a railex service shall be posted by being handed to an officer of the Post Office on duty at the counter at a post office which is also an express delivery office.

(2) A letter shall not be posted for transmission by a railex service:

(*a*) as a registered postal packet, or

(*b*) if it contains coin or jewellery.

(3) No postal packet other than a letter may be transmitted by a railex service.

(4) The delivery of a letter transmitted by a railex service to the addressee from the railway station to which it was conveyed by railway will be by special messenger meeting the train if, but only if, it arrives at that station at a time when a messenger is on duty.

Redirection by the public

28.—(1) Any postal packet (other than a business reply packet and a postage forward parcel) may be redirected from its original address, or any substituted address, to the same addressee at any other address in the British postal area or the Republic of Ireland.

(2) Any postal packet (other than a parcel) so redirected on the day of its delivery at the address from which it is redirected, or on the day next following (Sundays, Christmas Day, Good Friday, and public holidays being disregarded for this purpose), shall be transmitted by post free of any charge or postage in respect of such transmission :

Provided that this paragraph shall not apply if before redirection the packet has been opened, or altered otherwise than by the substitution of a new address, or if the name of the addressee has been obscured by any adhesive label used to indicate the new address.

(3) Subject to paragraph (2), there shall be charged on each redirection of a postal packet, and (if not previously paid) paid by the addressee on the delivery of the packet, the following additional postage and fees :

(*a*) (i) In the case of a recorded delivery packet redirected to an address in the British postal area, additional postage at the appropriate rate as if the transmission of the packet to the new address were a fresh transmission by post together with an additional recorded delivery fee of 9d. ;

(ii) In the case of any other unregistered postal packet (including an unregistered parcel), the said additional postage ;

(*b*) In the case of a registered postal packet (including a registered parcel), the said additional postage together with an additional minimum registration fee :

Provided that (without prejudice to his general power of remission under regulation 54) the Postmaster General may remit such additional postage and (where applicable) registration fee in the case of a parcel redirected within the period mentioned in paragraph (2), if the parcel is redirected to an address served from the same delivery office or to an address within the same local parcel delivery area, and may remit such additional registration fee as aforesaid in the case of a registered parcel redirected within such period where the parcel is redirected to an address which is not served as aforesaid.

(4) (*a*) A second class letter or printed packet which is redirected and to which paragraph (2) of this regulation applies may be withheld from despatch or delivery until any subsequent despatch or delivery.

(*b*) Any letter which is redirected and to which paragraph (3) of this regulation applies may be withheld from despatch or delivery until any subsequent despatch or delivery unless before it is redirected there is paid the additional postage mentioned in that paragraph at the rate specified in or fixed under Schedule 1 appropriate for its transmission as a first class letter together with any fee chargeable under the said paragraph.

Evasion of postage by redirection

29.—(1) In any case where the Postmaster General considers that a packet, purporting to be redirected, has been posted as a redirected packet with a view to evading the payment of any postage chargeable by law upon such packet, he may, before the delivery of such packet, require the addressee (who shall furnish proof of identity to the satisfaction of the Postmaster General) to sign a receipt for the same.

(2) Any redirected packet which appears to have been opened before being redirected, and any packet which purports to be redirected, but which appears to have been treated in a manner designed to evade the payment of any postage chargeable thereon by law, shall be dealt with and charged as an unpaid packet of the same description or otherwise dealt with as the Postmaster General may think fit.

Poste restante

30. The following provisions shall apply to postal packets addressed to a post office to be called for :

(a) Except as the Postmaster General may otherwise decide, the service is provided only for the convenience of travellers.

(b) The address of such packets shall include the words "To be called for" or "Poste Restante".

(c) Such packets shall not be addressed to an addressee designated by a fictitious name, or by initials only, or by a Christian name without a surname.

(d) The Postmaster General may refuse to deliver any such packet to a caller unless he is satisfied of the caller's identity.

(e) Such packets shall not be retained at the post office for delivery to the caller for more than 14 days, unless the Postmaster General shall otherwise decide in relation to any particular packet or class or description of packets.

(f) The Postmaster General may refuse or cease to retain for delivery to the caller any such packet the retention of which would in his opinion involve an abuse of the service, or which contravenes paragraphs (b) or (c), or which is addressed to a post office at which the service is not available.

(g) The sender may add to the address of any such packet a request that the packet may, if not called for within the time specified in the request, be returned to the sender or some person designated by him ; and (subject to paragraph (e)) at the expiration of such time the packet shall be returned as specified in the request.

(h) The provisions of these regulations as to the return of postal packets shall apply to any such packet which the Postmaster General refuses or ceases to retain for delivery to the caller.

Rebate postings of second class letters and printed packets

31.—(1) The Postmaster General may make arrangements with the senders of second class letters or printed packets for the acceptance and transmission of such letters or packets as a rebate posting under this regulation.

(2) A rebate posting shall consist of a consignment of not less than 4,501 second class letters or not less than 4,501 printed packets all sent by the same sender, each (except where the Postmaster General otherwise allows) being identical with the others in size and shape and in the nature of its contents.

(3) Unless the Postmaster General in any particular case otherwise allows in writing, a person who proposes to make a rebate posting shall make application therefor to the Postmaster General on a prescribed postal form at least 24 hours before the time at which he wishes to make the posting.

(4) Without prejudice to the generality of regulation 25(2), the sender shall comply with such conditions as the Postmaster General may consider appropriate in the particular case as to:

(*a*) the manner in which the postage on the individual postal packets comprised in the rebate posting is to be paid ;

(*b*) the sorting and assembly of the individual postal packets by the sender into groups according to their addresses ;

(*c*) the manner, time, day, and office at which the rebate posting is to be delivered to the Post Office for transmission ;

(*d*) any incidental or supplemental matters for which the Postmaster General may consider it expedient to provide.

(5) Where the Postmaster General accepts a rebate posting for transmission under this regulation, and the sender complies with the said conditions, the Postmaster General shall refund to the sender or allow him in account:

(*a*) Where the number of the postal packets comprised in the rebate posting is between 4,501 and 4,999 (inclusive), the amount by which the total postage charged on those packets exceeds the net payment in respect of 5,000 postal packets. For the purpose of this paragraph, the net payment in respect of 5,000 postal packets means the total postage which would be charged on 5,000 postal packets similar to those comprised in the particular rebate posting less the amount which would be refunded or allowed in account in respect of such 5,000 packets under paragraph (*b*) if they were accepted as a rebate posting for transmission under this regulation and the sender complied with the said conditions.

(*b*) Where the number of the postal packets comprised in the rebate posting is between 5,000 and 22,222 (inclusive), one tenth of the total postage charged on those packets.

(*c*) Where the number of the postal packets comprised in the rebate posting is between 22,223 and 24,999 (inclusive), the amount by which the total postage charged on those packets exceeds the net payment in respect of 25,000 postal packets. For the purpose of this paragraph, the net payment in respect of 25,000 postal packets means the total postage which would be charged on 25,000 postal packets similar to those comprised in the particular rebate posting less the amount which would be refunded or allowed in account of respect of such 25,000 packets under paragraph (*d*) if they were accepted as a rebate posting for transmission under this regulation and the sender complied with the said conditions.

(*d*) Where the number of the postal packets comprised in the rebate posting is between 25,000 and 234,375 (inclusive), one fifth of the total postage charged on those packets.

(*e*) Where the number of the postal packets comprised in the rebate posting is between 234,376 and 249,999 (inclusive), the amount by which the total postage charged on those packets exceeds the net payment in respect of 250,000 postal packets. For the purpose of this paragraph, the net payment in respect of 250,000 postal packets means the total postage which would be charged on 250,000 postal packets similar to those comprised in the particular rebate posting less the amount which would be refunded or allowed in account in respect of such 250,000 packets under paragraph (*f*) if they were accepted as a rebate posting for transmission under this regulation and the sender complied with the said conditions.

    (*f*) Where the number of the postal packets comprised in the rebate posting exceeds 249,999, one quarter of the total postage charged on those packets.

(6) The Postmaster General may defer for such time as he thinks expedient the despatch or delivery of postal packets accepted for transmission as a rebate posting under this regulation.

Transmission of postal packets in bulk

32.—(1) The Postmaster General may make arrangements with any senders of unregistered postal packets (other than cash on delivery packets) for their acceptance and transmission as bulk postings under this regulation and such arrangements shall operate and continue in force at such times and during such periods as the Postmaster General may from time to time consider expedient.

(2) The senders of packets under this regulation shall comply with such conditions as the Postmaster General may consider appropriate either generally or in the particular case and regulation 20(1) shall not apply to any such packets which are parcels.

(3) There shall be charged and paid on packets accepted for transmission under this regulation such rates of postage as the Postmaster General may fix; and different rates may be fixed for different circumstances.

(4) Postage on packets accepted for transmission under this regulation shall be paid and denoted in such manner and at such time as the Postmaster General may require or permit and regulation 10(3) shall not apply to such packets.

(5) The provisions of regulations 26, 27 and 40 shall not apply to any packet transmitted under this regulation.

PART VI—REGISTRATION AND COMPENSATION

Registration

33.—(1) Subject to the provisions of these regulations, any postal packet other than a second class letter or a printed packet may be registered.

(2) There shall be charged and paid for the registration of any such postal packet the minimum registration fee, or, if the sender so elects, one of the higher registration fees specified in the first column of Part I of Schedule 4.

Conditions as to registered packets

34.—(1) The conditions set out in Part II of Schedule 4 shall be complied with in relation to a registered postal packet.

(2) For the purpose of section 9 of the Crown Proceedings Act 1947 the expression "sender" means the person on whose behalf the postal packet is posted but does not include a person at whose request the article or any of the articles contained in the postal packet is sent by the first mentioned person by post.

Receipts for registered packets

35. On the delivery of a registered postal packet the recipient shall give a written receipt therefor in the prescribed form. Where such a receipt is not obtained, the packet may nevertheless be delivered, or may be withheld and dealt with or disposed of in such manner as the Postmaster General may think fit.

Compulsory registration

36.—(1) If any postal packet having the word "registered", or any other word, phrase, or mark conveying the impression that the packet is registered or intended to be registered, written or impressed on it or on its envelope or cover, is found in the post or left at a post office, and the packet has not been registered, it shall be registered (whether or not it is eligible for registration under regulation 33(1)), and may be detained for that purpose at any post office through which it shall pass.

(2) Where an unregistered postal packet is found when in the post to contain:

(*a*) any uncrossed postal order in which the name of the payee has not been inserted; or

(*b*) any cheque or dividend warrant which is uncrossed and payable to bearer; or

(*c*) any bearer security (including a share warrant, scrip or subscription certificate, bond or relative coupon); or

(*d*) any bank note or currency note, being current in the British postal area or elsewhere; or

(*e*) any unobliterated postage or revenue stamp available for current use in the British postal area or elsewhere (except a revenue stamp embossed or impressed on an instrument which has been executed); or

(*f*) any National Savings stamp; or

(*g*) any coupon, voucher, token, card, stamp or similar document, exchangeable (singly or with any other such documents) for money, goods or services; or

(*h*) coin or jewellery;

of a total value of 10s. or over, the packet shall be registered (whether or not it is eligible for registration under regulation 33(1)), and may be detained for that purpose at any post office through which it passes. In this paragraph the expression "value", except in relation to jewellery, means face value.

(3) Any postal packet which is subject to compulsory registration under paragraph (1) or paragraph (2) shall be forwarded to the addressee or tendered to the sender (as the case may be) charged with the minimum registration fee and, in the case of a second class letter, an additional sum equal to the difference between the amount of the postage paid thereon and the amount of the postage which would have been payable if the letter had been posted as a first class letter. The amount (if any) of the postage which may have been prepaid in respect of any packet other than a second class letter in excess of the ordinary postage and (in the case of a recorded delivery packet) the fee of 9d. paid thereon, shall be accepted in payment or part payment (as the case may be) of such registration fee. If the said excess amount is greater than the minimum registration fee, the packet shall be forwarded or tendered as aforesaid charged with the highest registration fee which the said excess amount covers, and the said excess amount shall be accepted in payment of such last mentioned registration fee.

(4) Where upon tender of such postal packet to the addressee or sender he refuses or fails to pay the charges to which the same has become liable by law, the packet may be dealt with or disposed of in such manner as the Postmaster General may think fit.

Compensation for registered packets

37.—(1) The maximum amount which shall be available for compensating persons aggrieved by the loss of or damage to a registered postal packet (including a packet which has been registered compulsorily under these regulations) and its contents shall be the amount specified in the second column of Part I of Schedule 4 opposite to the amount of the registration fee paid or charged in respect of the packet.

(2) For the purpose of this regulation any fee payable under regulation 28 on redirection of the packet shall be disregarded.

Compensation for unregistered parcels

38. If any article of pecuniary value enclosed in, or forming part of, an unregistered parcel be lost or damaged whilst in the custody of the Postmaster General, the Postmaster General may pay to any person who may, in the opinion of the Postmaster General, establish a reasonable claim to compensation (having regard to the nature of the article, the care with which it was packed, and other circumstances) such sum, not exceeding £5, in respect of such parcel as he may think just.

Compensation for unregistered express packets

39. If any article of pecuniary value enclosed in, or forming any part of, an unregistered express packet, which is conveyed by special messenger throughout its whole course in the post, be lost or damaged whilst in the custody of the Postmaster General, the Postmaster General may pay to the person who may, in the opinion of the Postmaster General, establish a reasonable claim to compensation (having regard to the nature of the article, the care with which it was packed, and other circumstances) such sum, not exceeding £5, in respect of such packet as he may think just.

PART VII—RECORDED DELIVERY

Recorded delivery service

40.—(1) Subject to the provisions of these regulations, any unregistered postal packet other than a parcel may be sent by the recorded delivery service.

(2) There shall be charged and paid on each recorded delivery packet, in addition to any postage and other charges payable on such packet, a fee of 9d.

(3) If an unregistered postal packet (other than a parcel) to which is attached a label as required by regulation 41(2), is found in the post or left at a post office, and the requirements of paragraph (1) or paragraph (3) of regulation 41 have not been complied with, the packet shall be forwarded to the addressee or tendered to the sender (as the case may be) charged with the recorded delivery fee of 9d., but the amount (if any) of the postage which may have been prepaid in respect of the packet in excess of the ordinary postage shall be accepted in payment or part payment (as the case may be) of such recorded delivery fee.

Conditions as to recorded delivery packets

41. The following conditions shall be complied with in relation to a recorded delivery packet:

(1) The packet shall:

    (*a*) be handed to an officer on duty at a post office; or

    (*b*) be handed to some officer of the Post Office authorised to receive recorded delivery packets though not on duty at a post office, and any recorded delivery packet which has been transmitted to its original address and which is redirected in pursuance of regulation 28 shall also be handed to such an officer as aforesaid.

(2) The sender of the packet shall complete such form, and shall attach to the packet such label in such position, as may be prescribed.

(3) On the posting of the packet the person handing over the packet shall obtain a receipt therefor.

(4) (*a*) The packet shall be made up in a reasonably strong cover appropriate to its contents, and (except in the case of a printed packet, packet consisting of articles for the use of the blind or a current registered newspaper) so that no part of the contents can be removed without either breaking or tearing the case, wrapper or cover or forcing two adhesive surfaces apart, or breaking a seal.

    (*b*) Any article contained in the packet shall be adequately packed as a protection against damage in course of transmission. In particular:

    (i) an article which is of a fragile nature shall be packed in a container of sufficient strength and shall be surrounded in that container with sufficient and suitable material to protect the article against the effects of concussion, pressure and knocks to which postal packets are ordinarily exposed in transmission, and the packet shall bear the words " FRAGILE WITH CARE " written conspicuously in capital letters on the face of the cover above the address;

    (ii) an article which is liable to be damaged by bending shall be packed in a container of sufficient strength to prevent the article from being bent in transmission, and the packet shall bear the words "DO NOT BEND" written conspicuously in capital letters on the face of the cover above the address.

(5) No postal packet to be transmitted as a recorded delivery packet shall contain:

    (i) any uncrossed postal order in which the name of the payee has not been inserted;

    (ii) any cheque or dividend warrant which is uncrossed and payable to bearer;

    (iii) any bearer security (including a share warrant, scrip or subscription certificate, bond or relative coupon);

    (iv) any bank note or currency note, being current in the British postal area or elsewhere;

    (v) any unobliterated postage or revenue stamp available for current use in the British postal area or elsewhere (except a revenue stamp embossed or impressed on an instrument which has been executed);

    (vi) any National Savings stamp;

(vii) any coupon, voucher, token, card, stamp or similar document, exchangeable (singly or with any other such documents) for money, goods or services;

(viii) coin or jewellery; or

(ix) any other article or articles of which the market value or aggregate market value exceeds £2.

(6) (a) Where a recorded delivery packet has been delivered and it is alleged that loss or abstraction of or damage to the contents or any of the contents of the packet occurred whilst it was in course of transmission by post, the following things shall be produced on demand for the Postmaster General's inspection, in the condition as nearly as possible in which they were when the packet was delivered:

(i) The receipt therefor obtained on posting the packet;

(ii) Where loss or abstraction is alleged, the cover of the packet;

(iii) Where damage is alleged, the cover of the packet, the damaged article, its packing material, and any container in which the damaged article was enclosed.

(b) Where it is alleged that a recorded delivery packet has not been delivered, the receipt therefor obtained on posting the packet shall be produced on demand for the Postmaster Generals' inspection.

Receipts for recorded delivery packets

42. On the delivery of a recorded delivery packet the recipient shall give a written receipt therefor in the prescribed form. Where such a receipt is not obtained, the packet may nevertheless be delivered, or may be withheld and dealt with or disposed of in such manner as the Postmaster General may think fit.

Compensation for recorded delivery packets

43. If any article of pecuniary value enclosed in, or forming part of, a recorded delivery packet be lost or damaged whilst in the custody of the Postmaster General, the Postmaster General may pay to any person from whom a claim for compensation shall be received, and who shall establish a reasonable claim to compensation (having regard to the nature of the article, the care with which it was packed, and other circumstances) such sum, not exceeding £2, in respect of such packet as he may think just:

Provided that no compensation shall be paid in respect of a packet which has been redirected from its original address, or any substituted address, to the same addressee at any other address in the Republic of Ireland.

PART VIII—CASH ON DELIVERY

Fees and conditions

44.—(1) There shall be charged and paid on each cash on delivery packet, in addition to the postage and other charges payable on such packet, a fee according to the scale of fees set out in Schedule 5.

(2) Cash on delivery packets (other than parcels) shall be registered.

(3) No trade charge exceeding £50 shall be collected under these regulations.

(4) The sender of a cash on delivery packet shall fill up, as far as required, the prescribed form (in these regulations referred to as "the trade charge form"), and shall mark the packet in such manner and with such particulars as the Postmaster General may require.

(5) The fee payable on a cash on delivery packet shall be paid by the sender and shall be indicated on the trade charge form.

Delivery of cash on delivery packets

45.—(1) A cash on delivery packet shall not be given up to the addressee, or opened at his request, until the trade charge and any postage or other charges due thereon have been paid.

(2) Where the trade charge on a cash on delivery packet exceeds £20 or the trade charge and the postage or other charges due in respect of such packet exceed that sum, the Postmaster General may give notice to the addressee of the arrival thereof and before delivery is effected require the addressee to pay the amount due within such period and at such office as may be specified in the notice.

Payment of trade charge to sender

46.—(1) The Postmaster General shall upon receiving the trade charge from the addressee remit the same to the sender of the packet, or a person named by him, by means of a trade charge money order forming part of the trade charge form or by such other means as the Postmaster General may think fit.

(2) Except where payment is made to a banker, the receipt for the amount of the trade charge which forms part of the trade charge form shall be signed by the sender of the packet, or by the person named by him to receive the amount or by a person duly authorised in that behalf by the sender or the person named by him.

(3) When a trade charge money order is made payable to a company, corporation or society, the receipt may be given by means of a stamp of the name of the company, corporation or society, to which is appended the signature of an officer of the company, corporation or society together with a description of his office.

Trade charge money orders—crossing

47.—(1) A trade charge money order shall be crossed and marked "not negotiable", and, except where the Postmaster General shall otherwise direct, shall be paid to a banker.

(2) The order may be crossed either:

(*a*) generally by the addition on its face of two parallel transverse lines, or

(*b*) specially by the addition on its face of the name of a banker between the two parallel transverse lines, in which case the order shall be deemed to be crossed to and shall be paid to that banker.

(3) A banker to whom a trade charge money order is crossed may again cross it to another banker as his agent for collection.

Trade charge money orders—payment to bankers

48. The following rules shall apply to the payment of a trade charge money order to a banker:

(1) A trade charge money order may be presented for payment by a banker at any office at which payment of such orders presented by a banker may from time to time be authorised by the Postmaster General.

(2) Where a trade charge money order is presented by a banker, the name of the banker by or on behalf of whom such order is presented, written or stamped by way of crossing or otherwise, upon the face of the order, shall be a good receipt to the Postmaster General for the amount of the trade charge.

(3) Where a trade charge money order has been presented for payment by a banker and has been paid or allowed to a banker and it is afterwards discovered that such order should not have been paid or allowed to such banker, the amount so paid or allowed may be deducted from any moneys which may thereafter become payable to such banker for or on account or in respect of Post Office money orders, and no objection shall be taken by any banker to such deduction.

Discharge to Crown by payment

49. The payment of the amount of a trade charge money order in accordance with these regulations, to whomsoever made, shall discharge the Crown and every officer of the Post Office from all liability whatsoever in respect of that order and payment of the amount thereof notwithstanding any forgery, fraud, mistake, loss, neglect or omission which may have been committed or have occurred in the procuring of the order or obtaining the payment thereof or otherwise in relation thereto.

Void trade charge money orders

50. After the expiration of 6 months from the last day of the month in which any trade charge money order is issued the order shall be absolutely void and of no effect, and the Postmaster General shall be under no liability to pay the order:

Provided that in such case the Postmaster General may, if he thinks fit, pay the amount of the order, although the order has become void, subject to a deduction of a sum equal to the sum payable under the Money Order Regulations 1967(a), for the renewal of a void money order.

PART IX—MISCELLANEOUS AND GENERAL

Stamping of paper

51. The fees to be paid to the Postmaster General for stamping any paper sent to him for the purpose of being stamped for use as cards to be transmitted as letters or as covers or envelopes of postal packets shall be at the rates specified in Schedule 6.

Jury summonses

52. The fee to be paid (over and above the postage) for the registration of a jury summons under section 11 of the Juries Act 1862(b) (which section relates to the procedure for serving jury summonses by post) shall be 1d.

(a) S.I. 1967/801 (1967 II, p. 2360).   (b) 1862 c. 107.

Variation of route

53. Where any postal packet from its size, weight, character, or condition is in the opinion of the Postmaster General unfit for transmission by the route by which such packet would ordinarily travel in the post, such packet may be detained and forwarded by such other route as the Postmaster General may think fit.

Remission of postage

54. The Postmaster General may remit in whole or in part any postage or other sums chargeable under these regulations in such cases or classes of case as he may determine.

Application of the regulations to packets to and from the Republic of Ireland

55. The provisions of these regulations shall apply to postal packets transmitted between the British postal area and the Republic of Ireland so far as relates to the posting, registration, conveyance, delivery and treatment of such postal packets under the authority of the Postmaster General, subject nevertheless to the following modifications, exceptions and additions:

(1) In the application of the definitions of "first class letter", "preferred envelope" and "preferred letter" in regulation 1(1), and of regulations 3 and 9 to postal packets posted in any part of the British postal area for transmission to the Republic of Ireland, the description of such packets, the rates of postage, and the shape and limits of size and weight specified in Schedule 7 shall be substituted for the descriptions, rates, shape and limits specified in Schedule 1.

(2) For regulation 21 there shall be substituted the following regulation:

"21.—(1) Postal packets intended to be transmitted by post between the British postal area and the Republic of Ireland shall not be posted, forwarded, conveyed or delivered except subject to such regulations as are referred to in section 16 of the Act.

(2) Where the sender of a parcel addressed to the Republic of Ireland desires that the parcel may be delivered to the addressee free of all customs duty and other charges thereon, the following rules shall apply to the parcel:

(a) The sender shall mark on the cover of the parcel the words "To be delivered free of charges".

(b) The sender shall pay at the time of posting such sum as the Postmaster General may require as a deposit in respect of the customs duty and other charges which may be due on the parcel at the time of delivery.

(c) The sender shall sign an undertaking in the prescribed form to pay to the Postmaster General on demand the amount of the customs duty and the said other charges, less the amount of the deposit paid.

(d) The Postmaster General shall furnish to the sender a certificate of posting bearing an acknowledgment that the said deposit has been paid.

(e) If the deposit paid exceeds the amount of the customs duty and the said other charges, the Postmaster General shall repay the balance to the sender.

(3) Where a postal packet received in the British postal area from the Republic of Ireland contains any article liable to customs duty, and the Postmaster General so directs, there shall be charged and paid by the addressee if the packet shall be delivered to him a fee of 2s. 9d. in respect of a parcel and of 1s. 9d. in respect of any other postal packet."

(3) Regulation 22 shall apply in respect of parcels and other postal packets received in the United Kingdom by post from the Republic of Ireland as it applies in respect of parcels received from the Channel Islands, with the substitution of a reference to regulation 21(3) for the reference to regulation 21(2) and with the addition at the end of regulation 22(4)(*b*) of the words "or (in the case of a postal packet other than a parcel) the postage and fees which would have been payable thereon if it had been posted as a fresh packet for transmission under the British Commonwealth and Foreign Post Regulations 1965(a), as amended (b), to the new address."

(4) (i) No postal packet shall be transmitted between the British postal area and the Republic of Ireland as a business reply packet, a postage forward parcel, a cash on delivery packet, an unaddressed packet or a recorded delivery packet.

(ii) The service relating to an express packet, in so far as it provides for the conveyance of the packet by special messenger throughout the whole of its course in the post, and the railex service, shall not apply to postal packets transmitted between the British postal area and the Republic of Ireland.

(iii) Regulation 31 shall not apply to postal packets transmitted between the British postal area and the Republic of Ireland.

(5) For regulation 34 there shall be substituted the following regulation:

"34. The conditions set out in Part II of Schedule 4 shall be complied with in relation to a registered postal packet posted in the British postal area for transmission to an addressee in the Republic of Ireland."

(6) For regulation 37 there shall be substituted the following regulation:

"37.—(1) If any article of pecuniary value enclosed in or, forming part of, a registered postal packet be lost or damaged whilst in the custody of the Postmaster General, the Postmaster General may pay to any person or persons who may, in the opinion of the Postmaster General, establish a reasonable claim to compensation (having regard to the nature of the article, the care with which it was packed, and other circumstances) such sum as he may think just:

Provided that if the registration fee paid in respect of the registered postal packet so lost or damaged as aforesaid is the minimum registration fee or one of the higher registration fees specified in column 1 of Part I of Schedule 4 (any of which higher registration fees may be paid by the sender) the sum paid by way of compensation shall not exceed the sum specified in column 2 of the said Part of the said Schedule opposite the amount of the registration fee paid.

(2) The compensation payable in respect of a registered parcel shall be in substitution for, and not in addition to, any compensation which would have been payable under these regulations in case the parcel had not been registered."

(a) S.I. 1965/1735 (1965 III, p. 4878).
(b) S.I. 1965/2173, 1966/912 (1965 III, p. 6371; 1966 II, p. 2185).

(7) In the application of regulation 38 to unregistered parcels transmitted between the British postal area and the Republic of Ireland, for "£5" there shall be substituted "£4".

(8) If any postal packet transmitted between the British postal area and the Republic of Ireland, being a packet which is subject to compulsory registration, shall be posted without registration no claim to compensation will be considered by the Postmaster General to arise in respect of the loss or damage (if any) of any article enclosed in or forming part of such packet.

(9) The decision of the Postmaster General on all questions arising between him and any person claiming payment in respect of the loss of or damage to any article enclosed in or forming part of a registered postal packet or a parcel transmitted between the British postal area and the Republic of Ireland shall be final and conclusive.

(10) Where the postage payable on any postal packet (other than a parcel) transmitted between the British postal area and the Republic of Ireland has not been, or has been insufficiently, prepaid by the sender, there shall be payable by the addressee on the delivery of the packet, or if the packet is refused or cannot for any other reason be delivered, by the sender, an amount equal to double the amount of the postage, or, as the case may be, of the deficiency.

Revocation and transitional provision

56.—(1) The Inland Post Regulations 1967(a) and the Inland Post Amendment (No. 1) Regulations 1968(b) are hereby revoked.

(2) Any rate of postage which has been fixed by the Postmaster General under the regulations hereby revoked, and which is in force at the commencement of these regulations, shall continue in force until superseded by a rate of postage fixed by the Postmaster General under these regulations.

Citation and commencement

57. These regulations may be cited as the Inland Post Regulations 1968, and shall come into operation on 16th September 1968.

Dated 5th August 1968.

John Stonehouse,
Her Majesty's Postmaster General.

(a) S.I. 1967/1416 (1967 III, p. 4077).   (b) S.I. 1968/533 (1968 I, p. 1278).

Regulations 3, 9

SCHEDULE 1

RATES OF POSTAGE AND LIMITS OF SIZE AND WEIGHT

Col. 1 Description of Postal Packet	Col. 2 Rates of Postage		Col. 3 Limits of Size	Col. 4 Limits of Weight
1. Letter (a) preferred letter	(a) (i) If transmitted as a first class letter ...	5d.	(a) Rectangular and oblong the longer side being at least 1.414 times the shorter. Length Max. 9¼ inches. Min. 5½ inches. Width Max. 4½ inches. Min. 3½ inches.	(a) Not exceeding 4 oz.
	(ii) If transmitted as a second class letter ...	4d.		
(b) any other letter	(b) (i) If transmitted as a first class letter—		(b) Length 2 feet. Width or depth 18 inches.	(b) (i) No limits.
	Weight not exceeding 4 oz.	Such rate, not exceeding 7d., as the Postmaster General may fix.	In roll form: Length plus twice diameter 3 feet 3 inches. Greatest dimension 2 feet 8 inches.	
	Weight exceeding 4 oz. but not exceeding 6 oz. ...	9d.		
	For each additional 2 oz. or part thereof up to a total weight of 1 lb. 8 oz. ...	3d.		
	For the next 8oz. or part thereof ...	1s. 0d.		
	For each additional 1lb. or part thereof thereafter	2s. 0d.		

Regulations 3, 9

SCHEDULE 1—continued

Col. 1 Description of Postal Packet	Col. 2 Rates of Postage		Col. 3 Limits of Size	Col. 4 Limits of Weight
	(b) (ii) If transmitted as a second class letter—			(b) (ii) Not exceeding 1lb. 8 oz.
	Weight not exceeding 4oz.	Such rate, not exceeding 6d., as the Postmaster General may fix.		
	Weight exceeding 4 oz. but not exceeding 6oz.	6d.		
	For each additional 2oz. or part thereof up to a total weight of 1lb. 2oz.	2d.		
	For each additional 2oz. or part thereof thereafter	1d.		
2. Printed packet		2s. 0d.	As for item 1(b).	Exceeding 1lb. 8oz. but not exceeding 2lb.
3. Current registered newspaper	Weight not exceeding 4oz....	4d.	As for item 1(b).	Not exceeding 2lb.
	Weight exceeding 4oz. but not exceeding 6oz.	6d.		
	For each additional 2oz. or part thereof up to a total weight of 1lb. 2oz. ...	2d.		

Regulations 3, 9

SCHEDULE 1—*continued*

Col. 1 Description of Postal Packet	Col. 2 Rates of Postage		Col. 3 Limits of Size	Col. 4 Limits of Weight
	For each additional 2oz. or part thereof thereafter up to a total weight of 1lb. 8oz. ...	1d.		
	Weight exceeding 1lb. 8oz. ...	2s. 0d.		
4. Articles for the use of the blind	No rate specified.		As for item 1(*b*).	Not exceeding 15lb.
5. Parcel: (*a*) ordinary	Weight not exceeding 1lb. 8oz.	2s. 6d.	Greatest length 3 feet 6 inches.	Not exceeding 22lb.
	Exceeding 1lb. 8oz. but not exceeding 2lb.	3s. 0d.	Greatest length and girth combined 6 feet (the girth to be measured round the thickest part).	
	Exceeding 2lb but not exceeding 6lb.	4s. 6d.		
	Exceeding 6lb. but not exceeding 10lb.	6s. 0d.		
	Exceeding 10lb. but not exceeding 14lb.	7s. 6d.		
	Exceeding 14lb. but not exceeding 18lb.	9s. 0d.		
	Exceeding 18lb.	10s. 6d.		
(*b*) local	The rate in paragraph (*a*) minus 1s.			
6. Business reply packet	The appropriate rate in item 1 or item 2 plus 1d.		As for item 1(*a*) or (*b*) as appropriate.	As for item 1(*a*) or (*b*) or item 2 as appropriate.
7. Postage forward parcel	The appropriate rate in item 5 plus 4d.		As for item 5.	As for item 5.

Regulation 25   **SCHEDULE 2**

Postal Facilities

1. Certificate of posting of an unregistered postal packet, other than a parcel ...   .   1d.

2. Certificate of posting of an unregistered parcel   ...   ...   No fee.

3. Duplicate certificate of posting of a registered postal packet   3d.

4. Advice of delivery of, or inability to deliver, a registered postal packet:
   - (a) if requested at time of posting ...   .   9d.
   - (b) if requested after posting   ...   .   1s. 0d.

5. Enquiry for a missing registered postal packet   ...   ...   1s. 0d.

   (*Note:* This charge is not payable if the charge for advice of delivery of, or inability to deliver, the packet has already been paid by the sender.

   The Postmaster General may refund the enquiry charge if he is satisfied that the packet was lost or seriously delayed while in his custody.)

6. Advice of delivery of, or inability to deliver, a recorded delivery packet:
   - (a) if requested at time of posting ...   .   9d.
   - (b) if requested after posting   ...   .   1s. 0d.

7. Enquiry for a missing recorded delivery packet   ...   ...   1s. 0d.

   (*Note:* This charge is not payable if the charge for advice of delivery of, or inability to deliver, the packet has already been paid by the sender.

   The Postmaster General may refund the enquiry charge if he is satisfied that the packet was lost or seriously delayed while in his custody.)

8. Receipt for bulk postings which have been prepaid in stamps:
   - For the first 1,000 items   ...   .   2s. 0d.
   - For each additional 1,000 or part thereof ...   .   4d.

9. Private Posting Boxes. Collection by the Postmaster General of postal packets (other than parcels) posted in a private posting box (provided by the person requesting the facility) of a design and in a position approved by the Postmaster General (not being a private roadside letter box in a rural postal delivery area):
   - (1) For initial period of one year or less:
     - (a) For one collection, on six or fewer weekdays in every week   ...   .   £4 0s. 0d.
     - (b) For one collection on Sundays   ...   .   £4 0s. 0d.
     - (c) For one collection, on six or fewer weekdays and on Sunday in every week ...   .   £6 0s. 0d.
     - (d) For each additional collection, on six or fewer weekdays in every week   ...   .   £2 0s. 0d.
     - (e) For each additional collection on Sundays ...   ...   £2 0s. 0d.

(*f*) Where the posting box is above or below ground floor—for each floor which the collector has to ascend or descend to make the collection ... ...   Such fee not exceeding £3 as the Postmaster General may fix, having regard to the facilities available for ascent and descent.

(*g*) Distance fee, payable where the private posting box is in a rural postal delivery area, and the collection in the opinion of the Postmaster General involves travelling in excess of the normal route of the collecting officer.   Such fee as the Postmaster General may fix, having regard to the cost of the excess travelling.

(2) For each subsequent full year ...   .   The fees chargeable under (1).

(3) For a subsequent part only of a year ...   .   A rateable proportion of the fees chargeable under (1).

10. **Private Boxes.** Provision by the Postmaster General of a private box (other than a lockable private box provided under item 11) at a delivery office within a town postal delivery area, or at any other Post Office at which the facility is available, in which postal packets are placed to await collection by the addressee or his agent instead of being delivered by postmen at the place of address:

A.—For initial period of one year or less:

(1) For Day Box, that is to say, where the postal packets are to be made available for collection by the addressee or his agent at or after the time of commencement of the first delivery, or the time of opening the public office (whichever is the earlier), and before 9.0 p.m. or the time of closing the public office (whichever is the earlier):

(*a*) Box for reception of postal packets other than parcels, or for reception of parcels only:

     London Postal Area   ... ...   £7   0s.   0d.

     Elsewhere:

         Head Office, Branch or District Office being a delivery office, or Salaried Sub-Office   ...   £7   0s.   0d.
         Other Sub-Office...   ... ...   £4   0s.   0d.

(*b*) Box for reception of all classes of postal packets:

     London Postal Area   ... ...   £14   0s.   0d.

     Elsewhere:

         Head Office, Branch or District Office being a delivery office, or Salaried Sub-Office   ...   £14   0s.   0d.

         Other Sub-Office...   ... ...   £8   0s.   0d.

(2) Additional fee for Day Box where the postal packets are additionally to be made available for collection by the addressee at or after 6.0 a.m. and before the time of commencement of the first delivery or the time of opening of the public office (whichever is the earlier).   An amount equal to the fee chargeable under (1).

(3) For Night Box, that is to say, where the postal packets are to be available for collection after 9.0 p.m. or the time of closing the public office (whichever is the earlier) and before 6.0 a.m. — Double the amount chargeable under (1).

(*Note:* If the box is used both as a Day Box and as a Night Box, the fee referred to in (3) is chargeable in addition to the fee referred to in (1) and (where applicable) the fee referred to in (2).)

(4) Diversion fee, payable in addition to the fees referred to in (1), (2) and (3) where the holder of the private box carries on business at different addresses and postal packets addressed to him at more than one address are to be placed in the private box for collection:

For each address (after the first) to which packets are addressed, and for each style (after the first) in which packets are addressed to each address (after the first)   ...   .   £6 0s. 0d.

B.—For each subsequent full year ...   . — The fees chargeable under paragraph A.

C.—For a subsequent part only of a year ...   . — A rateable proportion of the fees chargeable under paragraph A.

11. **Lockable Private Boxes.** Provision by the Postmaster General of a lockable private box and key therefor at any post office at which the facility is available, being a box in which certain postal packets (other than parcels) addressed to the box number or to premises designated by the renter are placed to await collection by the renter or his agent.

For every year or part thereof   ...   .   £2 0s. 0d.

Each duplicate or replacement key ...   .   10s. 0d.

Note: Registered packets, recorded delivery packets, packets on which a charge or fee is due, and packets which for any reason cannot be placed in the box, if addressed to the box number or the designated address, will be held by the postmaster to await collection by the renter or his agent instead of being placed in the box for collection.

12. **Private Bags.** Use of a private bag, that is to say, a bag or other receptacle (provided by the owner with the approval of the Postmaster General) in which postal packets for or from a particular address (i) in a town postal delivery area may be collected or posted by the owner or his agent, or (ii) in a rural postal delivery area, may either be collected and posted by the owner or his agent or be delivered at the place of address and collected therefrom by the Postmaster General:

A.—For initial period of one year or less:

(1) Where the address concerned is in a town postal delivery area:

Use of bag:

(a) For posting postal packets other than parcels or for posting parcels only   ...   .   £3 0s. 0d.

(b) For posting all classes of postal packets   ...   £6 0s. 0d.

(c) For posting and collecting postal packets:

(i) if facilities under item 11 are not provided.	The fee appropriate under (a) or (b), plus the appropriate fee under item 10 A(1) as if the bag were a private box.
(ii) if facilities under item 11 are provided ...	The fee appropriate under (a) or (b) plus a fee of £2.

(2) Where the address concerned is in a rural postal delivery area:

(a) Bag collected and posted by the owner or his representative:

(i) Bag made up for one collection, on seven or fewer days of the week	£3 0s. 0d.
(ii) Bag made up for more than one collection, on seven or fewer days of the week.	£3 0s. 0d. plus £2 0s. 0d. for each making-up after the first.
(iii) Additional fee where the bag is made available for collection at or after 6.0 a.m., and before the time of commencement of the first delivery or the time of opening of the public office (whichever is the earlier) ...	£3 0s. 0d.

(b) Bag delivered and collected by the Postmaster General:

(i) Once a day on seven or fewer days of the week	£3 0s. 0d.
(ii) Twice a day on seven or fewer days of the week	£6 0s. 0d.

(*Note:* The fees referred to in (b) are payable even though the bag is used only for the delivery of postal packets or only for their posting.)

(c) Distance fee, payable where the bag is collected by the Postmaster General from an address in a rural postal delivery area, and the collection in the opinion of the Postmaster General involves travelling in excess of the normal route of the collecting officer.	Such fee as the Postmaster General may fix, having regard to the cost of the excess travelling.
(3) Diversion fee, payable in addition to the fees chargeable under (1) or (2) in the circumstances referred to in item 10 A (4).	As item 10 A (4).
B.—For each subsequent full year	The fees chargeable under paragraph A.
C.—For a subsequent part only of a year	A rateable proportion of the fees chargeable under paragraph A.

13. Redirection by the Post Office. Redirection of postal packets from their original address to the same addressee at another address:

A.—Where the original address is a business address and the addressee has permanently ceased to occupy the premises to which the packets are addressed, or where the original address is not a business address:

(1) For a period not exceeding 3 months ... ...   No fee.

(2) For a period exceeding 3 months:

(*a*) For the first 12 months or part thereof after the first 3 months, for each addressee ... ...   5s. 0d.

(*b*) For each subsequent period of 12 months or part thereof, for each addressee ... ...   10s. 0d.

(*Note:* (i) Where the original address is a private residence and postal packets addressed to several members of one family bearing the same surname are all to be redirected to one other address, the addressees are to be regarded together as constituting one addressee for the purpose of the fee payable under (2).

(ii) See also regulation 5 as to additional postage on parcels.)

B.—Where the original address is a business address and the addressee has temporarily ceased to occupy the premises to which the packets are addressed:

For each continuous period not exceeding 14 days ...   10s. 0d.

14. Diversion of Postal Packets. Delivery of postal packets addressed to the addressee's private address at his business address, or of postal packets addressed to one or more business addresses at another business address of the same addressee or at his private address, where the fee mentioned in item 13 is not applicable:

For each address from which packets are diverted, and for each style after the first in which packets are addressed to each such address:

(1) For initial period of one year or less ... ...   £6 0s. 0d.

(2) For each subsequent full year ... ...   £6 0s. 0d.

(3) For a subsequent part only of a year ... ...   A rateable proportion of the fee chargeable under (2).

15. Delivery at Post Office. Retention at a delivery office of postal packets (other than those addressed to a post office to be called for in accordance with regulation 30) and delivery to the addressee or his agent on his calling therefor:

(1) For postal packets of all classes where the appropriate delivery office is in a rural postal area:

           annual fee ... £3 0s. 0d.

(2) For registered postal packets and recorded delivery packets only, whether the appropriate delivery office is in a rural postal area or a town postal area:

           annual fee ... £1 10s. 0d.

Note:

(*a*) These annual fees are not charged if the addressee is the holder of a Private Box or Lockable Private Box at the post office concerned, or the holder of a Private Bag used for the collection of postal packets from that post office.

(*b*) The addressee may at his option, instead of paying the annual fee, pay the search fee under item 16 for each separate search.

16. Search Fee. Search made at a delivery office at the request of the addressee or his agent to ascertain whether any postal packets for a particular address are available for delivery:

for each search   6d.

Note: This fee is not charged:

(a) if the search is for postal packets addressed to a post office to be called for in accordance with regulation 30;

(b) if the addressee is the holder of a Private Box or Lockable Private Box at the post office concerned, or the holder of a Private Bag used for the collection of postal packets from that post office; or

(c) if the addressee has paid the annual fee under item 15 in respect of the period within which the search is made.

17. Temporary Retention. Withholding of postal packets from delivery at the request of the addressee:

(1) For a period not exceeding five consecutive weekdays at Easter or Christmas or on the occasion of a local holiday, or not exceeding three consecutive weekdays at Whitsun or August Bank Holiday (Sunday being disregarded).   No fee.

(2) For any other period, unbroken except by a Sunday, up to two months.   Such sum not exceeding £1 as the Postmaster General may fix.

18. Floor Fee. For delivery of postal packets for a business address at a floor other than the ground floor, or (where the addressee is not in occupation of the ground floor) at a floor other than the floor occupied by the addressee which is nearest to the ground floor:

For each extra floor to which the delivery officer has to ascend or descend to make the delivery, per annum ...   Such fee not exceeding £3 as the Postmaster General may fix, having regard to the facilities available for ascent and descent.

19. Separation Fee. For separating postal packets addressed to a particular Department of the addressee from other postal packets addressed to the addressee at the same address, and delivering them separately to that Department:

For each Department to which postal packets are separately delivered (in addition to the floor fee where item 18 applies), per annum ... ...   £7 0s. 0d.

20. Special Collections. Special collections from an address in a rural postal delivery area:

(1) For initial period of one year or less:

(a) for one collection, on seven or fewer days of the week ... ...   £1 0s. 0d.

(b) For each additional collection, on seven or fewer days of the week... ... ...   £1 0s. 0d.

(c) Distance fee, payable where the collection in the opinion of the Postmaster General involves travelling in excess of the normal route of the collecting officer.   Such fee as the Postmaster General may fix, having regard to the cost of the excess travelling.

(2) For each subsequent full year ... ... The fees chargeable under (1).

(3) For a subsequent part only of a year ... ... A rateable proportion of the fees chargeable under (1).

21. Private Roadside Letter Boxes. Delivery into or collection from a locked private roadside letter box in a rural postal delivery area, or both delivery and collection:

(1) For initial period of one year or less:

(a) Delivery only, where the box need not be unlocked for this purpose ... ... No fee.

(b) Delivery only, where the box has to be unlocked for this purpose; collection only; or delivery and collection:

(i) For one visit, on seven or fewer days of the week 7s. 6d.

(ii) For each additional visit, on seven or fewer days of the week ... ... 7s. 6d.

(2) For each subsequent full year ... ... The fees chargeable under (1).

(3) For a subsequent part only of a year ... ... A rateable proportion of the fees chargeable under (1).

SCHEDULE 3

EXPRESS DELIVERY SERVICES

Col. 1 Service	Col. 2 Fees	Col. 3 Limit of Size and Weight	Col. 4 Provisions
1. Conveyance by special messenger throughout the whole course of the packet in the post.	3s. a mile or part of a mile in addition to any fees or other sums ordinarily payable.	—	(1) The distance on which the mileage fee is charged includes the distance between the express delivery office which provides the service and the point where the conveyance of the packet begins. (2) When the special messenger has to deliver for the same sender two or more postal packets for the same or different addressees at the same or different addresses, the sum of 4d. is charged for each packet after the first, in addition to a single mileage fee for the whole journey. (3) The service is not available on Sunday or (except in Scotland) on Good Friday and Christmas Day; in Scotland the service is not available on New Year's Day.
2. Conveyance by special messenger from the office of delivery at the request of the addressee.	3s. a mile or part of a mile in addition to any postage, fees or other sums ordinarily payable.	As specified in Schedule 1.	(1) When an addressee requests the delivery by special messenger of more than one postal packet from the normal postal delivery office an additional charge of 6d. is made for every 10 packets (or less than 10 packets) after the first. The Postmaster General may in his discretion include in the delivery all postal packets which may be held for the addressee and in such case the same additional charge shall be paid by the addressee as would have been payable if such postal packets had been included in the delivery at the request of the addressee. (2) Where more than one search has to be made at the office of delivery for the packet or packets to which the request relates, a charge of 6d. is payable for each search after the first. (3) If no postal packet to which the request relates is found, and a messenger is sent to inform the applicant to that effect, the fee set out in Col. 2 is payable for this service, and is charged on the single distance between the office of delivery and the applicant's address. (4) Provision (3) of item 1 applies.

Col. 1 Service	Col. 2 Fees	Col. 3 Limit of Size and Weight	Col. 4 Provisions
3. Conveyance by special messenger of a postal packet from the office of delivery at the request of the sender.	3s. for delivery on weekdays in addition to any postage, fees or other sums ordinarily payable. 6s. in addition to the above for delivery on Sundays.	As specified in Schedule 1.	(1) For delivery on Sunday the service operates for postal packets (other than parcels) posted on Saturday for delivery on Sunday, but that service is available only between certain places. (2) Second class letters and printed packets will not be accepted in this service.
4. Conveyance by special messenger of a postal packet through part only of its course in the post, in any case where neither item 2 nor item 3 applies.	3s. a mile or part of a mile in addition to any postage, fees or other sums ordinarily payable.	As specified in Schedule 1.	(1) Provisions (1) and (3) of item 1 apply. (2) When the service is used for the conveyance of a postal packet to an office of collection for subsequent transmission by ordinary post, the payment for the express service shall be by means of postage stamps affixed to a postal form. (3) Second class letters and printed packets will not be accepted in this service.
5. Hire of cab or other vehicle for conveyance.	The amount expended by the Postmaster General.	—	This charge may be incurred at the request of the sender in respect of items 1, 3 or 4 in this Schedule, or at the request of the addressee in respect of item 2, or at the discretion of the Postmaster General, and is payable in addition to any other sums payable in respect of the packet.
6. Packet charged for on an omnibus, tramcar or trolley vehicle by which it is conveyed.	The amount expended by the Postmaster General.	—	This charge is payable in addition to any other sums payable in respect of the packet.

Col. 1 Service	Col. 2 Fees	Col. 3 Limit of Size and Weight	Col. 4 Provisions
7. Waiting fee.	1s. for each 10 minutes, or part of 10 minutes, beyond the first 10 minutes.	—	This fee is payable when the messenger is detained at the request of the sender or the addressee or in the course of the service the messenger is performing.
8. Railex.	£1.	If posted in Northern Ireland or the Channel Islands not exceeding 2 oz., in all other cases not exceeding 1 lb.	(1) The charge covers conveyance by railway and service by Post Office messenger. (2) Provision (3) of item 1 applies.

SCHEDULE 4

REGISTERED POSTAL PACKETS

PART I

Col. 1 Registration Fee (In addition to any ordinary postage)	Col. 2 Maximum Compensation
s. d. 3 0 (minimum registration fee)	£ 100
3 3	200
3 6	300
3 9	400

PART II

CONDITIONS WHICH MUST BE COMPLIED WITH

1. A packet for tranmission by registered post shall:

(a) be handed for registration to an officer on duty at a post office; or

(b) be handed for registration to some officer of the Post office authorised to receive packets for registration though not on duty at a post office,

and any registered postal packet which has been transmitted to its original address, and which is redirected in pursuance of regulation 28, shall also be handed to such an officer as aforesaid.

2.—(1) Subject to the provisions of these regulations the fee chargeable for the registration of the packet, and any other sum chargeable thereon, shall be prepaid.

(2) On the posting of the packet the person handing over the packet shall obtain a certificate bearing thereon an acknowledgement that the registration fee has been paid.

(3) Where a registered postal packet which has been transmitted to its original address is redirected, paragraphs (1) and (2) shall not apply, and, if the person tendering the packet for registration does not prepay any sum chargeable on the packet, a certificate of posting stating that the said sum has not been paid shall be obtained.

3.—(1) A packet for transmission by registered post shall be made up in a reasonably strong cover appropriate to its contents.

(2) Except in the case of a packet consisting of articles for the use of the blind, or a current registered newspaper:

(a) the packet shall be fastened with wax, gum or other adhesive substance, or where suitable, securely tied with string which is sealed with wax or which is secured at each end by means of a lead, steel or strong metal seal crushed with a press;

(b) where the packet is fastened by means of strips of adhesive paper or tape each strip shall have printed, stamped or written on it the trade mark, name or initials of the sender or the name or initials of the person who tenders the packet for transmission;

(c) where the packet is fastened by means of strips of adhesive tape the tape shall (except as the Postmaster General may otherwise permit) be transparent and uncoloured;

(d) the packet shall be so made up that no part of the contents can be removed without either breaking or tearing the case, wrapper or cover or forcing two adhesive surfaces apart or breaking a seal.

(3) Any article contained in the packet shall be adequately packed as a protection against damage in course of transmission. In particular:

(a) an article which is of a fragile nature shall be packed in a container of sufficient strength and shall be surrounded in that container with sufficient and suitable material to protect the article against the effects of concussion, pressure and knocks to which postal packets are ordinarily exposed in transmission, and the packet shall bear the words "FRAGILE WITH CARE" written conspicuously in capital letters on the face of the cover above the address;

(b) an article which is liable to be damaged by bending shall be packed in a container of sufficient strength to prevent the article from being bent in transmission, and the packet shall bear the words "DO NOT BEND" written conspicuously in capital letters on the face of the cover above the address.

(4) If the packet contains coin the coin shall be packed in such a way that it cannot move about and coin of a total value in excess of £5 shall not be enclosed in any one postal packet.

(5) The following articles, if tendered for tranmission by registered post, shall (except as the Postmaster General may otherwise permit) be enclosed in one of the registered letter envelopes sold by the Post Office and be tendered for transmission by registered letter post:

(a) any uncrossed postal order in which the name of the payee has not been inserted;

(b) any cheque or dividend warrant which is uncrossed and payable to bearer;

(c) any bearer security (including a share warrant, scrip or subscription certificate, bond or relative coupon);

(d) any bank note or currency note, being current in the British postal area or elsewhere;

(e) any unobliterated postage or revenue stamp available for current use in the British postal area or elsewhere (except a revenue stamp embossed or impressed on an instrument which has been executed);

(f) any National Savings stamp;

(g) any coupon, voucher, token, card, stamp or similar document, exchangeable (singly or with any other such document) for money, goods or services;.

(h) coin.

(6) The address of the person to whom the packet is to be transmitted shall be written fully and correctly on the cover or on a label securely affixed to such cover by gum or other adhesive substance.

4. A postal packet containing any paper money which is not an article of a kind referred to in condition 3(5), if tendered for transmission by registered post, shall be tendered for transmission by registered letter post.

5. No packet for transmission by registered post shall contain any article or thing which by or under any enactment or these regulations it is unlawful to send by post.

6. Where a registered postal packet has been delivered and it is alleged that loss or abstraction of or damage to the contents or any of the contents of the packet

occurred whilst it was in course of transmission by post, the following things shall be produced on demand for the Postmaster General's inspection, in the condition as nearly as possible in which they were when the packet was delivered:

(*a*) Where loss or abstraction is alleged, the cover of the packet;

(*b*) Where damage is alleged, the cover of the packet, the damaged article, its packing material, and any container in which the damaged article was enclosed.

Regulation 44 — SCHEDULE 5

CASH ON DELIVERY PACKETS

SCALE OF FEES

Trade Charge						Fee
						s. d.
Not exceeding £10	...	...	...	...	...	3 6
Exceeding £10 but not exceeding £25		...	...	...		4 0
„ £25 „ „ „ £50	...		...		...	4 6

SCHEDULE 6   Regulation 51

FEES FOR STAMPING PAPER FOR USE AS CARDS, COVERS OR ENVELOPES

	Non-Glossy paper	Glossy paper
(1) Paper for use as cards to be transmitted as letters:		
A. For the first one thousand or part of one thousand stamps impressed on any one consignment of paper sent to the Postmaster General:		
(i) If three stamps or less are impressed on each single piece of paper	£1 0s. 0d.	£1 5s. 0d.
(ii) If four or five stamps are impressed on each single piece of paper	15s. 0d.	£1 0s. 0d.
(iii) If six or more stamps are impressed on each single piece of paper	10s. 0d.	12s. 6d.
B. For each additional one hundred or part of one hundred stamps impressed on the same consignment of paper	One tenth of the fees referred to in A.	

	Non-gummed paper	Gummed paper
(2) Paper for use as covers:		
A. For the first one thousand or part of one thousand stamps impressed on any one consignment of paper sent to the Postmaster General:		
(i) If three stamps or less are impressed on each single piece of paper	£1 0s. 0d.	£1 5s. 0d.
(ii) If four or five stamps are impressed on each single piece pf paper	15s. 0d.	£1 0s. 0d.
(iii) If six or more stamps are impressed on each single piece of paper	10s. 0d.	12s. 6d.
B. For each additional one hundred or part of one hundred stamps impressed on the same consignment of paper	One tenth of the fees referred to in A.	
(3) Paper for use as envelopes:		
A. For the first one thousand or part of one thousand stamps impressed on any one consignment of paper sent to the Postmaster General	15s. 0d.	
B. For each additional one hundred or part of one hundred stamps impressed on the same consignment of paper	1s. 6d.	

(NOTE: For the purpose of this Schedule, if two or more stamps are impressed in order that they may together denote postage of the amount which the Postmaster General has been requested to denote on each card, cover or envelope (as the case may be), they shall together be regarded as one stamp.)

SCHEDULE 7

RATES OF POSTAGE AND LIMITS OF SIZE AND WEIGHT FOR POSTAL PACKETS

TO BE TRANSMITTED TO THE REPUBLIC OF IRELAND

Regulation 55

Col. 1 Description of Postal Packet	Col. 2 Rates of Postage	Col. 3 Limits of Size	Col. 4 Limits of Weight
1. Letter			
(a) preferred letter	(i) If transmitted as a first class letter ... 5d. (ii) If transmitted as a second class letter ... 4d.	(a) Rectangular and oblong, the longer side being at least 1.414 times the shorter. Length Max. 9¼ inches. Min. 5½ inches. Width Max. 4½ inches. Min. 3½ inches.	(a) Not exceeding 4oz.
(b) any other letter	(i) If transmitted as a first class letter— Weight not exceeding 4 oz. ... ... Such rate, not exceeding 7d., as the Postmaster General may fix. Weight exceeding 4 oz. but not exceeding 6oz. ... ... 9d. For each additional 2oz. or part thereof up to a total weight of 1lb. 8oz. ... 3d. For the next 8oz. or part thereof ... 1s. 0d.	(b) Length 2 feet. Width or depth 18 inches. In roll form: Length plus twice diameter 3 feet 3 inches. Greatest dimension 2 feet 8 inches.	(b) (i) No limits.

Regulation 55

SCHEDULE 7—continued

Col. 1 Description of Postal Packet	Col. 2 Rates of Postage	Col. 3 Limits of Size	Col. 4 Limits of Weight
	For each additional 1lb. or part thereof thereafter ...... 2s. 0d.		
	(b) (ii) If transmitted as a second class letter—		(b) (ii) Not exceeding 1lb. 8oz.
	Weight not exceeding 4oz. ... ... Such rate, not exceeding 6d., as the Postmaster General may fix.		
	Weight exceeding 4oz. but not exceeding 6oz. ... ... 6d.		
	For each additional 2oz. or part thereof up to a total weight of 1lb. 2oz. ... 2d.		
	For each additional 2oz. or part thereof thereafter ... ... 1d.		
2. Printed packet	2s 0d.	As for item 1(b).	Exceeding 1lb. 8oz. but not exceeding 2lb.

SCHEDULE 7—*continued*

Regulation 55

Col. 1 Description of Postal Packet	Col. 2 Rates of Postage		Col. 3 Limits of Size	Col. 4 Limits of Weight
3. Current registered newspaper	Weight not exceeding 4oz. ...	4d.	As for item 1(*b*).	Not exceeding 2lb.
	Weight exceeding 4oz. but not exceeding 6oz. ...	6d.		
	For each additional 2oz. or part thereof up to a total weight of 1lb. 2oz.	2d.		
	For each additional 2oz. or part thereof thereafter up to a total weight of 1lb. 8oz. ... Weight exceeding 1lb. 8oz. ...	1d. 2s. 0d.		
4. Articles for the use of the blind	No rate specified.		As for item 1(*b*).	Not exceeding 15lb.
5. Parcel	Weight not exceeding 1lb. 8oz.	2s. 6d.	Greatest length 3 feet 6 inches.	Not exceeding 22lb.
	Exceeding 1lb. 8oz. but not exceeding 2lb.	3s. 0d.	Greatest length and girth combined 6 feet (the girth to be measured round the thickest part).	
	Exceeding 2lb. but not exceeding 6lb.	4s. 6d.		
	Exceeding 6lb., but not exceeding 10lb.	6s. 0d.		
	Exceeding 10lb. but not exceeding 14lb.	7s. 6d.		
	Exceeding 14lb. but not exceeding 18lb.	9s. 0d.		
	Exceeding 18lb.	10s. 6d.		

EXPLANATORY NOTE

(This Note is not part of the Regulations.)

These Regulations, which come into effect on 16th September 1968, consolidate and amend the Inland Post Regulations 1967 and the Inland Post Amendment (No. 1) Regulations 1968.

The principal changes are as follows:—

1. A choice is provided between a first and second class service for letters weighing up to $1\frac{1}{2}$ lbs., with provision for lower postage rates for second class letters (the despatch or delivery of which may be deferred). A letter is defined as meaning any postal packet except a printed packet, a packet consisting of articles for the use of the blind, a current registered newspaper, a parcel, an unaddressed packet or a petition or address to Her Majesty or to either House of Parliament.

2. Letters over $1\frac{1}{2}$ lbs. in weight may only be sent by the first class letter service.

3. New letter postage rates are introduced, and the first weight step is raised to 4 oz. in both the first and second class services.

4. The Postmaster General is empowered to fix a higher postage rate (not exceeding 7d. for a first class letter or 6d for a second class letter) for minimum weight letters which do not conform to the conditions of size, shape and material for a preferred letter.

5. There is a service for printed packets weighing not less than $1\frac{1}{2}$ lb. nor more than 2 lb. each.

6. Special rates of postage are no longer provided for postcards or sample packets (both of which now come within the definition of a letter).

7. The supplementary services of registration and express delivery at the request of the sender will not be available for second class letters or printed packets. Rebates for bulk postings will be given in the second class letter and printed packet services only. Articles for the use of the blind may still be sent free of postage and will not be subject to deferment. Current registered newspapers in course of distribution will be charged (a) if not exceeding 4oz. at the same rate as second class preferred letters, (b) if between 4 oz. and $1\frac{1}{2}$ lb., at the same rate as other second class letters, and (c) if over $1\frac{1}{2}$ lb., at the same rate as printed packets; but they will not be subject to deferment.

8. The regulations providing for the acceptance and transmission of parcels in bulk are extended to cover any unregistered postal packets (other than cash on delivery packets).

9. Customs clearance fees for mail from the Channel Islands and the Irish Republic are increased, and a storage fee is introduced for incoming parcels from those places which are not cleared within 28 days.

STATUTORY INSTRUMENTS

1968 No. 1254

POST OFFICE

The British Commonwealth and Foreign Post Amendment (No. 3) Regulations 1968

Made - - - -	*5th August* 1968
Laid before Parliament	*20th August* 1968
Coming into Operation	*16th September* 1968

I, the Right Honourable John Thomson Stonehouse, M.P., Her Majesty's Postmaster General, by virtue of the powers conferred on me by sections 5, 8, 15 and 81 of the Post Office Act 1953(a) (as amended or substituted by section 28 of and the Schedule to the Post Office Act 1961 (b)), and of all other powers enabling me in this behalf, do hereby make the following regulations:

Interpretation

1.—(1) These regulations shall be read as one with the British Commonwealth and Foreign Post Regulations 1965(c) (hereinafter called "the principal regulations"), as amended (d).

(2) The Interpretation Act 1889(e) applies for the interpretation of these regulations as it applies for the interpretation of an Act of Parliament.

Letters and postcards

2. For Parts 1 and 2 of Schedule 1 to the principal regulations (which Parts specify the rates of postage on certain letters and postcards) there shall be substituted the following:

PART 1

Rates of postage under regulation 3(1)

1. Letter not exceeding 1 oz. in weight	5d.
2. Letter exceeding 1 oz. in weight:	
for the first ounce	5d.
for each additional ounce or fractional part thereof	2d.
3. Single postcard	5d.
4. Reply postcard—on each half	5d.

PART 2

Rates of postage under regulation 3(2)

1. Letter not exceeding 1 oz. in weight	4d.
2. Letter exceeding 1 oz. in weight:	
for the first ounce	4d.
for each additional ounce or fractional part thereof	2d.
3. Single postcard	4d.
4. Reply postcard—on each half	4d.

(a) 1953 c. 36.   (b) 1961 c. 15.
(c) S.I. 1965/1735 (1965 III, p. 4878).
(d) S.I. 1965/2173, S.I. 1966/912, (1965 III, p. 6371; 1966 II, p. 2185).
(e) 1889 c. 63.

Specified countries or places

3.—(1) In Schedule 2 to the principal regulations, as amended **(a)**, (which Schedule specifies the countries or places in respect of which certain rates of postage and limits of weight and size apply):

(*a*) in Part I:

(i) the words "Aden and the Protectorate of South Arabia" shall be deleted;

(ii) for the words "Mauritius and Dependencies" there shall be substituted the word "Mauritius";

(iii) immediately before the word "Pakistan" there shall be inserted the word "Nigeria".

(*b*) Part 2 shall be deleted.

(*c*) For the heading "Part 3" there shall be substituted the heading "Part 2".

(2)(*a*) In regulation 3(1)(*a*) of the principal regulations, for the words "Part 1 or Part 2 of Schedule 2" there shall be substituted the words "Part 1 of Schedule 2".

(*b*) In regulation 3(1)(*b*) of the principal regulations, for the words "Part 1, Part 2 or Part 3 of Schedule 2", there shall be substituted the words "Part 1 or Part 2 of Schedule 2".

Certain outgoing packets

4. For Part 1 of Schedule 3 to the principal regulations (which Part specifies the rates of postage under regulation 4) there shall be substituted the following:

PART 1

Rates of postage under regulation 4

Printed packet:

(*a*) not exceeding 2oz. in weight	2d.
(*b*) exceeding 2oz. in weight:	
for the first 2oz.	2d.
for the next 2oz. or fractional part thereof	1d.
for each additional 4oz. or fractional part thereof	3d.

Bulk postage

5. For regulation 10(1)(*a*) of the principal regulations, as substituted **(b)**, (which regulation prescribes the postage payable on printed packets transmitted in bulk) there shall be substituted the following:

"(*a*) on every bag containing nothing but printed packets to which regulation 4 applies, postage at the rate of 1s. for each 1lb. weight, or fractional part thereof, of the bag and its contents, less 5%";

Articles liable to duty

6. In regulation 15(3) of the principal regulations, as amended **(b)**, (which paragraph prescribes the fee payable in respect of incoming postal packets containing articles liable to customs duty), for "1s. 6d." there shall be substituted "1s. 9d."

(a) S.I. 1965/2173, S.I. 1966/912, (1965 III, p. 6371; 1966 II, p. 2185).
(b) S.I. 1966/912 (1966 II, p. 2185).

Despatch of certain packets

7. For regulation 22 of the principal regulations there shall be substituted the following regulation:

"22. Without prejudice to the generality of regulation 44, any printed packet, sample packet or Phonopost packet may be withheld from despatch until any subsequent despatch."

Compensation for registered packets

8. In regulation 34 of the principal regulations (which prescribes the maximum compensation which the Postmaster General may pay in respect of registered postal packets (other than insured letters or boxes) and their contents), for the sum "£2 18s. 0d." in both places where it occurs there shall be substituted the sum "£3 8s. 0d."

Compensation fees and maximum compensation for insured letters

9. For Schedule 5 to the principal regulations (which specifies the compensation fees payable in respect of, and the maximum compensation which may be paid for the loss of or damage to, outgoing insured letters), there shall be substituted the following:

SCHEDULE 5
Regulations 36 and 37

INSURED LETTERS—COMPENSATION FEES AND MAXIMUM COMPENSATION

Compensation fees		Maximum compensation			Compensation fees		Maximum compensation		
s.	d.	£.	s.	d.	s.	d.	£.	s.	d.
	2	28	0	0	2	6	224	0	0
	4	42	0	0	2	8	238	0	0
	6	56	0	0	2	10	252	0	0
	8	70	0	0	3	0	266	0	0
	10	84	0	0	3	2	280	0	0
1	0	98	0	0	3	4	294	0	0
1	2	112	0	0	3	6	308	0	0
1	4	126	0	0	3	8	322	0	0
1	6	140	0	0	3	10	336	0	0
1	8	154	0	0	4	0	350	0	0
1	10	168	0	0	4	2	364	0	0
2	0	182	0	0	4	4	378	0	0
2	2	196	0	0	4	6	392	0	0
2	4	210	0	0	4	8	400	0	0

Citation and commencement

10. These regulations may be cited as the British Commonwealth and Foreign Post Amendment (No. 3) Regulations 1968, and shall come into operation on 16th September 1968.

Dated 5th August 1968.

John Stonehouse,
Her Majesty's Postmaster General.

EXPLANATORY NOTE
(This Note is not part of the Regulations.)

These Regulations, which come into operation on 16th September 1968, amend the regulations relating to postal packets (other than parcels) sent to or received from British Commonwealth or foreign countries (except the Republic of Ireland). The principal amendments are as follows:

(1) The rates of insurance for insured letters and boxes are adjusted in favour of senders.

(2) The maximum amounts of compensation payable in respect of lost or damaged registered packets (other than insured letters or insured boxes) are increased.

(3) Various rates of postage and a charge for service are altered. The following table sets out the principal changes:

Category of correspondence or service	Present charges	New charges
1. Outgoing mail		
Letters— Commonwealth		
First oz.	4d.	5d.
Each additional oz.	1½d.	2d.
Postcards— Commonwealth:	3d. single 6d. reply paid	5d. single 10d. reply paid
Printed papers, reduced rate		
Posted singly—		
First 2 oz.	2d.	2d.
Next 2 oz.	1½d.	1d.
Subsequent weight steps	1½d. per 2 oz.	3d. per 4oz.
Posted in bulk—		
First lb.	1s. 1d.	1s. 0d.
Each additional lb.	1s. 0d. less 5% of the total postage	1s. 0d. less 5% of the total postage
2. Incoming mail posted by HM Forces overseas		
Letters—		
First oz.	3d.	4d.
Each additional oz.	1½d.	2d.
Postcards—		
Single	2d.	4d.
Reply paid	4d.	8d.
3. Service		
Post Office fee for customs clearance	1s. 6d.	1s. 9d.

STATUTORY INSTRUMENTS

1968 No. 1255

POST OFFICE

The British Commonwealth and Foreign Parcel Post Amendment (No. 3) Regulations 1968

Made - - - -	*5th August* 1968
Laid before Parliament	*20th August* 1968
Coming into Operation	*16th September* 1968

I, The Right Honourable John Thomson Stonehouse, M.P., Her Majesty's Postmaster General, by virtue of the powers conferred on me by sections 5, 8, 15 and 81 of the Post Office Act 1953(a) (as amended or substituted by section 28 of and the Schedule to the Post Office Act 1961(b)), and of all other powers enabling me in this behalf, do hereby make the following regulations:

Interpretation

1.—(1) These regulations shall be read as one with the British Commonwealth and Foreign Parcel Post Regulations 1965(c) (hereinafter called "the principal regulations"), as amended (d).

(2) The Interpretation Act 1889(e) applies for the interpretation of these regulations as it applies for the interpretation of an Act of Parliament.

Rates of postage

2. In regulation 3(1) of the principal regulations (which paragraph prescribes the maximum rate of postage on outgoing parcels other than air parcels) for "£4" there shall be substituted "£5".

Fees for customs clearance

3. In regulation 7 of the principal regulations, as amended (f), (which regulation prescribes the further fee payable in respect of incoming parcels containing dutiable articles), for "2s. 6d." there shall be substituted "2s. 9d."

Insurance and compensation

4. For Schedule 2 to the principal regulations, as substituted(d), there shall be substituted the following:

(a) 1953 c. 36.   (b) 1961 c. 15.
(c) S.I. 1965/1734 (1965 III, p. 4859).
(d) S.I. 1965/2172, 1966/913 (1965 III, p. 6368; 1966 II, p. 2190).
(e) 1889 c. 63.   (f) S.I. 1966/913 (1966 II, p. 2190).

Regulations 20 and 21

SCHEDULE 2

INSURANCE AND COMPENSATION

PART I

Insured Parcels

Insurance fee	Maximum compensation	Insurance fee	Maximum compensation	Insurance fee	Maximum compensation
s. d.	£	s. d.	£	s. d.	£
3 2	28	4 10	168	6 10	336
3 4	42	5 0	182	7 0	350
3 6	56	5 2	196	7 2	364
3 8	70	5 4	210	7 4	378
3 10	84	5 6	224	7 6	392
4 0	98	5 8	238	7 8	400
4 2	112	5 10	252		
4 4	126	6 0	266		
4 6	140	6 2	280		
4 8	154	6 4	294		
		6 6	308		
		6 8	322		

PART II

Uninsured Parcels

Weight of Parcel	Maximum compensation
	£ s. d.
Not exceeding 2lb.	1 7 0
Exceeding 2lb. but not exceeding 7lb. (see Note below) ...	2 1 0
Exceeding 7lb but not exceeding 11lb	3 8 0
Exceeding 11lb but not exceeding 22lb	5 9 0

Note.—Where the relative postal arrangement provides for a first weight step of 3lb., the maximum compensation payable in respect of a parcel of a weight not exceeding 3lb. is £1 7s. 0d.

Parcels in bond

5. In regulation 24 of the principal regulations, as amended **(a)**, (which regulation provides, and prescribes fees, for certain facilities in respect of incoming parcels in bond) there shall be inserted immediately after paragraph (3) the following paragraph:

"(3A) Where notice has been given under regulation 9(1) of the Postal Packets (Customs and Excise) Regulations 1966**(b)**, as amended **(c)**, requiring entry to be made of the goods in a parcel in bond and the parcel remains in bond for a period of more than 28 days after the date of such notice, there shall be charged on the parcel (in addition to any other fees payable under these Regulations) a fee, not exceeding 27s., calculated at the rate of 1s. for each day or part of a day in excess of the said period of 28 days during which the parcel remains in bond as aforesaid; and the fee shall be paid by the addressee."

Citation and commencement

6. These regulations may be cited as the British Commonwealth and Foreign Parcel Post Amendment (No. 3) Regulations 1968, and shall come into operation on 16th September 1968.

Dated 5th August 1968.

John Stonehouse,
Her Majesty's Postmaster General.

EXPLANATORY NOTE

(This Note is not part of the Regulations.)

These Regulations, which come into operation on 16th September 1968, amend the regulations relating to parcels sent to or received from British Commonwealth or foreign countries (except the Republic of Ireland). The principal changes are as follows:

(1) The maximum postage chargeable on outgoing surface parcels is raised from £4 to £5.

(2) The insurance fees for outgoing parcels are adjusted in favour of senders.

(3) The amounts of compensation payable for uninsured parcels are increased.

(4) The Customs clearance fee for parcels is raised from 2s. 6d. to 2s. 9d.

(5) A new fee is introduced in respect of incoming parcels awaiting clearance at the postal Customs depot after a free period of 28 days.

(a) S.I. 1966/913 (1966 II, p. 2190).   **(b)** S.I. 1966/66 (1966 I, p. 134).
(c) S.I. 1968/931 (1968 II, p. 2440).

STATUTORY INSTRUMENTS

1968 No. 1256

TELEGRAPHS

The Telephone Regulations 1968

Made - - -	*5th August* 1968
Laid before Parliament	*20th August* 1968
Coming into Operation	*1st October* 1968

ARRANGEMENT OF REGULATIONS

PART V

CALL CHARGES

PART VI

SERVICES AND FACILITIES

PART VII

RADIOPHONE SERVICE

PART VIII

GENERAL CONDITIONS OF SERVICE TO SUBSCRIBERS

PART IX

GENERAL

51. Calculation of rentals.
52. Measurement of length of lines.
53. Liability for call office and other charges.
54. Evidence.
55. Remission of charges.
56. Service of notices, etc.
57. Misuse of the telephone system.
58. Non-liability of Post Office.
59. Consent or approval of the Postmaster General.
60. Construction.
61. Revocation and transitional provisions.
62. Citation and commencement.

I, The Right Honourable John Thomson Stonehouse, M.P., Her Majesty's Post-Master General, by virtue of the power vested in me by section 1 of the Telephone Act 1951(a), as amended by sections 16 and 28 of the Post Office Act 1961(b), and of every other power enabling me in this behalf, do hereby make the following regulations :

PART I

INTERPRETATION AND EXTENT

1.—(1) In these regulations, except so far as the contrary is provided or the context otherwise requires, the following expressions have the meanings hereby respectively assigned to them :—

"agreement" means an agreement made by the Postmaster General with any person for the provision of telephone service ;

"alarm call" means a call made to an installation from a telephone exchange in accordance with regulation 34 ;

(a) 1951 c. 52.   (b) 1961 c. 15.

"the appropriate telephone exchange", in relation to an exchange line, means the telephone exchange which in the opinion of the Postmaster General is the appropriate telephone exchange to serve that exchange line ;

"automatic extension" means an extension terminated on the automatic equipment of a private automatic branch exchange ;

"the British Islands" means the United Kingdom, the Channel Islands, and the Isle of Man ;

"business line" means a line provided under these regulations which is regarded as a business line in accordance with regulation 4 ;

"call office" means a telephone (other than a telephone forming part of an installation) which is available to the public for the purpose of sending and receiving telephonic messages, and where the context so requires includes the building or other external covering which houses such telephone ;

"certified" means certified by the Postmaster General ;

"change of apparatus" means the substitution for any equipment or apparatus provided for a subscriber of any other equipment or apparatus ;

"chargeable length" has the meaning assigned to it by regulation 52 ;

"coin box line" means an exchange line in respect of calls from which the Postmaster General requires sums of money to be placed in a coin collecting box provided by him ;

"exchange line" means a circuit provided as part of an installation for the purpose of connecting that installation with a telephone exchange, not being a circuit provided as a private circuit or part of a private circuit ;

"exclusive line" means an exchange line of which no part is used continuously in common with any other subscriber ;

"external extension" means an extension other than an internal extension ;

"external removal" means any removal of equipment or apparatus provided for a subscriber from one position to another, other than an internal removal ;

"external station", in relation to a house exchange system, means a station other than an internal station ;

"fixed time call" means a call booked in advance for connection at a specified time in accordance with regulation 29 ;

"house exchange system" (abbreviation "HES") means an installation comprising a number of stations each capable of being telephonically connected with any of the others or with an exchange line by the operation of press buttons, and includes any special extension provided as part thereof ;

"installation" means equipment or apparatus provided by the Postmaster General for a subscriber, either as means of telephonic communication wholly or in part through the medium of a public telephone system under the Postmaster General's control, or as a private circuit ;

"internal extension" and "internal private circuit" respectively mean an extension and a private circuit connecting points within the same building between which there is some means of access wholly within the building, and for the purpose of this definition where there is between separate buildings a tunnel or covered bridge which in the opinion of the Postmaster General is large enough for use by pedestrian traffic such buildings and such tunnel or bridge shall all be treated as being one building ;

"internal removal" means the removal of any equipment or apparatus provided for a subscriber from one position to another position within the same building, being positions between which there is some means of access wholly within the building, and for the purpose of this definition where there is between separate buildings a tunnel or covered bridge which in the opinion of the Postmaster General is large enough for use by pedestrian traffic such buildings and such tunnel or bridge shall all be treated as being one building ;

"internal station", in relation to a house exchange system, means a main station, and a station in the same building as a main station, provided that there is some means of access between those stations wholly within the building, and for the purpose of this definition where there is between separate buildings a tunnel or covered bridge which in the opinion of the Postmaster General is large enough for use by pedestrian traffic such buildings and such tunnel or bridge shall all be treated as being one building ;

"local call" means a call made to an installation or telephone which is served by :

(i) the local exchange, or

(ii) a telephone exchange in the same telephone group as the local exchange, or

(iii) a telephone exchange in a telephone group which is regarded as adjacent to that of the local exchange ;

"local exchange", in relation to a call, means the telephone exchange serving the installation or telephone from which the call is made ;

"main station", in relation to a house exchange system, means a station at which incoming calls from the telephone exchange are received ;

"minimum period of service" has the meaning assigned to it by regulation 8(1) ;

"party line" means a shared line ;

"personal call" means a call booked for the specified purpose of communication with a particular person or otherwise in accordance with regulation 30 ;

"the Postmaster General's system" means the public telephone system under the control of the Postmaster General ;

"private automatic branch exchange" (abbreviation "PABX") means a private branch exchange the whole or part of which is operated by means of automatic switches ;

"private branch exchange" (abbreviation "PBX") means switching apparatus designed to provide intercommunication between extensions connected with that apparatus and between those extensions and exchange lines, but does not include a house exchange system ;

"private circuit" means equipment and apparatus provided by the Postmaster General for a subscriber as means of telephonic communication otherwise than through the medium of the public telephone system under the Postmaster General's control, the termination of which at one end at least consists of a telephone or a telephone switchboard ;

"private manual branch exchange" (abbreviation "PMBX") means a private branch exchange the whole of which is manually operated ;

"radiophone system" means a system primarily designed for providing telephones in vehicles with telephone service through a public telephone system by means of a wireless telegraphy link between those telephones and a station for wireless telegraphy forming part of the public telephone system ;

"rental" means any charge in respect of equipment or apparatus which is fixed by or under these regulations or by an agreement as the case may be and is payable periodically ;

"rural party line scheme" means the scheme whereby not less than three and not more than twelve subscribers in rural areas only were offered telephone service by means of a party line at special rates of rental ;

"shared line" means an exchange line, some part whereof is used continuously in common with another subscriber or other subscribers ;

"special extension" means an extension provided as part of a house exchange system, whereby calls can be made from a telephone on that extension to the main station or main stations only, and not directly to any of the other stations ;

"station", in relation to a house exchange system, means a telephone capable of being connected with any of the other telephones comprised in the system or with an exchange line by the operation of press buttons, but does not include a telephone on a special extension ;

"subscriber" means a person on whose application the Postmaster General provides telephone service by means of an installation under these regulations or under an agreement, and includes where the context so requires an applicant for telephone service which is to be provided by means of an installation under these regulations, and also includes the personal representatives of a deceased subscriber ;

"the subscriber trunk dialling facility" means the facility whereby users of certain installations and telephones can obtain certain trunk calls without the intervention of the local operator by dialling a combination of figures, or of letters and figures, beginning with "O" ;

"subscriber's premises" means any premises in or on which an installation or part of an installation is situated, being either (a) premises in the possession or occupation or under the control of the person who is the subscriber in respect of the installation or of a person for whose use the installation or part thereof is provided on the application of the subscriber, or (b) premises connected telephonically with such premises as aforesaid by means of an extension or private circuit comprised in the installation ;

"telegraphic line" means a telegraphic line as defined in the Telegraph Act 1878(a), and in addition a telegraph as defined in the Telegraph Act 1869(b);

"telephone" (in expressions relating to calls made from or to a telephone) includes automatic apparatus for making calls or giving messages, or for answering calls or recording messages ;

"telephone exchange" means switching equipment and apparatus which forms part of the public telephone system provided by the Postmaster General or provided by a person licensed in that behalf by him, and is operated by the Postmaster General or that person for the purpose of affording telephonic communication through the medium of that system, and where the context so requires includes the building, vehicle, or other external covering which houses such equipment and apparatus ;

"telephone service" means the enjoyment of means of telephonic communication ;

"terminal exchange", in relation to a call, means the telephone exchange serving the installation or telephone to which the call is made ;

(a) 1878 c. 76. (b) 1869 c. 73.

2n

"trunk barring equipment" means equipment associated with telephone instruments and exchange lines on which the subscriber trunk dialling facility is available, for the purpose of preventing or restricting the making of trunk calls from such instruments, either at all times while the equipment is fitted, or at such times as the equipment is switched into circuit at the telephone instrument ; but does not include equipment for preventing all outgoing calls from being made from a particular telephone instrument ;

"trunk call" means any call to which regulation 20 applies other than a local call.

(2) In these regulations, except so far as the contrary is provided or the context otherwise requires, references to anything being or having been done by or under these regulations or any of them shall be construed as including references to that thing being or having been done by or under any previous Telephone Regulations, or by or under the corresponding regulation therein.

(3) References in Part III (Transitional Provisions) of the Telephone Regulations 1951(a) to any provisions of those regulations which are re-enacted, with or without modifications, by these regulations, shall be construed as references to those provisions as so re-enacted.

(4) The Interpretation Act 1889(b) applies for the interpretation of these regulations as it applies for the interpretation of an Act of Parliament, and as if these regulations and the regulations hereby revoked were Acts of Parliament.

(5) These regulations shall extend to Northern Ireland and the Isle of Man.

PART II

PROVISION OF TELEPHONE SERVICE, EQUIPMENT AND APPARATUS

Application of Part II

2. This part of these regulations applies to the provision by the Postmaster General of telephone service, not being telephone service provided under an agreement or by means of a call office.

Provision of telephone service

3. Telephone service shall be provided by means of an installation consisting of such equipment and apparatus as the Postmaster General from time to time considers appropriate, regard being had to the subscriber's requirements and the interests of the public telephone system as a whole.

Business lines

4.—(1) Subject to the following provisions of this regulation where immediately before the commencement of these regulations the rental in respect of an exchange line provided for a subscriber otherwise than under an agreement was being charged at the business rate as specified in Part 1 of Schedule 3 to the Telephone Regulations 1965(c), and the line continues to be so provided, the line shall be regarded as a business line.

(2) In the case of an exchange line first provided (otherwise than under an agreement) after the commencement of these regulations, the Postmaster General may determine that it shall be regarded as a business line and shall notify the subscriber of such determination, either in the relative application form furnished by him under regulation 5 or by other notice in writing.

(a) S.I. 1951/2075 (Rev. XXII p. 369: 1951 II, p. 697).   (b) 1889 c. 63.
(c) S.I. 1965/225 (1965 I, p. 518).

Provided that where before the commencement of these regulations a subscriber has applied for an exchange line and the Postmaster General has notified him in writing that the business rate of rental will be chargeable in respect thereof, or that the line will be regarded as a business line, and the line is not provided until after the commencement of these regulations, this paragraph shall not require the Postmaster General to give the subscriber notification if he determines under this paragraph that the line shall be regarded as a business line.

(3) The Postmaster General may at any time determine in respect of an exchange line which is regarded as a business line that the said line shall cease to be so regarded and shall notify the subscriber of such determination by notice in writing.

(4) In determining whether or not an exchange line shall be regarded as a business line the Postmaster General shall take into account all the circumstances of the case including the purposes (whether residential or otherwise) for which the premises at which telephone service is or is to be provided are being used or are in the Postmaster General's opinion likely to be used, and, in a case where the premises are being used partly for residential purposes and partly for other purposes, the purposes (whether social and domestic, or otherwise) for which the installation of which the exchange line forms part is being used or is in the Postmaster General's opinion likely to be used.

Method of application and contents of application form

5.—(1) Application for telephone service to be provided, or for the installation provided to be altered or removed, or for equipment or apparatus to be added thereto or taken therefrom, shall if the Postmaster General so requires be made on a form furnished by him and signed by the subscriber.

(2) The Postmaster General may include in an application form furnished by him under this regulation:—

(a) a statement of the component parts of the installation which is to be provided by him, or of the component parts which are to be added to or taken from the installation already provided by him, in pursuance of the application;

(b) a statement of the current rate or amount of any rental or other charges which are to be paid in respect of the component parts of the installation and are fixed by these regulations; and

(c) statements of such other matters as the Postmaster General thinks expedient.

(3) The Postmaster General shall notify the subscriber, either in the relative application form or by other notice in writing, of the rate or amount of any rental or other charges which are to be paid in respect of the component parts of the installation and are fixed by the Postmaster General under these regulations.

Conditions relating to particular installations

6.—(1) The following terms and conditions shall apply respectively in relation to telephone service provided under these regulations by means of installations which are of the following descriptions or are provided in the following circumstances:—

(a) where the installation is intended to be connected with telephone equipment or apparatus provided otherwise than by the Postmaster General, the terms and conditions set out in Part 1 of Schedule 1;

(b) where the installation consists of or includes an extension between switch-boards, the term or condition set out in Part 2 of Schedule 1 ;

(c) where the installation consists of or includes an external extension connecting premises occupied by the subscriber with premises occupied by another person, the term or condition set out in Part 3 of Schedule 1 ;

(d) where the installation is a private circuit, the terms and conditions set out in Part 4 of Schedule 1 ;

(e) where the installation is connected with an answering set provided by the Postmaster General, the term or condition set out in Part 5 of Schedule 1 ;

(f) subject to regulation 14 of the Telephone Regulations 1951, where telephone service is provided by means of an exclusive line not being a business line the term or condition that the telephone service provided thereby may at any time if the Postmaster General so decides be provided by means of a shared line.

(2) The Postmaster General may from time to time direct that the following terms and conditions shall apply in relation to the telephone service provided under these regulations by means of an installation in the following circumstances : —

(a) where in the opinion of the Postmaster General the premises at which telephone service is or is to be provided are subject to abnormal risk of fire or explosion, the terms and conditions set out in Schedule 2 ;

(b) where the circumstances are such that the Postmaster General considers that any special terms or conditions should apply for the prevention of injury to persons or for the protection of the installation or of any other equipment or apparatus of the Postmaster General, or in order to restrict the use of the installation or any part thereof to the purposes for which it was designed, such terms and conditions as the Postmaster General may determine in the particular case.

(3) Where the Postmaster General gives any direction under this regulation, he shall notify the subscriber thereof either in the relative application form furnished by the Postmaster General under regulation 5 or by other notice in writing.

Termination of service by notice

7.—(1) Subject to the provisions of these regulations, at any time after an installation has been connected for use : —

(a) the Postmaster General may, after giving to the subscriber at least one month's notice in writing of his intention so to do, cease to provide telephone service by means of the installation ; or

(b) the subscriber may give to the Postmaster General notice requiring him to cease to provide telephone service by means of the installation.

(2) If the Postmaster General gives a notice under paragraph (1), the liability of the subscriber to pay rental in respect of the installation shall cease on the expiration of the notice, without prejudice to any liability of his which has previously accrued.　If the subscriber gives a notice under paragraph (1), his liability to pay rental in respect of the installation shall cease on the expiration of 7 days from the date on which the Postmaster General receives the notice, or on the expiration of the notice, whichever is the later, without prejudice to any liability of the subscriber which has previously accrued or which may arise under regulation 8.

(3) This regulation shall not relieve the subscriber from liability to pay rental in respect of the installation for any period during which the Postmaster General, after giving or receiving a notice under paragraph (1), continues at the request of the subscriber to provide telephone service by means of the installation.

(4) Where the subscriber gives a notice under paragraph (1), the Postmaster General may cease to provide telephone service by means of the installation as soon after he receives the notice as he considers practicable :

Provided that, without prejudice to any other powers of the Postmaster General under these regulations, if the subscriber in his notice specifies a date on which it is to take effect, the Postmaster General shall not cease to provide telephone service under this paragraph before that date, unless the subscriber after giving the notice requests him so to do.

(5) The Postmaster General shall repay to the subscriber or allow him in account the appropriate proportion of any rental paid in advance in respect of a period ending after the date on which his liability to pay rental ceases by virtue of this regulation.

(6) In this regulation the word "installation" means in a case where the circumstances so require equipment or apparatus forming part of an installation.

(7) This regulation shall have effect subject to regulation 51.

Premature cesser of service

8.—(1) The Postmaster General may for the purpose of this regulation determine in respect of any installation a period (in these regulations referred to as "the minimum period of service"), beginning with the day on which the installation was connected for use, and shall notify the subscriber thereof either in the relative application form furnished by the Postmaster General under regulation 5 or by other notice in writing.

(2) Where, after an installation has been connected for use, it ceases to be provided before the expiration of the minimum period of service as a result of a notice given by the subscriber in accordance with regulation 7 or regulation 17(3), or otherwise at the instance of the subscriber, he shall pay on such cesser, towards recompensing the Postmaster General for loss of revenue by way of charges in respect of the provision of the installation, such sum (if any) as may be assessed by the Postmaster General in accordance with the following provisions of this regulation :

Provided that such sum shall not be payable where the installation ceases to be provided as a result of a notice given by the subscriber to the Postmaster General in consequence of an increase in the rate of rental payable in respect of the installation by virtue of regulation 11(1), being a notice given before or within fourteen days after the date on which the increase takes effect or is due to take effect.

(3) Such sum shall not exceed the amount of rental which would have been payable for the installation in respect of the period from the date when the installation ceases to be provided to the end of the minimum period of service, if the installation had been provided for the whole of the first mentioned period and if the rates of rental applicable to the installation at the time when it ceased to be provided had remained unchanged to the end of that period ; and in assessing the said sum the Postmaster General shall make such allowance (if any) as he may consider reasonable for any use which he is able to make of the

work done in installing the equipment and apparatus comprised in the installation, and of the equipment and apparatus, for the purpose of providing at the same premises telephone service for any person other than the subscriber.

(4) Nothing in this regulation shall prevent the Postmaster General from ceasing to provide telephone service by means of the installation under regulation 7 or under regulation 41, or from suspending or terminating such service under regulation 44 or regulation 57, before the expiration of the minimum period of service.

(5) In the foregoing paragraphs of this regulation the word "installation" means in a case where the circumstances so require equipment or apparatus forming part of an installation.

(6) Where at the request of the subscriber equipment or apparatus is added to an installation, the Postmaster General may at his discretion either determine a minimum period of service in respect of only the added equipment or apparatus (including any additional or substituted switching equipment which the Postmaster General considers it necessary or desirable to provide in consequence), or determine a fresh minimum period of service in respect of the whole installation including the added equipment or apparatus and any such switching equipment.

Cancellation of application for service

9.—(1) Where work done by the Postmaster General for the purpose of installing equipment or apparatus for the benefit of a subscriber is rendered abortive for that purpose before the connection of the equipment or apparatus for use by the cancellation of the application or in consequence of anything done, omitted, permitted, or suffered by the subscriber, he shall pay towards recompensing the Postmaster General for the cost incurred by him in doing the work a sum assessed by the Postmaster General in accordance with the following provisions of this regulation.

(2) Such sum shall not exceed whichever is the smaller of the following amounts :—

(*a*) the cost incurred by the Postmaster General in doing the work ;

(*b*) the total amount which would have been payable by way of rental for the minimum period of service in respect of the equipment or apparatus if it had been connected for use and provided for the whole of that period and if the rates of rental specified in the application form in respect of it, or otherwise notified to the subscriber before the work was begun, had been applicable to the installation during the whole of that period;

and in assessing the said sum the Postmaster General shall make such allowance (if any) as he may consider reasonable for any use which he is able to make of the said work in providing at the same premises telephone service for any person other than the subscriber.

PART III

RENTALS

Application of Part III

10. This part of these regulations applies to installations provided by the Postmaster General otherwise than under an agreement.

Rental for installations

11.—(1) The subscriber shall pay in respect of an installation rental at the rate applicable under the following provisions of this regulation.

(2) The rate of rental in respect of an installation shall be the total of the rates which, in respect of each component part thereof, are either specified in the appropriate Schedule hereto, or are fixed by the Postmaster General as hereinafter provided.

(3) Where the installation includes one or more exchange lines, and the installation was not provided under the rural party line scheme, the appropriate Schedule shall be Schedule 3.

(4) Where the installation includes any exchange line served by a telephone exchange by which less than twenty subscribers are for the time being served, and telephone service is at the request of the subscriber provided by means of that exchange line through the medium of another telephone exchange at hours during which telephone service is not provided by the first mentioned telephone exchange, the rate of rental in respect of the exchange line shall be increased by 7s. 6d. a quarter.

(5) Where the installation is a private circuit, the appropriate Schedule shall be Schedule 4.

(6) Where a private circuit is provided for non-continuous use, and at the request of the subscriber the circuit is so provided at a time or on a day which has not been fixed as a time or day on which service is regularly provided for that subscriber, he shall pay in respect of the period of the additional use such charge as the Postmaster General may fix.

(7) Provided that where—

(*a*) neither of the said Schedules is appropriate to the installation, or

(*b*) no rate is specified in the appropriate Schedule in respect of a particular component part of the installation, or

(*c*) the Postmaster General considers that, in order to meet the subscriber's requirements, it is necessary for the installation or any component part thereof to consist of non-standard equipment or apparatus or to be constructed by non-standard or exceptionally expensive methods of construction, or

(*d*) the subscriber requires the installation or any component part thereof to be provided for a period of less than one year, or

(*e*) the installation is a private circuit connecting three or more points in such manner as to provide communication between all such points simultaneously, or is a private circuit providing communication with a place outside the British Islands,

the Postmaster General may fix the rate of rental in respect of that installation or that component part as the case may be.

Variation of rental fixed by the Postmaster General

12. The Postmaster General may from time to time increase or reduce any rate of rental which was fixed by him under regulation 11(7) by notice in writing to the subscriber, and such increase or reduction shall take effect on the date specified in the notice, being a date which in the case of an increase of a rate of rental shall be not less than two months after the date of service of the notice.

PART IV

NON-PERIODIC CHARGES

Application of Part IV

13. This part of these regulations applies in respect of telephone service provided by the Postmaster General under these regulations or under an agreement:

Provided that where any provision in this part of these regulations is inconsistent with an agreement the agreement shall prevail.

Connection charge

14.—(1) The subscriber shall pay a connection charge in respect of the installation, connection for use, or provision of each of the items of equipment or apparatus specified in Schedule 5.

(2) The amount of the connection charge shall be such as the Postmaster General shall fix:

Provided that, except where the Postmaster General has fixed the rate of rental for the equipment or apparatus concerned under regulation 11(7), that amount shall not exceed the aggregate of the amounts specified in Schedule 5 in relation to the equipment and apparatus concerned.

(3) Where telephone service has been suspended wholly or in part or an installation has been disconnected under the provisions of these regulations, and the telephone service is restored or the installation is re-connected, the subscriber shall pay a re-connection charge of 10s., and no connection charge shall be payable under the foregoing paragraphs of this regulation in respect of the re-connection if the installation re-connected consists of the same equipment and apparatus as before the suspension or disconnection occurred.

Special construction

15.—(1) Where at the request of the subscriber any equipment or apparatus or any part thereof provided by the Postmaster General is of a more expensive type, or of a greater length, or installed in a more expensive manner, than the Postmaster General having regard to his normal methods of construction considers appropriate, or where at such request the installation or connection for use of any equipment or apparatus is effected wholly or partly outside such hours as the Postmaster General may from time to time determine to be normal working hours, the subscriber shall pay such sum as the Postmaster General may fix, not exceeding the certified excess cost incurred by him in complying with such request.

(2) Where the Postmaster General considers that any equipment or apparatus to be provided by him within the curtilage of the premises at which telephone service is or is to be provided will be subject to abnormal risks of damage or depreciation by reason of the presence within that curtilage of electric lines or plant or any inflammable, explosive, dangerous or deleterious substances or things, or by reason of the carrying on of any operations within that curtilage, and accordingly provides equipment or apparatus fitted with special protection against those risks, or of a more expensive type, or of a greater length, or installed in a more expensive manner, than would otherwise have been the case, the subscriber shall if the Postmaster General so requires pay such sum as the Postmaster General may fix, not exceeding the certified excess cost thereby incurred by him.

(3) Any sum payable under this regulation shall be payable in addition to any rental or other charge or sum payable under these regulations in respect of the equipment or apparatus.

Single payment charge

16.—(1) The subscriber shall make a single payment in respect of the provision of each of the items of equipment or apparatus specified in Schedule 6, in addition to any rental or other charge or sum payable in respect thereof.

(2) The amount of the single payment shall be :

(*a*) where the item is of a colour, design, and size for the time being determined by the Postmaster General to be standard, the amount specified in relation thereto in Schedule 6 ;

(*b*) otherwise, such amount as the Postmaster General may fix.

Removals and changes of apparatus

17.—(1) Subject to the following paragraphs of this regulation, the subscriber shall pay :—

(*a*) for the internal removal of any item of equipment or apparatus specified in Schedule 7, such charge as the Postmaster General shall fix not exceeding the sum specified in relation to that item in Schedule 7 ;

(*b*) for any other internal removal, and for any external removal, such charge as the Postmaster General may fix not exceeding the certified cost incurred by him in effecting the removal.

(2) Subject as aforesaid, where on the application of the subscriber the Postmaster General effects a change of apparatus :—

(*a*) if the subscriber has applied for a private branch exchange or a private exchange or a switchboard to be provided in substitution for another, the subscriber shall pay for the change of apparatus a charge equal to one half of the sum specified or referred to in Schedule 5 in relation to the first-mentioned private branch exchange or private exchange or switchboard ;

(*b*) the subscriber shall pay for any other change of apparatus such charge as the Postmaster General may fix, not exceeding the sum of £1 10s. in respect of each item of equipment or apparatus substituted.

(3) (*a*) In any case in which a subscriber whose telephone service is provided under these regulations applies for any internal or external removal or change of apparatus, the Postmaster General may if he thinks fit require that the removal or change of apparatus be effected under sub-paragraph (*b*) or sub-paragraph (*c*) of this paragraph, instead of under paragraph (1) or paragraph (2) of this regulation ; and in that event no charge shall be payable under the said paragraph (1) or paragraph (2).

(*b*) Where the Postmaster General requires that the removal or change of apparatus be effected under this sub-paragraph, the subscriber shall give notice to the Postmaster General under regulation 7 requiring him to cease to provide telephone service by means of the whole of the installation concerned, and shall apply under regulation 5 for telephone service to be provided by means of a fresh installation or fresh installations.

(*c*) Where the Postmaster General requires that the removal or change of apparatus be effected under this sub-paragraph, the subscriber shall give notice to the Postmaster General under regulation 7 requiring him to cease to provide telephone service by means of the equipment or apparatus which the subscriber wishes to be removed from one position to another or to be substituted by other equipment or apparatus, and shall apply under regulation 5 for telephone service to be provided by means of equipment or apparatus in that other position, or by means of equipment or apparatus substituted for that which was comprised in the said notice, as the case may be.

(d) A notice given by the subscriber under sub-paragraph (b) or sub-paragraph (c) of this paragraph may be expressed to expire on that date on which telephone service shall first be provided by means of the fresh or altered installation as the case may be.

(4) In any case in which the Postmaster General is of the opinion that the cost which he will incur in effecting any removal in respect of which a sum is specified or referred to in Schedule 7, or any change of apparatus, will be exceptionally large, he may give notice to the subscriber accordingly ; and if the subscriber then confirms his application and the removal or change of apparatus is effected, the subscriber shall pay the certified cost so incurred by the Postmaster General instead of a charge fixed under paragraph (1) of this regulation or a charge prescribed by or fixed under paragraph (2) of this regulation.

(5) Where any charges are payable in respect of an internal or external removal or a change of apparatus under paragraphs (1), (2) or (4) of this regulation, no connection charges shall be payable under regulation 14 in respect of the removal or the change of apparatus.

(6) If the subscriber cancels an application for an internal or external removal or a change of apparatus before the removal or change has been fully effected and the equipment or apparatus connected for use, the subscriber shall pay the certified cost of the work which has been done and has been rendered abortive by reason of the cancellation, and, if the subscriber requests that the installation should be restored to the condition in which it was before that work was begun, and re-connected for use, the certified cost of such restoration and re-connection.

Charges for outside normal hours repair work

18. If the subscriber requests the Postmaster General to carry out work to remedy a fault in an installation or any part thereof outside such hours as the Postmaster General may from time to time determine to be normal working hours, and the Postmaster General accedes to such request, the subscriber shall pay in respect of any work done outside such hours as aforesaid in remedying or attempting to remedy the fault a charge calculated and fixed in such manner as the Postmaster General may determine. The Postmaster General shall from time to time publish particulars of such manner of determination in the London, Edinburgh, and Belfast Gazettes or otherwise as he may determine.

PART V

CALL CHARGES

Telephone groups

19.—(1) For the purposes of regulation 20 and Schedule 8 the Postmaster General shall classify telephone exchanges into groups (herein referred to as "telephone groups"), and shall determine in relation to each telephone group: (a) what other telephone groups are to be regarded as adjacent to it, and (b) the point (herein referred to as "the group centre") which is to be used for measuring distances for the purposes of regulation 20 and Schedule 8.

(2) (a) Where owing to the distance of a call office from the telephone exchange by which it is served the Postmaster General considers it inappropriate that the

charges for calls made from or to the call office should be determined by reference to that telephone exchange, he may direct either that for the purposes of regulation 20 and Schedule 8 some other telephone exchange shall be regarded as the telephone exchange serving the call office, or that for those purposes the call office shall itself be regarded as a telephone exchange serving the telephone therein ; and in such cases the expressions "local exchange" and "terminal exchange" (as defined in regulation 1(1)) shall be construed accordingly.

(b) Where the Postmaster General directs under the preceding sub-paragraph that a call office shall be regarded as a telephone exchange, he shall include it in a telephone group under paragraph (1).

(3) The Postmaster General shall supply to every subscriber on demand a list of the telephone exchanges which are for the time being either in the same telephone group as the exchange by which the subscriber's installation is served or in the telephone groups which are regarded as adjacent to that group.

Inland call charges

20.—(1) This regulation applies to calls other than those to which regulation 21, 24(2), or 25 applies.

(2) The charges for local calls shall be as follows :

(a) Where the call is made from an installation or telephone on which the subscriber trunk dialling facility is available, or would be available but for a request from the subscriber that it should be withheld, the charge shall be at the rate specified in item 1 of Table A in the appropriate Part of Schedule 8, whether the called number is dialled by the caller or not.

(b) Otherwise, the charge shall be the sum specified in relation to the call in item 1 of Table B in the appropriate Part of Schedule 8 : Provided that the Postmaster General may fix the charge for the call at a rate not exceeding the total of the last mentioned sum for the first three minutes of the call's duration plus 3d. for each three minutes or part thereof after the first three minutes.

(3) The charges for trunk calls shall be as follows :

(a) Where the call is obtained by means of the subscriber trunk dialling facility, the charge shall be at the rate specified in item 2 of Table A in the appropriate Part of Schedule 8.

(b) Otherwise (whether or not the subscriber trunk dialling facility is available on the installation or telephone from which the call is made), the charge shall be at the rate specified in item 2 of Table B in the appropriate Part of Schedule 8.

(4) The rates specified in Tables A in Schedule 8 shall be applied as follows : the charge for the call shall be the sum of the number of charge units, each of the value specified at the head of the table, which is appropriate having regard to the duration of the call, one charge unit being charged for each period of time specified in the second column of the table opposite to the appropriate category of call, and any odd fraction of such period being treated as one such period.

(5) The charges specified in Part 3 of Schedule 8 do not include the charge which the person licensed to operate the local exchange may make in respect of the use of a call office or coin box telephone provided by that person.

(6) In this regulation references to the appropriate Part of Schedule 8 are references to the Part which is appropriate to the particular call having regard to the headings to the said Parts, and in Schedule 8 the expression "the distance between the group centres concerned" means the distance between the group centre of the telephone group which includes the local exchange and the group centre of the telephone group which includes the terminal exchange.

Charges for foreign and other calls

21.—(1) The charges for calls (other than calls to which regulation 24(2) or 25 applies) which involve the use of the Postmaster General's system, and which:

(a) are made from a place within the United Kingdom or the Isle of Man to a place outside the British Islands, or to a ship or aircraft, or to a telephone on a radiophone system ; or

(b) are made from a ship or aircraft registered in any part of the British Islands and are transmitted by wireless telegraphy over the first part of their course to a station for wireless telegraphy established on land within the British Islands ; or

(c) are made from a telephone within the United Kingdom or the Isle of Man which is on a radiophone system ;

shall be such as the Postmaster General may fix.

(2) The Postmaster General shall from time to time publish the charges so fixed in the London, Edinburgh and Belfast Gazettes or in such other manner as he may determine.

(3) In addition to the charge fixed under paragraph (1), there shall be charged and paid by the caller for every such call which is made from a call office of the Postmaster General the sum of 1s., unless an additional charge on account of the call's being so made is included in the charge for the call which is fixed under paragraph (1).

Calls from coin box lines

22.—(1) In the case of calls made from a coin box line provided by the Postmaster General and services and facilities for which application is made by means of such a coin box line, there shall be placed in the coin collecting box on the said line in respect of every call, service or facility such sum as would be payable therefor if the same were made or applied for by a caller at a call office.

(2) The sums so collected in the coin collecting box shall be the property of the subscriber, who in respect of any period for which an account is rendered shall pay to the Postmaster General for the calls, services and facilities referred to in paragraph (1) an amount equivalent to the aggregate of the sums recorded during the said period by the Postmaster General as having been so collected, less a rebate on the sums recorded as having been so collected for calls, calculated at such rates as the Postmaster General may fix.

(3) The Postmaster General may fix different rates of rebate in relation to different classes of call and different circumstances.

(4) The Postmaster General shall publish in the London, Edinburgh and Belfast Gazettes or in such other manner as he may determine a statement of the rates at which rebates are to be allowed to coin box line subscribers under paragraph (2) of this regulation.

(5) The sum payable under this regulation by a coin box line subscriber shall be in substitution for any charges which would otherwise be payable by him in respect of the said calls, services and facilities.

Reduction of charges at certain times

23. Any sums payable under these regulations in respect of calls of any description may be reduced at such times or during such periods as the Postmaster General may from time to time direct.

Limit of user, and contract calls

24.—(1) Calls for a period exceeding three minutes may be allowed at the discretion of the Postmaster General, but no person shall be entitled as of right to continue a call for a period exceeding three minutes.

(2) Nothing in these regulations shall preclude the Postmaster General from providing under a contract a call at a fixed time at a rate differing from the charge fixed by or under these regulations or a series of such calls, or a call to which regulation 25 applies.

Calls made by means of special equipment, etc.

25. Where for the purpose of any call the Postmaster General provides :—

(*a*) special equipment or apparatus affording sound reproduction of higher quality than that afforded by the ordinary public telephone system ; or

(*b*) means of simultaneous communication between three or more telephones ; or

(*c*) equipment or apparatus to facilitate the recording or broadcasting of messages ;

the charge for the call shall, subject to the terms of any contract for the provision of the call or of such equipment or apparatus or means of communication, be such as the Postmaster General may fix.

PART VI

SERVICES AND FACILITIES

General

26.—(1) The services and facilities referred to in this part of these regulations (including the services and facilities referred to in paragraph (3) and (4) of this regulation) may be provided by the Postmaster General at such times, during such periods, in such circumstances, and by means of such telephone exchanges, call offices or installations or classes thereof as the Postmaster General may from time to time consider expedient. The charges, terms and conditions determined by or under this part of these regulations shall apply to such services and facilities in so far as they are so provided.

(2) Regulations 29 and 30 shall not apply in relation to calls to which regulation 21, 24(2) or 25 applies.

(3) The charges applicable to any services and facilities provided in relation to calls to which regulation 21 applies, including the charges for the attempt to connect such calls in cases where communication between the person calling and the person called is not established by reason of the refusal of either of those persons to accept the call, shall (unless fixed by these regulations) be such

as the Postmaster General may fix. The Postmaster General shall from time to time publish the charges so fixed by him in the London, Edinburgh and Belfast Gazettes or in such other manner as he may determine.

(4) The charges applicable to any services and facilities provided in relation to calls to which regulation 24(2) or 25 applies shall, subject to the terms of any such contract as is mentioned in those regulations, be such as the Postmaster General may fix.

Temporary disconnection of telephone service

27.—(1) Telephone service provided by means of an installation may be temporarily disconnected either wholly or partially at the request of the subscriber or a person using the installation. The subscriber shall pay a charge of 10s. in respect of each exchange line on each occasion on which such line is so disconnected.

(2) The rental in respect of the installation shall continue to be payable in respect of any period during which the telephone service is so disconnected.

(3) Telephone service which has been so disconnected may be reconnected without payment of a re-connection charge.

Temporary transfer and interception of calls

28.—(1) All incoming calls to an exchange line may on the request of the subscriber or a person using the exchange line be transferred, during such period as may be specified in the request, to another exchange line (whether or not provided for the subscriber) which is served by the same telephone exchange, or be intercepted during such period at the telephone exchange and the caller informed of the telephone number of an exchange line (whether or not provided for the subscriber) at which the subscriber can be found or a message can be left for him. The subscriber in respect of the first mentioned exchange line shall pay the following charges for this service:

(a) for any number of days or parts of a day (whether or not consecutive) all falling within any one period of three months, £4

or (b) for each separate continuous period, 2s. per day or part of a day (subject to a minimum charge of 10s.),

whichever of the said charges in (a) and (b) shall be the less.

(2) Where an exchange line has ceased to be provided, all incoming calls to the line may on the written request of the person for whom it was previously provided be intercepted at the telephone exchange and the caller given the information mentioned in paragraph (1). This service may be given during such period (not exceeding twelve months) as may be specified in the request, but not after the telephone number previously allocated to the line has been allocated to another exchange line. No charge shall be payable for this service in respect of the period for which rental has been paid for the exchange line which has ceased to be provided but in respect of any subsequent period the person for whom the line was previously provided shall pay for this service a charge of £4 for each three months or part of three months.

Fixed time calls—British Islands

29.—(1) Subject to the provisions of this regulation, a subscriber or a person using an installation or a caller at a call office (in this regulation referred to as "the applicant") may book a call (including a personal call) in advance for connection at a specified time.

(2) A fixed time call which is to be made from a call office or a coin box line shall be booked from that call office or that coin box line. Any other fixed time call may be booked from any telephone or in writing. The Postmaster General may refuse to accept a booking if in his opinion notice of insufficient length has been given.

(3) A booking charge of 6d. shall be paid in respect of an application for a fixed time call in addition to the charge for the call.

(4) The booking charge for a fixed time call which is to be made from an installation shall be paid by the subscriber in respect of the installation from which the call is to be made. The booking charge for a fixed time call which is to be made from a call office shall be paid by the applicant at the time when the call is booked.

(5) Without prejudice to the generality of regulation 55, the Postmaster General may at his discretion remit the whole or part of the booking charge in respect of an application for a fixed time call, if the application for the call is cancelled by the applicant before the call is connected, or if the call is connected more than ten minutes after the specified time.

(6) The Postmaster General may at his discretion and without charge allow the applicant to alter the time specified by him for connection of a fixed time call.

Personal calls—British Islands

30.—(1) Subject to the provisions of this regulation, a person using an installation or a caller at a call office (in this regulation referred to as "the applicant") may book a call to a specified telephone number for the specified purpose of communication with a particular person identified by name or by such description as the Postmaster General may consider sufficient, or for connection to a particular department, correspondence reference, code number or extension number.

(2) The applicant when booking a personal call may specify :—

(*a*) one or more alternative telephone numbers after the first at which the person required may be found ;

(*b*) one or more substitutes for the person required, who may be found at the first of any specified alternative telephone number or numbers ; or

(*c*) two persons who may be found at the first or any specified alternative telephone number or numbers, with the requirement that unless both of them are available to speak the call is not to be connected.

(3) Subject to the following paragraphs of this regulation, a personal charge of 2s. shall be paid in respect of the application for a personal call, whether or not the call is connected.

(4) The personal charge shall be payable in addition to any other charges payable under these regulations for or in respect of the call or the application therefor.

(5) No personal charge shall be payable if the telephone exchange operator is unable to establish communication with the specified telephone number, or (as the case may be) is able to establish communication with none of the specified telephone numbers.

(6) The personal charge (if any) in respect of the application for a personal call which is also a fixed time call shall be payable in the manner in which the booking charge is payable under regulation 29(4).

(7) Where the applicant is unaware of the telephone number of a person required or of a substitute for him, the applicant may specify the address or alternative addresses of the person concerned, and in that event this regulation shall have effect as if the applicant had specified the telephone number or alternative telephone numbers (as the case may be) at which the person concerned might be found.

Transferred charge calls—British Islands

31.—(1) A person making a call to an installation may request the telephone exchange operator that the amount payable in respect of the call shall be charged to and payable by the person who is the subscriber in respect of the called installation, and if the person answering from the called installation consents to such request before the call is established, the amount payable in respect of the call and the transfer fee of 6d. shall be charged and payable accordingly.

(2) A person making a call to a call office may request the telephone exchange operator that the amount payable in respect of the call shall be payable by the person answering from the call office, and if the person so answering consents to such request, the amount payable in respect of the call and the transfer fee of 6d. shall be paid by that person in cash placed in the coin collecting box of the call office before the call is established.

(3) A person making a call from a coin box line or a call office to an installation may, before the termination of the call, request the telephone exchange operator that the duration of the call may be extended for a further period beyond the period in respect of which payment was made in cash, and that the amount payable in respect of such further period may be charged to and payable by the person who is the subscriber in respect of the called installation, or the person answering from the called installation may make the like request ; and (provided in the former case that the person so answering consents to the request) the amount payable in respect of the extended period of the call and the transfer fee of 6d. shall in either case be charged and payable accordingly.

(4) A person making a call from a coin box line or a call office to a call office may, before the termination of the call, request the telephone exchange operator that the duration of the call may be extended for a further period beyond the period in respect of which payment was made in cash, and that the amount payable in respect of such further period shall be payable by the person receiving the call, or the person receiving the call may make the like request ; and (provided in the former case that the person receiving the call consents to the request) the amount payable in respect of the extended period of the call and the transfer fee of 6d. shall in either case be paid by the person receiving the call in cash placed in the coin collecting box of the call office before the duration of the call is extended.

(5) Provided that where any call referred to in the foregoing paragraphs of this regulation is a personal call made from a coin box line or a call office, the

personal charge shall be paid in advance in cash placed in the coin collecting box by the person making the application for the call, and shall not be made payable by any other person by virtue of the foregoing paragraphs of this regulation.

(6) In any case in which the charge for a call made payable by another person under paragraph (1) or paragraph (2) falls within item 1 in Table B in Part I of Schedule 8, that item shall be read as if the sum specified in paragraph (b) thereof were specified also in paragraph (a) thereof.

(7) This regulation shall apply only to calls made through the Postmaster General's system from an installation or telephone on land (whether in a fixed location or not) within the British Islands to another such installation or telephone.

(8) For the purpose of the application of this regulation to calls which are made in either direction between :—

(a) an installation or telephone on the said system, or a telephone on the telephone system of any Authority providing service under licence from the Postmaster General, and

(b) a telephone on the telephone system of any Authority providing service as aforesaid,

references to the Postmaster General in the definition of the expressions "coin box line" and "installation" in regulation 1(1) shall include references to such Authority, and the expression "subscriber" shall include a person for whom such Authority provides telephone service.

Transferred charge calls—elsewhere

32.—(1) A person making a call from the United Kingdom or the Isle of Man to a place outside the British Islands in respect of which the transferred charge service is available may request that the call charges should be reversed ; and if the Telephone Authority providing service there or the Post Office operator obtains from the person answering on the called telephone his consent to such request before the call is established, and the call is established, no call charge or service charge shall be payable under these regulations in respect of the call or the transferred charge service.

(2) Where the call is not established (whether or not such consent has been obtained), or where such consent is not obtained and the call is established as an ordinary call, there shall be charged and paid under these regulations such service charge (if any) as the Postmaster General may fix, in addition in the latter case to the charge in respect of the call.

(3) Where a person making a call to the United Kingdom or the Isle of Man from a place outside the British Islands, or a ship or aircraft registered in any part of the British Islands, being a place, ship or aircraft in respect of which the transferred charge service is available, requests that the call charges shall be reversed, and the person answering from the called telephone consents to such request before the call is established, and the call is established, there shall be charged and paid under these regulations :

(a) where the call is made from a place, such call charge and such service charge (if any) as the Postmaster General may fix ;

(b) where the call is made from a ship or aircraft, the charge for the call fixed by the Postmaster General under regulation 21(1) and such service charge (if any) as the Postmaster General may fix.

The said charges shall be payable by the like person and in the like manner as if they were charges in respect of a call made from the called telephone, but not so as to make payable the additional charges referred to in regulation 21(3) where the called telephone is a call office.

(4) Where a person making a call to the United Kingdom or the Isle of Man from a ship or aircraft registered in any part of the British Islands, being a ship or aircraft in respect of which the transferred charge service is available, requests that the call charges shall be reversed, and either :

(*a*) the call is not established, or

(*b*) the consent of the person answering from the called telephone to such request is not obtained and the call is established as an ordinary call,

there shall be charged under these regulations and paid by the caller in the ship or aircraft such service charge (if any) as the Postmaster General may fix in addition in the latter case to the charge for the call.

(5) The Postmaster General shall publish as provided by regulation 26(3) the charges fixed by him under this regulation.

Credit card calls

33.—(1) The Postmaster General may issue to any subscriber he thinks fit on the subscriber's request a credit card under the authority of which, subject to the provisions of this regulation, any holder of the card may make calls from telephones other than the subscriber's telephone on terms that notwithstanding anything elsewhere in these regulations the call charges will be payable by the subscriber.

(2) On the expiry of a credit card the Postmaster General may if he thinks fit issue to the subscriber a credit card by way of renewal thereof unless the subscriber has requested the Postmaster General not to do so.

(3) The subscriber shall make periodical payments for the credit card service at the rate of 5s. per quarter in respect of each separate credit card number allocated to him, and in addition if more than one credit card bearing the same number is issued by the Postmaster General, the subscriber shall make periodical payments at the rate of 2s. 6d. per quarter for each credit card issued other than the first. These regulations shall apply in relation to such payments as if they were rental payable in respect of the subscriber's installation.

(4) A person wishing to make a credit card call under the authority of a credit card issued by the Postmaster General shall ask the appropriate telephone service operator to connect the call as a credit card call, and shall quote the number shown on the credit card.

(5) Credit card calls may be made under the authority of a credit card issued by the Postmaster General :

(*a*) from any telephone on the Postmaster General's system to any telephone to which calls may be made from the first mentioned telephone ;

(*b*) from any telephone in a ship or aircraft registered in any part of the British Islands, if the call is transmitted by wireless telegraphy over the first part of its course to a station for wireless telegraphy established on land within the British Islands ;

(*c*) from any telephone on the telephone system of any Authority providing service under licence from the Postmaster General ;

(*d*) from any telephone on the telephone system of any Authority providing service in any country outside the British Islands to any telephone in the British Islands;

provided, in cases (*b*) and (*d*), that the call involves the use of the Postmaster General's system, and in cases (*b*), (*c*) and (*d*) that an arrangement has been made between the Postmaster General and the other Telephone Authority concerned, or (as the case may be) between the Postmaster General and the person licensed by him under the Wireless Telegraphy Act 1949(a) to use the station in the ship or aircraft, permitting credit card calls of the description concerned to be made by the holders of credit cards issued by the Postmaster General.

(6) The subscriber to whom the credit card was issued shall pay to the Postmaster General on demand the following charges in respect of calls made as credit card calls by any holder of the credit card:

(*a*) Where the call is of the description referred to in sub-paragraphs (*a*) (*b*) or (*c*) of paragraph (5), the charge shall be 6d. (except in the case of a call made to a place outside the British Islands) and in addition such call charge and such service charge (if any) as would have been payable if the call had been made otherwise than as a credit card call: Provided that:

(i) where the call charge which would have been so payable falls within item 1 in Table B in Part I of Schedule 8, that item shall be read as if the sum specified in paragraph (*b*) thereof were specified also in paragraph (*a*) thereof;

(ii) where the telephone from which the call was made was a coin box line provided by the Postmaster General or a similar line provided by an Authority providing service under licence from the Postmaster General, the call charge and the service charge shall be that which would have been payable by the caller;

(iii) where the call was made from a telephone on the telephone system of any Authority providing service under licence from the Postmaster General to another telephone on that system, and the charge for any calls of that description is included in the rental for the first mentioned telephone, the call charge for the credit card call shall be that which would have been payable if such rental had not included the charge for any calls.

(*b*) Where the call is of the description referred to in sub-paragraph (*d*) of paragraph (5), the charge shall be such call charge and such service charge (if any) as the Postmaster General may fix.

(7) The Postmaster General shall publish as provided by regulation 26(3) the charges fixed by him under the last foregoing sub-paragraph.

(8) (*a*) Where there is an arrangement between the Postmaster General and an Authority providing telephone service under licence from the Postmaster General or providing such service in any country outside the British Islands, whereby the holders of credit cards issued by that Authority to its subscribers may make calls from telephones on the Postmaster General's system on terms that the call charges will be paid by those subscribers, the following sub-paragraph shall apply.

(*b*) A person who satisfies the Postmaster General that he is the holder of a current credit card issued by such Authority, and that the telephone to which he wishes to make a call is one to which he may make credit card calls under the arrangement, may make the call as a credit card call from any telephone on the

---

(a) 1949 c. 54

Postmaster General's system ; and in that case no call charge, service charge or other charge shall be payable under these regulations by the caller or by the person who is the subscriber in respect of the telephone from which the call is made.

(9) This regulation shall apply to services and facilities requested on the authority of a credit card and to the charges in respect of such services and facilities, as it applies to credit card calls and to the charges in respect thereof.

Alarm calls

34.—(1) A person using an installation or a caller at a call office may apply for an alarm call to be made from a telephone exchange to an installation at a specified time of the day or night.

(2) If the alarm call service is available in relation to that application, there shall be charged and paid in respect of the application :

(*a*) where the subscriber trunk dialling facility is available on the installation or at the call office from which the application is made, or (in the case of an application made from an installation) would be available but for a request from the subscriber that it should be withheld: a sum equal to twelve times the charge unit specified in Schedule 8 Part 1 Table A, or four times the charge unit specified in Schedule 8 Part 2 Table A, according to whichever Part would be appropriate to the application if it were an ordinary call;

(*b*) otherwise: a sum equal to eight times the sum specified in item 1 of Schedule 8 Part I Table B or six times the sum specified in item 1 of Schedule 8 Part 2 Table B according to whichever Part would be appropriate to the application if it were an ordinary call.

No charge shall be payable in respect of the alarm call itself.

(3) Where an application is made from an installation, otherwise than by means of a coin box line, for an alarm call to be made to another installation, the charge shall be paid by the person who is the subscriber in respect of the latter installation.

Advice of duration and charge

35.—(1) The Postmaster General may supply particulars of the duration of or the charge for a call, or of both such duration and charge, on the request of the person who is the subscriber in respect of the installation from which the call was made or of any other person using such installation or, in the case of a transferred charge call, on the request of the person who is the subscriber in respect of the called telephone or of any other person using such telephone.

(2) There shall be charged and paid for this service in respect of each call from a place within the British Islands to a place within the British Islands of which particulars are supplied, the sum of 6d.; and in respect of each other call of which particulars are supplied, the sum of 2s.

Additional particulars of calls charged individually

36.—(1) Where the Postmaster General provides or has provided for a subscriber a statement of the charges for individual calls made from the subscriber's installation, or for transferred charge calls made to that installation, or for credit card calls made by a holder of a credit card issued to the subscriber, he may on the request of the subscriber supply to him, either in the statement or subsequently, particulars of all or any of the following matters in relation to all or any of the calls :

(*a*) the duration of the call ;

(*b*) the telephone number of the called telephone, or of the telephone from which a transferred charge call was made ;

(*c*) the telephone exchange serving the called telephone, or serving the telephone from which a transferred charge call was made ;

(*d*) the name of the place of destination of a telegram originated by a call from the subscriber's installation ;

(*e*) the telephone numbers of the telephones from and to which a credit card call was made ;

(*f*) the telephone exchanges serving the telephones from and to which a credit card call was made.

(2) There shall be charged and paid for this service a charge at the rate of 2s. for each twenty-five calls in relation to which additional particulars are supplied as aforesaid on any one occasion, the charge in relation to calls made in each separate month being calculated separately, and odd fractions of twenty-five calls being reckoned as twenty-five.

Application of telegraph facilities

37.—(1) A person using an installation or a caller at a call office may give to the appropriate Post Office operator a telephonic message for further transmission to the addressee as a written telegram.

(2) This facility shall be subject to the provisions of these regulations and the statutory regulations for the time being in force relating to written telegrams, and shall be subject to the charges respectively payable thereunder for the telephone call involved and for the transmission and delivery of every message.

Directory enquiries

38.—(1) Where a caller who asks to be informed of the telephone number of a subscriber is unable to give such details of the name or names and the address of that subscriber as the Postmaster General may request, the Postmaster General may search for such information and whether or not the information requested by the caller is obtained by the search, the caller shall if the Postmaster General so requires pay a search fee of 1s.

(2) Where a caller asks to be informed of the name and address or the name or address of a subscriber, the Postmaster General may search for such information and whether or not the information requested by the caller is obtained by the search the caller shall if the Postmaster General so requires pay all or any of the following charges, namely, a search fee of 1s. and a charge or charges in respect of any trunk call or calls made in order to obtain such information calculated in the case of a call or calls made by the caller himself at the rate for trunk calls made otherwise than by means of the subscriber trunk dialling facility specified in the appropriate part of Schedule 8 and in the case of a call or calls made by the Postmaster General at the said rate as if the call or calls had been made by the caller himself from the telephone from which he asks for such information.

Part VII

Radiophone Service

Radiophone service

39.—(1) Subject to the provisions of this regulation, telephone service may be provided through a radiophone system to a person who is licensed under the Wireless Telegraphy Act 1949 to establish and use a station for wireless telegraphy, whether in a vehicle or elsewhere, for the purpose of sending and receiving calls between a telephone associated with that station and a station for wireless telegraphy forming part of the Postmaster General's system. In this regulation such telephone service is referred to as "radiophone service", such person as "the licensee", and such telephone as "a radiotelephone".

(2) The licensee shall pay in respect of each station of the licensee a subscription for radiophone service (in addition to the charges for calls, services and facilities obtained by means of the radiophone service) at the rate of £7 10s. 0d. per quarter, or part thereof.

(3) Subject to the exceptions and modifications set out in Schedule 9 these regulations shall apply to any radiophone service as if the licensee were a subscriber, the subscription a rental in respect of an installation, and a radiotelephone an installation.

(4) Nothing in this regulation shall apply to radiophone service provided under an agreement entered into before the 1st January 1965 (the date of coming into force of regulation 3 of the Telephone Amendment (No. 4) Regulations 1964(**a**)) so long as that agreement remains in force.

Part VIII

General Conditions of Service to Subscribers

Application of Part VIII

40. This part of these regulations applies in respect of telephone service provided by means of an installation, whether under these regulations or under an agreement :

Provided that where any provision in this part of these regulations is inconsistent with an agreement the agreement shall prevail.

General powers of the Postmaster General

41. Without prejudice to any other power or right of the Postmaster General he may at his discretion :—

(*a*) refuse, or cease, in consequence of any difficulty in obtaining or maintaining on terms acceptable to the Postmaster General any wayleave for an appropriate telegraphic line, to provide under these regulations or under an agreement any telephone service which would involve or involves the use of that line ;

(*b*) disconnect an installation from one shared line or telephone exchange and connect it with any other shared line or telephone exchange ;

(*c*) make any alteration in an installation ;

(*d*) alter a subscriber's telephone number, or the name of the telephone exchange serving an installation, or both ;

(**a**) S.I. 1964/1451 (1964 III, p. 3373).

(e) use any part or parts of an installation (including any exclusive line) provided for a subscriber under these regulations or under an agreement for any purpose (including the provision of services to other persons) involving the carrying of electric currents over such part or parts of the installation at frequencies different from those used for the purpose of that subscriber's telephone service.

Power to require security

42. The Postmaster General may, from time to time, either before or after providing an installation under these regulations or before or after making an agreement, require the payment of a deposit of such amount as he thinks necessary by way of security for the payment of the rental or other charges payable or to become payable by the subscriber, and the subscriber shall pay such deposit within such time as the Postmaster General may direct. The Postmaster General may retain such deposit so long as the installation continues to be provided for the subscriber.

Charges payable by subscribers

43.—(1) Subject to the provisions of these regulations, all charges in respect of calls made from an installation, and in respect of services and facilities rendered at the request or with the authority of persons using an installation, shall be payable on demand by the person who is the subscriber in respect of the installation.

(2) Any rental payable under these regulations or under an agreement in respect of an installation or of each component part thereof shall commence on the date when the installation or component part is connected for use.

(3) Any rental payable under these regulations or under an agreement shall be payable at such intervals and on such dates (whether in advance or in arrear, or partly in advance and partly in arrear) as the Postmaster General may from time to time decide either in relation to the installation for which the rental is payable or generally, and shall be payable by the person who is the subscriber in respect of that installation.

(4) Subject to the provisions of these regulations, any other sum payable under these regulations or under an agreement in respect of any equipment or apparatus shall be payable on demand by the person who is the subscriber in respect thereof.

(5) The charges for calls of any class, or of any combination of classes, may be aggregated and included as a single item in any account rendered to a subscriber.

(6) This regulation shall have effect subject to regulation 51.

Default by subscribers

44.—(1) If a subscriber—

(i) fails to pay when due any rental or other sum (including any sum required by way of deposit) payable by him under these regulations or under an agreement or under the statutory telex regulations for the time being in force or under an agreement made by the Postmaster General with the subscriber for or relating to the provision of telex service ; or

(ii) has a receiving order made against him or in Scotland is sequestrated, or becomes insolvent or makes any composition or arrangement with or assignment for the benefit of his creditors, or, being a company, goes into liquidation, whether voluntary or compulsory, or has a receiver of any assets appointed ; or

(iii) fails to observe or perform any of the provisions of these regulations or of an agreement, or any obligation on his part arising thereunder,

the Postmaster General may (without prejudice to any other right or remedy) :

(a) without notice, wholly or in part suspend telephone service provided by means of all or any of the subscriber's installations (whether such installations are provided under these regulations or under agreements) and if he shall think fit so to do disconnect all or any of such installations from the telephone exchange ; and, in addition or alternatively,

(b) summarily terminate the telephone service provided by means of all or any of such installations under these regulations after giving to the subscriber notice in writing of his intention so to do ; and, in addition or alternatively,

(c) summarily determine such agreements or any of them by notice in writing to that effect.

(2) On the termination under the provisions of this regulation of telephone service by means of an installation provided under these regulations, the subscriber shall pay, in addition to any other sums payable under these regulations up to the date of such termination, a sum equal to one month's rental, or to the rental which would have been payable for the installation in respect of the period from that date to the end of the minimum period of service at the rates in force at the date of such termination, whichever is the greater, credit being allowed to the subscriber for the appropriate proportion of any rental paid in advance in respect of a period ending after that date.

(3) On the determination of any agreement under the provisions of this regulation, the subscriber shall pay, in addition to any other sums payable under such agreement up to the date of its determination, a sum equal to one month's rental or to the rental for the period from the date of determination to the end of the initial term of the agreement at the rates in force at the date of determination, whichever is the greater, credit being allowed to the subscriber as aforesaid.

Subscriber's responsibility for installation

45.—(1) Every installation provided under these regulations or under an agreement is and shall at all times remain the property of the Postmaster General, and the subscriber shall be responsible for the safety of all such parts thereof as are in or on the subscriber's premises, fair wear and tear only excepted.

(2) The subscriber shall pay the following sums in respect of the replacement of any such parts of the installation as aforesaid which at any time are lost, stolen or destroyed, and the replacement or repair of any such parts which are damaged otherwise than by way of fair wear and tear :—

(a) in respect of the replacement of any such parts which are specified in Schedule 10, the sums specified in that Schedule in relation to those parts ; and (*b*) in respect of the repair of any such parts which are so specified, or the replacement or repair of any such parts which are not so specified, the certified cost incurred by the Postmaster General in replacing or repairing those parts.

Provided that in any case to which sub-paragraph (*b*) of this paragraph applies, the Postmaster General may substitute a charge not exceeding 10s. for the certified cost referred to in that sub-paragraph.

(3) The Postmaster General may remove the installation within such time as he thinks fit after the cesser or termination of provision of telephone service by means thereof or the determination of the relative agreement by any means, and the subscriber's obligations under paragraphs (1) and (2) shall continue until the installation has either been so removed or been provided for another subscriber at the same premises.

Permission to enter property

46.—(1) Every subscriber shall permit officers of the Post Office (or, when required by the Postmaster General so to do, procure permission for them from any other person whose permission is requisite) to enter at all reasonable times upon the subscriber's premises for the purpose of constructing, inspecting, maintaining, altering, or removing the installation or any part thereof and to have access at all reasonable times to all such parts of the installation as may be in or on the subscriber's premises.

(2) Every officer of the Post Office who desires to enter upon the subscriber's premises as aforesaid shall produce, if required so to do, some duly authenticated document showing his identity and authority.

Attachments etc.

47.—(1) A subscriber shall not, without the written consent of the Postmaster General :

(*a*) alter or remove an installation or any part thereof, or obliterate or deface any marks thereon ;

(*b*) place or use in any manner or position in relation to an installation any thing that may have a harmful effect on the installation or on the use of the installation for the purposes for which it was provided or on the quality of the telephone service ; or

(*c*) permit or suffer any other person except an officer of the Post Office so to do.

(2) A subscriber shall not :

(*a*) attach any thing to an installation, or place any thing in electrical connection therewith ; or

(*b*) place or use any thing in such a manner or position in relation to an installation that it transmits or enables to be transmitted any message or other communication to or from the installation ; or

(*c*) permit or suffer any other person except an officer of the Post Office so to do,

unless it is provided by the Postmaster General for that purpose, or unless it is, or is of a type which is, for the time being approved by the Postmaster General for that purpose in accordance with the next following paragraph.

(3) The Postmaster General may from time to time publish in such manner as he may think fit lists of the types of things which are for the time being approved by him for the purposes of paragraph (2), and may give to a subscriber in writing approval for those purposes of any thing which is not for the time being included in any such list.

(4) The subscriber shall, on being required by the Postmaster General so to do, forthwith cease to use and remove anything which has been attached, connected, placed or used as mentioned in paragraph (2) whether by the subscriber or by another person and whether or not it is approved or is of a type which is approved as aforesaid, and anything which has been placed in such manner or position in relation to an installation that in the opinion of the Postmaster General its use has had or may have a harmful effect on the installation or on the use of the installation for the purposes for which it was provided or on the quality of the telephone service.

Subscriber not to assign service or agreement

48.—(1) A subscriber shall not, except with the written consent of the Postmaster General, assign, dispose of or part with telephone service provided under these regulations, or assign or dispose of his agreement, or assign, dispose of or part with any benefit or advantage under this agreement.

(2) A subscriber who fails to comply with this regulation shall (without prejudice to any other right or remedy of the Postmaster General) continue to be liable for all rental, charges and sums due and to become due in respect of the installation, and in respect of calls made therefrom and services and facilities rendered at the request or with the authority of persons using the installation.

Supply of electricity

49.—(1) If and when required so to do by the Postmaster General, a subscriber shall provide at his own expense in all respects a continuous supply (at a pressure not exceeding 250 volts subject to any percentage variation allowed by the Electricity Supply Regulations 1937, or any regulations amending or superseding the same) of the electricity required by the Postmaster General for the installing, operation and maintenance of the installation or any part thereof. Such electricity shall be supplied at such point or points and by means of such wires fitted with such sockets or other means of connection and provided with such connection to earth and with such fusible cut-outs and other protective devices as the Postmaster General may from time to time require.

(2) The subscriber shall pay the certified cost incurred by the Postmaster General from time to time of making such alterations to the installation as the Postmaster General considers necessary to conform to any change made otherwise than by the Postmaster General in the method of supplying the electricity to the installation or in the kind of electric current used, or to prevent injurious affection to the installation by electric lines or plant erected on the subscriber's premises.

Telephone directories

50.—(1) Subject to the provisions of this regulation, the Postmaster General may make an entry in respect of every exchange line in such of the telephone directories from time to time published by him or on his behalf as he considers appropriate, and every such entry may be made in such terms, form, manner and order as the Postmaster General thinks fit.

(2) A subscriber may apply to the Postmaster General in writing for a special entry in respect of a specified exchange line provided for him to be made in a telephone directory in terms or in a form mentioned in Schedule 11 ; and if the Postmaster General accedes to the application the following provisions of this regulation shall apply.

(3) The subscriber shall pay for the facilities referred to in paragraph (2) a periodic charge at the annual rate, or, as the case may be, the total of the annual rates, specified or provided for in Schedule 11 in relation to the facility and the telephone directory concerned.

(4) The period in respect of which the said charge shall be payable shall begin on the first day of the month in which is published the first issue of the telephone directory in which effect is given to the application, and shall end as provided in the next following paragraph.

(5) The subscriber may at any time by notice in writing to the Postmaster General withdraw an application made under paragraph (2), and the said period shall end on the first day of the month in which is published the next subsequent issue of the telephone directory concerned, whether effect is given to the notice of withdrawal in that issue or not ; and if no such notice is given, the said period shall end on the date when the subscriber's liability to pay rental in respect of the exchange line concerned ceases.

(6) The said charge shall be payable at such intervals (not being longer than a year) and on such dates (whether in advance or in arrear, or partly in advance and partly in arrear) as the Postmaster General may from time to time decide either in relation to a particular entry or exchange line or generally ; and on the termination of the period referred to in paragraph (4) the Postmaster General shall repay to the subscriber or allow him in account the appropriate proportion of any instalment paid in advance in respect of a period ending after such termination.

(7)(a) In this regulation and in Schedule 11 : —

"telephone directory" does not include any directory in which the entries are classified according to the trades or professions of the subscribers ;

"main telephone directory" means the London Postal Area Telephone Directory published in numbered parts and the Outer London and Provincial Telephone Directory published in numbered sections ;

"business telephone directory" means a telephone directory published in addition to the main telephone directory and any local telephone directory, containing entries relating to certain business lines in a particular geographical area and to certain exchange lines in such an area provided under an agreement which the Postmaster General regards as business lines ;

"local telephone directory" means a telephone directory containing entries relating to a particular geographical area, not being either a part or section of the main telephone directory or a business telephone directory ;

"main entry" means a single entry relating to the exchange line or lines provided for a subscriber at one address ;

"extra entry" means an entry additional to a main entry, and relating to the exchange line or lines to which that main entry relates ;

"extra word" means any word which the Postmaster General permits to be included in an entry on condition that the extra charge specified in Schedule 11 is payable therefor.

(*b*) References in this regulation to an issue of a directory being a directory which is published in parts or sections, shall be construed as references to the issue of the part or section which is or would be appropriate to the particular entry or exchange line.

(*c*) Where an issue of a directory is dated by a reference to a month and year appearing therein or thereon, that issue shall be deemed to have been published on the first day of the month referred to.

PART IX

GENERAL

Calculation of rentals

51. The Postmaster General may if he thinks fit determine that the following rules shall apply for the purpose of calculating the rental payable in respect of any period at a quarterly rate under these regulations or under an agreement for an installation (other than a private circuit), or each component part of such an installation :

(*a*) Each quarter shall be deemed to begin on the first day of such month as the Postmaster General may determine.

(*b*) Each complete month in an incomplete quarter shall be treated as one third of a quarter.

(*c*) Each day in an incomplete month in the period shall be treated as one twenty-eighth of a complete month, but for the purpose of this rule such of the days between the 28th of the month and the last day of the month (inclusive) as fall within the period shall be treated together as one day.

(*d*) Odd fractions of a penny amounting to ½d. or more shall be charged as 1d. and those amounting to less than ½d. shall be disregarded.

Measurement of length of lines

52. For the purpose of these regulations, the chargeable length of any exchange line, extension, or private circuit, or of any part thereof, shall be the distance measured between such points and in such manner as the Postmaster General may consider appropriate, and in particular (but without prejudice to the generality of the foregoing provision) the chargeable length of any extension or private circuit whereof the terminal points are more than 25 miles apart may be calculated by reference to the distance (measured as hereinbefore provided) between the telephone exchanges which in the opinion of the Postmaster General are the appropriate telephone exchanges to serve the areas in which the premises connected by means of the extension or private circuit are respectively situated.

Liability for call office and other charges

53. Except as otherwise provided by these regulations :

(*a*) all charges in respect of calls made from a call office and in respect of services and facilities rendered at the request of a caller from a call office shall if the Postmaster General so requires be prepaid by the caller, and otherwise shall be payable by the caller to the Postmaster General on demand.

(*b*) All charges in respect of calls made from a telephone in a ship or aircraft registered in any part of the British Islands, and in respect of services and facilities rendered at the request of a caller from such a telephone, shall be payable by the caller on demand to the person licensed by the Postmaster General under the Wireless Telegraphy Act 1949 to use the station for wireless telegraphy in the ship or aircraft, and the latter person shall account for such charges to the Postmaster General in accordance with the licence and any other relative arrangements between him and the Postmaster General.

(c) All other charges and sums payable under these regulations shall be payable to the Postmaster General on demand.

Evidence

54.—(1) In any proceedings by or against the Crown in relation to any rental, charge or sum payable under these regulations or under an agreement :—

(a) where the person alleged by the Crown to be liable for payment of that rental, charge or sum has not disputed in writing his liability therefor within 30 days of the service on him of an account including that rental, charge or sum, the production of a certified account of that rental, charge or sum shall be conclusive evidence of the amount thereof and of the liability of that person for payment thereof ;

(b) in any other case, the production of a certified account thereof shall be sufficient evidence unless the contrary is proved that the rental, charge or sum is payable in respect of the installation referred to in the account, and that the amount thereof is as stated in the account ; and the production of a Post Office telephone exchange ticket recording a call made or a service or facility afforded shall unless the contrary is proved be sufficient evidence of the facts recorded thereon.

(2) A certified statement (whether or not included in a certified account) :—

(a) of the cost or excess cost incurred by the Postmaster General in relation to any matter whereof the certified cost or certified excess cost is referred to in these regulations,

(b) of the component parts of which an installation consisted on any specified date or during any specified period,

(c) of the date on which an installation or any part of an installation provided under these regulations or under an agreement was connected for use,

(d) of any distance for the purpose of regulation 20(3) or 52, or

(e) that a ticket produced is a Post Office telephone exchange ticket,

shall for all purposes (including the purposes of any proceedings by or against the Crown) be sufficient evidence, unless the contrary is proved, of the facts therein stated.

(3) A copy of the London, Edinburgh or Belfast Gazette containing any notice published therein by the Postmaster General in accordance with regulation 21 or 26 shall be conclusive evidence of the facts stated in the notice.

Remission of charges

55. The Postmaster General may remit in whole or in part any rental, charge or sum payable or paid by virtue of these regulations.

Service of notices, etc.

56. Any notice, account, statement, direction or other document which may be given, rendered or made by the Postmaster General under or for any purpose of these regulations or an agreement shall be deemed to have been duly given, rendered or made and served if left at or sent by registered post or by the recorded delivery service to the address at or in connection with which the relevant telephone service is required or provided, or the address stated in the relative application form or agreement as the subscriber's address, or an address notified to the Postmaster General by the subscriber as an address to which accounts may be sent, or the subscriber's usual or last known place of abode or business in the British Islands.

Misuse of the telephone system

57.—(1) A person shall not use the Postmaster General's system :—

(a) for sending any message or communication which is offensive or abusive or of an indecent, obscene or menacing character to an officer of the Post Office or to any other person, or

(b) for the persistent making of telephone calls without reasonable cause or for the making of telephone calls for the purpose of causing annoyance, inconvenience, or needless anxiety to an officer of the Post Office or any other person, or

(c) for the making of any telephone call otherwise than by the method appropriate to the telephone from which the call is made, according to the Postmaster General's published instructions to subscribers and to users of call offices.

(2) The Postmaster General may interrupt and terminate any telephonic message or communication of, and may refuse to give the means of telephonic communication to, any person who contravenes this regulation, and shall not in any such case be bound to return any sums paid in respect of the message or communication, and may suspend without notice the telephone service of any subscriber whose installation is used as aforesaid, either at the time the installation is so used or at any time thereafter, and may continue such suspension unless and until such assurance is received as the Postmaster General may deem sufficient that there will be no further contravention of the provisions of paragraph (1) :

Provided that no action taken under this regulation shall prejudice any other right or remedy of the Postmaster General.

Non-liability of Post Office

58.—(1) Neither the Crown nor the Postmaster General nor any other officer of the Post Office shall incur any liability for or on account of or in respect of any loss or damage sustained by reason of any interruption or failure of communication or suspension of service by means of any installation, or any failure or error in connection with the taking or giving of messages by officers of the Post Office, or any omission or insertion of or error in any entry in a telephone directory published by or on behalf of the Postmaster General.

(2) A subscriber shall not be entitled to any abatement or rental in connection with any of the matters aforesaid.

Consent or approval of the Postmaster General

59. Any consent or approval of the Postmaster General referred to in these regulations shall be revocable and may be given subject to such terms and conditions as the Postmaster General may think fit.

Construction

60. Without prejudice to regulation 24(2), nothing contained in or done under Part II of these regulations, or done under or pursuant to any term or condition contained in or determined under these regulations, and no request for a call, service or facility for which the charge, terms or conditions are fixed or determined by or under these regulations, shall constitute or lead to the formation of a contract between the Postmaster General and any other person ; and nothing contained in or done under Part II of these regulations or regulation 17 shall be construed as implying that the Postmaster General is under any obligation to provide equipment or apparatus for the purpose of affording means of telephonic communication, or to effect an internal or external removal or a change of apparatus.

Revocation and transitional provisions

61.—(1) The regulations mentioned in Schedule 12 are hereby revoked.

(2) Any charges for calls, services or facilities which have been fixed by the Postmaster General under the regulations hereby revoked, and which are in force at the commencement of these regulations, shall continue in force without further publication until superseded by charges fixed by the Postmaster General under these regulations.

Citation and commencement

62.—(1) These regulations may be cited as "the Telephone Regulations 1968".

(2) These regulations shall come into operation on the 1st October 1968.

Dated 5th August 1968.

John Stonehouse,
Her Majesty's Postmaster General.

Regulation 6

SCHEDULE 1

TERMS AND CONDITIONS APPLICABLE TO PARTICULAR INSTALLATIONS

Regulation 6(1)(*a*)

PART 1

1. The telephone equipment and apparatus provided otherwise than by the Postmaster General (in this Part of this Schedule referred to as "the private equipment") shall not be connected directly or indirectly with an exchange line unless the Postmaster General notifies the subscriber in writing that in his opinion it is capable of working efficiently in connection therewith and the standard of transmission afforded by it is acceptable to him.

2. The private equipment (including any extension circuits) shall be so arranged that efficient calling and clearing signals shall under all circumstances be automatically given to the telephone exchange serving the installation. Circuit diagrams of the private equipment shall be furnished to the Postmaster General for written approval before the private equipment is connected as aforesaid with an exchange line and after such connection no alteration to any of the electrical circuits or to any other part of the private equipment shall be made without the written approval of the Postmaster General.

3. As a means of connecting the installation with the private equipment, the subscriber shall supply and maintain connection blocks of such description and in such positions as shall be approved in writing by the Postmaster General. The subscriber shall provide facilities for testing and shall not notify the Postmaster General of a fault unless tests have indicated that it did not originate from the private equipment. The subscriber shall pay the certified cost incurred by the Postmaster General as a result of any notification of a fault if it is found that the fault originated from the private equipment.

4. The Postmaster General may at any time inspect and test the private equipment for all purposes relating to the Postmaster General's system, and especially in regard to:—

(*a*) efficient speaking;

(*b*) efficient signalling; and

(*c*) satisfactory mechanical construction and condition.

5. The Postmaster General may at any time require the subscriber to have effected at the subscriber's expense any alterations or additions to the private equipment which in the opinion of the Postmaster General are rendered necessary by any change or development of the Postmaster General's system.

6. The private equipment shall be maintained by the subscriber in an efficient working condition and shall be operated by the subscriber efficiently. The Postmaster General's decision as to whether this condition has been complied with shall be final and conclusive.

7. Except with the consent in writing of the Postmaster General there shall not be used in connection with the installation:—

(*a*) an extension from any switchboard forming part of the private equipment to a point beyond a radius of five miles from the telephone exchange serving the installation;

(*b*) an extension from that switchboard for the use of any person other than the subscriber; or

(*c*) a telephone which is available to the public for the purpose of sending and receiving telephonic messages.

PART 2

An extension between switchboards shall not be used for originating a call to a telephone exchange. It shall be used only for:—

(1) calls between the two switchboards which it connects;

(2) calls between any circuit (other than an exchange line) connected with one of the switchboards and any such circuit connected with the other switchboard;

(3) calls between either of the said switchboards and any circuit (other than an exchange line) connected with the other switchboard; and

(4) calls received at one of the said switchboards over an exchange line and extended to the other switchboard or by way thereof to an extension connected therewith: Provided that the use of the said extension for this purpose may be prohibited by the Postmaster General at any time by notice in writing to that effect.

Regulation 6(1)(*c*)

PART 3

Neither the subscriber nor any other person shall receive any consideration either directly or indirectly in return for or otherwise howsoever on account of the use of the external extension by or on behalf of any person other than the subscriber or the person in the occupation of the premises connected by means of the external extension with the premises occupied by the subscriber. The term "consideration" includes besides money or money's worth the giving or withholding of business or any other advantage or benefit of any kind or description.

Regulation 6(1)(*d*)

PART 4

1. Except as otherwise provided by any licence granted by the Postmaster General to the subscriber under the Telegraph Acts 1863 to 1962, or with the consent in writing of the Postmaster General, neither the subscriber nor any other person shall receive any consideration either directly or indirectly in return for or otherwise howsoever on account of the use of the private circuit by or on behalf of any person other than the subscriber or any of the respective persons whose premises are for the time being connected by means of the private circuit with the premises occupied by the subscriber. The term "consideration" includes besides money or money's worth the giving or withholding of business or any other advantage or benefit of any kind or description.

2. Except with the consent in writing of the Postmaster General, the total electrical power applied to the private circuit by the subscriber shall not at any instant exceed 5 milliwatts where alternating current is used. In the case of direct current working the voltage applied to the private circuit shall not exceed 50 volts and the current in the line shall not exceed 60 milliamperes. Where interrupted direct current working is adopted the subscriber shall insert suitable spark gap quenches and low pass filters to prevent any noise induction into other circuits.

3. Except with the consent in writing of the Postmaster General, the subscriber shall not directly or indirectly connect any exchange line with the private circuit or permit or suffer any exchange line to be so connected.

4. If the subscriber with the consent of the Postmaster General connects with the private circuit any equipment or apparatus provided otherwise than by the Postmaster General, the subscriber shall if required supply and maintain connection blocks of such description and in such positions as shall be approved by the Postmaster General. The subscriber shall supply facilities for testing and shall not notify the Postmaster General of a fault unless tests have indicated that it did not originate from the said equipment or apparatus. The subscriber shall pay the certified cost incurred by the Postmaster General as a result of any notification of a fault if it is found that the fault originated from the said equipment or apparatus.

Regulation 6(1)(e)

PART 5

Any recorded announcement made by means of the Answering Set shall be limited to the following matters or any of them:

(i) a statement that the call is being answered by a telephone answering machine;

(ii) the telephone number and identity of the subscriber;

(iii) an explanation of the subscriber's absence;

(iv) a statement of his expected time of return;

(v) an alternative telephone number at which the subscriber may be called or at which messages may be left for him;

(vi) any other matter which is approved by the Postmaster General, either specifically or by general description.

SCHEDULE 2

Regulation 6(2)(*a*)

TERMS AND CONDITIONS WHICH MAY BE APPLIED TO
PARTICULAR INSTALLATIONS

1. The subscriber shall not permit the provision by any officer of the Post Office of any equipment or apparatus at any point where under ordinary circumstances an explosion could be caused by heat, a naked light, a flame or sparks.

2. If owing to exceptional circumstances an explosive mixture should accumulate at any part of the subscriber's premises the subscriber shall not permit any such officer to begin or continue work of any kind whatsoever on or in the vicinity of such part of the subscriber's premises until the explosive mixture has been dispersed, whether or not an explosion could be caused by such work.

3. Subject to condition 5, the subscriber shall indemnify the Crown against all actions, proceedings and claims by whomsoever brought or made in respect of any loss, damage or injury attributable directly or indirectly to any explosion or fire on the subscriber's premises.

4. Subject to condition 5, the subscriber shall not be entitled to recover from the Crown in respect of any loss, damage or injury sustained or suffered by the subscriber through, as a result of, or consequential upon any explosion or fire attributable directly or indirectly to anything done or omitted by any such officer or to any property of the Postmaster General on the subscriber's premises.

5. If the subscriber shall have observed conditions 1 and 2, conditions 3 and 4 shall not apply in relation to any explosion or fire proved by the subscriber to have been caused by the omission of any such officer to observe instructions given by the subscriber under conditions 1 or 2.

Regulation 11(3)   SCHEDULE 3

RENTALS

The rates quoted in this Schedule are quarterly rates.

PART 1

Exchange lines served by the appropriate telephone exchange

		£	s.	d.
1.	Exclusive line ... ... {	4	0	0
		3	15	0
		(Note)		
2.	Shared line	3	10	0

Note:— The lower of the two rates applies only where the line is a business line and is provided for connection with a private branch exchange belonging to and maintained by the subscriber.

PART 2

Exchange lines served by a telephone exchange other than the appropriate telephone exchange

1. The rate of rental for the exchange line which would be applicable under Part 1 if the line were served by the appropriate telephone exchange,

plus

2. The rate of rental which would be applicable under item 1(*a*) of Part 4 to an external extension between the exchange by which the line is served and the appropriate telephone exchange,

plus

3. Where the exchange by which the line is served and the appropriate telephone exchange are in different telephone groups (see reg. 19)... ... ... £12 10s. 0d.

PART 3

Internal Extensions

		£	s.	d.
1.	Plan 1, 1A, 1B or 1C		14	0
2.	Plan 2			
	Two main stations		10	0
	Each associated extension		14	0
3.	Plan 3...	1	5	0
4.	Plan 4 (Plug and 2 sockets)		8	0
	Each additional socket...		2	0
	Each plug-in telephone after the first		12	0
5.	Plan 5 or 5A...	2	10	0
6.	Plan 7 or 7A...	1	15	0
7.	Plan 8	1	0	0
8.	Plan 8A	1	16	0
9.	Plan 9	1	5	0
10.	Plan 10 including apparatus for interception of one exchange line	1	10	0
	Apparatus associated with Plan 10 extension for interception of additional exchange lines: per line		6	0
11.	Plan 11	1	8	0
12.	Plan 12 or 12A	1	5	0
13.	Plan 105 or 105A	2	15	0
14.	Plan 107 or 107A	2	0	0
15.	Plan 108 or 108A	2	0	0
16.	Internal extension terminated on a socket		8	0
17.	Plug-in telephone for use with an internal extension terminated on a socket		12	0
18.	Any other internal extension		15	0

SCHEDULE 3 (cont.)

PART 4

External extensions (other than an external extension on a house exchange system (HES))

		£ s. d.
1.Mileage rate:		
(a) For an external extension other than a Plan 9 extension:		
Chargeable length:		
Up to 1 furlong...	... ...	1 0 0
Over 1 furlong up to 2 furlongs	... ...	2 0 0
Over 2 furlongs up to 3 furlongs	... ...	3 0 0
Over 3 furlongs up to 4 furlongs	... ...	4 0 0
Over 4 furlongs up to 6 furlongs	... ...	5 10 0
Over 6 furlongs up to 8 furlongs	... ...	7 0 0
And so on by ¼ mile steps	... ...	And so on by £2 steps
Over 1½ miles up to 1¾ miles ...	... ...	12 15 0
Over 1¾ miles up to 2 miles	... ...	14 10 0
And so on by ¼ mile steps	... ...	And so on by £1.10s. steps
Over 3 miles up to 3½ miles	... ...	23 10 0
And so on by ½ mile steps	... ...	And so on by £3 steps
Over 5 miles up to 6 miles	... ...	37 10 0
And so on by 1 mile steps	... ...	And so on by £5 steps
Over 30 miles up to 35 miles ...	... ...	175 0 0
And so on by 5 mile steps	... ...	And so on by £20 steps
Over 50 miles up to 60 miles ...	... ...	262 10 0
And so on by 10 mile steps	... ...	And so on by £25 steps
Over 200 miles up to 210 miles	... ...	632 10 0
And so on by 10 mile steps	... ...	And so on by £20 steps
Over 300 miles up to 325 miles	... ...	837 10 0
And so on by 25 mile steps	... ...	And so on by £25 steps
Over 400 miles ...	... ...	937 10 0
(b) For a Plan 9 extension...	... ...	Double the rate appropriate under (a) above.
2. Additional rate for external plan extensions:		
Plan 1A or 1C ...	... ...	14 0
Plan 7 or 7A ...	... ...	1 15 0
Plan 9 ...	... ...	1 5 0
Plan 105 or 105A	... ...	2 15 0
Plan 107 or 107A	... ...	2 0 0
3. Additional rate for each external extension not exceeding 4 furlongs chargeable length (other than a plan extension or an external extension terminated at both ends on apparatus belonging to and maintained by the subscriber)		15 0

SCHEDULE 3 (*cont.*)

PART 5

Private branch exchanges (PBX) and associated equipment

	£	s.	d.
1. PBX:			
(a) PMBX switchboard:			
(1) Other than a multiple type:			
Size:			
1 + 3	3	0	0
2 + 4	4	0	0
2 + 6	5	0	0
3 + 7 or 3 + 9...	8	0	0
3 + 12	10	0	0
3 + 12 (panel type)	11	0	0
3 + 10 or 5 + 20	13	0	0
4+18	16	0	0
5+25 (panel type)	22	0	0
10+30	25	0	0
10+50	30	0	0
10+60	35	0	0
(2) Multiple type: each section	42	10	0
(3) Stand-by power supply equipment:			
For use with PMBX switchboard (other than a multiple type) size:			
3+12	9	0	0
3+12 (panel type)	10	0	0
4+18	12	0	0
5+25 (panel type)	12	0	0
(b) PABX Type 1:			
Size:			
4+15	55	0	0
5+24	65	0	0
7+35	75	0	0
10+49	85	0	0
(c) PABX Type 2:			
Size:			
4+15	70	0	0
5+24	80	0	0
7+35	90	0	0
10+49	100	0	0
(d) PABX Types 5 or 6:			
Size:			
3+10	50	0	0
5+20	60	0	0
(e) PABX other than 1 to 6:			
Size:			
Up to 30 automatic extensions	35	0	0
31—50 automatic extensions	55	0	0

SCHEDULE 3 (cont.)

PART 5 (cont.)

	£ s. d.
2. Special additional switchboard for secret working connected with a PBX in the same building	The appropriate rental specified in Item 1
plus, in respect of each exchange line connected to such switchboard	9 0
plus, in respect of each extension connected to such switchboard	15 0
3. Special additional switchboard for night working connected with a PMBX in the same building	The appropriate rental specified in Item 1
plus, in respect of each exchange line and each extension connected with such switchboard	9 0
4. Special additional switchboard for night working connected with a PMBX in another building	The appropriate rental specified in Item 1
plus, in respect of each exchange line and each extension connected with such switchboard	1 10 0
5. Special equipment for night working from a particular extension connected with a PABX other than Types 1 to 6 in the same building	2 0 0
6. Special equipment to provide direct night exchange line service on a PABX Type 1: in respect of each exchange line connected for night service...	10 0
7. Special equipment to provide direct night exchange line service on a PABX Type 2:	1 0 0
8. Multiphone switchboard	6 0 0
plus, in respect of additional equipment (where required) for providing ancillary working on an exchange line or private circuit	1 10 0
9. Key and lamp unit and associated equipment: Key and lamp unit with one operator's circuit	3 0 0
Two Key and lamp units with one operator's circuit ...	4 10 0

SCHEDULE 3 *(cont.)*

PART 5 *(cont.)*

	£	s.	d.
Auxiliary apparatus: Whichever one of the following rates of rental is appropriate in relation to the number of exchange lines			
1 to 5 lines	3	0	0
6 to 10 lines	4	10	0
11 to 15 lines	6	0	0
16 to 20 lines	7	10	0
Amplifier 23d	5	0	0
10. Ringing lead from telephone exchange to subscriber's premises for providing power ringing	1	0	0
11. Ringing converter	1	0	0
12. Ringing vibrator	1	0	0
13. Transformer for power ringing	1	0	0
14. Howler cord circuit		8	0
15. Apparatus for recalling the operator at a magneto PBX... ...		2	3
plus: in respect of each exchange line connected with the PBX ...		2	3
in respect of each extension connected with the PBX ...			9
16. Wiring in excess of 15 yards supplied to connect the manual and automatic switching apparatus of a PABX provided by the Postmaster General (other than a PABX Type 1 to 6)		6	0
17. Apparatus for affording direct connection between extensions on a PABX provided by the Postmaster General (other than a PABX Type 1 to 6) and on exchange line connected with the PABX ...		15	0
18. Apparatus for affording direct connection between extensions on one PABX provided by the Postmaster General (other than a PABX Type 1 to 6) and extensions on another such PABX over an extension between the two PABXs	1	10	0
19. Message waiting facility at a PBX: per extension		13	0

Note: The appropriate rentals for the exchange lines and extensions are payable in addition to the rentals specified in this Part.

SCHEDULE 3 (cont.)

PART 6

Instruments for use by an operator at a private branch exchange (PBX)

	If provided instead of the operator's standard instrument supplied by the Postmaster General with the relative PBX		If provided in addition to the operator's standard instrument supplied by the Postmaster General with the relative PBX	
	s.	d.	s.	d.
1. Handset type telephone ...	—		10	0
2. Handset portion only of handset type telephone	5	0	5	0
3. Breastplate transmitter and single headgear receiver (where the standard instrument supplied by the Postmaster General with the relative PBX is a handset type telephone or the handset portion only of a handset type telephone)	12	0	12	0
4. Breastplate transmitter and single headgear receiver (where the standard instrument supplied by the Postmaster General with the relative PBX is a breastplate transmitter and single headgear receiver)	—		10	6
5. Breastplate transmitter and double headgear receiver (where the standard instrument supplied by the Postmaster General with the relative PBX is a handset type telephone or the handset portion only of a handset type telephone)	15	0	15	0
6. Breastplate transmitter and double headgear receiver (where the standard instrument supplied by the Postmaster General with the relative PBX is a breastplate transmitter and single headgear receiver)	—		15	0

SCHEDULE 3 (*cont.*)

PART 6 (*cont.*)

	If provided instead of the operator's standard instrument supplied by the Postmaster General with the relative PBX		If provided in addition to the operator's standard instrument supplied by the Postmaster General with the relative PBX	
	s.	d.	s.	d.
7. Lightweight headset (where the standard instrument supplied by the Postmaster General with the relative PBX is a handset type telephone or the handset portion only of a handset type telephone):				
Type No. 1	12	0	12	0
Type No. 2	15	0	15	0
8. Lightweight headset (where the standard instrument supplied by the Postmaster General with the relative PBX is a lightweight headset No. 1, or has been replaced by a lightweight headset No. 1):				
Type No. 1	—		12	0
Type No. 2	3	0	15	0

SCHEDULE 3 (cont.)

PART 7

Components forming part of a house exchange system (HES)

	£ s. d.
1. Internal or external station:	
HES No. 1	2 0 0
HES No. 2	2 10 0
HES No. 3 (Keymaster 1+5)...	2 10 0
HES No. 4 (Keymaster 2+10)	3 0 0
2. Additional apparatus for second main station ...	1 5 0
3. Internal special extension	The rate applicable under Item 1
4. Internal extension between HES and PBX ...	15 0
5. External special extension	The rate applicable under Item 1, plus mileage rate applicable under Item 1(a) of Part 4
6. External extension between HES and PBX ...	15 0 plus mileage rate applicable under Item 1(a) of Part 4

SCHEDULE 3 (cont.)

PART 8

Miscellaneous Equipment and Apparatus

	£	s.	d.
1. Coin box		2 10	0
2. Emergency press button on coin box		5	0
3. Autodial No. 1 (25 line size)		9	0
4. Autodial No. 2 (50 line size)		12	0
5. Breastplate transmitter:			
In addition to or instead of standard transmitter		9	0
6. Headgear receiver:			
In addition to or instead of standard receiver:			
Single		5	0
Double		8	0
7. Breastplate transmitter and single headgear receiver combined:			
In addition to or instead of standard instrument		12	0
8. Breastplate transmitter and double headgear receiver combined:			
In addition to or instead of standard instrument		15	0
9. Extension bell:			
Trembler 2½ inch (Battery operated)		3	0
Trembler 4 inch (Battery operated)		10	0
Trembler 6 inch (Battery operated)		10	0
Trembler 12 inch (Battery operated)	1	0	0
Trembler 6 inch (Mains operated)		10	0
Trembler 10 inch (Mains operated)		15	0
Magneto 2½ inch		3	0
Magneto Cow gong		3	0
Magneto 4 inch		3	0
Magneto 6 inch		6	0
Switchboard internal buzzer		5	0
10. Hooter (Mains operated)		15	0
11. Apparatus used in connection with the provision of telephone service to ships in dock:			
10 yards of cable or part thereof		3	0
Each additional 10 yards or part thereof		3	0
Weatherproof plug and socket		6	0
12. Special protective apparatus:			
Flameproof wall telephone No. 149	1	10	0
Flameproof table telephone No. 266	1	10	0
Flameproof telephone with reference number in the 700 series	2	10	0
Flameproof relay		18	0
Flameproof plugs and sockets (2 of each)	1	13	0
Flameproof magneto bell	1	0	0

SCHEDULE 3 (cont.)

PART 8 (cont.)

	£	s.	d.
Flameproof mains bell...	1	13	0
Cable Pyrotenax 25 yards in length (or less)		11	0
Cable Polythene 25 yards in length (or less)		11	0
Conduit 25 yards in length (or less)	1	0	0
13. Drop indicator on continuous ringing bell circuit		5	0
14. Eyeball or drop indicator		5	0

15. Apparatus (other than lamp circuit and lamp) to provide mains voltage lamp signal on exchange line or extension:

	£	s.	d.
Discontinuous signal		12	0
Continuous signal (press button control)		12	0
Optional switchhook control		9	0

Plus, if provided by the Postmaster General:

	£	s.	d.
in respect of the lamp circuit (except the lamp)		7	0
in respect of the lamp		1	6

	£	s.	d.
16. Low voltage lamp signal on exchange line or extension		5	0
17. Trimphone		7	6
18. Pendant telephone (including separate dialling unit where necessary)		8	0
19. Plug and socket in lieu of normal telephone termination strip ...		4	0
20. Watch receiver		2	0
21. Handset with transistor amplifier (Handset No. 4 or 5)		10	0
22. Speakerset No. 1	2	10	0
Speakerset No. 2		15	0
23. Faint speech amplifier	1	0	0

24. Loudspeaking telephone:

	£	s.	d.
No. 1	2	10	0
No. 2	6	0	0
No. 3	4	0	0
No. 4	7	10	0
25. Voice operated signalling unit (Unit signalling No. 5)	1	10	0
26. Footswitch to provide transmitter cut-out in association with a breastplate or fixed transmitter and headgear receiver or with a lightweight headset		3	0

SCHEDULE 3 (*cont.*)

PART 8 (*cont.*)

	£	s.	d.
27. Meters at subscriber's premises for measuring call units:			
(a) Clock type meter		15	0
(b) Cyclometer type meter			
(i) Reset type (showing call units for individual calls) ...	1	0	0
		(Note)	
(ii) Non-reset type (showing cumulative total of call units) ...	1	0	0
		(Note)	
(c) Switch to enable a clock type or cyclometer type of meter to be connected to any of a number of selected exchange lines			
in respect of each exchange line (other than the first) to which the meter can be connected by means of the switch ...		7	0
28. Answering set No. 1		6	0	0
29. Answering set No. 2	13	10	0
30. Lightweight headset No. 1		12	0
31. Lightweight headset No. 2		15	0
32. Trunk barring equipment:			
In respect of each exchange line with which the equipment is associated	1	10	0

Note: Where a pair of meters comprising a reset type meter and a non-reset type meter is provided there will be a combined rental of £1 per quarter.

SCHEDULE 4

RENTALS—PRIVATE CIRCUITS

	Rate per annum
	£ s. d.
1. Private circuit provided for continuous use	
(1) Internal private circuit consisting of two telephones with a connecting pair of wires	5 0 0
(2) Internal private circuit terminated on a switchboard at one end and a telephone or another switchboard at the other	3 0 0

	Chargeable length of circuit	Rate per annum
		£ s. d.
(3) Private circuit other than an internal private circuit		
(a) Basic point to point speech type circuit	Up to 1 furlong	4 0 0
	Over 1 furlong up to 2 furlongs	8 0 0
	Over 2 furlongs up to 3 furlongs	12 0 0
	Over 3 furlongs up to 4 furlongs	16 0 0
	Over 4 furlongs up to 6 furlongs	22 0 0
	Over 6 furlongs up to 8 furlongs	28 0 0
	And so on by ¼ mile steps	And so on by £6 steps
	Over 1½ miles up to 1¾ miles	45 0 0
	Over 1¾ miles up to 2 miles	50 0 0
	Over 2 miles up to 2¼ miles	54 0 0
	And so on by ¼ mile steps	And so on by £4 steps

SCHEDULE 4 (*cont.*)

		Chargeable length of circuit	Rate per annum
			£ s. d.
(3)(*a*) (*cont.*)	... ...	Over 3 miles up to 3½ miles	74 0 0
		And so on by ½ mile steps	And so on by £8 steps
		Over 5 miles up to 6 miles	114 0 0
		And so on by 1 mile steps	And so on by £16 steps
		Over 30 miles up to 35 miles	550 0 0
		And so on by 5 mile steps	And so on by £50 steps
		Over 50 miles up to 60 miles	800 0 0
		And so on by 10 mile steps	And so on by £100 steps
		Over 200 miles up to 210 miles	2,280 0 0
		And so on by 10 mile steps	And so on by £80 steps
		Over 300 miles up to 325 miles	3,100 0 0
		And so on by 25 mile steps	And so on by £100 steps
		Over 400 miles	3,500 0 0
(3)(*b*) Speech type circuit for private switched network ...		Up to 1 furlong	4 0 0
		Over 1 furlong up to 2 furlongs	8 0 0
		Over 2 furlongs up to 3 furlongs	12 0 0
		Over 3 furlongs up to 4 furlongs	16 0 0
		Over 4 furlongs up to 6 furlongs	22 0 0

SCHEDULE 4 (cont.)

Chargeable length of circuit	Rate per annum
	£ s. d.
(3)(b) (cont.)	
Over 6 furlongs up to 8 furlongs	28 0 0
And so on by ¼ mile steps	And so on by £6 steps
Over 3 miles up to 3½ miles	88 0 0
And so on by ½ mile steps	And so on by £12 steps
Over 5 miles up to 6 miles	146 0 0
Over 6 miles up to 7 miles	168 0 0
And so on by 1 mile steps	And so on by £20 steps
Over 27 miles up to 28 miles	586 0 0
And so on by 1 mile steps	And so on by £16 steps
Over 30 miles up to 35 miles	670 0 0
And so on by 5 mile steps	And so on by £50 steps
Over 50 miles up to 60 miles	920 0 0
And so on by 10 mile steps	And so on by £100 steps
Over 200 miles up to 210 miles	2,400 0 0
And so on by 10 mile steps	And so on by £80 steps
Over 300 miles up to 325 miles	3,220 0 0
And so on by 25 mile steps	And so on by £100 steps

SCHEDULE 4 *(cont.)*

	Chargeable length of circuit	Rate per annum
		£ s. d.
(3)(*b*) *(cont.)*	Over 400 miles	3,620 0 0
(3)(*c*) Low loss speech type circuit for private switched network	Up to 1 furlong	8 0 0
	Over 1 furlong up to 2 furlongs	16 0 0
	Over 2 furlongs up to 3 furlongs	24 0 0
	Over 3 furlongs up to 4 furlongs	32 0 0
	Over 4 furlongs up to 6 furlongs	44 0 0
	Over 6 furlongs up to 8 furlongs	56 0 0
	And so on by ¼ mile steps	And so on by £12 steps
	Over 1½ miles up to 1¾ miles	90 0 0
	Over 1¾ miles up to 2 miles	100 0 0
	Over 2 miles up to 2¼ miles	108 0 0
	And so on by ¼ mile steps	And so on by £8 steps
	Over 3 miles up to 3½ miles	148 0 0
	And so on by ½ mile steps	And so on by £16 steps
	Over 5 miles up to 6 miles	216 0 0
	And so on by 1 mile steps	And so on by £20 steps
	Over 14 miles up to 15 miles	395 0 0

SCHEDULE 4 (*cont.*)

Chargeable length of circuit	Rate per annum
	£ s. d.
And so on by 1 mile steps	And so on by £19 steps
Over 25 miles up to 26 miles	604 0 0
And so on by 1 mile steps	And so on by £16 steps
Over 30 miles up to 35 miles	720 0 0
And so on by 5 mile steps	And so on by £50 steps
Over 50 miles up to 60 miles	970 0 0
And so on by 10 mile steps	And so on by £100 steps
Over 200 miles up to 210 miles	2,450 0 0
And so on by 10 mile steps ...	And so on by £80 steps
Over 300 miles up to 325 miles	3,270 0 0
And so on by 25 mile steps	And so on by £100 steps
Over 400 miles	3,670 0 0

(3)(*c*) (*cont.*) ... ...

(4) Additional rate per annum for each private circuit mentioned in (3) above not exceeding 4 furlongs chargeable length 3 0 0

2. Private circuit provided for non-continuous use (basic point to point speech type circuit).

(1) In respect of the parts of the circuit which lie between

(*a*) the termination of the circuit at one end thereof and the telephone exchange to which that end is continuously connected

and (*b*) the termination of the circuit at the other end thereof and the telephone exchange with which that end is continuously connected:

the appropriate rental prescribed in Schedule 4, Item (3)(*a*), as if each of the said parts of the circuit was a separate private circuit provided for continuous use

SCHEDULE 4 (*cont.*)

(2) In respect of the part of the circuit which lies between the telephone exchanges mentioned in paragraph (1):

the following rental assessed in relation to the period during which the said part of the circuit is provided exclusively for the use of the subscriber as a private circuit

Distance between the telephone exchanges mentioned in paragraph (1)	Annual rental for use at the same time or times on any one fixed day of the week			
	Monday to Friday 8 A.M. to 6 P.M.		Monday to Friday 6 P.M. to 8 A.M. Saturday and Sunday All day	
	First 2 consecutive hours or part of 2 hours	Each additional consecutive ½ hour or part of ½ hour	First 2 consecutive hours or part of 2 hours	Each additional consecutive ½ hour or part of ½ hour
	£ s.	£ s.	£ s.	£ s.
Up to 15 miles	8 0	1 0	8 0	1 0
Over 15 miles up to 25 miles	12 0	1 10	9 0	1 2
Over 25 miles up ,, 35 ,,	18 0	2 6	10 0	1 6
Over 35 miles up ,, 50 ,,	24 0	3 0	12 0	1 10
Over 50 miles up ,, 75 ,,	30 0	3 16	15 0	1 18
Over 75 miles up ,, 100 ,,	42 0	5 6	21 0	2 12
Over 100 miles up ,, 125 ,,	54 0	6 16	27 0	3 8
Over 125 miles up ,, 175 ,,	72 0	9 0	36 0	4 10
Over 175 miles up ,, 250 ,,	90 0	11 6	45 0	5 12
Over 250 miles	108 0	13 10	54 0	6 16

SCHEDULE 4 (*cont.*)

	Rate per annum
	£ s. d.
3. Internal extension forming part of a private circuit:	The rate per annum equivalent to the quarterly rate applicable under Schedule 3 to an internal extension of the same description.
4. External extension forming part of a private circuit:	The rate applicable under this Schedule as if the extension were a separate private circuit.
5. Equipment and apparatus forming part of a private circuit, excluding the line or lines and one telephone instrument or simple manual switchboard termination at each end of each line:	
For each additional telephone instrument:	... ... 1 10 0
For each additional simple manual switchboard termination:	... ... 1 10 0
For each switch combination (bell, 3-way switch, and indicator):	... ... 1 10 0
For each private manual exchange switchboard or private automatic exchange:	The rate per annum equivalent to the quarterly rate applicable under Part 5 of Schedule 3 to a PMBX switchboard or PABX of the corresponding type and size.
For each other item of equipment or apparatus:	The rate per annum equivalent to the quarterly rate applicable under Schedule 3 for that item.

Regulation 14   **SCHEDULE 5**

CONNECTION CHARGES

	Maximum charges £ s. d.
1. Exchange line of which the chargeable length does not exceed 3 miles	20 0 0
2. Exchange line of which the chargeable length exceeds 3 miles	The charge specified in Item 1 plus £5 per furlong or part thereof by which the chargeable length exceeds 3 miles.
3. Internal private circuit (Note A)	2 0 0
4. Internal extension:	
Plan 1 or 1A	2 0 0
Plan 2—two main stations	2 0 0
each associated extension	2 0 0
Plan 4—two sockets	2 0 0
each additional socket	2 0 0
Plan 5 or 5A	5 0 0
Plan 7 or 7A	3 0 0
Plan 8 or 8A	3 0 0
Plan 9	3 0 0
Plan 10 (including apparatus for intercepting one exchange line)	4 0 0
Apparatus associated with Plan 10 extension for interception of additional exchange lines: per line	2 0 0
Plan 12A	2 0 0
Plan 105 or 105A	5 0 0
Plan 107 or 107A	3 0 0
Plan 108 or 108A	3 0 0
Any other internal extension	2 0 0
5. External extension, or private circuit other than an internal private circuit (Note A): Chargeable length:	
Up to 4 furlongs	5 0 0
Over 4 furlongs up to 10 miles	10 0 0
Over 10 miles up to 15 miles	15 0 0
Over 15 miles up to 30 miles	20 0 0
Over 30 miles up to 50 miles	30 0 0
Over 50 miles up to 100 miles	40 0 0
Over 100 miles	50 0 0
6. HES:	
For each station	8 0 0
For each internal special extension...	2 0 0
For each external special extension...	The appropriate charge specified in Item 5.

SCHEDULE 5 (*cont.*)

	Maximum charges £ s. d.
For each internal extension between a HES and a PBX...	2 0 0
For each external extension between a HES and a PBX...	The appropriate charge specified in Item 5.
7. PBX:	
(a) PMBX switchboards:	
(1) Other than a multiple type:	
Size:	
1+3	6 0 0
2+4	8 0 0
2+6	10 0 0
3+7 or 3+9	16 0 0
3+12	20 0 0
3+12 (panel type)	22 0 0
3+10 or 5+20	26 0 0
4+18 ·	32 0 0
5+25 (panel type)	44 0 0
10+30	50 0 0
10+50	60 0 0
10+60	70 0 0
(2) Multiple type: each section	170 0 0
(3) Stand-by power supply equipment:	
For use with PMBX switchboard (other than multiple type)	
Size:	
3+12	18 0 0
3+12 (panel type)	20 0 0
4+18	24 0 0
5+25 (panel type)	24 0 0
(b) PABX Type 1:	
Size:	
4+15	110 0 0
5+24	130 0 0
7+35	150 0 0
10+49	170 0 0
(c) PABX Type 2:	
Size:	
4+15	140 0 0
5+24	160 0 0
7+35	180 0 0
10+49	200 0 0
(d) PABXs Types 5 or 6:	
Size:	
3+10	100 0 0
5+20	120 0 0
8. Private exchange (forming part of a private circuit)	The charge for the corresponding equipment specified in Item 7.

SCHEDULE 5 (*cont.*)

	Maximum charges
	£ s. d.
9. Speakerset No. 1	2 0 0
Speakerset No. 2	1 0 0
10. Faint speech amplifier	2 0 0
11. Loudspeaking telephone (all types)...	2 0 0
12. Meters at subscriber's premises for measuring call units:	
Cyclometer type meter:	
(i) Reset type (showing call units for individual calls)	2 0 0 (Note B)
(ii) Non-reset type (showing cumulative total of call units)	2 0 0 (Note B)
13. Answering set No. 1	2 0 0
Answering set No. 2	2 0 0
14. Coin box	4 0 0
15. Key and lamp unit and associated equipment:	
Key and lamp unit with one operator's circuit ...	6 0 0
Two key and lamp units with one operator's circuit	9 0 0
Whichever one of the following rates of rental is appropriate in relation to the number of exchange lines:	
Auxiliary apparatus:	
1 to 5 lines	6 0 0
6 to 10 lines	9 0 0
11 to 15 lines	12 0 0
16 to 20 lines	15 0 0
Amplifier 23d	2 0 0
16. Extension bells, hooters and buzzers:	
(a) Provided internally	2 0 0
(b) Provided externally	5 0 0
17. Special protective apparatus: ...	
Flameproof wall telephone No. 149	2 0 0
Flameproof table telephone No. 266	2 0 0
Flameproof telephone with reference number in the 700 series	2 0 0
Flameproof plugs and sockets (2 of each)... ...	2 0 0
Flameproof magneto bell	2 0 0
Flameproof mains bell	2 0 0
18. Drop indicator on continuous ringing bell circuit ...	1 0 0
19. Eyeball or drop indicator	1 0 0
20. Watch receiver	1 0 0

SCHEDULE 5 (*cont.*)

	Maximum charges
	£ s. d.
21. Multiphone switchboard:	12 0 0
Indicator, switch and socket for providing ancillary working on one exchange line	2 0 0
Indicator, switch and socket for providing ancillary working on one private circuit	2 0 0
22. Apparatus (other than lamp circuit) to provide mains voltage lamp signal on exchange line or extension:	
Discontinuous signal	2 0 0
Continuous signal (press button control) ...	2 0 0
plus, if lamp circuit provided by the Postmaster General	5 0 0
23. Message waiting facility at a PBX; per extension...	2 0 0
24. Special equipment to provide direct night exchange line service on a PABX 1:	
in respect of each exchange line connected for night service	2 0 0
25. Special equipment to provide direct night exchange line service on a PABX 2...	2 0 0

Note A: These charges for private circuits are additional to the charges for extensions and terminal equipment forming part of the private circuits.

Note B: Where a reset type meter and a non-reset type meter are ordered at the same time there will be a combined charge of £2.

Regulation 16   SCHEDULE 6

SINGLE PAYMENT CHARGES

	£	s.	d.
1. Telephone with reference number in 700 series	1	0	0
2. Wall bracket	1	10	0
3. Instrument cord			
Up to 10 feet in length...	No	charge	
Over 10 feet in length	1	0	0
4. Multiple cord for house exchange system:			
Over 6 feet and up to 10 feet long	2	0	0
Over 10 feet and up to 15 feet long	2	10	0
5. Dial for telephone on PMBX	1	10	0
6. Key for coin box		2	0
7. Buzzer (in lieu of a telephone bell)...	1	10	0
8. Transmitter cut-out key	1	10	0
9. Duplicate key for optional barring equipment associated with a telephone instrument		2	0
10. Duplicate battery, drop indicator and other subsidiary or minor apparatus for which no rental is payable	1	10	0
11. Lightweight headset No. 1 or No. 2:			
In respect of each manual switchboard or each switchboard section which is modified for use with the lightweight headset... ...	5	0	0
In respect of each other item of apparatus which is so modified...	2	0	0
12. Telephone instrument with which trunk barring equipment is associated:			
(a) for permanent barring	3	0	0
(b) for optional barring	5	0	0
13. Special protective apparatus:			
Box, Protector, CD 408	2	10	0

SCHEDULE 7   Regulation 17(1)(a)

INTERNAL REMOVAL CHARGES

	£	s.	d.
1. Telephone instrument, not being a station on a HES. (This charge includes the removal of a bell connected with the telephone, and the removal of a switch, indicator and batteries provided for an associated extension bell where the extension bell itself is not removed)	3	0	0
2. Apparatus associated with Plan 10 extension for interception of exchange lines: per line	2	0	0
3. Extension bell, or other bell except where covered by Item 1 ...,	1	10	0
4. Reversal of position of main and extension telephones	3	0	0
5. Coin box	2	0	0
6. Socket	2	0	0
7. Answering set No. 1	2	0	0
Answering set No. 2	2	0	0
8. Change of indicator number on switchboard	1	10	0
9. Each other minor item of equipment or apparatus	1	10	0
10. PBX:			
(a) PMBX switchboard:			
(1) Other than a multiple type:			
Size:			
1+3	6	0	0
2+4	8	0	0
2+6	10	0	0
3+7 or 3+9	16	0	0
3+12	20	0	0
3+12 (panel type)	22	0	0
3+10 or 5+20	26	0	0
4+18	32	0	0
5+25 (panel type)	44	0	0
10+30	50	0	0
10+50	60	0	0
10+60	70	0	0
(2) Multiple type: each section	85	0	0
(3) Stand-by power supply equipment:			
For use with PMBX switchboard (other than a multiple type)			
Size:			
3+12	18	0	0
3+12 (panel type)	20	0	0
4+18	24	0	0
5+25 (panel type)	24	0	0
(b) PABX Type 1:			
Size:			
4+15	110	0	0
5+24	130	0	0

SCHEDULE 7 (cont.)

	£	s.	d.
7+35	150	0	0
10+49	170	0	0
(c) PABX Type 2:			
Size:			
4+15	140	0	0
5+24	160	0	0
7+35	180	0	0
10+49	200	0	0
(d) PABX Types 5 or 6:			
Size:			
3+10	100	0	0
5+20	120	0	0
(e) PABX other than Types 1 to 6:			
Size:			
Up to 30 automatic extensions	70	0	0
31—50 automatic extensions	110	0	0

11. Private exchange (forming part of private circuit) ... ... — The charge for the corresponding equipment specified in Item 10.

12. Key and lamp unit and associated equipment:

	£	s.	d.
Key and lamp unit with one operator's circuit	3	0	0
Two key and lamp units with one operator's circuit	4	10	0
Auxiliary apparatus:			
Whichever one of the following rates of rental is appropriate in relation to the number of exchange lines:			
1 to 5 lines	3	0	0
6 to 10 lines	4	10	0
11 to 15 lines	6	0	0
16 to 20 lines	7	10	0
Amplifier 23d	1	10	0

13. Speakerset No. 1 ... ... 2 0 0
    Speakerset No. 2 ... ... 1 0 0

Regulation 20

SCHEDULE 8

INLAND CALL CHARGES

PART 1

Where the local exchange is operated by the Postmaster General: charge to the subscriber for a call made from an installation, otherwise than by means of a coin box line

TABLE A

Charge unit: 2d.

								Time for each charge unit
1.	Local call	...	...	...	...	...	...	...	240 seconds
2.	Trunk call: where the distance between the group centres concerned:—								
	(a) does not exceed 35 miles							24 ,,
	(b) exceeds 35 miles but does not exceed 50 miles							12 ,,
	(c) exceeds 50 miles							8 ,,

TABLE B

1. Local call:

   (a) where the call is made from an exchange line (not being a business line) which is being provided under these regulations ... ... 2½d.

   (b) in any other case ... ... 3d.

	For the first 3 minutes or part of 3 minutes	For each minute or part of a minute after the first 3 minutes
	s. d.	s. d.
2. Trunk call: where the distance between the group centres concerned:—		
(a) does not exceed 35 miles	1 6	6
(b) exceeds 35 miles but does not exceed 50 miles	2 6	10
(c) exceeds 50 miles	4 0	1 4

SCHEDULE 8

PART 2

Where the local exchange is operated by the Postmaster General: charge to the caller for a call made from a call office or from a coin box line.

TABLE A

Charge unit: 6d.

		Time for each charge unit
1.	Local call	360 seconds
2.	Trunk call: where the distance between the group centres concerned:—	
	(a) does not exceed 35 miles	48 ,,
	(b) exceeds 35 miles but does not exceed 50 miles	24 ,,
	(c) exceeds 50 miles	16 ,,

TABLE B

1. Local call ... ... 4d.

		For the first 3 minutes or part of 3 minutes	For each 3 minutes or part of 3 minutes after the first 3 minutes
		s. d.	s. d.
2.	Trunk call: where the distance between the group centres concerned:—		
	(a) does not exceed 35 miles	2 6	1 6
	(b) exceeds 35 miles but does not exceed 50 miles	3 6	2 6
	(c) exceeds 50 miles	5 0	4 0

SCHEDULE 8 (*cont.*)

PART 3

Where the local exchange is operated by a person licensed by the Postmaster General in that behalf and the terminal exchange is not operated by that person.

TABLE A

Charge unit: 2d.

	Time for each charge unit
1. Call to an installation or telephone served by an exchange in an adjacent telephone group:—	
(a) made otherwise than from a call office or coin box telephone	240 seconds
(b) made from a call office or coin box telephone	180 ,,
2. Trunk call: where the distance between the group centres concerned:—	
(a) does not exceed 35 miles	24 ,,
(b) exceeds 35 miles but does not exceed 50 miles	12 ,,
(c) exceeds 50 miles	8 ,,

TABLE B

		Call made otherwise than from a call office or coin box telephone		Call made from a call office or coin box telephone
1. Call to an installation or telephone served by an exchange in an adjacent telephone group ... ... 3d.				
		For the first 3 minutes or part of 3 minutes	For each minute or part of a minute after the first 3 minutes	For each 3 minutes or part of 3 minutes
		s. d.	s. d.	s. d.
2. Trunk call: where the distance between the group centres concerned:—				
(a) does not exceed 35 miles		1 6	6	1 6
(b) exceeds 35 miles but does not exceed 50 miles ...		2 6	10	2 6
(c) exceeds 50 miles ...		4 0	1 4	4 0

Regulation 39   **SCHEDULE 9**

EXCEPTIONS AND MODIFICATIONS TO THESE
REGULATIONS IN THEIR APPLICATION TO RADIOPHONE SERVICE

1. *Exceptions*

The following regulations shall not apply;

> 3, 6, 7(5) and (6), 8 to 17 inclusive, 20, 22, the second sentence of 27(1), 27(3), 28
> to 30 inclusive, 32, 34, 35, 41(b), (c) and (e), 43(2) and (4), 44(2) and (3), 45 to
> 47 inclusive, 49, 51(b), (c) and (d), 52 and 53(a) and (b).

2. *Modifications*

Regulation 5.   The following regulation shall be substituted:
"5.   Application for radiophone service shall if the Postmaster General so
requires be made on a form furnished by him and signed by the licensee."

Regulation 7.   In paragraph (2), for the words after "cease" in the sixth line to the
end of the paragraph there shall be substituted the words "at the end of the quarter
in which the Postmaster General receives the notice or if the notice expires subsequently, at the end of the quarter in which the notice expires."

Regulation 42.   For the words "an installation" and the words "the installation"
there shall be substituted the words "radiophone service".

Regulation 50.   For the words "exchange line" wherever they occur there shall be
substituted the word "radiotelephone".

Regulation 45   **SCHEDULE 10**

REPLACEMENT CHARGES

	£	s.	d.
1. Telephone instrument (other than HES instrument):			
(i) Complete instrument with dial	5	0	0
(ii) Complete instrument without dial	4	0	0
(iii) Handset	1	10	0
(iv) Case...	1	0	0
2. Dials, Automatic:			
Complete dial	2	0	0
3. Miscellaneous apparatus:			
(a) Instrument cord (other than multiple type cord) over			
10 feet in length	1	0	0
(b) Coin box lock	1	0	0

SCHEDULE 11   Regulation 50

CHARGES FOR FACILITIES IN RESPECT OF TELEPHONE DIRECTORIES

PART 1

Main Telephone Directory

Special entries	Annual Rate	
	London Postal Area Telephone Directory	Outer London and Provincial Telephone Directory
	£ s.	£ s.
1. Main entry in heavy type	6 0	4 0 (maximum rate)
2. Extra entry in ordinary type	2 0	1 0
3. Extra entry in heavy type	8 0	5 0 (maximum rate)
4. Entry containing supplementary information (additional to words of description allowed for businesses): for each word in the entry	1 0	1 0
5. Entry in a part or section of the main telephone directory other than the appropriate part or section in which the main entry is made: in ordinary type ... ... in heavy type	4 0 10 0	4 0 8 0 (maximum rate)

Note. Where the rate is referred to as the maximum rate, the rate is such amount as the Postmaster General may fix in respect of the directory concerned not exceeding the maximum specified.

PART 2

Business Telephone Directory

Special entries	Annual Rate
	£ s.
1. Main entry in heavy type	8 0
2. Extra entry in ordinary type	2 0
3. Extra entry in heavy type	10 0
4. Entry containing supplementary information (additional to words of description allowed for businesses): for each word in the entry	1 0
5. Main entry for exchange line in respect of which no free entry is made: in ordinary type	4 0
in heavy type	8 0

PART 3

Local Telephone Directory

Special entries	Annual Rate
	£ s.
1. Main entry in heavy type	1 10
2. Extra entry in ordinary type where there is no corresponding extra entry in main directory	1 0
3. Extra entry in heavy type:	
(*a*) where there is a corresponding extra entry in ordinary or heavy type in the main telephone directory ...	1 10
(b) where there is no corresponding extra entry in the main telephone directory	2 10
4. Entry containing one or more additional words which are not included in a corresponding entry in the main telephone directory: ... ... for each additional word	12
5. Entry in a local telephone directory other than the appropriate local telephone directory in which the main entry is made:	
in ordinary type	2 0
in heavy type	3 10

Regulation 61   **SCHEDULE 12**

REGULATIONS REVOKED

The Telephone Regulations 1965(a).
The Telephone Amendment (No. 1) Regulations 1965(b).
The Telephone Amendment (No. 2) Regulations 1966(c).
The Telephone Amendment (No. 3) Regulations 1967(d).
The Telephone Amendment (No. 4) Regulations 1968(e).

EXPLANATORY NOTE

(This Note is not part of the Regulations.)

These Regulations consolidate with amendments the Telephone Regulations 1965, the Telephone Amendment (No. 1) Regulations 1965, the Telephone Amendment (No. 2) Regulations 1966, the Telephone Amendment (No. 3) Regulations 1967, the Telephone Amendment (No. 4) Regulations 1968.

(a) S.I. 1965/225 (1965 I, p. 518).   (b) S.I. 1965/1191 (1965 II, p. 3388).
(c) S.I. 1966/857 (1966 II, p. 2042).   (d) S.I. 1967/433 (1967 I, p. 1369).
(e) S.I. 1968/593 (1968 I, p. 1362).

The principal amendments are as follows:

1. *Rentals*

   (*a*) The rates for residential lines are increased by 10s. There is no increase for business lines which means that residential and business lines have the same rental.

   (*b*) The rates for most types of internal and external extensions are increased.

   (*c*) The rates for most private branch exchange switchboards and associated equipment are increased.

   (*d*) The rates for most items of miscellaneous equipment and apparatus are increased.

   (*e*) Different rates in relation to the type of circuit are prescribed for private circuits provided for continuous use and a two part method of charging rental is introduced in relation to circuits provided for non continuous use at stated times.

2. *Connection and Single Payment, Charges*

   The connection charges and charges for providing some items of equipment are increased.

3. *Internal Removal Charges*

   The charges for removing some items of equipment within the same building (or connected buildings) are increased.

4. *Call Charges*

   The charges for most calls are increased at certain times.

5. *Services and Facilities*

   The charges for most services and facilities in relation to calls are increased (in some cases by means of a change in the method of charging).

6. *Outside normal hours repair work*

   Charges are authorised for work done outside normal hours at the subscriber's request to remedy a fault in his installation.

7. *Directory enquiries*

   (*a*) A charge is authorised for supplying the telephone number of a subscriber where the caller is unable to give adequate details.

   (*b*) A new facility is introduced which enables a caller to be supplied with the name and address of a subscriber for an appropriate charge.

8. *Telephone directories*

   The charges for entries in telephone directories are increased and some facilities extended.

STATUTORY INSTRUMENTS

1968 No. 1257

TELEGRAPHS

The Telephone (Channel Islands) Regulations 1968

Made - - -	*5th August* 1968
Laid before Parliament	*20th August* 1968
Coming into Operation	*1st October* 1968

I, The Right Honourable John Thomson Stonehouse, M.P., Her Majesty's Postmaster General, by virtue of the power vested in me by section 1 of the Telephone Act 1951(a) as extended to the Channel Islands by the Telephone (Channel Islands) Order 1952(b) and as amended by sections 16 and 28 of the Post Office Act 1961(c) and of every other power enabling me in this behalf, do hereby make the following regulations, that is to say:—

Interpretation

1.—(1) In these regulations, except so far as the contrary is provided or the context otherwise requires, the following expressions have the meanings hereby respectively assigned to them:—

"the British Islands" means the United Kingdom, the Channel Islands and the Isle of Man;

"call office" means a telephone available to the public for the purpose of sending and receiving telephonic messages, not being a subscriber's telephone;

"coin box telephone" means a telephone (not being a call office) in respect of calls from which the States of the Island of Jersey or the States of the Island of Guernsey require sums of money to be placed in a coin collecting box provided by them;

"fixed time call" means a call booked in advance for connection at a specified time in accordance with regulation 8;

"the Guernsey system" means the public telephone system within the bailiwick of Guernsey worked by the States of the Island of Guernsey under licence from the Postmaster General;

"the Hull system" means the public telephone system worked by the Corporation of Kingston-upon-Hull under licence from the Postmaster General;

"the Jersey system" means the public telephone system within the Island of Jersey worked by the States of the Island of Jersey under licence from the Postmaster General;

"personal call" means a call booked for the specified purpose of communication with a particular person or otherwise in accordance with regulation 9;

"the Postmaster General's system" means the public telephone system under the control of the Postmaster General;

(a) 1951 c. 52.   (b) S.I. 1952/163 (1952 III, p. 3401).   (c) 1961 c. 15.

" radiophone system " means a system primarily designed for providing telephones in vehicles with telephone service through a public telephone system by means of a wireless telegraphy link between those telephones and a station for wireless telegraphy forming part of the public telephone system;

" telephone " (in expressions relating to calls made from or to a telephone) includes automatic apparatus for making calls or giving messages, or for answering calls or recording messages.

(2) The Interpretation Act 1889(a) applies for the interpretation of these regulations as it applies for the interpretation of an Act of Parliament, and as if these regulations and the regulations hereby revoked were Acts of Parliament.

Application

2. Except as provided in regulations 10 and 11, these regulations shall apply only to calls made from telephones on the Jersey system or the Guernsey system which involve the use of the Postmaster General's system, and to services and facilities provided in relation to such calls.

Call charges

3.—(1) The charges for calls other than calls to which regulation 4 or regulation 6 applies shall be as follows:—

(a) Where the call is obtained by means of the subscriber trunk dialling facility, the charge shall be at the rate of 3d. for each period of 12 seconds or fraction of such period.

(b) Otherwise (whether or not the subscriber trunk dialling facility is available on the telephone from which the call is made), the charge shall be at the appropriate rate specified in the Schedule hereto.

(2) The charges referred to in paragraph (1) do not include the charge which the States of the Island of Jersey or the States of the Island of Guernsey may make in respect of the use of a call office or a coin box telephone provided by them.

Charges for foreign and other calls

4.—(1) The charges for calls (other than calls to which regulation 6 applies) which are made to a place outside the British Islands, or to a ship or aircraft, or to a telephone on a radiophone system, shall be such as the Postmaster General may fix.

(2) The charges so fixed by the Postmaster General shall not include the charge referred to in regulation 3 (2).

(3) The Postmaster General shall notify the charges so fixed to the States of the Island of Jersey and the States of the Island of Guernsey.

Reduced rate calls

5. Any sums payable under these regulations in respect of calls of any description may be reduced at such times or during such periods as the Postmaster General may from time to time direct.

Calls made by means of special equipment, etc.

6.—(1) Where there is provided for the purpose of any call:—

(a) special equipment or apparatus affording sound reproduction of higher quality than that afforded by the ordinary public telephone system; or

---

(a) 1889 c. 63.

(*b*) means of simultaneous communication between three or more telephones; or

(*c*) equipment or apparatus to facilitate the recording or broadcasting of messages;

the charge for the call shall, subject to the terms of any contract with the Postmaster General for the provision of the call or of such equipment or apparatus or means of communication, be such as the Postmaster General may fix.

(2) The charge so fixed by the Postmaster General shall not include the charge referred to in regulation 3 (2).

Services and facilities

7.—(1) The services and facilities referred to in paragraphs (3) and (4) of this regulation and in regulations 8, 9, 10, 11 and 13 may be provided by the Postmaster General at such times, during such periods, in such circumstances, and by means of such telephones and telephone exchanges or classes thereof as the Postmaster General may from time to time consider expedient. The charges, terms and conditions determined by or under these regulations shall apply to such services and facilities in so far as they are so provided.

(2) Regulations 8, 9 and 13 shall not apply in relation to calls to which regulation 6 applies.

(3) The charges applicable to any services and facilities provided in relation to calls to which regulation 4 applies, and the charges for the attempt to connect such calls in cases where communication between the person calling and the person called is not established by reason of the refusal of either of those persons to accept the call, shall (unless fixed by these regulations) be such as the Postmaster General may fix and notify to the States of the Island of Jersey and the States of the Island of Guernsey.

(4) The charges applicable to any services or facilities provided in relation to any calls to which regulation 6 applies, shall, subject to the terms of any such contract as is mentioned in that regulation, be such as the Postmaster General may fix.

(5) The Postmaster General may permit the States of the Island of Jersey or the States of the Island of Guernsey to exercise on his behalf any discretion which is exercisable by him by virtue of paragraph (2), (5) or (6) of regulation 8 or paragraph (1) of regulation 9.

Fixed time calls

8.—(1) Subject to the provisions of this regulation, a person (in this regulation referred to as "an applicant") may book calls (including personal calls) in advance for connection at a specified time to a specified telephone number on the Postmaster General's system or the Hull system.

(2) A fixed time call which is to be made from a call office or a coin box telephone shall be booked from that call office or that coin box telephone. Any other fixed time call may be booked from any telephone or in writing. The Postmaster General may refuse to accept a booking if in his opinion notice of insufficient length has been given.

(3) A booking charge of 6d. shall be paid in respect of an application for a fixed time call in addition to the charge for the call.

(4) The booking charge for a fixed time call which is to be made from a subscriber's telephone shall be paid by the subscriber in respect of the telephone from which the call is to be made. The booking charge for a fixed time call which is to be made from a call office shall be paid by the applicant at the time when the call is booked.

(5) The Postmaster General may at his discretion remit the whole or part of the booking charge in respect of an application for a fixed time call if the application for the call is cancelled by the applicant before the call is connected, or if the call is connected more than ten minutes after the specified time.

(6) The Postmaster General may at his discretion and without charge allow the applicant to alter the time specified by him for connection of a fixed time call.

Personal calls

9.—(1) Subject to the provisions of this regulation, a person (in this regulation referred to as " the applicant ") may book a call to a specified telephone number on the Postmaster General's system or the Hull system, for the specified purpose of communication with a particular person identified by name or by such description as the Postmaster General may consider sufficient, or for connection to a particular department, correspondence reference, code number or extension number.

(2) The applicant when booking a personal call may specify:

  (*a*) one or more alternative telephone numbers after the first at which the person required may be found;

  (*b*) one or more substitutes for the person required, who may be found at the first or any specified alternative telephone number or numbers; or

  (*c*) two persons who may be found at the first or any specified alternative telephone number or numbers, with the requirement that unless both of them are available to speak the call is not to be connected.

(3) Subject to the following paragraphs of this regulation, a personal charge of 2s. shall be paid in respect of the application for a personal call, whether or not the call is connected.

(4) The personal charge shall be payable in addition to any other charges payable for or in respect of the call or the application therefor.

(5) No personal charge shall be payable if the telephone exchange operator is unable to establish communication with the specified telephone number, or (as the case may be) is able to establish communication with none of the specified telephone numbers.

(6) The personal charge (if any) in respect of the application for a personal call which is also a fixed time call shall be payable in the manner in which the booking charge is payable under Regulation 8 (4).

(7) Where the applicant is unaware of the telephone number of a person required or of a substitute for him, the applicant may specify the address or alternative addresses of the person concerned, and in that event this regulation shall have effect as if the applicant had specified the telephone number or alternative telephone numbers (as the case may be) at which the person concerned might be found.

Transferred charge calls—British Islands

10.—(1) A person making a call to a subscriber's telephone may request the telephone exchange operator that the amount payable in respect of the call shall be charged to and payable by the person who is the subscriber in respect of the called telephone, and if the person answering from the called telephone consents to such request before the call is established, the amount payable in respect of the call and the transfer fee of 6d. shall be charged and payable as if the call had been made from the called telephone.

(2) A person making a call to a call office may request the telephone exchange operator that the amount payable in respect of the call shall be payable by the person answering from the call office, and if the person so answering consents

to such request, the amount payable in respect of the call and the transfer fee of 6d. shall be paid by that person in cash placed in the coin collecting box of the call office before the call is established.

(3) A person making a call from a coin box telephone or a call office to a subscriber's telephone may, before the termination of the call, request the telephone exchange operator that the duration of the call may be extended for a further period beyond the period in respect of which payment was made in cash, and that the amount payable in respect of such further period may be charged to and payable by the person who is the subscriber in respect of the called telephone, or the person answering from the called telephone may make the like request; and (provided in the former case that the person so answering consents to the request) the amount payable in respect of the extended period of the call and the transfer fee of 6d. shall in either case be charged and payable as if the amount had been an amount payable in respect of a call made from the called telephone.

(4) A person making a call from a coin box telephone or a call office to a call office may, before the termination of the call, request the telephone exchange operator that the duration of the call may be extended for a further period beyond the period in respect of which payment was made in cash, and that the amount payable in respect of such further period shall be payable by the person receiving the call, or the person receiving the call may make the like request; and (provided in the former case that the person receiving the call consents to the request) the amount payable in respect of the extended period of the call and the transfer fee of 6d. shall in either case be paid by the person receiving the call in cash placed in the coin collecting box of the call office before the duration of the call is extended.

(5) Where any call referred to in the foregoing paragraphs of this regulation is a personal call made from a coin box telephone or a call office, the personal charge shall be paid in advance in cash placed in the coin collecting box by the person making the application for the call, and shall not be made payable by any other person by virtue of the foregoing paragraphs of this regulation.

(6) This regulation shall apply only to calls made in either direction between a telephone on the Jersey system or the Guernsey system, and a telephone on land (whether in a fixed location or not) on the Postmaster General's system or the Hull system.

(7) For the purpose of this regulation, where the context so requires or admits references in these regulations to a subscriber shall include references to a subscriber to the Postmaster General's system and a subscriber to the Hull system, and the reference to the States of the Island of Jersey and the States of the Island of Guernsey in the definition of " coin box telephone " in regulation 1 shall include references to the Postmaster General and the Corporation of Kingston-upon-Hull.

(8) For the purpose of the application of this regulation to calls made to a telephone on a radiophone system of the Postmaster General, such telephone shall be deemed to be a subscriber's telephone, and the person holding a Radiophone Service Licence under the Wireless Telegraphy Act 1949(a) in respect of it shall be deemed to be the subscriber.

(9) In this regulation the expression " the amount payable in respect of the call " shall, in relation to calls made from a call office or coin box telephone on the Jersey system or the Guernsey system, include the charge which the States of the Island of Jersey or the States of the Island of Guernsey may make in respect of the use of the call office or coin box telephone.

(a) 1949 c. 54.

Transferred charge calls—elsewhere

11.—(1) A person making a call from the Channel Islands to a place outside the British Islands in respect of which the transferred charge service is available may request that the call charges should be reversed; and if the Telephone Authority providing service in the latter place, or the operator in the Channel Islands, or the Post Office operator, obtains from the person answering on the called telephone his consent to such request before the call is established, and the call is established, no call charge or service charge shall be payable under these regulations in respect of the call or the transferred charge service.

(2) Where the call is not established (whether or not such consent has been obtained), or where such consent is not obtained and the call is established as an ordinary call, there shall be charged and paid under these regulations such service charge (if any) as the Postmaster General may fix, in addition in the latter case to the charge in respect of the call.

(3) Where a person making a call to the Channel Islands from a place outside the British Islands, or a ship or aircraft registered in any part of the British Islands, being a place, ship or aircraft in respect of which the transferred charge service is available, requests that the call charges shall be reversed, and the person answering from the called telephone consents to such request before the call is established, and the call is established, there shall be charged and paid under these regulations:

(a) where the call is made from a place, such call charge and such service charge (if any) as the Postmaster General may fix;

(b) where the call is made from a ship or aircraft, the charge for the call fixed by the Postmaster General under the Telephone Regulations 1968**(a)**, and such service charge (if any) as the Postmaster General may fix.

The said charges shall be payable by the like person and in the like manner as if they were charges in respect of a call made from the called telephone, but not so as to make payable the charge referred to in regulation 3 (2) where the called telephone is a call office or a coin box telephone.

(4) Where a person making a call to the Channel Islands from a ship or aircraft registered in any part of the British Islands, being a ship or aircraft in respect of which the transferred charge service is available, requests that the call charges shall be reversed, and either:

(a) the call is not established, or

(b) the consent of the person answering from the called telephone to such request is not obtained and the call is established as an ordinary call,

there shall be charged under these regulations and paid by the caller in the ship or aircraft such service charge (if any) as the Postmaster General may fix, in addition in the latter case to the charge for the call.

(5) The Postmaster General shall notify the charges fixed by him under this regulation to the States of the Island of Jersey and the States of the Island of Guernsey.

Credit card calls

12.—(1) Where:

(a) the States of the Island of Jersey or the States of the Island of Guernsey have issued to a subscriber a credit card, under the authority of which a holder of the card may make calls or certain classes of call from telephones other than the subscriber's telephone on terms that the call charges will be payable by the subscriber, or

(a) S.I. 1968/1256 (1968 II, p. 3448).

(b) the Postmaster General or any other Authority providing telephone service outside the Channel Islands has issued a credit card with like effect to a subscriber to the Postmaster General's system or to the system of that Authority, and there is in force an arrangement between the Postmaster General or that Authority and the States of the Island of Jersey or the States of the Island of Guernsey (as the case may be) whereby a holder of such card may make calls or certain classes of call under the authority of such card from telephones on the Jersey system or the Guernsey system (as the case may be);

then if a call involving the use of the Postmaster General's system is duly made as a credit card call under the authority of a current credit card from a telephone in the Channel Islands, no call charge or service charge shall be payable under these regulations by the caller or by the person who is the subscriber in respect of the telephone from which the call is made.

(2) This regulation shall apply to services and facilities requested on the authority of a credit card and to the charges in respect of such services and facilities, as it applies to credit card calls and to the charges in respect thereof.

Advice of duration and charge

13.—(1) Particulars of the duration of or the charge for a call, or of both such duration and charge, may be supplied on the request of the person who is the subscriber in respect of the telephone from which the call was made or of any other person using such telephone or in the case of a transferred charge call, on the request of the person who is the subscriber in respect of the called telephone or of any other person using such telephone.

(2) There shall be charged and paid for this service in respect of each call to or from a place within the British Islands of which particulars are supplied, the sum of 6d.; and in respect of each other call of which particulars are supplied, the sum of 2s.

Payment of charges

14.—(1) Subject to the provisions of these regulations, and without prejudice to the terms of any licence by the Postmaster General to the States of the Island of Jersey or the States of the Island of Guernsey to carry on telephonic business or to any agreement or arrangement between the Postmaster General and the said States relating to such business, the charges fixed by or under these regulations for calls made from telephones on the Jersey system and for services and facilities in relation to such calls shall be paid to the States of the Island of Jersey, and the charges so fixed for calls made from telephones on the Guernsey system and for services and facilities in relation to such calls shall be paid to the States of the Island of Guernsey.

(2) Subject as aforesaid, the said charges for calls made from a subscriber's telephone and for services and facilities in relation to such calls shall be paid by that subscriber on demand, and those for calls made from a call office and for services and facilities in relation to such calls shall be paid in advance by the person making the call.

Revocation

15. The Telephone (Channel Islands) Regulations 1963(a), the Telephone (Channel Islands) Amendment (No. 1) Regulations 1963(b), the Telephone (Channel Islands) Amendment (No. 2) Regulations 1966(c), and the Telephone (Channel Islands) Amendment (No. 3) Regulations 1966(d) are hereby revoked.

(a) S.I. 1963/230 (1963 I, p. 205). (b) S.I. 1963/607 (1963 I, p. 722).
(c) S.I. 1966/437 (1966 I, p. 935). (d) S.I. 1966/858 (1966 II, p. 2046).

Citation and commencement

16. These regulations may be cited as " The Telephone (Channel Islands) Regulations 1968 " and shall come into operation on the 1st October 1968.

Dated 5th August 1968.   *John Stonehouse,*

                   Her Majesty's Postmaster General.

Regulation 3

THE SCHEDULE

Call made otherwise than from a call office or coin box telephone		Call made from a call office or coin box telephone
For the first three minutes or part of three minutes	For each minute or part of a minute after the first three minutes	For each three minutes or part of three minutes
s. d. 4 0	s. d. 1 4	s. d. 4 0

EXPLANATORY NOTE
(*This Note is not part of the Regulations*)

These Regulations consolidate with amendments the Telephone (Channel Islands) Regulations 1963, the Telephone (Channel Islands) Amendment (No. 1) Regulations 1963, the Telephone (Channel Islands) Amendment (No. 2) Regulations 1966, and the Telephone (Channel Islands) Amendment (No. 3) Regulations 1966.

The principal amendments are as follows:

1. The charges for calls to the mainland obtained by subscriber trunk dialling are increased.

2. Other calls to the mainland will be charged for at uniform rates irrespective of distance; this will result in an increase in the charge for such calls of not more than 125 miles.

3. The additional charge for a personal call is increased to 2s.

4. The additional charge for certain transferred charge calls is increased to 6d.

5. The charge for supplying particulars of the duration of or the charge for a call to a place within the British Islands is increased to 6d. and a charge of 2s. is prescribed for providing this service in respect of a call to a place outside the British Islands.

STATUTORY INSTRUMENTS

1968 No. 1258

TELEGRAPHS

The Telex Amendment (No. 1) Regulations 1968

Made - - -		*5th August* 1968
Laid before Parliament		*20th August* 1968
Coming into Operation		*1st October* 1968

I, The Right Honourable John Thomson Stonehouse, M.P., Her Majesty's Postmaster General, by virtue of the power vested in me by section 1 of the Telegraph Act 1962(a) and of every other power enabling me in this behalf, do hereby make the following regulations:

Interpretation

1.—(1) These regulations shall be read as one with the Telex Regulations 1965(b) (hereinafter called "the principal regulations").

(2) The Interpretation Act 1889(c) applies for the interpretation of these regulations as it applies for the interpretation of an Act of Parliament.

Connection charges

2.—(1) The following regulation shall be inserted immediately after regulation 1 of the principal regulations:

"1A.—(1) The subscriber shall pay a connection charge in respect of the installation, connection for use, or provision of each of the items of equipment or apparatus specified in Schedule 4.

(2) The amount of the connection charge shall be such as the Postmaster General shall fix but shall not exceed the aggregate of the amounts specified in Schedule 4 in relation to the equipment and apparatus concerned.

(3) Where telex service has been suspended wholly or in part or an installation has been disconnected under the provisions of these regulations, and the telex service is restored or the installation is re-connected, the subscriber shall pay a re-connection charge of £1, and no connection charge shall be payable under the foregoing paragraphs of this regulation in respect of the re-connection if the installation consists of the same equipment and apparatus as before the suspension or disconnection occurred."

(2) The Schedule set out in Schedule 1 hereto shall be inserted after Schedule 3 to the principal regulations.

Call charges

3. For Schedule 1 to the principal regulations (which specifies the rates of charge for inland calls) there shall be substituted the Schedule set out in Schedule 2 hereto.

(a) 1962 c. 14.   (b) S.I. 1965/1192 (1965 II, p. 3390).   (c) 1889 c. 63.

Call offices

4. For regulation 3(1)(a) of the principal regulations (which regulation provides for additional charges in respect of calls made from call offices) there shall be substituted the following:

"(*a*) for every call which is made from a call office, the sum of 2s. 6d. and".

Citation and commencement

5. These regulations may be cited as the Telex Amendment (No. 1) Regulations 1968, and shall come into operation on 1st October 1968.

Dated 5th August 1968.

John Stonehouse,

Her Majesty's Postmaster General.

SCHEDULE 1

SCHEDULE INSERTED AFTER SCHEDULE 3 OF THE PRINCIPAL REGULATIONS

Regulation 1*A*

SCHEDULE 4

CONNECTION CHARGES

		Maximum charges £ s. d.
1.	Telex line (and teleprinter where provided)	10 0 0
2.	Additional Teleprinter	10 0 0
3.	Auto transmitter	10 0 0
4.	Printing reperforator	10 0 0
5.	Keyboard perforator	10 0 0
6.	Automatic error detection unit	10 0 0
7.	Character detection unit	10 0 0

SCHEDULE 2

SCHEDULE 1 TO THE PRINCIPAL REGULATIONS AS SUBSTITUTED BY

THESE REGULATIONS

Regulation 2

Inland Call Charges

TABLE A

Description of call	Charge
1. A call in respect of which the sending station and receiving station are within the same telex area	2d. plus 2d. for each minute or part of a minute after the first minute.
2. Any other call: if the distance between the telex centre of the sending station and the telex centre of the receiving station:	
(a) does not exceed 35 miles	2d. plus 2d. for each minute or part of a minute after the first minute.
(b) exceeds 35 miles but does not exceed 75 miles	2d. plus 2d. for each 30 seconds or part of 30 seconds after the first 30 seconds.
(c) exceeds 75 miles	2d. plus 2d. for each 15 seconds or part of 15 seconds after the first 15 seconds.

TABLE B

Description of call	For the first 3 minutes or part of 3 minutes	For each minute or part of a minute after the first 3 minutes
	s. d.	s. d.
1. A call in respect of which the sending station and the receiving station are within the same telex area	6	2
2. Any other call: if the distance between the telex centre of the sending station and the telex centre of the receiving station:		
(a) does not exceed 35 miles	6	2
(b) exceeds 35 miles but does not exceed 75 miles	1　0	4
(c) exceeds 75 miles	2　0	8

EXPLANATORY NOTE

(This Note is not part of the Regulations.)

These Regulations amend the Telex Regulations 1965. The principal amendments are:

1. the introduction of connection charges for major items of equipment and apparatus;

2. changes to Inland Call charges;

3. the fixing of 2s. 6d. as the additional sum payable on a call made from a call office.

STATUTORY INSTRUMENTS

1968 No.1262

CRIMINAL PROCEDURE, ENGLAND AND WALES

The Criminal Appeal Rules 1968

Made - - - -	31*st July* 1968
Laid before Parliament	14*th August* 1968
Coming into Operation	1*st September* 1968

ARRANGEMENT OF RULES

SCHEDULES

SCHEDULE 1—Forms.

Form 1 Judge's certificate.

Form 2 Notice of appeal or application for leave of court.

Form 3 Grounds of applications for extension of time, leave to appeal against conviction and leave to appeal against sentence.

Form 4 Notice of application for bail.

Form 5 Notice of application for leave to be present.

Form 6 Notice of application for reception of evidence.

Form 7 Recognizance of appellant.

Form 8 Recognizance of appellant's surety.

Form 9 Recognizance of appellant pending retrial.

Form 10 Recognizance of appellant's surety pending retrial.

Form 11 Certificate by Registrar of conditions of bail.

Form 12 Certificate of Registrar that all recognizances taken.

Form 13 Witness Order.

Form 14 Notice of abandonment of proceedings.

Form 15 Application for determination by Court of Appeal.

Form 16 Warrant directing conveyance of appellant to hospital.

Form 17 Notice of application for leave to appeal to the House of Lords.

Form 18 Recognizance of defendant on appeal to House of Lords.

Form 19 Recognizance of defendant's surety on appeal to House of Lords.

SCHEDULE 2—Rules revoked.

We, the Rule Committee of the Supreme Court, in pursuance of the powers conferred upon us by section 99 of the Supreme Court of Judicature (Consolidation) Act 1925(a), section 2(5) of the Criminal Appeal Act 1966(b), and section 46 of the Criminal Appeal Act 1968(c), hereby make the following rules of court:—

Certificate of trial judge

1.—(1) The certificate of the judge of the court of trial under section 1(2), 12 or 15(2) of the Act that a case is a fit case for appeal shall be in Form 1.

(2) The certificate shall be forwarded forthwith to the Registrar, whether or not the person to whom the certificate relates has applied for a certificate.

(3) A copy of the certificate shall be forwarded forthwith to the person to whom the certificate relates or to his legal representative.

Notice of appeal and application for extension of time

2.—(1) Notice of appeal or of an application for leave to appeal under Part I of the Act shall be given by completing Part 1 of Form 2 and so much of Part 2 thereof as relates to the notice and serving it on the Registrar.

(a) 1925 c. 49.   (b) 1966 c. 31.   (c) 1968 c. 19.

(2)(*a*) A notice of appeal or of an application for leave to appeal shall be accompanied by a notice in Form 3 containing the grounds of the appeal or application.

(*b*) If the appellant has been convicted of more than one offence, the notice in Form 3 shall specify the convictions or sentences against which the appellant is appealing or applying for leave to appeal.

(*c*) The grounds of an appeal or application set out in Form 3 may, with the consent of the court, be varied or amplified within such time as the court may allow.

(3)(*a*) Notice of an application to extend the time within which notice of appeal or of an application for leave to appeal may under Part I of the Act be given shall be given by completing so much of Part 2 of Form 2 as relates to the application and by giving notice of appeal or of an application for leave to appeal in accordance with the foregoing provisions of this Rule.

(*b*) Notice of an application to extend the time within which notice of appeal or of an application for leave to appeal may under Part I of the Act be given shall specify the grounds of the application.

(4) An appellant who is appealing or applying for leave to appeal against conviction shall specify in Form 3 any exhibit produced at the trial which he wishes to be kept in custody for the purposes of his appeal.

(5) Forms 2 and 3 shall be signed by, or on behalf of, the appellant.

(6) If Form 2 or Form 3 is not signed by the appellant and the appellant is in custody, the Registrar shall, as soon as practicable after receiving the form, send a copy of it to the appellant.

(7) In the case of an appellant who does not require leave to appeal or who is given leave to appeal, a notice of application for leave to appeal shall be treated as a notice of appeal; and in the case of an appellant who requires leave to appeal but who serves on the Registrar notice of appeal, the notice of appeal shall be treated also as an application for leave to appeal.

Application for bail, leave to be present or reception of evidence

3.—(1) Notice of an application by the appellant—

(*a*) to be admitted to bail pending the determination of his appeal or pending his retrial shall be in Form 4 and, unless notice of appeal or of an application for leave to appeal has previously been given, shall be accompanied by such a notice;

(*b*) to be given leave by the court to be present at proceedings for which such leave is required shall be in Form 5;

(*c*) that a witness who would have been a compellable witness at the trial be ordered to attend for examination by the court shall be in Form 6;

(*d*) that the evidence of a witness be received by the court shall be in Form 6;

and shall be served on the Registrar.

(2) An application as aforesaid may be made to the court orally.

Bail

4.—(1) Where the court directs the admission of an appellant to bail pending the determination of his appeal or pending his retrial, the court shall determine the number of sureties, if any, the amount in which he and any sureties are to be bound and the conditions to be endorsed on the recognizances with a view to the recognizances being taken subsequently.

(2) The recognizance of an appellant shall be in Form 7 and that of a surety in Form 8, except that in relation to an appellant admitted to bail pending his retrial his recognizance shall be in Form 9 and that of a surety in Form 10.

(3) Any such recognizance may be entered into before the Registrar, a justice of the peace, the clerk of a magistrates' court, a member of a police force either of or above the rank of inspector or in charge of a police station or, in the case of an appellant who is in custody, before the person having custody of him.

(4) The Registrar, if he does not take the recognizances, shall issue a certificate in Form 11 showing the conditions of the recognizances and the amounts in which the appellant and any sureties are to be bound; and a person authorised to take a recognizance under this Rule shall not be required to take it without production of such a certificate as aforesaid.

(5) A person authorised to take the recognizance of a surety under this Rule shall not do so unless he is satisfied that the person entering into the recognizance is, in all the circumstances, a suitable person to do so.

(6) Where a recognizance is taken under this Rule by a person other than the Registrar, that person shall send it to the Registrar.

(7) A person taking a recognizance under this Rule shall give a copy thereof to the person entering into the recognizance.

(8) The person having custody of an appellant shall—

    (*a*) on receipt of a certificate in Form 12 signed by the Registrar stating that the recognizances of any sureties required by the court have been taken or on being otherwise satisfied that all such recognizances have been taken, and

    (*b*) on being satisfied that the appellant has entered into his recognizance,

release the appellant.

(9) Where the court has granted bail pending retrial, the Registrar on receipt of all the recognizances shall forward them to the clerk of the court before which the appellant is to be retried.

Variation or revocation of bail

5.—(1) Where the court grants the application of an appellant to be admitted to bail pending the determination of his appeal or pending his retrial, the court may at any time reduce the amount in which it is proposed that he or any surety should be bound or dispense with any of the sureties or modify any condition specified by the court.

(2)(*a*) Where an appellant is released on bail pending the determination of his appeal or pending his retrial, the court may at any time, without prejudice to their power to order the forfeiture of his recognizance or that of any of his sureties or to a constable's power of arrest under section 23 of the Criminal Justice Act 1967(**a**), order his arrest and recommittal to custody.

(*b*) Where an appellant is recommitted to custody, the person having custody of him shall forthwith notify the Registrar of the fact.

(*c*) An appellant who has been recommitted to custody under this Rule may again be admitted to bail under these Rules.

(3) In this Rule any reference to the court shall include a reference to a judge of the court.

Forfeiture of bail

6.—(1) Where an appellant is admitted to bail pending the determination of his appeal or pending his retrial and he does not comply with the conditions endorsed on his recognizance, the court may order his recognizance and that of any of his sureties to be forfeited.

(2) Such an order shall fix a term of imprisonment which the person whose recognizance is forfeited is to undergo if the sum which he is liable to pay is not duly paid or recovered and may—

(*a*) allow time for the payment of such sum;

(*b*) direct payment of such sum by instalments of such amounts and on such dates respectively as may be specified in the order;

(*c*) discharge the recognizance or may reduce the amount due thereunder.

Custody of exhibits

7.—(1) On a conviction on indictment or on a coroner's inquisition the proper officer of the court of trial shall, subject to any directions of the judge of the court of trial, make arrangements for any exhibit at the trial which in his opinion may be required for the purposes of an appeal against conviction to be kept in the custody of the court, or given into the custody of the person producing it at the trial or any other person for retention, until the expiration of 35 days from the date of conviction.

(2) Where an appellant has given notice of appeal, or of an application for leave to appeal, against conviction, the Registrar shall inform the proper officer of the court of the notice and give directions concerning the continued retention in custody of any exhibit which appears necessary for the proper determination of the appeal or application.

(3) Where the court orders an appellant to be retried, it shall make arrangements pending his retrial for the continued retention in custody of exhibits.

(4) Any arrangements under this Rule may include arrangements for the inspection of an exhibit by an interested party.

Supply of documentary and other exhibits

8.—(1) The Registrar shall, on request, supply to the appellant or respondent copies of documents or other things required for the appeal and in such case may make charges in accordance with scales and rates fixed for the time being by the Treasury.

(2) The Registrar shall, on request, make arrangements for the appellant or respondent to inspect any document or other thing required for the appeal.

(3) This Rule shall not apply to the supply of the transcripts of any proceedings or part thereof.

(**a**) 1967 c. 80.

Examination of witness by court

9.—(1) An order of the court to a person to attend for examination as a witness shall be in Form 13 and shall specify the time and place of attendance.

(2) The evidence of a witness taken before an examiner shall be taken in like manner as depositions are taken in proceedings before a magistrates' court acting as examining justices.

Abandonment of proceedings

10.—(1) An appeal or an application for leave to appeal under Part I of the Act may be abandoned before the hearing of the appeal or application by serving on the Registrar notice thereof in Form 14.

(2) The notice shall be signed by, or on behalf of, the appellant.

(3) The Registrar shall, as soon as practicable after receiving a notice under this Rule, send a copy of it, endorsed with the date of receipt, to the appellant, to the Secretary of State and to the proper officer of the court of trial.

(4) Where an appeal or an application for leave to appeal is abandoned, the appeal or application shall be treated as having been dismissed or refused by the court.

Hearing by single judge

11.—(1) A judge of the court shall, for the purpose of exercising any of the powers referred to in section 31(2) of the Act or Rule 5, sit in such place as he appoints, and may sit otherwise than in open court.

(2) A party in any proceedings under the said section 31(2) or the said Rule may be represented by counsel or solicitor.

Determination by full court

12.—(1) Where a judge of the court has refused an application on the part of an appellant to exercise in his favour any of the powers referred to in section 31(2) of the Act, the appellant may have the application determined by the court by serving a notice in Form 15 on the Registrar within fourteen days, or such longer period as a judge of the court may fix, from the date on which notice of the refusal was served on him by the Registrar.

(2) A notice in Form 15 shall be signed by, or on behalf of, the appellant.

(3) If the notice is not signed by the appellant and the appellant is in custody, the Registrar shall, as soon as practicable after receiving the notice, send a copy of it to the appellant.

(4) If such a notice is not served on the Registrar within the said 14 days or such longer period as a judge of the court may fix, the application shall be treated as having been refused by the court.

Enforcement of fines

13.—(1) Where the court imposes a fine on an appellant, the court shall make an order fixing a term of imprisonment, not exceeding twelve months, which the appellant is to undergo if the fine is not duly paid or recovered.

(2) Such an order may—

(a) allow time for the payment of the fine;

(b) direct payment of the fine by instalments of such amounts and on such dates respectively as may be specified in the order.

Dismissal of appeal against hospital order

14. If the court dismisses an appeal or an application for leave to appeal by an appellant who is subject to a hospital order under the Mental Health Act 1959(a) or an order under section 5(1) of the Criminal Procedure (Insanity) Act 1964(b) or the court affirms the order and the appellant has been released on bail pending his appeal, the court shall give such directions as it thinks fit for his conveyance to the hospital from which he was released on bail and for his detention, if necessary, in a place of safety as defined in section 80 of the Mental Health Act 1959 pending his admission to the said hospital.

Notice of determination of court

15.—(1) The Registrar shall, as soon as practicable, serve notice of any determination by the court or by any judge of the court under section 31 of the Act on any appeal or application by an appellant on—

(a) the appellant;

(b) the Secretary of State;

(c) any person having custody of the appellant;

(d) in the case of an appellant detained under the Mental Health Act 1959 the responsible authority.

(2) The Registrar shall, as soon as practicable, serve notice on the proper officer of the court of trial of the order of the court disposing of an appeal or application for leave to appeal.

(3) In this Rule the expression "responsible authority" means—

(a) in relation to a patient liable to be detained under the said Act of 1959 in a hospital or mental nursing home, the managers of the hospital or home as defined in section 59(1) of that Act; and

(b) in relation to a patient subject to guardianship, the responsible local health authority as defined in subsection (4) of that section.

Reference by Home Secretary

16. Where the Secretary of State refers a point to the court under section 17(1)(b) of the Act, the court may consider the point in private.

Sittings in vacation

17. The Lord Chief Justice shall determine the days on which the court shall, if necessary, sit during vacations; and the court shall sit on such days in accordance with arrangements made by the Lord Chief Justice after consultation with the Master of the Rolls.

(a) 1959 c. 72.   (b) 1964 c. 84.

Record of proceedings at trial

18.—(1) Except as provided by this Rule, the whole of any proceedings in respect of which an appeal lies (with or without leave) to the court shall be recorded by means of shorthand notes or, with the permission of the Lord Chancellor, by mechanical means.

(2) Where such proceedings are recorded by means of shorthand notes, it shall not be necessary to record—

(*a*) the opening or closing addresses to the jury on behalf of the prosecution or an accused person unless the judge of the court of trial otherwise directs, or

(*b*) any other part of such proceedings which the judge of the court of trial directs need not be recorded.

(3) Where it is not practicable for such proceedings to be recorded by means of shorthand notes or by mechanical means, the judge of the court of trial shall direct how and to what extent the proceedings shall be recorded.

(4) The permission of the Lord Chancellor may contain conditions concerning the custody, and supply of transcripts, of a recording made by mechanical means.

Transcripts

19.—(1) A transcript of the record of any proceedings or part thereof in respect of which an appeal lies, with or without leave, to the court and which are recorded in accordance with the provisions of Rule 18—

(*a*) shall, on request, be supplied to the Registrar or any interested party, on payment of such charge, if any, as may be fixed for the time being by the Treasury;

(*b*) may, on request, be supplied to any other person, on payment of such sum as may be agreed between that person and the person supplying the transcript.

(2) Without prejudice to the provisions of paragraph (1) of this Rule, the Registrar may, on request, supply to any interested party a transcript of the record of any proceedings or part thereof which is in his possession for the purposes of the appeal or application in question and in such case may make charges in accordance with scales and rates fixed for the time being by the Treasury:

Provided that in the case of an interested party who has been given legal aid under section 73(5) of the Criminal Justice Act 1967 for the purpose of the appeal or any proceedings preliminary or incidental thereto such a transcript shall be supplied free.

Verification of record of proceedings

20.—(1) An official shorthand writer who takes shorthand notes of any proceedings or part thereof before the court of trial in respect of which an appeal lies (with or without leave) to the court shall—

(*a*) at the beginning of the notes state the name of the parties to the proceedings;

(*b*) in the case of shorthand notes of part of any proceedings, state the part concerned;

(*c*) record his name in the notes;

(*d*) retain the shorthand notes for not less than five years.

(2)(*a*) Verification of a transcript of the shorthand notes taken by an official shorthand writer of any proceedings or part thereof before the court of trial in respect of which an appeal lies (with or without leave) to the court shall be by a certificate by the person making the transcript that—

(i) he has made a correct and complete transcript of the notes to the best of his skill and ability; and

(ii) the notes were either taken by him and were to the best of his skill and ability a complete and correct account of those proceedings or part thereof or were taken by another official shorthand writer.

(*b*) Verification of a transcript of the record of the proceedings or part thereof if recorded by mechanical means shall be by—

(i) a certificate by the person making the transcript that he has made a correct and complete transcript of the recording to the best of his skill and ability; and

(ii) a certificate by a person responsible for the recording or a successor that the recording records so much of the proceedings as is specified in the certificate.

(*c*) Verification of a transcript of the record of the proceedings or part thereof if recorded in any other way shall be by—

(i) a certificate by the person who made the record that he recorded the proceedings or part thereof to the best of his ability; and

(ii) a certificate by the person making the transcript that he has made a correct and complete transcript of the record to the best of his skill and ability.

Service of documents

21.—(1) For the purpose of these Rules service of a document may be effected—

(*a*) in the case of a document to be served on the Registrar—

(i) in the case of an appellant who is in custody, by delivering it to the person having custody of him, or

(ii) by delivering it to the Registrar, or

(iii) by addressing it to him and leaving it at his office in the Royal Courts of Justice, London, W.C.2, or

(iv) by sending it by post addressed to him at the said office;

(*b*) in the case of a document to be served on a body corporate by delivering it to the secretary or clerk of the body at its registered or principal office or sending it by post addressed to the secretary or clerk of the body at that office;

(*c*) in the case of a document to be served on any other person—

(i) by delivering it to the person to whom it is directed, or

(ii) by leaving it for him with some person at his last known or usual place of abode, or

(iii) by sending it by post addressed to him at his last known or usual place of abode.

(2) A person having custody of an appellant to whom a document is delivered in pursuance of paragraph (1)(*a*)(i) of this Rule shall endorse on it the date of delivery and cause it to be forwarded forthwith to the Registrar.

The Registrar

22.—(1) The Registrar may require the court of trial to furnish the court with any assistance or information which it may require for the purpose of exercising its jurisdiction.

(2)(*a*) The Registrar shall give as long notice in advance as reasonably possible of the date on which the court will hear any appeal or application by an appellant to—
  (i) the appellant,
  (ii) any person having custody of the appellant, and
  (iii) any other interested party whom the court requires to be represented at the hearing.

(*b*) This paragraph shall not apply to proceedings before a judge of the court under section 31 of the Act or Rule 5.

Appeal to the House of Lords

23.—(1) An application to the court—
  (*a*) for leave to appeal to the House of Lords under Part II of the Act or section 13 of the Administration of Justice Act 1960(**a**);
  (*b*) to extend the time within which an application may be made by the defendant to the House of Lords or the court under section 34(1) of the Act or that subsection as applied by section 13(4) of the Administration of Justice Act 1960;
  (*c*) by the defendant to be given leave to be present on the hearing of the appeal or of any proceedings preliminary or incidental thereto;
  (*d*) by the defendant to be admitted to bail pending the appeal;
shall either be made orally immediately after the decision of the court from which an appeal lies to the House of Lords or notice thereof shall be in Form 17 and shall be served on the Registrar.

(2) Where the court directs the admission of a defendant to bail pending his appeal, the court shall determine the number of sureties, if any, the amount in which he and any sureties are to be bound and the conditions to be endorsed on the recognizances with a view to the recognizances being taken subsequently.

(3) The recognizance of a defendant shall be in Form 18 and that of a surety in Form 19.

(4) Paragraphs (3) to (8) of Rule 4 and Rules 5 and 6 shall apply with respect to a recognizance taken under this Rule as they apply with respect to a recognizance taken under those Rules with the necessary modifications.

(5) An application to the court for leave to appeal to the House of Lords under Part II of the Act or section 13 of the Administration of Justice Act 1960 may be abandoned before the hearing of the application by serving on the Registrar notice to that effect.

(6) For the purpose of having an application determined by the court in pursuance of section 44 of the Act, Rules 11 and 12 shall apply with the necessary modifications.

(7) Rule 15 shall apply to a determination under Part II of the Act or section 13 of the Administration of Justice Act 1960 with the necessary modifications.

(8) Rules 8, 19(2) and 22 shall apply in relation to an appeal under Part II

(**a**) 1960 c. 65.

of the Act or section 13 of the Administration of Justice Act 1960 as they apply in relation to an appeal under Part I of the Act, except that any reference to section 31 of the Act shall be construed as a reference to section 44 of the Act.

(9) In this Rule any reference to a defendant includes an appellant under section 13 of the Administration of Justice Act 1960.

Forms

24.—(1) Any reference in these Rules to a form means a reference to a form set out in Schedule 1 to these Rules.

(2) The forms set out in Schedule 1 to these Rules or forms substantially to the like effect may be used with such variations as the circumstances may require.

Definitions

25.—(1) In these Rules, unless the context otherwise requires—

" the Act " means the Criminal Appeal Act 1968;

" appellant " means an appellant under Part I of the Act, including a person who has given notice of application for leave to appeal;

" court " means the Criminal Division of the Court of Appeal;

" interested party " means the Director of Public Prosecutions or a person who is a defendant or prosecutor in proceedings in respect of which an appeal lies (with or without leave) to the court or who is named in, or immediately affected by, an order made by the judge of the court of trial in such proceedings;

" judge of the court " means judge of the court or of the Queen's Bench Division of the High Court;

" official shorthand writer " means a person appointed by or on behalf of the Lord Chancellor to take shorthand notes of criminal proceedings in a court of trial;

" Registrar " means the Registrar of criminal appeals of the court;

" shorthand " means any method of recording other than in longhand by means of symbols where the recording is made by a person either by hand or by the use of a machine.

(2) Any reference in these Rules to a Rule means a reference to a Rule contained in these Rules.

(3) The Interpretation Act 1889(a) shall apply to the interpretation of these Rules as it applies to the interpretation of an Act of Parliament and as if these Rules and the Rules revoked by these Rules were Acts of Parliament.

Repeals

26.—(1) Subject to paragraph (2) of this Rule, the Rules set out in Schedule 2 to these Rules are hereby revoked.

(2) The revocations effected by paragraph (1) of this Rule shall not affect the operation of the Rules so revoked in relation to a person who before the coming into operation of these Rules has given notice of appeal or of an application for leave to appeal; and these Rules shall not apply to such an appeal or application or proceedings preliminary or incidental to such an appeal.

(a) 1889 c. 63.

Citation and commencement

27.—(1) These Rules may be cited as the Criminal Appeal Rules 1968.

(2) These Rules shall come into operation on 1st September 1968.

Dated 31st July 1968.

Gardiner, C.
Parker of Waddington, C.J.
Denning, M.R.
J. E. S. Simon, P.
Cyril Salmon, L.J.
Fenton Atkinson, L.J.
Geoffrey Cross, J.
N. Browne-Wilkinson
M. D. L. Worsley
W. O. Carter
A. E. Cox
Arthur J. Driver

SCHEDULE 1
FORMS

R.1

FORM 1

CRIMINAL APPEAL ACT 1968

Judge's certificate
R. v.

Particulars of trial

Full name of person tried...

Name of court..

Offences for which person tried..

Decision of court—

*Delete
if
inapplicable

*convicted of...

*unfit to plead

*verdict of not guilty by reason of insanity

Date of decision of court...

I certify that the case is a fit case for appeal on the ground that:—

Signed...
Judge of the court of trial.

Date...

FORM 2   R.2

CRIMINAL APPEAL ACT 1968

Notice of appeal or application for leave to appeal

To the Registrar,
Criminal Appeal Office,
Royal Courts of Justice,
Strand,
London, W.C.2.

PART 1

Particulars of appellant:

Full names: Forenames   Surname   Age on conviction
(Block letters)

Address:
(If detained give address
where detained and, if
detained in prison, give
prison number)

Court where tried and/or sentenced:
(see note 3)

Dates of appearances at the   Name of
Court including dates of   Court
conviction (if convicted
at the Court) and sentence   Name of
                                     Judge

Particulars of offences of which convicted: whether convicted on
indictment or by a magistrates' court: particulars of sentences and
orders: (see notes 4, 5)

Offences	Convicted on indictment or by magistrates' court	Sentences and orders
....	....	....
....	....	....
....	....	....
....	....	....
....	....	....

Offences taken into consideration when sentenced

Total sentence

PART 2

The appellant is applying for (see note 8)—

*Delete
if
inapplicable

*Extension of time in which to give notice of application for leave to appeal

*Leave to appeal against conviction

*Leave to appeal against sentence

*Bail

*Leave to be present at hearing

*Leave to call witnesses

Signed...   Received in the
                    (Appellant)   Criminal Appeal
                                                                               Office

Date   ....   Date   ....

This notice was handed in by the appellant to-day

Signed...
                                        [Prison Officer]

Date   ....

Notes

1. This form should be sent to the Registrar within 28 days from the date of conviction, sentence, verdict or finding appealed against. If the appellant is in custody the form should be handed to the prison authority (or other person having custody) for forwarding to the Registrar; and the date of handing-in should be recorded on the form. The period of 28 days cannot be extended except by leave of the court and the reasons for the delay will be required.

2. The grounds of the application or of the appeal must be given on Form 3 and must accompany this form.

3. No appeal to the Court of Appeal lies from a magistrates' court. For the purposes of an appeal to the Court of Appeal the court where the appellant is tried and/or sentenced is always a court of assize or a court of quarter sessions.

4. Particulars of all convictions and sentences against which the appellant has a right of appeal (with or without leave) must be given in Part 1 of the form. A person can appeal against conviction only if he was convicted on indictment. A person can appeal against sentence only if the sentence was passed for an offence of which he was convicted on indictment or for which he was dealt with by a court of assize or quarter sessions as set out in section 10 of the Criminal Appeal Act 1968.

If the appeal is against a verdict of not guilty by reason of insanity or a finding of disability, Part 2 should be adapted accordingly.

5. Separate forms should be submitted for convictions or sentences which do not arise in the same proceedings.

6. The form must be signed by the appellant or on his behalf.

7. The notice will be treated as a notice of appeal in the case of an appellant who does not require leave to appeal, e.g., where a certificate has been granted by the trial judge, or in the case of an appellant who is given leave to appeal by the Court of Appeal.

8. An application for leave to be present, bail, or leave to call a witness must be supported by the appropriate form. Such an application can be made subsequently.

FORM 3   R.2

CRIMINAL APPEAL ACT 1968

Grounds of applications for extension of time,
leave to appeal against conviction and leave
to appeal against sentence

To the Registrar,   Criminal Appeal Office
Criminal Appeal Office,
Royal Courts of Justice,   Reference number
Strand,
London, W.C.2.

Full names of appellant: Forenames   Surname
(Block letters)

Give the name of the solicitor and/or counsel (if any) who represented the appellant at assizes or quarter sessions:
Solicitor   Counsel

List the documents sent with this form:

The applications are for:—

   *Extension of time in which to give notice of application for *Delete
   leave to appeal against *conviction and *sentence   if
                                                                  inapplicable
   *Leave to appeal against conviction of the following offences:—

   *Leave to appeal against the following sentences or orders:—

The grounds are as follows:—

The applications should be dealt with in the order shown above
and each offence and/or each sentence or order should be dealt
with separately: see notes 6 and 7 on reverse. The grounds
must be signed by or on behalf of the appellant.

Signed..   For use in the Criminal
              (Appellant)   Appeal Office

Date   ....   Received

Notes

1. This form must accompany Form 2 and must be completed as fully as is practicable at that time. If further grounds need to be given to amend or amplify the grounds given on this form, they should be forwarded to the Registrar on a form which can be obtained from him, or if the appellant is in custody from the person having custody of him. Grounds of application must not be set out in letters to the Registrar.

2. If this form relates to more than one application or to both an application and an appeal, they should be dealt with separately and in order.

3. An appellant who is applying for extension of time within which to give notice of appeal or of application for leave to appeal, must give the reasons for the delay: he must also give details of the appeal or application for leave to appeal.

4. An appellant who is applying for leave to appeal against conviction, must set out each conviction against which he is applying for leave to appeal, and the grounds of the application. The grounds may be the same for each conviction.

5. If the appellant requires, for the purposes of his appeal against conviction, any exhibits produced at his trial, he should specify them in the form.

6. An appellant who is applying for leave to appeal against sentence, must set out each sentence against which he is applying for leave to appeal, and the grounds of the application. The grounds may be the same for each sentence.

7. An appellant who is applying for leave to appeal against conviction and sentence, must deal with each conviction and each sentence separately.

8. This notice will be treated as a notice of appeal in a case in which leave to appeal is not required.

9. If the appeal or application is against a verdict of not guilty by reason of insanity or a finding of disability, references in this form to a conviction should be construed as references to such a verdict or finding.

10. An appellant who is applying for leave to appeal against sentence and wishes to call a witness to give evidence in mitigation should give his name and address. However, the Registrar is not responsible for arranging the attendance of the witness.

11. Documents sent with this form should be specified in the space provided.

12. If some application has been made on an earlier occasion, the Criminal Appeal reference number should be given.

R.3(1)(*a*)

FORM 4
CRIMINAL APPEAL ACT 1968
Notice of application for bail

To the Registrar,   Criminal Appeal Office
Criminal Appeal Office,
Royal Courts of Justice,   Reference number
Strand, London, W.C.2.

Particulars of appellant:

                        Forenames   Surname

Full names:
(Block letters)

Address:
(Where detained and, if
detained in prison, give
prison number)

Give the appellant's address if bail were granted, and the amount
of the recognizance in which he would agree to be bound.
Address if granted bail
Amount of recognizance offered   £.........................

Give the names, addresses and occupations of two persons who
might act as sureties if bail were granted and the amounts of the
recognizances in which they might agree to be bound.
1st Surety:
Name, address, occupation
Amount of recognizance offered   £.........................
2nd Surety:
Name, address, occupation
Amount of recognizance offered   £.........................

If bail was granted before trial or sentence state:—
Amount of recognizances:
      Appellant   Sureties
£ ....   £......................... and £.........................
Were the sureties the persons named above?
What, if any, special conditions were imposed?

The appellant applies for bail pending appeal/retrial on the
following grounds:—

Signed...   For use in the Criminal
           (Appellant)   Appeal Office

Date ....   Received

Notes

1. This form must accompany or follow Form 2. If this form follows Form 2 the Criminal
Appeal reference number must be given. An application for bail may be made whether or not
Form 2 contained an application for bail.
2. An application for bail will be considered in the light of the grounds of appeal or application
for leave to appeal. Accordingly, it is usual for the application for bail to be submitted to the
court or judge together with the other applications and the transcript of the proceedings at
the trial. This imposes some delay. Generally, strong grounds of appeal or application for
leave to appeal have to be shown before bail is granted.
3. Do not repeat the grounds of appeal or application for leave to appeal as the grounds for
bail. Mention any special other grounds which the judge or court might consider, e.g., medical
reasons.
4. Time spent on bail does not count towards sentence.
5. This form must be signed by, or on behalf of, the appellant.

R.3(1)(*b*)

FORM 5

CRIMINAL APPEAL ACT 1968

Notice of application for leave to be present

To the Registrar,
Criminal Appeal Office,
Royal Courts of Justice,
Strand,
London, W.C.2.

Criminal Appeal Office

Reference number

Particulars of appellant:
Full names: Forenames
(Block letters)

Surname

Address:
(Where detained and, if
detained in prison, give
prison number)

The appellant applies to be given leave by the Court of Appeal
to be present at proceedings for which such leave is required.
The special reasons for the application (see note 4) are as follows:—

Signed..

(Appellant)

For use in the Criminal
Appeal Office

Date   ....

Received

Notes

1. Form 5 is required for an application for leave to be present at the hearing of an application for leave to appeal or an appeal on grounds involving a question of law alone. This form must accompany or follow Form 2. If it follows Form 2 the Criminal Appeal reference number must be given.

2. Subject to note 3, Form 5 is not required, and the appellant if in custody is entitled to be present, on the hearing of an appeal by a certificate of the trial judge that the case is fit for appeal, on a reference by the Home Secretary, or by leave of the Court of Appeal.

3. Form 5 is required in the case of an appellant detained in consequence of a verdict of not guilty by reason of insanity or a finding of disability. The appellant is not entitled to be present at the hearing of any proceedings unless leave to be present is given.

4. The court grants leave to be present only in exceptional cases.

5. An appellant who is not in custody may attend a hearing before the full court and need not apply for leave. Proceedings before a single judge are in private.

FORM 6   R.3(1)(c), (d)

CRIMINAL APPEAL ACT 1968

Notice of application for reception of evidence

To the Registrar,
Criminal Appeal Office,
Royal Courts of Justice,
Strand,
London, W.C.2.

Full names of appellant..

Criminal appeal reference number (except where this form

   accompanies Form 2)..

Where detained...

Prison no..

Name and address of witness..

....

....

....

Do you want a witness order?   Yes/No

Was the witness called at the trial?   Yes/No

The witness can now give the following evidence (which he did not
   give at the trial):—

The evidence was not given at the trial for the following reasons:—

Signed...

Date ....

Notes

1. Notice of the application may be given whether or not it was given on Form 2.

2. A separate form must be used for each witness.

3. A witness cannot be called without the leave of the Court of Appeal. Before giving leave
to call a witness, the court will consider, with other matters, whether the evidence if received
would afford any ground for allowing the appeal, whether the evidence is likely to be credible,
and whether there is a reasonable explanation for failure to adduce the evidence at the trial.
Do not set out in the form the evidence which the witness gave at the trial.

4. Do not apply in respect of a witness in mitigation of sentence only.

R.4(2)   FORM 7

CRIMINAL APPEAL ACT 1968
Recognizance of appellant

I, ... (hereinafter called the appellant) acknowledge that I owe to our Sovereign Lady The Queen the sum of ...., payment thereof to be enforced against me by due process of law if I fail to comply with the condition[s] endorsed hereon.

Signed ....

Address   at   which ....
appellant proposes
to reside pending ....
appeal

....

....

Taken before me the .... day of ...., 19   ,

at ....

Signed ....

Office[1] ....

(*Endorsement*)

Condition[s]

The condition[s] of this recognizance is [are] that if the appellant appears before the Criminal Division of the Court of Appeal, unless the court otherwise orders, at each and every hearing of his appeal and at the final determination thereof, then this recognizance shall be void, but otherwise shall remain in full force[2].

(1) The recognizance may be taken by the Registrar of the Criminal Division of the Court of Appeal, a Justice of the Peace, the clerk of a magistrates' court or a member of a police force of or above the rank of inspector or in charge of a police station or the person having custody of the appellant.

(2) Conditions appearing to the court to be likely to result in the appellant's appearance at the time and place required, or to be necessary in the interests of justice or for the prevention of crime may be added.

FORM 8   R.4(2)

CRIMINAL APPEAL ACT 1968

Recognizance of appellant's surety

I, ... acknowledge that I owe

to our Sovereign Lady The Queen the sum of................................,

payment thereof to be enforced against me by due process of law

if .... detained in ....

fails to comply with the condition endorsed hereon.

Signed..

Address ....

....

....

....

Taken before me the............................ day of ...., 19 ,

at..

Signed..

Office(1) ....

(*Endorsement*)

Condition

The condition of this recognizance is that if the said........................

.... appears before the Criminal Division of the

Court of Appeal, unless the court otherwise orders, at each and

every hearing of his appeal and at the final determination thereof,

then this recognizance shall be void, but otherwise shall remain in

full force.

(1) The recognizance may be taken by the Registrar of the Criminal Division of the Court of
Appeal, a Justice of the Peace, the clerk of a magistrates' court or a member of a police force
of or above the rank of inspector or in charge of a police station.

R.4(2)

FORM 9

CRIMINAL APPEAL ACT 1968

Recognizance of appellant pending retrial

I, ... (hereinafter called the appellant) acknowledge that I owe to our Sovereign Lady The Queen the sum of ...., payment thereof to be enforced against me by due process of law if I fail to comply with the conditions endorsed hereon.

Signed..

Address at which ....
appellant proposes ....
to reside pending ....
retrial ....

....

Taken before me the .... day of ...., 19 ,

at..

Signed..

Office[1] ....

(*Endorsement*)

Condition[s]

The condition[s] of this recognizance is/are that if the appellant appears in person at and before the court of ....
for the [county] of .... on such date and at such time and place as may be notified to him by the proper officer of the court and there surrenders himself into custody and takes his trial upon any indictment preferred against him, then this recognizance shall be void, but otherwise shall remain in full force[2].

(1) The recognizance can be taken by the Registrar of the Criminal Division of the Court of Appeal, a Justice of the Peace, the clerk of a magistrates' court, a member of a police force of or above the rank of inspector or in charge of a police station, or the person having custody of the appellant.

(2) Conditions appearing to the court to be likely to result in the appellant's appearance at the time and place required, or to be necessary in the interests of justice or for the prevention of crime may be added.

FORM 10   R.4(2)

CRIMINAL APPEAL ACT 1968

Recognizance of appellant's surety pending retrial

I, ... acknowledge that I owe

to our Sovereign Lady The Queen the sum of..,

payment thereof to be enforced against me by due process of law

if .... (*insert name of principal*)

fails to comply with the condition endorsed hereon.

Signed..

Address ....

....

....

....

Taken before me the............................... day of ...., 19 ,

at..

Signed..

Office[(1)] ....

(*Endorsement*)

Condition

The condition of this recognizance is that if the said...............................

.... appears in person at and before the court

of .... for the [county] of

.... on such date and at such

time and place as may be notified to him by the proper officer

of the court and there surrenders himself into custody and takes

his trial upon any indictment preferred against him, then this

recognizance shall be void, but otherwise shall remain in full

force.

(1) The recognizance may be taken by the Registrar of the Criminal Division of the Court
of Appeal, a Justice of the Peace, the clerk of a magistrates' court or a member of a police
force of or above the rank of inspector or in charge of a police station.

R.4(4)

FORM 11

CRIMINAL APPEAL ACT 1968

Certificate by Registrar of conditions of bail

I hereby certify that the court has granted bail and has fixed

the amount of the recognizance to be entered into by.............................

....

detained in .... at the sum

of .... and .... suret   in ....

[each] conditioned for the appearance of the said.................................

.... before the Criminal Division of the Court of

Appeal, unless the court otherwise orders, at each and every

hearing of his appeal and at the final determination thereof [*or*

at and before the court of .... for the [county]

of .... on such date and at such time and place

as may be notified to him by the proper officer of the court to

stand his trial upon any indictment preferred against him].*

Signed..

Registrar of the Criminal Division
of the Court of Appeal.

*Add, in the case of the appellant, any other conditions specified by the court.

FORM 12 R.4(8)

CRIMINAL APPEAL ACT 1968

Certificate of Registrar that all recognizances taken

I hereby certify that the recognizances of the sureties of

.... detained in ....

have been taken.

Signed..

Registrar of the Criminal Division
of the Court of Appeal.

Date

FORM 13

CRIMINAL APPEAL ACT 1968

Witness Order

R. v. .... (Appellant)

To .... of ....

On the application of the appellant/prosecutor the Criminal Division of the Court of Appeal has ordered you to attend for examination as a witness upon the appeal of the appellant:

You are therefore hereby ordered to attend before [the said court] on the .... day of ...., 19 , at the hour of .... in the .... noon to give evidence [and to produce the following document[s] or thing[s]]:

Dated the .... day of ...., 19 .

Signed..

Registrar of the Criminal Division
of the Court of Appeal.

FORM 14   R.10

CRIMINAL APPEAL ACT 1968

Notice of abandonment of proceedings

To the Registrar,
Criminal Appeal Office,
Royal Courts of Justice,
Strand,
London, W.C.2.

Full names of appellant...

Criminal appeal reference number........................... ....

The appellant hereby abandons

*Delete one
or other
alternative.

*all proceedings in the Criminal Division of the Court of Appeal

*the following proceedings in the Criminal Division of the
Court of Appeal, namely,—

Signed..

Date ....

Notes

1. Where an appeal or application for leave to appeal is abandoned, the appeal or application is treated as having been dismissed or refused by the Court of Appeal.

2. If the appellant wishes to abandon several proceedings in the Court of Appeal for which there are more than one criminal appeal reference number, a separate notice of abandonment should be given in respect of each reference number.

3. The notice may be signed by, or on behalf of, the appellant.

R.12   FORM 15

CRIMINAL APPEAL ACT 1968

Application for determination by Court of Appeal

To the Registrar,
Criminal Appeal Office,
Royal Courts of Justice,
Strand,
London, W.C.2.[1]

Full names of appellant...

Criminal appeal reference number...

Whereas the appellant's application for [2]—

    (*a*) extension of the time within which notice of appeal/leave to appeal may be given;

    (*b*) leave to appeal;

    (*c*) bail;

    (*d*) leave to be present in court at the hearing of—
        (i) the application for leave to appeal
        (ii) the appeal;

    (*e*) a witness order,

has been refused by a single judge, the appellant applies to have such of the foregoing applications as are specified below[3] determined by the Criminal Division of the Court of Appeal[4]—

    (*a*) extension of the time within which notice of appeal/leave to appeal may be given;

    (*b*) leave to appeal;

    (*c*) leave to be present in court at the hearing of—
        (i) the application for leave to appeal
        (ii) the appeal;

    (*d*) bail;

    (*e*) a witness order.

Signed[5] ....

Date ....

(1) This form must be sent to the Registrar within fourteen days from the date on which notice of the refusal of the application by the single judge was served on the appellant by the Registrar, or such longer period as the judge may have fixed.

(2) Cross out all except the applications which have been refused.

(3) Cross out all except the application(s) which the appellant wishes to have determined by the Court of Appeal.

(4) If the appellant wishes to submit to the Court of Appeal any arguments not mentioned in the applications refused by the single judge, they should be set out overleaf.

(5) The notice must be signed by, or on behalf of, the appellant.

Page 2

Additional reasons

FORM 16 R.14

CRIMINAL APPEAL ACT 1968

Warrant directing conveyance of appellant to hospital

To the Governor and prison officers of..

and to the Managers of the hospital of..

Whereas .... an appellant in the Criminal Division of the Court of Appeal who is subject to a hospital order has been admitted to bail pending his appeal:

And whereas the Court has determined that the appeal be dismissed (*or as the case may be*):

You, the said prison officers, are hereby directed to convey the appellant to a place of safety pending his admission to the hospital

of.. :

And you, the Governor, Managers or other person having charge of the place of safety to which the appellant has been conveyed, to detain him pending his admission to the said hospital:

And you, the Managers of the said hospital and any person authorised in writing by you, to convey the appellant from the place of safety to the said hospital.

Signed..

Date

R.23(1)

FORM 17

CRIMINAL APPEAL ACT 1968

*Notice of application for leave to appeal to the
House of Lords*

To the Registrar,
Criminal Appeal Office,
Royal Courts of Justice,
Strand,
London, W.C.2.

Full names of the defendant...

Criminal appeal reference number...

Date of decision of the Criminal Division of the Court of Appeal

....

Name and address of place at which defendant detained or, if not

detained, defendant's address...

....

....

The defendant/prosecutor will apply to the Court of Appeal

*Delete
if
inapplicable

*to certify that a point of law of general public importance is
involved in the decision of the Court of Appeal

and if the court so certifies

*for leave to appeal to the House of Lords against the decision
of the Court of Appeal

*to extend the time within which an application to the court or
the House of Lords for leave to appeal to the House of Lords
may be made

*to be given leave to be present on the hearing of the appeal or
any proceedings preliminary or incidental thereto

*to be admitted to bail pending the appeal.

Grounds of appeal or application.

Signed...

Date ....

Notes

1. This form should be sent to the Registrar within fourteen days from the decision of the
Court of Appeal. This period may, on the application of a defendant, be extended. In the
case of such an application the reasons for the delay should be explained.

2. In the case of an application for leave to appeal state the point involved in the decision of
the Court of Appeal which the appellant wishes the court to certify as a point of law of general
public importance.

FORM 18   R.23(3)

CRIMINAL APPEAL ACT 1968

*Recognizance of defendant on appeal to
House of Lords*

I, ... (hereinafter called the defendant) acknowledge that I owe to our Sovereign Lady The Queen the sum of ...., payment thereof to be enforced against me by due process of law if I fail to comply with the condition[s] endorsed hereon[1].

Signed..

Address at which ....

defendant proposes ....

to reside pending ....

appeal: ....

Taken before me the .... day of ...., 19 ,

at...

Signed..

Office[1]...

(*Endorsement*)

Condition[s]

The condition[s] of this recognizance is [are] that if the defendant, unless the House of Lords otherwise directs, surrenders himself to such person and at such time and place as may be directed by the Criminal Division of the Court of Appeal, then this recognizance shall be void, but otherwise shall remain in full force[2].

(1) The recognizance can be taken by the Registrar of the Criminal Division of the Court of Appeal, a Justice of the Peace, the clerk of a magistrates' court, a member of a police force of or above the rank of inspector or in charge of a police station, or the person having custody of the defendant.

(2) Conditions appearing to the court to be likely to result in the defendant's appearance at the time and place required, or to be necessary in the interests of justice or for the prevention of crime may be added.

R.23(3)

FORM 19

CRIMINAL APPEAL ACT 1968

Recognizance of defendant's surety on appeal to
House of Lords

I,.. acknowledge that I owe

to our Sovereign Lady The Queen the sum of ....,

payment thereof to be enforced against me by due process of law

if .... (*insert name of principal*)

fails to comply with the condition endorsed hereon.

Signed...

Address ....

....

....

....

Taken before me the .... day of ...., 19 ,

at..

Signed..

Office[1] ....

(*Endorsement*)

Condition

The condition of this recognizance is that if the said............................

...., unless the House of Lords otherwise

directs, surrenders himself to such person and at such time and

place as may be directed by the Criminal Division of the Court of

Appeal, then this recognizance shall be void, but otherwise shall

remain in full force.

(1) The recognizance may be taken by the Registrar of the Criminal Division of the Court of
Appeal, a Justice of the Peace, the clerk of a magistrates' court or a member of a police force
of or above the rank of inspector or in charge of a police station.

SCHEDULE 2
Rule 26

RULES REVOKED

Rules	References
The Criminal Appeal Rules 1908	S.R. & O. 1908/227 (Rev. V, p. 352: 1908, p. 239).
The Criminal Appeal Rules 1908, Additional Rule dated 27th March 1908	S.R. & O. 1908/277 (Rev. V, p. 400: 1908, p. 291).
The Criminal Appeal Rules 1958	S.I. 1958/652 (1958 I, p. 396).
The Criminal Appeal Rules 1960	S.I. 1960/1260 (1960 I, p. 862).
The Criminal Appeal (No. 2) Rules 1960	S.I. 1960/2325 (1960 I, p. 879).
The Criminal Appeal Rules 1964	S.I. 1964/1211 (1964 II, p. 2800).
The Criminal Appeal Rules 1967	S.I. 1967/1811 (1967 III, p. 4838).

EXPLANATORY NOTE
(This Note is not part of the Rules.)

These Rules make fresh provision, in place of the Criminal Appeal Rules 1908 as amended which are hereby revoked, for regulating the practice and procedure of the Criminal Division of the Court of Appeal and for the recording of proceedings in courts of assize and quarter sessions and the supply and verification of transcripts of the record of such proceedings.

STATUTORY INSTRUMENTS

1968 No. 1263

TERMS AND CONDITIONS OF EMPLOYMENT

The Redundancy Fund (Advances out of the National Loans Fund) (No. 2) Order 1968

Laid before Parliament in draft

Made - - - -	*2nd August* 1968
Coming into Operation	16th *August* 1968

The Secretary of State with the consent of the Treasury in exercise of her powers under section 35(2) of the Redundancy Payments Act 1965(a) and of all other powers enabling her in that behalf hereby makes the following Order, a draft of which has been laid before Parliament and approved by a resolution of each House of Parliament.

1.—(1) This Order may be cited as the Redundancy Fund (Advances out of the National Loans Fund) (No. 2) Order 1968 and shall come into operation on 16th August 1968.

(2) The Redundancy Fund (Advances out of the National Loans Fund) Order 1968(b) is hereby revoked.

2. The Interpretation Act 1889(c) shall apply to the interpretation of this Order as it applies to the interpretation of an Act of Parliament, and as if this Order and the Order hereby revoked were Acts of Parliament.

3. The aggregate amount outstanding at any time during the period of two years beginning on 16th August 1968 by way of principal in respect of sums advanced under the said section 35 out of the National Loans Fund for the purposes of the Redundancy Fund shall not exceed £20 million.

29th July 1968.

Barbara Castle,
First Secretary of State and Secretary of State
for Employment and Productivity.

We consent.

Harry Gourlay,
B. K. O'Malley,
Two of the Lords Commissioners of Her
Majesty's Treasury.

2nd August 1968.

(a) 1965 c. 62.   (b) S.I. 1968/599 (1968 I, p. 1368).   (c) 1889 c. 63.

EXPLANATORY NOTE

(This Note is not part of the Order.)

This Order increases to £20 million the aggregate amount that may be outstanding at any time during the period of two years beginning on 16th August 1968 by way of principal in respect of sums advanced out of the National Loans Fund for the purposes of the Redundancy Fund, and revokes the Redundancy Fund (Advances out of the National Loans Fund) Order 1968 which increased the said aggregate amount from £12 million to £15 million for a period of one year beginning on 25th April 1968.

STATUTORY INSTRUMENTS

1968 No. 1264

TERMS AND CONDITIONS OF EMPLOYMENT

The Redundancy Fund Increase of Contributions Order 1968

Laid before Parliament in draft

Made - - - - 2nd August 1968

Coming into Operation 2nd September 1968

The Secretary of State with the consent of the Treasury in exercise of her powers under section 27(3) of the Redundancy Payments Act 1965(a) and of all other powers enabling her in that behalf hereby makes the following Order, a draft of which has been laid before Parliament and approved by a resolution of each House of Parliament.

1.—(1) This Order may be cited as the Redundancy Fund Increase of Contributions Order 1968 and shall come into operation on the 2nd September 1968.

(2) The Redundancy Fund Contributions Order 1966(b) is hereby revoked.

2. The Interpretation Act 1889(c) shall apply to the interpretation of this Order as it applies to the interpretation of an Act of Parliament, and as if this Order and the Order hereby revoked were Acts of Parliament.

3. In respect of any contribution week beginning on or after 2nd September 1968 section 27(2) of the Redundancy Payments Act 1965 shall have effect as if for the sums therein specified there were substituted respectively the sum of one shilling and threepence in the case of a man and of sevenpence in the case of a woman.

29th July 1968.

Barbara Castle,
**First Secretary of State and Secretary of State
for Employment and Productivity.**

We consent.

Harry Gourlay,

B. K. O'Malley,

Two of the Lords Commissioners of
2nd August 1968. **Her Majesty's Treasury.**

EXPLANATORY NOTE

(This Note is not part of the Order.)

This Order which comes into operation on 2nd September 1968 increases the weekly redundancy fund contributions from tenpence to one shilling and threepence in the case of a man and from fivepence to sevenpence in the case of a woman.

(a) 1965 c. 62.   (b) S.I. 1966/1461 (1966 III, p. 3961).   (c) 1889 c. 63.

STATUTORY INSTRUMENTS

1968 No. 1265

LEGAL AID AND ADVICE, ENGLAND

The Legal Aid in Criminal Proceedings (Assessment of Resources) Regulations 1968

Made - - - -	*2nd August* 1968
Laid before Parliament	*13th August* 1968
Coming into Operation	*1st October* 1968

ARRANGEMENT OF REGULATIONS

1. General.
2. Resources of persons other than applicant or legally assisted person.
3. Assessment of resources on applications for legal aid.
4. Assessment of resources for contribution orders.
5. Assessment of income.
6. Assessment of capital.
7. Disclosure of increase in resources.
8. Interpretation.
9. Citation and commencement.

In pursuance of the powers conferred upon me by section 78 of the Criminal Justice Act 1967(a), I hereby, with the consent of the Treasury, make the following Regulations:—

General

1. The resources and commitments of any person may be assessed in accordance with the provisions of these Regulations by—

    (*a*) the court empowered to make a legal aid order or a contribution order, as the case may be, in the particular case, by virtue of section 73 or 76(4) of the Act; or

    (*b*) any person entitled to sit as a member of that court; or

    (*c*) the proper officer of that court,

hereinafter referred to as "the assessor".

Resources of persons other than applicant or legally assisted person

2.—(1) In assessing the resources and commitments of any person for the purpose of deciding whether he is eligible for legal aid or should make any payment or contribution in respect of legal aid ordered or to be ordered, the assessor (without prejudice to the other provisions of these Regulations)—

    (*a*) may treat as the resources or commitments of that person any resources or commitments of his spouse unless it would in the circumstances of the case be unreasonable or impracticable for the spouse to make available his resources to that person;

    (*b*) when the application is made by or on behalf of an infant, may take into account the resources and commitments of all or any of the

---

(a) 1967 c. 80.

following persons as the assessor, having regard to the circumstances, including the age and resources of the infant, may decide—

(i) any person who under section 22 of the Ministry of Social Security Act 1966(a) is liable to maintain the infant, or would be so liable if the infant were under the age of sixteen;

(ii) any person having the care and control of the infant, not being a person having such care and control by reason of any contract or for some temporary purpose:

Provided that for the purposes of this Regulation the expression "person" shall not include the Minister of Social Security or a local authority or a fit person under the Children and Young Persons Act 1933(b).

(2) The resources of an infant shall include any sums payable under an order of the court or under any arrangement to any person for the maintenance of such infant.

Assessment of resources on applications for legal aid

3.—(1) In determining whether an applicant's means are such that he should be given legal aid under Part IV of the Act, in respect of all or part of the costs which he is likely to incur, or whether he shall be required to make a payment on account of any contribution which may be ordered under section 75(3) of the Act, the assessor shall assess, in accordance with the provisions of this Regulation, the resources of any person whose resources are to be taken into account.

(2) In making such determination, the assessor shall consider any statement of means submitted by any person and shall have regard to the costs likely to be incurred by such person if legal aid is not ordered and to the resources immediately available to such person at the date of the application which could, and ought reasonably to, be used to meet such costs, after such person has provided for all necessary commitments.

(3) In assessing the resources available to such person, the assessor shall not have regard to any capital which could not be realised, or on the security of which money could not be raised, in time to enable legal representation or advice to be obtained.

(4) Where it appears desirable in the interests of justice to make a legal aid order, such an order shall not be refused if—

(a) the applicant, or his spouse with whom he is living, is in receipt of a supplementary pension or allowance payable under the Ministry of Social Security Act 1966; or

(b) the applicant's resources at the date of the application which are immediately available do not exceed £25, or, where the applicant is married and living with his spouse, the joint resources of the applicant and his spouse which are immediately available do not exceed £40; or

(c) where the applicant is an infant, any person referred to in Regulation 2(1)(b) of these Regulations whose resources are taken into account by the assessor is in receipt of such a supplementary pension or allowance, or the resources of such person at the date of the application which are immediately available do not exceed £25, or, where such person is married and living with his spouse, the joint resources of that person and his spouse which are immediately available do not exceed £40.

(a) 1966 c. 20.   (b) 1933 c. 12.

Assessment of resources for contribution orders

4.—(1) In determining whether a legally assisted person shall be required to make a contribution under section 76 of the Act (whether in respect of the whole or part of the costs incurred) the assessor shall, in making his assessment of the resources of any person, have regard to—

(a) that person's likely income determined in accordance with Regulation 5 of these Regulations during the period of twelve months from the date of assessment;

(b) such part, if any, of that person's capital determined in accordance with Regulation 6 of these Regulations as it seems reasonable to the assessor to take into account.

(2) No legally assisted person shall be required to make a contribution as aforesaid if—

(a) he or any person referred to in Regulation 2(1) of these Regulations whose resources are taken into account by the assessor is in receipt of a supplementary pension or allowance payable under the Ministry of Social Security Act 1966; or

(b) during the period of twelve months prior to the date of assessment—

(i) the income from all sources of the legally assisted person or any person referred to in Regulation 2(1)(b) of these Regulations whose resources are taken into account by the assessor after deducting income tax and national insurance contributions was £250 or less and his capital was £25 or less;

(ii) where any of the persons referred to in sub-paragraph (b) (i) is married and living with his spouse, the joint income of that person and his spouse after the deductions referred to in sub-paragraph (b) (i) was £450 or less and their joint capital is £40 or less.

Assessment of income

5.—(1) In assessing a person's likely income, the assessor may, where appropriate, have regard to any income received by him at any time during a period between a date twelve months prior to the submission of his statement of means and the date of assessment.

(2) The income of a person from any trade or business or gainful occupation other than employment at a wage or salary shall be deemed to be the profits therefrom which will accrue during the period of twelve months from the date of assessment, and in calculating such profits the assessor may have regard to the profits of the last accounting period for which accounts have been made up.

(3) In assessing the income of any person there shall be deducted reasonable sums in respect of—

(a) the total amount of tax which it is estimated would be payable by him if his income for the period of assessment were his income for a fiscal year;

(b) his national insurance contributions for that period;

(c) expenses incurred in connection with his employment at a wage or salary;

(d) his annual outgoings in respect of accommodation including—

(i) the rent, after deducting the proceeds of sub-letting any part of the premises;

(ii) rates, repairs and insurance;

(iii) any instalments (whether of interest or capital) payable in respect of a mortgage debt or heritable security charged on the house in which he resides or on any interest therein after deducting the proceeds of sub-letting any part of the premises;

(e) the maintenance of his spouse or former spouse, children whom he is liable to maintain and his dependent relatives, whether living with him or not;

(f) any other matter for which he must, or reasonably may, provide.

(4) In assessing income from any source the assessor may disregard such amount as he considers to be reasonable to disregard, having regard to the nature of the income or to any other circumstances.

Assessment of capital

6.—(1) Subject to the provisions of this Regulation, in assessing the capital of any person there shall be included the amount or value of every resource of a capital nature belonging to him on the date of the assessment.

(2) So far as such resource does not consist of money, the amount or value thereof shall be taken to be the amount which that resource would realise if sold in the open market or, if there is only a restricted market for the resource, the amount which it would realise in that market, after deduction of any expenses incurred in the sale, or, if such amount cannot be ascertained, an amount which appears to the assessor to be reasonable.

(3) In assessing such capital, there shall be wholly disregarded—

(a) any death grant paid under the provisions of section 39 of the National Insurance Act 1965(a);

(b) any maternity grant which a woman is paid under the provisions of section 23 of the said Act;

(c) save in exceptional cases, the personal clothing of the person, the household furniture and effects of the dwelling-house occupied by him and the personal tools and equipment of his trade.

(4) If account is taken of the value of any dwelling-house in which a person resides, the amount taken into account shall not exceed one half of the amount by which the value of the dwelling-house, after deducting therefrom the amount of any incumbrances charged thereon, exceeds £3,000.

Disclosure of increase in resources

7. Before the assessor determines whether a contribution order should be made, the applicant or legally assisted person shall disclose to him any material change in his resources since submission of his statement of means.

Interpretation

8.—(1) In these Regulations—

"the Act" means the Criminal Justice Act 1967;

"applicant" and "application" are used with reference not only to an application for legal aid but also to an offer of legal aid made by a court without any such application;

(a) 1965 c. 51.

"date of assessment" means the date on which the court empowered to make the contribution order first assesses the means of the legally assisted person, or, if before such an assessment is made, the Supplementary Benefits Commission is requested to inquire into the means of such person, the date on which such request was made;

"national insurance contributions" means contributions payable under the National Health Service Contributions Act 1965(a), the National Insurance Act 1965, the National Insurance (Industrial Injuries) Act 1965(b), or any scheme made under either of the two last-mentioned Acts;

"proper officer" means the Clerk of the Parliaments, the Registrar of Criminal Appeals, the clerk of assize or of the peace or the justices' clerk (as the case may be);

"statement of means" means a statement of means submitted by an applicant for legal aid or, where the applicant is an infant, submitted by a person liable to maintain or having the care and control of the applicant.

(2) The Interpretation Act 1889(c) shall apply to the interpretation of these Regulations as it applies to the interpretation of an Act of Parliament.

(3) References in these Regulations to any enactment or subordinate instrument shall include references to such enactment or subordinate instrument as amended from time to time.

Citation and commencement

9. These Regulations may be cited as the Legal Aid in Criminal Proceedings (Assessment of Resources) Regulations 1968 and shall come into operation on 1st October 1968.

James Callaghan,
One of Her Majesty's Principal
Secretaries of State.

31st July 1968.

We consent,

B. K. O'Malley,
E. Alan Fitch,
Two of the Lords Commissioners of
Her Majesty's Treasury.

2nd August 1968.

(a) 1965 c. 54.   (b) 1965 c. 52.   (c) 1889 c. 63.

EXPLANATORY NOTE

(This Note is not part of the Regulations.)

Part IV of the Criminal Justice Act 1967 makes fresh provision for the granting of legal aid in criminal proceedings. These Regulations make provision for the assessment of the resources of any person when the court is considering whether it is proper to make a legal aid order under section 73 or a contribution order under section 76 of the Criminal Justice Act 1967. Regulation 1 lays down who may make such an assessment. Regulation 2 relates to persons (other than the applicant or legally assisted person) whose resources may be taken into consideration. Regulation 3 relates to the assessment of resources on an application for legal aid and Regulation 4 relates to the assessment of resources in connection with the question whether or not a contribution order should be made. Regulation 5 relates to the assessment of income and Regulation 6 to that of capital. Regulation 7 requires an applicant to disclose any material change in his resources which arises after he has submitted a statement of means.

STATUTORY INSTRUMENTS

1968 No. 1266

MAGISTRATES' COURTS

The Justices' Clerks (Accounts) Regulations 1968

Made - - - -	*2nd August* 1968
Coming into Operation	*1st October* 1968

In pursuance of the power conferred upon me by section 27(9) of the Justices of the Peace Act 1949(**a**), I hereby, with the concurrence of the Treasury, make the following Regulations:—

1.—(1) Regulation 1(1) of the Justices' Clerks (Accounts) Regulations 1953(**b**), as amended (**c**), shall be amended by the addition of the following sub-paragraph:—

"(*c*) all sums received by a justices' clerk in his capacity as an appropriate authority under Part IV of the Criminal Justice Act 1967(**d**).".

(2) Paragraphs (1) and (2) of Regulation 3 of the said Regulations shall be amended by the substitution for the words "by a responsible authority" of the words "by an authority acting as a responsible authority under section 27 of the Act".

(3) At the end of Regulations 5(1) and 6(1)(*a*) of the said Regulations there shall be added the words "and section 79(8) of the Criminal Justice Act 1967".

(4) Regulation 6(1)(*b*) of the said Regulations shall be amended by the substitution for the words "under the said subsection" of the words "as aforesaid".

(5) There shall be substituted for the Schedule to the said Regulations the Schedule to these Regulations.

2. These Regulations may be cited as the Justices' Clerks (Accounts) Regulations 1968 and shall come into operation on 1st October 1968.

James Callaghan,
One of Her Majesty's Principal
Secretaries of State.

31st July 1968.

We concur,

B. K. O'Malley,
E. Allan Fitch,

Two of the Lords Commissioners
of Her Majesty's Treasury.

2nd August 1968.

(**a**) 1949 c. 101.   (**b**) S.I.1953/493 (1953 I, p. 1006).
(**c**) The relevant instrument is S.I. 1965/705 (1965 I, p. 2197).   (**d**) 1967 c. 80.

SCHEDULE

RETURN OF FINES, FEES, LEGAL AID CONTRIBUTIONS AND ANY OTHER SUMS PAYABLE TO
THE SECRETARY OF STATE UNDER SECTION 27(1) OF THE JUSTICES OF THE PEACE ACT 1949
AND SECTION 79(8) OF THE CRIMINAL JUSTICE ACT 1967

Quarter Ended.................................19......   Borough of ⎫

                                       or

County of...   Petty Sessional ⎬ ....
                                         Division of ⎭

	Total amount received during quarter	Arrears outstanding at end of quarter
PART I *Fines* (other than fines required to be returned under Part II) which constitute Exchequer moneys within the meaning of section 27 of the Justices of the Peace Act 1949	£ s. d.	£ s. d.
PART II *Fines* which constitute Exchequer moneys within the meaning of section 27 of the Justices of the Peace Act 1949, but which by virtue of an appropriation in aid made by direction of the Treasury under paragraph (3) of section 2 of the Public Accounts and Charges Act 1891 are payable by the Secretary of State to the Minister of Transport		
PART III *Fines* (not constituting Exchequer moneys) payable to the Secretary of State under section 27(1) of the Justices of the Peace Act 1949, all fees and any other sums so payable £ s. d. (i) Total amount of fines and fees (ii) Sums (other than fees) payable to the Secretary of State under section 27(1)(*b*) of the Justices of the Peace Act 1949		
PART IV *Legal aid* contributions payable to the Secretary of State under section 79(8) of the Criminal Justice Act 1967		
TOTALS	*	

*NOTE.—If this total does not agree with the total of the sums remitted to the Secretary of State in respect of the quarter a letter of explanation should be sent with this Return.

SUMS REMITTED TO THE SECRETARY OF STATE IN RESPECT OF THE QUARTER			
	£	s.	d.
First payment			
Second payment			
Third payment			
TOTAL			

I certify that this Return is correct

Date... ....
                                                              Clerk to the Justices

NOTES

1. In accordance with Regulation 6 of the Justices' Clerks (Accounts) Regulations 1953, a Return in duplicate in the Form annexed must be sent to the Secretary of State not later than 21st January, 21st April, 21st July and 21st October in each year for the quarter ending at the expiration of the preceding month. The Return should be forwarded to the Finance Department, Home Office, Tolworth Tower, Surbiton, Surrey, using the prepaid labels supplied.

2. The Return *must* be made up to the end of the quarter to which it relates.

3. The Return concerns only fines, fees, legal aid contributions and other sums which are payable to the Secretary of State under section 27 of the Justices of the Peace Act 1949 and section 79(8) of the Criminal Justice Act 1967. Fines which under any enactment are payable to the Commissioners of Customs and Excise, or to any officer of theirs or person appointed by them, will continue to be so paid by justices' clerks; these fines are not payable to the Secretary of State and will therefore not be included in any Part of this Return.

4. The Return is in four Parts. Part I is for fines payable to the Secretary of State (other than fines required to be returned under Part II) which constitute Exchequer moneys within the meaning of section 27 of the Justices of the Peace Act 1949. "Exchequer moneys" is defined in section 27(10) as meaning moneys which, if section 27 had not been passed, would be paid into the Exchequer or to any Government department or person on behalf of Her Majesty by virtue of a specific provision to that effect made by or under any Act or would have been so paid but for any local or other special right or privilege of whatever origin. Fines imposed under statutes passed on or after 1st April 1953 may also constitute Exchequer moneys within the meaning of section 27 by virtue of an appropriate provision made in the particular statute.

Part II is for fines payable to the Secretary of State which constitute Exchequer moneys within the meaning of section 27 but which by virtue of an appropriation in aid made by direction of the Treasury under section 2(3) of the Public Accounts and Charges Act 1891, are payable by the Secretary of State to the Minister of Transport.

Sums paid by way of fixed penalty under section 80 of the Road Traffic Regulation Act 1967 are to be treated as if they were fines imposed on summary conviction for the offence to which they relate. The Part in which such sums should be included therefore depends on the Act creating the offence.

Part III is for other fines payable to the Secretary of State, all fees and any other sums so payable.

Part IV is for legal aid contributions payable under contribution orders made by magistrates' courts and other courts, which are payable to the Secretary of State under section 79(8) of the Criminal Justice Act 1967.

Parts I and II should show the amounts of the fines imposed; the amounts entered should not include any sums ordered to be paid as costs, damages or compensation.

5. Parts I, II and IV are divided as follows:—

(a) the total sums received by the justices' clerk during the quarter and payable to the Secretary of State;

(b) the arrears outstanding at the end of the quarter.

Part III is similarly divided as regards the total received and the arrears, but the total received is to be divided between (i) fines and fees and (ii) sums other than fees payable to the Secretary of State under section 27(1)(b) of the Justices of the Peace Act 1949 (under head (ii) there may be included sums received by the clerk in previous quarters, for example an unclaimed periodical payment).

EXPLANATORY NOTE

(This Note is not part of the Regulations.)

These Regulations amend the Justices' Clerks (Accounts) Regulations 1953 so as to provide that justices' clerks shall account for legal aid contributions under the Criminal Justice Act 1967 made by legally assisted persons to them, as the collecting authority, in the same way as they account for other sums paid to them and governed by those Regulations.

STATUTORY INSTRUMENTS

1968 No. 1271 (S. 134)

CLEAN AIR

The Clean Air (Measurement of Grit and Dust) (Scotland) Regulations 1968

Made - - - -	*1st August* 1968
Laid before Parliament	*15th August* 1968
Coming into Operation	*2nd September* 1968

In exercise of the powers conferred on me by section 7(2) as read with section 34(1) of the Clean Air Act 1956(a) and of all other powers enabling me in that behalf, I hereby make the following regulations:—

1. These regulations may be cited as the Clean Air (Measurement of Grit and Dust) (Scotland) Regulations 1968 and shall come into operation on 2nd September 1968.

2. The Interpretation Act 1889(b) applies for the interpretation of these regulations as it applies for the interpretation of an Act of Parliament.

3. Where, by virtue of a direction served by the local authority under section 7(1) of the Clean Air Act 1956, the provisions of subsection (2) of that section apply to a furnace, the occupier of the building in which the furnace is situated shall comply with the requirements set out in the schedule hereto.

William Ross,
One of Her Majesty's Principal
Secretaries of State.

St. Andrew's House,
Edinburgh, 1.
1st August 1968.

SCHEDULE

ADAPTATIONS TO CHIMNEYS AND PROVISION AND MAINTENANCE OF APPARATUS

1.—(1) Where the occupier receives not less than 6 weeks' notice in writing from the local authority requiring adaptations to the chimney serving a furnace and the provision of apparatus for the purpose of making and recording the measurements of grit and dust emitted from the furnace, he shall, within the period specified in the notice, make such adaptations to the chimney as are necessary for the making and recording of such measurements by one of the methods described in British Standard 3405, 1961, published by the British Standards Institution, and provide the apparatus therein mentioned.

(2) All apparatus provided for the purpose of this paragraph shall be maintained in good working order.

(a) 1956 c. 52.   (b) 1889 c. 63.

MAKING AND RECORDING MEASUREMENTS

2.—(1) When the requirements of paragraph 1 of this Schedule have been complied with the occupier, on receiving not less than 28 days' notice in writing from the local authority requiring him to make and record measurements of grit and dust emitted from a furnace, shall within the period specified in the notice, make and record such measurements in accordance with the method detailed in pages 13 to 26 of the publication "Measurement of Solids in Flue Gases" by P.G.W. Hawksley, S. Badzioch and J.H. Blackett, published in 1961 by the British Coal Utilisation Research Association.

(2) Before making any measurements the occupier shall give to the local authority not less than 48 hours' notice in writing of the date on which and the time at which he proposes to commence to do so.

(3) The occupier shall, in relation to each chimney to which these regulations apply, keep a written record containing the following particulars—

(a) the date on which any measurements were made;

(b) the number of furnaces discharging into the chimney on that date;

(c) the measurements in terms of pounds per hour of grit and dust emitted, and in the case of solid fuel fired boilers the percentage of grit contained in the solids emitted;

and shall transmit a copy of such particulars to the local authority within 7 days from the making of the measurements in respect of which the particulars are recorded.

(4) A notice served for the purpose of this paragraph may require the making of measurements from time to time or at stated intervals:

Provided that an occupier shall not be required by the notice to make measurements in respect of any one chimney more than once in any period of 3 months except to the extent that the local authority have reasonable cause to believe that the true level of emission of grit and dust cannot be determined without the making of more frequent measurements.

3. Anything requried to be done by an occupier under the provisions of this schedule may be done on his behalf by any other person.

EXPLANATORY NOTE

(*This Note is not part of the Regulations.*)

Under Section 7 of the Clean Air Act 1956 occupiers of buildings in which certain furnaces are situated may be directed by the local authority to make and record measurements of the grit and dust emitted from the furnace in accordance with requirements prescribed by the Secretary of State. These Regulations prescribe the requirements to be observed.

British Standard 3405, 1961, may be obtained from British Standards Institution, British Standards House, 2 Park Street, London, W.1, and "Measurements of Solids in Flue Gases" may be obtained from the British Coal Utilisation Research Association, Randalls Road, Leatherhead, Surrey.

STATUTORY INSTRUMENTS

1968 No. 1275

INCOME TAX

The Capital Allowances (Relevant Grants) Order 1968

Made - - - *29th July* 1968

Whereas it appears to the Treasury that the grants specified in this Order are made towards expenditure and for purposes corresponding respectively to expenditure towards which and purposes for which grants may be made in pursuance of schemes under Sections 1 and 6 of the White Fish and Herring Industries Act 1953(**a**) as amended by Sections 3 and 37 of the Sea Fish Industry Act 1962(**b**) (being enactments amended by Section 28 of the Industrial Development Act 1966)(**c**) :

Now, therefore, the Treasury in pursuance of powers conferred on them by Section 83(4) of the Capital Allowances Act 1968(**d**) hereby make the following Order :—

1. The following grants are hereby declared to be relevant for the purposes of the withholding or withdrawal of investment and initial allowances, that is to say—

(*a*) any grant made by the Ministry of Agriculture for Northern Ireland in respect of any expenditure incurred on or after 17th Jaunary 1966 or of any expenditure incurred before that date so far as it consists of a sum paid after that date in respect of the purchase of new fishing boats, the improvement of fishing boats, or the purchase and installation of new engines for fishing boats ; and

(*b*) any grant made under the Fishing Vessels (Grants) Act (Northern Ireland) 1967(**e**).

2. This Order may be cited as the Capital Allowances (Relevant Grants) Order 1968.

Joseph Harper,

E. Alan Fitch,
Two of the Lords Commissioners
of Her Majesty's Treasury.

29th July 1968.

(**a**) 1953 c. 17. (**b**) 1962 c. 31.
(**c**) 1966 c. 34. (**d**) 1968 c. 3.
(**e**) 1967 c. 8 (N.I.).

EXPLANATORY NOTE

(This Note is not part of the Order.)

Section 83(4) of the Capital Allowances Act 1968 re-enacts Section 35(3) of the Finance Act 1966 which entitles the Treasury to prescribe grants as "relevant" with the consequence that expenditure in respect of which the grant is paid will be disqualified from investment and initial allowances for tax purposes. This instrument so prescribes grants under the Fishing Vessels (Grants) Act (Northern Ireland) 1967 and grants made under the extra statutory scheme which preceded that Act in respect of payments made on or after 17th January 1966 towards the cost of acquisition and improvement of fishing vessels.

STATUTORY INSTRUMENTS

1968 No. 1280

PURCHASE TAX

The Temporary Importation (Printed Forms) Regulations 1968

Made - - - -	*9th August* 1968
Laid before Parliament	*15th August* 1968
Coming into Operation	*19th August* 1968

The Commissioners of Customs and Excise in pursuance of the powers conferred on them by section 40 of the Customs and Excise Act 1952(**a**) as applied by section 25(1) of the Purchase Tax Act 1963(**b**) and all other powers enabling them in that behalf, hereby make the following Regulations : —

1. If any goods being printed forms are imported into the United Kingdom and the importer satisfies the Commissioners—

(*a*) that the forms—

(i) are owned abroad ;

(ii) have been supplied free of charge to the importer solely for the purpose of recording information required by the owner ; and

(iii) are intended to be re-exported, and

(*b*) that the importer will comply with these Regulations and any conditions which the Commissioners may impose in respect of the forms,

the forms may be delivered without payment of any purchase tax chargeable thereon ; and purchase tax shall continue not to be payable if these Regulations and the conditions imposed by the Commissioners and any other conditions which they may thereafter impose with respect to the forms shall continue to be complied with.

2. The importer shall at the time of importation—

(*a*) produce the forms to the officer for examination,

(*b*) deposit in accordance with the officer's directions such sums of money or other security as the officer may require to secure the purchase tax and compliance with these Regulations and any conditions imposed by the Commissioners.

3. (*a*) While in the United Kingdom the forms shall not be (or be offered to be) sold, and shall, if the officer so requires, be produced to him for inspection.

(*b*) The importer shall keep such records relating to the forms as the officer may require ; and shall furnish him with such information and produce to him such records and other documents relating to the forms and their use as the officer may require.

(*c*) The forms shall be re-exported from the United Kingdom within twelve months from the date of their importation or within such other period as the Commissioners may allow ; and the importer shall furnish proof of such re-exportation if the officer so requires.

(**a**) 1952 c. 44.   (**b**) 1963 c. 9.

Provided that the Commissioners may, subject to such conditions as they may see fit to impose, permit the destruction of the forms in lieu of re-exportation provided that the importer makes prior application to them for such permission.

4. (*a*) In these Regulations—

" officer " means the proper officer of customs and excise ;

" owner " includes any person beneficially interested in the forms, and cognate expressions shall be construed accordingly ;

" owned abroad " means owned by a person who in the opinion of the Commissioners is principally resident abroad and whose principal place of business is abroad or by a corporation incorporated abroad whose principal place of business is abroad ;

(*b*) The Interpretation Act 1889(a) shall apply for the interpretation of these Regulations as it applies for the interpretation of an Act of Parliament.

5. These Regulations may be cited as the Temporary Importation (Printed Forms) Regulations 1968, and shall come into operation on the 19th August 1968.

K. B. Pepper,
Commissioner of Customs and Excise.

9th August 1968.
King's Beam House,
Mark Lane,
London, E.C.3.

EXPLANATORY NOTE
(*This Note is not part of the Order.*)

These Regulations provide for the admission without payment of purchase tax of printed forms which are temporarily imported for completion and return abroad.

(**a**) 1889 c. 63.

STATUTORY INSTRUMENTS

1968 No. 1281

EDUCATION, ENGLAND AND WALES

LOCAL GOVERNMENT, ENGLAND AND WALES

The Schools (Amendment) Regulations 1968

Made - - -	*7th August* 1968
Laid before Parliament	*19th August* 1968
Coming into Operation	*1st September* 1968

The Secretary of State for Education and Science, in exercise of the powers conferred upon him by section 33 of the Education Act 1944(a), as amended by the Secretary of State for Education and Science Order 1964(b), and by section 3(4) of the Local Government Act 1958(c), hereby makes the following regulations:—

Citation, commencement and interpretation

1.—(1) These regulations may be cited as the Schools (Amendment) Regulations 1968 and shall come into operation on 1st September 1968.

(2) The Interpretation Act 1889(d) shall apply for the interpretation of these regulations as it applies for the interpretation of an Act of Parliament.

Employment of unqualified persons

2. Subject to regulation 3, the provisions of the Schools Regulations 1959(e) as amended (f) (in these regulations called " the principal regulations ") relating to the employment of persons who are not qualified teachers shall have effect subject to the following amendments:—

(a) in regulation 17(1) for the expression " temporary assistant teacher " there shall be substituted the expression " student teacher " and for the reference to Part I of the schedule to the Training of Teachers (Local Education Authorities) Regulations 1959(g) there shall be substituted a reference to paragraph 3 of schedule 2 to the Training of Teachers Regulations 1967(h);

(a) 1944 c. 31.
(b) S.I. 1964/490 (1964 I, p. 800).
(c) 1958 c. 55.
(d) 1889 c. 63.
(e) S.I. 1959/364 (1959 I, p. 1584).
(f) The relevant amending instrument is S.I. 1964/1311 (1964 II, p. 2984).
(g) S.I. 1959/395 (1959 I, p. 1590).
(h) S.I. 1967/792 (1967 II, p. 2319).

(b) for regulation 18 there shall be substituted—

" 18. A person who is not a qualified teacher may be employed to give instruction in any art or skill or in any subject or group of subjects (including any form of vocational training) the teaching of which requires special qualifications or experience if, in the case of each such appointment,—

(a) he satisfies the authority as to his qualifications or, as the case may be, experience and as to his health and physical capacity for teaching; and

(b) no qualified teacher is available to give the instruction.";

(c) in paragraph 1 of schedule II, for the expression " temporary assistant teacher " there shall be substituted the expression " student teacher "; and

(d) in paragraph 3(a) of that schedule, for the expression " an occasional teacher " there shall be substituted the words " a person employed by virtue of regulation 18 ".

Transitory provisions

3. Nothing in paragraph (a) or (b) of regulation 2 shall prevent the employment during the two years ending on 31st August 1970—

(a) as a temporary assistant teacher in accordance with regulation 17 of the principal regulations, of a person who was so employed at any time before 1st September 1968;

(b) as an occasional teacher in accordance with regulation 18 of the principal regulations, of a person who was so employed at any time before 1st September 1968;

and accordingly paragraphs (c) and (d) of regulation 2 shall not apply in the case of any such person.

Probationary service

4.—(1) In respect of any teacher first employed after 31st August 1968 paragraph 2(a) of schedule II to the principal regulations shall have effect subject to—

(a) the substitution for the words " of one year " of the words " which in the case of a full-time teacher who has satisfactorily completed a course of training specified in schedule I shall be one year and in the case of any other teacher shall be two years "; and

(b) the insertion after the words " more than one year " of the words " or as the case may be two years ".

(2) In paragraph 2(c) of the schedule after the word " not " there shall be inserted the words " without the approval of the Secretary of State " and at the end there shall be added " and in the case of any teacher whose further employment is approved by the Secretary of State under this subparagraph the preceding provisions of this paragraph shall apply to the initial period of such further employment as if it were the initial period of his service as a qualified teacher."

Dismissal and exclusion of teachers

5. For paragraphs 4 and 5 of schedule II to the principal regulations there shall be substituted—

"Restriction on employment of teachers

4. A person who is on grounds of misconduct or conviction of a criminal offence determined by the Secretary of State to be unsuitable for employ-

ment as a teacher or suitable for employment as such only to a limited extent, shall not be employed as a teacher or, as the case may be, shall be employed as such only to the extent determined by the Secretary of State.

Reporting of termination of employment of teachers

5. If the engagement of a teacher is terminated whether by dismissal or resignation on account of misconduct or conviction of a criminal offence, the facts shall be reported to the Secretary of State."

Application to special schools

6. The references to the provisions of regulations 17 and 18 of, and of the Second Schedule to, the principal regulations which are contained in regulation 16 of the Handicapped Pupils and Special Schools Regulations 1959(a) as amended (b) shall be construed as references to those provisions as amended by these regulations.

Given under the Official Seal of the Secretary of State for Education and Science on 7th August 1968.

Edward Short,

(L.S.) Secretary of State for Education and Science.

EXPLANATORY NOTE
(This Note is not part of the Regulations.)

These provisions amend the regulations relating to the employment as teachers in county and voluntary schools and special schools of persons who are not qualified teachers. They permit the employment of certain student teachers and specialists and, subject to transitory provisions, bring to an end the provisions for the employment of temporary assistant teachers and occasional teachers. They also extend the period of probationary service for certain teachers and make drafting amendments to the provisions relating to the dismissal and exclusion of teachers.

(a) S.I. 1959/365 (1959 I, p. 1024).
(b) The amending Regulations are not relevant to the subject matter of these Regulations.

STATUTORY INSTRUMENTS

1968 No. 1283

AGRICULTURE

AGRICULTURAL GRANTS, GOODS AND SERVICES

The Small Farm (Business Management) Scheme 1968

Laid before Parliament in draft

Made - - - *7th August* 1968

Coming into operation 1st *September* 1968

The Minister of Agriculture, Fisheries and Food, in pursuance of sections 1, 4 and 6 of the Agriculture (Small Farmers) Act 1959(a) and all other powers enabling him in that behalf, with the approval of the Treasury, hereby makes the following scheme, a draft of which has been laid before Parliament and approved by resolution of each House of Parliament :—

Citation, extent and commencement

1. This scheme, which may be cited as the Small Farm (Business Management) Scheme 1968, shall apply to England and Wales and Northern Ireland and shall come into operation on 1st September 1968.

Interpretation

2.—(1) In this scheme, unless the context otherwise requires—

"the Act" means the Agriculture (Small Farmers) Act 1959 ;

"approved" means approved by the Minister ;

"basic programme" means any approved programme other than a complete programme ;

"complete programme" means such programme, expressly approved as a complete programme, as is in the opinion of the Minister best calculated to increase the efficiency of the business to which it relates, namely a business for which such adequate records have been kept before the day on which the programme is submitted to the Minister for approval as to make it unlikely in his opinion that the programme will subsequently require substantial modification in the light of records kept or disclosed after that day ;

"the Minister" means the Minister of Agriculture, Fisheries and Food ;

(a) 1959 c. 12.

"programme" means a programme of not less than three years' duration for increasing the efficiency of a small farm business, comprised of yearly plans for each of three consecutive specified years, every such plan containing a requirement that such farm business records, specified in the programme, shall be kept as appear to the Minister to be appropriate having regard to all the circumstances of the business ;

"the scheme of 1965" means the Small Farm (Business Management) Scheme 1965(**a**) ;

"small farm business" means a trade or business consisting in, or such part of any trade or business as consists in, the carrying out of agricultural operations on land comprised in the business, where the amount of that land under crops or grass, excluding any rough grazing land, does not exceed 150 acres ;

"small farm business to which this scheme applies" has the meaning assigned to it by paragraph 3 of this scheme ;

"the small farmer schemes" means the Small Farmer (England and Wales and Northern Ireland) Scheme 1959(**b**) and the Small Farmer (England and Wales and Northern Ireland) Scheme 1962(**c**).

(2) The Interpretation Act 1889(**d**) shall apply to the interpretation of this scheme as it applies to the interpretation of an Act of Parliament.

Classes of small farm business to which this scheme applies

3. This scheme applies to a small farm business where the amount of land under crops or grass, excluding any rough grazing land, comprised in the business is not less than 20 acres, and the standard labour requirements of the business calculated in accordance with the Schedule to this scheme are not less than 250 standard man-days a year.

Grants payable for approved programmes

4. Subject to the provisions of this scheme, where the person carrying on a small farm business to which this scheme applies has, within the period commencing with 1st September 1968 and ending with 31st August 1969, submitted to the Minister a programme in respect of the business, and the Minister has approved the programme for the purposes of the scheme, the Minister may in connection with the carrying out of the programme pay grants in respect of the general purposes of the farm business to the person for the time being carrying on the business.

Restrictions on approval of programmes

5.—(1) No programme shall be approved under this scheme in relation to a small farm business unless on the day on which the programme is submitted to the Minister for approval—

(*a*) the amount of land under crops or grass, excluding any rough grazing land, comprised in the business is not more than 125 acres, and

---

(**a**) S.I. 1965/1554 (1965 II, p. 4534).   (**b**) S.I. 1959/474 (1959 I, p. 200).
(**c**) S.I. 1962/1690 (1962 II, p. 2098).   (**d**) 1889 c. 63.

(*b*) the standard labour requirements of the business calculated in accordance with the Schedule to this scheme are not more than 600 standard man-days a year.

(2) Where any person carrying on a small farm business has received a grant in respect of that business under section 65 of the Agriculture Act 1967(**a**) (which enables grants to be made for keeping farm business records)—

(*a*) a programme in respect of that business may not be approved under this scheme unless it is a complete programme, and

(*b*) paragraph 7(4) of this scheme shall not apply to such a programme.

Circumstances in which grant may be paid

6.—(1) A grant under this scheme may be paid on the completion to the satisfaction of the Minister of each of the three yearly plans comprised in an approved programme.

(2) The maximum period in respect of which such a grant may be paid shall be three years from the date of the commencement of the year specified in the programme for the carrying out of the plan to which the grant relates, but without prejudice to section 5 of the Act (which relates to the revocation of programmes where there has been unreasonable delay, etc.) it shall nevertheless be a condition of payment of grant under this scheme that the plan to which the grant relates shall be completed within two years of the said date :

Provided that in cases where failure to complete the plan within the said period of two years has been caused mainly by factors outside the control of the person carrying on the business the Minister may extend the time for completion up to a maximum of one additional year.

Amounts of grants

7.—(1) The amounts of grant payable in connection with the carrying out of a basic programme shall be as follows :—

On completion of the first yearly plan ...	£50, plus £2 per acre, up to a maximum of 100 acres.
On completion of the second yearly plan ...	£50.
On completion of the third yearly plan ...	£50.

(2) The amounts of grant payable in connection with the carrying out of a complete programme shall be as follows :—

On completion of the first yearly plan ...	£50, plus £2 per acre, up to a maximum of 100 acres.
On completion of the second yearly plan ...	£50, plus £3 10s. per acre, up to a maximum of 100 acres.
On completion of the third yearly plan ...	£50, plus £3 per acre, up to a maximum of 100 acres.

(a) 1967 c. 22.

(3) Where a yearly plan comprised in a basic programme has been completed to the satisfaction of the Minister, and he has received such extracts from the records required to be kept in accordance with that plan as he is entitled to receive under this scheme, if he is satisfied that the next following yearly plan comprised in the programme, either unmodified, or having been modified in accordance with this scheme in such a way as has been agreed between him and the person carrying on the business, is best calculated to increase the efficiency of the business, having regard to the information obtained from such records, then on completion of that following yearly plan the Minister may pay grant at the rate which would have been payable if that plan had been comprised in a complete programme.

(4) Where a person has failed to complete a plan relating to the second or third year of a programme but has carried out such parts of the plan as require the keeping of records, the Minister may nevertheless pay him grant at the appropriate rate for a plan forming part of a basic programme

(5)(a) In this paragraph "per acre", in relation to any yearly plan, means per acre of the average amount of land under crops or grass, excluding any rough grazing land, comprised in the small farm business to the satisfaction of the Minister during the year to which the plan relates, fractions of an acre being rounded down to the nearest quarter of an acre and all land in respect of which grant has been paid by virtue of a scheme made under section 2 of the Agriculture and Horticulture Act 1964(a) being disregarded.

(b) Any increase or decrease in the amount of land under crops or grass, excluding any rough grazing land, comprised in the business shall at once be notified to the Minister by the person carrying on the business.

Supplementary conditions

8. It shall be a condition of the making of a payment to any person under this scheme that—

(a) there shall be an application in writing, in such form as the Minister may require, for the Minister's approval of any programme proposed to be carried out;

(b) there shall be no substantial modification of a programme except with the consent of the Minister on the application of the person for the time being carrying on the small farm business to which the programme relates;

(c) subject to the provisions of paragraphs 6(2) and 7(4) hereof the programme shall be properly carried out without any avoidable delay;

(d) any person authorised by the Minister in that behalf shall be given reasonable facilities to inspect any land, livestock, works or operations to which the programme relates and shall be given in respect of the programme all such information as the Minister may reasonably require for the purposes of the scheme;

(e) such records of the business as relate to the duration of the programme or to the three preceding years shall on reasonable notice be produced to a person authorised by the Minister, and extracts from records kept in pursuance of a requirement in the programme shall be submitted to the Minister in such form and at such times as he may require.

(a) 1964 c. 28.

Abatement where grant previously paid

9.—(1) Subject to the following provisions of this paragraph, it shall be a condition of the making of a payment to a person under this scheme that the sum of the grants payable under the foregoing provisions of this scheme in connection with the carrying out of the programme to which the payment relates shall be reduced by—

(*a*) the aggregate of all farm business grants paid to him under the small farmer schemes or either of them ;

(*b*) the aggregate of all field husbandry grants paid to him under the small farmer schemes or either of them in respect of any of the land comprised in the small farm business to which the programme relates ;

(*c*) the aggregate of the residual values of all field husbandry grants paid under the small farmer schemes or either of them to any other person in respect of any of the land comprised in the said small farm business ; and

(*d*) the aggregate of all grants paid to him in connection with the carrying out of a programme under the scheme of 1965 or any other programme under this scheme.

(2) For the purposes of this paragraph—

(*a*) the residual value of a field husbandry grant shall be the amount of such grant reduced by 25 per cent. for each complete year in excess of 3 years between the date of the commencement of the farm business plan in respect of which the grant was payable and the date on which the person to whom grant is payable under this scheme commenced to carry on the small farm business ;

(*b*) where a field husbandry grant has been paid partly in respect of land which is comprised in the small farm business and partly in respect of other land, the grant shall be apportioned by the Minister ;

(*c*) payment of a grant to a person includes the payment of a grant which in the opinion of the Minister is substantially paid for the benefit of that person, notwithstanding that the payment is nominally made to some other person ;

(*d*) where a grant has been paid to a partnership or otherwise to persons jointly, the Minister may apportion the grant between the members of the partnership or such other persons in such manner as he thinks appropriate, having regard to their respective interests, and any part of a grant so apportioned to a person shall be deemed to have been paid to him.

Other limitations

10.—(1) No person shall receive a grant in connection with the carrying out of a programme under this scheme if at any time while he is carrying out that programme he is also carrying out a farm business plan under either of the small farmer schemes, or a programme under the scheme of 1965, or is keeping farm business records with a view to obtaining a grant under section 65 of the Agriculture Act 1967.

(2) If a person is carrying out two or more programmes under this scheme at the same time, he may receive grants in respect of only one such programme.

In Witness whereof the Official Seal of the Minister of Agriculture, Fisheries and Food is hereunto affixed on 30th July 1968.

(L.S.)   *Cledwyn Hughes,*
                          Minister of Agriculture, Fisheries and Food.

Approved on 7th August 1968.

E. Alan Fitch,
Joseph Harper,
Two of the Lords Commissioners of
Her Majesty's Treasury.

SCHEDULE

Paragraphs 3 and 5

In this schedule "business" means a trade or business consisting in, or such part of a trade or business as consists in, the carrying out of agricultural operations on land comprised in it.

1. The standard labour requirements of a business on any day shall be expressed in standard man-days calculated, except as is otherwise provided in the succeeding paragraphs, by multiplying respectively the number of standard man-days set out in the table below in relation to any kind of crop or livestock therein mentioned by the total number of acres (or other units to which the standard man-days are related in the table) of that kind of crop, or the average of the numbers of that kind of livestock, shown to the satisfaction of the Minister to be comprised in the business during the 12 months immediately preceding the date to which the calculation relates, adding together the results so obtained and increasing the total by 15 per cent.

2. Where a crop is grown for a person other than the person carrying on the business under a contract with that other person by which he carries out any part of the cultivations necessary for growing or harvesting the crop, the number of standard man-days attributable to that crop shall be reduced to such figure as the Minister considers reasonable, having regard to the proportion of the cultivations carried out by the person carrying on the business.

3. Where double cropping is practised on land comprised in the business, the area of both crops shall be included in the calculation.

4. Agisted livestock shall be deemed to be comprised in the business while they are on land comprised in the business, and not otherwise.

5. A cow of a dairy type which suckles calves shall be classified as a beef cow.

6. The number of livestock comprised in the business shall not include calves less than 7 days old, unweaned piglets, or unweaned lambs.

7. The number of pigs fattened or reared on land comprised in the business shall be the total number of pigs so fattened or reared during the 12 months immediately preceding the date to which the calculation relates.

8. The number of any kind of poultry (other than laying birds and male birds for breeding) shall be the total number of that kind of poultry kept on the land comprised in the business during the 12 months immediately preceding the date to which the calculation relates.

9. If the Minister is satisfied that by reason of special circumstances the area of crops, or of any kind of crop, or the number of livestock, or of any kind of livestock, comprised in the business during any period of 12 months mentioned in the preceding paragraphs is unrepresentative of the area or number respectively usually comprised in the business, such other area or number shall be taken as is, in the opinion of the Minister, shown by the person for the time being carrying on the business to be representative of the area or number usually comprised in the business.

TABLE

CROPS

	Standard man-days (per acre)
Wheat	2½
Barley	2½
Oats	3½
Mixed corn	3½
Rye, for threshing	3½
Rye, for grazing	1½
Arable silage	3
Beans and peas for stockfeeding	3
Potatoes, seed	20
Potatoes, ware	18
Turnips and swedes for stockfeeding	11
Sugar beet	12½
Fodder beet	12½
Mangolds	11
Rape (or Cole)	1½
Kale, for grazing	1½
Cabbage, kale (other than for grazing), savoys and kohl rabi, for stockfeeding	6
Vetches or tares	3½
Hops	100
Cider orchards	10
Orchards (other than cider)	
Seven years old and over	25
Under seven years old	10
Derelict orchards	¼
Small fruit: Under orchard trees	30
Not under orchard trees—	
Strawberries	70
Raspberries	90
Currants (black)	50
Currants (red and white)	45
Gooseberries	45
Loganberries and cultivated blackberries	80

	Standard man-days (per acre unless otherwise indicated)
Vegetables for human consumption—	
Brussels sprouts	25
Cabbage	17
Kale and sprouting broccoli	17
Cauliflower	17
Carrots	17
Parsnips	21
Turnips and swedes	21
Beetroot (red beet)	35
Broad beans	30
Peas, green for pulling	30
Peas, for vining or harvesting dry	4½
Lettuce, grown in the open	10
Tomatoes, grown in the open	50
Other vegetables (including rhubarb)	50
Hardy nursery stock	50
Bulbs and flowers in the open	100
Other crops in the open (including all crops grown for seed except cereals, potatoes and grass)	3
Bare fallow	½
Grass (including clover, lucerne and sainfoin)—	
for mowing	1½
for grazing	¼
for seed	4½
Mushrooms (per 100 sq. ft.)	3½
Crops under glass (per 100 sq. ft.)	3½

LIVESTOCK

	Standard man-days (per head per annum)
Dairy cows in milk or in calf and heifers in milk	12
Beef cows	4
Bulls	7
Other cattle	2½
Upland sheep	¼
Lowland sheep	¾
Breeding sows and gilts	4
Boars	4
Pigs fattened or reared for breeding	½
Poultry—laying birds and male birds for breeding	0.20
—broilers produced and young birds (other than day-old chicks) sold for fattening	0.01
—other poultry sold for slaughter, or reared for flock replacement	0.05

EXPLANATORY NOTE

(This Note is not part of the Scheme.)

This scheme, which is made under section 1 of the Agriculture (Small Farmers) Act 1959, provides for the making of grants to a person carrying on a small farm business in England, Wales or Northern Ireland if he carries out with the approval of the Minister of Agriculture, Fisheries and Food a three year programme for increasing the efficiency of the business. Every programme must provide for the keeping of farm business records.

The scheme applies to programmes submitted for approval during the period from 1st September 1968 to 31st August 1969. To be eligible, a small farm business must comprise not less than 20, nor more than 150, acres of land under crops or grass, and have standard labour requirements of not less than 250 standard man-days a year. At the time the programme is submitted for approval the acreage must not be more than 125, nor the standard man-days more than 600.

Grants are made in respect of the general purposes of the business. The rates differ in the second and third years of a programme, according to its nature. Where records have already been kept, so that it is possible to formulate a complete programme from the outset, the higher rate of grant will be payable on completion of each year's plan. Otherwise there will be a basic programme, attracting the same rate in the first year, but lower rates in subsequent years conditional only on the keeping of records. A basic programme can be amended by agreement to take account of the records, and if the Minister is satisfied that the plan is then best calculated to increase the efficiency of the business, having regard to the records, he can pay grant at the higher rate in the second and third years.

The scheme replaces the Small Farm (Business Management) Scheme 1965 (S.I. 1965/1554), under which programmes may be submitted for approval during the three years ending 31st August 1968. A person is ineligible for grant under this scheme if he is keeping records under the Farm Business Recording Scheme, and if he has already participated in that scheme he can only undertake a complete programme under this scheme. Otherwise, apart from the shorter period during which programmes may be submitted, and some minor drafting amendments, the scheme is substantially the same as its predecessor.

STATUTORY INSTRUMENTS

1968 No. 1284

PENSIONS

The Pensions Increase (Approved Schemes) (Local Government) Regulations 1968

Made - - - -	*7th August* 1968
Laid before Parliament	*16th August* 1968
Coming into Operation	*21st August* 1968

The Minister of Housing and Local Government, in exercise of the powers conferred upon him by section 3(2)(*b*)(ii) and (4) of the Pensions (Increase) Act 1965(a) and of all other powers enabling him in that behalf, with the consent of the Treasury, hereby makes the following regulations:—

Title and commencement

1. These regulations may be cited as the Pensions Increase (Approved Schemes) (Local Government) Regulations 1968, and shall come into operation on 21st August 1968.

Interpretation

2.—(1) In these regulations, unless the context otherwise requires—

"the Act of 1937" means the Local Government Superannuation Act 1937 (b);

"the Act of 1965" means the Pensions (Increase) Act 1965;

"average remuneration", in relation to a person, means the annual average of the remuneration of his employment as assessed for the purposes of calculating the employer's superannuation contribution during the last 3 years of his reckonable service;

"contributory employee" means a contributory employee within the meaning of section 3(1) of the Act of 1937 to whom the provisions of the Local Government Superannuation (Benefits) Regulations 1954(c) (other than regulation 17) apply;

"dependant", in relation to a woman, means a person who is to the satisfaction of the relevant local authority wholly or mainly supported by that woman and who either has not attained the age of 16 years or is receiving instruction or undergoing training as referred to in section 1(5) of the Pensions (Increase) Act 1959(d) (as applied by section 1(2) of the Act of 1965);

"Health Service Regulations" means the National Health Service (Superannuation) Regulations 1961(e);

"local authority" has the meaning assigned to it by section 40 of the Act of 1937;

(a) 1965 c. 78.	(b) 1937 c. 68.	(c) S.I. 1954/1048 (1954 II, p. 1595).
(d) 1959 c. 50.		(e) S.I. 1961/1441 (1961 II, p. 2824).

"minimum pensionable age", in relation to a person, means the earliest age at which he could have become entitled to a pension (other than a pension payable consequent on physical or mental infirmity) if in his employment he had been a contributory employee;

"the Minister" means the Minister of Housing and Local Government;

"notional pension", in relation to a person, has the meaning assigned to it by regulation 5 of these regulations;

"reckonable service", in relation to a person, has the meaning assigned to it by the schedule to these regulations;

"relevant local authority", in relation to a person, means the local authority by whom an allowance will be payable under regulation 6 hereof if the conditions set out in regulation 4 are satisfied;

"statutory pension increases" means the benefits conferred by—

(i) section 1 of the Pensions (Increase) Act 1952(a);

(ii) section 1 of the Pensions (Increase) Act 1956(b);

(iii) section 1 of the Pensions (Increase) Act 1959;

(iv) sections 1 and 2 of the Pensions (Increase) Act 1962(c); and

(v) section 1 of the Act of 1965,

on persons whose superannuation benefits are regulated under the Superannuation Act 1965(d);

"superannuation scheme" means the Federated Superannuation Scheme for Nurses and Hospital Officers and any other scheme approved by the Treasury for the purposes of section 3 of the Act of 1965.

(2) The Interpretation Act 1889(e) shall apply to the interpretation of these regulations as it applies to the interpretation of an Act of Parliament.

(3) In these regulations, unless the context otherwise requires, references to any enactment or regulations shall be construed as references to that enactment or those regulations as amended or extended by any other enactment or regulations.

Effect of these regulations

3. These regulations shall apply for the payment to persons described in regulation 4 hereof of the allowances described in regulation 6, being allowances which appear to the Minister to be appropriate having regard to the statutory pension increases.

Persons to whom the regulations apply

4.—(1) These regulations shall apply to any person who—

(a) has retired from the employment of a local authority at or after minimum pensionable age or on account of physical or mental infirmity; and

(b) immediately before so retiring—

(i) was subject to a superannuation scheme; and

(ii) had completed 10 years' reckonable service; and

(a) 1952 c. 45.   (b) 1956 c. 39.   (c) 11 & 12 Eliz. 2. c. 2.   (d) 1965 c. 74.   (e) 1889 c. 63.

(c) has received or has become entitled to receive payment of any retirement benefit under a superannuation scheme; and

(d) either—

   (i) has attained the age of 60 years; or

   (ii) has retired on account of physical or mental infirmity, or is to the satisfaction of the relevant local authority disabled by physical or mental infirmity or permanently incapacitated by such infirmity from engaging in any regular full-time employment; or

   (iii) is a woman who has at least one dependant.

(2) For the purposes of the preceding paragraph, a person who was entitled to receive, and received, payment of any retirement benefit under a superannuation scheme within 12 months of minimum pensionable age shall be deemed to have attained that age.

Notional pension

5.—(1) There shall be ascribed to each person to whom these regulations apply a notional pension calculated on the following basis—

(a) for each year of reckonable service, one eightieth of his average remuneration; and

(b) for any additional part of a year of reckonable service which amounts to or exceeds 6 months, one one hundred and sixtieth of his average remuneration.

(2) In calculating a notional pension any fraction of a pound shall be treated as a whole pound.

(3) Where the amount of a notional pension ascribed to any person does not exceed £26 a year, these regulations shall not apply to him.

Payments of benefits equivalent to statutory pension increases

6.—(1) A local authority may, in respect of any period beginning on or after 1st July 1966, pay to any person to whom these regulations apply and who—

(a) was employed by them on the day when his reckonable service ended or

(b) was employed on that day by some other authority to whom the first mentioned authority are, or are deemed in accordance with paragraph (2) hereof to be, the successor,

an allowance equal to the statutory pension increases which would have been payable to him if he had been eligible under the Superannuation Act 1965 for a pension of the same amount as his notional pension, beginning on the day after the termination of his reckonable service.

(2) For the purposes of this regulation, a local authority shall be deemed to be the successor to any other local authority where the last-mentioned authority has been dissolved and the larger part of their area has been transferred to the first-mentioned authority; and any question as to who are the successor authority for the said purposes shall, in default of agreement, be determined by the Minister.

SCHEDULE

Regulation 2(1)

Meaning of Reckonable Service

1. Subject to the provisions of this schedule, a person's reckonable service shall be a period equivalent to the aggregate of any periods of employment which have both—

    (*a*) been spent in any employment described in paragraph 2 of this schedule and

    (*b*) become reckonable under a superannuation scheme as described in paragraph 3 of this schedule.

2. The employments to which paragraph 1 of this schedule relates are—

    (i) employment under a local authority or a local authority within the meaning of section 34 of the Local Government Superannuation (Scotland) Act 1937(a);

    (ii) employment under any voluntary organisation, undertakers or body, any employees of which are or are treated as contributory employees or local Act contributors under section 15 of the Local Government Superannuation Act 1953(b) or section 7 of the Superannuation (Miscellaneous Provisions) Act 1948(c);

    (iii) employment under an authority which was or was deemed to be an employing authority for the purposes of the Health Service Regulations or the National Health Service (Superannuation) (Scotland) Regulations 1961(d);

    (iv) employment in which the person was subject to any regulations or scheme made under section 2 of the Local Government (Superannuation) Act (Northern Ireland) 1950(e), or section 61 of the Health Services Act (Northern Ireland) 1948(f), or section 54 of the National Health Service (Isle of Man) Act 1948 (an Act of Tynwald);

    (v) employment in the civil service of the State;

    (vi) employment by a district nursing association during any period when a local health authority had arrangements with, or paid contributions to, that association under Part III of the National Health Service Act 1946(g).

3. For the purposes of paragraph 1 of this schedule a period of employment shall be deemed to have become reckonable under a superannuation scheme if—

    (*a*) during such period the person was subject to a superannuation scheme and the contributions authorised or required to be paid by the employer were duly paid, or

    (*b*) such period was taken into account in calculating a sum in the nature of a transfer value paid to that scheme under rules made under section 2 of the Superannuation (Miscellaneous Provisions) Act 1948 or under the Health Service Regulations, or any corresponding provision in force in Scotland, Northern Ireland or the Isle of Man:

    Provided that—

        (i) so much of any period referred to in sub-paragraph (*b*) as consisted of non-contributing service shall be reckonable under this paragraph at half its actual length, and

        (ii) so much of any such period as consisted of part-time service shall be reckonable under this paragraph as though it were whole-time service for a proportionately reduced period.

(a) 1937 c. 69.   (b) 1953 c. 25.   (c) 1948 c. 33.   (d) S.I. 1961/1398 (1961 II, p. 2697).
           (e) 1950 c. 10(N.I.).   (f) 1948 c. 3(N.I.).   (g) 1946 c. 81.

4. For the purposes of regulation 4(*b*)(ii) of these regulations, there may be added to the service described in paragraph 1 of this schedule any period of previous service which would have been reckonable under regulation 22 of the Health Service Regulations (which provides for the reckoning of qualifying service in certain cases) or any corresponding provision in force in Scotland, Northern Ireland or the Isle of Man.

5. For the purposes of paragraph 3(*a*) of this schedule no account shall be taken of any period of employment preceding a break of 12 months or more during which the person was not in employment described in paragraph 2 hereof.

Given under the official seal of the Minister of Housing and Local Government on 1st August 1968.

(L.S.) *Anthony Greenwood,*

Minister of Housing and Local Government.

We consent to these regulations.

E. Alan Fitch,

Joseph Harper,

Two of the Lords Commissioners of Her Majesty's Treasury.

7th August 1968.

EXPLANATORY NOTE

(*This Note is not part of the Regulations.*)

Certain persons who retired from local government employment elected to secure their superannuation benefits through schemes which operated by way of insurance policies to produce lump sums or annuities, or both, upon retirement. These Regulations provide for the payment of allowances corresponding broadly to the increases for which they would have been eligible under the Pensions (Increase) Acts 1952, 1956, 1959, 1962 and 1965 had they been pensionable as contributory employees under local government superannuation.

The relevant schemes are the Federated Superannuation Scheme for Nurses and Hospital Officers and any other scheme approved for this purpose by the Treasury.

The conditions of entitlement combine, with necessary modifications, the conditions for a local government pension and the conditions for increases under the Pensions (Increase) Acts. The principal of these are, broadly, that the person—

(i) completed 10 years' qualifying service in local government employment or certain types of related employment, or the National Health Service, or the civil service;

(ii) retired in circumstances in which a contributory employee could have retired with a pension;

(iii) has attained the age of 60 years, or is incapacitated, or is a woman who has a dependant.

The allowances are payable, as from 1st July 1966, upon a notional pension, which is an amount (defined in regulation 5) corresponding broadly to the pension the person would have received if he had been a contributory employee to whom the Local Government Superannuation (Benefits) Regulations 1954 applied, and entitled to reckon all his service during which he was within the Federated Superannuation Scheme for Nurses and Hospital Officers or other approved scheme.

Retrospective payment is authorised by section 3(4) of the Pensions (Increase) Act 1965.

1968 No. 1285

PENSIONS

The Pensions Increase (Approved Schemes) (National Health Service) Regulations 1968

Made - - - -	*7th August* 1968	
Laid before Parliament	*16th August* 1968	
Coming into Operation	*21st August* 1968	

The Minister of Health, in exercise of the powers conferred upon him by section 3(2)(*b*)(i) and (4) of the Pensions (Increase) Act 1965(a) and of all other powers enabling him in that behalf, with the consent of the Treasury, hereby makes the following regulations:—

Title and commencement

1. These regulations may be cited as the Pensions Increase (Approved Schemes) (National Health Service) Regulations 1968, and shall come into operation on 21st August 1968.

Interpretation

2.—(1) In these regulations, unless the context otherwise requires—

" the Act of 1965 " means the Pensions (Increase) Act 1965 ;

" average remuneration ", in relation to a person, means the annual average of his remuneration as it would have been calculated if he had been superannuable under the Regulations in respect of his reckonable service ;

" dependant ", in relation to a woman, means a person who is to the satisfaction of the Minister wholly or mainly supported by that woman and who either has not attained the age of 16 years or is receiving instruction or undergoing training as referred to in section 1(5) of the Pensions (Increase) Act 1959(b) (as applied by section 1(2) of the Act of 1965) ;

" employing authority " means an authority which is, or is deemed to be, an employing authority for the purposes of the Regulations ;

" minimum pensionable age ", in relation to a person, means the earliest age at which he could have become entitled to a pension (other than a pension payable consequent on physical or mental infirmity) if he had been superannuable under the Regulations ;

" the Minister " means the Minister of Health ;

" notional pension ", in relation to a person, has the meaning assigned to it by regulation 5 of these regulations ;

" reckonable service ", in relation to a person, has the meaning assigned to it by the schedule to these regulations ;

(a) 1965 c. 78.	(b) 1959 c. 50.

" the Regulations " means the National Health Service (Superannuation) Regulations 1961(a) as amended(b) ;

" statutory pension increases " means the benefits conferred by—

(i) section 1 of the Pensions (Increase) Act 1952(c) ;

(ii) section 1 of the Pensions (Increase) Act 1956(d) ;

(iii) section 1 of the Pensions (Increase) Act 1959 ;

(iv) sections 1 and 2 of the Pensions (Increase) Act 1962(e) ; and

(v) section 1 of the Act of 1965,

on persons whose superannuation benefits are regulated under the Superannuation Act 1965(f) ;

" superannuation scheme " means the Federated Superannuation Scheme for Nurses and Hospital Officers and any other scheme approved by the Treasury for the purposes of section 3 of the Act of 1965 ;

" superannuable under the Regulations ", in relation to a person, means entitled to participate in the superannuation benefits provided by the Regulations (other than regulations 43 and 45).

(2) The Interpretation Act 1889(g) shall apply to the interpretation of these regulations as it applies to the interpretation of an Act of Parliament.

(3) In these regulations, unless the context otherwise requires, references to any enactment or regulations shall be construed as references to that enactment or those regulations as amended or extended by any other enactment or regulations.

Effect of these regulations

3. These regulations shall apply for the payment to persons described in regulation 4 hereof of the allowances described in regulation 6, being allowances which appear to the Minister to be appropriate having regard to the statutory pension increases.

Persons to whom the regulations apply

4.—(1) These regulations shall apply to any person who—

(a) has ceased to be employed by an employing authority on or after attaining minimum pensionable age or on account of physical or mental infirmity ; and

(b) immediately before ceasing to be so employed—

(i) was subject to a superannuation scheme ; and

(ii) had completed 10 years' reckonable service ; and

(c) has received or has become entitled to receive payment of any retirement benefit under a superannuation scheme ; and

(d) either—

(i) has attained the age of 60 years ; or

(ii) has retired on account of physical or mental infirmity, or is to the satisfaction of the Minister disabled by physical or mental infirmity or permanently incapacitated by such infirmity from engaging in any regular full-time employment ; or

(iii) is a woman who has at least one dependant.

(a) S.I. 1961/1441 (1961 II, p. 2824).   (b) S.I. 1966/1523 (1966 III, p. 4309).   (c) 1952 c. 45.
(d) 1956 c. 39.   (e) 11 & 12 Eliz. 2. c. 2.   (f) 1965 c. 10.   (g) 1889 c. 63.

(2) For the purposes of the preceding paragraph, a person who was entitled to receive, and received, payment of any retirement benefit under a superannuation scheme within 12 months of minimum pensionable age shall be deemed to have attained that age.

Notional pension

5.—(1) There shall be ascribed to each person to whom these regulations apply a notional pension calculated on the following basis—

(a) for each year of reckonable service, one eightieth of his average remuneration ; and

(b) for any additional fraction of a year of reckonable service which exceeds 6 months, one one hundred and sixtieth of his average remuneration.

(2) In calculating a notional pension any fraction of a pound shall be treated as a whole pound.

(3) Where a person is receiving a supplementary payment under regulation 46(3) of the Regulations (which provides for supplementary payments in the case of certain officers), the amount of his notional pension shall be reduced by such amount as the Minister may determine as representing that part of the supplementary payment which is referable to employment under an employing authority on and after 5th July 1948.

(4) Where the amount of a notional pension ascribed to any person does not exceed £26 a year, these regulations shall not apply to him unless he is receiving a supplementary payment as referred to in paragraph (3) of this regulation.

Payments of benefits equivalent to statutory pension increases

6. The Minister shall, in respect of any period beginning on and after 1st July 1966, pay to any person to whom these regulations apply an allowance equal to the statutory pension increases which would have been payable to him if he had been eligible under the Superannuation Act 1965 for a pension of the same amount as his notional pension, beginning on the day after the last day of his reckonable service.

SCHEDULE Regulation 2(1)

Meaning of reckonable service

1. Subject to the provisions of this schedule, a person's reckonable service shall be a period equivalent to the aggregate of any periods of employment which—

(a) have been spent in any employment described in paragraph 2 of this schedule and

(b) have become reckonable under a superannuation scheme as described in paragraph 3 of this schedule.

2. The employments to which paragraph 1 of this schedule relates are—

(i) employment under an employing authority or an authority which was, or was deemed to be, an employing authority for the purposes of the National Health Service (Superannuation) (Scotland) Regulations 1961(a) ;

(ii) employment in which the person was subject to any regulations or scheme made under section 2 of the Local Government (Superannuation) Act (Northern Ireland) 1950(b), section 61 of the Health Services Act (Northern Ireland) 1948(c) or section 54 of the National Health Service (Isle of Man) Act 1948 (an Act of Tynwald) ;

(a) S.I. 1961/1398 (1961 II, p. 2697). (b) 1950 c. 10 (N.I.). (c) 1948 c. 3 (N.I.).

(iii) employment in the civil service of the State ;

(iv) employment under an employing authority or a local Act authority within the meaning of section 1(3) of the Local Government Superannuation Act 1937(a) or section 1(6) of the Local Government Superannuation (Scotland) Act 1937(b) ;

(v) employment by a district nursing association during any period when a local health authority had arrangements with, or paid contributions to, that association under Part III of the National Health Service Act 1946(c).

3. For the purposes of paragraph 1 of this schedule a period of employment shall be deemed to have become reckonable under a superannuation scheme if—

(a) during such period the person was subject to a superannuation scheme and the contributions authorised or required to be paid by the employer were duly paid, or

(b) such period was taken into account in calculating a sum in the nature of a transfer value paid to that scheme under the Regulations or any corresponding provision in force in Scotland, Northern Ireland or the Isle of Man or under rules made under section 2 of the Superannuation (Miscellaneous Provisions) Act 1948(d) :

Provided that—

(i) so much of any period referred to in sub-paragraph (b) as consisted of non-contributing service shall be reckonable under this paragraph at half its actual length, and

(ii) so much of any such period as consisted of part-time service shall be reckonable under this paragraph as though it were whole-time service for a proportionately reduced period.

4. For the purposes of regulation 4(1)(b)(ii) of these regulations, there may be added to the service described in paragraph 1 of this schedule any period of previous service which would have been reckonable under regulation 22 of the Regulations (which provides for the reckoning of qualifying service in certain cases) or any corresponding provision in force in Scotland, Northern Ireland or the Isle of Man.

5. For the purposes of paragraph 3(a) of this schedule no account shall be taken of any period of employment preceding a break of 12 months or more during which the person was not in employment described in paragraph 2 hereof

Given under the official seal of the Minister of Health on 1st August 1968.

(L.S.)

Kenneth Robinson,
Minister of Health.

We consent to these regulations.

E. Alan Fitch,
Joseph Harper,
Two of the Lords Commissioners of
Her Majesty's Treasury.

7th August 1968.

(a) 1937 c 68.   (b) 1937 c. 69.   (c) 1946 c. 81.   (d) 1948 c. 33.

EXPLANATORY NOTE

(This Note is not part of the Regulations.)

Certain persons who retired from employment in the National Health Service elected to secure their superannuation benefits through schemes which operated by way of insurance policies to produce lump sums or annuities, or both, upon retirement. These Regulations provide for the payment of allowances corresponding broadly to the increases for which they would have been eligible under the Pensions (Increase) Acts 1952, 1956, 1959, 1962 and 1965 had they been pensionable under the National Health Service Superannuation Scheme.

The relevant schemes are the Federated Superannuation Scheme for Nurses and Hospital Officers and any other scheme approved for this purpose by the Treasury.

The conditions of entitlement combine, with necessary modifications, the conditions for a health service pension and the conditions for increases under the Pensions (Increase) Acts. The principal of these are, broadly, that the person—

(i) completed 10 years' qualifying service in health service or local government employment or certain types of related employment or the civil service ;

(ii) retired in circumstances in which a person subject to the health service scheme could have retired with a pension ;

(iii) has attained the age of 60 years, or is incapacitated, or is a woman who has a dependant.

The allowances are payable, as from 1st July 1966, upon a notional pension, which is an amount (defined in regulation 5) corresponding broadly to the pension the person would have received if he had been in the health service scheme and entitled to reckon under that scheme certain service during which he was within the Federated Superannuation Scheme for Nurses and Hospital Officers or any other approved scheme.

Retrospective payment is authorised by section 3(4) of the Pensions (Increase) Act 1965.

STATUTORY INSTRUMENTS

1968 No. 1296

EDUCATION, ENGLAND AND WALES

The University and Other Awards (Amendment) Regulations 1968

Made - - -	*12th August* 1968
Laid before Parliament	*22nd August* 1968
Coming into Operation	*1st September* 1968

The Secretary of State for Education and Science, in exercise of the powers conferred upon him by sections 1 and 4 of the Education Act 1962(a) as amended by the Secretary of State for Education and Science Order 1964(b), hereby makes the following regulations:—

Citation, commencement and interpretation

1.—(1) These regulations may be cited as the University and Other Awards (Amendment) Regulations 1968 and shall come into operation on 1st September 1968.

(2) The Interpretation Act 1889(c) shall apply for the interpretation of these regulations as it applies for the interpretation of an Act of Parliament.

Effect of regulations

2. These regulations shall have effect for the amendment of the University and Other Awards Regulations 1965(d) as amended by the University and Other Awards Amending Regulations 1966(e) and the University and Other Awards Amending Regulations 1967(f); and any reference to a regulation, paragraph or schedule not otherwise identified is a reference to that regulation, paragraph or schedule in those regulations as so amended.

Meaning of "termination of marriage"

3. For the purposes of these regulations a person's marriage is to be treated as having been terminated, not only by the death of the other spouse or the annulment or dissolution of the marriage by an order of a court of competent jurisdiction, but also by virtue of the parties to the marriage ceasing to live together, whether or not an order for their separation has been made by any court.

Conditions

4. In regulation 4 for the words "condition that" there shall be substituted the words "conditions that (*a*)" and at the end of the regulation there shall be added—"and (*b*) as regards any course beginning after 30th November 1968, the applicant or his parent gives the authority a written undertaking that, where any sum is paid in pursuance of the award before the end of the year in

---

(a) 1962 c. 12.
(b) S.I. 1964/490 (1964 I, p. 800).
(c) 1889 c. 63.
(d) S.I. 1965/1404 (1965 II, p. 4134).
(e) S.I. 1966/985 (1966 II, p. 2360).
(f) S.I. 1967/209 (1967 I, p. 353).

respect of which the sum is payable, he will if called upon to do so repay or, as the case may be, pay to the authority the amount by which that sum exceeds the grant payable in respect of that year."

Exceptions

5. In regulation 5—

    (*a*) in paragraph (*a*) there shall be omitted the expression "full-time" and the words from "as a teacher" to the end of the paragraph shall be omitted; and

    (*b*) after paragraph (*a*) there shall be inserted as a new paragraph—

        "(*aa*) a person who has attended any full-time course or successfully completed any part-time course (not being a course in preparation for an educational qualification prescribed by or under these regulations) whether in the United Kingdom or elsewhere, being respectively a full-time course of further education of not less than two years' duration or a part-time course of a kind described in regulation 10(2)(*a*) and (*b*) of the Further Education (Local Education Authorities) Regulations 1959(**a**) as amended (**b**), or a comparable full-time or part-time course outside the United Kingdom."

Period of award

6. After paragraph (3) of regulation 7 there shall be inserted as a new paragraph—

    "(3A) Notwithstanding paragraphs (2) and (3) above, in a case to which either of those paragraphs would apart from this paragraph apply an authority may after consultation with the academic authorities terminate the award if it is satisfied that when the holder applied for the award he did not intend to complete the course to which the application related."

Payments

7.—(1) In regulation 8 for the words "to or for the benefit of the holder" there shall be substituted the words "in pursuance".

(2) At the end of regulation 8 there shall be added as a new paragraph—

    "(2) Payments in respect of fees may be made to the academic authorities but subject thereto all payments shall be made to the award holder."

(3) After regulation 8 there shall be inserted as a new regulation—

"*Minimum award*

    8A—(1) Subject to paragraph (2) below and to regulations 18 and 19(2) the authority shall in respect of each year pay in pursuance of the award the sum of £50 or a grant calculated in accordance with the following provisions of these regulations, whichever is the greater.

    (2) The sum of £50 mentioned in paragraph (1) above shall not be payable in respect of an award holder who holds a State Scholarship or any award from a Government department or other public body or is in receipt of any payment (whether by way of salary or otherwise) from his employer being a scholarship, award or payment of a sum not less than the maximum payments for which he is eligible under regulations 9 and 10; and accordingly

---

(a) S.I. 1959/393 (1959 I, p. 1577).
(b) The relevant amending instruments are S.I. 1961/1582, 1964/490, 1965/2, 1966/1432 (1961 II, p. 3245; 1964 I, p. 800; 1965 I, p. 3; 1966 III, p. 3789).

in its application to such a person paragraph (1) shall have effect with the omission of the words "the sum of £50 or" and "whichever is the greater".."

(4) Regulation 17 is hereby revoked.

Maintenance

8.—(1) At the beginning of regulation 10 there shall be inserted the words "(1) Subject to paragraph (2) below" and at the end of the paragraph there shall be added as a new paragraph—

"(2) Payments shall be made under this regulation at the rate of £275 for each year to a married woman who resides in the matrimonial home unless—

(*a*) her husband is incapacitated and dependent on her; or

(*b*) he is attending a course of full-time education at any university, establishment of further education or college of education. "

(2) The rate of payments specified by regulation 10 shall be increased in accordance with the following table:—

Paragraph	Present rate £	New rate £
(*a*)	370	395
(*b*)	275	290
(*c*)	340	360
(*d*)	275	290
(*e*)	370	420

Additional payments

9.—(1) The rate of payments specified by regulation 11(1) shall be increased in accordance with the following table:—

Subparagraph	Present rate £ s. d.			New rate £ s. d.		
(*a*)		17	6	1	0	0
(*a*)		10	0		11	6
(*b*)	1	0	0	1	2	6
(*c*)		17	6	1	0	0
(*c*)		10	0		11	6
(*d*)		17	6	1	0	0

(2) A payment in pursuance of regulation 11(1)(*e*) in respect of a course outside the United Kingdom shall be at the discretion of the authority unless the academic authorities have certified that if he did not attend it the award holder would not be eligible to complete the course in respect of which the award is held; and accordingly in its application to any course outside the United Kingdom in respect of which no such certificate has been given that subparagraph shall be read as if for the word "shall" there were substituted the word "may".

(3) In regulation 11(2) for the reference to £5 there shall be substituted a reference to £5 10*s.* 0*d*.

Dependants

10.—(1) The rate of payments specified by regulation 12(2) shall be varied in accordance with the following table:—

Subparagraph	Present rate £	New rate £
(a)	190	210
(b)	80	90
(c)	60	50
(d)	55	45
(e)	65	75

(2) In regulation 12(3) there shall be inserted after the word "dependant" where it first occurs the words "received during the year".

(3) After regulation 12(5) there shall be inserted as a new paragraph—
"(5A) Payments under this regulation in respect of dependants outside the United Kingdom shall be at the discretion of the authority."

Older students

11. In regulation 14—

(a) for the words from "has regularly supported himself" to "gross yearly income" there shall be substituted the words "has in each of any three of the six years immediately preceding that year earned a gross income";

(b) after the words "25 per cent. above" there shall be inserted the words "the sum of £360 and" and the reference to regulation 10 shall be omitted; and

(c) for the references to £20 and £100 there shall be substituted references to £24 and £120 respectively.

Reductions in respect of income

12. In regulation 15(2)—

(a) after subparagraph (a) there shall be inserted as a new subparagraph—
"(aa) the first £200 of any such income as is described in the first proviso to paragraph 2(a) of schedule 2 in the case of an award holder who—
(i) has no parent living;
(ii) is not such a person as is described in any subparagraph of regulation 16(2)"; and

(b) at the end of subparagraph (f) there shall be added the words "and any benefit under the Ministry of Social Security Act 1966"(a).

Women students

13. After regulation 15 there shall be inserted as a new regulation—

"*Women students*

15A. Notwithstanding the preceding provisions of these regulations (and in particular regulations 12 and 15)—

(a) if the award holder is a woman to whom any payment is required by regulation 12(2) to be made and whose marriage has terminated, whether before or during the course, then—
(i) the sum to be disregarded under regulation 15(2)(a) shall be £200 instead of £100; or
(ii) an additional payment of £100 shall be made to her under regulation 12(2); or

---

(a) 1966 c. 20.

(iii) in the case of an award holder to whom regulation 14 applies, an additional payment shall be made to her under that regulation—

whichever is the most favourable to the award holder;

(b) an award holder who is a widow may elect that, in place of the payments that would otherwise be made to her under regulation 12(2) in respect of any dependent child, in calculating her income there shall be disregarded £300 in respect of her first dependent child and £100 in respect of every other dependent child;

(c) payments in respect of a woman whose marriage terminates during the course shall be made after the termination of her marriage at a rate not lower than the rate at which they were made before the termination."

Parental contribution

14.—(1) In regulation 16(2) there shall be inserted after the words "award holder" the words "whose parent cannot be traced nor in respect of one".

(2) In schedule 2—

(a) in paragraph 1 for the words from "balance of income" to the end of the paragraph there shall be substituted the words "as follows:—if the balance of income is not less than £900 the parental contribution shall be £20 with the addition of £1 for every complete £10 by which the balance exceeds £900"; and accordingly Part II of the schedule shall be omitted;

(b) the first proviso to paragraph 2(a) shall apply in respect of a person of full age as it applies in respect of an infant and accordingly the references in that proviso to an infant shall be construed as including references to a person of full age;

(c) in paragraph 3(d) there shall be inserted immediately after the words "national insurance contributions" the words "and graduated pension contributions";

(d) a deduction shall be made under paragraph 4(a) or (b) only if the parents ordinarily live together;

(e) paragraph 4(c) shall apply to any other parent whose marriage has terminated as it applies to a widow or widower; and

(f) the maximum deduction under paragraph 5(a) shall be reduced from £200 to £100.

Sandwich courses

15. In regulation 19(2)—

(a) for the words "regulation 17 shall not apply and the regulations hereinafter specified shall be modified as follows" there shall be substituted the words "in respect of any year in which the award holder is required by the academic authorities to undertake any such course of experience as is described in paragraph (1) above, regulation 8A(1) shall not apply but the authority shall pay a grant calculated in accordance with the other provisions of these regulations subject to the following modifications"; and

(b) for the reference in subparagraphs (a) and (f) to £35 there shall be substituted references to £36.

Designated courses

16. In schedule 1—

   (*a*) in paragraph 2 the word "first" shall be inserted before the word "degree";

   (*b*) paragraph 4 shall be omitted; and

   (*c*) in paragraph 6 subparagraphs (*a*), (*f*), (*g*), (*h*), (*k*) and (*n*) shall be omitted and for the reference in subparagraph (*m*) to the Royal Scottish Academy of Music there shall be substituted a reference to the Royal Scottish Academy of Music and Drama.

Interpretation of 1965 regulations

17. Any reference in the University and Other Awards Regulations 1965 as amended to a provision of those regulations shall be construed as a reference to that provision as amended by any other regulations, including these regulations.

Given under the Official Seal of the Secretary of State for Education and Science on 12th August 1968.

(L.S.)

Edward Short,
Secretary of State for Education and
Science.

EXPLANATORY NOTE

(This Note is not part of the Regulations.)

These regulations alter the rates at which payments are made to students in pursuance of awards bestowed under the University and Other Awards Regulations 1965 as amended. They also make other minor amendments to those regulations.

STATUTORY INSTRUMENTS

1968 No. 1298 (S. 136)

PENSIONS

The Pensions Increase (Approved Schemes) (Local Government) (Scotland) Regulations 1968

Made - - - -	25th July 1968
Laid before Parliament	20th August 1968
Coming into Operation	21st August 1968

In exercise of the powers conferred on me by section 3(2)(*b*)(ii) and (4) of the Pensions (Increase) Act 1965(**a**) and of all other powers enabling me in that behalf, with the consent of the Treasury, I hereby make the following regulations:—

Citation and commencement

1. These regulations may be cited as the Pensions Increase (Approved Schemes) (Local Government) (Scotland) Regulations 1968, and shall come into operation on 21st August 1968.

Interpretation

2.—(1) In these regulations, unless the context otherwise requires—

"the Act of 1937" means the Local Government Superannuation (Scotland) Act 1937(**b**);

"the Act of 1965" means the Pensions (Increase) Act 1965;

"average remuneration", in relation to a person, means the annual average of the remuneration of his employment as assessed for the purposes of calculating the employer's superannuation contribution during the last 3 years of his reckonable service;

"contributory employee" means a contributory employee within the meaning of section 3(1) of the Act of 1937 to whom the provisions of the Local Government Superannuation (Benefits) (Scotland) Regulations 1954(**c**) (other than regulation 17) apply;

"dependant", in relation to a woman, means a person who is to the satisfaction of the relevant local authority wholly or mainly supported by that woman and who either has not attained the age of 16 years or is receiving instruction or undergoing training as referred to in section 1(5) of the Pensions (Increase) Act 1959(**d**) (as applied by section 1(2) of the Act of 1965);

"Health Service Regulations" means the National Health Service (Superannuation) (Scotland) Regulations 1961(**e**);

"local authority" has the meaning assigned to it by section 34 of the Act of 1937;

"minimum pensionable age", in relation to a person, means the earliest age at which he could have become entitled to a pension (other than a pension payable consequent on physical or mental infirmity) if in his employment he had been a contributory employee;

(a) 1965 c. 78.   (b) 1937 c. 69.   (c) S.I. 1954/1059 (1954 II, p. 1632).
(d) 1959 c. 50.   (e) S.I. 1961/1398 (1961 II, p. 2697).

"notional pension", in relation to a person, has the meaning assigned to it by regulation 5 of these regulations;

"reckonable service", in relation to a person, has the meaning assigned to it by the schedule to these regulations;

"relevant local authority", in relation to a person, means the local authority by whom an allowance will be payable under regulation 6 hereof if the conditions set out in regulation 4 are satisfied;

"statutory pension increases" means the benefits conferred by
    (i) section 1 of the Pensions (Increase) Act 1952(a);
    (ii) section 1 of the Pensions (Increase) Act 1956(b);
    (iii) section 1 of the Pensions (Increase) Act 1959;
    (iv) sections 1 and 2 of the Pensions (Increase) Act 1962(c); and
    (v) section 1 of the Act of 1965,

on persons whose superannuation benefits are regulated under the Superannuation Act 1965(d);

"superannuation scheme" means the Federated Superannuation Scheme for Nurses and Hospital Officers and any other scheme approved by the Treasury for the purposes of section 3 of the Act of 1965.

(2) The Interpretation Act 1889(e) shall apply for the interpretation of these regulations as it applies for the interpretation of an Act of Parliament.

(3) In these regulations, unless the context otherwise requires, references to any enactment or regulations shall be construed as references to that enactment or those regulations as amended or extended by any other enactment or regulations.

Effect of these regulations
3. These regulations shall apply for the payment to persons described in regulation 4 hereof of the allowances described in regulation 6, being allowances which appear to the Secretary of State to be appropriate having regard to the statutory pension increases.

Persons to whom the regulations apply
4.—(1) These regulations shall apply to any person who—

(a) has retired from the employment of a local authority at or after minimum pensionable age or on account of physical or mental infirmity; and

(b) immediately before so retiring—
    (i) was subject to a superannuation scheme, and
    (ii) had completed 10 years' reckonable service; and

(c) has received or has become entitled to receive payment of any retirement benefit under a superannuation scheme; and

(d) either—
    (i) has attained the age of 60 years; or
    (ii) has retired on account of physical or mental infirmity or is to the satisfaction of the relevant local authority disabled by physical or mental infirmity or permanently incapacitated by such infirmity from engaging in any regular full-time employment; or
    (iii) is a woman who has at least one dependant.

(2) For the purposes of the preceding paragraph, a person who was entitled to receive, and received, payment of any retirement benefit under a superannuation scheme within 12 months of minimum pensionable age shall be deemed to have attained that age.

(a) 1952 c. 45.   (b) 1956 c. 39.   (c) 11 & 12 Eliz. 2, c. 2.
(d) 1965 c. 74.   (e) 1889 c. 63.

Notional pension

5.—(1) There shall be ascribed to each person to whom these regulations apply a notional pension calculated on the following basis—

(a) for each year of reckonable service, one eighteeth of his average remuneration; and

(b) for any additional part of a year of reckonable service which amounts to or exceeds 6 months, one one hundred and sixtieth of his average remuneration.

(2) In calculating a notional pension any fraction of a pound shall be treated as a whole pound.

(3) Where the amount of a notional pension ascribed to any person does not exceed £26 a year, these regulations shall not apply to him.

Payments of benefits equivalent to statutory pension increases

6.—(1) A local authority may, in respect of any period beginning on or after 1st July 1966, pay to any person to whom these regulations apply and who—

(a) was employed by them on the day when his reckonable service ended, or

(b) was employed on that day by some other authority to whom the first-mentioned authority are, or are deemed in accordance with paragraph (2) hereof to be, the successor,

an allowance equal to the statutory pension increases which would have been payable to him if he had been eligible under the Superannuation Act 1965 for a pension of the same amount as his notional pension, beginning on the day after the termination of his reckonable service.

(2) For the purposes of this regulation, a local authority shall be deemed to be the successor to any other local authority where the last-mentioned authority has been dissolved and the larger part of their area has been transferred to the first-mentioned authority; and any question as to who are the successor authority for the said purposes shall, in default of agreement, be determined by the Secretary of State.

William Ross,
One of Her Majesty's Principal
Secretaries of State.

St. Andrew's House,
Edinburgh, 1.
23rd July 1968.
We consent,

J. McCann,
Harry Gourlay,
Two of the Lords Commissioners of
Her Majesty's Treasury.

25th July 1968.

Regulation 2(1) SCHEDULE

Meaning of reckonable service

1. Subject to the provisions of this schedule, a person's reckonable service shall be a period equivalent to the aggregate of any periods of employment which—

(a) have been spent in any employment described in paragraph 2 of this schedule and

(b) have become reckonable under a superannuation scheme as described in paragraph 3 of this schedule.

2. The employments to which paragraph 1 of this schedule relates are—

(i) employment under a local authority or a local authority within the meaning of section 40 of the Local Government Superannuation Act 1937(a);

(ii) employment under any voluntary organisation, undertakers or body, any employees of which are or are treated as contributory employees or local Act contributors under section 15 of the Local Government Superannuation Act 1953(b) or section 7 of the Superannuation (Miscellaneous Provisions) Act 1948(c);

(iii) employment under an authority which is or is deemed to be an employing authority for the purposes of the Health Service Regulations or the National Health Service (Superannuation) Regulations 1961(d);

(iv) employment in which the person was subject to any regulations or scheme made under section 2 of the Local Government (Superannuation) Act (Northern Ireland) 1950(e) or section 61 of the Health Services Act (Northern Ireland) 1948(f) or section 54 of the National Health Service (Isle of Man) Act 1948 (an Act of Tynwald);

(v) employment in the civil service of the State; and

(vi) employment by a district nursing association during any period when a local health authority had arrangements with, or paid contributions to, that association under Part III of the National Health Service (Scotland) Act 1947(g).

3. For the purposes of paragraph 1 of this schedule a period of employment shall be deemed to have become reckonable under a superannuation scheme if—

(a) during such period the person was subject to a superannuation scheme and the contributions authorised or required to be paid by the employer were duly paid, or

(b) such period was taken into account in calculating a sum in the nature of a transfer value paid to that scheme under rules made under section 2 of the Superannuation (Miscellaneous Provisions) Act 1948 or under the Health Service Regulations, or any corresponding provision in force in England and Wales, Northern Ireland or the Isle of Man:

Provided that—

(i) so much of any period referred to in sub-paragraph (b) as consisted of non-contributing service shall be reckonable under this paragraph at half its actual length, and

(ii) so much of any such period as consisted of part-time service shall be reckonable under this paragraph as though it were whole-time service for a proportionately reduced period.

4. For the purposes of regulation 4(1)(b)(ii) of these regulations, there may be added to the service described in paragraph 1 of this schedule any period of previous service which would have been reckonable under regulation 24 of the Health Service Regulations (which provides for the reckoning of qualifying service in certain cases) or any corresponding provision in force in England and Wales, Northern Ireland or the Isle of Man.

5. For the purposes of paragraph 3(a) of this schedule no account shall be taken of any period of employment preceding a break of 12 months or more during which the person was not in employment described in paragraph 2 hereof.

EXPLANATORY NOTE

(This Note is not part of the Regulations.)

Certain persons who retired from local government employment elected to secure their superannuation benefits through schemes which operated by way of insurance policies to produce lump sums or annuities, or both, upon retirement.

(a) 1937 c. 68.   (b) 1953 c. 25.   (c) 1948 c. 33.
(d) S.I. 1961/1441 (1961 II, p. 2824).   (e) 1950 c. 10 (N.I.).
(f) 1948 c. 3 (N.I.).   (g) 1947 c. 27.

These Regulations provide for the payment of allowances corresponding broadly to the increases for which they would have been eligible under the Pensions (Increase) Acts 1952, 1956, 1959, 1962 and 1965 had they been pensionable as contributory employees under local government superannuation.

The relevant schemes are the Federated Superannuation Scheme for Nurses and Hospital Officers and any other scheme approved for this purpose by the Treasury.

The conditions of entitlement combine, with necessary modifications, the conditions for a local government pension and the conditions for increases under the Pensions (Increase) Acts. The principal of these are, broadly, that the person—

(i) completed 10 years' qualifying service in local government employment or certain types of related employment, or the National Health Service, or the civil service;

(ii) retired in circumstances in which a contributory employee could have retired with a pension;

(iii) has attained the age of 60 years or is incapacitated or is a woman who has a dependant.

The allowances are payable, as from 1st July 1966, upon a notional pension, which is an amount (defined in Regulation 5) corresponding broadly to the pension the person would have received if he had been a contributory employee to whom the Local Government Superannuation (Benefits) (Scotland) Regulations 1954 applied, and entitled to reckon all his service during which he was within the Federated Superannuation Scheme for Nurses and Hospital Officers or other approved scheme.

Retrospective payment is authorised by Section 3(4) of the Pensions (Increase) Act 1965.

STATUTORY INSTRUMENTS

1968 No. 1299 (S.137)

PENSIONS

The Pensions Increase (Approved Schemes) (National Health Service) (Scotland) Regulations 1968

Made - - -	*25th July* 1968
Laid before Parliament	*20th August* 1968
Coming into Operation	*21st August* 1968

In exercise of the powers conferred on me by section 3(2)(*b*)(i) and (4) of the Pensions (Increase) Act 1965(a) and of all other powers enabling me in that behalf, and with the consent of the Treasury, I hereby make the following regulations:—

Citation and commencement

1. These regulations may be cited as the Pensions Increase (Approved Schemes) (National Health Service) (Scotland) Regulations 1968, and shall come into operation on 21st August 1968.

Interpretation

2.—(1) In these regulations, unless the context otherwise requires—

"the Act of 1965" means the Pensions (Increase) Act 1965;

"average remuneration", in relation to a person, means the annual average of his remuneration as it would have been calculated if he had been superannuable under the Regulations in respect of his reckonable service;

"dependant", in relation to a woman, means a person who is to the satisfaction of the Secretary of State wholly or mainly supported by that woman and who either has not attained the age of 16 years or is receiving instruction or undergoing training as referred to in section 1(5) of the Pensions (Increase) Act 1959(b) (as applied by section 1(2) of the Act of 1965);

"employing authority" means an authority which is, or is deemed to be, an employing authority for the purposes of the Regulations;

"minimum pensionable age", in relation to a person, means the earliest age at which he could have become entitled to a pension (other than a pension payable consequent on physical or mental infirmity) if he had been superannuable under the Regulations;

"notional pension", in relation to a person, has the meaning assigned to it by regulation 5 of these regulations;

"reckonable service", in relation to a person, has the meaning assigned to it by the schedule to these regulations;

"the Regulations" means the National Health Service (Superannuation) (Scotland) Regulations 1961(c);

(a) 1965 c. 78.   (b) 1959 c. 50.   (c) S.I. 1961/1398 (1961 II, p. 2697).

"statutory pension increases" means the benefits conferred by
  (i) section 1 of the Pensions (Increase) Act 1952(a) ;
  (ii) section 1 of the Pensions (Increase) Act 1956(b) ;
  (iii) section 1 of the Pensions (Increase) Act 1959 ;
  (iv) sections 1 and 2 of the Pensions (Increase) Act 1962(c) ; and
  (v) section 1 of the Act of 1965,

on persons whose superannuation benefits are regulated under the Super-annuation Act 1965(d) ;

"superannuation scheme" means the Federated Superannuation Scheme for Nurses and Hospital Officers and any other scheme approved by the Treasury for the purposes of section 3 of the Act of 1965 ;

"superannuable under the Regulations", in relation to a person, means entitled to participate in the superannuation benefits provided by the Regulations (other than regulations 44 and 46).

(2) The Interpretation Act 1889(e) shall apply for the interpretation of these regulations as it applies for the interpretation of an Act of Parliament.

(3) In these regulations, unless the context otherwise requires, references to any enactment or regulations shall be construed as references to that enactment or those regulations as amended, extended or applied by any other enactment or regulations.

Effect of these regulations

3. These regulations shall apply for the payment to persons described in regulation 4 hereof of the allowances described in regulation 6, being allowances which appear to the Secretary of State to be appropriate having regard to the statutory pension increases.

Persons to whom the regulations apply

4.—(1) These regulations shall apply to any person who—
  (*a*) has ceased to be employed by an employing authority on or after attaining minimum pensionable age or on account of physical or mental infirmity ; and
  (*b*) immediately before ceasing to be so employed—
    (i) was subject to a superannuation scheme, and
    (ii) had completed 10 years' reckonable service ; and
  (*c*) has received or has become entitled to receive payment of any retirement benefit under a superannuation scheme ; and
  (*d*) either—
    (i) has attained the age of 60 years ; or
    (ii) has retired on account of physical or mental infirmity or is to the satisfaction of the Secretary of State disabled by physical or mental infirmity or permanently incapacitated by such infirmity from engaging in any regular full-time employment ; or
    (iii) is a woman who has at least one dependant.

(2) For the purposes of the preceding paragraph, a person who was entitled to receive, and received, payment of any retirement benefit under a super-annuation scheme within 12 months of minimum pensionable age shall be deemed to have attained that age.

(**a**) 1952 c. 45.   (**b**) 1956 c. 39.   (**c**) 11 & 12 Eliz 2. c. 2.
(**d**) 1965 c. 74.   (**e**) 1889 c. 63.

Notional pension

5.—(1) There shall be ascribed to each person to whom these regulations apply a notional pension calculated on the following basis—

    (*a*) for each year of reckonable service, one eightieth of his average remuneration ; and

    (*b*) for any additional fraction of a year of reckonable service which exceeds 6 months, one one-hundred-and-sixtieth of his average remuneration.

(2) In calculating a notional pension any fraction of a pound shall be treated as a whole pound.

(3) Where a person is receiving a supplementary payment under regulation 47(3) of the Regulations (which provides for supplementary payments in the case of certain officers), the amount of his notional pension shall be reduced by such amount as the Secretary of State may determine as representing that part of the supplementary payment which is referable to employment under an employing authority on and after 5th July 1948.

(4) Where the amount of a notional pension ascribed to any person does not exceed £26 a year, these regulations shall not apply to him unless he is receiving a supplementary payment as referred to in paragraph. (3) of this regulation.

Payments of benefits equivalent to statutory pension increases

6. The Secretary of State shall, in respect of any period beginning on and after 1st July 1966, pay to any person to whom these regulations apply an allowance equal to the statutory pension increases which would have been payable to him if he had been eligible under the Superannuation Act 1965 for a pension of the same amount as his notional pension, beginning on the day after the last day of his reckonable service.

William Ross,
One of Her Majesty's Principal
Secretaries of State.

St. Andrew's House,
    Edinburgh, 1.
23rd July 1968.

J. McCann,
Harry Gourlay,
We consent,
Two of the Lords Commissioners of
Her Majesty's Treasury.

25th July 1968.

SCHEDULE

Regulation 2(1)

MEANING OF RECKONABLE SERVICE

1. Subject to the provisions of this schedule, a person's reckonable service shall be a period equivalent to the aggregate of any periods of employment which—

    (*a*) have been spent in any employment described in paragraph 2 of this schedule and

    (*b*) have become reckonable under a superannuation scheme as described in paragraph 3 of this schedule.

2. The employments to which paragraph 1 of this schedule relates are—

    (i) employment under an employing authority or an authority which was, or was deemed to be, an employing authority for the purposes of the National Health Service (Superannuation) Regulations 1961(a) ;

(a) S.I. 1961/1441 (1961 II, p. 2824).

 (ii) employment in which the person was subject to any regulations or scheme made under section 2 of the Local Government (Superannuation) Act (Northern Ireland) 1950(a), section 61 of the Health Services Act (Northern Ireland) 1948(b) or section 54 of the National Health Service (Isle of Man) Act 1948 (an Act of Tynwald) ;

 (iii) employment in the civil service of the State ;

 (iv) employment under an employing authority or a local Act authority within the meaning of section 1(6) of the Local Government Superannuation (Scotland) Act 1937(c) or section 1(3) of the Local Government Superannuation Act 1937(d).

 (v) employment by a district nursing association during any period when a local health authority had arrangements with, or paid contributions to, that Association under Part III of the National Health Service (Scotland) Act 1947(e).

3. For the purposes of paragraph 1 of this schedule a period of employment shall be deemed to have become reckonable under a superannuation scheme if—

 (a) during such period the person was subject to a superannuation scheme and the contributions authorised or required to be paid by the employer were duly paid, or

 (b) such period was taken into account in calculating a sum in the nature of a transfer value paid to that scheme under the Regulations or any corresponding provision in force in England and Wales, Northern Ireland or the Isle of Man or under rules made under section 2 of the Superannuation (Miscellaneous Provisions) Act 1948(f).

Provided that—

 (i) so much of any period referred to in sub-paragraph (b) as consisted of non-contributing service shall be reckonable under this paragraph at half its actual length, and

 (ii) so much of any such period as consisted of part-time service shall be reckonable under this paragraph as though it were whole-time service for a proportionately reduced period.

4. For the purposes of regulation 4(1)(b)(ii) of these regulations, there may be added to the service described in parargaph 1 of this schedule any period of previous service which would have been reckonable under regulation 24 of the Regulations (which provides for the reckoning of qualifying service in certain cases) or any corresponding provision in force in England and Wales, Northern Ireland or the Isle of Man.

5. For the purposes of paragraph 3(a) of this schedule no account shall be taken of any period of employment preceding a break of 12 months or more during which the person was not in employment described in paragraph 2 hereof.

EXPLANATORY NOTE

(This Note is not part of the Regulations.)

 Certain persons who retired from employment in the National Health Service in Scotland elected to secure their superannuation benefits through schemes which operated by way of insurance policies to produce lump sums or annuities, or both, upon retirement. These Regulations provide for the payment of allowances corresponding broadly to the increases for which they would have been eligible under the Pensions (Increase) Acts 1952, 1956, 1959, 1962 and 1965 had they been pensionable under the National Health Service Superannuation Scheme.

(a) 1950 c. 10 (N.I.).   (b) 1948 c. 3 (N.I.).   (c) 1937 c. 69.
(d) 1937 c. 68.   (e) 1947 c. 27.   (f) 1948 c. 33.

The relevant schemes are the Federated Superannuation Scheme for Nurses and Hospital Officers and any other scheme approved for this purpose by the Treasury.

The conditions of entitlement combine, with necessary modifications, the conditions for a health service pension and the conditions for increases under the Pensions (Increase) Acts. The principal of these are, broadly, that the person—

(i) completed 10 years' qualifying service in health service or local government employment or certain types of related employment or the civil service ;

(ii) retired in circumstances in which a person subject to the health service scheme could have retired with a pension ;

(iii) has attained the age of 60 years or is incapacitated, or is a woman who has a dependant.

The allowances are payable, as from 1st July 1966, upon a notional pension which is an amount, defined in regulation 5, corresponding broadly to the pension the person would have received if he had been in the health service scheme and entitled to reckon under that scheme certain service during which he was within the Federated Superannuation Scheme for Nurses and Hospital Officers or any other approved scheme.

Retrospective payment is authorised by section 3(4) of the Pensions (Increase) Act 1965.

STATUTORY INSTRUMENTS

1968 No. 1300 (S.138)

AGRICULTURE

AGRICULTURAL GRANTS, GOODS AND SERVICES

The Small Farm (Business Management) (Scotland) Scheme 1968

Laid before Parliament in draft

Made - - -	*7th August* 1968
Coming into Operation	*1st September* 1968

In exercise of the powers conferred on me by sections 1, 4 and 6 of the Agriculture (Small Farmers) Act 1959(a) and of all other powers enabling me in that behalf and with the approval of the Treasury, I hereby make the following scheme, a draft of which has been laid before Parliament and approved by resolution of each House of Parliament :—

Citation, extent and commencement

1. This scheme, which may be cited as the Small Farm (Business Management) (Scotland) Scheme 1968, shall apply to Scotland and shall come into operation on 1st September 1968.

Interpretation

2.—(1) In this scheme, unless the context otherwise requires—

"the Act" means the Agriculture (Small Farmers) Act 1959 ;

"approved" means approved by the Secretary of State ;

"basic programme" means any approved programme other than a complete programme ;

"complete programme" means such programme, expressly approved as a complete programme, as is in the opinion of the Secretary of State best calculated to increase the efficiency of the business to which it relates, namely a business for which such adequate records have been kept before the day on which the programme is submitted to the Secretary of State for approval as to make it unlikely in his opinion that the programme will subsequently require substantial modification in the light of records kept or disclosed after that day ;

(a) 1959 c.12.

"crofter" means a crofter within the meaning of the Crofters (Scotland) Acts 1955 and 1961(a);

"eligible occupier" means a person who is for the time being an eligible occupier within the meaning of the Crofting Counties Agricultural Grants (Scotland) Scheme 1961(b), the Crofting Counties Agricultural Grants (Scotland) Scheme 1963(c) or the Crofting Counties Agricultural Grants (Scotland) Scheme 1965(d) and, except in the case of a person who is a subtenant as is mentioned in section 14(1)(c) of the Crofters (Scotland) Act 1961, who has been offered a grant under any of the said schemes;

"programme" means a programme of not less than three years' duration for increasing the efficiency of a small farm business, comprised of yearly plans for each of three consecutive specified years, every such plan containing a requirement that such farm business records, specified in the programme, shall be kept as appear to the Secretary of State to be appropriate having regard to all the circumstances of the business;

"relevant land" means any land comprised in a small farm business other than land occupied by any person as a crofter or as an eligible occupier;

"the scheme of 1965" means the Small Farm (Business Management) (Scotland) Scheme 1965(e);

"small farm business" means a trade or business consisting in, or such part of any trade or business as consists in, the carrying out of agricultural operations on land comprised in the business, where the amount of that land under crops or grass, excluding any rough grazing land, does not exceed 150 acres;

"small farm business to which this scheme applies" has the meaning assigned to it by paragraph 3 of this scheme;

"the small farmers schemes" means the Small Farmers (Scotland) Scheme 1959(f) and the Small Farmers (Scotland) Scheme 1962(g).

(2) The Interpretation Act 1889(h) shall apply for the interpretation of this scheme as it applies for the interpretation of an Act of Parliament.

Classes of small farm business to which this scheme applies

3. This scheme applies to a small farm business where the amount of relevant land under crops or grass, excluding any rough grazing land, comprised in the business is not less than 20 acres, and the standard labour requirements of the business calculated in accordance with the Schedule to this scheme are not less than 250 standard man-days a year.

Grants payable for approved programmes

4. Subject to the provisions of this scheme, where the person carrying on a small farm business to which this scheme applies has, within the period commencing with 1st September 1968 and ending with 31st August 1969, submitted to the Secretary of State a programme in respect of the business, and the Secretary of State has approved the programme for the purposes of the scheme, the Secretary of State may in connection with the carrying out of the programme pay grants in respect of the general purposes of the farm business to the person for the time being carrying on the business.

(a) 3 & 4 Eliz. 2.c. 21; 1961 c.58.　　(b) S.I. 1961/2266 (1961 III, p. 3973).
(c) S.I. 1963/1294 (1963 II, p. 2240).　(d) S.I. 1965/1519 (1965 II, p. 4399).
(e) S.I. 1965/1576 (1965 II, p. 4590).　(f) S.I. 1959/573 (1959 I, p. 212).
(g) S.I. 1962/1700 (1962 II, p. 2114).　(h) 1889 c.63.

Restrictions on approval of programmes

5.—(1) No programme shall be approved under this scheme in relation to a small farm business unless on the day on which the programme is submitted to the Secretary of State for approval—

(*a*) the amount of relevant land under crops or grass, excluding any rough grazing land, comprised in the business is not more than 125 acres, and

(*b*) the standard labour requirements of the business calculated in accordance with the Schedule to this scheme are not more than 600 standard man-days a year.

(2) Where any person carrying on a small farm business has received one or more grants in respect of that business under section 65 of the Agriculture Act 1967(**a**) (which enables grants to be made for the keeping of farm business records)—

(*a*) a programme in respect of that business may not be approved under this scheme unless it is a complete programme ; and

(*b*) paragraph 7(4) of this scheme shall not apply to such a programme.

Circumstances in which grant may be paid

6.—(1) A grant under this scheme may be paid on the completion to the satisfaction of the Secretary of State of each of the three yearly plans comprised in an approved programme.

(2) The maximum period in respect of which such a grant may be paid shall be three years from the date of the commencement of the year specified in the programme for the carrying out of the plan to which the grant relates, but without prejudice to section 5 of the Act (which relates to the revocation of programmes where there has been unreasonable delay, etc.) it shall nevertheless be a condition of payment of grant under this scheme that the plan to which the grant relates shall be completed within two years of the said date :

Provided that in cases where failure to complete the plan within the said period of two years has been caused mainly by factors outside the control of the person carrying on the business the Secretary of State may extend the time for completion up to a maximum of one additional year.

Amounts of grants

7.—(1) The amounts of grant payable in connection with the carrying out of a basic programme shall be as follows :—

On completion of the first yearly plan ... £50, plus £2 per acre, up to a maximum of 100 acres.

On completion of the second yearly plan ... £50.

On completion of the third yearly plan ... £50.

(2) The amounts of grant payable in connection with the carrying out of a complete programme shall be as follows :—

On completion of the first yearly plan ... £50, plus £2 per acre, up to a maximum of 100 acres.

On completion of the second yearly plan ... £50, plus £3 10s. per acre, up to a maximum of 100 acres.

On completion of the third yearly plan ... £50, plus £3 per acre, up to a maximum of 100 acres.

(a) 1967 c.22.

(3) Where a yearly plan comprised in a basic programme has been completed to the satisfaction of the Secretary of State and he has received such extracts from the records required to be kept in accordance with that plan as he is entitled to receive under this scheme, if he is satisfied that the next following yearly plan comprised in the programme, either unmodified, or having been modified in accordance with this scheme in such a way as has been agreed between him and the person carrying on the business, is best calculated to improve the efficiency of the business, having regard to the information obtained from such records, then on completion of that following yearly plan the Secretary of State may pay grant at the rate which would have been payable if that plan had been comprised in a complete programme.

(4) Where a person has failed to complete a plan relating to the second or third year of a programme but has carried out such parts of the plan as require the keeping of records, the Secretary of State may nevertheless pay him grant at the appropriate rate for a plan forming part of a basic programme.

(5)(a) In this paragraph "per acre", in relation to any yearly plan, means per acre of the average amount of relevant land under crops or grass, excluding any rough grazing land, comprised in the small farm business to the satisfaction of the Secretary of State during the year to which the plan relates, fractions of an acre being rounded down to the nearest quarter of an acre and all land in respect of which grant has been paid by virtue of a scheme made under section 2 of the Agriculture and Horticulture Act 1964(a) being disregarded.

(b) Any increase or decrease in the amount of land under crops or grass, excluding any rough grazing land, comprised in the business shall at once be notified to the Secretary of State by the person carrying on the business.

Supplementary conditions

8. It shall be a condition of the making of a payment to any person under this scheme that—

(a) there shall be an application in writing, in such form as the Secretary of State may require, for the Secretary of State's approval of any programme proposed to be carried out;

(b) there shall be no substantial modification of a programme except with the consent of the Secretary of State on the application of the person for the time being carrying on the small farm business to which the programme relates;

(c) subject to the provisions of paragraphs 6(2) and 7(4) hereof the programme shall be properly carried out without any avoidable delay;

(d) any person authorised by the Secretary of State in that behalf shall be given reasonable facilities to inspect any land, livestock, works or operations to which the programme relates and shall be given in respect of the programme all such information as the Secretary of State may reasonably require for the purposes of the scheme;

(e) such records of the business as relate to the duration of the programme or to the three preceding years shall on reasonable notice be produced to a person authorised by the Secretary of State and extracts from records kept in pursuance of a requirement in the programme shall be submitted to the Secretary of State in such form and at such times as he may require.

(a) 1964 c.28.

Abatement where grant previously paid

9.—(1) Subject to the following provisions of this paragraph, it shall be a condition of the making of a payment to a person under this scheme that the sum of the grants payable under the foregoing provisions of this scheme in connection with the carrying out of the programme to which the payment relates shall be reduced by—

(a) the aggregate of all farm business grants paid to him under the small farmers schemes or either of them ;

(b) the aggregate of all field husbandry grants paid to him under the small farmers schemes or either of them in respect of any of the relevant land comprised in the small farm business to which the programme relates ;

(c) the aggregate of the residual values of all field husbandry grants paid under the small farmers schemes or either of them to any other person in respect of any of the relevant land comprised in the said small farm business ;
and

(d) the aggregate of all grants paid to him in connection with the carrying out of a programme under the scheme of 1965 or any other programme under this scheme.

(2) For the purposes of this paragraph—

(a) the residual value of a field husbandry grant shall be the amount of such grant reduced by 25 per cent. for each complete year in excess of 3 years between the date of the commencement of the farm business plan in respect of which the grant was payable and the date on which the person to whom grant is payable under this scheme commenced to carry on the small farm business ;

(b) where a field husbandry grant has been paid partly in respect of relevant land which is comprised in the small farm business and partly in respect of other land, the grant shall be apportioned by the Secretary of State ;

(c) payment of a grant to a person includes the payment of a grant which in the opinion of the Secretary of State is substantially paid for the benefit of that person, notwithstanding that the payment is nominally made to some other person ;

(d) where a grant has been paid to a partnership or to persons jointly, the Secretary of State may apportion the grant between the members of the partnership or such other persons in such manner as he thinks appropriate, having regard to their respective interests, and any part of a grant so apportioned to a person shall be deemed to have been paid to him.

Other limitations

10.—(1) No person shall receive a grant in connection with the carrying out of a programme under this scheme if at any time while he is carrying out that programme he is also carrying out a farm business plan under either of the small farmers schemes or a programme under the scheme of 1965 or is keeping farm business records with a view to obtaining grant under section 65 of the Agriculture Act 1967.

(2) If a person is carrying out two or more programmes under this scheme at the same time, he may receive grant in respect of only one such programme.

William Ross,
One of Her Majesty's Principal
Secretaries of State.

1st August 1968.

We approve,

E. Alan Fitch,
Joseph Harper,
Two of the Lords Commissioners of
Her Majesty's Treasury.

7th August 1968.

Paragraphs 3 and 5

SCHEDULE

In this Schedule "business" means a trade or business consisting in, or such part of a trade or business as consists in, the carrying out of agricultural operations on relevant land comprised in it.

1. The standard labour requirements of a business on any day shall be expressed in standard man-days calculated, except as is otherwise provided in the succeeding paragraphs, by multiplying respectively the number of standard man-days set out in the following table in relation to any kind of crop or livestock therein mentioned by the total number of acres (or other units to which the standard man-days are related in the table) of that kind of crop, or the average of the numbers of that kind of livestock, shown to the satisfaction of the Secretary of State to be comprised in the business during the 12 months immediately preceding the date to which the calculation relates, adding together the results so obtained and increasing the total by 15 per cent.

2. Where a crop is grown for a person other than the person carrying on the business under a contract with that other person by which he carries out any part of the cultivations necessary for growing or harvesting the crop, the number of standard man-days attributable to that crop shall be reduced to such figure as the Secretary of State considers reasonable, having regard to the proportion of the cultivations carried out by the person carrying on the business.

3. Where double cropping is practised on land comprised in the business, the area of both crops shall be included in the calculation.

4. Livestock taken into pasture in return for a money payment shall be deemed to be comprised in the business while they are on land comprised in the business, and not otherwise.

5. A cow of a dairy type which suckles calves shall be classified as a beef cow.

6. The number of livestock comprised in the business shall not include calves less than 7 days old, unweaned piglets, or unweaned lambs.

7. The number of pigs fattened or reared on land comprised in the business shall be the total number of pigs so fattened or reared during the 12 months immediately preceding the date to which the calculation relates.

8. The number of any kind of poultry (other than laying birds and male birds for breeding) shall be the total number of that kind of poultry kept on the land comprised in the business during the 12 months immediately preceding the date to which the calculation relates.

9. If the Secretary of State is satisfied that by reason of special circumstances the area of crops, or of any kind of crop, or the number of livestock, or of any kind of livestock, comprised in the business during any period of 12 months mentioned in the preceding paragraphs is unrepresentative of the area or number respectively usually comprised in the business, such other area or number shall be taken as is, in the opinion of the Secretary of State, shown by the person for the time being carrying on the business to be representative of the area or number usually comprised in the business.

TABLE

CROPS

	Standard man-days (per acre unless otherwise indicated)
Wheat	2½
Barley	2½
Oats	3½
Mixed Corn	3½
Rye, for threshing	3½
Rye, for grazing	1½
Arable silage	3
Beans and peas for stockfeeding	3
Potatoes, seed	20
Potatoes, ware	18
Turnips and swedes for stockfeeding	11
Sugar beet	12½
Fodder beet	12½
Mangolds	11
Rape (or Cole)	1½
Kale, for grazing	1½
Cabbage, kale (other than for grazing), savoys and kohl rabi, for stockfeeding	6
Vetches or tares	3½
Orchards	
Seven years old and over	25
Under seven years old	10
Derelict orchards	¼
Small fruit: Under orchard trees	30
Not under orchard trees—	
Strawberries	70
Raspberries	90
Currants (black)	50
Currants (red and white)	45
Gooseberries	45
Loganberries and cultivated blackberries	80
Vegetables for human consumption—	
Brussels sprouts	25
Cabbage	17
Kale and sprouting broccoli	17
Cauliflower	17
Carrots	17
Parsnips	21
Turnips and swedes	21
Beetroot (red beet)	35
Broad beans	30
Peas, green for pulling	30
Peas, for vining or harvesting dry	4½
Lettuce, grown in the open	10
Tomatoes, grown in the open	50
Other vegetables (including rhubarb)	50

	Standard man-days (per acre unless otherwise indicated)
Hardy nursery stock	50
Bulbs and flowers in the open	100
Other crops in the open (including all crops grown for seed except cereals, potatoes and grass)	3
Bare fallow	½
Grass (including clover, lucerne and sainfoin)—	
for mowing	1½
for grazing	¼
for seed	4½
Mushrooms (per 100 sq. ft.)	3½
Crops under glass (per 100 sq. ft.)	3½

LIVESTOCK

	Standard man-days (per head per annum)
Dairy cows in milk or in calf and heifers in milk	12
Beef cows	4
Bulls	7
Other cattle	2½
Upland sheep	¼
Lowland sheep	¾
Breeding sows and gilts	4
Boars	4
Pigs fattened or reared for breeding	½
Poultry—	
Laying birds and male birds for breeding	0.20
broilers produced and young birds (other than day-old chicks) sold for fattening	0.01
other poultry sold for slaughter, or reared for flock replacement	0.05

EXPLANATORY NOTE

(This Note is not part of the Scheme.)

This Scheme, made under Section 1 of the Agriculture (Small Farmers) Act 1959, provides for the making of grants to a person carrying on a small farm business in Scotland if he carries out with the approval of the Secretary of State a three year programme for increasing the efficiency of the business. Every programme must provide for the keeping of farm business records.

The Scheme applies to programmes submitted for approval during the period from 1st September 1968 to 31st August 1969. To be eligible, a small farm business must comprise not less than 20, and not more than 150, acres of land under crops or grass, and have standard labour requirements of not less than 250 standard man-days a year. At the time the programme is submitted for approval the acreage must be not more than 125, and the standard man-days not more than 600.

Grants are made in respect of the general purposes of the business. The rates differ in the second and third years of a programme, according to its nature. Where records have already been kept, so that it is possible to formulate a complete programme from the outset, the higher rate of grant will be payable on completion of each year's plan. Otherwise there will be a basic programme, attracting the same rate in the first year, but lower rates in subsequent years conditional only on the keeping of records. A basic programme can be amended by agreement to take account of the records, and if the Secretary of State is satisfied that the plan is then best calculated to increase the efficiency of the business, having regard to the records, he can pay grant at the higher rate in the second and third years.

The Scheme replaces the Small Farm (Business Management) (Scotland) Scheme 1965, under which programmes may be submitted for approval during the three years ending 31st August 1968. A person is ineligible for grant under this Scheme if he is keeping records under the Farm Business Recording Scheme, and if he has already participated in that scheme he can only undertake a complete programme under this Scheme. Otherwise, apart from the shorter period during which programmes may be submitted, the Scheme is substantially the same as its predecessor.

STATUTORY INSTRUMENTS

1968 No. 1309

REGISTRATION OF BIRTHS, DEATHS, MARRIAGES, ETC.

ENGLAND AND WALES

The Registration of Births, Deaths and Marriages (Fees) (Amendment) Order 1968

Made - - - -	14*th August* 1968
Laid before Parliament	14*th August* 1968
Coming into Operation	15*th August* 1968

The Minister of Health in exercise of the powers conferred on him by section 5 of, and schedule 3 to, the Public Expenditure and Receipts Act 1968(a) and of all other powers enabling him in that behalf, hereby makes the following order :—

Title, commencement and interpretation

1.—(1) This order may be cited as the Registration of Births, Deaths and Marriages (Fees) (Amendment) Order 1968 and shall come into operation on 15th August 1968.

(2) The Interpretation Act 1889(b) shall apply to the interpretation of this Order as it applies to the interpretation of an Act of Parliament.

Amendment of Registration of Births, Deaths and Marriages (Fees) Order 1968

2. In article 1 of the Registration of Births, Deaths and Marriages (Fees) Order 1968(c) for the date 16th August 1968 there shall be substituted the date 1st October 1968.

Given under the official seal of the Minister of Health on 14th August 1968.

(L.S.)

Julian Snow,
Parliamentary Secretary,
Ministry of Health.

EXPLANATORY NOTE

(This Note is not part of the Order.)

This Order corrects a mistake in the Registration of Births, Deaths and Marriages (Fees) Order 1968 and provides that that Order shall come into force on 1st October 1968 instead of on 16th August 1968.

(a) 1968 c. 14. (b) 1889 c. 63. (c) S.I. 1968/1242(1968 II, p. 3354).

STATUTORY INSTRUMENTS

1968 No. 1310

BRITISH NATIONALITY

The British Nationality (People's Republic of Southern Yemen) Order 1968

Made - - -	13*th August* 1968
Coming into Operation	14*th August* 1968

In exercise of the powers conferred upon me by paragraph 1 of the Schedule to the Aden, Perim and Kuria Muria Islands Act 1967(**a**), I hereby make the following Order:—

1. For the purposes of paragraph 1 of the Schedule to the Aden, Perim and Kuria Muria Islands Act 1967 (which provides, subject to exceptions, for the loss, on such date as may be specified by order, of citizenship of the United Kingdom and Colonies by a person possessing on that date such nationality or citizenship as is so specified by reason of his connection with a territory designated by the order)—

   (*a*) the People's Republic of Southern Yemen shall be a designated territory;

   (*b*) in relation thereto the specified nationality shall be Southern Yemeni nationality, and

   (*c*) in relation thereto the specified date shall be 14th August 1968.

2. This Order may be cited as the British Nationality (People's Republic of Southern Yemen) Order 1968 and shall come into operation on 14th August 1968.

James Callaghan,
One of Her Majesty's Principal
Secretaries of State.

Home Office,
 Whitehall.
13th August 1968.

(**a**) 1967 c. 71.

EXPLANATORY NOTE

(This Note is not part of the Order.)

This Order, read with the Schedule to the Aden, Perim and Kuria Muria Islands Act 1967, provides, with effect from 14th August 1968, that a person possessing the nationality of the People's Republic of Southern Yemen by reason of his connection therewith shall cease to be a citizen of the United Kingdom and Colonies unless his case falls within paragraph 3 of the Schedule to the 1967 Act.

STATUTORY INSTRUMENTS

1968 No. 1314

TELEGRAPHS

The Wireless Telegraphy (General Licence Charges) Regulations 1968

Made - - -	*15th August* 1968
Laid before Parliament	*22nd August* 1968
Coming into Operation	*1st October* 1968

I, The Right Honourable John Thomson Stonehouse, M.P., Her Majesty's Postmaster General, with the consent of the Treasury, by virtue of the power vested in me by section 2 of the Wireless Telegraphy Act 1949(a), by the said section as extended to the Channel Islands by the Wireless Telegraphy (Channel Islands) Order 1952(b), and by the said section as extended to the Isle of Man by the Wireless Telegraphy (Isle of Man) Order 1952(c), and of every other power enabling me in this behalf, do hereby make the following regulations, that is to say :—

Interpretation

1.—(1) In these regulations, except so far as the context otherwise requires, the following expressions have the meanings hereby respectively assigned to them :—

"the Act" means the Wireless Telegraphy Act 1949 ;

"aircraft station" means a station for wireless telegraphy established in an aircraft ;

"amateur station" means a station for wireless telegraphy established and used, as part of the self-training of the licensee in communication by wireless telegraphy, for the purpose of communication with other stations similarly established and used ; and "amateur television station" shall be construed accordingly ;

"coast station" means a station for wireless telegraphy on land which is established or licensed by the Government of the State in which it is situated to send and receive public correspondence and other messages to and from any ship station, but does not include a station which is licensed only to send and receive messages to and from a limited number of ship stations ;

"demonstration licence" means a licence of the description specified in item 5 in Part 1 of the Schedule hereto ;

"base station" means a station for wireless telegraphy established at a fixed location ;

"licence" means a wireless telegraphy licence granted under section one of the Act, not being either :—

(a) a licence of a type wholly or mainly intended to meet the needs of persons desiring to use, in a private dwellinghouse and without making any charge to other persons, apparatus not designed or adapted for emission (as opposed to reception), or

---

(a) 1949 c. 54.   (b) S.I. 1952/1900 (1952 III, p. 3414).
(c) S.I. 1952/1899 (1952 III, p. 3418).

(b) any other licence to which the Wireless Telegraphy (Broadcast Licence Charges) Regulations 1967(a) or any regulations amending or replacing the same apply ;

"mobile station" means a station for wireless telegraphy which is not a base station ;

"private mobile radio licence" means a licence of the description specified in item 9 of Part 1 of the Schedule hereto ;

"ship station" means a station for wireless telegraphy established in a vessel which is not permanently moored ;

"special service station" means a station for wireless telegraphy which provides, for the benefit of shipping generally, all or any of the following services : —

notices to navigators, meteorological bulletins, medical advices, standard frequencies and time signals ;

"radionavigation station" means a station for wireless telegraphy which provides for the benefit of shipping generally a service to enable ships to determine their distance from, or their position or bearing in relation to, any object ;

and other expressions have the same meaning as they have in the Act.

(2) The Interpretation Act 1889(b) applies for the interpretation of these regulations as it applies for the interpretation of an Act of Parliament and as if these regulations and the regulations hereby revoked were Acts of Parliament.

Issue fees

2. On the issue of a licence of a type and description specified in the Schedule hereto, the licensee shall pay an issue fee of the amount specified in relation to that type and description of licence in the said Schedule, whatever may be the duration of the licence.

Renewal fees

3.—(1) On every occasion when, by virtue of a term or provision in the licence, a licence of a type and description specified in Part 1 of the Schedule hereto would cease to be in force on a particular date unless a renewal fee were paid, and the licensee desires that the licence should remain in force for a further period after that date, he shall pay on or before that date, in respect of the period following, a renewal fee of the amount specified in relation to that type and description of licence in the said Schedule.

(2) So long as any licence of a type and description specified in Part 2 of the Schedule hereto remains in force, the licensee shall pay in advance in each year on or before the date specified in the licence, in respect of the year following, a renewal fee of the amount specified in relation to that type and description of licence in the said Schedule.

Other issue and renewal fees

4. On the issue or renewal of any licence which is not of a type or description specified in the Schedule hereto, the licensee shall pay an issue or renewal fee of such amount as may in the particular case appear to the Postmaster General to be proper.

(a) S.I. 1967/1566 (1967 III, p. 4341).   (b) 1889 c. 63.

Fees on variation of certain licences

5.—(1) Whenever a demonstration licence is varied by the addition of one or more stations for wireless telegraphy to those for the time being comprised in the licence, the licensee shall pay a fee at the following rate in respect of each additional station :—

	£	s.	d.
Where the date of the variation is more than 8 months before the next date on which the licence would cease to be in force if a renewal fee were not paid	4	10	0
Where the former date is more than 4 months but not more than 8 months before the latter date	3	0	0
Where the former date is not more than 4 months before the latter date	1	10	0

(2) Whenever a private mobile radio licence is varied by the addition of one or more stations for wireless telegraphy to those for the time being comprised in the licence, the licensee shall pay a fee at the following rate in respect of each additional station :—

	£	s.	d.
Where the date of the variation is more than 8 months before the next date on which the licence would cease to be in force if a renewal fee were not paid	2	5	0
Where the former date is more than 4 months but not more than 8 months before the latter date	1	10	0
Where the former date is not more than 4 months before the latter date	0	15	0

(3) Whenever a licence to which regulation four applies (not being a licence granted in pursuance of section four of the Act) is so varied, the licensee shall pay a fee of such amount as may in the particular case appear to the Postmaster General to be proper.

General

6. On the revocation or variation of a licence no part of any fee already paid or due to be paid shall be refunded or cease to be due unless the Postmaster General so determines.

Revocation

7. The Wireless Telegraphy (General Licence Charges) Regulations 1954(a) and the Wireless Telegraphy (General Licence Charges) Amendment (No. 1) Regulations 1957(b) are hereby revoked.

Citation and Commencement

8. These regulations shall come into operation on the 1st day of October 1968, and may be cited as the Wireless Telegraphy (General Licence Charges) Regulations 1968.

Dated 5th August 1968.

John Stonehouse,
Her Majesty's Postmaster General.

We consent to these regulations.

B. K. O'Malley,
Harry Gourlay,
15th August 1968.
Two of the Lords Commissioners of
Her Majesty's Treasury.

(a) S.I. 1954/439 (1954 II, p. 2376).   (b) S.I. 1957/978 (1957 II, p. 2544).

THE SCHEDULE

Part I

Type of Licence	Description of Licence	Issue Fee	Renewal Fee
1. Amateur (Sound) Licence A	A licence to establish and use, on specified frequency bands which include bands below 144 Megacycles a second, an amateur station otherwise than in a moving vehicle, vessel or aircraft, for the purpose of sending to and receiving from other amateur stations messages (but not visual images) of the class or classes specified in the licence.	£3	£3
2. Amateur (Sound) Licence B	A licence to establish and use, on specified frequency bands above 144 megacycles a second, an amateur station otherwise than in a moving vehicle, vessel or aircraft, for the purpose of sending to and receiving from other amateur stations messages (but not visual images) of the class or classes specified in the licence.	£3	£3
3. Amateur (Sound Mobile) Licence	A licence to establish and use (otherwise than on the sea or within any estuary, dock or harbour) an amateur station in any vehicle or vessel for the purpose of sending to and receiving from other amateur stations messages (but not visual images) of the class or classes specified in the licence.	£3 or, if the licence is expressed to be supplemental to an Amateur (Sound) Licence A or Amateur (Sound) Licence B, £1 10s.	£3 or, if the licence is expressed to be supplemental to an Amateur (Sound) Licence A or Amateur (Sound) Licence B, £1 10s.
4. Amateur (Television) Licence.	A licence to establish and use an amateur television station for the purpose of sending visual images to and receiving visual images from other amateur television stations.	£3	£3
5. Demonstration Licence.	A licence to establish and use specified sending and receiving stations for wireless telegraphy for the purpose of sending and receiving, between the stations, or between one or some of the stations and another or others of them, spoken test messages for demonstrating the apparatus comprised in the stations in the course of the licensee's business as manufacturer of or dealer in such apparatus (not being a licence authorising the transmission of messages directly between base stations).	At the rate of £4 10s. for each station comprised in the licence.	At the rate of £4 10s. for each station comprised in the licence on the last date on which the renewal fee is payable.

Type of Licence	Description of Licence	Issue Fee	Renewal Fee
6. Induction Communication Licence	A licence to establish and use, within a specified frequency band not being above 315 kilocycles a second, sending and receiving stations for wireless telegraphy operating only on the induction field, the number whereof is not limited by the licence, for the purpose of sending and receiving messages between the stations, or between one or some of the stations and another or others of them (not being a licence authorising the transmission of messages directly between base stations).	£3	£3
7. Model Control Licence.	A licence to establish and use a station for wireless telegraphy for the purpose of controlling the movement of a model vehicle, vessel or aircraft, by means of the emission of electro-magnetic energy from sending apparatus, and the reception of such energy by receiving apparatus in the model.	£1 10s.	£1 10s.
8. Police and Fire Service Licence.	A licence to establish and use sending and receiving stations for wireless telegraphy, the number whereof is not limited by the licence, for the purpose of sending and receiving spoken messages concerning the operation of Police or Fire Services.	£3	£3
9. Private Mobile Radio Licence.	A licence to establish and use, on specified frequencies not being below 30 megacycles a second, specified sending and receiving stations for wireless telegraphy (whether or not the licence also authorises the establishment and use of receiving stations for wireless telegraphy for the purpose of monitoring messages sent between the stations) for the purpose of sending and receiving spoken messages concerning the business of the licensee between the stations, or between one or some of the stations and another or others of them (not being a licence authorising the transmission of messages which are originated at one base station direct to another base station and which are not messages intended for onward transmission by that other base station to a mobile station).	At the rate of £4 for each of the first two stations comprised in the licence and £2 5s. for each of the other stations comprised in the licence.	At the rate of £4 for each of the first two of the stations comprised in the licence on the last date on which the renewal fee is payable and £2 5s. for each of the other stations comprised in the licence on the said date.

Type of Licence	Description of Licence	Issue Fee	Renewal Fee
10. Private Mobile Radio (Limited Period) Licence	A licence to establish and use, for a period not exceeding twenty-eight days, specified sending and receiving stations for wireless telegraphy, (using for emission either the frequency of 85.875 megacycles a second at any base station and the frequency of 72.375 megacycles a second at any mobile station, or the frequency of 167.2 megacycles a second at any base station, and the frequency of 172.0 megacycles a second at any mobile station or the frequency 456.925 megacycles a second at any base station and the frequency 462.425 megacycles a second at any mobile station, for the purpose of sending and receiving spoken messages concerning the business of the licensee between the stations, or between one or some of the stations and another or others of them (not being a licence authorising the transmission of messages which are originated at one base station direct to another base station and which are not messages intended for onward transmission by that other base station to a mobile station).	£1 10s.	—
11. Radar (Land) Station Licence.	A licence to establish and use a Radar sending and receiving station for wireless telegraphy at a place on land specified in the licence, for sending and receiving signals for the purposes of the determination of position, bearing or distance, or for the gaining of information as to the presence, absence, position or motion of any object or of any objects of any class.	£1 10s.	£1 10s.
12. Radio Beacon Licence.	A licence to establish and use a sending station for wireless telegraphy for sending signals by automatic means for the purpose of indicating to any ship or to any aircraft (as the case may be) the position bearing or distance of the station in relation thereto (whether or not the licence also authorises the establishment and use of receiving stations for wireless telegraphy as specified in the licence for monitoring the signals sent by the sending station).	£1 10s.	£1 10s.

Type of Licence	Description of Licence	Issue Fee	Renewal Fee
13. Radio Microphone Licence	A licence to establish and use mobile and base stations, the number whereof is not limited by the licence, for the purpose of sending from the mobile stations spoken messages or music for relay by public address system or for recording by means of sound recording apparatus and of receiving such messages or music by the base stations.	£3	£3
14. Radio Paging Licence.	A licence to establish and use, on specified frequencies not being below 26.1 megacycles a second, specified sending stations for wireless telegraphy, and receiving stations for wireless telegraphy the number whereof is not limited by the licence, for the purpose of sending and receiving messages concerning the business of the licensee (not being a licence authorising the transmission of messages which are originated at one base station direct to another base station and which are not messages intended for onward transmission by that other base station to a mobile station).	£4 10s.	£4 10s.
15. Ship (Receiving Only) Licence.	A licence to establish and use in a ship a receiving station for wireless telegraphy for the purpose of receiving messages sent from coast stations, ship stations, aircraft stations, special service stations, and radionavigation stations for general reception by ship stations or for reception by the said station, and messages sent by authorised broadcasting stations.	£2 10s.	£2 10s.
16. Testing and Development (Radiating) Licence.	A licence to establish a sending and receiving station for wireless telegraphy and, for the purpose of testing or developing the wireless telegraphy apparatus from time to time comprised in the station or in the other stations specified in the licence, to use the station for sending and receiving test messages to and from those other stations and sending test messages intended solely for reception within the room in which the first mentioned station is situate and receiving the same.	£3	£3

Type of Licence	Description of Licence	Issue Fee	Renewal Fee
17. Testing and Development (Supressed Radiation) Licence.	A licence to establish a sending and receiving station for wireless telegraphy and, for the purpose of testing or developing the wireless telegraphy apparatus from time to time comprised in the station, to use the station for sending test messages intended solely for reception within the room in which the station is situate and receiving the same, and for receiving test messages from the other stations specified in the licence.	£1 10s.	£1 10s.
18. Training Establishment Licence.	A licence to establish a sending and receiving station for wireless telgraphy and, for the purpose of instructing pupils in the theory and practice of wireless telegraphy, to use the station for sending messages intended solely for reception within the room in which the station is situate, and for receiving such messages and messages of any other classes specified in the licence—whether or not the licence in addition authorises the establishment and use of a radar station for wireless telegraphy.	£3	£3

Part II

Type of Licence	Description of Licence	Issue Fee	Renewal Fee
1. Aircraft Licence.	A licence to establish and use a sending and receiving station for wireless telegraphy in an aircraft for the purpose of sending messages, and receiving messages sent for general reception by aircraft stations or for reception by the said station and messages sent by authorised broadcasting stations.	£2 10s.	£2 10s.

PART II

Type of Licence	Description of Licence	Issue Fee	Renewal Fee
2. Ship Licence.	A licence to establish and use a sending and receiving station for wireless telegraphy in a ship for the purpose of (*a*) sending messages to coast stations, ship stations, and aircraft stations, and (*b*) receiving messages sent from coast stations, ship stations, aircraft stations, special service stations, and radionavigation stations for general reception by ship stations or for reception by the said station, and messages sent by authorised broadcasting stations — whether or not the licence in addition authorises the establishment and use of stations for wireless telegraphy in lifeboats or other survival-craft associated with or normally carried by the ship, or of a radar station for wireless telegraphy in the ship.	£3 10s.	£3 10s.

EXPLANATORY NOTE

(*This Note is not part of the Regulations.*)

These Regulations consolidate with amendments the Wireless Telegraphy (General Licence Charges) Regulations, 1954 and the Wireless Telegraphy (General Licence Charges) Amendment (No. 1) Regulations, 1957. The Regulations provide for the issue and renewal fees payable in respect of wireless telegraphy licences, other than the sound and television broadcast receiving licences and broadcast relay station licences which are covered by the Wireless Telegraphy (Broadcast Licence Charges) Regulations, 1967.

Issue and renewal fees for standard form licences are specified in the Schedule.

Regulation 5 fixes the fees payable when a demonstration licence or a private mobile radio licence is varied by the addition of a wireless telegraphy station.

Increases are made in all the fees specified in the Regulations which are consolidated, and fees are prescribed for some additional forms of licence.

The Regulations also enable the Postmaster General to fix the issue fee, renewal fee and (except as regards an experimental licence) the variation fee payable in respect of any special licence which is not on one of the standard forms referred to in the Schedule.

STATUTORY   INSTRUMENTS

1968 No. 1315

THEATRES

The Theatres (Licence Application Fees) Order 1968

Made - - - -	*13th August* 1968
Laid before Parliament	*22nd August* 1968
Coming into Operation	*26th August* 1968

In exercise of the powers conferred on me by paragraph 3(1) of Schedule 1 to the Theatres Act 1968(a), I hereby make the following Order:—

1.—(1) The fee payable under paragraph 3(1) of Schedule 1 to the Theatres Act 1968 by an applicant for the grant or renewal of a licence under that Act for a period of a year or a shorter specified period shall be £5 except that, where the specified period does not exceed 3 months and 3 weeks, the fee so payable shall be determined in accordance with the next following paragraph.

(2) Where the specified period does not exceed 3 months and 3 weeks, the fee so payable shall be the aggregate of—

(a) £1 5s. 0d. for each complete month or part of a month exceeding 3 weeks included in the period, and

(b) 7s. 6d. for each complete week or part of a week so included and not taken into account under the preceding sub-paragraph.

2.—(1) The fee payable under paragraph 3(1) of Schedule 1 to the Theatres Act 1968 by an applicant for the grant of a licence under that Act in respect of one or more particular occasions shall be 7s. 6d. except that, where the particular occasions fall on more than 7 different days, the fee so payable shall be determined in accordance with the next following paragraph.

(2) Where the particular occasions fall on more than 7 different days, the fee so payable shall be of the like amount as would be payable if the application were for the grant of a licence for a specified period equal to the aggregate number of days on which those occasions fall.

3. The fee payable under paragraph 3(1) of Schedule 1 to the Theatres Act 1968 by an applicant for the transfer of a licence under that Act shall be £1 5s. 0d. except that the fee so payable shall not exceed that which would be payable if the application were for the grant of a licence for the residue of the period for which, or the residue of the occasions in respect of which, the licence is in force.

(a) 1968 c. 54.

2t

4. In this Order a reference to a week is a reference to a period of 7 days and a reference to a month is a reference to a period of 4 weeks.

5. This Order may be cited as the Theatres (Licence Application Fees) Order 1968 and shall come into operation on 26th August 1968.

James Callaghan,
One of Her Majesty's Principal
Secretaries of State.

Home Office,
Whitehall.
13th August 1968.

EXPLANATORY NOTE

(This Note is not part of the Order.)

Paragraph 3(1) of Schedule 1 to the Theatres Act 1968 provides that on applying for the grant, renewal or transfer of a licence under that Act a person shall pay such fee as may be prescribed, except that no fee shall be payable on an application for the grant or transfer of an occasional licence if the licensing authority are satisfied that the play to be performed is of an educational or other like character or the performance is for charitable or other like purposes.

This Order prescribes the fees payable under paragraph 3(1). In particular, the application fee in respect of the grant or renewal of an annual licence is £5 (Article 1(1)), that in respect of the grant of an occasional licence covering not more than 7 days is 7*s*. 6*d*. (Article 2(1)) and that in respect of the transfer of a licence may not exceed 25*s*. 0*d*. (Article 3).

STATUTORY INSTRUMENTS

1968 No. 1316

CIVIL AVIATION

The Carriage by Air (Sterling Equivalents) Order 1968

Made - - -	*12th August* 1968
Coming into Operation	*1st September* 1968

The Board of Trade, in exercise of their powers under section 4(4) of the Carriage by Air Act 1961(**a**) and under that provision as applied by Article 6 of the Carriage by Air Acts (Application of Provisions) Order 1967(**b**), as having effect by virtue of the Transfer of Functions (Civil Aviation) Order 1966(**c**) and of all other powers enabling them in that behalf hereby order as follows:

1. This Order may be cited as the Carriage by Air (Sterling Equivalents) Order 1968 and shall come into operation on 1st September 1968.

2. The amounts shown in column 2 of the following Table are hereby specified as amounts to be taken for the purposes of Article 22 in the First Schedule to the Carriage by Air Act 1961 and of that Article as applied by the Carriage by Air Acts (Application of Provisions) Order 1967 as equivalent to the sums respectively expressed in francs on the same line in column 1 of that Table:

TABLE

Amount of francs	Sterling equivalent		
	£	s.	d.
250	6	18	$2\frac{3}{8}$
5,000	138	4	0
125,000	3,454	19	0
250,000	6,909	18	0
875,000	24,184	12	11

J. H. Riddoch,
An Under Secretary of the
Board of Trade.

12th August 1968.

(**a**) 1961 c. 27.   (**b**) S.I. 1967/480 (1967 I, p. 1475).
(**c**) S.I. 1966/741 (1966 II, p. 1732).

EXPLANATORY NOTE

(This Note is not part of the Order.)

This Order specifies the sterling equivalents of amounts expressed in gold francs as the limit of the air carrier's liability under the Warsaw Convention of 1929, and under that Convention as amended by the Hague Protocol of 1955, as well as under corresponding provisions applying to carriage by air to which the Convention and Protocol do not apply.

The amounts have been converted into sterling at 291s. 8d. per fine ounce troy, i.e. on the basis of the gold value of the pound sterling as declared by the United Kingdom to the International Monetary Fund.

STATUTORY INSTRUMENTS

1968 No. 1319

WAGES COUNCILS

The Wages Regulation (Shirtmaking) (Amendment) Order 1968

Made - - -	*15th August* 1968	
Coming into Operation	*11th September* 1968	

Whereas the Secretary of State has received from the Shirtmaking Wages Council (Great Britain) the wages regulation proposals set out in the Schedule hereto;

Now, therefore, the Secretary of State in exercise of her powers under section 11 of the Wages Councils Act 1959(a), and of all other powers enabling her in that behalf, hereby makes the following Order:—

1. This Order may be cited as the Wages Regulation (Shirtmaking) (Amendment) Order 1968.

2.—(1) In this Order the expression " the specified date " means the 11th September 1968, provided that where, as respects any worker who is paid wages at intervals not exceeding seven days, that date does not correspond with the beginning of the period for which the wages are paid, the expression " the specified date " means, as respects that worker, the beginning of the next such period following that date.

(2) The Interpretation Act 1889(b) shall apply to the interpretation of this Order as it applies to the interpretation of an Act of Parliament.

3. The wages regulation proposals set out in the Schedule hereto shall have effect as from the specified date.

Signed by order of the Secretary of State.
15th August 1968.

A. A. Jarratt,
Deputy Under Secretary of State,
Department of Employment and Productivity.

(a) 1959 c. 69. (b) 1889 c. 63.

SCHEDULE

STATUTORY MINIMUM REMUNERATION

The Wages Regulation (Shirtmaking) Order 1966(a) (Order S.(66)) shall have effect as if in the Schedule thereto for Parts II and III there were substituted the following Parts:—

" PART II

MALE WORKERS

GENERAL MINIMUM TIME RATES AND PIECE WORK BASIS TIME RATES

	Column 1 General minimum time rates	Column 2 Piece work basis time rates
Paragraph 2. Subject to the provisions of this Schedule, the general minimum time rates set out in Column 1 of this paragraph are payable to male time workers and the piece work basis time rates set out in Column 2 are applicable to male workers when employed on piece work, as follows:—	Per hour s. d.	Per hour s. d.
(1) SPECIAL OR MEASURE CUTTERS, PATTERN CUTTERS OR PATTERN TAKERS, who are employed as such during the whole or a substantial part of their time and have had after the age of 18 years not less than three years' employment as a cutter of any class specified in this or the next following sub-paragraph including not less than two years as a measure cutter	5 11	6 3
(2) CUTTERS, aged 21 years or over, who are employed as such during the whole or a substantial part of their time and have had not less than four years' employment as a cutter of any class specified in this or the last preceding sub-paragraph	5 9	6 0¾
(3) TIE CUTTERS, aged 22 years or over, who are employed during the whole or a substantial part of their time in tie cutting and have had at least five years' experience therein	5 11	6 3
(4) TIE CUTTERS (not being workers to whom sub-paragraph (3) applies) aged 21 years or over, who are employed during the whole or a substantial part of their time in tie cutting and have had at least four years' experience therein	5 9	6 0¾

(a) S.I. 1966/786 (1966 II, p. 1806).

	Column 1 General minimum time rates	Column 2 Piece work basis time rates
	Per hour s. d.	Per hour s. d.
(5) ALL OTHER MALE WORKERS being aged—		
21 years or over	5 5	
20 and under 21 years	4 7	
19 „ „ 20 „	4 2	
18 „ „ 19 „	3 $9\frac{1}{4}$	
17 „ „ 18 „	3 5	
16 „ „ 17 „	3 0	
under 16 years	2 7	

PART III
FEMALE WORKERS

GENERAL MINIMUM TIME RATES

Paragraph 3.

(1) Subject to the provisions of this Schedule, the general minimum time rates payable to female time workers are as follows:—

Per hour
s. d.

(a) CONVEYOR BELT MACHINISTS (that is to say, female persons employed in machining any work conveyed direct to or from them on a mechanical conveyor belt) not being learners to whom (b) of this sub-paragraph applies ... ... 4 $1\frac{1}{2}$

(b) LEARNERS during the following periods of employment in the trade:—

1st six months	2	$3\frac{1}{2}$
2nd six months	2	6
2nd year	3	0
3rd year	3	$4\frac{1}{4}$

Provided that a worker who enters, or has entered the trade for the first time at or over the age of 18 years shall be treated for the purposes of this paragraph as though she had, at the date of her entry, completed one year of employment as a learner.

(c) ALL OTHER WORKERS (including home-workers) .. 4 0

(2) For the purpose of determining the period of a learner's employment in the trade and the date on which she ceases to be a learner, there shall be reckoned as employment in the trade any employment in any branch of the trade or in the making, wherever carried on, of overalls for male or female persons.

PIECE WORK BASIS TIME RATES   Paragraph 4.

Per hour
s. d.

The piece work basis time rate applicable to a female worker of any age (including home-workers) employed on piece work is .. 4 $3\frac{1}{2}$ ”

EXPLANATORY NOTE
(This Note is not part of the Order.)

This Order, which has effect from 11th September 1968, amends the Wages Regulation (Shirtmaking) Order 1966 (Order S.(66)) by increasing the statutory minimum remuneration fixed by that Order.

New rates are printed in italics.

STATUTORY INSTRUMENTS

1968 No. 1320

WAGES COUNCILS

The Wages Regulation (Wholesale Mantle and Costume) Order 1968

Made	-	-	-	15th August 1968
Coming into Operation			13th September 1968	

Whereas the Secretary of State has received from the Wholesale Mantle and Costume Wages Council (Great Britain) the wages regulation proposals set out in the Schedule hereto ;

Now, therefore, the Secretary of State in exercise of her powers under section 11 of the Wages Councils Act 1959(a), and of all other powers enabling her in that behalf, hereby makes the following Order :—

1. This Order may be cited as the Wages Regulation (Wholesale Mantle and Costume) Order 1968.

2.—(1) In this Order the expression "the specified date" means the 13th September 1968, provided that where, as respects any worker who is paid wages at intervals not exceeding seven days, that date does not correspond with the beginning of the period for which the wages are paid, the expression "the specified date" means, as respects that worker, the beginning of the next such period following that date.

(2) The Interpretation Act 1889(b) shall apply to the interpretation of this Order as it applies to the interpretation of an Act of Parliament and as if this Order and the Order hereby revoked were Acts of Parliament.

3. The wages regulation proposals set out in the Schedule hereto shall have effect as from the specified date and as from that date the Wages Regulation (Wholesale Mantle and Costume) Order 1966(c) as amended by Schedule 2 to the Wages Regulation (Wholesale Mantle and Costume) (Holidays) Order 1967(d) shall cease to have effect.

Signed by order of the Secretary of State.

15th August 1968.

A. A. Jarratt,
Deputy Under Secretary of State,
Department of Employment and Productivity.

SCHEDULE

The following minimum remuneration shall be substituted for the statutory minimum remuneration fixed by the Wages Regulation (Wholesale Mantle and Costume) Order 1966 (Order W.M. (75)) as amended by Schedule 2 to the Wages Regulation (Wholesale Mantle and Costume) (Holidays) Order 1967 (Order W.M. (78.)).

(a) 1959 c. 69.
(c) S.I. 1966/1494 (1966 III, p. 4122).

(b) 1889 c. 63.
(d) S.I. 1967/1363 (1967 III, p. 4019).

STATUTORY MINIMUM REMUNERATION

PART I

GENERAL

1. The minimum remuneration payable to a worker to whom this Schedule applies for all work except work to which a minimum overtime rate applies under Part IV of this Schedule is:—

   (1) in the case of a time worker, the general minimum time rate payable to the worker under Part II or Part III of this Schedule;

   (2) in the case of a worker employed on piece work, piece rates each of which would yield, in the circumstances of the case, to an ordinary worker at least the same amount of money as the piece work basis time rate applicable to the worker under Part II or Part III of this Schedule.

PART II

MALE WORKERS

GENERAL MINIMUM TIME RATES AND PIECE WORK BASIS TIME RATES

2. Subject to the provisions of this Schedule, the general minimum time rates payable to male workers with the qualifications specified in Column 2 of the next following Table when employed on time work and the piece work basis time rates applicable to such workers when employed on piece work are those set out in Columns 3 and 4 respectively of the said Table.

Column 1	Column 2	Column 3	Column 4
		General Minimum Time Rates	Piece Work Basis Time Rates
Class of Worker	Qualifying Period of Employment or Age of Worker	Per hour s. d.	Per hour s. d.
(1) MEASURE CUTTER, that is to say, a person employed in any process of measure cutting who is capable of taking a complete set of measures and of cutting all garments for a female person from patterns.	Not less than three years' employment after the age of 18 years as a measure cutter, but excluding designing.	5 9¼	6 1½

(2) CUTTER or TRIMMER, that is to say, a person substantially employed in one of more of the following processes:—

  (a) marking-in or marking-up cloth or linings or other materials;

  (b) laying-up, hooking-up or folding cloth or linings or other materials;

  (c) cutting cloth or linings or other materials or cutting out patterns of any description to be used afterwards for the cutting out of garments; and

  (d) dividing (that is to say, the process ordinarily carried on by cutters or their assistants of dividing, parting or separating the parts of garments after being cut and of assembling them into suitable bundles for making up),

other than a measure cutter to whom the minimum rates specified in (1) of this Table apply or a knife cutter or knifeman.

> Not less than three years' employment after the age of 18 years as a cutter of any of the classes specified in Column 1 or as a knifeman.
>
> 5   7½   5   11¼

(3) KNIFE CUTTER or KNIFEMAN, that is to say, a person wholly or mainly employed on band, electric or hand-knife processes.

> Not less than three years' employment after the age of 18 years as a cutter of any of the classes specified in Column 1 or as a knifeman.
>
> 5   7½   5   11¼

(4) FITTER-UP, that is to say, a person employed in fitting-up (which is a process between that of cutting and that of sewing, baisting or machining, and which consists of preparing or fitting accurately the various parts of the garments before being baisted, sewn or machined, such work of preparing or fitting being always done by shears or knives or other cutting appliances—sewing, baisting or machining forming no part or process of fitting-up).

> Not less than three years' employment after the age of 18 years as a fitter-up or tailor.
>
> 5   7½   5   11¼

(5) TAILOR, that is to say, a person employed in sewing by hand in a process of:—

  (a) making a garment or portion of a garment, or

  (b) altering, repairing, renovating or re-making a garment or portion of a garment, when such process is carried out in a factory.

> Not less than three years' employment after the age of 18 years as a tailor.
>
> 5   7½   5   11¼

(6) PRESSER, that is to say, a person employed in pressing-off by hand or by machine.

> Not less than three years' employment after the age of 18 years in the processes of pressing-off or under-pressing.
>
> 5   7½   5   11¼

(7) MACHINIST, that is to say, a person employed in machining other than as a plain machinist and capable of machining any one garment or portion of a garment.

> Not less than three years' employment after the age of 18 years as a machinist.
>
> 5   7½   5   11¼

Column 1	Column 2	Column 3	Column 4
Class of Worker	Qualifying Period of Employment or Age of Worker	General Minimum Time Rates	Piece Work Basis Time Rates
		Per hour s. d.	Per hour s. d.
(8) PASSER, that is to say, a person employed in examining garments, either in the course of being made up or upon completion.	Not less than three years' employment after the age of 18 years as a passer or tailor.	5 7½	5 11¼
(9) UNDER-PRESSER, that is to say, a person employed in pressing processes other than pressing-off.	Not less than three years' employment after the age of 18 years as an under-presser or presser.	5 4	5 8
(10) PLAIN MACHINIST, that is to say, a person employed in the process of making up plain sleeves, facings, linings, inside pockets, quilting or padding.	Not less than three years' employment after the age of 18 years as a plain machinist or machinist.	5 4	5 8
(11) WAREHOUSEMAN, that is to say, a person employed, wholly or mainly, upon one or more of the operations of assembling, keeping, storing and distributing stock, and cutting off lengths of cloth, linings or other materials.	Not less than three years' employment as a warehouseman after the age of 18 years.	5 5½	5 9¼
(12) PACKER, that is to say, a person employed, wholly or mainly, in packing goods and materials.	Not less than three years' employment as a packer after the age of 18 years.	5 4½	5 8½
(13) LEARNERS (as defined in paragraph 11)	Aged 21 years or over	5 1½	5 6¼
	„ 20 and under 21 years	4 7¼	
	„ 19 „ „ 20 „	4 2¼	
	„ 18 „ „ 19 „	3 9½	
	„ 17 „ „ 18 „	3 5¼	
	„ 16 „ „ 17 „	2 11¾	
	„ under 16 years	2 6¼	
Provided that the general minimum time rate payable during his first year's employment to a learner who enters or has entered the trade for the first time at or over the age of 19 years shall be	(a) Aged under 21 years	3 11	
	(b) „ 21 years or over	4 3¼	

Part III

FEMALE WORKERS

GENERAL MINIMUM TIME RATES

3. Subject to the provisions of this Schedule, the general minimum time rates payable to female time workers are as follows:—

	Per hour s. d.
(1) CONVEYOR BELT MACHINISTS (that is to say, female workers employed in machining any work conveyed directly to or from them on a mechanical conveyor belt), not being learners to whom (3) of this paragraph applies	4 1

(2) CUTTERS, TRIMMERS or FITTER-UP being workers aged—

	Per hour s. d.
Under 19 years	3 11½
19 and under 20 years	4 0
20 years or over	4 0½

Provided that where the worker is employed as a cutter, trimmer or fitter-up for the first time at or over the age of 19 years the general minimum time rate payable during the first two months of such employment shall be 1d. per hour less than the general minimum time rate otherwise payable.

(3) LEARNERS (as defined in paragraph 11) during the following periods of employment in the trade—

	Per hour s. d.
First six months	2 3¼
Second six months	2 6¼
Second year	3 0
Third year	3 5

Provided that a worker who enters or has entered the trade for the first time at or over the age of 18 years shall be treated for the purposes of this paragraph as though she had, at the date of her entry, completed one year of employment as a learner.

	Per hour s. d.
(4) ALL OTHER WORKERS	3 11½

PIECE WORK BASIS TIME RATES

4. The piece work basis time rates applicable to female workers employed on piece work are as follows:—

	Per hour s. d.
(1) Workers employed as CUTTERS, TRIMMERS or FITTERS-UP being workers aged—	
Under 19 years	4 3
19 and under 20 years	4 3½
20 years or over	4 4
(2) ALL OTHER WORKERS (including home-workers) ...	4 3

PART IV

OVERTIME AND WAITING TIME

ALL WORKERS OTHER THAN ALTERATION HANDS WHO ARE NORMALLY REQUIRED TO ATTEND ON 6 DAYS IN THE WEEK

NORMAL NUMBER OF HOURS

5. Subject to the provisions of this Part of this Schedule, the minimum overtime rates set out in paragraph 6 are payable to workers other than alteration hands referred to in paragraphs 7 and 8 in respect of any time worked—

    (1) in excess of the hours following, that is to say,

        (*a*) in any week ...   .   40 hours

        (*b*) on any day other than a Saturday, Sunday or customary holiday—

            where the normal working hours exceed $8\frac{1}{2}$ ...   ...   9 hours

            or

            where the normal working hours are more than 8 but not more than $8\frac{1}{2}$ ...   . $8\frac{1}{2}$ hours

            or

            where the normal working hours are not more than 8 ...   8 hours

    (2) on a Saturday, Sunday or customary holiday.

MINIMUM OVERTIME RATES

6.—(1) Minimum overtime rates are payable to a worker other than an alteration hand referred to in paragraphs 7 and 8 as follows:—

    (*a*) on any day other than a Sunday or customary holiday—

        (i) for the first 2 hours of overtime worked   time-and-a-quarter

        (ii) for the next 2 hours   ...   .   time-and-a-half

        (iii) thereafter   ...   .   double time

    (*b*) on a Sunday or customary holiday—

        for all time worked   ...   .   double time

    Provided that where it is the practice in a Jewish undertaking for the employer to require attendance on Sunday instead of Saturday the provisions of this paragraph shall apply as if in such provisions the word "Saturday" were substituted for "Sunday", except where such substitution is unlawful.

    (*c*) in any week, exclusive of any time in respect of which any minimum overtime rate is payable under the foregoing provisions of this sub-paragraph—

        for all time worked in excess of 40 hours   ...   time-and-a-quarter

    (2) The minimum overtime rates set out in sub-paragraph (1) (*a*) or (*b*) of this paragraph are payable in any week whether or not the minimum overtime rate set out in sub-paragraph (1) (*c*) is also payable.

ALTERATION HANDS WHO ARE NORMALLY REQUIRED TO ATTEND ON 6 DAYS IN THE WEEK

NORMAL NUMBER OF HOURS

7. Subject to the provisions of this Part of this Schedule, the minimum overtime rates set out in paragraph 8 are payable to workers who are normally required to attend on 6 days in the week and who are employed solely in the alteration (including repairing and renovating) of any of the garments specified in inclusion

(1) in paragraph 13 and who are employed in or about a shop engaged in the retail sale of the garments so specified in respect of any time worked—

　(1) in excess of the hours following, that is to say,

(a) in any week	40 hours
(b) on any day other than a Saturday, Sunday or customary holiday	8 hours
(c) on a Saturday, not being a customary holiday ...	4 hours

　(2) on a Sunday or customary holiday.

MINIMUM OVERTIME RATES

8.—(1) Minimum overtime rates are payable to a worker who is normally required to attend on 6 days in the week and who is employed solely in the alteration (including repairing and renovating) of any of the garments specified in inclusion (1) in paragraph 13 and who is employed in or about a shop engaged in the retail sale of the garments so specified as follows:—

　(a) on any day other than a Saturday, Sunday or customary holiday—

(i) for the first 2 hours worked in excess of 8 hours	time-and-a-quarter
(ii) for the next 2 hours	time-and-a-half
(iii) thereafter	double-time

　(b) on a Saturday, not being a customary holiday—

(i) for the first 4 hours worked in excess of 4 hours	time-and-a-half
(ii) thereafter	double time

　(c) on a Sunday or customary holiday—

for all time worked	double time

　(d) in any week, exclusive of any time in respect of which any minimum overtime rate is payable under the foregoing provisions of this sub-paragraph—

for all time worked in excess of 40 hours ...	time-and-a-quarter

(2) The minimum overtime rates set out in sub-paragraph (1) (a), (b) or (c) of this paragraph are payable in any week whether or not the minimum overtime rate set out in sub-paragraph (1) (d) is also payable.

(3) Where the employer normally requires the worker's attendance on Sunday and not on Saturday, for the purposes of this Part of this Schedule (except where such attendance is unlawful) Saturday shall be treated as a Sunday and, subject to the provisions of sub-paragraph (4) of this paragraph, Sunday shall be treated as a Saturday.

(4) Where an ordinary week-day is substituted for Saturday or, in a case where the provisions of sub-paragraph (3) of this paragraph apply, for Sunday, as the worker's weekly short day, for the purposes of this Part of this Schedule (except where such substitution is unlawful) that ordinary week-day shall be treated as a Saturday, and Saturday or Sunday, as the case may be, shall be treated as an ordinary week-day.

9. In this Part of this Schedule—

　(1) The expression "customary holiday" means—

　　(a) (i) In England and Wales—

　　　　Christmas Day (or, if Christmas Day falls on a Sunday, such week-day as may be appointed by national proclamation, or, if none is so appointed, the next following Tuesday), Boxing Day, Good Friday, Easter Monday, Whit Monday (or where another day is substituted therefor by national proclamation, that day), August Bank Holiday, and one other day (being a day of the week on which the worker normally works for the employer) in the course of a calendar year, to be fixed by the employer and notified to the worker not less than three weeks before the holiday;

(ii) In Scotland—

New Year's Day (or, if New Year's Day falls on a Sunday, the following Monday);

the local Spring holiday;

the local Autumn holiday;

and four other days (being days of the week on which the worker normally works for the employer) in the course of a calendar year, to be fixed by the employer and notified to the worker not less than three weeks before the holiday;

or (b) in the case of each of the said days a day substituted by the employer therefor, being a day recognised by local custom as a day of holiday in substitution for the said day.

(2) The expressions "time-and-a-quarter", "time-and-a-half" and "double time" mean respectively—

(a) in the case of a time worker, one and a quarter times, one and a half times and twice the general minimum time rate otherwise payable to the worker;

(b) in the case of a male worker aged 21 years or over who is employed on piece work or of a female worker (not being a learner) who is employed on piece work,

(i) a time rate equal respectively to one quarter, one half and the whole of the piece work basis time rate applicable to the worker and in addition thereto,

(ii) the piece rates otherwise payable to the worker under paragraph 1 (2);

(c) in the case of a male worker aged less than 21 years who is employed on piece work or of a female learner who is employed on piece work,

(i) a time rate equal respectively to one quarter, one half and the whole of the general minimum time rate which would be payable if the worker were a time worker and a minimum overtime rate did not apply and in addition thereto,

(ii) the piece rates otherwise payable to the worker under paragraph 1 (2).

WAITING TIME

10.—(1) A worker is entitled to payment of the minimum remuneration specified in this Schedule for all time during which he is present on the premises of his employer unless he is present thereon in any of the following circumstances:—

(a) without the employer's consent, express or implied;

(b) for some purpose unconnected with his work and other than that of waiting for work to be given to him to perform;

(c) by reason only of the fact that he is resident thereon;

(d) during normal meal times in a room or place in which no work is being done and he is not waiting for work to be given to him to perform.

(2) The minimum remuneration payable under sub-paragraph (1) of this paragraph to a piece worker when not engaged on piece work is that which would be payable if he were a time worker.

Part V

INTERPRETATION

11. In this Schedule—

(1) A FEMALE CUTTER, TRIMMER or FITTER-UP is a worker substantially occupied in one or more of the following processes:—

(a) marking-in or marking-up cloth or linings or other materials;

(b) laying-up, hooking-up or folding cloth or linings or other materials;

(c) cutting cloth or linings or other materials;

(d) trimming (that is to say, the process as ordinarily carried on of cutting and assembling together the linings and fittings of garments);

(e) dividing (that is to say, the process as ordinarily carried on by cutters or their assistants, of dividing, parting or separating the parts of garments after being cut, and of assembling them into suitable bundles for making-up); and

(f) fitting-up (which is a process between that of cutting and that of sewing, baisting, or machining, and which consists of preparing and fitting accurately the various parts of the garment before being baisted, sewn or machined, such work of preparing and fitting being always done by shears or knives or other cutting appliances—sewing, baisting or machining forming no part or process of fitting-up).

(2) A LEARNER is a worker who:—

(a) is employed during the whole or a substantial part of his time in learning any branch or process of the trade by an employer who provides him with reasonable facilities for such learning; and

(b) does not work in a room used for dwelling purposes, except where he is in the employment of his parent or guardian.

(3) "THE TRADE" means the trade of wholesale mantle and costume making as specified in paragraph 13.

RECKONING OF EMPLOYMENT

12. For the purpose of determining whether a worker has completed any period of employment specified in paragraph 2 or paragraph 3, there shall be taken into account—

(1) any such employment as a worker in relation to whom there operated one or more of the following Wages Councils (or of the Trade Boards which respectively preceded them), that is to say, the Wholesale Mantle and Costume Wages Council (Great Britain), the Retail Bespoke Tailoring Wages Councils for England and Wales and for Scotland and the Readymade and Wholesale Bespoke Tailoring Wages Council (Great Britain) and

(2) in the case of a male worker employed as a cutter of any description or as a knifeman any such employment in the rubberised waterproof trade.

APPLICABILITY OF STATUTORY MINIMUM REMUNERATION

13. This Schedule applies to workers in relation to whom the Wholesale Mantle and Costume Wages Council (Great Britain) operates, that is to say, workers employed in Great Britain in wholesale mantle and costume making as specified in the Regulations made by the Minister of Labour and dated 20th November 1919, with respect to the constitution and proceedings of the Trade Board for the Wholesale Mantle and Costume Trade (Great Britain)(a), namely:—

"Women's, girls' and children's ready-made and wholesale bespoke tailoring, and all women's, girls' and children's retail bespoke tailoring carried on in a factory where garments are made up for three or more retail establishments,

---

(a) S.R. & O. 1919/2218 (1919 II, p. 576).

and any other branch of women's, girls' and children's tailoring which is not included within the scope of the Trade Boards (Tailoring) Order 1919(a),

including:—

(1) All operations and processes of cutting, making or finishing by hand or machine of coats, costumes, tailored skirts, coat-frocks, mantles, service clothing or similar garments made by tailoring processes;

(2) (a) The altering, repairing, renovating or remaking of any of the above-mentioned tailored garments, except where included within the scope of the Retail Bespoke Tailoring Trade Board;

(b) The cleaning of such garments where carried out in association with or in conjunction with the altering, repairing, renovating or remaking of the garments;

(3) The lining with fur of any of the above-mentioned garments where carried out in association with or in conjunction with the making of such garments;

(4) (a) All processes of embroidery or decorative needlework where carried on in association with or in conjunction with the making, altering, repairing, renovating or remaking of any of the above-mentioned tailored garments other than hand-embroidery or hand-drawn thread work on garments made of linen or cotton or of mixed linen and cotton;

(b) The following processes if done by machine, namely, thread-drawing, thread clipping, top-sewing, scalloping, nickelling and paring;

(5) Warehousing, packing and all other operations incidental to or appertaining to any of the above-mentioned branches of tailoring,

but excluding:—

(1) Those branches of women's or girls' bespoke tailoring, and all operations or processes covered by the Trade Boards (Tailoring) Order 1919;

(2) The making of head-gear;

(3) The making of rubberised or oilskin garments;

(4) Warehousing, packing and other similar operations carried on in shops mainly engaged in the retail distribution of articles of any description that are not made on the premises."

EXPLANATORY NOTE

(This Note is not part of the Order.)

This Order, which has effect from 13th September 1968, sets out the statutory minimum remuneration payable in substitution for that fixed by the Wages Regulation (Wholesale Mantle and Costume) Order 1966 (Order W.M. (75)), which is revoked.

New provisions are printed in italics.

(a) S.R. & O. 1919/1201 (1919 II, p. 528).

STATUTORY INSTRUMENTS

1968 No. 1321

WAGES COUNCILS

The Wages Regulation (Wholesale Mantle and Costume) (Holidays) Order 1968

Made - - -	*15th August* 1968
Coming into Operation	*13th September* 1968

Whereas the Secretary of State has received from the Wholesale Mantle and Costume Wages Council (Great Britain) the wages regulation proposals set out in the Schedule hereto ;

Now, therefore, the Secretary of State in exercise of her powers under section 11 of the Wages Councils Act 1959(**a**), and of all other powers enabling her in that behalf, hereby makes the following Order :—

1. This Order may be cited as the Wages Regulation (Wholesale Mantle and Costume) (Holidays) Order 1968.

2.—(1) In this Order the expression "the specified date" means the 13th September 1968, provided that where, as respects any worker who is paid wages at intervals not exceeding seven days, that date does not correspond with the beginning of the period for which the wages are paid, the expression "the specified date" means, as respects that worker, the beginning of the next such period following that date.

(2) The Interpretation Act 1889(**b**) shall apply to the interpretation of this Order as it applies to the interpretation of an Act of Parliament and as if this Order and the Order hereby revoked were Acts of Parliament.

3. The wages regulation proposals set out in the Schedule hereto shall have effect as from the specified date and as from that date the Wages Regulation (Wholesale Mantle and Costume) (Holidays) Order 1967(**c**) shall cease to have effect.

Signed by order of the Secretary of State.
15th August 1968.

A. A. Jarratt,
Deputy Under Secretary of State,
Department of Employment and Productivity.

(**a**) 1959 c. 69.   (**b**) 1889 c. 63.
(**c**) S.I. 1967/1363 (1967 III, p. 4019).

SCHEDULE

HOLIDAYS AND HOLIDAY REMUNERATION

The following provisions as to holidays and holiday remuneration shall be substituted for the provisions as to holidays and holiday remuneration set out in the Wages Regulation (Wholesale Mantle and Costume) (Holidays) Order 1967 (Order W.M. (78)).

PART I

APPLICATION

1.—(1) This Schedule applies to every worker (other than a homeworker) for whom statutory minimum remuneration has been fixed.

(2) For the purposes of this Schedule a homeworker is a worker who works in his own home or in any other place not under the control or management of the employer.

PART II

CUSTOMARY HOLIDAYS

2.—(1) An employer shall allow to every worker in his employment to whom this Schedule applies a holiday (hereinafter referred to as a "customary holiday") in each year on the days specified in the following sub-paragraph, provided that the worker has been in his employment for a period of not less than six weeks immediately preceding the customary holiday and has worked for the employer during the whole or part of that period and is in his employment on the day of the customary holiday.

(2) The said customary holidays are:—
 (a) (i) in England and Wales—
   Christmas Day (or, if Christmas Day falls on a Sunday, such week-day as may be appointed by national proclamation, or, if none is so appointed, the next following Tuesday), Boxing Day, Good Friday, Easter Monday, Whit Monday (or where another day is substituted therefor by national proclamation, that day), August Bank Holiday and one other day (being a day of the week on which the worker normally works for the employer) in the course of a calendar year, to be fixed by the employer and notified to the worker not less than three weeks before the holiday;

 (ii) in Scotland—
   New Year's Day (or, if New Year's Day falls on a Sunday, the following Monday);
   the local Spring holiday;
   the local Autumn holiday; and
   four other days (being days of the week on which the worker normally works for the employer) in the course of a calendar year, to be fixed by the employer and notified to the worker not less than three weeks before the holiday;

 or (b) in the case of each of the said days a day substituted by the employer therefor, being a day recognised by local custom as a day of holiday in substitution for the said day.

(3) Notwithstanding the preceding provisions of this paragraph, an employer may (except where in the case of a woman or young person such a requirement would be unlawful) require a worker who is otherwise entitled to any customary holiday under the foregoing provisions of this Schedule to work theron and, in lieu of any such holiday on which he so works for the employer, the worker shall be entitled to be allowed a day's holiday (hereinafter referred to as a "holiday in lieu of a customary holiday") on a week-day within the period of four weeks next ensuing.

(4) A worker who is required to work on a customary holiday shall be paid:—
 (a) for all time worked thereon at the minimum rate then appropriate to the worker for work on a customary holiday; and

 (b) in respect of the holiday in lieu of the customary holiday, holiday remuneration in accordance with paragraph 6.

PART III

ANNUAL HOLIDAY

3.—(1) Subject to the provisions of this paragraph and of paragraph 4, in addition to the holidays specified in Part II of this Schedule, an employer shall between the date on which the provisions of this Schedule become effective and 30th September 1968 and between 6th April and 30th September in each succeeding year, allow a holiday (hereinafter referred to as an "annual holiday") to every worker in his employment to whom this Schedule applies, who has been employed by him during the 12 months immediately preceding the commencement of the holiday season in that year for any of the periods of employment (calculated in accordance with the provisions of paragraph 10) specified in the following table, and the duration of the annual holiday shall in the case of each such worker be related to that period as follows:—

Workers with a normal working week of 6 days		Workers with a normal working week of 5 days or less	
Period of employment	Duration of annual holiday	Period of employment	Duration of annual holiday
At least 48 weeks	18 days	At least 48 weeks	15 days
„ „ 46 „	17 „	„ „ 45 „	14 „
„ „ 44 „	16 „	„ „ 42 „	13 „
„ „ 42 „	15 „	„ „ 39 „	12 „
„ „ 40 „	14 „	„ „ 36 „	11 „
„ „ 38 „	13 „	„ „ 33 „	10 „
„ „ 36 „	12 „	„ „ 30 „	9 „
„ „ 34 „	11 „	„ „ 27 „	8 „
„ „ 31 „	10 „	„ „ 24 „	7 „
„ „ 28 „	9 „	„ „ 21 „	6 „
„ „ 25 „	8 „	„ „ 18 „	5 „
„ „ 22 „	7 „	„ „ 15 „	4 „
„ „ 19 „	6 „	„ „ 12 „	3 „
„ „ 16 „	5 „	„ „ 8 „	2 „
„ „ 13 „	4 „	„ „ 4 „	1 day
„ „ 10 „	3 „		
„ „ 7 „	2 „		
„ „ 4 „	1 day		

(2) Notwithstanding the provisions of the last foregoing sub-paragraph—

(a) the number of days of annual holiday which an employer is required to allow to a worker in respect of a period of employment during the 12 months immediately preceding 6th April in any year shall not exceed in the aggregate *three times the number of days constituting the worker's normal working week*;

(b) where before 17th September in any holiday season a worker and his employer enter into an agreement in writing that the worker shall be allowed after the end of the holiday season and before 6th April next following, days of holiday not exceeding twice the number of days constituting his normal working week, being the whole or part of the annual holiday for which he has qualified under this paragraph, any such days of annual holiday may, subject to the provisions of paragraph 4, be allowed in accordance with the agreement and if so allowed shall be treated for the purposes of this Schedule as having been allowed during the holiday season;

(c) the duration of the worker's annual holiday during the holiday season ending on 30th September 1968 shall be reduced by any days of holiday with pay (not being days of customary holiday) which have been allowed to him by the employer during the period from and including 6th April 1968 to the date on which the provisions of this Schedule become effective.

(3) In this Schedule the expression "holiday season" means in relation to an annual holiday during the year 1968, the period commencing on 6th April 1968 and ending on 30th September 1968, and in relation to each subsequent year, the period commencing on 6th April and ending on 30th September in that year.

4.—(1) Subject to the provisions of this paragraph, an annual holiday under this Schedule shall be allowed on consecutive working days and days of holiday shall be treated as consecutive notwithstanding that a day of holiday allowed to a worker under Part II of this Schedule or a day upon which he does not normally work for the employer intervenes.

(2) (*a*) Where the number of days of annual holiday for which a worker has qualified exceeds the number of days constituting his normal working week, but does not exceed twice that number, the holiday may be allowed in two periods of consecutive working days; so, however, that when a holiday is so allowed, one of the periods shall consist of a number of such days not less than the number of days constituting the worker's normal working week.

(*b*) Where the number of days of annual holiday for which a worker has qualified exceeds twice the number of days constituting his normal working week the holiday may be allowed as follows:—

   (i) as to two periods of consecutive working days, each such period not being less than the period constituting the worker's normal working week, during the holiday season; and

   (ii) as to any additional days, on working days which need not be consecutive, to be fixed by the employer, either during the holiday season or within the period ending on 8th January immediately following the holiday season.

(3) Where a day of holiday allowed to a worker under Part II of this Schedule immediately precedes a period of annual holiday or occurs during such a period then, notwithstanding the foregoing provisions of this paragraph, the duration of that period of annual holiday may be reduced by one day and in such a case one day of annual holiday may be allowed on any working day (other than the worker's weekly short day) falling within the holiday season or, by agreement between the employer and the worker or his representative, after the holiday season but before the beginning of the next following holiday season.

(4) Subject to the foregoing provisions of this paragraph, any day of annual holiday under this Schedule may be allowed on a day on which the worker is entitled to a day of holiday or to a half-holiday under any enactment other than the Wages Councils Act 1959.

5. An employer shall give to a worker reasonable notice of the commencing date or dates and of the duration of his annual holiday. Such notice may be given individually to the worker or by the posting of a notice in the place where the worker is employed.

PART IV

HOLIDAY REMUNERATION

A—CUSTOMARY HOLIDAYS AND HOLIDAYS IN LIEU OF
CUSTOMARY HOLIDAYS

6.—(1) For each day of holiday (including a holiday falling on a Saturday) to which a worker is entitled under Part II of this Schedule he shall be paid by the employer as holiday remuneration whichever of the following amounts is the greater:—

   (*a*) one-fifth of the average weekly earnings of the worker during the 12 months ended on 5th April immediately preceding the holiday, such average weekly earnings to be determined by dividing, by the number of weeks of employment with the employer during the said period, the total remuneration paid to him by the employer during that period:

      Provided that when Good Friday or Easter Monday in England and Wales or the local Spring holiday in Scotland (or days substituted therefor under the provisions of sub-paragraph (2)(*b*) of paragraph 2 or holidays in lieu of such customary holidays) fall after 5th April in any year, the holiday remuneration for any such holiday under this sub-paragraph shall be one-fifth of the average weekly earnings of the worker during the 12 months ended on 5th April in the preceding calendar year;

or (b) the appropriate statutory minimum remuneration to which he would have been entitled as a time worker if the day had not been a day of holiday and he had been employed on work for which statutory minimum remuneration is payable:

   (i) in the case of a worker normally employed for more than 30 hours a week, for 8 hours, or

   (ii) in the case of a worker normally employed for 30 hours a week or less, for 4 hours.

(2) Notwithstanding the provisions of sub-paragraph (1) of this paragraph, payment of the said holiday remuneration is subject to the condition that the worker (unless excused by the employer or absent by reason of the proved illness of, or accident to, the worker) presents himself for employment at the usual starting hour on the first working day following the holiday:

Provided that when two customary holidays occur on successive days (or so that no working day intervenes) the said condition shall apply only to the second customary holiday.

(3) Where a worker normally works in the week on every week-day except Saturday, he shall be paid in respect of any Saturday on which he would have been entitled to a holiday under Part II of this Schedule if it had been a day on which he normally worked, a sum equivalent to the holiday remuneration he would have been entitled to receive had he been allowed a holiday on that day.

(4) Holiday remuneration in respect of any customary holiday shall be paid by the employer to the worker on the pay-day on which the wages for the first working day following the customary holiday are paid.

(5) Holiday remuneration in respect of any holiday in lieu of a customary holiday shall be paid on the pay-day on which the wages are paid for the first working day following the holiday in lieu of a customary holiday: Provided that the said payment shall be made immediately upon the termination of the worker's employment if he ceases to be employed before being allowed such holiday in lieu of a customary holiday and in that case the conditions specified in sub-paragraph (2) of this paragraph shall not apply.

B–ANNUAL HOLIDAY

7.—(1) Subject to the provisions of paragraph 8, a worker qualified to be allowed an annual holiday under this Schedule shall be paid as holiday remuneration by his employer in respect thereof, on the last pay-day preceding such annual holiday, whichever of the following amounts is the greater:—

(a) an amount equal to *three fifty-seconds* of the total remuneration paid by the employer to the worker during the 12 months ended on 5th April immediately preceding the holiday; or

(b) one day's holiday pay (as defined in paragraph 11) in respect of each day of annual holiday.

(2) Where, under the provisions of paragraph 4, an annual holiday is allowed in more than one period the holiday remuneration shall be apportioned accordingly.

8. Where any accrued holiday remuneration has been paid by the employer to the worker (in accordance with paragraph 9 of this Schedule or under the provisions of Order W.M. (78)) in respect of employment during any of the periods referred to in that paragraph or that Order, the amount of holiday remuneration payable by the employer in respect of any annual holiday for which the worker has qualified by reason of employment during the said period shall be reduced by the amount of the said accrued holiday remuneration unless that remuneration has been deducted from a previous payment of holiday remuneration made under the provisions of this Schedule or of Order W.M. (78).

ACCRUED HOLIDAY REMUNERATION PAYABLE ON TERMINATION OF EMPLOYMENT

9.—(1) Where a worker ceases to be employed by an employer after the provisions of this Schedule become effective, the employer shall, immediately on the termination of the employment, pay to the worker accured holiday remuneration in accordance with this paragraph.

(2) Accrued holiday remuneration shall be payable in accordance with the following table if the worker has in the 12 months commencing on 6th April 1967, and thereafter in any period of 12 months commencing on 6th April been employed for any of the periods of employment specified in that table.

(3) Accrued holiday remuneration is not payable in respect of any period of employment for which the worker has been allowed or become entitled to be allowed an annual holiday under this Schedule.

(4) Subject to the provisions of sub-paragraph (5) hereof, where a worker has been allowed in a holiday season part only of the annual holiday for which he has qualified under this Schedule or under Order W.M. (78) and his employment is terminated before he becomes entitled to the rest of that holiday the accrued holiday remuneration payable shall be:—

(a) in the case of a worker who has qualified for days of annual holiday exceeding twice the number of days constituting his normal working week and who has been allowed as days of annual holiday not less than twice the number of days constituting his normal working week, or, where the circumstances in sub-paragraph (3) of paragraph 4 are applicable, that number of days reduced by one:—

(i) in respect of the days of holiday for which he has qualified during the 12 months ended on 5th April immediately preceding the termination of his employment, the holiday remuneration due in respect thereof calculated in accordance with the provisions of paragraph 7 less the amount received by him in respect of the part of the holiday which has been allowed; and

(ii) in respect of any period of employment since the said 5th April, the amount calculated in accordance with the following table;

(b) in the case of any other worker, the appropriate amount under the following table in respect of the qualifying period of employment less the amount received by the worker in respect of that part of the holiday which has been allowed.

(5) Any accrued holiday remuneration payable under the provisions of this paragraph shall be reduced by the amount of any accrued holiday remuneration already paid by the employer to the worker in pursuance of this Order or Order W.M. (78) in respect of the same period of employment or part thereof.

TABLE OF ACCRUED HOLIDAY REMUNERATION

Column 1 — Period of employment calculated in accordance with the provisions of paragraph 10	Column 2 — Workers with a normal working week of 6 days — Accrued holiday remuneration	Column 3 — Workers with a normal working week of 5 days or less — Accrued holiday remuneration	Column 4
At least 48 weeks	Three times the amount in Col. 4	Three times the amount in Col. 4	The amount which the worker would be entitled to receive from his employer, at the date of the termination of his employment, for one week's work, if working his normal working week and the number of daily hours normally worked by him (exclusive of overtime) and if paid as a time worker at the appropriate rate of statutory minimum remuneration for work for which statutory minimum remuneration is payable and at the same rate for any work for which such remuneration is not payable.
" " 46 "	Two and five-sixths times the amount in Col. 4	Two and four-fifths times the amount in Col. 4	
" " 45 "	Two and two-thirds "	Two and four-fifths times the amount in Col. 4	
" " 44 "	Two and two-thirds "	Two and three-fifths "	
" " 42 "	Two and one-half "	Two and three-fifths "	
" " 40 "	Two and one-third "	Two and two-fifths "	
" " 39 "	Two and one-sixth "	Two and two-fifths "	
" " 38 "	Two and one-sixth "	Two and one-fifth "	
" " 36 "	Twice the amount in Col. 4	Two and one-fifth "	
" " 34 "	One and five-sixths times the amount in Col. 4	Twice the amount in Col. 4	
" " 33 "	One and two-thirds "	Twice the amount in Col. 4	
" " 31 "	One and two-thirds "	One and four-fifths times the amount in Col. 4	
" " 30 "	One and one-half "	One and four-fifths "	
" " 28 "	One and one-half "	One and three-fifths "	
" " 27 "	One and one-third "	One and three-fifths "	
" " 25 "	One and one-third "	One and two-fifths "	
" " 24 "	One and one-sixth "	One and two-fifths "	
" " 22 "	One and one-sixth "	One and one-fifth "	
" " 21 "	The amount in Col. 4	One and one-fifth "	
" " 19 "	The amount in Col. 4	The amount in Col. 4	
" " 18 "	Five-sixths of the amount in Col. 4	The amount in Col. 4	
" " 16 "	Five-sixths "	Four-fifths of the amount in Col. 4	
" " 15 "	Two-thirds "	Four-fifths "	
" " 13 "	Two-thirds "	Three-fifths "	
" " 12 "	One-half "	Three-fifths "	
" " 10 "	One-third "	Two-fifths "	
" " 8 "	One-third "	Two-fifths "	
" " 7 "	One-third "	One-fifth "	
" " 4 "	One-sixth "	One-fifth "	

(6) Notwithstanding the provisions of the foregoing table, the accrued holiday remuneration payable to a worker who has been employed by the employer for the whole of the 12 months ended on 5th April immediately preceding the termination of his employment shall be as follows:—

(*a*) in respect of that 12 months an amount equal to the holiday remuneration for the days of annual holiday for which he has qualified, calculated in accordance with the provisions of sub-paragraph (1) of paragraph 7; and

(*b*) in respect of any period of employment since the said 5th April, the amount calculated in accordance with the foregoing table.

PART V

GENERAL

10. For the purpose of calculating any period of employment qualifying a worker for an annual holiday or for any accrued holiday remuneration under this Schedule, the worker shall be treated—

(1) as if he were employed for a week in respect of any week in which—

(*a*) in the case of a worker other than a part-time worker, he has worked for the employer for not less than 20 hours and has performed some work for which statutory minimum remuneration is payable;

(*b*) in the case of a part-time worker, he has worked for the employer and has performed some work for which statutory minimum remuneration is payable;

(*c*) in the case of any worker—

(i) he has worked for the employer for less than 20 hours by reason of the proved illness of, or accident to, the worker or for a like reason has been absent throughout the week (provided that the number of weeks which may be treated as weeks of employment for such reason shall not exceed four in the aggregate in any such period); or

(ii) he has been suspended throughout the week owing to shortage of work (provided that the number of weeks which may be treated as weeks of employment for such reason shall not exceed six in the aggregate in any such period);

(2) as if he were employed on any day of holiday allowed under the provisions of this Schedule, or of Order W.M. (78), and on any other day of holiday with pay, and for the purposes of the provisions of sub-paragraph (1) of this paragraph, a worker who is absent on such a holiday shall be treated as having worked thereon for the employer on work for which statutory minimum remuneration is payable,

(*a*) where the holiday is a customary holiday, or a holiday in lieu of a customary holiday, for 8 hours if the worker is normally employed for more than 30 hours a week or for 4 hours if he is normally employed for 30 hours a week or less, or

(*b*) where the holiday is a day of annual holiday or any other day of holiday with pay, for the number of hours ordinarily worked by him on that day of the week.

11. In this Schedule, unless the context otherwise requires, the following expressions have the meanings hereby respectively assigned to them, that is to say:—
"NORMAL WORKING WEEK" means the number of days on which it has been usual for the worker to work in a week in the employment of the employer in the 12 months immediately preceding the commencement of the holiday season or, where under paragraph 9 accrued holiday remuneration is payable on the termination of the employment, in the twelve months immediately preceding the date of the termination of the employment:
Provided that—

(1) part of a day shall count as a day;

(2) no account shall be taken of any week in which the worker did not perform any work for which statutory minimum remuneration has been fixed.

"ONE DAY'S HOLIDAY PAY" means the appropriate proportion of the remuneration which the worker would be entitled to receive from his employer at the date of the annual holiday or at the termination of the employment, as the case may require, for one week's work if working his normal working week and the number of daily hours normally worked by him (exclusive of overtime) and if paid as a time worker at the appropriate rate of statutory minimum remuneration for work for which statutory minimum remuneration is payable and at the same rate for any work for which such remuneration is not payable, and in this definition "appropriate proportion" means—

where the worker's normal working week is six days   ...   ...   one-sixth

where the worker's normal working week is five days   ...   ...   one-fifth

where the worker's normal working week is four days or less   ...   one-quarter.

"PART-TIME WORKER" means a worker who normally works for the employer for less than 20 hours a week by reason only of the fact that he does not hold himself out as normally available for work for more than the number of hours he normally works in the week.

"STATUTORY MINIMUM REMUNERATION" means minimum remuneration (other than holiday remuneration) fixed by a wages regulation order.

"WAGES REGULATION ORDER" means a wages regulation order made by the Secretary of State to give effect to proposals submitted to her by the Council. "WEEK" means "pay week".

12. The provisions of this Schedule are without prejudice to any agreement for the allowance of any further holidays with pay or for the payment of additional holiday remuneration.

EXPLANATORY NOTE

(This Note is not part of the Order.)

This Order, which has effect from 13th September 1968, sets out the holidays which an employer is required to allow to workers and the remuneration payable for those holidays, in substitution for the holidays and holiday remuneration fixed by the Wages Regulation (Wholesale Mantle and Costume) (Holidays) Order 1967 (Order W.M. (78)), which Order is revoked.

New provisions are printed in italics.

STATUTORY INSTRUMENTS

1968 No. 1327

WAGES COUNCILS

The Wages Regulation (Dressmaking and Women's Light Clothing) (England and Wales) Order 1968

Made - - - 16th *August* 1968
Coming into Operation 20th *September* 1968

Whereas the Secretary of State has received from the Dressmaking and Women's Light Clothing Wages Council (England and Wales) the wages regulation proposals set out in the Schedule hereto ;

Now, therefore, the Secretary of State in exercise of her powers under section 11 of the Wages Councils Act 1959(a), and of all other powers enabling her in that behalf hereby makes the following Order :—

1. This Order may be cited as the Wages Regulation (Dressmaking and Women's Light Clothing) (England and Wales) Order 1968.

2.—(1) In this Order the expression "the specified date" means the 20th September 1968, provided that where, as respects any worker who is paid wages at intervals not exceeding seven days, that date does not correspond with the beginning of the period for which the wages are paid, the expression "the specified date" means, as respects that worker, the beginning of the next such period following that date.

(2) The Interpretation Act 1889(b) shall apply to the interpretation of this Order as it applies to the interpretation of an Act of Parliament and as if this Order and the Order hereby revoked were Acts of Parliament.

3. The wages regulation proposals set out in the Schedule hereto shall have effect as from the specified date and as from that date the Wages Regulation (Dressmaking and Women's Light Clothing) (England and Wales) Order 1966(c) shall cease to have effect.

Signed by order of the Secretary of State.

16th August 1968.

A. A. Jarratt,

Deputy Under Secretary of State,

Department of Employment and Productivity.

(a) 1959 c. 69.   (b) 1889 c. 63.
(c) S.I. 1966/855 (1966 II, p. 1998).

SCHEDULE

The following minimum remuneration shall be substituted for the statutory minimum remuneration fixed by the Wages Regulation (Dressmaking and Women's Light Clothing)(England and Wales) Order 1966(a)) (Order W.D. (82)), as amended by Schedule 2 to the Wages Regulation (Dressmaking and Women's Light Clothing) (England and Wales) (Holidays) Order 1967(b).

STATUTORY MINIMUM REMUNERATION

PART I

GENERAL

1.—(1) The minimum remuneration payable to a worker to whom this Schedule applies for all work except work to which a minimum overtime rate applies under Part V of this Schedule is:—

(a) in the case of a time worker, the hourly general minimum time rate;

(b) in the case of a worker employed on piece work, piece rates each of which would yield, in the circumstances of the case, to an ordinary worker at least the same amount of money as the hourly piece work basis time rate or, where no piece work basis time rate is applicable, at least the same amount of money as the hourly general minimum time rate which would be applicable if the worker were a time worker.

(2) In this Schedule:—

"hourly general minimum time rate" means the general minimum time rate applicable to the worker under Part II or Part III of this Schedule divided by 40.

"hourly piece work basis time rate" means the piece work basis time rate applicable to the worker under Part II or Part III of this Schedule divided by 40.

"per week" means per week of 40 hours.

PART II

RETAIL BESPOKE BRANCH
FEMALE WORKERS
GENERAL MINIMUM TIME RATES

2. Subject to the provisions of this Schedule, the general minimum time rates applicable to female workers in the retail bespoke branch, in Areas A, B and C respectively, are as follows:—

	Area A Per week s. d.	Area B Per week s. d.	Area C Per week s. d.
(1) BODICE, COAT, SKIRT, GOWN OR BLOUSE HANDS, aged 20 years or over, who—			
having worked for 2½ years in the said branch in one or more of the occupations of learner, apprentice or improver and for at least 2 years in the said branch thereafter, take bodices, coats, skirts, gowns or blouses direct from the fitter in an establishment in which a fitter is employed and make them up without supervision other than the general supervision of the fitter or the workroom foreman or forewoman...	152 6	160 0	165 0

(a) S.I. 1966/855 (1966 II, p. 1998).   (b) S.I. 1967/1601 (1967 III, p. 4401).

	Area A Per week		Area B Per week		Area C Per week	
	s.	d.	s.	d.	s.	d.

(2) LEARNERS (as defined in paragraph 19) during the following periods of employment in the retail bespoke branch:—

	Area A		Area B		Area C	
1st year	75	0	78	4	90	10
2nd year	99	2	104	2	114	2
6 months then next ensuing	110	0	116	8	130	0

Provided that a learner who enters, or has entered, the trade for the first time at or over the age of 18 years shall be treated for the purposes of this paragraph as though she had, at the date of her entry, completed her first year's employment as a learner in the said branch.

	Area A		Area B		Area C	
(3) All other workers	141	8	150	0	158	4

RECKONING EMPLOYMENT IN THE WHOLESALE MANUFACTURING BRANCH

3. Where a worker has been employed in the wholesale manufacturing branch, one half of the period of such employment shall be treated for the purposes of this Part of this Schedule as employment in the retail bespoke branch.

DEFINITION OF AREAS

4. For the purposes of this Part of this Schedule:—

Area A—comprises each area in England and Wales which at the date of the 1961 census was administered by

(1) a Rural District Council or

(2) a Municipal Borough Council or an Urban District Council having according to the said census a population of less than 10,000,

but does not include any area within the Metropolitan Police District.

Area B—comprises the whole of England and Wales except Area A and Area C.

Area C—comprises the Metropolitan Police District, as defined in the London Government Act 1963, the City of London, the Inner Temple and the Middle Temple.

MALE WORKERS

GENERAL MINIMUM TIME RATES

5. Subject to the provisions of this Schedule, the general minimum time rates applicable to male workers in the retail bespoke branch are as follows:—

	Per week	
	s.	d.
Aged 21 years or over	212	6
„ 20 and under 21 years	182	6
„ 19 „ „ 20 „	165	0
„ 18 „ „ 19 „	147	6
„ 17 „ „ 18 „	130	10
„ 16 „ „ 17 „	111	8
„ under 16 years	90	10

Provided that the general minimum time rate applicable during his first year's employment in the trade to a worker who enters, or has entered, the trade for the first time at or over the age of 19 years shall be—

During the 1st six months of such employment	148	4
„ „ 2nd „ „ „ „ „	156	8

PIECE WORK BASIS TIME RATE

Per week
s. d.

6. The piece work basis time rate applicable to a male worker of any age employed in the retail bespoke branch on piece work is *228 4*

PART III

WHOLESALE MANUFACTURING BRANCH
FEMALE WORKERS
GENERAL MINIMUM TIME RATES

7. Subject to the provisions of this Schedule, the general minimum time rates applicable to female workers in the wholesale manufacturing branch are as follows:—

Per week
s. d.

(1) CONVEYOR BELT MACHINISTS (that is to say, female workers employed in machining any work conveyed directly to and from them on a mechanical conveyor belt) not being learners to whom (2) of this paragraph applies *165 0*

(2) LEARNERS (as defined in paragraph 19) during the following periods of employment in the wholesale manufacturing branch:—

1st year	...	*94 2*
2nd year	...	*115 10*
6 months then next ensuing	...	*132 6*

Provided that a learner who enters, or has entered, the trade for the first time at or over the age of 18 years shall be treated for the purposes of this paragraph as though she had, at the date of her entry, completed her first year's employment as a learner in the said branch.

(3) All other workers *158 4*

RECKONING EMPLOYMENT IN THE RETAIL BESPOKE BRANCH

8. Where a worker has been employed in the retail bespoke branch, one half of the period of such employment shall be treated for the purposes of this Part of this Schedule as employment in the wholesale manufacturing branch.

PIECE WORK BASIS TIME RATE

Per week
s. d.

9. The piece work basis time rate applicable to a female worker of any age employed in the wholesale manufacturing branch on piece work is ... *171 8*

MALE WORKERS
GENERAL MINIMUM TIME RATES

10. Subject to the provisions of this Schedule, the general minimum time rates applicable to male workers in the wholesale manufacturing branch are as follows:—

Per week
s. d.

(1) CUTTERS aged 21 years or over who have had at least 4 years' experience as cutters in the wholesale manufacturing branch *232 6*

(2) All other workers:—

Aged 21 years or over	...	*212 6*
„ 20 and under 21 years	...	*185 0*
„ 19 „ „ 20 „	...	*167 6*
„ 18 „ „ 19 „	...	*150 0*
„ 17 „ „ 18 „	...	*134 2*
„ 16 „ „ 17 „	...	*113 4*
„ under 16 years	...	*94 2*

Per week
s. d.

Provided that the general minimum time rate applicable during his first year's employment in the trade to a worker who enters, or has entered, the trade for the first time at or over the age of 19 years shall be—

During the 1st six months of such employment *148 4*
„ „ 2nd „ „ „ „ „ *156 8*

PIECE WORK BASIS TIME RATES

11. The piece work basis time rates applicable to male workers employed in the wholesale manufacturing branch on piece work are as follows:—

Per week
s. d.

(1) CUTTERS aged 21 years or over who have had at least 4 years' experience as cutters in the wholesale manufacturing branch *249 2*

(2) All other workers *228 4*

PART IV

EXPERIENCE UNDER THE GOVERNMENT VOCATIONAL TRAINING SCHEME

12. Where any worker has completed a full course of training as a machinist or as a hand sewer under the Government Vocational Training Scheme for resettlement training such period of training shall, for the purpose of reckoning the period of the worker's employment in the trade, be treated as though it were

(1) in the case of a female worker, a period of three years' employment as a learner in the branch of the trade in which she is employed, or

(2) in the case of a male worker, a period of at least one year's employment in the trade.

PART V

RETAIL BESPOKE BRANCH AND WHOLESALE MANUFACTURING BRANCH

OVERTIME AND WAITING TIME

ALL WORKERS OTHER THAN ALTERATION HANDS WHO ARE NORMALLY REQUIRED TO ATTEND ON 6 DAYS IN THE WEEK

NORMAL NUMBER OF HOURS

13. Subject to the provisions of this Part of this Schedule, the minimum overtime rates set out in paragraph 14 are payable to workers in any branch of the trade, other than alteration hands referred to in paragraphs 15 and 16, in respect of any time worked—

(1) in excess of the hours following, that is to say,

(a) in any week ... ... 40 hours

(b) on any day other than a Saturday, Sunday or customary holiday—

where the normal working hours exceed 8½ ... ... 9 hours

or

where the normal working hours are not more than 8½ ... 8½ hours

(2) on a Saturday, Sunday or customary holiday.

MINIMUM OVERTIME RATES

14.—(1) Minimum overtime rates are payable to a worker in any branch of the trade other than an alteration hand referred to in paragraphs 15 and 16 as follows:—

    (a) on any day other than a Sunday or customary holiday—

        (i) for the first 2 hours of overtime worked   ...   time-and-a-quarter

        (ii) for the next 2 hours   ...   .   time-and-a-half

        (iii) thereafter   ...   .   double time

    (b) on a Sunday or customary holiday—

        for all time worked   ...   .   double time

        Provided that where it is the practice in a Jewish undertaking for the employer to require attendance on Sunday instead of Saturday the provisions of this paragraph shall apply as if in such provisions the word "Saturday" were substituted for "Sunday", except where such substitution is unlawful.

    (c) in any week, exclusive of any time in respect of which any minimum overtime rate is payable under the foregoing provisions of this sub-paragraph—

        for all time worked in excess of 40 hours ...   ...   time-and-a-quarter

(2) The minimum overtime rates set out in sub-paragraph (1) (a) or (b) of this paragraph are payable in any week whether or not the minimum overtime rate set out in sub-paragraph (1) (c) is also payable.

(3) Where a worker employed in the retail bespoke branch of the trade normally attends work on a Saturday, instead of on another week-day, for the purposes of this Part of this Schedule that other week-day shall be treated as a Saturday and Saturday as another week-day.

ALTERATION HANDS WHO ARE NORMALLY REQUIRED TO ATTEND ON 6 DAYS IN THE WEEK

NORMAL NUMBER OF HOURS

15. Subject to the provisions of this Part of this Schedule, the minimum overtime rates set out in paragraph 16 are payable to workers in any branch of the trade who are normally required to attend on six days in the week and who are employed solely in the alteration (including repairing and renovating) of any of the articles specified in inclusion (1) in paragraph 21 and who are employed in or about a shop engaged in the retail sale of the articles so specified, as follows:—

    (1) in any week,

        for all time worked in excess of ...   .   40 hours

    (2) on any day other than a Saturday, Sunday or a customary holiday,

        for all time worked in excess of   ...   .   8 hours

    (3) on a Saturday, not being a customary holiday,

        for all time worked in excess of   ...   .   4 hours

    (4) on a Sunday or a customary holiday ...   . for all time worked.

MINIMUM OVERTIME RATES

16.—(1) Subject to the provisions of this Part of this Schedule, minimum overtime rates are payable to a worker in any branch of the trade who is normally required to attend on six days in the week and who is employed solely in the alteration (including repairing and renovating) of any of the articles specified in inclusion (1) in paragraph 21 and who is employed in or about a shop engaged in the retail sale of the articles so specified, as follows:—

2u

(5) A learner means a female worker who is employed by an employer who provides her with reasonable facilities for learning, practically and efficiently, one of the branches of the trade or the various processes involved in the making of any of the articles specified in the definition of the trade set out in paragraph 21.

PART VII

APPLICABILITY OF STATUTORY MINIMUM REMUNERATION

20. This Schedule shall not apply to—

   (a) machinists

   (b) hand sewers

during any period in respect of which they are in receipt of allowances as provided under the Government Vocational Training Scheme for resettlement training if they are trainees who have been placed by the Department of Employment and Productivity with the employer for a period of approved training and if the requirements of the said Scheme are duly complied with.

21. Subject to the provisions of paragraph 20, this Schedule applies to workers in relation to whom the Dressmaking and Women's Light Clothing Wages Council (England and Wales) operates, that is to say, workers employed in England and Wales in those branches of the Women's Clothing Trade which are specified in Regulation 1 of the Trade Boards (Dressmaking and Women's Light Clothing Trade, England and Wales) (Constitution and Proceedings) Regulations 1928(a), excluding any processes or operations included in the appendix to the Trade Boards (Shirtmaking) Order 1920(b).

   The said branches of the women's clothing trade are specified in the said Regulations as follows:—

   Those branches of the women's clothing trade that are engaged in the making of non-tailored garments, namely, the making from textile or knitted fabrics of (a) non-tailored wearing apparel (other than hand-kerchiefs) worn by women or girls, or by children without distinction of sex, or (b) boys' ready-made washing suits or sailor suits, where carried out in association with or in conjunction with the making of garments to be worn by women or girls or by children without distinction of sex;

   INCLUDING:—

   (1) All operations and processes of cutting, making or finishing by hand or machine of dresses, non-tailored skirts, wraps, blouses, blouse-robes, jumpers, sports-coats, neckwear, tea-gowns, dressing gowns, dressing jackets, pyjamas, under-clothing, underskirts, aprons, overalls, nurses' and servants' caps, juvenile clothing, baby-linen or similar non-tailored articles;

   (2) The making of field bonnets, sun-bonnets, boudoir caps or infants' millinery where carried on in association with or in conjunction with the making of any of the articles mentioned in paragraph (1) above;

   (3) (a) The altering, repairing, renovating or re-making of any of the above-mentioned articles;

   (b) The cleaning of any of the above-mentioned articles, where carried on in association with or in conjunction with the altering, repairing, renovating or re-making of such garments;

   (a) S.R. & O. 1928/628 (1928, p. 1265).   (b) S.R. & O. 1920/711 (1920 II, p. 790).

(4) All processes of embroidery or decorative needlework where carried on in association with or in conjunction with the making, altering, repairing, renovating or re-making of such articles other than hand embroidery or hand-drawn thread work on articles made of linen or cotton or of mixed linen and cotton;

(5) The following processes if done by machine:—thread-drawing, thread-clipping, top-sewing, scalloping, nickelling and paring;

(6) Laundering, smoothing, folding, ornamenting, boxing, packing, warehousing or other operations incidental to or appertaining to the making, altering, repairing, renovating or re-making of any of the above-mentioned articles;

BUT EXCLUDING:—

(a) The making of knitted articles; the making of under-clothing, socks and stockings, from knitted fabrics; and the making from knitted fabrics of articles mentioned in paragraphs (1) and (2) above, where carried on in assocaition with or in conjunction with the manufacture of the knitted fabrics;

(b) The making of gloves, spats, gaiters, boots, shoes and slippers;

(c) The making of headgear, other than the articles mentioned in paragraph (2) above;

(d) The branches of trade covered by the Trade Boards (Corset) Order 1919(a);

(e) The making of rubberised or oilskin garments;

(f) The making of women's collars and cuffs and of nurses' stiff washing belts where carried on in association with or in conjunction with the making of men's or boys' shirts or collars;

(g) Warehousing, packing and other similar operations carried on in shops mainly engaged in the retail distribution of articles of any description that are not made on the premises.

EXPLANATORY NOTE

(This Note is not part of the Order.)

This Order, which has effect from 20th September 1968, sets out the statutory minimum remuneration payable in substitution for that fixed by the Wages Regulation (Dressmaking and Women's Light Clothing) (England and Wales) Order 1966 (Order W.D. (82)), which Order is revoked.

New provisions are printed in italics.

(a) S.R. & O. 1919/570 (1919 II, p. 509).

STATUTORY INSTRUMENTS

1968 No. 1328

WAGES COUNCILS

The Wages Regulation (Dressmaking and Women's Light Clothing) (England and Wales) (Holidays) Order 1968

Made - - -	16*th August* 1968
Coming into Operation	20*th September* 1968

Whereas the Secretary of State has received from the Dressmaking and Women's Light Clothing Wages Council (England and Wales) the wages regulation proposals set out in the Schedule hereto ;

Now, therefore, the Secretary of State in exercise of her powers under section 11 of the Wages Councils Act 1959(**a**), and of all other powers enabling her in that behalf hereby makes the following Order :—

1. This Order may be cited as the Wages Regulation (Dressmaking and Women's Light Clothing) (England and Wales) (Holidays) Order 1968.

2.—(1) In this Order the expression "the specified date" means the 20th September 1968, provided that where, as respects any worker who is paid wages at intervals not exceeding seven days, that date does not correspond with the beginning of the period for which the wages are paid, the expression "the specified date" means, as respects that worker, the beginning of the next such period following that date.

(2) The Interpretation Act 1889(**b**) applies to the interpretation of this Order as it applies to the interpretation of an Act of Parliament and as if this Order and the Order hereby revoked were Acts of Parliament.

3. The wages regulation proposals set out in the Schedule hereto shall have effect as from the specified date and as from that date the Wages Regulation (Dressmaking and Women's Light Clothing) (England and Wales) (Holidays) Order 1967(**c**) shall cease to have effect.

Signed by order of the Secretary of State.

A. A. Jarratt,

Deputy Under Secretary of State,

16th August 1968.

Department of Employment and Productivity.

(**a**) 1959 c. 69.   (**b**) 1889 c. 63.
(**c**) S.I. 1967/1601 (1967 III, p. 4401).

SCHEDULE

HOLIDAYS AND HOLIDAY REMUNERATION

The following provisions as to holidays and holiday remuneration shall be substituted for the provisions as to holidays and holiday remuneration set out in the Wages Regulation (Dressmaking and Women's Light Clothing) (England and Wales) (Holidays) Order 1967 (hereinafter referred to as "Order W.D.(85)").

PART I

APPLICATION

1.—(1) This Schedule applies to every worker (other than a homeworker) for whom statutory minimum remuneration has been fixed.

(2) For the purposes of this Schedule a homeworker is a worker who works in his own home or in any other place not under the control or management of the employer.

PART II

CUSTOMARY HOLIDAYS

2.—(1) An employer shall allow to every worker in his employment to whom this Schedule applies a holiday (hereinafter referred to as a "customary holiday") in each year on the days specified in the following sub-paragraph, provided that the worker has been in his employment for a period of not less than eight weeks immediately preceding the customary holiday and has worked for the employer during the whole or part of that period and is in his employment on the day of the customary holiday.

(2) The said customary holidays are:—

(a) Christmas Day (or, if Christmas Day falls on a Sunday, such week day as may be appointed by national proclamation, or, if none is so appointed, the next following Tuesday), Boxing Day, Good Friday, Easter Monday, Whit Monday (or where another day is substituted therefor by national proclamation, that day), August Bank Holiday and one other day (being a day of the week on which the worker normally works for the employer) in the course of each calendar year, to be fixed by consultation between the employer or his representative and the worker or his representative and notified to the worker not less than three weeks before the holiday, or

(b) in the case of each of the said days, a day substituted by the employer therefor, being a day recognised by local custom as a day of holiday in substitution for the said day.

(3) Notwithstanding the preceding provisions of this paragraph, an employer may (except where in the case of a women or young person such a requirement would be unlawful) require a worker who is otherwise entitled to any customary holiday under the foregoing provisions of this Schedule to work thereon and, in lieu of any such holiday on which he so works for the employer, the worker shall be entitled to be allowed a day's holiday (hereinafter referred to as a "holiday in lieu of a customary holiday") on a week day within the period of four weeks next ensuing.

(4) A worker who is required to work on a customary holiday shall be paid:—

(a) for all time worked thereon at the minimum rate then appropriate to the worker for work on a customary holiday; and

(b) in respect of the holiday in lieu of the customary holiday, holiday remuneration in accordance with paragraph 6.

PART III

ANNUAL HOLIDAY

3.—(1) Subject to the provisions of this paragraph and of paragraph 4, in addition to the holidays specified in Part II of this Schedule, an employer shall:—

(a) between the date on which the provisions of this Schedule become effective and 30th September 1968, allow a holiday (hereinafter referred to as an "annual holiday") to every worker in his employment to whom this Schedule applies, who has been employed by him during the 12 months immediately preceding the commencement of the holiday season for any of the periods of employment (calculated in accordance with the provisions of paragraph 10) specified below, and the duration of the annual holiday shall in the case of each such worker be related to that period as follows:—

Workers with a normal working week of 6 days		Workers with a normal working week of 5 days or less	
Period of employment	Duration of annual holiday	Period of employment	Duration of annual holiday
At least 48 weeks　　　.. 　..	16 days	At least 48 weeks　　.. 　..	14 days
,,　,,　46　,,　　.. 　..	15 ,,	,,　,,　45　,,　　.. 　..	13 ,,
,,　,,　43　,,　　.. 　..	14 ,,	,,　,,　42　,,　　.. 　..	12 ,,
,,　,,　40　,,　　.. 　..	13 ,,	,,　,,　39　,,　　.. 　..	11 ,,
,,　,,　37　,,　　.. 　..	12 ,,	,,　,,　36　,,　　.. 　..	10 ,,
,,　,,　35　,,　　.. 　..	11 ,,	,,　,,　33　,,　　.. 　..	9 ,,
,,　,,　32　,,　　.. 　..	10 ,,	,,　,,　30　,,　　.. 　..	8 ,,
,,　,,　29　,,　　.. 　..	9 ,,	,,　,,　27　,,　　.. 　..	7 ,,
,,　,,　26　,,　　.. 　..	8 ,,	,,　,,　24　,,　　.. 　..	6 ,,
,,　,,　24　,,　　.. 　..	7 ,,	,,　,,　20　,,　　.. 　..	5 ,,
,,　,,　21　,,　　.. 　..	6 ,,	,,　,,　16　,,　　.. 　..	4 ,,
,,　,,　18　,,　　.. 　..	5 ,,	,,　,,　12　,,　　.. 　..	3 ,,
,,　,,　15　,,　　.. 　..	4 ,,	,,　,,　8　,,　　.. 　..	2 ,,
,,　,,　12　,,　　.. 　..	3 ,,	,,　,,　4　,,　　.. 　..	1 day
,,　,,　8　,,　　.. 　..	2 ,,		
,,　,,　4　,,　　.. 　..	1 day		

(*b*) between 6th April 1969 and 30th September 1969, and between 6th April and 30th September in each succeeding year, allow a holiday (hereinafter referred to as an "annual holiday") to every worker in his employment to whom this Schedule applies, who has been employed by him during the 12 months immediately preceding the commencement of the holiday season for any of the periods of employment (calculated in accordance with the provisions of paragraph 10) specified below, and the duration of the annual holiday shall in the case of each such worker be related to that period as follows:—

Workers with a normal working week of 6 days		Workers with a normal working week of 5 days or less	
Period of employment	Duration of annual holiday	Period of employment	Duration of annual holiday
At least 48 weeks	18 days	At least 48 weeks	15 days
„ „ 46 „	17 „	„ „ 45 „	14 „
„ „ 44 „	16 „	„ „ 42 „	13 „
„ „ 42 „	15 „	„ „ 39 „	12 „
„ „ 40 „	14 „	„ „ 36 „	11 „
„ „ 38 „	13 „	„ „ 33 „	10 „
„ „ 36 „	12 „	„ „ 30 „	9 „
„ „ 34 „	11 „	„ „ 27 „	8 „
„ „ 31 „	10 „	„ „ 24 „	7 „
„ „ 28 „	9 „	„ „ 21 „	6 „
„ „ 25 „	8 „	„ „ 18 „	5 „
„ „ 22 „	7 „	„ „ 15 „	4 „
„ „ 19 „	6 „	„ „ 12 „	3 „
„ „ 16 „	5 „	„ „ 8 „	2 „
„ „ 13 „	4 „	„ „ 4 „	1 day
„ „ 10 „	3 „		
„ „ 7 „	2 „		
„ „ 4 „	1 day		

(2) Notwithstanding the provisions of the last foregoing sub-paragraph—

    (*a*) (i) the number of days of annual holiday which an employer is required to allow to a worker in respect of a period of employment during the 12 months immediately preceding 6th April 1968 shall not exceed in the aggregate—

        in the case of a worker with a normal working week of four days or more, twice the number of days constituting the worker's normal working week, plus four days; and

        in the case of a worker with a normal working week of less than four days, three times the number of days constituting the worker's normal working week; and

    (ii) the number of days of annual holiday which an employer is required to allow to a worker in respect of a period of employment during the 12 months immediately preceding 6th April 1969 and during the 12 months immediately preceding 6th April in any succeeding year shall not exceed in the aggregate *three times the number of days constituting the worker's normal working week;*

    (*b*) where before 17th September in any holiday season a worker and his employer enter into an agreement in writing that the worker shall be allowed after the end of the holiday season and before 6th April next following, days of holiday not exceeding twice the number of days constituting his normal working week, being all or part of the annual holiday for which he has qualified under this paragraph, any such days of annual holiday may, subject to the provisions of paragraph 4, be allowed in accordance with the agreement and if so allowed shall be treated for the purpose of this Schedule as having been allowed during the holiday season;

(*c*) the duration of the worker's annual holiday during the holiday season ending on 30th September 1968 shall be reduced by any days of holiday with pay (not being days of customary holiday) which have been allowed to him by the employer during the period from and including 6th April 1968 to the date on which the provisions of this Schedule become effective.

(3) In this Schedule the expression "holiday season" means in relation to an annual holiday during the year 1968, the period commencing on 6th April 1968 and ending on 30th September 1968, and in relation to an annual holiday during the year 1969 and each subsequent year, the period commencing on 6th April and ending on 30th September in that year.

4.—(1) Subject to the provisions of this paragraph, an annual holiday under this Schedule shall be allowed on consecutive working days and days of holiday shall be treated as consecutive notwithstanding that a day of holiday allowed to a worker under Part II of this Schedule or a day upon which he does not normally work for the employer intervenes.

(2) (*a*) Where the number of days of annual holiday for which a worker has qualified exceeds the number of days constituting his normal working week, but does not exceed twice that number, the holiday may be allowed in two periods of consecutive working days; so, however, that when a holiday is so allowed, one of the periods shall consist of a number of such days not less than the number of days constituting the worker's normal working week.

(*b*) Where the number of days of annual holiday for which a worker has qualified exceeds twice the number of days constituting his normal working week the holiday may be allowed as follows:—

(i) as to two periods of consecutive working days, each such period not being less than the period constituting the worker's normal working week, during the holiday season; and

(ii) as to any additional days, on working days which need not be consecutive, to be fixed by agreement between the employer or his representative and the worker or his representative, either during the holiday season or on any working day before the beginning of the next following holiday season.

(3) Where a day of holiday allowed to a worker under Part II of this Schedule immediately precedes a period of annual holiday or occurs during such a period then, notwithstanding the foregoing provisions of this paragraph, the duration of that period of annual holiday may be reduced by one day and in such a case one day of annual holiday may be allowed on any working day in the holiday season, or by agreement between the employer and the worker or his representative, on any working day before the beginning of the next following holiday season.

(4) Subject to the provisions of sub-paragraph (1) of this paragraph, any day of annual holiday under this Schedule may be allowed on a day on which the worker is entitled to a day of holiday or to a half-holiday under any enactment other than the Wages Councils Act 1959.

5. An employer shall give to a worker reasonable notice of the commencing date or dates and of the duration of his annual holiday. Such notice may be given individually to the worker or by the posting of a notice in the place where the worker is employed.

PART IV

HOLIDAY REMUNERATION

A—CUSTOMARY HOLIDAYS AND HOLIDAYS IN LIEU OF CUSTOMARY HOLIDAYS

6.—(1) For each day of holiday (including a holiday falling on a Saturday) to which a worker is entitled under Part II of this Schedule he shall be paid by the employer as holiday remuneration whichever of the following amounts is the greater:—

(a) (i) in the case of a worker employed in the retail bespoke branch of the trade whose normal working week exceeds five days, two-elevenths

(ii) in the case of all other workers, one-fifth ... ...

of the average weekly earnings of the worker during the 12 months ended on 5th April immediately preceding the holiday, such average weekly earnings to be determined by dividing, by the number of weeks of employment with the employer during the said period, the total remuneration paid to him by the employer during that period:

Provided that when Good Friday or Easter Monday (or days substituted therefor under the provisions of sub-paragraph (2) (b) of paragraph 2 or holidays in lieu of such customary holidays) fall after 5th April in any year, the holiday remuneration for any such holiday under this sub-paragraph shall be two-elevenths or one-fifth, as the case may require, of the average weekly earnings of the worker during the 12 months ended on 5th April in the preceding calendar year; or,

(b) the appropriate statutory minimum remuneration to which he would have been entitled as a time worker if the day had not been a day of holiday and he had been employed on work for which statutory minimum remuneration is payable:—

(i) in the case of a worker normally employed for more than 30 hours a week, for 8 hours, or

(ii) in the case of a worker normally employed for 30 hours a week or less, for 4 hours.

(2) Notwithstanding the provisions of sub-paragraph (1) of this paragraph, payment of the said holiday remuneration is subject to the condition that the worker (unless excused by the employer or absent by reason of the proved illness of, or accident to, the worker) presents himself for employment at the usual starting hour on the first working day following the holiday:

Provided that when two customary holidays occur on successive days (or so that no working day intervenes) the said condition shall apply only to the second customary holiday.

(3) Where a worker normally works in the week on every week-day except Saturday, he shall be paid in respect of any Saturday on which he would have been entitled to a holiday under Part II of this Schedule if it had been a day on which he normally worked, a sum equivalent to the holiday remuneration he would have been entitled to receive had he been allowed a holiday on that day.

(4) Holiday remuneration in resect of any customary holiday shall be paid by the employer to the worker on the pay-day on which the wages for the first working day following the customary holiday are paid.

(5) Holiday remuneration in respect of any holiday in lieu of a customary holiday shall be paid on the pay-day on which the wages are paid for the first working day following the holiday in lieu of a customary holiday: Provided that the said payment shall be made immediately upon the termination of the worker's employment if he ceases to be employed before being allowed such holiday in lieu of a customary holiday and in that case the condition specified in sub-paragraph (2) of this paragraph shall not apply.

B—ANNUAL HOLIDAY

7.—(1) Subject to the provisions of paragraph 8, a worker qualified to be allowed an annual holiday under this Schedule shall be paid as holiday remuneration by his employer in respect thereof, on the last pay-day preceding such annual holiday, whichever of the following amounts is the greater:—

(a) (i) in respect of the annual holiday to be allowed during the 1968 holiday season an amount equal to fourteen two-hundred-and-sixtieths of the total remuneration paid by the employer to the worker in the 12 months ended on 5th April 1968; and

(ii) in respect of the annual holiday to be allowed during the 1969 holiday season and during the holiday season in each succeeding year an amount equal to *three fifty-seconds* of the total remuneration paid by the employer to the worker in the 12 months ended on 5th April immediately preceding the holiday season; or

(b) one day's holiday pay (as defined in paragraph 11) in respect of each day of annual holiday.

(2) Where, under the provisions of paragraph 4, an annual holiday is allowed in more than one period the holiday remuneration shall be apportioned accordingly.

8. Where any accrued holiday remuneration has been paid by the employer to the worker (in accordance with paragraph 9 of this Schedule or under the provisions of Order W.D. (85)) in respect of employment during any of the periods referred to in that paragraph or that Order, the amount of holiday remuneration payable by the employer in respect of any annual holiday for which the worker has qualified by reason of employment during the said period shall be reduced by the amount of the said accrued holiday remuneration unless that remuneration has been deducted from a previous payment of holiday remuneration made under the provisions of this Schedule or of Order W.D. (85).

ACCRUED HOLIDAY REMUNERATION PAYABLE ON TERMINATION OF EMPLOYMENT

9.—(1) Where a worker ceases to be employed by an employer after the provisions of this Schedule become effective, the employer shall, immediately on the termination of the employment, pay to the worker accrued holiday remuneration in accordance with this paragraph.

(2) Accrued holiday remuneration shall be payable in accordance with the following table if the worker has in the 12 months commencing on 6th April 1967, and thereafter in any period of 12 months commencing on 6th April been employed for any of the periods of employment specified in that table.

(3) Accrued holiday remuneration is not payable in respect of any period of employment for which the worker has been allowed or become entitled to be allowed an annual holiday under this Schedule.

(4) Subject to the provisions of sub-paragraph (5) hereof, where a worker has been allowed in a holiday season part only of the annual holiday for which he has qualified under this Schedule or under Order W.D. (85) and his employment is terminated before he becomes entitled to the rest of that holiday the accrued holiday remuneration payable shall be:—

(a) in the case of a worker who has qualified for days of annual holiday exceeding twice the number of days constituting his normal working week and who has been allowed as days of annual holiday not less than twice the number of days constituting his normal working week, or, where the circumstances in sub-paragraph (3) of paragraph 4 are applicable, that number of days reduced by one:—

(i) in respect of the days of holiday for which he has qualified during the 12 months ended on 5th April immediately preceding the termination of his employment, the holiday remuneration due in respect thereof calculated in accordance with the provisions of paragraph 7 less the amount received by him in respect of the part of the holiday which has been allowed; and

(ii) in respect of any period of employment since the said 5th April, the amount calculated in accordance with the following table;

(b) in the case of any other worker, the appropriate amount under the following table in respect of the qualifying period of employment less the amount received by the worker in respect of that part of the holiday which has been allowed.

(5) Any accrued holiday remuneration payable under the provisions of this paragraph shall be reduced by the amount of any accrued holiday remuneration already paid by the employer to the worker in pursuance of this Order or Order W.D. (85) in respect of the same period of employment or part thereof.

TABLE OF ACCRUED HOLIDAY REMUNERATION

A. In respect of employment during the 12 months ended on 5th April 1968.

Column 1 — Period of employment calculated in accordance with the provisions of paragraph 10	Column 2 — Workers with a normal working week of 6 days. Accrued holiday remuneration	Column 3 — Workers with a normal working week of 5 days or less. Accrued holiday remuneration	Column 4
At least 48 weeks	Two and two-thirds times the amount in Col. 4	Two and four-fifths times the amount in Col. 4	The amount which the worker would be entitled to receive from his employer, at the date of the termination of his employment, for one week's work, if working his normal working week and the number of daily hours normally worked by him (exclusive of overtime) and if paid as a time worker at the appropriate rate of statutory minimum remuneration for work for which statutory minimum remuneration is payable and at the same rate for any work for which such remuneration is not payable.
" 46 "	Two and one-half "	Two and three-fifths "	
" 45 "	Two and one-third "	Two and three-fifths "	
" 43 "	Two and one-third "	Two and two-fifths "	
" 42 "	Two and one-sixth "	Two and two-fifths "	
" 40 "	Two and one-sixth "	Two and one-fifth "	
" 39 "	Twice the amount in Col. 4	Two and one-fifth "	
" 37 "	Twice the amount in Col. 4	Twice the amount in Col. 4	
" 36 "	One and five-sixths times the amount in Col. 4	Twice the amount in Col. 4	
" 35 "	One and five-sixths "	One and four-fifths times the amount in Col. 4	
" 33 "	One and two-thirds "	One and four-fifths "	
" 32 "	One and two-thirds "	One and three-fifths "	
" 30 "	One and one-half "	One and three-fifths "	
" 29 "	One and one-half "	One and two-fifths "	
" 27 "	One and one-third "	One and two-fifths "	
" 26 "	One and one-third "	One and one-fifth "	
" 24 "	One and one-sixth "	One and one-fifth "	
" 21 "	The amount in Col. 4	One and one-fifth "	
" 20 "	The amount in Col. 4	The amount in Col. 4	
" 18 "	Five-sixths of the amount in Col. 4	The amount in Col. 4	
" 16 "	Five-sixths "	Four-fifths of the amount in Col. 4	
" 15 "	Two-thirds "	Four-fifths "	
" 12 "	One-half "	Three-fifths "	
" 8 "	One-third "	Three-fifths "	
" 4 "	One-sixth "	Two-fifths "	
		One-fifth "	

TABLE OF ACCRUED HOLIDAY REMUNERATION (continued)

B. In respect of employment during the 12 months ending on 5th April 1969 and during each succeeding 12 months ending on 5th April.

Column 1 — Period of employment calculated in accordance with the provisions of paragraph 10	Column 2 — Workers with a normal working week of 6 days — Accrued holiday remuneration	Column 3 — Workers with a normal working week of 5 days or less — Accrued holiday remuneration	Column 4
At least 48 weeks	Three times the amount in Col. 4	Three times the amount in Col. 4	The amount which the worker would be entitled to receive from his employer, at the date of the termination of his employment, for one week's work, if working his normal working week and the number of daily hours normally worked by him (exclusive of overtime) and if paid as a time worker at the appropriate rate of statutory minimum remuneration for work for which statutory minimum remuneration is payable and at the same rate for any work for which such remuneration is not payable.
,, 46 ,,	Two and five-sixths times the amount in Col. 4	Two and four-fifths times the amount in Col. 4	
,, 45 ,,	Two and two-thirds ,,	Two and four-fifths times the amount in Col. 4	
,, 44 ,,	Two and two-thirds ,,	Two and three-fifths ,,	
,, 42 ,,	Two and one-half ,,	Two and three-fifths ,,	
,, 40 ,,	Two and one-third ,,	Two and two-fifths ,,	
,, 39 ,,	Two and one-sixth ,,	Two and two-fifths ,,	
,, 38 ,,	Two and one-sixth ,,	Two and one-fifth ,,	
,, 36 ,,	Twice the amount in Col. 4	Two and one-fifth ,,	
,, 34 ,,	One and five-sixths times the amount in Col. 4	Twice the amount in Col 4	
,, 33 ,,	One and two-thirds ,,	Twice the amount in Col 4	
,, 31 ,,	One and two-thirds ,,	One and four-fifths times the amount in Col. 4	
,, 30 ,,	One and one-half ,,	One and four-fifths times the amount in Col. 4	
,, 28 ,,	One and one-half ,,	One and three-fifths ,,	
,, 27 ,,	One and one-third ,,	One and three-fifths ,,	
,, 25 ,,	One and one-third ,,	One and two-fifths ,,	
,, 24 ,,	One and one-sixth ,,	One and two-fifths ,,	
,, 22 ,,	One and one-sixth ,,	One and one-fifth ,,	
,, 21 ,,	The amount in Col. 4	One and one-fifth ,,	
,, 19 ,,	The amount in Col. 4	The amount in Col. 4	
,, 18 ,,	Five-sixths of the amount in Col. 4	The amount in Col. 4	
,, 16 ,,	Five-sixths ,,	Four-fifths of the amount in Col. 4	
,, 15 ,,	Two-thirds ,,	Four-fifths ,,	
,, 13 ,,	Two-thirds ,,	Three-fifths ,,	
,, 12 ,,	One-half ,,	Three-fifths ,,	
,, 10 ,,	One-half ,,	Two-fifths ,,	
,, 8 ,,	One-third ,,	Two-fifths ,,	
,, 7 ,,	One-third ,,	One-fifth ,,	
,, 4 ,,	One-sixth ,,	One-fifth ,,	

(6) Notwithstanding the provisions of the foregoing table, the accrued holiday remuneration payable to a worker who has been employed by the employer for the whole of the 12 months ended on 5th April immediately preceding the termination of his employment shall be as follows:—

(*a*) in respect of that 12 months an amount equal to the holiday remuneration for the days of annual holiday for which he has qualified, calculated in accordance with the provisions of sub-paragraph (1) of paragraph 7; and

(*b*) in respect of any period of employment since the said 5th April, the amount calculated in accordance with the foregoing table in this paragraph.

PART V

GENERAL

10. For the purpose of calculating any period of employment qualifying a worker for an annual holiday or for any accrued holiday remuneration under this Schedule, the worker shall be treated—

(1) as if he were employed for a week in respect of any week in which—

(*a*) in the case of a worker other than a part-time worker, he has worked for the employer for not less than 20 hours and has performed some work for which statutory minimum remuneration is payable;

(*b*) in the case of a part-time worker, he has worked for the employer and has performed some work for which statutory minimum remuneration is payable;

(*c*) in the case of any worker—
   (i) he has worked for the employer for less than 20 hours by reason of the proved illness of, or accident to, the worker or for a like reason has been absent throughout the week (provided that the number of weeks which may be treated as weeks of employment for such reason shall not exceed four in the aggregate in any such period); or
   (ii) he has been suspended throughout the week owing to shortage of work (provided that the number of weeks which may be treated as weeks of employment for such reason shall not exceed six in the aggregate in any such period);

(2) as if he were employed on any day of holiday allowed under the provisions of this Schedule, or of Order W.D. (85), and on any other day of holiday with pay, and for the purposes of the provisions of sub-paragraph (1) of this paragraph, a worker who is absent on such a holiday shall be treated as having worked thereon for the employer on work for which statutory minimum remuneration is payable,

(*a*) where the holiday is a customary holiday, or a holiday in lieu of a customary holiday, for 8 hours if the worker is normally employed for more than 30 hours a week or for 4 hours if he is normally employed for 30 hours a week or less, or

(*b*) where the holiday is a day of annual holiday or any other day of holiday with pay, for the number of hours ordinarily worked by him on that day of the week.

11. In this Schedule, unless the context otherwise requires, the following expressions have the meanings hereby respectively assigned to them, that is to say:—
"NORMAL WORKING WEEK" means the number of days on which it has been usual for the worker to work in a week in the employment of the employer in the 12 months immediately preceding the commencement of the holiday season or, where under paragraph 9 accrued holiday remuneration is payable on the termination of the employment, in the 12 months immediately preceding the date of the termination of the employment:

Provided that—

(1) part of a day shall count as a day;

(2) no account shall be taken of any week in which the worker did not perform any work for which statutory minimum remuneration has been fixed.

"ONE DAY'S HOLIDAY PAY" means the appropriate proportion of the remuneration which the worker would be entitled to receive from his employer at the date of the annual holiday or at the termination of the employment, as the case may require, for one week's work if working his normal working week and the number of daily hours normally worked by him (exclusive of overtime) and if paid as a time worker at the appropriate rate of statutory minimum remuneration for work for which statutory minimum remuneration is payable and at the same rate for any work for which such remuneration is not payable, and in this definition "appropriate proportion" means—

where the worker's normal working week is six days   ..   ..   one-sixth
where the worker's normal working week is five days   ..   ..   one-fifth
where the worker's normal working week is four days or less ... one-quarter.

"PART-TIME WORKER" means a worker who normally works for the employer for less than 20 hours a week by reason only of the fact that he does not hold himself out as normally available for work for more than the number of hours he normally works in the week.

"RETAIL BESPOKE BRANCH OF THE TRADE" means that branch of the trade in which the employer supplies the garment direct to the individual wearer and employs the worker direct.

"STATUTORY MINIMUM REMUNERATION" means minimum remuneration (other than holiday remuneration) fixed by a wages regulation order.

"WAGES REGULATION ORDER" means a wages regulation order made by the Secretary of State to give effect to proposals submitted to her by the Wages Council.

"WEEK" means "pay week".

12. The provisions of this Schedule are without prejudice to any agreement for the allowance of any further holidays with pay or for the payment of additional holiday remuneration.

EXPLANATORY NOTE

(This Note is not part of the Order.)

This Order which has effect from 20th September 1968, sets out the holidays which an employer is required to allow to workers and the remuneration payable for those holidays in substitution for the holidays and holiday remuneration fixed by the Wages Regulation (Dressmaking and Women's Light Clothing) (England and Wales) (Holidays) Order 1967 (Order W.D. (85)), which Order is revoked.

New provisions are printed in italics.

STATUTORY INSTRUMENTS

1968 No. 1333

INDUSTRIAL TRAINING

The Industrial Training (Engineering Board) Order 1968

Made	- - -	20th August 1968
Laid before Parliament		29th August 1968
Coming into Operation		3rd September 1968

The Secretary of State after consultation with the Engineering Industry Training Board and with organisations and associations of organisations appearing to be representative respectively of substantial numbers of employers engaging in the activities hereinafter mentioned and of substantial numbers of persons employed in those activities and with the bodies established for the purpose of carrying on under national ownership industries in which the said activities are carried on to a substantial extent and in exercise of her powers under section 9 of the Industrial Training Act 1964(a) and of all other powers enabling her in that behalf hereby makes the following Order:—

Citation, commencement and interpretation

1.—(1) This Order may be cited as the Industrial Training (Engineering Board) Order 1968 and shall come into operation on 3rd September 1968.

(2) In this Order—

(*a*) " the Act " means the Industrial Training Act 1964;

(*b*) " the Board " means the Engineering Industry Training Board;

(*c*) " Levy Order " includes the Industrial Training Levy (Engineering) Order 1965(b), the Industrial Training Levy (Engineering) Order 1967(c), and the Industrial Training Levy (Engineering) (No. 2) Order 1967(d);

(*d*) " the 1967 Order " means the Industrial Training (Engineering Board) Order 1967(e);

(*e*) " the principal Order " means the Industrial Training (Engineering Board) Order 1964(f).

(3) The Interpretation Act 1889(g) shall apply to the interpretation of this Order as it applies to the interpretation of an Act of Parliament and as if this Order, the principal Order and the 1967 Order were Acts of Parliament.

Revocation

2. The 1967 Order is hereby revoked.

Activities of the Board

3. The activities in relation to which the Board exercises the functions conferred by the Act upon industrial training boards shall, in lieu of the activities specified in Schedule 1 to the principal Order (as amended by the 1967 Order),

---

(a) 1964 c. 16.	(b) S.I. 1965/1263 (1965 II, p. 3592).
(c) S.I. 1967/332 (1967 I, p. 1152).	(d) S.I. 1967/1427 (1967 III, p. 4127).
(e) S.I. 1967/279 (1967 I, p. 999).	(f) S.I. 1964/1086 (1964 II, p. 2402).

(g) 1889 c. 63.

be the activities specified in the Schedule to this Order, and accordingly in the principal Order the latter Schedule shall be substituted for the former Schedule.

Transitional provisions

4.—(1) The chairman and other members of the Board on the day upon which this Order comes into operation shall continue to be members of the Board and to hold and vacate their offices in accordance with the terms of the instruments appointing them to be members.

(2) The provisions of this Order shall not—

(*a*) extend the operation of a Levy Order;

(*b*) affect the operation of a Levy Order in relation to the assessment of an employer within the meaning of that Order in respect of an establishment that was engaged in the relevant levy period wholly or mainly in activities included in the Schedule to this Order;

(*c*) affect the operation of any assessment notice served by the Board under the provisions of a Levy Order before the date upon which this Order comes into operation or any appeal or other proceedings arising out of any such notice.

Signed by order of the Secretary of State.

20th August 1968.

Roy Hattersley,
Joint Parliamentary Under Secretary of State,
Department of Employment and Productivity.

SCHEDULE

THE ENGINEERING INDUSTRY

1. Subject to the provisions of this Schedule, the activities of the engineering industry are the following activities in so far as they are carried out in Great Britain:—

(*a*) the manufacture of—

(i) articles wholly or mainly from metal or tungsten carbide;

(ii) articles wholly or mainly from any combination of either metal and plastics material or of metal and tungsten carbide;

(iii) vehicle bodies;

(iv) aircraft or hovercraft;

(v) articles embodying a lens or prism;

(vi) primary cells, batteries or electric accumulators;

(vii) electric cables, electric filament lamps, electric discharge lamps or photographic flashbulbs;

(viii) thermionic, cold cathode or photo-cathode valves or tubes, cathode-ray tubes or electric capacitors or resistors;

(ix) printed or micro-electronic circuits, devices using ferrite or quartz crystals for electrical purposes or semi-conductor or piezo-electric devices;

(x) patterns or models constructed for engineering or metal casting purposes·

(*b*) the installation, testing, inspection or repair of any articles or other products above-mentioned;

(*c*) the painting or paint spraying of any articles specified in head (i), (ii), (iii), (iv) or (x) of sub-paragraph (*a*) of this paragraph;

(*d*) the casting in non-ferrous metal (other than gold, silver or platinum) of sculptured figures;

(*e*) the following operations or processes that is to say—

(i) the reduction of virgin aluminium, the production of secondary-based aluminium or of aluminium alloys or the manufacture of aluminium powder or paste and, when carried out by an employer engaged substantially in any of the said operations, the production or processing of any other non-ferrous metal;

(ii) the smelting or refining of copper or copper alloys;

(iii) the rolling, drawing, extruding or forging of non-ferrous metal and, when carried out by an employer engaged substantially in any such operation, any refining of metal incidental thereto;

(*f*) the following operations or processes, that is to say—

(i) any process of metal preparation including mechanical or chemical cleaning;

(ii) tempering, case-hardening and annealing or other process of metal treatment;

(iii) electro-plating, anodising, polishing, burnishing, vitreous or stove enamelling or other metal finishing process;

(*g*) the machining of carbon articles;

(*h*) the erection of—

(i) the main framework of buildings, being framework of metallic construction; or

(ii) other structures consisting wholly or mainly of metal, not being either structures forming part of a building, electric lines or structures designed for the support thereof, walls, fencing, hoardings, exhibition stands, scaffolding or contractors' plant;

(*i*) the preparation of engineering drawings;

(*j*) the assembly of electric blankets;

(*k*) the hiring out by an employer of individuals in his employment to persons engaging in any of the foregoing activities, where the said individuals are to be employed in such activities;

(*l*) any activities, being—

(i) related activities incidental or ancillary to principal activities of the engineering industry; or

(ii) activities undertaken in the administration, control or direction of one or more establishments, being establishments engaged wholly or mainly in principal activities of that industry, in related activities incidental or ancillary thereto, or in the administration, control or direction of one or more other establishments engaged in such principal or related activities; and carried out, in either case, by the employer engaged in those principal activities or, where that employer is a company, by the company or by an associated company of the company;

(*m*) any activities of industry or commerce (other than engineering activities) carried out at or from an establishment mainly engaged—

(i) in engineering activities; or

(ii) in engineering activities and in activities described in the Appendix to this Schedule, but to a greater extent in engineering activities than in activities described in that Appendix in relation to any one industry.

2. Notwithstanding anything contained in this Schedule, there shall not be included in the activities of the engineering industry:—

(*a*) the activities of any establishment engaged—

(i) mainly in activities not being engineering activities or activities described in the Appendix to this Schedule; or

(ii) to a less extent in engineering activities than in activities described in that

Appendix in relation to any one industry;

(b) the activities of any establishment engaged wholly or mainly in related activities, being activities—

    (i) incidental or ancillary to the activities of one or more establishments (in this sub-paragraph hereafter referred to as " the principal establishment ") engaged wholly or mainly in any activities not being principal activities of the engineering industry; and

    (ii) carried out by the employer carrying on the principal establishment or, where that employer is a company, by the company or by an associated company of the company;

(c) the activities of any establishment engaged wholly or mainly in one or more activities of a kind specified in an entry in the second column of the next following Table (being activities undertaken in relation to all or any of the products comprised in the group specified in the corresponding entry in the third column of that Table) or in two or more of such entries:

TABLE

Item No.	Activities	Group of Products
1.	Production and, when carried out in association therewith, casting.	Iron and steel.
2.	Production when carried out in association with the production of iron or steel.	Iron or steel forgings.
3.	Annealing or heat treatment, when carried out in association with the production of iron or steel.	Steel.
4.	Rolling for the purpose of reducing the cross-sectional area thereof.	Iron or steel products.
5.	Production from iron or steel.	Bright bars, hot finished tubes and hot finished pipes.
6.	Production where the employer (or an associated company of the employer, being a company) is mainly engaged in the production of iron or steel and in the production from iron or steel of hot finished tubes or hot finished pipes.	Cold finished tubes and cold finished pipes.
7.	Manipulation or fabrication when carried out by an employer or associated company described in item 6.	Tubes and pipes.
8.	Production.	Tinplate, terneplate, iron or steel wire and steel wire ropes.
9.	Production when carried out in association with any activities above-mentioned in this Table.	Galvanised or other coated steel sheets.
10.	Cutting and bending for the purposes of any operations in building work or civil engineering work.	Reinforcing steel.
11.	Erection, repair or dismantling.	Walls, fencing, hoardings and scaffolding.
12.	Manufacture.	Industrialised building components or sections and prefabricated buildings or sections of buildings, being components, sections, and buildings framed in wood.

Item No.	Activities	Group of Products
13.	Construction on the premises in which they are to be installed and prefabrication elsewhere by the employer engaged in their installation.	Shop, office or similar fittings.
14.	Erection or dismantling.	Exhibition stands.
15.	Installation, testing, inspection, maintenance or repair.	Contractors' plant.
16.	Preparation.	Drawings for the purpose of the construction of the hull of a ship.
17.	The operations following when carried out at or from a yard, a dry dock (including the precincts thereof), a harbour or a wet dock—	
	(a) construction, fitting out, reconstruction, repair, refitting, painting or finishing.	Ships and floating constructions.
	(b) scaling, scurfing or cleaning.	Ships' boilers.
	(c) scaling, chipping or shot blasting.	Ships' hulls.
	(d) shot blasting.	Ships' tanks.
18.	Construction (including any fitting out) elsewhere than at a place mentioned in item 17.	Ships.
19.	Not being mainly by an engineering process, manufacture or repair.	Furniture.
20.	Manufacture, repair or tuning.	Pianofortes, harpsichords, spinets, clavichords, pipe-organs and organ pipes.
21.	Manufacture.	Springs and spring units being products for use in beds, divans, divan bases, mattresses or furniture or in seating of any kind.
22.	Manufacture.	Brushes (not being carbon brushes), brooms and painters' rollers.
23.	Manufacture.	Fishing rods and golf clubs.
24.	Assembly, installation, cleaning or repair.	Venetian blinds.
25.	Repair except when the establishment is engaged wholly or mainly in the manufacture or repair of motor vehicle bodies.	Motor vehicles and trailers drawn by motor vehicles.
26.	Maintenance or repair.	Agricultural or horticultural machinery and equipment.
27.	Inspection, maintenance, repair or overhaul (not being operations carried out by the manufacturer of the product).	Aircraft, parts of aircraft and such of the equipment of aircraft as is necessary for the airworthiness thereof.
28.	Processing (not being an activity mentioned in any of the heads (iii) to (x) of paragraph 1(a) of this Schedule).	Plastics material.
29.	Manufacture or re-covering.	Printers' rollers.
30.	Manufacture.	Rubber stamps.
31.	Manufacture.	Ball point pens, fountain pens and propelling pencils.

Item No.	Activities	Group of Products
32.	Production or refining (not being activities specified in paragraph 1(*e*) of this Schedule).	Non-ferrous metal.
33.	Any activities in printing.	Metal products not being either metal plates for use in the manufacture of metal containers or electrical circuits.
34.	Assembly.	Creasing, cutting or scoring formes or forming tools for use in the manufacture from paper of either folding cartons or (for use in connection with the display of goods) showcards or other printed products.
35.	Selling.	Hearing aids.
36.	Installation, testing, inspection or repair, being operations carried out in furtherance of an agreement made between a person carrying on the business of selling or hiring out audio or video receiving apparatus or of operating a broadcast relay station and a person to whom such apparatus has been sold or hired or who is a sub-subscriber to the service provided from such a station.	Audio or video receiving apparatus and transmission lines connected with such apparatus,
37.	Manufacture or repair.	Footwear.
38.	Manufacture or repair.	Components for footwear not being components consisting wholly or mainly of metal.
39.	Manufacture or repair.	Attaché, brief, despatch or executive cases, suitcases, trunks and any similar receptacles of a kind used for personal or domestic purposes, not being cases, trunks or other receptacles consisting wholly or mainly of metal.
40.	Manufacture or repair.	Holdalls, rucksacks, satchels, cycle, shopping or sports bags, handbags, wallets, purses, and (not being products mentioned in item 39 of this Table) any similar receptacles of a kind used for personal or domestic purposes.
41.	Manufacture or repair.	The following products, not being products consisting wholly or mainly of metal, that is to say, cases and other containers for glasses or for optical, photographic, cinematographic, measuring, checking, precision, medical or surgical instruments or apparatus and jewel, toilet or similar cases.
42.	Manufacture.	The following products, not being products consisting wholly or mainly of metal, that is to say, baby harnesses, straps of any kind and trouser, costume or dress belts.

Item No.	Activities	Group of Products
43.	Manufacture.	Collars and leashes (not being products consisting wholly or mainly of metal) for dogs or cats.
44.	Manufacture or repair.	Wearing apparel other than head-gear.
45.	Manufacture or repair.	Jewellery.
46.	Manufacture (not being an activity specified in paragraph 1(e)(iii) of this Schedule), plating or assaying.	Any products wholly or mainly of gold, silver or platinum or of an alloy that includes any such metal.
47.	Cutting or polishing.	Diamonds.
48.	Manufacture or repair.	Artificial teeth, dentures and orthodontic appliances.
49.	Manufacture or repair.	Glasses and the frames thereof.
50.	Manufacture or repair.	Artificial flowers, folding push-cars, lampshades, pencils, perambulators, and toys and games.
51.	Repair.	Any barrels, kegs or drums designed for packaging.

(d) any operations in building work or civil engineering work, or (being operations undertaken in, upon, above or under a building, or the close, curtilage or precincts thereof, or a civil engineering work or the site of a building or such a work) in the provision or continued provision for the building, civil engineering work or site of water, gas, electricity, lighting, heating, ventilation or air-conditioning;

(e) the activities of—

(i) the Electricity Council, the Central Electricity Generating Board or an Area Electricity Board;

(ii) the North of Scotland Hydro-Electric Board or the South of Scotland Electricity Board;

(iii) the Gas Council or an Area Gas Board;

(iv) a harbour authority when acting in that capacity;

(v) a local authority, or a joint board or joint committee of such authorities;

(vi) statutory water undertakers within the meaning of the Water Act 1945(a) or regional water boards or water development boards within the meaning of the Water (Scotland) Act 1967(b), being the activities of such undertakers or boards in the exercise of their powers or duties as such; or

(vii) the United Kingdom Atomic Energy Authority;

(f) when carried out by the National Coal Board any activities specified in paragraph 1(b) of this Schedule;

(g) when carried out by the London Transport Board any activities (not being design or drawing or the training of employees or apprentices) to which paragraph 1(l) of this Schedule applies, or the activities of any establishment of that Board engaged wholly or mainly in the repair of motor vehicle bodies;

(h) the activities of any company, association or body that is required by its constitution to apply its profits, if any, or other income in promoting its objects and is prohibited thereby from paying any dividend to its members, and that has for its sole or principal object or among its principal objects the provision of facilities for any of the purposes mentioned in section 15(1) of the Disabled Persons (Employment) Act 1944(c) (which relates to the provision for registered persons who are seriously disabled of work or training);

(i) any work, occupation or training that is provided in accordance with arrangements made by a local authority under the Disabled Persons (Employment)

(a) 1945 c. 42.   (b) 1967 c. 78.   (c) 1944 c. 10.

Act 1958(a) or any other enactment that authorises or requires the provision of arrangements for persons suffering from illness, severe physical defect or disability or from mental disorder, or for persons who have been suffering from illness or whose care is undertaken with a view to preventing them from becoming ill, or for old people;

(*j*) any operations carried out by a person undergoing a course of training as a seagoing officer or rating under an agreement in writing with an employer in the shipping industry or with any organisation of employers in that industry or with any association of such organisations; or

(*k*) the supply of food or drink for immediate consumption.

3. In this Schedule unless the context otherwise requires:—

" agricultural or horticultural machinery and equipment " means any machinery, plant, equipment or appliance designed primarily or adapted for use in agriculture or horticulture, but does not include a self-propelled road vehicle which is designed primarily for the carriage of persons or of loads;

" aircraft " means any heavier than air aircraft;

" articles " includes any parts or components of articles, being parts or components made wholly or mainly from metal or tungsten carbide or from any combination of either metal and plastics material or of metal and tungsten carbide;

" audio or video receiving apparatus " does not include apparatus used or intended for use on a ship;

" broadcast relay station " means a station for the re-transmission by cable or wire, to the customers of the persons operating the station, of broadcast radio or television programmes which those persons receive either by cable or wire or by wireless from the persons who broadcast the programmes;

" building work " means the construction, alteration, repair or demolition of a building or part of a building or of any erection in the nature of a building, but does not include any activities to which paragraph 1(*h*) of this Schedule applies or the installation, testing, inspection or repair of machinery or plant, not being contractors' plant;

" civil engineering work " means the construction or demolition of a railway-line, siding or monorail, the construction, structural alteration, repair or demolition of any aerodrome, airport, bridge, road, viaduct, dock, harbour, pier, quay, wharf, coast protection, river or drainage work, aqueduct, canal, inland navigation, reservoir, waterworks, bore-hole, well (other than an oil well), filter bed, sewage works, sewer, cooling tower or pond, tunnel, heading, adit, chimney, furnace, carbonising or gas-making plant, nuclear or thermal power station, hydro-electric station, electric line or any structure designed for its support, cable trench or duct, oil refinery, pipe-line or defence installation, the sinking of a shaft or bore-hole in a mine of coal, stratified ironstone, shale or fire-clay, the construction of a road below ground in such a mine, the construction of a swimming pool or other bathing place or of a playing field or ground for sporting or recreational purposes, the laying out of a cemetery or the preparation of the site, or the laying down of a foundation or sub-structure, in connection with any of the said operations or with the erection of structural metalwork, but does not include any activities to which paragraph 1(*h*) of this Schedule applies or the installation, testing, inspection or repair of machinery or plant, not being contractors' plant;

" company " includes any body corporate, and " subsidiary " has the same meaning as by virtue of section 154 of the Companies Act 1948(b) it has for the purposes of that Act;

" contractors' plant " means machinery, plant or equipment of a kind used or intended for use in operations on the site of any building work or civil engineering work, but does not include lorries, ready-mixed concrete vehicles or other mechanically propelled vehicles mainly used for the carriage of goods on roads;

" electric line " means a wire or wires, conductor or other means used for the

---

(a) 1958 c. 33.   (b) 1948 c. 38.

purpose of conveying, transmitting, or distributing electricity, or any apparatus connected therewith;

" engineering activities " means any one or more of the principal activities of the engineering industry and the activities included in that industry by virtue of paragraph 1(*l*) of this Schedule;

" engineering process " means any one or more of the following and any similar processes when applied to metal, that is to say—

    (i) machining, grinding or bevelling;

    (ii) casting, forging, stamping, pressing, piercing or bending;

    (iii) sheet metal working, blacksmithing, welding or soldering;

    (iv) stove enamelling;

" floating constructions " does not include hovercraft;

" furniture " means furniture of a type commonly used for bank, church, domestic, educational, garden, hospital, laboratory or office purposes, whether or not supplied for those purposes and whether designed to be free-standing or to be fixed to a building, but does not include awnings, inside or outside blinds, or clocks;

" glasses " means any appliances designed to correct, remedy or relieve any defect of sight, and includes spectacles of the kind known as sunglasses;

" harbour authority " means a harbour authority within the meaning of the Harbours Act 1964(a);

" hearing aids " means any appliances designed to correct, remedy or relieve any defect of hearing;

" hovercraft " means a vehicle which is designed to be supported when in motion wholly or partly by air expelled therefrom to form a cushion of which the boundaries include the ground, water or other surface beneath the vehicle;

" iron " and " steel " include respectively alloy iron and alloy steel containing in each case more than 55 per cent. of pure iron by weight;

" jewellery " includes any article of personal adornment (whether or not containing stones) but does not include clock or watch movements;

" manufacture " includes assembly and any process or operation incidental or appertaining to manufacture or assembly;

" motor vehicles " means mechanically propelled vehicles intended or adapted for use on roads, and includes tramcars and trolley vehicles, but does not include implements for cutting grass that are not capable of being used or adapted for any other purpose, or contractors' plant;

" non-ferrous metal " means any metal not being iron or steel, and includes an alloy of any such metal;

" office premises " has the same meaning as in section 1(2) of the Offices, Shops and Railway Premises Act 1963(b);

" pipe-line " means a pipe or system of pipes (together with any apparatus or works associated therewith) for the conveyance of anything, but does not include a pneumatic despatch tube;

" plastics material " means any material (other than synthetic rubber of any kind) made wholly or mainly by addition, polyaddition, condensation, polycondensation, polymerisation, copolymerisation, esterification, or other similar chemical process, or regenerated or modified cellulose, or hardened proteins or natural resin modified by fusion or esterification, and includes any such material reinforced by glass fibres or bonding glass fibres;

" principal activities of the engineering industry " means activities which, subject to the provisions of paragraph 2 of this Schedule, are specified in paragraph 1, other than sub-paragraphs (*l*) and (*m*) thereof, as activities of the engineering industry;

" processing " in relation to plastics material means any of the following

---

(a) 1964 c.40.   (b) 1963 c.41.

operations, that is to say, masticating, compounding, mixing, calendering, extruding, moulding, pressing, thermoforming, blowing, casting, dipping, coating, encapsulating, heat sealing, laminating, filament winding, machining (other than stitching), cutting, vulcanising or foaming;

" production " includes any process or operation incidental or appertaining to production;

" related activities " means any of the following activities, that is to say—

(i) research, development, design or drawing;

(ii) buying, selling, letting out on hire, testing, advertising, packing, distribution, transport or any similar operations;

(iii) operations of a kind performed at office premises or laboratories, or at stores, warehouses or similar places;

(iv) cleaning, washing or garaging vehicles or carrying out running repairs or minor adjustments thereto;

(v) training of employees or apprentices;

" repair " includes all or any of the operations of repair, reconditioning, modification, alteration or conversion or the replacement of a part, but does not include cleaning or washing vehicles or carrying out running repairs or minor adjustments thereto;

" ship " includes any description of ship, vessel, boat or other floating craft, but does not include a hovercraft or an article that is inflatable by air, gas or liquid;

" toys and games " does not include sports requisites or coin or disc operated machines;

" vehicle bodies " includes motorcycle sidecars, invalid carriages and bodies for caravans.

4.—(1) References in this Schedule to the provisions of any enactment shall be construed as references to those provisions as amended by or under any subsequent enactment.

(2) For the purposes of this Schedule two companies shall be taken to be associated companies if one is a subsidiary of the other or both are subsidiaries of a third company, and " associated company " shall be construed accordingly.

APPENDIX

The activities that would be included in an industry specified in Column 1 hereof by virtue of the industrial training order specified in the corresponding entry in Column 2, if the provisions specified in Column 3 were omitted from that order.

Column 1	Column 2	Column 3
The wool, jute and flax industry	The Industrial Training (Wool Industry Board) Order 1964 as amended by the Industrial Training (Wool, Jute and Flax Board) Order 1968(a)	Schedule 1 Paragraph 1(s)
The iron and steel industry	The Industrial Training (Iron and Steel Board) Order 1964(b)	Schedule 1 Paragraph 1(j)
The construction industry	The Industrial Training (Construction Board) Order 1964 as amended by the Industrial Training (Construction Board) Order 1967(c)	Schedule 1 Paragraph 1(l)
The shipbuilding industry	The Industrial Training (Shipbuilding Board) Order 1964(d)	Schedule 1 Paragraph 1(d)
The ceramics, glass and mineral products industry	The Industrial Training (Ceramics, Glass and Mineral Products Board) Order 1965(e)	Schedule 1 Paragraph 1(n)

Column 1	Column 2	Column 3
The furniture and timber industry	The Industrial Training (Furniture and Timber Industry Board) Order 1965 (f)	Schedule 1 Paragraph 1(r)
The man-made fibres producing industry	The Industrial Training (Man-made Fibres Producing Industry Board) Order 1966(g)	Schedule 1 Paragraph 1(d)
The carpet industry	The Industrial Training (Carpet Board) Order 1966(h)	Schedule 1 Paragraph 1(d)
The knitting, lace and net industry	The Industrial Training (Knitting, Lace and Net Industry Board) Order 1966(i)	Schedule 1 Paragraph 1(j)
The cotton and allied textiles industry	The Industrial Training (Cotton and Allied Textiles Board) Order 1966(j)	Schedule 1 Paragraph 1(p)
The agricultural, horticultural and forestry industry	The Industrial Training (Agricultural, Horticultural and Forestry Board) Order 1966(k)	Schedule 1 Paragraph 1(m)
The road transport industry	The Industrial Training (Road Transport Board) Order 1966(l)	Schedule 1 Paragraph 1(o)
The hotel and catering industry	The Industrial Training (Hotel and Catering Board) Order 1966(m)	Schedule 1 Paragraph 1(e)
The civil air transport industry	The Industrial Training (Civil Air Transport Board) Order 1967(n)	Schedule 1 Paragraph 1(h)
The petroleum industry	The Industrial Training (Petroleum Board) Order 1967(o)	Schedule 1 Paragraph 1(h)
The rubber and plastics processing industry	The Industrial Training (Rubber and Plastics Processing Board) Order 1967(p)	Schedule 1 Paragraph 1(k)
The chemical and allied products industry	The Industrial Training (Chemical and Allied Products Board) Order 1967(q)	Schedule 1 Paragraph 1(s)
The printing and publishing industry	The Industrial Training (Printing and Publishing Board) Order 1968(r)	Schedule 1 Paragraph 1(n)
The paper and paper products industry	The Industrial Training (Paper and Paper Products Board) Order 1968(s)	Schedule 1 Paragraph 1(j)
The distributive industry	The Industrial Training (Distributive Board) Order 1968(t)	Schedule 1 Paragraph 1(h)
The food, drink and tobacco industry	The Industrial Training (Food, Drink and Tobacco Board) Order 1968(u)	Schedule 1 Paragraph 1(q)

(a) S.I. 1964/907, 1968/898 (1964 II, p. 1928; 1968 II, p. 2376).
(b) S.I. 1964/949 (1964 II, p. 2127).
(c) S.I. 1964/1079, 1967/924 (1964 II, p. 2384; 1967 II, p. 2757).
(d) S.I. 1964/1782 (1964 III, p. 3928).
(e) S.I. 1965/1391 (1965 II, p. 4062).
(f) S.I. 1965/2028 (1965 III, p. 5998).
(g) S.I. 1966/143 (1966 I, p. 257).
(h) S.I. 1966/245 (1966 I, p. 499).
(i) S.I. 1966/246 (1966 I, p. 506).
(j) S.I. 1966/823 (1966 II, p. 1907).
(k) S.I. 1966/969 (1966 II, p. 2333).
(l) S.I. 1966/1112 (1966 III, p. 2712).
(m) S.I. 1966/1347 (1966 III, p. 3669).
(n) S.I. 1967/263 (1967 I, p. 968).
(o) S.I. 1967/648 (1967 I, p. 2032).
(p) S.I. 1967/1062 (1967 II, p. 3151).
(q) S.I. 1967/1386 (1967 III, p. 4049).
(r) S.I. 1968/786 (1968 II, p. 2185).
(s) S.I. 1968/787 (1968 II, p. 2194).
(t) S.I. 1968/1032 (1968 II, p. 2709).
(u) S.I. 1968/1033 (1968 II, p.2721).

EXPLANATORY NOTE

(This Note is not part of the Order.)

This Order re-defines the activities in relation to which the Engineering Industry Training Board exercises its functions. The Board was established on 23rd July 1964 by the Industrial Training (Engineering Board) Order 1964. Its activities were re-defined by the Industrial Training (Engineering Board) Order 1967, which Order is now revoked.

Amongst the activities henceforth to be excluded from the engineering industry, in relation to which the Board exercises its functions, are those of establishments engaged wholly or mainly in—

(a) the manufacture or repair of perambulators, folding push-cars or organ pipes or, otherwise than by an engineering process, furniture;

(b) the manufacture of components (not being metal) for footwear;

(c) the repair or reconditioning of barrels, kegs and drums designed for packaging.

The activities of local authorities are also excluded from the engineering industry.

STATUTORY INSTRUMENTS

1968 No. 1334

NATIONAL HEALTH SERVICE, ENGLAND AND WALES

HOSPITAL AND SPECIALIST SERVICES

The National Health Service (Designation of London Teaching Hospitals) Amendment (No. 1) Order 1968

Made - - - *20th August* 1968

Coming into Operation *9th September* 1968

The Minister of Health, in exercise of the powers conferred on him by sections 11 and 75 of the National Health Service Act 1946(**a**) and of all other powers enabling him in that behalf, and after consultation with the University of London, hereby orders as follows :—

1. This order may be cited as the National Health Service (Designation of London Teaching Hospitals) Amendment (No. 1) Order 1968 and shall come into operation on 9th September 1968.

2. The Interpretation Act 1889(**b**) shall apply to the interpretation of this Order as it applies to the interpretation of an Act of Parliament.

3. In column 2 of the First Schedule to the National Health Service (Designation of London Teaching Hospitals) Order 1957(**c**) as amended (**d**) the words "The Fulham Maternity Hospital, Parsons Green, S.W.6." shall be deleted.

4. Any officer employed immediately before 1st July 1968 at or for the purposes of the said Fulham Maternity Hospital who suffers loss of employment or loss or diminution of emoluments which is attributable to the closure of that hospital shall be entitled to have his case considered for the payment of compensation at the like rate and in the like manner and subject to the like conditions as if he had been entitled to claim compensation under the Local Government (Executive Councils) (Compensation) Regulations 1964(**e**) as amended (**f**) and those regulations (except regulations 3, 4 and 5 thereof) shall apply for this purpose as if they had been set out in this order with the modifications that—

(*a*) references to the "material date" shall be construed as references to 1st July 1968, and

(*b*) references to "any such provision as is mentioned in regulation 4 of these regulations" shall be construed as references to this order, and

(*c*) at the end of regulation 7(1)(*b*) there shall be added the words or 14th October 1968 whichever is the later.".

(**a**) 1946 c.81. (**b**) 1889 c.63.
(**c**) S.I. 1957/488 (1957 I, p.1452). (**d**) The relevant amending instrument is S.I. 1959/518 (1959 I, p.1817).
(**e**) S.I. 1964/1177 (1964 II, p.2696). (**f**) S.I. 1966/254 (1966 I, p.653).

Given under the official seal of the Minister of Health on 20th August 1968.

L.S.

J. *Hauff*,
Under Secretary,
Ministry of Health.

EXPLANATORY NOTE

(*This Note is not part of the Order.*)

This Order deletes the Fulham Maternity Hospital from the group of hospitals designated by the Minister of Health as a teaching hospital under the name of Charing Cross Hospital. The Order also makes provision for compensation in certain cases to officers affected by the closure of the hospital.

STATUTORY INSTRUMENTS

1968 No. 1335

SUGAR

The Sugar (Rates of Surcharge and Surcharge Repayments) (No. 5) Order 1968

Made - - - -	*20th August* 1968
Laid before Parliament	*21st August* 1968
Coming into Operation	*22nd August* 1968

The Minister of Agriculture, Fisheries and Food, in exercise of the powers conferred on him by sections 7(4), 8(6) and 33(4) of the Sugar Act 1956(a) having effect subject to the provisions of section 3 of, and Part II of Schedule 5 to, the Finance Act 1962(b), and of all other powers enabling him in that behalf, with the concurrence of the Treasury, on the advice of the Sugar Board, hereby makes the following order:—

1.—(1) This order may be cited as the Sugar (Rates of Surcharge and Surcharge Repayments) (No. 5) Order 1968; and shall come into operation on 22nd August 1968.

(2) The Interpretation Act 1889(c) shall apply for the interpretation of this order as it applies for the interpretation of an Act of Parliament.

2. Notwithstanding the provisions of Article 2 of the Sugar (Rates of Surcharge and Surcharge Repayments) (No. 4) Order 1968(d), the rates of surcharge payable under and in accordance with the provisions of section 7 of the Sugar Act 1956, having effect as aforesaid, in respect of sugar and invert sugar imported or home produced or used in the manufacture of imported composite sugar products shall on and after 22nd August 1968 be those rates specified in Schedule 1 to this order.

3. For the purpose of section 8(3)(b) of the Sugar Act 1956, having effect as aforesaid, the rates of surcharge repayments in respect of invert sugar produced in the United Kingdom from materials on which on or after 22nd August 1968 sugar duty has been paid or, by virtue of paragraph 1 of Part II of Schedule 5 to the Finance Act 1962, is treated as having been paid shall, notwithstanding the provisions of Article 3 of the Sugar (Rates of Surcharge and Surcharge Repayments) (No. 4) Order 1968 be those specified in Schedule 2 to this order.

(a) 1956 c. 48. (b) 1962 c. 44.
(c) 1889 c. 63. (d) S.I. 1968/1124 (1968 II, p. 3092).

In Witness whereof the Official Seal of the Minister of Agriculture Fisheries and Food is hereunto affixed on 19th August 1968.

(L.S.)　　　　　　　　　　　　　　　　　　*R. P. Fraser,*

Authorised by the Minister.

We concur.

20th August 1968.

Joseph Harper,

E. Alan Fitch,

Two of the Lords Commissioners of Her Majesty's Treasury.

SCHEDULE 1

PART I

SURCHARGE RATES FOR SUGAR

Polarisation	Rate of Surcharge per cwt.	
	s.	d.
Exceeding—		
99°	37	4
98° but not exceeding 99°	35	2·4
97° ,, ,, ,, 98°	34	4·1
96° ,, ,, ,, 97°	33	5·4
95° ,, ,, ,, 96°	32	6·6
94° ,, ,, ,, 95°	31	7·9
93° ,, ,, ,, 94°	30	9·1
92° ,, ,, ,, 93°	29	10·4
91° ,, ,, ,, 92°	28	11·6
90° ,, ,, ,, 91°	28	0·8
89° ,, ,, ,, 90°	27	2·1
88° ,, ,, ,, 89°	26	3·3
87° ,, ,, ,, 88°	25	6·4
86° ,, ,, ,, 87°	24	9·4
85° ,, ,, ,, 86°	24	1·4
84° ,, ,, ,, 85°	23	5·3
83° ,, ,, ,, 84°	22	9·2
82° ,, ,, ,, 83°	22	1·2
81° ,, ,, ,, 82°	21	6
80° ,, ,, ,, 81°	20	10·8
79° ,, ,, ,, 80°	20	3·7
78° ,, ,, ,, 79°	19	8·5
77° ,, ,, ,, 78°	19	1·3
76° ,, ,, ,, 77°	18	6·2
Not exceeding 76°	17	11

Part II

Surcharge Rates for Invert Sugar

Sweetening matter content by weight	Rate of Surcharge per cwt.
	s. d.
70 per cent. or more	23 8
Less than 70 per cent. and more than 50 per cent.	17 0
Not more than 50 per cent.	8 4

SCHEDULE 2

Surcharge Repayment Rates for Invert Sugar

Sweetening matter content by weight	Rate of Surcharge Repayment per cwt.
	s. d.
More than 80 per cent.	28 0
More than 70 per cent. but not more than 80 per cent.	23 8
More than 60 per cent. but not more than 70 per cent.	17 0
More than 50 per cent. but not more than 60 per cent.	13 6
Not more than 50 per cent. and the invert sugar not being less in weight than 14 lb. per gallon	8 4

EXPLANATORY NOTE

(This Note is not part of the Order.)

This order prescribes—

(a) increases equivalent to 2s. 4d. per cwt. of refined sugar in the rates of surcharge payable on sugar and invert sugar which become chargeable with surcharge on or after 22nd August 1968;

(b) correspondingly increased rates of surcharge repayment in respect of invert sugar produced in the United Kingdom from materials on which surcharge has been paid.

STATUTORY   INSTRUMENTS

1968 No. 1336

SUGAR

The Composite Sugar Products (Surcharge and Surcharge Repayments—Average Rates) (No. 5) Order 1968

Made - - - -	*20th August* 1968
Laid before Parliament	*21st August* 1968
Coming into Operation	*22nd August* 1968

Whereas the Minister of Agriculture, Fisheries and Food (hereinafter called " the Minister ") has on the recommendation of the Commissioners of Customs and Excise (hereinafter called " the Commissioners ") made an order(a) pursuant to the powers conferred upon him by sections 9(1) and 9(4) of the Sugar Act 1956(b), having effect subject to the provisions of section 3 of, and Part II of Schedule 5 to, the Finance Act 1962(c) and to the provisions of section 52(2) of the Finance Act 1966(d), providing that in the case of certain descriptions of composite sugar products surcharge shall be calculated on the basis of an average quantity of sugar or invert sugar taken to have been used in the manufacture of the products, and that certain other descriptions of composite sugar products shall be treated as not containing any sugar or invert sugar, and that in the case of certain descriptions of goods in the manufacture of which sugar or invert sugar is used, surcharge repayments shall be calculated on the basis of an average quantity of sugar or invert sugar taken to have been so used:

Now, therefore, the Minister, on the recommendation of the Commissioners and in exercise of the powers conferred upon him by sections 9(1), 9(4) and 33(4) of the Sugar Act 1956, having effect as aforesaid, and of all other powers enabling him in that behalf, hereby makes the following order:—

1.—(1) This order may be cited as the Composite Sugar Products (Surcharge and Surcharge Repayments—Average Rates) (No. 5) Order 1968; and shall come into operation on 22nd August 1968.

(2) The Interpretation Act 1889(e) shall apply for the interpretation of this order as it applies for the interpretation of an Act of Parliament.

2. Surcharge payable on or after 22nd August 1968 under and in accordance with the Sugar Act 1956, having effect as aforesaid, in respect of sugar and invert sugar used in the manufacture of the descriptions of imported composite sugar products specified in column 2 of Schedule 1 to this order shall, notwithstanding the provisions of the Sugar (Rates of Surcharge and Surcharge Repayments) (No. 5) Order 1968(f) and the Composite Sugar Products (Surcharge and Surcharge Repayments—Average Rates) (No. 4) Order 1968(a), be calculated by reference to the weight or value, as the case may be, of the products at the rates specified in relation thereto in column 3 of the said Schedule.

(a) S.I. 1968/1125 (1968 II, p. 3095).   (b) 1956 c. 48.   (c) 1962 c. 44.
(d) 1966 c. 18.   (e) 1889 c. 63.   (f) S.I. 1968/1335(1968 II, p. 3708).

3. Imported composite sugar products other than those of a description specified in Schedules 1 and 2 to this order shall be treated as not containing any sugar or invert sugar for the purposes of surcharge payable on or after 22nd August 1968.

4. Surcharge repayments payable on and after 22nd August 1968 under and in accordance with the provisions of section 8 of the Sugar Act 1956, having effect as aforesaid, in respect of sugar and invert sugar used in the manufacture of the descriptions of goods specified in column 1 of Schedule 3 to this order shall, notwithstanding the provisions of the Sugar (Rates of Surcharge and Surcharge Repayments) (No. 5) Order 1968(a) and the Composite Sugar Products (Surcharge and Surcharge Repayments—Average Rates) (No. 4) Order 1968(b), be calculated by reference to the quantity of the goods at the rates specified in relation thereto in column 2 of the said Schedule.

In Witness whereof the Official Seal of the Minister of Agriculture, Fisheries and Food is hereunto affixed on 20th August 1968.

(L.S.)

R. P. Fraser,
Authorised by the Minister.

SCHEDULE 1

In this Schedule:—

" Tariff heading " means a heading or, where the context so requires, a subheading of the Customs Tariff 1959 (see paragraph (1) of Article 1 of the Import Duties (General) (No. 4) Order 1968(c)).

" Per cent." means, where it occurs in relation to any rate of surcharge, per cent. of the value for customs duty purposes of the product to which it relates.

Tariff heading	Description of Imported Composite Sugar Products	Rate of Surcharge
		per cwt. s. d.
04.02	Milk and cream, preserved, concentrated or sweetened containing more than 10 per cent. by weight of added sweetening matter	16 7
17.02 (B) (2) and 17.05 (B)	Syrups containing sucrose sugar, whether or not flavoured or coloured, but not including fruit juices containing added sugar in any proportion:—	
	containing 70 per cent. or more by weight of sweetening matter	23 8
	containing less than 70 per cent., and more than 50 per cent., by weight of sweetening matter...	17 0
	containing not more than 50 per cent. by weight of sweetening matter	8 4

(a) S.I. 1968/1335 (1968 II, p. 3708).   (b) S.I. 1968/1125 (1968 II, p. 3095).
(c) S.I. 1968/679 (1968 I, p. 1519).

Tariff heading	Description of Imported Composite Sugar Products	Rate of Surcharge
		per cwt. s. d.
17.02 (F) ...	Caramel:—	
	Solid	37 4
	Liquid	26 2
17.04	Sugar confectionery, not containing cocoa	30 4
18.06	Chocolate and other food preparations containing cocoa:—	
	Chocolate couverture not prepared for retail sale; chocolate milk crumb, liquid	16 7
	Chocolate milk crumb, solid	20 5
	Other	21 8
		per cent.
19.08	Pastry, biscuits, cakes and other fine bakers' wares containing added sweetening matter:—	
	Biscuits	8
	Other	$4\frac{4}{5}$
20.01	Vegetables and fruit, prepared or preserved by vinegar or acetic acid, containing added sweetening matter	$11\frac{1}{2}$
20.03	Fruit preserved by freezing, containing added sugar	4
		per cwt. s. d.
20.04	Fruit, fruit-peel and parts of plants, preserved by sugar (drained, glacé or crystallised)	24 6
20.05	Jams, fruit jellies, marmalades, fruit purée and fruit pastes, being cooked preparations, containing added sweetening matter	23 6
		per cent.
20.06	Fruit otherwise prepared or preserved, containing added sweetening matter:—	
	Ginger	16
	Other	4

SCHEDULE 2

Tariff heading	Description of Imported Composite Sugar Products
17.05 (A) and (B)	Sugar and invert sugar, flavoured or coloured.

SCHEDULE 3

Description of goods	Rate of surcharge repayment per bulk barrel of 36 gallons
Lager	1s. 6·7d.
All beer other than lager	1s. 4·7d.

EXPLANATORY NOTE

(*This Note is not part of the Order.*)

This order provides for increases on and after 22nd August 1968 in the average rates of surcharge payable on imported composite sugar products of the descriptions specified in Schedule 1 and in the average rates of surcharge repayment in respect of exported goods of the descriptions specified in Schedule 3. These correspond to the increases in surcharge rates effected by the Sugar (Rates of Surcharge and Surcharge Repayments) (No. 5) Order 1968 (S.I. 1968/1335). Provision is also made for certain imported composite sugar products to be treated as not containing any sugar or invert sugar.

STATUTORY INSTRUMENTS

1968 No. 1342

ENTERTAINMENT

The Theatrical Employers Registration (Amendment) Rules 1968

Made	- - -	*20th August* 1968
Coming into Operation		*1st October* 1968

In exercise of the powers conferred on me by sections 3, 4 and 13 of the Theatrical Employers Registration Act 1925(**a**), as amended by the Miscellaneous Fees (Variation) Order 1968(**b**) and the Miscellaneous Fees (Variation) (Scotland) Order 1968(**c**), I hereby make the following Rules :—

1. For Rule 12 of the Theatrical Employers Registration Rules 1925(**d**) there shall be substituted the following Rule :—

"**12.**—(1) The following fees shall be payable to the registration authority :—

for each registration	£6 ;
for each issue of a copy of a certificate of registration ...	10s. ;
for each inspection of the register of theatrical employers kept by the registration authority	5s. .

(2) The following fee shall be payable to the Secretary of State :—

for each inspection of the copies of register entries kept by the Secretary of State	5s.".

2. These Rules may be cited as the Theatrical Employers Registration (Amendment) Rules 1968 and shall come into operation on 1st October 1968.

James Callaghan,
One of Her Majesty's Principal
Secretaries of State.

Home Office,
Whitehall.

20th August 1968.

(**a**) 1925 c. 50. (**b**) S.I. 1968/170 (1968 I, p. 399).
(**c**) S.I. 1968/248 (1968 I, p. 758).
(**d**) S.R. & O. 1925/1146 (Rev. XXII, p. 525: 1925, p. 1600).

EXPLANATORY NOTE

(This Note is not part of the Rules.)

These Rules increase the fees payable on the registration of a theatrical employer under the Theatrical Employers Registration Act 1925, for a copy of a certificate of registration and an inspection of the register entries.

STATUTORY INSTRUMENTS

1968 No. 1344

CIVIL DEFENCE

The Civil Defence (Compensation) (General) Regulations 1968

Made - - - -	*21st August* 1968
Laid before Parliament	*30th August* 1968
Coming into Operation	*1st September* 1968

ARRANGEMENT OF REGULATIONS

PART V

RETIREMENT COMPENSATION AND PAYMENTS ON DEATH

PART VI

ADJUSTMENT, REVIEW AND COMPOUNDING OF COMPENSATION

PART VII

PROCEDURE AND MISCELLANEOUS

Schedule

In pursuance of the powers conferred on me by section 4 of the Public Expenditure and Receipts Act 1968(a), I hereby make the following Regulations:—

PART I

PRELIMINARY

Citation and commencement

1. These Regulations may be cited as the Civil Defence (Compensation) (General) Regulations 1968 and shall come into operation on 1st September 1968.

(a) 1968 c. 14.

Interpretation

2.—(1) In these Regulations, unless the context otherwise requires, the following expressions have the meanings hereby respectively assigned to them, that is to say:—

"accrued pension", in relation to a pensionable officer who has suffered loss of employment, means—

(*a*) if his last relevant pension scheme provided benefits in which he had a right to participate, the pension to which he would have become entitled in respect of his pensionable service according to the method of calculation, modified where necessary in accordance with Regulation 18(2), prescribed by that scheme if, at the date on which he ceased to be subject to that scheme, he had attained normal retiring age and complied with any requirement of that scheme as to a minimum period of qualifying service or contribution and completed any additional contributory payments or payments in respect of added years which he was in the course of making; and

(*b*) in any other case, such portion of the pension (if any) of which he had reasonable expectations as the compensating authority consider equitable, having regard to his age, the length of his employment at the date of loss and all the other circumstances of the case;

"accrued retiring allowance", in relation to a pensionable officer who has suffered loss of employment, means—

(*a*) if his last relevant pension scheme provided benefits in which he had a right to participate, any lump sum payment to which he would have become entitled in respect of his pensionable service according to the method of calculation, modified where necessary in accordance with Regulation 18(2), prescribed by that scheme if, at the date on which he ceased to be subject to that scheme, he had attained normal retiring age and complied with any requirement of that scheme as to a minimum period of qualifying service or contribution and completed any additional contributory payments or payments in respect of added years which he was in the course of making; and

(*b*) in any other case, such portion of the lump sum payment (if any) of which he had reasonable expectations as the compensating authority consider equitable, having regard to his age, the length of his employment at the date of loss and all the other circumstances of the case;

"accrued incapacity pension" and "accrued incapacity retiring allowance" have the same respective meanings as "accrued pension" and "accrued retiring allowance" except that the reference to a person's attaining normal retiring age shall be construed as a reference to his becoming incapable of discharging efficiently the duties of his employment by reason of permanent ill-health or infirmity of mind or body;

"added years" in relation to a person who suffers loss of employment means—

(*a*) in the case of a contributory employee or local Act contributor any additional years of service reckonable by him in his employment immediately prior to the loss in question under Regulation 12 of the Local Government Superannuation (Benefits) Regulations 1954(**a**) as amended(**b**), or, in Scotland, under Regulation 12 of the Local Government Superannuation (Benefits) (Scotland) Regulations 1954(**c**) as amended(**d**), or any corresponding provision of a local Act scheme, or those Regu-

---

(**a**) S.I. 1954/1048 (1954 II, p. 1595).   (**b**) S.I. 1955/1041 (1955 II, p. 1825).
(**c**) S.I. 1954/1059 (1954 II, p. 1632).   (**d**) S.I. 1955/1226 (1955 II, p. 1831).

lations or any such provision as aforesaid as applied by or under any enactment, and includes any additional years of service which, having been granted under any such provision or under any similar provision contained in any other enactment or scheme, have subsequently become and are reckonable under or by virtue of rules made under section 2 of the Superannuation (Miscellaneous Provisions) Act 1948(a), or any other enactment; and

(b) in the case of any other person, any additional years of service, similar to those mentioned in paragraph (a) of this definition, reckonable by him under the pension scheme associated with the employment he has lost;

"additional contributory payments" means—

(a) additional contributory payments of the kind referred to in section 2(3) and (4) of the Local Government Superannuation Act 1953(b); or

(b) any similar payments made under a local Act scheme or other pension scheme as a condition of reckoning any period of employment as service or as a period of contribution for the purposes of the scheme, or, where the scheme provides for the reckoning of non-contributing service, as contributing service for the purposes of the scheme; or

(c) any payments made for the purpose of increasing the length at which any period of service or of contribution would be reckonable for the purpose of calculating a benefit under a local Act scheme; or

(d) any payments similar to any of those mentioned in the foregoing sub-paragraphs made in pursuance of rules made under section 2 of the Superannuation (Miscellaneous Provisions) Act 1948 or in pursuance of any arrangements in that behalf made by an officer of a local authority in respect of a person employed under such an officer for the purposes of the functions of the local authority;

"compensating authority" in relation to any person who has suffered loss of employment or loss or diminution of emoluments means—

(a) in the case of a person who, immediately before the material date, was employed as an officer of a relevant local authority or under such an officer for the purposes of the functions of the local authority, that local authority;

(b) in the case of a person who, immediately before the material date, was employed by any authority on behalf of any (but not more than one) relevant local authority under Regulation 3 of the Civil Defence (General) Regulations 1949(c) or Regulation 4 of the Civil Defence (General) (Scotland) Regulations 1949(d), that local authority;

(c) in any other case, such local authority or other body as the Secretary of State may determine;

"compensation question" means a question—

(a) as to a person's entitlement to compensation for loss of employment, or for loss or diminution of emoluments; or

(b) as to the manner of a person's employment or the comparability of his duties;

"contributory employee" and "local Act contributor" have the same meaning as in the Local Government Superannuation Act 1937(e) or, in Scotland, as in the Local Government Superannuation (Scotland) Act 1937(f);

(a) 1948 c. 33.
(b) 1953 c. 25.
(c) S.I. 1949/1432 (1949 I, p. 637).
(d) S.I. 1949/1416 (1949 I, p. 642).
(e) 1937 c. 68.
(f) 1937 c. 69.

"emoluments" means all salary, wages, fees and other payments paid or made to an officer as such for his own use, and also the money value of any apartments, rations or other allowances in kind appertaining to his employment, but does not include payments for overtime or other work undertaken voluntarily which are not a usual incident of his employment, or payments under any Warrant of the Secretary of State relating to the payment of bounty, or any allowances payable to him to cover the cost of providing office accommodation or clerical or other assistance, or any travelling or subsistence allowance or other moneys to be spent, or to cover expenses incurred, by him for the purposes of his employment; and "net emoluments", in relation to any employment, means the annual rate of the emoluments of that employment less such part of those emoluments as the officer was liable to contribute under a pension scheme, and in relation to any employment which has been lost or the emoluments of which have been diminished, the expression means the annual rate of emoluments as aforesaid immediately before the loss or diminution, as the case may be:

Provided that, where fees or other variable payments were paid to an officer as part of his emoluments during any period immediately preceding the loss or diminution, the amount in respect of fees or other variable payments to be included in the annual rate of emoluments shall be the annual average of the fees or other payments paid to him during the period of five years immediately preceding the loss or diminution, or such other period as the compensating authority may think reasonable in the circumstances;

"enactment" means any Act or any instrument made under an Act;

"local authority" (except in the expression "relevant local authority") means, in England and Wales, the council of a county, county borough, metropolitan borough, London borough, county district, rural parish or borough included in a rural district, the Greater London Council, the Common Council of the City of London and the council of the Isles of Scilly, any two or more of those authorities acting jointly and any joint committee, combined authority or joint board and a police authority for a county, a borough or a combined police area; and means, in Scotland, any county council, town council or district council including any joint committee or joint board of such authorities appointed under any enactment, order or scheme;

"long-term compensation" means compensation payable in accordance with the provisions of Part IV of these Regulations for loss of employment or loss or diminution of emoluments;

"material date" in relation to any person who has suffered loss of employment or loss or diminution of emoluments means—

(a) for the purposes of Regulation 3, 16th January 1968; and

(b) for any other purpose of these Regulations, 1st April 1968 or the date on which the loss or diminution occurred, whichever is the earlier;

"minimum pensionable age" means, in relation to a pensionable officer, the earliest age at which, under his last relevant pension scheme, he could have become entitled to a pension, other than a pension payable in consequence of his redundancy or the termination of his employment in the interests of efficiency or his incapacity to discharge efficiently the duties of his employment by reason of permanent ill-health or infirmity of mind or body;

"national service" means service which is relevant service within the meaning of the Reserve and Auxiliary Forces (Protection of Civil Interests) Act 1951(a), and includes service immediately following such service as aforesaid, being service in any of Her Majesty's naval, military or air forces pursuant to

(a) 1951 c. 65.

a voluntary engagement entered into with the consent of the authority or person under whom an officer held his last relevant employment;

"normal retiring age" means, in the case of a pensionable officer to whom an age of compulsory retirement applied by virtue of any enactment to which he was subject in the employment which he has lost or the emoluments of which have been diminished or by virtue of the conditions of that employment, that age, and, in any other case, the age of sixty-five years if the officer is a male, or sixty years if the officer is a female;

"officer" includes the holder of any place, situation or employment;

"pensionable officer", in relation to a person who has suffered loss of employment or loss or diminution of emoluments, means a person who immediately before such loss or diminution was subject to a pension scheme;

"pension scheme", in relation to a pensionable officer, means any form of arrangement associated with his employment for the payment of superannuation benefits, whether subsisting by virtue of Act of Parliament, trust, contract or otherwise; and "last relevant pension scheme", in relation to a pensionable officer, means the pension scheme to which he was last subject before suffering loss of employment or loss or diminution of emoluments;

"reckonable service", in relation to a person, means any period of wholetime or part-time employment in any relevant employment and includes any period of war service or national service undertaken on his ceasing to hold any such employment but does not include employment of which account has been taken, or is required to be taken, in calculating the amount of any superannuation benefit to which he has become entitled;

"relevant employment" means employment—

(a) under the Crown or in the service of a local authority, or local valuation panel in Great Britain; or

(b) by any authority or body for the purposes of the Crown or of local government in Great Britain; or

(c) under any officer employed as mentioned in paragraph (a) or (b) of this definition for the purposes of the functions of the employing authority or body; or

(d) preceding any of the foregoing employments which was reckonable for the purposes of any pension scheme associated with the employment which has been lost or in which a loss or diminution of emoluments has been suffered; or

(e) in such other employment as the Secretary of State may, in the case of any named officer, approve,

but, except as provided in Regulations 6(1) and 12(1), does not include service in the armed forces of the Crown;

"relevant local authority" means—

(a) in England and Wales, a county council, a county borough council, the Greater London Council, the Common Council of the City of London, a London borough council, the council of the Isles of Scilly or the council of any of the following county districts, that is to say, the cities of Cambridge and Peterborough and the boroughs of Chesterfield, Scunthorpe and Swindon;

(b) in Scotland—

(i) the joint council of the counties of Moray and Nairn or of the counties of Perth and Kinross; or

(ii) the council of any other county; or

(iii) the town council of a large burgh within the meaning of the Local Government (Scotland) Act 1947(**a**); or

(iv) a joint civil defence committee appointed under Regulation 1(*b*) of the Civil Defence (General) (Scotland) Regulations 1949;

"resettlement compensation" means compensation payable in accordance with Part III of these Regulations for loss of employment;

"retirement compensation" means compensation payable in accordance with the provisions of Regulation 19, 20, 21 or 22;

"tribunal" means a tribunal established under section 12 of the Industrial Training Act 1964(**b**);

"war service" means war service within the meaning of the Local Government Staffs (War Service) Act 1939(**c**), the Teachers Superannuation (War Service) Act 1939(**d**) (or, in Scotland, the Education (Scotland) (War Service Superannuation) Act 1939(**e**), the Police and Firemen (War Service) Act 1939(**f**) or employment for war purposes within the meaning of the Superannuation Schemes (War Service) Act 1940(**g**) and includes any period of service in the First World War in the armed forces of the Crown or in the forces of the Allied or Associated Powers if such service immediately followed a period of relevant employment and was undertaken either compulsorily or with the permission of the employer in that employment.

(2)(*a*) Where under any provision of these Regulations an annual value is to be assigned to a capital sum or a capital value to an annual amount, the annual or capital value shall be ascertained in accordance with the tables set out in the Schedule to these Regulations in so far as they provide for the particular case.

(*b*) For the purpose of determining the application of the said tables the headings and the note to each table shall be treated as a part of the table.

(*c*) Where the said tables do not provide for a case in which an annual value is to be assigned to a capital sum or a capital value to an annual amount, the annual or capital value shall be such as may be agreed between the compensating authority and the person to whom the capital sum or annual amount is payable.

(3) Unless the context otherwise requires, references in these Regulations to the provisions of any enactment shall be construed as references to those provisions as amended, re-enacted or modified by any subsequent enactment.

(4) References in these Regulations to a numbered Regulation shall, unless the reference is to a regulation of specified regulations, be construed as references to the Regulation bearing that number in these Regulations.

(5) References in any of these Regulations to a numbered paragraph shall, unless the reference is to a paragraph of a specified Regulation, be construed as references to the paragraph bearing that number in the first mentioned Regulation.

(6) The Interpretation Act 1889(**h**) shall apply for the interpretation of these Regulations as it applies for the interpretation of an Act of Parliament.

PART II

ENTITLEMENT TO COMPENSATION

Persons to whom the Regulations apply

3.—(1) Subject to paragraph (2), these Regulations shall apply to any person who was employed immediately before the material date for the whole or for part only of his time—

(a) 1947 c. 43.	(b) 1964 c. 16.
(c) 1939 c. 94.	(d) 1939 c. 95.
(e) 1939 c. 96.	(f) 1939 c. 103.
(g) 1940 c. 26.	(h) 1889 c. 63.

(a) as an officer of a local authority or under such an officer for the purposes of the functions of the local authority; or

(b) by any authority on behalf of a local authority under Regulation 3 of the Civil Defence (General) Regulations 1949 or Regulation 4 of the Civil Defence (General) (Scotland) Regulations 1949.

(2) These Regulations shall not apply to any member of a fire brigade of a class prescribed, by the Firemen's Pension Scheme for the time being in force under section 26 of the Fire Services Act 1947(a), for the purposes of section 2 of the Fire Services Act 1951(b).

Grounds of entitlement to compensation

4. Subject to the provisions of these Regulations, any person to whom these Regulations apply and who suffers loss of employment or loss or diminution of emoluments which is attributable to the revocation or amendment of any regulations made under section 2 of the Civil Defence Act 1948(c) shall be entitled to have his case considered for the payment of compensation under these Regulations, and such compensation shall be determined in accordance with these Regulations.

PART III

RESETTLEMENT COMPENSATION

Resettlement compensation for loss of employment

5. The compensating authority shall, subject to the provisions of these Regulations, pay resettlement compensation to any person to whom these Regulations apply and who satisfies the conditions set out in Regulation 6.

Conditions for payment of resettlement compensation

6.—(1) Without prejudice to any other requirement of these Regulations, the conditions for the payment of resettlement compensation to any person are that—

(a) he has, not later than ten years after the material date, suffered loss of employment attributable to the revocation or amendment of any regulations made under section 2 of the Civil Defence Act 1948;

(b) he had not at the date of the loss attained normal retiring age;

(c) he had been for a period of three years immediately before the material date continuously engaged (disregarding breaks not exceeding in the aggregate six months) for the whole or part of his time in relevant employment; and for this purpose the expression "relevant employment" includes any period of national service immediately following such employment;

(d) he has made a claim for such compensation in accordance with the provisions of Part VII of these Regulations not later than thirteen weeks after the loss of employment which is the cause of his claim, or thirteen weeks after the coming into operation of these Regulations, whichever is the later;

(e) the loss of employment which is the cause of his claim has occurred for some reason other than misconduct or incapacity to perform such duties as, immediately before the loss, he was performing or might reasonably have been required to perform; and

(f) he has not, subject to paragraph (3), been offered any reasonably comparable employment under the Crown or in the service of a local authority.

(a) 1947 c. 41.   (b) 1951 c. 27.
(c) 12, 13 & 14 Geo. 6. c. 5.

(2) In ascertaining for the purposes of this Regulation whether a person has been offered employment which is reasonably comparable with the employment which he has lost, no account shall be taken of the fact that the duties of the employment offered are in relation to a different service from that in connection with which his employment was held or are duties which involve a transfer of his employment from one place to another within England and Wales or, as the case may be, within Scotland.

(3) No account shall be taken for the purposes of this Regulation of an offer of employment where the compensating authority are satisfied—

(a) that acceptance would have involved undue hardship to the person, or

(b) that he was prevented from accepting the offer by reason of ill-health or other circumstances beyond his control.

Amount of resettlement compensation

7.—(1) The amount of resettlement compensation which may be paid to a person shall, for each week for which such compensation is payable, be a sum ascertained by taking two-thirds of the weekly rate of the net emoluments which that person has lost and deducting therefrom, in addition to the items mentioned in Regulation 32(3) and (4), such of the following items as may be applicable—

(a) unemployment, sickness or injury benefit under any Act relating to National Insurance claimable by him in respect of such week (excluding any amount claimable by him in resp ct of a dependant); and

(b) two-thirds of the net emoluments received by him in respect of such week from work or employment undertaken as a result of the loss of employment.

(2) For the purposes of this Regulation the weekly rate of a person's net emoluments shall be deemed to be seven three hundred and sixty-fifths of those emoluments.

Period for payment of resettlement compensation

8. Subject to the provisions of these Regulations, resettlement compensation shall be payable to a person only in respect of the period of thirteen weeks next succeeding the week in which he lost the employment in respect of which his claim has been made or, in the case of a person who has attained the age of forty-five years, the said thirteen weeks and one additional week for every year of his age after attaining the age of forty-five years and before the date of the loss of employment, subject to a maximum addition of thirteen such weeks.

Additional provisions relating to resettlement compensation

9.—(1) Resettlement compensation shall be payable to a person at intervals equivalent to those at which the emoluments of his employment were previously paid or at such other intervals as may be agreed between the person and the compensating authority.

(2) Resettlement compensation shall be terminated by the compensating authority—

(a) if without reasonable cause the recipient fails to comply with any of the provisions of Regulation 10, or

(b) if on being requested to do so, he fails to satisfy the compensating authority that, so far as he is able, he is seeking suitable employment.

Claimant for resettlement compensation to furnish particulars of employment

10. Every person claiming or in receipt of resettlement compensation shall (after as well as before the compensation begins to be paid)—

   (*a*) forthwith supply the compensating authority in writing with particulars of any employment which he obtains or of any change in his earnings from any such employment, and

   (*b*) if the compensating authority so require, so long as he is out of employment and is not receiving sickness or injury benefit, register with the Department of Employment and Productivity.

PART IV

LONG-TERM COMPENSATION FOR LOSS OF

EMPLOYMENT OR LOSS OR DIMINUTION OF EMOLUMENTS

Long-term compensation

11. The compensating authority shall, subject to the provisions of these Regulations, pay long-term compensation to any person to whom these Regulations apply and who satisfies the conditions set out in Regulation 12.

Conditions for payment of long-term compensation

12.—(1) Without prejudice to any other requirement of these Regulations, the conditions for the payment of long-term compensation to any person are that—

   (*a*) he has, not later than ten years after the material date, suffered loss of employment or loss or diminution of emoluments attributable to the revocation or amendment of any regulations made under section 2 of the Civil Defence Act 1948;

   (*b*) he had not, save as is provided in Regulation 28, at the date of the loss or diminution attained normal retiring age;

   (*c*) he had been, for a period of not less than eight years immediately before the material date, continuously engaged (without a break of more than twelve months at any one time) for the whole or part of his time in relevant employment; and for this purpose the expression "relevant employment" includes any period of national service immediately following such employment;

   (*d*) he has made a claim for such compensation in accordance with the provisions of Part VII of these Regulations not later than two years after the loss or diminution which is the cause of the claim or two years after the coming into operation of these Regulations, whichever is the later; and

   (*e*) if the cause of the claim for compensation is loss of employment—
      (i) the loss has occurred for some reason other than misconduct or incapacity to perform such duties as, immediately before the loss, he was performing or might reasonably have been required to perform; and
      (ii) he has not been offered any reasonably comparable employment under the Crown or in the service of a local authority.

(2) Regulation 6(2) and (3) (which relate to offers of employment) shall apply for the purposes of this Regulation in ascertaining whether a person has been offered reasonably comparable employment.

(3) Claims for long-term compensation for loss of employment shall in all respects be treated as claims for such compensation for the loss of emoluments occasioned thereby and the provisions of these Regulations shall apply to all such claims accordingly.

Factors to be considered in determining payment of long-term compensation

13.—(1) For the purpose of determining whether long-term compensation for loss or diminution of emoluments is payable to any person and, if so, the amount of the compensation (subject to the limits set out in these Regulations), the compensating authority shall have regard to such of the following factors as may be relevant, that is to say—

(a) the conditions upon which the person held the employment which he has lost, including in particular its security of tenure, whether by law or practice;

(b) the emoluments and other conditions, including security of tenure, whether by law or practice, of any work or employment undertaken by the person as a result of the loss of employment;

(c) the extent to which he has sought suitable employment and the emoluments which he might have acquired by accepting other suitable employment offered to him;

(d) all the other circumstances of his case.

(2) In ascertaining for the purposes of paragraph (1)(c) whether a person has been offered suitable employment, Regulation 6(2) and (3) shall apply as they apply for the purpose of ascertaining whether employment is reasonably comparable with employment which has been lost.

Amount of long-term compensation payable for loss of emoluments

14.—(1) Long-term compensation for loss of emoluments shall, subject to the provisions of these Regulations, be payable until the normal retiring age or death of a person to whom it is payable, whichever first occurs, and shall not exceed a maximum annual sum calculated in accordance with the provisions of paragraphs (2) to (4).

(2) The said maximum annual sum shall, subject as hereinafter provided, be the aggregate of the following sums, namely—

(a) for every year of the person's reckonable service, one-sixtieth of the net emoluments which he has lost; and

(b) in the case of a person who has attained the age of forty years at the date of the loss, a sum calculated in accordance with the provisions of paragraph (3) appropriate to his age at that date,

but the said maximum annual sum shall in no case exceed two-thirds of the net emoluments which the person has lost.

(3) The sum referred to in paragraph (2)(b) shall be—

(a) in the case of a person who has attained the age of forty years but has not attained the age of fifty years at the date of the loss, the following fraction of the net emoluments which he has lost—

(i) where his reckonable service is less than ten years, one-sixtieth for each year of such service after attaining the age of forty years; or

(ii) where his reckonable service amounts to ten years but is less than fifteen years, one-sixtieth for each year of such service after attaining the age of forty years and one additional sixtieth; or

(iii) where his reckonable service amounts to fifteen years but is less than twenty years, one-sixtieth for each year of such service after

attaining the age of forty years and two additional sixtieths; or
(iv) where his reckonable service amounts to twenty years or more,
one-sixtieth for each year of such service after attaining the age
of forty years and three additional sixtieths;

but the sum so calculated shall not in any case exceed one-sixth of the
said net emoluments;

(b) in the case of a person who has attained the age of fifty years but has
not attained the age of sixty years at the date of the loss, one-sixtieth
of the said net emoluments for each year of his reckonable service
after attaining the age of forty years, up to a maximum of fifteen such
years; and

(c) in the case of a person who has attained the age of sixty years at the
date of the loss, one-sixtieth of the said net emoluments for each year of
his reckonable service after attaining the age of forty-five years.

(4) Where a person has become entitled (whether immediately or prospectively on attaining some greater age) to a superannuation benefit by way of
annual amounts under a pension scheme associated with the employment which
he has lost, the maximum annual sum referred to in paragraph (1) shall be the
maximum sum calculated under paragraphs (2) and (3) as if he had not become
so entitled.

(5) Where long-term compensation is payable in respect of any period and
resettlement compensation has also been paid in respect of that period, the
long-term compensation shall be limited to the amount (if any) by which it
exceeds the resettlement compensation paid as aforesaid.

(6) Long-term compensation shall be payable to a person at intervals equivalent to those at which the emoluments of his employment were previously
paid or at such other intervals as may be agreed between the person and the
compensating authority.

Long-term compensation for diminution of emoluments

15. Long-term compensation for diminution of emoluments in respect
of any employment shall, subject to the provisions of these Regulations, be
awarded and paid in accordance with the following provisions:—

(a) the compensation shall consist of an annual sum which shall be payable
to a person at intervals equivalent to those at which the emoluments of
his employment are or were previously paid or at such other intervals
as may be agreed between the person and the compensating authority,
and shall, subject to the provisions of these Regulations, be payable
until normal retiring age or death, whichever first occurs; and

(b) the said annual sum shall not exceed the maximum annual sum which
could have been awarded under Regulation 14 if the person had suffered
loss of employment and of emoluments equivalent to the amount of the
diminution:

Provided that no compensation shall be payable if the emoluments have
been diminished by less than 2½ per cent.

Date from which long-term compensation is to be payable

16.—(1) Long-term compensation shall be payable with effect from the date
of the claim or from any earlier date permitted by the succeeding provisions
of this Regulation.

(2) Where a claim for long-term compensation is duly made within thirteen
weeks of the occurrence of the loss or diminution which is the cause of the claim,

the award shall be made retrospective to the date on which the loss or diminution occurred.

(3) Where a claim for long-term compensation is made after the expiry of the period mentioned in paragraph (2), the award may, at the discretion of the compensating authority, be made retrospective to a date not earlier than thirteen weeks prior to the date on which the claim was made:

Provided that if the compensating authority are satisfied that the failure to make the claim within the period mentioned in paragraph (2) was due to ill-health or other circumstances beyond the claimant's control, the award may be made retrospective to a date not earlier than that on which the loss or diminution occurred.

PART V

RETIREMENT COMPENSATION AND PAYMENTS ON DEATH

Entitlement to retirement compensation and other payments

17.—(1) The compensating authority shall, subject to the provisions of these Regulations, pay retirement compensation to any person to whom this Part of these Regulations applies, and shall make the other payments for which provision is made in Regulations 25 to 29.

(2) Save as is provided in Regulation 28, this Part of these Regulations applies to a pensionable officer who satisfies the conditions set out in Regulation 12.

(3) Regulation 13 shall apply in relation to retirement compensation as it applies in relation to long-term compensation.

Additional factors governing payment of retirement compensation

18.—(1) Where retirement compensation is payable under any one of Regulations 19, 20, 21 and 22, such compensation shall not be payable under any other of those Regulations.

(2) If a person has attained the age of forty years at the date on which he lost his employment or suffered a diminution of his emoluments, the compensating authority, in calculating the amount of the retirement compensation payable to him, shall credit him with additional years of service or an additional period of contribution on the following basis, namely—

    (*a*) two years, whether or not he has completed any years of service after attaining the age of forty years, and

    (*b*) two years for each of the first four completed years of his reckonable service between the date when he attained the age of forty years and the date of the loss or diminution, and

    (*c*) one year for each such year of service after the fourth,

but the additional years of service or period of contribution so credited shall not exceed the shortest of the following periods, namely—

    (i) such number of years as, when added to his pensionable service, would amount to the maximum period of such service which would have been reckonable by him had he continued in his employment until attaining normal retiring age, or

    (ii) the number of years of his reckonable service, or

    (iii) fifteen years;

and in calculating the amount of any retirement compensation payable to him any period so added shall be aggregated with any years of service or period of contribution entailing reduction of the relevant pension or retiring allowance because of a retirement pension payable under section 30 of the National Insurance Act 1965(a).

(3) When retirement compensation is awarded, or when an award is reviewed under Regulation 34, the additional compensation payable in consequence of any years of service or period of contribution credited to a person under paragraph (2) may be reduced or withheld to such an extent as the compensating authority may think reasonable having regard to the pension scheme (if any) associated with any further employment obtained by him.

(4) If under his last relevant pension scheme the amount of any benefit to which a person might have become entitled could have been increased at the discretion of the authority administering the pension scheme or of any other body, the compensating authority may increase, to an extent not exceeding that to which his accrued pension, accrued retiring allowance, accrued incapacity pension or accrued incapacity retiring allowance might have been increased or supplemented, the corresponding component of any retirement compensation payable to him; and in this connection the compensating authority shall have regard to the terms of any relevant resolutions of the authority or body with regard to the increase of benefits and to the provision of any enactment protecting the interests of that person.

(5) If under his last relevant pension scheme a person would have been entitled to surrender a proportion of any pension which might have become payable to him in favour of his spouse or any dependant, then, if he so desires and informs the compensating authority by notice in writing accordingly within one month after becoming entitled to retirement compensation under these Regulations, he may surrender a proportion of so much of the said compensation as is payable by way of an annual sum on the like terms and conditions and in consideration of the like payments by the compensating authority as if the said annual sum were a pension to which he had become entitled under the said pension scheme.

(6) In calculating for the purposes of Regulation 19, 20 or 21 the amount of the annual sum which is equal to a person's accrued pension, no account shall be taken of any reduction falling to be made in that pension by reason of the provisions of any Act relating to National Insurance until the person reaches the age at which under his last relevant pension scheme the pension would have been so reduced.

(7) In paragraph (2) the expression "reckonable service" includes any period of employment of which account has been taken or is required to be taken in calculating the amount of any superannuation benefit to which a person has become entitled under a pension scheme associated with the employment which he has lost or, as the case may be, the employment in which his emoluments were diminished.

Retirement compensation for loss of emoluments payable to pensionable officer on attainment of normal retiring age

19. Subject to the provisions of these Regulations, when a person to whom this Part of these Regulations applies reaches normal retiring age, the retirement compensation payable to him for loss of emoluments shall be—

    (*a*) an annual sum equal to the amount of his accrued pension, and

    (*b*) a lump sum equal to the amount of his accrued retiring allowance (if any).

(a) 1965 c. 51.

Retirement compensation payable to pensionable officer on his becoming incapacitated or reaching minimum pensionable age

20.—(1) Where a person to whom this Part of these Regulations applies and who has suffered loss of employment before attaining what would have been his normal retiring age—

(*a*) becomes incapacitated in circumstances in which, if he had continued in the employment which he has lost, he would have become entitled to a pension under his last relevant pension scheme; or

(*b*) attains the age which, had he continued to serve in the employment which he has lost, would have been his minimum pensionable age,

he shall be entitled on the happening of either event to claim, in lieu of any compensation to which he would otherwise be entitled under these Regulations—

(i) in the case mentioned in head (*a*) of this paragraph, an annual sum equal to the amount of his accrued incapacity pension and a lump sum equal to the amount of his accrued incapacity retiring allowance (if any), and

(ii) in the case mentioned in head (*b*) of this paragraph, an annual sum equal to the amount of his accrued pension and a lump sum equal to the amount of his accrued retiring allowance (if any),

subject however to the conditions specified in paragraph (5).

(2) On receipt of a claim under paragraph (1) the compensating authority shall consider whether the claimant is a person to whom that paragraph applies, and within thirteen weeks after the date of the receipt of the claim—

(*a*) if they are satisfied that he is not such a person, they shall notify him in writing accordingly; or

(*b*) if they are satisfied that he is such a person, they shall assess the amount of compensation payable to him and notify him in writing accordingly,

and any such notification shall, for the purposes of these Regulations, be deemed to be a notification by the authority of a decision on a claim for compensation.

(3) A compensating authority may require any person who makes a claim under head (*a*) of paragraph (1) to submit himself to a medical examination by a registered medical practitioner selected by that authority, and, if they do so, they shall also offer the person an opportunity of submitting a report from his own medical adviser as a result of an examination by him, and the authority shall take that report into consideration together with the report of the medical practitioner selected by them.

(4) If a person wishes to receive compensation under this Regulation, he shall so inform the compensating authority in writing within one month from the receipt of a notification under paragraph (2) or, where the claim has been the subject of an appeal, from the decision of the tribunal thereon; and the compensation shall be payable as from the date on which the compensating authority received the claim.

(5) The calculation of compensation under this Regulation shall be subject to the following conditions—

(*a*) where the compensating authority, by virtue of Regulation 18, have credited the person with additional years of service or an additional period of contribution, no account shall be taken of any additional years or period beyond the number of years which he could have served, had he not lost his employment, before the date on which the claim was received by the compensating authority; and

(*b*) if, by reason of any provision of the relevant pension scheme for a minimum benefit, the amount of any such pension or retiring allowance is in excess of that attributable to the person's actual service, no account shall be taken of any such additional years or period except to the extent (if any) by which they exceed the number of years represented by the difference between his actual service and the period by reference to which the minimum benefit has been calculated; and

(c) if the number of years by reference to which an accrued incapacity pension or accrued incapacity retiring allowance is to be calculated is less than any minimum number of years of qualifying service prescribed by the relevant pension scheme, the amount of such pension or retiring allowance shall, notwithstanding any minimum benefit prescribed by the pension scheme, not exceed such proportion of such minimum benefit as the number of years of pensionable service bears to the minimum number of years of qualifying service.

Option to take retirement compensation prematurely

21.—(1) If a person to whom this Part of these Regulations applies has suffered loss of employment after attaining the age of fifty years and so requests the compensating authority by notice in writing, he shall be entitled, as from the date on which the compensating authority receive such notice, to an annual sum equal to the amount of his accrued pension and a lump sum equal to the amount of his accrued retiring allowance (if any), and in that event he shall not be entitled to receive any further payment of long-term compensation after that date:

Provided that—

(i) in calculating the amount of the compensation payable to a person who has given such notice as aforesaid no account shall be taken of any additional years of service or period of contribution credited to him under Regulation 18; and

(ii) where the person has claimed long-term compensation the said notice shall be given not later than two years after the determination of the claim or, where the determination has been reviewed under Regulation 34(3), not later than two years after the review.

(2) Regulation 20(2) shall apply in relation to a notice given under the last foregoing paragraph as it applies to a claim made under paragraph (1) of that Regulation.

(3) Where an annual sum is payable under this Regulation in respect of any period and resettlement compensation is also payable in respect of that period, the said annual sum shall be limited to the amount (if any) by which it exceeds the resettlement compensation payable as aforesaid.

Retirement compensation for diminution of emoluments

22. Regulations 19 and 20 shall apply to a person to whom this Part of these Regulations applies and who has suffered a diminution of his emoluments, as if he had suffered loss of employment and of emoluments equivalent to the amount of the diminution:

Provided that no compensation shall be payable—

(i) if the emoluments have been diminished by less than 2½ per cent.; or

(ii) if the person has continued to pay superannuation contributions as if his emoluments had not been diminished.

Superannuation contributions

23.—(1) A person entitled to retirement compensation under Regulation 19, 20 or 21 shall pay to the compensating authority an amount equal to any sum which was paid to him by way of return of superannuation contributions, including any interest, after ceasing to be employed, and the compensating authority may at his request repay that amount to him at any time before he becomes entitled as aforesaid, but if that amount is not paid to the compensating authority, or is repaid by them to the person, the compensation shall be reduced by an annual amount the capital value of which is equal to the amount of the said superannuation contributions.

(2) For the purposes of this Regulation the expression "superannuation contributions" shall include payments made by the person in respect of added years and any additional contributory payments made by him.

(3) Any sums paid to a compensating authority under this Regulation in respect of returned contributions shall, except in so far as they are repaid to the officers concerned, be applied for the payment of compensation which the authority is liable to pay under this Part of these Regulations.

Retirement compensation of a person who obtains further pensionable employment

24.—(1) Where a person to whom this Part of these Regulations applies, after suffering loss of employment or diminution of emoluments, enters employment in which he is subject to a pension scheme and thereafter becomes entitled to reckon for the purposes of that scheme any service or period of contribution which falls to be taken into account for the purpose of assessing the amount of any retirement compensation payable to him, his entitlement to retirement compensation shall be reviewed and no retirement compensation shall be payable in respect of such service or period unless the annual rate of the emoluments to which he was entitled immediately before such loss or diminution exceeds the annual rate on entry of the emoluments of the new employment by more than $2\frac{1}{2}$ per cent. of such first mentioned emoluments, and any retirement compensation so payable to him shall, in so far as it is calculated by reference to remuneration, be calculated by reference to the difference between the said annual rates:

Provided that this paragraph shall not operate to increase the amount of any retirement compensation payable in respect of diminution of emoluments beyond the amount which would have been payable if the person had attained normal retiring age immediately before he ceased to hold the employment in which he suffered the diminution of emoluments.

(2) No retirement compensation shall be payable in the circumstances mentioned in paragraph (1) if the person has continued to pay superannuation contributions as if his emoluments had not been diminished.

Compensation payable to widow or dependants of a claimant

25.—(1) Payments in accordance with this Regulation and Regulations 26 and 27 shall be made to or for the benefit of the widow, child or other dependant or to the personal representatives of a person to whom this Part of these Regulations applies.

(2) If the widow, child or other dependant of that person might have become entitled to a pension under his last relevant pension scheme, the widow, child or other dependant, as the case may be, shall be entitled to receive an annual sum equal to the prescribed proportion of any retirement compensation by way of annual amounts payable to the person under Regulation 19, 20 or 21 immediately before his death or, if he dies before becoming entitled to receive compensation under any of those Regulations, the prescribed proportion of the compensation by way of annual amounts which he would have received under Regulation 20 had he become entitled thereto immediately before his death:

Provided that—
    (i) where any retirement compensation has been surrendered under Regulation 18(5) or compounded under Regulation 35, any sum

payable under this Regulation shall be calculated as if such surrender or compounding had not taken place;

(ii) where the pension scheme provides for payment of the pension to any person on behalf of a child or other dependant, any annual sum payable as aforesaid to a child or other dependant shall be paid to that person on behalf of the child or dependant in the like manner and for the like period as is provided in the pension scheme;

(iii) in calculating the sum payable as aforesaid, it shall be assumed that the retirement compensation payable, or which would have been payable, to a person under Regulation 19, 20 or 21 was such sum as would have been payable if the accrued pension or accrued incapacity pension had not been reduced by reason of the provisions of any Act relating to National Insurance.

(3) Any annual sum payable to or for the benefit of a widow, child or other dependant under this Regulation shall cease to be payable in any circumstances in which a corresponding pension under the pension scheme referred to in paragraph (2) would have ceased to be payable.

(4) Except where the compensation has been reduced under Regulation 23, compensation payable under this Regulation and Regulation 26 shall in the aggregate be reduced by an amount the capital value whereof is equal to the amount of any superannuation contributions as defined in Regulation 23(2) returned to the person in respect of whom the compensation is payable and either not paid to the compensating authority or repaid to him by the compensating authority, the compensation under each such Regulation being reduced in proportion to the capital value of each amount.

(5) This Regulation shall apply in the case of a person who has suffered a diminution of emoluments with the substitution of references to diminution of emoluments for references to loss of employment, and the annual sum payable to a widow, child or other dependant of such a person shall be calculated as if he had lost emoluments equivalent to the amount of the diminution:
Provided that no sum shall be payable under this paragraph—
(i) if the emoluments have been diminished by less than $2\frac{1}{2}$ per cent.; or
(ii) if the person has continued to pay superannuation contributions as if his emoluments had not been diminished.

(6) In this Regulation "prescribed proportion" means the proportion which, under the relevant pension scheme, the pension payable to the widow, child or other dependant of any person, as the case may be, bears to the person's pension.

Compensation where death grant would have been payable

26.—(1) If the widow or the personal representatives of a person to whom this Part of these Regulations applies, or trustees empowered by such a person to stand possessed of any benefit under his last relevant pension scheme, might have become entitled to a death grant under that scheme, she or they, as the case may be, shall be entitled to receive a sum calculated in accordance with the provisions of Regulation 25(4) and paragraph (2) of this Regulation.

(2) The amount of the sum referred to in paragraph (1) shall be ascertained in accordance with the method of calculation prescribed by the last relevant pension scheme for the ascertainment of death grant as if the person had died immediately before losing his employment, subject to the following modifications—

(a) except where the person had been in receipt of retirement compensation under Regulation 21, account shall be taken of any additional years of service or period of contribution credited to him under Regulation 18(2)—

    (i) in the case of a person who had been in receipt of retirement compensation under Regulation 20, to the extent of the period between the loss of employment and the date of the claim made under that Regulation; and

    (ii) in any other case, to the extent of the period between the loss of employment and the person's death;

  (b) if the number of years of the person's service or period of contribution is less than the minimum number of years of qualifying service or period prescribed by the pension scheme for the receipt of a death grant, the said sum shall not exceed such proportion of the death grant calculated as aforesaid as the number of years of the person's pensionable service or period of contribution bears to the minimum number of years of qualifying service or period prescribed by the pension scheme; and

  (c) there shall be deducted from such sum the amount of any retirement compensation paid to the person under Regulation 19, 20 or 21, or, where any part of the compensation had been surrendered under Regulation 18(5), the amount which would have been so paid but for any such surrender.

(3) For the purpose of calculating such death grant, an annual sum payable to or for the benefit of a widow, child or other dependant under Regulation 25 shall be deemed to be a pension payable to or for the benefit of the widow, child or dependant, as the case may be.

(4) This Regulation shall apply in the case of a person who has suffered a diminution of emoluments with the substitution of references to diminution of emoluments for references to loss of employment, and the sum payable to the widow or personal representatives of such a person shall be calculated as if he had lost emoluments equivalent to the amount of the diminution:

Provided that no sum shall be payable under this paragraph—

    (i) if the emoluments have been diminished by less than $2\frac{1}{2}$ per cent.; or

    (ii) if the person has continued to pay superannuation contributions as if his emoluments had not been diminished.

Balance payable to claimant's widow or personal representatives

27.—(1) If no annual sum is payable to the widow, child or other dependant of any person under Regulation 25 and no sum is payable under Regulation 26 and the person dies before he has received in the aggregate by way of retirement compensation a sum equivalent to the amount of any contributions repaid by him under Regulation 23, together with compound interest thereon calculated at the rate of 3 per cent. per annum with half-yearly rests up to the date of his death as from the 1st April or the 1st October following the half year in which the amount was paid, there shall be paid to his personal representatives the difference between the aggregate amount received by way of retirement compensation as aforesaid and the said equivalent sum.

(2) If an annual sum becomes payable to a widow under Regulation 25 and on her re-marriage or death the sum ceases to be payable, and any sum payable to a child or other dependant under that Regulation has ceased to be payable, and if the aggregate amount of the payments which were made as aforesaid, to her husband by way of retirement compensation and to the widow or personal representatives under Regulation 26 is less than a sum equivalent to the amount which would have been payable to the personal representatives under that

Regulation if no annual sum had been payable under Regulation 25, there shall be paid to her or her personal representatives the difference between such aggregate amount and the said equivalent sum.

(3) For the purposes of this Regulation a person who has surrendered any part of his retirement compensation under Regulation 18(5) shall be deemed to have received during any period the amount of compensation for that period which he would have received but for any such surrender.

Compensation payable to non-pensionable officer on reaching retiring age

28.—(1) Where a person who is not a pensionable officer is receiving long-term compensation for loss of employment and attains normal retiring age, the compensating authority may, if satisfied that the person would, but for the loss, have continued in the employment he has lost for a substantial period beyond that age, continue to pay compensation to him for the remainder of his life at half its former rate.

(2) Where a person who is not a pensionable officer suffers loss of employment on or after attaining normal retiring age, the compensating authority may, if satisfied that the person would in the normal course have continued in the employment he has lost for a further substantial period, pay compensation to him for the remainder of his life at half the rate to which he would have been entitled under Regulation 14 had he not attained normal retiring age at the date on which he lost his employment.

Persons subject to policy schemes

29.—(1) Regulations 19, 20, 21, 22 and 26 shall not apply to a person (in this Regulation referred to as a "policy scheme participant") who had been participating in a scheme associated with his employment for providing superannuation benefits by means of contracts or policies of insurance, and who, after the loss of his employment or the diminution of his emoluments, continued to participate in that scheme, or became entitled to a benefit or prospective benefit thereunder other than a return of contributions.

(2) If a policy scheme participant has lost his employment, the compensating authority may, if the relevant scheme so permits, make such payments to or in respect of him, whether by way of the payment of premiums or otherwise, as are actuarially equivalent to the amounts by which his retirement compensation might have been increased under Regulation 18(2) or (4) had he been a person to whom Regulation 19, 20 or 21 applied.

(3) If a policy scheme participant has suffered a diminution of his emoluments, the compensating authority may, if the relevant scheme so permits, make such payments to or in respect of him, whether by way of the payment of premiums or otherwise, as will secure to him the like benefits as if his emoluments had not been diminished.

(4) If a policy scheme participant becomes entitled to a benefit under such a scheme as is mentioned in paragraph (1) before reaching normal retiring age, the compensating authority may reduce any long-term compensation payable to him by the amount of such benefit.

Intervals for payment of compensation under Part V

30. Any compensation awarded as an annual sum under this Part of these Regulations to or in respect of any person shall be payable at intervals equivalent to those at which the corresponding benefit would have been payable under the person's last relevant pension scheme or at such other intervals as may be agreed between the person entitled to receive the compensation and the compensating authority.

PART VI

ADJUSTMENT, REVIEW AND COMPOUNDING OF COMPENSATION

Adjustment of compensation where superannuation benefit is also payable

31.—(1) Where any period of service of which account was taken in calculating the amount of any compensation payable under Part IV or V of these Regulations is subsequently taken into account for the purpose of calculating the amount of any superannuation benefit payable to or in respect of any person in accordance with a pension scheme associated with any employment undertaken subsequent to the loss of employment or diminution of emoluments which was the subject of the claim for compensation, the compensating authority may in accordance with this Regulation withhold or reduce the compensation payable in respect of any period for which such superannuation benefit is being received.

(2) If the part of any superannuation benefit by way of annual amounts which is attributable to a period of service mentioned in paragraph (1) equals or exceeds the part of any compensation by way of annual amounts which is attributable to the same period, that part of the compensation may be withheld, or, if such part of the superannuation benefit is less than such part of the compensation, the compensation may be reduced by an amount not exceeding such part of the superannuation benefit.

(3) In the case of a death benefit payable in respect of any person, the sum payable under Regulation 26 may be reduced by an amount not greater than the proportion of the death benefit which the period of service mentioned in paragraph (1) bears to the total period of service of which account was taken in the calculation of the death benefit.

(4) In addition to any reduction authorised by paragraph (2) or (3), if, in the circumstances mentioned in paragraph (1), compensation by way of annual amounts is attributable in part to any provision of the relevant pension scheme for a minimum benefit, the compensation may be reduced by an amount not exceeding that part.

(5) Where any additional years of service or period of contribution have been credited to a person under Regulation 18(2), if the number of such years or such period is equal to or less than the period spent in the subsequent employment mentioned in paragraph (1), the compensation by way of annual amounts may be reduced (in addition to any other reduction authorised by this Regulation) by an amount not exceeding that attributable to the additional years or period so credited or, if the number of such years or such period is greater than the period spent in the subsequent employment, by such proportion of that amount as the period spent in the subsequent employment bears to the number of additional years or the period so credited.

(6) Where compensation has been calculated in accordance with Regulation 24, the provisions of this Regulation shall apply only in relation to such part (if any) of the superannuation benefit as is attributable to annual emoluments in excess of those to which the person was entitled on entering the new employment referred to in Regulation 24.

(7) Where compensation is payable in respect of diminution of emoluments, the provisions of this Regulation shall apply only in relation to such part (if any) of the superannuation benefit as is attributable to annual emoluments in excess of those to which the person was entitled immediately prior to the diminution.

Reduction of compensation in certain cases

32.—(1) If under a person's last relevant pension scheme any benefit for which the scheme provided would have been subject to reduction or suspension on his taking up other specified employment, any retirement compensation to which he is entitled for loss of employment or diminution of emoluments shall, where such employment is taken up, be reduced or suspended in the like manner and to the like extent:

Provided that in calculating the amount of the reduction there shall be aggregated with the emoluments of the employment taken up the amount of any superannuation benefit by way of annual amounts payable to the person under a pension scheme associated with the employment which he has lost or, as the case may be, the employment in which the emoluments were diminished.

(2) There shall be deducted from the retirement compensation payable to any person any additional contributory payments remaining unpaid at the date when he suffered loss of employment; and any such payments not recovered at the date of his death shall be deducted from any compensation payable in respect of that person under Regulation 25, 26 or 27.

(3) Where a person is entitled to compensation under these Regulations and the circumstances are such that he is also entitled to—

(a) a redundancy payment under the Redundancy Payments Act 1965(a), or

(b) any similar payment in consequence of the loss of his employment under any contract or arrangement with the authority by whom he was employed (other than payments by way of a return of contributions under a pension scheme), or

(c) any payment under or by virtue of the provisions of any enactment relating to the reinstatement in civil employment of persons who have been in the service of the Crown,

the compensation which would, apart from this paragraph become due to the person, whether by instalments or lump sum or both, shall in the aggregate be reduced by the amount of the payments referred to in this paragraph.

(4) Where compensation under these Regulations is payable to or in respect of any person, and that person or his widow, child or other dependant or his personal representatives is or are also entitled (whether immediately or on the person's attaining some greater age) to a superannuation benefit under a pension scheme associated with the employment which he has lost—

(a) any instalment of such compensation which is payable in respect of any period shall be reduced by the amount of the instalment of such superannuation benefit which is payable in respect of the same period; and

(b) any such compensation which is payable as a lump sum shall be reduced by the amount of any lump sum superannuation benefit.

(5) For the purposes of paragraph (4) no account shall be taken of any sum payable in consequence of the surrender by any person of part of his superannuation benefit under any provision in that behalf in the relevant pension scheme with a view to obtaining or increasing allowances for his widow, child or other dependant; and the person shall be deemed to have received during any period the amount of superannuation benefit which he would have received but for any such surrender.

(6) Where in any week a person is entitled to long-term compensation for loss or diminution of emoluments and is also entitled to unemployment,

sickness or injury benefit under any Act relating to National Insurance, other than a benefit claimable by him in respect of a dependant, there shall be deducted from the long-term compensation payable for that week a sum equal to the amount by which the aggregate of such National Insurance benefits claimable in respect of that week and the weekly rate at which the long-term compensation would be payable but for this Regulation exceeds two-thirds of the weekly rate of the net emoluments of the employment which he has lost or in which the emoluments have been diminished:

Provided that this paragraph shall not apply in relation to any such sickness or injury benefit in so far as—

(i) an equivalent sum is deducted from the emoluments of his current employment, and

(ii) such deduction from those emoluments has not occasioned an increase in his long-term compensation.

(7) In paragraph (6) the expression "weekly rate" means seven three hundred and sixty-fifths of the relevant annual rate.

Notification of change of circumstances

33. Where—

(a) a pensionable officer after suffering loss of employment or diminution of emoluments enters any employment referred to in Regulation 24 or becomes entitled to any superannuation benefit on ceasing to hold such employment, or

(b) a person entitled to long-term compensation enters employment the remuneration whereof is payable out of public funds, or ceases to hold such employment, or receives any increase in his remuneration in such employment, or

(c) a person entitled to retirement compensation enters employment in which the compensation is subject to reduction or suspension under Regulation 32, or ceases to hold such employment, or receives any increase in his remuneration in such employment, or

(d) a person entitled to long-term compensation starts to receive any benefit, any increase in benefit or any further benefit under any Act relating to National Insurance,

he shall forthwith inform the compensating authority in writing of that fact.

Review of awards of long-term or retirement compensation

34.—(1) The compensating authority shall, within a period of two years afte-the date on which any decision on a claim for long-term or retirement compensa-tion for loss of employment (other than compensation payable under Regulation 21) is notified to a claimant under Regulation 36, or within such longer period as is specified in the subsequent provisions of this Regulation, and at intervals of not more than six months, review their decision or, where the claim has been the subject of an appeal, the decision of the tribunal, and these Regulations shall apply in relation to any such review as they apply in relation to the initial determination of the claim; and on such review, in the light of any material change in the cirumstances of the case, compensation may be awarded, or compensation previously awarded may be increased, reduced or discontinued, subject to the limits set out in these Regulations.

(2) The person to whom the decision relates may require the compensating authority to carry out the review mentioned in paragraph (1) at any time within the period of two years mentioned in that paragraph if he considers that there

has been a change in the circumstances of his case which is material for the purposes of these Regulations.

(3) The compensating authority shall carry out a review in accordance with paragraph (1), notwithstanding the expiration of the period mentioned in that paragraph, if—

(a) the emoluments of employment or work undertaken as a result of the loss of employment were taken into account in determining the amount of any compensation awarded, and

(b) such employment or work has been lost or the emoluments thereof reduced, otherwise than by reason of misconduct or incapacity to perform such duties as the person might reasonably have been required to perform, and

(c) the compensating authority are satisfied that such loss or reduction is causing him hardship,

and where any decision is so reviewed, the decision shall be subject to further review in accordance with paragraph (1) as if the review carried out under this paragraph had been the initial determination of the claim.

(4) Paragraphs (1) and (2) shall apply in relation to any decision on a claim for long-term or retirement compensation in respect of diminution of emoluments as they apply in relation to any decision mentioned in paragraph (1):
Provided that—

(i) where the person to whom the decision relates ceases to hold the employment in which his emoluments were diminished, a review shall be held within three months after that date, but no further review shall be held after the expiry of that period, and

(ii) while that person continues to hold that employment, there shall be no limit to the period within which a review may take place.

(5) Notwithstanding anything contained in the foregoing provisions of this Regulation, the compensating authority shall review a decision (whether of the authority or the tribunal) on a claim for long-term compensation for loss of employment or diminution of emoluments after the expiration of any period within which a review is required to be made if at any time—

(a) the person to whom the decision relates becomes engaged in employment (hereinafter referred to as his "current employment") the remuneration whereof is payable out of public funds and which he has undertaken subsequent to the loss or diminution, and

(b) the aggregate of the net emoluments of his current employment, any superannuation benefit by way of annual amounts payable to him in respect of the employment which he has lost or the employment in which his emoluments have been diminished and the long-term compensation payable to him exceeds the net emoluments of the employment which he has lost or, as the case may be, in which the emoluments have been diminished.

(6) The compensating authority shall further review any decision reviewed under paragraph (5) whenever the net emoluments of the person's current employment are increased.

(7) If on any review under paragraph (5) or (6) the compensation is reduced, it shall not be reduced below the amount by which the net emoluments of the person's current employment, together with any superannuation benefit by way of annual amounts payable to him in respect of the employment which he has

lost or the employment in which his emoluments have been diminished, falls short of the net emoluments of the employment he has lost or, as the case may be, in which the emoluments have been diminished.

(8) The compensating authority shall give to a person to whom a decision relates not less than fourteen days' notice of any review of that decision to be carried out under this Regulation unless the review is carried out at his request.

(9) Nothing in this Regulation shall preclude the making of any adjustment of compensation required by Regulation 31 or 32.

Compounding of awards

35.—(1) In a case where an annual sum which has been or might be awarded under these Regulations does not exceed £26, the compensating authority may, at their discretion, compound their liability in respect thereof by paying a lump sum equivalent to the capital value of the annual sum and, if any lump sum payment has been or might be awarded in addition to such annual sum under Regulation 19, 20, 21 or 22, the compensating authority may likewise discharge their liability in respect thereof by an immediate payment.

(2) In any other case, if the person who has been awarded long-term or retirement compensation requests them to do so, the compensating authority may, after having regard to the state of health of that person and the other circumstances of the case, compound up to one quarter of their liability to make payments under the award (other than payments to a widow, child or other dependant under Regulation 25) by the payment of an equivalent amount as a lump sum or, where any compensation has been awarded as a lump sum, by increasing that compensation to such equivalent amount; and in calculating for this purpose the liability of the authority to make such payments, account shall be taken of the annual value of lump sum payments of compensation.

(3) The making of a composition under paragraph (2) in relation to an award of long-term or retirement compensation shall not prevent the subsequent making of a composition under paragraph (1) in relation to that award, but, subject as aforesaid, not more than one composition may be made in relation to any award.

Part VII
Procedure And Miscellaneous

Procedure on making claims

36.—(1) Every claim for compensation under these Regulations and every request for a review of an award of long-term or retirement compensation shall be made in accordance with this Regulation.

(2) Every such claim and request shall be made to the compensating authority in a form approved by the Secretary of State, and shall state whether any other claim for compensation has been made by the claimant under these Regulations.

(3) Resettlement compensation shall be claimed separately from any other form of compensation claimable under these Regulations.

(4) The compensating authority shall consider any such claim or request in accordance with the relevant provisions of these Regulations and shall notify the person making the claim or request in writing of their decision—

    (*a*) in the case of a claim for resettlement compensation, not later than one month after the receipt of the claim, and

    (*b*) in the case of a claim for, or request for the review of an award of, compensation under Part IV or V of these Regulations, not later than thirteen weeks after the receipt of the claim or request, and

(c) in any other case, as soon as possible after the decision;
but the decision of a compensating authority shall not be invalidated by reason of the fact that notice of the decision is given after the expiry of the period mentioned in this paragraph.

(5) Every notification of a decision by the compensating authority (whether granting or refusing compensation or reviewing an award, or otherwise affecting any compensation under these Regulations) shall contain a statement—

(a) giving reasons for the decision;

(b) showing how any compensation has been calculated and, in particular, if the amount is less than the maximum which could have been awarded under these Regulations, showing the factors taken into account in awarding that amount; and

(c) directing the attention of the claimant to his right under Regulation 42, if he is aggrieved by the decision, to institute proceedings before a tribunal and giving him the address to which the application instituting such proceedings should be sent.

Claimants to furnish information

37.—(1) Any person claiming or receiving compensation or whose award of compensation is being reviewed shall furnish all such information as the compensating authority may at any time reasonably require; and he shall verify the same in such manner, including the production of books or of original documents in his possession or control, as may be reasonably so required.

(2) Any such person shall, on receipt of reasonable notice, present himself for interview at such place as the compensating authority may reasonably require; and any person who attends for interview may, if he so desires, be represented by his adviser.

Procedure on death of claimant

38.—(1) In the event of the death of a claimant or of a person who, if he had survived, could have been a claimant, a claim for compensation under these Regulations may be continued or made, as the case may be, by his personal representatives.

(2) Where any such claim is continued or made as aforesaid by personal representatives, the personal representatives shall, as respects any steps to be taken or thing to be done by them in order to continue or make the claim, be deemed for the purposes of these Regulations to be the person entitled to claim, but, save as aforesaid, the person in whose right they continue or make the claim shall be deemed for the purposes of these Regulations to be such person, and the relevant provisions of these Regulations shall be construed accordingly:

Provided that the compensating authority may in any such case extend the period within which a claim is required to be made by Regulation 6 or 12.

Calculation of service

39.—(1) For the purpose of determining the amount of any compensation payable in respect of the loss of an office to which, or of any two or more offices to which in the aggregate, a person devoted substantially the whole of his time, any previous period of part-time employment shall be treated as though it were whole-time employment for a proportionately reduced period.

(2) For the purpose of making any calculation under these Regulations in respect of a person's reckonable service, all periods of such service shall be aggregated and, except where reference is made to completed years of service, if the aggregated service includes a fraction of a year, that fraction shall, if it equals or exceeds six months, be treated as a year, and shall in any other case be disregarded.

Emoluments of part-time employments

40. In ascertaining for the purposes of these Regulations whether, and how far, the remuneration of alternative employment falls short of emoluments which have been lost where those emoluments were payable in respect of two or more part-time employments, the remuneration of the alternative employment or of the aggregate of two or more such employments shall be apportioned in the proportion which the emoluments of the part-time employments bore to each other.

Compensation not assignable

41. Subject to any statutory provision in that behalf, any compensation to which a person becomes entitled under these Regulations shall be paid by the compensating authority and shall be payable to, or in trust for, the person who is entitled to receive it, and shall not be assignable:

Provided that, without prejudice to any other right of recovery, any compensation paid in error may be recovered by the compensating authority by deduction from any compensation payable under these Regulations.

Right of appeal from decision of compensating authority

42.—(1) Every person who is aggrieved by any decision of the compensating authority with respect to a compensation question or by any failure on the part of the compensating authority to notify him of any such decision within the appropriate time prescribed by these Regulations, may within thirteen weeks of the notification to him of the decision or the expiry of the prescribed time, as the case may be, institute proceedings for the determination of the question by a tribunal in accordance with—

(a) in England and Wales, the Industrial Tribunals (Employment and Compensation) Regulations 1967(a); and

(b) in Scotland, the Industrial Tribunals (Employment and Compensation) (Scotland) Regulations 1967(b),

and these Regulations; and the tribunal shall determine the question accordingly.

(2) For the purpose of any such proceedings a person or persons may be appointed to sit with the tribunal as assessor or assessors.

(3) The compensating authority shall give effect to the decision of a tribunal subject to any modifications that may be required in consequence of any appeal from that decision on a point of law.

James Callaghan,

One of Her Majesty's Principal
Secretaries of State.

Home Office,
   Whitehall.
21st August 1968.

(a) S.I. 1967/361 (1967 I, p. 1205).   (b) S.I. 1967/362 (1967 I, p. 1220).

Regulation 2(2) **SCHEDULE**

TABLE I

Table showing the capital value of an annual amount of £1 payable for life

Age	Capital value of £1 per annum payable for life	
	Female	Male
	£ s. d.	£ s. d.
Under 35	15 11 0	15 3 0
35 and under 40	15 2 0	14 12 0
40 and under 45	14 11 0	13 19 0
45 and under 50	13 18 0	13 2 0
50	13 9 0	12 11 0
51	13 5 0	12 7 0
52	13 2 0	12 3 0
53	12 18 0	11 18 0
54	12 14 0	11 14 0
55	12 10 0	11 9 0
56	12 6 0	11 5 0
57	12 2 0	11 0 0
58	11 18 0	10 15 0
59	11 13 0	10 10 0
60	11 8 0	10 5 0
61	11 4 0	10 0 0
62	10 19 0	9 14 0
63	10 14 0	9 9 0
64	10 8 0	9 3 0
65	10 3 0	8 18 0
66	9 18 0	8 12 0
67	9 12 0	8 7 0
68	9 7 0	8 1 0
69	9 1 0	7 16 0
70	8 15 0	7 10 0

NOTE:—This table is for use in connection with Regulation 35(1) and (2) for the compounding of annual retirement compensation which a person is currently entitled to receive under Regulation 19, 20, 21 or 22. Where the compensation is payable before age 60 (females), 65 (males) but will be reduced on the attainment of that age (in connection with National Insurance pension) the table should be used in conjunction with Table II, i.e. Table II should be used for valuing that part of the compensation which ceases to be payable at 60 (65) and this table should be used for valuing the remainder.

TABLE II

Table showing the capital value of an amount of £1 per annum ceasing
at age 60 (females), 65 (males)

Age						Capital Value					
						Female			Male		
						£	s.	d.	£	s.	d.
Under 35	...	...	...	...	...	13	8	0	14	2	0
35 and under 40	...	...	...	...	...	12	5	0	13	3	0
40 and under 45	...	...	...	...	...	10	14	0	11	19	0
45 and under 50	...	...	...	...	...	8	13	0	10	8	0
50 ...	...	...	...	...	...	7	3	0	9	6	0
51 ...	...	...	...	...	...	6	12	0	8	18	0
52 ...	...	...	...	...	...	6	0	0	8	9	0
53 ...	...	...	...	...	...	5	7	0	7	19	0
54 ...	...	...	...	...	...	4	13	0	7	10	0
55 ...	...	...	...	...	...	3	18	0	6	19	0
56 ...	...	...	...	...	...	3	3	0	6	8	0
57 ...	...	...	...	...	...	2	6	0	5	17	0
58 ...	...	...	...	...	...	1	9	0	5	4	0
59 ...	...	...	...	...	...		10	0	4	11	0
60 ...	...	...	...	...	...	—			3	17	0
61 ...	...	...	...	...	...	—			3	2	0
62 ...	...	...	...	...	...	—			2	6	0
63 ...	...	...	...	...	...	—			1	8	0
64 ...	...	...	...	...	...	—				10	0

NOTE:—This table is for use in connection with Regulation 35(1) and (2) for the compounding of any part of annual retirement compensation which will cease to be payable on the attainment of age 60 (females), 65 (males). Table I should be used in relation to the remainder of such compensation, i.e. the part which is payable for life—see note on that table.

TABLE III

Table showing the capital value of an annual amount of £1 payable to a
widow until death or remarriage

Age of widow at date of widowhood	Capital value of £1 per annum as at date of widow-hood	Age of widow at date of widowhood	Capital value of £1 per annum as at date of widow-hood
	£ s. d.		£ s. d.
20	6 0 0	45	11 18 0
21	6 0 0	46	12 1 0
22	6 0 0	47	12 3 0
23	6 0 0	48	12 5 0
24	6 0 0	49	12 6 0
25	6 5 0	50	12 6 0
26	6 12 0	51	12 6 0
27	6 19 0	52	12 5 0
28	7 6 0	53	12 4 0
29	7 13 0	54	12 3 0
30	8 0 0	55	12 1 0
31	8 8 0	56	11 19 0
32	8 15 0	57	11 16 0
33	9 2 0	58	11 13 0
34	9 8 0	59	11 10 0
35	9 15 0	60	11 6 0
36	10 1 0	61	11 3 0
37	10 6 0	62	10 19 0
38	10 11 0	63	10 14 0
39	10 16 0	64	10 8 0
40	11 1 0	65	10 3 0
41	11 5 0	66	9 18 0
42	11 9 0	67	9 12 0
43	11 12 0	68	9 7 0
44	11 15 0	69	9 1 0
		70	8 15 0

NOTE:—This table is for use in connection with Regulation 35(1) for compounding
annual compensation payable to a widow under Regulation 25. It should also be
used, where a reduction of compensation under Regulation 25(4) falls to be apportioned
between the compensation payable under that Regulation and under Regulation 26,
for ascertaining the capital value of annual compensation to a widow.

TABLE IV

Table showing the annual amount payable for life equivalent in value
to a lump sum of £100

Age	Annual sum, payable for life, equal in value to a lump sum of £100	
	Female	Male
	£ s. d.	£ s. d.
Under 35	6 8 7	6 12 0
35 and under 40	6 12 5	6 17 0
40 and under 45	6 17 5	7 3 4
45 and under 50	7 3 11	7 12 8
50	7 8 8	7 19 4
51	7 10 11	8 1 11
52	7 12 8	8 4 7
53	7 15 0	8 8 1
54	7 17 6	8 10 11
55	8 0 0	8 14 8
56	8 2 7	8 17 9
57	8 5 3	9 1 10
58	8 8 1	9 6 0
59	8 11 8	9 10 6
60	8 15 5	9 15 1
61	8 18 7	10 0 0
62	9 2 8	10 6 2
63	9 6 11	10 11 8
64	9 12 4	10 18 7
65	9 17 0	11 4 9
66	10 2 0	11 12 7
67	10 8 4	11 19 6
68	10 13 11	12 8 5
69	11 1 0	12 16 5
70	11 8 7	13 6 8

NOTE:—This table is for use in connection with Regulation 23(1) for ascertaining the annual amount by which retirement compensation under Regulation 19, 20 or 21 is to be reduced where a claimant has not paid to the compensating authority an amount equal to any sum paid to him by way of superannuation contributions or that amount has been repaid to him by the compensating authority at his request. It should also be used in connection with Regulation 35(2) for calculating for the purposes of that paragraph the annual value of retirement compensation awarded as a lump sum.

TABLE V

Table showing the annual amount payable to a widow until death or remarriage equivalent in value to a lump sum of £100

Age of widow at date of widowhood	Annual amount equal in value to a lump sum of £100			Age of widow at date of widowhood	Annual amount equal in value to a lump sum of £100		
	£	s.	d.		£	s.	d.
20	16	13	4	45	8	8	1
21	16	13	4	46	8	6	0
22	16	13	4	47	8	4	7
23	16	13	4	48	8	3	3
24	16	13	4	49	8	2	7
25	16	0	0	50	8	2	7
26	15	3	0	51	8	2	7
27	14	7	9	52	8	3	3
28	13	14	0	53	8	3	11
29	13	1	5	54	8	4	7
30	12	10	0	55	8	6	0
31	11	18	1	56	8	7	4
32	11	8	7	57	8	9	6
33	10	19	9	58	8	11	8
34	10	12	9	59	8	13	11
35	10	5	2	60	8	17	0
36	9	19	0	61	8	19	5
37	9	14	2	62	9	2	8
38	9	9	7	63	9	6	11
39	9	5	2	64	9	12	4
40	9	1	0	65	9	17	0
41	8	17	9	66	10	2	0
42	8	14	8	67	10	8	4
43	8	12	5	68	10	13	11
44	8	10	3	69	11	1	0
				70	11	8	7

NOTE:—This table is for use in connection with Regulation 25(4) for ascertaining the annual amount by which compensation to a widow is to be reduced in the circumstances described in that paragraph. If a reduction is required to be apportioned between compensation payable under Regulations 25 and 26, the capital value of annual compensation to a widow should be ascertained by reference to Table III.

TABLE VI

Table showing, according to the outstanding period of long-term compensation, the capital value of each £100 of the total amount of long-term compensation compounded

Outstanding number of complete years of long-term compensation	Capital value of each £100 of the total amount of long-term compensation	
	Female	Male
	£ s. d.	£ s. d.
0	98 8 0	98 4 0
1	95 4 0	94 16 0
2	92 2 0	91 10 0
3	89 4 0	88 6 0
4	86 8 0	85 8 0
5	83 16 0	82 14 0
6	81 6 0	80 2 0
7	78 18 0	77 14 0
8	76 14 0	75 8 0
9	74 12 0	73 4 0
10	72 12 0	71 4 0
11	70 12 0	69 6 0
12	68 16 0	67 10 0
13	67 0 0	65 14 0
14	65 6 0	64 2 0
15	63 14 0	62 10 0
16	62 2 0	61 0 0
17	60 12 0	59 12 0
18	59 4 0	58 4 0
19	57 16 0	56 18 0
20	56 10 0	55 12 0
21	55 4 0	54 8 0
22	54 0 0	53 4 0
23	52 16 0	52 0 0
24	51 12 0	50 18 0
25	50 10 0	49 18 0
26	49 8 0	48 18 0
27	48 8 0	47 18 0
28	47 8 0	46 18 0
29	46 8 0	45 18 0
30	45 10 0	45 0 0

NOTE:—This table is for use in connection with Regulation 35(1) and (2) for compounding awards of long-term compensation under Part IV of these Regulations. The total amount of the annual long-term compensation which is to be compounded must first be calculated, i.e. the amount which the person would receive on account of that compensation or the part of it which is to be compounded, if it were paid until "normal retiring age" (as defined in these Regulations). For each £100 so calculated, the lump sum payment will be the amount shown in the table according to the number of complete years in the period between the date of compounding and "normal retiring age".

EXPLANATORY NOTE

(This Note is not part of the Regulations.)

1. These Regulations, made under section 4 of the Public Expenditure and Receipts Act 1968, provide for the payment of compensation to or in respect of persons who suffer loss of employment or loss or diminution of emoluments which is attributable to the revocation or amendment of any regulations made under section 2 of the Civil Defence Act 1948.

2. Part I of the Regulations contains definitions. Part II specifies the persons to whom the Regulations apply and the grounds of entitlement to compensation. The Regulations apply to persons employed whole-time or part-time by or on behalf of a local authority (except persons subject to the Firemen's Pension Scheme).

3. The compensation payable is—

(*a*) resettlement compensation for loss of employment (Part III of the Regulations);

(*b*) long-term compensation for loss of employment or loss or diminution of emoluments (Part IV);

(*c*) retirement compensation for loss of employment or loss or diminution of emoluments (Part V);

(*d*) compensation to the widow, child or other dependant or to the personal representatives of a claimant who was a pensionable officer (Part V).

4. Resettlement compensation is payable for a period not exceeding 26 weeks to officers with at least three years' service in relevant employment. The qualifying conditions and factors to be considered are set out in Regulation 6. The method of calculating the amount of compensation is contained in Regulation 7.

5. Long-term and retirement compensation is payable to officers with at least eight years' service in relevant employment. The qualifying and other conditions are set out in Regulation 12.

6. The method of calculating the maximum amount of long-term compensation is laid down in Regulations 14 (loss of employment) and 15 (diminution of emoluments). This amount is a proportion, not exceeding two-thirds, of the net emoluments lost or of the amount by which emoluments have been diminished, as the case may be. This compensation is payable from a date determined under Regulation 16 and can be payable up to normal retiring age. In the case of a non-pensionable officer, compensation not exceeding one-half of the rate of long-term compensation may be paid beyond normal retiring age (Regulation 28).

7. Retirement compensation payable to a pensionable officer is based upon his accrued pension rights (Regulations 19 and 22) supplemented in the case of persons aged 40 or over at the date of loss by the addition of notional years of service (Regulation 18). Special provision is made for any persons whose pension arrangements are by way of policies of insurance (Regulation 29). Retirement compensation is ordinarily payable from normal retiring age but in certain circumstances is payable earlier (Regulations 20 and 21).

8. Compensation is payable to the widow, child or other dependant or to the personal representatives or trustees of a claimant who dies where such persons would have benefited under the relevant pension scheme (Regulations 25 to 27).

9. Part VI of the Regulations provides for long-term and retirement compensation to be reviewed and for awards to be varied in the light of changing circumstances (Regulation 34). It also contains provisions for the adjustment, suspension and compounding of compensation in certain circumstances.

10. Part VII contains provisions relating to the procedure for making claims and notifying decisions, and confers upon a claimant who is aggrieved by a decision on a compensation question or the failure of a compensating authority to notify their decision a right to refer the question for determination by a tribunal established under section 12 of the Industrial Training Act 1964.

STATUTORY INSTRUMENTS

1968 No. 1352

IRON AND STEEL

The Iron and Steel Arbitration Tribunal (Appointed Day) Order 1968

Made - - - *13th August* 1968

I, Gerald, Baron Gardiner, Lord High Chancellor of Great Britain, in exercise of the powers conferred on me by section 32 of the Iron and Steel Act 1967(a), hereby make the following Order :—

1. The day appointed for the purpose of section 32 of the Iron and Steel Act 1967 shall be 3rd September 1968.

2. This Order may be cited as the Iron and Steel Arbitration Tribunal (Appointed Day) Order 1968.

Dated 13th August 1968.

Gardiner, C.

EXPLANATORY NOTE

(*This Note is not part of the Order.*)

This Order appoints 3rd September 1968 as the day on which the Arbitration Tribunal established under the Iron and Steel Act 1949 is to be re-established.

(a) 1967 c.17.

STATUTORY INSTRUMENTS

1968 No. 1353

EDUCATION, ENGLAND AND WALES

The Teachers' Superannuation (Amending) Regulations 1968

Made - - -	*22nd August* 1968
Laid before Parliament	*30th August* 1968
Coming into Operation	*1st September* 1968

The Secretary of State for Education and Science, with the consent of the Treasury and after consultation with representatives of local education authorities and of teachers appearing to him to be likely to be affected, in exercise of of the powers conferred upon him by section 1 of the Teachers' Superannuation Act 1967(**a**), hereby makes the following Regulations :—

1.—(1) These Regulations may be cited as the Teachers' Superannuation (Amending) Regulations 1968 and shall come into operation on 1st September 1968.

(2) The Teachers' Superannuation Regulations 1967(**b**), the Teachers' Superannuation (Amending) Regulations 1967(**c**), the Teachers' (Part-time) Superannuation Regulations 1967(**d**) and these Regulations may be cited together as the Teachers' Superannuation Regulations 1967 and 1968.

2.—(1) In these Regulations the expression "the principal Regulations" means the Teachers' Superannuation Regulations 1967 and these Regulations shall be construed as one with those Regulations.

(2) The Interpretation Act 1889(**e**) shall apply for the interpretation of these Regulations as it applies for the interpretation of an Act of Parliament.

3. Except as in these Regulations expressly provided, amendment of the principal Regulations by these Regulations shall not—

(*a*) affect the previous operation of the principal Regulations or anything duly done or suffered under those Regulations ;

(*b*) affect any right, obligation or liability acquired, accrued or incurred under the principal Regulations before the coming into operation of these Regulations; or

(*c*) cause any annual superannuation allowance, additional superannuation allowance, gratuity or other benefit, or any increase thereof, to be payable from a date earlier than that on which these Regulations come into operation.

(**a**) 1967 c. 12.   (**b**) S.I. 1967/489 (1967 I, p. 1562).
(**c**) S.I. 1967/948 (1967 II, p. 2904)   (**d**) 1967/1286 (1967 II, p. 3721).
(**e**) 1889 c. 63.

4. In regulation 7 of the principal Regulations (which relates to the employments and occupations which are qualifying service for the purposes of those Regulations) after paragraph (*b*) there shall be inserted the following paragraph:—

> "(bb) any employment or occupation which, having been reckonable service or external service or reckonable as such, has ceased for any reason to be such service or to be so reckonable".

5.—(1) In regulation 16 of the principal Regulations (which relates to exclusion from reckonable service) sub-paragraph (*b*) of paragraph (1) shall cease to have effect.

(2) In the case of a person who immediately before 1st April 1967 was employed in services which was not treated as contributory service by virtue of section 3(2) of the Act of 1945—

> (*a*) his service in the same employment shall not be reckonable service ; and

> (*b*) any other service as a teacher of a kind specified in Part I of Schedule 1 to the principal Regulations—

>> (i) in which he becomes employed not more than one year after leaving that employment or after leaving any subsequent employment not treated as reckonable service by virtue of this regulation ; and

>> (ii) in respect of which he would, but for an election made under this paragraph, be subject to a superannuation scheme of a kind specified in paragraph 2(2) of Schedule 2 to the Act of 1967

> shall not be reckonable service unless within three months of becoming employed therein he otherwise elects by notice in writing to the Secretary of State and the body administering the superannuation scheme to which he would otherwise be subject.

(3) A person who—

> (*a*) immediately before 1st April 1967 was employed in service which was not treated as contributory service by virtue of section 3(2) of the Act of 1945 ;

> (*b*) before the coming into operation of these Regulations became employed in other service as a teacher of a kind specified in Part I of Schedule 1 to the principal Regulations ; and

> (*c*) could, if paragraph (2) above had been included in the principal Regulations and regulation 16(1)(*b*) omitted therefrom, have continued by virtue of that paragraph to be subject to a superannuation scheme of a kind therein mentioned

may within three months of the date of the coming into operation of these Regulations elect by notice in writing to the Secretary of State that his service shall from that date not be reckonable service.

6.—In Regulation 24 of the principal Regulations (which relates to emoluments) for paragraph (*a*) there shall be substituted the following paragraph:—

> "(*a*) the value (not exceeding one-sixth of the cash salary of the teacher) of a dwelling-house or other residential accommodation provided free of rent and the value of any heat, light, water or other services supplied free in connection therewith which, in the opinion of the Secretary of State, it is not practicable or convenient to convert into a cash salary ;"

7.—In regulation 43 of the principal Regulations (which relates to the duration of annual superannuation allowances) for paragraph (2) there shall be substituted the following paragraph:—

"(2) An annual superannuation allowance payable to a teacher by virtue of regulation 41(1)(*b*) shall begin to accrue on whichever of the following two days shall be the later, that is to say—

(*a*) the day following that on which the teacher ceases to be employed in reckonable service or external service ; or

(*b*) the day six months before the date of the last report of a duly qualified medical practitioner of which the Secretary of State took account in forming the opinion that the teacher had become permanently incapable through infirmity of mind or body of serving efficiently as a teacher in reckonable service."

8. In regulation 52 of the principal Regulations (which relates to avoidance of duplicate pensions) for the reference in paragraph (4)(*b*) to regulation 42 there shall be substituted a reference to regulation 43.

9. Regulation 70 of the principal Regulations (which relates to organisers) shall be amended as follows :—

(*a*) the existing regulation, amended as in this regulation provided, shall be paragraph (1) ;

(*b*) at the end of sub-paragraph (*a*) of paragraph (1) there shall be added the following : —

"(iii) a person employed by a body specified in paragraph (2) below who, before becoming so employed, was employed for not less than three years in reckonable service or class A external service and who, within three months of becoming so employed, with the agreement of the Secretary of State and his employer, elects by notice in writing to the Secretary of State that this Part shall apply to him ;" and

(*c*) after paragraph (1) there shall be added the following paragraph : —

"(2) The following are the bodies referred to in paragraph (1)(*a*)(iii) above, that is to say—

The City and Guilds of London Institute
The Associated Examining Board."

10. In regulation 74 of the principal Regulations (which relates to teachers in admitted schools) for the reference in paragraph (3) to paragraph (2)(*e*) there shall be substituted a reference to paragraph (2)(*a*).

11. For regulation 86 of the principal Regulations there shall be substituted the following regulations :—

"Contributions

86.—(1) The contributions payable by a services education officer shall be the aggregate of the contributions payable in respect of him under sections 3 and 5 of the Act of 1967 and no contributions shall be payable by any person as the employer of such an officer.

(2) For the purposes of determining the amount of the contributions payable by a services education officer his salary for any period shall be such salary, exclusive of any London allowance, as he would have received in respect of that period if he were affected by an order made under section 2 of the Remuneration of Teachers Act 1965(**a**).

(**a**) 1965 c. 3.

(3) So much of the contributions paid by a services education officer as is equal to six per cent of his salary shall be treated as contributions paid by a teacher and the remainder shall be treated as contributions paid by an employer.

(4) Any question arising under this regulation as to the amount of the salary for any period of a services education officer shall be decided by the Secretary of State and his decision thereon shall be final."

12. In Part I of Schedule 2 to the principal Regulations (which Part specifies the kinds of service which are class A external service for the purposes of those Regulations) for paragraph 1 there shall, with effect from the date on which regulations made under section 1 of the Teachers' Superannuation (Scotland) Act 1968(a) come into operation, be substituted the following paragraph :—

"1. Reckonable service within the meaning of regulations made under section 1 of the Teachers' Superannuation (Scotland) Act 1968."

13. Part III of Schedule 2 to the principal Regulations (which Part specifies the kinds of service which are class C external service for the purposes of those Regulations) shall be amended as follows :—

(a) for paragraph 24 there shall be substituted the following paragraph :—
"24. Employment after reckonable service in employment to which interchange rules made by the Secretary of State for the time being apply" ; and

(b) at the end there shall be added the following paragraph :—
"27. Pensionable service as a clerk in holy orders or as a regular minister of any religious denomination."

14. In Schedule 3 to the principal Regulations (which specifies the employments and occupations which are qualifying service for the purposes of those Regulations) paragraph 1 shall cease to have effect.

Given under the Official Seal of the Secretary of State for Education and Science on 14th August 1968.

(L.S.)

G. H. Andrew,
Permanent Under-Secretary of State
for Education and Science.

We concur.
22nd August 1968.

E. Alan Fitch,
B. K. O'Malley,
Two of the Lords Commissioners of
Her Majesty's Treasury.

EXPLANATORY NOTE
(This Note is not part of the Regulations.)

These regulations improve, and correct minor defects in, the Teachers' Superannuation Regulations 1967. In particular, Regulation 5 allows teachers who under earlier legislation had been permitted to remain subject to local government superannuation to continue to do so notwithstanding a change of employment.

(a) 1968 c. 12

STATUTORY INSTRUMENTS

1968 No. 1354

AGRICULTURE

The Price Stability of Imported Products (Rates of Levy No. 3) Order 1968

Made	-	-	-	*12th August* 1968
Coming into Operation				*13th August* 1968

The Minister of Agriculture, Fisheries and Food, in exercise of the powers conferred upon him by section 1(2), (4), (5), (6) and (7) of the Agriculture and Horticulture Act 1964(a) and of all other powers enabling him in that behalf, hereby makes the following order:—

1. This Order may be cited as the Price Stability of Imported Products (Rates of Levy No. 3) Order 1968; and shall come into operation on 13th August 1968.

2.—(1) In this order—

" the Principal Order " means the Price Stability of Imported Products (Levy Arrangements) Order 1966(b), as amended by any subsequent order and if any such order is replaced by any subsequent order the expression shall be construed as a reference to such subsequent order;

AND other expressions have the same meaning as in the Principal Order.

(2) The Interpretation Act 1889(c) shall apply to the interpretation of this order as it applies to the interpretation of an Act of Parliament.

3. In accordance with and subject to the provisions of Part II of the Principal Order (which provides for the charging of levies on imports of certain specified commodities)—

(a) the rate of general levy for such imports into the United Kingdom of any specified commodity as are described in column 2 of Part I of the Schedule to this order in relation to a tariff heading indicated in column 1 of that Part shall be the rate set forth in relation thereto in column 3 of that Part;

(b) the rate of country levy for such imports into the United Kingdom of any specified commodity as are described in column 2 of Part II of the Schedule to this order in relation to a tariff heading indicated in column 1 of that Part shall be the rate set forth in relation thereto in column 3 of that Part.

4. The Price Stability of Imported Products (Rates of Levy No. 2) Order 1968(d) shall be amended by deleting from column 2 of Part II of the Schedule thereto (which Part specifies a rate of country levy on imports of wheat grown in France or Sweden and consigned to the United Kingdom from that country) the words " which has been grown in the French Republic and consigned to the United Kingdom from that country or ".

In Witness whereof the Official Seal of the Minister of Agriculture. Fisheries and Food is hereunto affixed on 12th August 1968.

(L.S.)

A. C. Sparks,
Authorised by the Minister.

(a) 1964 c. 28.   (b) S.I. 1966/936 (1966 II, p. 2271).   (c) 1889 c. 63.
(d) S.I. 1968/1225 (1968 II, p. 3286).

SCHEDULE

PART I

1 Tariff Heading	2 Description of Imports	3 Rate of General Levy
		per ton s. d.
10·01	Imports of:— Denatured wheat	10 0

PART II

1 Tariff Heading	2 Description of Imports	3 Rate of Country Levy
		per ton s. d.
10·01	Imports of:— Denatured wheat which has been grown in and con- signed to the United Kingdom from Belgium, the French Republic, the Kingdom of the Netherlands or the Kingdom of Sweden	10 0

EXPLANATORY NOTE

(This Note is not part of the Order.)

This Order, which comes into operation on 13th August 1968, fixes rates of levy to be charged (in accordance with and subject to the provisions of the Principal Order) as follows:—

(*a*) a general levy of 10s. per ton on imports of denatured wheat; and

(*b*) a country levy of 10s. per ton on imports of denatured wheat which has been grown in and consigned to the United Kingdom from Belgium, France, the Netherlands or Sweden.

The Order also amends the Price Stability of Imported Products (Rates of Levy No. 2) Order 1968 to remove the country levy fixed by that order on imports of wheat grown in France and consigned to the United Kingdom from that country.

STATUTORY INSTRUMENTS

1968 No. 1355

WAGES COUNCILS

The Wages Regulation (Cotton Waste Reclamation) Order 1968

Made - - - *22nd August* 1968

Coming into Operation 11th September 1968

Whereas the Secretary of State has received from the Cotton Waste Reclamation Wages Council (Great Britain) the wages regulation proposals set out in the Schedule hereto;

Now, therefore, the Secretary of State in exercise of her powers under section 11 of the Wages Councils Act 1959(**a**), and of all other powers enabling her in that behalf, hereby makes the following Order:—

1. This Order may be cited as the Wages Regulation (Cotton Waste Reclamation) Order 1968.

2.—(1) In this Order the expression "the specified date" means the 11th September 1968, provided that where, as respects any worker who is paid wages at intervals not exceeding seven days, that date does not correspond with the beginning of the period for which the wages are paid, the expression "the specified date" means, as respects that worker, the beginning of the next such period following that date.

(2) The Interpretation Act 1889(**b**) shall apply to the interpretation of this Order as it applies to the interpretation of an Act of Parliament and as if this Order and the Order hereby revoked were Acts of Parliament.

3. The wages regulation proposals set out in the Schedule hereto shall have effect as from the specified date and as from that date the Wages Regulation (Cotton Waste Reclamation) Order 1965(**c**) shall cease to have effect.

Signed by order of the Secretary of State.
22nd August 1968.

C. J. Maston,
Assistant Under Secretary of State,
Department of Employment and Productivity.

(**a**) 1959 c. 69.   (**b**) 1889 c. 63.
(**c**) S.I. 1965/2135 (1965 III, p. 6273).

SCHEDULE

The following minimum remuneration shall be substituted for the statutory minimum remuneration fixed by the Wages Regulation (Cotton Waste Reclamation Order) 1965 (Order C.W. (75)).

STATUTORY MINIMUM REMUNERATION

PART I
GENERAL

1. The minimum remuneration payable to a worker to whom this Schedule applies for all work except work to which a minimum overtime rate applies under Part III of this Schedule is:—

(1) in the case of a time worker, the general minimum time rate payable to the worker under Part II of this Schedule;

(2) in the case of a worker employed on piece work, piece rates each of which would yield, in the circumstances of the case, to an ordinary worker at least the same amount of money as the general minimum time rate which would be payable to the worker under Part II of this Schedule if he were a time worker.

PART II
GENERAL MINIMUM TIME RATES
MALE WORKERS

2. The general minimum time rates payable to male workers are as follows:—

	Per hour	
	s.	d.
Aged 21 years or over	4	6
„ 20 and under 21 years	4	3
„ 19 „ „ 20 „	4	1¼
„ 18 „ „ 19 „	3	8½
„ 17 „ „ 18 „	3	6¼
„ 16 „ „ 17 „	3	1¾
„ under 16 years	2	11¼

FEMALE WORKERS

3. The general minimum time rates payable to female workers are as follows:—

	Per hour	
	s.	d.
(1) Aged 18 years or over	3	10
„ 17 and under 18 years	3	5½
„ 16 „ „ 17 „	3	1¼
„ under 16 years	2	11¼

PART III
OVERTIME AND WAITING TIME—ALL WORKERS
MINIMUM OVERTIME RATES

4.—(1) Subject to the provisions of this paragraph, minimum overtime rates are payable to any worker as follows:—

(a) on any day other than a Saturday, Sunday or customary holiday—

(i) for the first 2 hours worked in excess of 9 hours ... time-and-a-quarter

(ii) thereafter ... ... time-and-a-half

(b) on a Saturday— ...

(i) for the first 2 hours worked ... ... time-and-a-quarter

(ii) thereafter ... ... time-and-a-half

(c) on a Sunday or a customary holiday,

for all time worked ... ... double-time

(d) in any week (exclusive of any time in respect of which any minimum overtime rate is payable under the foregoing provisions of this sub-paragraph)—

    (i) for the first 2 hours worked in excess of 41 hours ... time-and-a-quarter

    (ii) thereafter   ...   . time-and-a-half

(2) Notwithstanding the provisions of (a)(i), (b)(i) and (d)(i) of sub-paragraph (1) of this paragraph, overtime at the rate of time-and-a-quarter shall not be paid for more than an aggregate of 2 hours worked in any week and any overtime so worked in excess of 2 hours in the aggregate shall be paid for at the overtime rate of time-and-a-half.

(3) In this paragraph the expression "customary holiday" means:—

  (a) (i) In England and Wales—
Christmas Day (or, if Christmas Day falls on a Sunday, such week day as may be appointed by national proclamation, or, if none is so appointed, the next following Tuesday), Boxing Day, Good Friday, Easter Monday, Whit Monday and August Bank Holiday.

    (ii) In Scotland—

New Year's Day (or, if New Year's Day falls on a Sunday, the following Monday);
the local Spring holiday;
the local Autumn holiday; and
    three other days (being days on which the worker normally works for the employer) in the course of a calendar year to be fixed by the employer and notified to the worker not less than three weeks before the holiday;

or (b) In the case of each of the said days (other than a day fixed by the employer in Scotland and notified to the worker as aforesaid) a day substituted by the employer therefor, being a day recognised by local custom as a day of holiday in substitution for the said day, or a day substituted by agreement between the employer and the worker or his representative.

(4) In this paragraph the expressions "time-and-a-quarter", "time-and-a-half" and "double time" mean respectively one and a quarter times, one and a half times, and twice the minimum remuneration payable to the worker for work to which a minimum overtime rate does not apply.

WAITING TIME

5.—(1) A worker is entitled to payment of the minimum remuneration specified in this Schedule for all time during which he is present on the premises of his employer, unless he is present thereon in any of the following circumstances:—

  (a) without the employer's consent, express or implied;

  (b) for some purpose unconnected with his work and other than that of waiting for work to be given to him to perform;

  (c) by reason only of the fact that he is resident thereon;

  (d) during normal meal times, in a room or place in which no work is being done, and he is not waiting for work to be given to him to perform.

(2) The minimum remuneration payable under sub-paragraph (1) of this paragraph to a piece worker when not engaged on piece work is that which would be payable if he were a time worker.

PART IV

APPLICABILITY OF STATUTORY MINIMUM REMUNERATION

6. This Schedule applies to workers in relation to whom the Cotton Waste Reclamation Wages Council (Great Britain) operates, that is to say, workers employed in Great Britain in the Cotton Waste Branch of the Waste Materials Reclamation trade as specified in the Schedule to the Trade Boards (Waste Materials Reclamation Trade, Great Britain) (Cotton Waste Branch) (Constitution

and Proceedings) Regulations 1929(a), which Schedule is as follows:—

"1. For the purposes of this Schedule the expression 'reclamation' means all operations (including the operations of willowing and garnetting) performed on any waste material or waste article.

The expression 'cotton waste establishment' means an establishment in which the operations specified in paragraphs 2(a) and 2(b) hereof and operations connected therewith constitute the principal business carried on.

The expression 'establishment' means any establishment or any branch or department of an establishment.

2. Subject to the provisions of this Schedule the Cotton Waste branch of the Waste Materials Reclamation trade consists of the following operations:—

(a) reclamation wherever performed of cotton waste;

(b) making engine cleaning waste;

(c) reclamation of any other waste material or article where performed in or in connection with a cotton waste establishment;

(d) making (whether from new or waste material) or repairing sacks or bags in a cotton waste establishment except where the bags are made or repaired:—

(i) otherwise than for use in the establishment; and

(ii) in an establishment wholly or mainly engaged in the making or repairing of sacks or bags;

and operations connected therewith.

3. Notwithstanding anything in this Schedule the following operations are not operations in the Cotton Waste branch of the Waste Materials Reclamation trade:—

(a) reclamation of any waste material or waste article in an establishment (other than a cotton waste establishment) in which that material or article is produced or is used as material for manufacture or as a container or wrapper for other articles manufactured in the establishment, and operations connected therewith;

(b) production of shoddy or mungo or wollen flock or any operations performed in an establishment in which the production of shoddy or mungo or wollen flock is the principal business carried on ;

(c) repairing or overhauling machinery or plant;

(d) collecting, transporting, packing, warehousing, or despatching when performed by workers in the direct employment of an employer who is not otherwise engaged in the Waste Materials Reclamation trade;

(e) cleaning or washing when performed in an establishment where the cleaning or washing is mainly of articles other than those specified in paragraph 2 hereof;

(f) cleaning of premises by charwomen;

(g) caretaking;

(h) clerical work;

(i) reclamation of cotton waste and making engine cleaning waste when performed in, or in connection with, a general waste materials establishment (as defined in the Schedule to the Trade Boards (Waste Materials Reclamation Trade, Great Britain) (General Waste Branch) (Constitution and Proceedings) Regulations 1933(b)), except where performed in or in connection with:—

(i) a branch or department of a general waste materials establishment which constitutes a cotton waste establishment, or

(ii) a branch or department of a cotton waste establishment which constitutes a general waste materials establishment."

(a) S.R. & O. 1929/3 (1929, p. 1378).

(b) S.R. & O. 1933/833 (Rev. XXIII, p. 497: 1933, p. 2056).

EXPLANATORY NOTE

(This Note is not part of the Order.)

This Order, which has effect from 11th September 1968, sets out the statutory minumum remuneration, payable in substitution for that fixed by the Wages Regulation (Cotton Waste Reclamation) Order 1965 (Order C.W. (75)) which Order is revoked.

New provisions are printed in italics.

STATUTORY INSTRUMENTS

1968 No. 1356

WAGES COUNCILS

The Wages Regulation (Cotton Waste Reclamation) (Holidays) Order 1968

Made	- - -	*22nd August* 1968
Coming into Operation		*11th September* 1968

Whereas the Secretary of State has received from the Cotton Waste Reclamation Wages Council (Great Britain) the wages regulation proposals set out in the Schedule hereto;

Now, therefore, the Secretary of State in exercise of her powers under section 11 of the Wages Councils Act 1959(a), and of all other powers enabling her in that behalf, hereby makes the following Order:—

1. This Order may be cited as the Wages Regulation (Cotton Waste Reclamation) (Holidays) Order 1968.

2.—(1) In this Order the expression "the specified date" means the 11th September 1968, provided that where, as respects any worker who is paid wages at intervals not exceeding seven days, that date does not correspond with the beginning of the period for which the wages are paid, the expression "the specified date" means, as respects that worker, the beginning of the next such period following that date.

(2) The Interpretation Act 1889(b) shall apply to the interpretation of this Order as it applies to the interpretation of an Act of Parliament and as if this Order and the Order hereby revoked were Acts of Parliament.

3. The wages regulation proposals set out in the Schedule hereto shall have effect as from the specified date and as from that date the Wages Regulation (Cotton Waste Reclamation) (Holidays) Order 1965(c) shall cease to have effect.

Signed by order of the Secretary of State.

22nd August 1968.

C. J. Maston,
Assistant Under Secretary of State,
Department of Employment and Productivity.

(a) 1959 c. 69.   (b) 1889 c. 63.
(c) S.I. 1965/2136 (1965 III, p. 6278).

SCHEDULE

The following provisions as to holidays and holiday remuneration shall be substituted for the provisions as to holidays and holiday remuneration set out in the Wages Regulation (Cotton Waste Reclamation) (Holidays) Order 1965 (hereinafter referred to as "Order C.W. (76)").

PART I

APPLICATION

1. This Schedule applies to every worker for whom statutory minimum remuneration has been fixed.

PART II

CUSTOMARY HOLIDAYS

2.—(1) An employer shall allow to every worker to whom this Schedule applies a holiday (hereinafter referred to as a "customary holiday") in each year on the days specified in the following sub-paragraph provided that the worker has been in his employment for a period of not less than 24 working days immediately preceding the customary holiday and (unless excused by the employer or absent by reason of the proved illness of, or accident to, the worker) has worked for the employer throughout the three working days on which work was available to him immediately preceding the customary holiday.

(2) The said customary holidays are:—

    (a) (i) In England and Wales—

        Christmas Day (or, if Christmas Day falls on a Sunday, such week day as may be appointed by national proclamation, or, if none is so appointed, the next following Tuesday), Boxing Day, Good Friday, Easter Monday, Whit Monday and August Bank Holiday;

      (ii) In Scotland—

        New Year's Day (or, if New Year's Day falls on a Sunday, the following Monday);

        the local Spring holiday;

        the local Autumn holiday; and

        three other days (being days on which the worker normally works for the employer) in the course of a calendar year to be fixed by the employer and notified to the worker not less than three weeks before the holiday;

    or (b) in the case of each of the said days (other than a day fixed by the employer in Scotland and notified to the worker as aforesaid) a day substituted by the employer therefor, being a day recognised by local custom as a day of holiday in substitution for the said day, or a day substituted therefor by mutual agreement between the employer and the worker or his representative.

(3) Notwithstanding the preceding provisions of this paragraph, an employer may (except where in the case of a woman or young person such a requirement would be unlawful) require a worker who is otherwise entitled to any customary holiday under the foregoing provisions of this Schedule to work thereon, and, in lieu of any holiday on which he so works, the employer shall allow to the worker a day's holiday (hereinafter referred to as a "holiday in lieu of a customary holiday") on a week day on which he would normally work for the employer, within the period of four weeks next ensuing.

(4) A worker who is required to work on a customary holiday shall be paid:—

    (a) for all time worked thereon, the statutory minimum remuneration then appropriate to the worker for work on a customary holiday; and

    (b) in respect of the holiday in lieu of the customary holiday, holiday remuneration in accordance with paragraph 6.

Part III

ANNUAL HOLIDAY

3.—(1) Subject to the provisions of paragraph 4, in addition to the holidays specified in Part II of this Schedule an employer shall, between the date on which this Order becomes effective and 30th September 1968, and between 1st May and 30th September in each succeeding year allow a holiday (hereinafter referred to as an "annual holiday") to every worker in his employment to whom this Schedule applies who has been employed by him during the 12 months immediately preceding the commencement of the holiday season for any of the periods of employment (calculated in accordance with the provisions of paragraph 10) set out in the table below and the duration of the annual holiday shall in the case of each such worker be related to his period of employment during that 12 months as follows:—

Workers with a normal working week of six days		Workers with a normal working week of five days or less	
Period of employment	Duration of annual holiday	Period of employment	Duration of annual holiday
At least 48 weeks	15 days	At least 48 weeks	13 days
" " 45 "	14 "	" " 45 "	12 "
" " 42 "	13 "	" " 42 "	11 "
" " 39 "	12 "	" " 39 "	10 "
" " 36 "	11 "	" " 36 "	9 "
" " 33 "	10 "	" " 32 "	8 "
" " 30 "	9 "	" " 28 "	7 "
" " 27 "	8 "	" " 24 "	6 "
" " 24 "	7 "	" " 20 "	5 "
" " 21 "	6 "	" " 16 "	4 "
" " 18 "	5 "	" " 12 "	3 "
" " 15 "	4 "	" " 8 "	2 "
" " 12 "	3 "	" " 4 "	1 day
" " 8 "	2 "		
" " 4 "	1 day		

(2) Notwithstanding the provisions of the foregoing sub-paragraph the number of days of annual holiday which an employer is required to allow to a worker in any holiday season shall not exceed *in the aggregate in the case of a worker with a normal working week of four days or more twice the number of days constituting the worker's normal working week, plus three days; and in the case of a worker with a normal working week of less than four days three times the number of days constituting the worker's normal working week.*

(3) The duration of the worker's annual holiday during the holiday season ending on 30th September 1968, shall be reduced by any days of annual holiday duly allowed to him by the employer under the provisions of Order C.W. (76) between 1st May 1968 and the date on which the provisions of this Schedule become effective.

(4) In this Schedule the expression "holiday season" means in relation to an annual holiday during the year 1968 the period commencing on 1st May 1968 and ending on 30th September 1968 and in relation to each subsequent year the period commencing on 1st May and ending on 30th September in that year.

4.—(1) Subject to the provisions of this paragraph, an annual holiday under this Schedule shall be allowed on consecutive working days, being days upon which the worker is normally called upon to work for the employer, and days of holiday shall be treated as consecutive notwithstanding that a Sunday, a customary holiday on which the worker is not reqired to work or a holiday in lieu of a customary holiday intervenes:

Provided that:—

(a) where the duration of an annual holiday which an employer is required to allow to a worker exceeds the number of days constituting the worker's normal working week *but does not exceed the period constituting twice his normal working week*, the said holiday may, by agreement between the employer and the worker or his representative, be allowed in two separate periods of such consecutive working days one of which shall be not less than the period of the worker's normal working week;

(b) *where the number of days of annual holiday for which a worker has qualified exceeds twice the number of days constituting his normal working week the holiday may be allowed as follows:—*

(i) *as to two periods of consecutive working days, each such period not being less than the period constituting the worker's normal working week, during the holiday season; and*

(ii) *as to any additional days, on working days which need not be consecutive, to be fixed by agreement between the employer and the worker or his representative, either during the holiday season or on any working day before the beginning of the next following holiday season;*

(c) one day of an annual holiday may be allowed on a non-consecutive working day (other than the worker's weekly short day) falling within the holiday season where the said annual holiday or, as the case may be, such separate period is allowed immediately after a customary holiday or so that such a holiday intervenes.

(2) Subject to the provisions of sub-paragraph (1) of this paragraph, any day of annual holiday under this Schedule may be allowed on a day on which the worker is entitled to a day of holiday or to a half holiday under any enactment other than the Wages Councils Act 1959.

5. An employer shall give to a worker reasonable notice of the commencing date or dates and duration of the period or periods of his annual holiday. Such notice may be given individually to the worker or by the posting of a notice in the place where the worker is employed.

PART IV

HOLIDAY REMUNERATION

A.—CUSTOMARY HOLIDAYS AND HOLIDAYS IN LIEU OF CUSTOMARY HOLIDAYS

6.—(1) Subject to the provisions of this paragraph, for each day of holiday to which a worker is entitled under Part II of this Schedule he shall be paid by the employer holiday remuneration equal to the amount, calculated at the appropriate rate of statutory minimum remuneration, to which he would have been entitled as a time worker if the day had not been a day of holiday and he had been employed on work for which statutory minimum remuneration is payable for the time usually worked by him on that day of the week:

Provided, however, that payment of the said holiday remuneration is subject to the condition that the worker (unless excused by the employer or absent by reason of the proved illness of, or accident to, the worker) works for the employer throughout the three working days on which work is available to him immediately following the customary holiday.

(2) The holiday remuneration in respect of any customary holiday shall be paid by the employer to the worker on the pay day on which the wages for the week including the last of the three working days aforesaid are paid.

(3) The holiday remuneration for any holiday in lieu of a customary holiday shall be paid on the pay day on which the wages are paid for the week including that holiday in lieu of a customary holiday: Provided that the said payment shall be made immediately upon the termination of the worker's employment in the case where he ceases to be employed before being allowed a holiday in lieu of a customary holiday to which he is entitled and in that case the proviso contained in sub-paragraph (1) of this paragraph shall not apply.

B.—ANNUAL HOLIDAY

7.—(1) Subject to the provisions of paragraph 8, a worker qualified to be allowed an annual holiday under this Schedule shall be paid by his employer in respect thereof, on the last pay day preceding such annual holiday, one day's holiday pay (as defined in paragraph 11) in respect of each day thereof.

(2) Where under the provisions of paragraph 4 an annual holiday is allowed in more than one period, the holiday remuneration shall be apportioned accordingly.

8. Where any accrued holiday remuneration has been paid by the employer to the worker in accordance with paragraph 9 of this Schedule or in accordance with the provisions of Order C.W. (76), in respect of employment during any of the periods referred to in that paragraph or that Order respectively, the amount of holiday remuneration payable by the employer in respect of any annual holiday for which the worker has qualified by reason of employment during the said period shall be reduced by the amount of the said accrued holiday remuneration unless that remuneration has been deducted from a previous payment of holiday remuneration made under the provisions of this Schedule or of Order C.W. (76).

ACCRUED HOLIDAY REMUNERATION PAYABLE ON TERMINATION OF EMPLOYMENT

9. Where a worker ceases to be employed by an employer after the provisions of this Schedule become effective the employer shall, immediately on the termination of the employment, pay to the worker as accrued holiday remuneration:—

(1) in respect of employment in the 12 months up to the preceding 30th April, a sum equal to the holiday remuneration for any days of annual holiday for which he has qualified, except days of annual holiday which he has been allowed or has become entitled to be allowed before leaving the employment; and

(2) in respect of any employment since the preceding 30th April, a sum equal to the holiday remuneration which would have been payable to him if he could have been allowed an annual holiday in respect of that employment at the time of leaving it:

Provided that where a worker is employed under a contract of service under which not less than one week's notice on either side is required to terminate the employment and the worker without the consent of his employer terminates his employment—

(a) without having given not less than one week's notice, or

(b) before one week has expired from the beginning of such notice,

the amount of accrued holiday remuneration payable to the worker shall be the amount payable under the foregoing provisions of this paragraph, less an amount equal to the holiday remuneration which would be payable to the worker for one day of annual holiday multiplied, in the case of (a) by the number of days constituting the worker's normal working week or, in the case of (b), by the number of days which at the termination of the employment would complete a normal working week commencing at the beginning of the notice.

PART V

GENERAL

10. For the purposes of calculating any period of employment qualifying a worker for an annual holiday or for any accrued holiday remuneration under this Schedule, the worker shall be treated:—

(1) as if he were employed for a week in respect of any week in which—

(a) he has worked for the employer for not less than 36 hours and has performed some work for which statutory minimum remuneration is payable; or (*b*) he has been absent throughout the week in the circumstances specified below, but not exceeding in the aggregate in the period of 12 months immediately preceding the commencement of the holiday season the following number of weeks—

where the absence is due to the proved illness of, or accident to, the worker ... ... 6 weeks

where the absence is due to suspension from work by reason of shortage of work ... ... 4 weeks

and

(2) as if he were employed on any day of holiday allowed under the provisions of this Schedule or of Order C.W. (76), and for the purposes of the provisions of sub-paragraph (1) of this paragraph, a worker who is absent on such a holiday shall be treated as having worked thereon the number of hours ordinarily worked by him for the employer on that day of the week on work for which statutory minimum remuneration is payable.

11. In this Schedule, unless the context otherwise requires, the following expressions have the meanings hereby respectively assigned to them, that is to say:—

"appropriate rate of statutory minimum remuneration" means:—

(1) in the case of a time worker, the rate of statutory minimum remuneration applicable to the worker, and

(2) in the case of a piece worker, the rate of statutory minimum remuneration which would be applicable to the worker if he were a time worker.

"normal working week" means the number of days on which it has been usual for the worker to work in a week in the employment of the employer during the 12 months immediately preceding the commencement of the holiday season or, where under paragraph 9 accrued holiday remuneration is payable on the termination of the employment, during the 12 months immediately preceding the date of the termination of the employment: Provided that—

(*a*) part of a day shall count as a day;

(*b*) no account shall be taken of any week in which the worker did not perform any work for which statutory minimum remuneration has been fixed.

"one day's holiday pay" means the appropriate proportion of the remuneration which the worker would be entitled to receive from his employer at the date of the annual holiday (or where the holiday is allowed in more than one period at the date of the first period) or at the termination of the employment, as the case may require, for one week's work if working his normal working week and the number of daily hours normally worked by him (exclusive of overtime) and if paid at the appropriate rate of statutory minimum remuneration for work for which statutory minimum remuneration is payable and at the same rate for any work for the same employer to which such remuneration does not apply, and in this definition "appropriate proportion" means—

Where the worker's normal working week is six days ... one-sixth

Where the worker's normal working week is five days ... one-fifth

Where the worker's normal working week is four days or less ... ... one-quarter

"statutory minimum remuneration" means minimum remuneration (other than holiday remuneration) fixed by a wages regulation order.

"wages regulation order" means a wages regulation order made by the Secretary of State to give effect to proposals submitted to her by the Wages Council.

"week" in paragraphs 3, 6 and 10 means "pay week".

12. The provisions of this Schedule are without prejudice to any agreement for the allowance of any further holidays with pay or for the payment of additional holiday remuneration.

EXPLANATORY NOTE

(This Note is not part of the Order.)

This Order, which has effect from the 11th September 1968, sets out the holidays which an employer is required to allow to workers and the remuneration payable for those holidays, in substitution for the holidays and holiday remuneration fixed by the Wages Regulation (Cotton Waste Reclamation) (Holidays) Order 1965 (Order C.W. (76)) which Order is revoked.

New provisions are printed in italics.

STATUTORY INSTRUMENTS

1968 No. 1357

WAGES COUNCILS

The Wages Regulation (Sack and Bag) Order 1968

Made - - -	*22nd August* 1968
Coming into Operation	16th September 1968

Whereas the Secretary of State has received from the Sack and Bag Wages Council (Great Britain) the wages regulation proposals set out in the Schedule hereto ;

Now, therefore, the Secretary of State in exercise of her powers under section 11 of the Wages Councils Act 1959(a), and of all other powers enabling her in that behalf, hereby makes the following Order : —

1. This Order may be cited as the Wages Regulation (Sack and Bag) Order 1968.

2.—(1) In this Order the expression "the specified date" means the 16th September 1968, provided that where, as respects any worker who is paid wages at intervals not exceeding seven days, that date does not correspond with the beginning of the period for which the wages are paid, the expression "the specified date" means, as respects that worker, the beginning of the next such period following that date.

(2) The Interpretation Act 1889(b) shall apply to the interpretation of this Order as it applies to the interpretation of an Act of Parliament and as if this Order and the Order hereby revoked were Acts of Parliament.

3. The wages regulation proposals set out in the Schedule hereto shall have effect as from the specified date and as from that date the Wages Regulation (Sack and Bag) Order 1967(c) shall cease to have effect.

Signed by Order of the Secretary of State.
22nd August 1968.

C. J. Maston,
Assistant Under Secretary of State,
Department of Employment and Productivity.

(a) 1959 c. 69.   (b) 1889 c. 63.
(c) S.I. 1967/639 (1967 I, p. 1917).

SCHEDULE

The following minimum remuneration shall be substituted for the statutory minimum remuneration fixed by the Wages Regulation (Sack and Bag) Order 1967 (Order S.B. (63)).

STATUTORY MINIMUM REMUNERATION

PART I

GENERAL

1. The minimum remuneration payable to a worker to whom this Schedule applies for all work except work to which a minimum overtime rate applies under Part IV of this Schedule is:—

   (1) in the case of a time worker, the general minimum time rate payable to the worker under Part II or Part III of this Schedule;

   (2) in the case of a male worker employed on piece work, piece rates each of which would yield, in the circumstances of the case, to an ordinary worker at least the same amount of money as the general minimum time rate which would be payable under Part II of this Schedule if he were a time worker;

   (3) in the case of a female worker employed on piece work, piece rates each of which would yield, in the circumstances of the case, to an ordinary worker at least the same amount of money as the piece work basis time rate applicable to the worker under Part III of this Schedule.

PART II

MALE WORKERS

GENERAL MINIMUM TIME RATES

2. The general minimum time rates payable to male workers are as follows:—

	Per hour
	s. d.

(1) Workers aged 21 years or over and employed during the whole or part of their time:—

   (*a*) as superintendents of packing presses (hand or machine) or as press foremen (hand or machine), or

   (*b*) in setting up or minding, or in setting up and minding, branding or printing machines or both such machines ...   4   9¾

Provided that the general minimum time rate payable during his first six months' employment in the trade to a worker who enters, or who has entered, the trade for the first time at or over the age of 21 years shall be   4   9

(2) All other workers aged

21 years or over	...	...	...	...	...	...	...	4	7
20 and under 21 years	...	...	...	...	...	...	4	1¾
19 „ „ 20 „ ...	...	...	...	...	...	...	3	9¼
18 „ „ 19 „ ...	...	...	...	...	...	...	3	5
17 „ „ 18 „ ...	...	...	...	...	...	...	2	9¾
16 „ „ 17 „ ...	...	...	...	...	...	...	2	5¾
under 16 years	...	...	...	...	...	...	...	2	3½

Provided that the general minimum time rate payable during his first two months' employment in the trade to a worker who enters, or who has entered, the trade for the first time at or over the age of 18 years shall be ½d. per hour less than the minimum rate otherwise payable under this sub-paragraph.

PART III

FEMALE WORKERS

GENERAL MINIMUM TIME RATES

3. The general minimum time rates payable to female workers are as follows:—

	Per hour
	s. d.

(1) Workers aged 18 years or over and employed as examiners of mended work, allocators, forewomen, hand sewers of heavy twill sacks and bags of 10 porter and upwards, selectors or graders of mixed loads or setters-up on branding machines ... **3 6¼**

Provided that the general minimum time rate payable during her first six months' employment in the trade to a worker who enters, or who has entered, the trade for the first time at or over the age of 18 years shall be **3 5¼**

(2) All other workers aged
18 years or over **3 5**
17 and under 18 years **2 9¼**
16 „ „ 17 „ **2 5¼**
under 16 years **2 3¼**

Provided that the general minimum time rate payable during her first two months' employment in the trade to a worker who enters, or who has entered, the trade for the first time at or over the age of 16 years shall be ½d. per hour less than the minimum rate otherwise payable under this sub-paragraph.

PIECE WORK BASIS TIME RATES

4. The piece work basis time rates applicable to female workers of any age employed on piece work are as follows:—

	Per hour
	s. d.

(1) Workers employed as examiners of mended work, allocators, forewomen, hand sewers of heavy twill sacks and bags of 10 porter and upwards, selectors or graders of mixed loads or setters-up on branding machines **3 8½**

(2) All other workers **3 7**

PART IV

OVERTIME AND WAITING TIME

MINIMUM OVERTIME RATES

5. Minimum overtime rates are payable to any worker, not being a male worker employed on piece work, as follows:—

(1) on any day other than a Saturday, Sunday or customary holiday—

(a) for the first 2 hours worked in excess of 8½ hours ... ... time-and-a-quarter
(b) thereafter ... ... time-and-a-half

Provided that, where the employer normally requires the worker's attendance on five days only in the week, the foregoing minimum overtime rates of time-and-a-quarter and time-and-a-half shall be payable after 9 and 11 hours' work respectively.

2x

(2) on a Saturday, not being a customary holiday—

    (*a*) where the worker is normally required to attend on six days in the week—

        for the first 2 hours worked in excess of 4 hours ... ... time-and-a-quarter

        thereafter ... ... time-and-a-half

    (*b*) where the worker is normally required to attend on five days only in the week—

        for the first 2 hours worked ... ... time-and-a-quarter

        thereafter ... ... time-and-a-half

(3) on a Sunday or a customary holiday—

    for all time worked ... ... double time

(4) in any week exclusive of any time for which a minimum overtime rate is payable under the foregoing provisions of this paragraph—

    for all time worked in excess of *41* hours ... time-and-a-quarter.

6. In this Part of this Schedule—

(1) the expressions "time-and-a-quarter", "time-and-a-half" and "double time" mean respectively—

    (*a*) in the case of a time worker, one and a quarter times, one and a half times and twice the general minimum time rate otherwise payable to the worker;

    (*b*) in the case of a female worker employed on piece work—

        (i) a time rate equal respectively to one-quarter, one-half and the whole of the piece work basis time rate otherwise applicable to the worker under Part III of this Schedule and, in addition thereto—

        (ii) the piece rates otherwise applicable to the worker under paragraph 1 (3).

(2) the expression "customary holiday" means

    (*a*) (i) in England and Wales—

Christmas Day (or, if Christmas Day falls on a Sunday, such weekday as may be appointed by national proclamation, or, if none is so appointed, the next following Tuesday), Boxing Day, Good Friday, Easter Monday, Whit Monday (or where another day is substituted therefor by national proclamation, that day), and August Bank Holiday;

        (ii) in Scotland—

New Year's Day and the following day:

    Provided that if New Year's Day falls on a Sunday the holidays shall be the following Monday and Tuesday, and if New Year's Day falls on a Saturday the holidays shall be New Year's Day and the following Monday;

the local Spring holiday;

the local Autumn holiday; and

two other days (being days on which the worker would normally work) in the course of a calendar year, to be fixed by the employer and notified to the worker not less than three weeks before the holiday;

or (*b*) in the case of each of the said days (other than a day fixed by the employer in Scotland and notified to the worker as aforesaid) such weekday as may be substituted therefor by the employer being either—

    (i) a day which is by local custom recognised as a day of holiday, or

    (ii) a day (being a day on which the worker would normally work) which falls within three weeks of the day for which it is substituted and is mutually agreed between the employer and the worker.

WAITING TIME

7.—(1) A worker is entitled to payment of the minimum remuneration specified in this Schedule for all time during which he is present on the premises of his employer unless he is present thereon in any of the following circumstances:—

(a) without the employer's consent, express or implied;

(b) for some purpose unconnected with his work and other than that of waiting for work to be given to him to perform;

(c) by reason only of the fact that he is resident thereon;

(d) during normal meal times in a room or place in which no work is being done and he is not waiting for work to be given to him to perform.

(2) The minimum remuneration payable under sub-paragraph (1) of this paragraph to a piece worker when not engaged on piece work is that which would be payable if he were a time worker.

Part V

APPLICATION

8. This Schedule applies to workers in relation to whom the Sack and Bag Wages Council (Great Britain) operates, namely, workers employed in Great Britain in the trade specified in the Schedule to the Trade Boards (Sack and Bag Trade, Great Britain) (Constitution and Proceedings) Regulations 1933(a), that is to say:—

The making from woven fabrics of corn sacks, flour sacks, coal sacks, sugar sacks, cement bags, sand bags, nail bags, potato bags, seed bags and similar sacks or bags, or the repairing thereof:

including:—

(a) the following and similar operations (whether performed by hand or machine) known in the trade as :—

(i) Folding (or hooking), cutting, machining, turning;

(ii) Brushing, selecting, mending;

(iii) Branding, tarring, bundling;

(b) the warehousing of, the packing of, and similar operations in regard to sacks or bags of the kind mentioned above when carried on in association with or in conjunction with the making or repairing thereof;

(c) the warehousing of, the packing of, and similar operations in regard to any other articles when carried on in or in association with or in conjunction with any business, establishment, branch or department mainly engaged in any of the operations mentioned in paragraph (b) above;

but excluding:—

(i) any of the operations mentioned above when carried on in association with or in conjunction with the weaving of jute, flax or hemp, or the dyeing, bleaching or finishing of jute, flax or hemp yarn or cloth;

(ii) any of the operations mentioned above when carried on in or in association with or in conjunction with any business, establishment, branch or department mainly engaged in a business in which the sacks or bags are used as containers for other articles the production or sale of which forms part of the business;

(a) S.R. & O. 1933/1157 (1933, p. 2052).

(iii) the making of rope-bound coal or coke sacks when carried on in association with or in conjunction with any business, establishment, branch or department engaged in the making of made-up textile articles other than sacks or bags, whether rope-bound or not, of the kind mentioned;

(iv) any of the operations mentioned in paragraph (*b*) above when carried on in or in association with or in conjunction with any business, establishment, branch or department mainly engaged in the warehousing of, the packing of, and similar operations in regard to made-up textile articles other than sacks or bags, whether rope-bound or not, of the kind mentioned;

(v) operations included in the Trade Boards (Waste Materials Reclamation) Order 1920(a).

EXPLANATORY NOTE

(This Note is not part of the Order.)

This Order, which has effect from 16th September 1968, sets out the statutory minimum remuneration payable in substitution for that fixed by the Wages Regulation (Sack and Bag) Order 1967 (Order S.B. (63)), which Order is revoked.

New provisions are printed in italics.

(a) S.R. & O. 1920/305 (1920 II, p. 794).

STATUTORY INSTRUMENTS

1968 No. 1358

WAGES COUNCILS

The Wages Regulation (Sack and Bag) (Holidays) Order 1968

Made - - -		*22nd August* 1968
Coming into Operation		16th September 1968

Whereas the Secretary of State has received from the Sack and Bag Wages Council (Great Britain) (hereinafter referred to as "the Wages Council") the wages regulation proposals set out in the Schedule hereto ;

Now, therefore, the Secretary of State in exercise of her powers under section 11 of the Wages Councils Act 1959(**a**), and of all other powers enabling her in that behalf, hereby makes the following Order : —

1. This Order may be cited as the Wages Regulation (Sack and Bag) (Holidays) Order 1968.

2.—(1) In this Order the expression "the specified date" means the 16th September 1968, provided that where, as respects any worker who is paid wages at intervals not exceeding seven days, that date does not correspond with the beginning of the period for which the wages are paid, the expression "the specified date" means, as respects that worker, the beginning of the next such period following that date.

(2) The Interpretation Act 1889(**b**), shall apply to the interpretation of this Order as it applies to the interpretation of an Act of Parliament and as if this Order and the Order hereby revoked were Acts of Parliament.

3. The wages regulation proposals set out in the Schedule hereto shall have effect as from the specified date and as from that date the Wages Regulation (Sack and Bag) (Holidays) Order 1963(**c**), shall cease to have effect.

Signed by Order of the Secretary of State.

22nd August 1968.

C. J. Maston,
Assistant Under Secretary of State,
Department of Employment and Productivity.

SCHEDULE

The following provisions as to holidays and holiday remuneration shall be substituted for the provisions as to holidays and holiday remuneration set out in the Wages Regulation (Sack and Bag) (Holidays) Order 1963 (hereinafter referred to as "Order S.B. (57)") as amended by Schedule 2 to the Wages Regulation (Sack and Bag) Order 1967(**d**) (Order S.B. (63)).

(**a**) 1959 c. 69. (**b**) 1889 c. 63.
(**c**) S.I. 1963/2040 (1963 III, p. 4287). (**d**) S.I. 1967/639 (1967 I, p. 1917).

PART I

APPLICATION

1.—(1) This Schedule applies to every worker (other than an outworker) for whom statutory minimum remuneration has been fixed.

(2) For the purposes of this Schedule an outworker is a worker who works in his own home or in some other place not under the control or management of the employer.

PART II

CUSTOMARY HOLIDAYS

2.—(1) An employer shall allow to every worker to whom this Schedule applies a holiday (hereinafter referred to as a "customary holiday") in each year on the days specified in the following sub-paragraph, provided that the worker was in his employment and (unless excused by the employer or absent by reason of the proved illness of, or accident to, the worker) has worked for the employer throughout the last working day on which work was available to him prior to the customary holiday.

(2) The said customary holidays are:—

(a) (i) In England and Wales—

Christmas Day (or, if Christmas Day falls on a Sunday, such weekday as may be appointed by national proclamation, or, if none is so appointed, the next following Tuesday), Boxing Day, Good Friday, Easter Monday, Whit Monday (or where another day is substituted therefor by national proclamation, that day), and August Bank Holiday;

(ii) In Scotland—
New Year's Day and the following day:
Provided that if New Year's Day falls on a Sunday the holidays shall be the following Monday and Tuesday, and if New Year's Day falls on a Saturday the holidays shall be New Year's Day and the following Monday;
the local Spring holiday;
the local Autumn holiday; and
two other days (being days on which the worker would normally work) in the course of a calendar year to be fixed by the employer and notified to the worker not less than three weeks before the holiday;

or (b) in the case of each of the said days (other than a day fixed by the employer in Scotland and notified to the worker as aforesaid) such weekday as may be substituted therefor by the employer being either—

(i) a day which is by local custom recognised as a day of holiday, or

(ii) a day (being a day on which the worker would normally work) which falls within three weeks of the day for which it is substituted and is mutually agreed between the employer and the worker.

(3) Notwithstanding the preceding provisions of this paragraph, where by reason of the circumstances in which the work is carried on in an establishment the allowing of the customary holiday is rendered impracticable, a worker may be required to work on a customary holiday (except where in the case of a woman or young person such a requirement would be unlawful) and, if so required, shall be paid for all time worked thereon the statutory minimum remuneration appropriate to him for work on a customary holiday.

PART III

ANNUAL HOLIDAY

3.—(1) Subject to the provisions of paragraph 4, in addition to the holidays specified in Part II of this Schedule an employer shall:—

(a) between the date on which this Schedule becomes effective and 30th September 1968, allow a holiday (hereinafter referred to as an "annual holiday") to every worker in his employment to whom this Schedule applies who has been employed by him during the 12 months immediately preceding the commencement of the holiday season for any of the periods of employment (calculated in accordance with the provisions of paragraph 10) set out in the table below and the duration of the annual holiday shall, in the case of each such worker, be related to his period of employment during that 12 months as follows:—

Workers with a normal working week of 6 days		Workers with a normal working week of 5 days or less	
Period of employment	Duration of annual holiday	Period of employment	Duration of annual holiday
At least 48 weeks	12 days	At least 48 weeks	10 days
„ „ 44 „	11 „	„ „ 43 „	9 „
„ „ 40 „	10 „	„ „ 38 „	8 „
„ „ 36 „	9 „	„ „ 33 „	7 „
„ „ 32 „	8 „	„ „ 28 „	6 „
„ „ 28 „	7 „	„ „ 24 „	5 „
„ „ 24 „	6 „	„ „ 19 „	4 „
„ „ 20 „	5 „	„ „ 14 „	3 „
„ „ 16 „	4 „	„ „ 9 „	2 „
„ „ 12 „	3 „		
„ „ 8 „	2 „		

(b) between 6th April 1969 and 30th September 1969, and in each succeeding year between 6th April and 30th September allow a holiday (hereinafter referred to as an "annual holiday") to every worker in his employment to whom this Schedule applies who has been employed by him during the 12 months immediately preceding the commencement of the holiday season for any of the periods of employment (calculated in accordance with the provisions of paragraph 10) set out in the table below and the duration of the annual holiday shall, in the case of each such worker, be related to his period of employment during that 12 months as follows:—

Workers with a normal working week of 6 days		Workers with a normal working week of 5 days or less	
Period of employment	Duration of annual holiday	Period of employment	Duration of annual holiday
At least 48 weeks	13 days	At least 48 weeks	11 days
„ „ 44 „	12 „	„ „ 44 „	10 „
„ „ 40 „	11 „	„ „ 40 „	9 „
„ „ 36 „	10 „	„ „ 35 „	8 „
„ „ 33 „	9 „	„ „ 31 „	7 „
„ „ 29 „	8 „	„ „ 27 „	6 „
„ „ 26 „	7 „	„ „ 22 „	5 „
„ „ 22 „	6 „	„ „ 18 „	4 „
„ „ 19 „	5 „	„ „ 14 „	3 „
„ „ 15 „	4 „	„ „ 9 „	2 „
„ „ 12 „	3 „		
„ „ 8 „	2 „		

(2) Notwithstanding the provisions of sub-paragraph (1) of this paragraph:—

(a) (i) the number of days of annual holiday which an employer is required to allow to a worker in the holiday season 6th April 1968 to 30th September 1968 shall not exceed in the aggregate twice the number of days constituting the worker's normal working week;

(ii) the number of days of annual holiday which an employer is required to allow to a worker in the holiday season 6th April 1969 to 30th September 1969 and in each succeeding year between 6th April and 30th September shall not exceed in the aggregate twice the number of days constituting the worker's normal working week, *plus one day;*

(b) the duration of the worker's annual holiday in the holiday season ending on 30th September 1968 shall be reduced by any days of annual holiday allowed to him by the employer under the provisions of Order S.B. (57) between 6th April 1968 and the date on which the provisions of this Schedule become effective.

(3) In this Schedule the expression "holiday season" means in relation to the year 1968 the period commencing on 6th April 1968 and ending on 30th September 1968, and, in each succeeding year, the period commencing on 6th April and ending on 30th September of the same year.

4.—(1) Subject to the provisions of this paragraph, an annual holiday shall be allowed on consecutive working days, being days on which the worker is normally called upon to work for the employer.

(2) Where the number of days of annual holiday for which a worker has qualified exceeds the number of days constituting his normal working week, the holiday may be allowed in two periods of consecutive working days; so, however, that when a holiday is so allowed, one of the periods shall consist of a number of such days not less than the number of days constituting the worker's normal working week.

(3) For the purposes of this paragraph, days of annual holiday shall be treated as consecutive notwithstanding that a day of holiday allowed to a worker under Part II of this Schedule or a day upon which he does not normally work for the employer intervenes.

(4) Where a day of holiday allowed to a worker under Part II of this Schedule immediately precedes a period of annual holiday or occurs during such a period and the total number of days of annual holiday required to be allowed in the period under the foregoing provisions of this paragraph, together with any such day of holiday allowed under Part II of this Schedule, exceeds the number of days constituting the worker's normal working week then, notwithstanding the foregoing provisions of this paragraph, the duration of that period of annual holiday may be reduced by one day and in such a case one day of annual holiday may be allowed on any working day (not being the worker's weekly short day) in the holiday season.

(5) Subject to the provisions of sub-paragraph (1) of this paragraph, any day of annual holiday under this Schedule may be allowed on a day on which the worker is entitled to a day of holiday or to a half-holiday under any enactment other than the Wages Councils Act 1959.

5. An employer shall give to a worker reasonable notice of the commencing date or dates and duration of the period or periods of his annual holiday. Such notice shall be given at least 21 days before the first day of the annual holiday or before the first day of each period of annual holiday, as the case may be, and may be given individually to the worker or by the posting of a notice in the place where the worker is employed.

PART IV

HOLIDAY REMUNERATION

A.—CUSTOMARY HOLIDAYS

6.—(1) Subject to the provisions of this paragraph, for each day of holiday to which a worker is entitled under Part II of this Schedule he shall be paid by the employer as holiday remuneration whichever of the following sums is the greater, that is to say either:—

> (a) a sum equal to the worker's average hourly earnings for the hours worked by him for the employer in the week immediately preceding that in which the holiday occurs; or

> (b) a sum equal to the hourly general minimum time rate (being statutory minimum remuneration) which is applicable to the worker (or which would be applicable to him if he were a time worker);

multiplied in either case by the number of hours (exclusive of overtime) normally worked by him for the employer on that day of the week.

(2) Payment of the said holiday remuneration is subject to the condition that the worker presents himself for employment at the usual starting hour on the first working day following the holiday and works throughout that day or, if he fails to do so, failure is by reason of the proved illness of, or accident to, the worker or with the consent of the employer.

(3) The holiday remuneration in respect of any customary holiday shall be paid by the employer to the worker on the pay day on which the wages for the week including the first working day following the customary holiday are paid.

B.—ANNUAL HOLIDAY

7.—(1) Subject to the provisions of this paragraph and of paragraph 8, a worker qualified to be allowed an annual holiday under this Schedule shall be paid as holiday remuneration by his employer in respect thereof, on the last pay day preceding such annual holiday:—

> (a) in respect of the annual holiday to be allowed during the holiday season commencing on 6th April 1968 an amount equal to 4 per cent. of the total remuneration paid by the employer to the worker during the 12 months immediately preceding the commencement of the holiday season;

> (b) in respect of the annual holiday to be allowed during the holiday season commencing on 6th April 1969 and during the holiday season in each succeeding year an amount equal to *4.4 per cent.* of the total remuneration paid by the employer to the worker during the 12 months immediately preceding the commencement of the holiday season.

(2) Where under the provisions of paragraph 4 an annual holiday is allowed in more than one period, the holiday remuneration shall be apportioned accordingly.

8. Where any accrued holiday remuneration has been paid by the employer to the worker (in accordance with paragraph 9 of this Schedule or with Order S.B. (57), as amended) in respect of employment during any of the periods referred to in that paragraph or that Order, the amount of holiday remuneration payable by the employer in respect of any annual holiday for which the worker has qualified by reason of employment during the said period shall be reduced by the amount of the said accrued holiday remuneration unless that remuneration has been deducted from a previous payment of holiday remuneration made under the provisions of this Schedule or of Order S.B. (57), as amended.

ACCRUED HOLIDAY REMUNERATION PAYABLE ON TERMINATION OF
EMPLOYMENT

9. Where a worker ceases to be employed by an employer after the provisions of this
Schedule become effective, the employer shall, immediately on the termination
of the employment (hereinafter called "the termination date"), pay to the worker
as accrued holiday remuneration:—

(1) in respect of employment in the 12 months up to and including 5th April immediately preceding the termination date, a sum equal to the holiday remuneration
for any days of annual holiday for which he has qualified except days of annual
holiday which he has been allowed or has become entitled to be allowed before
leaving the employment; and

(2) in respect of any employment since 5th April immediately preceding the termination date, an amount equal to *4.4 per cent.* of the total remuneration paid by
the employer to the worker since that date:

Provided that no worker shall be entitled to the payment by his employer of accrued
holiday remuneration if he is dismissed on the grounds of industrial misconduct and
is so informed by the employer at the time of dismissal.

PART V

GENERAL

10. For the purpose of calculating any period of employment qualifying a worker
for an annual holiday under this Schedule, the worker shall be treated—

(1) as if he were employed for a week in respect of any week in which—

(*a*) in the case of a worker other than a part-time worker, he has worked
for the employer for not less than 24 hours and has performed some
work for which statutory minimum remuneration is payable;

(*b*) in the case of a part-time worker, he has worked for the employer
and has performed some work for which statutory minimum remuneration
is payable;

(*c*) (i) in the case of a worker other than a part-time worker, he has worked
for the employer for less than 24 hours by reason of the proved
illness of, or accident to, the worker or, in the case of any worker,
for a like reason he has been absent throughout the week:
Provided that the number of weeks which may be treated
as weeks of employment for such reason shall not exceed
four in the aggregate in any such period; or

(ii) in the case of any worker, he has been suspended throughout
the week owing to shortage of work:
Provided that the number of weeks which may be treated
as weeks of employment for such reason shall not exceed
four in the aggregate in any such period:

(2) as if he were employed on any day of holiday allowed under the provisions
of this Schedule, or of Order S.B. (57), as amended, and for the purposes of
the provisions of sub-paragraph (1) of this paragraph, a worker who is absent
on any such holiday shall be treated as having worked thereon for the employer on work for which statutory minimum remuneration is payable for the
number of hours normally worked by him on that day of the week.

DEFINITIONS

11. In this Schedule, unless the context otherwise requires, the following expressions
have the meanings hereby respectively assigned to them, that is to say:—

"AVERAGE HOURLY EARNINGS" means the total remuneration
paid by the employer to the worker in the week preceding the holiday divided
by the number of hours (including overtime) worked for the employer in that
week:

Provided that where a worker has been allowed any day as holiday in that week he shall be deemed to have worked thereon for the number of hours normally worked by him on that day of the week.

"NORMAL WORKING WEEK" means the number of days on which it has been usual for the worker to work in a week in the employment of the employer in the 12 months immediately preceding the commencement of the holiday season, or, where under paragraph 9 accrued holiday remuneration is payable on the termination of the employment, in the 12 months immediately preceding the termination date:

Provided that—

(1) part of a day shall count as a day;

(2) no account shall be taken of any week in which the worker did not perform any work for which statutory minimum remuneration has been fixed.

"PART-TIME WORKER" means a worker who normally works for the employer for less than 24 hours a week by reason only of the fact that he does not hold himself out as normally available for work for more than the number of hours he normally works in the week.

"STATUTORY MINIMUM REMUNERATION" means minimum remuneration (other than holiday remuneration) fixed by a wages regulation order made by the Secretary of State to give effect to proposals submitted to her by the Wages Council.

"TOTAL REMUNERATION" means any payments paid or payable to the worker under his contract of employment, for time worked or piece work done by him, holiday remuneration, any productivity, long service or other bonus payable to the worker on a weekly, fortnightly or monthly basis and merit payments so payable but does not include any other payments.

"WEEK" means "pay week".

12. The provisions of this Schedule are without prejudice to any agreement for the allowance of any further holidays with pay or for the payment of additional holiday remuneration.

EXPLANATORY NOTE

(This Note is not part of the Order.)

This Order, which has effect from 16th September 1968, sets out the holidays which an employer is required to allow to workers and the remuneration payable for those holidays in substitution for the holidays and holiday remuneration set out in the Wages Regulation (Sack and Bag) (Holidays) Order 1963 (Order S.B. (57)), as amended by Schedule 2 to the Wages Regulation (Sack and Bag) Order 1967 (Order S.B. 63)). Order S.B. (57) is revoked.

New provisions are printed in italics.

STATUTORY INSTRUMENTS

1968 No. 1362 (C.15)

NATIONAL HEALTH SERVICE, ENGLAND AND WALES

PUBLIC HEALTH, ENGLAND AND WALES

NATIONAL ASSISTANCE SERVICES

The Health Services and Public Health Act 1968 (Commencement No. 1) Order 1968

Made - - - *23rd August* 1968

The Minister of Health, in exercise of the powers conferred on him by section 79(2) of the Health Services and Public Health Act 1968(a), and of all other powers enabling him in that behalf, hereby orders as follows:—

1. This Order may be cited as the Health Services and Public Health Act 1968 (Commencement No. 1) Order 1968.

2. The appointed day for the coming into force of the provisions of the Health Services and Public Health Act 1968 specified in Schedule 1 to this Order in their application to England and Wales shall be 9th September 1968.

3. The appointed day for the coming into force of the provisions of the Health Services and Public Health Act 1968 specified in Schedule 2 to this Order in their application to England and Wales shall be 1st October 1968.

(a) 1968 c. 46.

SCHEDULE 1
PROVISIONS COMING INTO FORCE 9TH SEPTEMBER 1968

Provisions of the Act	Subject matter of provisions
Section 5	Power of the Minister to designate certain hospitals in England and Wales as university hospitals.
Section 6	Power of Board of Governors of a teaching hospital to administer services outside the hospital.
Section 8	Amendments as to association with universities of provision of hospital and specialist services.
Section 10	Midwifery services.
Section 11	Health visiting and district nursing.
Section 12	Prophylaxis, care and after-care.
Section 17	Alteration of references to services provided in accordance with arrangements under section 41 of the National Health Service Act 1946(a).
Section 18(3)	Facilities for provision of ophthalmic services to be available at health centres.
Section 20	Redefinition of "dispensing optician" and "ophthalmic optician" for the purposes of the National Health Service Act 1946.
Section 21(2) and (3)	Additional pharmaceutical services for which facilities can be made available at health centres and prohibition of employment there of registered pharmacists.
Section 22	Use of health centres by practitioners.
Section 24	Power of Executive Councils to supply goods and materials to persons providing certain services.
Section 25	Disqualification of practitioners and others disqualified in Northern Ireland.
Section 30	Certificates for exemption from prescription charges.
Section 31	Power of the Minister to make services available and, in certain circumstances, to provide them otherwise than for purposes of hospital and specialist services.
Section 32	Power of the Minister to dispose of goods and, in certain circumstances, to produce or manufacture them otherwise than for purposes of hospital and specialist services.
Section 33	Provision of vehicles for persons suffering from physical defect or disability.

(a) 1946 c. 81.

Sch. 1 (*continued*)

Provisions of the Act	Subject matter of provisions
Section 34	Superannuation of officers of hospitals outside national health service used for providing hospital and specialist services.
Section 35	Compensation for loss of employment, etc., attributable to re-organisation of provision of hospital services, etc.
Section 36	Payment of allowances and remuneration to members of certain bodies established by or under the National Health Service Act 1946 and members of certain other bodies.
Section 39	Power to recover cost of replacing appliances where the replacement is necessitated by lack of care.
Section 40	Accommodation for persons displaced in course of development for purposes of the Acts relating to the national health service or to mental health.
Section 42	Orders and regulations under Part I.
Section 43	Interpretation of Part I.
Section 44	Extension of power under the National Assistance Act 1948(a) of local authority to provide accommodation.
Section 46	Application of Part II to the Isles of Scilly.
Section 59	Extension of power of user by Crown of patented invention to user for certain health services.
Section 61	Welfare foods.
Section 62	Hover vehicles brought within the scope of Acts relating to public health and food and drugs.
Section 63	Provision of instruction for officers of hospital authorities and other persons employed, or contemplating employment, in certain activities connected with health or welfare.
Section 64	Financial assistance by the Minister of Health to certain voluntary organisations.
Section 65	Financial and other assistance by local authorities to certain voluntary organisations.
Section 66	Payments in respect of travelling expenses of visitors to patients in special hospitals.
Section 67	Power of the Minister of Health to purchase goods for supply to local authorities and Executive Councils.

(a) 1948 c. 29.

Provisions of the Act	Subject matter of provisions
Section 68	Amendment of Mental Health Act 1959(a) in case where functions under Part IV thereof of a county council are delegated.
Section 77	Expenses and receipts.
Section 78 (1) and schedule 3—Except so far as amendments to enactments or schemes refer specifically to sections 13 and 45 of the Health Services and Public Health Act 1968.	Consequential amendments and repeals.
Section 78 (2) and schedule 4 to the extent set out in the Appendix hereto.	
Section 79	Short title, citation, commencement, and extent.
Schedule 2—Part I	Enactments of the National Health Service Act 1946 applied for the purposes of Part I.

(a) 1959 c. 72.

APPENDIX TO SCHEDULE 1

REPEALS TAKING EFFECT ON THE 9TH SEPTEMBER, 1968

Chapter	Short Title	Extent of Repeal
9 & 10 Geo. 6. c. 81.	The National Health Service Act 1946.	In section 11, in subsection (9) in paragraph (i), the words "and compensation", except in relation to an order made in consequence of the occurrence, before the coming into operation of section 35 of this Act, of any of the events mentioned in paragraphs (a) to (c) of that subsection.
		Section 22(5).
		Section 23.
		In section 28, subsection (1) subsection (2) (except in relation to services provided before the coming into operation of section 12 of this Act) and subsection (3).
		In section 31, in subsection (5), the words "and their compensation by the Minister", except in relation to an order made under subsection (2), (3) or (4) of that section before the coming into operation of section 35 of this Act or an order made before the coming into operation of that section revoking an order made under any of those subsections.
		In section 40(2) (e), the words "and also for the remuneration of members of the Board".
		Section 48.
		Section 54(5).
		In section 63, the words from "or by any voluntary" to "1959".
		In Schedule 1, in paragraph 2, the words from "and for the making of such payments" onwards.
		In Schedule 3, in Part IV, paragraphs 2(c) and 5.
		In Schedule 6, paragraph 3(b).
		In Schedule 7, paragraph 6(b).
11 & 12 Geo. 6. c. 29.	The National Assistance Act 1948.	Section 26(6).
		Section 30(2).
		Section 31(3), except in relation to councils of county districts in England and Wales.

Chapter	Short Title	Extent of Repeal
12, 13 & 14 Geo. 6. c. 93	The National Health Service (Amendment) Act 1949.	In section 21, the words "or ophthalmic or dispensing optician", and the words "or optician". Section 22. In the Schedule, in Part I, the words from "In subsection (5) of section 54" to "(including travelling, and subsistence expenses)", the words from "In paragraph 2 of the First Schedule" to "usual place of residence" and the words from "At the end of the said Part IV" onwards (except so far as those words relate to the constitution of Executive Councils the term of office of chairmen and the duties of medical officers of health).
14 & 15 Geo. 6. c. 53	The Midwives Act 1951.	In section 11(2), the words "or maternity nurses".
1 & 2 Eliz. 2. c. 47	The Emergency Laws (Miscellaneous Provisions) Act 1953.	Section 6(4).
7 & 8 Eliz. 2. c. 72	The Mental Health Act 1959.	Sections 6 and 7. Section 153(3). In Schedule 6, paragraph 1. In Schedule 7, the amendment of section 63 of the National Health Service Act 1946.
9 & 10 Eliz. 2. c. 43	The Public Authorities (Allowances) Act 1961.	Sections 4, 5 and 6.
10 & 11 Eliz. 2. c. 24	The National Assistance Act 1948 (Amendment) Act 1962.	As respects England and Wales, in section 1(1), subsection (3) of the section substituted for section 31 of the National Assistance Act 1948, except in relation to councils of county districts.
1963 c. 33	The London Government Act 1963.	Section 45(4). Section 46(3).
1964 c.xxxv.	The Newcastle upon Tyne Corporation Act 1964.	Section 29.
1967 c. 39	The National Health Service (Family Planning) Act 1967.	In section 2, subsection (2) from the beginning to "section, and". In section 3(1)(a), the words "or section 61 of the Local Government Act 1958"(a).

(a) 1958 c. 55.

SCHEDULE 2

PROVISIONS COMING INTO FORCE 1ST OCTOBER 1968

Provisions of the Act	Subject matter of provisions
Section 47	Redefinition of "notifiable disease".
Section 48	Cases of notifiable disease and food poisoning to be reported to local authority.
Section 49	Supply of forms for purposes of section 48.
Section 50	Fees for certificates under section 48.
Section 51	Reimbursement of fees in certain cases.
Section 52	Powers of local authority to extend category of notifiable diseases.
Section 53	Power of a justice of the peace to order examination of person believed to be a carrier of a notifiable disease.
Section 54	Power of a justice of the peace to order medical examination of group of persons believed to comprise a carrier of a notifiable disease.
Section 55	Construction of references to medical examination.
Section 56	Construction of section 143 of Public Health Act 1936(a).
Section 57	Interpretation of Part III.
Section 58	Extent of Part III.
Section 69	Repeal of section 172 of the Public Health Act 1936.
Section 70	Copy of notice under section 242 of the Public Health Act 1936 to be sent to health authority if it is not the local authority.
Section 78 (2) and schedule 4 to the extent set out in the Appendix hereto.	Repeals.

(a) 1936 c. 49.

APPENDIX TO SCHEDULE 2

REPEALS TAKING EFFECT ON THE 1ST OCTOBER, 1968

Chapter	Short Title	Extent of Repeal
26 Geo. 5 & 1 Edw. 8. c. 49	Public Health Act 1936	Sections 144 to 146 and section 172.
9 & 10 Geo. 6. c. 81	The National Health Service Act 1946.	In Schedule 10 the words from "Where the local authority" to "by the local health authority".
12, 13 & 14 Geo. 6. c. 93	The National Health Service (Amendment) Act 1949.	In the Schedule, in Part I, the words from "At the end of the said Part IV" onwards so far as they relate to the duties of medical officers of health.
4 & 5 Eliz. 2. c. 16	Food and Drugs Act 1955.	Section 26.

Given under the official seal of the Minister of Health on 23rd August, 1968.

(L.S.)

Kenneth Robinson,
Minister of Health.

EXPLANATORY NOTE

(This note is not part of the Order.)

This Order appoints 9th September 1968 as the appointed day for the coming into force of the provisions of the Health Services and Public Health Act 1968 listed in Schedule 1 to the Order, and 1st October 1968 as the appointed day for the coming into force of the provisions of the Act listed in Schedule 2 to the Order.

STATUTORY INSTRUMENTS

1968 No. 1363

PENSIONS

The Superannuation (Judicial Offices) Rules 1968

Made - - - -	*22nd August* 1968
Laid before Parliament	*29th August* 1968
Coming into Operation	*30th August* 1968

The Treasury, in exercise of the powers conferred on them by section 38 of the Superannuation Act 1965(a), and of all other powers enabling them in that behalf, hereby make the following Rules:—

Superannuation benefits for persons who have served in more than one judicial office

1.—(1) Where—

(*a*) a person has been continuously employed in two or more judicial offices; and

(*b*) he retires from, or dies while still serving in, the last of those offices in such circumstances that superannuation benefits are payable to or in respect of him under the enactments relating to such last office, or would be so payable if he had served in such office for the minimum qualifying period required by those enactments; and

(*c*) he elects, or, if he has died, his personal representatives elect, that these Rules shall apply in relation to him,

then, subject to the provisions of these Rules, there may be paid to or in respect of him the superannuation benefits specified in Rule 2 of these Rules.

(2) Where a person is employed continuously in two or more judicial offices service in which may be aggregated for the purposes of the pension enactments relating to the last of them, he shall be deemed for the purposes of these Rules to have been employed solely in the last of those offices during the whole of the period of his service in those offices.

(3) For the purposes of these Rules, a person shall be deemed to have been continuously employed in two judicial offices, notwithstanding that he has not transferred directly from the first office to the second, if he became employed in the second office within 31 days of ceasing to be employed in the first or within such longer period as the Treasury may allow in any particular case.

(a) 1965 c. 74.

(4) These Rules shall not apply in relation to a person—

(*a*) by or in respect of whom an election is made under section 4 of the Judicial Pensions Act 1959(a) (which contains special provisions as to holders of certain high judicial offices who are former holders of other judicial offices); or

(*b*) who retires from a judicial office having become eligible for superannuation benefits by virtue of a provision of any enactment under which the holder of a judicial office who is required to vacate his office at a time related to the attainment of a particular age becomes eligible for superannuation benefits if he retires before attaining that age otherwise than on grounds of ill-health.

(5) An election under this Rule shall be made within the period of three months beginning with the retirement or death, as the case may be, of the person by or in respect of whom it is made, and shall be made in writing addressed to the Treasury.

Amount of benefits

2.—(1) Where a person by or in respect of whom an election is made under Rule 1 of these Rules has served continuously in not more than two judicial offices, the benefits payable to or in respect of him shall—

(*a*) if at the time of his retirement or death the salary of the second of those offices is not less than the salary of the first, be equal to the benefits which would have been payable to or in respect of him under the enactments relating to the first office if he had continued to serve in that office until his retirement or death at the salary then payable to a holder of that office; or

(*b*) if at the time of his retirement or death the salary of the second of those offices is less than the salary of the first, be equal to whichever are the more favourable of the following:—

(i) the benefits which would have been payable to or in respect of him under the enactments relating to the second office if his service in the first office had been service in the second office, or

(ii) the benefits which would have been payable to or in respect of him under the enactments relating to the first office if he had retired from that office on grounds of ill-health on the date when he ceased to hold that office.

(2) Where a person by or in respect of whom an election is made under Rule 1 of these Rules has served continuously in not less than three judicial offices, the benefits payable to or in respect of him shall be equal to whichever are the most favourable of the following:—

(*a*) the benefits which would have been payable to or in respect of him under paragraph (1) of this Rule if the first of his last three judicial offices were the first office referred to in that paragraph, his service in the second of those offices were service in the third of those offices, and the third of those offices were the second office referred to in that paragraph;

(*b*) the benefits which would have been payable to or in respect of him under paragraph (1) of this Rule if his service in only the last two of his judicial offices were taken into account; or

(a) 1959 c. 9 (8 & 9 Eliz. 2).

(*c*) the benefits which would have been payable to or in respect of him under paragraph (1) of this Rule if his service in only the first two of his last three judicial offices were taken into account.

(3) Where a judicial office in which a person has been employed ceases to exist before the time of his retirement or death, then, for the purpose of calculating the amount of the benefits payable to or in respect of him under this Rule, the salary of that office shall be taken to be such amount as the Treasury may determine to be the salary which would have been payable in respect of that office if it had continued to exist at the time of his retirement or death.

(4) Where a person has been employed in a judicial office in such circumstances that, if he had retired from that office, a person other than the Crown would have been liable under any enactment to contribute to any pension or other benefit payable in respect of his service in that office, the length of any period of his service which would, apart from this paragraph, include the period of his service in that office shall, for the purpose of calculating the amount of any benefits for the purposes of this Rule, be reduced by the length of the period of his service in that office.

(5) Where a person has been employed in a judicial office in such circumstances that, if he had retired from that office, a person other than the Crown would have been liable under any enactment, by reason of his having previously been employed in another office, to contribute to any pension or other benefit for which he would have been eligible on his retirement from the judicial office, the length of any period of his service which would, apart from this paragraph, include the period of his service in that other office shall, for the purpose of calculating the amount of any benefits for the purposes of this Rule, be reduced by the length of the period of his service in that other office.

(6) Where any benefits are paid under these Rules in respect of a person's service in a judicial office, no superannuation benefit shall be paid in respect of that service under the enactments relating to that office.

Exception from the application of the Rules

3. If the application of these Rules would put a particular individual in a position less advantageous than that in which he would have been if the Rules did not apply in relation to him they shall not be so applied.

Interpretation

4.—(1) In these Rules, unless the context otherwise requires, the expression "judicial office" means any of the offices listed, or treated by virtue of any enactment as listed, in Schedule 1 to the Administration of Justice (Pensions) Act 1950(a), but does not, in relation to any person, include any such office if the Superannuation Act 1965 applies to him in respect of his service in that office.

(2) Any reference in these Rules to the provisions of any enactment shall be construed, unless the context otherwise requires, as a reference to those provisions as amended or re-enacted by any subsequent enactment.

(3) The Interpretation Act 1889(b) shall apply for the interpretation of these Rules as it applies for the interpretation of an Act of Parliament.

(a) 1950 c. 11 (14 & 15 Geo. 6).   (b) 1889 c. 63.

Citation and commencement

5. These Rules may be cited as the Superannuation (Judicial Offices) Rules 1968, and shall come into operation on 30th August 1968.

E. Alan Fitch,

B. K. O'Malley,

Two of the Lords Commissioners
of Her Majesty's Treasury.

22nd August 1968.

EXPLANATORY NOTE

(This Note is not part of the Rules.)

These Rules provide for the pension payable to or in respect of a person who has served in two or more judicial offices to be based on his aggregate service in those offices instead of on his service only in the last office held by him.

Where it is desired that the Rules shall apply, the person concerned or, if he has died, his personal representatives must make an election within three months of his retirement or death.

When such an election is made in respect of a person who has served in two judicial offices, the Rules provide for the pension to be calculated normally by reference to his aggregate service in those offices and the salary and pension scale of the first of the two offices. Where, however, the salary of the second office is less than that of the first, the pension will be calculated by whichever is the more favourable of the following methods:—

(*a*) by reference to his aggregate service in both offices and the salary and pension scale of the second office, or

(*b*) by reference to his service in the first office only and the salary and pension scale of the first office.

STATUTORY INSTRUMENTS

1968 No. 1364

NATIONAL HEALTH SERVICE, ENGLAND AND WALES

The National Health Service (Executive Councils) (Supply) Regulations 1968

Made - - -	*23rd August* 1968
Laid before Parliament	*30th August* 1968
Coming into Operation	*9th September* 1968

The Minister of Health in exercise of the powers conferred on him by section 24(1) of the Health Services and Public Health Act 1968(a), and of all other powers enabling him in that behalf, hereby makes the following regulations:—

1.—(1) These regulations may be cited as the National Health Service (Executive Councils) (Supply) Regulations 1968 and shall come into operation on 9th September 1968.

(2) The Interpretation Act 1889(b) applies to the interpretation of these regulations as it applies to the interpretation of an Act of Parliament.

2. The goods and materials specified in Column 1 of the Schedule hereto, being goods and materials which it appears to the Minister it is necessary or expedient for a person providing the service specified in Column 2 of the said Schedule in relation to such goods and materials to have for the purpose of providing that service, are hereby prescribed for the purposes of the said section 24(1).

SCHEDULE

Column 1	Column 2
Sterile disposable hypodermic syringes	General Medical Services under Part IV of the National Health Service Act 1946(c)
Sterile disposable hypodermic needles	General Medical Services under Part IV of the National Health Service Act 1946(c)

Given under the official seal of the Minister of Health on 23rd August 1968.

(L.S.)

Kenneth Robinson,
Minister of Health.

(a) 1968 c. 46.   (b) 1889 c. 63.   (c) 1946 c. 81.

EXPLANATORY NOTE

(This Note is not part of the Regulations.)

These Regulations prescribe goods and materials which an Executive Council, subject to the consent of the Minister of Health and on terms which he and the Treasury may approve, may supply to practitioners as part of their arrangements for the provision in their area of general medical services under Part IV of the National Health Service Act 1946.

STATUTORY INSTRUMENTS

1968 No. 1365

PUBLIC HEALTH, ENGLAND AND WALES

The Public Health (Fees for Notifications of Infectious Disease) Order 1968

Made - - -	*23rd August* 1968
Laid before Parliament	*30th August* 1968
Coming into Operation	*1st October* 1968

The Minister of Health, in exercise of the powers conferred on him by section 50(1) of the Health Services and Public Health Act 1968(a) and of all other powers enabling him in that behalf, hereby directs and orders as follows:—

Title and commencement

1. This order may be cited as the Public Health (Fees for Notifications of Infectious Disease) Order 1968 and shall come into operation on 1st October 1968.

Interpretation

2.—(1) In this order "local authority" has the same meaning as in the Public Health Act 1936(b).

(2) The Interpretation Act 1889(c) shall apply to the interpretation of this order as it applies to the interpretation of an Act of Parliament.

Fees for certificates of notification

3. A local authority shall pay to a medical practitioner a fee of five shillings for each certificate duly sent by him to their medical officer of health under section 48 of the Health Services and Public Health Act 1968 (which requires a medical practitioner to notify any case or suspected case of notifiable disease or food poisoning by certificate to the medical officer of health):

Provided that no fee shall be payable for a certificate sent by a medical practitioner serving for the time being in the naval, military or air forces of the Crown or in any women's service administered by the Defence Council.

Given under the official seal of the Minister of Health on 23rd August 1968.

(L.S.)

Kenneth Robinson,
Minister of Health.

(a) 1968 c. 46. (b) 1936 c. 49. (c) 1889 c. 63.

EXPLANATORY NOTE

(*This Note is not part of the Order.*)

Section 48 of the Health Services and Public Health Act 1968 provides that a medical practitioner shall notify any case or suspected case of notifiable disease or food poisoning to the medical officer of health for the district. This Order requires the local authority for the district to pay the medical practitioner a fee of five shillings for each certificate of notification, except a certificate sent by a medical practitioner serving in the forces.

STATUTORY INSTRUMENTS

1968 No. 1366

PUBLIC HEALTH, ENGLAND AND WALES

The Public Health (Infectious Diseases) Regulations 1968

Made - - - -	*23rd August* 1968
Laid before Parliament	*30th August* 1968
Coming into Operation	*1st October* 1968

The Minister of Health, in exercise of the powers conferred on him by section 143 (as extended by section 56 of the Health Services and Public Health Act 1968(a)) and section 283(2) of, and paragraph 1 of Schedule 1 to, the Public Health Act 1936(b) and section 108 of the Local Government Act 1933(c), and of all other powers enabling him in that behalf, hereby makes the following regulations:—

PART I

PRELIMINARY

Title and commencement

1. These regulations may be cited as the Public Health (Infectious Diseases) Regulations 1968 and shall come into operation on 1st October 1968.

Interpretation

2.—(1) In these regulations, unless the context otherwise requires—

"the Act of 1936" means the Public Health Act 1936;

"the Act of 1961" means the Public Health Act 1961(d)

"the Act of 1968" means the Health Services and Public Health Act 1968;

"certificate" means a certificate required by section 48 of the Act of 1968 to be sent by a medical practitioner to a medical officer of health;

"Chief Medical Officer" means the Chief Medical Officer to the Ministry of Health;

"county district" means a non-county borough or an urban district or rural district;

"district" means the district of a local authority (and includes part of a district);

"local authority" means—

   (a) as respects a county borough or county district, the council thereof;

   (b) as respects a London borough, the council of the borough;

   (c) as respects the City of London, the Common Council; and

   (d) as respects the Inner Temple and the Middle Temple, the Sub-Treasurer and the Under-Treasurer thereof respectively;

"the Minister" means the Minister of Health;

"notifiable disease" has the same meaning as in section 343(1) of the Act of 1936 (as amended by section 47 of the Act of 1968);

"ophthalmia neonatorum" means a purulent discharge from the eyes of an infant, commencing within 21 days from the date of birth;

(a) 1968 c. 46.	(b) 1936 c. 49.
(c) 1933 c. 51.	(d) 1961 c. 64.

"port health authority" means a port health authority constituted by an order made, or having effect as if made, by the Minister under section 2 of the Act of 1936, and includes the port health authority for the Port of London as constituted under section 41 of the London Government Act 1963(a);

"port health district" means the district of a port health authority;

"public health enactments" means the enactments relating to the notification of disease and to notifiable disease which are set out for purposes of reference in schedule 1;

"relevant medical officer of health", in relation to a county district, means the medical officer of health of any county within which the county district is wholly or partly situated, and in relation to a port health district means the medical officer of health of any county, county borough or London borough within which the port health district is wholly or partly situated.

(2) In these regulations, unless the context otherwise requires, references to any enactment, order or regulation shall be construed as references to that enactment, order or regulation as amended, extended or applied by or under any other enactment, order or regulation, including these regulations.

(3) Any reference in these regulations to a numbered schedule shall be construed as a reference to the schedule bearing that number in these regulations.

(4) The Interpretation Act 1889(b) shall apply to the interpretation of these regulations as it applies to the interpretation of an Act of Parliament, and as if these regulations and the regulations hereby revoked were Acts of Parliament.

Enforcement and publication

3.—(1) These regulations shall be enforced and executed—

(a) in a district, by the local authority thereof; and

(b) in a port health district, by the port health authority thereof, so far as these regulations are in terms applicable thereto.

(2) Every local authority shall send to any medical practitioner who after due enquiry is ascertained to be practising in their district—

(a) a copy of these regulations and

(b) a copy of sections 47 to 49 of the Act of 1968.

PART II

PROVISIONS AS TO NOTIFICATION OF DISEASE AND NOTIFIABLE DISEASES

Public health enactments applied to certain diseases

4.—(1) There shall apply to any disease mentioned in column (1) of schedule 2 such of the public health enactments as are listed in column (2) thereof against the name of that disease, subject in the case of tuberculosis to the modifications specified therein.

(2) In schedule 2 (without prejudice to the provisions of regulation 2(2) of these regulations) references to section 38 of the Act of 1961 (as amended) are to that section as amended by section 53 of the Act of 1968, and references to the said section 38 (as originally enacted) are to that section as originally enacted and not as so amended.

(a) 1963 c. 33.　　　　　　　　　(b) 1889 c. 63.

Form of certificates

5. The form set out in schedule 3, or a form substantially to the like effect, shall be the form of certificate.

Cases of infectious disease to be specially reported

6.—(1) In this regulation "quarantinable disease" means plague, cholera, yellow fever, smallpox, typhus or relapsing fever.

(2) Without prejudice to paragraph (3) of this regulation, a medical officer of health shall immediately inform the Chief Medical Officer of—

    (*a*) any case or suspected case of a quarantinable disease and

    (*b*) any serious outbreak of any disease (including food poisoning),

which to his knowledge has occurred in his district or port health district; and in the case of a county district or port health district he shall similarly inform any relevant medical officer of health.

(3) A medical officer of health who receives a certificate in respect of any case of—

    (*a*) a quarantinable disease, or

    (*b*) leprosy, or

    (*c*) malaria contracted naturally in Great Britain,

shall immediately send a copy to the Chief Medical Officer.

Weekly and quarterly returns

7.—(1) Subject to the provisions of paragraph (3) of this regulation, a medical officer of health shall, in respect of his district or port health district, send to the Registrar General by post every week in time to ensure its delivery on Monday, or the morning of Tuesday at the latest, a return, in such form as the Minister may from time to time require, of the number of cases of each disease (including food poisoning and suspected food poisoning but excluding leprosy) notified to him during the week ended on the preceding Friday night; and the medical officer of health of a county district shall send a copy of the return to any relevant medical officer of health.

(2) Subject to the provisions of paragraph (3) of this regulation, a medical officer of health of a district shall send to the Registrar General by post every three months, not later than 21st January, 21st April, 21st July and 21st October in every year, a return, in such form as the Minister may from time to time require, of the cases referred to in the preceding paragraph which have been notified to him during the preceding three months, showing separately the final number of cases after any correction of diagnosis subsequently made by the notifying medical practitioner or by the medical practitioner in charge of the patient; and the medical officer of health of a county district shall send a copy of the return to any relevant medical officer of health.

(3) Where, pursuant to section 48(2)(*b*) or 48(3)(*a*) of the Act of 1968, a copy of a certificate is sent by the medical officer of health of one district to the medical officer of health of another district, the case to which that certificate relates shall not be included in any return of the first-mentioned medical officer and shall be included in the returns of the last-mentioned medical officer.

PART III

PREVENTING SPREAD OF DISEASE

Provisions for preventing the spread of certain diseases

8.—(1) The provisions of schedule 4 shall have effect in relation to typhus and relapsing fever.

(2) The provisions of schedule 5 shall have effect in relation to food poisoning and to typhoid, paratyphoid and other salmonella infections, amoebic and bacillary dysentery, and staphylococcal infections likely to cause food poisoning.

Immunisation and vaccination

9. Where a case of any notifiable disease or of any disease mentioned in schedule 2 (other than tuberculosis) occurs in a district or port health district, the medical officer of health of that district or port health district and of any adjacent district or port health district may, if he considers it in the public interest, vaccinate or immunise, without charge, any person in his district or port health district who has come or may have come or may come in contact with the infection and is willing to be vaccinated or immunised.

Measures against infected rats

10. Where a local authority or port health authority have reason to believe that rats in their district or port health district are threatened by or infected with plague, or are dying in unusual numbers, they shall report the matter to the Chief Medical Officer and take measures for destroying all rats in the district or port health district and for preventing rats from gaining entry to buildings.

PART IV

GENERAL

Confidentiality of documents

11. Any certificate, or copy, and any accompanying or related document, shall be sent in such a manner that its contents cannot be read during transmission; and the information contained therein shall not be divulged to any person except—

(a) so far as is necessary for compliance with the requirements of any enactment (including these regulations), or

(b) for the purposes of such action as any medical officer of health considers reasonably necessary for preventing the spread of disease.

Compensation

12. Section 278(1) and (2) of the Act of 1936 (which provides for compensation for damage resulting from the exercise of powers under that Act) shall extend to anything done by a local authority or port health authority in pursuance of these regulations.

Revocation

13. There are hereby revoked—

(a) the regulations specified in schedule 6;

(b) paragraphs (3) and (7) of regulation 15 (Duties) of the Public Health Officers Regulations 1959(a); and

(c) paragraphs (3) and (6) of regulation 12 (Duties) of the Public Health Officers (Port Health Districts) Regulations 1959(b).

(a) S.I. 1959/962 (1959 I, p. 1605).
(b) S.I. 1959/963 (1959 II, p. 2125).

Regulations 2(1) and 4   **SCHEDULE I**

LIST OF THE PUBLIC HEALTH ENACTMENTS

In the Act of 1936—

Section 148	(Penalty on exposure of persons and articles);
Section 149	(Persons suffering from notifiable disease not to carry on occupation to danger of others);
Section 150	(Child liable to convey notifiable disease may be ordered not to attend school);
Section 151	(Local authority may require list of day scholars at school where notifiable disease exists);
Section 152	(Restrictions on sending or taking infected articles to laundry or public wash-house, or to cleaners);
Section 153	(Power to prohibit home work on premises where notifiable disease exists);
Section 155	(Provisions as to library books);
Section 156	(Infectious matter not to be placed in dustbins);
Section 157	(Provisions as to the letting of houses, or rooms in hotels, after recent case of notifiable disease);
Section 158	(Persons ceasing to occupy house to disclose to owner any recent case of notifiable disease, and to disinfect);
Section 159	(Provision as to use of public conveyance by persons suffering from notifiable disease);
Section 160	(Duty of owner, etc. of public conveyance in regard to cases of notifiable disease);
Section 163	(Restrictions in certain cases of removal of bodies of persons dying in hospital);
Section 164	(Avoidance of contact with body of person who suffered from notifiable disease);
Section 165	(Wake not to be held over body of person who suffered from notifiable disease);
Section 169	(Provision for removal to hospital of persons suffering from notifiable disease where serious risk of infection being spread);
Section 170	(Power of justice to order detention in hospital of infected person without proper lodging to return to).

In the Act of 1961—

Section 38	(Power of justice to order a medical examination);
Section 39	(Information to be furnished by occupier in case of notifiable disease or food poisoning);
Section 40	(Exclusion of children from places of entertainment or assembly);
Section 41	(Compensation for stopping employment to prevent spread of disease).

In the Act of 1968—

Section 48	(Cases of notifiable disease and food poisoning to be reported to local authority);
Section 49	(Supply of forms for purposes of section 48);
Section 50	(Fees for certificate under section 48);
Section 51	(Reimbursement of fees in certain cases);
Section 54	(Power of justice of peace to order medical examination of group of persons believed to comprise a carrier of a notifiable disease).

Regulation 4   SCHEDULE 2

PUBLIC HEALTH ENACTMENTS APPLIED TO PARTICULAR DISEASES

(1) Disease	(2) Enactments applied
Acute encephalitis Acute meningitis Acute poliomyelitis	In the Act of 1936— sections 148 to 153, 156 to 160, 164, 165, 169 and 170; In the Act of 1961— sections 38 (as originally enacted) and 39 to 41; In the Act of 1968— sections 48 to 51.
Diphtheria Dysentery (amoebic or bacillary) Infective jaundice Paratyphoid fever Typhoid fever	In the Act of 1936— sections 148 to 153, 156 to 160, 164, 165, 169 and 170; In the Act of 1961— sections 38 (as amended) and 39 to 41; In the Act of 1968— sections 48 to 51 and 54.
Anthrax	In the Act of 1936— sections 148 to 153, 156 to 160, 163 to 165, 169 and 170; In the Act of 1961— sections 38 (as originally enacted), 39 and 41; In the Act of 1968— sections 48 to 51.
Leprosy	In the Act of 1936— sections 148 to 150, 153, 157, 158, 164, 169 and 170; In the Act of 1961— sections 38 (as originally enacted) and 41; In the Act of 1968— sections 48 to 51.

(1) Disease	(2) Enactments applied

Leptospirosis
 	
Measles
 	
Whooping cough
	In the Act of 1936—
	    sections 148 to 153, 156 to 160, 164, 165,
	    169 and 170;
	
	In the Act of 1961—
	    sections 38 (as originally enacted), 39 and 41;
	
	In the Act of 1968—
	    sections 48 to 51.

Malaria
 	
Tetanus
 	
Yellow fever
	In the Act of 1961—
	    sections 38 (as originally enacted) and 39;
	
	In the Act of 1968—
	    sections 48 to 51.

Ophthalmia neonatorum	In the Act of 1936—
	    sections 148, 152 and 156;
	
	In the Act of 1968—
	    sections 48 to 51.

Scarlet fever	In the Act of 1936—
	    sections 148 to 153, 156 to 160, 164, 165,
	    169 and 170;
	
	In the Act of 1961—
	    sections 38 (as amended), 39 and 41;
	
	In the Act of 1968—
	    sections 48 to 51 and 54.

Tuberculosis	In the Act of 1936—
	    sections 148 to 153, 156 to 158, 164 and 165;
	    and sections 155, 169 and 170 shall apply
	    to tuberculosis of the respiratory tract in an
	    infectious state;
	
	In the Act of 1961—
	    sections 38 (as originally enacted) and 39 to
	    41;
	
	In the Act of 1968—
	    sections 49 to 51; and section 48 shall apply
	    where the opinion of the medical practitioner
	    that a person is suffering from tuberculosis
	    is formed from evidence not derived solely
	    from tuberculin tests.

Regulation 5

SCHEDULE 3

FORM OF CERTIFICATE

NOTIFICATION OF INFECTIOUS DISEASE OR FOOD POISONING

To the Medical Officer of Health.

I hereby certify and declare that in my opinion the person named below is suffering from the disease stated.

Counterfoil	No.

Date of Notification.......

Name.......

Date of Birth.......

Disease.......

Date of onset.......

Patient at:—

No.

AGE	DISEASE	See Noe*	DATE OF ONSET
SEX			

*NOTE
When the form is used for a case of food poisoning enter "F.P." (or "F.P. suspected") unless the case is diagnosed as one of specific disease (e.g. dysentery) which is required to be notified as such.

NAME (in full)

Full address where patient now is:—

If patient is at present in a hospital,
(a) the address in full from which the patient was admitted is:—

(b) in my opinion the disease was/was not contracted in the hospital. (Delete whichever does not apply)

Additional particulars required in cases of certain diseases.

Ophthalmia Neonatorum	Date of birth....... Name and address of parent or other person in charge of the child
Malaria	Mark "X" where applicable
Acute Meningitis	Contracted— (Abroad .... / In this country .... If induced— (Therapeutically....... / (Accidentally.......
Acute Poliomyelitis	Causal organism if known....... P N-P Paralytic or non-paralytic (Ring symbol which applies) [PARALYTIC means that there are or have been signs of weakness and paralysis of muscles either permanent or transient. NON-PARALYTIC means that there have been no such signs].
Acute Encephalitis	I P-I Infective or Post-infectious (Ring symbol which applies) If post-infectious state preceding infection below. ....
Tuberculosis	Organ or part affected.......
Date	Signature of Doctor Address

Regulation 8(1)   SCHEDULE 4

TYPHUS AND RELAPSING FEVER

Measures by local authority

1. The medical officer of health of a district shall, if he thinks it necessary, report any case of typhus or relapsing fever in his district to the local authority who may, by notice in writing, require—

(*a*) that such measures as may be specified in the notice shall be immediately taken to the satisfaction of the medical officer of health to obtain the complete destruction of lice on the person and clothing of every occupant of the building of which the patient is an inmate, and to secure the destruction of lice or their products in the building; and

(*b*) the temporary segregation, for a period to be specified in the notice, of other inmates of the building or of other persons recently in contact with the patient until their persons and clothing have been completely freed from lice.

Addressing of notices

2. The notice may be addressed to the head of the family to which the patient belongs, to any person in charge of or in attendance on the patient, to any other person in the building of which the patient is an inmate, or to the occupier of the building, and also to any person with whom the patient has recently been in contact.

Authorisation of medical officer of health

3.—(1) A local authority may authorise the medical officer of health generally to issue any notice on their behalf under this schedule in relation to any particular case if in his opinion it is immediately and urgently necessary for him to do so for the purpose of preventing the spread of infection.

(2) The medical officer of health shall at the earliest opportunity report any case dealt with under such an authorisation, and the action taken by him, to the local authority.

Regulation 8(2)   SCHEDULE 5

FOOD POISONING AND FOOD BORNE INFECTIONS

Measures by local authority

1.—(1) If a medical officer of health, after considering the information available to him, forms the opinion—

(*a*) that a person in the district—
  (i) is suffering from food poisoning which may be caused by an infection or
  (ii) is suffering from, or is shown to be a carrier of, any infection mentioned in paragraph 5 of this schedule, and

(*b*) that it is desirable for the protection of the public health that measures should be taken to prevent the spread of infection,

he shall report to the local authority accordingly.

(2) On receipt of such a report, the local authority may by notice in writing—

(*a*) require the person concerned to discontinue or to refrain from engaging in any occupation connected with food until they notify him that the risk of causing infection is removed;

(*b*) require that such measures shall be taken for the protection of the public health as are specified in the notice, being measures which in the opinion of the medical officer of health are desirable to prevent the spread of infection by the person concerned; and

(c) require the assistance of any other person reasonably able to assist in securing compliance with any requirement under this paragraph;

and if the person concerned is already engaged in any occupation connected with food, the local authority shall send a copy of any notice served on him under this paragraph to his employer, if any, and to any other person reasonably able to assist in securing compliance with any requirement under this paragraph.

Suspected carriers in food trade

2.—(1) If a medical officer of health has reason to believe that a person engaged in any trade or business connected with food may be a carrier of any infection mentioned in paragraph 5 of this schedule, he shall report to the local authority accordingly.

(2) The local authority may give notice in writing to the reponsible manager of the trade or business concerned that for the purpose of preventing the spread of infection they consider it necessary for the medical officer of health or a medical officer acting on his behalf to make a medical examination of that person, and the responsible manager shall give to the medical officer of health all reasonable assistance in the matter.

Authorisation of medical officer of health

3.—(1) A local authority may authorise the medical officer of health generally to issue any notice on their behalf under this schedule in relation to any particular case if in his opinion it is immediately and urgently necessary for him to do so for the purpose of preventing the spread of infection.

(2) The medical officer of health shall at the earliest opportunity report any case dealt with under such an authorisation, and the action taken by him, to the local authority.

Definition of terms

4. In this schedule—

    (a) "connected with food", in relation to an occupation, trade or business, means connected with the preparation or handling of food or drink for human consumption; and

    (b) the reference to making a medical examination shall be construed as including a reference to making bacteriological tests and similar investigations.

Infections to which this schedule applies

5. The infections referred to in paragraphs 1 and 2 of this schedule are typhoid, paratyphoid and other salmonella infections, amoebic and bacillary dysentery, and staphylococcal infections likely to cause food poisoning.

SCHEDULE 6   Regulation 13

REVOCATIONS

Regulations revoked	References
The Public Health (Notification of Infectious Diseases) Regulations Order 1900	S.R. & O. 1900/695 (Rev. XVIII, p.761: 1900, p.774).
The Public Health (Prevention of Infectious and Epidemic Diseases) Regulations Order 1910	S.R. & O. 1910/1165 (Rev. XVIII, p.800: 1910, p.632).
The Public Health (Small-pox Prevention) Regulations 1917	S.R. & O. 1917/146 (Rev. XVIII, p.804: 1917, p.935).
The Public Health (Notification of Infectious Disease) Regulations 1918	S.R. & O. 1918/67 (Rev. XVIII, p.763: 1918 II, p.688).

Regulations revoked	References
The Public Health (Cerebro-Spinal Fever) Regulations 1919	S.R. & O. 1919/767 (Rev. XVIII, p.795: 1919 II, p.365).
The Public Health (Ophthalmia Neonatorum) Regulations 1926	S.R. & O. 1926/971 (Rev. XVIII, p.767: 1926, p.1180).
The Public Health (Treatment of Infectious Disease) Regulations 1934	S.R. & O. 1934/674 (Rev. XVIII, p.796: 1934 II, p.132).
The Public Health (Ophthalmia Neonatorum) Amendment Regulations 1937	S.R. & O. 1937/35 (Rev. XVIII, p.767: 1937, p.1949).
The Measles and Whooping Cough Regulations 1940	S.R. & O. 1940/204 (Rev. XVIII, p.790: 1940 I, p.891).
The Measles and Whooping Cough (Amendment) Regulations 1948	S.I. 1948/421 (Rev.XVIII, p.790: 1948 I, p.3597).
The Public Health (Acute Poliomyelitis, Acute Encephalitis, and Meningococcal Infection) Regulations 1949	S.I. 1949/2259 (1949 I, p.3543).
The Puerperal Pyrexia Regulations 1951	S.I. 1951/1081 (1951 II, p.315).
The Public Health (Tuberculosis) Regulations 1952	S.I. 1952/704 (1952 III, p.2736).
The Public Health (Infectious Diseases) Regulations 1953	S.I. 1953/299 (1953 II, p.1691).
The Acute Rheumatism Regulations 1953	S.I. 1953/1928 (1953 II, p.1688).
The Puerperal Pyrexia (Amendment) Regulations 1954	S.I. 1954/1691 (1954 II, p.1846).
The Acute Rheumatism (Amendment) Regulations 1957	S.I. 1957/8 (1957 II, p.1932).
The Acute Rheumatism (Amendment) Regulations 1958	S.I. 1958/17 (1958 II, p.2012).
The Acute Rheumatism (Amendment) Regulations 1959	S.I. 1959/213.
The Public Health (Infectious Diseases) Amendment Regulations 1960	S.I. 1960/1989 (1960 II, p.2802).
The Public Health (Leprosy) Regulations 1966	S.I. 1966/12 (1966 I, p.13).
The Public Health (Infective Jaundice) Regulations 1968	S.I. 1968/861 (1968 I, p. 2287).

Given under the official seal of the Minister of Health on 23rd August 1968.

(L.S.)

Kenneth Robinson,
Minister of Health.

EXPLANATORY NOTE
(This Note is not part of the Regulations.)

These Regulations consolidate with amendments all previous Regulations relating to the notification and prevention of infectious disease except the Public Health (Prevention of Tuberculosis) Regulations 1925.

Certain infectious diseases were defined as notifiable diseases by the Public Health Act 1936, and all sections relating to the prevention and notification of disease in that Act and in the Public Health Act 1961 applied automatically to them. Regulations made under the Act of 1936 applied various of those sections, mainly relative to notification, to other infectious diseases, and authorised certain measures for preventing the spread of disease. The Health Services and Public Health Act 1968 has amended the list of notifiable diseases and certain relevant sections of the earlier Acts.

These Regulations—
(i) apply specific sections of the three Acts to the diseases listed below;
(ii) prescribe the duties of a medical officer of health with respect to notifications and to returns and reports of disease, superseding certain provisions in the Public Health Officers Regulations 1959 and the Public Health Officers (Port Health Districts) Regulations 1959;
(iii) authorise certain measures for preventing the spread of disease.

The diseases for which provision is made by these regulations are—

Acute encephalitis	Diphtheria	Paratyphoid fever
Acute meningitis	Infective jaundice	Scarlet fever
Acute poliomyelitis	Leprosy	Tetanus
Amoebic dysentery	Leptospirosis	Tuberculosis
Anthrax	Malaria	Typhoid fever
Bacillary dysentery	Measles	Whooping cough
	Ophthalmia neonatorum	Yellow fever

The principal changes from the earlier Regulations are—
(a) any obligation to notify a case of disease now rests solely on a medical practitioner;
(b) changes and additions are made to the list of diseases which are to be notified and of the sections which apply to each disease (as set out in schedule 2); in particular, acute primary pneumonia, acute influenzal pneumonia, acute rheumatism and puerperal pyrexia are no longer to be notified, and tetanus and yellow fever require for the first time to be notified;
(c) leptospirosis, hitherto to be notified only in certain areas, is to be notified throughout England and Wales;
(d) the powers of a medical officer of health of a district to vaccinate contacts of persons suffering from smallpox have been extended to other diseases;
(e) all documents relating to notifications are to be treated as confidential;
(f) the powers of a local authority to require a person to stop work, in order to prevent spread of infection, are extended to permit action in cases of food poisoning.

The regulations come into force on the same day as the relevant sections of the Health Services and Public Health Act 1968—namely, 1st October 1968.

STATUTORY INSTRUMENTS

1968 No. 1373

PENSIONS

The Superannuation (Miscellaneous Provisions) Act 1967, s.15 (Appointed Day) Order 1968

Made - - - *23rd August* 1968

In pursuance of section 15 of the Superannuation (Miscellaneous Provisions) Act 1967(a), I hereby make the following Order :—

1. 1st November 1968 shall be the appointed day for the purposes of section 15 of the Superannuation (Miscellaneous Provisions) Act 1967.

2. This Order may be cited as the Superannuation (Miscellaneous Provisions) Act 1967, s.15 (Appointed Day) Order 1968.

James Callaghan,
One of Her Majesty's Principal
Secretaries of State.

Home Office,
  Whitehall.
23rd August 1968.

EXPLANATORY NOTE

(This Note is not part of the Order.)

This Order appoints 1st November 1968 as the effective date for the purposes of section 15 of the Superannuation (Miscellaneous Provisions) Act 1967, which relates to the superannuation of the civil staff of the metropolitan police, and the justices' clerks for the inner London area and other officers employed by the committee of magistrates for that area.

(a) 1967 c. 28.

STATUTORY INSTRUMENTS

1968 No. 1374

DIPLOMATIC AND INTERNATIONAL IMMUNITIES AND PRIVILEGES

The Commonwealth Countries and Republic of Ireland (Immunities) (Amendment) (No. 2) Order 1968

Made - - - -	*26th August* 1968
Laid before Parliament	*30th August* 1968
Coming into Operation	*31st August* 1968

At the Court at Balmoral, the 26th day of August 1968

Present,

The Queen's Most Excellent Majesty in Council

Her Majesty, in exercise of the powers conferred on Her by section 1(2) of the Diplomatic Immunities (Commonwealth Countries and Republic of Ireland) Act 1952(a) and of all other powers enabling Her in that behalf, is pleased, by and with the advice of Her Privy Council, to order, and it is hereby ordered, as follows :—

1.—(1) This Order may be cited as the Commonwealth Countries and Republic of Ireland (Immunities) (Amendment) (No. 2) Order 1968.

(2) This Order shall come into operation on 31st August 1968.

(3) The Interpretation Act 1889(b) shall apply, with the necessary adaptations, for the interpretation of this Order as it applies for the interpretation of an Act of Parliament.

2. In Part I of Schedule 1 to the Commonwealth Countries and Republic of Ireland (Immunities) (No. 2) Order 1967(c) before the sub-heading "Australia" shall be inserted the sub-heading "The associated states", followed by the entry :—

"The Commissioner of the Eastern Caribbean Governments,

The Trade Secretary,

The Welfare Officer.".

N. E. Leigh.

(a) 1952 c. 18. (b) 1889 c. 63. (c) S.I. 1967/815 (1967 II, p. 2431).

EXPLANATORY NOTE

(This Note is not part of the Order.)

This Order adds three additional offices to Part I of Schedule 1 to the Commonwealth Countries and Republic of Ireland (Immunities) (No. 2) Order 1967, namely the Commissioner of the Eastern Caribbean Governments who is the representative in the United Kingdom of the associated states established by the West Indies Act 1967 and the Trade Secretary and Welfare Officer. It confers on the persons holding these offices the like immunity from suit and legal process and the like inviolability of official archives as are accorded to consular officers of a foreign sovereign Power, and restricts powers of entry into the official premises of such persons.

1968 No. 1375

FUGITIVE CRIMINAL

The Fugitive Offenders (Overseas Territories) (No. 2) Order 1968

Made - - - - *26th August* 1968
Laid before Parliament *30th August* 1968
Coming into Operation *6th September* 1968

At the Court at Balmoral, the 26th day of August 1968

Present,

The Queen's Most Excellent Majesty in Council

Her Majesty, in exercise of the powers conferred upon Her by sections 17 and 20 of the Fugitive Offenders Act 1967(a), is pleased, by and with the advice of Her Privy Council, to order, and it is hereby ordered, as follows :—

1.—(1) This Order may be cited as the Fugitive Offenders (Overseas Territories) (No. 2) Order 1968. *(Citation and Commencement.)*

(2) This Order shall come into operation on 6th September 1968.

2. The Interpretation Act 1889(b) shall apply, with the necessary adaptations, for the purpose of interpreting this Order and otherwise in relation thereto as it applies for the purpose of interpreting, and in relation to, Acts of Parliament. *(Interpretation.)*

3. Each of the Orders in Council specified in Schedule 1 hereto is amended in the manner set out in Schedule 2 hereto. *(Amendment of certain Orders in Council.)*

N. E. Leigh

SCHEDULE 1

Article 3.

Title	Reference
The Fugitive Offenders (Bahama Islands) Order 1967	S.I. 1967/1904 (1967 III, p. 5204).
The Fugitive Offenders (Bermuda) Order 1967	S.I. 1967/1905 (1967 III, p. 5215).
The Fugitive Offenders (British Honduras) Order 1967	S.I. 1967/1906 (1967 III, p. 5226).
The Fugitive Offenders (British Indian Ocean Territory) Order 1968	S.I. 1968/183 (1968 I, p. 499).
The Fugitive Offenders (British Solomon Islands Protectorate) Order 1967	S.I. 1967/1907 (1967 III, p. 5237).

(a) 1967 c. 68.   (b) 1889 c. 63.

Title	Reference
The Fugitive Offenders (Cayman Islands) Order 1968	S.I. 1968/112 (1968 I, p. 306).
The Fugitive Offenders (Falkland Islands and Dependencies) Order 1968	S.I. 1968/113 (1968 I, p. 317).
The Fugitive Offenders (Fiji) Order 1967	S.I. 1967/1908 (1967 III, p. 5248).
The Fugitive Offenders (Gibraltar) Order 1967	S.I. 1967/1909 (1967 III, p. 5259).
The Fugitive Offenders (Gilbert and Ellice Islands) Order 1967	S.I. 1967/1910 (1967 III, p. 5270).
The Fugitive Offenders (Hong Kong) Order 1967	S.I. 1967/1911 (1967 III, p. 5281).
The Fugitive Offenders (Montserrat) Order 1967	S.I. 1967/1913 (1967 III, p. 5303).
The Fugitive Offenders (Pitcairn) Order 1968	S.I. 1968/884 (1968 II, p. 2321).
The Fugitive Offenders (St. Helena) Order 1968	S.I. 1968/184 (1968 I, p. 510).
The Fugitive Offenders (Seychelles) Order 1967	S.I. 1967/1914 (1967 III, p. 5314).
The Fugitive Offenders (Sovereign Base Areas of Akrotiri and Dhekelia) Order 1967	S.I. 1967/1916 (1967 III, p. 5336).
The Fugitive Offenders (Turks and Caicos Islands) Order 1968	S.I. 1968/185 (1968 I, p. 521).
The Fugitive Offenders (Virgin Islands) Order 1967	S.I. 1967/1915 (1967 III, p. 5325).

Article 3.   SCHEDULE 2

1. In subsection 5(1) in the Schedule all the words from "by or on behalf of the Government of the United Kingdom" down to the end of the subsection shall be deleted and the following shall be substituted therefor—

"by or on behalf of the Government, in the case of the United Kingdom, the Republic of Ireland or a designated Commonwealth country, or the Governor in the case of a United Kingdom dependency, of the country in which the person to be returned is accused or was convicted".

2. Paragraphs (a) and (d) of subsection 19(2) in the Schedule shall be revoked.

EXPLANATORY NOTE

(This Note is not part of the Order.)

This Order amends the Orders specified in Schedule 1 thereto (whereby the Fugitive Offenders Act 1967 was extended with modifications to certain overseas territories) by deleting certain modifications in the construction of the term "Governor" which are no longer required. The Order also makes some minor drafting amendments.

STATUTORY INSTRUMENTS

1968 No. 1376

AFRICA

The Swaziland (Compensation and Retiring Benefits) Order 1968

Made - - - -	*26th August* 1968
Laid before Parliament	*30th August* 1968
Coming into Operation	*Immediately before* 6th September 1968

At the Court at Balmoral, the 26th day of August 1968

Present,

The Queen's Most Excellent Majesty in Council

Her Majesty, by virtue and in exercise of all the powers in that behalf by the Foreign Jurisdiction Act 1890(a) or otherwise in Her Majesty vested, is pleased, by and with the advice of Her Privy Council, to order, and it is hereby ordered, as follows:—

1.—(1) This Order may be cited as the Swaziland (Compensation and Retiring Benefits) Order 1968. *Citation and commencement.*

(2) This Order shall come into operation immediately before 6th September 1968.

2.—(1) In this Order "the general compensation scheme" means the general scheme of retirement benefits for pensionable officers who are designated officers for the purposes of the Overseas Service (Swaziland) Agreement 1962 that was published by the Government of Swaziland on 11th March 1968. *Interpretation.*

(2) The Interpretation Act 1889(b) shall apply, with the necessary adaptations, for the purpose of interpreting this Order and otherwise in relation thereto as it applies for the purpose of interpreting, and in relation to, Acts of Parliament of the United Kingdom.

3. The provisions contained in the Schedule to this Order shall have effect in relation to the public service of Swaziland. *Application of Schedule.*

4.—(1) Where any officer or authority has before the commencement of this Order in pursuance of any provision of the general compensation scheme given any permission or consent or prescribed any condition or granted any benefit or made any payment or made any declaration or done any other thing for the purposes of that scheme, that permission, consent, condition, benefit, payment, declaration or other thing shall be deemed to have been given, prescribed, granted, made or done, as the case may be, under the corresponding provision of the Schedule to this Order, and the provisions of that Schedule shall have effect accordingly. *Transitional provisions.*

(a) 1890 c. 37.   (b) 1889 c. 63.

(2) Where any officer has before the commencement of this Order in pursuance of any provision in the general compensation scheme given any undertaking or given or received any notice or retired or received any benefit he shall, provided that any conditions prescribed or deemed to have been prescribed by or under the Schedule to this Order are satisfied, be deemed to have given that undertaking, to have given or received that notice, or to have retired, or to have been granted or received that benefit, as the case may be, under the corresponding provision in that Schedule, and the provisions of that Schedule shall have effect accordingly.

(3) Any officer who has, before the commencement of this Order, been required under the provisions of the general compensation scheme, to retire to facilitate the localisation of the public service of Swaziland shall, for the purposes of the Schedule to this Order, be deemed to have retired under section 17 of the Swaziland Independence Order 1968(a).

(4) The notice prescribed by the general compensation scheme to be given by officers who elect to retire from the public service shall be deemed to have been prescribed by the appropriate Service Commission under paragraph 4 of the Schedule to this Order ; any declaration made by Her Majesty's Commissioner for Swaziland under the general compensation scheme as to whether an officer has been or is required to retire in the circumstances described in paragraph 5 of that Schedule shall be deemed to have been made by the appropriate Service Commission under that paragraph.

(5) Any conditions or notices prescribed by the appropriate Service Commission for the purpose of paragraph 4 or paragraph 9(2) of the Schedule to this Order shall be not less favourable to any officer than any conditions or notices prescribed by or for the purpose of the corresponding provision of the general compensation scheme.

Modified application. **5.** If the Government of the United Kingdom and the Government of Swaziland agree that, in their application to any officer, the foregoing provisions of this Order and the provisions of the Schedule thereto shall have effect subject to such modifications or exceptions as those Governments may agree, then those provisions shall have effect accordingly.

N. E. Leigh.

SCHEDULE

COMPENSATION AND RETIREMENT BENEFITS FOR CERTAIN OFFICERS IN THE PUBLIC SERVICE OF SWAZILAND

Interpretation. **1.**—(1) In this Schedule, unless the context otherwise requires—

" appropriate law " in relation to an officer in the public service means the law in force in Swaziland that governs the grant of pensions, gratuities and other like benefits in respect of the service of that officer in the public service ;

" appropriate Service Commission "—

(a) in relation to an officer who can be removed from his office by the Judicial Service Commission, means that Commission ; and

(b) in any other case, means the Public Service Commission ;

(a) S.I. 1968/1377(1968) II, p. 3838).

" entitled officer " means an officer in the public service who on the operative date has not attained the age of fifty-five years and who—

(a) was before the operative date selected for appointment to an office in the public service being a pensionable office for the purposes of the appropriate law ; or

(b) was on the operative date the substantive holder of an office that was at that date a pensionable office for the purposes of the appropriate law ; and

(c) is a designated officer for the purposes of the Overseas Service (Swaziland) Agreement 1962 ; and

(d) has since the operative date been the substantive holder of an office service in which may during his tenure thereof be taken into account in computing his pension under the appropriate law ; and

(e) has been confirmed in his appointment, where his appointment is subject to confirmation,

and includes an officer in the public service on and since the operative date to whom the provisions of the Oversea Superannuation Scheme (Consolidation) Regulations apply ;

" General Orders " means the General Orders of the Government ;

" Government " means the Government of Swaziland ;

" operative date " means 1st April 1968 ;

" Oversea Superannuation Scheme (Consolidation) Regulations " means any regulations so entitled made by a Secretary of State ;

" pensionable emoluments " means emoluments that may be taken into account in computing the pension of an officer under the appropriate law ;

" pensionable service " means the aggregate amount of service that may be taken into account for the purpose of computing the pension of an officer under the appropriate law or the Oversea Superannuation Scheme (Consolidation) Regulations, as the case may be, and in the case of an officer to whom the Oversea Superannuation Scheme (Consolidation) Regulations apply includes service that could be taken into account for the purpose of computing pensions under the Pensions Proclamation of Swaziland(a) ;

" public service " means the public service of Swaziland ;

" substantive holder " in relation to any office includes a person serving in that office on probation but does not include a person (other than a person serving under a probationary agreement) serving in that office for a specified term under a contract.

(2) For the purposes of this Schedule—

(a) a person shall not be regarded as holding any office on the operative date if on that date he was on leave of absence pending his retirement otherwise than under this Schedule ;

(b) a person whose office has been abolished and who retires in consequence of the abolition of his office shall be deemed to be the substantive holder of that office during the period between the date on which the office was abolished and the date of expiration of any leave of absence granted to him pending his retirement ;

(a) Chapter 57 of the Revised Laws of Swaziland 1959.

(c) when an officer on probation is required to retire—

(i) under section 17 of the Swaziland Independence Order 1968 ;

(ii) to facilitate the introduction of constitutional changes ;

(iii) in consequence of injury or ill-health ;

(iv) in consequence of the abolition of his office or for the purpose of facilitating improvements in the organisation of that part of the public service to which he belongs by which greater economy or efficiency may be effected ; or

(v) on the grounds of age in accordance with the provisions of the appropriate law,

he shall be deemed to have been confirmed in his appointment immediately before the day upon which he was given notice requiring him to retire ;

(d) subject to the provisions of head (a) of this sub-paragraph, an officer who satisfies the conditions specified in heads (a) or (b) and (c) and (e) of the definition of " entitled officer " in sub-paragraph (1) of this paragraph, and who has, before the date of the commencement of this Order retired or died, shall be deemed to have become entitled to compensation under paragraph 2 of this Schedule and the provisions of this Schedule shall have effect in relation to such officer as if he were an entitled officer immediately before such retirement or death.

(3) For the purposes of calculating the compensation to which an officer is entitled under this Schedule, where the officer is seconded to the service of another government or authority on the date in relation to which the assessment is made he shall be deemed to have such annual pensionable emoluments on that date as he would have had on that date if he had not been so seconded but had continued until that date to hold the office in the public service that he was holding immediately before his secondment and had been granted all increments and other increases of salary for which he would thus have been eligible.

(4) Where an officer was on any date appointed or selected for appointment to an office in the public service upon transfer from pensionable employment under the Government of the United Kingdom in a public office as defined by the Superannuation Act 1892(a) and for any period thereafter was entitled to return to such pensionable employment he shall not for the purposes of this Schedule be regarded as having been on that date appointed or, as the case may be, selected for appointment as the substantive holder of an office in the public service but shall for those purposes be regarded as having been so appointed or selected on the date on which he ceases to be entitled to return to such pensionable employment if on that date he was holder of an office in the public service.

(5) An entitled officer who is required to retire and who, immediately before being so required, acted for a period of six months to the satisfaction of the appropriate Service Commission in a pensionable office, the pensionable emoluments of which were higher than those of the office of which he was the substantive holder, shall be deemed to be confirmed in the pensionable office in which he was acting.

(a) 1892 c. 40.

(6) The provisions of this Schedule shall, in relation to an entitled officer who is a judge of the High Court of Swaziland, have effect as if—

(*a*) references to the age of fifty-five years were references to the age of sixty-two years ;

(*b*) references to Table I of the Annex to this Schedule were references to Table II of that Annex.

2.—(1) Subject to the provisions of this Schedule, every entitled officer shall, on the operative date or, in the case of a person who becomes an entitled officer after that date, on the date on which he becomes an entitled officer, become entitled to compensation which shall be assessed in accordance with the provisions of this paragraph and at each assessment shall be calculated by multiplying the amount of his annual pensionable emoluments on the date in relation to which the assessment is made by the appropriate factor and the resulting amount, or twenty-four thousand rands, whichever is the less, shall be the amount to which he is entitled.

Entitlement to compensation.

(2) The compensation of each entitled officer under this paragraph shall, if it has not already been provisionally assessed, be provisionally assessed as soon as is reasonably practicable after the commencement of this Order or, in the case of a person who becomes an entitled officer after the commencement of this Order, as soon as is reasonably practicable after that person becomes an entitled officer, and for that purpose the date in relation to which the assessment is to be made shall, subject to the provisions of paragraph 5(2) of this Schedule, be the operative date or, in the case of a person who becomes an entitled officer after the operative date, the date on which that person became an entitled officer.

(3) The compensation under this paragraph of each person who is serving as an entitled officer shall be provisionally re-assessed upon each anniversary of the date in relation to which his compensation was provisionally assessed and shall be finally assessed upon his retirement or death while still serving as an entitled officer, and for the purposes of this sub-paragraph the date in relation to which the assessment is to be made shall be such date (not being earlier than the date in relation to which his compensation was provisionally assessed or later than the date upon which his compensation is provisionally re-assessed or finally assessed, as the case may be) as is most advantageous in relation to the officer.

(4) When the compensation of any entitled officer is provisionally assessed or re-assessed or is finally assessed, he (or, in the case of an officer who has died, his personal representatives) shall thereupon be given a statement showing the amount of the compensation to which, in accordance with that provisional assessment or re-assessment or final assessment, he is entitled.

(5) In this paragraph " the appropriate factor " in relation to an officer means the factor obtained from Table I of the Annex to this Schedule that is appropriate to the age and pensionable service of that officer on the date in relation to which the assessment is to be made in completed years and months or, if it is more favourable to the officer, reckoned in completed years without regard to parts of a year.

Payment of
compensa-
tion.

3.—(1) When the compensation of an entitled officer has been provisionally assessed, a payment shall be made to that officer, which—

(a) in the case of an entitled officer who has undertaken after the operative date, otherwise than in relation to his promotion in the public service, to serve as such upon such conditions and for a period of not less than twenty-four months, shall be an amount equal to the amount of the compensation or four thousand rands, whichever is the less ;

(b) in any other case, shall be an amount equal to the amount of the compensation as so assessed or, if that amount exceeds two thousand rands, then one-sixth of the amount of compensation or two thousand rands, whichever is the greater:

Provided that if an entitled officer gives such an undertaking after a payment has been made to him under this sub-paragraph, but not later than twelve months after the date in relation to which his compensation was provisionally assessed, he shall be paid as soon as is reasonably practicable after the date on which he gave that undertaking and in any case within three months of that date, an amount which when added to the amount already paid to him equals the amount he would have been paid under this sub-paragraph if he had given that undertaking before any payment had been made to him under this sub-paragraph.

(2) Subject to the provisions of paragraph 12 of this Schedule, a further payment shall be made to every person who has become entitled to compensation under paragraph 2 of this Schedule and who has not already received the whole of that compensation (whether that person is serving as an entitled officer or has retired) upon each anniversary of the date in relation to which his compensation was assessed under sub-paragraph (2) of that paragraph, which—

(a) in the case of a payment made upon the first, second, third or fourth anniversary, shall be an amount equal to the appropriate fraction of the balance of compensation then outstanding ; and

(b) in the case of a payment made upon the fifth or any later anniversary, shall be an amount equal to the balance of compensation then outstanding:

Provided that—

(i) where the balance of compensation outstanding upon the first, second, third or fourth anniversary exceeds one thousand rands and, in the case of an officer to whom sub-paragraph (1)(a) of this paragraph applies, where that balance, if added to the amount of compensation already paid under this paragraph, would exceed four thousand rands, an amount equal to the appropriate fraction of that balance or eight hundred rands, whichever is the greater, shall be paid ;

(ii) where the balance so outstanding is less than one thousand rands, or, in the case of an officer to whom sub-paragraph (1)(a) of this paragraph applies, where that balance exceeds one thousand rands but would not, if added to the amount of compensation already paid under this paragraph, exceed four thousand rands, an amount equal to that balance shall be paid.

(3) In this section " the appropriate fraction "—

(a) in relation to an assessment made upon the first anniversary, means one-fifth ;

(b) in relation to an assessment made upon the second anniversary, means one-quarter ;

(c) in relation to an assessment made upon the third anniversary, means one-third ; and

(d) in relation to an assessment made upon the fourth anniversary, means one-half.

4.—(1) Subject to the provisions of this paragraph, an entitled officer Retirement. may, after giving such notice as may be prescribed by the appropriate Service Commission, retire at any time.

(2) An entitled officer who has given notice of his intention to retire under this paragraph on any date may, with the consent of the appropriate Service Commission, withdraw the notice at any time before that date.

(3) No entitled officer shall retire under this paragraph without the permission of the appropriate Service Commission:

Provided that the Commission shall not withhold permission unless disciplinary proceedings are being taken, or are about to be taken, against the officer and those proceedings might lead to his dismissal.

(4) An entitled officer—

(a) who is permitted to retire by reason of injury or ill health ;

(b) who is required to retire on or after his attainment of any age prescribed by law ;

(c) who is required to retire in consequence of the abolition of his office or for the purpose of facilitating improvements in the organisation of the part of the public service to which he belongs by which greater economy or efficiency may be effected ;

(d) who is required to retire in the public interest ;

(e) who is required to retire under section 17 of the Swaziland Independence Order 1968 ; or

(f) in the case of a woman officer, who is required to retire upon her marriage,

shall be deemed to have retired under this paragraph.

5.—(1) This paragraph shall apply to any entitled officer who is Retirement declared by the appropriate Service Commission to be an officer on required to retire in order to facilitate the introduction of constitutional constitutional changes ; and every such officer who so retires shall be deemed to have grounds. retired under this Schedule.

(2) The date in relation to which the compensation of an officer to whom this paragraph applies is to be assessed under paragraph 2(2) of this Schedule shall be such date in the period beginning on the date on which he was given notice requiring him to retire or the operative date, whichever is the earlier, and ending on the date of his retirement, as is most advantageous in relation to the officer.

(3) An officer to whom this paragraph applies shall as soon as reasonably practicable be paid a disturbance grant equal to one quarter of his annual pensionable emoluments at his retirement.

Special gratuity on the death of certain officers.

6.—(1) Where an entitled officer dies and it is lawful under the provisions of the appropriate law for a gratuity to be granted to his personal representatives there shall be granted to his personal representatives either that gratuity or a gratuity equal to the maximum gratuity that could have been granted to that officer under the provisions of paragraph 10 to this Schedule if he had retired under this Schedule at the date of his death, whichever is the greater.

(2) Where an entitled officer to whom the Oversea Superannuation Scheme (Consolidation) Regulations apply dies and a gratuity is payable to his personal representatives under those Regulations, there shall be granted to his personal representatives a gratuity equal to the amount produced by subtracting the amount of the gratuity payable under those Regulations from the amount of the maximum gratuity which could have been granted to that officer under paragraph 10 of this Schedule if that paragraph and the Pensions Proclamation had applied to him and he had retired under this Schedule at the date of his death.

(3) The Permanent Secretary, Ministry of Finance, may direct that instead of being paid to the personal representatives, any gratuity payable under this paragraph shall be paid to one of the dependants of the deceased or to two or more of those dependants in such proportions as the Permanent Secretary may think fit.

Officers reappointed to U.K. service.

7.—(1) This paragraph applies to an entitled officer who has retired under this Schedule and—

(a) who was transferred to the public service from pensionable employment under the Government of the United Kingdom either in a public office as defined by the Superannuation Act 1892 or in employment pensionable under the Federated Superannuation System for Universities ; and

(b) who not later than twelve months after he retired has (other than as the result of a competition conducted by the Civil Service Commissioners of the United Kingdom) returned to such pensionable employment.

(2) A person to whom this paragraph applies shall cease to be entitled to compensation under paragraph 2 of this Schedule, but shall be entitled to compensation of an amount equal to—

(a) one-half of the amount he would receive if he were entitled to compensation under paragraph 2 of this Schedule ; or

(b) the amount he would receive if he were entitled to compensation under paragraph 8 of this Schedule, having been transferred to the pensionable employment referred to in sub-paragraph (1)(b) of this paragraph on the date on which he retired,

whichever is the less.

(3) If the provisions of this paragraph become applicable to any person, his compensation shall forthwith be re-assessed, and—

(a) if the amount of compensation as so re-assessed exceeds the amount he has already received under this Schedule, the balance of compensation then outstanding shall be paid, together with any unpaid interest that has accrued under this Schedule before the re-assessment, in the manner prescribed by paragraph 3 of this Schedule for the payment of compensation assessed under paragraph 2 of this Schedule ; or

(b) if the amount of compensation he has already received under this Schedule exceeds the amount of compensation to which he is entitled under this paragraph, the excess shall forthwith become repayable, but in any such case any interest received on account of such excess shall not be repayable.

8.—(1) This paragraph applies to an entitled officer who is transferred from the public service— *Transfer to other public service.*

(a) to the service of a government or authority that is a Scheduled Government for the purposes of Part III of the Swaziland Pensions Regulations in circumstances in which he remains eligible for the grant of a pension under the appropriate law upon his eventual retirement ;

(b) to service in the office of Governor in such circumstances that he is or may become eligible for a pension under the Governors' Pensions Act 1957(a):

Provided that—

(a) it does not apply to an officer to whom paragraph 7 of this Schedule applies ;

(b) it applies to any officer—

(i) who, but for the provisions of paragraph 1(4) of this Schedule, would be an entitled officer ; and

(ii) who, in the opinion of the appropriate Service Commission, would have had a reasonable prospect of becoming an entitled officer if no constitutional changes had been introduced ; and

(iii) who, unless prevented by circumstances beyond his control, serves for a period of not less than two years residential service beginning on the operative date ; and

(iv) who returns to pensionable employment under the Government of the United Kingdom in a public office as defined in the Superannuation Act 1892,

as if he were an entitled officer.

(2) An officer to whom this paragraph applies shall cease to be entitled to compensation under paragraph 2 of this Schedule, but if the amount of his annual pensionable emoluments immediately before his transfer exceeds the amount of the annual emoluments payable to him immediately after his transfer (being emoluments that may be taken into account for the purposes of his pension under the law or regulations relating to his service in that other public service) he shall be entitled to compensation equal to—

(a) the amount of the excess multiplied by the appropriate factor ; or

(b) the amount he would receive if he were entitled to compensation under paragraph 2 of this Schedule, having retired on the date of his transfer,

whichever is the less.

(a) 1957 c. 62.

(3) If the provisions of this paragraph become applicable to any person, his compensation shall forthwith be re-assessed, and—

(*a*) if the amount of compensation as so re-assessed exceeds the amount he has already received under this Schedule, the balance of compensation then outstanding shall be paid, together with any unpaid interest that has accrued under this Schedule before the re-assessment, in the manner prescribed by paragraph 3 of this Schedule for the payment of compensation assessed under paragraph 2 of this Schedule ; or

(*b*) if the amount of compensation which has already been received under that paragraph exceeds the amount of compensation to which he is entitled under this paragraph, the excess shall forthwith become repayable, but in any such case any interest received on account of such excess shall not be repayable.

(4) In this paragraph " the appropriate factor " in relation to an officer means the factor obtained from Table III of the Annex to this Schedule that is appropriate to the age of the officer at the date of his transfer reckoned in completed years and completed months.

Penalties for breach of undertakings.

9.—(1) If an entitled officer who has given an undertaking for the purposes of paragraph 3(1)(*a*) of this Schedule ceases to serve in accordance with the terms of that undertaking at any time before the end of the period to which the undertaking relates otherwise than with the consent of the Government or by reason of his death, his retirement in circumstances beyond his control or his transfer to other public service in the circumstances described in paragraph 8 of this Schedule, then the amount of compensation to which he would otherwise be entitled under paragraph 2 of this Schedule shall be reduced by an amount equal to one-half per centum for each month or part of a month during that period in which he has not served in accordance with the undertaking, or four hundred rands, whichever is the less.

(2) If an entitled officer has been granted promotion in the public service after the operative date upon his giving an undertaking to serve upon such conditions as may be prescribed by the appropriate Service Commission for a period of not less than twenty-four months ceases to serve in accordance with the terms of that undertaking at any time before the end of the period to which the undertaking relates otherwise than with the consent of the Government or by reason of his death or his retirement in circumstances beyond his control, then the amount of compensation to which he is entitled under paragraph 2 of this Schedule shall be re-assessed and the amount of his compensation shall be determined as if his annual pensionable emoluments in relation to the date of his promotion or any subsequent date were the amount of the pensionable emoluments which would have been taken in accordance with Regulation 18 of the Swaziland Pensions Regulations for the purpose of computing his pension if he had retired on that date.

(3) If any of the provisions of this paragraph become applicable to any entitled officer, his compensation shall be re-assessed accordingly and paid in accordance with paragraph 3 of this Schedule and if the amount of compensation he has already received under that paragraph exceeds the amount of compensation to which he is entitled under the re-assessment the excess shall forthwith become repayable.

10.—(1) Subject to the provisions of paragraphs 17 and 19 of this Grant of pensions and gratuities. Schedule, an entitled officer, on his retirement under this Schedule, may be granted at his option (such option to be exercised in accordance with the provisions of Regulation 24 of the Swaziland Pensions Regulations) either—

 (*a*) a pension of such amount as may be granted under the appro- priate law ;

 (*b*) a reduced pension equal to such fraction as he may desire of the pension that may be granted under the appropriate law (not being, in the case of an officer who retires within twelve years of the operative date, less than the permitted fraction) together with a gratuity equal to the annual amount of the remaining fraction of that pension multiplied by the appropriate factor ; or

 (*c*) in the case of an officer who retires not less than twelve years after the operative date, a gratuity equal to the annual amount of the pension that may be granted under the appropriate law multiplied by the appropriate factor.

(2) For the purposes of this paragraph an officer shall be deemed to be eligible for the grant of a pension under the appropriate law—

 (*a*) notwithstanding that he may have retired before attaining the age specified in the appropriate law as qualifying him for the grant of a pension ; and

 (*b*) notwithstanding that he may not have completed at the date of his retirement the period of qualifying service required by the appropriate law to render him eligible for the grant of a pension.

(3) Where an officer retires by reason of injury or ill health in cir- cumstances in which he could under the appropriate law be granted an additional pension the provisions of this paragraph shall have effect in relation to that officer as if references to the pension that may be granted under the appropriate law included references to that additional pension.

(4) Where an officer to whom this paragraph applies retires in con- sequence of the abolition of his office or for the purpose of facilitating improvements in the organisation of the part of the public service to which he belongs by which greater economy or efficiency may be effected in circumstances in which he could under the appropriate law be granted an additional pension, the provisions of this paragraph shall have effect in relation to that officer as if references to the pen- sion that may be granted under the appropriate law did not include references to that additional pension.

(5) For the purposes of this paragraph the amount of the pension or gratuity that an officer who is required to retire in the circum- stances described in paragraph 4(4)(*c*) or (*e*) or paragraph 5(1) of this Schedule or on the grounds of age before attaining the age of fifty-five years may be granted under the appropriate law shall be calculated by reference to the full annual pensionable emoluments enjoyed by him on the date immediately prior to his retirement.

(6) If an officer has not exercised the option conferred upon him by sub-paragraph (1) of this paragraph within the period in which it is required to be exercised he shall be deemed to have opted for the grant of a pension of such amount as may be granted under the appropriate law.

(7) In this paragraph—

" the appropriate factor " in relation to an officer means the factor obtained from Table IV of the Annex to this Schedule that is appropriate to the age of that officer on the date immediately prior to his retirement reckoned in completed years and completed months ;

" the permitted fraction "—

(a) in relation to an officer who retires within one year of the operative date, means three-quarters ;

(b) in relation to an additional pension granted on account of injury under Regulation 23(1) of the Swaziland Pensions Regulations, means three-quarters ; and

(c) subject to head (b) of this definition, in relation to an officer who retires within not less than one and not more than twelve years of the operative date, means such fraction as is obtained by subtracting one-sixteenth for each complete year of his pensionable service after the operative date from three-quarters :

Provided that in reckoning for the purposes of this sub-paragraph the years of pensionable service of an officer who is granted leave of absence pending his retirement, leave of absence granted in respect of service prior to the operative date the enjoyment of which had on the operative date been deferred shall not be taken into account.

Special gratuity for certain officers.

11.—(1) Subject to the provisions of paragraphs 17 and 19 of this Schedule, where any entitled officer to whom Part III of the Swaziland Pensions Regulations applies retires under this Schedule and is granted by any government or other authority that is a Scheduled Government for the purposes of that Part both a pension and a gratuity, having elected to receive that pension and that gratuity in lieu of a pension of greater amount, he may be granted (in addition to any gratuity that may be granted to him under paragraph 10 of this Schedule) a gratuity equal to the amount (if any) by which the amount produced by—

(i) subtracting the annual amount of the pension granted to him by the Scheduled Government from the annual amount of the pension that would have been granted to him by that Goverment had he not elected to receive the gratuity granted to him by the Scheduled Government ; and

(ii) multiplying the resulting amount by the appropriate factor,

exceeds the amount of the gratuity granted to him by the Scheduled Government.

(2) Subject to the provisions of paragraphs17 and 19 of this Schedule, where an entitled officer to whom the provisions of the Oversea Superannuation Scheme (Consolidation) Regulations apply retires under this Schedule and is granted under those Regulations a pension and a lump sum—

(a) he may be granted a gratuity equal to the amount produced by subtracting that lump sum from the sum arrived by multiplying by the appropriate factor one-quarter of the annual amount of the pension he would have received if his pension had been calculated under the Pensions Proclamation ; and

(b) he may be granted (in addition to any gratuity that may be granted to him under head (a) of this sub-paragraph) at his option—

    (i) on assigning to the Government a part of the annual amount of the pension granted to him under those Regulations (not being in the case of an officer who retires within twelve years of the operative date, more than the permitted fraction); or

    (ii) in the case of an officer who retires not less than twelve years after the operative date, on assigning the whole of the annual amount of such pension,

a gratuity equal to the amount of his pension so assigned multiplied by the appropriate factor ; such option to be exercised in accordance with the provisions of Regulation 24 of the Swaziland Pensions Regulations.

(3) In this paragraph—

" the appropriate factor " has the same meaning as in paragraph 10 of this Schedule ;

" the permitted fraction "—

    (a) in relation to an officer who retires within not less than one year but within two years of the operative date, means one-twelfth ;

    (b) in relation to an officer who retires within not less than two years of the operative date, means the fraction obtained by adding one-twelfth for each completed year of his pensionable service after the operative date to one-twelfth:

Provided that in reckoning for the purposes of this sub-paragraph the years of pensionable service of an officer who is granted leave of absence pending his retirement leave of absence granted in respect of service prior to the operative date enjoyment of which had on the operative date been deferred shall not be taken into account.

12.—(1) Whenever—

    (a) a person who has become entitled to compensation under paragraph 2 of this Schedule but who has not already received the whole of that compensation (and in the case of an entitled officer whether he is still serving as such or has already retired) attains the age of fifty-five years, or dies before attaining that age ;

    (b) an entitled officer who has not already received the whole of the compensation to which he is entitled under paragraph 2 retires in the circumstances described in paragraph 4(4)(a), (c) or (d) of this Schedule before he has attained that age or is required to retire in the circumstances described in paragraph 4(4)(b) of this Schedule: or

    (c) an entitled officer who has not already received the whole of the compensation to which he is entitled under paragraph 2 of this Schedule retires in any other circumstances before he has attained that age but on or after the fifth anniversary of the operative date or, in the case of a person who became an entitled officer after that date, of the date on which he became an entitled officer,

the balance then outstanding of the compensation to which he is entitled shall be paid to that person or, if that person is dead, to his personal representatives.

Special provisions as to payment of compensation.

(2) Whenever an entitled officer, who has not already received the whole of the compensation to which he is entitled under paragraph 2 of this Schedule, is required to retire under section 17 of the Swaziland Independence Order 1968 before attaining the age of fifty-five years, the balance then outstanding of the compensation to which he is entitled under that paragraph shall be paid to him—

(a) if notice requiring him to retire is given to him while he is engaged upon a tour of residential service, before his departure from Swaziland ; or

(b) if such notice is given to him while on leave of absence after completing a tour of residential service, as soon as reasonably practicable after the date upon which such notice is given to him.

(3) Whenever an officer, who has not already received the whole of the compensation to which he is entitled under paragraph 2 of this Schedule, is required to retire in the circumstances described in paragraph 5(1) of this Schedule, the balance then outstanding of the compensation to which he is entitled under that paragraph shall be paid to him as soon as practicable after the date of the notice requiring him to retire.

(4) The Permanent Secretary, Ministry of Finance, may direct that instead of any payment being made to the personal representatives of a deceased person payment shall be made to one of the dependants of the deceased or two or more of those dependants in such proportions as the Permanent Secretary may think fit.

(5) Whenever any payment of compensation becomes due under this Schedule interest at the rate of five per centum per annum shall accrue from day to day—

(a) in cases where the compensation has not been finally assessed, during the period between the date on which the amount of the compensation was last due to be assessed and the date on which the next following assessment is to be made ;

(b) in cases where the compensation has been finally assessed, during the period between the date on which that payment of compensation became due and the date on which the next following payment of compensation will become due,

upon any part of the compensation that did not then become payable and that interest shall become payable at the end of the period during which it accrued :

Provided that, for the purpose of calculating interest under this sub-paragraph the compensation to which the officer is entitled shall be deemed to have been provisionally assessed, and the first instalment thereof paid to the officer, on the operative date.

(6) When the compensation of an entitled officer is finally assessed under paragraph 2(3) of this Schedule upon his retirement, in addition to the interest payable under sub-paragraph (5) of this paragraph that officer shall be paid a sum equal to the interest that would, if the balance of compensation due to him on the date of his retirement had not been paid and provision had been made for interest at the rate of five per centum per annum to accrue from day to day on that balance, have accrued upon that balance during the period between the date of his retirement and the next anniversary of the operative date.

13.—(1) This paragraph shall apply to an entitled officer (not being Leave and an officer to whom paragraph 17 of this Schedule applies) who is subsistence required to retire under section 17 of the Swaziland Independence Order allowance. 1968 or paragraph 5 of this Schedule:

Provided that sub-paragraph (3)(*a*) of this paragraph shall also apply to an entitled officer who is required to retire in the circumstances described in paragraph 4(4)(*c*) of this Schedule.

(2) An officer to whom this paragraph applies who is on leave of absence after completing a tour of residential service when he is required to retire shall—

(i) if the period of leave on full pensionable emoluments for which he is eligible on the date upon which he is given notice requiring him to retire is less than six months, be granted such additional leave on full pensionable emoluments as will bring the aggregate period of such leave of absence from that date up to six months ;

(ii) if he returns to Swaziland to settle his affairs, he shall be paid a subsistence allowance at the rate prescribed by General Orders for the period of his stay in Swaziland or twenty-one days, whichever is the less.

(3) An officer to whom this paragraph applies who is not on leave of absence after completing a tour of residential service when he is required to retire—

(*a*) shall not be required to depart from Swaziland on leave of absence pending his retirement until the expiration of a period of six months from the date upon which he was given notice requiring him to retire ;

(*b*) shall, if the period of leave on full pensionable emoluments for which he is eligible is less than six months, be granted such additional leave on full pensionable emoluments as will bring the aggregate period of such leave of absence pending his retirement up to six months.

14.—(1) Where an entitled officer who is on leave of absence after Passages completing a tour of residential service gives notice of his intention to and retire under paragraph 4 of this Schedule, then— baggage facilities.

(*a*) if he returns to Swaziland at the requirement of the Government and is willing to undertake a further tour of residential service of not less than six months ; or

(*b*) if he returns to Swaziland to settle his affairs and is willing to undertake a further tour of residential service of not less than twelve months,

he shall be provided with appropriate passages and appropriate baggage facilities for himself and his family in respect of his and their return journey to Swaziland and in respect of his and their journey from Swaziland consequential upon his retirement ; and in any other case (whether or not he returns to Swaziland) he shall be provided with appropriate baggage facilities for himself and his family for the purpose of removing his and their effects from Swaziland.

(2) Where an entitled officer who is on leave of absence after completing a tour of residential service is required to retire under section 17

of the Swaziland Independence Order 1968 or under paragraph 5 of this Schedule he shall, if he returns to Swaziland to settle his affairs, be provided with appropriate passages in respect of his return journey to Swaziland and his subsequent journey from Swaziland; and in any case (whether or not he returns to Swaziland) he shall be provided with appropriate baggage facilities for himself and his family for the purpose of removing his and their effects from Swaziland.

(3) Where an entitled officer who is not on leave of absence after completing a tour of residential service gives notice of his intention to retire under paragraph 4 of this Schedule or is required to retire under section 17 of the Swaziland Independence Order 1968 or under paragraph 5 of this Schedule, he shall be provided with appropriate passages for himself and his family in respect of his and their journey from Swaziland (if any) consequential upon his retirement; and in any case (whether or not such passages are provided) he shall be provided with appropriate baggage facilities for himself and his family for the purpose of removing his and their effects from Swaziland.

(4) Where an entitled officer who has given the undertaking referred to in paragraph 3(1)(*a*) or in paragraph 9(2) of this Schedule returns to Swaziland at the requirement of the Government to undertake a further tour of residential service of not more than twelve months in order to fulfil such undertaking and is willing to undertake such a tour, he shall be provided with appropriate passages and appropriate baggage facilities for himself and his family in respect of his and their return journey to Swaziland and in respect of his and their journey from Swaziland.

(5) In this paragraph "appropriate passages" and "appropriate baggage facilities", in relation to an entitled officer or, as the case may be, to the family of an entitled officer, mean respectively such passages and such baggage facilities as an officer of his status is entitled to under General Orders for the purpose of travelling to Swaziland in order to begin a tour of residential service or, as the case may be, for the purpose of travelling from Swaziland when retiring from the public service, having attained the age of fifty-five years and having completed such a tour.

Disciplinary proceedings and dismissal.

15.—(1) When disciplinary proceedings are taken, or are about to be taken, against any person who is serving as an entitled officer and those proceedings might lead to his dismissal, the payment of compensation under this Schedule and interest thereon shall be withheld pending the determination of those proceedings.

(2) Where any person who is serving as an entitled officer is dismissed, any compensation that he has not already received may, with the approval of the appropriate Service Commission, be withheld.

Place of payment and rate of exchange.

16. Any compensation, gratuity, disturbance grant or interest payable under this Schedule to an officer or to his personal representatives or dependants shall be paid, in accordance with any request made from time to time by such officer, his personal representatives or his dependants, as the case may be, in any of the following countries—

(*a*) in the United Kingdom;

(*b*) in Swaziland;

(c) in the country from which the officer was recruited or where he intends to reside ;

(d) in the case of payment to the personal representatives of an officer or his dependants, in the country in which the personal representatives or the dependants, as the case may be, reside ; or

(e) in such other country as the officer or his personal representatives or dependants may, with the concurrence of the Permanent Secretary, Ministry of Finance, select,

in the currency of the country in which payment is to be made ; and, where payment is to be made in a country other than Swaziland, the amount of the payment shall be such as would produce, at the official rate of exchange prevailing at the date of the payment, the amount in sterling of the compensation, gratuity, disturbance grant or interest as calculated at the official rate of exchange prevailing on the operative date.

17.—(1) An entitled officer who, before he receives his initial payment of compensation, gives notice of retirement under paragraph 4 of this Schedule, or is required to retire in any of the circumstances described in paragraph 4(1) or paragraph 5(1) of this Schedule may at his option (such option to be exercised within three months of the commencement of this Order or, in the case of an officer who was not an entitled officer on the operative date, within three months of the date on which he became an entitled officer) become an officer to whom this paragraph applies. *Right to opt for abolition terms.*

(2) An officer to whom this paragraph applies shall not be entitled to compensation under this Schedule or be granted a pension, gratuity or disturbance grant under this Schedule but, subject to the provisions of paragraph 19 of this Schedule may, on his retirement under this Schedule, be granted such benefits as may be granted under the appropriate law to an officer whose office has been abolished.

(3) An officer to whom this paragraph applies shall repay the amount of any compensation that may have been paid to him.

18.—(1) If an entitled officer becomes at any time after the commencement of this Order a citizen of Swaziland by virtue of his own act he shall thereupon cease to be an entitled officer. *Aquisition of citizenship by entitled officer.*

(2) If any person ceases to be an entitled officer by virtue of this paragraph, the amount of compensation (if any) he has received under this Schedule shall forthwith become repayable, but in any such case any interest received shall not be repayable.

19. The provisions of the appropriate law shall, subject to the provisions of this Schedule, apply in relation to the grant of any pension or gratuity under this Schedule and to any pension or gratuity granted thereunder as they apply in relation to the grant of a pension or gratuity, and to any pension or gratuity granted, under the appropriate law : *Application of appropriate law.*

Provided that section 10 of the Pensions Proclamation or any law amending or replacing that section shall not apply in relation to any pension granted under the provisions of this Schedule.

20. Any compensation, gratuity or disturbance grant payable under any of the provisions of this Schedule shall be exempt from tax under *Exemption from tax.*

any law in force in Swaziland relating to the taxation of incomes or imposing any other form of taxation.

Exercise of options.

21. Any option exercisable by any person for the purposes of this Schedule—

(a) shall be irrevocable after the end of the period within which it is to be exercised ;

(b) shall be exercised by notice in writing to the appropriate Service Commission ;

(c) shall be deemed to have been exercised on the date on which the notice is received:

Provided that the appropriate Service Commission may, if it thinks fit, generally or in respect of a particular person and subject or not to conditions, extend the period for the exercise of an option.

ANNEX

INSTRUCTIONS FOR OBTAINING THE APPROPRIATE FACTOR FROM

TABLE I

I. Read off from the Table the factors for officer's age at his last birthday and his—

(a) completed years of service,

(b) completed years of service plus one year.

II. Subtract I(a) from I(b), divide the difference by twelve and multiply the result by the number of completed months of service, if any, in excess of the completed years of service.

III. Add I(a) and II.

IV. Repeat steps to III for the officer's age at his next birthday.

V. Divide the difference between III and IV by twelve and multiply by the number of completed months of age, if any, since the officer's last birthday.

VI. If IV is greater than III, add V to III.
If IV is less than III subtract V from III.

VI is the factor required.

INSTRUCTIONS FOR OBTAINING THE APPROPRIATE FACTOR FROM
TABLE II, III OR IV

I. Read off from the Table the factors for the officer's age—

(a) at his last birthday ;

(b) at his next birthday.

II. Divide the difference between I(a) and I(b) by twelve and multiply by the number of completed months of age since the last birthday.

III. If I(b) is greater than I(a), add II to I(a).
If I(b) is less than I(a), subtract II from I(a).

III is the factor required.

In calculating factors by interpolation in respect of Tables I to III the calculations should be rounded off to two decimal points and where this results in a difference of point nought one in either direction such difference should be ignored.

THE SCHEDULE, PARAGRAPH 2

TABLE I

Age of Officer	Factor when length of service is								
	2 years	3 years	4 years	5 years	6 years	7 years	8 years	9 years	10 years or more
21	·11	·16							
2	·12	·19	·25						
3	·14	·21	·28	·36					
4	·16	·24	·32	·40	·49				
25	·18	·27	·36	·46	·55	·64			
6	·20	·31	·41	·51	·61	·71	·82		
7	·23	·34	·45	·56	·68	·79	·90	1·02	
8	·25	·38	·50	·63	·76	88	1·01	1·13	1·26
9	·28	·42	·56	·70	·85	·99	1·13	1·27	1·41
30	·32	·48	·64	·80	·97	1·13	1·29	1·45	1·61
1	·37	·56	·74	·93	1·12	1·30	1·49	1·67	1·86
2	·43	·65	·87	1·08	1·30	1·52	1·74	1·95	2·17
3	·50	·76	1·01	1·26	1·51	1·76	2·02	2·27	2·52
4	·58	·87	1·16	1·45	1·74	2·03	2·32	2·61	2·90
35	·65	·98	1·31	1·64	1·96	2·29	2·62	2·94	3·27
6	·72	1·08	1·44	1·80	2·16	2·52	2·88	3·24	3·60
7	·77	1·16	1·55	1·94	2·32	2·71	3·10	3·48	3·87
8	·82	1·22	1·63	2·04	2·45	2·86	3·26	3·67	4·08
9	·84	1·27	1·69	2·11	2·53	2·95	3·38	3·80	4·22
40	·86	1·29	1·72	2·14	2·57	3·00	3·43	3·86	4·29
1	·86	1·29	1·72	2·15	2·58	3·01	3·44	3·87	4·30
2	·85	1·28	1·70	2·12	2·55	2·98	3·40	3·82	4·25
3	·83	1·24	1·65	2·06	2·48	2·89	3·30	3·72	4·13
4	·79	1·18	1·57	1·96	2·36	2·75	3·14	3·54	3·93
45	·73	1·10	1·46	1·83	2·20	2·56	2·93	3·29	3·66
6	·67	1·01	1·34	1·68	2·02	2·35	2·69	3·02	3·36
7	·61	·92	1·22	1·53	1·84	2·14	2·45	2·75	3·06
8	·55	·83	1·10	1·38	1·66	1·93	2·21	2·48	2·76
9	·49	·74	·98	1·23	1·48	1·72	1·97	2·21	2·46
50	·43	·64	·86	1·08	1·29	1·50	1·72	1·94	2·15
1	·36	·54	·72	·90	1·09	1·27	1·45	1·63	1·81
2	·29	·43	·57	·72	·86	1·00	1·14	1·29	1·43
3	·20	·30	·40	·50	·60	·70	·80	·90	1·00
4	·10	·15	·20	·25	·30	·35	·40	·45	·50
55 and above ...	Nil	Nil	Nil	Nil	Nil	Nil	Nil	Nil	Nil

THE SCHEDULE, PARAGRAPHS 1(6) and 2

TABLE II

AGE OF OFFICER						FACTOR
55	...	...	...	...	...	2·50
56	...	...	...	...	...	2·27
57	...	...	...	...	...	2·04
58	...	...	...	...	...	1·76
59	...	...	...	...	...	1·42
60	...	...	...	...	...	1·00
61	...	...	...	...	...	·50
62 and above			...	...	...	Nil

NOTE: (a) These factors apply where the judge has at least ten years service.

(b) The factor corresponding to the judge's age in years and completed months should be obtained by interpolation.

THE SCHEDULE, PARAGRAPH 8

TABLE III

AGE						FACTOR
30 and under		...	...	...	...	5·00
31 ...	...	...	...	...	...	5·08
32 ...	...	...	...	...	...	5·21
33 ...	...	...	...	...	...	5·47
34 ...	...	...	...	...	...	5·90
35 ...	...	...	...	...	...	6·56
36 ...	...	...	...	...	...	7·44
37 ...	...	...	...	...	...	8·10
38 ...	...	...	...	...	...	8·53
39 ...	...	...	...	...	...	8·79
40 ...	...	...	...	...	...	8·92
41 ...	...	...	...	...	...	9·00
42 ...	...	...	...	...	...	8·92
43 ...	...	...	...	...	...	·77
44 ...	...	...	...	...	...	8·40
45 ...	...	...	...	...	...	7·61
46 ...	...	...	...	...	...	6·39
47 ...	...	...	...	...	...	5·60
48 ...	...	...	...	...	...	5·23
49 ...	...	...	...	...	...	5·08
50 and above		...	...	...	...	5·00

THE SCHEDULE, PARAGRAPHS 10 AND 11

TABLE IV

AGE OF OFFICER	FACTOR	AGE OF OFFICER	FACTOR
25 and under	17·08	40	15·07
26	16·97	41	14·90
27	16·86	42	14·73
28	16·74	43	14·55
29	16·62	44	14·36
30	16·50	45	14·17
31	16·38	46	13·97
32	16·25	47	13·76
33	16·12	48	13·54
34	15·98	49	13·32
35	15·84	50	13·08
36	15·70	51	12·84
37	15·55	52	12·59
38	15·40	53 and above	12·50
39	15·24		

EXPLANATORY NOTE

(This Note is not part of the Order.)

This Order makes provision for compensation and retiring benefits for certain officers in the public service of Swaziland.

STATUTORY INSTRUMENTS

1968 No. 1377

AFRICA

The Swaziland Independence Order 1968

Made - - - -	*26th August* 1968	
Laid before Parliament	*30th August* 1968	
Coming into Operation	*Immediately before*	
	6th September 1968	

At the Court at Balmoral, the 26th day of August 1968

Present,

The Queen's Most Excellent Majesty in Council

Her Majesty, by virtue and in exercise of the powers in that behalf by the Foreign Jurisdiction Act 1890(a) or otherwise in Her Majesty vested, is pleased, by and with the advice of Her Privy Council, to order, and it is hereby ordered, as follows :—

Citation and commence-ment.

1.—(1) This Order may be cited as the Swaziland Independence Order 1968.

(2) This Order shall come into operation immediately before 6th September 1968 :

Provided that the King may at any time after 30th August 1968 exercise any of the powers conferred upon him by section 5(3) of this Order or section 58 of the Constitution to such extent as may be necessary or expedient to enable the Constitution to function from 6th September 1968.

Interpreta-tion.

2.—(1) In this Order—

"the Constitution" means the Constitution of the Kingdom of Swaziland set out in the Schedule to this Order ;

"the existing House of Assembly" means the House of Assembly established by the existing Orders ;

"the existing laws" means any Acts of the Parliament of the United Kingdom, Orders of Her Majesty in Council, any Acts of the Parliament of Swaziland, proclamations, rules, regulations, orders or other instruments having effect as part of the law of Swaziland at the commencement of this Order but does not include any Order revoked by this Order ;

"the existing Orders" means the Orders revoked by section 3(1) of this Order ;

"the existing Senate" means the Senate established by the existing Orders.

(2) The provisions of sections 137 to 144 of the Constitution shall apply for the purpose of interpreting sections 1 to 19 of this Order

(a) 1890 c. 37.

and otherwise in relation thereto as they apply for the purpose of interpreting and in relation to the Constitution.

3.—(1) The Swaziland Constitution Order 1967(a), the Swaziland Constitution (Amendment) Order 1967(b) and the Swaziland Constitution (Amendment) Order 1968(c) are revoked with effect from the commencement of this Order. *Revocations.*

(2) The Emergency Powers Order in Council 1939(d) and the United Kingdom Forces (Jurisdiction of Colonial Courts) Order 1965(e) and any Order in Council amending those Orders shall cease to have effect as part of the law of Swaziland at the commencement of this Order.

(3) The Swaziland (Appeals to Privy Council) Order 1967(f) is revoked with effect from the commencement of this Order.

4. Subject to the provisions of this Order, the Constitution shall come into effect in Swaziland at the commencement of this Order. *Establishment of Constitution.*

5.—(1) The revocation of the existing Orders shall be without prejudice to the continued operation of any existing laws made, or having effect as if they had been made, under any of those Orders ; and any such laws shall have effect on and after the commencement of this Order as if they had been made in pursuance of the Constitution and shall be construed with such modifications, adaptations, qualifications and exceptions as may be necessary to bring them into conformity with the Swaziland Independence Act 1968(g) and this Order. *Existing laws.*

(2) Where any matter that falls to be prescribed or otherwise provided for under the Constitution by Act of Parliament or by any authority or person is prescribed or provided for by or under an existing law (including any amendment to any such law made under this section) or is otherwise prescribed or provided for immediately before the commencement of this Order by or under the existing Orders, that prescription or provision shall, as from that day, have effect (with such modifications, adaptations, qualifications and exceptions as may be necessary to bring it into conformity with the Swaziland Independence Act 1968 and this Order) as if it had been made under the Constitution by Act of Parliament or, as the case may require, by the authority or person.

(3) The King may, by order published in the Gazette, at any time before 6th March 1969 make such amendments to any existing law (other than the Swaziland Independence Act 1968 or this Order) as may appear to him to be necessary or expedient for bringing that law into conformity with the provisions of this Order or otherwise for giving effect or enabling effect to be given to those provisions.

(4) An order made under subsection (3) of this section may provide that any grant, lease or other disposition of minerals and mineral oils subsisting on 5th September 1968 shall be deemed, with effect from 6th September 1968, to include such provisions (being provisions which on 5th September 1968 attach to that grant, lease or disposition by virtue of any law) as may be specified in that order.

(a) S.I. 1967/241 (1967 I, p. 857).   (b) S.I. 1967/975 (1967 II, p. 2950).
(c) S.I. 1968/727 (1968 II, p. 2105).   (d) See S.I. 1952 I, at p. 621.
(e) S.I. 1965/1203 (1965 II, p. 3422).   (f) S.I. 1967/246 (1967 I, p. 944).
(g) 1968 c. 56.

(5) An order made under this section may be amended or revoked by Act of Parliament or, in relation to any existing law affected thereby, by any other authority having power to amend, repeal or revoke that existing law.

(6) The provisions of this section shall be without prejudice to any powers conferred by this Order or any other law upon any person or authority to make provision for any matter, including the amendment or repeal of any existing law.

Existing offices.

6.—(1) The persons who immediately before the commencement of this Order hold office as Prime Minister or other Minister or Assistant Minister shall, as from the commencement of this Order, hold the like offices as if they had been appointed thereto in accordance with the provisions of the Constitution and shall be deemed to have taken and subscribed any necessary oath under the Constitution.

(2) Where any other office has been established by or under the existing Orders or any existing law and the Constitution establishes a similar or an equivalent office any person who, immediately before the commencement of this Order, holds or is acting in the former office shall, so far as is consistent with the provisions of the Constitution, be deemed, as from the commencement of this Order, to have been appointed to hold or to act in the latter office in accordance with the provisions of the Constitution and to have taken and subscribed any necessary oaths under the Constitution:

Provided that any person who under the existing Orders or any existing law would have been required to vacate his office at the expiration of any period or on the attainment of any age shall vacate his office under the Constitution at the expiration of that period or upon the attainment of that age.

(3) The provisions of this section shall be without prejudice to any powers conferred by or under the Constitution upon any person or authority to make provision for the abolition of offices and the removal from office of persons holding or acting in any office.

Senate.

7.—(1) The persons who, immediately before the commencement of this Order, are members of the existing Senate having been elected as such by the existing House of Assembly shall be deemed, as from the commencement of this Order, to have been elected as Senators in pursuance of section 39 of the Constitution ; and the persons who, immediately before the commencement of this Order, are members of the existing Senate having been appointed as such by the King shall be deemed, as from the commencement of this Order, to have been appointed as Senators in pursuance of section 38 of the Constitution ; and those persons shall, subject to the provisions of subsection (3) of this section, hold their seats in the Senate in accordance with the Constitution.

(2) The persons who, immediately before the commencement of this Order, are Speaker and Deputy Speaker of the existing Senate shall be deemed, as from the commencement of this Order, to have been elected as President and Deputy President of the Senate, respectively, in pursuance of section 47 of the Constitution and shall hold their offices in accordance with the Constitution.

(3) Any person deemed by subsection (1) of this section to be a member of the Senate established by the Constitution who is not

a citizen of Swaziland on 6th September 1968 shall not be required until 6th March 1969 to vacate his seat in the Senate on the grounds that he is not a citizen of Swaziland, but he shall vacate his seat on that date if he is not then such a citizen.

8.—(1) The persons who, immediately before the commencement of this Order, are elected members of the existing House of Assembly shall be deemed, as from the commencement of this Order, to have been elected as members of the House of Assembly in pursuance of section 41 of the Constitution ; and the persons who, immediately before the commencement of this Order, are nominated members of the existing House of Assembly shall be deemed, as from the commencement of this Order, to have been nominated as members of the House of Assembly in pursuance of section 42 of the Constitution ; and those persons shall, subject to the provisions of subsection (3) of this section, hold their seats in the House of Assembly in accordance with the Constitution. *House of Assembly.*

(2) The persons who, immediately before the commencement of this Order, hold the offices of Speaker and Deputy Speaker of the existing House of Assembly shall be deemed, as from the commencement of this Order, to have been elected as Speaker and Deputy Speaker, respectively, in pursuance of section 48 of the Constitution and shall hold those offices in accordance with the Constitution.

(3) Any person deemed by subsection (1) of this section to be a member of the House of Assembly established by the Constitution who is not a citizen of Swaziland on 6th September 1968 shall not be required until 6th March 1969 to vacate his seat in the House of Assembly on the grounds that he is not a citizen of Swaziland, but he shall vacate his seat on that date if he is not then such a citizen.

9. Until such time as it is otherwise provided under section 55 of the Constitution, the respective boundaries of the constituencies established by that section shall be those prescribed in the Electoral Provisions Regulations 1966 made under section 2 of the Swaziland (Electoral Provisions) Order 1966(a). *Constituencies.*

10. Any person who, by virtue of the provisions of section 7 or 8 of this Order, is from the commencement of this Order a member of the Senate or of the House of Assembly established by the Constitution shall be deemed to have taken and subscribed any necessary oath under the Constitution. *Oaths of members of Parliament.*

11. The rules of procedure of the existing Senate and of the existing House of Assembly in force immediately before the commencement of this Order shall, until it is otherwise provided by the Senate or the House of Assembly respectively in pursuance of section 78 of the Constitution, be the rules of procedure of the Senate and the House of Assembly established by the Constitution, but they shall be construed with such modifications, adaptations, qualifications and exceptions as may be necessary to bring them into conformity with the Constitution. *Rules of procedure.*

12. Notwithstanding anything contained in section 59(2) of the Constitution (but subject to subsection (3) of that section) Parliament unless sooner dissolved shall stand dissolved on 6th July 1972. *Dissolution of Parliament.*

(a) S.I. 1966/1179 (1966 III, p. 3054).

Pending proceedings.

13.—(1) All proceedings commenced or pending before the High Court or the Court of Appeal immediately before the commencement of this Order may be carried on before the High Court or the Court of Appeal, as the case may be, established by the Constitution.

(2) Any decision given before the commencement of this Order by the High Court or the Court of Appeal shall, for the purpose of its enforcement or for the purpose of any appeal therefrom, have effect after the commencement of this Order as if it were a decision of the corresponding court established by the Constitution.

Transitional provisions relating to existing Commissions.

14. Any power that, immediately before the commencement of this Order, is vested in a Commission established by any of the existing Orders and that, under that Order, is then delegated to some other person or authority shall be deemed to have been delegated to that person or authority from the commencement of this Order in accordance with the provisions of the Constitution; and any proceedings commenced or pending before any such Commission immediately before the commencement of this Order may be carried on before the appropriate Commission established by the Constitution.

Remuneration of certain officers.

15. Until such time as a salary and allowances are prescribed by Act of Parliament, there shall be paid to the holder of any office to which section 131 of the Constitution applies a salary and allowances calculated at the same rate as the salary and allowances payable immediately before the commencement of this Order to the holder of the office corresponding thereto.

Rights, property, etc.

16. For the avoidance of doubt it is hereby declared that the revocation of the existing Orders shall not affect any right, liability, obligation, property or assets vested in the Government of the Kingdom of Swaziland or any person by virtue of section 89 of the Constitution set out in the Schedule to the Swaziland Constitution Order 1967 or by virtue of section 10A or 10B of that Order as inserted by section 2 of the Swaziland Constitution (Amendment) Order 1968.

Compulsory retirement to facilitate appointment of local candidates.

17.—(1) If the Prime Minister so requests, the authorities having power to make appointments in any branch of the public service shall consider whether there are more local candidates suitably qualified for appointment to, or promotion in, that branch than there are vacancies in that branch that could appropriately be filled by such local candidates; and those authorities, if satisfied that such is the case, shall, if so requested by the Prime Minister, select officers in that branch to whom this section applies and whose retirement would in the opinion of those authorities cause vacancies that could appropriately be filled by such suitably qualified local candidates as are available and fit for appointment and inform the Prime Minister of the number of officers so selected; and if the Prime Minister specifies a number of officers to be called upon to retire (not exceeding the number of officers so selected), those authorities shall nominate that number of officers from among the officers so selected and by notice in writing require them to retire from the public service; and any officer who is so required to retire shall retire accordingly.

(2) Any notice given under subsection (1) of this section requiring any officer to retire from the public service shall—

(*a*) in the case of an officer who, when he receives the notice, is on leave of absence upon the completion of a tour of duty, specify the date upon which he shall so retire which shall not be earlier than the expiration of six months from the date when he receives the notice or, if his leave of absence would otherwise expire later, when it would otherwise expire ; and

(b) in the case of any other officer, specify the period, which shall be not less than six months from the date when he receives the notice, at the expiration of which he shall proceed upon leave of absence pending retirement :

Provided that, with the consent of the officer, the notice may specify an earlier date or, as the case may be, a shorter period.

(3) This section applies to any officer who holds a pensionable public office (other than the office of judge of the Court of Appeal, judge of the High Court, Attorney-General or Director of Audit) and is for the time being an entitled officer for the purposes of the Swaziland (Compensation and Retiring Benefits) Order 1968(a) or the Non-Designated Expatriate Pensionable Officers' (Retirement Benefits) Act, 1968(b).

18.—(1) The provisions of this section shall have effect for the purpose of enabling an officer to whom this section applies or his personal representatives to appeal against any of the following decisions, that is to say :— *Appeals in respect of certain decisions affecting pensions benefits.*

(a) a decision of the appropriate Commission to give such concurrence as is required by subsection (1) or (2) of section 124 of the Constitution in relation to the refusal, withholding, reduction in amount or suspending of any pensions benefits in respect of such an officer's service as a public officer ;

(b) a decision of any authority to remove such an officer from office if the consequence of the removal is that any pensions benefits cannot be granted in respect of the officer's service as a public officer ; or

(c) a decision of any authority to take some other disciplinary action in relation to such an officer if the consequence of the action is, or in the opinion of the authority might be, to reduce the amount of any pensions benefits that may be granted in respect of the officer's service as a public officer.

(2) Where any such decision as is referred to in the preceding subsection is taken by any authority, the authority shall cause to be delivered to the officer concerned, or to his personal representatives, a written notice of that decision stating the time, not being less than twenty-eight days from the date on which the notice is delivered, within which he, or his personal representatives, may apply to the authority for the case to be referred to an Appeals Board.

(3) If application is duly made within the time stated in the notice, the authority shall notify the Prime Minister in writing of that application and the Prime Minister shall thereupon appoint an Appeals Board consisting of—

(a) one member selected by the Prime Minister ;

(b) one member selected by an association representative of public officers or a professional body, nominated in either case by the applicant ; and

(a) S.I. 1968/1376 (1968 II, p. 3817).   (b) Swaziland Act No. 15 of 1968.

(c) one member selected by the two other members jointly (or, in default of agreement between those members, by the Judicial Service Commission) who shall be the chairman of the Board.

(4) The Appeals Board shall enquire into the facts of the case, and for that purpose—

(a) shall, if the applicant so requests in writing, hear the applicant either in person or by a legal representative of his choice, according to the terms of the request, and shall consider any representations that he wishes to make in writing ;

(b) may hear any other person who, in the opinion of the Board, is able to give the Board information on the case ; and

(c) shall have access to, and shall consider, all documents that were available to the authority concerned and shall also consider any further document relating to the case that may be produced by or on behalf of the applicant or the authority.

(5) When the Appeals Board has completed its consideration of the case, then—

(a) if the decision that is the subject of the reference to the Board is such a decision as is mentioned in paragraph (a) of subsection (1) of this section, the Board shall advise the appropriate Commission whether the decision should be affirmed, reversed or modified and the Commission shall act in accordance with that advice ; and

(b) if the decision that is the subject of the reference to the Board is such a decision as is referred to in paragraph (b) or paragraph (c) of subsection (1) of this section, the Board shall not have power to advise the authority concerned to affirm, reverse or modify the decision but—

(i) where the officer has been removed from office the Board may direct that there shall be granted all or any part of the pensions benefits that, under any law, might have been granted in respect of his service as a public officer if he had retired voluntarily at the date of his removal and may direct that any law with respect to pensions benefits shall in any other respect that the Board may specify have effect as if he had so retired ; and

(ii) where some other disciplinary action has been taken in relation to the officer the Board may direct that, on the grant of any pensions benefits under any law in respect of the officer's service as a public officer, those benefits shall be increased by such amount or shall be calculated in such manner as the Board may specify in order to offset all or any part of the reduction in the amount of those benefits that, in the opinion of the Board, would or might otherwise be a consequence of the disciplinary action,

and any direction given by the Board under this paragraph shall be complied with notwithstanding the provisions of any other law.

(6) In this section—

" pensions benefits " has the meaning assigned to that expression in section 123 of the Constitution; and "legal representative" means a person lawfully in or entitled to be in Swaziland and entitled to practise as an advocate or attorney in Swaziland.

(7) This section applies to any officer who holds a pensionable public office and is for the time being an entitled officer for the purposes of the Swaziland (Compensation and Retiring Benefits) Order 1968 or the Non-Designated Expatriate Pensionable Officers' (Retirement Benefits) Act 1968.

19.—(1) This Order may be altered by Act of Parliament in the same manner as the provisions of the Constitution, other than provisions mentioned in Schedule 4 to the Constitution, may be so altered: Alteration of this Order.

Provided that this section and sections 4, 7, 8, 9, 12, 15, 17 and 18 of this Order may be altered only in the manner in which the provisions of the Constitution mentioned in Part I of Schedule 4 to the Constitution may be altered.

(2) Section 134(3) of the Constitution shall apply for the purpose of construing references in this section to any provision of this Order and to the alteration of any such provision as it applies for the purpose of construing references in section 134 of the Constitution to any provision of the Constitution and to the alteration thereof.

N. E. Leigh.

THE SCHEDULE TO THE ORDER

CHAPTER I

THE KINGDOM AND ITS CONSTITUTION

Section
1. The Kingdom and its territory.
2. The Constitution.

CHAPTER II

PROTECTION OF FUNDAMENTAL RIGHTS AND FREEDOMS OF THE INDIVIDUAL

3. Fundamental rights and freedoms of the individual.
4. Protection of right to life.
5. Protection of right to personal liberty.
6. Protection from slavery and forced labour.
7. Protection from inhuman treatment.
8. Protection from deprivation of property.
9. Protection against arbitrary search or entry.
10. Provisions to secure protection of law.
11. Protection of freedom of conscience.
12. Protection of freedom of expression.
13. Protection of freedom of assembly and association.
14. Protection of freedom of movement.
15. Protection from discrimination on the grounds of race, etc.
16. Derogations from fundamental rights and freedoms under emergency powers.
17. Enforcement of protective provisions.
18. Declarations of emergency.
19. Interpretation and savings.

CHAPTER III

CITIZENSHIP

CHAPTER IV

THE MONARCHY

CHAPTER V

PARLIAMENT

PART 1

Composition of Parliament

PART 2

Summoning, prorogation and dissolution

CHAPTER VI

LEGISLATION AND PROCEDURE IN PARLIAMENT

CHAPTER VII

THE EXECUTIVE

CHAPTER VIII

LAND AND MINERALS

CHAPTER IX

THE JUDICATURE

PART 1

The High Court

PART 2

The Court of Appeal

PART 3

Judicial Service Commission

CHAPTER X

THE PUBLIC SERVICE

SCHEDULE 1 TO THE CONSTITUTION
SUMMONING AND PROCEDURE OF JOINT SITTINGS OF SENATE AND HOUSE OF ASSEMBLY

SCHEDULE 2 TO THE CONSTITUTION
OATHS

SCHEDULE 3 TO THE CONSTITUTION
MATTERS WHICH SHALL CONTINUE TO BE REGULATED BY SWAZI LAW AND CUSTOM

SCHEDULE 4 TO THE CONSTITUTION
SPECIALLY ENTRENCHED PROVISIONS AND ENTRENCHED PROVISIONS

THE CONSTITUTION OF THE KINGDOM OF SWAZILAND

CHAPTER I

THE KINGDOM AND ITS CONSTITUTION

The Kingdom and its territory.

1.—(1) Swaziland is a sovereign independent Kingdom.

(2) The territory of Swaziland comprises all the areas that immediately before 6th September 1968 were comprised in the former protected state of Swaziland together with such other areas as may from time to time be declared by Act of Parliament to form part of Swaziland.

The Constitution.

2. This Constitution is the supreme law of Swaziland and if any other law is inconsistent with this Constitution, that other law shall to the extent of the inconsistency, be void.

CHAPTER II

PROTECTION OF FUNDAMENTAL RIGHTS AND FREEDOMS OF THE INDIVIDUAL

Fundamental rights and freedoms of the individual.

3. Whereas every person in Swaziland is entitled to the fundamental rights and freedoms of the individual, that is to say, the right, whatever his race, tribe, place of origin, political opinions, colour, creed or sex, but subject to respect for the rights and freedoms of others and for the public interest, to each and all of the following, namely—

(a) life, liberty, security of the person and the protection of the law ;

(b) freedom of conscience, of expression and of assembly and association ; and

(c) protection for the privacy of his home and other property and from deprivation of property without compensation,

the provisions of this Chapter shall have effect for the purpose of affording protection to those rights and freedoms subject to such limitations of that protection as are contained in those provisions, being limitations designed to ensure that the enjoyment of the said rights and freedoms by any individual does not prejudice the rights and freedoms of others or the public interest.

Protection of right to life.

4.—(1) No person shall be deprived of his life intentionally save in execution of the sentence of a court in respect of a criminal offence under the law of Swaziland of which he has been convicted.

(2) Without prejudice to any liability for a contravention of any other law with respect to the use of force in such cases as are hereinafter mentioned, a person shall not be regarded as having been deprived of his life in contravention of this section if he dies as the result of the use of force to such extent as is reasonably justifiable in the circumstances of the case—

(a) for the defence of any person from violence or for the defence of property ;

(b) in order to effect a lawful arrest or to prevent the escape of a person lawfully detained ;

(c) for the purpose of suppressing a riot, insurrection or mutiny ; or

(d) in order to prevent the commission by that person of a criminal offence,

or if he dies as the result of a lawful act of war.

5.—(1) No person shall be deprived of his personal liberty save as may be authorised by law in any of the following cases, that is to say— *Protection of right to personal liberty.*

(a) in execution of the sentence or order of a court, whether established for Swaziland or some other country, in respect of a criminal offence of which he has been convicted ;

(b) in execution of the order of a court punishing him for contempt of that court or of another court or tribunal ;

(c) in execution of the order of a court made to secure the fulfilment of any obligation imposed on him by law ;

(d) for the purpose of bringing him before a court in execution of the order of a court ;

(e) upon reasonable suspicion of his having committed, or being about to commit, a criminal offence under the law of Swaziland ;

(f) in the case of a person who has not attained the age of eighteen years, for the purpose of his education or welfare ;

(g) for the purpose of preventing the spread of an infectious or contagious disease ;

(h) in the case of a person who is, or is reasonably suspected to be, of unsound mind, addicted to drugs or alcohol, or a vagrant, for the purpose of his care or treatment or the protection of the community ;

(i) for the purpose of preventing the unlawful entry of that person into Swaziland, or for the purpose of effecting the expulsion, extradition or other lawful removal of that person from Swaziland or for the purpose of restricting that person while he is being conveyed through Swaziland in the course of his extradition or removal as a convicted prisoner from one country to another ; or

(j) to such extent as may be necessary in the execution of a lawful order requiring that person to remain within a specified area within Swaziland or prohibiting him from being within such an area, or to such extent as may be reasonably justifiable for the taking of proceedings against that person relating to the making of any such order, or to such extent as may be reasonably justifiable for restraining that person during any visit that he is permitted to make to any part of Swaziland in which, in consequence of any such order, his presence would otherwise be unlawful.

(2) Any person who is arrested or detained shall be informed as soon as reasonably practicable, in a language that he understands, of the reasons for his arrest or detention.

(3) Any person who is arrested or detained—

(a) for the purpose of bringing him before a court in execution of the order of a court ; or

(b) upon reasonable suspicion of his having committed, or being about to commit, a criminal offence, and who is not released, shall be brought without undue delay before a court ; and where he is not brought before a court within forty-eight hours of his arrest or from the commencement of his detention, the burden of proving that the person arrested or detained has been brought before a court without undue delay shall rest upon any person alleging that the provisions of this subsection have been complied with.

(4) Where any person is brought before a court in execution of the order of a court in any proceedings or upon any suspicion of his having committed or being about to commit an offence, he shall not be there-after further held in custody in connection with those proceedings or that offence save upon the order of a court.

(5) If any person arrested or detained as mentioned in paragraph (*b*) of subsection (3) of this section is not tried within a reasonable time, then, without prejudice to any further proceedings that may be brought against him, he shall be released either unconditionally or upon reason-able conditions, including in particular such conditions as are reasonably necessary to ensure that he appears at a later date for trial or for pro-ceedings preliminary to trial.

(6) Any person who is unlawfully arrested or detained by any other person shall be entitled to compensation therefor from that other person or from any other person or authority on whose behalf that other person was acting.

Protection from slavery and forced labour.

6.—(1) No person shall be held in slavery or servitude.

(2) No person shall be required to perform forced labour.

(3) For the purposes of this section, the expression " forced labour " does not include—

(*a*) any labour required in consequence of the sentence or order of a court ;

(*b*) labour required of any person while he is lawfully detained which, though not required in consequence of the sentence or order of a court, is reasonably necessary in the interests of hygiene or for the maintenance of the place at which he is detained ;

(*c*) any labour required of a member of a disciplined force in pur-suance of his duties as such or, in the case of a person who has conscientious objections to service as a member of a naval, military or air force, any labour that that person is required by law to perform in place of such service ;

(*d*) any labour required during a period of public emergency or in the event of any other emergency or calamity that threatens the life or well-being of the community, to the extent that the requiring of such labour is reasonably justifiable, in the circumstances of any situation arising or existing .during that period or as a result of that other emergency or calamity, for the purpose of dealing with that situation ; or

(*e*) any labour reasonably required as part of reasonable and normal communal or other civic obligations.

7.—(1) No person shall be subjected to torture or to inhuman or degrading punishment or other treatment. Protection from inhuman treatment.

(2) Nothing contained in or done under the authority of any law shall be held to be inconsistent with or in contravention of this section to the extent that the law in question authorises the infliction of any description of punishment that was lawful in Swaziland immediately before 6th September 1968.

8.—(1) No property shall be compulsorily taken possession of, and no interest in or right over property shall be compulsorily acquired, except where the following conditions are satisfied, that is to say— Protection from deprivation of property.

(a) the taking of possession or acquisition is necessary in the interests of defence, public safety, public order, public morality, public health, town and country planning or the development or utilisation of any property in such manner as to promote the public benefit ;

(h) the necessity therefor is such as to afford reasonable justification for the causing of any hardship that may result to any person having an interest in or right over the property ; and

(c) provision is made by a law applicable to that taking of possession or acquisition for the prompt payment of full compensation.

(2) Every person having an interest in or right over property which is compulsorily taken possession of or whose interest in or right over any property is compulsorily acquired shall have a right to direct access to the High Court for—

(a) the determination of his interest or right, the legality of the taking of possession or acquisition of the property, interest or right, and the amount of any compensation to which he is entitled ; and

(b) the purpose of obtaining prompt payment of that compensation :

Provided that if any law for the time being in force in Swaziland so provides in relation to any matter referred to in paragraph (a) of this subsection the right of access shall be by way of appeal (exercisable as of right at the instance of the person having the interest in or right over the property) from a tribunal or authority, other than the High Court, having jurisdiction under any law to determine that matter.

(3) No person who is entitled to compensation under this section shall be prevented from remitting, within a reasonable time after he has received any amount of that compensation, the whole of that amount (free from any deduction, charge or tax made or levied in respect of its remission) to any country of his choice outside Swaziland.

(4) Nothing contained in or done under the authority of any law shall be held to be inconsistent with or in contravention of the last foregoing subsection to the extent that the law in question authorises—

(a) the attachment, by order of a court, of any amount of compensation to which a person is entitled in satisfaction of the judgment of a court or pending the determination of civil proceedings to which he is a party ; or

(b) the imposition of reasonable conditions relating to the form in which any amount of compensation is to be remitted.

(5) Nothing contained in or done under the authority of any law (including the common law) shall be held to be inconsistent with or in contravention of subsection (1) or subsection (2) of this section—

(a) to the extent that the taking of possession or acquisition of any property is permitted by the law in question—

(i) in satisfaction of any tax, duty, rate, cess or other impost ;

(ii) by way of penalty for breach of the law or forfeiture in consequence of a breach of the law ;

(iii) as an incident of a lease, tenancy, mortgage, charge, bill of sale, pledge or contract ;

(iv) in the execution of judgments or orders of a court in proceedings for the determination of civil rights or obligations ;

(v) in circumstances where it is reasonably necessary to do so because the property is in a dangerous state or injurious to the health of human beings, animals or plants or because of the risk that the property is likely to spread an infectious or dangerous disease ;

(vi) in consequence of any law with respect to prescription or the limitation of actions ; or

(vii) for so long only as may be necessary for the purposes of any examination, investigation, trial or inquiry or, in the case of land, for the purposes of the carrying out thereon of work of soil conservation or the conservation of other natural resources or work relating to agricultural development or improvement (being work relating to such development or improvement that the owner or occupier of the land has been required, and has without reasonable excuse refused or failed, to carry out),

except so far as that provision or, as the case may be, the thing done under the authority thereof is shown not to be reasonably justifiable in a democratic society ; or

(b) to the extent that the law in question makes provision for the taking of possession or acquisition of—

(i) enemy property ;

(ii) property of a deceased person, a person of unsound mind or a person who has not attained the age of twenty-one years, for the purpose of its administration for the benefit of the persons entitled to the beneficial interest therein ;

(iii) property of a person adjudged insolvent or a body corporate in liquidation for the purpose of its administration for the benefit of the creditors of the insolvent or body corporate and, subject thereto, for the benefit of other persons entitled to the beneficial interest in the property ; or

(iv) property subject to a trust, for the purpose of vesting the property in persons appointed as trustees under the instrument creating the trust or by a court or, by order of a court, for the purpose of giving effect to the trust.

(6) Nothing contained in or done under the authority of any law shall be held to be inconsistent with or in contravention of this section to the extent that the law in question makes provision for the compulsory taking possession of any property or the compulsory

acquisition of any interest in or right over property where that property, interest or right is vested in a body corporate, established by law for public purposes, in which no moneys have been invested other than moneys provided by any legislature in Swaziland.

9.—(1) Except with his own consent, no person shall be subjected to the search of his person or his property or the entry by others on his premises.

Protection against arbitrary search or entry.

(2) Nothing contained in or done under the authority of any law shall be held to be inconsistent with or in contravention of this section to the extent that the law in question makes provision—

(*a*) (i) that is reasonably required in the interests of defence, public safety, public order, public morality, public health, town and country planning, the development and utilisation of mineral resources, or the development or utilisation of any other property in such a manner as to promote the public benefit ; or

(ii) that is reasonably required for the purpose of promoting the rights or freedoms of other persons ; or

(*b*) that authorises an officer or agent of the Government or of a local government authority, or of a body corporate established by law for public purposes, to enter on the premises of any person in order to inspect those premises or anything thereon for the purpose of any tax, rate or due or in order to carry out work connected with any property that is lawfully on those premises and that belongs to that Government, authority, or body corporate, as the case may be ; or

(*c*) that authorises, for the purpose of enforcing the judgment or order of a court in any civil proceedings, the entry upon any premises by order of a court,

except so far as, in respect of paragraph (*b*) or paragraph (*c*) of this subsection, that provision or, as the case may be, the thing done under the authority thereof is shown not to be reasonably justifiable in a democratic society.

10.—(1) If any person is charged with a criminal offence, then, unless the charge is withdrawn, the case shall be given a fair hearing within a reasonable time by an independent and impartial court established by law.

Provisions to secure protection of law.

(2) Every person who is charged with a criminal offence—

(*a*) shall be presumed to be innocent until he is proved or has pleaded guilty ;

(*b*) shall be informed as soon as reasonably practicable, in a language that he understands and in detail, of the nature of the offence charged ;

(*c*) shall be given adequate time and facilities for the preparation of his defence ;

(*d*) shall be permitted to defend himself before the court in person or by a legal representative of his own choice ;

(*e*) shall be afforded facilities to examine in person or by his legal representative the witnesses called by the prosecution before the court and to obtain the attendance and carry out the examination of witnesses to testify on his behalf before the court on the same conditions as those applying to witnesses called by the prosecution ; and

(f) shall be permitted to have without payment the assistance of an interpreter if he cannot understand the language used at the trial of the charge,

and, except with his own consent, the trial shall not take place in his absence unless he so conducts himself as to render the continuance of the proceedings in his presence impracticable and the court has ordered him to be removed and the trial to proceed in his absence.

(3) When a person is tried for any criminal offence, the accused person or any person authorised by him in that behalf shall, if he so requires and subject to payment of such reasonable fee as may be prescribed by law, be given within a reasonable time after judgment a copy for the use of the accused person of any record of the proceedings made by or on behalf of the court.

(4) No person shall be held to be guilty of a criminal offence on account of any act or omission that did not, at the time it took place, constitute such an offence, and no penalty shall be imposed for any criminal offence that is severer in degree or description than the maximum penalty that might have been imposed for that offence at the time when it was committed.

(5) No person who shows that he has been tried by a competent court for a criminal offence and either convicted or acquitted shall again be tried for that offence or for any other criminal offence of which he could have been convicted at the trial for that offence, save upon the order of a superior court in the course of appeal or review proceedings relating to the conviction or acquittal.

(6) No person shall be tried for a criminal offence if he shows that he has been pardoned for that offence.

(7) No person who is tried for a criminal offence shall be compelled to give evidence at the trial.

(8) Any court or other adjudicating authority prescribed by law for the determination of the existence or extent of any civil right or obligation shall be established by law and shall be independent and impartial ; and where proceedings for such a determination are instituted by any person before such a court or other adjudicating authority, the case shall be given a fair hearing within a reasonable time.

(9) All proceedings of every court for the determination of the existence or extent of any civil right or obligation shall be held in public.

(10) All proceedings of every adjudicating authority, other than a court,—

(a) for the determination of the existence or extent of any civil right to trade or carry on a business or occupation ; or

(b) for the determination of the existence or extent of any civil right or obligation which on 6th September 1968 it is within the original jurisdiction of the High Court to determine,

shall be held in public.

(11) Notwithstanding the provisions of subsections (9) and (10) of this section a court or other adjudicating authority—

(a) may, unless it is otherwise provided by Act of Parliament, exclude from its proceedings persons other than the parties and their legal representatives to such extent as the court or other adjudicating authority may consider necessary or expedient—

    (i) in circumstances where publicity may prejudice the interests of defence, public safety, public order, justice, or public morality or would prejudice the welfare of persons under the age of eighteen years or the protection of the private lives of the persons concerned in the proceedings ; or

    (ii) in interlocutory proceedings ;

(b) shall, if it so prescribed by a law that is reasonably required in the interests of defence, public safety, public order, justice, public morality, the welfare of persons under the age of eighteen years or the protection of the private lives of the persons concerned in the proceedings, exclude from its proceedings persons, other than the parties and their legal representatives, to such extent as is so prescribed.

(12) Nothing contained in or done under the authority of any law shall be held to be inconsistent with or in contravention of—

(a) paragraph (a) of subsection (2) of this section to the extent that the law in question imposes upon any person charged with a criminal offence the burden of proving particular facts ;

(b) paragraph (d) of subsection (2) of this section to the extent that the law in question prohibits legal representation before a Swazi court or before any court or authority hearing appeals from such a court ;

(c) paragraph (e) of subsection (2) of this section to the extent that the law in question imposes conditions that must be satisfied if witnesses called to testify on behalf of an accused person are to be paid their expenses out of public funds ; or

(d) subsection (5) of this section to the extent that the law in question authorises a court to try a member of a disciplined force for a criminal offence notwithstanding any trial and conviction or acquittal of that member under the disciplinary law of that force, so, however, that any court so trying such a member and convicting him shall in sentencing him to any punishment take into account any punishment awarded him under that disciplinary law.

(13) In the case of any person who is held in lawful detention, the provisions of subsection (1), paragraphs (d) and (e) of subsection (2) and subsection (3) of this section shall not apply in relation to his trial for a criminal offence under the law regulating the discipline of persons held in such detention.

(14) In this section " criminal offence " means a criminal offence under the law of Swaziland, and " proceedings " in relation to a court or adjudicating authority includes the announcement of the decision of the court or adjudicating authority.

11.—(1) Except with his own consent, no person shall be hindered in the enjoyment of his freedom of conscience, and for the purposes of this section freedom of conscience includes freedom of thought and of religion, freedom to change his religion or belief, and freedom, either alone or in community with others, and both in public and in private, to manifest and propagate his religion or belief in worship, teaching practice and observance.

Protection of freedom of conscience.

(2) Every religious community shall be entitled, at its own expense, to establish and maintain places of education and to manage any place of education which it wholly maintains ; and no such community shall be prevented from providing religious instruction for persons of that community in the course of any education provided at any place of education which it wholly maintains or in the course of any education which it otherwise provides.

(3) Except with his own consent (or, if he is a minor, the consent of his guardian), no person attending any place of education shall be required to receive religious instruction or to take part in or attend any religious ceremony or observance if that instruction, ceremony or observance relates to a religion that he does not profess.

(4) No person shall be compelled to take any oath which is contrary to his religion or belief or to take any oath in a manner which is contrary to his religion or belief.

(5) Nothing contained in or done under the authority of any law shall be held to be inconsistent with or in contravention of this section to the extent that the law in question makes provision—

(a) that is reasonably required in the interests of defence, public safety, public order, public morality or public health ; or

(b) that is reasonably required for the purpose of protecting the rights and freedoms of other persons, including the right to observe and practise any religion or belief without the unsolicited intervention of members of any other religion or belief.

(6) References in this section to a religion shall be construed as including references to a religious denomination, and cognate expressions shall be construed accordingly.

Protection of freedom of expression.

12.—(1) Except with his own consent, no person shall be hindered in the enjoyment of his freedom of expression, that is to say, freedom to hold opinions without interference, freedom to receive ideas and information without interference, freedom to communicate ideas and information without interference (whether the communication be to the public generally or to any person or class of persons) and freedom from interference with his correspondence.

(2) Nothing contained in or done under the authority of any law shall be held to be inconsistent with or in contravention of this section to the extent that the law in question makes provision—

(a) (i) that is reasonably required in the interests of defence, public safety, public order, public morality or public health ; or

(ii) that is reasonably required for the purpose of protecting the reputations, rights and freedoms of other persons or the private lives of persons concerned in legal proceedings, preventing the disclosure of information received in confidence, maintaining the authority and independence of the courts or regulating the technical administration or the technical operation of telephony, telegraphy, posts, wireless broadcasting or television ; or

(b) that imposes restrictions upon public officers,

except so far as that provision or, as the case may be, the thing done under the authority thereof is shown not to be reasonably justifiable in a democratic society.

13.—(1) Except with his own consent, no person shall be hindered in the enjoyment of his freedom of assembly and association, that is to say, his right to assemble freely and associate with other persons and in particular to form or belong to trade unions or other associations for the protection of his interests.

(2) Nothing contained in or done under the authority of any law shall be held to be inconsistent with or in contravention of this section to the extent that the law in question makes provision—

(*a*) (i) that is reasonably required in the interests of defence, public safety, public order, public morality or public health ;

(ii) that is reasonably required for the purpose of protecting the rights or freedoms of other persons ; or

(*b*) that imposes restrictions upon public officers,

except so far as that provision or, as the case may be, the thing done under the authority thereof is shown not to be reasonably justifiable in a democratic society.

(3) Without prejudice to the generality of subsection (2) of this section, nothing contained in or done under the authority of any law shall be held to be inconsistent with or in contravention of this section to the extent that the law in question makes provision—

(*a*) for the registration of trade unions, employers organisations, companies, partnerships or co-operative societies including provision relating to the procedure for registration, prescribing qualifications for registration and authorising refusal of registration on the grounds that the prescribed qualifications are not fulfilled:

Provided that in the case of trade unions or employers associations the grounds for refusal of registration provided for by virtue of this paragraph are only that—

(i) the qualifications relating to the maximum or minimum number of members are not fulfilled ;

(ii) the persons whom it is the purpose of the trade union or employers association to represent are already adequately represented by a registered trade union or employers association ; or

(iii) the rules of the trade union or employers association contain discriminatory provisions (as defined in section 15 of this Constitution) ; or

(*b*) for prohibiting or restricting the performance of any function or the carrying on of any business by any such association as is mentioned in paragraph (*a*) of this subsection which is not registered.

14.—(1) No person shall be deprived of his freedom of movement, that is to say, the right to move freely throughout Swaziland, the right to reside in any part of Swaziland, the right to enter Swaziland, the right to leave Swaziland and immunity from expulsion from Swaziland.

(2) Any restriction on a person's freedom of movement that is involved in his lawful detention shall not be held to be inconsistent with or in contravention of this section.

(3) Nothing contained in or done under the authority of any law shall be held to be inconsistent with or in contravention of this section to the extent that the law in question makes provision—

(*a*) for imposing restrictions on the movement or residence within Swaziland of any person or on any person's right to leave Swaziland that are reasonably required in the interests of defence, public safety or public order ;

(*b*) for imposing restrictions on the movement or residence within Swaziland or on the right to leave Swaziland of persons generally or any class of persons that are reasonably required in the interests of defence, public safety, public order, public morality or public health, and except so far as that provision or, as the case may be, the thing done under the authority thereof is shown not to be reasonably justifiable in a democratic society ;

(*c*) for imposing restrictions, by order of a court, on the movement or residence within Swaziland of any person or on any person's right to leave Swaziland either in consequence of his having been found guilty of a criminal offence under the law of Swaziland or for the purpose of ensuring that he appears before a court at a later date for trial of such a criminal offence or for proceedings preliminary to trial or for proceedings relating to his extradition or lawful removal from Swaziland.

(*d*) for imposing restrictions on the freedom of movement of any person who is not a citizen of Swaziland ;

(*e*) for imposing restrictions on the acquisition or use by any person of any property in Swaziland that are reasonably required in the interests of defence, public safety, public order, public morality or public health ;

(*f*) for imposing restrictions on the movement or residence within Swaziland of any person who holds or is acting in any public office ;

(*g*) for the removal of a person from Swaziland to be tried or punished in some other country for a criminal offence under the law of that other country or to undergo imprisonment in some other country in execution of the sentence of a court in respect of a criminal offence under the law of Swaziland of which he has been convicted ; or

(*h*) for the imposition of restrictions on the right of any person to leave Swaziland that are reasonably required in order to secure the fulfilment of any obligation imposed on that person by law.

(4) If any person whose freedom of movement has been restricted by virtue of such a provision as is referred to in paragraph (*a*) of subsection (3) of this section so requests at any time during the period of that restriction not earlier than three months after the order imposing that restriction was made or three months after he last made such a request, as the case may be, his case shall be reviewed by an independent and impartial tribunal presided over by a person appointed by the Chief Justice from among persons entitled to practise in Swaziland as advocates or attorneys.

(5) On any review by a tribunal in pursuance of subsection (4) of this section of the case of any person whose freedom of movement has been restricted, the tribunal may make recommendations concerning the

necessity or expediency of continuing that restriction to the authority by whom it was ordered and, unless it is otherwise provided by law, that authority shall not be obliged to act in accordance with any such recommendations.

15.—(1) Subject to the provisions of subsections (4), (5), (6) and (9) of this section, no law shall make any provision that is discriminatory either of itself or in its effect.

(2) Subject to the provisions of subsections (7), (9) and (10) of this section, no person shall be treated in a discriminatory manner by any person acting in the performance of any public function conferred by any law or otherwise in the performance of the functions of any public office or any public authority.

Protection from discrimination on the grounds of race, etc.

(3) In this section the expression " discriminatory " means affording different treatment to different persons attributable wholly or mainly to their respective descriptions by race, tribe, place of origin, political opinions, colour or creed whereby persons of one such description are subjected to disabilities or restrictions to which persons of another such description are not made subject, or are accorded privileges or advantages which are not accorded to persons of another such description.

(4) Subsection (1) of this section shall not apply to any law so far as that law makes provision—

(*a*) with respect to persons who are not citizens of Swaziland or companies which are not registered in Swaziland ;

(*b*) for the application in the case of members of a particular race or tribe of customary law with respect to any matter to the exclusion of any law with respect to that matter which is applicable in the case of other persons ; or

(*c*) whereby persons of any such description as is mentioned in subsection (3) of this section may be subjected to any disability or restriction or may be accorded any privilege or advantage which, having regard to its nature and to special circumstances pertaining to those persons or to persons of any other such description, is reasonably justifiable in a democratic society.

(5) Subsection (1) of this section shall not apply to the Poll Tax Proclamation(**a**), the African Tax Proclamation(**b**), the African Tax (Consolidation) Proclamation 1963(**c**), as in force on 5th September 1968, or to any order made under the Swazi Administration Proclamation(**d**) which is in force on that date:

Provided that if any such Proclamation or order is amended on or after 6th September 1968 in such a way as to increase the discrimination made in the Proclamation or order or to impose a new discrimination, the provisions of this subsection shall cease to apply to that Proclamation or order.

(6) Nothing contained in any law shall be held to be inconsistent with or in contravention of subsection (1) of this section to the extent that it makes provision with respect to standards or qualifications (not being standards or qualifications specifically relating to race, tribe, place

---

(**a**) Revised laws of Swaziland 1959, c. 108.
(**b**) Revised laws of Swaziland 1959, c. 109.   (**c**) Proclamation No. 13 of 1963.
(**d**) Revised laws of Swaziland 1959, c. 60.

of origin, political opinions, colour or creed) to be required of any person who is appointed to any public office, any office in a disciplined force, any office in the service of a local government authority or any office in a body corporate established by any law for public purposes.

(7) Subsection (2) of this section shall not apply to anything which is expressly or by necessary implication authorised to be done by any such provision of law as is referred to in subsection (4) of this section.

(8) Subject to the provisions of subsection (9) of this section, no person shall be treated in a discriminatory manner in respect of access to shops, hotels, lodging-houses, public restaurants, eating-houses, beer halls or places of public entertainment or in respect of access to places of public resort maintained wholly or partly out of public funds or dedicated to the use of the general public.

(9) Nothing contained in or done under the authority of any law shall be held to be inconsistent with or in contravention of this section to the extent that the law in question makes provision whereby persons of any such description as is mentioned in subsection (3) of this section may be subjected to any restriction on the rights and freedoms guaranteed by sections 9, 11, 12, 13 and 14 of this Constitution, being such a restriction as is authorised by section 9(2), section 11(5), section 12(2), section 13(2), section 13(3) or paragraph (a) or (b) of section 14(3), as the case may be.

(10) Nothing in subsection (2) of this section shall affect any discretion relating to the institution, conduct or discontinuance of civil or criminal proceedings in any court that is vested in any person by or under any law for the time being in force in Swaziland.

Derogations from fundamental rights and freedoms under emergency powers.

16.—(1) Nothing contained in or done under the authority of a law shall be held to be inconsistent with or in contravention of section 5 or section 15 of this Constitution to the extent that the law authorises the taking during any period of public emergency of measures that are reasonably justifiable for dealing with the situation that exists in Swaziland during that period.

(2) When a person is detained by virtue of a power exercised in the absolute discretion of any authority and conferred by any such law as is referred to in subsection (1) of this section (not being a person who is detained because he is a person who, not being a citizen of Swaziland, is a citizen of a country with which Swaziland is at war or has been engaged in hostilities against Swaziland in association with or on behalf of such a country or otherwise assisting or adhering to such a country) the following provisions shall apply, that is to say:—

(a) he shall, as soon as reasonably practicable and in any case not more than five days after the commencement of his detention, be furnished with a statement in writing in a language that he understands specifying in detail the grounds upon which he is detained;

(b) not more than fourteen days after the commencement of his detention, a notification shall be published in the Gazette stating that he has been detained and giving particulars of the provision of law under which his detention is authorised;

(c) not more than one month after the commencement of his detention and thereafter during his detention at intervals of not more than six months, his case shall be reviewed by an independent and impartial tribunal established by law and presided over by a person appointed by the Chief Justice from among persons entitled to practise in Swaziland as advocates or attorneys ;

(d) he shall be afforded reasonable facilities to consult a legal representative of his own choice who shall be permitted to make representations to the tribunal ; and

(e) at the hearing of his case by the tribunal he shall be permitted to appear in person or by a legal representative of his own choice.

(3) On any review by a tribunal in pursuance of this section of the case of a detained person, the tribunal may make recommendations concerning the necessity or expediency of continuing his detention to the authority by which it was ordered but, unless it is otherwise provided by law, that authority shall not be obliged to act in accordance with any such recommendations.

17.—(1) If any person alleges that any of the foregoing provisions of this Chapter has been, is being, or is likely to be, contravened in relation to him (or, in the case of a person who is detained, if any other person alleges such a contravention in relation to the detained person) then, without prejudice to any other action with respect to the same matter which is lawfully available, that person (or that other person) may apply to the High Court for redress. *Enforcement of protective provisions.*

(2) The High Court shall have original jurisdiction—

(a) to hear and determine any application made in pursuance of subsection (1) of this section ;

(b) to determine any question which is referred to it in pursuance of subsection (3) of this section,

and may make such orders, issue such writs and give such directions as it may consider appropriate for the purpose of enforcing or securing the enforcement of any of the provisions of this Chapter.

(3) If in any proceedings in any court subordinate to the High Court any question arises as to the contravention of any of the provisions of this Chapter, the person presiding in that court may, and shall if any party to the proceedings so requests, refer the question to the High Court unless, in his judgment, which shall be final, the raising of the question is merely frivolous or vexatious.

(4) Where any question is referred to the High Court in pursuance of subsection (3) of this section the High Court shall give its decision upon the question and the court in which the question arose shall dispose of the case in accordance with that decision or, if that decision is the subject of an appeal to the Court of Appeal in accordance with the decision of the Court of Appeal.

(5) No appeal shall lie, without the leave of the Court of Appeal, from any determination by the High Court that an application made in pursuance of subsection (1) of this section is merely frivolous or vexatious.

(6) Provision may be made by or under an Act of Parliament for conferring upon the High Court such powers in addition to those conferred by this section as may appear to be necessary or expedient for the purpose of enabling that court more effectively to exercise the jurisdiction conferred upon it by this section.

(7) The Chief Justice may make rules for the purposes of this section with respect to the practice and procedure of the High Court (including rules with respect to the time within which applications to that court may be made).

Declarations of emergency.

18.—(1) The King may, by proclamation which shall be published in the Gazette, declare that a state of emergency exists for the purposes of this Chapter.

(2) A declaration under subsection (1) of this section, if not sooner revoked, shall cease to have effect—

(a) in the case of a declaration made when Parliament is sitting or has been summoned to meet within seven days, at the expiration of a period of seven days beginning with the date of publication of the declaration ;

(b) in any other case, at the expiration of a period of twenty-one days beginning with the date of publication of the declaration,

unless, before the expiration of that period, it is approved by a resolution passed at a joint sitting of the Senate and the House of Assembly.

(3) Subject to the provisions of subsection (4) of this section, a declaration approved by a resolution passed at a joint sitting of the Senate and the House of Assembly under subsection (2) of this section shall continue in force until the expiration of a period of six months beginning with the date upon which it was so approved or until such earlier date as may be specified in the resolution :

Provided that approval of the declaration may be extended for periods of not more than six months at a time by a resolution passed at a joint sitting of the Senate and the House of Assembly.

(4) A declaration approved under this section may at any time be revoked by a resolution passed at a joint sitting of the Senate and the House of Assembly.

(5) A resolution for the purpose of subsections (2) or (3) of this section shall not be passed at a joint sitting unless it is supported by a majority of all the members of the Senate and the House of Assembly.

(6) The provisions of Schedule 1 to this Constitution shall apply with respect to the summoning and procedure of a joint sitting of the Senate and the House of Assembly for the purpose of this section.

Interpretation and savings.

19.—(1) In this Chapter, unless the context otherwise requires—

" contravention ", in relation to any requirement, includes a failure to comply with that requirement, and cognate expressions shall be construed accordingly ;

" court " means a court of law having jurisdiction in Swaziland, but does not include, save in sections 4 and 6 of this Constitution, a court established by a disciplinary law ;

" disciplinary law " means a law regulating the discipline of any disciplined force ;

" disciplined force " means—

(a) a naval, military or air force ;

(b) the Swaziland Police Force ; or

(c) the Swaziland Prison Service ;

" legal representative " means a person lawfully in or entitled to be in Swaziland and entitled to practise as an advocate or attorney in Swaziland ;

" member ", in relation to a disciplined force, includes any person who, under the law regulating the discipline of that force, is subject to that discipline ;

" a period of public emergency " means any period during which Swaziland is at war or a declaration of a state of emergency is in force under section 18 of this Constitution ;

" property " means property, movable or immovable, corporeal or incorporeal, of any description whatever including Swazi nation land and minerals and mineral oils in Swaziland, and any right or interest held, in relation to minerals or mineral oils in Swaziland, by any person under any grant, lease or other disposition lawfully made.

(2) Nothing contained in section 10(2) or 16(2) of this Constitution shall be construed as entitling a person to legal representation at public expense.

(3) Nothing contained in sections 12, 13 or 15 of this Constitution shall be construed as precluding the inclusion in the terms and conditions of service of public officers of reasonable requirements as to their communication or association with other persons or as to their movements or residence.

(4) In relation to any person who is a member of a disciplined force of Swaziland, nothing contained in or done under the authority of the disciplinary law of that force shall be held to be inconsistent with or in contravention of any of the provisions of this Chapter other than sections 4, 6 and 7.

(5) In relation to any person who is a member of a disciplined force that is not a disciplined force of Swaziland and who is present in Swaziland in pursuance of arrangements made between the Government of Swaziland and another Government or an international organisation, nothing contained in or done under the authority of the disciplinary law of that force shall be held to be inconsistent with or in contravention of any of the provisions of this Chapter.

(6) No measures taken in relation to a person who is a member of a disciplined force of a country with which Swaziland is at war and no law, to the extent that it authorises the taking of any such measures, shall be held to be inconsistent with or in contravention of any of the provisions of this Chapter.

CHAPTER III

CITIZENSHIP

Persons who become citizens on 6th September 1968.

20. Every person who, on 5th September 1968, is a citizen of the former protected state of Swaziland by virtue of any of the provisions of Chapter XI of the former Constitution shall, on 6th September 1968, be a citizen of Swaziland.

Persons born in Swaziland after 5th September 1968.

21. Every person born in Swaziland on or after 6th September 1968 shall, if his father is a citizen of Swaziland, become a citizen of Swaziland at the time of his birth.

Persons born outside Swaziland after 5th September 1968.

22. Every person born outside Swaziland on or after 6th September 1968 shall, if his father is a citizen of Swaziland and is domiciled in Swaziland, become a citizen of Swaziland at the time of his birth.

Persons entitled to be registered as citizens.

23.—(1) Subject to the provisions of this section, any of the following persons shall be entitled, upon making application in such manner as may be prescribed by Act of Parliament, to be registered as a citizen of Swaziland—

(*a*) any woman who is married to a person who is a citizen of Swaziland ;

(*b*) any woman whose marriage has been terminated by death or dissolution if the person to whom she was married was a citizen of the former protected state of Swaziland or a citizen of Swaziland or would but for his death have been a citizen of the former protected state of Swaziland by virtue of section 127(*a*) or (*b*) of the former Constitution ;

(*c*) any person one of whose parents is a citizen of Swaziland or was, at the date of the death of such parent, a citizen of Swaziland or a citizen of the former protected state of Swaziland ;

(*d*) any person who is certified, by writing under the hand of the Nggwenyama or the Secretary to the Swazi National Council, to have " khonta'd ", that is to say, to have been accepted as a Swazi in accordance with Swazi law and custom ;

(*e*) any person born in Swaziland on or after 6th September 1968 who was stateless at the time of his birth and is stateless at the time of the application and who is not entitled to acquire as of right the citizenship of his father or his mother.

(2) A person who has not attained the age of twenty-one years (other than a woman who is or has been married) may not himself make an application under subsection (1) of this section, but an application may be made on his behalf by his parent or guardian.

(3) A person registered as a citizen of Swaziland under this section shall be a citizen by registration from the date on which he is so registered.

Citizenship by naturalisation.

24.—(1) Subject to the provisions of this section, the Minister responsible for citizenship may, upon application made by any person who has attained the age of twenty-one years, grant a certificate of naturalisation to that person if satisfied—

> (a) that he has been ordinarily and lawfully resident in Swaziland—
>> (i) throughout the period of twelve months immediately preceding the date of the application ; and
>> (ii) during the seven years immediately preceding the said period of twelve months, for periods amounting in the aggregate to not less than four years or, in the case of a Commonwealth citizen, for periods amounting in the aggregate to not less than three years ; and
> (b) that he is of good character ; and
> (c) that he has an adequate knowledge of at least one of the following languages—
>> (i) English ;
>> (ii) siSwati ; and
> (d) that he intends, if the certificate is granted, to continue to reside in Swaziland.

(2) Provision may be made by Act of Parliament empowering the Minister responsible for citizenship to grant a certificate of naturalisation to any person who has not completed the periods of residence specified in subsection (1)(a) of this section, but is otherwise qualified under that subsection, if the Minister thinks fit in the circumstances of any particular case.

(3) A certificate of naturalisation shall not be granted to any person under this section until he has taken the oath of allegiance set out in Schedule 2 to this Constitution or such other oath as may be prescribed.

(4) A person to whom a certificate of naturalisation is granted shall be a citizen by naturalisation from the date on which the certificate is so granted.

25.—(1) Every person who under this Constitution or any other law is a citizen of Swaziland or under any enactment for the time being in force in any country to which this section applies is a citizen of that country shall, by virtue of that citizenship, have the status of a Commonwealth citizen. *Commonwealth citizens.*

(2) Every person who is a British subject without citizenship under the British Nationality Act 1948(a), continues to be a British subject under section 2 of that Act or is a British subject under the British Nationality Act 1965(b) shall, by virtue of that status, have the status of a Commonwealth citizen.

(3) Save as may be otherwise provided by Act of Parliament, the countries to which this section applies are the United Kingdom and Colonies, Canada, Australia, New Zealand, India, Pakistan, Ceylon, Ghana, Malaysia, Nigeria, Cyprus, Sierra Leone, Tanzania, Jamaica, Trinidad and Tobago, Uganda, Kenya, Malawi, Malta, Zambia, The Gambia, Singapore, Guyana, Lesotho, Botswana, Barbados, Mauritius and Southern Rhodesia.

26.—(1) Subject to the provisions of this Chapter, provision may be made by Act of Parliament relating to the acquisition of citizenship of Swaziland by registration or naturalisation. *Provision by Act of Parliament.*

(a) 1948 c. 56.   (b) 1965 c. 34.

(2) Provision may be made by Act of Parliament for depriving of his citizenship of Swaziland any person who is such a citizen by registration or naturalisation.

(3) Provision may be made by Act of Parliament for the renunciation by any person of his citizenship of Swaziland.

Interpretation.

27.—(1) Any reference in this Chapter to the father of a person shall, in relation to any person born out of wedlock, be construed as a reference to the mother of that person.

(2) Any reference in this Chapter to a citizen by registration shall include a reference to any person who is a citizen by virtue of section 20 of this Constitution and acquired citizenship of the former protected state of Swaziland under section 128 of the former Constitution and any reference in this Chapter to a citizen by naturalisation shall include a reference to any person who is a citizen by virtue of section 20 of this Constitution and acquired citizenship of the former protected state of Swaziland under section 129 of the former Constitution.

(3) For the purposes of this Chapter, a person born aboard a registered aircraft, or aboard an unregistered aircraft of the Government of any country, shall be deemed to have been born in the place in which the aircraft was registered or, as the case may be, in that country.

(4) Any reference in this Chapter to the national status or domicile of the father of a person at the time of that person's birth shall, in relation to a person born after the death of his father, be construed as a reference to the national status or domicile of the father at the time of the father's death ; and where that death occurred before 6th September 1968 such a reference to the national status shall be construed as a reference to the national status the father of a person would have had if he had died on 6th September 1968.

CHAPTER IV

The Monarchy

The office of King.

28.—(1) The King of Swaziland is the Head of State.

(2) The King shall do all things that belong to his office in accordance with the provisions of this Constitution and of all other laws for the time being in force.

Succession to the throne of Swaziland.

29. When an announcement is made to the Swazi nation in accordance with Swazi law and custom that the office of King is vacant by reason of the death of the holder thereof or any other cause, such person as, in accordance with Swazi law and custom, is declared to be King shall become King.

The Regent.

30.—(1) Until the King has been installed, that is to say, until he has publicly assumed the functions and responsibilities of King in accordance with Swazi law and custom, or during any period when he is by reason of absence from Swaziland or any other cause unable to perform the functions of his office, those functions shall be performed, save as otherwise provided in this section, by the Ndlovukazi acting as Regent.

(2) If the Regent is unable for any reason to perform the functions of such office, a person shall be authorised, in accordance with Swazi law and custom (hereinafter referred to as " an authorised person "), to perform on her behalf her functions under subsection (1) of this section.

31.—(1) The King shall be paid such emoluments and shall have such Civil List as may be prescribed by Act of Parliament. The King's emoluments and Civil List.

(2) The emoluments of the King and his Civil List shall be a charge on and paid out of the Consolidated Fund and shall not be reduced during the King's continuance in office.

32.—(1) The Ndlovukazi shall, in respect of any period during which she acts as Regent, be entitled to such remuneration as may be prescribed by Act of Parliament. Remuneration of Regent and of authorised person.

(2) An authorised person shall be entitled to such remuneration as may be prescribed by Act of Parliament.

(3) Any remuneration prescribed under subsection (1) or (2) of this section shall be a charge on and paid out of the Consolidated Fund and shall not be reduced during the Ndlovukazi's continuance in office as Regent or, as the case may be, during the period in which an authorised person is acting under section 30(2) of this Constitution.

33.—(1) The King shall be entitled to immunity from taxation in respect of his emoluments and Civil List, all income accruing to him in his private capacity and all property owned by him in his private capacity. Immunities of King and Ndlovukazi.

(2) The Ndlovukazi shall be entitled to immunity from taxation in respect of her emoluments or any income accruing to her in her private capacity and all property owned by her in her private capacity.

(3) The King and the Ndlovukazi shall be entitled to immunity from compulsory acquisition of all property owned by them in their private capacities.

34. An authorised person shall be entitled to immunity from taxation in respect of any remuneration to which he is entitled under section 32 of this Constitution, and all income accruing to him in his private capacity during any period in which he is performing on behalf of the Ndlovukazi her functions as Regent, and, in so far as the taxation relates to the period concerned, all property owned by him in his private capacity. Immunities of authorised person.

35.—(1) Whilst any person holds the office of King, he shall be entitled to immunity from suit and legal process in any civil cause in respect of all things done or omitted to be done by him in his private capacity, to immunity from criminal proceedings in respect of all things done or omitted to be done by him either in his official capacity or in his private capacity and to immunity from being summoned to appear as a witness in any civil or criminal proceeding. Protection of King and of Ndlovukazi in respect of legal proceedings.

2aa

(2) The Ndlovukazi shall be entitled to immunity from suit and legal process in any civil cause in respect of all things done or omitted to be done by her in her private capacity, to immunity from criminal proceedings in respect of all things done or omitted to be done by her in her official capacity or in her private capacity and to immunity from being summoned to appear as a witness in any civil or criminal proceedings.

(3) Where provision is made by law limiting the time within which proceedings of any description may be brought against any person, the period during which that person has held the office of King or Ndlovukazi shall not be taken into account in calculating the period of time prescribed by that law which determines whether any such proceedings as are mentioned in subsection (1) or (2), as the case may be, of this section may be brought against that person.

(4) For the avoidance of doubt it is hereby declared that any right, interest or function vested in the Nggwenyama in relation to Swazi nation land or minerals or mineral oils in Swaziland is so vested in him, in his capacity as Nggwenyama, and not as King or in his private capacity.

Oaths by King, etc.

36.—(1) The King shall, at his installation as King, take and subscribe the oath for the due execution of his office which is set out in Schedule 2 to this Constitution.

(2) The Ndlovukazi shall, before commencing to act as Regent, take and subscribe the oath of allegiance and the oath for the due execution of the office of Regent which are set out in Schedule 2 to this Constitution.

(3) The oaths referred to in the foregoing provisions of this section shall be administered to the King or the Ndlovukazi by the Chief Justice (or, in the absence of the Chief Justice, by a judge of the Court of Appeal or some other judge of the High Court) in the presence of such of the judges of the Court of Appeal, such of the other judges, if any, of the High Court and such Ministers of the Government as are able to attend.

CHAPTER V

PARLIAMENT

PART 1

Composition of Parliament

Establishment of Parliament.

37. There shall be a Parliament which shall consist of a Senate and a House of Assembly.

Composition of Senate.

38.—(1) Subject to the provisions of this section, the Senate shall consist of twelve members (in this Constitution referred to as "Senators") who shall be elected or appointed in accordance with this section.

(2) If any person who is not a Senator is elected to be President or Deputy President of the Senate he shall, by virtue of holding the office of President or Deputy President, as the case may be, be a member of the Senate in addition to the twelve members aforesaid.

(3) Six Senators shall be elected by the members of the House of Assembly entitled to vote in the manner prescribed by section 39 of this Constitution.

(4) The remaining six Senators shall be appointed by the King, acting in his discretion, in accordance with subsection (5) of this section.

(5) The Senators appointed by the King shall be persons who, in the opinion of the King after consultation with such bodies as he may consider appropriate,—

(a) are able by reason of their special knowledge or practical experience to represent economic, social or cultural interests not already adequately represented in Parliament ; or

(b) are, by reason of their particular merit, able to contribute substantially to the good government of Swaziland.

(6) Notwithstanding any other provision of this section, the power of the King to appoint six Senators shall not be so exercised as to deny a majority in the Senate to the party or coalition of parties which is in the majority in the House of Assembly and, accordingly, that power shall be exercised after the election of the Senators referred to in subsection (3) of this section.

39. The Senators elected by the members of the House of Assembly shall be elected, in such manner as may be prescribed by or under any law, in accordance with the system of proportional representation by means of the single transferable vote. Method of election of Senators.

40.—(1) Subject to the provisions of this section, the House of Assembly shall consist of twenty-four elected members, six nominated members and the Attorney-General. Composition of House of Assembly.

(2) If any person who is not a member of the House is elected to be Speaker or Deputy Speaker thereof he shall, by virtue of holding the office of Speaker or Deputy Speaker, as the case may be, be a member of the House of Assembly in addition to the members specified in subsection (1) of this section.

41. Swaziland shall, in accordance with the provisions of section 55 of this Constitution, be divided into eight constituencies and each constituency shall elect three members to the House of Assembly in such manner as, subject to the provisions of this Constitution, may be prescribed by or under any law. Elected members of House of Assembly.

42. The nominated members of the House of Assembly shall be appointed by the King, acting in his discretion, after consultation with such bodies as he may consider appropriate and after taking account of any interests not already adequately represented in the House: Nominated members of House of Assembly.

Provided that the power of appointment shall not be so exercised as to deprive the party or coalition of parties which has a majority among the elected members of the House of that majority.

43. Subject to the provisions of section 44 of this Constitution, a person shall be qualified to be elected or appointed as a Senator or to be elected as an elected member or appointed as a nominated member Qualifications for membership of Parliament.

of the House of Assembly if, and shall not be qualified to be so elected or appointed unless, he—

(a) is ordinarily resident in Swaziland ;

(b) is a person qualified for registration as a voter ; and

(c) has been so registered in any constituency.

Disqualifications for membership of Parliament.

44.—(1) No person shall be qualified to be elected or appointed as a Senator or to be elected as an elected member or appointed as a nominated member of the House of Assembly who—

(a) is, by virtue of his own act, under acknowledgment of allegiance, obedience or adherence to a foreign power or state ;

(b) is a member of the armed forces of Swaziland or is holding or acting in any public office, or is holding or acting in any other office established by or under any law that may be prescribed ;

(c) is a party to, or is a partner in a firm or a director or manager of a company which is a party to, any subsisting Government contract, and has not made the appropriate disclosure of the nature of the contract and his interest, or the interest of the firm or company, therein :

Provided that the provisions of this paragraph shall not apply in the case of a Senator or a nominated member of the House of Assembly if he is appointed as such without his consent being obtained prior to the appointment ;

(d) is an unrehabilitated insolvent or an undischarged bankrupt, having been adjudged or otherwise declared an insolvent or a bankrupt under any law for the time being in force in any country ;

(e) is certified to be insane or otherwise adjudged to be of unsound mind under any law for the time being in force in Swaziland ;

(f) is, for an offence which is a criminal offence under the law of Swaziland, under sentence of death imposed on him by a court in any country, or is, for such an offence, under a sentence of imprisonment (by whatever name called) for a term of or exceeding six months, including a suspended sentence, imposed on him by such a court or substituted by the competent authority for some other sentence imposed on him by such a court ;

(g) has at any time been, for an offence which is a criminal offence under the law of Swaziland, under a sentence of imprisonment for a term of or exceeding six months (other than a suspended sentence which has not been enforced) imposed on him by a court in any country or substituted by competent authority for some other sentence imposed on him by such a court :

Provided that if two years or more have elapsed since the termination of the sentence of imprisonment, the person shall not be disqualified for membership of Parliament by reason only of such sentence ;

(h) is disqualified for membership of the Senate or House of Assembly under any law for the time being in force relating to offences connected with elections ; or

(i) in the case of an elected member of the House of Assembly, holds, or is acting in, any office, the functions of which involve any responsibility for, or in connection with, the conduct of any election or the compilation or revision of any electoral register.

(2) For the purposes of paragraph (c) of subsection (1) of this section the appropriate disclosure of the nature of and interest in a Government contract shall be—

(a) in the case of an elected Senator, disclosure to the elected members of the House of Assembly through the Speaker of the House before the election is held under section 39 of this Constitution ;

(b) in the case of an appointed Senator or a nominated member of the House of Assembly, disclosure to the King before the appointment is made ;

(c) in the case of an elected member of the House of Assembly, disclosure during the period commencing with the notification of the writ for the election in the Gazette and ending three days before the date of the election, by publication of a notice in English in the Gazette and in English and siSwati in a newspaper circulating in Swaziland.

45. A Senator or a member of the House of Assembly shall vacate his seat as such if, but only if,— *Tenure of seats of members of Parliament.*

(a) Parliament is dissolved ;

(b) he resigns his seat by writing under his hand addressed to the President or Speaker of the chamber ;

(c) he is absent from two consecutive meetings of the Senate or, as the case may be, the House of Assembly, without having obtained before the termination of either meeting from the President or Speaker, or other person presiding, permission to be or to remain absent therefrom ;

(d) in the case of a Senator or nominated member who was appointed without his consent being obtained prior to the appointment, he is at the time of his appointment a party to, or is a partner in a firm or a director or manager of a company which is a party to, a subsisting Government contract and has not within one week after his appointment been exempted by the King, by writing under his hand, from vacating his seat ;

(e) he becomes a party to any Government contract, or if any firm in which he is a partner or any company of which he is a director or manager becomes a party to any such contract, or if he becomes a partner in a firm or a director or manager of a company which is a party to any such contract:

Provided that, if in the circumstances it appears to them to be just to do so, the Senate may by resolution exempt a Senator and the House of Assembly may by resolution exempt a member of the House from vacating his seat under the provisions of this paragraph, if the member, before becoming a party to the contract or before or as soon as practicable after becoming otherwise interested in the contract (whether as a partner in a firm or as a director or manager of a company), discloses to the President of the Senate or the Speaker of the House, as the case may be, the nature of the contract and his interest, or the interest of the firm or company, therein ;

(f) he ceases to be qualified for registration as a voter ;

(g) he ceases to be ordinarily resident in Swaziland ;

(*h*) he becomes a member of the other chamber of Parliament ;

(*i*) any circumstances arise that, if he were not a Senator or a member of the House of Assembly, would cause him to be disqualified for election or appointment thereto by virtue of paragraph (*a*), (*b*), (*d*), (*e*), (*h*) or (*i*) of section 44(1) of this Constitution ; or

(*j*) the circumstances mentioned in section 46 of this Constitution arise.

Vacation of seats on sentence, etc. **46.**—(1) Subject to the provisions of this section, if a Senator or an elected member or a nominated member of the House of Assembly is, for an offence which is a criminal offence under the law of Swaziland, sentenced by a court in any country to death or to imprisonment (by whatever named called) for a term of or exceeding six months, including a suspended sentence, he shall forthwith cease to perform his functions as a Senator or member of the House, and his seat therein shall become vacant at the expiration of a period of thirty days thereafter:

Provided that the President of the Senate or the Speaker of the House, as the case may be, may, at the request of the member, from time to time extend that period for thirty days to enable the member to pursue any appeal in respect of his conviction or sentence, so however that extensions of time exceeding in the aggregate one hundred and eighty days shall not be granted without the approval of the Senate or House signified by resolution.

(2) If at any time before the Senator or member vacates his seat he receives a free pardon or his conviction is set aside or his sentence is reduced to a term of imprisonment of less than six months or a punishment other than imprisonment is substituted, his seat in the Senate or House of Assembly shall not become vacant under the provisions of this section, and he may again perform his functions as a Senator or member of the House of Assembly.

President and Deputy President of Senate. **47.**—(1) When the Senate first meets after any general election and before it proceeds to the despatch of any other business, it shall elect a person to be the President of the Senate ; and if the office of President falls vacant at any time before the next dissolution of Parliament, the Senate shall elect as soon as practicable another person to that office.

(2) At any time after the election of a President the Senate may, if it thinks fit, elect a person to be the Deputy President of the Senate ; and if the office of Deputy President falls vacant at any time before the next dissolution of Parliament, the Senate may, if it thinks fit, elect another person to that office.

(3) The President or Deputy President may be elected either from among the Senators who are not Ministers or Assistant Ministers or from among persons who are not Senators:

Provided that a person who is not a Senator shall not be elected as President or Deputy President if he would be disqualified to be a Senator by virtue of paragraph (*d*), (*e*), (*f*), (*g*) or (*h*) of section 44(1) of this Constitution.

(4) A person shall vacate the office of President or Deputy President—

(*a*) if, having been elected from among the Senators, he ceases to be a Senator otherwise than by a dissolution of Parliament or if he is appointed to be a Minister or an Assistant Minister or if he is required, by virtue of section 46 of this Constitution, to cease to perform his functions as a Senator ;

(*b*) in the case of a President or Deputy President who was elected from among persons who were not Senators, if any circumstances arise which would cause him to be disqualified to be President or Deputy President under the proviso to subsection (3) of this section ;

(*c*) when the Senate first sits after any dissolution of Parliament ;

(*d*) if he is removed from office by a resolution of the Senate supported by the votes of not less than two-thirds of all the Senators ; or

(*e*) in the case of the Deputy President, if he is elected as President.

(5) A person holding the office of President or Deputy President may resign his office by writing under his hand addressed to the Senate and the office shall become vacant when the writing is received by the Clerk to the Senate.

(6) During any period when a person holding the office of the Deputy President is acting as President of the Senate in accordance with section 49 of this Constitution he shall not perform the functions of Deputy President.

48.—(1) When the House of Assembly first meets after any general election and before it proceeds to the despatch of any other business, it shall elect a person to be the Speaker of the House of Assembly ; and if the office of Speaker falls vacant at any time before the next dissolution of Parliament, the House shall elect as soon as practicable another person to that office.

Speaker and Deputy Speaker of House of Assembly.

(2) At any time after the election of a Speaker the House of Assembly may, if it thinks fit, elect a person to be the Deputy Speaker of the House of Assembly ; and if the office of Deputy Speaker falls vacant at any ·time before the next dissolution of Parliament, the House may, if it thinks fit, elect another person to that office.

(3) The Speaker or Deputy Speaker may be elected either from among the members of the House (other than the Attorney-General or Ministers or Assistant Ministers) or from among persons who are not members of the House:

Provided that a person who is not a member of the House shall not be elected as Speaker or Deputy Speaker if he would be disqualified to be a member of the House by virtue of paragraph (*d*), (*e*), (*f*), (*g*) or (*h*) of section 44(1) of this Constitution.

(4) A person shall vacate the office of Speaker or Deputy Speaker of the House of Assembly—

(*a*) if, having been elected from among the members of the House, he ceases to be a member otherwise than by the dissolution of Parliament or if he is appointed to be a Minister or Assistant

Minister or Attorney-General or if he is required, by virtue of section 46 of this Constitution, to cease to perform his functions as a member of the House ;

(b) in the case of a Speaker or Deputy Speaker who was elected from among persons who were not members of the House, if any circumstances arise which would cause him to be disqualified to be Speaker or Deputy Speaker under the proviso to subsection (3) of this section ;

(c) when the House first sits after any dissolution of Parliament ;

(d) if he is removed from office by a resolution of the House supported by the votes of not less than two-thirds of all the members thereof ; or

(e) in the case of the Deputy Speaker, if he is elected as Speaker.

(5) A person holding the office of Speaker or Deputy Speaker may resign his office by writing under his hand addressed to the House and the office shall become vacant when the writing is received by the Clerk to the House.

(6) During any period when a person holding the office of the Deputy Speaker is acting as Speaker of the House of Assembly in accordance with section 49 of this Constitution he shall not perform the functions of Deputy Speaker.

Acting President and Speaker. **49.**—(1) During any period when the office of President or Speaker is vacant or the holder of the office of President or Speaker is absent from Swaziland or is for any other reason unable to perform the functions of his office, the Senate or the House of Assembly, as the case may be, may elect a person (not being a Minister, an Assistant Minister or the Attorney-General) from among the members of the chamber to act as President or Speaker until a President or Speaker has been elected or, as the case may be, the President or Speaker has resumed the functions of his office.

(2) During any period when the office of Deputy President or Deputy Speaker is vacant or the holder of the office of Deputy President or Deputy Speaker is absent from Swaziland or is acting as President or Speaker or is for any other reason unable to perform the functions of his office, the Senate or the House of Assmbly, as the case may be, may elect a person (not being a Minister, an Assistant Minister or the Attorney-General) from among the members of the chamber to act as Deputy President or Deputy Speaker until a Deputy President or Deputy Speaker has been elected or, as the case may be, the Deputy President or Deputy Speaker has resumed the functions of his office.

(3) The provisions of sections 47(4) and 47(5) of this Constitution shall apply in relation to a person elected under this section to act as President or Deputy President of the Senate as they apply in relation to the holder of the office of President or Deputy President ; and the provisions of sections 48(4) and 48(5) of this Constitution shall apply in relation to a person elected under this section to act as Speaker or Deputy Speaker as they apply in relation to the holder of the office of Speaker or Deputy Speaker.

50.—(1) There shall be a Clerk to the Senate and a Clerk to the House of Assembly.

Clerks to Senate and House of Assembly and their staffs.

(2) The offices of the Clerk to the Senate and the Clerk to the House of Assembly and of the members of their staffs shall be offices in the public service.

(3) Nothing in this section shall be construed as preventing the appointment of one person to the offices of Clerk to the Senate and Clerk to the House of Assembly or the appointment of one person to any office on the staff of the Clerk to the Senate and any office on the staff of the Clerk to the House of Assembly.

51.—(1) Subject to the provisions of section 52 of this Constitution, a person shall be qualified to be registered as a voter for the purpose of elections of elected members of the House of Assembly if, and shall not be so qualified unless, he has attained the age of twenty-one years and is a citizen of Swaziland.

Qualifications of voters.

(2) A person shall be entitled to be registered in one constituency only.

52. No person shall be qualified to be registered as a voter, or to vote, if—

Disqualifications of voters.

(a) he is certified to be insane or otherwise adjudged to be of unsound mind under any law for the time being in force in Swaziland ;

(b) he is, for an offence which is a criminal offence under the law of Swaziland, under sentence of death imposed on him by a court in any country, or is, for such an offence, under a sentence of imprisonment (by whatever name called) for a term of or exceeding six months imposed on him by such a court or substituted by competent authority for some other sentence imposed on him by such a court ; or

(c) he is disqualified for registration as a voter under any law for the time being in force in Swaziland relating to offences connected with elections.

53.—(1) Any person who is registered as a voter shall be entitled to vote at any election of a member to the House of Assembly and, in the case of any general election, be entitled to cast one vote for each of any three candidates for election:

Right to vote at elections.

Provided that (except in so far as may otherwise be prescribed) no such person shall be entitled so to vote if on the date prescribed for polling he is for any reason unable to attend in person at the place and time prescribed for polling.

(2) No person shall vote at any election for a constituency who is not registered as a voter in that constituency.

54.—(1) There shall be a Delimitation Commission which shall be appointed by the Judicial Service Commission in the circumstances specified in section 55(3) of this Constitution and which shall consist of a chairman and two other members.

Delimitation Commission.

(2) The chairman and the other members of the Commission shall be appointed by the Judicial Service Commission.

(3) The chairman shall be appointed from among the judges of the High Court.

(4) No person shall be qualified to be appointed as one of the other members of the Commission if—

(*a*) he is a Senator or member of the House of Assembly or is nominated for election to the House of Assembly ;

(*b*) he is the holder of an office in any organisation that sponsors or supports, or that has at any time sponsored or supported, a candidate for election as a member of a Legislative Council established for Swaziland by Order of Her Majesty in Council or of the Senate or House of Assembly established by this Constitution or the former Constitution ;

(*c*) during the period of five years immediately preceding the date of the appointment—

(i) he has been a member of a Legislative Council or of a Senate or House of Assembly established as aforesaid ;

(ii) he has been nominated for election to a Legislative Council or Senate or House of Assembly established as aforesaid ; or

(iii) he has been the holder of an office in such an organisation as is referred to in paragraph (*b*) of this subsection ; or

(*d*) he is a public officer, other than a judge of the High Court or the Court of Appeal:

Provided that a person shall not be so disqualified by reason only that he has been Speaker of a Legislative Council established as aforesaid or has been Speaker of the House of Assembly or Speaker of the Senate established as aforesaid having been elected as such from outside the House of Assembly or, as the case may be, the Senate.

(5) Subject to the provisions of this section, the office of a member of the Commission shall become vacant—

(*a*) when an order of the Commission is published in the Gazette in accordance with the provisions of section 55(5) of this Constitution ; or

(*b*) if any circumstances arise that, if he were not a member of the Commission, would cause him to be disqualified to be appointed as such under subsection (4) of this section.

(6) A member of the Commission shall not enter upon the duties of his office until he has taken and subscribed the oath of allegiance and the oath for the due execution of his office that are set out in Schedule 2 to this Constitution or such other oaths as may be prescribed.

(7) In the exercise of its functions under this Constitution the Commission shall not be subject to the direction or control of any other person or authority.

(8) The Commission may by regulation or otherwise regulate its own procedure and, with the consent of the Prime Minister, may confer powers or impose duties on any public officer or on any authority of the Government for the purpose of the exercise of its functions.

(9) The Commission may, subject to its rules of procedure, act notwithstanding any vacancy in its membership or the absence of any member and its proceedings shall not be invalidated by the presence or participation of any person not entitled to be present at or to participate in those proceedings:

Provided that any decision of the Comission shall require the concurrence of a majority of all its members.

55.—(1) For the purpose of the election of elected members of the Constit-House of Assembly Swaziland shall be divided into eight constituencies uencies. having such boundaries as may be prescribed by order made by the Delimitation Commission.

(2) All constituencies shall contain as nearly equal numbers of adult inhabitants as appears to the Commission to be reasonably practicable but the Commission may depart from this principle to such extent as it considers expedient in order to take account of the following factors, that is to say—

(a) the density of population, and in particular the need to ensure the adequate representation of sparsely populated rural areas;

(b) the means of communication;

(c) geographical features; and

(d) the boundaries of existing administrative areas.

(3) The Judicial Service Commission shall appoint a Delimitation Commission in the following circumstances, that is to say—

(a) whenever a census of the population of Swaziland has been held in pursuance of any law and the report of that census has been published;

(b) whenever provision has been made altering the number of constituencies or the number of seats of elected members in the House of Assembly; or

(c) on the expiration of not less than five nor more than ten years after the Commission last reviewed the boundaries of the constituencies in accordance with the provisions of this section.

(4) Whenever the Delimitation Commission has been appointed in any of the circumstances specified in subsection (3) of this section it shall forthwith carry out a review of the boundaries of the constituencies into which Swaziland is divided and may (and in the circumstances specified in subsection (3)(b) shall), by order, alter the boundaries in accordance with the provisions of this section to such extent as it thinks desirable in the light of those circumstances and that review.

(5) Every order made by the Delimitation Commission under this section shall be published in the Gazette and shall come into effect upon the next dissolution of Parliament after it was made.

(6) For the purposes of subsection (2) of this section the number of inhabitants of any part of Swaziland shall be ascertained by reference to the latest census of the population held in pursuance of any law.

56.—(1) The High Court shall have jurisdiction to hear and determine Decision of any question whether— questions as to member-

(a) any person has been validly elected as a Senator by the members ship of of the House of Assembly; Parliament.

(b) any person has been validly appointed as a Senator by the King ;

(c) any person has been validly elected as an elected member of the House ;

(d) any person has been validly appointed as a nominated member of the House by the King ;

(e) any person who has been elected as President or Deputy President of the Senate or as Speaker or Deputy Speaker of the House from among persons who were not members thereof was qualified to be so elected ; or

(f) the seat in the Senate or House of any member thereof has become vacant.

(2) An application to the High Court may be made for the determination of any question—

(a) under subsection (1)(a) of this section, by any elected member of the House of Assembly or by the Attorney-General ;

(b) under subsection (1)(b) of this section, by any Senator or by the Attorney-General ;

(c) under subsection (1)(c) of this section, by any person who was a candidate at or entitled to vote in the election to which the application relates or by the Attorney-General ;

(d) under subsection (1)(d) of this section, by any elected or nominated member of the House or by the Attorney-General ;

(e) under subsection (1)(e) of this section, by any Senator or elected or nominated member of the House, as the case may be, or by the Attorney-General ;

(f) under subsection (1)(f) of this section, by any Senator or elected or nominated member of the House, as the case may be, or by the Attorney-General, or, in the case of the seat of an elected member of the House, by any person registered in some constituency as a voter in elections of elected members of the House,

and, if it is made by a person other than the Attorney-General, the Attorney-General may intervene and may then appear or be represented in the proceedings.

(3) Provision may be made by Act of Parliament with respect to—

(a) the circumstances and manner in which and the conditions upon which any application may be made to the High Court for the determination of any question under this section ; and

(b) the powers, practice and procedure of the High Court in relation to any such application,

but, subject to any provision in that behalf made by Act of Parliament under this subsection, the practice and procedure of the High Court in relation to any such application shall be regulated by rules made by the Chief Justice.

(4) The determination by the High Court of any question under this section shall not be subject to appeal.

(5) In the exercise of his functions under this section, the Attorney-General shall not be subject to the direction or control of any other person or authority.

57.—(1) In this Part of this Chapter "Government contract" means a contract with the Government for or on account of the public service the consideration for which exceeds two hundred rand or which forms part of a larger transaction or series of transactions in respect of which the amount or value, or the aggregate amount or value, of the consideration exceeds two hundred rand. Interpretation.

(2) For the purpose of this Part of this Chapter—

(a) two or more terms of imprisonment that are required to be served consecutively shall be regarded as a single term of imprisonment for the aggregate period of those terms ;

(b) references to a sentence of imprisonment shall not include a sentence of imprisonment in lieu of a fine.

PART 2

Summoning, prorogation and dissolution

58.—(1) Each session of Parliament shall be held at such place within Swaziland and begin at such time (not being later than twelve months from the end of the preceding session if Parliament has been prorogued or fourteen days from the holding of a general election of elected members of the House of Assembly if Parliament has been dissolved) as the King may appoint. Sessions of Parliament, etc.

(2) Subject to the provisions of subsection (1) of this section, the sittings of each chamber of Parliament shall be held at such time and place as that chamber may, by its rules of procedure or otherwise, determine.

59.—(1) The King may at any time prorogue or dissolve Parliament. Prorogation and dissolution of Parliament.

(2) Subject to the provisions of subsection (3) of this section, Parliament, unless sooner dissolved, shall continue for five years from the date when the House of Assembly first meets after any dissolution of Parliament and shall then stand dissolved.

(3) At any time when Swaziland is at war the period of five years specified in subsection (2) of this section may be extended by Act of Parliament for not more than twelve months at a time:

Provided that the life of Parliament shall not be extended under this subsection for more than five years.

(4) In the exercise of his power to dissolve Parliament, the King shall act in accordance with the advice of the Prime Minister:

Provided that—

(a) if the Prime Minister recommends a dissolution and the King considers that the government of Swaziland can be carried on without a dissolution and that dissolution would not be in the interests of Swaziland, he may refuse to dissolve Parliament ;

(b) if the House of Assembly passes a resolution of no confidence in the Government of Swaziland and the Prime Minister does not within three days thereafter either resign or advise a dissolution, the King may dissolve Parliament ; and

(c) if the office of Prime Minister is vacant and the King considers that there is no prospect of his being able within a reasonable time to find a person who is the leader of a party or a coalition of parties that will command the support of a majority of the members of the House of Assembly, he shall dissolve Parliament.

Recalling the Senate and House of Assembly in case of emergency.

60. If, between a dissolution of Parliament and the next ensuing general election of elected members of the House of Assembly, an emergency arises of such a nature that in the opinion of the King, after consultation with the Prime Minister, it is necessary for the two chambers of Parliament to be summoned before that general election can be held, the King may, after consultation with the Prime Minister, by proclamation published in the Gazette, summon the preceding chambers of Parliament as constituted immediately before the said dissolution, and those chambers shall thereupon be deemed (except for the purposes of section 61 of this Constitution) not to have been dissolved but shall be deemed (except as aforesaid) to be dissolved on the date on which the next ensuing general election of elected members of the House of Assembly is held.

Elections.

61.—(1) A general election of elected members of the House of Assembly shall be held at such time within three months after every dissolution of Parliament as the King shall appoint by proclamation published in the Gazette.

(2) Where the seat of any elected member of the House of Assembly becomes vacant for any cause other than a dissolution of Parliament the King shall, unless Parliament is sooner dissolved, issue a writ for the holding of an election to fill that vacancy returnable not later than six months after the occurrence of the vacancy.

CHAPTER VI

LEGISLATION AND PROCEDURE IN PARLIAMENT

Power to make laws.

62.—(1) Subject to the provisions of this Constitution, the King and Parliament may make laws for the peace, order and good government of Swaziland.

(2) Subsection (1) of this section shall not apply to the matters specified in Schedule 3 to this Constitution, which shall continue to be regulated by Swazi law and custom:

Provided that, with the consent of the Swazi National Council signified in writing under the hand of the Secretary of that Council, the King and Parliament may make laws with respect to any such matter that is specified in the writing.

Oaths to be taken by members of Parliament.

63.—(1) Every member of either chamber of Parliament shall, before taking his seat in that chamber, take and subscribe before the chamber the oath of allegiance that is set out in Schedule 2 to this Constitution or such other oath as may be prescribed, but a member may before taking and subscribing that oath take part in the election of the President or Speaker of the chamber.

(2) Any person elected as President or Deputy President or Speaker or Deputy Speaker of a chamber of Parliament shall, if he has not

already taken and subscribed the oath of allegiance under subsection (1) of this section, take and subscribe that oath before the chamber before entering upon the duties of his office.

64.—(1) There shall preside at any sitting of the Senate—

(a) the President of the Senate ;

(b) in the absence of the President and in circumstances in which the rules of procedure of the Senate authorise the Deputy President to preside, the Deputy President ; or

(c) in the absence of the President and a Deputy President authorised as aforesaid to preside, such other Senator as the Senate may elect for the purpose of presiding at the sitting.

(2) References in this section to circumstances in which the President or Deputy President is absent include references to circumstances in which the office of President or Deputy President is vacant.

65.—(1) There shall preside at any sitting of the House of Assembly—

(a) the Speaker of the House of Assembly ;

(b) in the absence of the Speaker and in circumstances in which the rules of procedure of the House of Assembly authorise a Deputy Speaker to preside, the Deputy Speaker ; or

(c) in the absence of the Speaker and a Deputy Speaker authorised as aforesaid to preside, such member as the House may elect for the purpose of presiding at the sitting.

(2) References in this section to circumstances in which the Speaker or Deputy Speaker is absent include references to circumstances in which the office of Speaker or Deputy Speaker is vacant.

66.—(1) If objection is taken by a Senator who is present that there are present in the Senate (besides the person presiding) fewer than six Senators and, after such interval as may be prescribed in the rules of procedure of the Senate, the person presiding ascertains that there are still fewer than six Senators present, he shall thereupon adjourn the Senate.

(2) If objection is taken by any member of the House of Assembly who is present that there are present in the House (besides the person presiding) fewer than twelve members of the House and, after such interval as may be prescribed in the rules of procedure of the House, the person presiding ascertains that there are still fewer than twelve members of the House present, he shall thereupon adjourn the House.

67.—(1) Save as otherwise provided in this Constitution, any question proposed for decision in either chamber of Parliament shall be deter- mined by a majority of the votes of the members thereof present and voting.

(2) A President elected from among persons who are Senators or a Speaker elected from among persons who are members of the House of Assembly or a member of either chamber of Parliament presiding in that chamber shall have an original but not a casting vote.

(3) A President or Deputy President of the Senate elected from among persons who are not Senators or a Speaker or Deputy Speaker of the House of Assembly elected from among persons who are not members of the House shall have no vote.

(4) The Attorney-General shall have no vote in the House of Assembly.

(5) If upon any question before either chamber the votes of the members are equally divided the motion shall be lost.

(6) The rules of procedure of either chamber of Parliament may make provision under which a member who votes upon a question in which he has a direct pecuniary interest shall be deemed not to have voted.

Right of Ministers, etc., to address other chamber of Parliament.

68. A Minister or an Assistant Minister who is a member of the House of Assembly or the Attorney-General shall be entitled to attend all meetings of the Senate and to take part in all proceedings thereof but he shall not be regarded as a member of, or be entitled to vote on any question before, the Senate ; and a Minister or an Assistant Minister who is a Senator shall be entitled to attend all meetings of the House of Assembly and to take part in all proceedings thereof but he shall not be regarded as a member of, or be entitled to vote on any question before, the House.

Unqualified persons sitting or voting.

69.—(1) Any person who sits or votes in either chamber knowing or having reasonable grounds for knowing that he is not entitled to do so shall be guilty of an offence and liable to a fine not exceeding one hundred rand, or such other sum as may be prescribed, for each day on which he so sits and votes in that chamber.

(2) Any prosecution for an offence under this section shall be instituted in the High Court and shall not be so instituted except by the Attorney-General.

Mode of exercise of power to make laws.

70.—(1) The power of the King and Parliament to make laws shall be exercised by bills—

(a) passed by both chambers of Parliament (that is to say, passed without amendments or with amendments agreed by both chambers) ;

(b) in the cases mentioned in sections 72, 73, 74 and 75(3) of this Constitution, passed by the House of Assembly ; or

(c) in the cases mentioned in sections 75(2), 76 and 134 of this Constitution, passed at a joint sitting of the Senate and the House of Assembly,

and assented to by the King.

(2) Subject to the provisions of sections 76 and 134(1)(e) of this Constitution, when a bill has been presented to the King for assent in pursuance of subsection (1) of this section, he shall signify that he assents or that he withholds assent—

(a) in the case of an Appropriation bill or a bill to alter this Constitution, forthwith ;

(b) in the case of any other bill, within thirty days.

(3) When a bill that has been duly passed is assented to in accordance with the provisions of this Constitution it shall become law and the King shall thereupon cause it to be published in the Gazette as a law.

(4) No law made by the King and Parliament shall come into operation until it has been published in the Gazette but the King and Parliament may postpone the coming into operation of any such law and may make laws with retrospective effect.

(5) All laws made by the King and Parliament shall be styled " Acts of Parliament " and the words of enactment shall be " Enacted by the King and the Parliament of Swaziland ".

71.—(1) A bill may be introduced in either chamber of Parliament: Introduction of bills, etc.

Provided that a money bill or a bill introduced in pursuance of section 62(2) of this Constitution shall not be introduced in the Senate.

(2) Except with the consent of the Cabinet signified by a Minister, neither chamber shall—

(*a*) proceed upon any bill (including any amendment to a bill) that, in the opinion of the person presiding, makes provision for any of the following purposes—

(i) for the imposition of taxation or the alteration of taxation otherwise than by reduction ;

(ii) for the imposition of any charge upon the Consolidated Fund or any other public fund of Swaziland or the alteration of any such charge otherwise than by reduction ;

(iii) for the payment, issue or withdrawal from the Consolidated Fund or any other public fund of Swaziland of any moneys not charged thereon or any increase in the amount of such a payment, issue or withdrawal ; or

(iv) for the composition or remission of any debt due to the Government ; or

(*b*) proceed upon any motion (including any amendment to a motion) the effect of which, in the opinion of the person presiding, would be to make provision for any of those purposes.

72.—(1) When a bill that is passed by the House of Assembly and that is certified by the Speaker of the House under subsection (2) of this section as an Appropriation bill is sent to the Senate it shall forthwith be introduced in the Senate and shall be passed by the Senate without delay ; and if it is not passed by the Senate by the end of the day after the day on which it was sent to the Senate or if it is passed by the Senate with amendments to which the House does not by then agree, the bill, with such amendments, if any, as may have been agreed to by both chambers, shall, unless the House of Assembly otherwise resolves, be presented to the King for assent. Limitation on powers of Senate with respect to appropriation bills.

(2) When a bill that in the opinion of the Speaker of the House of Assembly is an Appropriation bill is sent to the Senate from the House it shall bear a certificate of the Speaker of the House that it is an Appropriation bill.

73.—(1) Subject to the provisions of section 74 of this Constitution, when a bill that is passed by the House of Assembly is certified by the Speaker of the House under subsection (2) of this section as a money bill other than an Appropriation bill and, having been sent to the Senate at least thirty days before the end of the session, is not passed by the Senate within thirty days after it is so sent or is passed by the Limitation on powers of Senate with respect to other money bills.

CHAPTER VII

THE EXECUTIVE

Executive authority of Swaziland.

79.—(1) Subject to the provisions of this Constitution, the executive authority of Swaziland shall vest in the King.

(2) Save as otherwise provided in this Constitution, that authority may be exercised by the King either directly or through officers or authorities of the Government of Swaziland.

(3) Nothing in this section shall prevent the conferment by Act of Parliament of functions on persons or authorities other than the King.

Ministers.

80.—(1) There shall be a Prime Minister who shall be appointed by the King.

(2) There shall be, in addition to the office of Prime Minister, the office of Deputy Prime Minister and such other offices of Minister of the Government as may be prescribed or, subject to the provisions of any law, established by the King, acting in accordance with the advice of the Prime Minister:

Provided that the number of offices of Minister other than the Prime Minister and Deputy Prime Minister shall not exceed eight.

(3) The King, acting in his discretion, shall appoint as Prime Minister the elected member of the House of Assembly who appears to him best able to command the support of a majority of the members of the House and shall, acting in accordance with the advice of the Prime Minister, appoint the other Ministers from among the elected or appointed members of either chamber.

(4) For the purposes of this section, during any period when Parliament is dissolved a person who was an elected or appointed member of either chamber immediately before the dissolution shall be regarded as continuing as an elected or appointed member, as the case may be, of that chamber.

Tenure of office of Ministers.

81.—(1) The King, acting in his discretion, may remove the Prime Minister from office—

(a) if a resolution of no confidence in the Government of Swaziland is passed by the House of Assembly ; or

(b) if, at any time between the holding of a general election of elected members of the House of Assembly and the date on which the House first meets thereafter, the King considers that, in consequence of changes in the membership of the House resulting from that election, the Prime Minister will not be able to command the support of a majority of the members of the House :

Provided that the King shall not remove the Prime Minister from office when a vote of no confidence has been passed by the House of Assembly unless three days have elapsed since the vote was passed and the King has decided not to dissolve Parliament under paragraph (b) of the proviso to section 59(4) of this Constitution.

(2) The office of Prime Minister or any other Minister shall become vacant—

(a) if he ceases to be a member of Parliament otherwise than by reason of a dissolution of Parliament;

(b) if, when Parliament first meets after a dissolution of Parliament, he is not then a member thereof ; or

(c) if he resigns from office.

(3) The office of a Minister other than the Prime Minister shall become vacant—

(a) if the King, acting in accordance with the advice of the Prime Minister, so directs ;

(b) if the Prime Minister resigns from office within three days after the passage by the House of Assembly of a resolution of no confidence in the Government or is removed from office under subsection (1) of this section ; or

(c) on the appointment of any person to the office of Prime Minister.

(4) If for any period the Prime Minister or any other Minister is unable by reason of the provisions of section 46 of this Constitution to perform his functions as a member of Parliament, he shall not during such period perform any of his functions as Prime Minister or a Minister, as the case may be.

82.—(1) There shall be a Cabinet of Ministers, consisting of the Prime Minister and the other Ministers. Cabinet.

(2) The function of the Cabinet shall be to advise the King in the government of Swaziland, and the Cabinet shall be collectively responsible to Parliament for any advice given to the King by or under the general authority of the Cabinet and for all things done by or under the authority of any Minister in the execution of his office.

(3) The provisions of subsection (2) of this section shall not apply in relation to--

(a) the appointment and removal from office of Ministers and Assistant Ministers, the assignment of responsibility to any Minister under section 83 of this Constitution, the authorisation of any Minister under section 84 of this Constitution to exercise the functions of the Prime Minister during absence or illness or the designation of an Assistant Minister as a Minister of State ; or

(b) the dissolution of Parliament.

83. The King, acting in accordance with the advice of the Prime Minister, may, by directions in writing, assign to the Prime Minister or any other Minister responsibility for the conduct (subject to the provisions of this Constitution and any other law) of any business of the government of Swaziland, including the administration of any department of government. Assignment of responsibilities to Ministers.

84.—(1) Whenever the Prime Minister is absent from Swaziland or is by reason of illness or the provisions of section 81(4) of this Constitution unable to exercise the functions conferred on him by this Constitution, those functions (other than the functions conferred by this section) shall be exercised by— Exercise of Prime Minister's functions during absence or illness.

(a) the Deputy Prime Minister ; or

(b) if the office of Deputy Prime Minister is vacant or the Deputy Prime Minister is absent from Swaziland or is by reason of illness or the provisions of section 81(4) of this Constitution unable to exercise the functions of the office of Prime Minister, by such other Minister as the King may, by directions in writing, authorise in that behalf.

(2) The powers of the King under this section shall be exercised by him in accordance with the advice of the Prime Minister or Deputy Prime Minister as the case may be:

Provided that if the Prime Minister and the Deputy Prime Minister are unable to exercise the functions of the office of Prime Minister by reason, as the case may be, of absence, illness or the provisions of section 81(4) of this Constitution, the King may exercise those powers acting in his discretion.

Exercise of King's functions.

85.—(1) In the exercise of his functions under this Constitution or any other law, the King shall, subject to the following provisions of this section, act in accordance with the advice of the Cabinet or a Minister acting under the general authority of the Cabinet.

(2) The provisions of subsection (1) of this section shall not apply in relation to the exercise by the King of—

(a) any function conferred upon him by this Constitution that is expressed to be exercisable by him in his discretion or in accordance with the advice of, or after consultation with, any person or authority other than the Cabinet ;

(b) any function conferred upon him by any other law that is expressed to be exercisable by him in his discretion or that he is otherwise authorised by such law to exercise without obtaining the advice of the Cabinet ; or

(c) the functions which the King is required to perform by section 100(3), 113(5) or 115(5) of this Constitution or paragraph 1(1) of Schedule 1 to this Constitution.

(3) (a) Where in any matter the King has received the advice of the Cabinet or a Minister for the purposes of subsection (1) of this section, he may, within the prescribed period, by writing under his hand require that, for reasons to be specified by him, the Prime Minister shall cause such advice to be reconsidered or, as the case may be, considered at a meeting of the Cabinet, and thereupon the following provisions shall apply—

(i) during the prescribed period no act in furtherance of that advice shall be done by any other person pending consideration thereof by the King unless the Prime Minister, by writing under his hand, has certified that on grounds of urgency such act should be done ;

(ii) a meeting of the Cabinet shall be held within seven days after the receipt by the Prime Minister of the requirement made by the King that the advice be reconsidered or considered, as the case may be ; and

(iii) if the Cabinet, having reconsidered or, as the case may be, considered the original advice tendered to the King, re-submits the same advice to him, the King shall forthwith act in accordance with that advice.

(b) For the purposes of this subsection, " the prescribed period " shall be the period of seven days commencing with the day upon which the King has received the advice in question or, if the King, by writing under his hand, so requires in any case before the expiration of the said period of seven days, the period of fourteen days commencing as aforesaid.

(4) Where the King is required by this Constitution to exercise any function after consultation with any person or authority other than the Cabinet, he shall not be obliged to exercise that function in accordance with the advice of that person or authority.

(5) Where the King is required by this Constitution to act in accordance with the advice of or after consultation with any person or authority, the question whether he has in any matter so acted shall not be called in question in any court of law.

86. The King, acting in his discretion, shall have the right to require the Prime Minister and other Ministers to consult with him on any matter relating to the government of Swaziland and the Prime Minister shall keep him fully informed concerning the general conduct of the government of Swaziland and shall furnish him with such information as he, acting in his discretion, may request in respect of any particular matter relating to the government of Swaziland. *King to be consulted and informed concerning matters of Government.*

87.—(1) The King, acting in accordance with the advice of the Prime Minister, may appoint Assistant Ministers, the number of whom shall not exceed the number of Ministers, to assist Ministers in the performance of their duties, from among the elected or appointed members of either chamber, and may, by directions in writing, designate not more than two Assistant Ministers as Ministers of State. *Assistant Ministers.*

(2) For the purpose of this section, during any period when Parliament is dissolved a person who was an elected or appointed member of either chamber immediately before that dissolution shall be regarded as continuing as an elected or an appointed member, as the case may be, of that chamber.

(3) The provisions of subsections (2), (3) and (4) of section 81 of this Constitution shall apply in relation to an Assistant Minister as they apply in relation to a Minister.

88. A Minister or an Assistant Minister shall not enter upon the duties of his office unless he has taken and subscribed the oath of allegiance and the oath for the due execution of his office that are set out in Schedule 2 to this Constitution or such other oaths as may be prescribed. *Oaths by Ministers.*

89.—(1) There shall be a Secretary to the Cabinet whose office shall be an office in the public service. *Secretary to Cabinet.*

(2) The Secretary to the Cabinet shall have charge of the Cabinet Office and shall be responsible, in accordance with such instructions as may be given to him by the Prime Minister, for arranging the business for, and keeping the minutes of, the meetings of the Cabinet and for conveying decisions of the Cabinet to the appropriate person or authority, and shall have such other functions as the Prime Minister may from time to time direct.

90. Where any Minister has been charged with responsibility for any department of government, he shall exercise general direction and control over that department and, subject to such direction and control, the department shall be under the supervision of a permanent secretary whose office shall be an office in the public service: *Direction of government departments.*

Provided that two or more government departments may be placed under the supervision of one permanent secretary, and any department of government in which the Minister charged with responsibility is assisted by one or more Ministers of State may be placed under the supervision of two permanent secretaries or such greater number of permanent secretaries as does not exceed the number of Ministers (including Ministers of State) in that department.

Attorney-General.

91.—(1) There shall be an Attorney-General whose office shall be a public office.

(2) The Attorney-General shall be the principal legal adviser to the Government of Swaziland and, for the due performance of his duties, entitled to be provided with all papers which are available to the members of the Cabinet or any committee thereof; and he shall have such other functions as may be conferred on him by this Constitution or any other law.

(3) The Attorney-General may, whenever requested so to do, advise the King on any matter of law relating to any function vested in the King by this Constitution or any other law.

(4) The Attorney-General shall have power in any case in which he considers it desirable so to do—

(a) to institute and undertake criminal proceedings against any person before any court (other than a court-martial) in respect of any offence alleged to have been committed by that person ;

(b) to take over and continue any such criminal proceedings that have been instituted or undertaken by any other person or authority ; and

(c) to discontinue at any stage before judgment is delivered any such criminal proceedings instituted or undertaken by himself or any other person or authority.

(5) The powers conferred on the Attorney-General by paragraphs (b) and (c) of subsection (4) of this section shall be vested in him to the exclusion of any other person or authority :

Provided that, where any other person or authority has instituted criminal proceedings, nothing in this subsection shall prevent the withdrawal of those proceedings by or at the instance of that person or authority and with the leave of the court.

(6) Notwithstanding the provisions of subsection (5) of this section, the powers of the Attorney-General under subsection (4) of this section may be exercised by him in person or by officers subordinate to him acting in accordance with his general or special instructions.

(7) For the purposes of this section, any appeal from any judgment in any criminal proceedings before any court, or any case stated or question of law reserved for the purpose of any such proceedings, to any other court shall be deemed to be part of those proceedings :

Provided that the power conferred on the Attorney-General by subsection (4)(c) of this section shall not be exercised in relation to any appeal by a person convicted in any criminal proceedings or to any case stated or question of law reserved at the instance of such a person.

(8) In the exercise of the functions vested in him by subsection (4) of this section, the Attorney-General shall not be subject to the direction or control of any other person or authority.

92.—(1) The King may— Prerogative of Mercy.

(a) grant to any person convicted of any offence under the law of Swaziland a pardon, either free or subject to lawful conditions ;

(b) grant to any person a respite, either indefinite or for a specified period, of the execution of any punishment imposed on that person for such an offence ;

(c) substitute a less severe form of punishment for any punishment imposed on any person for such an offence ; and

(d) remit the whole or part of any punishment imposed on any person for such an offence or of any penalty or forfeiture otherwise due to the Government on account of such an offence.

(2) There shall be a Committee on the Prerogative of Mercy which shall consist of—

(a) three Ministers appointed by the King, acting in his discretion, one of whom shall be appointed by the King, acting as aforesaid, to be the chairman ; and

(b) the Attorney-General.

(3) An appointed member of the Committee shall vacate his seat on the Committee—

(a) at the expiration of the term of his appointment (if any) specified in the instrument of his appointment ;

(b) if his appointment is revoked by the King, acting in his discretion ; or

(c) if he ceases to be a Minister.

(4) In the exercise of the powers conferred upon him by subsection (1) of this section, the King shall act in accordance with the advice of the Committee.

(5) The Committee shall not be summoned except by the authority of the chairman.

(6) The chairman or, in his absence, such member of the Committee as the chairman may designate in that behalf shall preside at meetings of the Committee.

(7) Subject to the provisions of this section, the Committee shall regulate its own procedure.

(8) The Committee may act notwithstanding any vacancy in its membership or the absence of any member, and the validity of the transaction of business by the Committee shall not be affected by the fact that some person who was not entitled to do so took part in the proceedings.

(9) Whenever any person has been sentenced to death by any court in Swaziland other than a court-martial, the chairman shall cause a report on the case by the judge who presided at the trial (or, if a report cannot be obtained from that judge, a report on the case by the Chief Justice), together with such other information derived from the

record of the case or elsewhere as he may require, to be taken into consideration at a meeting of the Committee so that the Committee may advise the King whether or not to exercise his powers under subsection (1) of this section in that case.

(10) The provisions of this section shall not apply in relation to any conviction by a court established under a law of a country other than Swaziland that has jurisdiction in Swaziland in pursuance of arrangements made between the Government of Swaziland and another Government or an international organisation relating to the presence in Swaziland of members of the armed forces of that other country or in relation to any punishment imposed in respect of any such conviction or any penalty or forfeiture resulting from any such conviction.

(11) Nothing in this section shall be construed as precluding an Act of Parliament from making provision of general application under which any sentence of imprisonment shall be reduced if such conditions (being conditions relating to good behaviour by the person on whom the sentence was imposed whilst serving that sentence) as are prescribed are fulfilled.

CHAPTER VIII

LAND AND MINERALS

Power to dispose of Government land.

93. Subject to the provisions of any law for the time being in force in Swaziland, the Government may exercise all rights of ownership over Government land accorded by law including the power to make grants, leases or other dispositions, subject to such rights and interests and to such conditions as the Government may think fit.

Swazi nation land.

94.—(1) All land which is vested in the Nggwenyama in trust for the Swazi nation shall continue so to vest subject to the provisions of this Constitution and to subsisting rights and interests which before 6th September 1968 have been granted to, or recognised as vested in, any person.

(2) The Nggwenyama in Libandla may exercise all rights of ownership over such land including the power to make grants, leases or other dispositions, subject to such rights and interests and to such conditions as he may think fit:

Provided that no right to mortgage such land shall be exercisable save and except by a mortgage registered against land acquired by purchase or grant.

(3) The rights and the powers conferred upon the Nggwenyama in Libandla by this section shall be subject to the provisions of any law for the time being in force in Swaziland but no such law shall operate to vest those rights or that power in any other person or authority.

(4) For the avoidance of doubt it is hereby declared that Swazi nation land is subject to compulsory acquisition for public purposes under the law for the time being in force relating to the compulsory acquisition of land for such purposes.

Minerals and mineral oils.

95.—(1) All minerals and mineral oils in, under or upon any land in Swaziland shall continue to vest in the Nggwenyama in trust for the Swazi nation, subject to any subsisting rights and interests which, before 6th September 1968, by or under any Order of Her Majesty in Council or any other law in force in Swaziland, or otherwise, have been granted to or recognised as vested in any other person.

(2) The Nggwenyama may make grants, leases or other dispositions conferring rights or interests in respect of minerals or mineral oils in Swaziland, but the Nggwenyama shall not exercise any such power except after consultation with the Minerals Committee established by subsection (3) of this section.

(3) There shall be a Minerals Committee which shall consist of not less than four nor more than six persons who shall be appointed by the Nggwenyama in Libandla.

(4) Such member of the Minerals Committee as the Nggwenyama, acting in his discretion, may designate in that behalf shall be chairman of the committee.

(5) The Minerals Committee shall not be summoned except upon the authority of the Nggwenyama.

(6) Subject to the provisions of this section, the Minerals Committee may regulate its own procedure.

96. In this Chapter "Nggwenyama in Libandla" means the Nggwenyama acting in accordance with the advice of his Libandla. Interpretation.

CHAPTER IX

THE JUDICATURE

PART 1

The High Court

97.—(1) There shall be a High Court for Swaziland and, subject to the provisions of this Chapter, the judges of the High Court shall be the Chief Justice and such number of puisne judges as may be prescribed. Establishment of High Court.

(2) The High Court shall be deemed to be duly constituted notwithstanding any vacancy in the office of any judge of that court.

98.—(1) The holder of the office of Chief Justice or any office of puisne judge of the High Court shall be appointed by the King, acting in accordance with the advice of the Judicial Service Commission. Appointment of judges of High Court.

(2) (*a*) A person shall not be qualified for appointment as a judge of the High Court unless—

(i) he is, or has been, a judge of a court having unlimited jurisdiction in civil and criminal matters in some part of the Commonwealth or in the Republic of Ireland or in any other country outside the Commonwealth that may be prescribed by Act of Parliament, or a court having jurisdiction in appeals from any such court; or

(ii) he is and has been, for a period in the aggregate of at least ten years, a barrister or advocate entitled to practise in any such court and has so practised for not less than ten years.

(*b*) For the purposes of this subsection, a barrister or advocate shall be regarded as entitled to practise, and as having practised as such, during any period in which he held office as a judge, magistrate, Attorney-General, Solicitor-General, Director of Public Prosecutions or Crown Counsel or State Counsel in any part of the Commonwealth or in a country outside the Commonwealth referred to in this subsection.

Tenure of office of judges of High Court. **99.**—(1) Subject to the provisions of this Chapter, a person holding the office of a judge of the High Court shall vacate that office on attaining the retiring age.

(2) Notwithstanding that he has attained the age at which he is required by the provisions of this section to vacate his office, a person may sit as a judge for the purpose of delivering judgment or doing any other thing in relation to proceedings which were commenced before him before he attained that age.

(3) A judge of the High Court may at any time resign his office.

(4) The office of any judge of the High Court shall not be abolished while there is a substantive holder thereof.

(5) For the purposes of subsection (1) of this section, the retiring age shall be the age of sixty-two years or such other age as may be prescribed by Act of Parliament:

Provided that—

(*a*) a provision of an Act of Parliament, to the extent that it alters the age at which judges of the High Court shall vacate their offices, shall not have effect in relation to a judge after his appointment unless he consents to its having effect;

(*b*) the King, acting in accordance with the advice of the Judicial Service Commission, may permit a judge who attains the age prescribed by or under this subsection to continue in office for such fixed period as may be agreed between the King and that judge, and in relation to that person the provisions of this Constitution shall have effect as if he would attain the retiring age on the expiration of the fixed term so agreed.

Removal of judges. **100.**—(1) A judge of the High Court may be removed from office only for inability to perform the functions of his office (whether arising from infirmity of body or mind or any other cause) or for misbehaviour, and shall not be removed except in accordance with the provisions of this section.

(2) If the King, acting in his discretion in the case of the Chief Justice and in accordance with the advice of the Chief Justice in the case of a puisne judge, considers that the question of removing a judge of the High Court from office for inability as aforesaid or misbehaviour ought to be investigated, then—

(*a*) the King, acting in his discretion, shall appoint a tribunal, which shall consist of a chairman and not less than two other members, selected by the King from among persons who hold or have held high judicial office;

(b) the tribunal shall enquire into the matter and report on the facts thereof to the King and advise the King whether the judge ought to be removed from office under this section for inability as aforesaid or for misbehaviour.

(3) Where a tribunal appointed under subsection (2) of this section advises the King that a judge of the High Court ought to be removed from office for inability as aforesaid or for misbehaviour, the King shall remove such judge from office.

(4) (a) All questions for decision by a tribunal appointed under subsection (2) of this section shall be decided by a majority of its members ; and the chairman shall have an original vote, and, if the votes are equally divided, a casting vote.

(b) The provisions of any law in force governing the procedure of commissions of enquiry shall apply to the tribunal as if the tribunal were a commission of enquiry, and references in that law to a commission shall be construed accordingly.

(c) Subject to the provisions of this subsection, the procedure to be followed by the tribunal shall be in the discretion of the tribunal.

(5) If the question of removing a judge of the High Court from office has been referred to a tribunal under subsection (2) of this section the King, acting in his discretion, may suspend the judge from performing the functions of his office, and any such suspension may at any time be revoked by the King and shall in any case cease to have effect if the tribunal recommends to the King that the judge should not be removed.

101. If the office of Chief Justice is vacant or if the Chief Justice is for any reason unable to perform the functions of his office, then until a person has been appointed to and has assumed the functions of that office or until the Chief Justice has resumed those functions, as the case may be, those functions shall be performed by such one of the judges of the Court of Appeal or of the puisne judges or by such other person qualified for appointment as a judge of the High Court as the King, acting in accordance with the advice of the Judicial Service Commission, may appoint for that purpose: *Acting Chief Justice.*

Provided that a person may be so appointed notwithstanding that he has attained the age prescribed for the purposes of section 99 of this Constitution.

102.—(1) If the office of a puisne judge is vacant or if a puisne judge is appointed to act as Chief Justice or is for any reason unable to perform the functions of his office or if the Chief Justice advises the King that the state of business in the High Court requires that the number of judges of the Court should be temporarily increased, the King, acting in accordance with the advice of the Judicial Service Commission, may appoint a person qualified for appointment as a judge of the High Court to act as a puisne judge. *Acting puisne judge.*

(2) If the Chief Justice has occasion to be absent from Swaziland for a period which he considers will be of short duration or is unable to perform the functions of his office for any other cause which he

considers will be of short duration, the Chief Justice may appoint a person qualified for appointment as a judge of the High Court to act as a puisne judge during such period as he may specify as the period of that absence or inability:

Provided that the period of an appointment under this subsection shall not exceed seven days.

(3) A person may be appointed to act as a puisne judge under this section notwithstanding that he has attained the age prescribed for the purposes of section 99 of this Constitution.

(4) A person appointed under subsection (1) of this section to act as a puisne judge shall, subject to the provisions of section 100 of this Constitution, continue to act until the expiration of the period of his appointment or, if no such period is specified, until his appointment is revoked by the King, acting in accordance with the advice of the Judicial Service Commission.

(5) A person appointed under subsection (2) of this section to act as a puisne judge shall, subject to the provisions of section 100 of this Constitution, continue to act until the expiration of the period of his appointment or until his appointment is revoked by the Chief Justice, whichever is the earlier.

(6) A person whose appointment to act as a puisne judge has expired or been revoked may, with the permission of the King, acting in accordance with the advice of the Chief Justice, continue to act as such for such a period as may be necessary to enable him to deliver judgment or to do any other thing in relation to proceedings that were commenced before him previously thereto.

Oaths by judges of High Court.

103. A judge of the High Court shall not enter upon the duties of his office unless he has taken and subscribed the oath of allegiance and the oath for the due execution of his office that are set out in Schedule 2 to this Constitution or such other oaths as may be prescribed.

Jurisdiction of High Court.

104.—(1) The High Court shall be a superior court of record and shall have—

(a) unlimited original jurisdiction in civil and criminal matters;

(b) such appellate jurisdiction as may be prescribed by or under any law for the time being in force in Swaziland;

(c) such revisional jurisdiction as the High Court possesses at the commencement of this Constitution in accordance with the provisions of this Constitution and any other law then in force in Swaziland; and

(d) such revisional jurisdiction, additional to the jurisdiction mentioned in paragraph (c) of this subsection, as may be prescribed by or under any law for the time being in force in Swaziland.

(2) Subject to the provisions of this Constitution, the Chief Justice may make rules for regulating the practice and procedure of the High

Court and such rules may (without prejudice to the generality of the foregoing provisions of this subsection) include provision for any of the following purposes—

(a) for regulating the sittings of the High Court and the selection of judges for any purpose;

(b) for prescribing forms and fees in respect of proceedings in the High Court and regulating the costs of and incidental to any such proceedings;

(c) for regulating the right of representation of persons concerned in any proceedings in the High Court;

(d) for prescribing the time within which any requirement of the rules is to be complied with;

(e) for prescribing and regulating the powers and duties of registrars and officers of the court.

(3) No rules of court made under this section which may involve an increase in the expenses of the High Court shall be made except with the concurrence of the Minister for the time being responsible for finance, but the validity of a rule of court shall not be called in question in any proceedings on the grounds that the concurrence of the Minister was not or does not appear to have been obtained.

(4) In this section any reference to revisional jurisdiction shall be construed as including a reference to jurisdiction to determine reserved questions of law and cases stated.

PART 2

The Court of Appeal

105.—(1) There shall be a Court of Appeal for Swaziland, styled the Swaziland Court of Appeal, which shall be a superior court of record. Establishment of Court of Appeal.

(2) The judges of the Court of Appeal shall be—

(a) the Judge President;

(b) such number of Justices of Appeal, being not less than two or more than four, as may be prescribed; and

(c) the Chief Justice and the puisne judges, if any, of the High Court.

(3) The Court of Appeal shall be duly constituted notwithstanding any vacancy among the judges of the Court.

106.—(1) The holder of the office of Judge President shall be appointed by the King, acting in accordance with the advice of the Judicial Service Commission. Appointment of judges of Court of Appeal.

(2) The holder of any office of Justice of Appeal shall be appointed by the King, acting in accordance with the advice of the Judge President.

(3) A person shall not be qualified for appointment as the Judge President or a Justice of Appeal unless he is or has been a judge of a court having unlimited jurisdiction in civil and criminal matters in a country which has been designated in that behalf by Act of Parliament or a court having jurisdiction in appeals from any such court.

(4) (*a*) Notwithstanding the provisions of section 107 of this Constitution and subject to the provisions of this subsection, it shall be lawful to appoint a person to hold the office of Judge President or Justice of Appeal for a period of three years.

(*b*) A person may be appointed under this subsection who has attained the age prescribed for the purposes of section 107 of this Constitution or who will attain that age before the expiration of the appointment.

(*c*) The period of an appointment under this subsection shall be fixed and the appointment shall not be revoked or otherwise terminated:

Provided that the appointment of a person holding office as a Justice of Appeal shall terminate if he is appointed to hold the office of Judge President, but in that case, if he is appointed under this subsection, the period of his appointment as Judge President shall terminate on the date upon which his appointment to be a Justice of Appeal would have expired.

(*d*) In relation to any person appointed under this subsection, the provisions of this Constitution shall have effect as if he would attain the age specified for the purposes of section 107 of this Constitution on the expiration of the period of his appointment.

Tenure of office of Judge President and of Justices of Appeal.

107.—(1) Subject to the provisions of this section, a person holding the office of Judge President or Justice of Appeal shall vacate that office on attaining the retiring age.

(2) Notwithstanding that he has attained the retiring age, a person may sit as a judge of the Court of Appeal for the purpose of delivering judgment or doing any other thing in relation to proceedings which were commenced before him before he attained that age.

(3) The Judge President or a Justice of Appeal may at any time resign his office.

(4) The office of Judge President or Justice of Appeal shall not be abolished while there is a substantive holder thereof.

(5) For the purposes of this section the retiring age shall be the age of sixty-two years or such other age as may be prescribed by Act of Parliament:

Provided that a provision of an Act of Parliament, to the extent that it alters the age at which judges of the Court of Appeal shall vacate their offices, shall not have effect in relation to a judge after his appointment unless he consents to its having effect.

(6) Section 100 of this Constitution shall apply in relation to persons holding or acting in the office of Judge President or Justice of Appeal as it applies in relation to a person holding or acting in the office of puisne judge of the High Court.

Acting judges of Court of Appeal.

108.—(1) If the office of Judge President is vacant or the Judge President is for any reason unable to perform the functions of his office then, until a person has been appointed to and has assumed the functions of that office or until the Judge President has resumed those functions, as the case may be, those functions shall be performed by such one of the other judges of the Court of Appeal or such other person qualified for appointment as a judge of the Court as the King, acting in accordance with the advice of the Judicial Service Commission, may appoint.

(2) If the office of any Justice of Appeal is vacant or if a Justice of Appeal is appointed to act as Judge President or is for any reason unable to perform the functions of his office or if the Judge President advises the King that the state of business in the Court of Appeal so requires, the King, acting in accordance with the advice of the Judge President, may appoint a person who is qualified for appointment as a Justice of Appeal to act as a Justice of Appeal.

(3) A person appointed under subsection (2) of this section to act as a Justice of Appeal shall, subject to the provisions of section 100 of this Constitution, continue to act for the period of his appointment or, if no such period is specified, until his appointment is revoked by the King, acting in accordance with the advice of the Judge President.

(4) A person, other than a Justice of Appeal, whose appointment to act as Judge President has expired or been revoked and a person whose appointment to act as a Justice of Appeal has expired or been revoked may, with the permission of the King, acting in accordance with the advice of the Judge President, continue to act as a judge of the Court of Appeal for such a period as may be necessary to enable him to give judgment or to do any other thing in relation with proceedings that were commenced before him previously thereto.

109. The Judge President and any Justice of Appeal shall not enter upon the duties of his office unless he has taken and subscribed the oath of allegiance and the oath for the due execution of his office that are set out in Schedule 2 to this Constitution or such other oaths as may be prescribed.

Oaths by judges of Court of Appeal.

110. The Court of Appeal may, in any case in which it appears to the Court to be expedient, call in the aid of one or more assessors with such special qualifications as the Court may think fit, and hear such case wholly or in part with the assistance of such assessors.

Appointment of assessors.

111.—(1) The Court of Appeal shall have—

Jurisdiction of Court of Appeal.

(a) such jurisdiction to hear and determine such appeals from the courts of Swaziland and such powers and authority as the Court of Appeal possesses at the commencement of this Constitution in accordance with the provisions of this Constitution and of any other law then in force in Swaziland ; and

(b) such jurisdiction to hear and determine appeals from the courts of Swaziland and such powers and authority (additional to the jurisdiction, powers and authority mentioned in paragraph (a) of this subsection) as may be prescribed by or under any law for the time being in force in Swaziland.

(2) Subject to the provisions of subsection (1) of this section, the Court of Appeal shall have, for all purposes of and incidental to the hearing and determination of any appeals in its jurisdiction, the power, authority and jurisdiction vested in the court from which the appeal is brought.

(3) Any decision of the Court of Appeal shall be enforced in like manner as if it were a judgment of the court from which the appeal was brought.

Practice and procedure on appeals.

112.—(1) Subject to the provisions of this Constitution, the Judge President may make rules for regulating the practice and procedure of the Court of Appeal with respect to appeals and, in connection with such appeals, for regulating the practice and procedure in any court from which such appeals are brought.

(2) Without prejudice to the generality of subsection (1) of this section, rules of court may be made for the following purposes—

(a) for regulating the sittings of the Court of Appeal, whether in divisions or otherwise, and the selection of judges for any purpose ;

(b) for regulating the right of representation of persons concerned in any proceedings in the Court of Appeal ;

(c) for prescribing cases in which, and conditions upon which, an appellant in a criminal appeal to the Court of Appeal shall be entitled to be present at the hearing of the appeal ;

(d) for providing for summary determination of any appeal which appears to the Court of Appeal to be frivolous or vexatious or to be brought for the purposes of delay ;

(e) for prescribing forms and fees in respect of proceedings in the Court of Appeal and regulating the costs of and incidental to any such proceedings ;

(f) for prescribing and regulating the powers and duties of registrars and officers of the Court of Appeal ;

(g) for prescribing the time within which any requirement of the rules is to be complied with ;

(h) for providing for a reference from a decision of a single judge to the Court of Appeal.

(3) Rules made under this section may fix the number of judges of the Court of Appeal who may sit for any purpose:

Provided that—

(a) an uneven number of judges shall sit, which, for the purposes of any final determination by the Court of Appeal other than the summary dismissal of an appeal, shall not be less than three ; and

(b) any determination by the Court of Appeal of any matter (whether final or otherwise) shall, where more than one judge sits, be according to the opinion of a majority of the judges who sit for the purpose of determining that matter.

(4) No rules of court made under this section which may involve an increase in the expenses of the Court of Appeal shall be made except with the concurrence of the Minister for the time being responsible for finance but the validity of a rule of court shall not be called in question in any proceedings on the grounds that the concurrence of the Minister was not or does not appear to have been obtained.

PART 3

Judicial Service Commission

Judicial Service Commission.

113.—(1) There shall be a Judicial Service Commission for Swaziland which shall consist of—

(a) the Chief Justice, who shall be chairman ;

(b) the chairman of the Public Service Commission ; and

(c) a member who shall be styled the appointed member and who shall be appointed by the King, acting in accordance with the advice of the Chief Justice, from among persons who hold or have held high judicial office:

Provided that if the office of Chief Justice is vacant or the Chief Justice is for any reason unable to perform the functions of his office and by reason of other vacancies in the Commission the Commission cannot act, then, until a person is appointed to hold or act in the office of Chief Justice, the Judge President (or if the office of Judge President is vacant or the Judge President is for any reason unable to perform the functions of his office a Justice of Appeal designated by the King, acting in his discretion) shall perform the functions of the chairman of the Commission.

(2) No person shall be qualified to be appointed as the appointed member if—

(a) he is a Senator or member of the House of Assembly or is nominated for election to the House of Assembly ;

(b) he is the holder of an office in any organisation that sponsors or supports, or that has at any time sponsored or supported, a candidate for election as a member of a Legislative Council established for Swaziland by Order of Her Majesty in Council or of the Senate or House of Assembly established by this Constitution or the former Constitution ;

(c) during the period of two years immediately preceding the date of the appointment—

(i) he has been a member of a Legislative Council or of a Senate or House of Assembly established as aforesaid ;

(ii) he has been nominated for election to a Legislative Council or Senate or House of Assembly established as aforesaid ; or

(iii) he has been the holder of an office in such an organisation as is referred to in paragraph (b) of this subsection ; or

(d) he is a public officer, other than a judge of the High Court or the Court of Appeal:

Provided that a person shall not be so disqualified by reason only that he had been Speaker of a Legislative Council established as aforesaid or had been Speaker of the House of Assembly or Speaker or President of the Senate established as aforesaid having been elected as such from outside the House of Assembly or, as the case may be, the Senate.

(3) Subject to the provisions of this section, the office of the appointed member shall become vacant—

(a) at the expiration of five years or such lesser period, not being less than two years, from the date of his appointment as may be specified in his appointment ; or

(b) if any circumstances arise that, if he were not the appointed member, would cause him to be disqualified to be appointed as such under subsection (2) of this section.

(4) The appointed member may be removed from office only for inability to exercise the functions of his office (whether arising from infirmity of body or mind or any other cause) or for misbehaviour and shall not be so removed except in accordance with the provisions of this section.

(5) The appointed member shall be removed from office by the King if the question of his removal from office has been referred to a tribunal appointed under subsection (6) of this section and the tribunal has recommended to the King that he ought to be removed from office for inability as aforesaid or for misbehaviour.

(6) If the Chief Justice represents to the King that the question of removing the appointed member under this section ought to be investigated, then—

(a) the King shall appoint a tribunal which shall consist of a chairman and not less than two other members, selected by the Chief Justice from among persons who hold or have held high judicial office ; and

(b) the tribunal shall enquire into the matter and report on the facts thereof to the King and recommend to him whether the appointed member ought to be removed under this section.

(7) If the question of removing the appointed member has been referred to a tribunal under this section, the King, acting in accordance with the advice of the Chief Justice, may suspend that member from the exercise of the functions of his office and any such suspension may at any time be revoked by the King, acting in accordance with such advice as aforesaid, and shall in any case cease to have effect if the tribunal recommends to the King that that member should not be removed.

(8) If the office of the appointed member is vacant or if the person holding that office is for any reason unable to exercise the functions of his office, the King, acting in accordance with the advice of the Chief Justice, may appoint a person who is qualified to be the appointed member to act as that member, and any person so appointed shall, subject to the provisions of subsection (3) of this section, continue to act until the office in which he is acting is filled or, as the case may be, until the holder thereof resumes his functions or until his appointment to act is revoked by the King, acting in accordance with the advice of the Chief Justice.

(9) The appointed member shall not enter upon the duties of his office until he has taken and subscribed the oath of allegiance and the oath for the due execution of his office in the form set out in Schedule 2 to this Constitution or such other oaths as may be prescribed.

(10) In the exercise of its functions under this Constitution, the Commission shall not be subject to the direction or control of any other person or authority.

(11) The Commission may by regulation or otherwise regulate its own procedure and, with the consent of the Prime Minister, may confer powers or impose duties on any public officer or on any authority of the Government for the purpose of the discharge of its functions.

(12) The Commission may, subject to its rules of procedure, act notwithstanding any vacancy in its membership or the absence of any member and its proceedings shall not be invalidated by the presence or participation of any person not entitled to be present at or to participate in those proceedings :

Provided that any decision of the Commission shall require the concurrence of a majority of all the members thereof.

114.—(1) The power to appoint persons to hold or act in any offices to which this section applies (including the power to confirm appointments), the power to exercise disciplinary control over persons holding or acting in such offices and the power to remove such persons from office shall vest in the Judicial Service Commission.

Appointment, etc., of judicial officers.

(2) The Judicial Service Commission may, by directions in writing and subject to such conditions as it thinks fit, delegate any of its powers under subsection (1) of this section to any one or more of the members of that Commission or to any person holding or acting in any office to which this section applies.

(3) The offices to which this section applies are—

(*a*) the office of Registrar or Assistant Registrar of the High Court ;

(*b*) the office of Registrar or Assistant Registrar of the Court of Appeal ;

(*c*) the office of magistrate ; and

(*d*) such other offices connected with any court as may be prescribed by Act of Parliament.

CHAPTER X

THE PUBLIC SERVICE

115.—(1) There shall be a Public Service Commission for Swaziland which shall consist of a chairman and not less than two nor more than four other members, who shall be appointed by the King, acting in accordance with the advice of the Judicial Service Commission.

Public Service Commission.

(2) No person shall be qualified to be appointed as a member of the Commission if—

(*a*) he is a Senator or member of the House of Assembly or is nominated for election to the House of Assembly ;

(*b*) he is the holder of an office in any organisation that sponsors or supports, or that has at any time sponsored or supported, a candidate for election as a member of a Legislative Council established for Swaziland by Order of Her Majesty in Council or of the Senate or House of Assembly established by this Constitution or the former Constitution ;

(*c*) during the period of two years immediately preceding the date of the appointment—

(i) he has been a member of a Legislative Council or of a Senate or House of Assembly established as aforesaid ;

(ii) he has been nominated for election to a Legislative Council or Senate or House of Assembly established as aforesaid ; or

(iii) he has been the holder of an office in such an organisation as is referred to in paragraph (*b*) of this subsection ; or

(*d*) he is a public officer, other than a judge of the High Court or the Court of Appeal :

Provided that a person shall not be so disqualified by reason only that he had been Speaker of a Legislative Council established as aforesaid or had been Speaker of the House of Assembly or Speaker or President of the Senate established as aforesaid having been elected as such from outside the House of Assembly or, as the case may be, the Senate.

(3) Subject to the provisions of this section, the office of a member of the Commission shall become vacant—

(a) at the expiration of five years or such lesser period, not being less than two years, from the date of his appointment as may be specified in his instrument of appointment ; or

(b) if any circumstances arise that, if he were not a member of the Commission, would cause him to be disqualified to be appointed as such under subsection (2) of this section.

(4) A member of the Commission may be removed from office only for inability to exercise the functions of his office (whether arising from infirmity of body or mind or any other cause) or for misbehaviour and shall not be so removed except in accordance with the provisions of this section.

(5) A member of the Commission shall be removed from office by the King if the question of his removal from office has been referred to a tribunal appointed under subsection (6) of this section and the tribunal has recommended to the King that he ought to be removed from office for inability as aforesaid or for misbehaviour.

(6) If the Prime Minister in the case of the chairman or the chairman in the case of any other member represents to the King that the question of removing a member of the Commission under this section ought to be investigated, then—

(a) the King shall appoint a tribunal which shall consist of a chairman and not less than two other members, selected by the Chief Justice from among persons who hold or have held high judicial office ; and

(b) the tribunal shall enquire into the matter and report on the facts thereof to the King and recommend to him whether the member ought to be removed under this section.

(7) If the question of removing a member of the Commission has been referred to a tribunal under this section, the King, acting in accordance with the advice of the Prime Minister, in the case of the chairman of the Commission or member for the time being acting as chairman, or acting in accordance with the advice of the chairman of the Commission, in the case of any other member, may suspend the chairman, acting chairman or other member from the exercise of the functions of his office and any such suspension may at any time be revoked by the King, acting in accordance with such advice as aforesaid, and shall in any case cease to have effect if the tribunal recommends to the King that the chairman, acting chairman or other member should not be removed.

(8) If the office of the chairman of the Commission is vacant or if the chairman is for any reason unable to exercise the functions of his office, those functions shall be performed by such one of the other members of the Commission as the King, acting in accordance with the advice of the Judicial Service Commission, may appoint.

(9) If at any time there are less than two members of the Commission besides the chairman or if any such member is acting as chairman or is for any reason unable to perform the functions of his office, then, the King, acting in accordance with the advice of the Judicial Service Commission, may appoint a person who is qualified to be appointed as a member of the Commission to act as a member, and any person so

appointed shall continue to act until his appointment is revoked by the King, acting in accordance with the advice of the Judicial Service Commission.

(10) A member of the Commission shall not enter upon the duties of his office until he has taken and subscribed the oath of allegiance and the oath for the due execution of his office in the form set out in Schedule 2 to this Constitution or such other oaths as may be prescribed.

(11) In the exercise of its functions under this Constitution, the Commission shall not be subject to the direction or control of any other person or authority:

Provided that the Commission shall act in a manner consistent with the general policy of the Government as conveyed to the Commission by the Prime Minister in writing.

(12) The Commission may by regulation or otherwise regulate its own procedure and, with the consent of the Prime Minister, may confer powers or impose duties on any public officer or on any authority of the Government for the purpose of the discharge of its functions.

(13) The Commission may, subject to its rules of procedure, act notwithstanding any vacancy in its membership or the absence of any member and its proceedings shall not be invalidated by the presence or participation of any person not entitled to be present at or to participate in those procedings:

Provided that any decision of the Commission shall require the concurrence of a majority of all the members thereof.

(14) Before tendering advice to the King for the purposes of any of the provisions of this section the Judicial Service Commission shall consult the Prime Minister.

116.—(1) Subject to the provisions of this Constitution, the power to appoint persons to hold or act in any offices in the public service (including power to confirm appointments), to exercise disciplinary control over persons holding or acting in such offices and to remove such persons from office shall vest in the Public Service Commission. _{Appointment, etc., of public officers.}

(2) The Public Service Commission may, by directions in writing and subject to such conditions as it thinks fit, delegate any of its powers under subsection (1) of this section to any member of the Commission or to any public officer.

(3) The provisions of this section shall not apply in relation to any of the following offices—

(a) the office of a judge of the High Court or Court of Appeal ;

(b) any office to which section 117 of this Constitution (which relates to Ambassadors, High Commissioners or principal representatives of Swaziland) applies ;

(c) any office to which section 118 of this Constitution (which relates to permanent secretaries and certain police officers) applies ;

(d) the office of Attorney-General ;

(e) except for the purpose of making appointments thereto or to act therein, the office of Director of Audit ;

(f) any office appointments to which is within the functions of the Judicial Service Commission ;

(g) offices in the Police Force and offices in the Prison Service, to the extent provided by sections 121 and 122 of this Constitution.

Appoint-
ment and
removal of
Ambassa-
dors, etc.

117.—(1) This section applies to the offices of Ambassador, High Commissioner or other principal representative of Swaziland in any other country or accredited to any international organisation.

(2) Subject to the provisions of subsections (3) and (4) of this section, power to appoint persons to hold the offices to which this section applies and to remove such persons from office shall vest in the King, acting in accordance with the advice of the Prime Minister.

(3) Before advising the King to appoint to any office to which this section applies any person who holds any public office which is not such an office the Prime Minister shall consult the Public Service Commission.

(4) Before or as soon as practicable after advising the King to remove from an office to which this section applies any person who prior to his appointment to that office (or, if he has held more than one such office in succession, to those offices) held any public office which is not such an office the Prime Minister shall refer the question of that person's removal to the Public Service Commission and obtain the Commission's report.

Appoint-
ment, etc.,
of per-
manent secre-
taries and
certain
police
officers.

118.—(1) This section applies to the office of the Secretary to the Cabinet, the office of the Commissioner of Police, the office of the Deputy Commissioner of Police, and the offices of permanent secretary.

(2) The power to appoint persons to hold or act in any office to which this section applies and, subject to the provisions of sub-section (3) of this section, to exercise disciplinary control over persons holding or acting in such offices and to remove such persons from office shall vest in the King, acting in accordance with the advice of the Prime Minister.

(3) Before advising the King to exercising any power under sub-section (2) of this section to exercise disciplinary control over or remove from office any person the Prime Minister shall refer the question of the exercise of those powers in that case to the Public Service Commission and the following provisions shall apply—

(*a*) the Prime Minister shall cause the person concerned to be furnished with a statement of the grounds upon which it is proposed to exercise those powers ;

(*b*) the Commission shall enquire into the facts of the case and shall, if the person concerned so requests, consider any representation that he wishes to make in person or in writing ;

(*c*) the Commission shall report its findings on the facts of the case and its recommendation concerning the exercise of any powers under subsection (2) of this section.

Appoint-
ment of
Attorney-
General.

119.—(1) The power to appoint a person to hold or act in the office of Attorney-General and to terminate the appointment of any person acting in the office of Attorney-General shall vest in the King, acting in accordance with the advice of the Judicial Service Commission.

(2) A person shall not be qualified for appointment to hold or act in the office of Attorney-General unless he is qualified to be appointed as a judge of the High Court or has practised as an advocate or attorney in Swaziland for not less than ten years.

120. The provisions of section 100 of this Constitution shall apply in relation to a person holding the office of Attorney-General or the office of Director of Audit as they apply in relation to a puisne judge of the High Court but as if there were substituted for any reference in those provisions to the Chief Justice a reference—

    (a) in the case of the Attorney-General, to the Judicial Service Commission ;

    (b) in the case of the Director of Audit, to the Public Service Commission.

121.—(1) In relation to any officer in the Police Force below the rank of Inspector, any power vested in the Public Service Commission by section 116 of this Constitution shall not apply to the extent to which that power is, by or under the provisions of any law in force in Swaziland, to be exercised by the Commissioner of Police or any other officer in the Police Force:

Provided that in the case of disciplinary proceedings an appeal shall lie to the Public Service Commission against the award by the Commissioner of Police or such other officer of the punishment of dismissal or of reduction in rank.

(2) The provisions of section 116(2) of this Constitution shall not apply in relation to offices in the Police Force.

122. The provisions of subsections (1) and (2) of section 121 of this Constitution shall apply to persons holding offices in the Prison Service below the rank of Chief Officer as they apply to persons holding offices in the Police Force below the rank of Inspector ; and, for the purposes of this section, those subsections shall have effect as if there were substituted for the words " Police Force " the words " Prison Service ", for the word " Inspector " the words " Chief Officer " and for the words " Commissioner of Police " the words " Director of Prisons ".

123.—(1) The law to be applied with respect to any pensions benefits that were granted to any person before 6th September 1968 shall be the law that was in force at the date on which those benefits were granted or any law in force at a later date that is not less favourable to that person.

(2) The law to be applied with respect to any pensions benefits (not being benefits to which subsection (1) of this section applies) shall—

    (a) in so far as those benefits are wholly in respect of a period of service as a public officer that commenced before 6th September 1968, be the law that was in force immediately before that day ; and

    (b) in so far as those benefits are wholly or partly in respect of a period of service as a public officer that commenced after 6th September 1968, be the law in force on the date on which that period of service commenced,

or any law in force at a later date that is not less favourable to that person.

(3) Where a person is entitled to exercise an option as to which of two or more laws shall apply in his case, the law for which he opts shall, for the purposes of this section, be deemed to be more favourable to him than the other law or laws.

(4) All pensions benefits (except so far as they are a charge on some other fund and have been duly paid out of that fund to the person or authority to whom payment is due) shall be a charge on the Consolidated Fund.

(5) Any person who is entitled to the payment of any pensions benefits and who is ordinarily resident outside Swaziland may, within a reasonable time after he has received that payment, remit the whole of it (free from any deduction, charge or tax made or levied in respect of its remission) to any country of his choice outside Swaziland:

Provided that nothing in this subsection shall be construed as preventing—

(a) the attachment, by order of a court, of any payment or part of any payment to which a person is entitled in satisfaction of the judgment of a court or pending the determination of civil proceedings to which he is a party to the extent to which such attachment is permitted by the law with respect to pensions benefits that apply in the case of that person ; or

(b) the imposition of reasonable conditions relating to the form in which any. payment is to be remitted.

(6) In this section " pensions benefits " means any pensions, compensation, gratuities or other like allowances for persons in respect of their service as public officers or for the widows, children, dependants or personal representatives of such persons in respect of such service.

(7) References in this section to the law with respect to pensions benefits include (without prejudice to their generality) references to the law regulating the circumstances in which such benefits may be granted or in which the grant of such benefits may be refused, the law regulating the circumstances in which any such benefits that have been granted may be withheld, reduced in amount or suspended and the law regulating the amount of any such benefits.

(8) For the purposes of this section—

(a) to the extent to which the emoluments attaching thereto were payable by Swaziland, the office of judge of the Basutoland, Bechuanaland Protectorate and Swaziland Court of Appeal ;

(b) to the extent aforesaid, the office of Registrar of the Basutoland, Bechuanaland Protectorate and Swaziland Court of Appeal, or other officer of that Court, for Swaziland ;

(c) to the extent aforesaid, any office under the High Commissioner for South Africa or the High Commissioner for Basutoland, the Bechuanaland Protectorate and Swaziland ;

(d) to the extent aforesaid, any office in the joint audit service of Basutoland, the Bechuanaland Protectorate and Swaziland ;

(e) to the extent aforesaid, the office of Agent for the High Commission Territories, Witwatersrand Agencies, or any office under the Agent or any office for the time being succeeding to the functions of any such office ; and

(f) to the extent aforesaid, any office in the service of such body, authority, department, service or other organisation as the King may designate by notice under his hand which shall be published in the Gazette,

shall be regarded as offices in the public service.

124.—(1) Where under any law any person or authority has a discretion— Power of Commissions in relation to pensions, etc.

    (*a*) to decide whether or not any pensions benefits shall be granted ; or

    (*b*) to withhold, reduce in amount or suspend any such benefits that have been granted,

those benefits shall be granted and may not be withheld, reduced in amount or suspended unless the appropriate Commission concurs in the refusal to grant the benefits or, as the case may be, in the decision to withhold them, reduce them in amount or suspend them.

(2) Where the amount of any pensions benefits that may be granted to any person is not fixed by law, the amount of the benefits to be granted to him shall be the greatest amount for which he is eligible unless the appropriate Commission concurs in his being granted benefits of a smaller amount.

(3) The appropriate Commission shall not concur under subsection (1) or subsection (2) of this section in any action taken on the ground that any person who holds or has held the office of judge of the High Court, judge of the Court of Appeal, Attorney-General or Director of Audit has been guilty of misbehaviour unless he has been removed from office by reason of such misbehaviour.

(4) In this section " the appropriate Commission " means—

    (*a*) in the case of benefits for which any person may be eligible in respect of the service in the public service of a person who, immediately before he ceased to be a public officer, was subject to the disciplinary control of the Judicial Service Commission or that have been granted in respect of such service, the Judicial Service Commission ; and

    (*b*) in any other case, the Public Service Commission.

(5) In this section " pensions benefits " means any pensions, compensation, gratuities or other like allowances for persons in respect of their service as public officers or for the widows, children, dependants or personal representatives of such persons in respect of such service.

(6) For the purposes of this section—

    (*a*) to the extent to which the emoluments attaching thereto were payable by Swaziland, the office of judge of the Basutoland, Bechuanaland Protectorate and Swaziland Court of Appeal ;

    (*b*) to the extent aforesaid, the office of Registrar of the Basutoland, Bechuanaland Protectorate and Swaziland Court of Appeal, or other officer of that Court, for Swaziland ;

    (*c*) to the extent aforesaid, any office under the High Commissioner for South Africa or the High Commissioner for Basutoland, the Bechuanaland Protectorate and Swaziland ;

    (*d*) to the extent aforesaid, any office in the joint audit service of Basutoland, the Bechuanaland Protectorate and Swaziland ;

    (*e*) to the extent aforesaid, the office of Agent for the High Commission Territories, Witwatersrand Agencies, or any office under the Agent or any office for the time being succeeding to the functions of any such office ; and (*f*) to the extent aforesaid, any office in the service of such body, authority, department, service or other organisation as the King may designate by notice under his hand which shall be published in the Gazette,

shall be regarded as offices in the public service.

Right of action for wrongful dismissal, etc.

125.—(1) If any person holding a public office is removed from office under any of the provisions of this Constitution, his removal as aforesaid shall be without prejudice to any right of action to which he may be entitled under the law for the time being in force in Swaziland for damages for wrongful dismissal or loss of status :

Provided that no such damages shall be recoverable if the holder of the office is offered appointment to another public office in respect of which the emoluments are not less than the emoluments of the office from which he is removed.

(2) The law relating to rights of action for damages for wrongful dismissal or loss of status shall not be altered to the disadvantage of a public officer during his continuance in office.

(3) Nothing in this section shall apply to the holder of the office of judge of the High Court, judge of the Court of Appeal, Attorney-General or Director of Audit or to any holder of an office to which section 117 of this Constitution applies who immediately prior to his appointment to that office (or if he has held more than one such office in succession, to those offices) was not the holder of a public office.

CHAPTER XI

FINANCE

Consolidated Fund.

126. All revenues or other moneys raised or received for the purposes of the Government of Swaziland (not being revenues or other moneys that are payable by or under this Constitution or any other law into some other fund established for a specific purpose or that may by or under any law be retained by the department of Government that received them for the purposes of defraying the expenses of that department) shall be paid into and form one Consolidated Fund.

Withdrawals from Consolidated Fund or other public funds.

127.—(1) No moneys shall be withdrawn from the Consolidated Fund except—

(*a*) to meet expenditure that is charged upon the Fund by this Constitution or by any other law in force in Swaziland ;

(*b*) where the issue of those moneys has been authorised by an Appropriation Act, by a supplementary estimate approved by resolution of the House of Assembly or in such manner and subject to such conditions as may be prescribed in pursuance of section 129 of this Constitution.

(2) No moneys shall be withdrawn from any public fund of Swaziland other than the Consolidated Fund or any Contingencies Fund established under section 130 of this Constitution unless the issue of those moneys has been authorised by or under a law.

(3) No moneys shall be withdrawn from the Consolidated Fund except in the manner prescribed.

(4) The deposit of any moneys forming part of the Consolidated Fund with a bank or with the Crown Agents for Oversea Governments and

Administrations or the investment of any such moneys in securities in which, under the law for the time being in force in Swaziland, trustees are authorised to invest, or the making of advances to such extent and in such circumstances as may be prescribed shall not be regarded as a withdrawal of those moneys from the Fund for the purposes of this section.

128.—(1) The Minister responsible for finance shall cause to be prepared and laid before both chambers, before or not later than thirty days after the commencement of each financial year, estimates of the revenues and expenditure of Swaziland for that year. *Authorisation of expenditure.*

(2) The heads of expenditure contained in the estimates for a financial year (other than expenditure charged upon the Consolidated Fund by this Constitution or any other law) shall be included in a bill to be known as an Appropriation bill which shall be introduced in the House of Assembly to provide for the issue from the Consolidated Fund of the sums necessary to meet that expenditure and the appropriation of those sums for the purposes specified in the bill.

(3) If in any financial year it is found—

(a) that the amount appropriated by the Appropriation Act for the purposes included in any head of expenditure is insufficient or that a need has arisen for expenditure for a purpose for which no amount has been appropriated by the Appropriation Act ; or

(b) that any moneys have been expended on any head of expenditure in excess of the amount appropriated for the purposes included in that head by the Appropriation Act or for a purpose for which no amount has been appropriated by the Appropriation Act,

a supplementary estimate showing the sums required or spent shall be laid before the House of Assembly and shall be included in a motion or motions seeking approval for the supplementary expenditure in such manner as the House shall prescribe.

(4) A final Supplementary Appropriation bill shall be introduced in the House of Assembly, not later than the end of the financial year next following, providing for the appropriation under each head of expenditure of any funds which it has proved necessary to spend in addition to those appropriated in the Appropriation Act.

129. If the Appropriation Act in respect of any financial year has not come into operation by the beginning of that financial year, the Minister responsible for finance may, to such extent and subject to such conditions as may be prescribed, authorise the withdrawal of moneys from the Consolidated Fund for the purpose of meeting expenditure necessary to carry on the services of the Government until the expiration of four months from the beginning of that financial year or the coming into operation of the Appropriation Act, whichever is the earlier: *Authorisation of expenditure in advance of appropriation.*

Provided that the expenditure so authorised for any service shall not exceed one quarter of the amount authorised for that service in the preceding year.

130.—(1) An Act of Parliament may make provision for the establishment of a Contingencies Fund and for authorising the Minister responsible for finance, if satisfied that there has arisen an urgent and unforeseen need for expenditure for which no other provision exists, to make advances from that Fund to meet that need. *Contingencies Fund.*

(2) Where any advance is made from the Contingencies Fund, a supplementary estimate shall be laid before the House of Assembly, and a bill or motion shall be introduced therein, as soon as possible, for the purpose of replacing the amount so advanced.

Remuneration of certain officers.

131.—(1) There shall be paid to the holders of the offices to which this section applies such salaries and such allowances as may be prescribed.

(2) The salaries and any allowances payable to the holders of the offices to which this section applies shall be a charge on and paid out of the Consolidated Fund.

(3) The salary payable to the holder of any office to which this section applies and his terms of office, other than allowances which, under the law for the time being in force relating to pensions, are not taken into account in computing pensions, shall not be altered to his disadvantage after his appointment.

(4) Where a person's salary or terms of office depend upon his option, the salary or terms for which he opts shall, for the purposes of sub-section (3) of this section, be deemed to be more advantageous to him than any others for which he might have opted.

(5) This section applies to the offices of judge of the High Court, judge of the Court of Appeal, appointed member of the Judicial Service Commission, member of the Public Service Commission, Attorney-General and Director of Audit.

Public debt.

132.—(1) All debt charges for which Swaziland is liable shall be a charge on and paid out of the Consolidated Fund.

(2) For the purposes of this section debt charges include interest, sinking fund charges, the repayment or amortisation of debt and all expenditure in connection with the raising of loans on the security of the revenues of Swaziland or the Consolidated Fund and on the service and redemption of debt thereby created.

Director of Audit.

133.—(1) There shall be a Director of Audit, whose office shall be a public office.

(2) The public accounts of Swaziland and of all officers, courts and authorities of the Government shall be audited and reported on by the Director of Audit and for that purpose the Director of Audit or any person authorised by him in that behalf shall have access to all books, records, reports and other documents relating to those accounts :

Provided that, if it is so provided by any law in the case of any body corporate directly established by law, the accounts of that body corporate shall be audited and reported on by such person as may be specified by or under that law.

(3) The Director of Audit shall submit his reports to the Minister responsible for finance, who shall cause them to be laid before both chambers.

(4) In the exercise of his functions under this Constitution the Director of Audit shall not be subject to the direction or control of any other person or authority.

CHAPTER XII

ALTERATION OF THE CONSTITUTION

134.—(1) This Constitution shall not be altered except in the following manner— Mode of altering this Constitution.

(a) the alteration shall be initiated by the introduction of a bill, expressly providing that the Constitution shall be so altered, in a joint sitting of the Senate and the House of Assembly summoned for the purpose in accordance with the provisions of Schedule 1 to this Constitution ;

(b) after the bill has been introduced in a joint sitting it shall be published in the Gazette and no further proceedings shall be taken on the bill in Parliament until the prescribed period has elapsed ;

(c) if, after the prescribed period has elapsed, the bill is passed at a joint sitting of the Senate and the House of Assembly it shall, subject to paragraphs (e) and (f) of this subsection, be submitted to the King for assent ;

(d) for the purpose of paragraph (c) of this subsection, if a bill contains provision for altering any of the specially entrenched provisions or entrenched provisions of this Constitution, the bill shall not be passed at a joint sitting of the Senate and the House of Assembly unless it is supported on its final reading by the votes of not less than three-quarters of all the members of both those chambers ;

(e) if the bill as passed at the joint sitting contains provision for altering any of the specially entrenched provisions of this Constitution that provision shall be submitted to a referendum, held in such manner as may be prescribed by Act of Parliament, at which every person who at the time when the referendum is held would be entitled to vote at an election of elected members of the House of Assembly but no other person is entitled to vote ; and unless that provision is approved on the referendum by not less than two-thirds of all the votes validly cast on that referendum the bill shall not be submitted to the King for assent ;

(f) when a bill to alter this Constitution is submitted to the King for assent it shall be accompanied by a certificate under the hand of the President of the Senate and the Speaker of the House of Assembly that the provisions of paragraphs (a), (b) and (d) of this subsection have been complied with and when a referendum has been held by a certificate of the officer in charge of the referendum stating the result of the referendum.

(2) A bill to alter this Constitution shall lapse—

(a) if it is not submitted for assent at the date of the conclusion of the next session of Parliament after the session in which it is introduced ;

(b) if on any reading of the bill in a joint sitting it is not passed ; or

(c) if, having been submitted to a referendum in accordance with subsection (1)(e) of this section, it is not approved in the manner provided by that subsection.

(3) In this section—

(*a*) references to any of the provisions of this Constitution include references to any law that amends or replaces that provision ; and

(*b*) references to the alteration of this Constitution or, as the case may be, to altering any provision include references—

(i) to revoking it with or without re-enactment thereof or the making of different provision in lieu thereof ;

(ii) to modifying it, whether by omitting or amending any of its provisions or inserting additional provisions in it or otherwise ; or

(iii) to suspending its operation for any period or terminating any such suspension.

(4) In this section—

" entrenched provisions " means any of the provisions of this Constitution specified in Part II of Schedule 4 to this Constitution ;

" prescribed period ", in relation to any bill containing provision to alter the entrenched provisions or the specially entrenched provisions of this Constitution, means a period of three months commencing from the introduction of the bill in a joint sitting and, in relation to any other bill means a period of one month commencing as aforesaid ;

" specially entrenched provisions " means any of the provisions of this Constitution specified in Part I of Schedule 4 to this Constitution.

CHAPTER XIII

MISCELLANEOUS

Swazi National Council.

135. Save as otherwise provided in this Constitution, the Swazi National Council, which consists of the Nggwenyama, the Ndlovukazi, and of all adult male Swazi, shall continue to exercise its function of advising the Nggwenyama on all matters regulated by Swazi law and custom and connected with Swazi traditions and culture ; and shall exercise such function either in Libandla or in Liqoqo, as the case may be, in accordance with Swazi law and custom.

Subordinate legislation.

136. An Act of Parliament may make provision conferring functions on a joint sitting of the chambers of Parliament with respect to any subordinate legislation (that is to say any instruments having the force of law made under an Act of Parliament) and for the summoning and procedure of a joint sitting for the purpose of the exercise of those functions.

References to public office, etc.

137.—(1) In this Constitution, unless the context otherwise requires, the expression " public office "—

(*a*) shall be construed as including the offices of judges of the High Court or Court of Appeal, the offices of members of all other courts of law in Swaziland (other than courts-martial), and the offices of members of the Police Force and of members of the Prison Service ; and (*b*) shall not be construed as including the offices of President or Deputy President of the Senate, Speaker or Deputy Speaker of the House of Assembly, Minister, Assistant Minister, Senator, member of the House of Assembly or member of any Commission established by this Constitution.

(2) For the purposes of this Constitution, a person shall not be regarded as holding a public office by reason only of the fact that he is in receipt of a pension or other like allowance in respect of public service.

138.—(1) In this Constitution, unless the context otherwise requires, a reference to the holder of an office by the term designating his office shall be construed as including a reference to any person for the time being lawfully acting in or exercising the functions of that office. *Acting appointments.*

(2) Where power is vested by this Constitution in any person or authority to appoint any person to act in or perform the functions of any office if the holder thereof is himself unable to perform those functions, no such appointment shall be called in question on the ground that the holder of the office was not unable to perform those functions.

139.—(1) References in this Constitution to the power to remove a public officer from his office shall be construed as including references to any power conferred by any law to require or permit that officer to retire from the public service and to any power or right to terminate a contract on which a person is employed as a public officer and to determine whether any such contract shall or shall not be renewed : *Removal from office.*

Provided that—

(*a*) nothing in this subsection shall be construed as conferring on any person or authority power to require a judge of the High Court or of the Court of Appeal or the Attorney-General or the Director of Audit to retire from the public service ; and

(*b*) any power conferred by any law to permit a person to retire from the public service shall, in the case of any public officer who may be removed from office by some person or authority other than a Commission established by this Constitution, vest in the Public Service Commission.

(2) Any provision in this Constitution that vests in any person or authority power to remove any public officer from his office shall be without prejudice to the power of any person or authority to abolish any office or to any law providing for the compulsory retirement of public officers generally or any class of public officer on attaining an age specified therein.

140. Save as otherwise provided in this Constitution, any person who has been appointed to any office established by this Constitution may resign from that office by writing under his hand addressed to the person or authority by whom he was appointed ; and the resignation shall take effect and the office shall accordingly become vacant— *Resignations.*

(*a*) at such time or on such date (if any) as may be specified in the writing ; or

(*b*) when the writing is received by the person or authority to whom it is addressed or by such other person as may be authorised by that person or authority to receive it, whichever is the later :

Provided that the resignation may be withdrawn before it takes effect if the person or authority to whom the resignation is addressed consents to its withdrawal.

Re-appointments and concurrent appointments. **141.**—(1) Where any person has vacated any office established by this Constitution, he may, if qualified, again be appointed or elected to hold that office in accordance with the provisions of this Constitution.

(2) Where a power is conferred by this Constitution upon any person to make any appointment to any office, a person may be appointed to that office notwithstanding that some other person may be holding that office, when that other person is on leave of absence pending the relinquishment of the office ; and where two or more persons are holding the same office by reason of an appointment made in pursuance of this subsection, then, for the purposes of any function conferred upon the holder of that office, the person last appointed shall be deemed to be the sole holder of the office.

Saving for jurisdiction of courts. **142.** No provision of this Constitution that any person or authority shall not be subject to the direction or control of any other person or authority in the exercise of any functions under this Constitution shall be construed as precluding a court of law from exercising jurisdiction in relation to any question whether that person or authority has performed those functions in accordance with this Constitution or any other law or should not perform those functions.

Power to amend and revoke instruments, etc. **143.** Where any power is conferred by this Constitution to make any order, regulation or rule, or to give any direction, the power shall be construed as including the power, exercisable in like manner, to amend or revoke any such order, regulation, rule or direction.

Interpretation. **144.**—(1) In this Constitution unless the context otherwise requires—

" Act of Parliament " means any law made by the King and Parliament ;

" the Commissioner of Police " means the officer, by whatever title called, commanding the Police Force ;

" the Commonwealth " means the countries that are independent members of the Commonwealth and territories for whose international relations any of those countries is wholly or in part responsible ;

" financial year " means the period of twelve months ending on the thirty-first day of March in any year or such other day as may be prescribed ;

" the former Constitution " means the Constitution of the Kingdom of Swaziland set out in the Schedule to the Swaziland Constitution Order 1967 as in force on 5th September 1968 ;

" the Gazette " means the Swaziland Government Gazette ;

" the Government " means the Government of Swaziland ;

" high judicial office " means the office of a judge of a court of unlimited jurisdiction in civil and criminal matters in some part of the Commonwealth or in the Republic of Ireland' or in any other country outside the Commonwealth that may be prescribed or the office of a judge of a court having jurisdiction in appeals from such a court ;

" the King " includes any person lawfully performing the functions of the King in accordance with Chapter IV of this Constitution ;

" Libandla " means a Council consisting of advisers of the Nggwenyama and of representatives of the Swazi nation or part of that nation, meeting to discuss any matters of communal concern in accordance with Swazi law and custom ;

" Liqoqo " means a Council the membership of which is in part elected by the Swazi National Council from among their number, in part selected by the Nggwenyama and in part traditionally appointed, and of which both the Nggwenyama and the Ndlovukazi are themselves members ;

" the Ndlovukazi " means the person appointed as Ndlovukazi under Swazi law and custom ;

" the Nggwenyama " means the person appointed as Nggwenyama under Swazi law and custom and includes any person for the time being exercising the functions of the Nggwenyama under Swazi law and custom ;

" oath " includes affirmation ;

" Parliament " means the Parliament of Swaziland established by this Constitution ;

" the Police Force " means the Swaziland Police Force and includes any other police force established in accordance with such provision as may be prescribed ;

" prescribed " means prescribed in a law: provided that, in relation to anything that may be prescribed only by Act of Parliament, it means so prescribed ;

" public office " means, subject to the provisions of section 137 of this Constitution, an office of emolument in the public service ;

" public officer " means the holder of any public office and includes a person appointed to act in any public office ;

" public service " means service in a civil capacity in respect of the government of Swaziland ;

" session " means, in relation to Parliament, the sittings of Parliament commencing when the House of Assembly first meets after any general election or when Parliament first meets after its prorogation at any time and terminating when Parliament is prorogued or is dissolved without having been prorogued ;

" sitting " means, in relation to a chamber, a period during which that chamber is sitting continuously without adjournment, and includes any period during which the chamber is in committee.

(2) Save as otherwise provided in this Constitution, the Interpretation Act 1889(a) shall apply, with the necessary adaptations, for the purpose of interpreting this Constitution and otherwise in relation thereto as it applies for the purpose of interpreting and in relation to Acts of the Parliament of the United Kingdom.

(a) 1889 c. 63.

SCHEDULE 1 TO THE CONSTITUTION

SUMMONING AND PROCEDURE OF JOINT SITTINGS OF SENATE AND
HOUSE OF ASSEMBLY

1.—(1) The King shall summon a joint sitting of the Senate and the House of Assembly—

(a) whenever he is informed by the Prime Minister that it is necessary in order that a joint sitting may deliberate and vote upon the question of approval, extending approval, or revocation of a declaration of a state of emergency under section 18 of this Constitution ;

(b) in the circumstances mentioned in section 75(2) or 76(2) of this Constitution ;

(c) whenever he is informed by the President of the Senate or the Speaker of the House of Assembly that a member of the Senate or the House of Assembly, as the case may be, has given notice of the introduction of a bill to alter the Constitution ; or

(d) whenever it is necessary in order that a joint sitting of the Senate and the House of Assembly may deliberate and vote upon a bill to alter the Constitution in accordance with section 134(1)(c) of this Constitution.

(2) Subject to sub-paragraph (4) of this paragraph, the summons of a joint sitting shall be by message to the Senate and the House of Assembly through the President or Speaker, as the case may be, and shall state the business which the sitting is summoned to transact and shall appoint a day for the joint sitting, being not more than fourteen days after the date of the message in the case of a sitting for the purpose mentioned in sub-paragraph (1)(a) of this paragraph and not more than twenty-one days after the message in any other case.

(3) The prorogation of Parliament shall not affect any business which a joint sitting of the Senate and the House of Assembly has, at the date of the prorogation, been summoned to transact in accordance with the provisions of this paragraph or which is then under consideration by a joint sitting, but, subject to the provisions of sub-paragraph (4) of this paragraph, any business pending for consideration or under consideration by a joint sitting when Parliament is dissolved shall lapse at the date of the dissolution.

(4) The provisions of section 60 of this Constitution (which relates to the recall of the chambers of Parliament after a dissolution) shall apply for the purpose of authorising the recall of members of those chambers in a joint sitting as it applies for authorising the recall of the chambers of Parliament.

2. The members of the Senate and the House of Assembly shall meet together in joint sitting on the day appointed and on any succeeding day or days that may be necessary and may deliberate and shall vote together upon the business the joint sitting was summoned to transact.

3. Where a joint sitting of the Senate and the House of Assembly is summoned for the purpose of deliberating and voting upon a bill in the circumstances mentioned in section 75(2) of this Constitution the following provisions shall apply—

(a) the members of the Senate and the House of Assembly may deliberate and shall vote together upon the bill as last proposed in the chamber in which it was introduced and upon such admissible amendments to the bill as may be proposed in the joint sitting ;

(b) if the bill, with such admissible amendments, if any, as are agreed to by the joint sitting, is affirmed by the joint sitting, the bill as so affirmed shall be deemed to have been duly passed ;

(c) for the purposes of this paragraph—

    (i) if the bill has not been passed by the chamber to which it was sent with amendments and returned to the chamber in which it was introduced, there shall be admissible only such amendments, if any, as are made necessary by the delay in the passage of the bill ;

    (ii) if the bill has been passed by the chamber to which it was sent with amendments and returned to the chamber in which it was introduced, there shall be admissible only such amendments, if any, as are made necessary by the delay in the passage of the bill and such other amendments as are relevant to the matters with respect to which the chambers have not agreed ;

    (iii) the decision of the person presiding in the joint sitting as to the amendments that are admissible under the provisions of this sub-paragraph shall be final.

4.—(1) Where a joint sitting of the Senate and the House of Assembly is summoned for the purpose of considering a bill referred back by the King in accordance with section 76(2) of this Constitution the following provisions shall apply—

(a) if the whole bill has been referred back, the joint sitting may deliberate and shall vote upon the bill as presented to the King for assent together with any amendment to any provision of the bill which may be proposed in the joint sitting ;

(b) if the bill has been referred back for consideration of provisions of the bill specified by the King, the joint sitting may deliberate and shall vote upon the bill as presented to the King for assent together with any admissible amendment which may be proposed in the joint sitting ;

(c) if the bill is affirmed with such amendments (if any) as are mentioned in the preceding sub-paragraphs and are agreed by the joint sitting, it shall be deemed to be duly passed.

(2) For the purposes of sub-paragraph (1)(b) of this paragraph there shall be admissible only amendments to the provisions specified by the King and such other amendments as are relevant to the matters contained in the King's message, and the decision of the person presiding in the joint sitting as to the amendments that are admissible shall be final.

5. The Speaker of the House of Assembly and the President of the Senate shall, in that order, preside alternately at joint sittings of the Senate and the House of Assembly and for the purpose of this paragraph the sitting or sittings necessary to dispose respectively of any motion for the purpose of section 18 of this Constitution, of the business relating to any bill referred to a joint sitting in accordance with section 75(2) or 76(2) of this Constitution, or of the business relating to any bill to alter the Constitution shall be regarded as a single sitting.

6. A joint sitting shall not be disqualified for the transaction of business by reason of any vacancy in the membership of either chamber.

7. If objection is taken by a member of either chamber who is present that there are present in that sitting (besides the person presiding) fewer than twenty-five members of the chambers of Parliament and, after such interval as may be prescribed in the rules of procedure applying to a joint sitting, the member presiding ascertains that there are still fewer than twenty-five members of the chambers of Parliament present, he shall thereupon adjourn the joint sitting.

8.—(1) Save as otherwise provided in this Constitution, any question proposed for decision in a joint sitting of the Senate and the House of Assembly shall be determined by a majority of the votes of the members of Parliament present and voting.

(2) A President elected from among persons who are Senators or a Speaker elected from among persons who are members of the House (whether or not he is presiding in a joint sitting) shall have an original but not a casting vote.

(3) A President or Deputy President of the Senate elected from among persons who are not Senators or a Speaker or a Deputy Speaker of the House of Assembly elected from among persons who are not members of the House shall have no vote.

(4) The Attorney-General shall have no vote.

(5) Subject to the provisions of sections 18(5) and 134(1)(d) of this Constitution, if upon any question before a joint sitting the votes of the persons entitled to vote are equally divided the motion shall be lost.

(6) If the rules of procedure of a chamber of Parliament make provision under which a member who votes upon a question in which he has a direct pecuniary interest shall be deemed not to have voted, those rules of procedure shall have effect for determining whether a member of that chamber has voted in a joint sitting.

9. Subject to the provisions of this Schedule, the rules of procedure for the time being of the House of Assembly shall apply, with the necessary modifications, for regulating any proceedings of a joint sitting under this Constitution which correspond to proceedings of the House of Assembly.

Sections 36, 54(6), 63, 88, 103, 109, 113(9) and 115(10).

SCHEDULE 2 TO THE CONSTITUTION

OATHS

(Oath or affirmation for the due execution of the office of King of Swaziland)

I .... do swear [or solemnly affirm] that I, in the office of King of Swaziland will, under the Constitution of the Kingdom of Swaziland, preserve, protect and defend the said Constitution ; that I will, as King, govern the people of Swaziland according to the said Constitution and the other laws of Swaziland ; and that I will, as King and so far as lies within my power, cause law and justice to be administered in mercy to the people of Swaziland.

So help me God. [To be omitted in affirmation.]

(Oath or affirmation for the due execution of the office of Regent)

I .... do swear [or solemnly affirm] that I, in the office of Regent of Swaziland, will, under the Constitution of the Kingdom of Swaziland, well and truly serve the King of Swaziland, his heirs and successors ; that I will, as Regent, preserve, protect and defend the said Constitution ; that I will, as Regent, govern the people of Swaziland according to the said Constitution and the other laws of Swaziland ; and that I will, as Regent and so far as lies within my power, cause law and justice to be administered in mercy to the people of Swaziland.

So help me God. [To be omitted in affirmation.]

(Oath or affirmation of allegiance)

I .... do swear [or solemnly affirm] that I will be faithful and bear true allegiance to King ...., his heirs and successors, according to law.

So help me God. [To be omitted in affirmation.]

(Oath or affirmation for due execution of office)

I .... do swear [or solemnly affirm] that I will well and truly serve King ...., his heirs and successors, in the office of [here insert the description of the office].

So help me God. [To be omitted in affirmation.]

(Judicial oath or affirmation)

I .... do swear [or solemnly affirm] that I will well and truly serve King ...., his heirs and successors, in the office of [here insert the description of the judicial office] and I will do right to all manner of people according to the law without fear or favour, affection or ill-will.

So help me God. [To be omitted in affirmation.]

SCHEDULE 3 TO THE CONSTITUTION

Section 62(2).

MATTERS WHICH SHALL CONTINUE TO BE REGULATED BY SWAZI LAW AND CUSTOM

(a) The office of Nggwenyama.

(b) The office of Ndlovukazi (the Queen Mother).

(c) The authorisation of a person to perform the functions of Regent for the purposes of section 30 of this Constitution.

(d) The appointment, revocation of appointment and suspension of Chiefs.

(e) The composition of the Swazi National Council, the appointment and revocation of appointment of members of the Council, and the procedure of the Council.

(f) The Ncwala Ceremony.

(g) The Libutfo (regimental) system.

SCHEDULE 4 TO THE CONSTITUTION

Section 134.

PART I

SPECIALLY ENTRENCHED PROVISIONS

(i) Chapter I;

(ii) Chapter II;

(iii) Sections 28, 29 and 30;

(iv) Sections 37, 56, 58, 59(1), 59(4), 60 and 61(1);

(v) Sections 62, 70(1), 70(2) and 70(3);

(vi) Sections 79(1), 79(2), 80(1), 80(3), 81, 82, 83, 84, 85, 86, 92(1), 92(2), 92(3) and 92(4);

(vii) Sections 94 and 95;

(viii) Sections 97, 98, 99, 100, 101, 102, 104, 105, 106, 107, 108, 113 and 114;

(ix) Sections 115 and 116;

(x) Sections 131, 133(1), 133(4), 134 and 135;

(xi) Chapter XIII in its application to any of the provisions referred to in this part of this Schedule;

(xii) Schedule 1 in its application to any of the provisions referred to in this part of this Schedule;

(xiii) Schedule 3;

(xiv) This Schedule.

PART II

ENTRENCHED PROVISIONS

(i) Sections 36, 38, 39, 40, 41, 42, 43, 44, 45, 46, 47, 48, 49, 54, 55, 59(2), 59(3) ;

(ii) Sections 71, 72, 73, 75, 77(1) and 78 ;

(iii) Sections 87, 91, 117, 118, 119, 120, 121, 122, 123, 124 and 125 ;

(iv) Sections 133(2) and 133(3) ;

(v) Chapter XIII in its application to any of the provisions referred to in this part of this Schedule ;

(vi) Schedule 1 in its application to any of the provisions referred to in this part of this Schedule.

EXPLANATORY NOTE

(This Note is not part of the Order.)

By virtue of the Swaziland Independence Act 1968 Her Majesty's jurisdiction will cease in Swaziland on 6 September 1968 and Swaziland will accordingly become an independent kingdom within the Commonwealth. This Order makes provision for a Constitution for Swaziland to come into effect on that day ; it includes provision for the exercise of the functions of the Head of State by the King of Swaziland, for the legislature, the executive government, the judicature and the public service. The Constitution also contains provisions relating to citizenship of Swaziland and fundamental rights and freedoms of the individual.

STATUTORY INSTRUMENTS

1968 No. 1378

CONSULAR RIGHTS AND PRIVILEGES

ADMINISTRATION OF ESTATES

The Consular Conventions (Union of Soviet Socialist Republics) Order 1968

Made - - -	*26th August* 1968
Laid before Parliament	*30th August* 1968
Coming into Operation	*22nd September* 1968

At the Court at Balmoral, the 26th day of August 1968

Present,

The Queen's Most Excellent Majesty in Council

Whereas by section 6(1) of the Consular Conventions Act 1949(a) (hereinafter referred to as "the Act") it is enacted that Her Majesty may by Order in Council direct that sections 1 and 2 of the Act (which provide for the exercise by consular officers of certain powers in relation to the property of deceased persons) shall apply to any foreign State specified in the Order, being a State with which a Consular Convention providing for matters for which provision is made by those sections has been concluded by Her Majesty:

And whereas such a Consular Convention between Her Majesty in respect of the United Kingdom of Great Britain and Northern Ireland and the Praesidium of the Supreme Soviet of the Union of Soviet Socialist Republics was signed at Moscow on 2nd December, 1965(b) and will enter into force on 22nd September 1968:

Now, therefore, Her Majesty, by virtue and in exercise of the powers in that behalf by the Act or otherwise in Her Majesty vested, is pleased, by and with the advice of Her Privy Council, to order, and it is hereby ordered, as follows:

1. Sections 1 and 2 of the Act shall apply to the Union of Soviet Socialist Republics.

2. This Order may be cited as the Consular Conventions (Union of Soviet Socialist Republics) Order 1968. It shall come into operation on 22nd September 1968.

N. E. Leigh.

(a) 1949 c. 29.   (b) Cmnd. 2910.

EXPLANATORY NOTE

(This Note is not part of the Order.)

This Order provides for the application of sections 1 and 2 of the Consular Conventions Act 1949 to the Soviet Union and enables Her Majesty to give effect to the provisions relating to administration of estates in the Consular Convention between the United Kingdom and the Soviet Union which was signed at Moscow on 2nd December 1965 (Cmnd. 2910).

The purport of sections 1 and 2 of the Act is stated in the preamble to this Order. Section 1 relates to England and, with the modifications contained in section 7 of the Act, to Northern Ireland; section 2 relates to Scotland.

1968 No. 1379

SOCIAL SECURITY

The Social Services (Northern Ireland Agreement) Order 1968

Made - - - *26th August* 1968

At the Court at Balmoral, the 26th day of August 1968

Present,

The Queen's Most Excellent Majesty in Council

Whereas by section 59(3) of the Finance Act 1968(a) it is provided that section 59 of that Act (which confirms the Social Services Agreement between the Treasury and the Ministry of Finance for Northern Ireland set out in Schedule 19 to that Act) shall not come into operation unless and until Her Majesty by Order in Council declares that a corresponding provision has been enacted by the Parliament of Northern Ireland:

And Whereas the Parliament of Northern Ireland has passed the Finance Act (Northern Ireland) 1968, and Her Majesty is satisfied that section 20 of that Act is such corresponding provision as aforesaid:

Now, therefore, Her Majesty, in pursuance of section 59(3) of the Finance Act 1968, is pleased, by and with the advice of Her Privy Council, to order, and it is hereby ordered, as follows:—

1. It is hereby declared that a provision corresponding to section 59 of the Finance Act 1968 has been enacted by the Parliament of Northern Ireland.

2. The Interpretation Act 1889(b) shall apply for the interpretation of this Order as it applies for the interpretation of an Act of Parliament.

3. This Order may be cited as the Social Services (Northern Ireland Agreement) Order 1968.

N. E. Leigh.

(a) 1968 c. 44.   (b) 1889 c. 63.

EXPLANATORY NOTE

(This Note is not part of the Order.)

The Treasury and the Ministry of Finance for Northern Ireland have entered into an Agreement dated 28th February 1968 (set out in Schedule 19 to the Finance Act 1968) which amends an Agreement of 11th February 1949 entered into with a view to assimilating the burdens on the Exchequers of the United Kingdom and Northern Ireland in respect of certain social and allied services. Confirmation of the Agreement of 28th February 1968 is given by section 59 of the Finance Act 1968, but that section is not to come into operation unless and until Her Majesty by Order in Council declares that a corresponding provision has been enacted by the Parliament of Northern Ireland. This Order declares that a corresponding provision has been so enacted.

STATUTORY INSTRUMENTS

1968 No. 1380

TAXES

The Special Charge Regulations 1968

Made - - - -	*26th August* 1968
Laid before the House of Commons	*30th August* 1968
Coming into Operation	*3rd September* 1968

The Commissioners of Inland Revenue, in exercise of the powers conferred on them by section 43(8) of the Finance Act 1968(a) and after consultation with the Council on Tribunals in so far as is required by section 8 of the Tribunals and Inquiries Act 1958(b) (as amended by section 3 of the Tribunals and Inquiries Act 1966(c)), hereby make the following Regulations:—

Citation and commencement

1. These Regulations may be cited as the Special Charge Regulations 1968 and shall come into operation on 3rd September 1968.

Interpretation

2.—(1) In these Regulations "Part IV" means Part IV of the Finance Act 1968, and references to sections and Schedules are references to sections of and Schedules to that Act unless some other Act is specified.

(2) The Interpretation Act 1889(d) shall apply to these Regulations as it applies to an Act of Parliament.

Trusts

3.—(1) Where under paragraph 7(3) of Schedule 15 a certificate is given by the Board to the person answerable for a trust that person may, by giving notice to the Board within 30 days of the date of the certificate, appeal to the Special Commissioners against the certificate (but only as respects the amount proper to be taken for the purpose of the certificate as the amount of the individual's investment income arising under the trust).

(2) All enactments which under section 43(7) apply to an appeal against an assessment to the special charge shall apply (with any necessary adaptations) to the appeal; and the certificate shall be varied as may be necessary to give effect to the determination of the appeal.

4. On the hearing of an appeal against an assessment to the special charge, a notice of charge issued under paragraph 5 of Schedule 15, a certificate issued under paragraph 7(3) of that Schedule, or a decision on any claim under Part IV to which section 9 of the Income Tax Management Act 1964(e) applies, any other person interested, that is to say the person originally chargeable, any person who has received a notice of charge under paragraph 5 of Schedule 15, or any person who has received a certificate under paragraph 7(3) of that

---

(a) 1968 c. 44. (b) 6 & 7 Eliz. 2. c. 66. (c) 1966 c. 43.
(d) 52 & 53 Vict. c. 63. (e) 1964 c. 37.

Schedule, shall, notwithstanding that he has not himself appealed, be entitled to appear or make representations in writing, and shall have the same rights as an appellant to be represented at the hearing;

Provided that a person answerable for a trust shall not be entitled to be heard or make representations in writing except on a question concerning income of the trust for which he is answerable.

5.—(1) Where—

(a) by reason of a reduction of an assessment to the special charge the amount of the special charge payable by the person originally chargeable is reduced, and

(b) the person originally chargeable has recovered any part of the special charge from the person answerable for a trust, under paragraph 3 of Schedule 15,

the person answerable for the trust shall be entitled to repayment under paragraph (2) of this Regulation of the amount by which the sum recovered from him exceeds the sum that would have been recoverable from him if the assessment had in the first instance been made in the reduced amount.

(2) Where the Board have given a certificate under paragraph 7(3) of Schedule 15 the repayment shall be made by the Board, and the amount repayable to the person originally chargeable shall be reduced accordingly; and in any other case the repayment shall be made by the person originally chargeable.

Interest

6. Where any amount of the special charge is repaid by the Board, there shall also be repaid any interest paid in respect of that amount.

7. Section 495(5) of the Income Tax Act 1952(a) and section 40(4) of the Finance Act 1967(b) (collection and recovery of interest on tax) shall apply to interest in respect of the special charge as they apply to interest charged under subsection (1) of the said section 495.

Close companies

8. Section 250(3), (4) and (5) and section 264 of the Income Tax Act 1952 (powers of obtaining information and of estimating income) shall apply for the purposes of apportionments and sub-apportionments under section 45(3) as they apply in relation to section 78 of the Finance Act 1965(c).

Exercise of functions

9. Functions relating to the administration and collection of the special charge may be exercised, subject to the Board's authority, by the Controller of Surtax and in his name; and any claim, application or notice to be made, given or sent to the Board in connection with the special charge shall be made, given or sent to the Controller of Surtax.

Service by post

10. Any notice or other document to be given, served, sent or delivered under Part IV, or under these Regulations, or under any enactment applied by Part IV or by these Regulations, may be served by post.

(a) 15 & 16 Geo. 6 & 1 Eliz. 2. c. 10.	(b) 1967 c. 54.
(c) 1965 c. 25.

By Order of the Commissioners of Inland Revenue.

J. Webb,
Secretary.

26th August 1968.

EXPLANATORY NOTE
(*This Note is not part of the Regulations.*)

These Regulations supplement the administrative provisions laid down by Part IV of the Finance Act 1968 for the Special Charge.

Regulations 3, 4 and 5 provide a supplementary procedure for appeals and repayments in cases where trusts are concerned.

Under Regulations 6, 7 and 8 certain existing provisions in the Income Tax Acts will apply for the collection of interest on the Special Charge, and for obtaining information in the case of close companies.

STATUTORY INSTRUMENTS

1968 No. 1381

CUSTOMS AND EXCISE
The Composite Goods Order 1968

Made - - -		*26th August* 1968
Laid before the House of Commons - -		*4th September* 1968
Coming into Operation		*5th September* 1968

Whereas the continued use of the Customs Tariff 1959, in classifying goods for customs purposes, has been authorised by the Import Duties (General) (No. 4) Order 1968(a) and the composite goods to which this Order applies (being imported composite goods) require to be classified accordingly:

And whereas it appears to the Treasury on the recommendation of the Commissioners of Customs and Excise that, in respect of composite goods of any description specified or indicated in this Order which are chargeable with duty in respect of hydrocarbon oil contained in them as a part or ingredient, it is inconvenient, and of no material advantage to the revenue or to importers of goods of any such description, to charge duty according to the quantity of hydrocarbon oil appearing to be used in the manufacture or preparation of the goods (as provided by section 259(1) of the Customs and Excise Act 1952(b), which section is in this Order referred to as "the principal section"):

Now, therefore, the Lords Commissioners of Her Majesty's Treasury by virtue of the powers conferred on them by Schedule 2 to the Finance Act 1957(c), hereby make the following Order:—

1. Any composite goods which, apart from small proportions of colouring matter or of additives, consist wholly of hydrocarbon oil shall be treated for the purpose of the duty of customs chargeable thereon as consisting wholly of hydrocarbon oil.

2. In the case of composite goods, other than those mentioned in Article 1 of this Order, which fall to be classified in any of the tariff subheadings indicated in the first column of the schedule to this Order (the general descriptions of which are indicated in the second column of that schedule) the duty of customs chargeable under the principal section in respect of hydrocarbon oils contained in the goods as a part or ingredient of them shall be calculated at the rates indicated in the third column of the schedule to this Order.

3. In this Order, unless the context otherwise requires, the following expressions have the meanings respectively assigned to them:—

(a) S.I. 1968/679 (1968 I, p. 1519).   (b) 1952 c. 44.
(c) 1957 c. 49.

"additive" means any substance commonly added in small proportions to hydrocarbon oils for the purpose of improving or modifying their quality or characteristics as fuel or as lubricants;

"composite goods" means goods which contain as a part or ingredient of them any article chargeable with hydrocarbon oil duty;

"hydrocarbon oils", "light oils" and "heavy oils" have the same meanings as in the Customs and Excise Act 1952;

"tariff subheading" means a subheading of the Customs Tariff 1959 as defined in Article 1(1) of the Import Duties (General) (No. 4) Order 1968.

4.—(1) This Order may be cited as the Composite Goods Order 1968.

(2) The Interpretation Act 1889**(a)** applies for the interpretation of this Order as it applies for the interpretation of an Act of Parliament.

(3) This Order shall come into operation on the 5th September 1968.

(4) The Composite Goods Order 1964**(b)** and the Composite Goods (Amendment) Order 1968**(c)** are hereby revoked.

> *B. K. O'Malley,*
> *Joseph Harper,*
> Two of the Lords Commissioners
> of Her Majesty's Treasury.

26th August 1968.

SCHEDULE

GOODS CHARGEABLE WITH HYDROCARBON OIL DUTY IN RESPECT OF HYDROCARBON OILS CONTAINED IN THEM AS A PART OR INGREDIENT.

Tariff Subheading	General description of goods	Rate per cent of the value of the goods
	(1) The following, containing light oils:—	
27.10(B) (1) ...	Preparations containing not less than 70 per cent. by weight of petroleum or shale oils.	8
34.03(B) (1) ...	Lubricating preparations containing less than 70 per cent. by weight of petroleum or shale oils.	8
38.18(B) (1) (a) ⎫ 38.18(B) (2) (a) ⎬	Composite solvents and thinners for varnishes and similar products.	8
	(2) The following, containing heavy oils:—	
36.08(C)	Firelighters	$4\frac{1}{2}$

(a) 1889 c. 63.   **(b)** S.I. 1964/1341 (1964 II, p. 3056).

(c) S.I. 1968/405 (1968 I, p. 1086).

EXPLANATORY NOTE

(*This Note is not part of the Order.*)

This Order imposes hydrocarbon oil duty at the rate of $4\frac{1}{2}$ per cent. *ad valorem* on imported firelighters containing heavy oil. It revokes, and replaces in consolidated form, the Orders mentioned in Article 4(4) of the Order, under which duty is imposed on certain other imported composite goods containing oil. This Order makes no change in the liability to duty of these other goods.

Taking account of section 6(3) of the Finance Act 1964, under which hydrocarbon oil duty is charged on imported goods containing oil as a part or ingredient only if they are goods which should be classed with oil according to their use, the Order provides that certain of the goods so classed shall be charged with duty as if they consisted wholly of hydrocarbon oil, and that others shall be charged with duty at the *ad valorem* rates shown in the Schedule to the Order.

STATUTORY INSTRUMENTS

1968 No. 1382

MERCHANT SHIPPING

The Shipping Contracts (Foreign Measures) Order 1968

Made - - - -	*26th August* 1968
Laid before Parliament	*29th August* 1968
Coming into Operation	*30th August* 1968

WHEREAS

(1) The North Atlantic Westbound Freight Association (hereinafter called "the Association") is an association of shipping lines for the purpose of providing regular services and stabilising freight rates from the United Kingdom and the Republic of Ireland to the Atlantic ports of the United States of America:

(2) The Association is governed by an agreement dated 4th October 1944, as currently amended, which provides, inter alia, for the settlement of disputes and complaints as to breaches of the agreement in manner therein set out:

(3) Complaint has been made by a member of the Association to the effect that a through service started by Container Marine Lines, a division of American Export Isbrandtsen Lines Inc., another member of the Association, between places in the United Kingdom and ports on the Atlantic coast of the United States of America is a breach of the said agreement:

(4) The Association and its member lines have initiated in the United Kingdom the procedure laid down in the said agreement for investigating the complaint:

(5) The Federal Maritime Commission of the United States of America have by Order served on 25th July 1968 directed the Association and its member lines to cease and desist from any further action under the Association's Conference arrangements with respect to the matter complained of:

(6) It appears to the Board of Trade that—

(a) the said Order of the Federal Maritime Commission is a measure taken by or under the law of a foreign country, the United States of America, for regulating or controlling terms or conditions of contracts or arrangements relating to the carriage of goods or passengers by sea ;

(b) insofar as the said Order applies to things done or to be done outside the territorial jurisdiction of the United States of America by persons carrying on business in the United Kingdom it constitutes an infringement of the jurisdiction which under international law belongs to the United Kingdom:

Now, therefore, the Board of Trade in exercise of their powers under section 1(1) of the Shipping Contracts and Commercial Documents Act 1964(**a**) as having effect by virtue of the Transfer of Functions (Shipping and Construction of Ships) Order 1965(**b**), and of all other powers enabling them in that behalf, hereby make the following Order—

1. Section 1 of the Shipping Contracts and Commercial Documents Act 1964 shall apply to the Order of the Federal Maritime Commission of the United States of America served on 25th July 1968 being the measure referred to above.

2. This Order may be cited as the Shipping Contracts (Foreign Measures) Order 1968 and shall come into operation on 30th August 1968.

Edmund Dell,
Minister of State,
Board of Trade.

26th August 1968.

EXPLANATORY NOTE

(This Note is not part of the Order.)

This Order, made under the Shipping Contracts and Commercial Documents Act 1964, applies section 1 of that Act (which enables the Board of Trade to give directions for maintaining the jurisdiction of the United Kingdom) to an Order of the Federal Maritime Commission of the United States of America directed to the North Atlantic Westbound Freight Association and its member lines.

(**a**) 1964 c. 87.   (**b**) S.I. 1965/145 (1965 I, p. 438).

STATUTORY INSTRUMENT

1968 No. 1383

CUSTOMS AND EXCISE

The Import Duties (General) (No. 8) Order 1968

Made - - - -	26th August 1968
Laid before the House of Commons	4th September 1968
Coming into Operation	5th September 1968

The Lords Commissioners of Her Majesty's Treasury, by virtue of the powers conferred on them by sections 1, 2 and 13 of the Import Duties Act 1958(a), and of all other powers enabling them in that behalf, on the recommendation of the Board of Trade hereby make the following Order:—

1. Schedule 1 to the Import Duties (General) (No. 4) Order 1968(b) (which Schedule by reference to the Customs Tariff 1959 sets out the import duties chargeable under the Import Duties Act 1958) shall be amended in accordance with the Schedule to this Order.

2.—(1) This Order may be cited as the Import Duties (General) (No. 8) Order 1968.

(2) The Interpretation Act 1889(c) shall apply for the interpretation of this Order as it applies for the interpretation of an Act of Parliament.

(3) This Order shall come into operation on 5th September 1968.

B. K. O'Malley,

Joseph Harper,

Two of the Lords Commissioners
of Her Majesty's Treasury.

26th August 1968.

SCHEDULE

Amendments of Schedule 1 to No. 4 Order of 1968

1. In Chapter 36, the following note shall be inserted after note 2:—

" 3. ' Heavy oils ' in subheading 36.08 (C) has the meaning given by section 195(1) of the Customs and Excise Act 1952 as for the time being in force."

2. In heading 36.08, the following subheading shall be inserted after subheading (B) and the existing subheading (C) shall accordingly become (D):—

" (C) Firelighters containing heavy oils   8%, in addition to   —   "
                                                    any hydrocarbon
                                                    oil duty.

(a) 1958 c. 6.   (b) S.I. 1968/679 (1968 I, p. 1519).   (c) 1889 c. 63.

3. In heading 90.07—

(*a*) in the heading, for the colon there shall be substituted " ; **photo-copying apparatus (not contact type):** ";

(*b*) the following subheading shall be inserted after subheading (B) and the existing subheading (C) shall accordingly become (D):—

" (C) Photo-copying apparatus 11 % — "
        (not contact type)

EXPLANATORY NOTE

(*This Note is not part of the Order.*)

The Composite Goods Order 1968 (S.I. 1968 No. 1381) imposes hydrocarbon oil (revenue) duty on imported firelighters containing heavy oil. This Order adds a new subheading for such firelighters to heading 36.08 of the Customs Tariff to preserve the existing level of protective duty (8 %).

To accord with a Classification Opinion of the Customs Co-operation Council, the Order also amends heading 90.07 of the Tariff by including photo-copying apparatus (not contact type) specifically within its scope. The present rate of import duty is preserved.

STATUTORY INSTRUMENTS

1968 No. 1384

CUSTOMS AND EXCISE

The Import Duties (Temporary Exemptions) (No. 4) Order 1968

Made -	*-*	*-*	*-*	26*th August* 1968
Laid before the				
House of Commons				4*th September* 1968
Coming into Operation				5*th September* 1968

The Lords Commissioners of Her Majesty's Treasury, by virtue of the powers conferred on them by sections 3(6) and 13 of the Import Duties Act 1958(**a**), and of all other powers enabling them in that behalf, on the recommendation of the Board of Trade hereby make the following Order:—

1.—(1) Until the beginning of 1st January 1969 or, in the case of goods in relation to which an earlier day is specified in Schedule 1 to this Order, until the beginning of that day, any import duty which is for the time being chargeable on goods of a heading of the Customs Tariff 1959 specified in that Schedule shall not be chargeable in respect of goods of any description there specified in relation to that heading.

(2) The period for which the goods of the headings of the Customs Tariff 1959 and descriptions specified in Schedule 2 to this Order are exempt from import duty shall be extended until the beginning of 1st January 1969, or in the case of goods in relation to which an earlier day is specified in that Schedule, until the beginning of that day.

(3) Any entry in column 2 in Schedule 1 or 2 to this Order is to be taken to comprise all goods which would be classified under an entry in the same terms constituting a subheading (other than the final subheading) in the relevant heading in the Customs Tariff 1959.

(4) For the purposes of classification under the Customs Tariff 1959, in so far as that depends on the rate of duty, any goods to which paragraph (1) or (2) above applies shall be treated as chargeable with the same duty as if this Order had not been made.

2.—(1) This Order may be cited as the Import Duties (Temporary Exemptions) (No. 4) Order 1968.

(2) The Interpretation Act 1889(**b**) shall apply for the interpretation of this Order as it applies for the interpretation of an Act of Parliament.

(3) This Order shall come into operation on 5th September 1968.

B. K. O'Malley,

Joseph Harper,

Two of the Lords Commissioners
of Her Majesty's Treasury.

26th August 1968.

(**a**) 1958 c. 6.   (**b**) 1889 c. 63.

SCHEDULE 1

GOODS TEMPORARILY EXEMPT FROM IMPORT DUTY

Tariff Heading	Description
28.39	Barium nitrate containing not more than 0·006 per cent. by weight of heavy metals calculated as Pb
29.04	Pentan-1-ol
29.14	Potassium sorbate Sodium formate
29.16	Butoxycarbonylmethyl butyl phthalate DL-Malic acid (until 7th November 1968)
29.21	Phenyl phosphorodichloridate
29.22	4,5-Dichloro-o-phenylenediamine
29.23	2-Amino-4,6-dichlorophenol (until 7th November 1968) 3,9-Di-(3-aminopropyl)-2,4,8,10-tetraoxaspiro[5,5]undecane
29.29	2-Chloro-4,6-xylylhydrazinium chloride (until 7th November 1968)
29.31	isoThiocyanatobenzene
29.35	2-[2-(4-Benzhydrylpiperazin-1-yl)ethoxy]ethanol dihydrochloride Methyl 3-amino-5,6-dichloropyrazine-2-carboxylate (until 7th November 1968) Pancuronium bromide
29.36	Chloramine T
29.37	Sulthiame
29.44	Novobiocin
70.20	Glass fibres, loose, unfelted, having a diameter not greater than 3 microns
73.15	Cold-rolled steel strip, with dressed edges, in coils, the strip being not less than 0·002 inch nor more than 0·040 inch in thickness and not less than 1/16 inch nor more than 4 inches in width, containing not less than 16 per cent. by weight nor more than 18 per cent. by weight of chromium and not less than 6 per cent. by weight nor more than 8 per cent. by weight of nickel and being of a tensile strength of not less than 120 tons per square inch (until 7th November 1968) Cold-rolled steel strip, with dressed edges, in coils, the strip being not less than 0·002 inch nor more than 0·007 inch in thickness and not less than 1/16 inch nor more than 1/4 inch in width, containing not less than 16 per cent. by weight nor more than 18 per cent. by weight of chromium and not less than 6 per cent. by weight nor more than 8 per cent. by weight of nickel and being of a tensile strength of not less than 115 tons per square inch (until 7th November 1968)
90.20	Beryllium metal windows of a thickness less than 0·004 inch for X-ray tubes

SCHEDULE 2

GOODS FOR WHICH EXEMPTION FROM IMPORT DUTY EXTENDED

Tariff Heading   *Description*

27.07   Naphthalene (until 7th November 1968)

28.18   Barium oxide (until 7th November 1968)

28.52   Mixed rare earth compounds containing not less than 3·5 per cent. by weight and not more than 9·0 per cent. by weight of combined fluorine estimated as F, and not less than 0·5 per cent. by weight and not more than 4·0 per cent. by weight of barium compounds estimated as BaSO$_4$; and of which not less than 10 per cent. by weight is retained by a sieve having a nominal width of aperture of 45 microns and conforming to British Standard 410:1962

29.01   Naphthalene (until 7th November 1968)

29.04   Tridecyl alcohol, mixed isomers (until 7th November 1968)

29.07   2,4,5-Trichlorophenol

29.14   3-(2-Chloroethoxy)-9α-fluoro-11β,21-dihydroxy-20-oxo-16α,17α-*iso*propylidenedioxypregna-3,5-diene-6-carbaldehyde 21-acetate

          Palmitoyl chloride containing:

              (*a*) not more than 100 parts per million by weight of phosphorus compounds calculated as P,

              (*b*) not more than 100 parts per million by weight of sulphur compounds calculated as S, and

              (*c*) not more than 10 parts per million by weight of heavy metals calculated as Pb (until 7th November 1968)

29.23   *NN*-Di-(2-hydroxypropyl)aniline

          1,2-Di-[*N*-methyl-*N*-3-(3,4,5-trimethoxybenzoyloxy)propylamino]-ethane dihydrochloride

31.02   Mixtures consisting of ammonium nitrate and ammonium sulphate and containing not less than 25 per cent. by weight and not more than 27 per cent. by weight of nitrogen expressed as N

38.19   Prepared catalysts, in the form of spheres, containing silver or silver oxide dispersed with alumina or silica or compounds thereof, and which contain not less than 7 per cent. by weight and not more than 20 per cent. by weight of total silver calculated as Ag (until 7th November 1968)

90.17   Endoradiosondes for the measurement of pH; and specialised receiving and recording apparatus therefor (until 7th November 1968)

EXPLANATORY NOTE

(This Note is not part of the Order.)

This Order provides that the goods listed in Schedule 1 shall be temporarily exempt from import duty, and those listed in Schedule 2 shall continue to be exempt from import duty, both until 1st January 1969, except for items for which an earlier day is specified.

STATUTORY INSTRUMENTS

1968 No. 1385

CUSTOMS AND EXCISE

The Import Duty Drawbacks (No. 7) Order 1968

Made - - - -	*26th August* 1968
Laid before the	
House of Commons	*4th September* 1968
Coming into Operation	*5th September* 1968

The Lords Commissioners of Her Majesty's Treasury, by virtue of the powers conferred on them by sections 9 and 13 of, and Schedule 5 to, the Import Duties Act 1958(a), and section 2(5) of the Finance Act 1965(b), and of all other powers enabling them in that behalf, on the recommendation of the Board of Trade hereby make the following Order :—

1. Schedule 1 to the Import Duty Drawbacks (No. 6) Order 1966(c) (which relates to the drawbacks to be allowed on the exportation of imported articles or goods incorporating them) as amended by paragraph 7 of Schedule 1 to the Import Duty Drawbacks (No. 5) Order 1968(d) shall be further amended by substituting for the entry relating to heading 90.07 of the Customs Tariff 1959 the following heading :—

" 90.07 (photographic cameras: photographic flashlight apparatus, photo-copying apparatus (not contact type)).	Allowable for all goods except tripods and other stands, pistol grips and photographic flashlight apparatus."

2.—(1) Schedule 2 to the said Order of 1966 (which relates to the drawbacks to be allowed on the exportation of goods produced or manufactured from imported articles) shall be amended as provided by the Schedule to this Order.

(2) In consequence of the amendments made by the Schedule to this Order, the following provisions of paragraph 2 of the Schedule to the Import Duty Drawbacks (No. 2) Order 1968(e) are hereby revoked, namely, in sub-paragraph (1), paragraphs (a) and (c) to (l), and sub-paragraph (2).

3.—(1) This Order may be cited as the Import Duty Drawbacks (No. 7) Order 1968.

(2) The Interpretation Act 1889(f) shall apply for the interpretation of this Order as it applies for the interpretation of an Act of Parliament.

(3) This Order shall come into operation on 5th September 1968.

B. K. O'Malley,
Joseph Harper,
Two of the Lords Commissioners of
Her Majesty's Treasury.

26th August 1968.

(a) 1958 c. 6.　　(b) 1965 c. 25.　　(c) S.I. 1966/921 (1966 II, p. 2207).
(d) S.I. 1968/930 (1968 II, p. 2432).　　(e) S.I. 1968/251 (1968 I, p. 763).　　(f) 1889 c. 63.

SCHEDULE

AMENDMENTS OF SCHEDULE 2 TO NO. 6 ORDER OF 1966

1. In the entry beginning "Furniture" inserted by paragraph 6 of the Schedule to the Import Duty Drawbacks (No. 8) Order 1966(a),—

(a) in column 2, at the beginning there shall be inserted " (A) " ;

(b) at the end of column 2, in columns 2 and 3 there shall be inserted the following :—

> " (B) Plywood of birch and beech, blockboard,   —."
> laminboard and battenboard, excluding ven-
> eered panels and sheets.

2.—(1) In the entry relating to linseed oil and goods made with linseed oil (other than printers' inks) as amended by paragraph 2(1) of the Schedule to the Import Duty Drawbacks (No. 2) Order 1968—

(a) in paragraph 1 (linseed oil and certain mixtures), in column 3, for " £10 7s. 2d. " (the rate of drawback per ton of linseed oil) there shall be substituted " £13 10s. 0d. " ;

(b) in paragraph 3 (mixtures containing cobalt linoleate), in column 3, for " 8s. 9d. " (the rate per 100 kg. of the mixture) there shall be substituted " 11s. 5d. " ;

(c) in paragraph 4 (linseed oil fatty acids), in column 3, for " £10 10s. 2d. " (the rate per ton of acids) there shall be substituted " £13 13s. 10d." ;

(d) in paragraph 5 (printed linoleum and floor cloth), in column 3, for " £1 9s. 5d. " (the rate per ton of linoleum or floor cloth) there shall be substituted " £1 18s. 5d. " ;

(e) in paragraph 6 (linoleum, not printed, manufactured on a base of jute canvas, cotton or spun rayon cloth), in column 3, for " £2 8s. 3d." (the rate per ton of linoleum) there shall be substituted " £3 2s. 10d. " ;

(f) in paragraph 7 (linoleum, not printed, manufactured on a base of bitumenised felt), in column 3, for " £1 12s. 4d. " (the rate per ton of linoleum) there shall be substituted " £2 2s. 2d. " ;

(g) in paragraph 8 (linoleum, not printed, manufactured on a base of resin coated paper felt), in column 3, for " £2 3s. 2d. " (the rate per ton of linoleum) there shall be substituted " £2 16s. 3d. " ;

(h) in paragraph 9 (cork carpets and linoleum composition), in column 3, for " £2 8s. 10d. " (the rate per ton of carpet or composition) there shall be substituted " £3 3s. 8d. " ;

(i) in paragraph 10 (felt base), in column 3, for " 6s. 1d. " (the rate per ton of felt base) there shall be substituted " 7s. 11d. " ;

(j) in paragraph 11 (oil baize and leather cloth), in column 3, for " £1 13s. 9d. " (the rate per ton of baize or leather cloth) there shall be substituted " £2 4s. 0d. " ;

(k) in paragraph 12 (blocks, tiles and similar articles), in column 3, for " £1 2s. 2d. " (the rate per ton of blocks, tiles or other articles) there shall substituted " £1 8s. 11d. ".

(2) In the entry relating to printers' inks and printing ink base, as amended by paragraph 2(2) of the Schedule to the said Order of 1968, in column 3, for " £10 7s. 2d. " (the rate of drawback per ton of linseed oil) there shall be substituted " £13 10s. 0d. ".

3. For the entry beginning " Syrups and treacles " there shall be substituted the following :—

> " Syrups and treacles.   Beet sugar and cane sugar,   —."
> solid, not qualifying for
> Commonwealth prefer-
> ence.

(a) S.I. 1966/1220 (1966 III, p. 3278).

EXPLANATORY NOTE

(This Note is not part of the Order.)

This Order—

(1) provides that there shall continue to be drawback of import duty in respect of certain photo-copying apparatus, notwithstanding the reclassication of those goods in a tariff heading (90.07) which would otherwise render them ineligible for drawback, and also corrects the description of goods for which drawback is allowable under that heading ;

(2) provides for the allowance of drawback of import duty on the exportation of furniture manufactured from certain imported plywood, blockboard, laminboard and battenboard ;

(3) revises the rates of drawback of import duty in respect of certain specified linseed oil and linseed oil goods manufactured from imported linseed or linseed oil ; and

(4) revokes the existing fixed rate of drawback of import duty for exported syrups and treacles and provides for drawback to be related to the duty paid on the imported sugar actually used in their manufacture.

STATUTORY INSTRUMENTS

1968 No. 1386

INDUSTRIAL TRAINING

The Industrial Training Levy (Rubber and Plastics Processing) Order 1968

Made - - -	*26th August* 1968
Laid before Parliament	*5th September* 1968
Coming into Operation	*9th September* 1968

The Secretary of State after approving proposals submitted by the Rubber and Plastics Processing Industry Training Board for the imposition of a levy on employers in the rubber and plastics processing industry and in exercise of her powers under section 4 of the Industrial Training Act 1964(a) and of all other powers enabling her in that behalf hereby makes the following Order :—

Title and commencement

1. This Order may be cited as the Industrial Training Levy (Rubber and Plastics Processing) Order 1968 and shall come into operation on 9th September 1968.

Interpretation

2.—(1) In this Order unless the context otherwise requires :—

(a) "an appeal tribunal" means an industrial tribunal established under section 12 of the Industrial Training Act 1964 ;

(b) "assessment" means an assessment of an employer to the levy ;

(c) "the Board" means the Rubber and Plastics Processing Industry Training Board ;

(d) "business" means any activities of industry or commerce ;

(e) "emoluments" means all emoluments assessable to income tax under Schedule E (other than pensions), being emoluments from which tax under that Schedule is deductible, whether or not tax in fact falls to be deducted from any particular payment thereof ;

(f) "employer" means a person who is an employer in the rubber and plastics processing industry at any time in the first levy period but does not include a person in whose case the number of persons in his employment in the said industry in the first base period is less than six ;

(g) "the first base period" means the period of twelve months that commenced on 6th April 1967 ;

(h) "the first levy period" means the period commencing with the day upon which this Order comes into operation and ending on 31st August 1969 ;

(a) 1964 c. 16.

(i) "the industrial training order" means the Industrial Training (Rubber and Plastics Processing Board) Order 1967(a) :

(j) "the levy" means the levy imposed by the Board in respect of the first levy period ;

(k) "notice" means a notice in writing ;

(l) "rubber and plastics processing establishment" means an establishment in Great Britain engaged in the first base period wholly or mainly in the rubber and plastics processing industry for a total of twenty-seven or more weeks or, being an establishment that commenced to carry on business in the first base period, for a total number of weeks exceeding one half of the number of weeks in the part of the said period commencing with the day on which business was commenced and ending on the last day thereof ;

(m) "the rubber and plastics processing industry" means any one or more of the activities which, subject to the provisions of paragraph 2 of Schedule 1 to the industrial training order, are specified in paragraph 1 of that Schedule as the activities of the rubber and plastics processing industry.

(2) Any reference in this Order to a person employed in the rubber and plastics processing industry or to a person employed at or from a rubber and plastics processing establishment shall in any case where the employer is a company be construed as including a reference to any director of the company (or any person occupying the position of director by whatever name he is called) who is required to devote substantially the whole of his time to the service of the company.

(3) In the case where a rubber and plastics processing establishment is taken over (whether directly or indirectly) by an employer in succession to, or jointly with, another person, a person employed at any time in the first base period at or from the establishment shall be deemed, for the purposes of this Order, to have been so employed by the employer carrying on the said establishment on the day upon which this Order comes into operation, and any reference in this Order to persons employed by an employer in the first base period shall be construed accordingly.

(4) Any reference in this Order to an establishment that commences to carry on business or that ceases to carry on business shall not be taken to apply where the location of the establishment is changed but its business is continued wholly or mainly at or from the new location, or where the suspension of activities is of a temporary or seasonal nature.

(5) The Interpretation Act 1889(b) shall apply to the interpretation of this Order as it applies to the interpretation of an Act of Parliament.

Imposition of the Levy

3.—(1) The levy to be imposed by the Board on employers in respect of the first levy period shall be assessed in accordance with the provisions of this Article.

(2) The levy shall be assessed by the Board separately in respect of each rubber and plastics processing establishment of an employer, but in agreement with the employer one assessment may be made in respect of any number of such establishments, in which case those establishments shall be deemed for the purposes of that assessment to constitute one establishment.

(a) S.I. 1967/1062 (1967 II, p. 3151).   (b) 1889 c. 63.

(3) Subject to the provisions of this Article, the levy assessed in respect of a rubber and plastics processing establishment of an employer shall be an amount equal to 0.75 per cent. of the sum of the emoluments of all the persons employed by the employer at or from that establishment in the first base period.

(4) The amount of the levy imposed in respect of a rubber and plastics processing establishment that ceases to carry on business in the first levy period shall be in the same proportion to the amount that would otherwise be due under paragraph (3) of this Article as the number of days between the commencement of the said levy period and the date of cessation of business (both dates inclusive) bears to the number of days in the said levy period.

(5) For the purposes of this Article no regard shall be had to the emoluments of any person engaged wholly in the supply of food or drink for immediate consumption.

Assessment Notices

4.—(1) The Board shall serve an assessment notice on every employer assessed to the levy, but one notice may comprise two or more assessments.

(2) The amount of any assessment payable under an assessment notice shall be rounded down to the nearest £1.

(3) An assessment notice shall state the Board's address for the service of a notice of appeal or of an application for an extension of time for appealing.

(4) An assessment notice may be served on the person assessed to the levy either by delivering it to him personally or by leaving it, or sending it to him by post at his last known address or place of business in the United Kingdom or, if that person is a corporation, by leaving it, or sending it by post to the corporation, at such address or place of business or at its registered or principal office.

Payment of the Levy

5.—(1) Subject to the provisions of this Article and of Articles 6 and 7, the amount of each assessment appearing in an assessment notice served by the Board shall be payable to the Board in three instalments, equal to one-tenth, two-fifths and one half of the said amount respectively, and the said instalments shall be due respectively one month, five months and eight months after the date of the notice.

(2) An instalment of an assessment shall not be recoverable by the Board until there has expired the time allowed for appealing against the assessment by Article 7(1) of this Order and any further period or periods of time that the Board or an appeal tribunal may have allowed for appealing under paragraph (2) or (3) of that Article or, where an appeal is brought, until the appeal is decided or withdrawn.

Withdrawal of Assessment

6.—(1) The Board may, by a notice served on the person assessed to the levy in the same manner as an assessment notice, withdraw an assessment if that person has appealed against that assessment under the provisions of Article 7 of this Order and the appeal has not been entered in the Register of Appeals kept under the appropriate Regulations specified in paragraph (5) of that Article.

(2) The withdrawal of an assessment shall be without prejudice to the power of the Board to serve a further assessment notice in respect of any establishment to which that assessment related and, where the withdrawal is made by

reason of the fact that an establishment has ceased to carry on business in the first levy period, the said notice may provide that the whole amount payable thereunder in respect of the establishment shall be due one month after the date of the notice.

Appeals

7.—(1) A person assessed to the levy may appeal to an appeal tribunal against the assessment within one month from the date of the service of the assessment notice or within any further period or periods of time that may be allowed by the Board or an appeal tribunal under the following provisions of this Article.

(2) The Board by notice may for good cause allow a person assessed to the levy to appeal to an appeal tribunal against the assessment at any time within the period of four months from the date of the service of the assessment notice or within such further period or periods as the Board may allow before such time as may then be limited for appealing has expired.

(3) If the Board shall not allow an application for extension of time for appealing, an appeal tribunal shall upon application made to the tribunal by the person assessed to the levy have the like powers as the Board under the foregoing paragraph.

(4) In the case of an establishment that ceases to carry on business in the first levy period on any day after the date of the service of the relevant assessment notice the foregoing provisions of this Article shall have effect as if for the period of four months from the date of the service of the assessment notice mentioned in paragraph (2) of this Article there were substituted the period of six months from the date of the cessation of business.

(5) An appeal or an application to an appeal tribunal under this Article shall be made in accordance with the Industrial Tribunals (England and Wales) Regulations 1965(**a**) as amended by the Industrial Tribunals (England and Wales) (Amendment) Regulations 1967(**b**) except where the establishment to which the relevant assessment relates is wholly in Scotland in which case the appeal or application shall be made in accordance with the Industrial Tribunals (Scotland) Regulations 1965(**c**) as amended by the Industrial Tribunals (Scotland) (Amendment) Regulations 1967(**d**).

(6) The powers of an appeal tribunal under paragraph (3) of this Article may be exercised by the President of the Industrial Tribunals (England and Wales) or by the President of the Industrial Tribunals (Scotland) as the case may be.

Evidence

8.—(1) Upon the discharge by a person assessed to the levy of his liability under an assessment the Board shall if so requested issue to him a certificate to that effect.

(2) The production in any proceedings of a document purporting to be certified by the Secretary of the Board to be a true copy of an assessment or other notice issued by the Board or purporting to be a certificate such as is mentioned in the foregoing paragraph of this Article shall, unless the contrary is proved, be sufficient evidence of the document and of the facts stated therein.

Signed by order of the Secretary of State.

26th August 1968.   *Roy Hattersley,*

Joint Parliamentary Under Secretary of State,
Department of Employment and Productivity.

(**a**) S.I. 1965/1101 (1965 II, p. 2805).   (**b**) S.I. 1967/301 (1967 I, p. 1040).
(**c**) S.I. 1965/1157 (1965 II, p. 3266).   (**d**) S.I. 1967/302 (1967 I, p. 1050).

EXPLANATORY NOTE
(*This Note is not part of the Order.*)

This Order, which is made by the Secretary of State for Employment and Productivity, gives effect to proposals submitted by the Rubber and Plastics Processing Industry Training Board for the imposition of a levy on employers in the rubber and plastics processing industry for the purpose of raising money towards the expenses of the Board.

The levy is to be imposed in respect of the first levy period commencing with the day upon which this Order comes into operation and ending on 31st August 1969. The levy will be assessed by the Board and there will be a right of appeal against an assessment to an industrial tribunal.

STATUTORY   INSTRUMENTS

1968 No. 1387 (C.16) (S.139)

NATIONAL HEALTH SERVICE, SCOTLAND

PUBLIC HEALTH, SCOTLAND

The Health Services and Public Health Act 1968 (Commencement No. 1) (Scotland) Order 1968

Made -   -   -   -   *22nd August* 1968

In exercise of the powers conferred on me by section 79(2) of the Health Services and Public Health Act 1968(**a**) I hereby make the following Order:—

1. This Order which shall extend to Scotland only, may be cited as the Health Services and Public Health Act 1968 (Commencement No. 1) (Scotland) Order 1968.

2. The following provisions of the Health Services and Public Health Act 1968 shall come into force on 9th September 1968:—

(1) Section 8 (Amendment of section 11 of the National Health Service (Scotland) Act 1947(**b**) (hereinafter referred to in this Order as the "1947 Act") as to association with universities of provision of hospital and specialist services).

(2) Section 10 (Midwifery services).

(3) Section 11 (Health visiting and district nursing).

(4) In Section 19 (General ophthalmic services) subsections (1) (7) and (8).

(5) Section 20 (Redefinition of "dispensing optician" and "ophthalmic optician").

(6) Section 21 (Amendment of section 15(6) of the 1947 Act as to facilities available at health centres).

(7) Section 24 (Power of Executive Councils to supply goods and materials to persons providing certain services).

(8) Section 25 (Amendment of section 43(6) of the 1947 Act as to the disqualification of practitioners and others already disqualified in Northern Ireland).

(9) Section 30 (Certificates for exemption from prescription charges).

(10) Section 31 (Power of the Secretary of State to make services available and, in certain circumstances, to provide them otherwise than for purposes of hospital and specialist services).

(**a**) 1968 c. 46.   (**b**) 1947 c. 27.

(11) Section 32 (Power of the Secretary of State to dispose of goods and, in certain circumstances, to produce or manufacture them otherwise than for purposes of hospital and specialist services).

(12) Section 33 (Provision of vehicles for persons suffering from physical defect or disability).

(13) Section 35 (Compensation for loss of employment, etc. attributable to re-organisation of provision of hospital services etc.).

(14) Section 37 (Payment of allowances and remuneration to members of certain bodies established by or under the 1947 Act and members of certain other bodies).

(15) Section 39 (Amendment of sections 3 and 45 of the 1947 Act as to power to recover cost of replacing appliances where the replacement is necessitated by lack of care).

(16) Section 40 (Accommodation for persons displaced in course of development for purposes of the Acts relating to the national health service or to mental health).

(17) Section 41 (Provision of practice accommodation).

(18) Section 42 (Orders and regulations).

(19) Section 43 and Schedule 2 (Interpretation of Part I and application of provisions of the 1947 Act).

(20) Section 44 (Extension of power under the National Assistance Act 1948(a) of local authority to provide accommodation elsewhere than in premises managed by them or another such authority).

(21) Section 59 (Extension of power of user by Crown of patented invention to user for certain health services).

(22) Section 61 (Welfare foods).

(23) Section 62 (Hover vehicles brought within scope of Acts relating to public health and food and drugs).

(24) Section 63 (Provision of instruction for officers of hospital authorities and other persons employed, or contemplating employment, in certain activities connected with health or welfare).

(25) Section 64 (Financial assistance by the Secretary of State to certain voluntary organisations).

(26) Section 65 (Financial and other assistance by local authorities to certain voluntary organisations).

(27) Section 66 (Payments in respect of travelling expenses of visitors to patients in State hospitals).

(28) Section 67 (Power of the Secretary of State to purchase goods for supply to local authorities and Executive Councils).

(29) Section 71 (Compensation for stopping employment to prevent spread of disease).

(30) Section 72 (Powers of sheriff, justice of the peace or magistrate to order a medical examination).

(a) 1948 c. 29.

(31) Section 73 (Power of medical officers of health to enter premises).

(32) Section 74 (Fees for certain certificates no longer payable under section 4 of the Infectious Disease (Notification) Act 1889(**a**).

(33) Section 75 (Correspondence of patients in State hospitals).

(34) Section 76 (Grants to certain authorities in respect of functions relating to imported food).

(35) Section 77 (Expenses and receipts).

(36) Section 78(1) and Schedule 3 (Consequential amendments) but except in so far as amendments to enactments refer specifically to sections 13 and 45 of the Health Services and Public Health Act, 1968.

(37) Section 78(2) and Schedule 4 (Repeals so far as consequential upon the coming into force of the foregoing sections and which are set out in the Schedule hereto).

(38) Section 79 (Short title, citation, commencement, and extent).

William Ross (sgd.)
One of Her Majesty's Principal
Secretaries of State.

St. Andrew's House,
Edinburgh, 1.
22nd August 1968.

SCHEDULE

Chapter	*Short Title*	*Extent of Repeal*
52 & 53 Vict. c. 72	The Infectious Disease (Notification) Act 1889	In section 4(2) the words "and shall pay" onwards.
60 & 61 Vict. c.38	The Public Health (Scotland) Act 1897	Section 45.
10 & 11 Geo. 6 c.27	The National Health Service (Scotland) Act 1947	In section 11, in subsection (10), in paragraph (i), the words "and compensation", except in relation to an order made in consequence of the occurrence, before the coming into operation of section section 35 of this Act, of any of the events mentioned in paragraphs (*a*) and (*b*) of that subsection.
		In section 22, subsection (3).
		Section 23.
		In section 27, subsection (3).
		In section 32, in subsection (5) the words "and their compensation by the Secretary of State" except

(**a**) 1889 c. 72.

Chapter	Short Title	Extent of Repeal
10 & 11 Geo. 6 c.27	The National Health Service (Scotland) Act 1947 —cont.	in relation to an order made under subsection (2), (3) or (4) of that section before the coming into operation of section 35 of this Act or an order made before the coming into operation of that section revoking an order made under any of those subsections.
		In section 39, in subsection (2)(*e*) the words "and also for the remuneration of members of the Board".
		Section 48.
		In section 54, subsection (3).
		In Schedule 1 in paragraph 2 the words from "and for the making of such payments" onwards.
		In Schedule 4 Part IV paragraphs 2(*c*) and 5.
		In Schedule 6, paragraph 4(*c*), the proviso to paragraph 4, and paragraph 8.
		In Schedule 7 paragraph 3(*b*).
		In Schedule 8 paragraph 6(*b*).
11 & 12 Geo. 6 c.29	The National Assistance Act 1948	Section 26(6).
		Section 30(2).
		Section 31(3).
		In section 33, in the proviso, the words from "and in subsection (3) of the said section thirty-one" to the end of the proviso.
12, 13 & 14 Geo. 6 c.93	The National Health Service (Amendment) Act 1949	In section 21, the words "or ophthalmic or dispensing optician", and the words "or optician".
		Section 22.
		In the Schedule, in Part II the words from "In subsection (3) of section 54" to "(including travelling and subsistence expenses)", the words from "in paragraph 2 of the First Schedule" to "set up as aforesaid", the words from "For sub-paragraph (*c*) of paragraph 2" to "usual place of residence", the words from "at the end of the said Part IV" to "such bodies", the words from "For sub-paragraph (*c*) of paragraph 4" to "any approved duty" and the words from "At the end of the said paragraph 4" onwards.
8 & 9 Eliz. 2 c.61	The Mental Health (Scotland) Act 1960	In Schedule 4, the amendment of section 63 of the National Health Service (Scotland) Act 1947.

Chapter	Short Title	Extent of Repeal
9 & 10 Eliz. 2 c. 43	The Public Authorities (Allowances) Act 1961	Sections 4, 5 and 6.
10 & 11 Eliz. 2 c.24	The National Assistance Act 1948 (Amendment) Act 1962	In section 1(1) the substituted subsection (3) of section 31 of the National Assistance Act 1948; and section 1(2).

EXPLANATORY NOTE

(This Note is not part of the Order.)

Section 79 of the Health Services and Public Health Act 1968 provides that its provisions shall come into force on such date as the Secretary of State may by Order appoint. This Order brings into force on 9th September 1968 those provisions of the Act which are set out in the Order. The Order extends only to Scotland.

STATUTORY INSTRUMENTS

1968 No. 1388

TAXES

The Selective Employment Tax (Payments to Public Bodies) (Variation) Order 1968

Made - - - -	*26th August* 1968
Laid before Parliament	*30th August* 1968
Coming into Operation	*2nd September* 1968

The Treasury, in exercise of the powers conferred on them by section 9(2) of the Selective Employment Payments Act 1966(**a**), and of all other powers enabling them in that behalf, hereby make the following Order:—

1.—(1) Part I of Schedule 1 to the Selective Employment Payments Act 1966 (which sets out the bodies to which section 3 of that Act applies) shall be amended—

(*a*) by adding at the end of paragraph 17 the words " and any wholly-owned subsidiary thereof " ; and

(*b*) by deleting paragraph 18.

(2) Part II of the said Schedule 1 (which sets out the excepted parts of undertakings) shall be amended—

(*a*) by adding after the words " Premises occupied by British Transport Hotels Ltd." the words " other than premises comprised in an establishment which satisfies the requirements of section 2(3A) of this Act " ; and

(*b*) by adding at the end of the said Part II the following words:—

" B.O.A.C. Restaurants Limited.

Pickfords Shipping and Forwarding Company Limited ".

(3) Part III of the said Schedule 1 (which sets out the parts of undertakings qualifying for premium) shall be amended by adding at the end thereof the words " B.O.A.C. Engine Overhaul Limited ".

2. The Interpretation Act 1889(**b**) shall apply for the interpretation of this Order as it applies for the interpretation of an Act of Parliament.

3. This Order may be cited as the Selective Employment Tax (Payments to Public Bodies) (Variation) Order 1968, and shall come into operation on 2nd September 1968.

B. K. O'Malley,
E. Alan Fitch,
Two of the Lords Commissioners
of Her Majesty's Treasury.

26th August 1968.

(a) 1966 c. 32.   (b) 1889 c. 63.

EXPLANATORY NOTE

(This Note is not part of the Order.)

This Order amends Schedule 1 to the Selective Employment Payments Act 1966, which relates to payments to certain public bodies. The effect of the Order is :

(1) to enable refunds of selective employment tax to be made for employment in those premises occupied by British Transport Hotels Ltd. which satisfy the requirements of section 2(3A) of the Act, as inserted by section 52 of the Finance Act 1968 ;

(2) to add B.O.A.C. Restaurants Limited and Pickfords Shipping and Forwarding Company Limited to the list of parts of undertakings in respect of which refunds of selective employment tax may not be made ; and

(3) to add B.O.A.C. Engine Overhaul Limited to the list of parts of undertakings which qualify for premium.

STATUTORY INSTRUMENTS

1968 No. 1389

PATENTS

The Patents Rules 1968

Made - - -	*27th August* 1968
Laid before Parliament	*12th September* 1968
Coming into Operation	*1st November* 1968

ARRANGEMENT OF RULES

(Any reference to a section is a reference to that section of the Patents Act 1949 as amended by the Patents Act 1957 and the Patents and Designs (Renewals, Extensions and Fees) Act 1961)

SCHEDULES

The Board of Trade, in pursuance of the powers conferred upon them by sections 94, 95 and 99 of the Patents Act 1949(a), as amended by the Patents Act 1957(b), and Patents and Designs (Renewals, Extensions and Fees) Act 1961(c) and the Patents (Fees Amendment) Order 1961(d), and of all other powers enabling them in that behalf, after consultation with the Council on Tribunals, and, as regards Rule 3 hereof, with the consent of the Treasury, hereby make the following Rules :—

Citation, Commencement and Interpretation

1. These Rules may be cited as the Patents Rules 1968 and shall come into operation on 1st November 1968.

2.—(1) In these Rules, unless the context otherwise requires—

"the Act" means the Patents Act 1949, as amended by the Patents Act 1957 and the Patents and Designs (Renewals, Extensions and Fees) Act 1961, and save where otherwise indicated, any reference to a section is a reference to that section of the Act ;

"Journal" means the Official Journal (Patents) published in accordance with Rule 143 ;

"Office" means the Patent Office ;

"register" means the register of patents kept under the provisions of section 73 ;

"United Kingdom" includes the Isle of Man.

(2) The Interpretation Act 1889(e) shall apply to the interpretation of these Rules as it applies to the interpretation of an Act of Parliament, and as if these Rules and the Rules hereby revoked were Acts of Parliament.

Fees and Forms

3. The fees to be paid in respect of any matters arising under the Act shall be those specified in Schedule I to these Rules and in any case where a form specified in that Schedule as the corresponding form in relation to any matter is required to be used that form shall be accompanied by the fee specified in respect of that matter.

4. The forms mentioned in these Rules are those set out in Schedule 2 to these Rules and such forms shall be used in all cases in which they are applicable and may be modified as directed by the Comptroller.

Documents

5.—(1) All documents and copies of documents, except drawings, filed at the Office shall, unless the Comptroller otherwise directs, be written, typewritten, lithographed or printed in the English language—

(a) upon strong white paper of a size approximately 13 inches by 8 inches ;

(b) in legible characters with a dark indelible ink ;

(c) with the lines widely spaced ;

(d) except in the case of statutory declarations and affidavits, on one side only ;

(a) 1949 c. 87.　　　　　　　　　　(b) 1957 c. 13.
(c) 1961 c. 25.　　　　　　　　　　(d) 1961/1499 (1961 II, p. 3050).
(e) 1889 c. 63.

(e) leaving a margin of at least $1\frac{1}{2}$ inches on the left-hand part thereof ; and

(f) in the case of each of the forms set out in Schedule 2 hereto, leaving a space of about 3 inches blank at the top of the form.

(2) Duplicate documents required under these Rules may be carbon copies of the original documents provided that they are on paper of good quality and the typing is black and distinct.

6. Any notice, application, or other document sent to the Office by post shall be deemed to have been given, made or filed at the time when the letter containing the document would be delivered in the ordinary course of post.

7. Every person concerned in any proceedings to which these Rules relate, and every patentee, shall furnish to the Comptroller an address for service in the United Kingdom and that address may be treated for all purposes connected with such proceedings or patent as the address of the person concerned in the proceedings or the patentee.

Agency

8.—(1) With the exception of documents mentioned in sub-rule (2) and unless the Comptroller otherwise directs in any particular case, all notices, applications or other documents filed under the Act may be signed by, and all attendances upon the Comptroller may be made by or through, an agent duly authorised to the satisfaction of the Comptroller.

(2) The following documents are excepted from sub-rule (1) :—the autho-risation of an agent ; an application for a patent, for the grant of a patent of addition in lieu of an independent patent, or for a complete specification to be treated as a provisional specification ; a notice of opposition ; and an application, request, notice, claim or declaration on any of the following forms, namely Patents Forms numbers 4, 6, 14, 15, 17 to 19, 27, 29, 32, 35, 38 to 40, 42 to 45, 47 to 50, 53 to 57, and 68.

(3) The Comptroller may refuse to recognise as such agent in respect of any business under the Act

(a) any individual whose name has been erased from, and not restored to, the register of patent agents, or who is for the time being suspended from acting as a patent agent ;

(b) any person who has been convicted of an offence under section 88 ;

(c) any person who is found by the Board of Trade (after being given an opportunity to be heard) to have been convicted of any such offence, or to have been guilty of any such misconduct, as, in the case of an individual registered in the register of patent agents, would render him liable to have his name erased therefrom ;

(d) any person, not being registered as a patent agent, who in the opinion of the Comptroller is engaged wholly or mainly in acting as agent in applying for patents in the United Kingdom or elsewhere in the name or for the benefit of a person by whom he is employed ;

(e) any company or firm, if any person whom the Comptroller could refuse to recognise as agent in respect of any business under the Act is acting as a director or manager of the company or is a partner in the firm.

Applications for the grant of patents

9.—(1) An application, other than a Convention application, shall be made on Patents Form No. 1 or, provided the application is made and signed by the applicant personally and not by a nominee, on the form reproduced at 1A in Schedule 3 hereto (being the form adopted for the purpose by the European Convention relating to the Formalities required for Patent Applications done at Paris on 11th December 1953).

(2) In the case of an application by the assignee of the person claiming to be the true and first inventor there shall be furnished at the time of filing such application, or within a period of three months thereafter, the declaration required by section 2 (2).

(3) A Convention application shall be made on Patents Form No. 1 Con. or, provided the application is made and signed by the applicant personally and not by a nominee, on the form reproduced at 1B in Schedule 3 hereto (being the form adopted for the purpose by the said European Convention).

(4) An application for the grant of a patent of addition in lieu of an independent patent shall be made on Patents Form No. 1 Add.

10. In the case of an application, other than a Convention application, by the personal representative of a deceased person who, immediately before his death, was entitled to make such an application, the probate of the will of the deceased, or the letters of administration of his estate, or an official copy of the probate or letters of administration, shall be produced at the Office in proof of the applicant's title to act as personal representative.

11.—(1) Except in the case of an application (other than a Convention application) which is accompanied by a complete specification, Patents Form No. 4 including a declaration as to the inventorship of the invention disclosed in the complete specification, shall be filed with the complete specification or subsequently at any time before the expiration of the period allowed by or under section 12 for putting the application in order.

(2) When so requested by the applicant the Comptroller may, if he sees fit, dispense with the said declaration.

12. Where, in pursuance of section 3 (3), the Comptroller allows a single complete specification to be proceeded with in respect of two or more applications in respect of which two or more complete specifications have been filed, the single complete specification may include any matter disclosed in any of the said specifications and shall be deemed to have been filed on such date, not earlier than the earliest date on which all the matter disclosed in the said single complete specification has been disclosed to the Office in or in connection with the applications, as the Comptroller may direct.

13.—(1) Where an applicant has made an application for a patent and, before the acceptance of the complete specification, makes a fresh application for a patent for matter included in the first mentioned application or in any specification filed in pursuance thereof, the Comptroller may direct that the fresh application or any specification filed in pursuance thereof shall be ante-dated to a date not earlier than the date of filing of the first mentioned application or specification if the applicant includes in the fresh application a request to that effect.

(2) Where an applicant having made an application for a patent subsequently discloses to the Office additional matter in connection therewith, and before the acceptance of the complete specification makes a fresh application for a patent in respect of the additional matter, the Comptroller may direct that the fresh application or any specification filed in pursuance thereof shall be ante-dated to a date not earlier than the date on which the matter was first disclosed to the Office if the applicant includes in the fresh application a request to that effect.

(3) The Comptroller may require such amendment of the complete specification filed in pursuance of either of the said applications as may be necessary to ensure that neither of the said complete specifications includes a claim for matter claimed in the other.

14. Where a complete specification has been filed pursuant to two or more applications accompanied by provisional specifications for inventions which the applicant believes to be cognate or modifications one of another and the Comptroller is of opinion that such inventions are not cognate or modifications one of another, the Comptroller may allow the complete specification to be divided into such number of complete specifications as may be necessary to enable the applications to be proceeded with as two or more separate applications for patents.

15.—(1) In addition to the specification filed with every Convention application, there shall be filed with the application, or within three months thereafter, a copy of the specification and drawings or documents filed in respect of the relevant application for protection in a Convention country or of each such application, duly certified by the official chief or head of the Patent Office of the Convention country, or otherwise verified to the satisfaction of the Comptroller.

(2) If any specification or other document relating to the application is in a foreign language, it shall be accompanied by a translation thereof verified by statutory declaration or otherwise to the satisfaction of the Comptroller.

16. Where a single Convention application has been made in respect of all or part of the inventions in respect of which two or more applications for protection have been made in one or more Convention countries, and the Examiner reports that the claims of the specification filed with the said Convention application relate to more than one invention, the Comptroller may allow one or more further applications to be filed and the specification to be divided into such number of specifications as may be necessary to enable two or more separate Convention applications to be proceeded with and may direct that the said applications be deemed to have been filed on the date of filing of the original application.

Drawings

17. Drawings, when supplied, shall be furnished in duplicate and shall accompany the provisional or complete specification to which they refer, except in the case provided for by Rule 24.

18.—(1) Drawings shall be hand-made or reproduced on white, hot-pressed, rolled or calendered strong drawing paper of smooth surface, good quality, and medium thickness, without washes or colours, in such a way as to admit of being clearly reproduced on a reduced scale by photography, or, without any intermediary steps, on a stereotype.

(2) Mounted drawings may not be used.

19.—(1) Drawings shall be on sheets which measure 13 inches from top to bottom and are either from 8 inches to 8¼ inches or from 16 inches to 16½ inches wide, and a clear margin of half an inch shall be left at the edges of the sheet.

(2) If there are more figures than can be shown on one of the smaller-sized sheets, two or more of these sheets shall be used unless the larger size is required by the size of any one figure.

(3) An exceptionally large figure may be continued on subsequent sheets.

(4) No more sheets shall be employed than are necessary.

(5) The figures shall be numbered consecutively without regard to the number of sheets, and shall as far as possible be arranged in numerical order, separated by a sufficient space to keep them distinct.

(6) Where figures on a number of sheets form in effect a single complete figure, they shall be so arranged that the complete figure can be assembled without concealing any part of another figure.

20. Drawings shall be prepared in accordance with the following requirements :—

(a) they shall be executed in durable, very dark markings ;
(b) each line shall be firmly and evenly drawn, sharply defined, and of the same strength throughout ;
(c) section lines, lines for effect, and shading lines shall be as few as possible, and shall not be closely drawn ;
(d) shading lines shall not contrast excessively in thickness with the general lines of the drawing ;
(e) sections and shading shall not be represented by solid black or washes ;
(f) they shall be on a scale sufficiently large to show the invention clearly, and only so much of the apparatus, machine, or article may appear as effects this purpose ;
(g) if the scale is given, it shall be drawn, and not denoted by words, and no dimensions may be marked on the drawings ;
(h) reference letters and numerals, and index letters and numerals used in conjunction therewith, shall be bold, distinct and not less than one-eighth of an inch in height ; the same letters or numerals shall be used in different views of the same parts, and where the reference letters or numerals are shown outside the parts referred to they shall be connected with the said parts by fine lines.

21.—(1) Drawings shall bear :—

(a) in the left-hand top corner the name of the applicant and, in the case of drawings filed with a complete specification after one or more pro- visional specifications, the numbers and years of the applications ;
(b) in the right-hand top corner the number of sheets of drawings sent and the consecutive number of each sheet, and the words "original" or "duplicate" as the case may require ;
(c) in the right-hand bottom corner the signature of the applicant or his agent.

(2) The title of the invention shall not appear on the drawings.

22.—(1) No descriptive matter shall appear on constructional drawings, but drawings in the nature of flow sheets may bear descriptive matter to show the materials used and the chemical or other reactions or treatments effected in carrying out the invention.

(2) Drawings showing a number of instruments or units of apparatus and their interconnections, either mechanical or electrical, where each such instru-

ment or unit is shown only symbolically, may bear such descriptive matter as is necessary to identify the instruments or units or their interconnections.

(3) No drawing or sketch, other than a graphic chemical formula or a mathematical formula, symbol or equation, shall appear in the verbal part of the specification and if such a formula, symbol or equation is used therein a copy thereof, prepared in the same manner as drawings, shall be furnished if the Comptroller so directs.

23. Drawings shall be delivered at the Office free from folds, breaks or creases which would render them unsuitable for reproduction by photography.

24. If an applicant desires to adopt the drawings filed with his provisional specification as the drawings or part of the drawings for his complete specification, he shall refer to them in the complete specification as those filed with the provisional specification.

Extension of the period for filing complete specification

25. A request for an extension of the period for filing a complete specification up to a period not exceeding fifteen months from the date of filing of the application shall be made on Patents Form No. 5.

Request for post-dating an application

26. Where an applicant for a patent desires that his application shall be post-dated in pursuance of the provisions of section 6 (3), he shall make a request on Patents Form No. 6.

Procedure under Sections 7, 8 and 9

27.—(1) When the Examiner, in making the investigation under section 7, reports that the invention so far as claimed in any claim of the complete specification has been published in any specification or other document falling within section 7 (1) or 7 (2), the applicant shall be so informed and shall be afforded an opportunity of amending his specification.

(2) If the Examiner finds that substantially the whole of the invention claimed has been published in one or more such specifications or documents he may, without continuing the investigation, make a provisional report to that effect.

(3) If the applicant re-files his specification and the Examiner is not satisfied either that the invention so far as claimed in any claim has not been published in any specification or other document cited by the Examiner or that the priority date of the claim is not later than the date on which the relevant document was published, the applicant shall be given an opportunity to be heard in the matter if he so requests.

(4) Whether or not the applicant has re-filed his specification, the Comptroller may appoint a hearing if he considers it desirable to do so, having regard to the time remaining for putting the application in order or other circumstances of the case.

(5) When a hearing is appointed, the applicant shall be given at least ten days' notice of the appointment or such shorter notice as appears to the Comptroller to be reasonable in the circumstances and shall as soon as possible notify the Comptroller whether he will attend the hearing.

(6) After hearing the applicant, or without a hearing if the applicant has not attended or has notified that he does not desire to be heard, the Comptroller may prescribe or permit such amendment of the specification as will be to his satisfaction and may refuse to accept the specification unless the amendment is made within such period as he may fix.

28.—(1) When the Examiner reports that the invention so far as claimed in any claim of the complete specification is claimed in any claim of any other complete specification falling within section 8 (1) or 8 (3), the applicant shall be so informed and shall be afforded an opportunity of amending, or submitting amendments of, his specification.

(2) If, when the applicant's specification is otherwise in order for acceptance, an objection under section 8 is outstanding, the Comptroller may accept the specification and allow a period of two months from the date of its publication for removing the objection.

(3) If an objection under section 8 is communicated to the applicant after acceptance of the specification, a period of two months from the date of the communication shall be allowed for removing the objection.

29.—(1) If the applicant so requests at any time, or if the Examiner is not satisfied that the objection has been met within the period prescribed by Rule 28, including any extension thereof which the Comptroller may allow, a time for hearing the applicant shall be appointed and the applicant shall be given at least ten days' notice of the appointment and shall, as soon as possible, notify the Comptroller whether he will attend the hearing.

(2) After hearing the applicant, or without a hearing if the applicant has not attended or has notified that he does not desire to be heard, the Comptroller may prescribe or permit such amendment of the specification as will be to his satisfaction and may direct that a reference to such other specification as he shall mention shall be inserted in the applicant's specification unless the amendment is made or agreed to within such period as he may fix.

30. The periods mentioned in Rules 28 and 29 may be extended if a request for such extension is made on Patents Form No. 7 at any time within the extended period specified in the request, provided that the total extension of either period allowed under this provision shall not exceed six months.

31. When, in pursuance of Rule 29, the Comptroller directs that reference to another specification shall be inserted in the applicant's complete specification, the reference shall be inserted after the claims and shall be in the following form :—

"Reference has been directed, in pursuance of section 8 of the Patents Act 1949, to specification No.   ".

32. An application under the proviso to section 79 (2), for disclosure of the result of a search made under sections 7 and 8, shall be made on Patents Form No. 8.

33. When in making the investigations under sections 7 and 8 it appears to the Examiner that the applicant's invention cannot be performed without substantial risk of infringement of a claim of another patent, the applicant shall be so informed and the procedure provided in Rules 28 to 30 shall apply.

34. When, pursuant to such procedure, the Comptroller directs that reference to a patent shall be inserted in the applicant's complete specification, the reference shall be inserted after the claims and shall be in the following form :—

"Reference has been directed in pursuance of section 9, subsection (1) of the Patents Act 1949, to patent No.   ".

35. An application under section 9 (2) for the deletion of a reference inserted pursuant to a direction under section 9 (1) shall be made on Patents Form No. 9, and shall state fully the facts relied upon in support of the application.

36. In the application of Rules 28 to 31, 33 and 34 to proceedings subsequent to the grant of the patent, references to the patentee shall be substituted for references to the applicant.

Putting Applications in order and acceptance of complete specifications (Sections 12 and 13)

37.—(1) There is hereby prescribed for the purposes of section 12(1) as the period within which an application for the grant of a patent is to be put in order for acceptance—

(a) in the case of an application for the grant of a patent filed before 1st January 1962, a period of three years and six months ;

(b) in the case of an application for the grant of a patent filed on or after that date but before 1st January 1964, a period of three years ;

(c) in the case of an application for the grant of a patent filed on or after 1st January 1964, a period of two years and six months.

(2) Where an application for the grant of a patent is post-dated under any of the provisions of the Act, it shall nevertheless be treated for the purpose of determining the relevant period prescribed for the purposes of section 12(1) as if it had not been so post-dated.

(3) A notice under section 12 (2) requesting an extension of the period allowable under section 12 (1) for putting an application in order shall be given on Patents Form No. 10.

(4) A notice under the proviso to section 13 (1) requesting postponement of the acceptance of a complete specification to a date later than twelve months from the date of its filing, shall be given on Patents Form No. 11.

38.—(1) After the date of the publication of a complete specification the application and specification as accepted together with the drawings and documents (if any) filed in pursuance of Rule 15 may be inspected at the Office upon payment of a fee prescribed by these Rules.

(2) The documents (if any) filed in pursuance of Rule 15 or photographic copies thereof may be made available for inspection without fee.

Opposition to grant of patent (Section 14)

39.—(1) A notice of opposition to the grant of a patent

(a) shall be given on Patents Form No. 12,

(b) shall state the ground or grounds on which the opponent intends to oppose the grant, and

(c) shall be accompanied by a copy thereof and shall be supported by a statement (in duplicate) setting out fully the nature of the opponent's interest, the facts upon which he relies and the relief which he seeks.

(2) A copy of the notice and of the statement shall be sent by the Comptroller to the applicant.

40. If the applicant desires to proceed with his application, he shall, within three months of the receipt of such copies, file a counterstatement setting out fully the grounds upon which the opposition is contested and deliver to the opponent a copy thereof.

41. The opponent may within three months from the receipt of the copy of the counterstatement file evidence in support of his case and shall deliver to the applicant a copy of the evidence.

42. Within three months from the receipt of the copy of the opponent's evidence or, if the opponent does not file any evidence, within three months from the expiration of the time within which the opponent's evidence might have been filed, the applicant may file evidence in support of his case and shall deliver to the opponent a copy of the evidence ; and within three months from the receipt of the copy of the applicant's evidence the opponent may file evidence confined to matters strictly in reply and shall deliver to the applicant a copy of the evidence.

43. No further evidence shall be filed by either party except by leave or direction of the Comptroller.

44.—(1) Copies of all documents, other than printed United Kingdom specifications, referred to in the notice of opposition or in any statement or evidence filed in connection with the opposition, authenticated to the satisfaction of the Comptroller, shall be furnished (in duplicate) for the Comptroller's use unless he otherwise directs. Such copies shall accompany the notice, statement or evidence in which they are referred to.

(2) Where a specification or other document in a foreign language is referred to, a translation thereof, verified by statutory declaration or otherwise to the satisfaction of the Comptroller, and one additional copy of the translation, shall also be furnished.

45.—(1) On completion of the evidence (if any), or at such other time as he may see fit, the Comptroller shall appoint a time for the hearing of the case, and shall give the parties at least fourteen days' notice of the appointment.

(2) If either party desires to be heard he shall notify the Comptroller on Patents Form No. 13 and the Comptroller may refuse to hear either party who has not filed the said form prior to the date of hearing.

(3) If either party intends to refer at the hearing to any publication not already mentioned in the proceedings, he shall give to the other party and to the Comptroller at least ten days' notice of his intention, together with details of each publication to which he intends to refer.

(4) After hearing the party or parties desiring to be heard or, if neither party desires to be heard, then without a hearing, the Comptroller shall decide the case and notify his decision to the parties giving reasons for his decision if so required by any party.

46. If in consequence of the proceedings the Comptroller directs that a reference to another patent shall be inserted in the applicant's specification under section 9 (1), the reference shall be as prescribed by Rule 34.

47. If the applicant notifies the Comptroller that he does not desire to proceed with the application, the Comptroller, in deciding whether costs should be awarded to the opponent, shall consider whether proceedings might have been avoided if the opponent had given reasonable notice to the applicant before the opposition was filed.

Procedure under Section 15

48. If at any time after the acceptance of a complete specification and before the grant of the patent it comes to the notice of the Comptroller, otherwise than in consequence of proceedings in opposition to the grant, that the invention so far as claimed in any claim of the complete specification has been published in any specification or other document falling within section 15 (1), the applicant shall be so informed and shall be allowed a period of two months within which to submit such amendment of his specification as will be to the Comptroller's satisfaction.

49.—(1) If the specification has not been amended to the Comptroller's satisfaction within the period allowed under Rule 48, including any extension thereof which the Comptroller may allow, a time for hearing the applicant shall be appointed, and the applicant shall be given at least ten days' notice of the appointment, and shall, as soon as possible, notify the Comptroller whether he will attend the hearing.

(2) After hearing the applicant, or without a hearing if the applicant has not attended or has notified that he does not desire to be heard, the Comptroller may prescribe or permit such amendment of the specification as will be to his satisfaction and may refuse to grant a patent unless the amendment is made or agreed to within such period as he may fix.

50. The periods mentioned in Rules 48 and 49 may be extended if a request for such extension is made on Patents Form No. 7 at any time within the extended period specified in the request, provided that the total extension of either period allowed under this provision shall not exceed six months.

Mention of inventor as such (Section 16)

51. A request by the applicant for a patent, or, if the actual deviser of the invention or of a substantial part thereof is not the applicant or one of the applicants, by the applicant and the said deviser, under section 16 (3) shall be made on Patents Form No. 14 and shall be accompanied by a statement setting out fully the facts relied upon.

52.—(1) A claim under section 16 (4) shall be made on Patents Form No. 15 and shall be accompanied by a statement setting out fully the facts relied upon.

(2) A copy of the claim and of the statement shall be sent by the Comptroller to every applicant for the patent (not being the claimant) and to any other person whom the Comptroller may consider to be interested and the claimant shall supply a sufficient number of copies for that purpose.

(3) The Comptroller may give such directions (if any) as he may think fit with regard to the subsequent procedure.

53. An application under section 16 (5) for an extension of the period for making a request or claim shall be made on Patents Form No. 16.

54.—(1) An application under section 16 (8) for a certificate shall be made on Patents Form No. 17 and shall be accompanied by a statement setting out fully the facts relied upon.

(2) A copy of the application and of the statement shall be sent by the Comptroller to each patentee (not being the applicant), to the person mentioned as the actual deviser, and to any other person whom the Comptroller may consider to be interested and the applicant shall supply a sufficient number of copies for that purpose.

(3) The Comptroller may give such directions (if any) as he may think fit with regard to the subsequent procedure.

55. Any mention of an actual deviser as inventor under section 16 (1) may be made in the patent after the name of the Comptroller, and on the complete specification at the head of Patents Form No. 3, and may be in the form "The inventor of this invention in the sense of being the actual deviser thereof within the meaning of section 16 of the Patents Act, 1949, is   of   ", or "The inventor of a substantial part of this invention in the sense of being the actual deviser thereof within the meaning of section 16 of the Patents Act, 1949, is of   ", as the case may require.

Procedure under Section 17

56.—(1) A claim under section 17 (1) that an application for a patent shall proceed in the name of the claimant or in the names of the claimant and the applicant or the other joint applicant or applicants shall be made on Patents Form No. 18 and shall be accompanied by a certified copy of any assignment or agreement upon which the claim is based.

(2) The original assignment or agreement shall also be produced for the Comptroller's inspection, and the Comptroller may call for such other proof of title or written consent as he may require.

57.—(1) An application under section 17 (5) by a joint applicant for the directions of the Comptroller as to the names or manner in which an application for a patent shall be proceeded with shall be made on Patents Form No. 19 and shall be accompanied by a statement setting out fully the facts upon which the applicant relies and the directions which he seeks.

(2) A copy of the application and statement shall be sent by the Comptroller to each other joint applicant and the person making the application under section 17 (5) shall supply a sufficient number of copies for that purpose.

(3) The Comptroller may give such directions as he may think fit with regard to the subsequent procedure.

Sealing and form of patent

58. A request for the sealing of a patent on an application shall be made on Patents Form No. 20.

59. The period within which a request for the sealing of a patent may be made under proviso (*a*) to section 19 (2) shall be two months from the final determination of the proceedings.

60.—(1) An application under section 19 (3) for the extension of the period for making a request for the sealing of a patent shall be made on Patents Form No. 21.

(2) Such extension shall not be more than three months.

61.—(1) An application under section 19 (4) for extension of the period for making a request for the sealing of a patent shall be made on Patents Form No. 22.

(2) Such extension shall not be more than six months on any one application under the subsection.

62. A patent shall be in the Form A or Form B (whichever is applicable) set out in Schedule 4 to these Rules, or such modification of either of these forms as the Comptroller directs.

Amendment of patent (*Section* 20)

63. An application under section 20 for the amendment of a patent shall be made on Patents Form No. 23 and shall be accompanied by evidence verifying the statements therein and by the Letters Patent.

Renewal fees (*Section* 22)

64. If it is desired, at the expiration of the fourth year from the date of a patent or of any succeeding year during the term of the patent, to keep the patent in force, Patents Form No. 24 accompanied by the prescribed renewal fee shall be filed before the expiration of that year ; Provided that, where a patent is sealed after the expiration of the fourth or any succeeding year, except in cases mentioned in Rule 69, Patents Form No. 24 in respect of the fifth and any succeeding year, may be filed at any time before the expiration of three months from the date of sealing the patent.

65. All or any of the prescribed annual renewal fees may be paid in advance.

66. A request for extension of the period for payment of any renewal fee shall be made on Patents Form No. 25.

67. On due compliance with the terms of Rule 64 the Comptroller shall issue a Certificate on Patents Form No. 26 that the prescribed fee has been duly paid.

68. At any time not less than one month before the date when any renewal fee will become due in respect of any patent, the Comptroller shall send to the patentee or patentees at his or their address or addresses for service, and to the address of the person or persons who paid the last renewal fee, a notice reminding him or them of the date when such fee will become due, and of the consequences of the non-payment thereof.

69. Where directions given by the Comptroller under section 18 (1) of the Act or under section 12 of the Atomic Energy Act 1946(**a**), prohibiting the publication of information with respect to an invention forming the subject of an application for a patent have been revoked and a patent is granted on the application, no renewal fees shall be payable in respect of any year which commenced in the period during which directions were in force.

Extension of term of patent (*Sections* 24 *and* 25)

70.—(1) An application to the Comptroller under section 24 or 25 for an Order extending the term of a patent shall be made on Patents Form No. 27.

(2) The application shall state the period of the extension which is sought and shall be supported by evidence setting out fully the facts relied upon, such evidence being filed either with the application or at any time within one month from the date thereof.

71. When an application is formally in order the Comptroller shall advertise it in two issues of the Journal and the applicant shall notify registered licensees and, in the case of an application under section 25, the patentee, of the advertisement.

72.—(1) At any time within two months from the date of the first advertisement of the application in the Journal any person may give notice of opposition.

(2) Such notice shall be on Patents Form No. 28, shall be accompanied by a copy thereof and shall be supported by a statement (in duplicate) setting out fully the nature of the opponent's interest, the grounds of opposition, and the relief which he seeks and evidence (in duplicate) of the facts upon which he relies.

(3) A copy of the notice, the statement and the evidence shall be sent by the Comptroller to the applicant, who, within three months from the receipt thereof, may file evidence confined to matters strictly in reply and shall deliver to the opponent a copy of the evidence.

73.—(1) An opponent shall be entitled on request made to the applicant within one month of the giving of the notice of opposition, to be supplied, at his own expense, by the applicant with a copy of the application and of the evidence filed in support.

(2) Within three months of the receipt of the copy of the evidence filed in support of the application, the opponent may file additional evidence and

---

(**a**) 1946 c. 80.

shall deliver to the applicant a copy of such evidence and, within three months of the receipt of the copy of the opponent's additional evidence, the applicant may file further evidence confined to matters strictly in reply and shall deliver to the opponent a copy of such evidence.

74. No further evidence shall be filed by either party except by leave or direction of the Comptroller.

75.—(1) On completion of the evidence or at such other time as he may see fit, the Comptroller shall appoint a time for the hearing of the case, and shall give the parties at least fourteen days' notice of the appointment.

(2) If either party desires to be heard he shall notify the Comptroller on Patents Form No. 13 and the Comptroller may refuse to hear either party who has not filed the said form prior to the date of the hearing.

(3) After hearing the party or parties desiring to be heard or, if neither party desires to be heard, then without a hearing, the Comptroller shall decide the case and notify his decision to the parties.

76. If no notice of opposition to the application is given the Comptroller shall, on the expiration of the period prescribed by Rule 72 (1), after hearing the applicant if desiring to be heard, decide the case and notify his decision to the applicant.

77. If at any stage of the application the Comptroller decides to refer the application for decision by the Court he shall notify the applicant and any opponent accordingly.

Restoration of lapsed patents and lapsed applications for patents (Sections 27 and 28)

78. An application under section 27 for restoration of a patent shall be made on Patents Form No. 29 and shall be accompanied by evidence in support of the statements made in the application.

79.—(1) If, upon consideration of the evidence, the Comptroller is not satisfied that a prima facie case for an order under section 27 has been made out, he shall notify the applicant accordingly and, unless within one month the applicant requests to be heard in the matter, the Comptroller shall refuse the application.

(2) If the applicant requests a hearing within the time allowed, the Comptroller after giving the applicant an opportunity of being heard shall determine whether the application may proceed to advertisement or whether it shall be refused.

80.—(1) At any time within two months of the advertisement of the application under section 27 (4), any person may give notice of opposition thereto on Patents Form No. 30.

(2) Such notice shall be accompanied by a copy thereof and shall be supported by a statement (in duplicate), setting out fully the nature of the opponent's interest and the facts upon which he relies.

(3) A copy of the notice and of the statement shall be sent by the Comptroller to the applicant.

81. Upon notice of opposition being given the provisions of Rules 40 to 45 shall apply.

82. If the Comptroller decides in favour of the applicant, he shall notify him accordingly, and require him to file Patents Form No. 31 together with

Patents Form No. 24 accompanied by fees to the amount of the unpaid renewal fees.

83. In every order of the Comptroller restoring a patent the following provision shall be inserted for the protection of persons who have begun to avail themselves of the patented invention between the date when the patent ceased to have effect and the date of the application :—

"(1) No action or other proceeding shall be commenced or prosecuted nor any damage recovered in respect of any manufacture, use, or sale of the invention the subject of the patent in the interim period as hereinafter defined by any person not being a licensee under the patent at the date when it ceased to have effect, the   , who after such date and before the   , the date of the application, has made, used, exercised or sold the invention the subject of the patent or has manufactured or installed any plant, machinery or apparatus claimed in the specification of the patent or for carrying out a method or process so claimed. Any such person shall be deemed to have so acted with the licence of the patentee and shall thereafter be entitled to continue to make, use, exercise or sell the invention without infringement of the patent to the extent hereinafter specified that is to say :—

(a) In so far as the complete specification of the patent claims an article (other than plant, machinery or apparatus or part thereof as specified under head (b) hereof) and any article so claimed has been manufactured by him during the said interim period, that particular article may at all times be used or sold.

(b) In so far as the complete specification claims any plant, machinery or apparatus or part thereof for the production of an article, then any particular plant, machinery or apparatus or part thereof so claimed, which has been manufactured or installed by him during the said interim period, and the products thereof, may at all times be used or sold and so that in the event of any such plant, machinery apparatus or part thereof being impaired by wear or tear or accidentally destroyed, a like licence shall extend to any replacement thereof and to the products of such replacement.

(c) In so far as the complete specification claims any process for the making or treating of any article or any method or process of testing, any particular plant, machinery or apparatus which during the said interim period has been manufactured or installed by him or exclusively or mainly used by him for carrying on such method or process may at all times be so used or continued to be so used and the products thereof may at all times be used or sold and so that in the event of any such plant, machinery or apparatus being impaired by wear or tear or accidentally destroyed a like licence shall extend to such method or process when carried on in any replacement of such plant, machinery or apparatus and to the products of the process so carried on.

(2) In the foregoing paragraph, "article" has the same meaning as in section 101 of the Patents Act 1949 and "the interim period" means the period between the date when the patent ceased to have effect and the date of this Order".

84. An application under section 28 for the sealing of a patent shall be made on Patents Form No. 32 and shall be accompanied by evidence in support of the statements made in the application.

85.—(1) If, upon consideration of the evidence, the Comptroller is not satisfied that a prima facie case for an order under section 28 has been made out he shall notify the applicant accordingly and unless within one month from that notification the applicant requests to be heard in the matter, the Comptroller shall refuse the application.

(2) If the applicant requests a hearing within the time allowed, the Comptroller, after giving the applicant an opportunity of being heard, shall determine whether the application may proceed to advertisement or whether it shall be refused.

86.—(1) At any time within two months of the advertisement of an application under section 28 (3) any person may give notice of opposition thereto on Patents Form No. 33.

(2) Such notice shall be accompanied by a copy thereof and shall be supported by a statement (in duplicate), setting out fully the nature of the opponent's interest and the facts upon which he relies.

(3) A copy of the notice and statement shall be sent by the Comptroller to the applicant.

87. Upon notice of opposition being given the provisions of Rules 40 to 45 shall apply.

88. If the Comptroller decides in favour of the applicant, he shall notify the applicant accordingy and require him to file Patents Form No. 34 together with Patents Form No. 20.

89. In every order of the Comptroller under section 28 for the sealing of a patent the same provision shall be inserted for the protection of persons who have begun to avail themselves of the invention between the date when the time allowed by or under section 19 for making the prescribed request for sealing expired, and the date of the application for an order for sealing, as are specified in Rule 83 for the protection of persons who have begun to avail themselves of a patented invention between the date when the patent ceased to have effect and the date of the application for restoration, there being substituted for references to the date when the patent ceased to have effect references to the date when the time allowed by or under section 19 for making the request for sealing expired.

Amendment of specification or application for patent

90. An application to the Comptroller for leave to amend an accepted complete specification under section 29 shall be made on Patents Form No. 35, and, subject to the proviso to section 29 (3), shall be advertised by publication of the application and the nature of the proposed amendment in the Journal, and in such other manner, if any, as the Comptroller may in each case direct.

91.—(1) Any person wishing to oppose the application shall, within one month from the date of the advertisement in the Journal, or such further period not exceeding three months from the said date as the Comptroller may in special cases allow, give notice to the Comptroller on Patents Form No. 36.

(2) Such notice shall be accompanied by a copy thereof and shall be supported by a statement (in duplicate) setting out fully the nature of the opponent's interest, the facts upon which he relies and the relief which he seeks. A copy of the notice and of the statement shall be sent by the Comptroller to the applicant.

92. Upon such notice of opposition being given and a copy thereof sent to the applicant the provisions of Rules 40 to 45 shall apply.

93. Unless the Comptroller otherwise directs, an application or proposal for amendment of an accepted complete specification shall be accompanied by a copy of the printed specification and drawings clearly showing in red ink the amendment sought.

94.—(1) An application for leave to amend a complete specification which has not been accepted, except when the amendment is made to meet an objection contained in an Examiner's report, shall be made on Patents Form No. 37.

(2) An application for leave to convert an application for a patent to a Convention application may be made at any time within twelve months from the date of the first application for protection in a Convention country and shall be made on Patents Form No. 38 Con.

(3) Any other application for leave to amend an application for a patent shall be made on Patents Form No. 38.

95. Where leave to amend a specification is given the applicant shall, if the Comptroller so requires, and within a time to be fixed by him, file a new specification and drawings as amended, which shall be prepared in accordance with Rules 5 and 18 to 23.

Application for the revocation of a patent
96.—(1) An application for the revocation of a patent shall :—
(a) be made on Patents Form No. 39,
(b) state the ground or grounds for the application, and
(c) be accompanied by a copy thereof and
shall be supported by a statement (in duplicate) setting out fully the nature of the applicant's interests, the facts upon which he relies, and the relief which he seeks.
(2) A copy of the application and of the statement shall be sent by the Comptroller to the patentee.

97. Upon such application being made and a copy thereof sent to the patentee the provisions of Rules 40 to 46 shall apply with such consequential adaptations as the case requires and in particular with the substitution of references to the patentee for references to the applicant and of references to the applicant for references to the opponent.

98. If the patentee offers under section 34 to surrender his patent, the Comptroller, in deciding whether costs should be awarded to the applicant for revocation, shall consider whether proceedings might have been avoided if the applicant had given reasonable notice to the patentee before the application was filed.

99. A notice of an offer by a patentee under section 34 to surrender his patent shall be given on Patents Form No. 40, and shall be advertised by the Comptroller in the Journal.

100.—(1) At any time within one month from the advertisement any person may give notice of opposition to the Comptroller on Patents Form No. 41, which shall be accompanied by a copy thereof and shall be supported by a statement (in duplicate) setting out fully the nature of the opponent's interest, the facts upon which he relies, and the relief which he seeks.

(2) A copy of the notice and of the statement shall be sent by the Comptroller to the patentee.

101. Upon such notice of opposition being given and a copy thereof sent to the patentee, the provisions of Rules 40 to 45 shall apply with the substitution of references to the patentee for references to the applicant.

Voluntary endorsement of patents "Licences of Right" (Sections 35 and 36)

102. An application under section 35 (1) for endorsement of a patent "Licences of Right" shall be made on Patents Form No. 42, and shall be accompanied by evidence verifying the statement in the application, and by the Letters Patent.

103. (1) An application under section 35 (2) (*a*) or section 35 (2) (*b*) for settlement of the terms of a licence under a patent endorsed "Licences of Right" shall be made on Patents Form No. 43, and shall be accompanied by a copy thereof and a statement (in duplicate) setting out fully the facts upon which the applicant relies, and the terms of the licence which he is prepared to accept or grant.

(2) A copy of the application and statement shall be sent by the Comptroller to the patentee or the person requiring a licence, as the case may be, who, if he does not agree to the terms set out in the statement, shall, within six weeks of the receipt of such copies, file a counterstatement setting out fully the grounds of his objection and send a copy thereof to the applicant.

(3) The Comptroller shall give such directions as he may think fit with regard to the filing of evidence and the hearing of the parties.

104. An application under section 36 (1) for the cancellation of an endorsement shall be made on Patents Form No. 44, and shall be accompanied by evidence verifying the statement in the application, and by Patents Form No. 24 accompanied by fees to the amount of the balance of all renewal fees which would have been payable if the patent had not been endorsed.

105. An application under section 36 (2) for the cancellation of an endorsement shall be made on Patents Form No. 45 within two months after the patent has been endorsed and shall be accompanied by a copy and a statement (in duplicate) setting out fully the nature of the applicant's interest, and the facts upon which he relies.

106.—(1) Every application under section 36 (1) or 36 (2) shall be advertised in the Journal, and the period within which notice of opposition to the cancellation of an endorsement may be given under section 36 (5) shall be one month after the advertisement.

(2) Such notice shall be given on Patents Form No. 46 and shall be accompanied by a copy thereof, and shall be supported by a statement (in duplicate) setting out fully the facts upon which the opponent relies and, in the case of opposition to an application under section 36 (1), the nature of his interest.

107.—(1) A copy of the notice and of the statement shall be sent by the Comptroller to the applicant for cancellation of the endorsement and thereafter Rules 40 to 45 shall apply.

(2) Where the Comptroller cancels the endorsement pursuant to section 36 (3), the patentee shall, within one month from the cancellation of the endorsement, file Patents Form No. 24 accompanied by fees to the amount of the balance of all renewal fees which would have been payable if the patent had not been endorsed.

Compulsory licence, compulsory endorsement of patent "Licences of Right" and revocation (Sections 37 to 45)

108. An application under section 37 for a licence under a patent or for endorsement of a patent "Licences of Right" shall be made on Patents Form No. 47.

109. An application under section 40 (1) for the endorsement of a patent "Licences of Right" or for the grant of a licence under a patent to a specified person shall be made on Patents Form No. 48.

110. An application under section 40 (3) for an Order of the Comptroller under section 40 (4) shall be made on Patents Form No. 49.

111. An application under section 42 for the revocation of a patent shall be made on Patents Form No. 50.

112. An application under section 37, section 40 or section 42 shall be accompanied by evidence verifying the statements in the application.

113.—(1) If upon consideration of the evidence the Comptroller is not satisfied that a prima facie case has been made out for the making of an order, he shall notify the applicant accordingly, and unless within one month the applicant requests to be heard in the matter the Comptroller shall refuse the application.

(2) If the applicant requests a hearing within the time allowed, the Comptroller, after giving the applicant an opportunity of being heard, shall determine whether the application may proceed to advertisement or whether it shall be refused.

114.—(1) If the Comptroller allows the application to proceed to advertisement, he shall direct the applicant to serve copies of the application and of the evidence filed in support thereof upon the patentee and any other persons appearing from the register to be interested in the patent and upon any other person on whom, in his opinion, copies should be so served.

(2) The time within which notice of opposition under section 43 (3) may be given shall be two months after the advertisement of the application under section 43 (2).

(3) Such notice shall be given on Patents Form No. 51, accompanied by a copy thereof, and shall be supported by evidence (in duplicate) verifying the statements made therein.

(4) The Comptroller shall send a copy of the notice and the evidence to the applicant and thereafter the provisions of Rule 42 (so far as they are applicable) and of Rules 43 to 45 shall apply.

115.—(1) An application under section 41 for a licence under a patent shall be made on Patents Form No. 52.

(2) The procedure to be followed in connection with such application shall be the same as that prescribed in Rules 112 to 114 for an application under section 37.

Directions to co-owners (*Section* 55)

116.—(1) An application for directions under section 55 (1) by a co-grantee or co-proprietor of a patent shall be made on Patents Form No. 53 and shall be accompanied by a statement setting out fully the facts upon which the applicant relies and the directions which he seeks.

(2) A copy of the application and of the statement shall be sent by the Comptroller to each other person registered as grantee or proprietor of the patent and the applicant shall supply a sufficient number of copies for that purpose.

(3) Thereafter the Comptroller may give such directions as he may think fit with regard to the subsequent procedure.

117.—(1) An application for directions under section 55 (2) by a co-grantee or co-proprietor of a patent shall be made on Patents Form No. 54, and shall be accompanied by a copy thereof, and a statement (in duplicate) setting out fully the facts upon which the applicant relies and the directions which he seeks.

(2) A copy of the application and of the statement shall be sent by the Comptroller to the person in default.

(3) Thereafter the Comptroller may give such directions as he may think fit with regard to the subsequent procedure.

Disputes as to inventions made by employees (Section 56)

118.—(1) An application under section 56 (1) to determine a dispute as to rights in an invention shall be made on Patents Form No. 55 and shall be accompanied by a copy thereof, together with a statement (in duplicate) setting out fully the facts of the dispute and the relief which is sought.

(2) A copy of the application and of the statement shall be sent by the Comptroller to the other party to the dispute, who, within three months after receipt thereof, shall file a counterstatement (in duplicate) setting out fully the grounds on which he disputes the right of the applicant to the relief sought.

(3) The Comptroller shall send a copy of this counterstatement to the applicant and thereafter, subject to such directions as the Comptroller may think fit to give, the provisions of Rules 41 to 45 shall apply with the substitution of references to the applicant for references to the opponent and references to the other party for references to the applicant.

Reference to Comptroller of disputes as to infringement (Section 67)

119. Where the parties to a dispute of the kind specified in section 67 (1) agree to refer the dispute to the Comptroller they shall give notice to him on Patents Form No. 56 giving full particulars of the matters which are in dispute, and of the matters on which the parties are in agreement.

120.—(1) The procedure set out in this Rule shall apply unless the only matter stated in the notice to be in dispute is the validity of any claim of the specification of the patent alleged to be infringed.

(2) The patentee or exclusive licensee (referred to in this and the next following Rule as the plaintiff), shall with such notice or within one month thereafter, file a statement (in duplicate) giving full particulars of his case on the matters in dispute.

(3) A copy of the plaintiff's statement shall be sent by the Comptroller to the other party to the dispute (referred to in this and the next following Rule as the defendant), who shall, within one month after receipt thereof, file a counterstatement setting out fully the grounds on which he contests the plaintiff's case and shall deliver to the plaintiff a copy thereof.

(4) If the defendant alleges in his counterstatement that any claim of the specification alleged by the plaintiff to have been infringed is not valid, the plaintiff, within one month after receipt of the copy of the counterstatement, shall file a further statement setting out fully the grounds on which he contests the defendant's allegation, and shall deliver to the defendant a copy thereof.

(5) The Comptroller may at any time require the statements to be amplified or amended to his satisfaction.

(6) Subject to such directions as the Comptroller may think fit to give the plaintiff may, within six weeks of filing his further statement, file evidence in support of his case, and shall deliver to the defendant a copy thereof, and thereafter the provisions of Rules 42 to 45 shall apply with the substitution of references to the plaintiff for references to the opponent and references to the defendant for references to the applicant.

121.—(1) The procedure set out in this Rule shall apply if the only matter stated in the notice to be in dispute is the validity of any claim of the specification alleged to be infringed.

(2) The defendant shall, with the notice, or within one month thereafter, file a statement (in duplicate) giving full particulars of the ground on which he alleges that the claim is invalid.

(3) A copy of the defendant's statement shall be sent by the Comptroller to the plaintiff, who shall, within one month after the receipt thereof, file a counterstatement giving full particulars of the grounds on which he contests the defendant's allegations, and shall deliver to the defendant a copy thereof.

(4) The Comptroller may at any time require the statements to be amplified or amended to his satisfaction.

(5) Subject to such directions as the Comptroller may think fit to give the defendant may within six weeks after the receipt of the copy of the plaintiff's counterstatement, file evidence in support of his case, and shall deliver to the plaintiff a copy thereof, and thereafter the provisions of Rules 42 to 45 shall apply with the substitution of references to the defendant for references to the opponent and references to the plaintiff for references to the applicant.

122. If the Comptroller decides that relief shall be granted, he may require the parties to supply him with such information or evidence as he considers to be necessary to assist him in assessing the amount of the damages.

Register of Patents (*Sections* 73 *and* 74)

123.—(1) Upon the sealing of a patent the Comptroller shall cause to be entered in the register the name, address, and nationality of the grantee as the patentee thereof, the title of the invention, the date of the patent, and the date of the sealing thereof, together with the address for service.

(2) The Comptroller may at any time enter in the register such other particulars as he may deem necessary.

124.—(1) A request by a patentee for the alteration of a name, nationality or address or address for service entered in the register in respect of his patent shall be made on Patents Form No. 57.

(2) Before acting on a request to alter a name or nationality, the Comptroller may require such proof of the alteration as he may think fit.

(3) If the Comptroller is satisfied that the request may be allowed, he shall cause the register to be altered accordingly.

125.—(1) An application for the registration of the title of any person becoming entitled by assignment, transmission or operation of law to a patent or to a share in a patent, or becoming entitled by virtue of a mortgage, licence or other instrument to any other interest in a patent, shall be made

    (a) in the case of an application under section 74 (1), by the person becoming so entitled on Patents Form No. 58 or Patents Form No. 59, and

    (b) in the case of an application under section 74 (2), by the assignor, mortgagor, licensor, or other party conferring the interest, on Patents Form No. 60 or Patents Form No. 61, as the case may be.

(2) Application may be made on Patents Form No. 62 for entry in the register of notification of any other document purporting to affect the proprietorship of a patent.

126.—(1) An official or certified copy of a document which is referred to in an application under Rule 125 and is a matter of record in the United Kingdom shall be produced to the Comptroller with the application.

(2) Unless the Comptroller otherwise directs, the original of any other document so referred to shall be produced to him with the application and a certified copy of any such document shall be filed.

127. Upon the issue of a certificate of payment under Rule 67, the Comptroller shall enter in the register the fact that the fee has been paid, and the date of payment as stated on the certificate.

128. Where an Order for the extension of the term of a patent under sections 23 or 24 or 25 contains a provision that persons claiming to be deemed to have acted with the licence of the patentee or exclusive licensee shall make application for entry of their claim upon the register, the application shall be made on Patents Form No. 63.

Correction of clerical errors (Section 76)

129. A request for the correction of a clerical error in an application for a patent or in any document filed in pursuance of such an application or in any patent or in the register, shall be made on Patents Form No. 64.

130. Where the Comptroller requires notice of the nature of the proposed correction to be advertised, the advertisement shall be made by publication of the request and the nature of the proposed correction in the Journal, and in such other manner (if any) as the Comptroller may direct.

131.—(1) Any person may, at any time within one month from the date of the advertisement in the Journal, give notice to the Comptroller of opposition to the proposed correction on Patents Form No. 65.

(2) Such notice shall be accompanied by a copy thereof and shall be supported by a statement (in duplicate) setting out fully the nature of the opponent's interest, the facts on which he relies, and the relief which he seeks.

(3) A copy of the notice and of the statement shall be sent by the Comptroller to the person making the request, and thereafter the provisions of Rules 40 to 45 shall apply.

132. Where, in accordance with section 76 (3), a hearing is appointed, at least fourteen days' notice of the appointment shall be given to the patentee or the applicant for a patent and to any other person to whom notice of the proposed correction has been given by the Comptroller.

Certificates and information

133. A request for a certificate of the Comptroller for the purposes of section 77 (1) shall be made on Patents Form No. 66.

134. Certified copies of any entry in the register, or certified copies of, or extracts from, patents, specifications, and other public documents in the Office, or of or from registers and other records kept there, may be furnished by the Comptroller on payment of the fees prescribed in Schedule 1 to these Rules.

135.—(1) A request under section 78 for information relating to any patent or application for a patent may be made

(a) as to when a complete specification following a provisional specification has been filed or when a period of fifteen months from the date of the application has expired and a complete specification has not been filed,

(b) as to when a complete specification is or will be published, or when an application for a patent has become void,

(c) as to when a patent has been sealed or when the time for requesting sealing has expired,

(d) as to when a renewal fee has been paid,

(e) as to when a patent has expired,

(f) as to when an entry has been made in the register or application has been made for the making of such entry, or

(g) as to when any application is made or action taken involving an entry in the register or advertisement in the Journal if the nature of the application or action is specified in the request,

(h) as to when any document filed in proceedings after acceptance of the complete specification may be inspected in accordance with the provisions of Rule 146.

(2) Any such request shall be made on Patents Form No. 67 and a separate form shall be used in respect of each item of information required.

Duplicate patent

136. An application under section 80 for a duplicate of a patent shall be made on Patents Form No. 68 and shall be accompanied by evidence setting out fully and verifying the circumstances in which the patent was lost or destroyed, or cannot be produced.

Evidence before Comptroller

137. Where under these Rules evidence is required to be filed it shall be by statutory declaration or affidavit unless otherwise expressly provided in these Rules.

138.—(1) The statutory declarations and affidavits required by these Rules, or used in any proceedings thereunder, shall be headed in the matter or matters to which they relate, and shall be divided into paragraphs consecutively numbered, and each paragraph shall so far as possible be confined to one subject.

(2) Every statutory declaration or affidavit shall state the description and true place of abode of the person making the same, and shall be written, typed, lithographed or printed.

139. The statutory declarations and affidavits shall be made and subscribed as follows—

(a) In the United Kingdom, before any justice of the peace, or any commissioner or other officer authorised by law in any part of the United Kingdom to administer an oath for the purpose of any legal proceedings ;

(b) In any other part of Her Majesty's dominions, or in any British protectorate or protected state or in any mandated territory as defined in the British Nationality Act 1948(a), or in any trust territory as so defined or in the Republic of Ireland, before any court, judge, justice of the peace, or any officer authorised by law to administer an oath there for the purpose of any legal proceedings ; and

(c) Elsewhere, before a British Minister, or person exercising the functions of a British Minister, or a Consul, Vice-Consul, or other person exercising the functions of a British Consul, or before a notary public, or before a judge or magistrate.

140. Any document purporting to have affixed, impressed or subscribed thereto or thereon the seal or signature of any person authorised by the last foregoing Rule to take a declaration, in testimony that the declaration was made and subscribed before him, may be admitted by the Comptroller without proof of the genuineness of the seal or signature or of the official character of the person or his authority to take the declaration.

141. At any stage of any proceedings before the Comptroller he may direct that such documents, information or evidence as he may require shall be furnished within such period as he may fix.

(a) 1948 c. 56.

Hearing in Scottish cases (*Section* 86)

142.—(1) Any party or parties to proceedings under sections 55 (1), 55 (2) or 56 (1) of the Act may request the Comptroller to direct that any hearing in such proceedings shall be held in Scotland.

(2) A request made under sub-rule (1) shall—

(*a*) be in writing ;

(*b*) be accompanied by a statement of facts setting out the grounds upon which the request is made ; and

(*c*) be lodged with the Comptroller at any time before the Comptroller issues notification to the parties that a hearing has been appointed, or, with the leave of the Comptroller, within 14 days thereafter.

(3) The Comptroller, upon a request being made under sub-rule (1) of this rule, shall forthwith intimate such request by sending a copy thereof together with the relevant statement of facts to any party to the proceedings who has not signed the request as a consenter thereto, and for the purpose of such intimation sufficient copies of the request and statement shall be lodged with the Comptroller by the party or parties making the request.

(4) Any party or parties to the proceedings having objection to a request intimated under sub-rule (3) may, within one month of such intimation, lodge with the Comptroller a counterstatement setting out the grounds upon which objection is taken, and the Comptroller shall forthwith intimate the objection by sending a copy of the counterstatement to any party who is not a signatory, and for the purpose of such intimation sufficient copies of the counterstatement shall be lodged with the Comptroller by the party or parties making the objection.

(5) Subject to the foregoing provisions the Comptroller may give such directions as he thinks fit with regard to the procedure to be followed in dealing with a request made under sub-rule (1) including any hearing thereon which may appear to him to be necessary.

(6) Where the Comptroller, after consideration of a request made under sub-rule (1), is satisfied, having regard to the balance of convenience in all the circumstances of the case, that any hearing thereon should be held in Scotland, he shall grant the request and issue such directions as shall seem to him appropriate.

(7) Any decision of the Comptroller under this Rule shall be final.

The Journal, Reports of Cases, and publication of documents

143.—(1) The Comptroller shall publish a journal containing particulars of applications for patents and other proceedings under the Act and any other information that he may deem to be generally useful or important.

(2) The journal shall be entitled "The Official Journal (Patents)".

(3) Unless the Comptroller otherwise directs, the journal shall be published weekly.

144. The Comptroller shall publish from time to time reports of such cases relating to patents, trade marks and registered designs as he may deem to be generally useful or important.

145. The Comptroller may arrange for the publication and sale of copies of specifications, drawings and other documents in the Office, and of indexes to and abridgments of such documents.

146.—(1) In addition to the documents mentioned in section 13 (2) and Rule 38 (1), and subject to the provisions of this Rule, the following documents shall be open to public inspection after the date of publication of the complete specification, that is to say, every Patents Form duly filed in pursuance of an application for a patent or in relation to a patent and every document filed with or sent to the Office after the said date for the purposes of any proceedings relating to a patent or an application for a patent.

(2) The following shall not be open to public inspection, namely, Patents Forms Nos. 8, 37, 66 and 67.

(3) (a) Where a document other than a Patents Form is filed or sent after the said date and the person filing or sending it so requests at the time of filing, the Comptroller may direct it to be treated as confidential.

(b) Where such a direction has been given and not withdrawn, nothing in this Rule shall be taken to authorise or require any person to be allowed to inspect the document to which the direction relates except by leave of the Comptroller.

(c) The Comptroller shall not withdraw any direction given under this Rule nor shall he give leave for any person to inspect any document to which a direction which has not been withdrawn relates without prior consultation with the person at whose request the direction was given, unless the Comptroller is satisfied that such prior consultation is not reasonably practicable.

(d) Where such a direction is given or withdrawn a record of the fact shall be filed with the document to which it relates.

Hours of business and excluded days (Section 98)

147.—(1) The following shall be excluded days for purposes of the transaction by the public of business of all classes under the Act :—

Christmas Day, Good Friday, the Saturday following Good Friday and all Sundays.

(2) Days which may, from time to time, be notified by a notice posted in a conspicious place in the Office shall be excluded days for purposes of the transaction of business of all classes or such class or classes as may be specified in the notice.

(3) All Saturdays, other than those falling within sub-rule (1) or (2), shall be excluded days for purposes of the transaction of all classes of business other than the filing of new applications for patents which are not Convention applications.

148. The Office shall be deemed to be closed at the following hours for the transaction of business of the classes specified—

(a) On weekdays other than Saturdays, at six o'clock for the filing of applications, forms and other documents, and at four o'clock for all other business ;

(b) On Saturdays, at one o'clock for the filing of new applications for patents which are not Convention applications.

Applications to and Orders of Court

149. Where an application to the Court under section 75 for rectification of the register has been made, the applicant shall forthwith serve an office copy of the application on the Comptroller, who shall enter a notice of the application on the register.

150. Where any Order has been made by the Court under the Act revoking a patent or extending the term of a patent, or allowing a patentee to amend his specification, or affecting the validity or proprietorship of a patent or any rights thereunder, the person in whose favour such order has been made shall file Patents Form No. 69 accompanied by an office copy of such order, and thereupon the specification shall be amended or the register rectified or altered as the case may be.

General

151. Except as otherwise provided in these Rules, before exercising any discretionary power given to him by the Act or these Rules adversely to an applicant for a patent or for amendment of a specification, the Comptroller shall give at least ten days' notice to the applicant of the time when he may be heard.

152. Any document filed in any proceedings before the Comptroller may, if he thinks fit, be amended, and any irregularity in procedure may be rectified, on such terms as he may direct.

153.—(1) Where by virtue of any of the Rules mentioned in sub-rule (2) of this Rule any notice of opposition or application for the revocation of a patent is required to be supported by a statement or evidence, such statement or evidence shall be filed on, or within 14 days after, the date on which the notice is given or the application is made.

(2) The Rules referred to in sub-rule (1) are Rules 39 (1), 72 (2), 80 (2), 86 (2), 91 (2), 96 (1), 100 (1), 106 (2), 114 (3) and 131 (2).

154. The times prescribed by these Rules for doing any act, or taking any proceeding thereunder, other than the times prescribed by Rules 37, 59, 72 (1), 80, 86, 100 and 106, may be extended by the Comptroller if he thinks fit, upon such notice to the parties and upon such terms, as he may direct, and such extension may be granted although the time has expired for doing such act or taking such proceeding.

155. Where, under these Rules, any person is required to do any act or thing, or any document or evidence is required to be produced or filed, and it is shown to the satisfaction of the Comptroller that from any reasonable cause that person is unable to do that act or thing, or that that document or evidence cannot be produced or filed, the Comptroller may, upon the production of such evidence and subject to such terms as he thinks fit, dispense with the doing of any such act or thing, or the production or filing of such document or evidence.

156. Where the hearing before the Comptroller of any dispute between two or more parties relating to any matter in connection with a patent or an application for a patent takes place after the date of the publication of the complete specification, the hearing of the dispute shall be in public unless the Comptroller, after consultation with those parties to the dispute who appear in person or are represented at the hearing, otherwise directs.

Revocation of existing Rules

157. The Patents Rules 1958(**a**), the Patents (Amendment) Rules 1964(**b**), the Patents (Amendment No. 2) Rules 1964(**c**), the Patents (Amendment) Rules 1966(**d**), the Patents (Amendment) Rules 1967(**e**) and the Patents (Amendment No. 2) Rules 1967(**f**), are hereby revoked :

Provided that the Patents Rules 1939(**g**), as amended by the Patents (Amendment) Rules 1942(**h**), and the Patents (Amendment) Rules 1946(**i**), shall continue to apply in relation to any matter to which by virtue of Schedule 3 to the Act the provisions of the Patents and Designs Acts 1907 to 1946(**j**), continue to apply.

(**a**) S.I. 1958/73 (1958 II, p. 1713).
(**b**) S.I. 1964/228 (1964 I, p. 423).
(**c**) S.I. 1964/1337 (1964 II, p. 3049).
(**d**) S.I. 1966/1482 (1966 III, p. 4092).
(**e**) S.I. 1967/392 (1967 I, p. 1322).
(**f**) S.I. 1967/1171 (1967 II, p. 3455).
(**g**) S.R. & O. 1939/858 (1939 II, p. 2453).
(**h**) S.R. & O. 1942/273 (1942 I, p. 705).
(**i**) S.R. & O. 1946/756 (1946 I, p. 1236).
(**j**) 1907 c. 29; 4 & 5 Geo. 5. c. 18; 1919 c. 80; 18 & 19 Geo. 5. c. 3; 1932 c. 32; 1938 c. 29; 1939 c. 32; 1942 c. 6 and 1946 c. 44.

27th August 1968.

Edmund Dell,
Minister of State,
Board of Trade.

We consent to the making of Rule 3 of these Rules.

26th August 1968.

B. K. O'Malley,
Joseph Harper,
Two of the Lords Commissioners
of Her Majesty's Treasury.

Rules 3 and 134   SCHEDULE 1

LIST OF FEES PAYABLE

			Corresponding Form
	£	s. d.	
1. On application for a patent	1	0 0	Patents Form No. 1 or Schedule 3 Form 1A.
2. On Convention application for a patent:— In respect of each application for protection in a Convention country	1	0 0	Patents Form No. 1 Con. or Schedule 3 Form 1B.
3. On filing specification:—			
Provisional	—		Patents Form No. 2.
Complete	14	0 0	Patents Form No. 3.
4. On application for grant of patent of addition in lieu of an independent patent	6	0 0	Patents Form No. 1 Add.
5. Declaration of inventorship of invention disclosed in complete specification ...	—		Patents Form No. 4.
6. For extension of the period for filing complete specification	3	10 0	Patents Form No. 5.
7. On request for the post-dating of an application under section 6(3)	3	10 0	Patents Form No. 6.
8. For extension of time under Rule 30 or 33 or 50:—			
Not exceeding one month	1	5 0	Patents Form No. 7.
Each succeeding month	1	5 0	,, ,, ,,
9. On application for result of search made under sections 7 and 8		1 0	Patents Form No. 8.
10. On application under section 9(2) for deletion of reference	1	5 0	Patents Form No. 9.
11. For extension of the period for putting an application in order:—			
Up to one month after the period allowed by section 12(1)	2	10 0	Patents Form No. 10.
Up to two months	5	0 0	,, ,, ,,
Up to three months	7	10 0	,, ,, ,,
12. For postponement of acceptance of complete specification:—			
Up to 13 months from date of filing of complete specification	2	10 0	Patents Form No. 11.
From 13 months to 14 months	2	10 0	,, ,, ,,
From 14 months to 15 months	2	10 0	,, ,, ,,
13. On notice of opposition to grant of patent. By opponent	2	10 0	Patents Form No. 12.
14. On hearing by Comptroller. By each party ...	2	10 0	Patents Form No. 13.
15. On a request under section 16(3)	1	5 0	Patents Form No. 14.
16. On a claim under section 16(4)	1	5 0	Patents Form No. 15.
17. On an application for extension of the period under section 16(5)	1	5 0	Patents Form No. 16.
18. On an application for a certificate under section 16(8)	2	10 0	Patents Form No. 17.
19. On a claim under section 17(1) for application to proceed in name of claimants ...	2	10 0	Patents Form No. 18.
20. On application for directions under section 17(5)	6	0 0	Patents Form No. 19
21. On a request for sealing of a patent	3	0 0	Patents Form No. 20.

	£	s.	d.	Corresponding Form
22. On application for extension of the period for requesting the sealing of a patent under section 19(3):—				
Not exceeding one month	2	10	0	Patents Form No. 21.
,, ,, two months	5	0	0	,, ,, ,,
,, ,, three months	7	10	0	,, ,, ,,
23. On application for extension of the period for requesting the sealing of a patent under section 19(4):—				
Not exceeding one month	1	5	0	Patents Form No. 22.
Each succeeding month		12	6	,, ,, ,,
24. On application under section 20 for amendment of a patent	6	0	0	Patents Form No. 23.
25. †On application for certificate of payment of renewal fee:—				
Before the expiration of the 4th year from the date of the patent and in respect of the 5th year	6	0	0	Patents Form No. 24.
Before the expiration of the 5th year from the date of the patent and in respect of the 6th year	7	0	0	,, ,, ,,
Before the expiration of the 6th year from the date of the patent and in respect of the 7th year	10	0	0	,, ,, ,,
Before the expiration of the 7th year from the date of the patent and in respect of the 8th year	12	0	0	,, ,, ,,
Before the expiration of the 8th year from the date of the patent and in respect of the 9th year	14	0	0	,, ,, ,,
Before the expiration of the 9th year from the date of the patent and in respect of the 10th year	17	0	0	,, ,, ,,
Before the expiration of the 10th year from the date of the patent and in respect of the 11th year	20	0	0	,, ,, ,,
Before the expiration of the 11th year from the date of the patent and in respect of the 12th year	22	0	0	,, ,, ,,
Before the expiration of the 12th year from the date of the patent and in respect of the 13th year	24	0	0	,, ,, ,,
Before the expiration of the 13th year from the date of the patent and in respect of the 14th year	26	0	0	,, ,, ,,
Before the expiration of the 14th year from the date of the patent and in respect of the 15th year	28	0	0	,, ,, ,,
Before the expiration of the 15th year from the date of the patent and in respect of the remainder of the term of the patent	30	0	0	,, ,, ,,
26. On extension of the period for payment of renewal fees:—				
Not exceeding one month	2	10	0	Patents Form No. 25.
,, ,, two months	5	0	0	,, ,, ,,

†One half only of these fees payable on patents endorsed " Licences of Right ".

		£	s.	d.	Corresponding Form
26.—*cont.*					
Not exceeding three months		7	10	0	Patents Form No. 25.
„ „ four months		10	0	0	„ „ „
„ „ five months		12	10	0	„ „ „
„ „ six months		15	0	0	„ „ „
27. Certificate of payment of renewal fee ...			—		Patents Form No. 26.
28. On application under section 24 or 25 for extension of term of patent		6	0	0	Patents Form No. 27.
29. On opposition to application for extension of term of patent		2	10	0	Patents Form No. 28.
30. On application for restoration of a patent ...		3	10	0	Patents Form No. 29.
31. On notice of opposition to application for restoration of patent		2	10	0	Patents Form No. 30.
32. Additional fee on resoration of patent ...		12	0	0	Patents Form No. 31.
33. On application under section 28 for sealing of patent		3	10	0	Patents Form No. 32.
34. On opposition to application under section 28		2	10	0	Patents Form No. 33.
35. Additional fee for sealing under section 28...		12	0	0	Patents Form No. 34.
36. On application to amend specification after acceptance:—					
Up to sealing. By applicant		3	10	0	Patents Form No. 35.
After sealing. By patentee		6	0	0	„ „ „
37. On notice of opposition to amendment. By opponent		2	10	0	Patents Form No. 36.
38. On application to amend specification not yet accepted		2	10	0	Patents Form No. 37.
39. On application to amend an application for a patent		2	10	0	Patents Form No. 38.
39a. Application for the conversion of an application for a patent to a Convention application under Rule 94(2)			—		Patents Form No. 38. Con.
40. On application for revocation of a patent under section 33		3	10	0	Patents Form No. 39.
41. On offer to surrender a patent under section 34			—		Patents Form No. 40.
42. On notice of opposition to surrender of a patent...		2	10	0	Patents Form No. 41.
43. On application for endorsement of patent "Licences of Right"		1	5	0	Patents Form No. 42.
44. On application for settlement of terms of licence under patent endorsed "Licences of Right"		6	0	0	Patents Form No. 43.
45. On application by patentee for cancellation of endorsement of patent "Licences of Right"		2	10	0	Patents Form No. 44.
46. On application for cancellation of endorsement "Licences of Right" ...		2	10	0	Patents Form No. 45.
47. On notice of opposition to cancellation of endorsement of patent "Licences of Right"		2	10	0	Patents Form No. 46.
48. On application under section 37 for grant of compulsory licence or endorsement of a patent "Licences of Right"		6	0	0	Patents Form No. 47.
49. On application under section 40(1) for endorsement of patent "Licences of Right" or grant of licence		6	0	0	Patents Form No. 48.
50. On application under section 40(3) for Order of Comptroller		6	0	0	Patents Form No. 49.

	£	s.	d.	Corresponding Form
51. On application under section 42 for revocation	6	0	0	Patents Form No. 50.
52. On opposition to application under section 37, 40, 41 or 42	2	10	0	Patents Form No. 51.
53. On application for licence under section 41	6	0	0	Patents Form No. 52.
54. On application under section 55(1) for directions of Comptroller	6	0	0	Patents Form No. 53.
55. On application under section 55(2) for directions of Comptroller	6	0	0	Patents Form No. 54.
56. On application under section 56(1) to determine dispute	6	0	0	Patents Form No. 55.
57. On reference of dispute to Comptroller under section 67(1)	6	0	0	Patents Form No. 56.
58. For altering name or nationality or address or address for service in register, for each patent...		6	0	Patents Form No. 57.
59. On application for entry of name of subsequent proprietor in the register, if made within six months from date of acquisition of proprietorship:—	1	5	0	Patents Form No. 58 or 60.
If made after the expiration of six months but within twelve months from the date of acquisition of proprietorship	3	0	0	,, ,, ,,
If made after expiration of twelve months from date of acquisition of proprietorship	3	10	0	,, ,, ,,
On each application covering more than one patent, the devolution of title being the same as in the first patent. For each additional patent		3	0	,, ,, ,,
60. On application for entry of notice of a mortgage or licence in the register, if made within six months from date of acquisition of interest or the sealing of the patent (whichever is the later)	1	5	0	Patents Form No. 59 or 61.
If made after expiration of six months but within twelve months from date of acquisition of interest or the sealing of the patent (whichever is the later) ...	3	0	0	,, ,, ,,
If made after expiration of twelve months from date of acquisition of interest or the sealing of the patent (whichever is the later)	3	10	0	,, ,, ,,
On each application covering more than one patent, the devolution of title being the same as in the first patent. For each additional patent...		3	0	,, ,, ,,
61. On application for entry of notification of a document in the register, if made within six months from date of document or the sealing of the patent (whichever is the later):—	1	5	0	Patents Form No. 62.
If made after expiration of six months but within twelve months from date of document or the sealing of the patent (whichever is the later)	3	0	0	,, ,, ,,

				Corresponding Form

	£	s.	d.	
61.—cont.				
If made after expiration of twelve months from date of document or the sealing of the patent (whichever is the later) ...	3	10	0	Patents Form No. 62
On each application covering more than one patent, for each additional patent referred to in the same document as the first patent		3	0	,, ,, ,,
62. On application for entry in the register of claim to a licence under a patent extended under section 23, 24 or 25	1	5	0	Patents Form No. 63.
63. On request to Comptroller to correct a clerical error:—				
Up to sealing		12	6	Patents Form No. 64.
After sealing	1	5	0	,, ,, ,,
64. On notice of opposition to the correction of a clerical error	1	5	0	Patents Form No. 65.
65. For certificate of Comptroller under section 77(1)		12	6	Patents Form No. 66.
66. On request for information as to a matter affecting a patent or an application therefor	1	5	0	Patents Form No. 67.
67. For duplicate of patent	3	10	0	Patents Form No. 68.
68. On notice of Order of Court		12	6	Patents Form No. 69.
69. On inspection of register or supply of an extract from register, or on inspection of original documents (other than provisional specifications), samples or specimens ...		2	6	
70. For typewritten office copies (every 100 words) (but never less than two shillings) ...		1	0	
71. For photographic office copies and office copies of drawings	Cost according to agreement			
72. For office copy of patent		5	0	
73. For certifying office copies, MSS., printed or photographic ... ... each		3	0	
74. On written enquiry as to whether a patent or patents is or are in force:—				
for one patent		1	0	
for each additional patent included in the same enquiry			6	

SCHEDULE 2

PATENTS FORM NO. 1   GENERAL FORMS   Rules 4 and 5(1)(f)

PATENTS ACT 1949

APPLICATION FOR PATENT

(To be accompanied by two copies of Patents Form No. 2 or of Patents Form No. 3)

NOTE.—This is a comprehensive form and parts inappropriate to a particular application should be cancelled. In the case of an application by the inventor, only sections 1, 4 and 6 of this form are appropriate, and section 5 if a Patent of Addition is applied for.

1. I/We (a) ....
....
....

....

(a) Insert (in full) name address and nationality of applicant(s).

am/are in possession of an invention which is described in the accompanying

(b) $\dfrac{\text{provisional}}{\text{complete}}$ specification under the title (c).............................

(b) Delete the words which are not applicable.

....

(c) Insert title of invention.

(b) $\left\{\begin{array}{l}\text{I} \\ \text{We} \\ \text{The said } (d)\end{array}\right.$..

(d) Insert name of inventor *if included at (a).*

claim . . to be the true and first inventor . . of the invention.

or

2. I/We believe (e) ....
....
....

....

(e) Insert (in full) name, address and nationality of inventor(s) *if not included at (a).*

to be the true and first inventor of the invention and

(b) $\left\{\begin{array}{l}\text{I} \\ \text{we} \\ \text{the said}\end{array}\right.$..

(b) $\left\{\begin{array}{l}\text{am} \\ \text{are} \\ \text{is}\end{array}\right\}$ the (b) $\left\{\begin{array}{l}\text{assignee . . of the said inventor . . in respect of the} \\ \text{right to make this application} \\ \text{personal representative . . of the said inventor . . .}\end{array}\right.$

3. The invention or a part of the invention was communicated to

(b) $\left\{\begin{array}{l}\text{me} \\ \text{us} \\ \text{the said}\end{array}\right.$..

....

by (f)..

(f) Insert (in full) name, address and nationality of communicator.

....

....

....

4. I/We declare that to the best of my/our knowledge and belief the state-ments made above are correct and there is no lawful ground of objection to the grant of a patent to me/us on this application and I/we pray that a patent may be granted to me/us for the said invention;

Use of the invention in the United Kingdom before the date of the application for a patent is a lawful ground of objection.

5. And I/we request that the patent may be granted as a patent of addition to (b) { patent No.................... { the patent to be granted on application No......................

6. And I/we request that all notices, requisitions, and communications relating to this application may be sent to..

(g) The address must be within the United Kingdom.

at (g) ....

....

(h) Delete if not applicable.

(h) who is/are hereby appointed to act for me/us.

(i) To be signed by applicant(s).

(i)..

....

....

Declaration to be signed by any person named as inventor who is not an applicant

....

I/We claim to be the true and first inventor(s) and assent to the making of this application

....

....

....

To the Comptroller,
    The Patent Office,
        25, Southampton Buildings,
            Chancery Lane, London, W.C.2.

PATENTS FORM NO. 1 CON.

PATENTS ACT 1949

CONVENTION APPLICATION FOR A PATENT
(To be accompanied by two copies of Patents Form No. 3)

NOTE:—This is a comprehensive form, and parts inappropriate to a particular application should be cancelled.

1. I/We (a) .... (a) Insert, in full, name,
.... address and
.... nationality of
.... applicant(s).

hereby declare that an application or applications for protection for an invention or inventions has or have been made in the following country or countries and on the following official date or dates, namely:—

in (b) .... on (c) ....   (b) Insert the
by (d) ....   name of the
Convention
.... country in
which the *first*
in (b) .... on (c) .... application
by (d) ....   was made.
.... (c) Insert the
official date
in (b) .... on (c) .... of the *first*
by (d) ....   application in
a Convention
.... country.

and that the said application or each of the said applications was the first (d) Insert name
application in a Convention country in respect of the relevant invention of applicant
by me/us or by any person from whom I/we derive title.   and (if not
included at (a))
address and
nationality.

2. I am/We are (e) the assignee . . of the said (d) .... Particulars of
.............................by virtue of (f).........................   any further
applications
.... should be given
on the back of
or (e) the personal representative . . of the said (d)........................... this form or on
a separate sheet.

3. I/We declare that to the best of my/our knowledge and belief there (e) Delete
is no lawful ground of objection to the grant of a patent to me/us on this whichever does
not apply.
application, and pursuant to subsection (2) (and subsection (3))of section 1
(f) Give
of the Act I/we pray that a patent may be granted to me/us with priority particulars of
founded on the above-mentioned application . . in a Convention country or the assignment.
countries as provided by subsection (4) of section 5, for the invention
described in the accompanying complete specification under the title

....
....

4. And I/we request that the patent may be granted as a patent of
           ⎧ patent No...........................
addition to (e) ⎨ the patent to be granted on
           ⎩ application No......................

5. And I/we request that all notices, requisitions, and communications
relating to this application may be sent to... (g) The address
must be
at (g) .... within the
United
.... Kingdom.

(h) who is/are hereby appointed to act for me/us.   (h) Delete if
(i)...   not applicable.
(i) To be signed
.... by applicant(s).
....

To the Comptroller.
   The Patent Office,
      25, Southampton Buildings,
         Chancery Lane, London, W.C.2.

PATENTS FORM NO. 1 ADD.

PATENTS ACT 1949

APPLICATION FOR THE GRANT OF A PATENT OF ADDITION IN LIEU OF AN INDEPENDENT PATENT

(a) State full name, address and nationality of patentee or patentees.

(a) I/We..
....
....
hereby request that patent No. .... of which I am/we are the patentee . . be revoked and that in lieu thereof a patent of addition to patent No. .... of which I am/we are also the patentee be granted to me/us, such patent of addition to bear the same date as the patent so revoked.

(b) To be signed by patentee.

(b)...
....
....

To the Comptroller,
   The Patent Office,
      25, Southampton Buildings,
         Chancery Lane, London, W.C.2.

PATENTS FORM NO. 2

PATENTS ACT 1949

PROVISIONAL SPECIFICATION
(To be furnished in duplicate)

(a) Insert title verbally agreeing with that in the application form.

(a) ....
....
....

(b) State (in full) name, address and nationality of applicant or applicants as in application form.

(b) I/We...
....
....
....
....
....
....

do hereby declare this invention to be described in the following statement:—

(c) Here begin description of the invention. The continuation of the specification should be on one side only of paper of the same size as this form with the lines well spaced and with a margin of one inch and a half on the left-hand part of the paper. The specification and the duplicate thereof must be signed at the end.

(c) ....
....
....
....
....
....
....
....
....
....
....
....
....

PATENTS FORM NO. 3

PATENTS ACT 1949

————

COMPLETE SPECIFICATION

(*To be furnished in duplicate*)

————

> Where priority as provided by subsection (2) or (3) of section 5 is desired in respect of one or more provisional specifications, quote No. or Nos. and date or dates.
>
> No............................
> Date ....

(a) ....

....

....

....

(a) Insert title of invention.

(b) I/We..

....

....

....

....

....

(b) State (in full) name, address and nationality of applicant or applicants as in application form.

do hereby declare the invention, for which I/we pray that a patent may be granted to me/us, and the method by which it is to be performed, to be particularly described in and by the following statement:—

(c) ....

....

....

....

....

....

....

....

....

....

....

(c) Here begin full description of invention. The continuation of the specification should be upon paper of the same size as this form, on one side only, with the lines well spaced and with a margin of one inch and a half on the left-hand part of the paper. The completion of the description should be followed by the words " What I (or we) claim is " after which should be written the claim or claims numbered consecutively (see note below).
The specification and the duplicate thereof must be signed at the end.

NOTE.—The claims must relate to a single invention, must be clear and succinct and must be fairly based on the matter disclosed in the specification. They should form in brief a clear statement of that which constitutes the invention. Applicants should be careful that their claims include neither more or less than they desire to protect by their patent. Any unnecessary multiplicity of claims or prolixity of language should be avoided. Claims should not be made for the efficiency or advantages of the invention.

PATENTS FORM NO. 4

PATENTS ACT 1949

DECLARATION AS TO INVENTORSHIP (SECTION 4 (5))

(a) Insert name(s) of applicant(s).

I/We (a)...
do hereby declare that the true and first inventor .. of the invention
disclosed in the complete specification filed in pursuance of my/our
application... numbered........................ and dated the.................. day of
...........................19... is/are:

(b) State name, address and nationality of inventor or of each inventor.

(b) ....
....
....
....

and that my/our right to apply for a patent for the invention as follows

(c) This need not be filled in if the inventor(s) named at (b) is or are an applicant or applicants, or if the right to apply is as stated on the application form.

(c) ....
....
....
....
....
....

(d) To be signed by applicant(s).

(d)...
....

Except in the case of a Convention Application, if any person named
as inventor at (b) above is not so named in the application or in any of
the applications, he must sign the following statement.

I assent to the invention referred to in the above declaration, being
included in the complete specification filed in pursuance of the stated
application(s).

....

To the Comptroller,
   The Patent Office,
      25, Southampton Buildings,
         Chancery Lane, London, W.C.2.

PATENTS FORM NO. 5

PATENTS ACT 1949

APPLICATION FOR EXTENSION OF THE PERIOD FOR FILING A COMPLETE SPECIFICATION

I/We hereby, in respect of application No.............dated........................,
request an extension of the period in which to file a complete specification
to a period not exceeding fifteen months from the date of the application.

(a) To be signed by applicant or applicants, or his or their agent.

(a)...
....
....

To the Comptroller,
   The Patent Office,
      25, Southampton Buildings,
         Chancery Lane, London, W.C.2.

PATENTS FORM NO. 6

PATENTS ACT 1949

REQUEST FOR THE POST-DATING OF AN APPLICATION UNDER SECTION 6 (3)

I/We hereby request that application No.........................filed on the
...................of...........................19......... be deemed to have been made
on the following date, namely, the..................of...........................19.........

(*a*)... (*a*) To be
signed by
.... applicant(s).

....

....

To the Comptroller,
The Patent Office,
25, Southampton Buildings,
Chancery Lane, London, W.C.2.

PATENTS FORM NO. 7

PATENTS ACT 1949

APPLICATION FOR EXTENSION OF TIME UNDER RULE 30 OR 33 OR 50

Application No......................dated..............................
I/We hereby apply for.....................month......... extension of time within
which

(*a*) to remove an objection under section 8 (Rule 28),

(*b*) agreement to the amendment of the specification or to the insertion
of a reference under Rule 29 or 33 may be notified,

(*c*) to submit an amendment under section 15 (Rule 48),

(*d*) agreement to the amendment of the specification under Rule 49 may
be notified.

(*a*), (*b*), (*c*) and
(*d*) Delete the
words which
are not
applicable.

(*e*)... (*e*) To be signed
by applicant
.... or applicants,
or his or their
.... agent.

To the Comptroller,
The Patent Office,
25, Southampton Buildings,
Chancery Lane, London, W.C.2.

PATENTS FORM NO. 8

PATENTS ACT 1949

APPLICATION UNDER SECTION 79 (2) FOR THE RESULT OF A SEARCH MADE UNDER SECTIONS 7 AND 8

I/We hereby request that I/we may be informed of the result of the search made under sections 7 and 8 in connection with Application for Patent No.....................................

(a) Insert name and full address to which information is to be sent.

(a) ....

....

To the Comptroller,

    The Patent Office,

        25, Southampton Buildings,

            Chancery Lane, London, W.C.2.

(This part to be filled in at the Patent Office.)

Result of the search made under sections 7 and 8 of the Patents Act, 1949, in connection with Application for Patent No....................................

Specifications or other publications cited as the result of the search made under section 7	Specifications cited as the result of the search made under section 8

NOTE.—Citations may be made during the examination of the specifications which are not relevant to the specification as accepted. Citations under section 7 are completed before acceptance of the specification, but citations under section 8 may be made subsequently.

PATENTS FORM No. 9

PATENTS ACT 1949

APPLICATION UNDER SECTION 9 (2) FOR DELETION OF REFERENCE

I/We (a)...

....

....

(a) State, in full, name and address of applicant(s).

hereby apply for deletion of the reference to patent No.............................
which has been inserted in the complete specification of my/our (b) (application for a) patent No............................. in pursuance of a direction
under section 9 (1).

(b) Delete the words in brackets if a patent has been granted.

The facts relied upon in support of this application are (c).........................

(c) The facts must be stated fully.

....

....

....

....

....

....

....

Communications should be sent to...

....

at (d) ....

....

(d) The address must be within the United Kingdom.

(e) who is/are hereby appointed to act for me/us.

(e) Delete if not applicable.

(f)..

....

....

(f) To be signed by applicant(s) or his or their authorised agent.

To the Comptroller,
    The Patent Office,
        25, Southampton Buildings,
            Chancery Lane, London, W.C.2.

PATENTS FORM No. 10

PATENTS ACT 1949

NOTICE OF DESIRE FOR EXTENSION OF THE PERIOD FOR PUTTING AN APPLICATION IN ORDER

I/We hereby give notice that I/we desire the period for putting in order Application No........................dated..to be extended to................................months from the date of filing of the complete specification.

(a) To be signed by applicant or applicants or his or their agent.

(a)...

....

....

To the Comptroller,
  The Patent Office,
    25, Southampton Buildings,
      Chancery Lane, London, W.C.2.

PATENTS FORM No. 11

PATENTS ACT 1949

REQUEST FOR POSTPONEMENT OF ACCEPTANCE OF COMPLETE SPECIFICATION

I/We hereby request a postponement of the acceptance of the complete specification of Application No...................dated.....................................
to a date not later than the expiration of.....................................months from the date of filing of the complete specification.

(a) To be signed by applicant or applicants or his or their agent.

(a)...

....

....

To the Comptroller,
  The Patent Office,
    25, Southampton Buildings,
      Chancery Lane, London, W.C.2.

PATENTS FORM NO. 12

PATENTS ACT 1949

NOTICE OF OPPOSITION TO GRANT OF PATENT (SECTION 14)

(To be accompanied by a copy, and a statement of case in duplicate)

(a) I/We...

....

....

....

hereby give notice of opposition to the grant of a patent upon application

No.................applied for by...

....

....

....

upon the ground (b)..

....

....

....

....

....

....

....

....

Communications should be sent to:.......................................

....

at (c) ....

....

(d) who is/are hereby appointed to act for me/us.

(e)...

....

(a) State full name and address.

(b) State upon which of the grounds of opposition permitted by section 14 of the Act the grant is opposed, and identify all specifications and other publications relied upon.

(c) The address must be within the United Kingdom.

(d) Delete if not applicable.

(e) To be signed by opponent(s).

To the Comptroller,
    The Patent Office,
        25, Southampton Buildings,
            Chancery Lane, London, W.C.2.

PATENTS FORM No. 13

PATENTS ACT 1949

NOTICE THAT HEARING BEFORE THE COMPTROLLER WILL BE ATTENDED

(a) State name
and address.

(b) Insert date
of Hearing.

(c) Give
particulars (i.e.,
number of
application or
patent, names
of parties and
nature of
proceedings).

(d) Signature.

(a) I/We...

....

hereby give notice that the Hearing fixed for the (b)...........................

in reference to (c)...

....

....will be attended by myself/ourselves

or by some person on my/our behalf.

(d)..

....

....

To the Comptroller,

The Patent Office,
    25, Southampton Buildings,
        Chancery Lane, London, W.C.2.

PATENTS FORM No. 14

PATENTS ACT 1949

REQUEST UNDER SECTION 16 (3)

(a) State (in
full) name,
address and
nationality of
applicant or
applicants for
the patent.

(b) Insert title
of invention.

(c) State the
name, address
and nationality
of the deviser
or devisers if
not included
at (a).

(d) Insert name
of deviser or
devisers.

(a) I/We...

....

....

who made Application No...................on the.....................................

....19........for the grant of a

patent for an invention the title of which is (b)..................................

....

and (c) I/we...

...., hereby

declare that the said (d)..

is/are the inventor ... in the sense of being the actual deviser ... of (a

substantial part of) the invention, and that the Application for the patent

is a direct consequence of his/their being such inventor..., and we hereby

request that the said (d)..

....

be mentioned as such inventor... in accordance with section 16.

A statement setting out the circumstances upon which we rely to justify

this request is attached.

Communications should be sent to..

(e) The address
must be within
the United
Kingdom.

(f) Delete if
not applicable.

(g) To be signed
by all the
persons making
the request.

....at (e)..................................

....

(f) who is/are hereby appointed to act for us.

(g)..

....

....

To the Comptroller,

The Patent Office,
    25, Southampton Buildings,
        Chancery Lane, London, W.C.2.

PATENTS FORM NO. 15

PATENTS ACT 1949

_____

CLAIM UNDER SECTION 16 (4)

_____

(To be accompanied by a copy or copies as required
by Rule 52)

(*a*) I ....

....

hereby declare that I am the inventor in the sense of being the actual

deviser of (a substantial part of) the invention entitled (*b*).............................

....

in respect of which Application No.....................................for patent was

made by (*c*)...   ....

....

on the...19.........., and that the application

for the patent is a direct consequence of my being such inventor, and I

hereby claim to be mentioned as such inventor in accordance with

section 16 (4).

A statement setting out the circumstances upon which I rely to justify

this claim is attached together with a copy/copies thereof as required by

Rule 52.

Communications should be sent to...

....

at (*d*)...

....

(*e*) who is/are hereby appointed to act for me.

(*f*)..

To the Comptroller,
    The Patent Office,
        25, Southampton Buildings,
           Chancery Lane, London, W.C.2.

(a) State (in full) name, address and nationality of the claimant.

(b) Insert title of invention.

(c) Insert name and address of applicant or applicants for the patent.

(d) The address must be within the United Kingdom.

(e) Delete if not applicable.

(f) To be signed by the claimant.

PATENTS FORM No. 16

PATENTS FORM No. 16

PATENTS ACT 1949

APPLICATION UNDER SECTION 16 (5)

(a) State (in full) name, address and nationality of the person or persons making this application.

(b) Insert name, address and nationality of applicant or applicants for the patent.

(c) Insert title of invention.

(d) The address must be within the United Kingdom.

(e) To be signed by the person or all the persons making the application or by his or their duly authorised agent.

(a) I/We...

....

hereby apply for an extension of time (not exceeding one month) for making a request under section 16 (3) (or a claim under section 16 (4)) in respect of Application No..........for a patent made by *(b)*.................................

....

on the........................19........., in respect of an invention the title of which is *(c)*..

....

Communications should be sent to...

at *(d)*...

....

(e)..

....

....

To the Comptroller,
   The Patent Office,
      25, Southampton Buildings,
         Chancery Lane, London, W.C.2.

PATENTS FORM No. 17

PATENTS ACT 1949

APPLICATION UNDER SECTION 16 (8)

(To be accompanied by copies as required by Rule 54)

(a) State (in full) name, address and nationality of the person or persons making this application.

(b) Insert the name of the person mentioned as the actual deviser.

(c) Insert title of invention.

(a) I/We...

....

hereby declare that *(b)*...

....

ought not to have been mentioned under section 16 as the inventor in the sense of being the actual deviser of (a substantial part of) the invention covered by Application No...................... dated the.................................

19........., and entitled *(c)*..

....

and I/we hereby apply for a certificate to that effect.

A statement setting out the circumstances upon which I/we rely to justify this Application is attached together with copies thereof as required by Rule 54.

Communications should be sent to...

(d) The address must be within the United Kingdom.

(e) Delete if not applicable.

(f) To be signed by all the persons making the application.

at *(d)*...

....

(e) who is/are hereby appointed to act for me/us

(f)..

....

....

To the Comptroller,
   The Patent Office,
      25, Southampton Buildings,
         Chancery Lane, London, W.C.2.

PATENTS FORM NO. 18

PATENTS ACT 1949

CLAIM UNDER SECTION 17 (1) TO PROCEED AS AN APPLICANT OR CO-APPLICANT

I/We (a)... (a) State name of claimant(s).

....

hereby request that the Patent Application No. (b)................................... (b) State the number and date of the
....dated .... application for patent.

made by (c)... (c) State name of the applicant or
.... applicants for patent.

may proceed in the name(s) of (d) .... (d) Insert (in full) name, address and
.... nationality of the person or
.... persons in whose name(s) it is requested
.... that the application
.:... shall proceed.

I/We claim to be entitled to proceed as applicant(s) for the patent by

virtue of (e).. (e) Give the particulars of such document,
.... giving its date and the parties
.... to the same, and showing
.... how the claim here made is
.... substantiated.

....

And in proof whereof I/we transmit the accompanying (f)..................... (f) State the nature of the document.
.... The certified copy should be written,

Communications should be sent to... type-written or printed on
at (g)... foolscap paper.

(h) who is/are hereby appointed to act for me/us. (g) The address must be within the United Kingdom.

(i)... (h) Delete if not applicable.
.... (i) To be signed by claimant(s).

(j) I/We...
(j) To be signed by the
consent to the above request.   applicant(s).
....

To the Comptroller,
    The Patent Office,
        25, Southampton Buildings,
            Chancery Lane, London, W.C.2.

PATENTS FORM NO. 19

PATENTS ACT, 1949

APPLICATION FOR DIRECTIONS UNDER SECTION 17 (5) AS TO PROCEEDING WITH AN APPLICATION FOR A PATENT IN CASE OF DISPUTE BETWEEN JOINT APPLICANTS

(To be accompanied by a statement of case and by copies of the application and statement as required by Rule 57)

(a) State name and address.

(*a*) I..

....

....

(b) State name and address of other applicant(s).

being a joint applicant with (*b*)...

....

....

in the application for a patent numbered...
hereby declare that a dispute has arisen between us and request that an order of the Comptroller be made giving directions for enabling the application to proceed.

Particulars of the matters in dispute are given in the annexed statement setting out the facts upon which I rely, and the relief which I seek.

(c) The address must be within the United Kingdom.

Communications should be sent to..

....at (*c*)...

....

....

(d) Delete if not applicable.

(e) Signature.

(*d*) who is hereby appointed to act for me.

(*e*)...

To the Comptroller,
    The Patent Office,
        25, Southampton Buildings,
           Chancery Lane, London, W.C.2.

PATENTS FORM NO. 20

PATENTS ACT 1949

REQUEST FOR THE SEALING OF A PATENT

(a) State name of applicant or applicants.

I/We (*a*)...

.... request

that a patent may be sealed on my/our

(b) Both these numbers to be inserted.

(*b*) Application No................................. and that the following may be
    Acceptance No.................................

entered on the Register as my/our address for service:—

(c) The address must be within the United Kingdom.

(*c*) ....

....

(d) Signature.

(*d*)...

To the Comptroller,
    The Patent Office,
        25, Southampton Buildings,
           Chancery Lane, London, W.C.2.

PATENTS FORM NO. 21

PATENTS ACT 1949

APPLICATION UNDER SECTION 19 (3) FOR EXTENSION OF THE PERIOD FOR MAKING A REQUEST FOR SEALING OF A PATENT

I/We hereby apply for..............................month.................................
extension of the period for making a request for the sealing of a patent
upon Application No...............................

(a)... *(a)* Signature

....

....

To the Comptroller,
  The Patent Office,
    25, Southampton Buildings,
      Chancery Lane, London, W.C.2.

PATENTS FORM NO. 22

PATENTS ACT 1949

APPLICATION UNDER SECTION 19 (4) FOR AN EXTENSION OF THE PERIOD FOR MAKING A REQUEST FOR THE SEALING OF A PATENT

I/We hereby apply for (a).................month......extension of the period *(a)* Not more than six months
for making a request for the sealing of a patent upon Application No.......... extension may be applied for
The circumstances in and grounds upon which this extension is applied at one time.
for are as follows (b):—... *(b)* The circumstances
.... and grounds must be stated in detail.
....
....
....
....

I/We hereby declare that
  (c) An extension of time of three months for making a request for sealing *(c)* and *(d)* Delete the
has been allowed under section 19 (3) and has not yet expired. words which
  (d) An extension of time of...............months for making a request for are not applicable.
sealing has been allowed under section 19 (4) and has not yet expired.

(e)... *(e)* Signature.

....

To the Comptroller,
  The Patent Office,
    25, Southampton Buildings,
      Chancery Lane, London, W.C.2.

PATENTS FORM NO. 23

PATENTS ACT 1949

APPLICATION UNDER SECTION 20 FOR AMENDMENT OF LETTERS PATENT

(To be accompanied by evidence verifying the statements made in this application)

(a) State name and address.

I/We (a)..

....

hereby request that Letters Patent No...............granted to.......................

....

(b) State name, address and nationality of person to whom patent should have been granted.

may be amended by substituting the name of (b)...................................

....

....

for the name of the grantee.

My/Our address for service in the United Kingdom is.............................

....

(c) Signature.

(c)..

To the Comptroller,

The Patent Office,
25, Southampton Buildings,
Chancery Lane, London, W.C.2.

PATENTS FORM NO. 24

[When stamped this Form must be at once sent to or left at the Patent Office]

PATENTS ACT 1949

PAYMENT OF RENEWAL FEE

(a) State name of person tendering the fee.

I/We (a)..

....

hereby transmit the fee prescribed for the continuation in force of

(b) Here insert name of patentee(s).

(b)...

Patent No...............for a further period of...................and request that

(c) Here insert full address.

the Certificate of Payment may be sent to me/us at (c)...........................

....

....

NOTE.—If the address given above is not that entered in the Register of Patents as the Patentee's Address for Service and it is desired to amend the entry in the Register, application therefor must be made on Patents Form No. 57.

To the Comptroller,

The Patent Office,
25, Southampton Buildings,
Chancery Lane, London, W.C.2.

PATENTS FORM NO. 25

PATENTS ACT 1949

REQUEST FOR EXTENSION OF THE PERIOD FOR PAYMENT OF RENEWAL FEE

I/We hereby apply for an extension of...............month(s) of the period prescribed for payment of the renewal fee of........................upon my/our Patent No............................

(a) ....   (a) State name
....   and full
....   address to
   which receipt
   is to be sent.

To the Comptroller,
   The Patent Office,
      25, Southampton Buildings,
         Chancery Lane, London, W.C.2.

PATENTS FORM NO. 26

PATENTS ACT 1949

CERTIFICATE OF PAYMENT OF RENEWAL FEE

Letters Patent No....................

This is to certify that..
did this............day of................................19......, make the prescribed payment of £...............in respect of a period of......................................
from......................................

The Patent Office,
   London.

PATENTS FORM NO. 27

PATENTS ACT 1949

APPLICATION UNDER SECTION 24 OR 25 FOR EXTENSION OF TERM OF PATENT

(To be accompanied by evidence in support of the application)

I/We (a)...   (a) State (in
....   full) name,
....   address and
   nationality
hereby apply for extension of the term of Patent No...............................for   of applicant
   or applicants.
(b)..   (b) Insert period
   for which
   Communications should be sent to...   extension is
....at (c)...   sought.
   (c) The address
....   must be within
   the United
(d) who is/are hereby appointed to act for me/us.   Kingdom.
                  (e)...   (d) Delete if
   not applicable.
....   (e) To be signed
   by the applicant
To the Comptroller,   or applicants.
   The Patent Office,
      25, Southampton Buildings,
         Chancery Lane, London, W.C.2.

PATENTS FORM NO. 28

PATENTS ACT 1949

NOTICE OF OPPOSITION TO APPLICANT FOR EXTENSION OF TERM OF PATENT

(To be accompanied by a copy, and evidence (in duplicate) in support of the opposition)

(a) State (in full) name, address and nationality of opponent or opponents.

I/We (a)..
....
....

hereby give notice of opposition to the application for extension of the term of Patent No........................

(b) The address must be within the United Kingdom.

Communications should be sent to..
....at (b)...
....
....

(c) Delete if not applicable.

(c) who is/are hereby appointed to act for me/us.

(d) To be signed by the opponent or opponents.

(d)...
....

To the Comptroller,
    The Patent Office,
        25, Southampton Buildings.
           Chancery Lane, London, W.C.2.

PATENTS FORM NO. 29

PATENTS ACT 1949

APPLICATION UNDER SECTION 27 FOR THE RESTORATION OF A PATENT

(To be accompanied by evidence verifying the statements made in this application)

(a) State name and address.

I/We (a)..
....
....

hereby apply for an order for the restoration of Patent No...........................

(b) State amount of fee.

(c) State date when fee was due.

The circumstances which led to the failure to pay the renewal fee of

(d) The circumstances must be stated in detail.

(b)........................on or before the (c)........................are as follows (d)
....
....
....
....
....
....
....
....
....

(e) The address must be within the United Kingdom.

Communications should be sent to..
....
at (e)...

(f) Delete if not applicable.

(f) who is/are hereby appointed to act for me/us.

(g) To be signed by applicant.

(g)...
....

To the Comptroller,
    The Patent Office,
        25, Southampton Buildings,
           Chancery Lane, London, W.C.2.

Patents Form No. 30

PATENTS ACT 1949

_____

NOTICE OF OPPOSITION TO AN APPLICATION UNDER SECTION 27 FOR THE RESTORATION OF A PATENT

_____

(To be accompanied by a copy, and a statement of case in duplicate)

I/We (a).. (a) State name and address.

....

....

....

hereby give notice of opposition to the application for restoration of Patent No......................for the following reason:...

....

....

....

....

Communications should be sent to..

....

at (b).. (b) The address must be within the United Kingdom.

(c) who is/are hereby appointed to act for me/us. (c) Delete if not applicable.

(d)... (d) Signature of opponent.

To the Comptroller,

The Patent Office,
25, Southampton Buildings,
Chancery Lane, London, W.C.2.

_____

Patents Form No. 31

PATENTS ACT 1949

_____

ADDITIONAL FEE ON AN APPLICATION UNDER SECTION 27 FOR RESTORATION OF A PATENT

_____

I/We (a).. (a) State name and address.

....

....

the applicant(s) for the restoration of Patent No...
hereby transmit the prescribed additional fee, together with Patents Form No. 24 in respect of the unpaid renewal fee(s).

(b)... (b) Signature of applicant(s)

To the Comptroller,

The Patent Office,
25, Southampton Buildings,
Chancery Lane, London, W.C.2.

PATENTS FORM NO. 32

PATENTS ACT 1949

APPLICATION UNDER SECTION 28 FOR THE SEALING OF A PATENT

(To be accompanied by evidence verifying the statements made in this application)

(a) State name and address.

I/We *(a)*..

....

....

the applicant(s) for a patent numbered..hereby apply for an order for a patent to be sealed thereon.

(b) State date when request was due.

The circumstances which led to the failure to make the prescribed request for sealing on or before the *(b)*..are as follows *(c)*...

(c) The circumstances must be stated in detail.

....

....

....

....

....

(d) The address must be within the United Kingdom.

Communications should be sent to..

....at *(d)*.......................................

(e) Delete if not applicable.

(e) who is/are hereby appointed to act for me/us.

(f) Signature.

(f)...

To the Comptroller,
 The Patent Office,
  25, Southampton Buildings,
   Chancery Lane, London, W.C.2.

PATENTS FORM NO. 33

PATENTS ACT 1949

NOTICE OF OPPOSITION TO AN APPLICATION UNDER SECTION 28 FOR THE SEALING OF A PATENT

(To be accompanied by a copy, and a statement of case in duplicate)

(a) State name and address.

I/We *(a)*..

....

hereby give notice of opposition to the application for the sealing of a patent on Application No..for the following reasons:— ....

....

....

....

....

....

(b) The address must be within the United Kingdom.

Communications should be sent to..

....at *(b)*.......................................

(c) Delete if not applicable.

(c) who is/are hereby appointed to act for me/us.

(d) Signature.

(d)...

To the Comptroller,
 The Patent Office,
  25, Southampton Buildings,
   Chancery Lane, London, W.C.2.

PATENTS FORM No. 34

PATENTS ACT 1949

ADDITIONAL FEE ON AN APPLICATION UNDER SECTION 28 FOR THE SEALING OF A PATENT

I/We (a).. (a) State name and address.

....

....

the applicant(s) for the sealing of a patent on Application No......................
hereby transmit the prescribed additional fee, together with Patents Form
No. 20 accompanied by the fee prescribed in respect of the making of the request
for sealing.

(b)... (b) Signature of applicants for sealing.

To the Comptroller,

    Patent Office,
        25, Southampton Buildings,
           London, W.C. 2.

PATENTS FORM No. 35

PATENTS ACT 1949

APPLICATION UNDER SECTION 29 FOR AMENDMENT OF A COMPLETE SPECIFICATION AFTER ACCEPTANCE

(a) I/We... (a) State full name and address of applicant or patentee.

....

....

....

seek leave to amend the complete specification No......................................
as shown in red ink in the copy of the printed specification hereunto
annexed.

(b) I/We declare that no action for infringement or proceeding before
the Court for revocation of the Patent is pending. (b) These words are to be struck out when a Patent has not been sealed.

My/Our reasons for making this amendment are in detail as follows:—

(c) .... (c) State full particulars of the reasons for seeking amendment. If this space is not sufficient the particulars may be continued on a separate sheet.

....

....

....

....

....

Communications should be sent to...
at (d).. (d) The address must be within the United Kingdom.

(e) who is/are hereby appointed to act for me/us. (e) Delete if not applicable.

(f)... (f) To be signed by applicant or patentee.

To the Comptroller,

    The Patent Office,
        25, Southampton Buildings,
           Chancery Lane, London, W.C.2.

PATENTS FORM NO. 36

PATENTS ACT 1949

NOTICE OF OPPOSITION TO AMENDMENT OF SPECIFICATION UNDER SECTION 29

(To be accompanied by a copy, and a statement of case in duplicate.)

(a) State full name and address.

(a) I/We...
....
....
....
....

hereby give notice of opposition to the proposed amendment of specification No..........................for the following reason:

....
....
....
....
....
....
....
....
....
....
....
....
....
....
....
....

Communications should be sent to...
....

(b) The address must be within the United Kingdom.

at (b)..

(c) Delete if not applicable.

(c) who is/are hereby appointed to act for me/us.

(d) To be signed by the opponent.

(d)..

To the Comptroller,
    The Patent Office,
        25, Southampton Buildings,
            Chancery Lane, London, W.C.2.

PATENTS FORM No. 37

PATENTS ACT 1949

APPLICATION FOR AMENDMENT OF A COMPLETE
SPECIFICATION NOT YET ACCEPTED

I/We (a)...
....
....
....

seek leave to amend the specification of Application No............................
of..as shown in red ink in the copy of the
original specification hereunto annexed.

My/Our reasons for making this amendment are as follows (b)
....
....
....
....
....

(c)...

To the Comptroller,
    The Patent Office,
        25, Southampton Buildings,
            Chancery Lane, London, W.C.2.

(a) State (in full) name and address of applicant or applicants.

(b) State reasons for seeking amendment.

(c) To be signed by applicant or applicants, or his or their agent.

PATENTS FORM No. 38

PATENTS ACT 1949

APPLICATION FOR AMENDMENT OF AN APPLICATION
FOR A PATENT

(a) I/We..
....
....
....

seek leave to amend my/our Application No..
of..as shown in red ink in the copy of
the original Application hereunto annexed.

My/Our reasons for making this amendment are as follows (b)
....
....
....
....
....

(c)...
....

To the Comptroller,
    The Patent Office,
        25, Southampton Buildings,
            Chancery Lane, London, W.C.2.

(a) State full name and address of applicant or applicants.

(b) State reasons for seeking amendment.

(c) To be signed by applicant or applicants.

PATENTS FORM NO. 38 CON.

PATENTS ACT 1949

APPLICATION FOR THE CONVERSION OF AN APPLICATION FOR A PATENT TO A CONVENTION APPLICATION UNDER RULE 94 (2)

(a) State full name and address of applicant or applicants.

I/We (a)...
....
....
....
seek leave to amend my/our Application No...of
....so as to convert it to a Convention
application as shown in red ink in the copy of the original Application hereunto annexed.

(b) To be signed by applicant or applicants.

(b)...
....
....

To the Comptroller,
   The Patent Office,
      25, Southampton Buildings,
         Chancery Lane, London, W.C.2.

PATENTS FORM NO. 39

PATENTS ACT 1949

APPLICATION UNDER SECTION 33 FOR THE REVOCATION OF A PATENT

(*To be accompanied by a copy, and a statement of case in duplicate*)

(a) State full name and address.

(a) I/We...
....
....
....
hereby apply for an Order for the revocation of Patent No...........................
on the following grounds:

(b) State upon which of the grounds the application is based and identify all specifications and other publications relied upon.*

(b)..
....
....
....
....
....
....

(c) If such action or proceeding is pending in any Court the application cannot be made without the leave of the Court.

(c) I/We declare that no action for infringement or proceeding in any
Court for the revocation of the patent is pending.
   Communications should be sent to...

(d) The address must be within the United Kingdom.

....at (d)..
....

(e) Delete if not applicable.

(e) who is/are hereby appointed to act for me/us.

(f) To be signed by applicant.

(f)...

To the Comptroller,
   The Patent Office,
      25, Southampton Buildings,
         Chancery Lane, London, W.C.2.

---

*Note: Such ground or grounds can only be one or more of the grounds on which the grant of a patent could have been opposed under section 14.

PATENTS FORM NO. 40

PATENTS ACT 1949

OFFER UNDER SECTION 34 TO SURRENDER A PATENT

(a) I/We...   *(a)* State full
....   name and
....   address.
....
....

hereby offer to surrender Patent No...

(b) I/We declare that no action for infringement or proceeding in any   *(b)* Delete if
Court for the revocation of the patent is pending.   any action or
  proceeding is

My/Our reasons for making this offer are as follows:.............................   pending, and
....   furnish full
  particulars of
....   such action
  or proceeding.

Communications should be sent to...
....at (c)..   *(c)* The address
  must be within
  the United

(d) who is/are hereby appointed to act for me/us.   Kingdom.

                     (e)..   *(d)* Delete if
  not applicable.

To the Comptroller,   *(e)* To be signed
  by the patentee.

    The Patent Office,

        25, Southampton Buildings,

            Chancery Lane, London, W.C.2.

PATENTS FORM NO. 41

PATENTS ACT 1949

NOTICE OF OPPOSITION UNDER SECTION 34 TO OFFER TO SURRENDER A PATENT

*(To be accompanied by a copy, and a statement of case
in duplicate)*

(a) I/We...   *(a)* State full
....   name and
  address.

hereby give notice of opposition to the offer to surrender Patent
No.............................for the following reason:..
....
....
....
....
....

Communications should be sent to...
....

at (b)..   *(b)* The address
....   must be within
  the United

(c) who is/are hereby appointed to act for me/us.   Kingdom.

               (d)..   *(c)* Delete if
  not applicable.

To the Comptroller,   *(d)* To be signed
  by the

    The Patent Office,   opponent.

        25, Southampton Buildings,

            Chancery Lane, W.C.2.

PATENTS FORM NO. 42

PATENTS ACT 1949

VOLUNTARY APPLICATION FOR ENDORSEMENT OF PATENT "LICENCES OF RIGHT"

(To be accompanied by evidence verifying the statement in the application and by the Letters Patent)

(*a*) State name and address.

I/We (*a*)...

....

hereby request that Patent No...may be endorsed " Licences of Right ".

I am/We are not precluded by contract from granting licences under the patent.

Communications should be sent to

(*b*) The address must be within the United Kingdom.

...................................at (*b*)...

(*c*) who is/are hereby appointed to act for me/us.

(*c*) Delete if not applicable.

(*d*)...

....

(*d*) To be signed by the patentee.

To the Comptroller,

The Patent Office,
25, Southampton Buildings,
Chancery Lane, London, W.C.2.

PATENTS FORM NO. 43

PATENTS ACT 1949

APPLICATION UNDER SECTION 35 (2) FOR SETTLEMENT OF TERMS OF LICENCE UNDER PATENT ENDORSED "LICENCES OF RIGHT"

(To be accompanied by a copy, and a statement of case in duplicate)

(*a*) State name and address.

I/We (*a*)...

....

....

hereby apply for settlement of the terms of a licence to be granted under Patent No.......................

I am/We are the

(*b*) (*c*) (*d*) Delete the two categories not applicable.

(*b*) patentee(s)

(*c*) person(s) requiring a licence

(*d*) holder(s) of a licence under the Patent granted before endorsement.

(*e*) Delete if the applicant is not the holder of a licence.

I/We (*e*) request that an Order may be made entitling me/us to exchange my/our existing licence for a licence to be granted upon the terms as settled.

Communications should be sent to...

(*f*) The address must be within the United Kingdom.

...................................at (*f*)...

....

(*g*) who is/are hereby appointed to act for me/us.

(*g*) Delete if not applicable.

(*h*)...

(*h*) Signature of applicant.

To the Comptroller,

The Patent Office,
25, Southampton Buildings,
Chancery Lane, London, W.C.2.

PATENTS FORM NO. 44

PATENTS ACT 1949

APPLICATION UNDER SECTION 36 (1) BY PATENTEE FOR CANCELLATION OF ENDORSEMENT OF A PATENT "LICENCES OF RIGHT"

(To be accompanied by evidence in support of the application)

I/We (a).. *(a)* State name and address.

....
hereby request that the endorsement of Patent No..................................
"Licences of Right" may be cancelled, and I/we enclose Patents Form
No. 24 accompanied by the balance of all renewal fees which would have been
payable if the patent had not been endorsed.

I/We declare (b) that there is no existing licence under the Patent, or *(b) (c)* Delete whichever is
(c) all the licensees consent to this application. not applicable.

Communications should be sent to... *(d)* The address must be within
....at (d)................................... the United Kingdom.

....
(e) who is/are hereby appointed to act for me/us. *(e)* Delete if not applicable.
(f)... *(f)* To be signed
.... by the patentee.

To the Comptroller,
    The Patent Office,
        25, Southampton Buildings,
            Chancery Lane, London, W.C.2.

PATENTS FORM NO. 45

PATENTS ACT 1949

APPLICATION UNDER SECTION 36 (2) BY ANY PERSON INTERESTED FOR CANCELLATION OF ENDORSEMENT OF PATENT "LICENCES OF RIGHT"

(To be accompanied by a copy, and a statement of case in duplicate)

I/We (a).. *(a)* State name and address.

....
hereby claim that the endorsement of Patent No.....................................
"Licences of Right" is and was at the time of the endorsement contrary
to a contract in which I am/we are interested and I/we request that such
endorsement may be cancelled.

Communications should be sent to... *(b)* The address must be within
....at (b)................................... the United Kingdom.

....
(c) who is/are hereby appointed to act for me/us. *(c)* Delete if not applicable.
(d)... *(d)* To be signed
.... by the
To the Comptroller, applicant(s).
    The Patent Office,
        25, Southampton Buildings,
            Chancery Lane, London, W.C.2.

PATENTS FORM NO. 46

PATENTS ACT 1949

NOTICE OF OPPOSITION BY PATENTEE OR BY ANY PERSON INTERESTED TO CANCELLATION OF ENDORSEMENT OF A PATENT "LICENCES OF RIGHT"

(To be accompanied by a copy, and a statement of case in duplicate.)

(*a*) State name and address.

I/We (*a*)..

hereby give notice of opposition to the application for the cancellation of the endorsement " Licences of Right " in respect of Patent No.....................

Communications should be sent to...

(*b*) The address must be within the United Kingdom.

....at (*b*)..

(*c*) Delete if not applicable.

(*c*) who is/are hereby appointed to act for me/us.

(*d*)To be signed by the opponent.

(*d*)...

To the Comptroller,

    The Patent Office,
        25, Southampton Buildings,
           Chancery Lane, London, W.C.2.

PATENTS FORM NO. 47

PATENTS ACT 1949

APPLICATION FOR COMPULSORY LICENCE OR FOR COMPULSORY ENDORSEMENT "LICENCES OF RIGHT"

(*a*) State name and address.

I/We (*a*)..

hereby apply for an Order of the Comptroller in respect of Patent No.............

(*b*) (*c*) Delete whichever is not applicable.

    (*b*) for a licence under the patent to be granted to me/us; or
    (*c*) for the endorsement of the patent " Licences of Right ",

(*d*) State the nature of the applicant's interest, the facts upon which he relies, and the grounds upon which the application is made.

for the following reasons:—(*d*)..
....
....
....
....
....
....
....
....
....
....
....

Communications should be sent to:—...

(*e*) The address must be within the United Kingdom.

....at (*e*)..

(*f*) Delete if not applicable.

(*f*) who is/are hereby appointed to act for me/us.

(*g*) To be signed by the applicant(s).

(*g*)...

To the Comptroller,

    The Patent Office,
        25, Southampton Buildings,
           Chancery Lane, London, W.C.2.

PATENTS FORM NO. 48

PATENTS ACT 1949

APPLICATION BY GOVERNMENT DEPARTMENT
UNDER SECTION 40 (1)

I/We (a)...   (a) State name
and address of
....   Department.

....

hereby apply for an Order of the Comptroller in respect of Patent No...........
    (b) for the endorsement of the patent " Licences of Right " or   (b) (c) Delete
    (c) for the grant of a licence under the patent to (d)...........................   whichever is
not applicable.

....   (d) Insert name,
address and
for the following reasons:—(e)..   nationality of
person to whom
....   licence is to
be granted.

....
    (e) State the
....   facts and
    My/Our address for service in the United Kingdom is...........................   grounds on
which the case
....   is based.

....
                             (f)...   (f) Signature
of applicant.

To the Comptroller,
    The Patent Office,
        25, Southampton Buildings,
            Chancery Lane, London, W.C.2.

PATENTS FORM NO. 49

PATENTS ACT 1949

APPLICATION UNDER SECTION 40 (3) BY A COMPETENT
AUTHORITY FOR AN ORDER UNDER SECTION 40 (4)

I/We (a)...   (a) State name
and address of
....   competent
authority.

....

....

hereby apply for an Order of the Comptroller in respect of Patent No...........
(b) for the cancellation or modification of conditions in a licence or licences   (b) (c) Delete
granted by the patentee under date...........................to........................   whichever is
                                                            ;   not applicable.

or (c) for the endorsement of the patent " Licences of Right " for the following reasons:—
(d)...   (d) State the
facts and
....   grounds upon
which the
....   application
is based.

....

....

....

    My/Our address for service in the United Kingdom is:—..........................

....

....
                             (e)...   (e) Signature
of applicant.
To the Comptroller,
    The Patent Office,
        25, Southampton Buildings,
            Chancery Lane, London, W.C.2.

PATENTS FORM No. 50

PATENTS ACT 1949

APPLICATION UNDER SECTION 42 FOR REVOCATION
OF A PATENT

(a) State name
and address.

I/We (a)..
....
....
....
....
hereby apply for the revocation of Patent No................for the following reasons:—

(b) State
the nature of
applicant's
interest, the
facts upon
which he relies
and the
grounds upon
which the
application
is made.

(b)..
....
....
....
....
....
....
....
....
....

Communications should be sent to..

(c) The address
must be within
the United
Kingdom.

....at (c)....................................
....
....

(d) Delete if
not applicable.

(d) who is/are hereby appointed to act for me/us.

(e) Signature.

(e)...

To the Comptroller,
     The Patent Office,
          25, Southampton Buildings,
               Chancery Lane, London, W.C.2.

PATENTS FORM No. 51

PATENTS ACT 1949

NOTICE OF OPPOSITION UNDER SECTION 43 TO AN APPLICATION FOR AN ORDER UNDER SECTION 37, 40, 41 OR 42

(To be accompanied by evidence verifying the statement at (f) below)

I/We (a)...   (a) State name and address.

....

hereby give notice of opposition to the application made in respect of

Patent No......................... by ....

....

....

    (b) for a licence under the patent

    (c) for the endorsement of the patent "Licences of Right"   (b) to (e) Delete whichever is not applicable.

    (d) for the grant of a licence to the person specified in the application

    (e) for the revocation of the patent under section 42.

My/Our grounds for opposing are (f).....................................   (f) Insert statement of grounds on which application is opposed.

....

....

....

....

....

....

Communications should be sent to...

.... at (g)...   (g) The address must be within the United Kingdom.

....

....

(h) who is/are hereby appointed to act for me/us.   (h) Delete if not applicable.

          (i)...   (i) Signature.

To the Comptroller,
    The Patent Office,
       25, Southampton Buildings,
          Chancery Lane, London, W.C.2.

PATENTS FORM No. 52

PATENTS ACT 1949

___

APPLICATION UNDER SECTION 41 FOR LICENCE

___

(a) State name
and address.

I/We *(a)*..
....
....
hereby apply for a licence under Patent No............................for the making,
using, exercising and vending the invention

(b) (c) (d)
Delete
whichever is
not applicable.

    (b) as food or medicine;
    (c) for the purposes of the production of food or medicine; or
    (d) as or as part of a surgical or curative device

(e) State nature
of applicant's
interest, and
the facts
relied upon.

for the following reasons:—*(e)*..
....
....
....
....
....

(f) The address
must be within
the United
Kingdom.

Communications should be sent to..
.... at *(f)*.....................................
....

(g) Delete if
not applicable.

(g) who is/are hereby appointed to act for me/us.

(h) Signature
of applicant.

          (h)..

To the Comptroller,
    The Patent Office,
        25, Southampton Buildings,
            Chancery Lane, London, W.C.2.

___

PATENTS FORM No. 53

PATENTS ACT 1949

___

APPLICATION FOR DIRECTIONS UNDER SECTION 55 (I)

___

*(To be accompanied by a statement of case and by copies of the
application and statement as required by Rule* 116)

(a) State name
and address.

I/We *(a)*..
....
hereby apply for the following directions in respect of Patent No...................

(b) State the
directions
sought.

(b) ....
....
....
....
....
....

(c) The address
must be within
the United
Kingdom.

Communications should be sent to..
.... at *(c)*.....................................
....

(d) Delete if
not applicable.

(d) who is/are hereby appointed to act for me/us.

(e) To be signed
by the patentee
seeking
directions.

          (e)..

To the Comptroller,
    The Patent Office,
        25, Southampton Buildings,
            Chancery Lane, London, W.C.2.

PATENTS FORM No. 54

PATENTS ACT 1949

APPLICATION FOR DIRECTIONS UNDER SECTION 55 (2)

*(To be accompanied by a copy and by a statement
of case in duplicate)*

I/We (a)..
....
....
....

(*a*) State name and address of patentee or joint patentees.

hereby apply for directions in respect of the failure of (b)............................
....

(*b*) State name of person in default.

to comply with the directions of the Comptroller given under section 55 (1)
on the..in the following matter: (c).....................
....
....

(*c*) State the directions sought.

Communications should be sent to..
....

at (*d*) ....
(e) who is/are hereby appointed to act for me/us.

(*d*) The address must be within the United Kingdom.

(f)..
....

(*e*) Delete if not applicable.

To the Comptroller,
    The Patent Office,
        25, Southampton Buildings,
            Chancery Lane, London, W.C.2.

(*f*) To be signed by the patentee.

PATENTS FORM No. 55

PATENTS ACT 1949

APPLICATION UNDER SECTION 56 TO DETERMINE A DISPUTE BETWEEN EMPLOYER AND EMPLOYEE AS TO RIGHTS IN AN INVENTION

*(To be accompanied by a copy and a statement in duplicate setting
out the facts of the dispute and the relief sought)*

I/We (a)..
....

(*a*) State name and address.

hereby declare that in respect of the rights in the invention for which
an application for a patent was made by..
....

and numbered..........................(b) and upon which a patent has been
granted, a dispute has arisen between me/us and (c)...................................
....

(*b*) Delete if a patent has not been granted.

(*c*) State name and address of other party to dispute.

and I/we hereby apply to the Comptroller to determine the dispute.
    The facts of the dispute, and the relief which I/we seek are set out
fully in the accompanying statement.
    Communications should be sent to..
at (d)..
....

(*d*) The address must be within the United Kingdom.

(e) who is/are hereby appointed to act for me/us.

(f)..
....

(*e*) Delete if not applicable.

(*f*) Signature.

To the Comptroller,
    The Patent Office,
        25, Southampton Buildings,
            Chancery Lane, London, W.C.2.

PATENTS FORM NO. 56

PATENTS ACT 1949

REFERENCE TO THE COMPTROLLER OF A DISPUTE AS TO INFRINGEMENT (SECTION 67)

(a) Insert, in full, name and address of patentee or exclusive licensee.

(b) Insert, in full, name and address of the other party to the dispute.

(c) Insert name as at (a).

(d) Delete whichever does not apply.

(e) Insert name as at (b).

(f) State full particulars of these matters. They may be given or continued on a separate sheet or sheets.

(g) The address must be within the United Kingdom.

(h) Delete if not applicable.

We (a)..

and (b)..

....
hereby refer to the Comptroller for determination of a dispute whether any claim of the specification of Patent No...............................of which the said (c)..
is/are the (d) (patentee...) (exclusive licensee...) has been infringed by anything done by the said (e)..
....or whether any such claim alleged to be infringed is valid.

The matters in dispute are (f)..

....

The matters on which we are in agreement are (f)..

....

....
(To be signed by the patentee or exclusive licensee)
Communications should be sent to..

....
at (g)..

....
(h) who is/are hereby appointed to act for me/us.

....
(To be signed by the other party to the dispute)
Communications should be sent to..

....
at (g)..
(h) who is/are hereby appointed to act for me/us.

....

To the Comptroller,
    The Patent Office,
        25, Southampton Buildings,
            Chancery Lane, London, W.C.2.

PATENTS FORM NO. 57

PATENTS ACT 1949

REQUEST FOR ALTERATION OF A NAME OR NATIONALITY OR AN ADDRESS OR AN ADDRESS FOR SERVICE IN THE REGISTER OF PATENTS

(a) State (in full) name and address of applicant or applicants.

(b) Strike out words not applicable.

(c) Insert name, nationality, or address or address for service, as the case may be.

(d) Signature of applicant or applicants.

In the matter of Patent No...............................

I/We (a)..

....

....
hereby request that the (b) name
                (b) nationality
                (b) address
                (b) address for service
now upon the Register of Patents may be altered to (c)...............................

....
(d)..

NOTE. Where the request is for alteration in a name or nationality, evidence of the alteration must be furnished.

To the Comptroller,
    The Patent Office,
        25, Southampton Buildings,
            Chancery Lane, London, W.C.2.

PATENTS FORM NO. 58

PATENTS ACT 1949

APPLICATION FOR ENTRY OF NAME OF PROPRIETOR OR CO-PROPRIETOR IN THE REGISTER OF PATENTS

I/We (a).. *(a)* Insert (in full) name, address and nationality.

....

....

hereby apply that you will enter my/our name in the Register of Patents as proprietor............(or co-proprietor............) of Patent No.......... at present registered in the name of (b)*.. *(b)* Give name of registered proprietor.

....

I/We claim to be so entitled by virtue of (c).. *(c)* Specify the particulars of such document giving its date, and the parties to the same, and showing how the claim here made is substantiated.

....

....

....

....

....

....

And in proof whereof I/we transmit the accompanying (d)....................... *(d)* Insert the nature of the document. The certified copy should be written, typewritten or printed on *foolscap paper on one side only.*

....with a certified copy thereof.

My/Our address for service in the United Kingdom is..............................

....

(e).. *(e)* Signature.

(f).. *(f)* State in what capacity the signatory is acting.

* If the application is in respect of more than one patent, the numbers thereof, as well as the particulars required at (b) above, should be given in a separate schedule which should be attached to this Form.

To the Comptroller,

    The Patent Office,

        25, Southampton Buildings,

            Chancery Lane, London, W.C.2.

PATENTS FORM NO. 59

PATENTS ACT 1949

APPLICATION FOR ENTRY OF NOTICE OF A MORTGAGE OR LICENCE IN THE REGISTER OF PATENTS

(a) Insert (in full) name, address and nationality.

I/We (a)..

....

....

hereby apply that you will enter in the Register of Patents a notice of the following interest in a patent:—

(b) Insert the nature of the claim, whether by way of mortgage or licence.

I/We claim to be entitled (b)..

....to an interest in

Patent No...* at present registered in the

(c) Give name of registered proprietor.

name of (c) ....

....

(d) Specify the particulars of such document, giving its date, and the parties to the same.

by virtue of (d)..

....

....

....

....

....

(e) Insert the nature of the document. The certified copy should be written, typewritten or printed on *foolscap paper on one side only.*

And in proof whereof I/we transmit the accompanying (e).....................

.... with a certified copy thereof.

My/Our address for service in the United Kingdom is.............................

....

(f) Signature.

(f).....................................

(g) State in what capacity the signatory is acting.

(g) ....

* If the application is in respect of more than one patent, the numbers thereof, as well as the particulars required at (c) and (d) above, should be given in a separate schedule which should be attached to this form.

To the Comptroller,

  The Patent Office,

    25, Southampton Buildings,

      Chancery Lane, London, W.C.2.

PATENTS FORM No. 60

PATENTS ACT 1949

APPLICATION UNDER SECTION 74 (2) BY ASSIGNOR FOR ENTRY OF NAME OF PROPRIETOR OR CO-PROPRIETOR IN THE REGISTER OF PATENTS

I/We (a)..   (a) Insert (in full) name and address.

....

....

hereby apply that you will enter the name(s) of (b).................................   (b) Insert name address and nationality of person(s) to be registered.

....

....

in the Register of Patents as proprietor (or part proprietor) of Patent No.........................* of which I am/we are the registered proprietor(s).

He is/they are entitled to the said patent or to a share therein by virtue of (c)...   (c) Specify the particulars of such document, giving its date, and the parties to the same, and showing how the claim here made is substantiated.

....

....

....

....

....

....

And in proof whereof I/we transmit the accompanying (d)......................   (d) Insert the nature of the document. The certified copy should be written, typewritten or printed on *foolscap paper on one side only.*

...............................with a certified copy thereof.

My/Our address for service in the United Kingdom is.............................

....

The address for service in the United Kingdom of the person(s) to be registered as proprietor or co-proprietor is:—...

....

(e)...   (e) Signature.

(f)...   (f) State in what capacity the signatory is acting.

* If the application is in respect of more than one patent, the numbers thereof, as well as the particulars required at (b) and (c) above, should be given in a separate schedule which should be attached to this Form.

To the Comptroller,

     The Patent Office,
         25, Southampton Buildings,
             Chancery Lane, London, W.C.2.

2ff

PATENTS FORM NO. 61

PATENTS ACT 1949

APPLICATION UNDER SECTION 74 (2) BY MORTGAGOR OR LICENSOR FOR ENTRY OF NOTICE OF A MORTGAGE OR LICENCE IN THE REGISTER OF PATENTS

(a) Insert (in full) name and address.

I/We (a)...

....

....

hereby apply that you will enter in the Register of Patents a notice of the

(b) Insert name, address and nationality of mortgagee or licensee.

following interest in a patent:—(b)..

....

(c) Insert the nature of the claim, whether by way of Mortgage or Licence.

He/They are entitled (c)...

....to an interest in Patent

No..*, of which I am/we are the registered

(d) Specify the particulars of such document, giving its date, and the parties to the same.

proprietor(s), by virtue of (d)..

....

....

....

....

....

....

(e) Insert the nature of the document. The certified copy should be written, typewritten or printed on *foolscap paper on one side only.*

And in proof whereof I/we transmit the accompanying (e).....................

.............................with a certified copy thereof.

My/Our address for service in the United Kingdom is............................

....

....

The address for service in the United Kingdom of the person(s) to be

registered as mortgagee or licensee is:—...

....

(f) Signature.

(f)...

(g) State in what capacity the signatory is acting.

(g)..

* If the application is in respect of more than one patent, the numbers thereof, as well as the particulars required at (c) and (d) above, should be given in a separate schedule which should be attached to this Form.

To the Comptroller,
    The Patent Office,
        25, Southampton Buildings,
            Chancery Lane, London, W.C.2.

PATENTS FORM NO. 62

PATENTS ACT 1949

APPLICATION FOR ENTRY OF NOTIFICATION OF DOCUMENT IN REGISTER OF PATENTS

I/We (a)... (a) Insert (in
....   full) name
transmit the accompanying (b)...   address and
....   nationality
....   of the party
....   benefiting under
....   the document.

(together with a certified copy thereof) (c) affecting the proprietorship of   (b) Specify the
particulars of
the document,
Patent No.................................* at present registered in the name of   giving its
nature, date,
and the parties
(d) ....   to the same.
....
....   (c) The certified
copy should
be written,
and request that a notification thereof may be entered in the Register of   typewritten or
printed on
Patents.   foolscap paper
(e)..   on one side only.

(f)..   (d) State name of
registered
proprietor.
* If the application is in respect of more than one patent the numbers and
particulars thereof should be given in a separate schedule which should be   (e) Signature.
attached to this Form.   (f) State in
what capacity
the signatory
is acting.

To the Comptroller,
The Patent Office,
25, Southampton Buildings,
Chancery Lane, London, W.C.2.

PATENTS FORM NO. 63

PATENTS ACT 1949

APPLICATION FOR ENTRY OF A CLAIM TO BE DEEMED A LICENSEE IN THE REGISTER OF PATENTS

I/We (a)..   (a) State name,
address and
....   nationality.
....
hereby apply that you will enter my/our claim to be deemed to have acted
with the licence of the patentee (exclusive licensee) in accordance with the
conditions in the Order dated..extending the
term of Patent No..............................
Evidence in support of my/our claim accompanies this application.
My/Our address for service in the United Kingdom is..............................
....
....
(b)..   (b) Signature.
To the Comptroller,
The Patent Office,
25, Southampton Buildings,
Chancery Lane, London, W.C.2.

PATENTS FORM No. 64

PATENTS ACT 1949

REQUEST FOR CORRECTION OF CLERICAL ERROR (SECTION 76)

(a) State full name and address.

I/We (a)..
....
....

(b) State whether in application, specification, entry in register, patent, or the particular relevant document.

hereby request that the clerical error(s) in the (b)...
relating to application/patent No......................................indicated in red ink
in the annexed copy of the said (b)...
or shown as follows:—

....
....
....
....

may be corrected.

Communications should be sent to..

(c) The address must be within the United Kingdom.

.... at (c)..
(d) who is/are hereby appointed to act for me/us.

(d) Delete if not applicable.

(e)..

To the Comptroller,

(e) To be signed by applicant or his authorised agent.

The Patent Office,
25, Southampton Buildings,
Chancery Lane, London, W.C.2.

PATENTS FORM No. 65

PATENTS ACT 1949

NOTICE OF OPPOSITION TO THE CORRECTION OF A CLERICAL ERROR

(To be accompanied by a copy, and a statement of case in duplicate.)

(a) State (in full) name and address.

I/We (a)..
....

hereby give notice of opposition to the correction of an alleged clerical
error in ....
....

which said correction has been applied for by...

The grounds upon which the said correction is opposed are as follows:—

....
....
....
....

Communications should be sent to..

(b) The address must be within the United Kingdom.

at (b) ....
(c) who is/are hereby appointed to act for me/us.

(c) Delete if not applicable.

(d)..

(d) To be signed by opponents.

To the Comptroller,

The Patent Office,
25, Southampton Buildings,
Chancery Lane, London, W.C.2.

PATENTS FORM NO. 66

PATENTS ACT 1949

REQUEST FOR CERTIFICATE OF COMPTROLLER

Patent (or Application) No...................... of 19......

....

I/We ....

of...

hereby request you to furnish me/us with your Certificate to the effect

that (a) .... *(a)* Here set out
the particulars
which the
Comptroller is
requested to
certify, and of
any copies of
documents
which are to be
annexed to the
Certificate,
stating also the
purpose for
which the
copies are
required.

(b) ....

(b) Name and
full address
to which
Certificate is
to be sent.

To the Comptroller,
   The Patent Office,
      25, Southampton Buildings,
         Chancery Lane, London, W.C.2.

PATENTS FORM NO. 67

PATENTS ACT 1949

REQUEST FOR INFORMATION AS TO A MATTER AFFECTING A PATENT OR AN APPLICATION THEREFOR

Patent (or Application) No. ....of 19......

I/We ....

of ....

hereby request you to furnish me/us with the following information
affecting the patent (or application) aforesaid:—

(a) ....

(a) Here set out
particulars as
to the matter
in respect of
which
information
is sought.

(b)...

(b) To be signed
by the person
or persons
seeking
information, or
by their agent.

To the Comptroller,
   The Patent Office,
      25, Southampton Buildings,
         Chancery Lane, London, W.C.2.

PATENTS FORM No. 68

PATENTS ACT 1949

APPLICATION FOR DUPLICATE OF LETTERS PATENT

(a) State date, number, and full name and address of grantee or grantees.

(b) Insert title of invention.

(c) State, in full, the circumstances of the case, *which must be verified by evidence.*

I/We have to inform you that the Letters Patent dated (a)..........................
No. .... granted to... for an
invention the title of which is (b) ....
....
has been lost or destroyed, or cannot be produced in the following
circumstances:— (c) ....
....
....
....

(d) State interest possessed by applicant or applicants in the Patent.

(e) Signature of patentee or patentees and full address to which the duplicate is to be sent.

I/We accordingly apply for the issue of a duplicate of such Letters
Patent. (d)

(e)...

To the Comptroller,
    The Patent Office,
        25, Southampton Buildings,
            Chancery Lane, London, W.C.2.

PATENTS FORM No. 69

PATENTS ACT 1949

APPLICATION FOR ENTRY OF ORDER OF COURT IN THE REGISTER

(a) State (in full) name and address of applicant or applicants.

I/We (a)..
....
....
....

(b) State the purport of the Order.

hereby transmit an office copy of an Order of the Court with reference
to (b) ....
....
....
....
....

(c) Signature.

(c)..

SCHEDULE 3

Rule 9(1) and (3)

FORMS ADOPTED BY THE EUROPEAN CONVENTION RELATING TO THE FORMALITIES REQUIRED FOR PATENT APPLICATIONS DONE AT PARIS ON 11TH DECEMBER, 1953 (Cmd. 9095).

1A   *(Form reproduced from Annex 1 of the Convention)*

APPLICATION FOR PATIENT

I/We the undersigned (1)..

*acting { in my/our own name...

on behalf of (2)..

Hereby make application for a patent for the invention described in the accompanying specification (and drawings) and entitled.............................

I/We, the applicant {

claim(s) to be the true (and first) inventor(s) of the invention

claim(s) the following of us (them), namely
    to be the true and first inventor(s)
(or)
believe(s)..to be the
true and first inventor(s)
(and)
claim(s) to be the { Assignee(s) / Personal / Representative(s) } of the inventor

by virtue of (3)...

I/We request that the patent may be granted as a (4)...........................

....

....

to Patent (5) { No. ....

Application No......................... dated.............................

(6)..

....

Dated this.........................day of.........................19...

....(Signature)

List of documents accompanying this application:

....

....

N.B.—Delete where not applicable or required.

INSTRUCTIONS

(1) Give the following particulars:

   (a) When this form is signed by the applicant(s), here insert his/their first names, surname(s), full address(es) and nationality(ies) or the name and full address where the applicant is not a physical person;

   (b) When the form is signed by a nominee of the applicant(s) here insert the first names, surnames and full address of the nominee.

(2) In the case (1) (b), insert here the particulars at (1) (a).
    Note: Nominees cannot apply in certain countries.*

(3) Here insert particulars of the assignment or other document.

(4) Here indicate the nature of the protection applied for e.g. independent patent, patent of importation, patent for an improvement, patent or certificate of addition.

(5) In the case of a divisional application or where otherwise applicable, insert here the number of the related patent, or, where the related patent application is still pending, the number and date of such application.

(6) Insert here, where necessary, any other relevant particulars such as the authorisation of an agent in the country in which the application is made, or, if no such agent is appointed an address for service in that country.

Nominee applications are not accepted in the United Kingdom.

1B   (*Form reproduced from Annex II of the Convention*)

CONVENTION APPLICATION FOR PATENT

I/We the undersigned (1)...

*acting { in my/our own name..

{ on behalf of (2)...

Hereby declare that (an) application(s) for protection for an invention or inventions has(ve) been made in the following country(ies) on the following date(s), namely:—

in .... on...

by ....

in .... on...

by ....

in .... on...

by ....

and that the said application or each of the said applications was the first application in a Convention country.

I am/We are the assignee(s) of the said..

or the personal representative(s) of the said..

by virtue of (3)..

I/We request that a patent may be granted with priority founded on the above-mentioned application(s) in a Convention country(ies) for the invention described in the accompanying specification (and drawings) and entitled

....

....

I/We request that the patent may be granted as a (4)..............................

....

to Patent (5) { No. ....

{ Application No........................dated............................

(6)...

....

Dated this...................................day of...............................19......

....(Signature)

List of documents accompanying this application:

....

....

N.B.—Delete where not applicable or required.

INSTRUCTIONS

(1) Give the following particulars:

(*a*) When this form is signed by the applicant(s), here insert his/their first names, surname(s), full address(es) and nationality(ies) or the name and full address where the applicant is not a physical person;

(*b*) When the form is signed by a nominee of the applicant(s) here insert the first names, surname and full address of the nominee.

Note: Nominees cannot apply in certain countries.*

(2) In the case (1) (*b*), insert here the particulars at (1) (*a*).

(3) Here insert particulars of the assignment or other document.

(4) Here indicate the nature of the protection applied for e.g. independent patent, patent of importation, patent for an improvement, patent or certificate of addition.

(5) In the case of a divisional application or where otherwise applicable insert here the number of the related patent or, where the related patent application is still pending, the number and date of such application.

(6) Insert here, where necessary, any other relevant particulars such as the authorisation of an agent in the country in which the application is made, or, if no such agent is appointed, an address for service in that country.

Nominee applications are not accepted in the United Kingdom.

Rule 62   **SCHEDULE 4**

                                   FORM OF PATENT

Form A

ELIZABETH the Second by the Grace of God of the United Kingdom of Great Britain and Northern Ireland and of Her other Realms and Territories, Queen, Head of the Commonwealth, Defender of the Faith: To all to whom these presents shall come greeting:

WHEREAS a request for the grant of a patent has been made by

for the sole use and advantage of an invention for

AND WHEREAS We, being willing to encourage all inventions which may be for the public good, are graciously pleased to condescend to the request:

KNOW YE, THEREFORE, that We, of our especial grace, certain knowledge, and mere motion do by these presents, for Us, our heirs and successors, give and grant unto the person(s) above named and any successor(s), executor(s), administrator(s) and assign(s) (each and any of whom are hereinafter referred to as the patentee) our especial licence, full power, sole privilege, and authority, that the patentee or any agent or licensee of the patentee and no others, may subject to the conditions and provisions prescribed by any statute or order for the time being in force at all times hereafter during the term of years herein mentioned, make, use, exercise and vend the said invention within our United Kingdom of Great Britain and Northern Ireland, and the Isle of Man, and that the patentee shall have and enjoy the whole profit and advantage from time to time accruing by reason of the said invention during the term of sixteen years from the date hereunder written of these presents: AND to the end that the patentee may have and enjoy the sole use and exercise and the full benefit of the said invention, We do by these presents for Us, our heirs and successors, strictly command all our subjects whatsoever within our United Kingdom of Great Britain and Northern Ireland, and the Isle of Man, that they do not at any time during the continuance of the said term either directly or indirectly make use of or put in practice the said invention, nor in anywise imitate the same, without the written consent, licence or agreement of the patentee, on pain of incurring such penalties as may be justly inflicted on such offenders for their contempt of this our Royal command, and of being answerable to the patentee according to the law for damages thereby occasioned:

PROVIDED ALWAYS that these letters patent shall be revocable on any of the grounds from time to time by law prescribed as grounds for revoking letters patent granted by Us, and the same may be revoked and made void accordingly:

PROVIDED ALSO that nothing herein contained shall prevent the granting of licences in such manner and for such considerations as they may by law be granted: AND lastly, We do by these presents for Us, our heirs and successors, grant unto the patentee that these our letters patent shall be construed in the most beneficial sense for the advantage of the patentee.

IN WITNESS whereof We have caused these our letters to be made patent as of the   day of
one thousand nine hundred and   and to be
sealed.

                                   Comptroller-General of Patents,
                                   Designs, and Trade Marks.

        Seal of
    Patent Office.

FORM OF PATENT OF ADDITION

Form B

ELIZABETH the Second by the Grace of God of the United Kingdom of Great Britain and Northern Ireland and of Her other Realms and Territories, Queen, Head of the Commonwealth, Defender of the Faith: To all to whom these presents shall come greeting:

WHEREAS a request for the grant of a patent has been made by

for the sole use and advantage of an invention for

and it has been further requested that the patent may be granted as a patent of addition to Patent No.   dated the
day of   19   (hereinafter referred to as the main patent):

AND WHEREAS We, being willing to encourage all inventions which may be for the public good, are graciously pleased to condescend to the request:

KNOW YE, THEREFORE, that We ,of our especial grace, certain knowledge, and mere motion do by these presents for Us, our heirs and successors, give, and grant unto the person(s) above named and any successor(s), executor(s), administrator(s) and assign(s) (each and any of whom are hereinafter referred to as the patentee) our especial licence, full power, sole privilege, and authority, that the patentee or any agent, or licensee of the patentee and no others, may subject to the conditions and provisions prescribed by any statute or order for the time being in force at all times hereafter during the term of years herein mentioned, make, use, exercise and vend the said invention within our United Kingdom of Great Britain and Northern Ireland, and the Isle of Man, and that the patentee shall have and enjoy the whole profit and advantage from time to time accruing by reason of the said invention during a term beginning on the date hereunder written of these presents and ending at the expiration of sixteen years from the   day of
one thousand nine hundred and   the date of said main patent:
AND to the end that the patentee may have and enjoy the sole use and exercise and the full benefit of the said invention, We do by these presents for Us, our heirs and successors, strictly command all our subjects whatsoever within our United Kingdom of Great Britain and Northern Ireland, and the Isle of Man, that they do not at any time during the continuance of the said term either directly or indirectly make use of or put in practice the said invention, nor in anywise imitate the same, without the written consent, licence or agreement of the patentee, on pain of incurring such penalties as may be justly inflicted on such offenders for their contempt of this our Royal command, and of being answerable to the patentee according to law for damages thereby occasioned:

PROVIDED ALWAYS that these letters patent shall be revocable on any of the grounds from time to time by law prescribed as grounds for revoking letters patent granted by Us, and the same may be revoked and made void accordingly:

PROVIDED ALSO that nothing herein contained shall prevent the granting of licences in such manner and for such considerations as they may by law be granted: AND lastly, We do by these presents for Us, our heirs and successors, grant unto the patentee that these our letters patent shall be construed in the most beneficial sense for the advantage of the patentee.

IN WITNESS whereof We have caused these our letters to be made patent as of the   day of
one thousand nine hundred and   and to be sealed.
                                   Comptroller-General of Patents,
                                   Designs, and Trade Marks.

Seal of
Patent Office.

EXPLANATORY NOTE

(This Note is not part of the Rules.)

These Rules consolidate and amend the Patents Rules 1958, the Patents (Amendment) Rules 1964, the Patents (Amendment No. 2) Rules 1964, the Patents (Amendment) Rules 1966, the Patents (Amendment) Rules 1967 and the Patents (Amendment No. 2) Rules 1967. The principal amendments are—

(1) a new Rule (Rule 146) makes provision for the documents therein described to be open to public inspection ;

(2) the Forms of Patents and Patents of Addition (Schedule 4) are modified.

STATUTORY INSTRUMENTS

1968 No. 1390

AGRICULTURE

The Price Stability of Imported Products (Rates of Levy No. 4) Order 1968

Made -	-	-	-	16*th August* 1968
Coming into Operation				19*th August* 1968

The Minister of Agriculture, Fisheries and Food, in exercise of the powers conferred upon him by section 1(2), (4), (5), (6) and (7) of the Agriculture and Horticulture Act 1964(a) and of all other powers enabling him in that behalf, hereby makes the following order:—

1. This Order may be cited as the Price Stability of Imported Products (Rates of Levy No. 4) Order 1968 ; and shall come into operation on 19th August 1968.

2.—(1) In this order—

" the Principal Order " means the Price Stability of Imported Products (Levy Arrangements) Order 1966(b), as amended by any subsequent order and if any such order is replaced by any subsequent order the expression shall be construed as a reference to such subsequent order ;

AND other expressions have the same meaning as in the Principal Order.

(2) The Interpretation Act 1889(c) shall apply to the interpretation of this order as it applies to the interpretation of an Act of Parliament.

3. In accordance with and subject to the provisions of Part II of the Principal Order (which provides for the charging of levies on imports of certain specified commodities)—

(*a*) the rate of general levy for such imports into the United Kingdom of any specified commodity as are described in column 2 of Part I of the Schedule to this order in relation to a tariff heading indicated in column 1 of that Part shall be the rate set forth in relation thereto in column 3 of that Part ;

(*b*) the rate of country levy for such imports into the United Kingdom of any specified commodity as are described in column 2 of Part II of the Schedule to this order in relation to a tariff heading indicated in column 1 of that Part shall be the rate set forth in relation thereto in column 3 of that Part.

4. The Price Stability of Imported Products (Rates of Levy No. 3) Order 1968(**d**) shall be amended by deleting article 3 thereof and the Schedule thereto.

In Witness whereof the Official Seal of the Minister of Agriculture, Fisheries and Food is hereunto affixed on 16th August 1968.

(L.S.)   *A. C. Sparks,*

Authorised by the Minister.

(a) 1964 c. 28.   (b) S.I. 1966/936 (1966 II, p. 2271).   (c) 1889 c. 63.
                (d) S.I. 1968/1354(1968 II, p. 3757).

SCHEDULE

PART I

1. Tariff Heading	2. Description of Imports	3. Rate of General Levy
		per ton £ s. d.
10.01	Imports of :— Denatured wheat	1 5 0

PART II

1. Tariff Heading	2. Description of Imports	3. Rate of Country Levy
		per ton £ s. d.
10.01	Imports of :— Denatured wheat which has been grown in and consigned to the United Kingdom from Belgium, the French Republic, the Kingdom of the Netherlands or the Kingdom of Sweden	1 5 0

EXPLANATORY NOTE

(This Note is not part of the Order.)

This Order, which comes into operation on 19th August 1968, increases from 10s. to 25s. per ton—

(*a*) the general levy on imports of denatured wheat ; and

(*b*) the country levy on imports of denatured wheat which has been grown in and consigned to the United Kingdom from Belgium, France, the Netherlands or Sweden.

STATUTORY INSTRUMENTS

1968 No. 1391

AGRICULTURE

The Price Stability of Imported Products (Rates of Levy No. 5) Order 1968

Made - - -		19*th August* 1968
Coming into Operation		20*th August* 1968

The Minister of Agriculture, Fisheries and Food, in exercise of the powers conferred upon him by section 1(2), (4), (5), (6) and (7) of the Agriculture and Horticulture Act 1964(**a**) and of all other powers enabling him in that behalf, hereby makes the following order:—

1. This order may be cited as the Price Stability of Imported Products (Rates of Levy No. 5) Order 1968; and shall come into operation on 20th August 1968.

2.—(1) In this order—
"the Principal Order" means the Price Stability of Imported Products (Levy Arrangements) Order 1966(**b**), as amended by any subsequent order and if any such order is replaced by any subsequent order the expression shall be construed as a reference to such subsequent order;
AND other expressions have the same meaning as in the Principal Order.

(2) The Interpretation Act 1889(**c**) shall apply to the interpretation of this order as it applies to the interpretation of an Act of Parliament and as if this order and the order hereby revoked were Acts of Parliament.

3. In accordance with and subject to the provisions of Part II of the Principal Order (which provides for the charging of levies on imports of certain specified commodities)—

(*a*) the rate of general levy for such imports into the United Kingdom of any specified commodity as are described in column 2 of Part I of the Schedule to this order in relation to a tariff heading indicated in column 1 of that Part shall be the rate set forth in relation thereto in column 3 of that Part;

(*b*) the rate of country levy for such imports into the United Kingdom of any specified commodity as are described in column 2 of Part II of the Schedule to this order in relation to a tariff heading indicated in column 1 of that Part shall be the rate set forth in relation thereto in column 3 of that Part.

4. The Price Stability of Imported Products (Rates of Levy No. 4) Order 1968(**d**) is hereby revoked.

In Witness whereof the Official Seal of the Minister of Agriculture, Fisheries and Food is hereunto affixed on 19th August 1968.

(L.S.)

R. J. E. Taylor,
Assistant Secretary.

(**a**) 1964 c. 28.
(**c**) 1889 c. 63.
(**b**) S.I. 1966/936 (1966 II, p. 2271).
(**d**) S.I. 1968/1390 (1968 II, p. 4041).

SCHEDULE

PART I

1. Tariff Heading	2. Description of Imports	3. Rate of General Levy
		per ton £ s. d.
10.01	Imports of :— Denatured wheat	1 10 0

PART II

1. Tariff Heading	2. Description of Imports	3. Rate of Country Levy
		per ton £ s. d.
10.01	Imports of:— Denatured wheat which has been grown in and consigned to the United Kingdom from Belgium, the French Republic, the Kingdom of the Netherlands or the Kingdom of Sweden ...	1 10 0

EXPLANATORY NOTE

(This Note is not part of the Order.)

This Order, which comes into operation on 20th August 1968, increases from 25s. to 30s. per ton—

(a) the general levy on imports of denatured wheat; and

(b) the country levy on imports of denatured wheat which has been grown in and consigned to the United Kingdom from Belgium, France, the Netherlands or Sweden.

The Price Stability of Imported Products (Rates of Levy No. 4) Order 1968 is revoked.

STATUTORY INSTRUMENTS

1968 No. 1397 (S.140)

NATIONAL HEALTH SERVICE, SCOTLAND

The National Health Service (Executive Councils) (Supply) (Scotland) Regulations 1968.

Made - - -	*22nd August* 1968
Laid before Parliament	*4th September* 1968
Coming into Operation	*9th September* 1968

In exercise of the powers conferred on me by section 24 of the Health Services and Public Health Act 1968(**a**), and of all other powers enabling me in that behalf I hereby make the following regulations:—

1.—(1) These Regulations may be cited as the National Health Service (Executive Councils) (Supply) (Scotland) Regulations 1968 and shall come into operation on 9th September 1968.

(2) The Interpretation Act 1889(**b**) applies for the interpretation of these regulations as it applies for the interpretation of an Act of Parliament.

2. The goods and materials specified in Column 1 of the Schedule hereto, being goods and materials which it appears to the Secretary of State it is necessary or expedient for a person providing the service specified in Column 2 of the said Schedule in relation to such goods and materials to have for the purpose of providing that service, are hereby prescribed for the purposes of the said section 24.

William Ross,

One of Her Majesty's Principal
Secretaries of State.

St. Andrew's House,
Edinburgh.
22nd August 1968.

(**a**) 1968 c. 46.	(**b**) 1889 c. 63.

SCHEDULE

Column 1	Column 2
Sterile disposable hypodermic syringes	General Medical Services under Pt. IV of the National Health Service (Scotland) Act 1947(a)
Sterile disposable hypodermic needles	- ditto -

EXPLANATORY NOTE

(This Note is not part of the Regulations.)

These Regulations prescribe goods and materials which an Executive Council, subject to the consent of the Secretary of State and on terms which he and the Treasury may approve, may supply to practitioners as part of their arrangements for the provision in their area of general medical services under Part IV of the National Health Service (Scotland) Act 1947.

(a) 1947 c. 27.

1968 No. 1399

EXCHANGE CONTROL

The Exchange Control (Scheduled Territories) (Amendment) (No. 2) Order 1968

Made - - -	*26th August* 1968
Laid before Parliament	*5th September* 1968
Coming into Operation	*6th September* 1968

The Treasury, in exercise of the powers conferred upon them by sections 1(3)(*b*) and 36(5) of the Exchange Control Act 1947(**a**), hereby make the following Order:—

1. Schedule 1 to the Exchange Control Act 1947, as amended by the Exchange Control (Scheduled Territories) Order 1967(**b**) and as further amended (**c**), shall be further amended by inserting after paragraph 28 the following paragraph:—

" 28A. Swaziland."

2. This Order shall extend to the Channel Islands, and any reference in this Order to the Exchange Control Act 1947 includes a reference to that Act as extended by the Exchange Control (Channel Islands) Order 1947(**d**).

3. The Interpretation Act 1889(**e**) shall apply for the interpretation of this Order as it applies for the interpretation of an Act of Parliament.

4. This Order may be cited as the Exchange Control (Scheduled Territories) (Amendment) (No. 2) Order 1968, and shall come into operation on 6th September 1968.

26th August 1968.

B. K. O'Malley,

Joseph Harper,

Two of the Lords Commissioners
of Her Majesty's Treasury.

EXPLANATORY NOTE

(This Note is not part of the Order.)

Under the Swaziland Independence Act 1968, Swaziland ceases, on 6th September, 1968, to be a protected state and attains independence. This Order amends the list of scheduled territories contained in Schedule 1 to the Exchange Control Act, 1947 by the inclusion of Swaziland by name; previously it was included in the list by virtue of being a protected state.

(**a**) 1947 c. 14.
(**b**) S.I. 1967/1767 (1967 III, p. 4736).
(**c**) S.I. 1968/333 (1968 I, p. 971).
(**d**) S.R. & O. 1947/2034 (Rev. VI, p. 1001: 1947 I, p. 660).
(**e**) 1889 c. 63.

STATUTORY INSTRUMENTS

1968 No. 1402

HARBOURS, DOCKS, PIERS AND FERRIES

The National Ports Council Provision of Funds (Variation) Scheme 1968 (Confirmation) Order 1968

Made - - - -	*27th August* 1968
Laid before Parliament	10*th September* 1968
Coming into Operation	16*th September* 1968

The Minister of Transport (hereinafter referred to as "the Minister") in exercise of the powers conferred upon him by section 4(5) and (7) of the Harbours Act 1964(**a**) (hereinafter referred to as "the Act") and of all other enabling powers hereby makes the following Order:—

1.—(1) The Minister hereby confirms the scheme submitted to him by the National Ports Council in pursuance of section 4(7) of the Act for the variation of the National Ports Council Provision of Funds Scheme 1965(**b**) as amended by the National Ports Council Provision of Funds (Variation) Scheme 1966(**c**) and the National Ports Council Provision of Funds (Variation) Scheme 1967(**d**).

(2) The scheme is set out in the Schedule to this Order and shall come into force on the date specified in Article 2(1) of this Order.

2.—(1) This Order may be cited as the National Ports Council Provision of Funds (Variation) Scheme 1968 (Confirmation) Order 1968 and shall come into operation on the 16th September 1968.

(2) The Interpretation Act 1889(**e**) shall apply for the interpretation of this Order as it applies for the interpretation of an Act of Parliament.

Given under the Official Seal of the Minister of Transport the 27th August 1968.

(L.S.)

Richard Marsh,
Minister of Transport.

(a) 1964 c. 40
(c) S.I. 1966/989 (1966 II, p. 2369).
(e) 52 & 53 Vict. c. 63.

(b) S.I. 1965/2196 (1965 III, p. 6417).
(d) 1967/1392 (1967 III, p. 4066).

SCHEDULE

NATIONAL PORTS COUNCIL

SCHEME UNDER SECTION 4 OF THE HARBOURS ACT 1964

The National Ports Council, in exercise of their powers under section 4 of the Harbours Act 1964, hereby make the following scheme:—

1. This scheme may be cited as the National Ports Council Provision of Funds (Variation) Scheme 1968.

2. The National Ports Council Provision of Funds Scheme 1965 as varied by the National Ports Council Provision of Funds (Variation) Scheme 1966 and the National Ports Council Provision of Funds (Variation) Scheme 1967 (hereinafter referred to as "the principal scheme") shall have effect as if in the schedule—

    (*a*) there were substituted for the words "Forth Conservancy Board" the words "Forth Ports Authority";

    (*b*) there were inserted immediately below the words "Port of Par Ltd" the words "Port of Tyne Authority";

    (*c*) the words "Gateshead Corporation", "Granton Harbour Ltd.", "Humber Conservancy Board", "Margate Pier and Harbour Co.", "Kirkcaldy Corporation", "Leith Dock Commission", "Newcastle Upon Tyne Corporation", "Southampton Harbour Board", "Tynemouth Corporation" and "Tyne Improvement Commission" were deleted.

3. As respects the accounting period beginning on 1st January 1969:—

    (*a*) the aggregate of the gross amount of dues received by the Forth Conservancy Board, Granton Harbour Limited, Kirkcaldy Corporation and the Leith Dock Commission respectively in the year ended on 31st December 1967 and the gross amount of dues received in that year by the British Transport Docks Board in respect of their undertakings which have been transferred to the Forth Ports Authority by the Forth Harbour Reorganisation Scheme 1966 shall be deemed for the purposes of article 3(2) of the principal scheme to be the gross amount of dues received by the Forth Ports Authority in the last financial year;

    (*b*) the aggregate of the gross amount of dues received by Gateshead Corporation, Newcastle Upon Tyne Corporation, Tynemouth Corporation and the Tyne Improvement Commission in the year ended on 31st December 1967 shall be deemed for the purposes of article 3(2) of the principal scheme to be the gross amount of dues received by the Port of Tyne Authority in the last financial year.

4.—(1) In this scheme any expression to which a meaning is attributed by the principal scheme shall, unless the context otherwise requires, have the meaning so attributed.

(2) The Interpretation Act 1889 shall apply for the interpretation of this scheme as it applies for the interpretation of an Act of Parliament.

EXPLANATORY NOTE

(This Note is not part of the Order.)

By this Order the Minister of Transport confirms a Scheme made and submitted to him by the National Ports Council under section 4 of the Harbours Act 1964 for varying the National Ports Council Provision of Funds Scheme 1965. The Variation Scheme as so confirmed is set out in the Schedule.

STATUTORY INSTRUMENTS

1968 No. 1404

AGRICULTURE

The Price Stability of Imported Products (Rates of Levy) (Amendment) Order 1968

Made - - - - *26th August* 1968
Coming into Operation *27th August* 1968

The Minister of Agriculture, Fisheries and Food, in exercise of the powers conferred upon him by section 1(2), (4), (5), (6) and (7) of the Agriculture and Horticulture Act 1964(a) and of all other powers enabling him in that behalf, hereby makes the following order :—

1.—(1) This Order may be cited as the Price Stability of Imported Products (Rates of Levy) (Amendment) Order 1968 ; and shall come into operation on 27th August 1968.

(2) The Interpretation Act 1889(b) shall apply to the interpretation of this order as it applies to the interpretation of an Act of Parliament.

2. The Price Stability of Imported Products (Rates of Levy No. 2) Order 1968(c) as amended(d) shall be further amended by deleting therefrom sub-paragraph (*b*) of article 3 thereof and Part II of the Schedule thereto.

In Witness whereof the Official Seal of the Minister of Agriculture, Fisheries and Food is hereunto affixed on 26th August 1968.

(L.S.)

R. J. E. Taylor,
Assistant Secretary.

EXPLANATORY NOTE

(*This Note is not part of the Order.*)

This Order, which comes into operation on 27th August 1968, amends the Price Stability of Imported Products (Rates of Levy No. 2) Order 1968 to remove the country levy fixed by that order on imports of wheat grown in Sweden and consigned to the United Kingdom from that country.

(a) 1964 c. 28.   (b) 1889 c. 63.   (c) S.I. 1968/1225 (1968 II, p. 3286).
(d) S.I. 1968/1354(1968 II, p. 3757).

STATUTORY INSTRUMENTS

1968 No. 1406

NATIONAL HEALTH SERVICE, ENGLAND AND WALES

The Health and Welfare Services (Provision of Instruction) Regulations 1968

Made - - - -	30*th August* 1968
Laid before Parliament	6*th September* 1968
Coming into Operation	9*th September* 1968

The Minister of Health, in exercise of the powers conferred on him by section 63 of the Health Services and Public Health Act 1968(a) and of all other powers enabling him in that behalf, with the approval of the Treasury, hereby makes the following regulations:—

1. These Regulations may be cited as the Health and Welfare Services (Provision of Instruction) Regulations 1968 and shall come into operation on 9th September 1968.

2. The Interpretation Act 1889(b) shall apply to the interpretation of these regulations as it applies to the interpretation of an Act of Parliament.

3. The classes of person described in the schedule hereto are hereby specified as classes for the purposes of section 63(1)(*b*) of the Health Services and Public Health Act 1968 (which enables the Minister of Health to provide instruction for persons of specified classes who are employed or contemplate employment in certain activities connected with health or welfare).

Regulation 3   **SCHEDULE**

Specified classes

Ancillary staff in general medical practices.

Chiropodists.

Dental auxiliaries.

Dental hygienists.

Dental technicians.

Employees of—

    (i) the Dental Estimates Board,
    (ii) Executive Councils,
    (iii) the Joint Pricing Committee for England,
    (iv) the Welsh Joint Pricing Committee.

(a) 1968 c. 46.   (b) 1889 c. 63.

Midwives.

Occupational therapists.

Ophthalmic opticians.

Registered dentists.

Registered medical practitioners.

Social workers.

Speech therapists.

Teachers of the mentally handicapped.

Given under the official seal of the Minister of Health on 26th August 1968.

L.S.   *Kenneth Robinson,*
                                       Minister of Health.

We approve these regulations.

                                       B. K. O'Malley,
                                       Joseph Harper,
                                       Two of the Lords Commissioners
30th August 1968.   of Her Majesty's Treasury.

EXPLANATORY NOTE
(This note is not part of the Regulations.)

Section 63(1) of the Health Services and Public Health Act 1968 enables the Minister of Health to provide instruction for (*a*) persons employed or contemplating employment under hospital authorities and (*b*) classes of person, to be specified in Regulations, who are employed or contemplating employment in certain other health or welfare services. These Regulations specify these classes of person, which include registered medical practitioners and dentists, ophthalmic opticians, employees of Executive Councils and other bodies set up under Part IV of the National Health Service Act 1946, ancillary staff in general medical practices and members of certain professions supplementary to medicine.

STATUTORY INSTRUMENTS

1968 No. 1407 (S.141)

NATIONAL HEALTH SERVICE, SCOTLAND

The Health and Welfare Services (Provision of Instruction) (Scotland) Regulations 1968

Made - - -		*26th August* 1968
Laid before Parliament		*6th September* 1968
Coming into Operation		*9th September* 1968

In exercise of the powers conferred on me by section 63 of the Health Services and Public Health Act 1968(**a**) and of all other powers enabling me in that behalf, and with the approval of the Treasury, I hereby make the following regulations:—

1. These regulations may be cited as the Health and Welfare Services (Provision of Instruction) (Scotland) Regulations 1968 and shall come into operation on 9th September 1968.

2. The Interpretation Act 1889(**b**) applies for the interpretation of these regulations as it applies for the interpretation of an Act of Parliament.

3. The classes of persons described in the schedule hereto are hereby specified as classes for the purposes of section 63(1)(**b**) of the Health Services and Public Health Act 1968 (which enables the Secretary of State to provide instruction for persons of specified classes who are employed or contemplate employment in certain activities connected with health and welfare).

St. Andrew's House,
Edinburgh, 1.
22nd August 1968.

William Ross,
One of Her Majesty's Principal
Secretaries of State.

We Approve.
26th August 1968.

B. K. O'Malley,
Joseph Harper,
Two of the Lords Commissioners
of Her Majesy's Treasury.

(**a**) 1968 c. 46.   (**b**) 1889 c. 63.

SCHEDULE

Specified classes

Ancillary staff in general medical practices
Chiropodists
Dental auxiliaries
Dental hygienists
Dental technicians
Employees of:—
    (i) The Scottish Dental Estimates Board
    (ii) Executive Councils
    (iii) the Drug Accounts Committee
Midwives
Occupational therapists
Ophthalmic opticians
Registered dentists
Registered medical practitioners
Social workers
Speech therapists
Teachers of the mentally handicapped

EXPLANATORY NOTE

(*This Note is not part of the Regulations.*)

Section 63(1) of the Health Services and Public Health Act 1968 enables the Secretary of State to provide instruction (*a*) for persons employed or contemplating employment under a hospital authority, and (*b*) for classes of persons to be specified in Regulations who are employed or contemplating employment in certain other health and welfare services. These Regulations specify the classes ; they include registered medical practitioners and dentists, ophthalmic opticians, employees of Executive Councils and other bodies set up under Part IV of the National Health Service (Scotland) Act 1947, ancillary staff in general medical practices, and members of certain of the professions supplementary to medicine.

STATUTORY INSTRUMENTS

1968 No. 1408

INSURANCE

The Insurance Companies (Accounts and Forms) Regulations 1968

Made - - - -	*29th August* 1968
Laid before Parliament	*11th September* 1968
Coming into Operation	*1st January* 1969

The Board of Trade, in pursuance of the powers conferred upon them by sections 4, 5, 7, 9, 13, 33 and 34 of the Insurance Companies Act 1958(**a**) as amended by the Companies Act 1967(**b**), hereby make the following Regulations:—

1. These Regulations apply to every insurance company to which the Insurance Companies Act 1958 as so amended applies other than a company which carries on in Great Britain no insurance business other than industrial assurance business (that Act as so amended being hereinafter referred to as " the Act ").

Accounts

2.—(1) The accounts of every company which are prepared in pursuance of section 4 of the Act and all statements, certificates and reports annexed thereto which by this Regulation or by Regulation 3, 4 or 6 are required or permitted to be so annexed shall give a true and fair view of the state of affairs of the company as at the end of its financial year and of the profit or loss of the company for the financial year:

Provided that such accounts, statements, certificates and reports shall not be deemed not to give such a true and fair view by reason only of the fact that the amount at which any asset of the company has been included in the balance sheet is less than the full value of that asset.

(2) Without prejudice to the general requirements of paragraph (1) of this Regulation there shall be shown, stated or included, as the case may be, in or in a note on the accounts of every company which are prepared in pursuance of section 4 of the Act or in a statement or report annexed thereto the matters and particulars which, by virtue of sections 196 and 197 of the Companies Act 1948(**c**) and sections 3 to 8 (inclusive) of the Companies Act 1967, would have been required to be so shown, stated or included if those accounts had been the accounts of a company within the meaning of the Companies Act 1948 laid before the company in general meeting and in addition—

> (*a*) the balance sheet and profit and loss account of a company which are so prepared shall comply with the requirements of Schedule 1 hereto so far as applicable thereto;
>
> (*b*) the revenue account of a composite company which is so prepared shall be in two parts, one part relating to the company's long-term business and the other part relating to the company's general business;

(**a**) 1958 c. 72. (**b**) 1967 c. 81.
(**c**) 1948 c. 38.

(c) the revenue account of a company which in the financial year carried on no insurance business other than long-term business and which is so prepared and that part of the revenue account of a composite company which relates to its long-term business and which is so prepared (each being hereinafter referred to as the "long-term business revenue account") shall be in the form set out in Part I of Schedule 2 hereto;

(d) the long-term business revenue account shall have annexed to it a statement relating to the company's long-term business for the financial year in the form set out in Part II of Schedule 2 hereto;

(e) the revenue account of a company which in the financial year carried on no insurance business other than general business and which is so prepared and that part of the revenue account of a composite company which relates to its general business and which is so prepared (each being hereinafter referred to as the " general business revenue account ") shall be in the form set out in Part III of Schedule 2 hereto: except that a company which at no time in the financial year carried on any general business other than marine, aviation and transport insurance business may prepare its general business revenue account in the form set out in Part IV of Schedule 2 hereto;

(f) a general business revenue account may have annexed to it a revenue statement in the form set out in Part IV of Schedule 2 hereto relating to any one or more of the categories of marine, aviation and transport insurance business (any statement so annexed being hereinafter referred to as a " three-year business revenue statement ");

(g) every general business revenue account shall have annexed to it a statement relating to the company's general business for the financial year in the form set out in Part V of Schedule 2 hereto (such statement being hereinafter referred to as the " general business premium analysis ");

(h) all amounts which are required to be shown in the accounts or in any statement, certificate or report annexed thereto which by this Regulation or by Regulation 3 or 4 is required or permitted to be so annexed shall be shown in sterling but may be shown to the nearer £1,000 and the basis on which foreign currencies have been converted into sterling, where the amount affected is material, shall be stated in a statement annexed to the accounts;

(i) for all items shown in the accounts or in any statement, certificate or report annexed thereto which by this Regulation or by Regulation 3 or 4 is required or permitted to be so annexed, other than a three-year business revenue statement or a general business revenue account prepared in the form of such a statement, there shall, except in the case of accounts relating to the first financial year of the company beginning after 31st December 1968, be shown the corresponding amounts for the immediately preceding financial year.

Certificates

3. There shall be annexed to every balance sheet of a company prepared in pursuance of section 4 of the Act a certificate signed by the secretary or manager, if any, and where there are more than two directors of the company by at least two of those directors, and where there are not more than two directors by all the directors, and such certificate shall state—

(a) whether or not, in the opinion of those signing the certificate, the value of the company's assets at the end of the financial year was in the aggregate at least equal to the aggregate of the amounts thereof shown in the balance sheet and, if for the purpose of giving this opinion any of the assets dealt with in the statement or report prepared in pursuance of paragraph 10 of Schedule 1 hereto have been valued at other than their market value, the basis on which each such valuation was made;

(*b*) whether or not, in their opinion, the aggregate of the market values at the end of the financial year of such of the company's realisable domestic assets as were free from any mortgage or charge together with the aggregate of the market values at that time of the company's equities of redemption in such of its realisable domestic assets as were mortgaged or charged otherwise than to secure the liabilities of a person other than the company was at least equal to the aggregate of the values at that time of the company's domestic liabilities (as defined in section 65(9) of the Companies Act 1967) to the extent that those liabilities were unsecured by mortgages or charges upon the company's realisable domestic assets; and for the purposes of this statement:

   (i) assets shall be deemed to be realisable domestic assets if they were, in the opinion of those signing the statement, realisable in the United Kingdom at the end of the financial year and the documents of title to which (where documents of title existed) were then in the United Kingdom,

   (ii) the extent to which a domestic liability of the company shall be deemed to be unsecured is the amount by which the value of that liability (as stated or included in the balance sheet) exceeds the market value at the end of the financial year of any realisable domestic assets of the company mortgaged or charged to secure that liability, and

   (iii) the reference to equities of redemption in assets mortgaged or charged shall, in relation to Scotland, be construed as a reference to rights to redeem such assets;

(*c*) in the case of a company which at the end of the financial year was carrying on general business—

   (i) the aggregate amount of the premiums as shown in the general business revenue account,

   (ii) the amount of the minimum solvency margin applicable to that company in the period immediately following the end of the financial year, and

   (iii) the amount by which, in their opinion, the aggregate of the amounts of the company's assets as stated in the balance sheet exceeded the company's liabilities at the end of the financial year after taking into account all prospective and contingent liabilities but not liabilities in respect of share capital.

4. In the case of a company which annexes a three-year business revenue statement to its general business revenue account or which prepares its general business revenue account in the form of such a statement there shall be contained in a note to that statement or account, as the case may be, a certificate signed by all the persons required to sign the certificate referred to in Regulation 3 stating—

(*a*) whether or not, in the opinion of those signing the certificate, the fund carried forward in that statement or account in relation to business transacted in the year of account is sufficient to meet all the liabilities outstanding at the end of the year of account in relation to that business (including those in respect of risks to be borne by the company after the end of the year of account in relation to that business), (*b*) whether or not, in their opinion, the total of the funds carried forward in that statement or account in relation to business transacted in the first year preceding the year of account is sufficient to meet all the liabilities outstanding at the end of the year of account in relation to that business,

(*c*) if funds are carried forward in that statement or account in relation to business transacted before the beginning of the first financial year preceding the year of account, whether or not, in their opinion, the total of the funds so carried forward is sufficient to meet all the liabilities outstanding at the end of the year of account in relation to that business, and

(*d*) if funds are not carried forward in that statement or account in relation to the business referred to in paragraph (*c*) of this Regulation, whether or not, in their opinion, the liabilities referred to in the said paragraph (*c*) have been adequately reinsured and the aggregate amount of premiums required to secure such reinsurance.

5. There shall be annexed to every balance sheet prepared in pursuance of section 4 of the Act being a balance sheet of a company which has at any time during the financial year carried on long-term business a certificate signed by an actuary stating whether or not, in his opinion, the aggregate amount of the liabilities of the company in relation to its long-term business as at the end of the financial year exceeded the aggregate amount of those liabilities as shown in the balance sheet.

6. There shall be annexed to every long-term business revenue account a certificate signed by all the persons required to sign the certificate referred to in Regulation 3 stating whether or not, in the opinion of those signing the certificate, any part of any long-term business fund has been used directly or indirectly for any purpose for which it should not have been used having regard to the provisions of section 3 of the Act and, where applicable, to the provisions of any instrument setting up the fund.

Audit

7.—(1) The accounts of every company which are prepared in pursuance of section 4 of the Act and every statement, certificate and report annexed thereto which by Regulation 2, 3, 4 or 6 are required or permitted to be so annexed shall be audited by a person who would be qualified to audit them (otherwise than by virtue of section 13 of the Companies Act 1967) if they were the accounts of a company within the meaning of the Companies Act 1948 laid before the company in general meeting and he shall make a report on them.

(2) The report shall state whether or not, in the auditors' opinion, the accounts and the statements and reports annexed thereto which by Regulation 2 are required or permitted to be so annexed have been properly prepared in accordance with the provisions of these Regulations and whether or not, in their opinion and according to the information and explanations they have received, the certificates annexed to the accounts in pursuance of Regulations 3, 4 and 6 have been properly prepared in accordance with the provisions of these Regulations and whether or not, in their opinion and according to the information and explanations they have received, it was reasonable for the persons giving those certificates to have arrived at the opinions therein stated.

(3) A copy of the auditors' report shall be annexed to each copy of the accounts deposited at the Board of Trade in pursuance of section 8 of the Act.

(4) Subsections (4), (5) and (6) of section 14 of the Companies Act 1967 shall apply for the purposes of the audit of the accounts of a company prepared in pursuance of section 4 of the Act and shall apply as if the words "(unless it is framed as a consolidated profit and loss account)" wherever they occur were

omitted and as if references to the profit and loss account included references to the revenue account.

General Business Reinsurance Summary

8. General business is hereby prescribed as a class of insurance business for the purposes of section 7 of the Act and every company which carries on such business shall prepare a statement of business of that class in the form set out in Part I of Schedule 3 hereto with respect to each financial year of the company.

Claim Frequency and Claim Settlement Analyses

9. The following classes of insurance business are hereby prescribed for the purposes of section 7 of the Act, that is to say, liability insurance business, marine, aviation and transport insurance business, motor vehicle insurance business, pecuniary loss insurance business, personal accident insurance business and property insurance business.

10. For the purposes of Regulations 11 and 12 the business of each class of insurance business prescribed by Regulation 9 carried on by a company in each country shall be classified by the company into risk groups. Each such risk group shall comprise risks insured by the company in carrying on that class of business in that country which, in the opinion of the directors, are not significantly dissimilar either by reference to the nature of the objects exposed to such risks or by reference to the nature of the cover against such risks given by the company:

Provided that, if the directors are of opinion that the risks insured by the company in carrying on that class of business in that country are not significantly dissimilar either by reference to the nature of the objects exposed to such risks or by reference to the nature of the cover against such risks given by the company, there shall for the purposes of Regulations 11 and 12 be only one risk group for that class of business in that country.

11.—(1) Subject to Regulation 13 every company shall, with respect to each financial year and in relation to each risk group of each of the classes of insurance business prescribed by Regulation 9 carried on by it in each country, prepare a statement of its business in the appropriate form set out in Part II of Schedule 3 hereto.

(2) For the purposes of this Regulation the appropriate form set out in Part II of Schedule 3 hereto shall, in relation to business dealt with in a three-year revenue statement for the financial year or in a general business revenue account for the financial year prepared in the form of such a statement, be Form Number 2 and in relation to any other business be Form Number 1.

12.—(1) Subject to Regulation 13 every company shall, with respect to each financial year and in relation to each risk group of each of the classes of insurance business prescribed by Regulation 9 carried on by it in each country, prepare statements of its business in the form set out in Part III of Schedule 3 hereto and separate such statements shall be prepared for each completed financial year of the company in which claims within that risk group originated being claims still outstanding at the beginning of the year of account.

(2) For the purposes of this Regulation the financial year of the company in which a claim shall be regarded as having originated is—

  (a) in relation to claims made in connection with business dealt with in a three-year business revenue statement for the year of account or in a general business revenue account for that year prepared in the form of such a statement, the financial year of the company in which the business to which the claim relates is, for the purposes of that statement or account, treated as having been transacted, and

(b) in relation to other claims, the financial year of the company in which the incident giving rise to the claim occurred.

13.—(1) No statement need be prepared under Regulation 11 or 12 with respect to any financial year of a company in relation to any country if the aggregate of the company's gross premiums for that year in respect of general business carried on by it in that country as shown or included in the general business premium analysis of the company for the financial year was less than $2\frac{1}{2}$ per cent of the aggregate of its gross premiums for that year in respect of general business carried on by it in all parts of the world (including that country) as so shown or included.

(2) No statement need be prepared under Regulation 11 or 12 with respect to any financial year of a company in relation to any class of insurance business prescribed by Regulation 9 carried on by the company in any country if the aggregate of the company's gross premiums for that year in respect of that class of business carried on by it in that country as so shown or included was less than £25,000.

(3) No statement need be prepared under Regulation 11 or 12 with respect to any financial year of a company if the aggregate of the company's gross premiums for that year in respect of its general business carried on in the United Kingdom as so shown or included was less than £25,000.

Summary of Changes in Ordinary Long-Term Insurance Business

14. Ordinary long-term insurance business is hereby prescribed as a class of insurance business for the purposes of section 7 of the Act and every company which carries on such business shall prepare a statement of business of that class in the form set out in Part IV of Schedule 3 hereto with respect to each financial year of the company.

Qualifications of an Actuary

15. Any person acting as an " actuary " within the meaning of section 33(1) of the Act shall be either—

(a) a Fellow of the Institute of Actuaries or of the Faculty of Actuaries, or

(b) such other person having actuarial knowledge as the Board of Trade may, on the application of a company, approve.

Actuary's Valuation Report

16. The form set out in Schedule 4 hereto is hereby prescribed as the form of abstract of the actuary's report in respect of ordinary long-term insurance business for the purposes of section 5(1)(b) of the Act.

Statement of Ordinary Long-Term Insurance Business valued

17. The form set out in Schedule 5 hereto is hereby prescribed as the form of statement of ordinary long-term insurance business for the purposes of section 5(2) of the Act.

Interpretation

18.—(1) In these Regulations, except where the context otherwise requires, the following expressions have the meanings hereby respectively assigned to them, that is to say—

" accounts " means the balance sheet, the profit and loss account and the revenue account;

" authorised unit trust scheme " has the same meaning as in the Prevention of Fraud (Investments) Act 1958(a);

" aviation hull insurance business" means the business of effecting and carrying out contracts of insurance—

    (i) upon aircraft, or upon the machinery, tackle, furniture or equipment of aircraft;

    (ii) upon goods, merchandise or property of any description whatever on board of aircraft other than cargo;

    (iii) upon the freight of, or any other interest in or relating to, aircraft;

    (iv) against damage arising out of, or in connection with, the use of aircraft, other than damage to cargo, including third party risks; or

    (v) against any other risks (not being transit risks) insurance against which is customarily undertaken in conjunction with, or as incidental to, the undertaking of such business as falls within this definition by virtue of any of the foregoing paragraphs;

" British Government authority " means Her Majesty's Government in the United Kingdom, the Government of Northern Ireland, the Government of the Isle of Man or a public or local authority or nationalised industry or undertaking in the United Kingdom or the Isle of Man;

" capital redemption contracts " means contracts falling within section 59(6)(c) of the Companies Act 1967;

" categories of marine, aviation and transport insurance business " are marine hull insurance business, aviation hull insurance business and transport insurance business;

" claims equalisation " means the amount set aside as at the end of the financial year of a company for the purpose of its being used to prevent exceptional fluctuations in the amounts charged to revenue in subsequent financial years in respect of claims under insurance contracts;

" claims outstanding " means the amount set aside as at the end of the financial year of a company to meet claims under contracts of insurance in respect of incidents occurring before the end of that year which have not been paid (including claims the amounts of which have not been determined and claims arising out of incidents which have not been notified to the company) and to meet expenses likely to be incurred in connection with the settlement of such claims;

" company " means an insurance company to which the Act applies not being one which carries on in Great Britain no insurance business other than industrial assurance business;

" composite company " means a company which carries on both long-term business and general business;

" equity share capital " has the meaning assigned to it by section 154(5) of the Companies Act 1948;

" gross premiums " means premiums after deduction of refunds and rebates of premium but before deduction of premiums for reinsurance ceded and commission payable by the company;

" investments " means—

    (i) shares or debentures, or

(a) 1958 c. 45.

    (ii) securities of any Government or public or local authority, or

    (iii) rights or interests (described whether as units or otherwise) in any shares or debentures or in any securities of a Government or public or local authority or which may be acquired under any unit trust scheme;

" land " includes any interest or right in or over land, and " freehold land " and " leasehold land " include, in relation to land situated outside the United Kingdom, property in respect of which the company has corresponding rights and, where the company is the lessee of any land and has an option to extend the lease, the duration of the lease shall be taken to include any period for which the company may, by the exercise of the option, extend the lease;

" long-term personal accident contracts " means contracts falling within section 59(6)(b) of the Companies Act 1967;

" marine hull insurance business " means the business of effecting and carrying out contracts of insurance—

    (i) upon vessels, or upon the machinery, tackle, furniture or equipment of vessels;

    (ii) upon goods, merchandise or property of any description whatever on board of vessels other than cargo;

    (iii) upon the freight of, or any other interest in or relating to, vessels;

    (iv) against damage arising out of, or in connection with, the use of vessels, other than damage to cargo, including third party risks;

    (v) against risks incidental to the construction, repair or docking of vessels, including third party risks; or

    (vi) against any other risks (not being transit risks) insurance against which is customarily undertaken in conjunction with, or as incidental to, the undertaking of such business as falls within this definition by virtue of any of the foregoing paragraphs;

" the minimum solvency margin " means, in relation to any company at any time, the amount by which the value of its assets must exceed the amount of its liabilities at that time if it is not, under section 13(1) of the Act, then to be deemed for the purposes of section 222 of the Companies Act 1948 to be unable to pay its debts;

" premiums " in relation to long-term business includes the consideration for the granting of an annuity;

" profit and loss account " means, in relation to a company not trading for profit, income and expenditure account;

" quoted investment " has the meaning assigned to it in Schedule 8 to the Companies Act 1948 and " unquoted investment " shall be construed accordingly;

" redeemable investments " means investments which must be redeemed or repaid at or before a particular date;

" reinsurance ceded " includes reinsurance retroceded;

" reinsurance recoveries " includes recoveries in connection with reinsurance retroceded;

" subsidiary " has the same meaning as in the Companies Act 1948;

" transport insurance business " means the business of effecting and carrying out contracts of insurance against transit risks (whether the transit is by sea, inland water, land or air, or partly one and partly another), including risks incidental to the transit insured from the commencement of the transit to the ultimate destination covered by the insurance;

" unearned premiums " means the amount set aside as at the end of the financial year of a company out of premiums in respect of risks to be borne by the company after the end of that year under contracts of insurance entered into before the end of that year;

" unexpired risks " means the amount set aside as at the end of the financial year of a company, in addition to unearned premiums, in respect of risks to be borne by the company after the end of that year under contracts of insurance entered into before the end of that year;

" unit trust scheme " has the same meaning as in the Prevention of Fraud (Investments) Act 1958;

" variable interest investments " means investments which are not fixed interest investments;

" year of account " means, in relation to a three-year business revenue statement, to a general business revenue account prepared in the form of such a statement or to any statement prepared under Regulation 8, 11 or 12, the financial year of the company with respect to which the statement is prepared;

" year of origin " means, in relation to any claim made against a company, the financial year of the company in which the claim is, for the purposes of Regulation 12, regarded as having originated.

(2) For the purposes of these Regulations—

    (i) an investment shall be deemed to be a fixed interest investment if it is an investment on which the dividend or interest payable is fixed or subject to a fixed minimum amount;

    (ii) investments shall be deemed to be guaranteed if the payment of interest or dividend thereon or the return of capital thereunder is guaranteed, and

    (iii) a loan shall be deemed to fall due for repayment, and an instalment of a loan shall be deemed to fall due for payment, on the earliest date on which the lender could require repayment or, as the case may be, payment if he exercised all options and rights available to him.

(3) Without prejudice to the provisions of section 31 of the Interpretation Act 1889(a), words and phrases used in these Regulations shall, except where the context otherwise requires, have the meanings assigned to them in the Act or in Part II of the Companies Act 1967.

(4) The Interpretation Act 1889 shall apply to the interpretation of these Regulations as it applies to the interpretation of an Act of Parliament.

Application to Scotland

19. In the application to Scotland of these Regulations—

" freehold land " means the *dominium utile* or, in the case of land other than feudal land, the ownership of land;

" leasehold land " means land held under a lease; and

" mortgage " means a heritable security within the meaning of the Conveyancing (Scotland) Act 1924(b), except that it includes a security constituted by an *ex facie* absolute disposition or assignation, and the expression " mortgaged " means burdened with a heritable security.

Application and Cesser of Existing Rules and Regulations

20.—(1) Regulations 2 to 7 (inclusive) of these Regulations shall not apply to the accounts of a company prepared in pursuance of section 4 of the Act

---

(a) 1889 c. 63.   (b) 1924 c. 27.

with respect to a financial year of the company beginning before 1st January 1969 or to the audit of such accounts and Regulation 2 of the Insurance Companies (Forms) Regulations 1958(a) and Rules 12, 17 and 18 of the Assurance Companies Rules 1950(b) shall not apply to the accounts of a company prepared in pursuance of section 4 of the Act with respect to a financial year of the company beginning after 31st December 1968 or to the audit of such accounts.

(2) No statement need be prepared by any company under Regulation 8 or 14 of these Regulations with respect to a financial year of the company beginning before 1st January 1969, no statement need be prepared by any company under Regulation 11 or 12 of these Regulations with respect to a financial year of the company beginning before 1st January 1970 and no statement need be prepared by any company under Regulation 5 of the Insurance Companies (Forms) Regulations 1958 with respect to a financial year beginning after 31st December 1969.

(3) Regulation 16 of these Regulations shall not apply to the abstract of the actuary's report of any investigation made in pursuance of section 5(1)(a) of the Act as at a date before 1st January 1969 and Regulation 3 of the Insurance Companies (Forms) Regulations 1958 shall not apply to the abstract of the actuary's report of any investigation so made as at a date after 31st December 1968.

(4) Regulation 17 of these Regulations shall not apply to any statement of insurance business prepared in pursuance of section 5(2) of the Act as at a date before 1st January 1969 and Regulation 4 of the Insurance Companies (Forms) Regulations 1958 shall not apply to any statement of insurance business so prepared as at a date after 31st December 1968.

Revocation

21. Rules 2 to 11 (inclusive) and Rules 13, 14 and 15 of the Assurance Companies Rules 1950 and the Assurance Companies (Amendment) Rules 1950(c) are hereby revoked.

Citation and Commencement

22. These Regulations may be cited as the Insurance Companies (Accounts and Forms) Regulations 1968 and shall come into operation on 1st January 1969.

Edmund Dell,
Minister of State,
Board of Trade.

29th August 1968.

SCHEDULE 1

PRELIMINARY

1. Part I of this Schedule applies to the balance sheet of every company, Part II thereof applies only to the balance sheet of a company which at no time during the financial year carried on long-term business, Part III thereof applies only to the

---

(a) S.I. 1958/1765 (1958 I, p. 1291).　　　(b) S.I. 1950/533 (1950 I, p. 1121).
(c) S.I. 1950/643 (1950 I, p. 1139).

SCHEDULE 1—*contd.*

balance sheet of a company which at no time during the financial year carried on general business, Part IV thereof applies only to the balance sheet of a composite company and Part V thereof applies to the profit and loss account of every company.

PART I

Provisions as to the balance sheet of every company

2.—(1) In arriving at amounts receivable in the balance sheet or in any statement or report annexed thereto, amounts currently receivable from any one person may be included net of amounts currently payable to that person and, in arriving at amounts payable in the balance sheet or in any such statement or report, amounts currently payable to any one person may be included net of amounts currently receivable from that person but, if this be done, there shall be stated by way of note in the balance sheet, or in any such statement or report, the fact that amounts payable and receivable have been shown on this basis.

(2) Subject to sub-paragraph (1) of this paragraph amounts receivable and amounts payable shall be shown in the balance sheet, or in any statement or report annexed thereto, as gross amounts.

3.—(1) Where the amount of any assets shown in the balance sheet or in any statement or report annexed thereto includes an amount of shares in a body corporate falling within any of the descriptions in sub-paragraph (3) of this paragraph or an amount of indebtedness to the company (whether on account of a loan or otherwise) of a person falling within any of those descriptions, in showing the amount of those assets such part of that amount as represents shares in and indebtedness of persons falling within each of those descriptions shall be separately distinguished.

(2) Where the amount of any liabilities shown in the balance sheet or in any statement or report annexed thereto includes an amount of indebtedness of the company (whether on account of a loan or otherwise) to a person falling within any of the descriptions in sub-paragraph (3) of this paragraph, in showing the amount of those liabilities such part of that amount as represents indebtedness to persons falling within each of those descriptions shall be separately distinguished.

(3) The descriptions referred to in the foregoing sub-paragraphs of this paragraph are the following:

(a) a subsidiary of the company;

(b) a body corporate of which the company is a subsidiary or which is the company's fellow subsidiary;

(c) a body corporate, not falling within either of the preceding heads of this sub-paragraph, which is controlled by the company;

(d) a body corporate, not falling within any of the preceding heads of this sub-paragraph, in which the company's assets are invested, the aggregate amount of such assets so invested (as stated or included in the accounts) being an amount which exceeds one tenth of the amount of the company's assets (as so stated);

(e) a body corporate, not falling within any of the preceding heads of this sub-paragraph, which is a member of a group of connected bodies corporate being bodies corporate in which or in some of which the company's assets are invested, the aggregate amount of such assets so invested in the members of the group (as stated or included in the accounts) being an amount which exceeds one tenth of the amount of the company's assets (as so stated);

(f) a body corporate, not falling within any of the preceding heads of this sub-paragraph, in which the company holds shares of any class comprised in the equity share capital of that body corporate exceeding in nominal value one tenth of the nominal value of the issued shares of that class;

(g) a person, not being a body corporate falling within any of the preceding heads of this sub-paragraph, the amount of whose indebtedness to the company (as stated or included in the accounts) exceeds one tenth of the amount of the company's assets (as so stated).

SCHEDULE 1—contd.

(4) For the purpose of this paragraph:

(a) a company shall be deemed to be a fellow subsidiary of another body corporate if both are subsidiaries of the same body corporate but neither is the other's;

(b) a company's assets shall be deemed to be invested in another body corporate to the extent that the company's assets consist of shares in or amounts owing (whether on account of a loan or otherwise) from that body corporate;

(c) " group of connected bodies corporate " means any body corporate which is the subsidiary of another or which has subsidiaries together with all other bodies corporate of which it is a subsidiary or a fellow subsidiary and its subsidiaries; and

(d) a body corporate shall be deemed to be controlled by the company if the company and all the officers of the company together are entitled to exercise, or control the exercise of, one third or more of the voting power at any general meeting of the body corporate.

4. The authorised share capital, issued share capital, liabilities and assets shall be summarised, with such particulars as are necessary to disclose the general nature of the assets and liabilities, and there shall be specified—

(a) any part of the issued capital that consists of redeemable preference shares, the earliest and latest dates on which the company has power to redeem those shares, whether those shares must be redeemed in any event or are liable to be redeemed at the option of the company and whether any (and, if so, what) premium is payable on redemption;

(b) so far as the information is not given in the profit and loss account, any share capital on which interest has been paid out of capital during the financial year, and the rate at which interest has been so paid;

(c) the amount of the share premium account;

(d) particulars of any redeemed debentures which the company has power to reissue.

5. There shall be stated under separate headings, so far as they are not written off,—

(a) the preliminary expenses;

(b) any expenses incurred in connection with any issue of share capital or debentures;

(c) any sums paid by way of commission in respect of any shares or debentures;

(d) any sums allowed by way of discount in respect of any debentures; and

(e) the amount of the discount allowed on any issue of shares at a discount.

6. The aggregate amount (before deduction of income tax) which is recommended for distribution by way of dividend shall be shown.

7. Where any liability of the company is secured otherwise than by operation of law on any assets of the company, the fact that that liability is so secured shall be stated, but it shall not be necessary to specify the assets on which the liability is secured.

8. Where any of the company's debentures are held by a nominee of or trustee for the company, the nominal amount of the debentures and the amount at which they are stated in the books of the company shall be stated.

9.—(1) The matters referred to in the following sub-paragraphs shall be stated by way of note, or in a statement or report annexed, if not otherwise shown.

(2) The number, description and amount of any shares in the company which any person has an option to subscribe for, together with the following particulars of the option, that is to say—

(a) the period during which it is exercisable;

(b) the price to be paid for shares subscribed for under it.

SCHEDULE 1—*contd.*

(3) The amount of any arrears of fixed cumulative dividends on the company's shares and the period for which the dividends or, if there is more than one class, each class of them are in arrear, the amount to be stated before deduction of income tax, except that, in the case of tax free dividends, the amount shall be shown free of tax and the fact that it is so shown shall also be stated.

(4) Where practicable the aggregate amount or estimated amount, if it is material, of contracts for capital expenditure, so far as not provided for and, where practicable, the aggregate amount or estimated amount, if it is material, of capital expenditure authorised by the directors which has not been contracted for.

10.—(1) There shall be shown in tabular form in a statement or report annexed to the balance sheet the following matters:

(*a*) in respect of fixed interest irredeemable investments—

    (i) the amount of such investments which were issued or guaranteed by a British Government authority,

    (ii) the amount of such investments which were issued or guaranteed by a Government or public or local authority not being a British Government authority, and

    (iii) the amount of such investments not falling within heads (i) and (ii) of this sub-paragraph distinguishing between those which are quoted investments and those which are not;

(*b*) in respect of fixed interest redeemable investments (other than those which must be redeemed within one year after the end of the financial year)—

    (i) the amount of such investments which were issued or guaranteed by a British Government authority,

    (ii) the amount of such investments which were issued or guaranteed by a Government or public or local authority not being a British Government authority, and

    (iii) the amount of such investments not falling within heads (i) and (ii) of this sub-paragraph distinguishing between those which are quoted investments and those which are not;

(*c*) the amount of variable interest investments (other than those which must be redeemed within one year after the end of the financial year) distinguishing between those which are quoted investments and those which are not;

(*d*) in respect of land:—

    (i) the amount of freehold land,

    (ii) the amount of leasehold land where the lease has not less than fifty years to run from the end of the financial year, and

    (iii) the amount of leasehold land where the lease has less than fifty years to run from the end of the financial year;

(*e*) in respect of mortgages and loans not falling within sub-paragraphs (*a*), (*b*) and (*c*) above and not being mortgages or loans which must be redeemed or repaid within one year after the end of the financial year:—

    (i) the amount of such loans which are secured on mortgages of residential property intended, at the time the loan was made, for occupation by the borrower,

    (ii) the amount of such loans otherwise secured on mortgages of land,

    (iii) the amount of such loans secured on mortgages of life insurance contracts made by the company but not secured upon mortgages of land,

    (iv) the amount of such loans secured otherwise than by mortgages of land or life insurance contracts made by the company, and

    (v) the amount of such loans as are unsecured;

(*f*) in respect of investments, mortgages and loans which must be redeemed or repaid within one year after the end of the financial year:—

    (i) the amount of such as consist of investments, and

    (ii) the amount of such as consist of mortgages or loans,

SCHEDULE 1—*contd.*

(g) the amount of deposits withdrawable only after notice of more than seven days and loans repayable only after such notice;

(h) the amount of deposits withdrawable at call or at notice of not more than seven days and loans repayable at call or after such notice;

(i) the amount of any other assets from which income has been derived in the financial year classified under appropriate headings;

(j) the aggregate of the amounts shown in pursuance of the preceding heads of this sub-paragraph;

(k) the amount of the company's income for the financial year (before deduction of United Kingdom and overseas taxation) that is ascribable to all the assets dealt with respectively by each of heads (a) to (i) of this sub-paragraph;

(l) the aggregate of the amounts shown in pursuance of head (k) of this sub-paragraph.

(2) In the case of a company which at any time in the financial year carried on long-term business—

(a) if that company also carried on other business in the financial year, in showing the amounts required to be shown by this paragraph, those amounts which do not relate only to the company's long-term business shall for each item be separately shown, and

(b) if that company maintains any separate long-term business fund to which a certain group of its assets is appropriated or if the company enters into insurance contracts the benefits of which are wholly or partly linked to the value of or the income from a certain group of its assets, in showing the amounts required to be shown by this paragraph, the amounts which relate to each such group of assets shall for each item be separately shown.

(3) If any amount which is required to be separately shown in the statement or report annexed to the balance sheet in pursuance of sub-paragraph (1) of this paragraph includes an amount of investments in a unit trust scheme which is not an authorised unit trust scheme, there shall be set out in tabular form in a note to that statement particulars relating to the trust property of that unit trust and the income therefrom in the financial year of the company corresponding to the particulars required to be stated in relation to the company's assets by sub-paragraph (1) of this paragraph showing amounts against each item which are attributable to the proportionate interest of the company in that trust property and income.

PART II

Additional provisions as to the balance sheet of a company carrying on general business but not long-term business

11.—(1) There shall be shown under separate headings:—

(a) in relation to business other than business dealt with in a three-year business revenue statement for the financial year or in a general business revenue account for that year prepared in the form of such a statement, the aggregate amounts set aside respectively for:

    (i) unearned premiums,

    (ii) unexpired risks,

    (iii) claims outstanding, and

    (iv) claims equalisation;

(b) the total of the funds, if any, carried forward in any three-year business revenue statement of the company for the financial year or in the general business revenue account of the company for the financial year if it be prepared in the form of such a statement;

(c) the amount payable to policy holders, brokers and agents including any amount payable in connection with reinsurance accepted by the company but excluding any amount payable in connection with claims under insurance contracts

SCHEDULE 1—*contd.*

(*d*) the amount payable to the company's reinsurers identifying any part of the amount of reinsurance premiums payable which has been retained by the company as a security for future claims against the company's reinsurers;

(*e*) the amount payable to persons carrying on insurance business (other than amounts payable in connection with reinsurance accepted and ceded);

(*f*) the amount of bank loans and overdrafts;

(*g*) the amount of loans made to the company, not being bank loans or overdrafts, which—

    (i) are repayable otherwise than by instalments and fall due for repayment after the expiration of the period of five years beginning with the day next following the expiration of the financial year; or

    (ii) are repayable by instalments any of which fall due for payment after the expiration of that period;

(*h*) the amount payable to other creditors classified under appropriate headings;

(*i*) other amounts set aside classified under appropriate headings.

(2) In relation to each loan falling within head (*g*) of sub-paragraph (1) of this paragraph, there shall be stated by way of note (if not otherwise stated) the terms on which it is repayable and the rate at which interest is payable thereon:

Provided that if the number of loans is such that, in the opinion of the directors, compliance with the foregoing requirement would result in a statement of excessive length, it shall be sufficient to give a general indication of the terms on which the loans are repayable and the rates at which interest is payable thereon.

(3) In showing the amounts required to be shown by sub-paragraph (1) of this paragraph, where an amount under any heading is not material, it need not be shown under a separate heading but, if it is not so shown, it shall be included with the amount under some other heading.

(4) If an amount is set aside for the purpose of its being used to prevent undue fluctuations in charges for taxation, it shall be stated.

12.—(1) There shall be shown under separate headings—

(*a*) the amount receivable from policy holders, brokers and agents including any amount receivable in connection with reinsurance accepted by the company identifying any part of the amount receivable by way of reinsurance premiums which has been retained by persons reinsured as a security for future claims against the company;

(*b*) the amount receivable from the company's reinsurers;

(*c*) the amount receivable from persons carrying on insurance business (other than amounts receivable in connection with reinsurance accepted or ceded);

(*d*) the aggregate amount of any outstanding loans made under the authority of provisos (*b*) and (*c*) of section 54(1) of the Companies Act 1948;

(*e*) the amount receivable from other debtors;

(*f*) cash on current account at bankers and in hand;

(*g*) if the amount of the goodwill and of any patents and trade marks or part of that amount is shown as a separate item in or is otherwise ascertainable from the books of the company, or from any contract for the sale or purchase of any property to be acquired by the company, or from any documents in the possession of the company relating to the stamp duty payable in respect of any such contract or the conveyance of any such property, the said amount so shown or ascertained so far as not written off or, as the case may be, the said amount so far as it is so shown or ascertainable and as so shown or ascertained, as the case may be;

(*h*) the aggregate of the amounts of the assets shown in the statement or report prepared in pursuance of paragraph 10 except to the extent that any such amount has been included in the amount shown under another heading;

SCHEDULE 1—*contd.*

(*i*) the amount of assets not included in the amounts shown under other headings classified under appropriate headings.

(2) Nothing in head (*g*) of the foregoing sub-paragraph shall be taken as requiring the amount of the goodwill, patents and trade marks to be stated otherwise than as a single item.

13.—(1) The matters referred to in the following sub-paragraphs shall be stated by way of note, or in a statement or report annexed, if not otherwise shown.

(2) Particulars of any charge on the assets of the company to secure the liabilities of any other person (other than liabilities arising under a contract of insurance), including, where practicable, the amount secured.

(3) The general nature of any other contingent liabilities not provided for (other than one arising under a contract of insurance) and, where practicable, the aggregate amount or estimated amount of those liabilities, if it is material.

(4) If a sum set aside for the purpose of its being used to prevent undue fluctuations in charges for taxation has been used during the financial year for another purpose, the amount thereof and the fact that it has been so used.

(5) If the amount carried forward for stock in trade or work in progress is material for the appreciation of the company's state of affairs or of its profit or loss for the financial year, the manner in which that amount has been computed.

(6) The basis on which the amount, if any, set aside for United Kingdom corporation tax is computed.

(7) The amount of that part of the amount of claims outstanding which has been set aside to meet claims and expenses likely to be incurred in connection with the settlement of claims arising out of incidents not notified to the company before the date on which the company's records for the financial year were closed.

PART III

Additional provisions as to the balance sheet of a company carrying on long-term business but not general business

14. The requirements of Part II of this Schedule shall apply and shall apply as if—

(i) for heads (*a*) and (*b*) of sub-paragraph (1) of paragraph 11 there were substituted the following:

" (*a*) the amount of each long-term business fund carried forward in the revenue account of the company for the financial year;

(*b*) the amount of claims admitted but not paid; " and

(ii) sub-paragraph (7) of paragraph 13 were omitted.

PART IV

Additional provisions as to the balance sheet of a composite company

15. The requirements of Part II of this Schedule shall apply and shall apply as if in head (*a*) of paragraph 11(1) after the words " the aggregate amounts set aside respectively " there were added the words " in relation to the company's general business ". In showing the amount of each item thus required to be shown and in stating any matter in relation to any amount thus required to be stated there shall be excluded any part of that amount which relates only to the company's long-term business and, in relation to each amount so excluded, that amount shall be separately shown, or the relevant matter in relation to that amount shall be separately stated, in the balance sheet or in a statement or report annexed thereto and the following amounts in relation to the company's long-term business shall also be so shown under separate headings, that is to say—

SCHEDULE 1—contd.

(a) the amount of each fund carried forward in the long-term business revenue account of the company for the financial year, and

(b) the amount of claims admitted but not paid.

PART V

Provisions as to the profit and loss account

16. There shall be shown—

(a) in the case of a company which at any time in the financial year carried on general business, the amounts respectively transferred to and transferred from the general business revenue account of the company for the financial year;

(b) in the case of a company which at any time in the financial year carried on long-term business, the amounts respectively transferred to and transferred from the long-term business revenue account of the company for the financial year;

(c) the amount of the interest on loans of the following kinds made to the company (whether on the security of debentures or not), namely, bank loans, overdrafts and loans which, not being bank loans or overdrafts,—

(i) are repayable otherwise than by instalments and fall due for repayment before the expiration of the period of five years beginning with the day next following the expiration of the financial year; or

(ii) are repayable by instalments the last of which falls due for payment before the expiration of that period;

and the amount of the interest on loans of other kinds so made (whether on the security of debentures or not);

(d) the amounts respectively provided for redemption of share capital and for redemption of loans;

(e) the amount of expenses of management not shown in the revenue account;

(f) the amount of taxation not shown in the revenue account;

(g) the amount of other expenditure not shown in the revenue account classified under appropriate headings;

(h) the aggregate amount of interest, dividends and rents (before deduction of tax) not shown in the revenue account;

(i) the amount of other income not shown in the revenue account classified under appropriate headings;

(j) the aggregate amount (before deduction of income tax) of the dividends paid and proposed.

17. The amount of any charge arising in consequence of the occurrence of an event in a preceding financial year and of any credit so arising shall, if not included in a heading relating to other matters, be stated under a separate heading.

18. The amount of the remuneration of the auditors shall be shown under a separate heading and, for the purposes of this paragraph, any sums paid by the company in respect of the auditors' expenses shall be deemed to be included in the expression " remuneration ".

19.—(1) The matters referred to in the following sub-paragraphs shall be stated by way of note, if not otherwise shown.

(2) The following amounts (whether or not the whole or any part thereof has been shown in the revenue account for the financial year) distinguishing in each case that part of that amount which relates only to the company's long-term business:—

(a) the amount of the charge to revenue for United Kingdom corporation tax,

(b) the amount of the charge for United Kingdom income tax, and

(c) the amount of the charge for taxation imposed outside the United Kingdom of profits, income and (so far as charged to revenue) capital gains.

SCHEDULE 1—*contd.*

(3) If the amount of the charge to revenue for United Kingdom corporation tax would have been greater but for relief from double taxation, the amount which it would have been but for such relief.

(4) The aggregate amount of the expenses of management (whether or not the whole or any part thereof has been shown in the revenue account of the company for the financial year) distinguishing that part of that amount which relates only to the company's long-term business.

(5) The basis on which the charge for United Kingdom corporation tax and United Kingdom income tax is computed.

(6) Any special circumstances which affect liability in respect of taxation of profits, income or capital gains for the financial year or liability in respect of taxation of profits, income or capital gains for succeeding financial years.

(7) Any material respects in which any items shown in the profit and loss account are affected—

    (*a*) by transactions of a sort not usually undertaken by the company or otherwise by circumstances of an exceptional or non-recurrent nature; or

    (*b*) by any change in the basis of accounting.

SCHEDULE 2

PART I

LONG-TERM BUSINESS REVENUE ACCOUNT of the [Name of Company] for the year ending

	Description of category of long-term business .... (each category in a separate column)	Total
	£	£
INCOME		
1. Fund brought forward		
2. Premiums (net of refunds, rebates and premiums for reinsurance ceded)		
3. Interest, dividends and rents (before tax)		
4. Other income (particulars to be specified)		
5. Total		
EXPENDITURE	£	£
6. Claims (net of reinsurance recoveries) ...		
7. Commission (net of commission on business ceded)		
8. Expenses of management		
9. Taxation		
10. Shareholders' share of distributable surplus transferred to Profit and Loss Account		
11. Other expenditure (particulars to be specified)		
12. Fund carried forward		
13. Total		

NOTES:

1. Amounts against each item are to be given in a separate column for each category of long-term business for which a separate fund is maintained.

2. Each amount shown against item 2 is to be analysed in or in a note to the Account, such analysis showing how much of that amount relates to each of the following categories of contract:

(a) life policies,

(b) annuities on human life,

(c) long-term personal accident contracts, and

(d) capital redemption contracts.

3. Each amount shown against item 6 is to be analysed in or in a note to the Account, such analysis showing how much of that amount consists of each of the following categories of payment:

(a) payments under life policies on death otherwise than by way of return of premiums,

(b) payments on the maturity of life policies otherwise than by way of return of premiums,

(c) payments by way of periodical endowment benefits,

(d) payments on the surrender of life policies otherwise than by way of return of premiums,

(e) payments made by way of return of premiums,

(f) payments on the separate surrender of bonuses attaching to life policies,

(g) annuity payments,

(h) payments under long-term personal accident contracts, and

(i) payments under capital redemption contracts.

SCHEDULE 2—*contd.*

PART II

LONG-TERM BUSINESS PREMIUM ANALYSIS of the [Name of Company] for the year ending

	Description of category of long-term business .... (each category in a separate column)	Total
	£	£
1. ANALYSIS OF PREMIUMS		
Gross premiums in respect of		
(*a*) U.K. business		
(*b*) Overseas business		
(*c*) Total		
2. ANALYSIS OF REINSURANCE CEDED		
(i) Reinsurance premiums in respect of		
(*a*) U.K. business		
(*b*) Overseas business		
(*c*) Total		
(ii) Reinsurance recoveries		
(iii) Commission (included in (i)) on reinsurance business ceded		

SCHEDULE 2—contd.

PART III

GENERAL BUSINESS REVENUE ACCOUNT of the [Name of Company] for the year ending

INCOME	Liability	Marine, Aviation and Transport		Motor Vehicle	Pecuniary Loss	Personal Accident	Property	Treaty Reinsurance Accepted (not dealt with in columns 1 to 7)	Total
		Categories dealt with in any revenue statement annexed	Categories not dealt with in any revenue statement annexed						
	1	2	3	4	5	6	7	8	9
	£	£	£	£	£	£	£	£	£
1. Unearned premiums brought forward		—							
2. Unexpired risks brought forward ...		—							
3. Claims outstanding brought forward...		—							
4. Claims equalisation brought forward...		—							
5. Fund brought forward	—		—	—	—	—	—	—	
6. Premiums (net of refunds, rebates and premiums for reinsurance ceded) ...									
7. Interest, dividends and rents (before tax)									
8. Other income (particulars to be specified)...									
9. Transfer from Profit and Loss account									
10. Total									

EXPENDITURE	£	£	£	£	£	£	£	£	£
11. Claims (net of salvage, reinsurance and other recoveries)									
12. Commission (net of commission on business ceded)									
13. Expenses of management									
14. Taxation									
15. Other expenditure (particulars to be specified)									
16. Unearned premiums carried forward	—								
17. Unexpired risks carried forward ...	—								
18. Claims outstanding carried forward	—								
19. Claims equalisation carried forward	—								
20. Fund carried forward	—	—	—	—	—	—	—		
21. Transfer to Profit and Loss account...									
22. Total									

Notes:

1. Facultative reinsurance business accepted is to be included in whichever is appropriate of columns 1 to 7.

2. The basis on which the amounts shown against items 1 and 16 respectively have been calculated is to be stated in a note on or statement annexed to the account and, if this be less accurate than the twenty-fourths method, the reason for its adoption is to be so stated.

3. The entries in column 2 are to be the same as the entries in column 9 of any three-year business revenue statement annexed.

4. If no three-year business revenue statement is annexed or if one only of the categories of marine, aviation and transport insurance business is dealt with in a three-year business revenue statement which is annexed, there is to be stated in a note on or a statement annexed to the general business revenue account how much of each amount shown in column 3 against items 6 and 11 respectively relate to each of those categories not dealt with in a three-year business revenue statement annexed.

5. If any amount shown in any column against items 1, 2, 3, 4 or 5 does not agree with the corresponding amount carried forward from the previous year's account a statement is to be given of the reasons for the difference.

SCHEDULE 2—contd.

PART IV

THREE-YEAR BUSINESS REVENUE STATEMENT of the [Name of Company] for the year ending

	Business transacted in 19.. and earlier years (i.e., before the commencement of the first year preceding the year of account)				Business transacted in 19.. (i.e., in the first year preceding the year of account)			Business transacted in 19.. (i.e., in the year of account)	Income and expenditure in 19.. (i.e., the year of account) [Total of Columns 3, 6 and 8]
	Income and expenditure in 19.. (i.e., the second year preceding the year of account)	Income and expenditure in 19.. (i.e., the first year preceding the year of account)	Income and expenditure in 19.. (i.e., the year of account)	Total of Columns 1, 2 and 3	Income and expenditure in 19.. (i.e., the first year preceding the year of account)	Income and expenditure in 19.. (i.e., the year of account)	Total of Columns 5 and 6	Income and expenditure in 19.. (i.e., the year of account)	
	1	2	3	4	5	6	7	8	9
	£	£	£	£	£	£	£	£	£
INCOME									
1. Fund brought forward ...				—			—		
2. Premiums (net of refunds, rebates and premiums for reinsurance ceded)									
(a) Marine hull insurance business ...									
(b) Aviation hull insurance business ...									
(c) Transport insurance business ...									
3. Interest, dividends and rents (before tax) ...									
4. Other income (particulars to be specified) ...									
5. Transfer from profit and loss account ...									
6. Total ...				—			—		

EXPENDITURE		£	£	£	£	£	£	£
7. Claims (net of salvage, reinsurance and other recoveries)	(a) Marine hull insurance business							
	(b) Aviation hull insurance business							
	(c) Transport insurance business							
8. Commission (net of commission on business ceded)								
9. Expenses of management								
10. Taxation								
11. Other expenditure (particulars to be specified)								
12. Fund carried forward			—		—			
13. Transfer to profit and loss account ...			—		—			
14. Total								

NOTES:

1. In showing any amount in column 3 against items 2 or 7 which includes an amount in respect of business transacted before the beginning of the second year preceding the year of account that part of that amount which relates to such business is to be distinguished in a note.

2. There is to be stated in a note or statement annexed the basis on which in completing the statement it has been determined in which year any business has been transacted.

3. If the amount shown in any column against item 1 does not agree with the corresponding amount carried forward from he previous year's statement a statement is to be given of the reasons for the difference.

SCHEDULE 2—*contd.*

PART V

GENERAL BUSINESS PREMIUM ANALYSIS
of the [Name of Company] for the year ending

	Liability	Marine, Aviation and Transport			Motor vehicle	Pecuniary loss	Personal accident	Property	Treaty reinsurance not dealt with in columns 1 to 8	Total
		Marine hull	Aviation hull	Transport						
	1	2	3	4	5	6	7	8	9	10
	£	£	£	£	£	£	£	£	£	£
1. ANALYSIS OF PREMIUMS										
(i) Gross premiums in respect of—										
(a) U.K. direct and facultative business ...	£	£	£	£	£	£	£	£	£	£
(b) U.K. reinsurance business other than facultative business									—	
(c) overseas direct and facultative business...									—	
(d) overseas reinsurance business other than facultative business										
(e) treaty reinsurance business in which U.K. and overseas components cannot be distinguished										
(f) total										
(ii) Premiums (net of refunds, rebates and premiums for reinsurance ceded)—										
(a) in respect of direct business and facultative reinsurance business accepted, by months in respect of contracts commencing in:										
Month 1									—	
" 2									—	
" 3										

     " 4

     " 5

     " 6

     " 7

     " 8

     " 9

     " 10

     " 11

     " 12

(b) in respect of treaty reinsurance business accepted, by quarters in respect of contracts commencing in:—

     First quarter

     Second quarter

     Third quarter

     Fourth quarter

2. ANALYSIS OF REINSURANCE CEDED

  (i) Reinsurance premiums in respect of:—

     (a) U.K. business ... ...

     (b) overseas business... ...

     (c) treaty reinsurance business in which U.K. and overseas components cannot be distinguished ... ...

     (d) total ... ...

  (ii) Reinsurance recoveries ... ...

  (iii) Commission on reinsurance business ceded

NOTES:

1. Amounts are to be shown in column 9 only in respect of business accepted or ceded by the company under treaties of reinsurance covering more than one class of insurance business in respect of which it is not practicable to distinguish individual classes of business. Amounts in respect of all other reinsurance business accepted or ceded are to be included in whichever is appropriate of columns 1 to 8.

2. Item 1(ii) is not required to be completed in respect of any category of marine, aviation and transport insurance business dealt with in a three-year business revenue statement annexed to the general business revenue account and that item is not required to be completed at all if the general business revenue account takes the form of a three-year business revenue statement.

SCHEDULE 3—*contd.*

FORM No. 2

For Board of Trade use	Company ref.	Country	Class	Risk group	Year
	200				

CLAIM FREQUENCY ANALYSIS of the [Name of Company]

Year of account ending on   19..

Country:	Class:	Risk group:
	insurance business	

		Business transacted in 19.. (i.e., the second financial year preceding the year of account) 1	Business transacted in 19.. (i.e., the first financial year preceding the year of account) 2	Business transacted in 19.. (i.e., the year of account) 3
A. Gross premiums in the year of account	1			
B. Number of claims (a) notified before the beginning of the year of account	2			
(b) notified during the year of account	3			
(c) notified up to the end of the year of account (a)+(b)	4			
(d) estimated to be notified after the end of the year of account	5			

N.B. See NOTES 1 to 4 and 8 on page 31.

SCHEDULE 3—*contd.*

NOTES to FORM No. 1 and FORM No. 2:

1. Particulars are to be given in connection with business other than reinsurance business accepted by the company under treaties of reinsurance.

2. Particulars of gross premiums are to be shown in sterling.

3. The number of claims shown is to include the number of claims which have been settled without payment.

4. If the period between the end of the year of account and the date on which the company's records for that year are closed is different from the corresponding period for the immediately preceding financial year particulars of the difference are to be stated.

NOTES to FORM No. 1 only:

5. The column headed " Units of Exposure " need be completed only in statements relating to motor vehicle insurance business. In completing this column exposure to risk is to be calculated in annual units and the number of units of exposure under any insurance contract is to be the product of the period (expressed in years) for which the contract was made and an appropriate measure of the cover provided by that contract selected by the company, the measure being either the sum insured under the contract or the number of homogeneous objects, persons or risks insured under the contract. Units of exposure are to be suitably described according to the measure selected. For example, where the measure is a vehicle, the number of units may be described as the number of vehicle/years, where the measure is a person, the number of units may be described as the number of person/years and, where the measure is the sum insured, the units may be described as the number of £1,000/years.

6. In apportioning gross premiums and exposure to risk for the purpose of completing heads A and B, periods of time are to be determined by a method not less accurate than that used for the purposes of the general business revenue account of the company for the year of account to determine the amount of unearned premiums carried forward for the class of business to which the statement relates.

7. The claim frequency in the year of account (head D) is to be the figure given against head C(e) divided by the number of units of exposure given against head A(c) and expressed as a percentage.

NOTE to FORM No. 2 only:

8. Business is to be treated as having been transacted in that financial year of the company in which it is treated as having been transacted for the purposes of the three-year business revenue statement for the year of account or for the purposes of the general business revenue account for the year of account if that has been prepared in the form of such a statement.

SCHEDULE 3—contd.
PART III

For Board of Trade use | 300

Company ref.   Country   Class   Risk group   Year of origin   Year of account   No. of claims

CLAIM SETTLEMENT ANALYSIS of the [Name of Company]
Year of account ending on .... 19..

Country: ....

Class: .... insurance business

Risk group: ....

Year of origin: ....

Total number of claims attributable to the year of origin: ....

Year	Number of claims closed in the year		Number of claims outstanding at the end of the year	Amount of payments made in the year in settlement or on account	Aggregate payments made up to the end of the year	Claims outstanding at the end of the year		Total amount paid and outstanding at the end of the year [Total of Columns 6 and 8]
	at no cost	at some cost				Payments on account included in column 6	Estimated payments remaining to be made	
1	2	3	4	5 £	6 £	7 £	8 £	9 £
Year of origin 19..								
Each intermediate financial year (see Note 3)								
Year of account 19..								

NOTES:

1. For the purposes of column 2 a claim is not to be regarded as settled at no cost if any expenses have been incurred by the company specifically in connection with consideration of that claim (e.g. legal, medical or assessment costs).

2. Claim payments are to be shown after deduction of salvage and other recoveries but without deduction of recoveries from reinsurers and they are to include costs directly attributable to individual claims (e.g. legal, medical or assessment costs).

3. The table is to be prepared so as to provide a separate line for each year between the year of origin and the year of account. Each year shown is to be numbered consecutively in column 1 beginning with the year of origin.

SCHEDULE 3—*contd.*

PART IV

SUMMARY OF CHANGES IN ORDINARY LONG-TERM BUSINESS of the [Name of Company] for the year ending   19..

(1) *Changes in business in force during the financial year.*

	Assurances		Deferred annuities		Annuities in payment	
	No. of contracts	Sums assured	No. of contracts	Amounts of annuity per annum	No. of contracts	Amounts of annuity per annum
		£		£		£
In force at beginning of year						
New business Net transfers and other alterations " on " Bonus allotted						
Total " on "						
Deaths Maturities Surrenders for cash Forfeitures Conversions to paid-up policies for reduced benefits Net transfers, expiries and other alterations " off "						
Total " off "						
In force at end of year						

NOTES:

(i) Separate statements are to be given for United Kingdom and overseas business.

(ii) Information in the form of the table is to cover all business other than that under group life or pension schemes and is to be net of reinsurance. For group business, the information need be given only in respect of business in force at the end of the year or, where appropriate, at the last preceding policy anniversaries, but in addition an estimate of the total number of persons covered by group life or pension schemes is to be given in a footnote. Where scheme business by individual policies is not kept separate from non-group business, it may be included in the table but if this is done the fact is to be stated.

(iii) Sums assured and amounts of annuity are to include vested bonuses throughout.

(iv) For decreasing temporary assurances an approximation to the current sum assured may be shown, but if this is done the fact is to be stated.

(v) Separate statements suitably modified are to be given in respect of capital redemption contracts and long-term personal accident contracts.

SCHEDULE 3—*contd.*

(2) *New business taken on in the financial year.*

	Number of contracts	Sums assured or amounts of annuity per annum	Annual premiums	Single premiums and considerations
		£	£	£
Assurances:—				
Non-group ...				
Group				
Total				
Deferred annuities:—				
Non-group				
Group				
Total				
Immediate annuities:—				
Non-group				
Group				
Total				
Other (to be specified) ...				

NOTES:

(i) Separate statements are to be given for United Kingdom and overseas business.

(ii) The amounts shown for group business are to include increments under existing schemes.

SCHEDULE 4

VALUATION REPORT on the [Name of Company] to be made and signed by the Actuary.

The following information is to be given, the answers to be numbered to accord with the numbers of the corresponding paragraphs:—

1. The date to which the investigation relates.

2. The date to which the previous investigation under section 5 of the Act related.

3. The general principles adopted in the valuation including specific reference to the following:—

   (i) the extent to which account has been taken of the nature and term of the assets available to meet the liabilities valued;

   (ii) if the net premium method has been used, whether and to what extent it has been modified and for what purpose the modification has been made;

   (iii) whether there were any negative values and, if so, the extent to which they were eliminated;

   (iv) whether any specific reserve has been made for future bonus and, if so, at what rate or rates.

4. The rates of interest used in the calculation showing which rates of interest have been used for which categories of business.

5.—(1) The mortality tables employed in the valuation showing which tables have been used for which categories of business.

(2) Where the tables employed have not been published, details of the rates of mortality used.

6.—(1) Where an explicit allowance is made in the valuation for future expenses and profits, particulars of the extent of the provision for each category of contract.

SCHEDULE 4—*contd.*

(2) Where the net premium method of valuation has been used, the proportion of the value of future office premiums implicitly reserved for expenses and profits for assurances with participation in profits, assurances without participation in profits, annuities with participation in profits and annuities without participation in profits respectively.

(3) The method by which provision is made for expenses after premiums have ceased or where no future premiums are payable or where the method of valuation does not take credit for future premiums as an asset.

(4) The provision made for premium rate guarantees and guaranteed options with particulars of each type of such guarantee or option given by the company.

7. Full particulars of long-term business reinsurance contracts entered into by the company and in force at any time during the period since the previous investigation corresponding to the particulars relating to the general business of an insurance company set out in Part I of Schedule 3 to these Regulations.

8. Separate valuation summaries in the form set out in Form No. 1 in the Appendix to this Schedule in respect of each separate fund for:

(i) direct business and reinsurance accepted;

(ii) reinsurance ceded.

9. The general principles on which the distribution of profits among policyholders and shareholders is made and whether these principles are determined by the instrument constituting the company or by its regulations or bye-laws or how otherwise.

10. Statements of the results of the valuation in the forms set out in Forms No. 2, 3 and 4 in the Appendix to this Schedule.

11. A statement of the categories of contract distinguished in the valuation summaries which will participate in any distribution of profits showing, where some only of the contracts in a particular category participate, the number of contracts so participating and the corresponding sums assured or amounts of annuity.

12. The value of the bonuses allocated which are respectively:—

(i) declared in the form of cash or in reduction of premium,

(ii) added to sums assured as reversionary bonuses,

(iii) added to annuities as reversionary bonuses, and

(iv) allocated by other methods (each method to be described and shown separately).

13. Any provision made for future payments of mortuary bonuses, that is, bonuses which have been declared as payable only in the event of claims arising during a specified period.

14. Particulars of the bonus declared for each category of contract, including the basis of calculation and the circumstances and the form in which the bonus is payable.

(N.B.—Wherever appropriate rates of bonus are to be expressed as a fraction of the attribute of the contract to which they are related, e.g., as rates per £100 of the sum assured and existing bonuses.)

15. Where the rates of bonus declared depend on the original term of the contract or on the period of years a contract has been in force or on the age of the life assured, specimen rates at 5-year intervals of original term or duration or at 10-year intervals of age, as the case may be.

16. Where any conditions attach to the allocation of bonus to any category of contract concerning the number of years premiums to be paid before a bonus vests or otherwise, particulars of such conditions in relation to each category of contract.

17. A statement of the practice regarding interim bonuses and the current rates of interim bonus where they differ from the bonus rates last declared.

SCHEDULE 4—contd.

APPENDIX TO SCHEDULE 4

Form No. 1. Valuation Summary.

Type of insurance	1 Number of contracts	2 Amount of sums assured or annuities per annum including vested reversionary bonuses	3 Amount of yearly premiums Office premiums	4 Amount of yearly premiums Net premiums	5 Value of sums assured or annuities per annum including vested reversionary bonuses	6 Value of yearly premiums Office premiums	7 Value of yearly premiums Net premiums	8 Amount of net liability
		£	£	£	£	£	£	£
Assurances								
(i) With participation in profits:								
Whole life								
Endowment								
Other types (to be specified)								
Miscellaneous								
Total assurances with profits...								
(ii) Without participation in profits								
Whole life								
Endowment								
Other types (to be specified)								
Miscellaneous								
Total assurances without profits								
Total assurances								
Adjustments (to be specified)...								
TOTAL OF THE RESULTS								
(a) United Kingdom business								

SCHEDULE 5

STATEMENT OF THE ORDINARY LONG-TERM INSURANCE BUSINESS of the [Name of Company] valued as at the   to be signed by the Actuary.

1.—(1) A statement for each category of contract which is separately distinguished in the valuation summaries is to be given in such one of the forms set out in Tables A, B, C and D in the Appendix to this Schedule as is appropriate to that category of contract or, in the case of a category of contract to which none of these forms is appropriate, in such form and containing such particulars as are sufficient to enable an independent assessment of the liabilities of the company's ordinary long-term business to be made. A separate statement is to be given in respect of each category for (i) direct business and reinsurance accepted and (ii) reinsurance ceded.

(2) Where contracts are written in currencies other than sterling, amounts in such currencies may be distinguished in the statements referred to in the foregoing sub-paragraph and expressed in those currencies provided that the " total " items in each statement are also given in sterling for each currency at the rate of exchange for that currency used for the purpose of preparing the valuation summaries.

(3) In the case of contracts the benefits of which are wholly or partly linked to the income from or the value of any group of the company's assets or wholly or partly calculated by reference to the yield from or the value of any descriptions of investments, the current sum assured or the amount of annuity and any guaranteed minimum amount payable are to be stated, the amounts being expressed in terms of currency or units as appropriate. In the case of contracts expressed in non-monetary units the sterling value of the units at 3-monthly intervals since the date of the previous statement prepared under section 5(2) of the Act are to be given in a supplement.

(4) In the case of a category of contract subject to premiums payable only for a limited term, the premiums are to be classified either—

(a) according to age, or

(b) according to the number of annual payments remaining to be made,

but if the premiums are classified according to age there is to be appended to the Table either a statement of the corresponding valuation factors required in calculating the value of future premiums or a statement of the average future period of payment of the premiums at each age.

2. In the case of a category of contract which in the directors' opinion is not significant in relation to the company's business as a whole, a statement may be prepared in the form set out in Table E in the Appendix to this Schedule and, if this be done, no statement need be prepared in pursuance of paragraph 1 of this Schedule for that category of contract:

Provided that advantage may be taken of this paragraph only to the extent that the net liability in respect of all categories of contract for which statements are not prepared in pursuance of paragraph 1 of this Schedule does not exceed 10 per cent of the aggregate net liability of the company's ordinary long-term insurance business.

3. Tables are to be given of the amounts currently allowed for the surrender of contracts and for the conversion of contracts to free paid-up contracts for whole life assurances, endowment assurances and deferred annuities respectively or statements given of the methods employed in calculating such surrender values or paid-up values with examples of the application of the method, in the case of whole life assurances, to contracts which have been in force for 1, 2, 3, 4, 5, 10, 15 and 20 years taken out at ages 20, 30, 40 and 50 respectively and, in the case of endowment assurances, to contracts for original terms of 10, 20 and 30 years maturing at age 65 in each case.

4. Particulars are to be given of any minimum surrender values or paid-up values guaranteed in the contracts, if these differ from the amounts currently allowed.

5. Where any of the surrender values or paid-up values referred to in paragraphs 3 and 4 are the minimum amounts prescribed under the Industrial Assurance Act 1923 or the Industrial Assurance and Friendly Societies Act 1929, this fact is to be stated.

SCHEDULE 5—*contd.*

6. Particulars of the premium rates being charged for new contracts offered in the United Kingdom, whether by prospectus or otherwise, at the date to which the statement relates are to be given.

7. The proportion of the total net liability of the company's ordinary long-term insurance business as shown in the valuation summaries represented by liabilities not matched by assets in the same currency is to be stated.

8.—(1) Statements are to be given in the form set out in Table F in the Appendix to this Schedule relating to the assets attributable to each ordinary long-term insurance business fund for which separate assets are maintained and, where there are contracts the benefits of which are wholly or partly linked to the income from or the value of a group of the assets attributable to an ordinary long-term insurance business fund, separate such statements are to be given in relation to each such group of assets and in relation to the remainder of the assets (if any) attributable to that fund.

(2) For those ordinary long-term insurance business funds for which separate assets are not maintained a statement in the form set out in Table F is to be given relating to all the assets regarded by the directors as available for meeting the combined liabilities of those funds.

(3) If any amount shown in a statement given in pursuance of this paragraph includes an amount of investments in a unit trust scheme which is not an authorised unit trust scheme a separate statement in the form set out in Table F is to be prepared in relation to the trust property of that unit trust scheme and the income therefrom, giving amounts against each item attributable to the proportionate interest of the company in that trust property and income.

SCHEDULE 5—contd.

APPENDIX TO SCHEDULE 5

TABLE A

Whole Life Assurances

Age (starting with the youngest)	Sums assured	Reversionary bonuses	Yearly office premiums
Total			

NOTES to Table A:
1. The information may be given for 5-year age groups.
2. An indication is to be given of how the age has been assessed.

TABLE B

Endowment Assurances

Year of maturity (starting with the nearest)	Sums assured	Reversionary bonuses	Yearly office premiums
Total			

NOTE to Table B: The information may be given for 5-year groups of year of maturity for contracts maturing more than 15 years after the valuation date.

SCHEDULE 5—*contd.*

TABLE C

Deferred Annuities

Year in which payment is due to commence (starting with the nearest)	Men			Women		
	Annual amount of annuities (excluding bonus)	Amount of bonus additions per annum	Yearly office premiums	Annual amount of annuities (excluding bonus)	Amount of bonus additions per annum	Yearly office premiums
Total						

NOTES to Table C:

1. The information may be given for 5-year groups of year of commencement.

2. The amount of annuity shown is to be the amount used in the calculation of the corresponding net liability shown in the relevant valuation summary. Where this amount is the amount purchased to the date of the valuation no office yearly premiums need be shown.

3. Separate tables are to be given in respect of business with a return of premiums on death before pension age and in respect of business with no such benefit, provided that one table only need be given for both these categories if that table contains sufficient additional information to enable the actuarial value of the death benefit to be estimated.

4. Where separate tables are not given for each age at which annuities are due to commence the proportion of the business relating to each age of commencement or the average age at commencement is to be stated.

5. Where retirement has been deferred beyond the age at which the annuity was due to commence, the basis on which the amount of annuity has been included is to be stated.

SCHEDULE 5—*contd.*

TABLE D

Annuities in Payment

Part I: Life annuities including annuities guaranteed for a term certain.

Age (starting with the youngest)	Amounts in payment per annum	
	Men	Women
Total		

Part II: Annuities payable for a term certain only.

Year in which payment ceases	Amount in payment per annum
Total	

NOTES to Table D:

1. For ages under 60 the information may be given for 5-year age groups.

2. The basis on which the age has been assessed is to be stated.

3. Annuities not yet payable, because retirement has been deferred beyond normal pension age, are to be recorded as deferred annuities.

TABLE E

Description of category of contract...

1. Total number of contracts...

2. Total of the sums assured or annual amounts of annuity £............................

3. Total reversionary bonuses £...

4. Total yearly office premiums £...

5. Total net liability £...

SCHEDULE 5—*contd.*

TABLE F

Assets at   19..   attributable to the company's ordinary long-term insurance business

PART I: Total assets

	Book value	Income on an annual basis
	£	£
1. Fixed interest irredeemable investments		
2. Fixed interest redeemable investments (other than those falling within item 6)		
3. Variable interest investments (other than those falling within item 6)		
4. Land		
5. Mortgages and other secured loans (other than those falling within items 1, 2, 3 or 6)		
6. Investments, mortgages and other secured loans maturing within one year after the date as at which the table is prepared— (*a*) Fixed interest redeemable investments ... ... (*b*) Other		
7. All other assets		
8. Total		

PART II: Classification of fixed interest redeemable investments

Year of redemption	Book value	Amount payable on redemption	Income on an annual basis
	£	£	£
Total			

NOTES to Table F:

1. The latest of any optional redemption years is to be given or a note appended stating how it has been assumed the option will be exercised. The information may be given for 5-year groups of year of redemption.

2. The annual income is to be shown before deduction of tax.

EXPLANATORY NOTE

(This Note is not part of the Regulations.)

These Regulations prescribe the contents of the accounts of insurance companies to be prepared under the Insurance Companies Acts 1958 to 1967 and make provision for the audit of those accounts. They also prescribe forms of statements of business to be prepared by insurance companies under those Acts and the form of the actuaries' reports on their long-term business.

STATUTORY INSTRUMENTS

1968 No. 1409

INSURANCE

The Insurance Companies Act 1958 (Section 4) (Appointed Day) Order 1968

Made - - - 29th August 1968

The Board of Trade, in pursuance of the powers conferred upon them by section 103(a) of the Companies Act 1967(a), hereby make the following Order:—

1. 1st January 1969 is hereby appointed as the day on which section 4 of the Insurance Companies Act 1958(b) shall apply to all insurance companies to which the said Act of 1958, as amended by section 70 of the Companies Act 1967, applies.

2. This Order may be cited as the Insurance Companies Act 1958 (Section 4) (Appointed Day) Order 1968.

29th August 1968.

Edmund Dell,
Minister of State.
Board of Trade.

EXPLANATORY NOTE

(This Note is not part of the Order.)

This Order appoints 1st January 1969 as the day on which an insurance company made subject to the Insurance Companies Act 1958 as a consequence of the extension of that Act to all classes of insurance business by section 70 of the Companies Act 1967 shall, subject to any modifications made by the Board of Trade under section 92 of the Companies Act 1967 in favour of that company, become obliged to prepare annual accounts in accordance with Regulations made under section 4 of the Insurance Companies Act 1958.

(a) 1967 c. 81.   (b) 1958 c. 72.

S.I. Nos. 1410 to 1412 are local: particulars of them will be found in Part III of the Volume.

APPENDIX
OF CERTAIN INSTRUMENTS
NOT REGISTERED AS S.I.

Orders in Council,
Letters Patent
and Royal Instructions

relating to the Constitutions etc. of
Overseas Territories or to appeals to the Judicial
Committee,

Royal Proclamations, etc.

CARIBBEAN AND NORTH ATLANTIC TERRITORIES

The British Honduras Letters Patent 1968

LETTERS PATENT passed under the Great Seal of the Realm amending the British Honduras Letters Patent 1964.

Dated: 11th June, 1968.

ELIZABETH THE SECOND, by the Grace of God of the United Kingdom of Great Britain and Northern Ireland and of Our other Realms and Territories Queen, Head of the Commonwealth, Defender of the Faith.

TO ALL TO WHOM THESE PRESENTS SHALL COME, GREETING!

Know Ye that We have declared and do hereby declare Our will and pleasure as follows:—

Citation, construction and commencement.

1.—(1) These Our Letters may be cited as the British Honduras Letters Patent 1968 and shall be construed as one with the British Honduras Letters Patent 1964(a) (hereinafter called "the principal Letters Patent").

(2) The principal Letters Patent and these Our Letters may be cited together as the British Honduras Letters Patent 1964 and 1968.

(3) These Our Letters shall be published in the Gazette and shall come into operation upon the date of such publication(b).

Amendment of Article 5(1) of principal Letters Patent.

2. Article 5 of the principal Letters Patent is amended by the deletion of paragraph (1) thereof and the substitution therefor of the following paragraph:—

"(1) During any period when the office of Governor is vacant or the Governor is absent from British Honduras or is for any other reason unable to perform the functions of his office, those functions shall, during Our pleasure, be assumed and performed by—

(a) such person as We may designate by instructions through a Secretary of State; or

(b) if there is no person in British Honduras so designated and able to perform those functions, the person who holds the substantive appointment of Financial Secretary; or

(c) if there is no person in British Honduras holding such appointment and able to perform those functions, the person who holds the substantive appointment of Attorney-General if the office of Attorney-General is a public office.".

Amendment of Article 21(1) of principal Letters Patent.

3. Paragraph (1) of Article 21 of the principal Letters Patent is amended by the substitution of the words "paragraph (2) of Article 11" for the words "paragraph (3) of Article 11".

Amendment of Article 36 of principal Letters Patent.

4. Article 36 of the principal Letters Patent is amended by the substitution of the words "under Article 11(2)" for the words "under Article 11(3)".

(a) S.I. 1964 I, p. 1136.   (b) Day published 20.7.68.

5. We do hereby reserve to Ourself full power and authority to amend or revoke these Presents.

Power reserved to Her Majesty.

In Witness whereof We have caused these Our Letters to be made Patent.

Witness Ourself at Westminster the eleventh day of June in the seventeenth year of Our Reign.

By Warrant under The Queen's Sign Manual.

Dobson.

ROYAL WARRANT

To amend the Royal Warrant of 19th September 1964, concerning pensions and other grants in respect of disablement or death due to service in the military forces during the 1914 World War and after 2nd September 1939.

ELIZABETH R.

Preamble

WHEREAS We deem it expedient to amend Our Warrant of 19th September 1964(a), as amended (b), concerning pensions and other grants in respect of disablement or death due to service in the military forces during the 1914 World War and after 2nd September 1939 (hereinafter referred to as "the 1964 Warrant"):

Our Will and Pleasure is that, notwithstanding anything in the 1964 Warrant, the following provisions of this Our Warrant shall take effect accordingly and, except in the cases stated in the Warrant of Her Majesty Queen Victoria of 27th October 1884, and except as otherwise provided by statute, shall be established and obeyed as the sole authority in the matters herein treated of.

Amendment of Schedule 6 to the 1964 Warrant, and transitional provisions

1.—(1) In Schedule 6 to the 1964 Warrant (rates of allowances payable in respect of disablement) there shall be made the amendments set out in Part I of the Appendix hereto.

(2) Where, by virtue of the provisions of paragraph (1) of this Article, the aggregate rate of additional unemployability or treatment allowances and allowances, if any, under the Family Allowances Act 1965 **(c)** or under any legislation in Northern Ireland or the Isle of Man corresponding to that Act, payable in respect of the children of a member of the military forces who qualify therefor at 7th October 1968 is, upon the coming into operation of the said paragraph, less than it was according to the rates in force on the said 7th October, then for the period for which the said aggregate rate in respect of those children or any remaining number of them continues to be less than it would have been had the said rates remained in force, the rate of additional unemployability or treatment allowances payable in respect of those children may be varied to the extent required to exclude the reduction in the said aggregate rate.

Amendment of Schedule 7 to the 1964 Warrant

2. In Schedule 7 to the 1964 Warrant (rates of pensions, other than widows' pensions, and allowances payable in respect of death) there shall be made the amendments set out at Part II of the Appendix hereto.

(a) S.I. 1964 III, p. 5257.
(b) The relevant amending Warrants are S.I. 1967 II, p. 3811; 1968 I, p. 1857.
(c) 1965 c. 53:

Amendment of Article 19 of the 1964 Warrant, and consequential amendment

3. In the 1964 Warrant, in Article 19 (allowance for lowered standard of occupation) there shall be made the amendment set out in paragraph 1 of Part III of the Appendix hereto, and in Article 33 (temporary allowances to widows and unmarried dependants who lived as wives of severely disabled pensioners) there shall be made the amendments set out in paragraph 2 of the said Part.

Article added to the 1964 Warrant, and consequential amendment

4. In the 1964 Warrant, after Article 59 there shall be added the Article set out in paragraph 3 of Part III of the Appendix hereto, and in Article 55 (interpretation of Part VI) there shall be made the amendment set out in paragraph 4 of the said Part.

Amendment of Article 60 of the 1964 Warrant

5. In Article 60 of the 1964 Warrant (payment of public claims out of pensions) there shall be made the amendment set out in paragraph 5 of the said Part.

Commencement

6.—(1) Subject to the following provisions of this Article, this Our Warrant shall come into operation on 5th August 1968.

(2) Article 1 shall come into operation in relation to an officer on 8th October 1968 and in relation to a soldier on 9th October 1968.

(3) Article 2 shall come into operation in relation to an officer on 8th October 1968 and in relation to a soldier on 14th October 1968.

Given at Our Court at St. James's, this twenty-fourth day of July 1968, in the 17th Year of Our Reign.

By Her Majesty's Command.

Judith Hart.

APPENDIX

PART I

Amendment of Schedule 6 to the 1964 Warrant

1. In Schedule 6 paragraph 5 (unemployability allowances) for head (iii) of sub-paragraph (*b*) there shall be substituted the following head:—

"(iii) increased allowance under
Article 17(4)(*f*)—

(*a*) in respect of the child, or
the elder or eldest of the
children, of a member .. £72 16s. per annum   28s. per week

(b) in respect of the second
child of a member .. £30 per annum 10s. per week
(c) in respect of each other child
of a member .. .. £30 per annum 8s. per week"

2. In Schedule 6 paragraph 9 (treatment allowances) for sub-paragraph (d) there shall be substituted the following sub-paragraph:—

"(d) increased additional allowance under Article 21(4) proviso (b)—
(i) in respect of the child, or the elder or eldest of the children, of a member .. £72 16s. per annum 28s. per week
(ii) in respect of the second child of a member .. £30 per annum 10s. per week
(iii) in respect of each other child of a member .. £30 per annum 8s. per week"

PART II

Amendment of Schedule 7 to the 1964 Warrant

In Schedule 7—

(a) for paragraph 5 (allowances in respect of children) there shall be substituted the following paragraph:—

"5. Allowances in respect of children—
(a) under Article 35(1)—
(i) in respect of the child, or the elder or eldest of the children, of a member .. £136 16s. per annum 49s. 6d. per week
(ii) in respect of each other child of a member—
(a) where the child qualifies for a family allowance under the Family Allowances Act 1965 or under any legislation in Northern Ireland or the Isle of Man corresponding to that Act .. .. £110 16s. per annum 39s. 6d. per week
(b) where the child does not so qualify .. £129 per annum 46s. 6d. per week

(b) under Article 35(3) .. .. £197 16s. per annum (maximum) where the child is 15 years of age or over—72s. 6d. per week (maximum)"

(b) for paragraph 6 (pension under Article 36 to a motherless or fatherless child) there shall be substituted the following paragraph:—

"6. Pension under Article 36 to a motherless or fatherless child—

(*a*) in respect of the child, or the elder or eldest of the children, of a member, and in respect of each other child of a member who does not qualify for a family allowance as aforesaid	£197 16*s*. per annum	(i) where the child is under 15 years of age— 49*s*. 6*d*. per week (ii) where the child is 15 years of age or over— 72*s*. 6*d*. per week
(*b*) in respect of each other child of a member who qualifies for a family allowance as aforesaid	£171 16*s*. per annum	(i) where the child is under 15 years of age— 39*s*. 6*d*. per week (ii) where the child is 15 years of age or over— 62*s*. 6*d*. per week"

PART III

1. *Amendment of Article 19 of the 1964 Warrant*

In Article 19 (allowance for lowered standard of occupation) for paragraph (3) there shall be substituted the following paragraph:—

"(3) An allowance under this Article shall not be payable to a member for any period in respect of which an allowance under Article 17(1)(i) is payable to him."

2. *Amendment of Article 33 of the 1964 Warrant*

In Article 33 (temporary allowances to widows and unmarried dependants who lived as wives of severely disabled pensioners) in paragraph (1) after the words "an allowance under Article 14 or Article 17(1)(i)" there shall be inserted the words "or, in the case of a member who was concurrently eligible for an allowance under Article 17(1)(i), Article 19 ", and in paragraph (ii) of the proviso to paragraph (2) for the words "retired pay or pension" there shall be substituted the words "retired pay, pension or allowances" and after the words "before 3rd September 1939" there shall be added the words "and a member who, being concurrently eligible for an allowance under Article 17(1)(i), was in receipt of an allowance under Article 19 shall be deemed in lieu thereof to have been in receipt of an allowance under Article 17(1)(i)".

3. *Article to be added to the 1964 Warrant*

"*Abatement of awards in respect of National Insurance and Industrial Injuries Benefits*

59A. Where a pension is awarded to or in respect of a person for any past period for which benefit under the National Insurance Acts 1965 to 1968 or the National Insurance (Industrial Injuries) Acts 1965 to 1968 or any legislation in Northern Ireland corresponding to those Acts has been paid to or in respect of that person, the total amount of pension so awarded may be abated by the amount by which the amount of benefit so paid exceeds what would have been payable for that period had the pension been concurrently payable."

4. *Amendment of Article 55 of the 1964 Warrant*

In paragraph (1) of Article 55 (interpretation of Part VI) for the words " Articles 56, 57, 60, 61, 62 and 64" there shall be substituted the words "Articles 56, 57, 59A, 60, 61, 62 and 64".

5. *Amendment of Article 60 of the 1964 Warrant*

In Article 60 (payment of public claims out of pensions) for paragraph (2) there shall be substituted the following paragraph:—

"(2) Where payment in respect of a pension is in arrears for any period and benefit under the Ministry of Social Security Act 1966(a) or benefit similar to the aforesaid benefit under any legislation in Northern Ireland or the Isle of Man corresponding to that Act has been paid for that period by reference to the requirements of the person to whom the payment is due, the amount by which the amount of benefit paid exceeds what would have been paid had the said payment not fallen into arrears shall be deemed to have been an overpayment for the purposes of paragraph (1) of this Article, and in the case of benefit paid under legislation in Northern Ireland or the Isle of Man as aforesaid shall for the purposes of that paragraph be repayable to the authority administering that benefit."

EXPLANATORY NOTE

(This Note is not part of the Royal Warrant.)

This Royal Warrant further amends the Royal Warrant of 19th September 1964.

Articles 1 and 2 make amendments which take account of the increases in family allowances made by the Family Allowances and National Insurance Act 1968 from 8th October 1968 and have the effect of adjusting the rates of children's pensions and allowances so that the pensions or allowances and (where payable) family allowances together will normally continue to provide the same total rate for each child as was payable immediately before the aforesaid increases came into force. Transitional provisions secure that the aggregate rate of existing awards will be maintained where this is more advantageous.

Article 3 makes amendments which enable an award of an allowance for lowered standard of occupation in payment to a pensioner who becomes unemployable to be continued if, exceptionally, it would be to his financial

---

(a) 1966 c.20.

disadvantage, having regard to any national insurance benefit concurrently payable, to transfer to unemployability supplement, and extend entitlement to an award of temporary allowances, at the rate which would have been payable had the pensioner been in receipt of unemployability supplement, to the widow, or unmarried dependant who lived as a wife, of such a pensioner.

Article 4 makes provision for the prevention of overlapping payments of war pension or allowances and national insurance benefit.

Article 5 extends the provisions for preventing overlapping payments of war pension or allowances and supplementary benefit, to Northern Ireland and the Isle of Man.

ORDER BY HER MAJESTY

To amend the Order of 24th September 1964, concerning pensions and other grants in respect of disablement or death due to service in the air forces during the 1914 World War and after 2nd September 1939.

ELIZABETH R.

Preamble

WHEREAS by Section 2 of the Air Force (Constitution) Act 1917(a) it is provided that it shall be lawful for Her Majesty, by order signified under the hand of a Secretary of State, to make orders with respect to the government, discipline, pay, allowances and pensions of the Air Force, and with respect to all other matters and things relating to the Air Force, including any matter by that Act authorised to be prescribed or expressed to be subject to orders or regulations:

AND WHEREAS Her Majesty deems it expedient to amend the Order dated 24th September 1964(b), as amended(c), concerning pensions and other grants in respect of disablement or death due to service in the air forces during the 1914 World War and after 2nd September 1939 (hereinafter referred to as " the 1964 Order "):

NOW, THEREFORE, Her Majesty, in exercise of the powers conferred upon Her as aforesaid and of all other powers whatsoever Her thereunto enabling, is pleased to order, and it is hereby ordered that, notwithstanding anything in the 1964 Order, the following provisions of this Order shall take effect accordingly and, except in the cases stated in the Order by His Majesty King George V of 13th January 1922, and except as otherwise provided by statute, shall be established and obeyed as the sole authority in the matters herein treated of.

Amendment of Schedule 6 to the 1964 Order, and transitional provisions

1.—(1) In Schedule 6 to the 1964 Order (rates of allowances payable in respect of disablement) there shall be made the amendments set out in Part I of the Appendix hereto.

(2) Where, by virtue of the provisions of paragraph (1) of this Article, the aggregate rate of additional unemployability or treatment allowances and allowances, if any, under the Family Allowances Act 1965(d) or under any legislation in Northern Ireland or the Isle of Man corresponding to that Act, payable in respect of the children of a member of the air forces who qualify therefor at 7th October 1968 is, upon the coming into operation of the said paragraph, less than it was according to the rates in force on the said 7th October, then for the period for which the said aggregate rate in respect of those children or any remaining number of them continues to be less than it would have been

---

(a) 7 & 8 Geo. 5.c. 51.   (b) S.I. 1964 III, p. 5361.
(c) The relevant amending Orders are S.I. 1967 II, p. 3831; 1968 I, p. 1861.
(d) 1965 c. 53.

had the said rates remained in force, the rate of additional unemployability or treatment allowances payable in respect of those children may be varied to the extent required to exclude the reduction in the said aggregate rate.

Amendment of Schedule 7 to the 1964 Order

2. In Schedule 7 to the 1964 Order (rates of pensions, other than widows' pensions, and allowances payable in respect of death) there shall be made the amendments set out at Part II of the Appendix hereto.

Amendment of Article 19 of the 1964 Order, and consequential amendment

3. In the 1964 Order, in Article 19 (allowance for lowered standard of occupation) there shall be made the amendment set out in paragraph 1 of Part III of the Appendix hereto, and in Article 33 (temporary allowances to widows and unmarried dependants who lived as wives of severely disabled pensioners) there shall be made the amendments set out in paragraph 2 of the said Part.

Article added to the 1964 Order, and consequential amendment

4. In the 1964 Order, after Article 59 there shall be added the Article set out in paragraph 3 of Part III of the Appendix hereto, and in Article 55 (interpretation of Part VI) there shall be made the amendment set out in paragraph 4 of the said Part.

Amendment of Article 60 of the 1964 Order

5. In Article 60 of the 1964 Order (payment of public claims out of pensions) there shall be made the amendment set out in paragraph 5 of the said Part.

Commencement

6.—(1) Subject to the following provisions of this Article, this Order shall come into operation on 5th August 1968.

(2) Article 1 shall come into operation in relation to an officer on 8th October 1968 and in relation to an airman on 9th October 1968.

(3) Article 2 shall come into operation in relation to an officer on 8th October 1968 and in relation to an airman on 14th October 1968.

By Her Majesty's Command.

Denis Healey,
Secretary of State.

Judith Hart,
Minister of Social Security.

26th July 1968.

APPENDIX

PART I

Amendment of Schedule 6 to the 1964 Order

1. In Schedule 6 paragraph 5 (unemployability allowances) for head (iii) of sub-paragraph (b) there shall be substituted the following head:—

"(iii) increased allowance under Article 17(4)(f)—

(a) in respect of the child, or the elder or eldest of the children, of a member ..	£72 16s. per annum	28s. per week
(b) in respect of the second child of a member ..	£30 per annum	10s. per week
(c) in respect of each other child of a member	£30 per annum	8s. per week"

2. In Schedule 6 paragraph 9 (treatment allowances) for sub-paragraph (d) there shall be substituted the following sub-paragraph:—

"(d) increased additional allowance under Article 21(4) proviso (b)—

(i) in respect of the child, or the elder or eldest of the children, of a member ..	£72 16s. per annum	28s. per week
(ii) in respect of the second child of a member ..	£30 per annum	10s. per week
(iii) in respect of each other child of a member ..	£30 per annum	8s. per week"

PART II

Amendment of Schedule 7 to the 1964 Order

In Schedule 7—

(a) for paragraph 5 (allowances in respect of children) there shall be substituted the following paragraph:—

"5. Allowances in respect of children—

(a) under Article 35(1)—

(i) in respect of the child, or the elder or eldest of the children, of a member ..	£136 16s. per annum	49s. 6d. per week
(ii) in respect of each other child of a member—		
(a) where the child qualifies for a family allowance under the Family Allowances Act 1965 or under any legislation in Northern Ireland or the Isle of Man corresponding to that Act	£110 16s. per annum	39s. 6d. per week

(b) where the child does not so qualify ..	£129 per annum	46s. 6d. per week
(b) under Article 35(3)	£197 16s. per annum (maximum)	where the child is 15 years of age or over—72s. 6d. per week (maximum)"

(b) for paragraph 6 (pension under Article 36 to a motherless or fatherless child) there shall be substituted the following paragraph:—

"6. Pension under Article 36 to a motherless or fatherless child—

(a) in respect of the child, or the elder or eldest of the children, of a member, and in respect of each other child of a member who does not qualify for a family allowance as aforesaid	£197 16s. per annum	(i) where the child is under 15 years of age— 49s. 6d. per week (ii) where the child is 15 years of age or over— 72s. 6d. per week
(b) in respect of each other child of a member who qualifies for a family allowance as aforesaid	£171 16s. per annum	(i) where the child is under 15 years of age— 39s. 6d. per week (ii) where the child is 15 years of age or over— 62s. 6d. per week"

PART III

1. Amendment of Article 19 of the 1964 Order

In Article 19 (allowance for lowered standard of occupation) for paragraph (3) there shall be substituted the following paragraph:—

"(3) An allowance under this Article shall not be payable to a member for any period in respect of which an allowance under Article 17(1)(i) is payable to him."

2. Amendment of Article 33 of the 1964 Order

In Article 33 (temporary allowances to widows and unmarried dependants who lived as wives of severely disabled pensioners) in paragraph (1) after the words "an allowance under Article 14 or Article 17(1)(i)" there shall be inserted the words "or, in the case of a member who was concurrently eligible for an allowance under Article 17(1)(i), Article 19", and in paragraph (ii) of the proviso to paragraph (2) for the words "retired pay or pension" there shall be substituted the words "retired pay, pension or allowances" and after the words "before 3rd September 1939" there shall be added the words "and a member who, being concurrently eligible for an allowance under Article 17(1)(i), was in receipt of an allowance under Article 19 shall be deemed in lieu thereof to have been in receipt of an allowance under Article 17(1)(i)".

3. *Article to be added to the* 1964 *Order*

"*Abatement of awards in respect of National Insurance and Industrial Injuries Benefits*

59A. Where a pension is awarded to or in respect of a person for any past period for which benefit under the National Insurance Acts 1965 to 1968 or the National Insurance (Industrial Injuries) Acts 1965 to 1968 or any legislation in Northern Ireland corresponding to those Acts has been paid to or in respect of that person, the total amount of pension so awarded may be abated by the amount by which the amount of benefit so paid exceeds what would have been payable for that period had the pension been concurrently payable."

4. *Amendment of Article* 55 *of the* 1964 *Order*

In paragraph (1) of Article 55 (interpretation of Part VI) for the words " Articles 56, 57, 60, 61, 62 and 64" there shall be substituted the words "Articles 56, 57, 59A, 60, 61, 62 and 64".

5. *Amendment of Article* 60 *of the* 1964 *Order*

In Article 60 (payment of public claims out of pensions) for paragraph (2) there shall be substituted the following paragraph:—

"(2) Where payment in respect of a pension is in arrears for any period and benefit under the Ministry of Social Security Act 1966(a) or benefit similar to the aforesaid benefit under any legislation in Northern Ireland or the Isle of Man corresponding to that Act has been paid for that period by reference to the requirements of the person to whom the payment is due, the amount by which the amount of benefit paid exceeds what would have been paid had the said payment not fallen into arrears shall be deemed to have been an overpayment for the purposes of paragraph (1) of this Article, and in the case of benefit paid under legislation in Northern Ireland or the Isle of Man as aforesaid shall for the purposes of that paragraph be repayable to the authority administering that benefit."

EXPLANATORY NOTE

(This Note is not part of the Order.)

This Order further amends the Order of 24th September 1964.

Articles 1 and 2 make amendments which take account of the increases in family allowances made by the Family Allowances and National Insurance Act 1968 from 8th October 1968 and have the effect of adjusting the rates of children's pensions and allowances so that the pensions or allowances and (where payable) family allowances together will normally continue to provide the same total rate for each child as was payable immediately before the aforesaid increases came into force. Transitional provisions secure that the aggregate rate of existing awards will be maintained where this is more advantageous.

Article 3 makes amendments which enable an award of an allowance for lowered standard of occupation in payment to a pensioner who becomes unemployable to be continued if, exceptionally, it would be to his financial disadvantage, having regard to any national insurance benefit concurrently

---

(a) 1966 c.20.

payable, to transfer to unemployability supplement, and extend entitlement to an award of temporary allowances, at the rate which would have been payable had the pensioner been in receipt of unemployability supplement, to the widow, or unmarried dependant who lived as a wife, of such a pensioner.

Article 4 makes provision for the prevention of overlapping payments of war pension or allowances and national insurance benefit.

Article 5 extends the provisions for preventing overlapping payments of war pension or allowances and supplementary benefit, to Northern Ireland and the Isle of Man.

At the Court at Buckingham Palace, the 26th day of July 1968

Present,

The Queen's Most Excellent Majesty in Council

WHEREAS by section 3 of the Naval and Marine Pay and Pensions Act 1865(a) it is enacted that all pay, wages, pensions, bounty money, grants or other allowances in the nature thereof, payable in respect of services in Her Majesty's naval or marine force to a person being or having been an officer, seaman or marine, or to the widow or any relative of a deceased officer, seaman or marine, shall be paid in such manner and subject to such restrictions, conditions and provisions, as are from time to time directed by Order in Council:

AND WHEREAS Her Majesty deems it expedient to amend the Order in Council dated 25th September 1964(b), as amended(c), concerning pensions and other grants in respect of disablement or death due to service in the naval forces during the 1914 World War and after 2nd September 1939 (hereinafter referred to as " the 1964 Order "):

NOW, THEREFORE, Her Majesty, in exercise of the powers conferred upon Her as aforesaid and of all other powers whatsoever Her thereunto enabling, is pleased, by and with the advice of Her Privy Council, to order, and it is hereby ordered, that, notwithstanding anything in the 1964 Order, the following provisions of this Order shall take effect accordingly and, except in the cases stated in the Order in Council of 19th December 1881, and except as otherwise provided by statute, shall be established and obeyed as the sole authority in the matters herein treated of.

Amendment of Schedule 6 to the 1964 Order, and transitional provisions

1.—(1) In Schedule 6 to the 1964 Order (rates of allowances payable in respect of disablement) there shall be made the amendments set out in Part I of the Appendix hereto.

(2) Where, by virtue of the provisions of paragraph (1) of this Article, the aggregate rate of additional unemployability or treatment allowances and allowances, if any, under the Family Allowances Act 1965(d) or under any legislation in Northern Ireland or the Isle of Man corresponding to that Act, payable in respect of the children of a member of the naval forces who qualify therefor at 7th October 1968 is, upon the coming into operation of the said paragraph, less than it was according to the rates in force on the said 7th October, then for the period for which the said aggregate rate in respect of those children or any remaining number of them continues to be less than it would have been had the said rates remained in force, the rate of additional unemployability or treatment allowances payable in respect of those children may be varied to the extent required to exclude the reduction in the said aggregate rate.

(a) 28 and 29 Vict. c. 73.   (b) S.I. 1964 III, p. 5466.
(c) The relevant amending Orders are S.I. 1967 II, p. 3851; 1968 I, p. 1865.
(d) 1965 c. 53.

Amendment of Schedule 7 to the 1964 Order

2.—In Schedule 7 to the 1964 Order (rates of pensions, other than widows' pensions, and allowances payable in respect of death) there shall be made the amendments set out at Part II of the Appendix hereto.

Amendment of Article 19 of the 1964 Order, and consequential amendment

3.—In the 1964 Order, in Article 19 (allowance for lowered standard of occupation) there shall be made the amendment set out in paragraph 1 of Part III of the Appendix hereto, and in Article 33 (temporary allowances to widows and unmarried dependants who lived as wives of severely disabled pensioners) there shall be made the amendments set out in paragraph 2 of the said Part.

Article added to the 1964 Order, and consequential amendment

4.—In the 1964 Order, after Article 59 there shall be added the Article set out in paragraph 3 of Part III of the Appendix hereto, and in Article 55 (interpretation of Part VI) there shall be made the amendment set out in paragraph 4 of the said Part.

Amendment of Article 60 of the 1964 Order

5.—In Article 60 of the 1964 Order (payment of public claims out of pensions) there shall be made the amendment set out in paragraph 5 of the said Part.

Commencement

6.—(1) Subject to the following provisions of this Article, this Order shall come into operation on 5th August 1968.

(2) Article 1 shall come into operation in relation to an officer on 8th October 1968 and in relation to a rating on 9th October 1968.

(3) Article 2 shall come into operation in relation to an officer on 8th October 1968 and in relation to a rating on 14th October 1968.

W. G. Agnew.

APPENDIX

PART I

Amendment of Schedule 6 to the 1964 Order

1. In Schedule 6 paragraph 5 (unemployability allowances) for head (iii) of sub-paragraph (*b*) there shall be substituted the following head:—

" (iii) increased allowance under Article 17(4)(f)—

(*a*) in respect of the child, or the elder or eldest of the children, of a member ...	£72 16s. per annum	28s. per week
(*b*) in respect of the second child of a member...	£30 per annum	10s. per week
(*c*) in respect of each other child of a member...	£30 per annum	8s. per week "

2. In Schedule 6 paragraph 9 (treatment allowances) for sub-paragraph (d) there shall be substituted the following sub-paragraph:—

" (d) increased additional allowance under Article 21(4) proviso (b)—

(i) in respect of the child, or the elder or eldest of the children, of a member ... ... £72 16s. per annum 28s. per week

(ii) in respect of the second child of a member ... ... £30 per annum 10s. per week

(iii) in respect of each other child of a member ... ... £30 per annum 8s. per week "

PART II
Amendment of Schedule 7 to the 1964 Order

In Schedule 7—

(a) for paragraph 5 (allowances in respect of children) there shall be substituted the following paragraph:—

" 5. Allowances in respect of children—

(a) under Article 35(1)—

(i) in respect of the child, or the elder or eldest of the children, of a member ... ...
(i) Commissioned Officer* or Nurse— £136 16s. per annum 49s. 6d. per week
(ii) Warrant Officer†— £130 16s. per annum

(ii) in respect of each other child of a member—

(a) where the child qualifies for a family allowance under the Family Allowances Act 1965 or under any legislation in Northern Ireland or the Isle of Man corresponding to that Act ...
(i) Commissioned Officer* or Nurse— £110 16s. per annum 39s. 6d. per week
(ii) Warrant Officer†— £104 16s. per annum

(b) where the child does not so qualify ... ...
(i) Commissioned Officer* or Nurse— £129 per annum 46s. 6d. per week
(ii) Warrant Officer†— £123 per annum

(b) under Article 35(3)—

(i) Commissioned Officer*— £197 16s. per annum (maximum)

where the child is 15 years of age or over— 72s. 6d. per week (maximum) "

(ii) Warrant Officer†—

(a) where the child is under 15 years of age— £136 16s. per annum (maximum)

(b) where the child is 15 years of age or over— £189 16s. per annum (maximum)

(b) for paragraph 6 (pension under Article 36 to a motherless or fatherless child) there shall be substituted the following paragraph:—

" 6. Pension under Article 36 to a motherless or fatherless child—

(a) in respect of the child, or the elder or eldest of the children, of a member, and in respect of each other child of a member who does not qualify for a family allowance as aforesaid   ...

(i) Commissioned Officer* or Nurse— £197 16s. per annum

(i) where the child is under 15 years of age— 49s. 6d. per week

(ii) Warrant Officer†— (a) where the child is under 15 years of age— £136 16s. per annum

(ii) where the child is 15 years of age or over— 72s. 6d. per week

(b) where the child is 15 years of age or over— £189 16s. per annum

(b) in respect of each other child of a member who qualifies for a family allowance as aforesaid ...   .

(i) Commissioned Officer* or Nurse— £171 16s. per annum

(i) where the child is under 15 years of age— 39s. 6d. per week

(ii) Warrant Officer†— (a) where the child is under 15 years of age— £110 16s. per annum

(ii) where the child is 15 years of age or over— 62s. 6d. per week "

(b) where the child is 15 years of age or over— £163 16s. per annum

PART III

1. *Amendment of Article 19 of the 1964 Order*

In Article 19 (allowance for lowered standard of occupation) for paragraph (3) there shall be substituted the following paragraph:—

"(3) An allowance under this Article shall not be payable to a member for any period in respect of which an allowance under Article 17(1) (i) is payable to him."

2. *Amendment of Article 33 of the 1964 Order*

In Article 33 (temporary allowances to widows and unmarried dependants who lived as wives of severely disabled pensioners) in paragraph (1) after the words "an allowance under Article 14 or Article 17(1)(i)" there shall be inserted the words "or, in the case of a member who was concurrently eligible for an allowance under Article 17(1)(i), Article 19" and in paragraph (ii) of the proviso to paragraph (2) for the words "retired pay or pension" there shall be substituted the words "retired pay, pension or allowances" and after the words "before 3rd September 1939" there shall be added the words "and a member who, being concurrently eligible for an allowance under Article 17(1)(i), was in receipt of an allowance under Article 19 shall be deemed in lieu thereof to have been in receipt of an allowance under Article 17(1)(i)."

3. *Article to be added to the 1964 Order*

"*Abatement of awards in respect of National Insurance and Industrial Injuries Benefits*

59A. Where a pension is awarded to or in respect of a person for any past period for which benefit under the National Insurance Acts 1965 to 1968 or the National Insurance (Industrial Injuries) Acts 1965 to 1968 or any legislation in Northern Ireland corresponding to those Acts has been paid to or in respect of that person, the total amount of pension so awarded may be abated by the amount by which the amount of benefit so paid exceeds what would have been payable for that period had the pension been concurrently payable."

4. *Amendment of Article 55 of the 1964 Order*

In paragraph (1) of Article 55 (interpretation of Part VI) for the words "Articles 56, 57, 60, 61, 62 and 64" there shall be substituted the words "Articles 56, 57, 59A, 60, 61, 62 and 64".

5. *Amendment of Article 60 of the 1964 Order*

In Article 60 (payment of public claims out of pensions) for paragraph (2) there shall be substituted the following paragraph:—

"(2) Where payment in respect of a pension is in arrears for any period and benefit under the Ministry of Social Security Act 1966 (a) or benefit similar to the aforesaid benefit under any legislation in Northern Ireland or the Isle of Man corresponding to that Act has been paid for that period by reference to the requirements of the person to whom the payment is due, the amount by which the amount of benefit paid exceeds what would have been paid had the said payment not fallen into arrears shall be deemed to have been an over-payment for the purposes of paragraph (1) of this Article, and in the case of

---

(a) 1966 c. 20.

Year and Number (or date)	Act or instrument	How affected
1925		
1146	Theatrical Employers Registration Rules 1925 (Rev. XXII, p. 525)	am., 1968/1342
1926	Fertilisers and Feeding Stuffs Act 1926 (c. 45)	sch. 1, 2, 4 **am.**, 1968/883
971	Public Health (Ophthalmia Neonatorum) Regs. 1926 (Rev. XVIII, p. 767)	r., 1968/1366
1927		
1185	Land Charges Fees O. 1927 (Rev. XI, p. 814)	r., 1968/677
1928		
668	Agricultural Credits Fees O. 1928 (Rev. I, p. 94)	r., 1968/678
1094	Post Office Annuity Regs. 1928 (Rev. IX, p. 763)	am., 1968/1003
1933		
1149	Savings Certificates Regs. 1933 (Rev. XV, p. 309)	am., 1968/995
1934		
674	Public Health (Treatment of Infectious Disease) Regs. 1934 (Rev. XVIII, p. 796)	r., 1968/1366
1936	Firearms (Amdt.) Act 1936 (c. 39) ...	s. 7 (N.I.) functions transfd. to Secy. of State, 1968/1200
	Public Health Act 1936 (c. 49) ...	s. 144 **mod.**, 1968/861
1937		
35	Public Health (Ophthalmia Neonatorum) Amdt. Regs. 1937 (Rev. XVIII, p. 767)	r., 1968/366
509	Public Health (Imported Food) Regs. (S.) 1937 (Rev. VIII, p. 127)	r., 1968/1181
993	Methylated Spirits (Sale by Retail) (S.) O. 1937 (Rev. XXI, p. 474)	am., 1968/1126
1938	Young Persons (Employment) Act 1938 (c. 69)	s. 5 **am.** (S.), 1968/1177, (E. and W.),1968/1242
1939		
9 Mar.	Emergency Powers O. in C. 1939 (see 1952 I, p. 621)	am., 1968/724 r. (Swaziland), 1968/1377

Year and Number (or date)	Act or instrument	How affected
1940 204	Measles and Whooping Cough Regs. 1940 (Rev. XVIII, p. 790)	r., 1968/1366
1944	Education Act 1944 (c. 31)	s. 94 **am.**, 1968/1242
1945 698	Provision of Milk and Meals Regs. 1945 (Rev. VI, p. 380)	**am.**, 1968/1251
1947	Exchange Control Act 1947 (c. 14) ...	sch. 1 **am.**, 1968/1399
	Local Govt. (S.) Act 1947 (c. 43) ...	ss. 219, 233 **am.**, 228 **replaced**, 1968/711
865	Factories (Luminising) Special Regs. 1947 (Rev. VII, p. 384)	r. (15.11.68), 1968/780
1774	Double Taxation Relief (Taxes on Income) (Cyprus) O. 1947 (Rev. X, p. 377)	**am.**, 1968/1097
2865	Double Taxation Relief (Taxes on Income) (Antigua) O. 1947 (Rev. X, p. 341)	**am.**, 1968/1096
2867	Double Taxation Relief (Taxes on Income) (Gambia) O. 1947 (Rev. X, p. 399)	**am.**, 1968/1099
2873	Double Taxation Relief (Taxes on Income) (Sierra Leone) O. 1947 (Rev. X, p. 492)	**am.**, 1968/1104
1948	Industrial Assurance and Friendly Societies Act 1948 (c. 39)	sch. 1 para. 7 **am.** (S.), 1968/1177, (E. and W.), 1242
421	Measles and Whooping Cough (Amdt.) Regs. 1948 (Rev. XVIII, p. 790)	r., 1968/1366
1434	Public Health (Imported Food) (Amdt.) (S.) Regs. 1948 (Rev. VIII, p. 127)	r., 1968/1181
1949	Marriage Act 1949 (c. 76)	ss. 27, 29, 31, 32, 41, 51, 57, 63–65 **am.**, 1968/1242
359	Double Taxation Relief (Taxes on Income) (Dominica) O. 1949 (1949 I, p. 2256)	**am.**, 1968/1098
366	Double Taxation Relief (Taxes on Income) (St. Lucia) O. 1949 (1949 I, p. 2289)	**am.**, 1968/1102
367	Double Taxation Relief (Taxes on Income (St. Vincent) O. 1949 (1949 I, p. 2296)	**am.**, 1968/1103
870	Food and Drugs (Whalemeat) (S.) Regs. 1949 (1949 I, p. 1760)	r., 1968/1181

Year and Number (or date)	Act or instrument	How affected
1949		
875	National Insurance (Members of the Forces) Regs. 1949 (1949 I, p. 2731)	r., 1968/827
1205	Water (Adaptation and Modification of the Local Govt. (S.) Act 1947) (S.) Regs. 1949 (1949 I, p. 4724)	r., 1968/711
2058	County Cts. Districts O. 1949 (1949 I, p. 955)	am., 1968/938
2259	Public Health (Acute Poliomyelitis, Acute Encephalitis, and Meningococcal Infection) Regs. 1949 (1949 I, p. 3543)	r., 1968/1366
1950	Shops Act 1950 (c. 28) ...	s. 35 am. (S.), 1968/1177, (E. and W.),1968/1242
198	Food and Drugs (Whalemeat) (Amdt.) (S.) Regs. 1950 (1950 I, p. 758)	r., 1968/1181
376	Coal Industry Nationalisation (Superannuation) Regs. 1950	am., 1968/748
533	Assurance Companies Rules 1950 (1950 I, p. 1121)	am. (1.1.69), 1968/1408
643	Assurance Companies (Amdt.) Rules 1950 (1950 I, p. 1139)	r. (1.1.69), 1968/1408
947	Water (Adaptation and Modification of the Local Govt. (S.) Act 1947) Amdt. (S.) Regs. 1950 (1950 II, p. 1509)	r., 1968/711
1596	Aerated Waters Wages Council (S.) Wages Regulation (No. 2) O. 1950 (1950 II, p. 1228)	r., 1968/752
1951		
1081	Puerperal Pyrexia Regs. 1951 (1951 II, p. 315)	r., 1968/1366
1720	National Insurance (Members of the Forces) Amdt. Regs. 1951 (1951 I, p. 1491)	r., 1968/827
1952		
194	Courts-Martial (Appeals) Rules 1952 (1952 I, p. 648)	r., 1968/1071
649	National Insurance (Members of the Forces) Amdt. Regs. 1952 (1952 II, p. 2188)	r., 1968/827
704	Public Health (Tuberculosis) Regs. 1952 (1952 III, p. 2736)	r., 1968/1366
1432	Detention Centre Rules 1952 (1952 I, p. 787)	am., 1968/1014
2184	National Insurance (Members of the Forces) Amdt. (No. 2) Regs. 1952 (1952 II, p. 2190)	r., 1968/827

Year and Number (or date)	Act or instrument	How affected
1953	Births and Deaths Registration Act 1953 (c. 20)	ss. 5–7, 9, 11–14, 20, 21, 24, 29–33 **am.**, 1968/1242
299	Public Health (Infectious Diseases) Regs. 1953 (1953 II, p. 1691)	**r.**, 1968/1366
493	Justices Clerks (Accounts) Regs. 1953 (1953 I, p. 1006)	**am.**, 1968/1266
1928	Acute Rheumatism Regs. 1953 (1953 II, p. 1688)	**r.**, 1968/1366
1954		
189	National Insurance (Maternity Benefit and Miscellaneous Provisions) Regs. 1954 (1954 I, p. 1387)	**am.**, 1968/827
370	Pedestrian Crossings Regs. 1954 (1954 II, p. 1948)	**am.**, 1968/1196
439	Wireless Telegraphy (General Licence Charges) Regs. 1954 (1954 II, p. 2376)	**r.**, 1968/1314
898	British Transport Commission (Male Wages Grades Pensions) Regs. 1954 (1954 I, p. 175)	**am.**, 1968/1249
1596	Registration (Births, Still births, Deaths and Marriages) Consolidated Regs. 1954 (1954 II, p. 1871)	**am.**, 1968/1241
1635	Exchange Control (Declarations and Evidence) O. 1954 (1954 I, p. 818)	**r.**, 1968/1232
1691	Puerperal Pyrexia (Amdt.) Regs. 1954 (1954 II, p. 1846)	**r.**, 1968/1366
1955		
1047	Pensions Commutation Regs. 1955 (1955 II, p. 1755)	**r.**, 1968/1163
1956	Therapeutic Substances Act 1956 (c. 25)	sch. 1 **am.**, 1968/906, 907
	Restrictive Trade Practices Act 1956 (c. 68)	s. 7 **am.**, 1968/1036
162	Rules of Procedure (Army) 1956 (1956 I, p. 213)	**am.**, 1968/1180
163	Rules of Procedure (Air Force) 1956 (1956 II, p. 2020)	**am.**, 1968/1173
619	Double Taxation Relief (Taxes on Income) (Federation of Rhodesia and Nyasaland) O. 1956 (1956 I, p. 1072)	**am.**, 1968/1101, 1106
894	Schools (S.) Code 1956 (1956 I, p. 735)	**am.**, 1968/1055
1657	Premium Savings Bonds Regs. 1956 (1956 I, p. 1489)	**am.**, 1968/994
1981	Imprisonment and Detention (Air Force) Rules 1956 (1956 II, p. 2118)	**am.**, 1968/874
1999	Police (S.) Regs. 1956 (1956 II, p. 1766)	**r.**, 1968/716

Year and Number (or date)	Act or instrument	How affected
1957	House of Commons Disqualification Act 1957 (c. 20)	sch. 2 **am.**, 1968/729
8	Acute Rheumatism (Amdt.) Regs. 1957 (1957 II, p. 1932)	**r.**, 1968/1366
336	Police (S.) Amdt. Regs. 1957 (1957 II, p. 1879)	**r.**, 1968/716
488	National Health Service (Designation of London Teaching Hospitals) O. 1957 (1957 I, p. 1452)	**am.**, 1968/1334
619	Matrimonial Causes Rules 1957 (1957 II, p. 2406)	**r.**, 1968/1244
742	Police (S.) Amdt. (No. 2) Regs. 1957 (1957 II, p. 1880)	**r.**, 1968/716
978	Wireless Telegraphy (General Licence Charges) Amdt. (No. 1) Regs. 1957 (1957 II, p. 2544)	**r.**, 1968/1314
1074	Motor Vehicles (International Circulation) O. 1957 (1957 II, p. 2154)	**am.**, 1968/1111
1781	Police (S.) Amdt. (No. 3) Regs. 1957 (1957 II, p. 1882)	**r.**, 1968/716
2011	Central Midwives Board for Scotland Rules 1957 Approval Instrument, 1957 (1957 I, p. 1381)	**r.**, 1968/694
2039	Police (S.) Amdt. (No. 4) Regs. 1957 (1957 II, p. 1883)	**r.**, 1968/716
1958		
17	Acute Rheumatism (Amdt.) Regs. 1958 (1958 II, p. 2012)	**r.**, 1968/1366
73	Patents Rules 1958 (1958 II, p. 1713)	**r.**, 1968/1389
473	Public Service Vehicles (Conditions of Fitness) Regs. 1958 (1958 II, p. 2014)	**am.**, 1968/824
652	Criminal Appeal Rules 1958 (1958 I, p. 396)	**r.**, 1968/1262
926	Public Service Vehicles (Equipment and Use) Regs. 1958 (1958 II, p. 2036)	**am.**, 1968/826
1192	Central Midwives Board for Scotland (Amdt.) Rules 1958, Approval Instrument, 1958 (1958 II, p. 1701)	**r.**, 1968/694
2009	Police (S.) Amdt. Regs. 1958 (1958 II, p. 1917)	**r.**, 1968/716
1959		
363	Schools Health Service Regs. 1959 (1959 I, p. 1582)	**am.**, 1968/1252
364	Schools Regs. 1959 (1959 I, p. 1584)...	**am.**, 1968/1281
747	Police (S.) Amdt. Regs. 1959 (1959 II, p. 2096)	**r.**, 1968/716
962	Public Health Officers Regs. 1959 (1959 I, p. 1605)	**am.**, 1968/1366

Year and Number (or date)	Act or instrument	How affected
1959		
963	Public Health Officers (Port Health Districts) Regs. 1959 (1959 II, p. 2125)	am., 1968/1366
1832	Direct Grant Schools Regs. 1959 (1959 I, p. 1034)	am., 1968/1148
1917	Police (S.) Amdt. (No. 2) Regs. 1959 (1959 II, p. 2098)	r., 1968/716
2201	Saint Vincent (Constitution) O. in C. 1959 (1959 I, p. 479)	am., 1968/1093
2257	Police (S.) Amdt. (No. 3) Regs. 1959 (1959 II, p. 2100)	r., 1968/716
1960	Ministers of the Crown (Parliamentary Secretaries) Act 1960 (9 & 10 Eliz. 2. c. 6)	sch. 1 am., 1968/729
69	Coal and Other Mines (Shafts, Outlets and Roads) Regs. 1960 (1960 II, p. 2028)	am., 1968/1037
369	Police (S.) Amdt. Regs. 1960 (1960 II, p. 2750)	r., 1968/716
726	Cinematograph Films (Collection of Levy) Regs. 1960 (1960 I, p. 555)	r., 1968/1077
819	Superannuation (Civil Service and N.I. Local Govt.) Transfer Rules 1960	am., 1968/779
910	Housing (Declaration of Unfitness) (S.) Regs. 1960 (1960 II, p. 1613)	r., 1968/955
1071	Trustee Savings Banks (Special Investments Regs. 1960 (1960 III, p. 3069)	r., 1968/1029
1143	Housing (Forms) (S.) Regs. 1960 (1960 II, p. 1617)	am., 1968/955
1185	Cinematograph Films (Collection of Levy) (Amdt.) Regs. 1960 (1960 I, p. 558)	r., 1968/1077
1260	Criminal Appeal Rules 1960 (1960 I, p. 862)	r., 1968/1262
1622	Police (S.) Amdt. (No. 2) Regs. 1960 (1960 II, p. 2751)	r., 1968/716
1989	Public Health (Infectious Diseases) Amdt. Regs. 1960 (1960 II, p. 2802)	r., 1968/1366
2325	Criminal Appeal (No. 2) Rules 1960 (1960 I, p. 879)	r., 1968/1262
2404	Police (S.) Amdt. (No. 3) Regs. 1960 (1960 II, p. 2753)	r., 1968/716
1961	Factories Act 1961 (c. 34)	s. 178 am. (S.), 1968/ 1177, (E. and W.), 1968/1242
275	Police (S.) Amdt. Regs. 1961	r., 1968/716
577	Double Taxation Relief (Taxes on Income) (Sweden) O. 1961	am., 1968/1105

Year and Number (or date)	Act or instrument	How affected
1961		
1015	Courts-Martial Appeal (Amdt.) Rules 1961	r., 1968/1071
1311	Police (S.) Amdt. (No. 2) Regs. 1961...	r., 1968/716
1902	Police (S.) Amdt. (No. 3) Regs. 1961...	r., 1968/716
2352	National Insurance (Members of the Forces) Amdt. Regs. 1961	r., 1968/827
1962	Education (S.) Act 1962 (c. 47) ...	s. 99 **am.**, 1968/1177
146	Central Midwives Bd. for Scotland (Amdt.) Rules 1961, Approval Instrt. 1962	r., 1968/694
667	Pensions Commutation (Amdt.) Regs. 1962	r., 1968/1163
800	Mental Health (Constitution of State Hospital Management Cttee.) (S.) O. 1962	**am.**, 1968/1010
874	Police (S.) Amdt. Regs. 1962	r., 1968/716
1402	Housing (Forms) (S.) Amdt. Regs. 1962	r., 1968/955
2544	Cinematograph Films (Collection of Levy) (Amdt. No. 2) Regs. 1962	r., 1968/1077
2741	Police (S.) Amdt. (No. 2) Regs. 1962 ...	r., 1968/716
1963	Purchase Tax Act 1963 (c. 9)	sch. 1 Pt. 1 **am.**, 1968/709
230	Telephone (Channel Is.) Regs. 1963 ...	r., 1968/1257
607	Telephone (Channel Is.) Amdt. (No. 1) Regs. 1963	r., 1968/1257
948	Local Govt. (Rate Product) (S.) Rules 1963	**am.**, 1968/754
999	Local Govt. (Compensation) Regs. 1963	**am.**, 1968/913
1026	Motor Vehicles (Driving Licences) Regs. 1963	**am.**, 1968/947
1375	Cinematograph Films (Collection of Levy) (Amdt. No. 3) Regs. 1963	r., 1968/1077
1376	Cinematograph Films (Distribution of Levy) Regs. 1963	**am.**, 1968/1076
1456	Therapeutic Substances (Manufacture of Preparations of Human Blood) Regs. 1963	**am.**, 1968/908
1781	Motor Cycles (Protective Helmets) Regs. 1963	r., 1968/844
2040	Wages Regulation (Sack and Bag) (Holidays) O., 9163	r., 1968/1358
2077	Police (S.) Amdt. Regs. 1963 ...	r., 1968/716
1964	Ministers of the Crown Act 1964 (c. 98)	sch. 2 Pt. II **am.**, 1968/729

Year and Number (or date)	Act or instrument	How affected
1964		
26	Water Officers (Compensation) Regs. 1964	**am.,** 1968/912
149	Police (S.) Amdt. Regs. 1964 ...	**r.,** 1968/716
205	Road Vehicles Lighting Regs. 1964 ...	**am.,** 1968/1247
228	Patents (Amdt.) Rules 1964	**r.,** 1968/1389
461	Police (S.) Amdt. (No. 2) Regs. 1964...	**r.,** 1968/716
504	National Insurance (Industrial Injuries) (Benefit) Regs. 1964	**am.,** 1968/1007
687	Price Stability of Imported Products (Minimum Import Price Levels) O. 1964	**r.,** 1968/1132
810	Price Stability of Imported Products (Minimum Import Price Levels) (Operative Date) O. 1964	**r.,** 1968/1132
840	Cereals (Guarantee Payments) O 1964	**am.,** 1968/767
907	Industrial Training (Wool Industry Bd.) O. 1964	**am.,** 1968/898
973	Police (S.) Amdt. (No. 3) Regs. 1964 ...	**r.,** 1968/716
990	Price Stability of Imported Products (Minimum Import Price Levels) (Amdt.) O. 1964	**r.,** 1968/1132
1002	Motorways Traffic (S.) Regs. 1964 ...	**am.,** 1968/960
1086	Industrial Training (Engineering Bd.) O. 1964	**am.,** 1968/1333
1211	Criminal Appeal Rules 1964	**r.,** 1968/1262
1222	Wages Regulation (Button Manufacturing) O. 1964	**r.,** 1968/742
1337	Patents (Amdt. No. 2) Rules 1964 ...	**r.,** 1968/1389
1341	Composite Goods O. 1964	**r.,** 1968/1381
1729	Fees of Appointed Factory Doctors (No. 1) O. 1964	**r.,** 1968/937
1890	Fees of Appointed Factory Doctors (No. 2) O. 1964	**r.,** 1968/937
1953	London Govt. (Compensation) Regs. 1964	**am.,** 1968/911
1969	Police (S.) Amdt. (No. 4) Regs. 1964 ...	**r.,** 1968/716
2077	Personal Injuries (Civilians) Scheme 1964	**am.,** 1968/1206
1 Jan.	British Honduras L.P. 1964 (1964 I, p. 1136)	**am.,** L.P. 11.6.68
19 Sept.	Disablement and Death Pensions etc. (Military), 1914 World War Service, and Service subsequent to 2 Sept. 1939, R. Warrant 1964. (1964 III, p. 5257)	**am.,** R. Warrant 24.7.68
24 Sept.	Disablement and Death Pensions etc. (Air Force), 1914 World War Service, and Service subsequent to 2 Sept. 1939, O. 1964 (1964 III, p. 5361)	**am.,** O. 26.7.68

SBN 11 840011 8

Index to Parts I and II

Year and Number (or date)	Act or instrument	How affected
1968		
26	Police Regs. 1968	**am.,** 1968/766, 1207
50	Police (S.) Amdt. Regs. 1968	**r.,** 1968/716
80	Exchange Control (Declarations and Evidence) (Amdt.) O. 1968	**r.,** 1968/1232
92	National Insurance (Industrial Injuries) (Benefit) Amdt. Regs. 1968	**r.,** 1968/1007
112	Fugitive Offenders (Cayman Is.) O. 1968	**am.,** 1968/1375
113	Fugitive Offenders (Falkland Is. and Dependencies) O. 1968	**am.,** 1968/1375
123	Wages Regulation (Road Haulage) (Amdt.) O. 1968	**r.,** 1968/1130
182	Bermuda Constitution O. 1968 ...	**am.,** 1968/726
183	Fugitive Offenders (British Indian Ocean Territory) O. 1968	**am.,** 1968/1375
184	Fugitive Offenders (St. Helena) O. 1968	**am.,** 1968/1375
185	Fugitive Offenders (Turks and Caicos Is.) O. 1968	**am.,** 1968/1375
218	Fertilisers and Feeding Stuffs Regs. 1968	**am.,** 1968/883
238	Sea Fisheries (S.) Byelaw (No. 77) 1967	**r.,** 1968/1011
239	Sea Fisheries (S.) Byelaw (No. 78) 1967	**r.,** 1968/1012
251	Import Duty Drawbacks (No. 2) O. 1968	**am.,** 1968/1385
405	Composite Goods (Amdt.) O. 1968 ...	**r.,** 1968/1381
533	Inland Post Amdt. (No. 1) Regs. 1968	**r.,** 1968/1253
593	Telephone Amdt. (No. 4) Regs. 1968...	**r.,** 1968/1256
599	Redundancy Fund (Advances out of National Loans Fund) O. 1968	**r.,** 1968/1263
600	Sea Fisheries (S.) Byelaw (No. 80) 1968	**r.,** 1968/1013
601	Goods Vehicles (Plating and Testing) Regs. 1968	**am.,** 1968/1169
727	Swaziland Constitution (Amdt.) O. 1968	**r.,** 1968/1377
679	Import Duties (General) (No. 4) O. 1968	**am.,** 1968/950, 1030, 1158, 1383, **am.** (*temp.*), 1968/1384
816	Awards and Settlements (Temporary Continuation of Standstill) (No. 1) O. 1968	**am.,** 1968/1188
861	Public Health (Infective Jaundice) Regs. 1968	**r.,** 1968/1366
884	Fugitive Offenders (Pitcairn) O. 1968	**am.,** 1968/1375
885	Southern Rhodesia (United Nations Sanctions) O. 1968	**r.,** 1968/1020
1242	Registration of Births, Deaths and Marriages (Fees) O. 1968	**am.,** 1968/1309
1225	Price Stability of Imported Products (Rates of Levy No. 2) O. 1968	**am.,** 1968/1404
1390	Price Stability of Imported Products (Rates of Levy No. 4) O. 1968	**r.,** 1968/1391

Year and Number (or date)	Act or instrument	How affected
1967		
1303	Fugitive Offenders (Extension) O. 1967	**r.** (Pitcairn, Henderson, Ducie and Oeno Is.), 1968/884 **r.** (New Hebrides), 1968/1091
1315	Police (Promotion) (Amdt.) Regs. 1967	**r.**, 1968/1074
1342	Police (S.) Amdt. (No. 2) Regs. 1967...	**r.**, 1968/716
1363	Wages Regulation (Wholesale Mantle and Costume) (Holidays) O. 1967	**r.**, 1968/1321
1416	Inland Post Regs. 1967	**r.**, 1968/1253
1559	Beef Cow Subsidy Payment (E. and W.) O. 1967	**am.**, 1968/967
1561	Beef Cow Subsidy Payment (S.) O. 1967	**am.**, 1968/983
1583	Exchange Control (Authorised Dealers and Depositaries) O. 1967	**am.**, 1968/1002
1601	Wages Regulation (Dressmaking and Women's Light Clothing) (E. and W.) (Holidays) O. 1967	**r.**, 1968/1328
1730	Fees of Appointed Factory Doctors (Amdt.) O. 1967	**r.**, 1968/937
1811	Criminal Appeal Rules 1967	**r.**, 1968/1262
1904	Fugitive Offenders (Bahamas Is.) O. 1967	**am.**, 1968/1375
1905	Fugitive Offenders (Bermuda) O. 1967	**am.**, 1968/1375
1906	Fugitive Offenders (British Honduras) O. 1967	**am.**, 1968/1375
1907	Fugitive Offenders (British Solomon Is. Protectorate) O. 1967	**am.**, 1968/1375
1908	Fugitive Offenders (Fiji) O. 1967 ...	**am.**, 1968/1375
1909	Fugitive Offenders (Gibraltar) O. 1967	**am.**, 1968/1375
1910	Fugitive Offenders (Gilbert and Ellice Is.) O. 1967	**am.**, 1968/1375
1911	Fugitive Offenders (Hong Kong) O. 1967	**am.**, 1968/1375
1913	Fugitive Offenders (Montserrat) O. 1967	**am.**, 1968/1375
1914	Fugitive Offenders (Seychelles) O. 1967	**am.**, 1968/1375
1915	Fugitive Offenders (Virgin Is.) O. 1967	**am.**, 1968/1375
1916	Fugitive Offenders (Sovereign Base Areas of Akrotiri and Dhekelia) O. 1967	**am.**, 1968/1375
1977	Beef Cow Subsidy Payment (N.I.) O. 1967	**am.**, 1968/968
1968	Firearms Act 1968 (c. 27)	**s.** 5, 12(2) functions transfd. to Secy. of State, 1968/1200 **ss.** 31, 34, 38 **am.**, 1968/1200

Year and Number (or date)	Act or instrument	How affected
1967		
241	Swaziland Constitution O., 1967 ...	r., 1968/1377
246	Swaziland (Appeals to Privy Council) O. 1967	r., 1968/1377
248	Southern Rhodesia (Prohibited Trade and Dealings) (Overseas Territories) (Amdt.) O. 1967	r. (certain territories), 1968/1094
279	Industrial Training (Engineering Bd.) O. 1967	r., 1968/1333
392	Patents (Amdt.) Rules 1967	r., 1968/1389
394	Southern Rhodesia (Prohibited Trade and Dealings) (Amdt.) O. 1967	r., 1968/885
433	Telephone Amdt. (No. 3) Regs. 1967...	r., 1968/1256
454	Milk (N.I.) (Amdt.) O. 1967	r., 1968/850
489	Teachers Superannuation Regs. 1967...	am., 1968/1353
556	Exchange Control (Specified Currency and Prescribed Securities) O. 1967	am., 1968/1233
639	Wages Regulation (Sack and Bag) O. 1967	r., 1968/1357
663	Wages Regulation (Aerated Waters) (S.) O. 1967	r., 1968/751
675	Export of Goods (Control) O. 1967 ...	am., 1968/845, 1073
757	Wages Regulation (Rope, Twine and Net) O. 1967	am., 1968/1051
765	Police (Promotion) Regs. 1967 ...	r., 1968/1074
815	Commonwealth Countries and Republic of Ireland (Immunities) (No. 2) O. 1967	am., 1968/1374
844	National Insurance (Assessment of Graduated Contributions) Regs. 1967	am., 1968/827
889	Cinematograph Films (Collection of Levy) (Amdt. No. 5) Regs. 1967	r., 1968/1077
944	Police (S.) Amdt. Regs. 1967 ...	r., 1968/716
975	Swaziland Constitution (Amdt.) O. 1967	r., 1968/1377
980	Irish Land (Finance) (Amdt.) Rules 1967	r., 1968/991
1019	Grading of Produce (Pears) Regs. 1967	am., 1968/1041
1020	Grading of Produce (Apples) Regs. 1967	am., 1968/1040
1021	Police (Discipline) (S.) Regs. 1967 ...	am., 1968/716
1171	Patents (Amdt. No. 2) Rules 1967 ...	r., 1968/1389
1265	National Insurance (Increase of Benefit and Miscellaneous Provisions) Regs. 1967	am., 1968/827
1294	Act of Sederunt (Alteration of Sheriff Ct. Fees) 1967	am., 1968/1166

Year and Number (or date)	Act or instrument	How affected
1966		
997	Building Control (Cost Limit Exemption) O. 1966	r., 1968/781
1003	National Insurance (Members of the Forces) Amdt. Regs. 1966	r., 1968/827
1081	Import Duty Drawbacks (No. 7) O. 1966	am., 1968/930
1083	Police (S.) Amdt. (No. 2) Regs. 1966...	r., 1968/716
1210	National Health Service (General Medical and Pharmaceutical Services) Regs. 1966	am., 1968/759
1220	Import Duty Drawbacks (No. 8) O. 1966	am., 1968/1157
1233	National Health Service (General Medical and Pharmaceutical Services) (S.) Regs. 1966	am., 1968/818
1244	Police (S.) Amdt. (No. 3) Regs. 1966 ...	r., 1968/716
1254	Air Navigation (Restriction of Flying) Regs. 1966	am., 1968/1045
1288	Motor Vehicles (Construction and Use) Regs. 1966	am., 1968/1248
1289	Motor Vehicles (Authorisation of Special Types) Gen. O. 1966	am., 1968/839
1461	Redundancy Fund Contributions O. 1966	r., 1968/1264
1471	Commons Registration (General) Regs. 1966	am., 1968/989
1482	Patents (Amdt.) Rules 1966	r., 1968/1389
1494	Wages Regulation (Wholesale Mantle and Costume) O. 1966	r., 1968/1320
1548	County Cts. (Bankruptcy and Companies Winding-up-Jurisdiction) O. 1966	am., 1968/939
1595	Southern Rhodesia (Prohibited Trade and Dealings) O. 1966	r., 1968/885
1619	Police (S.) Amdt. (No. 4) Regs. 1966 ...	r., 1968/716
21 Dec.	Mauritius Constitution O. 1966 (1966 III, p. 5190)	r., O. 4.3.68 (II, p. 1871)
1967	General Rate Act 1967 (c. 9)	sch. 9 paras. 12, 13 am., 1968/1066
18	Southern Rhodesia (Prohibited Trade and Dealings) (Overseas Territories) O. 1967	r. (certain territories), 1968/1094
79	Import Duties (General) (No. 1) O. 1967	r., 1968/679
99	Southern Rhodesia (Prohibited Trade and Dealings) (Amdt.) O. 1967	r., 1968/885

Year and Number (or date)	Act or instrument	How affected
1966		
159	Overseas Service (Pensions Supplement) Regs. 1966	am., 1968/745
292	Southern Rhodesia (Prohibited Exports) (Sugar) O. 1966	r., 1968/885
407	Southern Rhodesia (Prohibited Exports) (Iron Ore) O. 1966	r., 1968/885
409	Motor Cycles (Protective Helmets) (Amdt.) Regs. 1966	r., 1968/844
428	Industrial Training (Wool, Jute and Flax Bd.) O. 1966	r., 1968/898
437	Telephone (Channel Is.) Amdt. (No. 2) Regs. 1966	r., 1968/1257
452	Superannuation (Civil Service and N.I. Local Govt.) Transfer (Amdt.) Rules 1966	am., 1968/779
484	Cereals (Guarantee Payments) (Amdt.) O. 1966	am., 1968/767
502	Therapeutic Substances (Manufacture of Hormone Products) Regs. 1966	am., 1968/907
505	Therapeutic Substances (Manufacture of Antibiotics) Regs. 1966	am., 1968/906
554	Wages Regulation (Road Haulage) O. 1966	r., 1968/1130
579	Local Land Charges Rules 1966 ...	am., 1968/1212
660	Southern Rhodesia (Prohibited Exports) (Asbestos) O. 1966	r., 1968/885
661	Southern Rhodesia (Prohibited Exports) (Pig Iron) O. 1966	r., 1968/885
667	Origin of Goods (Republic of Ireland) Regs. 1966	am., 1968/988, 1223
727	Post Office Savings Bank Regs. 1966...	am., 1968/1064
759	Registration of Births, Deaths and Marriages (Local Registration Authies; Officers) Compensation (S.) Regs. 1966	am., 1968/1087
786	Wages Regulation (Shirtmaking) O. 1966	am., 1968/1319
855	Wages Regulation (Dressmaking and Women's Light Clothing) (E. and W.) O. 1966	r., 1968/1327
857	Telephone Amdt. (No. 2) Regs. 1966...	r., 1968/1256
858	Telephone (Channel Is.) Amdt. (No. 3) Regs. 1966	r., 1968/1257
921	Import Duty Drawbacks (No. 6) O. 1966	am., 1968/930, 1157, 1385
966	Police (S.) Amdt. Regs. 1966 ...	r., 1968/716
975	Offices, Shops and Railway Premises Act 1963 (Exemption No. 4) O. 1966	r., 1968/1183

Year and Number (or date)	Act or instrument	How affected
1965		
1803	Trustee Savings Banks (Rate of Interest) O. 1965	r., 1968/765
1861	Turks and Caicos Is. (Constitution) O. 1965	am., 1968/728
1881	Continental Shelf (Jurisdiction) O. 1965	r., 1968/892
1887	Water Officers (Compensation) (S.) Regs. 1965	am., 1968/848
1895	Motor Cycles (Protective Helmets) (Amdt.) Regs. 1965	r., 1968/844
1899	Police (S.) Amdt. (No. 3) Regs. 1965...	r., 1968/716
1971	Molluscan Shellfish (Control of Deposit) O. 1965	am., 1968/1164
1976	Rent Regulation (Forms etc.) (E. and W.) Regs. 1965	am., 1968/1080
2042	Rent Regulation (Forms etc.) (S.) Regs. 1965	am., 1968/1081
2135	Wages Regulation (Cotton Waste Reclamation) O. 1965	r., 1968/1355
2136	Wages Regulation (Cotton Waste Reclamation) (Holidays) O. 1965	r., 1968/1356
2140	Southern Rhodesia (Petroleum) O. 1965	r., 1968/885
1966	Rating Act 1966 (c. 9)	s. 7 **am.** (S.), 1968/1079
	Ministry of Social Security Act 1966 (c. 20)	sch. 2 para. 23 **am.**, 1968/759, 818
		sch. 2 para. 9, 10 **replaced**, 1968/1118
		sch. 2 para. 11, 12, 13 **am.**, 1968/1118
	Docks and Harbours Act 1966 (c. 28)	sch. 1 **am.**, 1968/1075
	Selective Employment Payments Act 1966 (c. 32)	s. 1 **am.**, 1968/1147
		sch. 1 pts. I, II, III **am.**, 1968/1388
	Arbitration (International Investment Disputes) Act 1966 (c. 41)	mod. (Guernsey), 1968/1199
12	Public Health (Leprosy) Regs. 1966 ...	r., 1968/1366
20	Wages Regulation (Rope, Twine and Net) (Holidays) O. 1966	r., 1968/1051
41	Southern Rhodesia (Prohibited Exports and Imports) O. 1966	r., 1968/885
42	Southern Rhodesia (Prohibited Exports) (Chrome) O. 1966	r., 1968/885
48	Town and Country Planning (Development Plans for Greater London) Regs. 1966	am., 1968/815
66	Postal Packets (Customs and Excise) Regs. 1966	am., 1968/931
115	Southern Rhodesia (Prohibited Exports) (Tobacco) O. 1966	r., 1968/885

Year and Number (or date)	Act or instrument	How affected
1964 25 Sept.	Disablement and Death Pensions etc. (Naval Forces), 1914 World War Services, and Services subsequent to 2 Sept. 1939, O. in C: 1964 (1964 III, p. 5466)	**am.,** O. in C. 26.7.68
1965	National Insurance Act 1965 (c. 51) ...	s. 4 **am.,** 1968/827 s. 99 mod. (N.I.), 1968/827 s. 91 **am.** (S.), 1968/1177, (E.and W.), 1968/1262
	Ministerial Salaries Consolidation Act 1965 (c. 58)	sch. 1 **am.,** 1968/729
	Redundancy Payments Act 1965 (c. 62)	s. 27 **am.,** 1968/1264
5	Price Stability of Imported Products (Minimum Import Price Levels) (Amdt.) O. 1965	**r.,** 1968/1132
40	National Insurance (Increase of Benefit and Miscellaneous Provisions) Regs. 1965	**am.,** 1968/827
225	Telephone Regs. 1965	**r.,** 1968/1256
321	A.S. (Rules of Ct., consolidation and amdt). 1965	**am.,** 1968/1016, 1150
536	Special Constables Regs. 1965 ...	**am.,** 1968/899
826	Police (S.) Amdt. Regs. 1965 ...	**r.,** 1968/716
836	River Authorities (Compensation) Regs. 1965	**am.,** 1968/914
1023	Superannuation (Teaching and Public Bds.) Interchange Rules 1965	**r.,** saving, 1968/1120
1191	Telephone Amdt. (No. 1) Regs. 1965	**r.,** 1968/1256
1192	Telex Regs. 1965	**am.,** 1968/1258
1203	U.K. Forces (Jurisdiction of Colonial Cts.) O. 1965	**r.** (Swaziland), 1968/1377
1227	Police (S.) Amdt. (No. 2) Regs. 1965...	**r.,** 1968/716
1352	Central Midwives Bd. for Scotland (Amdt.) Rules 1965 Approval Instrument 1965	**r.,** 1968/694
1404	University and Other Awards Regs. 1965	**am.,** 1968/1296
1412	Milk (N.I.) O. 1965	**am.,** 1968/850
1578	Price Stability of Imported Products (Minimum Import Price Levels) (Amdt. No. 2) O. 1965	**r.,** 1968/1132
1734	British Commonwealth and Foreign Parcel Post Regs. 1965	**am.,** 1968/1255
1735	British Commonwealth and Foreign Post Regs. 1965	**am.,** 1968/1254
1776	Rules of the Supreme Ct. 1965 ...	**am.,** 1968/1244